Personal Financial Planning: Theory and Practice

12TH EDITION

COLLEGE FOR FINANCIAL PLANNING®
A KAPLAN COMPANY

At press time, this edition contains the most complete and accurate information currently available. Due to the nature of advanced designation examinations, however, information may have been added recently to the actual test that does not appear in this edition. Please contact the publisher to verify that you have the most current edition.

This publication is designed to provide accurate and authoritative information in regard to the subject matter covered. It is sold with the understanding that the publisher is not engaged in rendering legal, accounting, or other professional services. If legal advice or other expert assistance is required, the services of a competent professional should be sought.

PERSONAL FINANCIAL PLANNING: THEORY AND PRACTICE, 12TH EDITION

Published by The College for Financial Planning, Inc.

10 9 8 7 6 5 4 3 2 1

ISBN: 978-1-0788-2906-9

About the Contributing Authors

Michael Angell, MS, CFP®, EA

- Associate Professor, The College for Financial Planning
- MS, Finance, The College for Financial Planning
- BS, Mathematics, Creighton University
- Federally licensed tax practitioner with a nationally recognized firm
- Former Registered Representative in Securities
- Over 20 years of experience in banking, insurance, investments, retirement planning, estate planning, and charitable philanthropic organizations
- Co-author of The College for Financial Planning/Kaplan's *CFP® Exam Prep Review Books 1–7*, 2020–2022
- Co-author of The College for Financial Planning/Kaplan's *CFP® Exam Required Education Course Materials* 2020–2022

Sara Stolberg Berkowicz, Ph.D., MS, CFP®, CDFA™

- Assistant Professor, The College for Financial Planning
- Ph.D., Personal Financial Planning, Kansas State University
- MS, Financial Planning, The College for Financial Planning
- BA, Political Science, State University of New York at Binghamton
- Mediator, Association for Conflict Resolution and Northwestern University
- Co-author of The College for Financial Planning/Kaplan's *CFP® Exam Prep Review Books 1–7*, 2020–2022
- Co-author of The College for Financial Planning/Kaplan's *CFP® Exam Required Education Course Materials* 2020–2022

Gary O. Clement, MSF, CFP®, CRPS®, CRPC®, AFC®, MPAS®

- Assistant Professor and Chair, Financial Planning Education, The College for Financial Planning
- MSFS, The College for Financial Planning
- BA, Mathematics, Cheyney University
- FINRA Series 7, 63, 3, 31, and 24 licenses
- Former Compliance Examiner for an international insurance and financial services company
- Former Financial Advisor for multiple national organizations
- Co-author of the College for Financial Planning/Kaplan's *Personal Financial Planning: Theory and Practice*, 12th edition textbook and instructor manual
- Co-author of The College for Financial Planning/Kaplan's *Personal Financial Planning: Cases and Applications*, 12th edition textbook and instructor manual
- Co-author of The College for Financial Planning/Kaplan's *CFP® Exam Required Education Course Materials* 2022
- Co-author of The College for Financial Planning/Kaplan's *CFP® Exam Prep Review Materials* 2022

Jennifer N. Coombs, MSF, CSRIC®, CRPC®

- Associate Professor, The College for Financial Planning
- MS Finance, The College for Financial Planning
- BS, Finance/Political Science, Clarkson University
- Co-author of The College for Financial Planning/Kaplan's *CFP® Exam Prep Review Books 1–7*, 2020–2022
- Co-author of The College for Financial Planning/Kaplan's *CFP® Exam Required Education Course Materials* 2020–2022

Timothy R. Greer, DBA, CEBS™, ChFC®, CLU®, RHU®, CASL®

- Adjunct Professor, The College for Financial Planning
- DBA, University of South Florida
- MBA, Quinnipiac University
- BA, Business Administration, Grove City College
- Licensed Property & Casualty and Life and Health Insurance Producer
- Senior Chief Petty Officer, United States Navy Reserve
- Co-author of The College for Financial Planning/Kaplan's *Personal Financial Planning: Theory and Practice*, 12th edition textbook and instructor manual
- Co-author of The College for Financial Planning/Kaplan's *Personal Financial Planning: Cases and Applications*, 12th edition textbook and instructor manual

- Co-author of The College for Financial Planning/Kaplan's *CFP® Exam Required Education Course Materials* 2020–2022
- Co-author of The College for Financial Planning/Kaplan's *CFP® Exam Prep Review Materials* 2022
- Co-author of The College for Financial Planning/Kaplan's Advisor Accelerator Materials 2022
- Co-author of The College for Financial Planning's *CFP® Exam Required Education Course Materials* 2015–2018
- Co-author of The College for Financial Planning's *CFP® Exam Prep Review Materials* 2015–2018
- Co-author of The College for Financial Planning's LUTCF® Materials 2015–2018
- Co-author of The College for Financial Planning's FFPN® Materials 2015–2016
- Co-author of The College for Financial Planning's CRPC® Materials 2016–2022

Mike Harris, CFP®, MPAS®, CRPC®, AAMS®, AWMA®, CMFC®, CRPC®

- Professor and Chair, Retirement Studies, The College for Financial Planning
- Former Senior Content Specialist, Kaplan Financial Education
- BS in management from the United States Air Force Academy, Colorado Springs, Colorado
- MDiv, Southwestern Baptist Theological Seminary
- MS, Financial Planning, College for Financial Planning
- Served in the United States Air Force for seven years in Oklahoma, California, Idaho, England, and New Mexico
- Former senior relationship manager for a large nonprofit organization
- Over 25 years of experience in the insurance and securities business
- Former general securities representative and life and health insurance agent
- Co-author of Kaplan University/Financial Education's *Personal Financial Education Cases and Applications*, 10th edition textbook and instructor guide
- Co-author of Kaplan University/Financial Education's *CFP® Exam Prep Review Books 1–7*, 2017–2018
- Co-author of The College for Financial Planning/Kaplan's *CFP® Exam Prep Review Books 1–7*, 2019–2022
- Co-author of Kaplan University/Financial Education's *CFP® Exam Required Education Course Materials* 2017
- Co-author of Kaplan's *CFP® Exam Required Education Course Materials* 2018–2019
- Co-author of The College for Financial Planning/Kaplan's *CFP® Exam Required Education Course Materials* 2020–2022

Daniel Johnson, MS, CFP®, EA

- Assistant Professor, The College for Financial Planning
- MS, Financial Planning, The College for Financial Planning
- BS, Finance, University of Minnesota Duluth
- Federally registered tax practitioner
- Creator of The College for Financial Planning/Kaplan's Sports & Entertainment - Accredited Wealth Management Advisor (SE-AWMA) designation, 2021–2022
- Co-author of The College for Financial Planning/Kaplan's *CFP® Exam Prep Review Books 1–7*, 2020–2022
- Co-author of The College for Financial Planning/Kaplan's *CFP® Exam Required Education Course Materials* 2020–2022

David Ness, JD, CFP®, AAMS®

- Adjunct Professor, The College for Financial Planning
- JD, Marquette University
- BS, Accounting, Bradley University
- Securities Industry Institute, Wharton School, University of Pennsylvania
- Former General Practice of Civil Law attorney
- Former wire house financial consultant
- Former President of two broker affiliated trust companies
- Certified Public Accountant (CPA) 1998–2008
- Co-author of The College for Financial Planning/Kaplan's *Personal Financial Planning: Theory and Practice*, 12th edition textbook and instructor manual
- Co-author of The College for Financial Planning/Kaplan's *Personal Financial Planning: Cases and Applications*, 12th edition textbook and instructor manual
- Co-author of The College for Financial Planning/Kaplan's *CFP® Exam Required Education Course Materials* 2020–2022
- Co-author of The College for Financial Planning/Kaplan's *CFP® Exam Prep Review Materials* 2022
- Author, *Keys to Planning for Long-Term Custodial Care* (Barron's Educational Series)

Cindy R. Riecke, MSF, CFP®, CRPC®, FPQP®, ChFC®, CLU®

- Professor, College for Financial Planning
- Former Senior Director, Kaplan Financial Education
- BS in Business Administration from Louisiana State University

- MSF from Purdue University Global
- CFP Board Council on Education, 2020
- CFP Board Ethics CE Advisory Group, 2017–2020
- Member of the Financial Planning Association
- Former Director of Marketing Development for an international insurance and financial services company
- Co-author of Kaplan Financial Education's *Personal Financial Planning Cases and Applications*, 5th–8th editions textbook and instructor manual
- Co-author of Kaplan University/Financial Education's *Personal Financial Planning Cases and Applications*, 9th Edition textbook and instructor manual
- Co-author of Kaplan Financial Education's *Personal Financial Planning Theory and Practice*, 4th–7th editions textbook and instructor manual
- Co-author of Kaplan University/Financial Education's *Personal Financial Planning Theory and Practice*, 8th Edition textbook and instructor manual
- Co-author of the *Kaplan Schweser Review for the CFP® Certification Examination*, 9th–13th editions
- Co-author of the *Kaplan Schweser Review for the CFP® Certification Examination, July–November 2010, March–November 2011*, and *2012–2013 Exams*
- Co-author of Kaplan University/Financial Education's *CFP® Exam Prep Review Books 1–7*, 2014–2018
- Co-author of The College for Financial Planning/Kaplan's *CFP® Exam Prep Review Books 1–7*, 2019–2020
- Co-author of the *Kaplan University/Kaplan Schweser Certification Examination Education Program*, 4th–11th Editions materials
- Co-author of Kaplan University/Financial Education's *CFP® Exam Required Education Course Materials* 2014–2017
- Co-author of Kaplan's *CFP® Exam Required Education Course Materials* 2018–2019
- Co-author of The College for Financial Planning/Kaplan's *CFP® Exam Required Education Course Materials* 2020–2022

Calvin Barclay Roper, III, DBA, MSF

- Assistant Professor, The College for Financial Planning
- DBA, Financial Management, California Southern University
- MS, Finance, The College for Financial Planning
- Co-author of The College for Financial Planning/Kaplan's *CFP® Exam Prep Review Books 1–7*, 2020–2022
- Co-author of The College for Financial Planning/Kaplan's *CFP® Exam Required Education Course Materials* 2020–2022

Scott N. Sayre, MS, CFP®, CFS®, ChSNC®

- Adjunct Professor, The College for Financial Planning
- MS, The College for Financial Planning
- BS, Business Management, Brigham Young University
- Financial Planning Manager for a national financial planning firm
- Former Director of Financial Planning and Chief Compliance Officer for a regional financial planning firm
- President, International Association of Financial Planners, Utah Chapter, 1993
- Chairman of the Board, International Association of Financial Planners, Utah Chapter, 1994
- Co-author of The College for Financial Planning/Kaplan's *Personal Financial Planning: Theory and Practice*, 12th edition textbook and instructor manual
- Co-author of The College for Financial Planning/Kaplan's *Personal Financial Planning: Cases and Applications*, 12th edition textbook and instructor manual
- Co-author of The College for Financial Planning/Kaplan's *CFP® Exam Required Education Course Materials* 2020–2022
- Co-author of The College for Financial Planning/Kaplan's *CFP® Exam Prep Review Materials* 2022

Christopher Woehrle, JD, LL.M

- Professor and Chair, Tax and Estate Planning, The College for Financial Planning
- Adjunct Professor, Widger School of Law, Villanova University
- LLM, Taxation, Villanova University
- JD, Villanova University
- AB, English, Cornell University
- Former Chair, Pensions and Retirement, The American College
- Member, Pennsylvania Bar
- Council for Advancement and Support of Education (CASE)
- Served in high-level positions managing planned giving and development for universities, the performing arts, and healthcare institutions
- Co-author of The College for Financial Planning/Kaplan's *CFP® Exam Prep Review Books 1–7*, 2020–2022
- Co-author of The College for Financial Planning/Kaplan's *CFP® Exam Required Education Course Materials* 2020–2022

Preface

Personal Financial Planning: Theory and Practice was written in response to numerous pleas from instructors and students requesting a fundamental financial planning textbook. Through this text, the contributing authors hope to convey their knowledge of financial planning and reflect their enthusiasm for the subject.

This text is written for graduate and undergraduate students who are interested in acquiring an in-depth understanding of personal financial planning from a professional planning viewpoint. The text is also intended to serve as a reference for practicing professional financial planners.

Content and Themes

The Financial Planner's Pyramid of Knowledge is depicted throughout this text. The base of the pyramid identifies the core knowledge that every financial planner should possess. Chapters 8–17 detail this foundation of knowledge on which a successful financial planning profession can be built. The second layer of the pyramid, presented in chapters 6 and 7, focuses on the basic financial planning tools a financial planner must be familiar with and capable of implementing. The third and fourth layers of the pyramid, presented in chapters 1–5, describe the basic financial planning skills every professional financial planner should possess. Finally, the pyramid's pinnacle explores the financial planning profession and the ethical responsibilities faced by a professional financial planner. Chapters 18 and 19 cover these topics.

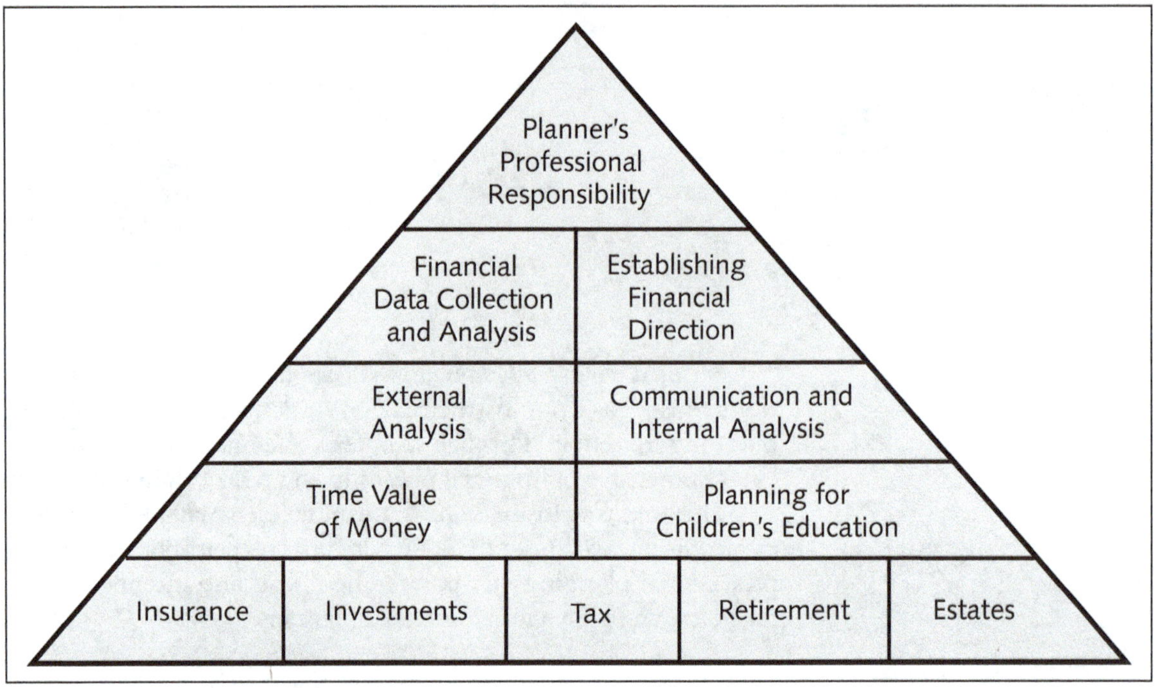

Throughout the text, two themes are identified. The first theme of the text is that personal financial planning is about attaining financial goals and managing financial risks. There are perhaps as many goals as there are clients. Generally, the majority of clients want to achieve one or more of the following goals: to attain financial security for themselves, to accumulate assets to fund their children's education, to save a specific lump sum to cover future expenditures, or to prepare their assets for transfer to heirs. There are many risks threatening the attainment of these goals, including disability, poor health, and untimely death. This text will identify these risks and present ways to manage them.

The second theme emphasized throughout the text is that the professional practice of personal financial planning emphasizes data collection and analysis. For the professional financial planner, this requires knowledge of external environmental influences and skill at data collection, interviewing, and administering questionnaires. Analytical skills are invaluable when applying time-value-of-money concepts and when preparing and analyzing personal financial statements. Excellent communication skills, including displaying empathy and using verbal and nonverbal pacing, are essential when dealing with clients. Finally, helping clients set reasonable goals that are objectively measurable in time and form and using good follow-up and evaluation skills are most valuable to the professional financial planner.

Special Features

A variety of tools and presentation methods are used throughout this text to assist in the learning process. The following are some of the features presented in this text that are designed to enhance the readers' understanding and learning process.

Section Break Features

- **The financial planner's pyramid of knowledge**—The financial planning pyramid is shown on every section break to focus the student's attention to the section topic. We have shaded the corresponding area on the pyramid to identify the broad knowledge topic discussed in the section. The pyramid's intricacies are discussed more fully in Chapter 1.
- **Knowledge level: In Brief**—The knowledge level In Brief section allows us to be more specific on the topics covered in the section. The topics are listed by difficulty, with the easier topics at the top, medium topics in the middle, and more difficult topics at the bottom. This was done to help the student be aware of and prepared for the difficulty of the topics. It also allowed us to give a brief keyword overview of the section.
- **Goal and risk identification**—Common goals and risks are identified on the section break to focus the reader's attention on the ever-present conflict between goal attainment and risk avoidance.
- **Data collection and analysis requirements**—Data collection and data analysis requirements are identified to help the reader become adept at identifying relevant information.

Chapter Features

- **Where on the Web**—Each chapter has a Where on the Web section that provides the reader with useful website domains.
- **Bold keywords**—Keywords appear in boldfaced type throughout the text to assist in the identification of important concepts and terminology. Keyword definitions appear in the margin for quick access to important concepts.
- **Examples**—Examples are used frequently to illustrate the concepts being discussed.
- **Exhibits**—The written text is enhanced and simplified by using exhibits where appropriate.

12th Edition Changes

- All tax numbers, tax tables, and threshold amounts have been updated through 2022.
- New content covering behavioral finance and client counseling has been included in this edition.
- The Insurance section has been updated to reflect 2022 inflation-adjusted dollar amounts that affect several key Social Security concepts, such as the Social Security wage base, the primary insurance amount (PIA), and the maximum family benefit. The discussion of Medicare has been updated to illustrate the impact of the 2022 Medicare premiums, copayments, and deductibles.
- The Investment section has been reorganized and edited in order to present the material in a more clear and concise manner.
- The Tax section has been updated for 2022 law changes released.
- Retirement statistics and limits have been updated for 2022.
- The Estate Planning section has been updated to reflect the federal transfer tax rates, exemptions, and credits that are in effect in 2022.

Contents

SECTION 1
IN BRIEF

- Personal financial planning
- The Financial Planner's Pyramid of Knowledge
- The external environment
- Communication skills of the financial planner
- Internal analysis
- Life cycle positioning

- Financial statement preparation
- Ratio analysis and comparison to benchmarks
- Trend analysis
- Sensitivity and risk analysis

- Establishing and defining the client-planner relationship
- Gathering information necessary to fulfill the engagement
- Analyzing and evaluating the client's current financial status
- Developing the recommendations
- Communicating the recommendations
- Implementing the recommendations
- Monitoring the recommendations
- Practicing within professional and regulatory standards

SECTION

1 Basic Financial Planning Skills

CHAPTERS

Risks

- Inadequate data collection
- Incorrect data analysis
- Miscommunication to client
- Poor strategy
- No client buy-in

Goals

- Establish appropriate mission statement
- Establish goals
- Establish objectives
- Select a strategy

Data Collection

- Economic information
- Legal information
- Personal information
- Financial information
- Tax returns
- Mission
- Goals
- Objectives
- Strategic alternatives

Data Analysis

- Economic analysis
- Personal financial analysis
- Savings analysis
- Investment analysis
- Risk tolerance of client
- Strategic alternatives

CHAPTER 1

Introduction to Personal Financial Planning

LEARNING OBJECTIVES

After learning the material in this chapter, you will be able to do the following:

- Define personal financial planning
- Discuss the benefits of personal financial planning
- Explain how the financial planning process promotes efficient allocation of a client's resources
- Explain how financial success is a relative concept
- Identify why people hire professional financial planners
- Describe the Financial Planner's Pyramid of Knowledge and explain the importance of each component

PERSONAL FINANCIAL PLANNING DEFINED

Personal financial planning
The process of formulating, implementing, and monitoring multifunctional decisions that enable an individual or family to achieve financial goals

Comprehensive **personal financial planning** is the process of formulating, implementing, and monitoring multifunctional decisions that enable an individual or family to achieve financial goals. Personal financial planning involves the management of personal financial risks through cost benefit analysis. It capitalizes on personal and financial strengths and opportunities while managing financial risks and weaknesses. Financial planning professionals and those studying financial planning should understand and appreciate the comprehensive nature of a competently prepared personal financial plan and what it is intended to accomplish for the person who implements it effectively.

BENEFITS OF PERSONAL FINANCIAL PLANNING

A financial plan integrates a financial mission, goals, and objectives into one cohesive plan that allocates financial resources consistently. Individuals and families with no formal financial plan actually have an informal financial plan, which is reflected by their historical pattern of financial decisions and financial behavior. For example, consistent late debt repayments suggest a pattern (plan), and such a pattern eventually leads to financial consequences. Conversely, consistent long-term savings and investment without any formal plan creates a pattern (plan) that also leads to financial consequences. The historical pattern of personal or family financial behavior is as difficult to change as is any other personal habit. Thus, the professional financial planner is not only a strategist and planner but may also be a counselor and a financial "therapist."

Benefits of personal financial planning

- *Goals identified are more likely to be achieved*
- *Helps to clearly identify risk exposures*
- *Is proactive rather than reactive*
- *Creates a framework for feedback, evaluation, and control*
- *Establishes measurable goals and expectations*
- *Develops an improved awareness of financial choices*
- *Provides an opportunity for an increased commitment to financial goals*

There are many **benefits of personal financial planning**. Perhaps the most important benefit is that goals identified and planned for are more likely to be achieved. The planning process helps clearly recognize risks that can undermine goals. Once identified, these risks can be managed with a variety of techniques. The financial planning process is one of learning, growing, and choosing wisely. The process is proactive rather than reactive, thus giving clients more control over their financial status. By using a more logical, systematic, and rational approach to decision making, clients make better strategic choices regarding the use of resources. The process also creates a framework for feedback, evaluation, and control. It establishes measurable goals and expectations that can be compared to actual results.

During the financial planning process, the client develops an improved awareness of financial choices and how internal and external environments affect those choices. The process also provides the client an opportunity to increase commitment to selected goals. When clients and their families understand what they want to achieve, why they want to accomplish it, and how and when it can be attained, they often take ownership of their financial plan and become more committed to it.

A comprehensive personal financial plan helps to establish rationality and reality and eliminate the client's unrealistic ideas and wishful thinking. For example, many people want to retire early and maintain their preretirement lifestyle while currently spending more than 100% of their personal disposable income with no plan to save or invest. A comprehensive personal financial plan will quickly demonstrate the irrationality of such an approach and assist the client in identifying those changes necessary to achieve a more realistic plan.

The financial planning process also brings financial order and discipline. This process instills confidence that goals can be achieved and identifies the behavioral changes necessary to accomplish those goals. It provides a forum for rationalizing the need for change and helps to view change as an opportunity rather than a threat.

Financially successful individuals—not necessarily those who are wealthy but rather those who meet their financial goals—tend to do more financial planning to prepare themselves for the inevitable changes in their internal and external environments. They tend to make more informed financial decisions. They also tend to better anticipate both the short- and long-term consequences of their decisions. Conversely, individuals who are not as financially successful tend to underestimate the value of planning and may attribute their lack of financial success to uncontrollable factors such as a poor economy, foreign competition, government interference, or just bad luck.

There are no absolutes in financial planning any more than there are absolutes about anything in the future. Financial planning will not guarantee desired results; however, it will increase the probability of clients achieving their financial goals. Clients who believe in financial planning generally learn the importance of managing the various risks that could have a negative impact on their plans.

FINANCIAL SUCCESS IS A RELATIVE CONCEPT

Financial success
For most individuals, financial success means accomplishing one's financial goals

Financial success means different things to different people. The fisherman who lives in a poor village in a developing country and has a slightly larger boat than most of the other local fishermen may feel financially successful. The millionaire whose friends are all billionaires may feel less financially successful. In a way, financial success is a comparison with the client's own benchmarks or standards. Thus, from the client's perspective, financial success is both relative and subjective. The professional financial planner needs to keep in mind that, to a particular client, financial success is a relative concept, the description of which may be subjectively determined by the client.

Subjectivity
Relating to the client's perception of reality

Objectivity
Relating to facts without distortion by personal feelings or prejudices

While **subjectivity** tends to dominate the client's thinking about financial success, **objectivity** should dominate the planner's thinking about financial planning. Accomplishing specific goals is objectively determined if objectively defined. Risks that exist in the external environment are objective and real to the professional planner. The client may have a subjective perception of the same risks. For example, the risk of untimely death can be measured actuarially, regardless of the subjective perception of the client. Another example of objectivity is recognizing the risk of permanent disability for a particular job. Consider an example of an NFL running back. The number of running backs who are disabled each year is a predictable percentage, league-wide. Regardless of how the players subjectively feel about their chances of suffering a disabling injury, it is mathematically objective that a certain percentage of running backs will be injured and will be unable to play in any given year. With full knowledge of this objective risk and its catastrophic financial consequences, a professional financial planner would strongly advise his running back client to purchase long-term disability insurance that pays benefits if the player is injured while playing professional football. Most professional planners would agree with that advice even though the policy premiums will be extremely high. The premiums are high because the insurers also understand the objective risks, and they set premiums that will cover losses and earn a profit.

RESOURCE ALLOCATION IN FINANCIAL PLANNING

Financial planning involves making financial choices and allocating scarce resources. People make choices because scarcity exists. At any moment in time, all people want the highest level of overall satisfaction from their choices. Most people are aware from an early

Personal utility curves
Economic curves that describe the satisfaction that an individual receives from a selected item or additional units of that item

Opportunity cost
The highest-valued alternative not chosen; represents what is forgone by choosing another alternative

age that there are alternative financial choices to be made, such as whether to consume today or defer consumption until later. The internal psychological analysis that people perform when they decide among alternatives is a subjective evaluation resulting from the application of their own **personal utility curves** to the alternatives identified and presented to them. Personal utility curves are subjectively based and reflect our knowledge, values, and beliefs and, therefore, may be quite different for each person. Some individuals place a high value on spending time alone, while some value spending time with others in social settings. If a client believes there is no tomorrow, he may as well consume today. If, however, he believes in a long future during which he plans not to work, he may be willing to forego consumption today, deferring those unconsumed resources for the future.

When making choices, we are faced with alternatives. Each alternative poses risks and consequences. Doing nothing is one alternative. The highest-valued alternative not chosen is called the **opportunity cost**. Opportunity cost represents what is forgone by choosing another alternative. For example, if a client chooses to spend $2,500 on a cruise as an alternative to saving for the future, the opportunity cost is the value of the $2,500 in the client's investment portfolio. Five years after taking the cruise, the client has fond memories and beautiful photos of the trip. Alternatively, had he not taken the cruise and invested the money in a well-structured investment portfolio for those five years, he might have significantly increased the value of his portfolio.

When choosing among alternatives, clients need a framework for comparison. When making comparisons, human nature tends to discount anything in the future in favor of immediate gratification. In the cruise example above, the client decided to spend the $2,500 now to take the cruise, even though he objectively knew that the money might increase significantly in five years if invested wisely. For this client, the current subjective satisfaction expected from taking the cruise is worth more today than the increased future value of the investment portfolio.

Once a financial planner presents a client with a framework of objective alternatives that identifies the opportunity cost associated with each choice, the client can make a more informed, more rational choice among alternatives. In this way, the financial planning process promotes efficient allocation of a client's resources and avoids commitment of resources to more costly, less rational choices.

WHY DO PEOPLE HIRE PROFESSIONAL FINANCIAL PLANNERS?

Many people seek the advice of professionals, such as doctors, lawyers, and accountants, on a regular basis. Generally, professionals have a more comprehensive knowledge of their subject field than does the public. In some cases, it is simply a matter of opportunity cost. It may be less expensive—in total satisfaction and cost—to retain an expert than to invest the time to learn to do it ourselves. We may lack the day-to-day cognitive references, financial benchmarks, and comparisons needed to know when a plan is competent or attainable. Even when people have a limited knowledge of financial planning, they may lack the confidence to make important decisions based on that limited knowledge. People hire professional financial planners because they believe that doing so is more effective and efficient than attempting to create and implement a financial plan on their own.

The public has a reasonable expectation that a professional financial planner is knowledgeable and competent in the financial planning field. The planner should have an understanding of objective risks in the environment, such as the risks of untimely death, health issues, disability, property loss, and negligence lawsuits and awards. The public can reasonably expect that a professional financial planner will have knowledge of life expectancies and, thus, an understanding of the average expected number of retirement years. Planners should know that in general it takes 60–80% of preretirement income to maintain a lifestyle during retirement. Planners should know that for low-income workers, Social Security may provide an adequate wage replacement, but for highly paid workers, it may only replace a small percentage of preretirement income. Professional planners should know the risk of inflation and its historical patterns. Planners should also know the historical investment returns for various classes of assets and which asset allocation choices have produced the best overall investment returns for selected risk levels. This text will broaden the professional financial planner's knowledge and skill base in all of these areas.

THE FINANCIAL PLANNER'S PYRAMID OF KNOWLEDGE

The Financial Planner's Pyramid of Knowledge, as depicted in Exhibit 1.1, is presented throughout this text. The Pyramid identifies the skills and basic tools that the financial planner must possess as well as the core topics of which the planner must be knowledgeable. Just as the strength of any structure depends on a solid foundation, the success of any professional financial planner relies on a well-built foundation of knowledge, competency, and skill. The base of the Financial Planner's Pyramid of Knowledge identifies the core knowledge and skill sets that every financial planner should possess. Collectively, these competencies make up the financial planner's toolkit—a foundation on which a successful profession in financial planning can be established. Out of necessity in this text, these skills, tools, and competencies are presented individually; however, they are not performed sequentially or independently. Rather, they are performed simultaneously throughout the many aspects of the financial planning process.

EXHIBIT 1.1 Financial Planner's Pyramid of Knowledge

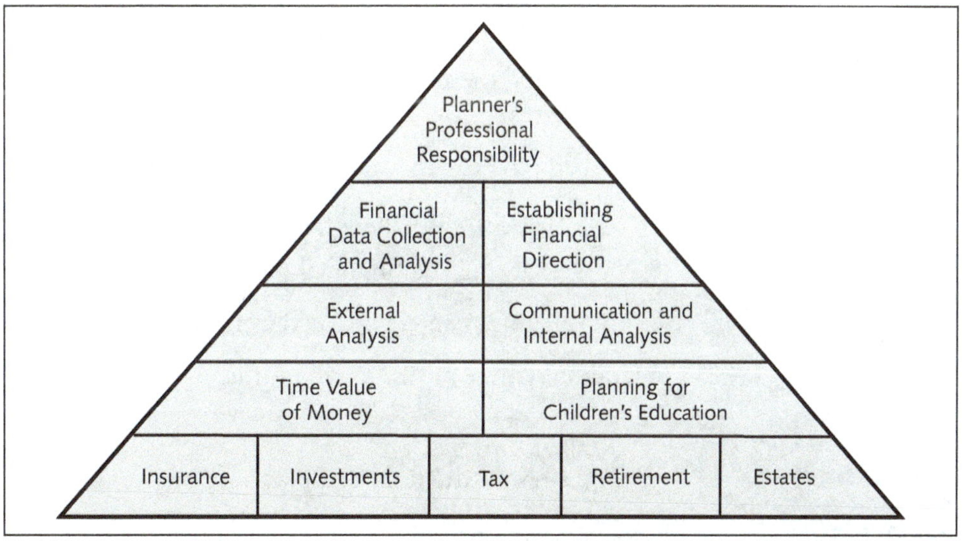

Throughout the text, we also focus on two themes. The first theme of the text is that personal financial planning involves attaining financial goals and managing financial risks. There are perhaps as many goals as there are clients. Generally, the majority of clients are looking to achieve one or more of the following goals: to attain financial security for themselves, to create an accumulation of assets to fund their children's education, to save a specific lump sum to cover future expenditures, or to prepare their assets for transfer to heirs. There are many risks threatening the attainment of these goals, including disability, ill health, or untimely death. The text will identify these risks and suggest ways for managing them.

The second theme emphasized throughout the text is that the professional practice of personal financial planning emphasizes data collection and analysis. For the professional financial planner, this requires a good education in external environmental influences and good data collection skills for interviewing and administering questionnaires. Analytical skills are invaluable when applying time value of money concepts and when preparing and analyzing personal financial statements. Excellent communication skills, including **emotional intelligence** and **active listening**, are essential when gathering information and communicating with clients. Finally, helping clients set reasonable goals that are objectively measurable in time and form and using good follow-up and evaluation techniques are most valuable to the professional financial planner.

Emotional intelligence
The ability to recognize and assess emotional expressions in themselves and their clients

Active listening
Paying full attention to what clients are saying and responding by paraphrasing their comments, thus gaining a full understanding of what clients are attempting to communicate

Basic Financial Planning Skills

The first section of the text explains that the practice of personal financial planning requires the financial planner to master good communication, data collection, and analysis skills. These skills are necessary when applying financial planning tools and working with clients. The planner must be aware that individuals generally progress through **financial phases** during their lives. These phases include the asset accumulation phase, the conservation/protection phase, and the distribution/gifting phase. These phases are not mutually exclusive. For example, a client may function in two phases simultaneously. If a professional planner can identify which phase or phases a client is in, the planner will have better insight into the client's financial behavior and a better understanding of the client's approach to goals and risks.

Financial phases
These phases include the asset accumulation phase, the conservation/protection phase, and the distribution/gifting phase

This section also identifies the process of establishing financial direction. The seven steps in the financial planning process are based on the eight job task domains of Certified Financial Planner Board of Standards, Inc.:

1. Understanding the client's personal and financial circumstances (Step 1)
2. Identifying and selecting goals (Step 2)
3. Analyzing the client's current course of action and potential alternative course(s) of action (Step 3)
4. Developing the financial planning recommendation(s) (Step 4)
5. Presenting the financial planning recommendation(s) (Step 5)
6. Implementing the financial planning recommendation(s) (Step 6)
7. Monitoring progress and updating (Step 7)

Practicing within professional and regulatory standards takes place throughout all seven steps.

The steps in the financial planning process are further discussed in Chapter 5.

A broad and enduring statement that identifies the client's long-term purpose for wanting a financial plan is called a **financial mission,** which begins the process. Once the mission has been identified and embraced, the planner must consider relevant internal and external environmental information. The planner should use objective analysis and rational judgment to guide the client to effective decision making. The client's **financial goals** are high-level statements of financial desires that may be for the short or the long term and the client's **financial objectives** are statements that contain time and measurement attributes, making them more specific than financial goals. These are then identi-

Financial mission
A broad and enduring statement that identifies the client's long-term purpose for wanting a financial plan

Financial goals
High-level statements of financial desires that may be for the short or the long term

Financial objectives
Statements of financial desire that contain time and measurement attributes, making them more specific than financial goals

fied and prioritized so that feasible alternative strategies can be created. After examining the alternatives, the planner helps the client select the optimal strategy. The recommendations will then be implemented and monitored, but this does not mean the process is finished. The responsible financial planner will then monitor the recommendations that were implemented by providing regular feedback to the client on the plan's performance. All of these activities should be performed in a professional manner and within any applicable regulatory standards.

Basic Financial Planning Tools

Time value of money
The concept that money received today is worth more than the same amount of money received sometime in the future

The second section of the text identifies two basic financial planning tools: **time value of money** and planning for children's education.

Chapter 6 discusses time value of money (TVM) concepts, one of the most useful and important concepts in finance and personal financial planning. The chapter includes in-depth discussions of TVM concepts, such as present value, future value, loan amortization, net present value (NPV) and internal rate of return (IRR), yield to maturity, debt management, and the inflation rate.

Chapter 7 covers developing a plan for funding children's education, which is a primary financial goal of many parents. Education funding is a common area of concern for those seeking financial planning advice, because paying for higher education is one of the largest financial burdens a family will face. In this discussion, the various issues that parents should consider when setting goals for financing their children's education are discussed. The types of financial aid information that can be gathered from a college's financial aid office are also examined, and the importance of the Expected Family Contribution (EFC) formula in student financial aid application is explained. Also discussed are the major student financial assistance programs available and how time value of money concepts are used to help calculate the cost of a child's education.

Core Topics

Chapters 8–11 are dedicated to insurance planning. Chapter 8 discusses the legal foundation of insurance and the transference of risks using insurance contracts. Chapter 9 identifies the risks associated with premature death, catastrophic illness, disability, and the need for long-term care. Also discussed is self-insurance, business uses of life insurance, health savings accounts (HSAs), Health Care Reimbursement Arrangements (HCRAs), equity indexed annuities (EIAs), and Section 1035 exchanges. Other employee benefits are also discussed. Chapter 10 identifies the risks to property and liability exposures. Chapter 11 covers Social Security and other types of social insurance.

Chapters 12–17 provide an introduction to investments, income tax, retirement, and estate planning. Chapter 12 and Supplements A, B, and C offer a discussion on investment planning. Chapter 12 introduces investment goals and the risks that threaten those goals and discusses modern portfolio theory and investment strategies. Supplement 12A discusses investing in lending securities, such as bonds. Supplement 12B covers equity securities, namely common and preferred stock. Supplement 12C discusses mutual funds.

Chapters 13 and 14 cover individual income tax and tax planning and the formation and taxation of business entities. Chapter 13 includes discussions on the objectives of the federal income tax law, the tax rate structures under which income can be taxed, how to perform tax calculations to determine a client's income tax liability, the types of IRS rulings issued as guidance to taxpayers, payroll taxes, the various civil penalties imposed on tax law violators, and the various tax-advantaged investment options available to taxpayers. Chapter 14 identifies the several types of business entities that a businessowner may choose as a legal form of business and characterizes each type of business entity with regard to formation requirements, operation, ownership restrictions, tax treatment, legal liability risk, and management operations. The chapter goes on to discuss the basic factors that a businessowner should consider when selecting a legal form of business and explains how each type of business entity differs with regard to simplicity of formation and operation, ownership restrictions, limited liability, management operations, and tax characteristics.

Chapters 15 and 16 discuss retirement planning. Chapter 15 identifies and explains the major factors that affect retirement planning. Chapter 16 provides an introduction to employer-sponsored and individual retirement plans, including qualified retirement plans, other tax-advantaged retirement plans, and nonqualified plans.

Chapter 17 presents the goals of efficient and effective wealth transfer, during life or at death, and the risks that are associated with such transfers. This chapter introduces estate planning, describes the estate planning process, discusses the objectives of and the benefits derived from planning an estate, lists the types of client information necessary to conduct this planning, and describes the probate process and its advantages and disadvantages. Chapter 17 also explains the gift and estate tax system, identifies the basic strategies for transferring wealth through gifting, explains the purpose of the federal estate tax, defines the marital deduction and how it affects estate planning, and discusses the various estate tax reduction techniques available.

The Financial Planning Profession

Chapter 18 describes the financial planning profession today and describes and differentiates financial institutions from individual financial professionals. The chapter outlines the methods of compensation and closes with ideas about developing and maintaining a practice. Chapter 19 covers the ethical responsibilities of a financial planner, provides a legal framework for malpractice and civil liability, and details the CFP Board Code of Ethics and Standards of Conduct (Code and Standards), which covers the Code of Ethics, duties owed to clients, CFP Board, Firms, and subordinates. In addition, the seven-step financial planning process outlined in the Code and Standards is discussed and analyzed.

WHERE ON THE WEB

Association for Financial Counseling and Planning Education **www.afcpe.org**

Barron's Online **www.barrons.com**

Bloomberg **www.bloomberg.com**

Certified Financial Planner Board of Standards, Inc. **www.cfp.net**

Financial Planning Association **www.fpanet.org**

Forbes Magazine **www.forbes.com**

Fortune Magazine **www.fortune.com**

Kiplinger **www.kiplinger.com**

Money Magazine **www.money.cnn.com**

National Association of Personal Financial Advisors **www.napfa.org**

Society of Financial Service Professionals **national.societyoffsp.org**

Wall Street Journal **www.wsj.com**

Yahoo Finance **www.finance.yahoo.com**

DISCUSSION QUESTIONS

1. What is personal financial planning?
2. What does it mean to consider financial success a relative concept?
3. How does the financial planning process promote efficient allocation of a client's resources?
4. Why do people hire professional financial planners?
5. What does the Financial Planner's Pyramid of Knowledge identify?
6. How can a client benefit from the personal financial planning process?
7. What concepts must the professional financial planner balance in order to create a successful financial plan?
8. Through what activities is the personal financial planner expected to guide the client?

CHAPTER 2

External Environmental Analysis

LEARNING OBJECTIVES

After learning the material in this chapter, you will be able to do the following:

- Differentiate between the external and internal environments in which financial planning occurs
- Discuss how external environmental factors link to the different areas of financial planning
- Give examples of how external environmental factors might affect clients from different economic levels
- Give reasons why external environmental analysis is important
- Explain how economic factors, such as interest rates, taxes, and inflation, affect areas of financial planning
- Define the several phases and important extreme points that make up a business cycle and describe their effect on the economy

- Calculate the inflation rate
- Define the consumer price index, the gross domestic product deflator, and the producer price index
- Explain how changes in monetary and fiscal policy affect the economy
- Discuss the different types of financial institutions and negotiable instruments
- Explain how FDIC coverage works
- Identify federal consumer protection/bankruptcy laws and give a brief description of each
- List federal programs that offer protection for workers on the job site
- Give examples of how other external environmental factors—social, technological, political, and taxation—affect a client's personal financial plan

THE EXTERNAL ENVIRONMENT

The success of a client's financial planning is affected by both internal and external environmental factors. Internal environmental forces, which will be examined fully in subsequent chapters, include a client's current and projected financial situation, risk tolerance, discipline regarding savings and investments, consumption patterns, and financial goals. Exhibit 2.1 shows how the internal environment fits within the external environment.

EXHIBIT 2.1 Internal and External Environments

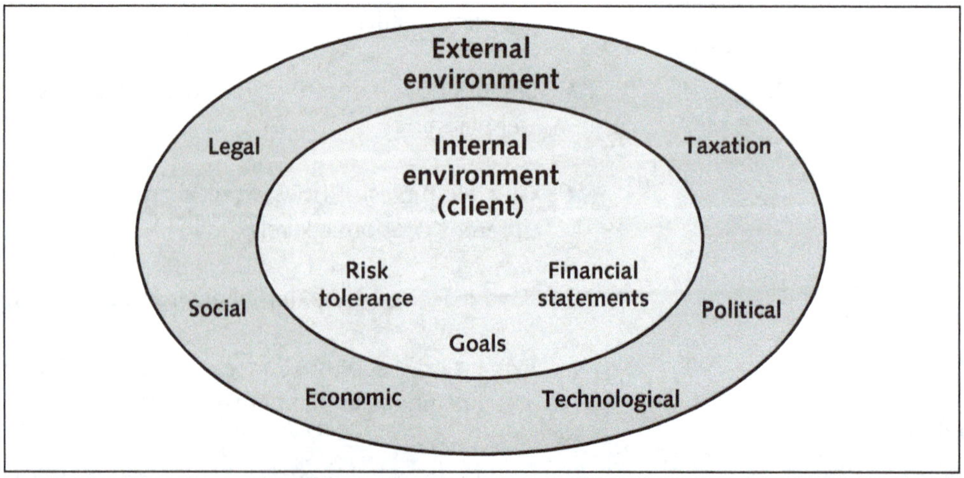

External environment
The whole complex of factors independent of the client that influence the financial planning process, including economic, legal, social, technological, political, and taxation factors

The **external environment** is made up of a variety of factors, or sub-environments, that are broad in scope but have at least some influence on the financial planning process. The external environment includes economic, legal, social, technological, political, and taxation factors. An abbreviated list of factors for each of the external environmental influences is presented in Exhibit 2.2.

EXHIBIT 2.2 Abbreviated List of External Factors*

Economic Factors	Legal Factors
Gross domestic product (GDP)	Antitrust acts
Inflation (Consumer Price Index)	Consumer protection acts
Interest rates	Bankruptcy acts
Trade payments	Securities acts
Consumer income/debt/spending	Forms of business organization
Unemployment	Employer/employee relations
Population age	Workers' compensation
Index of leading economic indicators	Continuation of benefits (COBRA)
	Social Security

Social Factors	Technological Factors
Age of population life expectancy	Current state of technology
Customs and beliefs	Creation of new technology
Attitudes and motivations	Human and business solutions
Status symbols/social institutions	Advances in service and engineering

Political Factors	Taxation Factors
Form of government	Income taxes (federal and state)
Political ideology/stability	Property taxes
Foreign trade policy	Transfer taxes (gift and estate)
Degree of government protectionism	Payroll taxes
	Sales taxes

*There are many other factors than those listed; however, a full discussion of all factors is beyond the scope of this text.

This chapter describes the external environment in which financial planning occurs. The external environment is characterized by opportunities and threats. For the financial planner, the purpose of studying the external environment is to scan for those opportunities and threats that may relate to particular clients and their financial goals. The financial planner may forecast external trends (or use experts to forecast trends) to help clients achieve goals and avoid external risks.

As stated previously, external environmental factors include economic, legal, social, technological, political, and taxation forces. Everyone is influenced by these forces to differing degrees as shown by the selected examples in Exhibit 2.3.

Because some clients are more affected by certain environmental factors than others, it is the financial planner's responsibility to decide the influences relevant to a particular client at a particular time.

EXHIBIT 2.3 External Environmental Impact on Financial Planning (Selected Examples)

Client's economic level	External Environmental Forces					
	Economic	Legal	Social	Political	Taxation	Technological
High income	• Gross domestic product • Interest rates	• Antitrust • Form of business organization	• Status symbols • Life expectancy	• Political ideology/ stability	• Income and transfer taxes • Property taxes	• Investments • Internet
Middle income	• Inflation • Interest rates	• Form of business organization • Employer/ employee relationships • Consumer protection • COBRA • Social Security	• Customs/ beliefs • Life expectancy	• Foreign trade policy	• Property taxes • Income taxes • Payroll taxes	• Investments • Jobs • Electronic tax filing • Internet
Low income	• Unemployment • Inflation	• Workers' compensation • Consumer protection • COBRA • Social Security	• Social institutions • Life expectancy • Customs/ beliefs	• Government protectionism	• Sales taxes • Payroll taxes	• Electronic tax filing • Internet

Analyzing the External Environment

External environmental analysis
The process of identifying and monitoring the environment in which a client lives and the opportunities and threats that are present

External environmental analysis is important for a variety of reasons.

- External trends and particular events play a significant role in changing the world and the behavior of individuals.
- Changes in external forces impact beliefs, economics, unemployment, inflation, and a society's well-being.
- The external environment shapes the way people live, work, spend, save, and reason.

Professional financial planners need to understand these forces and should develop a method for staying abreast of the changes in the external environment.

When performing an external environmental analysis, the financial planner must determine the relevance of one or more external environmental factors for each client. The relevance of such factors may depend on the client's age, goals, net worth, or income. Consider the following examples.

EXAMPLE Bryan is 70 years old and married, has five adult children and seven grandchildren, and has a net worth of $25 million. One of his goals is to leave as much money as he can to his heirs. Because the tax environment incorporates gift taxes, estate taxes, generation-skipping transfer taxes, and in some cases state inheritance taxes, the tax environment is highly relevant to Bryan's personal financial planning.

EXAMPLE Xu, age 36, is married, has three young children, and has debts in excess of her assets. She was injured on the job and may never return to work. Although the tax environment may have some relevance to Xu, it will be a minor influence relative to Bryan's circumstances. The legal environment, which addresses consumer protection, bankruptcy, workers' compensation, Medicaid, COBRA, Social Security disability benefits, and civil lawsuits, may be of utmost importance to Xu.

Why Study the External Environment?

Regular observation and monitoring of the external environment is essential to providing high-quality financial planning services to clients. Financial planners may study the external environment formally or informally. Formal study will usually include university-level courses in economics, taxation, political science, sociology, and the legal environment. The external environment may also be studied informally using a variety of sources, such as general economic and business periodicals, books, academic and professional journals, websites, newspapers, government statistical studies, and by obtaining environmental briefings from various information providers. Financial planners should also take continuing professional education courses to stay abreast of the ever-changing external environment.

The Economic and Legal Environments

The external environment—particularly the economic and legal environment—exerts far-reaching yet often subtle influence on accomplishing financial goals and reducing risks. For example, consider an economic environment characterized by low interest rates, modest growth, and low inflation. Such an environment is ideal for businesses to prosper and for investors to achieve excellent investment returns with relatively moderate levels of risk. Alternatively, periods of high interest rates and growing inflation are not as suitable for businesses, investors, or retirees, who, living on fixed incomes, are losing purchasing power. The legal environment, especially consumer protection, is important because it establishes the legal rules by which consumers must abide and creates the legal rights to which consumers are entitled.

IMPORTANCE OF THE ECONOMIC ENVIRONMENT

Of all the external environments, the economic environment has the most direct influence on personal financial planning. The economic environment includes many factors, such as gross domestic product, inflation rates, interest rates, trade payments, consumer income/debt/spending, unemployment, population age, and the index of leading economic indicators. Interest rates, inflation, unemployment, and gross domestic product play a key role in real investment returns and, therefore, in the attainment of financial goals.

Professional financial planners must understand the current economic environment to better forecast the economic future. By identifying the opportunities and threats that lie ahead, planners can help clients adapt to that future. The planner needs an understanding of the current economy's general condition, the current interest rate environment, the current inflation rate, and recent changes in monetary and fiscal policy. The planner must have the ability to anticipate each element's behavior and its potential effect on a client's financial plan. Exhibit 2.4 illustrates several selected economic factors and their relationship to various areas of financial planning.

EXHIBIT 2.4 The Economic Environment and Financial Planning

Selected Economic Factors	Financial Planning Areas Affected	How They Are Affected
Interest rates	Investment returns	Inversely
	Purchasing power and, therefore, the costs of goods and services in the future including education, retirement funding, and health care	Inversely
Taxes	Redistribution of income through government	Directly
	Production of goods	Inversely
	Distribution of wealth	Directly
Inflation	The cost of goods, services, money, and unemployment	Directly
Unemployment	Wage rates and other costs/expansion/contraction/consumption	Inversely
Monetary and fiscal policy	Economic expansion/contraction/expectations	Directly

Remember, these economic factors are not mutually exclusive but interrelated. As Exhibit 2.4 illustrates, one economic factor may influence several areas of financial planning in different ways. Professional financial planners need to interpret the external economic environment accurately so they can adjust their clients' financial plans accordingly.

The General Economy

The economy is a resource-allocation market system that achieves its objectives through a pricing mechanism. Prices are essentially determined in the marketplace at the point where supply and demand reach equilibrium. If supply or demand is affected, prices will change.

In the News

When the Pope lifted the ban on eating meat on Friday for Catholics in 1966, the average price per pound of fish dropped 12.5%. However, with the current awareness of health issues, the price of fish has risen faster than general inflation. Thus, if demand is affected, prices will also be affected. (Frederick W. Bell, "The Pope and the Price of Fish," American Economic Review 58 [December 1968]: 1346–1350)

Demand
The quantity of a particular good that people are willing to buy; usually dependent on price

Demand curve
The graphic depiction that illustrates the relationship between a particular good's price and the quantity demanded

Demand

The **demand** for a particular good is the quantity people are willing to buy. Demand is heavily dependent on price. The **demand curve** (Exhibit 2.5) illustrates the general relationship between a particular good's price and the quantity demanded.

EXHIBIT 2.5 The Demand Curve

Substitution effect
The phenomenon in which consumers substitute less expensive goods for similar, more expensive goods; this is one of two reasons why the demand curve slopes downward

Changes in quantity demanded
The movements along the demand curve in response to a change in price

Downward sloping demand indicates that if the price increases, the quantity demanded will fall. Conversely, when the price falls, quantity demanded increases. There are two reasons demand declines when the price increases. The first is that consumers will substitute other, less expensive goods when the price for a particular good rises. This phenomenon is called the **substitution effect**. The second reason demand declines is that consumers curb consumption when prices rise. For example, assume Exhibit 2.5 shows the demand curve for Malik's consumption of ice cream. If the price of ice cream is $5 per pint, Malik will consume 15 pints of ice cream. However, if the price of ice cream increases to $8 per pint, Malik will consume only 10 pints of ice cream. Malik could substitute cupcakes for ice cream or simply reduce his overall consumption of desserts. These movements along the demand curve in response to a change in price are called **changes in quantity demanded.**

Change in demand
This occurs when the entire curve shifts to the right or left as the quantity demanded at each price level changes

When the entire curve shifts to the right or the left, we say that there is a **change in demand**. When the curve shifts, quantity demanded at each price level changes. The average income or standard of living is a key determinant of demand. As incomes increase, individuals demand and purchase more goods at each price level. The size of the market and the price and availability of related, substitute goods also influence the demand for a particular good.

EXHIBIT 2.6 Effects of Selected Events on the Demand Curve

Event	Effect on Demand Curve
Increase in the price of the good	Downward movement along the demand curve
Increase in average income	Upward (right) shift of demand curve
Increase in population	Upward shift of demand curve
Increase in the price of related goods	Upward shift of demand curve
Increase in the price of complement goods	Downward (left) shift of demand curve
Increase in taste preference	Upward shift of demand curve
Increases in price and economic expectations	Upward shift of demand curve

The opposite event (e.g., a decrease in average income) will result in an opposite effect on the demand curve (downward shift in the demand curve). Any changes or influences other than the price of a good cause a shift in the demand curve. Price changes simply cause movement along the demand curve.

Supply

Supply
The quantity of a particular good businesses are willing to produce or sell

Supply curve
Depicts the general relationship between the market price of a particular good and the quantity supplied

The **supply** of a particular good is the quantity businesses are willing to produce and sell. The **supply curve** (Exhibit 2.7) depicts the general relationship between the market price of a particular good and the quantity supplied.

EXHIBIT 2.7 The Supply Curve

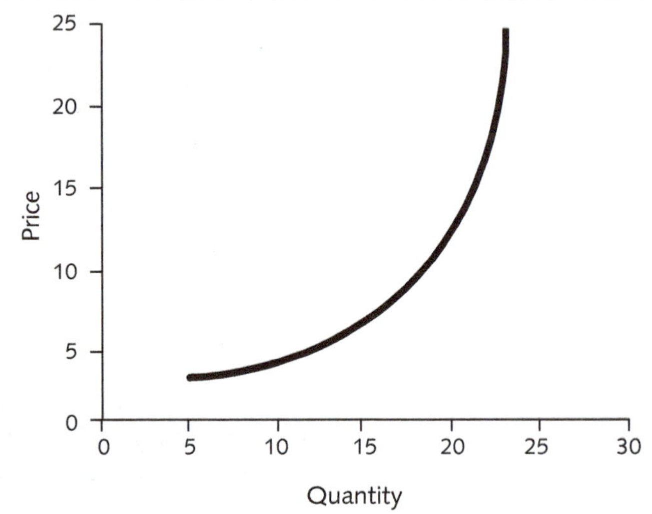

EXHIBIT 2.8 Effects of Selected Events on the Supply Curve

Event	Effect on Supply Curve
Increase in the price of the good	Upward movement along the supply curve
Increase in technology	Upward (right) shift of supply curve
Increase in input prices	Downward (left) shift of supply curve
Increase in the price of related goods	Upward shift of supply curve

Law of diminishing marginal utility
As the rate of consumption increases, the marginal utility derived from consuming additional units of a good will decline

Marginal utility
The additional utility received from the consumption of an additional unit of a good

Diminishing Marginal Utility

The **law of diminishing marginal utility** states that as the rate of consumption increases, the marginal utility derived from consuming additional units of a good will decline. **Marginal utility** is the additional utility received from the consumption of an additional unit of a good. For example, if Eddie's favorite food is steak, he might eat steak often. However, if Eddie ate steak for *n* consecutive days for dinner, the enjoyment, or utility, that he received from the dinner would be higher the first day than on the last.

Price elasticity
The quantity demanded of a good in response to changes in that good's price; a good is elastic when its quantity demanded responds greatly to price changes (luxuries) and inelastic when its quantity demanded responds little to price changes (necessities)

Price Elasticity

Price elasticity is the quantity demanded of a good in response to changes in that good's price. The percentage of change in quantity demanded divided by the percentage of change in price is a relative measure of price elasticity (PE). The formula for elasticity of demand is as follows:

$$\frac{\text{\% Change in Quantity Demanded}}{\text{\% Change in Price}} = \frac{\left(\dfrac{Q_1 - Q_0}{Q_0}\right)}{\left(\dfrac{P_1 - P_0}{P_0}\right)}$$

Goods differ in their elasticity. A good is elastic when its quantity demanded responds greatly to price changes (PE > 1). Luxuries such as movie tickets and liquor could be considered elastic because they are, generally, highly price sensitive. A good is inelastic when its quantity demanded responds little to price changes (PE < 1). Milk and electricity, considered necessities by some, will remain in demand no matter what the price. **Unit-elastic demand** exists when the percentage of change in quantity demanded is exactly equal to the percentage of change in price, ignoring the direction of the change (PE = 1).

Unit-elastic demand
The percentage of change in quantity demanded is exactly equal to the percentage of change in price, ignoring the direction of the change (PE = 1); a change in price results in no change to total revenue

EXAMPLE Assume that in a given year U.S. gasoline consumption was 2.563 million gallons per day at an average price of \$1.53 per gallon. Several years later, the average price of gasoline rose to \$2.27 per gallon, and consumption was 3.288 million barrels per day. We can calculate the price elasticity (PE) of gasoline for this period as follows:

$$\frac{\text{\% Change in Quantity Demanded}}{\text{\% Change in Price}} = \frac{\left(\frac{3.288 - 2.563}{2.563}\right)}{\left(\frac{2.27 - 1.53}{1.53}\right)} = \frac{28.29\%}{48.37\%} = .585$$

Because PE < 1, we conclude that the demand for this period's gasoline is inelastic.

Price elasticity can also have an effect on a company's total revenues. When the demand for a good is price inelastic, a price decrease reduces total revenues. When the demand is price elastic, a price decrease increases total revenue. In the case of unit-elastic demand, a price decrease results in no change in total revenue.

EXAMPLE Consider a gas company that derives its revenues from the price of gasoline (an inelastic good). The company typically sells 1 million gallons per day at \$5.50 per gallon. This translates into sales of \$5.5 million per day. If the price of gasoline increases to \$6 per gallon, revenues increase to \$6 million per day, giving the company an extra \$500,000 of revenue.

With inelastic goods, the demand curve becomes vertical because the price has no effect on the quantity demanded. However, the curve may shift right or left depending on various factors.

EXAMPLE To explain unit-elastic demand and its effects on company revenues, consider a grocer selling apples for \$1 per pound. He typically sells 500 pounds a week for a gross revenue of \$500. One week, he decided to raise the price of apples to \$2 per pound and only ended up selling 250 pounds and maintaining a gross revenue of \$500. Because the change in price had no effect on total revenue, this good is said to be perfectly unit-elastic.

Equilibrium

Equilibrium
The state of the market where quantity demanded equals quantity supplied

In a competitive market, prices are free to adjust to changes in supply and consumer demand. When the price of a good is such that the quantity supplied equals the quantity demanded, the market for that good is said to be in **equilibrium**. The conditions of a competitive market encourage price movement toward equilibrium. For example, if more apples are grown than are demanded, the price for apples will fall, which will encourage consumers to buy. Similarly, if consumers are demanding more bananas than producers are supplying, the price of bananas will rise, discouraging consumers from buying. These adjustments continue until the market prices of apples and bananas achieve equal quantities of supply and demand—equilibrium.

EXHIBIT 2.9 Equilibrium

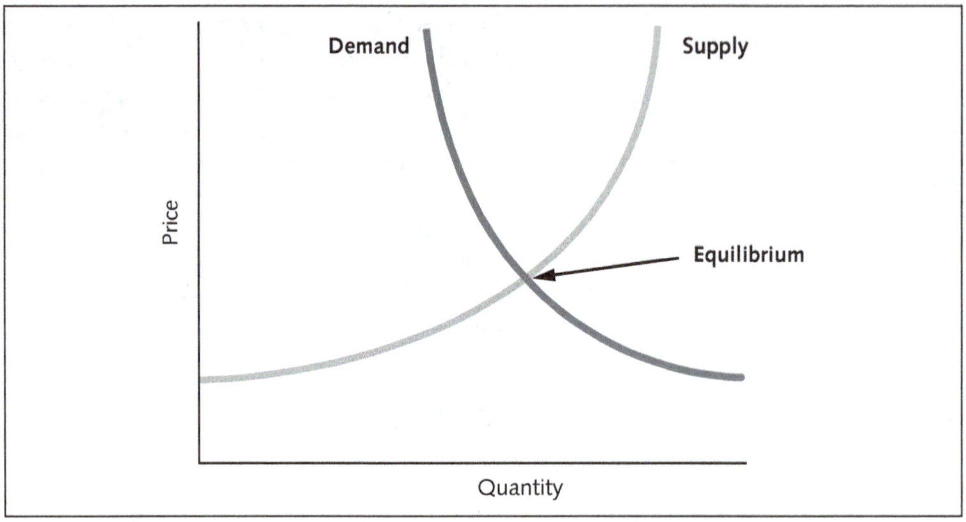

Business Cycles

Business cycles
Swings in total national output, income, and employment marked by widespread expansion or contraction in many sectors of the economy

Business cycles are swings in total national output, income, and employment marked by widespread expansion or contraction in many sectors of the economy. These cycles generally occur because of shifts in aggregate demand. The financial planner should be familiar with the impact of business cycles on the economy, as different investments will not perform the same during various phases of a business cycle. For example, cyclical industries such as the automobile or housing industry generally perform well during an economic expansion and poorly during a contraction.

The business cycle (as depicted in Exhibit 2.10) consists of two general phases, expansion and contraction, and two points, peak and trough. Each phase of the business cycle passes into the next phase and is characterized by different economic conditions.

The expansion phase ends and moves into the contraction phase at the upper turning point, or peak. Similarly, the contraction phase gives way to expansion at the lower turning point, or trough. The emphasis here is not so much on high or low business activity as on the dynamic aspects of the rise and fall of business activity.

EXHIBIT 2.10 A Hypothetical Business Cycle

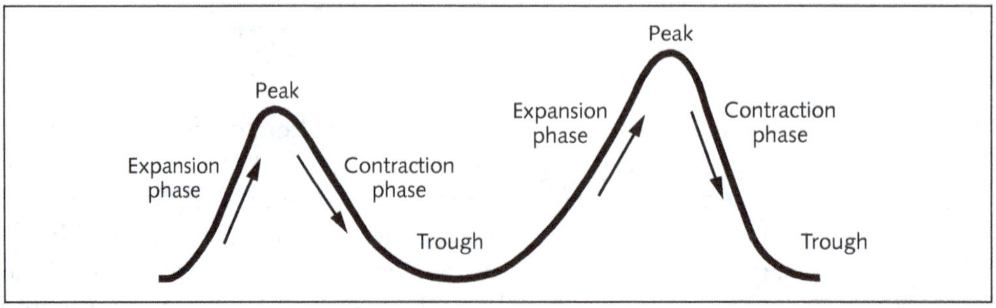

Note: The actual business cycle is not as symmetrical as drawn here. The pattern is more irregular and unpredictable. See Exhibit 2.12 for an illustration of the changes in the actual business cycle.

Expansion phase
One of the two general business cycle phases characterized by a rise in business sales, growth of the gross domestic product, and a decline in unemployment

Peak
The point in the business cycle that appears at the end of the expansion phase when most businesses are operating at full capacity and gross domestic product is increasing rapidly

Contraction phase
One of the two general business cycle phases characterized by a fall in business sales, decreased growth of the gross domestic product, and increased unemployment

Trough
The point in the business cycle that appears at the end of the contraction phase when most businesses are operating at their lowest capacity levels and the gross domestic product is at its lowest

Recession
A decline in real gross domestic product for two or more successive quarters

Depression
A persistent recession that brings a severe decline in economic activity

Business Cycle Components and Their Effect on the Economy

The **expansion phase** leads to the peak. During the expansion phase, business sales rise, gross domestic product (GDP)—which is the value of all goods and services produced in the United States—grows, and unemployment declines.

The **peak** appears at the end of the expansion phase when most businesses are operating at full capacity and GDP is increasing rapidly. The peak is the point at which GDP is at its highest and exceeds the long-run average GDP. Usually employment levels also peak at this point. (See Exhibit 2.11 for a depiction of the relationship between long-run GDP and the business cycle.)

The **contraction phase** leads to the trough. During the contraction phase, business sales fall, GDP growth falls, and unemployment increases.

The **trough** occurs at the end of the contraction phase where businesses are generally operating at their lowest capacity. The trough point is characterized by the lowest GDP growth. Unemployment is rapidly increasing and finally peaks when sales fall rapidly.

Recession is a decline in real GDP for two or more successive quarters characterized by the following:

- Declining consumer purchases
- Expanding business inventories
- Decreasing capital investment
- Decreasing demand for labor
- High unemployment
- Falling commodity prices
- Decreasing business profits
- Falling interest rates due to reduced demand for money

Depression is a persistent recession that brings a severe decline in economic activity.

EXHIBIT 2.11 The Business Cycle and GDP

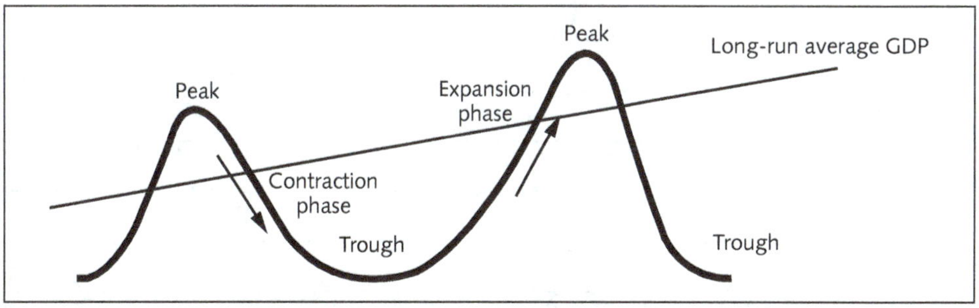

While there are many economic variables that fluctuate during the business cycle, certain economic variables always show greater fluctuation than others. **Capital formation** rises and falls significantly with expansion and contraction, usually leading the trend. **Durable goods**, also a trend leader, are subject to highly erratic patterns of demand. It is the economy's durable, or capital, goods sector that by far shows the greatest cyclical fluctuation. There is good reason to believe that the movement of durable goods represents key causes in the direction of expansion or contraction. **Consumption movements**, which lag behind trends, seem to be the effect of the business cycle phase rather than the cause.

Capital formation
Production of buildings, machinery, tools, and other equipment that will help economic participants produce in the future

Durable goods
Products that are not consumed or quickly disposed of and can be used for several years, such as automobiles, furniture, and computers

Consumption movements
Economic variables that fluctuate during the business cycle; describe changes in consumer purchases

Business Cycle Theories

Two opposing types of theories attempt to explain the fluctuations in the business cycle: external theories and internal theories. External theories find the root of the business cycle in the fluctuations of something outside the economic system, such as wars, revolutions, political events, rates of population growth and migration, discoveries of new resources, scientific and technological discoveries, and innovation. Internal theories look for mechanisms within the economic system that give rise to self-generating business cycles. Thus, every expansion breeds recession and contraction. Every contraction, in turn, breeds revival and expansion in a quasi-regular, repeating, never-ending chain. Each peak and valley, however, is higher than the last and leads to growth in the economy over the long term despite the business cycle.

Actual Business Cycle

The actual business cycle for the United States as depicted below has averaged growth of approximately 3% per year. Growth, as measured by gross domestic product (GDP), will exceed the average in some years, whereas in other years growth will be less than the average. Exhibit 2.12 illustrates the actual change in GDP as a percentage. Note that the graph appears to move horizontally across the page. However, because all years except four have positive growth, the amount of business done has actually increased virtually every year since 1932. At a 3% average growth rate, American business was 11.3 times larger in 2014 than in 1932.

EXHIBIT 2.12 Annual Change in Gross Domestic Product 1932–2019

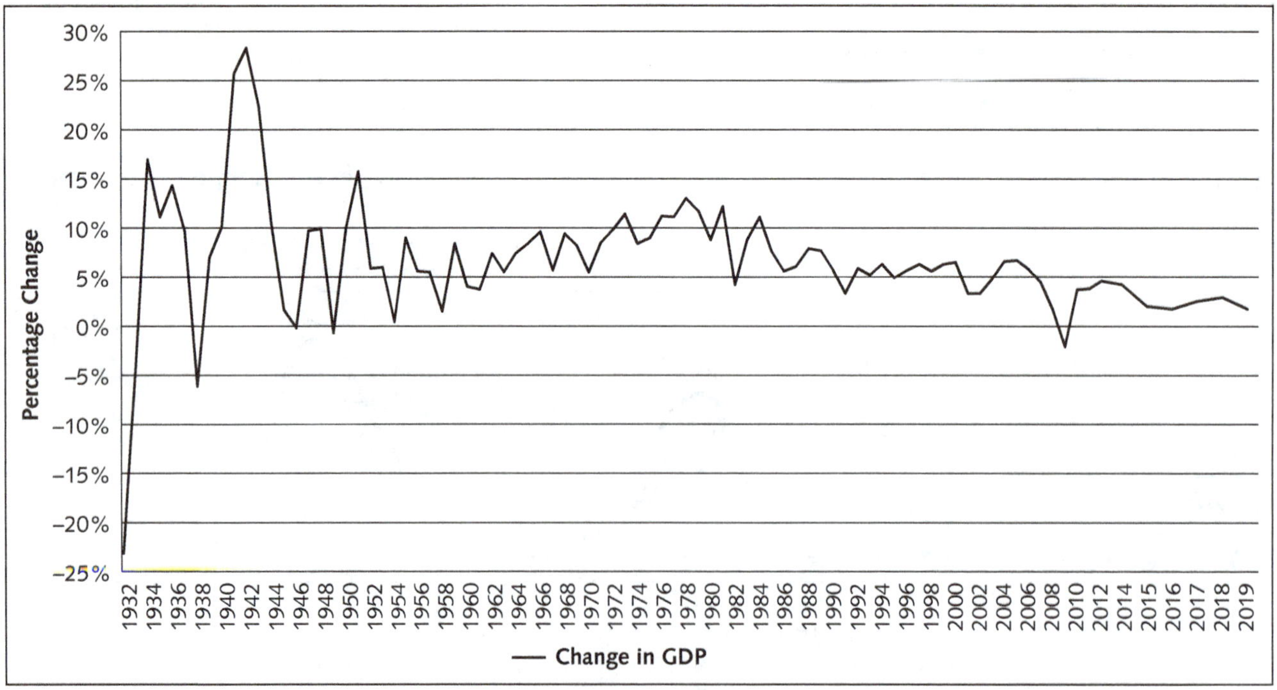

Source: U.S. Department of Commerce Bureau of Economic Analysis, www.bea.gov/national/index.htm (accessed May 20, 2020).

Inflation

Inflation
An increase in the price level of goods and services

Deflation
The opposite of inflation; it occurs when the general level of prices is falling

Disinflation
A decline in the rate of inflation

Moderate inflation
Inflation characterized by slowly rising prices

Galloping inflation
Inflation that occurs when money loses its value very quickly, and real interest rates can be negative 50% or 100% per year

Inflation is another important element affecting the economic environment. Inflation is an increase in the price of goods and services. Inflation increases the cost of buying a home, durable goods, and consumption goods. For retirees on fixed incomes, substantial increases in inflation can dramatically affect their financial plan. Likewise, for wage earners, the rate of inflation may sometimes be greater than the individual's wage increases, resulting in a loss of purchasing power. Professional financial planners need to understand how the rate of inflation is calculated, how it affects the economy, and how it is measured.

The opposite of inflation is **deflation**, which occurs when the general level of prices is falling. **Disinflation** is the term used to denote a decline in the rate of inflation. **Moderate inflation** is characterized by slowly rising prices. **Galloping inflation** occurs when money loses its value very quickly, and real interest rates can be negative 50% or 100% per year. During a period of galloping inflation, people hold only the absolute minimum of cash needed for daily transactions. Financial markets are in turmoil or disappear, and funds are generally allocated by rationing rather than by interest rates. People hoard goods, buy houses, and never lend money at the low nominal interest rate. Remember, though, that during periods of inflation, all prices and wages do not increase at the same rate.

Calculating Inflation

Inflation denotes a rise in the general level of prices. The rate of inflation is the rate of change in the general price level and is calculated as follows:

Inflation rate (year *t*):

$$\frac{\text{Price level (year } t) - \text{Price level (year } t-1)}{\text{Price level (year } t-1)} \times 100$$

EXAMPLE Last year Abby paid $30,000 for her college tuition. This year Abby will pay $31,500 for tuition, with the increase solely attributable to inflation. Calculate the inflation rate for Abby's education expense.

Answer: The inflation rate attributable to Abby's increase in tuition is 5%, calculated as follows.

$$\frac{\$31{,}500 - \$30{,}000}{\$30{,}000} \times 100 = 5\%$$

Effects of Inflation

Unexpected inflation causes a redistribution of income and wealth among different classes of people in our economy. Changes are created in the relative prices and outputs of different goods or sometimes in output and employment for the economy as a whole. The major redistributive impact of inflation occurs through its effect on the real value of people's wealth. In general, unanticipated inflation redistributes wealth from creditors to debtors. Said another way, unanticipated or unforeseen inflation helps those who have previously borrowed money and hurts those who have loaned money. An unanticipated decline in inflation has the opposite effect. If, however, inflation is anticipated, prices adjust as expected and there is little redistribution of wealth.

Inflation affects the real economy in two specific areas: total output and economic efficiency. The relationship between prices and output is not necessarily direct. Inflation may be associated with a higher or a lower level of output and employment. Generally, the higher the inflation rate, the greater the changes in relative prices of goods. Distortions occur when price changes accelerate relative to changes in costs and demand.

Real interest rate adjustment
The rate of interest expressed in dollars of constant value (adjusted for inflation) and equal to the nominal interest rate, less the rate of inflation

If inflation persists for a long period, markets begin to adapt, and an allowance for inflation is built into the market interest rate. This is known as the **real interest rate adjustment**. This phenomenon is consistent with anticipated price increases.

Measures of Inflation

Price index
A weighted average of the prices of numerous goods and services (e.g., the Consumer Price Index, the gross domestic product deflator, the gross national product deflator, and the Producer Price Index)

A **price index** is a weighted average of the prices of numerous goods and services. The best known price indexes are the Consumer Price Index (CPI), the gross domestic product (GDP) deflator, the gross national product (GNP) deflator, and the Producer Price Index (PPI).

Consumer Price Index (CPI)
A price index that measures the cost of a market basket of consumer goods and services purchased for day-to-day living

The **Consumer Price Index (CPI)** measures the cost of a market basket of consumer goods and services, including prices of food, clothing, housing, property taxes, fuels, transportation, medical care, college tuition, and other commodities purchased for day-to-day living. The CPI is constructed by weighting each price according to the economic importance of the commodity in question. Each item is assigned a fixed weight proportional to its relative importance in consumer expenditure budgets.

Gross domestic product (GDP)
The value of all goods and services produced in the country; GDP is the broadest measure of the general state of the economy

The **gross domestic product (GDP)** is the market value of final goods and services produced within a country over a specific period, usually a year. The GDP deflator is the ratio of nominal GDP to real GDP and gives an overall measure of prices in the economy. Real GDP only measures increases or decreases in production output. Nominal GDP is affected by changes in prices as well as increases and decreases in production. The GDP deflator is a broader price index than the CPI. In addition to consumer goods, the GDP deflator includes prices for capital goods and other goods and services purchased by businesses and government.

Exhibit 2.13 presents data for both the CPI and GDP deflator. Even though the two indexes are based on different market baskets of goods with different base years, the two measures of the annual rate of inflation are quite similar. The differences between these two measures of inflation have been small, usually only a few tenths of a percentage point per year. The closeness of the two rates is not a surprise because consumer spending makes up about two-thirds of GDP.

EXHIBIT 2.13 Consumer Price Index and GDP Deflator Percentage Change 1986–2019

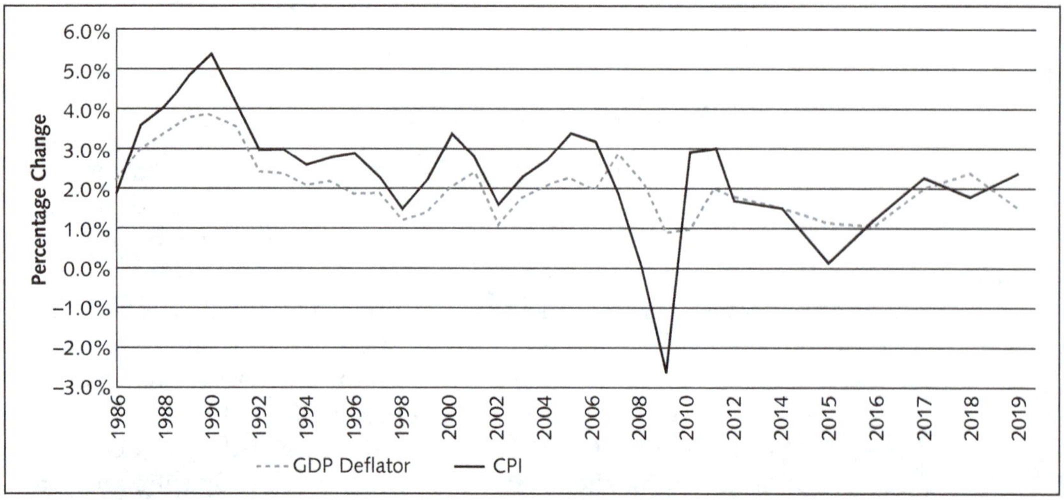

Sources: U.S. Department of Labor and http://data.worldbank.org/indicator/NY.GDP.DEFL.KD.ZG (accessed May 20, 2020).

Price indexes are not problem-free. The cost of living, as estimated by the CPI, is considered overestimated in the situation where consumers substitute relatively inexpensive goods for relatively expensive goods. The CPI does not accurately capture changes in the quality of goods. Although the CPI is modified from time to time, the CPI is not corrected for quality improvements in goods and services.

The GNP deflator is the ratio of nominal gross national product to real gross national product. The difference between gross domestic product and gross national product is subtle. GDP measures goods and services produced within the country, regardless of the citizenship of the owners. For example, automobiles produced at a Honda plant in Ohio would be included in the United States' GDP. GNP, on the other hand, measures goods and services produced by citizens of the country regardless of where they are produced. For example, wages paid to an American working for Honda in Tokyo would be included in GNP but not in GDP.

Producer Price Index (PPI)
A group of indexes that measures the average change in the selling prices received by domestic producers of goods and services over time

The **Producer Price Index (PPI)** is the oldest continuous statistical series published by the Labor Department. It is a group of indexes that measures the average change in the selling prices received by domestic producers of goods and services over time. PPIs measure price change from the perspective of the seller, in contrast with the Consumer Price Index (CPI), which measures price change from the purchaser's perspective. Sellers' and purchasers' prices may differ due to sales and excise taxes, distribution costs, and government subsidies.

For professional planners, the CPI is a good proxy for overall consumer price changes. However, due to the general nature of the market basket of goods described previously, it is likely that many clients' inflation experience will be different from the general CPI. Consider the fact that many people have fixed-rate mortgages rather than rent; thus the cost of the housing payment (principal and interest) associated with the mortgage payment is unaffected by inflation. The property taxes and insurance costs on the home, however, are subject to inflation, as are any maintenance or repair costs. Also consider that some households will need to factor in the effect of inflation on their savings plans for their children's education, whereas other households are relatively unaffected by the costs of higher education. The planner with clients on a fixed income can review a line-item budget to determine which costs are subject to inflation and adjust their overall financial plan accordingly. Having seen some of the more dominant ways individuals are affected by inflation, realize that all individuals are affected in a consequential way by inflation because they pay for groceries, clothing, automobiles, fuel, and medical care.

Monetary and Fiscal Policy

Monetary policy and fiscal policy exert far-reaching influence on the economic environment. Competent financial planners must identify changes in monetary and fiscal policy that will be the most beneficial and most detrimental to their client's financial goals and objectives. Once identified, the planner should forecast the likelihood of the important policy changes and adjust the financial plan accordingly.

Federal Reserve (Fed)
The banking and financial system developed under the Federal Reserve Act of 1913; it makes the basic policy decisions that regulate the country's money and banking systems

Monetary Policy

The **Federal Reserve (Fed)** is charged with three primary responsibilities:

1. To maintain sustainable long-term economic growth
2. To maintain price levels that are supported by that economic growth
3. To maintain full employment

The Fed goes about its mission primarily using the tools of monetary policy. The Fed controls the money supply, which enables it to significantly impact short-term interest rates. The Fed will follow a loose, or easy, monetary policy when it wants to increase the money supply and thus expand the level of income and employment. In times of inflation and when it wants to constrict the money supply, the Fed will follow a tight monetary policy.

Reserve requirement *The percentage of deposit liabilities that must be held in reserve by a member bank of the Federal Reserve; as the reserve requirement is increased, less money is available to be loaned, resulting in a restriction of the money supply*

Easy monetary policy When the Fed wants to stimulate the money supply, it lowers the cost of short-term loans to commercial banks. The money supply increases, resulting in the circulation of more money. This leads to more funds available for banks to lend and, ultimately, to a decline in short-term interest rates.

Tight monetary policy When the Fed wants to tighten the money supply, it raises the cost of short-term borrowing for commercial banks. The money supply is restricted, resulting in less money available for banks to lend. This leads to an increase in short-term interest rates.

The Fed has several methods for controlling the money supply, including adjusting the reserve requirements, adjusting the Federal Reserve discount rates, and using open market operations.

The **reserve requirement** for a member bank of the Federal Reserve is the percentage of deposit liabilities that must be held in reserve. As this requirement is increased, less money is available to be loaned to customers, resulting in a restriction of the money supply. Conversely, as reserve requirements are decreased, more money is made available for loans.

Federal Reserve discount rate *The rate at which Federal Reserve member banks can borrow funds to meet reserve requirements; the Fed will lower the discount rate when it wants to increase the money supply*

The **Federal Reserve discount rate** is the rate at which member banks can borrow funds from the Federal Reserve to meet reserve requirements. When the Fed raises the discount rate, it increases short-term borrowing costs and discourages member banks from borrowing funds. This causes the money supply to contract. The Fed will lower the discount rate when it wants to increase the money supply. Banks are able to borrow funds at lower rates and lend more money, which increases the money supply.

Note that the Federal Reserve discount rate is the borrowing rate from the Federal Reserve, and differs from the federal funds rate, which is the overnight lending rate between member banks.

Open market operations *The process by which the Federal Reserve purchases and sells government securities in the open market*

Open market operations is the process by which the Federal Reserve purchases and sells government securities in the open market. The Fed buys government securities to cause more money to circulate, resulting in lower interest rates, increased lending, and growth of the money supply. The Fed sells government securities to restrict the money supply. As investors purchase government securities, more money leaves circulation, which increases interest rates and decreases lending.

Fiscal Policy

Fiscal policy *Taxation, expenditures, and debt management of the federal government*

Taxation, expenditures, and debt management of the federal government is called **fiscal policy**. Economic growth, price stability, and full employment are other goals that may be pursued by changes in fiscal policy.

Changes in taxation affect corporate earnings, disposable earnings, and the overall economy. As tax rates increase, corporations' after-tax income declines, which reduces their ability to pay dividends. This may cause the price for equities to decrease. Tax rate increases also reduce an individual's disposable income and limit the amount of money entering the economy. The demand for tax-free investments is also influenced by changes in taxation levels. As increases in proportional tax rates occur, the attractiveness of tax-free instruments also increases, reducing yields.

Deficit spending *Occurs when governmental expenditures exceed the government's tax collections*

Deficit spending occurs when governmental expenditures exceed tax collections. By selling debt securities to the public to finance deficits, Treasury securities compete with other issuers of debt securities. This demand drives the value of debt down because of the increased supply of debt, causing the yields on debt instruments to rise to meet competition.

Discount rate
Interest rate charged by the Federal Reserve on a loan made to a member bank

Nominal interest rate
Stated interest rate without considering the effect of inflation

Real interest rate
Nominal interest rate considering the effect of inflation

The Nature of Interest Rates

The economic environment is greatly influenced by interest rates. Decreases in interest rates are often followed by periods of economic expansion, whereas increases are generally followed by economic contractions. Investment returns and purchasing power are just two of the areas that are affected by the rise and fall of interest rates. Simply stated, the interest rate is the price of money. The **discount rate** is the interest rate charged by the Fed on a loan that it makes to a member bank. The **nominal interest rate** is the stated interest rate without considering the effect of inflation. The return on investments in terms of real goods and services is a real interest rate measure. The return in terms of dollars is an absolute measure. The real interest rate measures the quantity of goods we receive tomorrow for goods forgone today. The **real interest rate** is obtained by correcting nominal or dollar interest rates for the rate of inflation.

Expansion and Recession

As discussed earlier, the economy is in a constant state of flux. Some economic factors tend to expand the economy, and others tend to contract the economy. In the following section, the factors that contribute to the economy's rise and fall are discussed.

Periods of economic expansion are characterized by high employment, high resource demand, and output in excess of the historical gross domestic product average of 3%. As the economy expands, real wages rise, as do real interest rates. Higher interest rates decrease capital expenditures, and higher resource costs increase overall costs and reduce aggregate demand, ultimately ending the expansionary period.

Periods of recession are characterized by high unemployment, low resource demand, falling real wages, and decreasing real interest rates. The economy eventually pulls itself out of recession as prices for money and resources fall.

Recall Exhibit 2.10 (the drawing of the business cycle) with its peaks and troughs. The peaks are simply the top of the expansion, and the troughs, the bottom of the recession. Each is characterized by high and low real interest rates and changes in nonfarm hourly payroll. Real interest rates are at their highest at the peak and at their lowest at the trough. The rate of change in nonfarm hourly labor costs is at its highest at peaks and at its lowest in troughs.

A reasonable question to ask at this point is whether the economy is self-correcting. It appears to be so, although slowly. This slowness is evidenced by a recession's prolonged high unemployment and below-capacity utilization. As a result of the belief that the economy is too slow to self-correct, there is widespread support for monetary and fiscal policy stimulation during periods of recession and, alternatively, for monetary and fiscal restriction during periods of excessive economic expansion. Thus, monetary and fiscal policy tools are used to guide the economy to stability and long-run prosperity. The degree of policy discretion remains controversial. Some economists believe in less discretion and more constant growth models, including the management of money supply, inflation, unemployment, and budget deficits, while others believe in greater discretion and aggressive monetary and fiscal management.

Index of leading economic indicators
A composite index of 10 variables that has had a reasonable track record in predicting recessions; it has accurately predicted every recession since 1950 but has also predicted five that did not happen

Forecasting the Economy—Index of Leading Economic Indicators

Can anyone successfully predict the future economy? Some say that monitoring the gross domestic product is useful in forecasting the economy. Others look to the **index of leading economic indicators**. Monitoring both GDP and the index may be the best approach to forecasting the economy.

GDP is the value of all goods and services produced in the country. It is the broadest measure of the general state of the economy. The historical growth rate is approximately 3%. Growth of GDP less than 2% is considered low and signals a possible recession. Growth in excess of 4% is robust and suggests the possibility of expansion. Monitoring GDP growth is useful in forecasting the peaks and troughs in the economy.

Another indication of future economic activity of which financial planners should be keenly aware is the index of leading economic indicators. This index is a composite index of 10 variables. It has had a reasonable track record in predicting recessions and has accurately predicted every recession since 1950 but has also predicted five that did not happen. When the index declines for three months in a row, it signals a slowdown in economic growth. The index only predicts the direction of economic activity and not the magnitude. The 10 components listed below make up the index.

1. Length of average work week in hours, manufacturing
2. Initial weekly claims for unemployment
3. New orders placed with manufacturers for consumer goods
4. Percentage of companies receiving slower deliveries from supplier
5. Contracts and orders for new plant and equipment
6. Permits for new housing starts
7. Interest rate spread, 10-year Treasury bond less federal funds rate
8. S&P 500 Index
9. Money supply (M2)
10. Index of consumer expectations

Lagging economic indicators
Economic statistics that fall or rise 3–12 months after the general economy

In addition to leading economic indicators, there are **lagging economic indicators**. These economic statistics fall or rise 3 to 12 months after the general economy. The lagging index gives a good picture of where the economy has been. The following are seven components of the lagging index for the United States:

1. Average duration of unemployment
2. Inventories to sales ratio, manufacturing and trade
3. Labor cost per unit of output, manufacturing
4. Average prime rate
5. Commercial and industrial loans
6. Consumer installment credit to personal income ratio
7. Consumer price index for services

Although the word *recession* for some investors may have a less-than-positive connotation in periods of declining economic growth, interest rates generally fall, making the purchases of fixed instruments prior to the decline in interest rates an attractive investment opportunity. Likewise, generally the best time to buy stocks and hold them through economic recovery may be when the economy is at its worst.

How fast should the economy be growing? At first, many people might think, "The faster the better." A quickly growing economy could lead to more business, more wealth, and more jobs. Everyone would win. However, over time, high growth rates have been found to be unsustainable because they can lead to higher inflation. This brings higher interest rates to fight inflation. Thus, unsustainable booms have been followed by harmful busts. One way to measure how fast an economy can grow in the medium term without causing inflation is the "potential GDP." When thinking about an economy, the sustainable rate of growth would most essentially be a combination of productivity growth plus labor force growth. Productivity is the GDP divided by the number of workers each year. For example, if labor productivity grows by 1% a year and the labor force grows by 2% a year, then the "potential GDP" for that economy would be 3%. If the economy was actually growing by 4%, then its growth would be unsustainable over the long term. Excess growth can eventually lead to inflation and higher interest rates to fight that inflation. However, when the actual GDP growth rate is above the potential GDP growth rate, the current unemployment should improve. On the other hand, if this economy was only growing at 1% (2% below potential GDP), inflation and interest rates will be low, but unemployment will be high.

Potential GDP is a useful concept for evaluating the growth rates of different countries. A country with a rapidly rising labor force should grow faster than a country with a slower growing labor force. Also, productivity enhancements help an economy grow. Potential GDP can also inform evaluations of how fast an economy should be growing now compared to former times. For example, China's labor force grew strongly during the 1990–2000s. As the labor force growth slows, either productivity must leap ahead or the economy will not be able to sustain the rapid growth rates of former years. Finally, comparing actual GDP growth to potential GDP growth can diagnosis if an economy is underperforming or is unsustainably high. That should be the starting point for any fiscal or momentary policy decisions. Finally, the best measure of potential GDP is real potential GDP. This is potential GDP with an adjustment to remove inflation.

IMPORTANCE OF THE LEGAL ENVIRONMENT

The legal environment is another component of the external environment that may have far-reaching influence on risk exposure and the accomplishment of financial goals. The rules of property ownership, consumer rights and protections, worker rights and protections, investor rights and protections, and the rules regarding formation of a business are established within this environment. With a high level of competence and knowledge of the legal environment, the personal financial planner can guide clients toward their financial goals while avoiding legal risks and protecting the clients' rights.

Torts

Tort
A private wrong; an infringement on the rights of another

A **tort** (private wrong) is an infringement on the rights of another. The wrongdoer, also known as a tortfeasor, creates a right in the damaged party to bring a civil action. Intentional torts—battery (harmful touching), assault (threat causing apprehension), libel (written falsehood), slander (oral falsehood), false imprisonment (unlawfully holding against will), trespass to land, invasion of privacy, and intentional infliction of emotional

Unintentional tort
Failure to act in a reasonably prudent manner, thereby causing harm to another

distress—are not covered by liability insurance. An **unintentional tort** results from negligence and is defined as the failure to act in a reasonably prudent manner, thereby causing harm to another. Elements of unintentional torts include duty, breach of duty, causation, and actual loss. When determining whether negligence is present, ask, "Did the person exercise the proper degree of care to carry out his duty, and if not, was that the cause of the actual loss suffered by the other party?" If so, the person performing the act may be liable for negligence.

Negligence

Negligence
The failure to act in a way that a reasonably prudent person would have acted under similar circumstances

Negligence is defined as the failure to act in a way that a reasonably prudent person would have acted under similar circumstances. Types of liability created from negligent behavior include the following:

- *Strict (absolute) liability*—Liability without regard to negligence or fault. It applies to damage resulting from some extraordinarily dangerous activity or other statutorily defined activity (e.g., product liability, hazardous materials, blasting operations). Negligence does not have to be proved; however, defenses may be allowed to refute or lessen liability. Workers are indemnified for employment-connected injuries regardless of who was at fault (e.g., workers' compensation). In these cases, negligence does not have to be proved on the part of the employer, nor are defenses permitted by the employer to refute or lessen liability.
- *Negligence per se*—The act itself constitutes negligence, thereby relieving the burden to prove negligence (e.g., drunk driving).

Res ipsa loquitur
"The act speaks for itself"; negligence can be assumed from the character of the outcome without evidence of wrongdoing on the part of the tortfeasor

Burden of proof is initially borne by the injured party. Standard of proof in most civil cases is the preponderance of the evidence (greater than 50%). Other concepts to consider include ***res ipsa loquitur*** ("the act speaks for itself"). *Res ipsa loquitur* is a doctrine of the law of negligence under which negligence can be assumed from the character of the outcome without evidence of wrongdoing on the part of the tortfeasor. For example, if an airplane crashes due to engine failure and, prior to takeoff, a maintenance company checked the engine, the maintenance company may be found negligent based on the concept of *res ipsa loquitor* even though there is not enough physical evidence to determine how or why the engine failed.

Damages

A tort can result in two forms of injury: bodily injury and property damage. Bodily injury may lead to medical expense, loss of income, pain and suffering, and mental anguish. The damages for bodily injury can be:

- special damages to compensate for measurable losses;
- general damages to compensate for intangible losses (pain and suffering); or
- punitive damages—amounts assessed against the negligent party as punishment.

Property damage is usually measured by the actual monetary loss.

Collateral source rule
Damages assessed against a negligent party should not be reduced simply because the injured party has other sources of recovery available

The **collateral source rule** holds that damages assessed against a negligent party should not be reduced simply because the injured party has other sources of recovery available such as insurance or employee benefits (health or disability insurance).

Vicarious Liability

Under the doctrine of **vicarious liability**, parents and guardians may be liable for the acts of minors and mentally incompetent people in their care. Likewise, employers may be vicariously liable for the acts of their employees.

Vicarious liability
One person may become legally liable for the torts of another (e.g., parent/child, employer/employee acting in the scope of employment)

Defenses to Negligence

There are various defenses available to alleged negligent parties that can relieve them of legal liability in spite of negligent behavior.

Assumption of the risk—The injured party fully understood and recognized the dangers that were involved in an activity and voluntarily chose to proceed. This defense is not available in all states.

Negligence on the part of the injured party—This can be either contributory negligence, where there is evidence that the injured party did not look out for his own safety, or comparative negligence, where the amount of damage is adjusted to reflect the injured party's proportion of contribution to the cause of the injury (same with multiple defendants). Contributory negligence theories usually cause the entire action to fail, thus effecting a harsh result. Many states allow recovery for that portion of damage not caused by the injured party (comparative negligence). The "last clear chance" rule may apply. This rule states that a claimant who is endangered by his own negligence may recover if the defendant had a last clear chance to avoid the accident and failed to do so.

Property Ownership

Property ownership rules are generally determined by individual states and will be discussed in Chapter 17: Introduction to Estate Planning.

Consumer Protection

Consumer protection laws are passed at both the state and federal levels. Federal laws preempt state laws where the state law provides less protection than the federal law. However, states do have the right to grant their citizens additional protection in excess of federal laws.

Federal Trade Commission (FTC)
The federal organization created in 1914 to keep competition free and fair and to protect U.S. consumers

Bait-and-switch promotion
Deceptive sales practice in which a business advertises a low price for an item in order to engage customers and then advise them that the advertised item is no longer available or is of substandard quality, attempting to entice the customers to purchase a more expensive product

Consumer protection laws accomplish their goals by affecting contractual obligations. Without the right to enforce contracts, there would certainly be less private enterprise. Thus, certain consumer protection laws allow for the rescission of illegal contracts and provide for monetary damages or injunctive relief for the injured party.

Federal consumer protection began with the creation of the **Federal Trade Commission (FTC)** in 1914. Its charge was to keep competition free and fair and to protect consumers. The FTC promotes competition through the enforcement of antitrust laws. It also ensures consumer protection by trade practice regulation prohibiting "unfair or deceptive acts or practices in commerce."

The FTC also prohibits the unfair and deceptive advertising of prices and practices, such as **bait-and-switch promotions**. Credit and packaging also fall under FTC regulation. Federal credit regulations are a response to the magnitude of credit transactions. The laws include the regulation of credit extension and discrimination and the collection and dissemination of credit report information. Laws also regulate consumer warranties and debt collection practices. What follows is a brief description of several FTC laws that have a direct effect on consumers.

EXHIBIT 2.14 The FTC and Federal Consumer Protection Laws

Law	Purpose
Fair Packaging and Labeling Act	Prohibit deceptive labeling and require disclosure
Equal Credit Opportunity Act	Prohibit discrimination in granting credit
Fair Credit Reporting Act	Regulate the consumer credit reporting industry
Fair Credit Billing Act	Regulate consumer credit billing practices
Truth in Lending Act	Require disclosure of terms
Magnuson-Moss Warranty Act	Regulate consumer product warranty
Fair Debt Collection Act	Prevent abusive or deceptive debt collection practices
Federal bankruptcy laws	Adjust consumer debt and allow for a fresh start
Consumer protection at state level	Protect against unfair business practices
Antitrust legislation	Prevent monopolistic price practices
Federal Trade Commission Act	Prohibit unfair and deceptive acts of commerce
Fair Debt Collection Practices Act	Prohibit bill collectors from using threatening or obscene language
Fair and Accurate Credit Transaction Act	Require nationwide consumer reporting agencies to provide free copies of credit reports annually
Credit Card Accountability Responsibility and Disclosure Act	Prohibit unfair practices designed to help consumers understand their credit transactions

The Equal Credit Opportunity Act of 1975 was designed to prohibit discrimination when extending credit to consumers. The law prohibits those to whom it applies from discouraging a consumer from seeking credit on the basis of sex, race, religion, marital status, national origin, or because of the receipt of welfare payments.

The Fair Credit Reporting Act applies to anyone preparing or using a credit report in connection with extending credit, selling insurance, or hiring or terminating an employee. The purpose of the law is to prevent unjust injury to an individual because of inaccurate or arbitrary information in a credit report. It is also designed to prevent undue invasion of privacy in the collection and dissemination of a person's credit record or information. The law gives consumers the right to require the reporting agency to reveal the information given in a credit report and the right to correct incorrect information or explain the consumer's version regarding disputed facts. The act is designed to cover credit-reporting agencies, not individual businesses. A consumer has 60 days to make a written request as to the nature of information received upon which an adverse credit decision was made. If challenged, the credit agency must investigate and respond to the consumer within 30 days of the challenge.

The Fair Credit Billing Act (FCBA) provides a mechanism for consumers to correct credit card billing errors. The consumer must provide a written billing complaint to a creditor within 60 days of receiving the alleged erroneous bill. The creditor must acknowledge the complaint within 30 days and explain the alleged error in writing or correct the error within two billing periods not to exceed 90 days.

The Consumer Credit Protection Act (also known as the Truth in Lending Act) imposes a duty on persons regularly extending credit to private individuals to inform those individuals fully as to the cost of the credit, including financial charges and the annual percentage rate of interest (APR). The purpose of the law is to promote informed decisions about the cost and use of credit.

The Magnuson-Moss Warranty Act covers express consumer warranties. The terms of the warranty must be simple and in readily understandable language, and if the price of the product is greater than $10, the warranty must be labeled as "full" or "limited."

The Fair Debt Collection Practices Act (FDCPA) applies to agencies and individuals whose primary business is the collection of debts for others. The law regulates collectors by prohibiting the collector from physically threatening the debtor or from using obscene language. The collector cannot falsely represent himself as an attorney or threaten the debtor with arrest or garnishment unless the collector can and intends to do so. The collector must disclose that he is a collector and must limit telephone calls to after 8:00 am and before 9:00 pm. The collector cannot telephone repeatedly with the intent to annoy the debtor. The collector cannot place collect calls to the debtor or use any unfair or unconscionable means to collect the debt.

The Fair and Accurate Credit Transaction Act (FACTA) passed in 2003 requires each of the nationwide consumer reporting companies—Equifax, Experian, and TransUnion—to provide a consumer with a free copy of his credit report, at his request, once every 12 months. Finally, the Credit Card Accountability Responsibility and Disclosure Act of 2009 (CARD Act) was enacted to establish fair practices and to enable consumers to better understand their credit transactions.

Bankruptcy
The financial condition when a debtor is determined by the court to be unable to pay creditors

Consumers and businesses receive further protection from creditors through the federal bankruptcy laws. **Bankruptcy** proceedings are held in a separate federal bankruptcy court with the filing of a voluntary (debtor) or involuntary (creditor-forced) petition. When a debtor is determined by the court to be unable to pay creditors, the court will provide or order relief in either liquidation (also known as Chapter 7) or adjusted debts (Chapter 13). Businesses and the self-employed may also enter bankruptcy under reorganization (Chapter 11). Debtor rehabilitation is the main objective of the bankruptcy proceeding allowing the consumer or business entity a fresh start.

With Chapter 7 bankruptcy, individuals are required to relinquish their assets to satisfy the claims of creditors. An individual is permitted, however, to retain certain assets because it is exempt under federal bankruptcy law or under the laws of the debtor's home state. These assets include interest in personal household goods; clothing, books, animals, and so forth. Once Chapter 7 bankruptcy is completed, most debts are discharged completely and the debtor is no longer responsible for their repayment; however, there are certain nondischargeable debts. These nondischargeable debts include back taxes (going back three years); those debts based upon fraud, embezzlement, misappropriation, or defalcation against the debtor acting in a fiduciary capacity; alimony; child support; intentional tort claims; property or money obtained by the debtor under fraudulent or false pretenses; student loans (unless paying the loan will impose an undue hardship on the debtor or the debtor's dependents); unscheduled claims (those not listed while filing for bankruptcy); claims from prior bankruptcy action in which the debtor was denied a discharge; consumer debts of more than $500 for luxury goods or services owed a single creditor within 40 days of relief; cash advances aggregating more than $1,000 as extensions of open-end consumer credit obtained by the debtor within 20 days of the order relief; and judgments or consent decrees awarded against the debtor for liability incurred as a result of the debtor's operation of a motor vehicle while intoxicated.

Chapter 13 bankruptcy tends to be more favorable for creditors because they receive at least some portion of what is owed to them. Chapter 7 bankruptcy does not guarantee that creditors will receive anything. To qualify for Chapter 13, the individual must be a wage earner or have regular income. Also, the debtor's noncontingent, liquidated, unsecured debts must amount to less than $465,275, and secured debts must amount to less than $1,362,800. Payments to creditors are reduced according to an established plan. The debtor is not required to relinquish assets in order to discharge debts.

In 2005, the Bankruptcy Abuse Prevention and Consumer Protection Act (BAPCPA) was passed. The act makes the abuse of the bankruptcy laws more difficult for those debtors who have the capacity to pay. It forces many consumers to file under Chapter 13 (adjustments of debts) rather than Chapter 7 (discharge of debts). The law also increases creditor protection for retirement accounts to those who declare bankruptcy. With BAPCPA 2005, all retirement plans (including non-ERISA plans, or IRAs) are protected in bankruptcy proceedings. Traditional and Roth IRAs are currently protected to a total value of $1,362,800 to $1,512,350, with adjustments for inflation made every three years (the next adjustments are in 2025 and 2028). SEP, SIMPLE, and rollover accounts are not subject to this exemption amount.

Certain states have moved to protect citizens from unfair and deceptive acts and practices by enacting legislation that closes gaps in federal law or provides additional protection for consumers under the state law. An example of such state consumer protection is state-ordered lemon laws dealing with defective new automobiles. This legislation creates public or private remedies for undesirable activities (illegal activities under the law). Public remedies include injunction, restitution, fines, and revocation of licenses. Private remedies include loss recovery, punitive damages, injunctions, rescission, and redhibition.

Antitrust legislation
Laws passed to protect consumers from monopolistic price practices and to protect investors by promoting fair competition

Monopoly
A single seller of a well-defined product with no valid substitutes

Oligopoly
Small number of rival seller firms; incentive to collude; high barrier to entry

The purpose of **antitrust legislation** is to protect consumers from monopolistic price practices and to protect investors by promoting fair competition. A **monopoly** is a single seller of a well-defined product with no valid substitute. Usually monopolies exist in industries with high barriers to entry, meaning it is cost prohibitive for new producers to enter the market. Because there is no competition, monopolies can control the market price of their products by adjusting output. Multiple sellers of goods can also engage in monopolistic practices when there is a small number of producers with a high incentive to collude. Such groups are called oligopolies. The Organization of Petroleum Exporting Countries (OPEC) is an example of an **oligopoly**. Some of the most important antitrust legislation includes the Sherman Act and the Clayton Act.

The Sherman Act states, "Every contract, combination...or conspiracy in restraint of trade is illegal." It also states, "Every person who shall monopolize or attempt to monopolize shall be guilty of a misdemeanor."

The Clayton Act contains several sections that regulate monopolization, pricing practices, and competition. The following four sections are of particular interest to financial planners.

Section 2 prohibits sellers from discriminating in price between similarly situated buyers of goods (not services) where the effect of such discrimination may be to substantially lessen competition or create a monopoly (Robinson-Patman Act). The objective is to prevent large firms from using predatory pricing practices to drive out small competitors. Section 3 states that persons engaged in commerce may not contract, lease, or sell where the effect of the contract, lease, or sale may be to substantially lessen competition or tend to create a monopoly. This legislation deals with tying contracts, exclusive dealing, and requirements contracts. Section 7 states that corporate mergers are illegal if they tend to create a monopoly in any line of business. Section 8 prohibits persons from being directors of competing corporations. Again, the legislation is intended to prohibit a lessening of competition.

The Federal Trade Commission Act protects consumers through trade practice regulation. The act prohibits unfair methods of competition in or affecting commerce or deceptive acts or practices in commerce. The Federal Trade Commission enforces the Clayton Act provisions on price discrimination, tying and exclusive contracts, mergers and acquisitions, and interlocking directories. The FTC Act is broader in scope than the Sherman Act or the Clayton Act and may be used to curtail activities that prevent fair competition but do not rise to the level regulated by the Sherman or Clayton Acts.

Worker Protection (Employer/Employee Relations)

Worker protection is another facet of the legal environment. There are two fundamental areas of worker protection: job safety and financial security. The reasons for these protections are the same as those for consumer protection, except that they apply specifically to employees.

The Occupational Safety and Health Act (OSHA) ensures safe and healthy working conditions for employees. The Secretary of Labor issues federal standards for safe employment environments to safeguard employees' health.

Workers' compensation acts are enacted both at the federal and state level and impose a form of strict liability on employers for accidental injuries occurring in the workplace. The legislation essentially removes the right of the injured employee to sue the employer for acts of ordinary negligence and replaces that right with the right to collect benefits—solely funded by employers—from an administrative agency. Workers' compensation protects against financial losses due to accidental injury, death, or disease resulting from employment. Generally, workers' compensation is the exclusive remedy to employment accidents. However, courts are now carving out exceptions to the exclusive remedy rule, recognizing that workers' compensation laws may not adequately compensate workers with the greatest injuries and for situations that exceed normal negligence on the employer's part.

Other federal programs that offer protection for workers are discussed in the following paragraphs.

Unemployment compensation is a federal and state financial security program that provides for temporary payments to workers who, through no fault of their own, become unemployed. Unemployment benefits are funded with a tax on employers based on an extensive rating system.

Social Security is a federal financial security program for providing some replacement income lost due to retirement, disability, and survivorship. Additionally, Social Security provides a death benefit and Medicare benefits, all of which are thoroughly discussed in Chapter 11.

The Employee Retirement Income Security Act (ERISA) was passed to protect the financial security of employees by protecting employee rights in qualified retirement plans. Chapter 16 discusses ERISA and qualified retirement plans.

The Consolidated Omnibus Budget Reconciliation Act of 1986 (COBRA) requires that employees and certain dependents of employees be allowed to continue their group health insurance coverage following a qualifying loss of coverage. Chapter 9 contains a discussion of COBRA.

Financial Institutions

Commercial Banks

Commercial banks are chartered under federal and state regulations. They offer numerous consumer services, such as checking, savings, loans, safe-deposit boxes, investment services, financial counseling, and automatic payment of bills. Depositors in a federally chartered commercial bank are protected against loss by the Federal Deposit Insurance Corporation (FDIC). The basic FDIC-insured amount of a depositor is $250,000. Deposits maintained in different categories of legal ownership are separately insured. A more detailed discussion of FDIC follows later in this section.

Savings and Loan Associations

The purpose of savings and loan associations (S&Ls), also known as thrift institutions, is to accept savings and provide home loans. They can also make installment loans for consumer products (e.g., automobiles and appliances). S&Ls may not provide demand deposits (such as checking accounts with a commercial bank); however, they may offer interest-bearing negotiable order of withdrawal (NOW) accounts, which are similar to demand deposit accounts. Accounts maintained at savings and loan associations are eligible for FDIC protection.

S&Ls are either mutual or corporate. The mutual savings and loans, which are more common, have the depositors as the actual owners of the association (shareowners).

Corporate savings and loans operate as corporations and issue common and preferred stock to denote ownership.

Mutual Savings Banks

A mutual savings bank (MSB) is similar to a savings and loan association (S&L). Historically, they accepted deposits in order to make housing loans, but they primarily compete for consumer loans and offer interest-bearing NOW accounts. Technically, the depositors of savings are the owners of the institution. MSBs are state chartered and have either FDIC insurance or a state-approved insurance. They are not, however, permitted in all states. Most are located in the Northeast.

Credit Unions

Credit unions are not-for-profit cooperative ventures. They are developed to pool the deposits of members. These funds are used to invest or lend to members/owners. Members are usually joined by a common bond such as work, union, or fraternal association, and regulations make it possible for people to remain members of a credit union after the common bond has been severed. Credit unions with federal charters have their accounts insured up to $250,000 through the National Credit Union Share Insurance Fund (NCUSIF), administered by the National Credit Union Administration (NCUA), that provides the same safety as deposits insured by the FDIC. Credit unions accept deposits and make loans for consumer products. They also make home loans. Employment-related credit unions typically use payroll deductions for deposits and loan repayments, often offer free term life insurance up to certain limits, and usually offer free credit life insurance.

Money Market Mutual Funds

A mutual fund is an investment company that raises money by selling shares to the public and investing the money in a diversified portfolio of securities. The investments are professionally managed with securities purchased and sold at the discretion of the fund manager. Many mutual fund companies have created money market mutual funds (MMMFs) that serve as money market accounts. The accounts can be used for cash management.

An MMMF is a mutual fund that pools the cash of many investors and specializes in earning a relatively safe and high return by buying securities that have short-term maturities (always less than one year). The average maturity for the portfolio cannot exceed 120 days (portfolios have an average maturity of ≤60 days). This reduces price swings so that the money funds maintain a constant share value. Securities are bought and sold almost daily in money markets that result in payment of the highest daily rates available to small investors. Money deposited in mutual funds is not insured by the federal government; however, MMMFs are considered extremely safe because of the high quality of the securities. Accounts in money market mutual funds provide a convenient and safe place to keep money while awaiting alternative investment opportunities.

Stock Brokerage Firms

A stock brokerage firm is a licensed financial institution that specializes in selling and buying investment securities. These firms usually receive a commission for the advice and assistance they provide. Commissions are based on the buy/sell orders they execute. Stock brokerage firms usually offer money market fund accounts where clients may place money while waiting to invest in stocks and bonds. Money held in a money market mutual fund at a stock brokerage firm is not insured against loss by any government agency; however, most brokerage firms purchase private insurance against such losses.

Financial Services Companies

Financial services companies are national or regional corporations that offer a number of financial services to consumers, including traditional checking, savings, lending, credit card accounts, and MMMFs as well as advice on investments, insurance, real estate, and general financial planning. Financial services companies are also referred to as nonbank banks because they provide limited traditional banking services, either accepting deposits or making commercial loans, but not both.

FDIC Insurance

Any person or entity can have FDIC insurance on a deposit. A depositor does not have to be a U.S. citizen or even a resident of the United States. The FDIC insures deposits in some, but not all, banks and savings associations. Federal deposit insurance protects deposits that are payable in the United States. The FDIC does not insure the following items:

- Deposits that are payable only overseas
- Securities, mutual funds, and similar types of investments
- Creditors (other than depositors) and shareholders of a failed bank or savings association
- Treasury securities (bills, notes, and bonds) purchased by an insured depository institution on a customer's behalf

All types of deposits received by a qualifying financial institution in its usual course of business are insured. For example, savings deposits, checking deposits, deposits in NOW accounts, Christmas club accounts, and time deposits (including certificates of deposit, or CDs) are all FDIC-insured deposits. The FDIC also insures the following:

- Cashiers' checks, money orders, officers' checks, and outstanding drafts
- Certified checks, letters of credit, and travelers' checks for which an insured depository institution is primarily liable, when issued in exchange for money or its equivalent, or for a charge against a deposit account

Deposits in different qualified institutions are insured separately. If an institution has one or more branches, however, the main office and all branch offices are considered to be one institution. Thus, deposits at the main office and at branch offices of the same institution are added when calculating deposit insurance coverage. Financial institutions owned by the same holding company but separately chartered are separately insured. The FDIC presumes that funds are owned as shown on the deposit account records of the insured depository institution. The basic FDIC insured amount of a depositor is $250,000. Accrued interest is included when calculating insurance coverage. Deposits maintained in different categories of legal ownership are separately insured. Accordingly, a depositor can have more than $250,000 insurance coverage in a single institution if the funds are owned and deposited in different ownership categories. The most common categories of ownership are single (or individual) ownership, joint ownership, and testamentary accounts. Separate insurance is also available for funds held for retirement and business purposes. Federal deposit insurance is not determined on a per-account basis. A depositor cannot increase FDIC insurance by dividing funds owned in the same ownership category among different accounts within the same institutions. The type of account (checking, savings, certificate of deposit, outstanding official checks, or other form of deposit) has no bearing on the amount of insurance coverage.

Single Ownership Accounts

A single (or individual) ownership account is an account owned by one person. Single ownership accounts include accounts in the owner's name; accounts established for the benefit of the owner by agents, nominees, guardians, custodians, or conservators; and accounts established by a business that is a sole proprietorship. All single ownership accounts (except retirement accounts) established by, or for the benefit of, the same person are added, and the total is insured up to a maximum of $250,000. If an individual owns and deposits funds in his own name but then gives another person the right to withdraw funds from the account, the account will generally be insured as a joint ownership account.

EXAMPLE Assume Justin Grant has the accounts listed below. Because the restaurant is Justin's sole proprietorship, its account is considered individually owned by Justin. In this case, $25,000 of Justin's accounts are uninsured by the FDIC.

Depositor	Account Type	Amount Deposited
Justin Grant	Savings account	$125,000
Justin Grant	CD	100,000
Justin Grant	NOW account	25,000
Justin's Restaurant (a sole proprietorship)	Checking	25,000
Total deposited		$275,000
Maximum amount of insurance available		($250,000)
Uninsured amount		$25,000

The Uniform Gifts to Minors Act is a state law that allows an adult to make an irrevocable gift to a minor. Funds given to a minor under the Uniform Gifts to Minors Act are held in the name of a custodian for the minor's benefit. The funds are added to any other single ownership accounts of the minor, and the total is insured up to a maximum of $250,000.

Joint Accounts

A joint account is an account owned by two or more individuals. They are insured separately from single ownership accounts if all of the following conditions are met.

- All co-owners must be natural persons. This means that legal entities such as corporations or partnerships are not eligible for joint account deposit insurance coverage.
- Each of the co-owners must have a right of withdrawal on the same basis as the other co-owners. For example, if one co-owner can withdraw funds on his signature alone but the other co-owner can withdraw funds only on the signature of both co-owners, then this requirement has not been satisfied; the co-owners do not have equal withdrawal rights. Likewise, if a co-owner's right to withdraw funds is limited to a specified dollar amount, the funds in the account will be allocated between the co-owners according to their withdrawal rights and insured as single ownership funds. So, for example, if $100,000 is deposited in the names of A and B, but A has the right to withdraw only up to $5,000 from the account, $5,000 is allocated to A and the remainder is allocated to B. The funds, as allocated, are then added to any other single ownership funds of A or B, respectively.

- Each of the co-owners must have personally signed a deposit account signature card. The execution of an account signature card is not required for certificates of deposit; deposit obligations evidenced by a negotiable instrument; or accounts maintained by an agent, nominee, guardian, custodian, or conservator, but the deposit must in fact be jointly owned.

The interests of each individual in all joint accounts he owns at the same FDIC-insured depository institution are added and insured up to $250,000. Each person's interest (or share) in a joint account is deemed equal unless otherwise stated on the deposit account records.

A deposit account held in two or more names that does not qualify for joint account deposit insurance coverage is treated as owned by each named owner as an individual, corporation, partnership, or unincorporated association, as the case may be, according to each co-owner's actual ownership interest. As such, each owner's interest is added to any other single ownership accounts or, in the case of a corporation, partnership, or unincorporated association, to other accounts of such entity, and the total is insured up to $250,000.

Business Accounts

Funds deposited by a corporation, partnership, or unincorporated association are FDIC-insured up to $250,000. Funds deposited by a corporation, partnership, or unincorporated association are insured separately from the personal accounts of the stockholders, partners, or members. To qualify for this coverage, the entity must be engaged in an independent activity. *Independent activity* means that the entity is operated primarily for some purpose other than to increase deposit insurance. Funds owned by a sole proprietorship are treated as the individually owned funds of the sole proprietor. Consequently, funds deposited in the name of the sole proprietorship are added to any other single ownership accounts of the sole proprietor, and the total is insured to $250,000.

Retirement Accounts

Retirement accounts established at FDIC-insured institutions also qualify for FDIC insurance. The total amount insured across all retirement accounts held at a single institution is limited to $250,000. This is provided that the IRA investments are assets eligible for FDIC coverage.

Negotiable Instruments

Negotiable instruments serve two important functions: they serve as an extension of credit and as substitute for money. For an instrument to be negotiable, it must have all of the following requirements on its face:

- In writing
- Signed by maker or drawer
- Contain an unconditional promise or order to pay
- State a fixed amount in money
- Payable on demand or at a definite time
- Payable to order or to bearer, unless it is a check

Commercial paper is a typical form of negotiable instrument, and there are several types.

The first type is known as a draft, and it has three parties in which one person or entity (drawer) orders another (drawee) to pay a third party (payee) a sum of money.

April 1, 2022

On April 1, 2022, pay to the order of Shahriar $1,000 plus 6% annual interest from April 1, 2023.

To: Acme Publications, Inc.

(signed) **Jose Garcia**

A check is a special type of draft that is payable on demand, and the drawee must be a bank. The check writer is the drawer.

A promissory note is another type of commercial paper that is a two-party instrument. With a promissory note, Party A (the maker) promises to pay a specified sum of money to Party B (the payee). The note may be payable on demand or at a definite time. The following example is a promissory note in which Teboho Darrow is the maker and Kristin Fourroux the payee.

April 1, 2022

I promise to pay to the order of Kristin Fourroux $1,000 plus 6% annual interest on April 1, 2023.

To: Acme Publications, Inc.

(signed) **Teboho Darrow**

Investor Protection

The *Securities Act of 1933* and the *Securities Exchange Act of 1934* were passed to protect investors and to regulate those providing investment services. Professional financial analysts should be familiar with both of these Acts and the related Acts that followed them.

The Securities Act of 1933 is primarily concerned with new issues of securities or issues in the primary market. The act forbids fraud and deception and requires that all relevant information on new issues be fully disclosed, that new securities be registered with the Securities and Exchange Commission (SEC), and that audited financial statements be filed with the registration statements. When sold, all securities must be accompanied by a prospectus.

Although the Securities Act of 1933 was limited to new issues, the Securities Exchange Act (SEA) of 1934 extended the regulation to securities sold in the secondary markets. The act provided the following.

- Establishment of the Securities and Exchange Commission—The SEC's primary function is to regulate the securities markets.
- Disclosure requirements for secondary market—Annual reports and other financial reports are required to be filed with the SEC before listing on the organized exchanges. These reports include the annual 10K report, which must be audited, and the quarterly 10Q report, which is not required to be audited.
- Registration of organized exchanges—All organized exchanges must register with the SEC and provide copies of their rules and bylaws.

- Credit regulation—Congress gave the Federal Reserve Board the power to set margin requirements for credit purchases of securities. This act also limited securities dealers' indebtedness to 20 times their owners' equity capital.
- Proxy solicitation—Specific rules governing solicitation of proxies were established.
- Exemptions—Securities of federal, state, and local governments, securities that are not traded across state lines, and any other securities specified by the SEC are exempt from registering with the SEC. This includes Treasury bonds and municipal bonds.
- Insider activities—A public report called an insider report must be filed with the SEC in every month that a change in the holding of a firm's securities occurs for an officer, director, or 10% or more of the shareholders. The SEA of 1934 forbids insiders profiting from securities held less than six months and requires these profits be returned to the organization. In addition, short sales are not permitted by individuals considered to be insiders.
- Price manipulation—The SEA of 1934 forbids price manipulation schemes such as wash sales, pools, circulation of manipulative information, and false and misleading statements about securities.

For a complete discussion on Regulatory Requirements, see Appendix C.

Forms of Business Organizations

Each state's legal environment establishes the forms of business organizations that may be created within that state. This chapter introduces the legal forms of business. A more detailed discussion of business organizations is covered in Chapter 14—Business Entities.

There are seven legal forms of organization that a business can use: sole proprietorship, general partnership, limited partnership, limited liability partnership, limited liability company, corporation, and S corporation.

- A sole proprietorship is a business owned by an individual who is personally liable for the obligations of the business.
- A general partnership is an association of two or more persons, who jointly control and carry on a business as co-owners for making a profit. The partners are personally liable for the obligations of the business.
- A limited partnership is an organization in which at least one partner is a general partner and at least one other is a limited partner with limited management participation and limited liability.
- A limited liability partnership (LLP) is usually a professional partnership (CPAs, attorneys) wherein the partners have limited liability to the extent of investment except where personally liable through malpractice. This form protects the individual assets of the partners who do not commit malpractice.
- A limited liability company (LLC) is an entity in which the owners, or members, have limited liability for debts and claims of the business even while participating in management. The governing document is called an operating agreement. Some states prohibit single member LLCs.

- A corporation (C Corporation) is a separate legal entity created by state law and operates under a common name through its elected management. Owners (shareholders) have limited liability.
- An S corporation is a domestic corporation with 100 shareholders or less; comprising individuals (excluding nonresident aliens), estates, certain trusts, and exempt organizations; and having no more than one class of stock.

There are several other forms of business organizations.

- A joint venture is an association formed to perform a single transaction or a series of similar transactions that, for tax purposes, is treated the same as a partnership (although no partnership tax return is filed).
- A syndicate or investment group consists of a number of persons who pool their resources to finance a business venture.
- A business trust involves a number of people who turn over management and legal title of property to one or more trustees who then distribute the profits to the participants (the beneficiaries of the trust).
- A cooperative is an association (may be incorporated) organized to provide an economic service to its members (or shareholders).

IMPORTANCE OF THE SOCIAL ENVIRONMENT

A society's culture affects the way a society lives and what it values. Culture changes slowly, but it does change. How does a changing social environment affect a client's financial plan? Financial planners must accurately assess the social environment and forecast the threats and opportunities that change will bring. Some of the characteristics of a changing social environment include the following:

- Advancing population age
- Increasing life expectancy
- Changing customs, norms, values, folkways, and morals
- Shifts in attitudes and motivations
- Dedication to or alienation from traditional religious beliefs
- Evolving global languages
- Acceptance or rejection of traditional status symbols and social institutions

One likely forecast for the United States is the flow of new cultures from around the globe into the workforce. These modern-day settlers bring new customs and cultures to be assimilated into this country. How they interpret the American dream may determine the country's future social environment.

Statistics show that the U.S. population is aging. At some point, retirees will outnumber active workers. The larger number of retirees will put additional pressure on the finances of the Social Security system. There will be new investment opportunities as our country is faced with the challenges of an aging population with increased life expectancies, geographic mobility, and financial freedom.

IMPORTANCE OF THE TECHNOLOGICAL ENVIRONMENT

Perhaps the most rapidly changing environment is that of technology. Technological advancement has affected our workplace, our homes, and our investment planning. Already, the internet, through large institutions, provides basic financial planning to anyone with access to a computer. Such assistance may include income tax preparation, credit assessment and counseling, mortgage qualification, education planning, preparation of basic personal financial statements, determination of investment selection for Section 401(k) plan contributions, and retirement planning. Why do these institutions provide these services, especially free of charge? The answer is to get more assets under management. Assets under management equals fee revenues. Such technology has displaced some financial planners who were providing the same service for persons in the same market niche. Astute financial planners learn to recognize how the technological environment can best serve them and their clients. Success comes from keeping a constant vigil on the characteristics that make up the technological environment:

- Current state of technology
- Information processing and communication
- Production equipment and processes
- Medical advances
- Creation of new technology
- New patents, trademarks, copyrights
- Human and business solutions
- Biotechnology
- Gene identification and cloning
- Advances in service and engineering

IMPORTANCE OF THE POLITICAL ENVIRONMENT

The political environment is especially important to risk analysis in investments. Political stability means less investment risk. To evaluate the political environment of any country, the financial planner should assess the country's:

- form of government;
- political ideology/stability;
- social unrest;
- relative strength of opposing political groups and views;
- foreign trade policy; and
- degree of government protectionism regarding foreign goods.

This analysis becomes increasingly important as the world moves to a global economy and investors try to diversify investment portfolios using worldwide investments.

IMPORTANCE OF THE TAXATION ENVIRONMENT

Taxation, in its many forms, leaves the taxpayer with less disposable income. In that sense, all taxes, including income taxes, estate transfer taxes, payroll taxes, property taxes, and sales taxes, have a dampening effect on consumer spending and consumption.

Many of the taxes we pay are the result of complex tax laws about which the average taxpayer has little knowledge or understanding. Enter the income tax expert, the transfer tax expert, and even the property tax expert—each offering a specialized knowledge and distinctive expertise.

Some of the taxes we pay are the result of economic choice, some from a lack of understanding of the alternatives. This is especially true in the area of transfer taxes (estate and gift taxes). If people were more keenly aware of the way to avoid transfer taxes, many would. Because of the potential burden of transfer taxes, there is a great opportunity to avoid these transfer taxes through competent tax planning.

The changing nature of taxes and tax legislation has the potential to broadly affect large segments of the financial planning community. Even though transfer taxes affect a small percentage of the U.S. population, those affected are the country's wealthiest. Many of these persons spend substantial amounts to avoid or mitigate the costs of transfer taxes. They spend this money with estate planners, lawyers, CPAs, and insurance professionals because it is cheaper to pay these professionals than to pay the tax. If the transfer tax were eliminated, many of the transaction costs associated with avoiding the transfer tax would also be eliminated. What would happen to the estate-planning bar? What would happen to the insurance professional who sells only multimillion-dollar second-to-die whole life policies? What would happen to the CPA who practices primarily or exclusively in the estate planning area? Perhaps many of the services, products, and devices used to avoid the transfer taxes would disappear.

The tax environment itself is constantly changing. Congress writes new tax laws as frequently as annually. If a professional financial planner is to assist clients in minimizing their legal taxes, thus giving them more disposable income for consumption, savings, and investments, the planner must have a basic education in taxation and must develop ways to remain current in the field.

WHERE ON THE WEB

Board of Governors of the Federal Reserve System **www.federalreserve.gov**

Bureau of Economic Analysis **www.bea.gov**

Bureau of the Fiscal Service **www.fiscal.treasury.gov**

Bureau of Labor Statistics **www.bls.gov**

CPI **www.bls.gov/cpi**

Department of Commerce **www.commerce.gov**

Economy at a Glance **stats.bls.gov/eag/eag.us.htm**

Lawlink (information on bankruptcy) **www.americanbar.org/groups/departments_offices/legal_technology_resources/**

National Council on Economic Education **www.councilforeconed.org/**

National Foundation for Credit Counseling **www.nfcc.org**

PPI **www.bls.gov/ppi**

U.S. Census Bureau **www.census.gov**

DISCUSSION QUESTIONS

1. How do the external and internal environments in which financial planning occur differ?
2. What are some examples of how each external environmental factor might affect clients from different economic levels?
3. Why is external environmental analysis so important?
4. How is the external environment analyzed?
5. Why is the economic environment so important to financial planning?
6. What is price elasticity?
7. What is unit-elastic demand?
8. What is marginal utility?
9. What is the law of diminishing marginal utility?
10. How do interest rates, taxes, and inflation affect areas of financial planning?
11. What are the components of the business cycle, and how do they affect the economy?
12. What is the formula for the inflation rate?
13. What are the Consumer Price Index, the gross domestic product deflator, and the Producer Price Index?
14. What is monetary policy?
15. What is fiscal policy?
16. What are the Federal Reserve's three economic goals?
17. What is the index of leading economic indicators?
18. For what is the index of leading economic indicators used?
19. How good is the index of leading economic indicators as a predictor?
20. What are 5 of the 10 components of the index of leading economic indicators?
21. What is negligence?
22. What are considered nondischargeable debts in Chapter 7 bankruptcy?
23. List some examples of federal consumer protection laws.
24. What are some examples of federal programs that offer protection for workers on the job site?
25. Identify two federal securities acts that protect investors.
26. How do the external environmental factors—social, technological, political, and taxation—affect a client's financial plan?

EXERCISES

1. Define the laws of supply and demand.
2. What does it mean if the demand for a product is inelastic?
3. What action might the Federal Reserve take if it wanted to lower interest rates?
4. What is the price adjustment process in a competitive market, and how does it shift?
5. What happens in the marketplace when the supply curve decreases or shifts to the left?
6. Describe what has occurred when the price of a particular product decreases and consumers buy more of that product.
7. Consumer demand for sugar at $.80 per pound results in 1,000 pounds sold. A drop in sugar's price to $.50 per pound results in 1,250 pounds sold. Is the demand for sugar inelastic, elastic, or unit elastic? (Ignore negative signs for PE calculations.)
8. If a substitute good is readily available for a product, is the product demand likely to be elastic or inelastic?
9. Give an example illustrating the law of downward-sloping demand.
10. An increase in the price of product A causes a decrease in the demand for product B. What is the relationship between the two products?
11. Describe reasons for a change in consumer demand.
12. Which of the following might cause an increase in supply?
    A. A decrease in productivity
    B. Fewer sellers in the marketplace
    C. More efficient technology
    D. A decrease in government subsidies
13. Identify several determinants of demand elasticity.
14. If the quantity supplied does not change significantly with a change in price, is the type of supply elastic or inelastic?
15. Define inflation.
16. How would someone living on a fixed income be affected by inflation?
17. When the economy is slowing and unemployment is increasing, what phase of the business cycle is the economy in?
18. Which of the following economic activities represent examples of monetary policy?
    A. The federal funds rate is increased.
    B. The Federal Reserve lowers bank reserve requirements.
    C. The Federal Open Market Committee sells securities.
19. What actions taken by the Fed will lead to increased money supply?
20. Identify the phases and points of a typical business cycle.
21. In a typical business cycle, which phases exhibit periods of increasing employment and increasing output?

PROBLEMS

1. Identify whether each of the following involves a shift in the demand curve or a change in the quantity demanded.
   A. Fish prices fall after Catholics are allowed to eat meat on Fridays.
   B. Auto sales decrease due to increased unemployment.
   C. Gasoline consumption increases as some gasoline taxes are lowered.
   D. After a drought occurs in Louisiana, crawfish sales decrease.

2. If the cost of one year of college education on January 1 of 2020, 2021, and 2022 is \$25,000, \$16,000, and \$27,500, respectively, what was the rate of education inflation for 2020 and 2021? What was the annualized education inflation rate from 2020 to 2022?

3. Erin has the following liquid assets on deposits with her bank, which is an FDIC-insured institution.

Account	Ownership	Balance
CD	Erin	\$200,000
Savings	Erin with spouse	\$50,000
IRA (money market deposit account)	Erin	\$75,000
Checking account	Erin	\$90,000

What is the total amount currently insured by the FDIC?

CHAPTER 3

Communication, Behavioral Finance, and Internal Environmental Analysis

LEARNING OBJECTIVES

After learning the material in this chapter, you will be able to do the following:

- Explain how a financial planner can successfully communicate respect, trust, and empathy to a client
- List several techniques that reduce the risk of misinterpretation and misunderstanding when communicating with a client
- Identify the effect of a client's learning style on the format and presentation of a financial plan
- Distinguish various types of interpersonal communication including linguistic signs and non-verbal communications

- Recognize active listening and response skills during in-person communications with clients
- Identify areas of potential financial conflict between spouse and/or family
- Communicate the importance of being transparent and agreeing on financial goals with spouse and/or family
- Select appropriate counseling and communication techniques for use with individual clients
- Demonstrate how a planner can develop a relationship of honesty and trust in client interactions
- Identify professional liability risks affecting the financial planner
- List the four phases of thinking through which a client often progresses in the financial planning process
- Describe the auditory learning style, the visual learning style, and the kinetic, or tactile, learning style by discussing how a client with each style prefers to learn
- Identify the five categories that make up a client's internal environment
- List the factors that make up life cycle positioning
- Name the life cycle phases through which most financial planning clients eventually progress
- Explain how a client's tolerance for risk; savings and consumption habits; views about employment, retirement, and leisure time; and attitudes on government (especially taxation) affect the setting of her financial goals
- Predict how behavioral psychology in terms of cognitive errors will affect a client's goals, perspective, understanding, decision-making process, and actions
- Determine the ways in which a client's emotional biases affect the selection of client goals and understanding
- Assess a client's risk tolerance, risk perception, risk capacity, attitudes, and beliefs to formulate recommendations that are consistent with personal preferences and financial needs
- Identify special needs that may influence the successful development of a client's financial plan
- Identify the financial statements and other information needed to develop an accurate assessment of a client's financial position
- Explain how a client's subjective perception of her financial position affects the objective reality of the financial position provided by a financial planner

COMMUNICATION SKILLS

The importance of a good working relationship between the personal financial planner and the client cannot be overemphasized. This relationship requires excellent interpersonal skills, proficient communication skills, and the ability to educate. As indicated in Exhibit 3.1, these skills are essential to achieving a successful financial plan. Specifically, they are required to efficiently gather accurate information from the client and to educate the client throughout the financial planning process. With a good working relationship, the client is more willing to share information and be less resistant to accepting a planner's advice. A solid relationship is one in which everyone involved is treated with respect, trust, and empathy.

EXHIBIT 3.1 Financial Planner's Pyramid of Knowledge

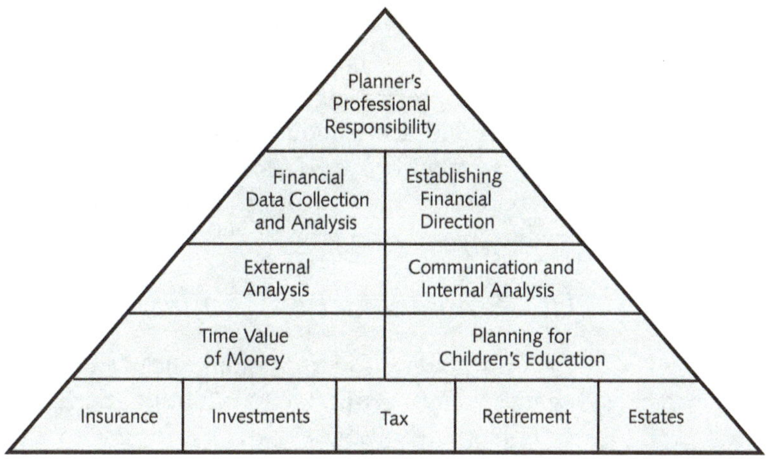

Be Respectful of Your Client

Respect can be conveyed in several ways. One obvious way is the manner in which the client is addressed. When first meeting a client, use a courteous title such as Mr., Ms., or Dr. If later the client indicates a preference to be called by a first name or some other nickname, that desire should be met. Listening to clients, not talking over them, and showing value for their time also portray respect. Always return phone calls when you say you will. Be on time for appointments. Let the client know how long a meeting is expected to last. If you are exceeding the allotted time, ask if the meeting should continue or be rescheduled for another time. These issues may seem elementary, but being mindful of them will assist in developing a professional relationship with your client.

Trust must be developed between the planner and the client. Trust has to be earned, but the process is expedited by showing evidence that others deem you trustworthy. Provide prospective clients with letters of reference from current clients (if permitted), especially those that cite specific examples of how they benefit from your skills. Take care to maintain confidentiality. Clients need to know that any information they share with you will remain strictly confidential. Therefore, if specific examples are provided, make sure the client knows that permission was received before any disclosure.

Respect is shown by being empathetic and viewing the client as an individual. Empathy is the identification with and understanding of another's circumstances, feelings, and motives. Remember that financial success is a relative concept. The client defines success subjectively. The client's definition is based on personal circumstances, feelings, and motives. The financial planner needs to understand the client's perspective and show regard for those views and values.

Communicate With Your Client

A financial planner cannot develop a good relationship with the client without first mastering communication skills. Communications between the financial planner and the client can be difficult because of subjectivity, paradigms, and unspoken words that lead to misinterpretation and misunderstanding.

For example, suppose the client states a desire to take at least one nice vacation each year. The keen financial planner might ask for the vacation destination. Suppose that destination is the Caribbean. The planner may now believe that enough information has been gathered to include this objective into the financial plan. However, enough information has probably not been gathered. The planner might assume the client intends to vacation for one week, because that is the norm in the United States. However, the client may be planning a month-long vacation. In addition, the planner does not know how the client plans to travel. Is she going to fly? If so, does she plan to fly first class or coach? In what type of accommodations does she plan to stay? As you can see, by attributing the financial planner's own standards or by assuming to know the client's standards, the goal of taking one nice vacation a year is easily misinterpreted. This misinterpretation may lead to inappropriate financial planning.

Use Communication Techniques

Fortunately, several communication techniques exist that can greatly reduce the chance of misinterpretation and misunderstanding. Here are a few techniques the financial planner should use when speaking with a client.

Keep the client informed. Tell the client what will happen, what is happening as it happens, and what has happened when it is completed. Although you may be very experienced in the financial planning process, the client is not. Consider the client's perspective. If he does not know what to expect, he will probably be apprehensive. If he is not informed of the significance of particular questions, he may resist answering them or provide only partial information.

Clarify statements and remove ambiguity. Avoid general statements by using clarification techniques such as restating, paraphrasing, and summarizing. Apply the ideas of "is" and "is not." For example, in describing the purpose of property insurance, you may state that property insurance *is* intended to help minimize loss in the event of a disaster. This type of insurance *is not* intended to eliminate loss in the event of a disaster.

Seek information to understand the client's situation and goals. Use open-ended questions to ascertain relevant information. Do not make assumptions. Question everything. Question the answers to the questions. When the client can no longer generate another answer, all the information the client has may be known. However, that does not mean the planner has all of the necessary information. As a result, the planner may need to obtain information from other sources.

Be specific. When communicating with the client, identify the "what, where, when, responsible party, and extent" to describe a task or a result. Avoid the use of slang and colloquialisms. Articulate goals in terms of time, place, and form. A financial plan is useless if it cannot be accurately and precisely communicated to the client.

Interpersonal communication
Understanding the application of verbal and nonverbal skills

Interpersonal communication, or communicating one on one, is important throughout the financial planning process. Mastering interpersonal communication skills involves understanding differences when communicating across generations, cultures, and genders, and will ensure that the listener understands and responds effectively to the communicator. Effective interpersonal communication involves the understanding and application of oral and nonverbal skills when interacting with clients. Proper use of these skills helps develop a relationship of honesty and trust between financial planners and their clients.

Body Language

Body language
Involves facial expressions, eye contact, gestures, and body posture

Financial planners should understand that all behavior is communication and relays a message to clients. **Body language** involves facial expressions, eye contact, gestures, and body posture; it actually impacts how clients receive messages more than any other type of communication. Facial expressions communicate emotions such as interest, agreement, excitement, fear, surprise, or contempt. Eye contact can indicate attention, interest, and engagement between planners and clients. Conversely, failure to make eye contact may be interpreted as disinterested, distracted, or discourteous.

Voice Pitch and Tone

Pitch
The sound quality of highness or lowness, the frequency of the sound wave

Tone
The inflection of voice or emphasis on certain words

The pitch and inflection of one's voice influence the message conveyed more than the actual spoken words. The **pitch** of one's voice is the sound quality of highness or lowness; it is primarily dependent on the frequency of the sound wave. Lower voice pitches are usually interpreted as conveying confidence, whereas higher pitches project uncertainty. The **tone** is the inflection of voice or emphasis on certain words and shows attitude, whether humor, anger, sincerity, or sarcasm.

Mirroring

Mirroring
Imitating client's gestures and physical positions, or using similar verbal styles

A financial planner who communicates effectively often uses the technique of **mirroring** to improve rapport with clients. This is accomplished by imitating clients' gestures and physical positions or by using a similar verbal style. In physical mirroring, the financial planner copies the clients' body language. In verbal mirroring, the financial planner imitates the clients' word use, tone of voice, and communication method. The financial planner's goal is not to mimic the clients' gestures exactly but to subtly adjust her own posture and disposition to those of her clients. This will communicate to clients that the financial planner accepts and is open to the clients' suggestions and ideas.

Planners must also develop the important skill of emotional intelligence, which includes the ability to recognize emotional expressions in themselves and their clients, as well as selecting socially appropriate responses to the circumstances and their clients' emotions. Active listening is also a key to effective communication. Planners should practice active listening by paying full attention to what their clients are saying and responding by paraphrasing the clients' comments. This will help planners fully understand what their clients are trying to communicate. Planners can also give leading responses that guide clients to give more details, making a meeting of the minds more likely. The most successful financial planners make their clients feel understood and are able to effectively discuss their clients' most sensitive money issues.

The Engagement Letter

Engagement letter
A tool of communication between client and financial planner that sets down in writing the information about any agreements or understandings obtained at client/planner meetings, including the plan of action for developing a financial plan, the expected outcome of the engagement, and the method of compensation

An **engagement letter** is a useful tool in communicating with your client. An engagement letter is written near the beginning of the client/planner relationship, usually following the first meeting. The letter should summarize the previous meeting(s) and conversations with the client. This includes the plan of action for developing a financial plan, the expected outcome of the engagement, and the methods and amounts of compensation. Exhibit 3.2 illustrates a sample engagement letter.

EXHIBIT 3.2 Sample Engagement Letter

(Date)

(Name of Client)
(Address of Client)

Dear (Name of Client):

Thank you for meeting with me on *(date)*. Per our discussions, I understand your goals are as follows:
1. *(list goal)*
2. *(list goal)*
3. *(list goal)*

This letter sets forth our understanding of the terms and objectives of our engagement to provide personal financial planning services to you. The scope and nature of the services to be provided are as follows:

1. **Review and Evaluation**
We will review and analyze all information furnished to us including:
(list items)

2. **Written Plan**
Based on our review and analysis, we will prepare a written analysis of your:
(list items)

We will also prepare, in writing, specific initial recommendations to address your concerns and issues, including goals, objectives, and risks with respect to:
(list items)

Our recommendations will include strategies based on our analysis of your circumstances. Where appropriate, we will include financial illustrations and financial projections to enhance your understanding of the potential outcomes of the alternatives.

We will meet with you to discuss our analysis and will provide you with a preliminary draft copy of our recommended strategies. You will be given an opportunity to concur with the preliminary recommendations or suggest modifications. Following agreement on your personal financial goals and the strategies to be used to achieve them, we will provide you with a finalized version of the plan.

3. **Fees**
Our fee for these services is based on our standard hourly rates and the number of hours required. We expect our fees to be no less than $__________ but not to exceed $__________. We will bill you beginning with our next regular billing cycle. The final payment will be adjusted to reflect actual time expended, not to exceed the maximum total amount quoted for the year, and will be due upon completion of the engagement.

4. **Implementation**
We will assist you in implementing the strategies that have been agreed upon. Accordingly, we will be available on an ongoing basis, by telephone or in person, to answer questions, to assist you or your other advisors to take necessary actions, and to make recommendations regarding these matters. We will bill you for these additional services based on time expended at our standard hourly rate.

5. **Limitation on Scope of Services**

These services are not intended to include:
(list items)

We will bill separately for any such additional services provided, based on time expended at our standard hourly rates.

If this letter correctly sets forth your understanding of the terms and objectives of the engagement, please so indicate by signing in the space provided below.

Respectfully yours,

(Name of Planner)
(Name of Firm)

The above letter sets forth my understanding of the terms and objectives of the engagement to provide personal financial planning services.

Signed: ____________________ Date: ________________

SOURCES OF MONEY CONFLICT AND PRINCIPLES OF COUNSELING

Financial behaviors and perspectives influence relationship satisfaction in marriages and families. It is important that financial planners provide recommendations based on goals that are mutually agreed-upon by couples. *How* partners speak to one another during conversations is equally as important as *what* they discuss. During meetings with clients, planners should be aware of behaviors that signal financial conflict:

- Arguing during sessions
- Discussing financial disagreements at home
- One partner speaking more frequently than the other
- One partner interrupting and/or speaking over the other
- Behaving in a way that represents nonverbal behaviors related to conflict (crossing arms, rolling eyes, sitting far from one another, no eye contact between partners)
- Criticizing or speaking sarcastically to the other partner

Sources of Financial Conflict

There are many reasons partners and family disagree about financial matters. Below are common circumstances that can be sources of financial conflict.

Family-of-origin treatment of money. Parents' financial circumstances and patterns may greatly influence their children's beliefs about money and how they value it. As adults, the money principles learned from their families can cause conflict with partners who have different viewpoints.

Inadequate communication. Money issues are common in families. Conflict can result from an inadequate cash flow to meet needs, but more often, a lack of communication regarding money is the source of financial difficulties. A planner cannot only facilitate healthy conversations regarding money, but can also give clients advice about how to make it a priority to communicate frequently.

Different risk tolerance levels. Married couples with dissimilar risk tolerance levels can present challenges during investment planning. Therefore, there must be open and honest discussion between the couple, facilitated by the planner, regarding how marital funds should be invested. Additionally, the retirement account balances of each spouse should be reviewed. If there are comparable amounts in each retirement account, it is often preferable for each spouse to invest according to their own individual risk tolerance. If, however, the account balances differ significantly, this practice will likely cause the couple's retirement portfolio to be too conservative or too aggressive.

Adult children. Many parents of adult children provide them some financial support. This is frequently a source of tension when parents do not agree about whether support should be given and, if so, the amount to be provided. Conflicts between parents and the adult children arise when expectations are not communicated. To minimize disagreements, it is important to establish realistic guidelines with the adult child, preferably in a written agreement with detailed terms.

Blended families. Couples who bring together children from previous marriages may want to consider a prenuptial agreement. This can assist them when planning how to merge financially the two families and setting expectations for how the assets and debt brought into the new family will be managed. Remarried couples should also take legal action (wills, trusts, etc.) to make certain that assets are distributed according to their wishes upon death.

Cultural differences. Cultural factors may also influence money conflict among family members, for example in cases where paternalism, centralized decision-making, and personalized family business structures are present.

Inheritances. Inheritances can create family conflict with children who are heirs to their relative's estate. What can be seen as inequality in the distribution of assets can affect the emotional and psychological aspects of family life. Therefore, planners may have clients who are facing a number of challenges and benefits when receiving inheritances.

THE IMPORTANCE OF TRANSPARENCY AND AGREEMENT ON FINANCIAL GOALS, COUNSELING, AND COMMUNICATION TECHNIQUES

Financial transparency promotes honesty and trust in relationships. For financial wellbeing among spouses and in families, those involved must be clear and unambiguous about income, spending, assets, and liabilities. Ideally, this should be the case even when couples have separate accounts, especially if there are common goals shared by partners.

Often, spouses and their families may struggle with transparency and shared financial planning when spouse wants to avoid money conflict over purchases concealed from their spouse or when a spouse wishes to hide that they are spending money on themselves or others. Planners should help clients understand that lack of transparency will likely sabotage the financial planning needed to meet shared goals. This conversation may be an uncomfortable, yet important, to have.

Couples who do not share financial values and goals are more likely to experience money conflict. For financial satisfaction, it is important that a couple share values and goals, or at least respect goals that differ and have agreement about how they should be met with their resources. When decisions related to family financial goals are discussed openly, the planner can make relevant recommendations that will put clients on track to meet the agreed-upon goals.

Communication Components

Financial planners who effectively communicate with their clients are better prepared to counsel their clients in a way that helps them achieve their goals. Communication is a process that includes several components:

- Sender: one who shares information with another person
- Message: the information shared
- Form: the method, or channel, of communication
- Receiver: one with whom information is shared

- Effect: receipt and understanding of the message
- Feedback: provided through language and writing
  - Both are a series of signs, with writing the best way to communicate feedback.

Counseling and Communication Techniques

Social Penetration Theory

The **social penetration theory**, originally created by Irwin Altman and Dalmas Taylor, outlines the four stages in which relationships, such as those between clients and their planners, develop and progress.

Stage 1: Orientation

Orientation, the first stage of social penetration, begins even before the first meeting between the client and the planner. Marketing messages, initial telephone or email communication, and the planner's office environment all influence how clients become familiar with the financial planning process.

When the planner and client meet for the first time, it is important to recognize the goal of the orientation stage: for the client and planner to determine if there is value in developing an ongoing relationship. Additionally, the goal is to develop general likeability, the beginning stages of trust, and to show that the planner can meet client needs and expectations.

Communication generally begins in a conversational manner. Typically, it is a general conversation that does not yet discuss the financial planning process. The client may feel cautious at this time and may speak in generalities instead of with substance and depth. Generally, the planner and client move towards Stage 2, Exploration, rather quickly.

Stage 2: Exploration

During **exploration**, clients and planners begin to discuss the financial planning process in more detail. This includes a discussion of the client's financial goals and perceptions, and also involves learning more about the client. For example, in this stage the planner seeks to understand the client's beliefs, attitudes, feelings, and perceptions. Understanding these client attributes will help the planner better understand and respond to the client in meaningful ways.

If the foundation for a trusting relationship is established in this stage, clients will begin to share their true feelings, concerns, and priorities. Conversations are more in-depth regarding clients' financial and personal circumstances; however, they are more comfortable and friendly at this point.

Stage 3: Affective Exchange

In the **affective exchange** stage, the planner-client relationship becomes one of significant trust. Without reservation, clients share their true feelings, aspirations, goals, and concerns in this stage. The relationship may become more of a friendship. This stage is represented by open disclosure, sincerity, and intimacy.

The planner will more fully understand the client's goals, deeply understand how their life experience plays into their financial planning process, and the planner will understand how to provide a comfortable space that helps clients fully express themselves.

Stage 4: Stable Exchange

Clients and planners move into the **stable exchange** phase when they have developed a consistent and established pattern together. The pattern is most often represented by open, uninhibited, friendly, and meaningful conversation.

In this stage, the planner demonstrates deep levels of empathy towards the client. They are generally able to anticipate questions, feelings, and behavioral tendencies. The client-planner relationship is strong and is expected to be long term. Honesty, trust, and mutual benefit are hallmarks of this stage.

Not all client-planner relationships will proceed through all four of these stages of social penetration. There is no "typical" timeline for how long the process will be. Each client-planner relationship will proceed in its own unique way.

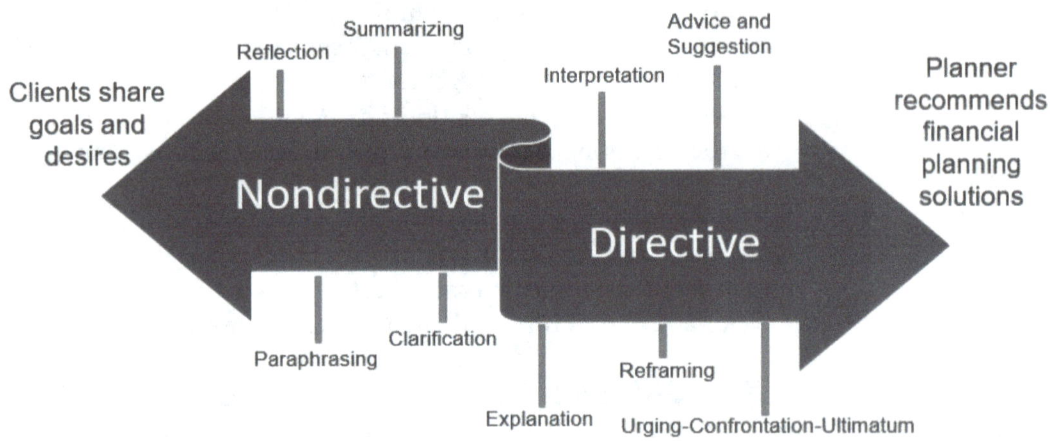

Nondirective and Directive Communication
Based on *Communication Essentials for Financial Planners: Strategies and Techniques* by John Grable and Joseph Goetz.

Nondirective Counseling Skills

Nondirective counseling skills are considered one of the following:

- **Nondirectional**—There is not a clear path forward in the conversation as established by the planner.
- **Client-centered**, or client-directed—There client is taking the lead in the focus and direction of the conversation.

Nondirective counseling skills encourage clients to reflect and share their goals, beliefs, traditions, cultural background, feelings, and concerns in a thorough and open manner. They allow planners to understand their clients better. They allow the planner to support clients in discussing their circumstances, challenges and financial plans thoroughly and comfortably. Some may assume that nondirective communication is not time effective or necessary; however, should understand that creating financial plans before thoroughly understanding the client's perspective, goals, beliefs, and concerns may lead to ineffective recommendations.

Types of Nondirective Counseling Skills

Clarification. **Clarification** is used to ensure the planner understands the client. The planner may request that clients clarify what they said, often by prefacing what needs clarification then asking a question.

EXAMPLE Clarification

The conversation below illustrates how the planner uses the clarification technique.

Client: (Tells the planner about how she would like to save for her children's college education and her retirement.)

Planner: I want to make sure I fully understood you when you told me about your savings goals for your children's college expenses. Will you tell me about your goals again with more information on what colleges you think they will attend and what expenses you'd like to save for?

Paraphrasing. When planners **paraphrase**, they use their words to express something that was said by their clients. This involves rephrasing clients' statements or restating their meanings. Paraphrasing contributes to helpful communication in three ways.

1. Planners ensure that they have heard their clients correctly.
2. Clients are given the opportunity to self-reflect.
3. Clients can provide correction if the planners paraphrased inaccurately.

Generally, there are two types of paraphrases, the first of which is the **restatement paraphrase**. Here, the planner essentially repeats what the client says in another way.

EXAMPLE Restatement Paraphrase

The restatement paraphrase technique is illustrated in the dialogue below.

Client: I'm concerned that if I invest in this mutual fund right now it will go down in value quickly, just like one of my other investments did.

Planner: Part of you expects that this mutual fund won't perform well, like your other investment...

Restatement paraphrase has limited value because its purpose simply is to clarify what the client has said.

The second type of paraphrase is the **meaning paraphrase**, which restates clients' statements in the context of what the planner believes the clients have in mind.

EXAMPLE Meaning Paraphrase

Here, the planner paraphrases to confirm that the meaning of what the client is saying is understood.

Client: I think I might need to look further into your stock recommendations.

Planner: You aren't sure you are ready to move forward at this point.

Additionally, the planner would likely depend upon nonverbal messages and previous exchanges when making this paraphrase of meaning.

Summarizing. In contrast to a paraphrase, a **summarization** is a brief outline of a discussion. Summaries allow the planner to verify that they are capturing clients' key goals, values, and intentions at that point in the dialogue.

EXAMPLE Summarizing

In the conversation below, to confirm that the planner understands the client's values and goals, he recaps what the client has said.

Client: (Shares her values and goals with the planner.)

Planner: Overall, when discussing what's important to you, I hear you say that you value an honest relationship with your planner and regular emails to update you on the progress of your financial plan development. Additionally, your two top goals are more diversification of your assets, and having your surviving family members maintain their standard of living when you pass away.

Reflection. **Reflection** involves mirroring the emotional state or mood of the client in words. This is important in building rapport with clients and fosters a relationship of trust. Additionally, it often helps clients confront challenges and work through them. Financial discussions often provoke feelings such as fear, excitement, distress, and guilt. It is important for the planner to follow the client's lead when choosing which feelings to reflect. The words the planner uses matter, especially when a client is emotional. Feeling reflections are often best employed when they are short and to the emotional point.

EXAMPLE Reflection

Here, the planner paraphrases to confirm that the meaning of what the client is saying is understood.

Client: I am so very angry my manager passed me up for a promotion! I have given my life to that company, and for what?!

Planner: I understand you're angry right now, really feel you deserved the promotion, and want to know why you didn't get it given your loyalty to the company.

Directive Counseling Skills

Directive counseling skills are financial planner centered or financial planner directed. The planner takes the lead in choosing how the conversation progresses when employing directive communication skills. The skills described here may better help planners recognize when, how, and why they should use a particular directive counseling technique.

At some point, all financial planning requires the planner to guide the clients toward their financial goals. This requires the planner to take the lead in choosing the focus and content of meetings with clients.

Types of Directive Counseling Skills

Interpretation. **Interpretation** involves helping clients understand their situations using financial terms and principles.

EXAMPLE Interpretation

Assume that the planner and client have been working together for some time and have an excellent relationship.

Client: Wow, I'm not sure why, but I am feeling really worried lately. My partner, Jordan, and I are spending money like crazy. I don't want to think about our budget. I'm sure we are waaay over on what we're spending on clothes.

Planner: Your anxiety is totally normal.

Client: Really???

Planner: Absolutely. Jordan usually does the back-to-school uniform shopping every year. This year, you went along and actually saw how much the clothes cost, which was a lot. What you think is a spending spree is normal for your family's clothing expenses at the start of a school year. And, remember, you budgeted for this increase, so it's all good.

Reframing. **Reframing** helps clients shift their perspectives by considering circumstances, feelings, or thoughts from another viewpoint. Planners use this skill when clients may benefit from information not previously considered. This can also relate to helping the clients see their present situation from a different, yet more beneficial perspective. Reframing is typically done in a non-confrontational manner.

EXAMPLE Reframing

Here, the planner reframes the client's current circumstances into an opportunity to learn from an unfortunate experience. Note that the planner's first sentence is paraphrasing in practice.

Client: Ugh. I feel like I've messed up my future because of all the poor financial decisions I've made.

Planner: It's really tough to go through how things have played out. Maybe there's another way to look at this. What have you learned from your financial challenges that will help you do better from here on out?

Explanation. An **explanation** is a descriptive statement used to make something more straightforward or understandable. When clients lack information, they often need to receive the missing information in a clear manner. Understanding financial concepts and principles may be especially challenging for clients with limited financial backgrounds. A *planner's* understanding of concepts is not sufficient; they should be explained to clients in a way that *they* understand.

Advice. This is giving **advice**, or direction, to a client. Advising is one of the most obvious and utilized directive skills that planners use. Note that although advice may seem to be what a client wants, but when given without thoroughly understanding the client's situation (through the use of nondirective counseling skills), advice may not be well received. In other words, what clients really need may be to explore thoroughly their situation before they receive advice on how to proceed.

Planners should inquire about what the client has already done in the past before providing advice. Additionally, clients may benefit from giving **advice with permission**. This directive counseling skill involves planners refraining from giving unsolicited advice. Rather, they should give clients guidance only if the clients agree to receive it. Thus, clients may feel more empowered and may consider themselves more involved in the financial decision-making process.

EXAMPLE Advice with Permission

The planner's statement below demonstrates how to approach a client by asking permission to give advice.

Clients: (Share their financial circumstances, including how they spend considerable amounts of money on expensive luxury items, such as cars and extravagant trips. They share with the planner that they want to spend much less and invest more.)

Planner: I have some idea about how you might move forward from here. Would you like to hear them or is there something else you'd like to talk about?

Suggestion. Although advice and suggestion seem very similar, **suggestion** is different because, unlike advice, it includes helping clients choose a course of action through their own initiative. In this case, clients are finding their own direction, with the planner's guidance, rather than the planner directly offering the direction. Another way to view the difference between advice and suggestion is that advice provides answers/direction; suggestion provides information. Planners often practice suggestion by bringing together multiple solutions, present the advantages and disadvantages of each, and then allow the client to choose among the alternatives.

Urging. **Urging** is prompting the client to take immediate action and is more directive than the previous examples of directive counseling skills. Urging is typically practiced in crises. Planners may turn to urging if nondirective communication has been ineffective. They are seeking to motivate clients extrinsically instead of motivating them to make their decisions independently. Urging should be used sparingly and only when absolutely needed. It is possible that planners who frequently urge their clients will develop weak, fragile, and distrustful relationships.

Confrontation. Planners directly sharing their disagreement with their clients is **confrontation**. This skill is normally utilized when there is high trust already developed in the relationship. It may be used when a client needs to be prompted into action. Remember, it can also backfire and lead to a weakening of the client-planner relationship. Additionally, sharing disagreement does not need to be forceful or hurtful. It can be done in a way that still honors the client's autonomy.

EXAMPLE Confrontation

The planner's response below represents the use of appropriate confrontation.

Client: (Reveals to the planner that she is going to make a significant investment in her brother's business that is financially unstable.)

Planner: I have to be honest with you here. I am concerned that the path you are about to take is too risky. I don't agree that it is a good choice to make. In the end, the decision is yours to make, but I feel it's my responsibility to be truthful with you.

Ultimatum. For the purpose of use in financial planning, an ultimatum is giving the choice to a client to change behavior immediately or the client-planner relationship will end. They are normally used when a client's behavior becomes dysfunctional and disruptive to a planner's practice and/or when is appears that ethical boundaries may be crossed by the client.

Counseling Theory

There are several approaches planners can take with their clients when providing counseling with the goal of helping them change their financial behavior. Examples of these approaches, which involve education and guidance, are introduced next.

Economic and resource approach. Clients are assumed to be rational and will change to the most favorable behavior if given the appropriate counseling. In this approach, the financial planner is the agent of change. The focus is on obtaining and analyzing quantitative data, such as cash flow, assets, and debt.

Classical economics approach. Clients choose among alternatives based on objectively defined cost-benefit and risk-return tradeoffs. The belief in this approach is that increasing financial resources or reducing financial expenditures results in improved financial outcomes.

Strategic management approach. A client's goals and values drive the client-planner relationship. Conducting a SWOT analysis (identifying strengths, weaknesses, opportunities, and threats) is done early in the financial planning process.

Cognitive-behavioral approach. Clients' attitudes, beliefs, and values influence their behavior. Planners use this approach attempt to substitute negative beliefs that lead to poor financial decisions with positive attitudes, which should result in better financial results.

Psychoanalytic approach. Based on the use of psychoanalytic theory, such as Freudian psychodynamic theory or Gestalt theory, this approach is not widely used by planners.

Politeness and Sensitivity

Politeness and sensitivity begin with planners understanding who they are as people. As planners better understand themselves, they open themselves up to better understanding their clients. The way planners view the world will influence their ability to respond politely and sensitively to clients. It is important for planners to learn about themselves as a cultural being. Everyone comes from their own unique background related to gender, ethnicity, sexual orientation, disability status, socioeconomic standing, political affiliations, educational backgrounds, and regional backgrounds. Much of the unintentional impoliteness and insensitivity results from individuals not thinking deeply enough about whom they are as people.

Sensitivity relates to planners' ability to respond thoughtfully to clients. Planners risk being insensitive when they make assumptions about clients. When planners assume that clients align with dominant culture perspectives, groups, and/or beliefs, there will likely be issues in the client-planner relationship.

Inclusion and Exclusion

It is important to deliver inclusive messages to clients. This means that a client's presence is acknowledged and considered important. For example, in a meeting where there are two financial professionals working with a client, it is important for them to use terminology that the client understands when speaking to one another. If the financial professionals speak to one another about financial concepts in a highly technical manner, the client may be implicitly excluded from the conversation.

Exclusion occurs any time clients feel that they are left out of a conversation or relationship. Exclusion can occur in subtle ways. Consider how planners could exclude an important part of a clients' identities if they assume clients were in heterosexual relationships when, in fact, they are in same sex relationships. Overall, it is important for planners to be thoughtful of their language so all clients are included.

DEVELOPING A CLIENT-PLANNER RELATIONSHIP OF HONESTY AND TRUST

Developing an Honest and Trusting Client-Planner Relationship

It stands to reason that clients must perceive their planner as trustworthy if the relationship is going to be productive. Client's trust in their planners is linked directly with the probability that they will implement recommendations made by these planners. Several factors contribute to a client-planner relationship of honesty and trust. Some of these factors are discussed below.

Counseling Skills

Many of the counseling skills addressed in the previous section foster honest and trusting relationships between planners and their clients. When clients feel heard, understood, and respected by their planners, they are more likely to trust them. Nondirective counseling skills are especially important when developing these relationships. Paraphrasing, summarizing, reflecting, and clarifying, along with the appropriate use of open-ended questions, are especially important in building trust and helping to place the client at ease. Additionally, these skills will lead the client to be more open when discussing their financial goals, beliefs, and challenges.

Cultural Implications

Understanding and responding sensitively to clients of all cultures is also needed for an honest and trusting client-planner relationship. Culture relates to the values, beliefs, practices, norms, roles, social regularities, and styles of communication that are learned and shared generationally. Planners who fail to consider the cultural preferences of their clients are likely to lack professional success.

It helps to recognize to what extent a client aligns with an individualist or collectivist cultural frame of reference. It is best to think of individualism and collectivism as a continuum (individualism at one end of the continuum and collectivism at the other end). These backgrounds influence the beliefs, actions, and attitudes that people hold.

Individualism. Clients who come from an individualist background tend to value independence and uniqueness. They may desire equal power dynamics in relationships. This could mean that they want a more collaborative and honest process with planners.

Collectivism. Clients who come from a collectivist background tend to value interdependence, social cooperation, conformity, and inclusivity. They may be more open to unequal and hierarchical power dynamics. This could mean that the client expects the planner to take the lead, be the expert, and provide recommendations. The client may be more hesitant to collaborate in the process.

These principles of collectivism and individualism are general and only begin to explain how culture influences trust and honesty. It is also important to note that there is great variety in how culture influences each individual, therefore nondirective counseling skills become essential in learning as much as possible about the worldviews, traditions, values, and beliefs of each client.

It is also important to note that determining a specific client's social risk tolerance is also influenced by culture. **Social risk** relates to the level that one is willing to engage openly with another person. It is especially important to keep social risk in mind at the initiation of relationships with new clients. Each client will have unique experiences and traditions regarding discussions with others. It may be taboo to talk openly about fears and worries for some, and completely normal for others.

PROFESSIONAL LIABILITY

As members of a profession, financial planners are expected to comply with ethical standards and perform their services in accordance with accepted principles and standards. Financial planners who fail to perform such duties may be civilly liable to their clients, for whom they have agreed to provide services, and to third parties, who may have relied upon statements the financial planner has prepared. Civil and criminal liability may also be imposed upon financial planners through statutes such as the federal securities laws.

Common Law Liability to Clients

Common law liability
Liability based on breach of contract, tort of negligence, or fraud

Common law liability to which a financial planner may be subject is based on breach of contract, tort of negligence, or fraud. The failure to perform one's contractual duties is a breach of contract for which one is liable to the party to whom the performance was to be rendered. Thus, if a financial planner has agreed to perform certain services for a client and fails to perform those contractual duties honestly, properly, and completely, the financial planner may be civilly liable. If there has been a breach of contract by a financial planner, courts may award compensatory damages as a remedy to the client.

A financial planner has a duty to exercise the same standard of care that a reasonably prudent and skillful financial planner in the community would exercise under similar circumstances. A violation of generally accepted principles and standards is sufficient evidence of negligence but a financial planner may comply with accepted principles and standards and still be negligent for failure to act with reasonable care. The financial planner, however, is not liable for errors in judgment if made according to accepted practices and with reasonable care or if the client's own negligence or intentional acts contributed significantly to the client's loss.

In an action based on fraud, the client must establish that the financial planner made a false representation of a material fact. The misrepresentation by the financial planner must have been made with the knowledge that it was false (actual fraud) or with reckless disregard for its truth or falsity (constructive fraud). For the fact to be deemed material, the financial planner must have intentionally made the misrepresentation to induce the client to act or discourage the client from acting, and the client must have been injured as a result of his reasonable reliance on the misrepresentation. Damages for common law liability will be equal to the actual or anticipated losses incurred by the client as a result of the breach of contract, negligent act, or fraud and may include the cost of securing the services of another financial planner.

Common Law Liability to Third Parties

Third parties are not clients of the financial planner but are persons who reasonably relied on documents prepared by the financial planner. Traditionally, in common law, a financial planner does not owe contractual duties to third parties unless they are direct parties to or third party beneficiaries of a contract for the planner's services. The financial planner may, however, be subject to tort liability, which is based on negligence in failing to exercise ordinary, reasonable care. If a third party is injured because he reasonably relied on documents prepared by a financial planner who failed to act with reasonable care, the financial planner may be liable and compensatory damages may be awarded.

Statutory Liability

Securities Act of 1933
Federal law that provides rules and regulations related to new issues of investment securities

The financial planner is subject to criminal liability imposed by the Securities Act of 1933, the Securities Exchange Act of 1934, the Investment Advisers Act of 1940 (discussed in Appendix C), and other federal statutes and state criminal codes. The **Securities Act of 1933** provides rules and regulations related to new issues of investment securities such as initial public offerings. Before the issuer can offer the securities to the public, a registration statement that includes financial statements of the firm must be filed with the Securities and Exchange Commission (SEC).

Securities Exchange Act of 1934
Federal law that provides rules and regulations related to the purchase and sale of investment securities in the secondary market

The **Securities Exchange Act of 1934** provides rules and regulations related to the purchase and sale of investment securities in the market after the initial offering. Under this act, persons are liable for false or misleading statements of material facts that are made in applications, reports, documents, and registration statements filed with the SEC. Liability is also imposed on financial planners who have access to material nonpublic information and trade in securities without making a disclosure. It is unlawful to use any manipulative or deceptive device in connection with the sale or purchase of securities such as attempting to defraud, making untrue statements of material facts, and omitting true statements of material facts. The financial planner will be liable to a person who was injured because he purchased or sold securities as a result of such misrepresentation.

Educate Your Client

A significant role of a personal financial planner is that of educator. The client may need to be taught the meaning of common financial planning terminology, such as the time value of money and opportunity costs. The professional financial planner should be an expert in the use of time value of money principles to assist clients in putting financial choices into a logical, systematic, and quantifiable framework. For most clients, the best understood time reference is today. The planner may project that the client will need $1 million at age 62 to quit working (achieve financial independence) and continue to maintain the same preretirement lifestyle. If the client is currently 35 years old, the million dollars and the 27 years until he will need the money may have little relevance. The planner can create relevance and understanding, however, by calculating the need in today's dollars. In this example, $1 million is equal to roughly $100,000 in invested assets or, alternatively, if the client has no investments, $731.25 will need to be saved each month. (This calculation was determined by assuming 324 months of saving $731.25 at an earnings rate of 9% per year to accumulate $1 million at age 62.) The reality of the $100,000 or the $731.25 each month is much more meaningful to the client than the distant $1 million. People understand today's realities and values much better than of those in the future.

Learning styles [auditory, visual, kinetic (or tactile)]
The conditions under which people learn best. Clients whose preferred learning style is auditory learn best by hearing information; clients who prefer a visual learning style learn best by reading and viewing; those who prefer a kinetic, or tactile, style learn best through manipulation and testing information

Clients may need education during the development of goals and objectives or the selection and implementation of the financial strategy. Undoubtedly, clients will need to be educated on many aspects of the financial planning process throughout the relationship. Therefore, the planner should understand how individuals learn. Learning is easier and more effective when people are taught in a manner conducive to their learning style. People who learn best by listening prefer the auditory learning style. Those who prefer to learn by seeing are visual learners. Kinetic, or tactile, learners learn best by doing. Most likely, clients will not know their preferred **learning style**. Exhibit 3.3 may help you gain a better understanding of a client's learning style.

EXHIBIT 3.3 Determining Learning Styles

If Your Client...	Her Learning Style is Most Likely ...	She Should be Educated by...
Talks about situations; expresses emotions verbally; enjoys listening but cannot wait to talk; tends to move lips or subvocalize when reading.	Auditory	Providing verbal instruction and repeating yourself often.
Seems to enjoy watching demonstrations; has intense concentration and ability to visually imagine information; writes things down and takes detailed notes; doodles and looks around studying the environment; often becomes impatient when extensive listening is involved.	Visual	Providing written information, especially charts, graphs, and pictures. This client learns best by studying alone.
Fidgets when reading; is easily distracted when not able to move; expresses emotions physically by jumping and gesturing; does not listen well and tries things out by touching, feeling, and manipulating; needs frequent breaks during meetings.	Kinetic or tactile	Providing exercises or assignments to perform. This client learns best by manipulating and testing information.

Understand the Client's Thinking Phase

The financial planner should be aware that the financial planning process can be both comforting and confusing to a client—comforting because action is being taken to accomplish goals but confusing because this is usually the time when the client realizes the magnitude of the planning choices and decisions required. The planner is responsible for assisting the client throughout this process and providing education and reassurance when necessary. Exhibit 3.4 depicts the common thinking phases that a client often progresses through while establishing a financial plan. The objective is for the client to achieve the high cognitive thinking phase. The financial planner should be knowledgeable about these common phases of thinking and assist the client in progressing through them while establishing financial direction. The planner should help the client transition from the outer edge of the circle to the inner circle in Exhibit 3.4.

EXHIBIT 3.4 Common Thinking Phases

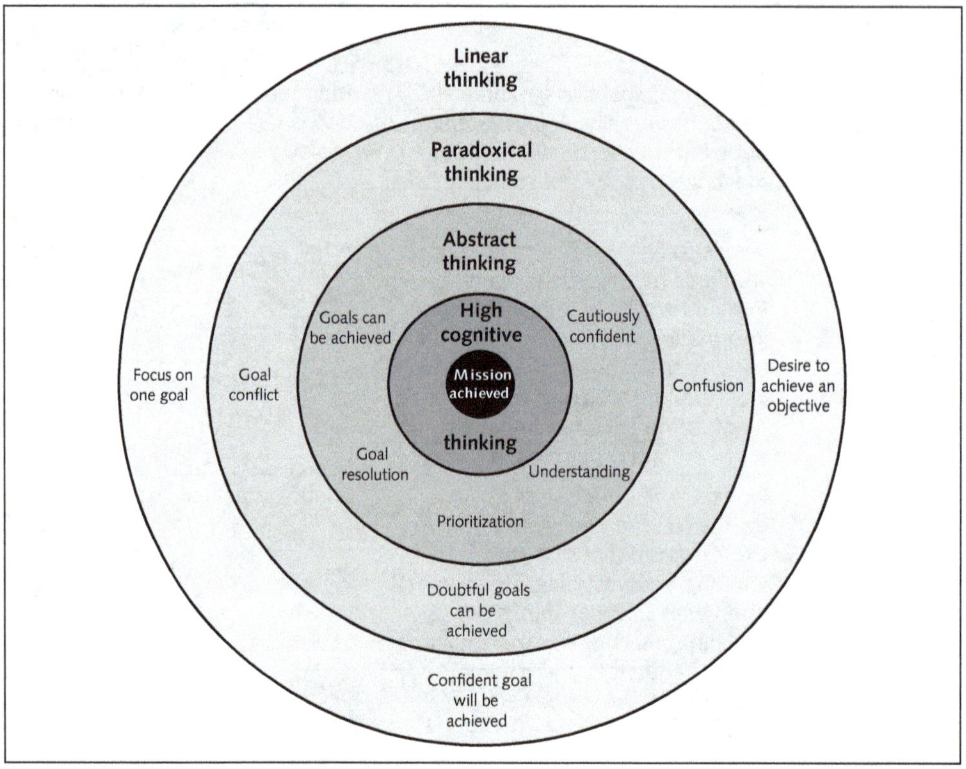

Linear Thinking

Generally, individuals who are just beginning to plan financially are in the outer phase of thinking, referred to as linear thinking. Focusing on accomplishing a particular goal or objective describes the concept of linear thinking. During this phase, an individual's financial plan is compartmentalized and simplistic. The primary interest is in achieving one or two narrow objectives. Confidence that objectives can and will be achieved is high. However, once the individual begins to face the reality that saving for one objective means forgoing funds in another area because funds are limited, confidence in the ability to achieve overall goals is often questioned and the person may give up. During this phase, the client may increase savings or set up a special savings account to save for something only to find that those funds must be used for day-to-day or unexpected expenses. Because of the frequent failure to achieve all goals, clients often give up the idea of developing a financial plan. However, if success is achieved in the linear phase, the client's thinking usually changes from linear to paradoxical.

Paradoxical Thinking

During this phase, the client begins to focus on several simultaneous objectives. As a result, it is during this phase in particular that people become frustrated. They may become overwhelmed with the amount of financial planning required and discover that many of their objectives are in conflict with each other. They often become uncertain of their ability to accomplish any of their financial objectives. Confusion, goal conflict, and ambiguity characterize the paradoxical thinking phase. During this phase an individual often seeks the advice of a financial planner. The financial planner can be of great comfort to clients during this phase by assuring them that goal conflict and confusion are common and can be overcome by good planning.

Abstract Thinking

The skilled financial planner can assist a client in advancing from paradoxical thinking to abstract thinking by providing education and encouragement. During the abstract thinking phase, clients begin to integrate elements of the financial plan into their day-to-day lives. They become aware of the consequences of their financial actions and can conceptually understand how savings and consumption decisions impact their financial plans. At this point, clients commonly become confident that identified goals and objectives can be achieved.

High Cognitive Thinking

The ultimate phase of development is the high cognitive thinking phase. The client becomes enlightened about the financial issues that exist in everyday life. Once this phase is achieved, clients have a great amount of control over their financial future. They are able to successfully integrate their entire financial plan into the other aspects of their lives. During this phase, the mission of achieving financial independence and avoiding catastrophic financial occurrences and financial dependence is most likely achieved.

The personal financial planner greatly increases the probability of developing an appropriate financial strategy and having it properly implemented if a good relationship with the client is established, communication skills are practiced, the client's preferred learning style is identified, and the financial planner understands the client's current phase of thinking.

INTERNAL ANALYSIS

The internal environment defines the way people live, work, spend, save, and think. Internal data about the client are needed to understand the environment in which the client exists and the strengths and weaknesses that are present. Once a good working relationship is developed with the client, and communication lines are open, it is easy to collect most of the internal data needed. The key is to know what information to collect and how to collect it efficiently and accurately. Internal data can be divided into five general categories, which include the following facts about the client:

- Life cycle position
- Attitudes and beliefs
- Special needs
- Financial position
- Perception of his financial situation

Life Cycle Positioning

Life cycle positioning
Using information about a client's age, marital status, dependents, income level, and net worth to help determine goals and risks

Life cycle positioning information is needed because it plays a significant role in affecting a client's goals and behaviors. It also suggests which financial risks currently exist. To identify the client's life cycle position, the planner needs to have the following information about the client:

- Age
- Marital status

- Dependents
- Income level
- Net worth

Age

Age is one of the most important and revealing factors in financial planning. Generally, young people give little thought to retirement goals or wealth-transfer goals. As people age, they become aware that adequate retirement income requires funding. At some time, they begin to seriously plan for this financial goal. In the recent past, it was common for people to become conscious about their "retirement reality" as late as age 50. Today, clients are beginning to become aware of this issue at a much younger age. Perhaps this is the result of the increased amount of readily available information on the cost of retirement and the necessity to plan early.

Marital Status

The second factor that affects goal determination is marital status. The desire to provide for one's dependents creates a host of goals to achieve and risks to avoid. Married couples commonly combine their future economic resources to jointly purchase assets, such as a house, by jointly committing to indebtedness. The purchase of a personal residence through indebtedness, which can be afforded only by combining both incomes, creates an interdependency of one spouse on the other. If one spouse were to suffer unemployment, untimely death, disability, or some other catastrophic event, the commitment to the repayment of the debt may not be met.

Dependents

A third factor affecting the creation of goals is the existence of dependents. Dependents may be children, grandchildren, or elderly parents. Parents commonly have goals of providing education for their children. Education can be an expensive goal that requires substantial expenditures made over a finite period. For example, the average total cost of a college education at a private university in the United States is currently about $55,800 per year, according to *Trends in College Pricing*, a 2021 report from the College Board. If we assume two children and four years in college, the current total cost of such an education would be about $446,000. Whatever the cost, it is probably a substantial amount, on a relative basis, for most 40-year-old clients to take on. Even public university education (in-state) is high—approximately $27,330 for each student per year. Not all parents feel obligated to provide their children with a college education. However, many parents do, and many more wish they were able to do so.

Grandchildren may also be considered dependents. People may have grandchildren as early as in their 30s but more commonly in their 50s or older. The significance of grandchildren is not that they are actual dependents; rather, that grandchildren may signal the initial phase of wealth transfer. Grandparents may find themselves with more assets and income than they feel necessary to sustain their lifestyle. At that point, they may begin to provide financially for their grandchildren.

Other examples of dependencies that affect goals are caring for an aging parent or providing special care to a handicapped child or sibling. Planners should realize that married people with children are not the only ones with dependents. Single, childless people also may have financial dependents by taking on the obligations of aging parents or other loved ones.

Income and Net Worth

Income and net worth are the last two factors concerning life cycle positioning. Substantial income suggests an opportunity to achieve financial goals, as long as the goals are realistic relative to the income. Lower income presents greater challenges in achieving financial security and financial independence. People with a low income and low net worth generally have a more difficult time overcoming financial setbacks. In contrast, a person with substantial net worth is generally less likely to suffer catastrophic consequences from a single financial setback. Substantial net worth also implies a need for increased management of assets and planning. The general rule is that the greater the income or net worth, the greater the interest in tax deferral or avoidance.

Life Cycle Phases and Characteristics

Life cycle phases
Intervals in a client's life cycle that tend to give a planner insight into the client's financial objectives and concerns (asset-accumulation, conservation/protection, and distribution/gifting phases)

As people progress through their lives, there is a tendency to move subtly but surely among financial objectives because of changes in personal financial circumstances. We have identified and labeled these **life cycle phases** and characteristics as the asset-accumulation phase, the conservation/protection phase, and the distribution/gifting phase. Although not all people move through these phases at the same rate, a sufficient percentage of people do, which enables financial planners to gain valuable insight into their clients' objectives and concerns by identifying which phase or phases their clients are in at a particular time. Exhibit 3.5 illustrates the life cycle phases and the typical characteristics of each phase.

EXHIBIT 3.5 Life Cycle Phases and Characteristics

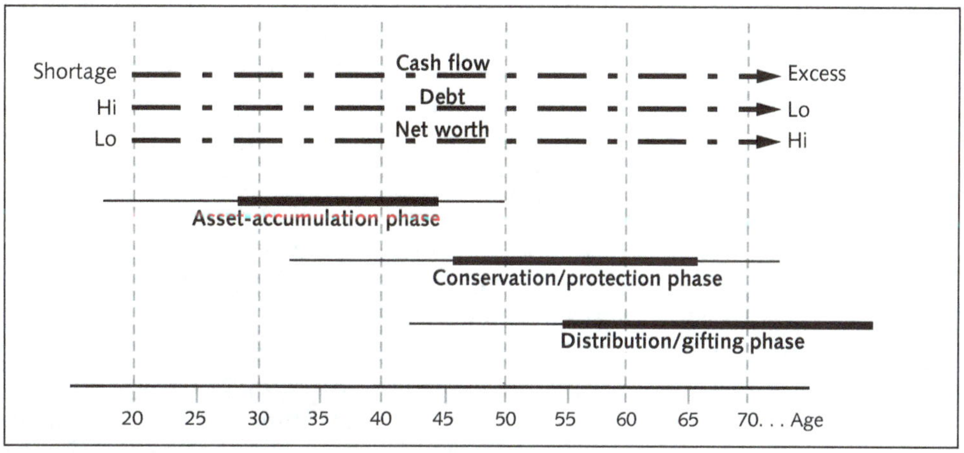

Asset Accumulation

Asset-accumulation phase
Life cycle phase through which clients pass; usually begins between the ages of 20 and 25 and lasts until about age 50, characterized by limited excess funds for investing, high degree of debt, and low net worth

The **asset-accumulation phase** usually begins somewhere between the ages of 20 and 25 and lasts until about age 50. The beginning of this phase is characterized by limited excess funds for investing, a relatively high degree of debt, and a low net worth. At the beginning of this phase, there is generally a low appreciation for the risks that exist. As the person moves through the asset-accumulation phase, cash for investments generally increases, the use of debt as a percentage of total assets decreases, and net worth increases.

Conservation/Protection

Conservation/protection phase
Life cycle phase through which clients pass characterized by an increase in cash flow, assets, and net worth, with some decrease in the proportional use of debt

The **conservation/protection phase** begins when one has acquired some assets, usually in the late 30s or 40s, and may last throughout the work life expectancy. This phase characterized by an increase in cash flow, assets, and net worth, with some decrease in the proportional use of debt. People generally become more risk averse as they acquire more assets. From an investments viewpoint, they are more concerned about losing what they have acquired than acquiring more. They become aware of and concerned with many of the risks they ignored at the beginning of the asset-accumulation phase, including an increased awareness of life's risks (e.g., untimely death, unemployment, and disability). This is not to say that they have completely left the asset-accumulation phase. At least at the beginning, they are simultaneously in both phases (trying to accumulate while trying not to lose what they have).

Making payments for children's education and saving for retirement frequently characterize the conservation/protection phase. It is the time when the client feels a real struggle between current-consumption needs and deferred-consumption necessities. It is also during this period that the client is most financially confused because of the conflicting goals and perceived risks. One of the financial planner's greatest opportunities to assist the client exists during this phase.

Distribution/Gifting

Distribution/gifting phase
Life cycle phase through which clients pass characterized by excess relative cash flows, low debt, and high relative net worth

The **distribution/gifting phase** begins subtly when the person realizes she can afford to spend money on things she never believed possible. The asset-accumulation and conservation/protection phases make this phase possible. At the beginning of this phase, the person is often simultaneously in both the asset-accumulation and conservation/protection phases. When parents purchase new cars for adult children, pay for a grandchild's private school tuition, or take themselves on relatively expensive vacations, they are likely in the distribution/gifting phase.

The distribution/gifting phase may begin as early as the late 40s and continue until death. Excess relative cash flows, low debt, and high relative net worth characterize this phase. At the onset of this phase, the client begins to feel financial pressures declining, starts to believe life is short and should be enjoyed, and cares less about material things. Now, clients start asking, "Where did yesterday go?" It is also during this period that life's risks are put into perspective. Frequently, during this phase, life insurance is reduced or dropped, deductibles are raised, and the client achieves more financial balance and confidence.

People are often in two life cycle phases simultaneously, although not necessarily to the same degree. By determining where the client is in terms of these phases, we can gain some insight about the person's financial goals, concerns, and behaviors, which will help serve the client better. Throughout the text, we will refer to whether the client, in a specific application, is predominantly in the asset-accumulation, conservation/protection, or distribution gifting phase, or some combination. We do so to put the client's goals and risks into perspective and gain insight into appropriate financial planning solutions.

Once life cycle positioning is completed, the experienced financial planner can develop a generic financial plan to meet clients' needs who are in similar life cycle phases. Exhibit 3.6 illustrates some generalized life cycle positions and the likely goals and risks associated with each. Remember, however, these are only generalizations. Although enough information has been obtained to begin developing a client's financial plan, much more information is required before an accurate financial plan can be developed for a particular individual.

EXHIBIT 3.6 Selected Life Cycle Positions and Related Goals and Risks

Life Cycle Position	Phase	Common Goals	Risks					
			L	H	D	LTC	P	LB
25- to 35-year-old single (S/25–35); modest income/ net worth	AAP	Savings; investment; wealth accumulation; personal residence; debt management	X	✓	✓	X	✓	✓
25- to 35-year-old married with young, dependent children (MWC/25–35); moderate income/net worth	AAP	Education funding; savings; investment; wealth accumulation; personal residence; debt management	✓	✓	✓	X	✓	✓
40- to 50-year-old with dependent children	AAP, CPP	Retirement planning; education funding; savings; investment; wealth accumulation; debt management	✓	✓	✓	X	✓	✓
62- to 68-year-old; retired with adult children and grandchildren	CPP, DGP	Estate planning	X	✓	X	?	?	✓

Key:
L = Life
H = Health
D = Disability
LTC = Long-term care
P = Property
LB = Liability

✓ = The risk is likely.
X = The risk is not likely.
? = The risk is possible.

AAP = Asset-accumulation phase
CPP = Conservation/protection phase
DGP = Distribution/gifting phase

Client data collection questionnaire
A survey used by financial planners to gather internal data from clients, such as their tolerance for risk and their personal perception of their financial situation, as well as tax-related data, Social Security numbers, information relating to their dependents, and so on

Life cycle positioning is one of the easiest types of internal data to collect. The client is usually comfortable providing this information because it is not too personal and the client probably expects to be asked such questions. This information may be gathered during a face-to-face meeting, a telephone meeting, or by using a **client data collection questionnaire** similar to the one in Appendix 3-A at the end of the chapter.

Attitudes and Beliefs

The second type of internal data identifies the client's attitudes and beliefs. Attitudes and beliefs are important because they play a significant role in affecting the goals and behaviors of individuals. Information that should be gathered includes the client's:

- risk tolerance levels;
- savings and consumption habits;
- views about employment, retirement, and leisure time; and
- attitude regarding government, especially taxation.

Risk Tolerance Levels

Risk tolerance
The level of risk exposure with which an individual is comfortable

Knowledge of **risk tolerance** levels helps the financial planner determine the types of investments and the style of risk management best suited for the client. The style of risk management refers to the degree to which insurance is sought for mitigation of small to moderate losses. Risk management involves balancing lower premiums and self-reliance for small losses with higher premiums and less loss exposure. Stated risk tolerance levels may be misinterpreted because they are subjective. The statement, "I am not very risk tolerant," may mean different things to different clients. Therefore, additional questioning is needed to ensure understanding. Implementing the communication techniques discussed earlier can assist the planner. In addition to using a client data collection questionnaire, a discussion of the client's past investment decisions can help in assessing the client's risk tolerance level. The concept of risk management will be emphasized throughout the text with special emphasis in the chapters on insurance and investments.

Savings and Consumption Habits

Information regarding a client's savings and consumption habits assists the planner in developing a successful strategic financial plan for the client. If the client does not have a history of consistently saving money, it would be wise to develop a strategy in which money is directed into savings prior to the client receiving a paycheck from the employer. Similarly, if the client has a history of making impulsive large-dollar purchases, it would be wise to discuss ways to institute barriers to this behavior. Historical behavior is the best indicator of future behavior. A good way to collect information about the client's savings and consumption habits is to ask the client detailed questions and to review inflows and outflows for previous years.

Views on Employment, Retirement, Leisure Time

A client's view of employment, retirement, and leisure time is often useful to a financial planner because it provides information about likely behavior. A person who is unhappy with his job or who places a high value on leisure time may be more likely to take spontaneous vacations. The financial planner may want to incorporate these likely-but-unplanned expenditures into the financial strategy. Suppose a client is 55 years old, married with no dependent children, and is unsatisfied with his employment situation. Although this client may intend to work until age 62, the financial planner should be aware that this client might decide to retire earlier than planned, if financially able. The skilled financial planner will develop a strategy that includes contingency plans for various possibilities. Information about a client's views is best gathered through question-and-answer sessions with the client.

Attitude Toward Government

The last type of information about a client's attitudes and beliefs is the attitude toward government fiscal responsibility and taxation. A client who believes that government expenditures are wise and useful to the public would probably be less resistant to taxation than a client who believes that government essentially wastes whatever money it receives. These attitudes toward tax and government translate into financial planning issues in numerous ways. Some clients ignore the role taxes play in financial planning. Other clients are tax conscious and simply view the tax environment as one in which they live and must take into consideration. Still other clients are so focused on tax minimization that they spend extraordinary time and resources on the tax minimization objective, sometimes to the detriment of other goals.

Special Needs

The third type of internal data to be gathered concerns the client's special needs. Special needs may include planning for divorce, remarriage, aging parents, disabled children, terminal illness, nontraditional families, career changes, and unemployment.

Divorce

The financial planner can assist divorcing couples in determining an equitable division of marital assets and planning for the financial changes that accompany the separation of a household. Sources of inflows and outflows may change dramatically, making a review of the client's budget necessary. Other areas for review include:

- legally changing a client's name, changing beneficiaries of retirement plans, and evaluation of retirement funds;
- amending wills and setting up trusts for the benefit of children;
- requiring life insurance from a former spouse for the benefit of the client or children and changing beneficiaries;
- maintaining or acquiring health insurance for the client or children;
- evaluating the need for disability or long-term care insurance; and
- requiring funding from a former spouse for college education of children and assessing education funding requirements.

Remarriage

Many of the areas discussed in divorce planning are relevant in financial planning for remarriage. Besides continuation of insurance for the client and children and review of beneficiary designations, the financial planner should make clients aware of income that will be unavailable after remarriage and discuss integration of families for estate planning and education funding. Frequently, divorce decrees halt alimony payments when the receiver remarries, and Social Security benefits available to the client on the basis of the ex-spouse's earnings generally disappear. Child support, payment of insurance premiums, retirement benefits, and other sources of income from the former spouse may diminish or be eliminated. Finding replacement sources of income or helping the client adjust to a different standard of living is an important role of the financial planner.

When remarriage combines families, the financial planner will have an even larger role. Estate planning and education funding must consider the new couple's relationship with children from each other's previous marriage. A range of questions should be asked, from "Who should inherit the house?" to "How much college tuition would the couple fund?" The financial planner can offer an objective view on the fairness of property gifting and education funding from the perspective of children and stepchildren.

Aging Parents

With the increase in life expectancy, adults may be caring for their aging parents and grandparents for 10 or 20 years. The financial planner can reduce stress for clients faced with prolonged care of an elderly family member by helping them discuss living wills, powers of attorney, and long-term care options with their parents, as well as by helping them prepare financially for medical and living expenses. Two tax advantages that may apply are deductibility of medical expenses paid by the client for a dependent parent and the dependent-care tax credit. Using a loan against life insurance and a reverse mortgage, whereby the homeowner uses the equity in the home to pay expenses, are options that can be discussed with the aging family member. In planning for the care of a client's parents, financial planners must act objectively and with sensitivity.

Disabled Dependents

Many Americans have a child or spouse with a disability. Often, the client with a special-needs dependent is the primary caregiver. The financial planner can assist the client in planning for continuous care for the life of the child or spouse. Wills may need to be modified to provide a custodian for the dependent. Trusts can be created to secure assets for care after the client's death. Second-to-die life insurance, which pays out after both parents have died, may be appropriate for disabled children.

Terminal Illness

Families of a loved one with a terminal illness may come to the financial planner in a state of shock or denial. The financial planner can benefit the terminally ill client and family by retaining a level of detachment and being proactive in addressing financial issues. At the same time, the financial planner must be considerate and empathetic of family members' feelings. Some financial planning topics to address include:

- Estimation of medical or assisted-living expenses for physician, pharmacy, hospital, home health, and hospice care
- Budgeting for medical expenses, loss of income from inability to work or desire not to work, and last wishes
- Coverage provided under health and disability insurance; COBRA options; and government benefits such as Medicare, Medicaid, and Social Security
- Using life insurance benefits through a policy's accelerated benefits clause or through a viatical settlement (the sale of life insurance to a third party)
- Review of investment portfolio goals and time horizons
- Availability of benefits from retirement plans
- Powers of attorney, wills, living wills, and beneficiaries

Nontraditional Families

Unmarried heterosexual couples, domestic partners, and other nontraditional families can benefit greatly from the services of a financial planner. Although same-sex spouses now enjoy the same federal tax benefits as traditional spouses, certain rights and advantages available to married couples are not available to unmarried couples, even if they live together as a family and share common goals. For example, unmarried couples do not qualify for married-filing-jointly income tax status, the unlimited marital deduction for estate taxes, survivorship benefits from Social Security, the ability to direct medical treatment for each other, and legal transfer of assets at death without a will or proper titling of property. It is common for employer-provided retirement benefits and health insurance to be available only to the employee, a spouse, or relative. Besides addressing these disadvantages, the financial planner can help nontraditional families take advantage of their tax status. Because they are not married, both members receive the single standard deduction and may qualify for head of household status, which would reduce their tax liability. Mortgage interest paid on a first and second home is tax deductible. For married couples, this means they can deduct interest on two homes. For unmarried couples, they each can deduct interest on two homes.

Career Change and Unemployment

Career changes and unemployment present similar challenges to the client and his family. The family budget will need revising. Inflows will be reduced, and outflows may increase for job hunting and the purchase of new business clothes, education or training, and resumé preparation. Severance packages and unemployment benefits will help replace lost income for a short period. Health, life, and disability insurance may be eliminated, or premiums may increase. Retirement plans and investment portfolios should be reviewed. The financial planner can assist the client in making these adjustments.

Financial Position

The fourth type of internal data needed is the client's current financial position. This information is so important that it is the focus of Chapter 4. The gathering of information on financial position is the most time consuming step for two reasons. First, the client often does not readily know the answers to the questions. Therefore, some information may need to be collected from third parties, such as stockbrokers, accountants, employers, and lawyers. Second, the financial planner may need to prepare the client's personal financial statements. Financial statements include the statement of financial position (known as a balance sheet when used by a business), the personal statement of cash flows (known as an income statement when used by a business), and the statement of changes in net worth.

Information that needs to be collected to develop these financial statements includes the following:

- Assets
  - Cash, checking accounts, savings accounts
  - Mutual funds, ownership of business, brokerage and retirement accounts
  - Personal residence, jewelry, art collection, automobile
- Liabilities
  - Credit card debt, student loans
  - Auto loan, home mortgage
- Inflows
  - Salaries, bonuses
  - Interest income, employer contributions to retirement plan
- Outflows
  - Rent or mortgage payments, utilities, groceries
  - Insurance premiums, payments on credit cards and other debts, taxes
  - Deposits to savings accounts and retirement plans, donations to charity

In addition to developing financial statements, the financial planner must collect information about the client's insurance policies and coverage, investments, retirement, and other employee benefits. The client's historical tax returns are useful, as is information about any wills, trusts, or other estate planning documents. The planner should be aware of any powers of attorney the client may possess or may have given to others. How to obtain each of these items and how to judge their relevance will be discussed fully in the following chapter.

Client's Perception of Financial Situation

The fifth and final type of internal data is the client's subjective evaluation of her own financial situation. This is how the client thinks she is doing. It allows the financial planner to compare the client's subjective perception to the objective reality of the situation. The greater the gap between the client's subjective perception and economic reality, the greater the education needed. This information may be gathered by using the client data collection questionnaire in Appendix 3-A at the end of this chapter.

A client's internal data changes over time. Therefore, the data should be regularly revisited. If a good client/planner relationship has been developed, the client will notify the financial planner when a major life change occurs. The financial planner, however, should not rely on the client for notification. A competent financial planner will contact the client with sufficient frequency (usually quarterly) to learn how the financial plan is working and to ask if any significant changes have occurred. Contacting clients by phone, email, or in writing should be done in addition to regularly scheduled face-to-face meetings.

WHERE ON THE WEB

Better Business Bureau **www.bbb.org**

CFP® Board Public Website **www.letsmakeaplan.org**

Consumer Federation of America **www.consumerfed.org**

USAGov (formerly known as the Federal Citizen Information Center) **www.usa.gov**

Federal Trade Commission **www.ftc.gov**

Financial Planning Association **www.onefpa.org**

National Endowment for Financial Education **www.nefe.org**

National Consumers League **www.fraud.org**

DISCUSSION QUESTIONS

1. How does a financial planner successfully communicate respect, trust, and empathy to a client?
2. Which techniques can be used to reduce the risk of misinterpretation and misunderstanding when communicating with a client?
3. What is the purpose of an engagement letter?
4. To what common law liabilities is the financial planner exposed?
5. How do the Securities Act of 1933 and the Securities Exchange Act of 1934 affect financial planners?
6. What four thinking phases does a client progress through during the financial planning process? What can the financial planner do to assist the client in progressing through the common thinking phases? In which phase is it most common for a client to seek the assistance of a financial planner? In which phase is the financial mission most likely to be achieved?
7. Define the auditory learning style, the visual learning style, and the kinetic learning style, and explain how a client with each style prefers to learn.
8. What five categories make up a client's internal environment?
9. Which factors make up a client's life cycle positioning?
10. What are the life cycle phases through which financial planning clients usually pass?
11. Explain how the following affect the setting of financial goals by the client:
    - Risk tolerance
    - Savings and consumption habits
    - Views about employment, retirement, and leisure time
    - Attitudes toward government (especially taxation)
12. What are the special needs that may influence the successful development of a client's financial plan?
13. Which financial statements are needed to develop an accurate assessment of a client's financial position? What other information is important?
14. How does a client's subjective perception of her financial position affect the objective reality of the financial position provided by a financial planner?
15. In 2014, the average cost of a new home in Kensington Square was $250,000. In 2017, to the disappointment of many prospective homeowners, the average home cost rose to $300,000. Then, in 2019, the average cost of a new home fell to $275,000. The reaction to the decreased cost was positive, though the new average cost was higher than the 2014 average cost of a new home. What is this behavior known as and why?
16. Arnie has accumulated $15,000 in a savings account over the last few years and has earmarked that money to buy a new car. His furnace breaks and requires $9,000 in repairs. Arnie is reluctant to spend the money in his savings account to make the repairs because he wants to use that money for a new car. Instead, he puts the $9,000 repair bill on his credit card at an annual interest rate of 23%. This is known as which type of behavior?

EXERCISES

1. Upon your first meeting, how should you address your client?
2. What are some techniques that can be used to clarify statements when speaking with a client?
3. Nancy is a financial planner. Her client, Mr. Martin, is 62 years old and retired. His Social Security and pension plan benefits barely cover his living expenses. His two assets are his personal residence and a brokerage account of $600,000 invested in conservative mutual funds. Nancy advises Mr. Martin to sell all of his mutual fund shares and invest the proceeds in commercial real estate. If Mr. Martin follows Nancy's advice and subsequently loses $300,000, will Nancy be liable for fraud?
4. If you noticed that your client was taking notes and occasionally doodling while you spoke with her, what would you assume her learning style to be? How would you go about educating her regarding financial planning information?
5. If your client is 30 years old, has no children, and has a moderate income and net worth, what are the risks he is most likely seeking to avoid?
6. If your clients are 73 years old, retired, and have adult children and grandchildren and a high net worth, which life cycle phase are they most likely in?
7. What might be the common financial goals of a client who is 24 years old and single with a modest income?

PROBLEMS

1. Write an engagement letter to conduct comprehensive personal financial planning for the Nelsons.
2. Identify their life cycle position and related risks most likely to affect the achievement of the Nelsons' goals.

NELSON FAMILY CASE SCENARIO

The Nelsons recently visited you, their financial planner. After initial discussions and completion of a client data questionnaire similar to the one presented in Appendix 3-A, you have gathered the following information. (The Nelson family will be used throughout the text for various examples and explanations.)

DANA AND DAVID NELSON

As of 1/1/2022

PERSONAL BACKGROUND AND INFORMATION

David Nelson (age 37) is a bank vice president. He has been employed by the bank for 12 years and has an annual salary of $70,000. Dana Nelson (age 37) is a full-time homemaker. David and Dana have been married for eight years. They have two children, John (age 6) and Gabrielle (age 3), and are expecting their third child in two weeks. They have always lived in this community and expect to remain in their current residence indefinitely.

GOALS (not prioritized)

- Save for college education
- Reduce debt
- Save for retirement
- Estate planning
- Invest wisely

APPENDIX 3-A: Client Data Questionnaire

Client Name________________________

Date_____________________________

PERSONAL INFORMATION

Your Full Name ____________________ Social Security No. ________________

U.S. Citizen? ❐ Yes ❐ No Date and Place of Birth ________________

Employer ____________________ Position ________________

Work Phone ____________________ Years with current employer ________________

Married ________ Single ________ Divorced ________

Spouse's Full Name (if married) ____________________ Social Security No. ________________

U.S. Citizen? ❐ Yes ❐ No Date and Place of Birth ________________

Employer ____________________ Position ________________

Work Phone ____________________ Years with current employer ________________

Home Address ____

Home Phone ____________________ Home Fax ________________

E-mail address ________________

Previous Marriages

Have you been previously married? ❐ Yes ❐ No Has your spouse been previously married? ❐ Yes ❐ No

Children

Name(s)	Date(s)of Birth	Social Security Number(s)	Tax Dependent
			❐ Yes ❐ No
			❐ Yes ❐ No
			❐ Yes ❐ No
			❐ Yes ❐ No

Grandchildren

Name(s)	Date(s)of Birth	Social Security Number(s)	Tax Dependent
			❐ Yes ❐ No
			❐ Yes ❐ No

Other Income Tax/Financial Dependents

Does anyone other than your children depend on you or your spouse for financial support? ❐ Yes ❐ No

If so, provide names, ages, and relationships: ________________________

____

____

Health Issues

Do you or any members of your family have serious health problems? ❐ Yes ❐ No

Describe: ____

Professional Advisers (include names, addresses, phone numbers, fax numbers, and e-mail addresses)

Attorney ____

Accountant (CPA) ____

Insurance Agent ____

Banker ____

Investment Adviser ____

Page 1 Initial _____ Date _____

APPENDIX 3-A: Client Data Questionnaire (cont.)

FINANCIAL PLANNING GOALS AND OBJECTIVES

Financial Objectives (Please select and indicate degree of importance)	Degree of Importance (1-high/5-low) 1	2	3	4	5
Retire and maintain preretirement lifestyle					
Retire early - Indicate age ___________					
Protection from risks to person/property/liability					
Provide education for children/grandchildren					
Major purchases (car, boat, second home)					
Establish an emergency fund					
Save more					
Invest for safety					
Invest for growth					
Invest for income					
Transfer of wealth					
Minimize income taxes					
Minimize transfer taxes (estates and gifts)					
Other:					

Page 2 Initial _____ Date _____

APPENDIX 3-A: Client Data Questionnaire (cont.)

ASSETS

Cash Accounts (indicate current ($) dollar balance for each account)

Type of Account	Your Name	Spouse's Name	Joint w/ Spouse	Other
Cash on hand				
Checking accounts				
Savings accounts				
CDs				
Money market funds				
Treasury securities				
U.S. Savings Bonds				
Total				

Brokerage Accounts (Stocks)

Name of Security	No. of Shares	Market Value

Mutual Funds (Stocks)

Name of Institution (Fund Name)	No. of Shares	Market Value

Mutual Funds (Bonds)

Name of Institution (Fund Name)	No. of Shares	Market Value

Bonds Owned

Name of Institution	Maturity Face Value	Market Value

Page 3 Initial _____ Date _____

APPENDIX 3-A: Client Data Questionnaire (cont.)

Stock Options and/or Stock Purchase Plans

Do you or your spouse participate in a company stock option plan or stock purchase plan? ❐ Yes ❐ No

Receivables (owed to you and/or your spouse)

Type	Description	Interest Rate	Amount	Maturity Date
Notes Receivable				
Other Receivables				

Retirement Accounts (indicate vested values)

Type	Description	Fair Market Value You	Fair Market Value Your Spouse
IRA – Regular			
IRA – Roth			
401(k) or 403(b) plan			
Keogh plan			
Pension plan			
Profit-sharing plan			
Employee stock bonus plan			
Employee stock ownership plan			
SEP			
SIMPLE			

Real Estate (Personal Use)

Address	Type*	State Located	Original Cost	Fair Market Value	Current Mortgage Amount

* PR = Personal Residence VH = Vacation Home

Real Estate (Held for Investment)

Address	Type*	State Located	Original Cost	Fair Market Value	Current Mortgage Amount

* R = Rental O = Other

Page 4 Initial _____ Date _____

APPENDIX 3-A: Client Data Questionnaire (cont.)

Closely Held Business Interest *(attach financial statement if available)*

Description	Type of Entity*	Date Acquired	Percentage Owned	Est. Fair Market Value

* P = Proprietorship PTR = Partnership S = S corporation C = C corporation LLC = Limited Liability Company

Any Other Investments

Description	Date Acquired	Est. Fair Market Value

Personal Use Property

Type	Estimated Fair Market Value
Furniture & household goods	
Jewelry & furs	
Automobiles	
Boats, aircraft	
Recreational vehicles	
Art & antiques	
Other collectibles (stamps, baseball cards)	
Other items of significant value	

Page 5 Initial _____ Date _____

APPENDIX 3-A: Client Data Questionnaire (cont.)

LIABILITIES

	Amount Owed		Monthly Payments	
	You	Spouse	You	Spouse
Bank Loans				
Student Loans				
Insurance Policy Loans				
Personal Loans				
Taxes Payable				
Installment Debt (Automobile)				
Credit Cards				
Other Unpaid Bills				
Alimony/Child Support Obligations				
Charitable Pledges				
Other (______________________)				
Other (______________________)				
Other (______________________)				

Page 6 Initial _____ Date _____

APPENDIX 3-A: Client Data Questionnaire (cont.)

INFLOWS

	You	Spouse	Joint
Employment Income			
Gross Salary			
Bonuses			
Commissions			
Other (Describe________________)			
Investment Income			
Taxable Interest			
Nontaxable Interest			
Dividends			
Net Rental Income			
Business Income			
Annuities			
Social Security Benefits			
Pension/Retirement Plan			
Other (Describe________________)			
Miscellaneous Income (Expected)			
Inheritances			
Alimony			
Child Support			
Other (Describe________________)			

Page 7 Initial _____ Date _____

APPENDIX 3-A: Client Data Questionnaire (cont.)

INSURANCE

Life Insurance (Bring in policies)

Type	Policy Owner	Face Amount	Cash Value	Beneficiary	Premium Paid by Employer/ You
Term – You					
Term - Your Spouse					
Permanent – You					
Permanent - Your Spouse					
Other - You (____________)					
Other - Your Spouse (______)					

General Insurance (Check the ones you have and bring in the policies and premium statements)

Type	
Dental	______
Health	______
Short-term disability	______
Long-term disability	______
Automobile (Property and Liability)	______
Homeowners/Renters	______
Specified Personal Property	______
Personal Umbrella Liability	______
Other (____________________________)	______
Other (____________________________)	______

Page 8 Initial _____ Date _____

APPENDIX 3-A: Client Data Questionnaire (cont.)

RETIREMENT PLANNING AND ESTATE PLANNING

At what age do you and your spouse plan to retire? ____________ You
____________ Spouse

Describe your plans for retirement. Include a description of your retirement lifestyle.

____
____
____
____
____
____
____

	You		Your Spouse	
	Yes	No	Yes	No
Do you have a recent will?	❒	❒	❒	❒
Are you planning to make any changes to the will?	❒	❒	❒	❒
Do you have an advance medical directive?	❒	❒	❒	❒
Have you given a power of attorney for healthcare and property?	❒	❒	❒	❒

Page 9 Initial _____ Date _____

CHAPTER 4

Personal Financial Statements (Preparation and Analysis)

LEARNING OBJECTIVES

After learning the material in this chapter, you will be able to do the following:

- Explain the need for financial statements
- Explain the need for financial statement preparation
- Identify and describe each financial statement, its content, and its objective
- Prepare financial statements
- Identify the tools of financial statement analysis
- Calculate ratios
- Perform financial statement analysis

- Identify the ratios used to determine debt utilization, liquidity, and asset performance
- Discuss the limitations of financial statement analysis
- Define fair market value
- Define liquidity
- List the necessary steps to create a budget
- Discuss the importance of debt management and differentiate between the types of home mortgages

INTRODUCTION

Personal financial statements serve as a fundamental planning tool for the financial planner by providing important financial information and giving the planner an opportunity to analyze the information and use the statements to assist the client in financial decision making. Financial statements are intended to provide information about financial resources available to the client, how these resources were acquired, and what the client has accomplished financially using these resources. Financial statements represent the scoring mechanism for recording and evaluating an individual's financial performance. Information obtained from financial statements can be used to analyze the financial well-being of the client and determine what factors influence the client's earnings and cash flows. Personal financial statements are different from business financial statements primarily in the valuation of assets. Business financial statements use historical values, and personal financial statements use current fair market values.

Financial statements typically used by individuals include the statement of financial position (known as a *balance sheet* when used by a business), the personal statement of cash flows (known as an income statement when used by a business), and the statement of changes in net worth. This chapter will include a discussion of these financial statements, how they are prepared, and where the data are obtained. The chapter provides examples illustrating the different financial statements based on the Nelson family introduced in the previous chapter. Information from the Nelsons is also used to demonstrate a thorough treatment of financial statement analysis including ratio analysis, vertical analysis, and growth analysis.

Decision-Making Uses of Financial Statements and Financial Statement Analysis

Personal financial statements provide planners, clients, and lenders the necessary information to make adequate financial decisions. Clients prepare personal budgets to assist in understanding their spending patterns, gain more control over their financial affairs, and improve the likelihood of reaching their financial goals. As we will see in this chapter, financial statements are used by clients to benchmark goal achievement, by planners to help clients decide financial direction, and by creditors and lenders to make decisions to extend, continue, or call indebtedness. Exhibit 4.1 presents financial actions using the different financial information that can be gathered, the most likely user of the information, and the types of decisions that can be made from gathering and analyzing the financial information.

EXHIBIT 4.1 Financial Information Collection and Analysis

Financial Actions	Likely User	Type of Decision
Preparing personal budgets	Client/planner	Basic planning
Evaluating spending patterns	Client/planner	Efficiency/effectiveness
Determining the financial solvency of the client	Client/planner/lender	Debt management
Determining whether financial goals are being achieved	Client/planner	Redirect or steady course
Determining whether the client is making adequate progress toward retirement	Client/planner	Capital needs analysis
Evaluating the relative risk and performance of the investment portfolio	Client/planner	Asset allocation
Evaluating the client's use and cost of debt	Client/planner/lender	Refinance
Determining the adequacy of income replacement insurance	Client/planner	Insurance/estate planning
Determining the adequacy of liquidity for estate planning	Client/planner	Liquidity at death
Evaluating net worth	Client/planner/lender	Lending
Financial statements required for loans	Lender	Lending

Financial Accounting Standards Board (FASB)
Nongovernmental board that sets the standards for financial statements and generally accepted accounting principles (GAAP)

Rules Regarding Financial Statements

The **Financial Accounting Standards Board** (FASB) is a nongovernmental board that sets the standards for financial statements and generally accepted accounting principles (GAAP). While GAAP generally applies to businesses, the principles are also useful in the development of personal financial statements. The objectives in following such accounting conventions include consistency and comparability in the preparation and presentation of financial statements. Therefore, objective rather than subjective judgments of value should be used in presentation and decision making.

Preparation of Financial Statements

A client is rarely able to provide the financial planner with a complete set of well-documented personal financial statements. The client often does not have the necessary documentation or a clear understanding of his current financial position. With that in mind, the planner can either personally prepare the client's financial statements or have someone else prepare them, usually the client's certified public accountant (CPA). Personally preparing and analyzing a client's financial statements provides the planner with a wealth of information and insight about the client. Because financial statement preparation and analysis are fundamental to financial planning, all competent financial planners should have a basic understanding of the terminology, evaluation and valuation methods, and current and relevant accounting and reporting principles to develop financial statements.

THE STATEMENT OF FINANCIAL POSITION

Statement of financial position
A list of assets, liabilities, and net worth

The **statement of financial position** is a listing of assets, liabilities, and net worth that depicts resources and tells how those resources were obtained or financed. The statement is a financial snapshot of the client at a moment in time (the date of the statement). Historically, the statement of financial position was the primary financial statement given to and relied upon by third parties, especially lenders. This statement was originally designed to meet the needs of creditors who wanted information about assets, collateral, and a person's ability to repay debts (net worth). Now, lenders generally require copies of all personal financial statements, not just the statement of financial position.

Statement of Financial Position Terms and Presentation Order

Assets
Property owned completely or partially by the client

Liquidity
The ability to buy or sell an asset quickly and at a known price

Current assets
Assets expected to be converted to cash within one year

Liability
Money owed by the client

Net worth
The amount of wealth or equity the client has in owned assets

An **asset** is property owned completely or partially by the client. Some examples of assets are cash, investments, personal residences, and automobiles. The classification of the list of assets on the statement of financial position is generally based on liquidity. **Liquidity** is the ability to buy or sell an asset quickly and at a known price. Assets expected to be converted to cash within one year are **current assets**. Therefore, cash and cash equivalents are presented first, followed by assets held as investments, and, finally, assets held for personal use.

A **liability** is money owed by the client. Some examples of liabilities are bank loans, student loans, automobile loans, credit card debt, home mortgages, and taxes owed. On the liability side, liabilities that will or should be paid within one year are presented as current liabilities in their expected order of payoff. Liabilities extending beyond a year are presented as long-term liabilities.

Net worth is the amount of wealth or equity the client has in owned assets. This is the amount of money that would remain after selling all owned assets at their estimated fair market values and paying off all liabilities. The client's net worth is calculated by taking the difference between total assets and total liabilities.

Traditionally, assets are listed on the left side of the statement of financial position and liabilities on the right side. The net worth is shown below liabilities on the right side. Depending on the client and the purpose of the statement of financial position, the categories may be subdivided into more detail. Regardless of the categorization of assets and liabilities, the statement must always balance. The basic statement of financial position formula is assets – liabilities = net worth.

EXHIBIT 4.2 Statement of Financial Position Format

Abbreviated Statement of Financial Position			
Cash and cash equivalents	$ xxx	Current liabilities	$ xxx
Investment assets	xxx	Long-term liabilities	xxx
Personal use assets	xxx	Total liabilities	$ xxx
		Net worth	xxx
Total assets	$ xxx	Total liabilities and net worth	$ xxx

Categories and Classifications of Assets

Cash and Cash Equivalents

Cash and cash equivalents include cash on hand, checking accounts, savings accounts, certificates of deposit, cash value in life insurance policies (if intended for current use as cash and cash equivalents; otherwise, classify permanent insurance policies as investments), money market accounts, income tax refunds due, and accounts receivable that are expected to be collected quickly. These are assets easily converted to cash for regular or emergency expenses and assets that are expected to convert to cash within one year.

Investment Assets

Investment assets include stocks, bonds, mutual funds, real estate, collectibles (e.g., stamps and art) held for investment, cash value in life insurance policies (if not intended for use as cash and cash equivalents), and interests in closely held corporations or businesses. Generally, investment assets are held for growth or income. Assets may also be distinguished in the statement of financial position as tax advantaged or not tax advantaged. This distinction is useful for tax and distribution purposes.

Personal Use Assets

Personal use assets include the personal residence, personal property (e.g., furniture and clothing) jewelry, automobiles, other vehicles, and recreational boats. These assets are generally long lived and are not expected to be liquidated in the short term but are to be used to maintain the client's quality of life.

EXHIBIT 4.3 Commonly Held Assets

Cash and Cash Equivalents	Investments	Personal Use Assets
■ Cash on hand	■ Stocks and bonds	■ Primary residence
■ Checking accounts	■ Certificates of deposit (1 year or more maturity)	■ Vacation home
■ Savings accounts	■ Mutual funds	■ Automobiles
■ Money market accounts	■ Real estate	■ Recreational equipment
■ Certificates of deposit (<1 year maturity)	■ Business ownership	■ Household items
	■ Cash value of life insurance (generally)	■ Jewelry
	■ Cash value of pensions	
	■ Retirement accounts	
	■ Collectibles	
	■ Annuities	
	■ Other investment vehicles	

Categories and Classifications of Liabilities

Current Liabilities

Current liability
Debt owed by the client that is expected to be paid off within the year (current ≤ 12 months)

Current liabilities include any short-term credit card debt and unpaid bills. These bills represent money the client currently owes. Unpaid credit card balances, taxes payable, bank loans, and other debts that will or should be paid off within one year are also considered current liabilities.

Long-Term Liabilities

Long-term liability
Debt extending beyond one year (long term > 12 months)

Long-term liabilities are debts that will not be paid off within one year, usually debts of larger assets. Generally, home loans, automobile loans, long-term notes payable, and student loans are considered long-term liabilities. When the debt is long term, the current portion due is listed under current liabilities.

EXHIBIT 4.4 Common Personal Liabilities

Current Liabilities	Long-Term Liabilities
■ Current portion of mortgages due	■ Primary residence mortgage
■ Utility bills due	■ Vacation home mortgage
■ Credit card balances due	■ Other mortgages
■ Insurance premiums due	■ Automobile loans
■ Taxes due	■ Home improvement loans
■ Medical bills due	■ Student loans
■ Repair bills due	■ Other loans

Valuation of Assets and Liabilities

For personal financial statements, assets and liabilities on the statement of financial position are stated at the current fair market value. Presenting assets and liabilities at fair market value is not an easy task. There are problems with the precise determination of fair market value for many of the assets listed. Liabilities are more straightforward in terms of valuation.

Fair market value (FMV)
The price at which an exchange will take place between a willing buyer and a willing seller, both reasonably informed and neither under duress to exchange

Fair market value (FMV) is defined as the price at which an exchange will take place between a willing buyer and a willing seller, both reasonably informed and neither under duress to exchange. Fair market value for certain assets like cash, cash equivalents, some investment account balances, and most liabilities is readily available from institutional statements or by contacting the institution holding the asset. For those assets, a determination can be made. However, for certain other assets, the determination of fair market value is difficult and may require an appraisal by an expert or an estimate by the client. In some cases, the cost of an appraisal is not warranted because the information gained by appraisal is not worth the cost. For example, a small change in the value of a personal residence from year to year may not be relevant to the financial statements, especially where the client has no intent to dispose of the personal residence. The same is true for the valuation of closely held business interests where there is no intent to dispose of the business interests. For liabilities, the FMV is the current payoff value.

The Nelson Family Statement of Financial Position

Exhibit 4.5 is the Nelsons' statement of financial position for December 31, 2021. Exhibit 4.6 is their statement of financial position for December 31, 2022. Notice the changes in net worth, assets, and liabilities. Even though these changes are readily apparent by comparing the numbers, there is no explanation as to what transactions caused those changes. This is one of the weaknesses of the statement of financial position.

For example, in Exhibits 4.5 and 4.6, ABC stock increased from $12,500 to $14,050. Did the Nelsons buy more stock? Did the value of the stock increase? Do the Nelsons still hold the same number of shares? The two statements of financial position do not reveal the answer to these questions. A comparison only reveals an increase in the Nelsons' total assets from $423,072 to $458,947 and an increase in their net worth from $207,626 to $241,573—an increase of $33,947. Is the increase good or bad? Obviously, an increase (for an asset) is better than a decrease, but what was the cause? Once again, the two statements of financial position do not reveal the answer. To answer these questions, other financial statements need to be prepared for the Nelsons: the personal statement of cash flows and the statement of changes in net worth. Once all of the financial statements are prepared, they can be analyzed to gain a better understanding of the underlying financial transactions that occurred during the year. All the financial statements for the Nelsons will be presented and analyzed in this chapter. As you will see, the statement of financial position does not tell the whole financial story.

EXHIBIT 4.5 Nelsons' Statement of Financial Position 12/31/2021

Dana and David Nelson
Statement of Financial Position
12/31/2021

ASSETS			**LIABILITIES AND NET WORTH**		
Cash/cash equivalents			**Current liabilities**		
JT	Checking account	$1,425	JT	Credit cards	$4,000
JT	Savings account	$950	JT	Mortgage on principal residence	$1,234
			David	Boat loan	$1,493
Total cash/cash equivalents		$2,375	**Total current liabilities**		$6,727
Invested assets			**Long-term liabilities**		
Dana	ABC stock	$12,500	JT	Mortgage on principal residence	$196,654
JT	Education fund	$14,000	David	Boat loan	$12,065
David	Section 401(k) plan	$32,197			
Total invested assets		$58,697	**Total long-term liabilities**		$208,719
Personal use assets			**Total liabilities**		**$215,446**
JT	Principal residence	$245,000			
JT	Automobile	$18,000			
David	Boat A	$25,000	**Net worth**		$207,626
Dana	Jewelry	$13,000			
JT	Furniture/household	$61,000			
Total personal use assets		$362,000			
Total assets		**$423,072**	**Total liabilities and net worth**		**$423,072**

Notes to financial statements:

- Assets are stated at fair market value.
- The ABC stock was inherited from Dana's aunt on November 15, 2021. Her aunt originally paid $20,000 for it on October 31, 2012. The fair market value at the aunt's death was $12,000.
- Liabilities are stated at principal only.
- JT = joint tenancy; client name = separate property

EXHIBIT 4.6 Nelsons' Statement of Financial Position 12/31/2022

Dana and David Nelson
Statement of Financial Position
12/31/2022

ASSETS			LIABILITIES AND NET WORTH		
Cash/cash equivalents			**Current liabilities**		
JT	Checking account	$1,268	JT	Credit cards	$3,655
JT	Savings account	$950	JT	Mortgage on principal residence	$1,370
Total cash/cash equivalents		$2,218	David	Boat loan	$1,048
			Total current liabilities		$6,073
Invested assets			**Long-term liabilities**		
Dana	ABC stock	$14,050	JT	Mortgage on principal residence	$195,284
JT	Education fund	$15,560	David	Boat loan	$16,017
David	Section 401(k) plan	$38,619	**Total long-term liabilities**		$211,301
David	XYZ stock	$10,000			
Total invested assets		$78,229			
Personal use assets			**Total liabilities**		$217,374
JT	Principal residence	$250,000			
JT	Automobile	$15,000			
David	Personal watercraft	$10,000			
David	Boat B	$30,000	**Net worth**		$241,573
Dana	Jewelry	$13,500			
JT	Furniture/household	$60,000			
Total personal use assets		$378,500			
Total assets		**$458,947**	**Total liabilities and net worth**		**$458,947**

Notes to financial statements:

- Assets are stated at fair market value.
- The ABC stock was inherited from Dana's aunt on November 15, 2021. Her aunt originally paid $20,000 for it on October 31, 2012. The fair market value at the aunt's death was $12,000.
- Liabilities are stated at principal only.
- JT = joint tenancy; client name = separate property

Valuation of Assets and Liabilities—The Nelsons

Reviewing the December 31, 2021, and the December 31, 2022, statements of financial position for the Nelsons, notice that the value of their personal residence has increased by $5,000 ($245,000 – $250,000). If we assume that there were no improvements to the residence, and that we did not have a real estate appraisal, what does the $250,000 value represent? Probably, the planner and client estimated inflation at 2% and rounded the increase in value to $5,000, assuming that real estate generally appreciates at the same rate as inflation. What are the relative merits of such estimation for valuation? If you have no plans to sell an asset but you need a valuation and no ready valuation is available, estimation is a reasonable idea. To rely on a financial statement, you must verify the valuations of important assets and liabilities. In reality, no individual is going to have an annual appraisal for a personal residence, furnishings, automobile, or other personal-use assets. Therefore, the reader of personal financial statements should be skeptical of the valuations given for personal-use assets.

There is always some imprecision in valuing certain assets and liabilities. The extent to which such imprecision is acceptable to the user depends on the particular use of the financial statements. It is frequently appropriate to have the client estimate a value, particularly for a personal residence. Usually clients know what houses have been selling for in their neighborhood and have no intent to dispose of the house. Likewise, it is reasonable to have the client estimate the value of an interest in a closely held business, especially when there is no current intent to dispose of the business interest. Precise valuation may be necessary when the financial statements are used to obtain a loan from a third party and that third party cannot, or will not, accept estimates. For example, if the client is refinancing a home, the mortgage lender may require an appraisal.

Information Sources

The financial planner needs to thoroughly review the client's various assets and liabilities in order to prepare the financial statements. The planner will need to access many different documents to determine valuation, payment schedules, and applicable interest concerns. The detail desired of the financial planning engagement will determine the thoroughness of the planner's assessment of these documents.

EXHIBIT 4.7 Sources and Types of Information for Statement of Financial Position

Source of Information	Types of Information Obtained from Source
Bank statements	Bank balances and possible loan creation or repayments
Investment account statements	Investment account balance and types
Life insurance statements	Cash value of life insurance and any indebtedness
Real estate purchase agreement	Purchase price of real estate
Mortgage notes	Indebtedness of real estate and terms of indebtedness
Auto purchase agreements	Purchase price of automobile
Auto notes	Terms of indebtedness for automobile
Employer benefit statements	Vested and nonvested account balance/options/ contributions by employee and employer to retirement plan
Credit card statements	Purchase price of use assets, balances of credit card indebtedness, payments, interest rates, late charges
Appraisals	Value of the appraised asset
Installment notes	Value of installment notes or liability and terms
Client	All documents and estimates of value regarding assets and liabilities

In the case of the assets and liabilities other than personal-use assets, a wide variety of sources and documents may be used to assist the financial planner in the preparation of the statement of financial position.

Exhibit 4.8 presents each account on the statement of financial position and the best source of information to determine the correct statement of financial position amount. In addition, alternative sources are presented where the cost/benefit of finding precise data does not warrant collection from the best source.

EXHIBIT 4.8 Statement of Financial Position Information by Account Type

Accounts and Account Balances	Best Source of Information for Valuation	Alternative Source
ASSETS		
Cash/cash equivalents		
Checking account	Bank statements	Client/planner estimate
Savings account	Bank statements	
Certificates of deposit	Bank statements	
Invested assets		
Stocks	Brokerage or investment statements	Client/planner estimate
Bonds	Brokerage or investment statements	
Mutual funds	Account statements	
Section 401(k) plan	Account statements	
Section 403(b) plan	Account statements	
IRA/SEP	Account statements	
Investment real estate	Appraisal if warranted	
Personal use assets		
Personal residence	Appraisal if warranted	Client/planner estimate
Personal furniture & fixtures	Appraisal if warranted	
Closely held business interests	Appraisal if warranted	Client/planner estimate
Automobiles	Blue book, bank, credit union	Client/planner estimate
LIABILITIES		
Current liabilities		
Credit card debt	Credit card statements	Client estimate
Bank loans	Lender	Client estimate
Long-term liabilities		
Mortgage loans	Amortization table/lender/ annual statements	Client/planner estimate
Auto loans	Coupon/lender	Client/planner estimate
Student loan(s)	Lender/annual statements	Client/planner estimate

Identification of Ownership of Assets and Liabilities

Financial planners find it useful to indicate the type of property ownership and the titling of assets and liabilities on the statement of financial position when preparing financial statements for married persons. Identifying ownership is especially helpful for estate planning and where one individual has separately owned property not subject to the claims of the other spouse's creditors.

Common abbreviations for property ownership and titling on personal statement of financial position are:

Client name = separate property for clients with joint statements
JT = property held jointly with survivorship rights with another (or others)
CP = community property of spouses

Footnotes to the Statement of Financial Position

Generally, footnotes are used to provide additional information or to clarify the item footnoted on the financial statements. Examples of common footnotes to the statement of financial position include:

- assets that are stated at fair market value;
- property title listings;
- existing contingent liabilities (guarantors/cosigned obligations); and
- additional notes regarding property that may be needed at a later date (e.g., basis of gifted property and date of asset acquisition).

THE PERSONAL STATEMENT OF CASH FLOWS

Personal statement of cash flows
Summary of the client's income and expenses during an interval of time, usually one year

The **personal statement of cash flows** presents a summary of the client's cash inflows and outflows during an interval, usually one year. The statement may focus on realized transactions; if so, this is helpful when comparing with budgeted financial goals. The statement may also be prepared pro forma (in advance) and, therefore, can be used for budgeting or projections. The basic equation used in the personal statement of cash flows is:

$$\text{inflows} - \text{outflows} = \text{net cash flow}$$

The bottom line on a personal statement of cash flows shows the amount of **net cash flow** available to the client. As defined in the equation, net cash flow represents the difference between the inflows and the outflows (including committed savings). This calculated cash flow may be a cash flow surplus or a cash flow deficit. Such surplus cash flow may be used for consumption, reduction of debt, additional savings, cash gifts, or the purchase of gifts. If such net positive cash flows are used to reduce debt or are added to savings, statement of financial position ratios will be improved. If the cash flow results in a cash flow deficit, the planner's analysis of the client's financial situation may result in planning opportunities the planner may discover to rectify the situation, creating a surplus.

Statement of Personal Cash Flows Terms and Order of Their Presentation

Inflows

Inflows
All monies received, usually in cash, from employment, investments, and other sources

Inflows include all monies received, usually in cash, from employment, investments, and other sources.

- Employment income includes wages, salaries, bonuses, and commissions.
- Investment income includes interest and dividends from savings and investment accounts, proceeds from the sale of assets, income from annuities, and any other investment-related activities.
- Other inflow sources may include Social Security benefits, child support, alimony, gifts, scholarships, tax refunds, pension income, and any other cash inflow that is received on a regular basis.

Savings

Savings
Deferred consumption

Savings is actually a cash outflow because it reduces income available for expenses. Savings is deferred consumption and will be treated as an increase to assets on the statement of financial position.

Outflows

Outflows
Recurring obligations, or monthly expenses paid

Fixed outflows/expenses
Outflows that remain constant over a period of time and over which the client has little control

Outflows are recurring obligations paid, or monthly expenses paid. The three main categories of outflows are fixed, variable, and discretionary.

Fixed outflows/expenses are expenses that remain constant over a period of time and over which the client has little control. Examples of fixed outflows include rent or mortgage payments, insurance premiums, tuition, and loan payments.

Variable outflows/expenses are outflows that fluctuate in amount from time to time over which the client has some control. Examples of variable outflows include food, utilities, and transportation costs.

Discretionary expenses are luxuries or expenses over which the client has complete control. Examples of discretionary expenses are vacations, entertainment expenses, and gifts. Furthermore, some clients do not consider regular donations to religious organizations to be discretionary but consider these outflows to be fixed.

Variable outflows/expenses
Outflows that fluctuate in amount from time to time over which the client has some control

Information Sources

Discretionary expenses
Luxuries or expenses over which the client has complete control

The financial planner will need to thoroughly review the client's various inflow sources and personal outflows to create the personal statement of cash flows. Exhibit 4.9 lists some of the more common sources of financial information that may be used in the collection of data for the preparation of the personal statement of cash flows.

EXHIBIT 4.9 Personal Inflows and Outflows—Sources

Inflows	Information Source
Salary	Form W-2/tax return
Interest (taxable)	Form 1099/tax return
Dividends	Form 1099
Outflows	**Information Source**
Savings	Bank statements/Section 401(k) plan statements/1099s
Food	Budget/check register/receipts/credit card statement
Clothing	Budget/check register/receipts/credit card statement
Child care	Budget/check register/receipts/credit card statement
Entertainment	Budget/check register/receipts/credit card statement
Utilities	Actual bills/check register/receipts
Auto maintenance	Budget/check register/receipts/credit card statement
Charitable contributions	Checks and receipts
Section 401(k) plan loan repayments	Participant statement
Credit card payments	Credit card statements
Mortgage payments	Mortgage statement
Automobile/boat loan	Loan agreement/check register
Insurance premiums	Invoice/policy/check register
Tuition and education expenses	Invoice/check stubs
Federal income tax (W/H)	Form W-2/tax return
State (and city) income tax	Form W-2/tax return
FICA	Form W-2/tax return
Property tax for real estate	Mortgage statement/check register

Exhibit 4.10 is the Nelsons' personal statement of cash flows showing their inflows, savings, outflows, and net cash flow for 2022.

EXHIBIT 4.10 Personal Statement of Cash Flows

Dana and David Nelson Personal Statement of Cash Flows For 2022		
INFLOWS		
Salary—David		**$70,000**
Investment income		
Interest income	$900	
Dividend income	$150	$1,050
Total inflows		**$71,050**
Savings		
Reinvestment (interest/dividends)	$1,050	
Section 401(k) plan deferrals	$3,803	
Education fund	$1,000	
Total savings		**$5,853**
Available for outflows		**$65,197**
OUTFLOWS		
Ordinary living expenses		
Food	$6,000	
Clothing	$3,600	
Child care	$600	
Entertainment	$1,814	
Utilities	$3,600	
Auto maintenance	$2,000	
Church	$3,500	
Total ordinary living expenses		**$21,114**
Debt payments		
Credit card payments principal	$345	
Credit card payments interest	$615	
Mortgage payment principal	$1,234	
Mortgage payment interest	$20,720	
Boat loan principal	$1,493	
Boat loan interest	$1,547	
Total debt payments		**$25,954**
Insurance premiums		
Automobile insurance premiums	$900	
Disability insurance premiums	$761	
Homeowners insurance premiums	$950	
Total insurance premiums		**$2,611**
Tuition and education expenses		**$1,000**
Taxes		
FICA and federal income tax (W/H)	$12,855	
State (and city) income tax	$820	
Property tax (principal residence)	$1,000	
Total taxes		**$14,675**
Total outflows		**$65,354**
Net cash flow (deficit)		**($157)**

Compromise in Information Reporting

The personal statement of cash flows is a compromise in information reporting. For an individual, the statement is almost a full cash flow statement. The exceptions, those transactions that are not considered income or expenses but are cash flows, are generally not included in the statement. For example, although conventional corporate accounting would include only the interest portion from any repayment of debt as an expense, personal financial statements commonly include both the principal and the interest in debt repayment as an expense or cash flow for the period (e.g., mortgage payments, credit card payments, and bank loan repayments).

The astute planner will notice that the personal statement of cash flows is neither an accrual statement nor a full cash flow statement. Because the statement is frequently prepared pro forma (in advance) and used as a budget, it is a presentation of recurring inflows and outflows presented in a conventional manner and is, therefore, a compromise. If it were a full statement of cash flows, it would have to consider the acquisition and disposition of all assets for and by cash.

The personal statement of cash flows generally does not consider the sale or purchase of assets during the period, nor does it consider employer matching contributions to qualified retirement accounts. As we will see, another financial statement must be prepared to present the complete financial picture of the client.

The Relationship of the Statement of Financial Position to the Personal Statement of Cash Flows

The statement of financial position represents the financial picture of the individual at a moment in time setting forth assets, liabilities, and net worth. The personal statement of cash flows presents recurring inflows, savings, outflows, and net cash flow over a period of time. The personal statement of cash flows provides a partial picture of what has happened between two statement of financial position dates. As discussed previously, neither statement by itself nor both when taken together present the entire financial picture of the individual. This deficiency creates the need for another financial statement—the statement of changes in net worth—to help further clarify the complete financial picture of the client.

THE STATEMENT OF CHANGES IN NET WORTH

Statement of changes in net worth
Summary of changes from one statement of financial position to the next

Throughout the preparation of the previously mentioned financial statements, we have tried to provide financial information useful to the client and the planner. We now need to be able to explain the changes in net worth between two statements of financial position. The financial statement that allows us to do this is called the **statement of changes in net worth.** To the extent that we have not been able to ascertain all of the exact changes in the net worth, this statement will allow us to do so. Examples of transactions or changes in account balances that would not be included in the personal statement of cash flows are listed below:

- Changes in value for assets due to either appreciation or depreciation
- If an asset other than cash is exchanged for some other assets (real estate for real estate)

- If assets other than cash are received by gift or inheritance (property)
- If assets other than cash are given to charities or noncharitable donees (automobiles, buildings, or investments)

EXAMPLE Below are some sample transactions and how the transactions affect net worth.

- The client buys $5,000 of furniture on credit. Assets (furniture) increase by $5,000 and liabilities (debt) increase by $5,000; no change in net worth.
- The client's IRA appreciates by $10,000 this year. Assets (IRA) increase by $10,000 and liabilities remain the same, so net worth increases by $10,000.
- The client buys a house for $200,000 with a 5% down payment and financing the balance. Assets decrease by $10,000 (cash) and increase by $200,000 (house), and liabilities increase by $190,000 (mortgage); no change in net worth.

Exhibit 4.11 depicts the statement of changes in net worth for the Nelsons. The Nelsons' net worth statement ties together the overall change in their net worth and reflects each noncash item that was altered during the year. Transactions that were not previously reported on the other statements include:

- an inheritance of $10,000 in XYZ stock from David's grandmother;
- appreciation in value of the jewelry, residence, ABC stock, education fund, and Section 401(k) plan;
- employer contribution to David's Section 401(k) plan ($2,100); and
- a gift of a table to Dana's mother ($1,000 value).

EXHIBIT 4.11 Statement of Changes in Net Worth

Dana and David Nelson Statement of Changes in Net Worth For the Year Ending 12/31/2022	
Additions to net worth	
Increases in assets:	
Inheritance	
XYZ stock	$10,000
Appreciation of assets:	
Jewelry	$500
Residence	$5,000
Adjustment from exchange:	
Boat B	$30,000
Purchase	
Personal watercraft	$10,000
Appreciation of investments:	
ABC stock	$500
Education fund	$560
Section 401(k) plan	$519
Increase of investment contributions:	
ABC stock	$1,050
Education fund	$1,000
Section 401(k) plan—employee contribution (deferrals)	$3,803
Section 401(k) plan—employer contribution (deferrals)	$2,100
Decrease in liabilities (debt repayments):	
Mortgage on principal residence	$1,234
Boat loan	$1,493
Credit card debt	$345
Total	**$68,104**
Reductions in net worth	
Decrease in assets:	
Checking account	($157)
Depreciation of assets:	
Auto	($3,000)
Gifts	
Table to mother	($1,000)
Adjustment from exchange:	
Boat A	($25,000)
Increase in liabilities	
Addition to boat loan	($5,000)
Total	**($34,157)**
Net change in net worth	**$33,947**

NELSON EXAMPLE RECAP

Recall that the statement of financial position for December 31, 2021, and the statement of financial position for December 31, 2022, do not show the same net worth. Based on this observation, we know that there were circumstances in which the overall financial status of the Nelsons changed during the year.

EXHIBIT 4.12 Spreadsheet Reconciliation of Changes in Net Worth

Asset	12/31/2021 Stmt of Fin Position	Change in Net Worth	12/31/2022 Stmt of Fin Position
Checking account	$1,425	($157)	$1,268
Savings account	$950		$950
ABC stock	$12,500	$1,550	$14,050
Education fund	$14,000	$1,560	$15,560
Section 401(k) plan	$32,197	$6,422	$38,619
XYZ stock	$0	$10,000	$10,000
Principal residence	$245,000	$5,000	$250,000
Automobile	$18,000	($3,000)	$15,000
Personal watercraft	$0	$10,000	$10,000
Boat A	$25,000	($25,000)	$0
Boat B	$0	$30,000	$30,000
Jewelry	$13,000	$500	$13,500
Furniture/household	$61,000	($1,000)	$60,000
Credit cards	($4,000)	$345	($3,655)
Mortgage on residence*	($197,888)	$1,234	($196,654)
Boat loan*	($13,558)	($3,507)	($17,065)
Net worth	**$207,626**	**$33,947**	**$241,573**

* Includes current and long-term liabilities

FINANCIAL ANALYSIS OF PERSONAL FINANCIAL STATEMENTS

Once the statement of financial position, personal statement of cash flows, and statement of changes in net worth have been properly prepared, financial statement analysis can be performed to gain insight into the financial strengths and weaknesses of the client. The financial planner may look upon this activity as a form of diagnosing the financial health of the client. Remember that financial analysis, while somewhat comprehensive, is only one tool of the competent financial planner. Financial analysis by its very nature is limited to the past and, therefore, is not necessarily predictive of the future. Even with its inherent limitations, however, financial statement analysis is a useful and powerful tool to gain insight into the financial well-being of the client.

We begin with a traditional approach to analyzing the financial statements and then broaden our analysis to improve our insights. Our traditional approach utilizes ratio, vertical, and growth analysis.

Financial statement analysis (in general) and ratio analysis (in particular) can assist us in answering the following questions about a client.

- Can the client financially withstand a sudden negative financial disruption to income (such as unemployment or loss of a significant asset)?
- Can the client meet short-term obligations?
- Does the client manage debt well?

- Does the client have an appropriate balance among various classes of expenditures relative to income?
- Is the client's income growing at an appropriate rate?
- Are the client's savings and savings rate appropriate for the given income and income growth?
- Is the client making a satisfactory total return on investments and savings?
- Is the client's net worth growing at an appropriate rate?
- Is the client making satisfactory progress toward funding retirement?

Ratio Analysis

Ratio analysis
The relationship or relative value of two characteristics used to analyze an individual's financial health and to conduct comparison and trend analysis

There are many financial ratios one might use to gain insight into the client's financial well-being. The ratios we have selected are only suggestions. Other financial planners may have ratios they use that we have not presented. Furthermore, some decisions require exhaustive **ratio analysis**, and other decisions are quite simple and may require only the calculation of a few simple ratios. Thus, there is no one set of ratios that needs to be used all of the time, nor is there a particular ratio that is always calculated. The ratios are used to clarify and improve the understanding of the data and are used in comparison with established benchmarks, such as those established in the mortgage lending industry, to make judgments as to their appropriateness for a particular client. We would expect, for example, that at higher income levels, there are greater amounts of savings and larger net worths. Therefore, we must be careful to compare the financial ratios of each individual with relevant benchmarks.

Financial statement analysis is both an art and a science. Although anyone can mathematically calculate ratios, the ability to understand the implications of those ratios and to motivate the client to take actions to affect those ratios where appropriate is truly an art. The art will only come with practice and experience.

Ratio analysis is intended to provide additional perspective on the financial statements. The selection of each numerator and denominator to calculate a particular ratio must be done with care. Not every ratio is relevant for every client. The objective of ratio analysis is twofold: to gain additional insight into the financial situation and behavior of the client and to generate questions for the client to answer to further gain such insight.

The ratios selected for discussion in this chapter are ones the authors have found to be particularly useful. The key to ratio analysis is whether the ratio answers the question asked and then whether there is some standard or benchmark to determine whether the result is appropriate for this particular client. Ratio analysis uses both the statement of financial position and the personal statement of cash flows.

Liquidity Ratios

Liquidity ratios measure the ability of the client to meet short-term financial obligations. They compare current financial obligations such as current liabilities or financial requirements to current assets or cash flows available to meet those financial obligations. These liquidity ratios include the emergency fund ratio and the current ratio.

The Emergency Fund Ratio The emergency fund ratio assists the planner in determining the ability of the client to withstand a sudden negative financial disruption to cash inflows. Such a financial disruption could occur as a result of a layoff, untimely death, disability, or some other event that causes the cash inflows to cease or be reduced. This ratio is calculated by comparing the amount of liquid assets to the monthly cash outflows/expenses of the client. The emergency fund ratio should generally be three to six months' of nondiscretionary cash outflows to accommodate unemployment, losses of significant assets, or other unexpected major expenditures.

Reviewing Exhibit 4.6, the statement of financial position dated December 31, 2022, the Nelsons had $2,218 in liquid assets. In reviewing the personal statement of cash flows, they have monthly outflows/expenses totaling $5,446 ($65,354 ÷ 12). A closer review of the monthly expenditures reveals that there are certain outflows that could be reduced if necessary. Assume that the following costs could be eliminated:

Child care[1]	$ 600
Entertainment	1,814
FICA and federal income taxes[2]	12,855
State and city taxes[2]	820
Eliminated cash outflows	$16,089

1 Dana is a full-time homemaker. In an emergency, child care costs could be eliminated unless the emergency is Dana's death.

2 If David lost his source of income, the Nelsons would not pay income taxes.

Thus, the real nondiscretionary monthly outflows/expenses are $4,105 ([$65,354 – $16,089] ÷ 12). (Note that in consultation with the Nelsons, the church contribution of $3,500 was not considered discretionary.) The emergency fund ratio (EFR) is calculated by dividing the current assets (numerator) by the monthly nondiscretionary outflows/expenses (denominator) to provide the result.

$$\text{Emergency fund ratio (EFR)} = \frac{\text{Current assets}}{\text{Monthly nondiscretionary expenses}} = \text{Target of 3 to 6 months}$$

$$\text{Nelsons' EFR } \frac{\$2{,}218}{\$4{,}105} = .54 \text{ months}$$

The emergency fund ratio of .54 months is substantially below the target goal of three to six months, suggesting a substantial risk to the overall financial plan. You may observe that the Nelsons could liquidate some of their investments or borrow from David's Section 401(k) plan in the event of an emergency. Although both observations are correct, this course of action would be disruptive to a long-term investment plan. Therefore, we would place building the emergency fund as one of our current objectives with a quantitative target of initially three months, and over a longer period of six months.

Although a client should strive to maintain a three- to six-month EFR using only current assets in the numerator, each client's situation is unique. Some clients may be at little risk of losing income to cover basic living expenses and may desire higher rates of return than can be achieved with checking and savings accounts. In such a case, substitutions for current assets may be made in the EFR calculation. For example, the client may be willing and able to sell marketable securities or obtain a low-interest line of credit.

The Current Ratio The current ratio examines the relationship between current assets and current liabilities. The current ratio indicates the ability to meet short-term obligations. This ratio is calculated by dividing current assets (numerator) by current liabilities (denominator).

$$\text{Current ratio (CR)} = \frac{\text{current assets}}{\text{current liabilities}} = \text{target of 1.0 to 2.0}$$

In reviewing the Nelsons' statement of financial position dated December 31, 2022, we find current assets of $2,218 and current liabilities of $6,073.

$$\text{Nelsons' CR} = \frac{\$2,218}{\$6,073} = .37$$

The current ratio of .37 is low relative to the target of 1.0 to 2.0 and suggests insufficient current assets, too many current liabilities, or some combination of both. Therefore, we would suggest increasing the current ratio to 1.0 over a reasonable period of time. By increasing the emergency fund ratio, the Nelsons may also increase the current ratio.

Debt Ratios and Debt Analysis

Debt ratios indicate how well the person manages debt. Debt is not inherently good or bad. All debt carries some cost, interest costs at least. Quality debt is low in cost and has a term structure that does not exceed the economic life of the asset that created the debt. When a person consistently repays debt as agreed, the repayment creates a history of good credit ratings, the borrower gains confidence in handling debt, and lenders gain confidence in extending credit to the borrower. Excessive debt or expensive debt is a warning sign that default risk is a serious threat. Determining exactly how much debt a person should have is impossible, but various ratios give signals as to the person's ability to handle debt and whether the person may be overextended. The initial debt ratios include total debt to net worth, long-term debt to net worth, debt to total assets, and long-term debt to total assets. These debt ratios are compared from one year to the next in order to identify trends, rather than having a particular target, as with liquidity ratios.

Total Debt to Net Worth

$$\text{Total debt to net worth} = \frac{\text{total debt}}{\text{net worth}}$$

The ratio indicates the portion of a person's assets derived from debt compared to net worth. Generally, we would expect the debt-to-net-worth ratio to decline over a person's lifetime.

Reviewing the two statements of financial position for the Nelsons (December 31, 2021, and December 31, 2022), we find the total debt-to-net-worth ratio to be:

$$12/31/2021 \quad \frac{\$215,446}{\$207,626} = 1.04$$

$$12/31/2022 \quad \frac{\$217,374}{\$241,573} = .90$$

The total debt ratio has improved this year, as a lower proportion of debt indicates less financial risk.

Long-Term Debt to Net Worth The long-term debt ratio removes short-term debt from the numerator to get a look at the long-term capital structure. The ratio is calculated as follows:

$$\text{Long-term debt to net worth} = \frac{\text{long-term debt}}{\text{net worth}}$$

Net worth should be increasing and long-term debt should be declining over time. Therefore, we expect a decreasing ratio when comparing one year to the next.

Again, after reviewing the two statements of financial position for the Nelsons, we find long-term debt to net worth ratio to be:

$$12/31/2021 \quad \frac{\$208{,}719}{\$207{,}626} = 1.01$$

$$12/31/2022 \quad \frac{\$211{,}301}{\$241{,}573} = .87$$

Note that the long-term debt-to-net-worth ratios are very close to the total debt to net worth ratios, which suggests that most of the Nelsons' debt is long term. An examination of the Nelsons' long-term debt reveals that the primary debt is the mortgage on the principal residence, which (as opposed to credit card debt) is generally considered high-quality debt.

Total Debt to Total Assets The ratio of total debt to total assets indicates the proportion of assets furnished by creditors as a percentage of total assets.

$$\text{Total debt to total assets} = \frac{\text{total debt}}{\text{total assets}}$$

Reviewing the Nelsons' two statements of financial position, we find total debt to total assets to be:

$$12/31/2021 \quad \frac{\$215{,}446}{\$423{,}072} = .51$$

$$12/31/2022 \quad \frac{\$217{,}374}{\$458{,}947} = .47$$

Once again, the ratio has modestly improved over the last year.

Long-Term Debt to Total Assets The long-term-debt-to-total-assets ratio is a numerator refinement on the previous ratio to focus on long-term debt as a proportion of total assets.

$$\text{Long-term debt to total assets} = \frac{\text{long-term debt}}{\text{total assets}}$$

Once again, we use the two statements of financial position for the Nelsons to determine the long-term debt to total assets:

$$12/31/2021 \quad \frac{\$208{,}719}{\$423{,}072} = .49$$

$$12/31/2022 \quad \frac{\$211{,}301}{\$458{,}947} = .46$$

The ratio has modestly declined. For the Nelsons, this decline does not add very much insight because of the debt mix. However, for a client with different debt mixes, this ratio could be very revealing.

Debt Analysis

The proper use of debt is to match the economic benefit period of the asset purchased with the repayment period of the debt such that the economic benefit period equals or exceeds the repayment period. We expect that there is a life cycle of indebtedness beginning at the asset accumulation phase, peaking sometime in the conservation/preservation phase, and declining rapidly during or before the gifting phase. Debt is useful for asset accumulation, but it has a cost. Once it is established that the person can manage debt well, lenders are willing to extend more debt up to the point where default risk is increased. At some point, persons who have acquired assets using debt wish to be out of debt to devote the repayment resources to other goals, such as saving for retirement.

Certain types of debt are often thought of as reasonable, such as student loans, mortgages, and auto loans. The underlying assets of education, housing, and transportation create long-lived economic benefits and are expensive. These assets are commonly purchased with some debt financing. Exhibit 4.13 presents the types of debts, the benefits created by those debts, the expected economic benefits period of the asset purchased, and the common repayment period. Many items may be purchased with credit cards; however, credit card debt is considered the worst kind of debt because of its potentially high costs. Many people use credit cards to purchase consumable goods and then find themselves repaying the debt long after the period of consumption. There are some positive ways to use credit cards, such as paying off the balance monthly without increasing overall debt.

EXHIBIT 4.13 Types of Debt: Economic Benefit and Repayment Periods

Type of Debt	Type of Benefit Created	Expected Benefit Period*	Common Repayment Period
Student loans	Education	Lifetime	10 years
Mortgage or principal residence	Shelter	40 years	15–30 years
Auto loans	Transportation	3–10 years	3–5 years
Bank loans	Various	Various	Various
Credit cards	Various[1]	Various	30 days to 1 year[2] or more

*Assumes asset held for entire economic life.

[1] Various, but typically consumption.

[2] If credit cards are paid at the minimum payment, the interest rate may be high (18–21%), and the debt will last a long time.

Consumer Debt Ratio—Non-housing Monthly Debt Service to Monthly Net Income One of the most commonly used debt management ratios is the consumer debt ratio. This is the ratio of monthly consumer debt payments to monthly net (after-tax) income. Generally, consumer debt refers to debt other than mortgage indebtedness and often includes debt incurred to service automobile and credit card purchases. A generally accepted rule in personal financial planning is that this ratio should not exceed 20%. The ratio is calculated as:

$$\text{Non-housing monthly debt payments} \div \text{Monthly net income} \leq 20\%$$

The Nelsons' consumer debt ratio is very good. At 6.97%, they are well below the 20% benchmark. The numerator consists of the credit cards payments and the boat loan payments.

$$\frac{(\$960 + \$3{,}040) \div 12}{[\$71{,}050 - (\$12{,}855 + \$820)] \div 12} = \frac{\$333.33}{\$4{,}781.25} = 6.97\%$$

Monthly Housing Costs to Monthly Gross Income Mortgage lenders are sophisticated lenders. They have benchmarks for loans secured with real estate used as a personal residence. The first such benchmark is:

$$\frac{\text{Monthly housing costs (PITI)}}{\text{Monthly gross income}} \leq 28\% \text{ monthly gross income}$$

P	=	principal
I	=	interest
T	=	taxes (real estate)
I	=	insurance

Housing costs
Principal and interest to pay the mortgage loan, real estate taxes, and homeowners insurance

Housing costs include the monthly principal and interest to repay the loan, real estate taxes, and homeowners insurance. This sum is divided by monthly gross income (income before taxes and other deductions). Generally, to issue a mortgage loan at prevailing market interest rates, lenders require this ratio to be less than or equal to 28%.

For the Nelsons:

$$\frac{(\$20{,}720 + \$1{,}234 + \$1{,}000 + \$950) \div 12}{\$71{,}050 \div 12} = \frac{\$1{,}992}{\$5{,}921} = 33.6\%$$

This ratio, which for the Nelsons significantly exceeds the benchmark of 28%, suggests that the Nelsons have taken on housing debt in excess of what is reasonable for their income.

Monthly Housing Costs and Other Debt Repayments to Monthly Gross Income The second ratio that lenders use adjusts the previous numerator to reflect all monthly debt repayments. This ratio should be less than or equal to 36%.

$$\frac{\text{Housing costs} + \text{other monthly debt pyts}}{\text{Monthly gross income}} \leq 36\% \text{ monthly gross income}$$

This ratio of housing costs and all other monthly debt repayments must be less than or equal to 36%. A mortgage applicant must generally meet both the requirements of the 28% benchmark and the 36% benchmark to qualify for a mortgage loan at the best interest rates.

For the Nelsons:

$$\frac{\text{Housing costs + credit cards + boat loan}}{\text{Monthly gross income}} \leq 36\% \text{ monthly gross income}$$

$$\frac{\$1{,}992 + [(\$960 + \$3{,}040) \div 12]}{\$71{,}050 \div 12} = \frac{\$2{,}325.33}{\$5{,}921} = 39.3\%$$

The Nelsons have also exceeded the second benchmark. This should serve as a warning sign that they have too much debt for their current income level. The second housing ratio is not grossly deficient (over the target). If the Nelsons paid off the credit cards and boat with invested assets, the second ratio would be within the established benchmark.

Because these ratios are so widely used by mortgage lenders for both initial mortgage indebtedness and for mortgage refinance, they are useful benchmark ratios to calculate for any client to determine whether the client is at risk of having too much debt. The ratios indicate that monthly housing nondiscretionary costs should not exceed 28% of monthly gross income and that all monthly debt repayments should not exceed 36% of monthly gross income. The second ratio suggests that if the full initial 28% of gross income is used for housing, there is only 8% of gross income left for auto loans, furniture loans, student loans, and monthly credit card repayments. Many clients tend to stretch beyond their means when buying a home and should be cautioned by the planner. These ratios can bring a sense of reality to a client regarding the debt picture and indebtedness decisions. For the Nelsons, when these ratios are reviewed in combination with the consumer debt ratio, it becomes clear that it is not consumer debt that is making their mortgage ratios exceed the benchmark but their housing costs.

Performance Ratios—Savings

Performance ratios are designed to assess the financial flexibility of the client as well as to assess the client's progress toward financial goal achievement. These ratios are the savings ratio and discretionary cash flow plus savings-to-gross-income ratio.

The Savings Ratio The savings ratio indicates the amount that is actually being saved as a percentage of gross income.

$$\frac{\text{Annual savings (personal and employer-related)}}{\text{Annual gross income}} = \text{annual rate of savings} = \text{target of } 10\%$$

The long-run savings rate for a client is the level of savings that has been achieved on a consistent basis and is reasonably likely to persist. The long-run combined savings rate should be about 10% of gross income if the client begins saving by age 30 expecting to retire at the age of 62. If saving begins later, retirement must be delayed or the savings rate must be increased. For example, beginning to save at age 40 and retiring at 65 would require a 15% savings rate. For these savings rates to be effective, there is also an earnings rate assumption of real market returns on a growth investment portfolio. Unfortunately, many clients do not save enough to create adequate retirement capital. Some clients also do not invest wisely and, therefore, do not achieve growth-oriented portfolio returns.

In reviewing the Nelsons' personal statement of cash flows, Exhibit 4.10, we have determined their savings rate to be:

$$\frac{\$5{,}853 + \$2{,}100}{\$71{,}050} = 11.2\%$$

The Nelsons have a good combined savings rate of 11.2%, which includes the 3% ($71,000 × 3% = $2,100) matching contribution from David's employer.

Net Cash Flows Plus Savings to Annual Gross Income This ratio indicates the amount that could be saved as opposed to what is saved. The ratio is calculated using net cash flow from the personal statement of cash flows and adding scheduled savings. This sum is then divided by total gross income.

$$\frac{\text{NCF + savings}}{\text{Annual gross income}} \geq 10\% \text{ target}$$

Reviewing the Nelsons' personal statement of cash flows, we determine that the ratio is:

$$\frac{(\$157) + \$5{,}853 + \$2{,}100}{\$71{,}050} = 11\%$$

Although this ratio is unrevealing for the Nelsons, it may be useful for other clients whose savings rate is lower or where there are significant discretionary cash flows.

Performance Ratios—Investments

Investment performance ratios are designed to assist the reader in understanding the returns on investments. They include income on investments, rate of return on investments, and investment assets to gross income.

Rate of Return on Investments (ROI) This ratio provides us with a return on investments that we can compare to a previously established benchmark or to an appropriate investment index. The numerator is the change in investment assets from one year to the next (ending investments [EI] – beginning investments [BI]) less any savings or gifts/inheritances received that went into investments. The denominator is the average invested assets. ROI is calculated as:

$$\frac{\text{EI} - \text{BI} - \text{savings} - \text{gifts received}}{\text{Average invested assets}} = \text{target of } 9 - 12\%$$

$$\frac{\text{BI} + \text{EI}}{2} = \text{Average invested assets}$$

Again, using the Nelsons' personal statement of cash flows and statement of financial position, the ROI is calculated to be:

$$\frac{\$78{,}229 - \$58{,}697 - \$7{,}953 - \$10{,}000}{(\$58{,}697 + \$78{,}229) \div 2} = \frac{\$1{,}579}{\$68{,}463} = 2.3\%$$

The rate of return on investments for the Nelsons for 2022 was 2.3%. While at first glance that may seem a poor rate of return, it will need to be compared with portfolios with similar asset allocations to determine exactly how the performance compared to a relevant benchmark. Obviously, it is a poor rate of return against the general benchmark of 9–12% needed annually to provide a sufficient capital base for retirement. It may, however, only represent one "down" year among many "up" years that exceeded the target.

Income on Investments The income on investments is calculated by dividing the income from investment returns by the average invested assets.

$$\frac{\text{Income from investment returns}}{\text{Average invested assets}} = \text{target depends on the client's situation}$$

Using the personal statement of cash flows and the statement of financial position for the Nelsons, we calculate their income on investments to be:

$$\frac{(\$900 + \$150)}{(\$58{,}697 + \$78{,}229) \div 2} = \frac{\$1{,}050}{\$68{,}463} = 1.5\%$$

The ratio of 1.5% indicates a low level of income from investments. A review of the rate of return on all investments, however, including any unrealized appreciation in investment assets, will provide additional information that may be useful regarding investment performance.

Investment Assets to Annual Gross Income Calculating investment assets as a percentage of annual gross income provides a peek into the issue of capital needed at retirement. A simple example will help us. Assume that a person about to retire has investment assets devoted to retirement of $1 million, has annual gross income of $100,000, and can invest at a rate of return of 10% with no inflation. The investment asset to income ratio is 10 ($1,000,000 ÷ $100,000), and the client can produce that income in perpetuity. We expect investment assets to be equal to or greater than 10 times preretirement income at normal retirement age. This ratio calculated over time helps us to benchmark the progress toward retirement. The ratio should be about three to four 10 years before retirement and about one 20 years before retirement.

$$\frac{\text{Investment assets}}{\text{Annual gross income}} = \text{Target depends on the client's situation and age}$$

Using the Nelsons' personal statement of cash flows and statement of financial position, the ratio is calculated as:

$$\frac{\$78{,}229}{\$71{,}050} = 1.10$$

This investment ratio is excellent for the Nelsons at their age if all the investment assets were held for retirement. Even when the education fund is deducted from the invested assets, the ratio equals .88, which is good progress toward retirement for their age. Exhibit 4.14 gives a summary of the ratio analysis for the Nelsons.

EXHIBIT 4.14 Summary of Ratio Analysis (Targets and Nelsons') Year End 12/31/2022

		Formula		Target	Nelsons'
Liquidity ratios					
Emergency fund ratio	=	current assets / monthly nondiscretionary expenses	=	3–6	.54
Current ratio	=	current assets / current liabilities	=	1–2	.37
Debt Ratios					
Total debt to net worth	=	total debt / net worth	=	*	.90
Long-term debt to net worth	=	long-term debt / net worth	=	*	.87
Total debt to total assets	=	total debt / total assets	=	*	.47
Long-term debt to total assets	=	long-term debt / total assets	=	*	.46
Consumer debt ratio	=	non-housing monthly debt payments / monthly net income	=	≤ 20%	6.97%
Monthly housing costs to monthly gross income	=	monthly housing costs / monthly gross income	=	≤ 28%	33.6%
Monthly housing costs and other debt repayments to monthly gross income	=	housing costs and debt repayments / monthly gross income	=	≤ 36%	39.3%
Savings ratios					
Savings ratio	=	personal saving and employer contribution / annual gross income	=	≤ 10%	11.2%
Net cash flow plus savings to annual gross income	=	net cash flow + savings / annual gross income	=	> 10%	11%
Performance ratios					
Income on investments	=	dividends and interest / average investments	=	*	1.5%
Return on investments	=	EI – BI – savings – gifts / average investments	=	9%–12%	2.3%
Investment assets to annual gross income	=	investment assets / annual gross income	=	*	1.10

*Target depends on the individual's age or investment objectives.

Vertical Analysis

Vertical Analysis and Common Size Analysis

Vertical analysis of financial statements presents each statement in percentage terms. Usually, the statement of financial position is presented with each item as a percentage of total assets, and the income statement is prepared with each item as a percentage of total income. Percentage items allow us to compare items over time when we have multiple-year financial statements for the same client.

The comparison of one statement on a percentage basis is called common size analysis because the percentages calculated ignore absolute dollars and provide information regarding the stability or instability of each account in percentage terms. Exhibit 4.15 presents the two statements of financial position in a vertical analysis format, and Exhibit 4.16 presents the Nelsons' personal statement of cash flows using vertical analysis.

EXHIBIT 4.15 Statement of Financial Position—Vertical Analysis

Dana and David Nelson Statement of Financial Position—Vertical Analysis 2022		12/31/21	12/31/22	Difference
ASSETS				
Cash/cash equivalents				
JT	Checking account	.34%	.28%	–.06%
JT	Savings account	.22%	.21%	–.01%
	Total cash/cash equivalents	.56%	.48%*	–.08%*
Invested assets				
Dana	ABC stock	2.96%	3.06%	.10%
JT	Education fund	3.31%	3.39%	.08%
JT	Section 401(k) plan	7.61%	8.42%	.81%
David	XYZ stock	.00%	2.18%	2.18%
	Total invested assets	**13.88%**	**17.05%**	**3.17%**
*Includes rounding differences				
Personal use assets				
JT	Principal residence	57.91%	54.47%	–3.44%
JT	Automobile	4.25%	3.27%	–.98%
David	Personal watercraft	.00%	2.18%	2.18%
David	Boat A	5.91%	.00%	–5.91%
David	Boat B	.00%	6.54%	6.54%
Dana	Jewelry	3.07%	2.94%	–.13%
JT	Furniture/household	14.42%	13.07%	–1.35%
	Total personal use assets	85.56%	82.47%	–3.09%
	Total assets	**100%**	**100%**	**0%**
LIABILITIES AND NET WORTH				
Current liabilities				
JT	Credit cards	.95%	.79%	–.16%
JT	Mortgage on principal residence	.29%	.30%	.01%
David	Boat loan	.35%	.23%	–.12%
	Total current liabilities	**1.59%**	**1.32%**	**–.27%**
Long-term liabilities				
JT	Mortgage on principal residence	46.48%	42.55%	–3.93%
David	Boat loan	2.85%	3.49%	.64%
Total long-term liabilities		49.33%	46.04%	–3.29%
Total liabilities		**50.92%**	**47.36%**	**–3.56%**
Net worth		**49.08%**	**52.64%**	**3.56%**
Total liabilities and net worth		**100%**	**100%**	**0%**

EXHIBIT 4.16 Personal Statement of Cash Flows

Dana and David Nelson
Personal Statement of Cash Flows—Vertical Analysis
For 2022

INFLOWS		
Salary—David		98.52%
Investment income		
Interest income	1.27%	
Dividend income	.21%	1.48%
Total Inflows		**100%**
Savings		
Reinvestment (interest/dividends)	1.48%	
Section 401(k) plan deferrals	5.35%	
Education fund	1.41%	
Total savings		**8.24%**
Available for outflows		**91.76%**
OUTFLOWS		
Ordinary living expenses		
Food	8.45%	
Clothing	5.07%	
Child care	.84%	
Entertainment	2.55%	
Utilities	5.07%	
Auto maintenance	2.81%	
Church	4.93%	
Total ordinary living expenses		**29.72%**
Debt payments		
Credit card payments principal	.48%	
Credit card payments interest	.87%	
Mortgage payment principal	1.74%	
Mortgage payment interest	29.16%	
Boat loan principal	2.10%	
Boat loan interest	2.18%	
Total debt payments		**36.53%**
Insurance premiums		
Automobile insurance premiums	1.27%	
Disability insurance premiums	1.07%	
Homeowners insurance premiums	1.34%	
Total insurance premiums		**3.67%**
Tuition and education expenses		**1.41%**
Taxes		
FICA and federal income tax (W/H)	18.09%	
State (and city) income tax	1.15%	
Property tax (principal residence)	1.41%	
Total taxes		**20.65%**
Total outflows		**91.98%**
Net cash flow (deficit)		**(.22%)**

Growth Analysis

The purpose of growth analysis is to calculate the growth rate of certain financial variables over time using time value of money tools. We expect that increases in gross income will exceed increases in the Consumer Price Index (CPI) by more than 1%. Exhibit 4.17 lists the financial variables for which growth rates should be calculated. The second column presents the growth rates that are appropriate for the particular financial variable.

EXHIBIT 4.17 Financial Variables and Growth Rates

Variable	Growth Rate
Inflation	Should equal CPI
Gross income	Should exceed CPI
Savings increase	Should exceed CPI
Savings rate	Should remain constant or increase
NCF + savings	Should grow modestly
Net worth	Should exceed CPI
Investment assets	Should grow exponentially due to combining returns and savings contributions

Limitations of Financial Statement Analysis

Inflation

Because inflation exists, comparing multiple reporting periods will require adjusting certain numbers either to current dollars (inflated dollars) or to some base percentage or index. Inflation reduces the comparability of multiperiod financial statements and ratios even when adjusted for the inflation. It is especially important to adjust growth rates for income and savings to real dollars. It is also useful to adjust nominal investment returns for inflation to determine real economic returns.

Use of Estimates

Whenever estimates of values are used, even if provided by expert appraisers, there is some risk that the estimated value is different from the actual fair market value. Such risks should be evaluated considering the purpose of the financial statement analysis. For example, net worth may be dependent on the estimated value of personal use assets (which are very difficult to value). Because net worth is used as a denominator for several ratios, an error in the denominator will affect the result of any ratio using that denominator.

Benchmarks

For corporations and industries, there are published financial statements and, therefore, clear benchmarks with which to compare ratios for companies in the same industry. Unfortunately, there are few published personal financial statements and, therefore, fewer clearly established benchmarks for individuals. Recall the housing mortgage ratios where benchmarks exist at 28% and 36% of gross income.

Sensitivity Analysis

Some ratios are more important than others. For example, the long-term savings rate and emergency fund ratio are critical, whereas the current ratio is less so. The relative size of the numerator and denominator may cause some ratios to be more sensitive to changes. Sensitivity analysis allows us to manipulate the numerators and denominators by small increments to determine the impact on the ratio.

Risk Analysis

Risk analysis examines the uncertainty of cash flows to the individual. Uncertainty regarding the asset side of the statement of financial position is called business or investment risk. Specifically, earnings may vary because of fluctuations in the value of investments and personal use assets. Financial risk is the risk on the liability side of the statement of financial position. Indebtedness is accompanied by fixed interest and principal repayments. There is always some risk as to whether debt repayments can be made. The debt/net worth ratio and other debt ratios help to measure the financial risk of the individual.

BUDGETING

Description

Planners and clients should remember that good budgeting is a learned phenomenon and, as such, there is a learning curve (the more you do it, the better you get at it). Budgeting requires planning for the expected, the recurring, and the supposedly unexpected (every month it's something). **Budgeting** is a process of projecting, monitoring, adjusting, and controlling future income and expenditures. It may be used to determine the wage replacement ratio for capital needs analysis for retirement where the client is sufficiently close to retirement to be able to estimate the retirement budget.

Budgeting
A process of projecting, monitoring, adjusting, and controlling future income and expenditures

Steps

1. Start with bank statements, checks, and check stubs for a twelve-month period. Create a spreadsheet of all expenditures by month and category. If needed, retrieve copies of credit card expenditure information for a twelve-month period to assist in determining the amounts and categories of expenditures.
2. Once the dollar amounts are determined per category and month, calculate these as a percentage of gross income. Analyze each category, looking for consistent percentage expenditures to develop a predictive model for that particular expenditure.
3. Identify which costs are sensitive to inflation and which are fixed. Examples include:
   - ordinary living expenses (e.g., food, clothing, and utilities);
   - home mortgage payments (interest);
   - credit card payments (interests); and
   - other interest-based payments (e.g., boat payments).

4. Forecast next year's income on a monthly basis.
5. Determine how much expenditures will amount to and in which months the expenditure will occur. Insurance bills are often paid annually or semiannually. If they arrive at the wrong time, they can create havoc with cash flows.
6. Project the budget for the next 12 months.
7. Compare actual expenditures for the month to expected expenditures. Adjust the next 11 months accordingly.
8. Continue to analyze, picking out specific expenditure categories that you can control. Utilities are an example of a cost that can be managed. Review cable/internet charges, and consider usage and possible alternatives.

Nelson Budgeting Plan

We are now going to look at how a budgeting plan would help the Nelsons achieve their financial goals. First we will look at the personal statement of cash flows to gauge what costs they are incurring against their income.

EXHIBIT 4.18 Personal Statement of Cash Flows

Dana and David Nelson
Personal Statement of Cash Flows
For 2022

INFLOWS		
Salary—David		**$70,000**
Investment income		
Interest income	$900	
Dividend income	$150	$1,050
Total inflows		**$71,050**
Savings		
Reinvestment (interest/dividends)	$1,050	
Section 401(k) plan deferrals	$3,803	
Education fund	$1,000	
Total savings		**$5,853**
Available for outflows		**$65,197**
OUTFLOWS		
Ordinary living expenses		
Food	$6,000	
Clothing	$3,600	
Child care	$600	
Entertainment	$1,814	
Utilities	$3,600	
Auto maintenance	$2,000	
Church	$3,500	
Total ordinary living expenses		**$21,114**
Debt payments		
Credit card payments principal	$345	
Credit card payments interest	$615	
Mortgage payment principal	$1,234	
Mortgage payment interest	$20,720	
Boat loan principal	$1,493	
Boat loan interest	$1,547	
Total debt payments		**$25,954**
Insurance premiums		
Automobile insurance premiums	$900	
Disability insurance premiums	$761	
Homeowners insurance premiums	$950	
Total insurance premiums		**$2,611**
Tuition and education expenses		**$1,000**
Taxes		
FICA and federal income tax (W/H)	$12,855	
State (and city) income tax	$820	
Property tax (principal residence)	$1,000	
Total taxes		**$14,675**
Total outflows		**$65,354**
Net cash flow (deficit)		**($157)**

The next step is to focus on the outflows and what percentage of available inflows they represent. It is also beneficial to break down the amounts further into monthly amounts.

EXHIBIT 4.19 Monthly Amounts

Available for Outflows (Monthly)	$5,433.08	Percentage of Available Income
OUTFLOWS (monthly—percentages rounded)		
Ordinary living expenses		
Food	$500	9.2%
Clothing	$300	5.5%
Child care	$50	.9%
Entertainment	$151.16	2.8%
Utilities	$300	5.5%
Auto maintenance	$167.67	3.1%
Church	$291.67	5.4%
Total ordinary living expenses	**$1,760.50**	**32.4%**
Debt payments		
Credit card payments principal	$28.75	.5%
Credit card payments interest	$51.25	.9%
Mortgage payment principal	$102.83	1.9%
Mortgage payment interest	$1,726.66	31.8%
Boat loan principal	$124.42	2.3%
Boat loan interest	$128.92	2.4%
Total debt payments	**$2,162.83**	**39.8%**
Insurance premiums		
Automobile insurance premiums	$75	1.4%
Disability insurance premiums	$63.42	1.2%
Homeowners insurance premiums	$79.16	1.5%
Total insurance premiums	**$217.58**	**4.1%**
Tuition and education expenses	**$83.33**	**1.5%**

We can now see which outflow percentages are higher than others and thus need greater control. This is where the planner and the client begin to discuss the control of costs and establish a budget. With the Nelsons' ordinary living expenses, we see that a large percentage is devoted to food, clothing, and utilities. These are expenses that can be controlled and managed in order to decrease overall expenditures. The planner would also discuss with the Nelsons what other living expenses could possibly be managed.

Debt payments and insurance premiums are also areas where proper management can control costs. There are several techniques that can decrease premium payments for insurance. For example, increasing deductibles and managing appropriate risks and coverage can have dramatic effects on the costs of premiums. Savings with insurance costs and ordinary living expenses can be used in several ways. They can be used toward savings, investments, emergency funds, self-insurance, or education funding, or they may be used to pay down large amounts of debt. A large portion of the Nelsons' outflows goes toward debt payments. They could use the savings to pay off their credit card debt or make additional principal payments on their boat or home. Mortgage payments have certain tax advantages associated with them, so depending on the situation, the planner should recommend paying off other debts first.

Once the Nelsons have agreed on certain cost controls, the planner can establish a projected monthly budget for next year. The budget should then be strictly adhered to and reviewed each month to make sure the goals of the budget are being met. Adjustments and restructuring can be done for those costs that are proving difficult to manage.

Saving and Consumption Habits

Information about a client's saving and consumption habits assists the planner in developing a successful strategic financial plan for the client. If the client does not have a history of saving money consistently, developing a strategy in which money could be directed into savings before the client receives a paycheck from his employer should be encouraged. Similarly, if the client has a history of making large dollar impulse purchases, creating barriers to discourage this tendency would be wise. Historical behavior is the best indicator of future behavior. Therefore, a good way to collect information about the client's saving and consumption habits is by asking the client about previous saving and consumption habits.

DEBT MANAGEMENT

Personal Use—Assets and Liabilities

Debt is appropriate when matched properly with the economic life of the asset and the ability to repay.

For example, the purchase of an automobile that is expected to be used for three years (36 months) has a maximum realistic economic life of five years (60 months). Ideally, it would be financed over 36 months but certainly no longer than 60 months.

A number of risks should be considered when taking on debt, including:

- a shorter than expected economic life;
- increasing cash outflows for repairs as the asset ages; and
- the change of the initial utility curves of the purchaser during the holding period unexpectedly reducing the overall utility of the asset.

Debt repayment cash flows should be matched to the economic life of the asset. Generally, the cash flows considered are not only the principal and interest to retire the debt. Also included are the cash flows associated with the increase in repairs and maintenance due to asset aging (both real and personal property) as well as the prospect of higher executory costs (insurance and taxes).

Either the cost of the replacement asset will have to be borne entirely by future cash flows or the current asset value will help to offset replacement costs. One question is whether the cost of the new asset is increasing in price more quickly than the old asset. Another question is whether the value of the old asset (exchange value to another buyer) is diminishing more quickly than the debt is being extinguished. If so, the purchaser of such an asset may find that he is in a negative equity position. This is the primary reason that lenders insist on down payments and generally establish a repayment schedule to ensure that the borrower will always be in a positive equity position. Such a position will reduce the likelihood that the borrower will abandon the property.

Home Mortgages

Types of home mortgages include:

- 30-year fixed mortgage;
- 15-year fixed mortgage;
- variable mortgage; and
- balloon mortgage.

Fixed-Rate Mortgages

Fixed-rate mortgages offer a level interest rate for the term of the loan and a fixed payment amortization schedule. An amortization schedule outlines the portion of each payment allocated to interest and the portion allocated to principal reduction. The payments are selected such that at the end of the term (i.e., 15 or 30 years), the principal is completely repaid.

EXAMPLE If John purchases his home using a 15-year fixed-rate mortgage of $120,000 with a 6.5% interest rate, he will pay 6.5% interest on the outstanding balance every month. His monthly payment will be $1,045.33 for the 15-year term of the loan. For the first month, John owes interest of 6.5% ÷ 12 = .5417% on $120,000, which equals $650. The remaining $395.33 will go toward repayment of the loan principal. After this payment, John owes $120,000 – $395.33 = $119,604.67. The $119,604.67 will be the new balance on which the 6.5% interest is calculated. Thus, for each subsequent payment the portion allocated to interest is reduced and the portion allocated to principal repayment is increased.

Variable-Rate Mortgages or Adjustable Rate Mortgages (ARMs)

With a variable-rate mortgage, or adjustable rate mortgage (ARM), the borrower is charged interest based on a benchmark such as the 90-day Treasury bill rate. The interest rate will change monthly on the basis of changes in the benchmark rate. Variable-rate mortgages typically have amortization schedules with fixed payments. The payment is determined by selecting an interest rate and calculating the payment necessary to retire a fixed-rate mortgage with that interest rate. Because the actual interest rate varies, the portion of the mortgage payment allocated to principal repayment will not always be greater than the previous month's allocation as under a fixed mortgage. If the actual interest rate is much higher than the rate used to calculate the mortgage payment, there will still be principal outstanding at the end of the term. In that case, the borrower will be required to repay the remaining balance in a lump sum. On the other hand, if the actual interest rate is much lower than the rate used to calculate the mortgage payment, the loan will be repaid before the end of the term.

EXAMPLE Samantha has a 2/6 ARM. Her 30-year mortgage interest rate is currently 4%. This means that Samantha's interest rate cannot increase more than 2% per year or 6% over the life of the loan. The maximum interest rate is 10%.

Many variable-rate mortgages limit the amount by which the interest rate can change on a monthly and yearly basis. For example, an ARM may state that the interest rate can only adjust by .5% each month and no more than 2% per year. Another common feature of adjustable rate mortgages is conversion from a fixed rate after a period of time, usually five to seven years. Most ARMs used for personal residences begin as fixed-rate mortgages and then convert to adjustable rate. The borrower pays a fixed rate of interest, usually lower than that for a comparable fixed-rate mortgage, for five to seven years, and then the interest rate adjusts monthly on the basis of the predetermined benchmark.

Balloon Mortgages

Besides the fixed-rate and variable-rate mortgages, a prospective homeowner may acquire a balloon mortgage. Balloon mortgages can have fixed or adjustable interest rates, but the term will be less than the period required to amortize the loan.

EXAMPLE Teresa obtains a seven-year balloon mortgage of $80,000 with a fixed interest rate of 5.75%. The lender determines Teresa's payments on the basis of a 30-year amortization, which results in a fixed monthly payment of $466.86. Teresa will pay $466.86 per month for seven years. At the end of the seventh year, the outstanding balance on Teresa's loan is $71,386.82. Because the term of the loan is seven years, Teresa will be required to pay off the remaining balance in a lump sum. Instead of paying cash, Teresa will probably refinance, replacing her original $80,000 loan with a new one for $71,386.82.

Mortgage Selection

Several issues must be addressed in the selection of mortgages. They include the length of time expected to stay in the house, cash flow capacity, and risk tolerance. A determination should be made of spread between yields after a quantitative analysis comparison of fixed-to-fixed rates and fixed-to-variable rates.

Historically, if the time expected to be in the house is short, an adjustable rate mortgage (ARM) is more likely the mortgage of choice. This is simply because most ARMs have a 2–3% lower interest rate than a 30-year fixed-rate mortgage and have 2/6 caps (2% maximum interest rate increase per year, 6% life of loan). The downside risk is the prospect of the interest rate increasing periodically, causing the payment to increase proportionally. An advantage of an ARM is that, because of the low initial interest rate, the principal and interest (P&I) payments are low relative to a 30-year fixed-rate mortgage. Therefore, potential borrowers may find it easier to qualify for a mortgage using the traditional lender hurdle rates of 28%/36%.

EXAMPLE When comparing a 15-year to a 30-year fixed rate mortgage, the interest rates will usually be about .5% different assuming the same down payment. The cash flows will differ depending on the interest rate and the size of the mortgage.

	Sales Price	Down Payment	Paid Closing Costs	Mortgage Amount	Term Months	Interest Rate	P & I Payment (rounded)
Fixed 30 Year	$180,000	$36,000	$5,760	$144,000	360	5.5%	$ 818
Fixed 15 Year	$180,000	$36,000	$5,760	$144,000	180	5.0%	$1,139
ARM 30 Year	$180,000	$36,000	$5,760	$144,000	360	3.0%	$ 607

Although the ARM has the current lowest payment, the risk is that at some point in the life of the ARM, the interest rate will be 9%, assuming a 2%/6% cap, at which time the monthly P&I payment would be $1,158.66 over a 30-year period. It should be pointed out that in this particular example, loan qualifying would be easier using the ARM because the initial payment is lower (assuming $200 per month taxes and $75 per month insurance).

- 30-year fixed rate: total monthly housing costs = $818 + $200 + $75 = $1,093; monthly gross income needed to qualify for loan = $1,093 ÷ .28 = $3,903.57.
- 15-year fixed rate: total monthly housing costs = $1,139 + $200 + $75 = $1,414; monthly gross income needed to qualify for loan = $1,414 ÷ .28 = $5,050.
- ARM: total monthly housing costs = $607 + $200 + $75 = $882; monthly gross income needed to qualify for loan = $882 ÷ .28 = $3,150.

If a client has a low tolerance for fluctuating payments, a fixed-rate mortgage should be selected. Assuming a higher risk tolerance, the planner will have to consider the length of expected ownership (shorter term will mitigate risk) and the opportunity cost of alternative investments. It is generally not appropriate to select an ARM (using the first-year teaser rate) simply to qualify for a loan and hope that cash flows will be sufficient to pay for any interest increases.

EXAMPLE The savings resulting from mortgage selection is a result of (1) the 15-year mortgage causing earlier retirement of the principal indebtedness and (2) the slightly lower interest rate. Many 30-year loans are selected simply as a necessity to meet lender qualification requirements. If no prepayment penalties exist, most of the savings can be achieved by paying a 30-year loan according to a 15-year amortization schedule.

	Number of Payments	Monthly Payment	Total Payments	Loan Principal	Interest Paid
Fixed 30 Year	360	$ 818	$294,480	$144,000	$150,480
Fixed 15 Year	180	$1,139	$205,020	$144,000	$ 61,020
Savings					$ 89,460

The total interest paid is determined by multiplying the amount of the payment by the number of payments and then subtracting the principal borrowed.

WHERE ON THE WEB

BankRate **www.bankrate.com**

Credit Union National Association **www.cuna.org**

Equifax **www.equifax.com**

USAGov (Formerly known as the Federal Citizen Information Center) **www.usa.gov**

DISCUSSION QUESTIONS

1. What is the relationship between GAAP/FASB and personal financial statements?
2. Describe some of the uses of personal financial statements.
3. What is the purpose of the statement of financial position?
4. What items are included on the statement of financial position?
5. Discuss the presentation of the statement of financial position (i.e., how items are listed and why).
6. What is the purpose of the personal statement of cash flows?
7. What items are included on the personal statement of cash flows?
8. Discuss the presentation of the personal statement of cash flows (i.e., how items are listed and why).
9. What is the purpose of the statement of changes in net worth?
10. What items are included on the statement of changes in net worth?
11. Discuss the presentation of the statement of changes in net worth (i.e., how items are listed and why).
12. What are the differences between long-term and current assets/liabilities?
13. Why are financial ratios important to financial planning?
14. What is the importance of keeping accurate and up-to-date financial statements?
15. What is fair market value?
16. What is liquidity?
17. Why do we prepare three different financial statements?
18. Discuss the importance of vertical analysis.
19. What are some of the limitations of personal financial statements?
20. What is the purpose of budgeting?
21. List the different types of home mortgages and their characteristics.

EXERCISES

1. What is the balancing equation for the statement of financial position?
2. What do current assets and current liabilities have in common?
3. Your client purchased new living room furniture for $6,500 last month. Which financial statement(s) would this purchase affect and how?
4. How would each of the following items affect net worth?
   A. Repayment of a loan using funds from a savings account
   B. Purchase of an automobile – 25% down payment/75% financed
   C. The S&P 500 increases, and the client has an S&P 500 index mutual fund
   D. Interest rates increase, and the client has a substantial bond portfolio
5. Lauren and Herb have the following assets and liabilities:

Liquid assets	$6,750
Investment assets	$16,250
Personal residence	$125,000
Current liabilities	$3,100
Long-term liabilities	$86,000

   Calculate their total assets, total liabilities, and net worth.

6. Calculate the current ratio based on the facts given in the previous question.
7. After reviewing Kenny and Jane's financial statements, the following information was determined:

Liquid assets	$3,976
Investment assets	$10,738
Annual nondiscretionary expenses	$13,913
Current liabilities	$9,247

   Calculate this couple's emergency fund ratio. Does the ratio fall within the target goal?

8. After reviewing Matt and Jennifer's personal statement of cash flows, the following information was determined:

Mortgage principal	$5,467
Mortgage interest	$21,500
Property tax	$2,000
Homeowners insurance premium	$1,800

   The couple has monthly gross income of $9,500. According to benchmarks set by mortgage lenders, has this couple taken on debt in excess of what is reasonable for their income?

9. In addition to the information given in Exercise 8, Matt and Jennifer had other annual debt payments of $11,600. Calculate the monthly housing costs and other debt repayments to monthly gross income ratio. Do Matt and Jennifer qualify for a mortgage loan?

10. Marisa and Bryant have the following assets and liabilities:

Checking account	$2,000
Personal residence	$125,000
Savings account	$3,000
CDs	$5,000
Automobile	$13,500
Stocks	$10,000
Mortgage	$80,000
Auto loan	$5,000

Determine their net worth.

11. Use the following items to determine total assets, total liabilities, net worth, total cash inflows, and total cash outflows:

Net monthly salary	$2,280
Rent	$750
Savings account balance	$2,000
Auto loan payment	$416
Money market mutual fund	$4,800
Clothing expense	$150
Value of home computer	$1,200
Groceries expense	$220
Entertainment expense	$130
Value of autos	$10,800
Student loan payment	$212
Utilities	$510
Laundry expense	$46
Insurance premium	$368
Balance of student loan	$8,625

Note: Inflow and outflow items are shown monthly.

12. The Coopers have a net worth of $250,000 before any of the following transactions:

- Paid off credit cards of $9,000 using a savings account
- Transferred $5,000 from checking to their Traditional IRAs
- Purchased $2,500 of furniture with credit

What is the Coopers' net worth after these transactions?

13. What are the advantages of performing vertical analysis on financial statements?

14. Explain how inflation limits financial statement analysis.

15. Bart has a history of making large dollar impulse purchases. As Bart's planner, what could you do to help remedy this situation?

PROBLEMS

1. Given the following information, develop a beginning-of-the-year statement of financial position.

Beginning date	January 1, 2022
End date	December 31, 2022
Client name	Frank and Lois Fox

	Beginning Balance	Ending Balance	Income/Expenses Amount (Yearly)
Section 401(k) plan deferrals			$750
Section 401(k) plan—Frank	$0	$1,500	
Section 403(b) plan deferrals			$990
Section 403(b) plan—Lois	$0	$990	
Auto loan	$15,432	$10,436	
Auto loan interest			$381
Auto loan principal			$4,996
Auto maintenance			$600
Automobile—Frank	$20,000	$18,000	
Automobile—Lois	$5,750	$5,175	
Automobile insurance premiums			$2,124
Checking	$10,000	$15,570	
Child support			$2,400
Clothing			$3,600
Credit card	$10,870	$10,417	
Credit card payments interest			$1,707
Credit card payments principal			$453
Entertainment			$4,200
FICA and federal income tax (W/H)			$11,449
Food			$4,800
Furniture/household	$36,000	$34,000	
Go-cart	$0	$1,200	
Homeowners insurance premiums			$534
Jewelry	$6,000	$6,100	
Maid/child care			$4,800
Mortgage on residence	$72,960	$72,164	
Mortgage payment interest			$5,808
Mortgage payment principal			$796
Personal residence	$85,000	$89,250	
Property tax (principal residence)			$850
Reinvestment in savings account/trust			$5,675
Salary—Frank			$25,000
Salary—Lois			$33,000
Savings	$13,500	$14,175	
Savings account/trust fund interest			$5,675
Trust fund	$100,000	$105,000	
Tuition and education expenses			$2,893
Utilities			$2,100

Additional transactions:

Made a joint gift of bedroom furniture with a fair market value of $2,000 to Frank's little sister
Section 401(k) plan employer match = 3% of income
Bought a go-cart for their son for $1,200

2. Use the data in Problem 1 to create a personal statement of cash flows.
3. Use the data in Problem 1 to create a statement of changes in net worth.
4. Use the data in Problem 1 to create an end-of-the-year statement of financial position.

5. Use the results from problems 1–4 to calculate the following ratios for year-end:
    a. Emergency fund
    b. Current ratio
    c. Total debt to net worth
    d. Long-term debt to net worth
    e. Total debt to total assets
    f. Long-term debt to total assets
    g. Monthly housing costs to monthly gross income
    h. Monthly housing costs and other debt repayments to monthly gross income
    i. Savings ratio
    j. Net cash flow plus savings to annual gross income
    k. Income on investments
    l. Return on investments
    m. Investment assets to annual gross income
6. Discuss the financial position of the Foxes as based on the ratios you calculated in the previous problem.
7. Prepare a vertical analysis of the end-of-the-year statement of financial position and the personal statement of cash flows for the Foxes.
8. Lisa recently bought a house for $150,000 using a fixed 30-year home loan with a 5% interest rate. She used 20% of the amount toward the down payment and paid the $5,000 in closing costs out of pocket. How much mortgage interest can Lisa expect to pay during the course of this loan?

CHAPTER 5

Establishing Financial Direction: The Financial Planning Process

LEARNING OBJECTIVES

After learning the material in this chapter, you will be able to do the following:

- Identify the seven steps of the financial planning process used to establish financial direction
- Assist clients in identifying an appropriate financial mission
- Gather client data and identify external and internal environmental information that is relevant for a particular client
- Assist clients in determining goals, expectations, and objectives
- Determine a client's financial status and analyze internal strengths and weaknesses, as well as external environmental opportunities and threats

- Develop a financial plan by formulating appropriate financial strategies
- Assist clients in analyzing and selecting the financial strategy that best meets their needs and desires
- Assist clients in implementing and monitoring their financial plans

THE FINANCIAL PLANNING PROCESS

The first step in the financial planning process, establishing and defining the client-planner relationship, has been discussed in Chapter 3. Once this step is completed, the financial planner now begins to establish financial direction by gathering the information necessary to fulfill the engagement and then analyzing and evaluating the client's current financial status. These steps, and the subsequent steps in the financial planning process, are illustrated in Exhibit 5.1.

EXHIBIT 5.1 The Financial Planning Process

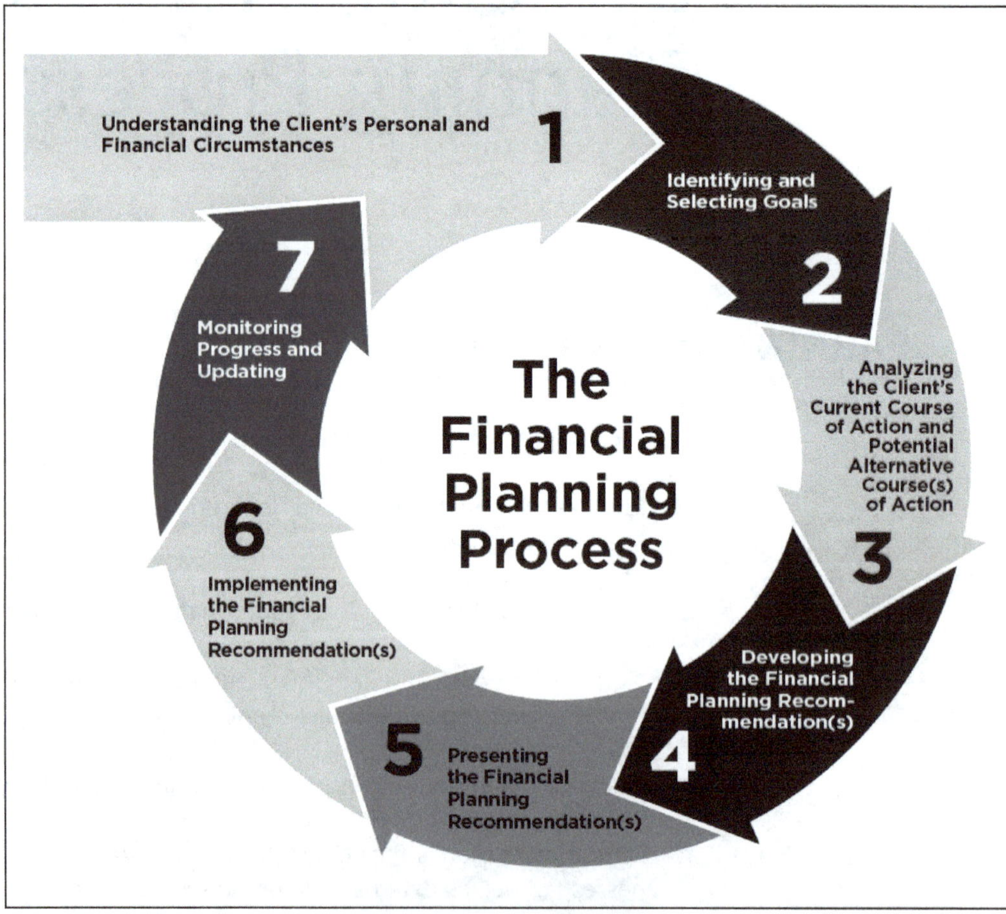

Source: CFP Board - Roadmap to the Code of Ethics and Standards of Conduct

Steps

1. Understanding the client's personal and financial circumstances.
2. Identifying and selecting goals.
3. Analyzing the client's current course of action and potential alternative course(s) of action.
4. Developing the financial planning recommendation(s).
5. Presenting the financial planning recommendation(s).
6. Implementing the financial planning recommendation(s).
7. Monitoring progress and updating.

The seven steps of the financial planning process are completed in sequential order because each step depends on the previous step. The elimination of any step may result in the loss of direction and, possibly, an inappropriate financial strategy. Furthermore, the financial planner must periodically monitor the external and internal environments so that changes in the environment may be responded to appropriately. Monitoring is a continuous and ongoing process that does not end once the plan has been implemented. Modifications to the plan must be made as changes in situations and circumstances require.

To establish financial direction in a manner that is concise and systematic, we recommend the use of the "Client/Planner Worksheet for Establishing Financial Direction" (Exhibit 5.2). The application of this worksheet will be demonstrated throughout this chapter. Notice that the worksheet has a header for the client's name and date, a footer for the planner's name, a section for the financial mission, a section for financial goals and objectives, and a section in which each goal or objective is identified and classified as a need or want, with the want objectives ranked from 1 (nice to have) to 5 (of great importance).

The process of interviewing the client and gathering necessary paperwork could take several weeks. Financial planners may find it helpful to ask the client to provide bank statements, pay stubs, investment account statements, and insurance policies at the data-gathering meeting. A completed client questionnaire may also be requested before the meeting. Having these support documents will speed the analysis phase and allow the planner to ask pointed questions during the data-gathering meeting.

EXHIBIT 5.2 Client/Planner Worksheet—Blank Form

Client/Planner Worksheet for
Establishing Financial Direction

Client Name______________________________ **Date**______________________

FINANCIAL MISSION

1. Educate the client as to what a financial mission is and the importance of it being broad and enduring.
2. Working with your client, develop a financial mission that your client is willing to embrace.

____

____

Financial Goals & Objectives

1. Discuss and explain common financial goals with client.
2. Identify goals the client is interested in achieving.
3. Write client objective under appropriate goal classification.
4. Ensure all "need" objectives have been identified and documented.
5. Classify each objective as a want or a need; remember to remain objective.
6. For each "want" objective, the client must assign a weight between 1 and 5 (1 = objective would be nice to have, 5 = objective is of great importance).

Goal:		
Objectives:	Need	Want
	•	•____
	•	•____
	•	•____

Goal		
Objectives:	Need	Want
	•	•____
	•	•____
	•	•____

Goal:		
Objectives:	Need	Want
	•	•____
	•	•____
	•	•____

Goal:		
Objectives:	Need	Want
	•	•____
	•	•____
	•	•____

Planner's Name ____________________________________

STEP 1: UNDERSTANDING THE CLIENT'S PERSONAL AND FINANCIAL CIRCUMSTANCES

As discussed in Chapter 3, financial planners must establish relationships of trust and open communication with their clients. During this first step of the financial planning process, the client-planner relationship is defined as expectations that are set for both parties. The financial planner discusses the services to be provided and the methods and sources of compensation. The parties also discuss decision-making and the duration of the relationship.

Financial mission
Broad and enduring statement that identifies the client's long-term purpose for creating a financial plan

At this meeting, the planner may help the client develop a financial mission statement. A **financial mission** is a broad and enduring statement that identifies the client's long-term purpose for creating a financial plan. Because the mission statement is broad and enduring, it should not change throughout the planning process. The purpose of a financial mission is twofold. First, it ensures a common understanding between the client and the planner as to why the financial plan is being created and implemented. Second, it provides a basis for the creation of feasible alternative goals, objectives, and strategies, and for selecting among strategic alternatives. Throughout this text, it is assumed that the financial mission for most clients is to achieve financial independence and avoid catastrophic financial occurrences that could result in financial dependence.

Appropriate financial planning requires a holistic approach. All aspects of a client's past, present, and projected financial situation need to be evaluated. It is inappropriate to focus only on one or two aspects of a client's situation because all aspects are interrelated and interdependent. This is why developing an appropriate financial mission is so important. The financial planner can use the "Client/Planner Worksheet for Establishing Financial Direction" to begin formalizing the financial planning process when working with the client.

Exhibit 5.3 identifies how the Nelsons, a couple introduced at the end of Chapter 3, might complete the Financial Mission section of the "Client/Planner Worksheet for Establishing Financial Direction." When completing the Financial Mission section, the first step is for the financial planner to communicate with and educate the client so that a realistic, enduring, and broad financial mission is developed. Once the client has adopted the mission, it should be documented on the worksheet. Throughout this chapter, we will assume the Nelsons have embraced the following mission: "To achieve financial independence and avoid catastrophic financial occurrences resulting in financial dependence."

EXHIBIT 5.3 Client/Planner Worksheet—Financial Mission

Client/Planner Worksheet for
Establishing Financial Direction

Client Name Dana and David Nelson **Date** February 16, 2023

FINANCIAL MISSION

1. Educate the client as to what a financial mission is and the importance of it being broad and enduring.
2. Working with your client, develop a financial mission that your client is willing to embrace.

To achieve financial independence and avoid catastrophic financial occurrences that may result in financial dependence.

Identifying Relevant Environmental Information

Once the client-planner relationship is established and the mission is adopted, the financial planner gathers data needed to analyze and evaluate the client's financial status. In this step, the financial planner identifies the relevant external and internal environmental information that applies to the client. The planner should apply the skills and information discussed in Chapter 2, External Environmental Analysis, to identify external environmental information that is current and relevant to the client. The planner must also be able to identify the relevant information that has been collected about the client. Lessons learned in Chapter 3, Communication and Internal Environmental Analysis, should also be applied during this step. It is important to keep the mission in mind to determine whether information is relevant. Only relevant information should be listed to keep the amount of information collected manageable. During this step, it is important to gather and list only the facts. Analysis will be conducted and conclusions will be drawn later while developing the SWOT Analysis, during Step 3: Analyzing the client's current course of action and potential alternative course(s) of action.

External and internal environmental information has been gathered and determined to be relevant to the Nelsons; it is listed next.

Relevant external environmental information is as follows.

- Mortgage rates are 5% for 30 years and 4.5% for 15 years, fixed.
- Gross domestic product (GDP) is expected to grow at less than 3%.
- Inflation is expected to be 2.6%.
- Expected return on investment is 8% for common stocks, 9% for small company stocks, and 1.1% for U.S. Treasury bills.
- College education costs are $15,000 per year ($75,000 for 5 years).

Relevant internal environmental information is as follows.

- David has been employed at the bank for 12 years, has a salary of $70,000, and they have a gross income of $71,050.
- The Nelsons are in the asset-accumulation phase.
- Relevant financial ratios, identified in Chapter 4, are as follows:
  - Current assets to monthly nondiscretionary expenses ratio is 0.54.
  - Housing costs to gross income ratio is 33.6%.
  - All debt payments to gross income ratio is 39.3%.
  - Annual savings to annual gross income ratio is 11.2%.
  - Investment asset ratio is 1.10 for the previous year.
- The entire family is insured under David's employer's health plan (PPO). For covered expenses, a $1,000 in-network deductible and a $2,000 out-of-network deductible apply, after which 80%/20% coinsurance applies in-network and 60%/40% applies out-of-network. There is a stop-loss limit of $20,000 annually in-network and $30,000 annually out-of-network. The entire monthly premium of $1,123.54 is paid by David's employer.
- David's employer provides group term life insurance equal to two times his current salary.
- David has a private disability insurance policy covering accidental disability for "own occupation" with a 30-day elimination period. The benefit is $2,700 per month until his normal Social Security retirement age. David pays the annual premium of $761.
- The Nelsons have a homeowners insurance (HO-3) policy with dwelling extension and replacement cost on contents. The deductible is $250 with an annual premium of $950.
- David currently contributes 5.43% of his salary into the company's Section 401(k) plan. The company contributes dollar-for-dollar up to 3%. David's maximum contribution is 16%. David's assets within the plan are currently earning 8.5%, based on his investment choices within the plan.
- David and Dana are in the 15% marginal federal income tax bracket.

STEP 2: IDENTIFYING AND SELECTING GOALS

Goals
High-level statements of financial desire that may be for the short term or the long term

Paradoxical thinking
The second phase of a client's thinking process when setting financial direction in which a client tries to focus on several simultaneous objectives, causing confusion, goal conflict, and ambiguity. The paradoxical thinking phase is where a client often seeks the advice of a financial planner.

The next part of the financial planning process is Step 2: Identifying and selecting goals. Goals are high-level statements of desires that may be for either the short term or the long term. Short-term goals are those that will occur within five years. Long-term goals are those that will occur sometime beyond five years. Identifying goals requires the client to consider all aspects of a financial plan. If all goals are identified and prioritized, the client is less likely to overlook some goals while focusing on others. Performing this process of defining and prioritizing goals, however, often results in the client entering the second common phase of thinking—**paradoxical thinking.** As the client advances to the paradoxical thinking level, he also may begin to become discouraged or frustrated with the process because of a new awareness of the extent of financial planning required to achieve multiple and often conflicting goals. During this phase, the planner should keep explanations simple and discuss goals in present dollar value terms because future value terms may be more difficult for the client to understand.

Goals are critical to the planning engagement because they define what the client wants to achieve and direct the overall process. If this stage of the process is not given the full attention it requires, the rest of the planning process lacks focus and becomes misguided.

Financial goals should be quantified in dollar amounts and have established time frames. Quantifying goals makes it easier to estimate required savings and establish patterns that lead to success. Several goals will include personal and economic assumptions. These assumptions may include, but are not limited to, the following:

- **Personal assumptions**, based on client-related variables, such as retirement age(s), life expectancy(ies), income needs, risk factors, time horizon, and special needs
- **Economic assumptions**, based on economic-based data or performance (current and/or historic), such as inflation rates and investment returns

The specific assumptions that are embedded in the plan require a collaborative exchange between the planner and the client. It is important to remember that the assumptions and goals will shift over time and that calculations are merely estimates. However, any decisions concerning material assumptions within the plan must be disclosed and vetted with the client.

An individual who seeks financial planning services is often motivated by a specific situation or set of circumstances. Early in the planning relationship, these motivating factors can be transformed into well-defined goals that the client aims to achieve. Although achieving these goals becomes central to the plan, the planner must account for issues that the client may not have considered independently. For example, a planner is responsible for conducting a risk analysis of the client's situation and instituting protection against events that can cause unanticipated financial difficulty, hindering long- or short-term goals as a result. If the client were to experience a period of disability, the ensuing financial losses could have consequences on short-term and long-term education planning goals. The planner must anticipate these risks and focus the attention of the client on the interrelated nature of every goal. In addition, personal financial planning should incorporate and responsibly manage financial needs that exist for all clients, such as retirement and estate planning. In the initial phase of the data-gathering process, a discussion must be held regarding these long-term needs, as well as implications of not addressing other issues immediately. After all goals, assumptions, timelines, and risks have been explored, the planner and client can collaborate to rank financial objectives in order of importance. In prioritizing one goal over another, the planner must take care to point out the impact to other goals that arise as a result of the choice.

Generally, financial goals can be divided into the following five categories, each of which will be discussed fully in subsequent chapters.

- *Insurance planning and employee benefits*—The goal is to mitigate the risks of catastrophic losses to persons, property, and liability by maintaining appropriate insurance coverage while paying efficient premiums. Also included in this category are benefits available to employees, including group life, health, and disability insurance.
- *Investment planning*—The goal is to save and invest to accumulate capital for retirement, wealth transfer, and other expenditure objectives, such as the purchase of personal property, education funding, lump-sum payments, and emergencies.
- *Tax planning*—The goal is to arrange income tax affairs to mitigate income tax liability and take advantage of incentives in the income tax law as appropriate.
- *Retirement planning*—The goal is to provide inflation-protected retirement income at an appropriate age for full life expectancy, conservatively estimated.
- *Estate planning*—The goal is to have a proper estate plan consistent with transfer goals.

The financial planner can again use the "Client/Planner Worksheet for Establishing Financial Direction" to assist in establishing financial goals. As the Nelsons' financial planner, you should work with and educate them so that they become familiar with the common financial goals. Next, you should assist them in identifying the goals they are interested in achieving. Once they understand the importance and interdependence of all common financial goals, the goals should be documented in the Financial Goals section of the worksheet. Exhibit 5.4 identifies the goals that are relevant to the Nelsons.

EXHIBIT 5.4 Establishing Financial Direction—Financial Goals

Client/Planner Worksheet for
Establishing Financial Direction

Client Name **Dana and David Nelson** Date **February 16, 2023**

FINANCIAL MISSION

1. Educate the client as to what a financial mission is and the importance of it being broad and enduring.
2. Working with your client, develop a financial mission that your client is willing to embrace.

To achieve financial independence and avoid catastrophic financial occurrences that may result in financial dependence.

Financial Goals and Objectives

1. Discuss and explain common financial goals with client.
2. Identify goals the client is interested in achieving.

Goal: Mitigate risk of catastrophic losses by maintaining appropriate insurance coverage while paying efficient premiums.		
Objectives:	**Need**	**Want**
	❐	❐____

Goal: Provide inflation-protected retirement income, assuming a life expectancy of 92 years of age.		
Objectives:	**Need**	**Want**
	❐	❐____

Goal: Develop an appropriate estate plan consistent with transfer goals.		
Objectives:	**Need**	**Want**
	❐	❐____

Goal: Arrange income tax affairs to minimize income tax liability and take advantage of tax law incentives.		
Objectives:	**Need**	**Want**
	❐	❐____

Goal: Accumulate capital, through saving and investing, for the purchase of personal property, education, and emergencies.		
Objectives:	**Need**	**Want**
	❐	❐____

Developing Financial Objectives

Goals are further defined by the development of financial objectives. Objectives are more specific than goals. Several objectives may be developed for each goal category and should include time and measurement attributes when appropriate.

The client usually engages in paradoxical thinking during this step. The client often becomes confused and frustrated because of the conflict between unlimited wants and limited resources. The planner can greatly assist the client by presenting information in a clear, concise, systematic, and objective manner.

Once objectives have been identified for each goal category, each objective must then be classified as either a want or a need. Generally, the client is more focused on identifying the want objectives. Therefore, the planner is responsible for ensuring that all of the need objectives are identified. To this end, the planner should keep the mission and relevant environmental factors in mind when assisting the client in the development of financial objectives.

Distinguishing between a want and need can be difficult for clients because subjectivity and strong desires become issues. This potential difficulty can be eliminated by asking two questions of each objective:

- Is this objective necessary to accomplish the financial mission?
- Does the law require that this objective be implemented?

If the answer to either of these questions is yes, the objective is a need. If the answer to both of these questions is no, the objective is a want.

For example, under the goal of protection against risk, the objectives of property insurance for an old car and auto liability coverage may have been identified. If the planner asks the questions above in reference to auto insurance, we find that in this case auto insurance is a want objective. Implementation of this objective is not necessary to accomplish the mission of achieving financial independence and avoiding catastrophic financial occurrences, nor does law require it because it is an older car and is paid for in full. However, liability insurance may be a need objective because state law requires all licensed automobile owners to carry liability insurance. If the Nelsons are involved in an accident for which they are at fault, lack of liability coverage will likely jeopardize their assets.

Objectives classified as wants are further analyzed by having the client attach weights to them. Assigning weights to objectives allows the planner and the client to objectively evaluate a subjective desire. A weight expresses the importance or desirability of an objective relative to the others by assigning it a number between 1 and 5. A 5 should be assigned to a want objective of great importance—something the client has a strong desire to achieve. A 1 should be assigned to a want objective that the client would like to have but could do without if the objective is not achieved. The weight assignment will be used during strategy selection to assist in determining which want objectives will be implemented. It is probable that not all of the want objectives will be achieved; however, all of the need objectives must be implemented to achieve the financial mission and comply with the law. Therefore, objectives classified as needs do not require weight assignment.

Exhibit 5.5 identifies a partial list of objectives that are important to the Nelsons. Throughout this chapter, we will address only a partial list of objectives in order to keep the amount of material manageable.

EXHIBIT 5.5 Client/Planner Worksheet—Financial Objectives

Client/Planner Worksheet for
Establishing Financial Direction

Client Name Dana and David Nelson **Date** February 16, 2023

FINANCIAL MISSION

1. Educate the client as to what a financial mission is and the importance of it being broad and enduring.
2. Working with your client, develop a financial mission that your client is willing to embrace.

To achieve financial independence and avoid catastrophic financial occurrences that may result in financial dependence.

Financial Goals & Objectives

1. Discuss and explain common financial goals with client.
2. Identify goals the client is interested in achieving.
3. Write client objective under appropriate goal classification.
4. Ensure all "need" objectives have been identified and documented.
5. Classify each objective as a "want" or a "need." Remember to remain objective.
6. For each "want" objective, the client must assign a weight between 1 and 5. (1 = objective would be nice to have, 5 = objective is of great importance).

Goal: Mitigate risk of catastrophic losses by maintaining appropriate insurance coverage while paying efficient premiums.		
Objectives:	**Need**	**Want**
Within 6 months, modify Life Insurance to include 20-year level term for $500,000.	✔	❐ ___
Within 6 months, modify Disability Insurance to include disability by sickness.	✔	❐ ___
Within 6 months, modify Health Insurance to include major medical with $10,000 deductible due to lifetime limit.	✔	❐ ___

Goal: Provide inflation-protected retirement income, assuming a life expectancy of 92 years of age.		
Objectives:	**Need**	**Want**
Retire at age 67 with an 80% wage replacement, thereby, maintaining lifestyle.	✔	❐ ___
Retire at age 62 with an 80% wage replacement, thereby, maintaining lifestyle.	❐	✔ 5

Goal: Develop an appropriate estate plan consistent with transfer goals.		
Objectives:	**Need**	**Want**
Develop a will for David, within three months.	✔	❐ ___
Develop a will for Dana, within three months.	✔	❐ ___

Goal: Arrange income tax affairs so that income tax liability is minimized and to take advantage of tax law incentives.		
Objectives:	**Need**	**Want**
Reduce tax payments to the minimum amount allowable by law.	❐	✔ 5
Within 2 months, increase contributions into Section 401(k) plan to ensure adequate retirement income and to reduce income tax liability.	✔	❐ ___

Goal: Accumulate capital, through saving and investing, for the purchase of personal property, education, and emergencies.		
Objectives:	**Need**	**Want**
Purchase a $200,000 home in Key West within 5 years.	❐	✔ 4
Save for college tuition so that money is available when John, Gabrielle, and new baby begin college.	❐	✔ 3
Purchase a new car in two years, twelve years, and at retirement.	❐	✔ 2
Eliminate credit card debt within six years.	❐	✔ 3

STEP 3: ANALYZING THE CLIENT'S CURRENT COURSE OF ACTION AND POTENTIAL ALTERNATIVE COURSE(S) OF ACTION

Analyzing and evaluating the client's current course of action and potential alternative course(s) of action, Step 3 of the financial planning process, employs knowledge from all financial disciplines:

- Insurance planning and employee benefits
- Investment planning
- Income tax planning
- Retirement planning
- Estate planning

SWOT analysis
An analysis that helps the financial planner understand how internal and external environmental factors impact the client's financial situation. The acronym SWOT stands for strengths, weaknesses, opportunities, and threats.

This step involves identifying strengths, weaknesses, opportunities, and threats. A **SWOT** (strengths, weaknesses, opportunities, and threats) **analysis** is a useful tool to assist the planner in converting several bits of relevant information into an understandable format. The analysis helps the planner understand how the internal and external environments impact the client's situation—a critical element to developing feasible and responsive strategies. A SWOT analysis is developed by listing the client's internal strengths and weaknesses and the external environment's opportunities and threats. Once the strengths, weaknesses, opportunities, and threats are identified, the planner systematically analyzes the SWOT list to assist in the generation of feasible alternative strategies.

When identifying strengths, the planner should consider the internal and financial data collected from the client. Client strengths, such as appropriate consumption and savings behaviors and positive attitudes and beliefs with regard to financial planning and financial stability, also should be considered. The planner should indicate whether the timing of the plan is appropriate to the client's goals and objectives and whether the client's subjective perception of her financial situation is similar to the planner's objective appraisal of the client's financial situation. The planner should consider areas in which the client has adequate insurance coverage for life, health, disability, long-term care, property, and liability. Finally, the financial ratios that meet or exceed recommended levels should be listed.

When identifying weaknesses, the planner again should consider the internal and financial data collected from the client. Client weaknesses, such as poor savings behaviors, unwise consumption habits, a poor attitude toward financial planning, special needs, and financial instability, should be identified. The planner should indicate whether the timing of the plan is appropriate for the client and whether the client's subjective perception of his financial situation is dissimilar to the objective financial situation. The planner should consider areas in which the client has inadequate insurance coverage for life, health, disability, long-term care, property, and liability. Finally, the financial ratios that do not meet recommended levels should be listed.

When identifying external environmental opportunities, the planner should consider monetary trends, favorable interest rates and inflation levels, technological breakthroughs, governmental controls, favorable changes in income tax rules, social attitudes toward businesses, and the emergence of new industries. The planner should also list favorable trends and forecasts that may positively impact the client's financial plan.

When identifying external environmental threats, the planner should consider unfavorable interest rates and inflation forecasts, technological breakthroughs, governmental controls, adverse changes in income tax rules, public distrust of businesses, and emergence of new industries. The planner also should list unfavorable trends and forecasts that may negatively impact the client's financial plan.

Using the Nelsons as an example, the following SWOT may be developed:

Strengths	■ David's job in a stable industry that provides the family with sufficient income ■ Net worth is reasonable for the Nelsons' ages ■ Investment assets-to-income ratio exceeds the target ratio for the Nelsons' ages
Weaknesses	■ Insufficient annual savings to drive goals ■ Inadequate life and disability insurance ■ Inappropriate investment risk ■ Too much debt ■ Unrealistic goals for current savings and investments ■ Deficient health insurance policy ■ No estate planning ■ Poor housing-cost-to-income ratio
Opportunities	■ Mortgage rates favorable for refinancing ■ High expected return on investments in stocks ■ Low expected inflation rate ■ Low current interest rates ■ Leading economic index signaling expansion
Threats	■ Current cost of college (room and board, tuition) is $15,000 per year per child ■ Slow economy and high unemployment; investments may not provide expected returns

STEP 4: DEVELOPING THE FINANCIAL PLANNING RECOMMENDATION(S)

Several financial, environmental, and internal client aspects must be considered and analyzed before feasible strategies can be formulated for the client and a financial plan developed. This is illustrated in Exhibit 5.6 below. Note that input from other advisors—an estate planning attorney, accountant or CPA, for example—is necessary in most cases.

EXHIBIT 5.6 Strategy Formulation

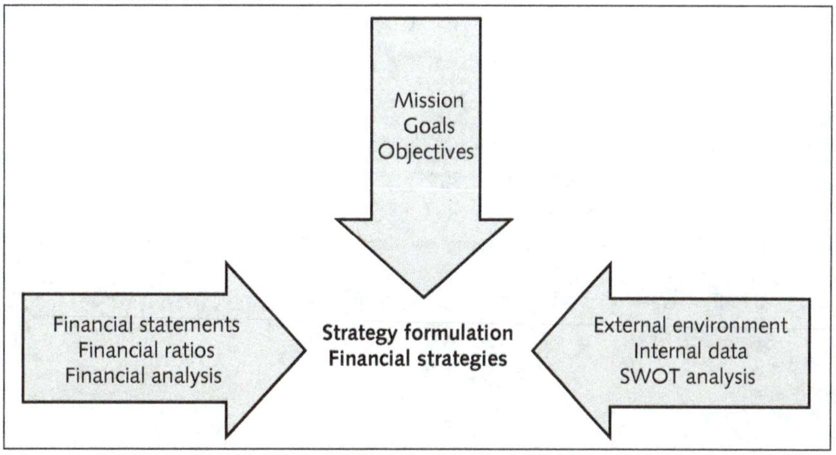

When developing the financial plan, the client's financial situation must be analyzed using financial data collection techniques (Chapter 4). The external environment and its effect on the client also must be considered (Chapter 2). In addition, the client's internal data and life cycle positioning must be understood (Chapter 3). Note that, throughout this process, the client's mission, goals, and objectives must remain central to the development of strategies.

When formulating feasible strategies, the planner should begin by developing an abbreviated income statement to identify the client's current cash flow situation. Then, the planner should identify the costs associated with implementing the need objectives and add the required cash outflows necessary to meet the need requirements to the existing cash flow. This will provide an estimate of the cash flow required to implement a plan that will accomplish the need objectives. Do not be concerned that the addition of these costs may cause the net cash flow to be negative. If a negative net cash flow exists, it may help bring the client into financial reality.

Using the Nelsons as an example and the initial income statement information gathered in Chapter 4, we can estimate the costs for implementing the need objectives.

EXHIBIT 5.7 Abbreviated Statement of Cash Flows

Income	$71,050
Savings	(5,853)
Ordinary living expenses	(21,114)
Other payments	(25,954)
Insurance payments	(2,611)
Tuition and education	(1,000)
Total taxes	(14,675)
Net cash flow (deficit)	$ (157)

The estimated costs for implementing the need objectives for the Nelsons are listed next.

Acquire appropriate amount of insurance

- Life—Add 20-year level term of $500,000, for an estimated cost of $500.
- Disability—Modify coverage to include disability by sickness, at an estimated cost of $1,400.
- Health—Add major medical with $10,000 deductible because of lifetime limit, at an estimated cost of $1,000.

Retire and maintain lifestyle

- David should save 10% of his salary due to his age. Because his company matches 3%, David should save at least 7% in his Section 401(k) plan. David is currently saving 5.43% ($3,803/$70,000). Therefore, he intends to increase his Section 401(k) plan savings by $1,099 (1.57%).
- By increasing his Section 401(k) plan contributions, David will reduce his tax payments by $165 ($1,099 @ 15% = $164.85 rounded to nearest dollar). Therefore, the change in cash flow is an increased outflow of $934 ($1,099 – $165).

Reduce debt

- The Nelsons should increase their payments toward their credit card debt; however, no estimated amounts will be identified at this time. This objective will be addressed when selecting a strategy with the client.

Prepare wills

- David and Dana should each create a will. The estimated cost of having a will drawn up is $500 each, for a total of $1,000.

The Nelsons currently have a cash flow deficit of $157; however, the implementation of all need objectives would increase the deficit by $4,834 [$2,900 for insurance, $934 for Section 401(k) plan contributions, $1,000 for wills] for a total deficit of $4,991 ($4,834 + $157).

EXHIBIT 5.8 Net Cash Flows After Implementation of Need Objectives

Net cash flow	$ (157)
Life insurance	(500)
Disability insurance	(1,400)
Health Insurance	(1,000)
Additional Section 401(k) plan contributions	(1,099)
Reduction of tax resulting from Section 401(k) plan contributions	165
Drafting of wills	(1,000)
Net cash flow after implementation of need objectives	$ (4,991)

Often, as in the case of the Nelsons, the analysis of the abbreviated income statement and the addition of costs associated with need objectives indicate a cash shortage. Therefore, either more cash inflow, less cash outflow, or a combination of the two is required. Common sources of available cash flows to increase inflows or reduce outflows include:

- cutting discretionary expenses such as entertainment, vacations, utilities, and charitable contributions;
- refinancing mortgages to reduce payment or decrease the debt term;
- raising insurance deductibles to reduce premiums;
- making use of tax-advantaged savings; and
- obtaining additional income from employment.

After determining the cash flow situation, including the implementation of need objectives, the next step is to develop strategies that (1) create a positive net cash flow; (2) at the same time, resolve weaknesses identified in the SWOT analysis; and (3) accomplish, at a minimum, the need objectives. Therefore, the planner should consider each of the common methods to increase cash inflow or reduce cash outflow, the opportunities identified in the SWOT analysis, and each of the objectives previously identified by the client and the planner.

While developing alternative strategies, the planner must determine how each strategy might affect cash flow and the client's objectives. Remember, all need objectives should be resolved first, and then the want objectives should be considered. These alternative strategies will be presented to the client and, with the assistance of the planner, the client will ultimately choose which strategy to implement.

Revisiting the SWOT analysis and taking advantage of the available external opportunities indicate that the Nelsons should refinance their home. Refinancing their home mortgage at 5% will reduce their annual mortgage payment by $9,206.04, or ($1,829.48 – $1,062.31) × 12. [Assume a 30-year mortgage at 5%: n = 360, i = 0.416667 (5 ÷ 12),

PV = 197,888 (includes the balance of closing costs not paid at closing), and PMT = 1.062.31.] During analysis of the financial statements and tax returns, it was discovered that the Nelsons' income taxes are currently overwithheld annually by $5,744. This type of discovery is common, and an adjustment to increase receivables will be made on a future balance sheet. The combination of refinancing the home and properly adjusting their income tax withholdings will increase the Nelsons' cash flow by $14,950.04.

If we now compare the total cash flow deficit of $4,991 to the newly found cash inflows of $14,950.04, we find that the Nelsons now have a positive net cash flow of $9,959.04. Some of this positive cash flow should be used to reduce credit card debt. The remainder of the cash flow may be used to achieve some of the want objectives, to create an emergency fund, or increase savings and investments. The expense for the wills is not a recurring expense and will add $1,000 to cash flow in future years.

Recall that the two want objectives most important to the Nelsons (each with a 5 ranking) were to minimize payment of income taxes and to retire at age 62. The next most important objective, with a 4 ranking, was to purchase a home in Key West, Florida.

The objective of minimizing the payment of income taxes was resolved while focusing on the need objectives. For David to retire at age 62, he will need the exceptional investment returns (greater than the 8.5% rate he is currently earning) on his retirement investments. Purchasing a $200,000 home in Key West will require annual savings of $6,684 for five years to create a 20% down payment, then monthly mortgage payments of $1,174.02 ($14,088 annually). (See Supplement at the end of this chapter for detailed calculations.)

The Nelsons have already taken advantage of refinancing and tax savings, so they must now consider cutting discretionary expenses, raising deductibles on insurance, or obtaining additional income. Raising deductibles is usually the next option considered because this strategy has little impact on daily life or the overall financial plan. Clients seem to be more resistant to cutting discretionary expenses or obtaining additional income because those options can have a significant impact on the clients' daily lives.

STEP 5: PRESENTING THE FINANCIAL PLANNING RECOMMENDATION(S)

When presenting a recommendation, the practitioner must make a reasonable effort to assist the client in understanding the client's current situation, the recommendation itself, and its impact on the ability to meet the client's goals, needs, and priorities. In doing so, the practitioner must avoid presenting the practitioner's opinion as fact.

The practitioner must communicate the factors critical to the client's understanding of the recommendations. These factors may include, but are not limited to, the following:

- Personal and economic assumptions
- Interdependence of recommendations
- Material advantages and disadvantages
- Risks
- Time sensitivity

The practitioner should indicate that while the recommendations may meet the client's goals, needs, and priorities, changes in personal and economic conditions could alter the projected progression of the plan. Changes include, but are not limited to, updates to monetary or fiscal policy, family status, career, investment performance, and/or health.

If there are conflicts of interest that have not been previously disclosed, these issues and their impact on the recommendations should be addressed at this time.

Presenting recommendations provides the practitioner an opportunity to further assess whether the potential options meet client expectations, whether the client is willing to act on the recommendations, and whether modifications are necessary.

Ideally, recommendations are written and prepared in a clear, understandable manner. Thorough and thoughtfully crafted recommendations can prepare the adviser to systematically walk the client through the decision-making process.

Abstract thinking
The third phase of a client's thinking process in establishing financial direction, in which a client becomes aware of the consequences of financial actions and understands how day-to-day savings and consumption decisions impact a financial plan

The selection of strategy recommendations is made simpler when analyzed in a quantitative manner. It also helps the client move on to the **abstract-thinking** level. The Strategy Selection Worksheet, shown in Exhibit 5.9, can assist in this analysis. During the evaluation of each alternative, the planner should discuss with the client actions that must be taken; what must occur to implement the strategy; and how the strategy might change the client's current consumption and savings behavior, existing savings rate, time horizon, and asset allocation.

While considering the previously mentioned issues, the client should answer the following questions with the planner's assistance:

- How easy can I implement this strategy?
- How committed am I to implementing this strategy, considering the required action and sacrifices?

The client should respond to each of these questions using a weighting scale of 1 to 5. For the first question, a 5 would indicate the strategy is *very easy* to implement. For the second, a 5 would indicate the client is *very committed* to implementing the strategy. The answer weightings of each question are multiplied to result in a ranking for that strategy. The strategies with the highest rankings are the ones most likely to be successful.

The ranking of the *want* objectives include one additional measure. The weight of the objective identified on the "Client/Planner Worksheet for Establishing Financial Direction" should be considered when obtaining the ranking for that strategy. Again, the strategies with the highest rankings are most likely to be successful and therefore should be seriously considered. Exhibit 5.9 indicates how the Nelsons may have completed the Strategy Selection Worksheet.

EXHIBIT 5.9 Strategy Selection Worksheet

Strategy Selection Worksheet

Client Name Dana and David Nelson **Date** February 16, 2023

a) List strategy options.
b) For each strategy option, indicate the objective(s) that is resolved.
c) Discuss, with the client, the impact of implementing the objective.
d) For each strategy option, the client should answer the following questions by ranking the answers 1 to 5.
   - ✓ How easy will it be to implement this strategy? (A 5 ranking indicates very easy to implement.)
   - ✓ How committed am I to implementing this strategy? (A 5 ranking indicates very committed.)
e) For "want" objectives, consider the original importance ranking that was identified when completing the **Client/Planner Worksheet**.

Strategy (Discuss how each strategy impacts relevant objectives)	**Benefits of Implementing Strategy**	**Behavior Change Required**	**Ease of Implementation**	**Commitment Level**	**Ranking**
Refinance Home	Increases annual cash flow by $9,206	None	5	5	25
Adjust tax withholdings	Increases annual cash flow by $5,744	None	5	5	25
Increase contributions to Section 401(k) plan	Takes advantage of tax-free savings	None, since other strategies will increase current cash flow	5	5	25
Raise Insurance Deductibles	Increases cash flow by $200	Acceptance of additional risk	5	3	15
Cut discretionary expenses	Increases annual cash flow by maximum of $2,414	Do not use paid babysitters, eliminate entertainment expenses, etc.	1	2	2
Dana acquires part-time job	Increases annual cash flow	Put Gabby in daycare	2	1	2
David acquires a second job	Increases annual cash flow	Spend less time with family	2	1	2

After completing the Strategy Selection Worksheet, the Nelsons have decided to refinance their home, adjust their tax withholdings, and increase David's contributions to the Section 401(k) plan. This increase in cash flow will allow them to meet all of their need objectives. They have also decided to use the surplus cash flow to reduce their credit card debt and to begin making deposits into an emergency fund. The Nelsons now realize that purchasing a vacation home in Key West is not reasonable at this time and have decided to revisit this objective in five years. David also realizes that retiring at age 62 may not be possible unless the investment objectives for retirement are achieved; however, he has made a commitment to increase his Section 401(k) plan contributions each time he gets a raise until he reaches the maximum allowable amount.

David and Dana do not want to raise their insurance deductibles because they enjoy the peace of mind of not having a considerable cash outlay in the event of an insurance claim. They do not want to acquire additional employment because spending time with family is very important to both of them.

Communicating the Recommendations

When the planner communicates recommendations to clients, it is important to engage them through meaningful interpersonal (one-on-one) communication. As recommendations are made, a planner becomes both an advisor—actually making the recommendations, and a counselor—offering professional guidance during the client's decision-making process. Active listening and emotional intelligence, both discussed in Chapter 1, are also critical. Planners should use open-ended questions to clarify clients' understanding of the plan recommendations. Refer to "Chapter 3: Communication and Internal Environmental Analysis" for more information regarding open-ended questions and other key communication techniques.

STEP 6: IMPLEMENTING THE FINANCIAL PLANNING RECOMMENDATION(S)

The financial planner is responsible for implementing the client's financial planning recommendation(s) *unless* specifically excluded from the Scope of Engagement. The client is responsible for accepting or rejecting recommendations. In the event that a planner does not have implementation responsibilities, the client and planner collaborate to determine whether implementation responsibilities are retained by the planner and/or delegated to the client or a team of specialists.

The practitioner's responsibilities may include, but are not limited to, the following:

- Identifying activities necessary for implementation
- Determining division of activities between the practitioner and the client
- Referring to other professionals
- Coordinating with other professionals
- Sharing of information as authorized
- Selecting and securing products and/or services

If there are conflicts of interest, sources of compensation, or material relationships with other professionals or advisers that have not been previously disclosed, such conflicts, sources, or relationships must be disclosed at this time.

When referring the client to other professionals or advisers, the financial planning practitioner must indicate the basis on which the practitioner believes the other professional or adviser may be qualified. If the practitioner is engaged by the client to provide only implementation activities, the scope of the engagement must be mutually defined in accordance with Step 1 of the Practice Standards. This scope may include matters such as the extent to which the practitioner will rely on information, analysis, or recommendations provided by others.

The financial planning practitioner must investigate products or services that reasonably address the client's needs. The products or services selected to implement the recommendation(s) must be suitable to the client's financial situation and consistent with the client's goals, needs, and priorities.

At all times, a planner must use professional judgment in selecting the products and services that are in the client's best interest. Professional judgment incorporates both qualitative and quantitative information.

Products and services selected by the practitioner may differ from those of other practitioners or advisers. More than one product or service may exist that can reasonably meet the client's goals, needs, and priorities.

The practitioner must make all disclosures required by applicable regulations.

Above all, the planner's role in coordinating the activities of the client and the other advisers is critical, for in the absence of implementation, the plan has minimal value.

STEP 7: MONITORING PROGRESS AND UPDATING

The purpose of Step 7 of the financial planning process is to clarify the role of the practitioner in the monitoring and updating process. By specifying this responsibility, the client's expectations are more likely to be in alignment with the level of oversight and updating that the practitioner intends to provide.

When engaged in monitoring and updating, the practitioner must make a reasonable effort to define and communicate the specific items that will be subject to oversight. By defining the items to be monitored, the frequency of monitoring, and the communication method(s), the client is provided reassurance and is able to appropriately set expectations.

The monitoring process may reveal the need to reinitiate steps of the financial planning process. Consequently, the current scope of the engagement may need to be modified.

Earlier in the financial planning process, the planner established a client file and a system for periodic review and revision. The scope of engagement defined the planner's role in monitoring. Due to liability concerns, many companies require that the planning engagement be terminated within a certain period, such as six months or one year, and that a new engagement must be created if the relationship continues past that point. If the planner is managing investments or products, the expectation is that the planner will monitor the performance of investments, products, and the general economic environment.

At regularly scheduled reviews with the client, the planner evaluates the progress toward the client's goals and whether shifts to the prior strategies and recommendations need to be made. In addition to economic or investment-related changes, the client's personal objectives, health status, income, or other circumstances may have changed. If this is the case, the financial planner returns to the early steps of the process, reevaluates

goals, and gathers additional data to make recommendations that meet the client's new requirements.

When changes in the economy, tax laws, or other issues arise that are likely to affect the client's financial situation, the planner informs the client that the implemented financial planning recommendations are being monitored for potential updates. Step 7 creates a cyclical process, allowing the updates that arise from monitoring to be smoothly integrated into the plan.

WHERE ON THE WEB

Association for Financial Counseling and Planning Education **www.afcpe.org**

Bloomberg **www.bloomberg.com**

Bureau of Economic Analysis (U.S. Department of Commerce) **www.bea.gov**

Bureau of Labor Statistics (U.S. Department of Labor) **www.bls.gov**

CPI Homepage (U.S.) **www.bls.gov/cpi**

Economy at a Glance (U.S.) **stats.bls.gov/eag/eag.us.htm**

Forbes Magazine **www.forbes.com**

National Association of Personal Financial Advisors **www.napfa.org**

Service Corps of Retired Executives **www.score.org**

U.S. Small Business Administration **www.sba.gov**

DISCUSSION QUESTIONS

1. What are the seven steps of the financial planning process?
2. What is the definition of a financial mission?
3. What are the main activities that take place during Step 2 of the financial planning process: Identifying and selecting goals?
4. What are the most common financial goals developed during the planning process?
5. How do financial goals and financial objectives differ?
6. Why must a financial planner keep abreast of the external environment?
7. How does client subjectivity affect the establishment of financial objectives?
8. What is the difference between *need* and *want* objectives?
9. What questions can be asked of financial objectives to determine if the objective is a *need* or a *want*?
10. What does the acronym SWOT stand for?
11. During Step 3 of the financial planning process—Analyzing the client's current course of action and potential alternative course(s) of action—how can a SWOT analysis be useful to a financial planner?
12. What must be considered when formulating planning alternatives?
13. What are common methods to increase cash inflow or reduce cash outflow?
14. What should be considered when selecting strategies to implement?
15. How can the planner improve the probability of successful implementation of strategies?
16. How often should the recommendations within a financial plan be monitored?

EXERCISES

1. Assume Nicholas and Ashley contacted you, a financial planner, to assist them in saving for a car, their children's education, and a boat. Which thinking phase are they probably demonstrating?
2. What would you do if a client came to you insisting that his financial mission was to buy a 1965 Mustang?
3. If you were working with a client to distinguish between a want and a need objective and the client wanted to categorize buying a vacation home as a need, what would you do?
4. What would you say or do to help clients in understanding the difference between a goal and an objective?

PROBLEMS

1. Assume your clients, Alex and Megan, have multiple objectives requiring monthly cash flows of $400, $250, $150, $750, and $325, respectively. Also assume that their current net cash flow per month is $380.
   A. What technique would you use to bring Alex and Megan into economic reality?
   B. How would you distinguish between *need* and *want* objectives?
   C. Where might you look for additional available cash flows to meet their objectives?

2. Assume Ben and Abby have hired you as their financial planner. Upon brief investigation, you collect the following information. The couple has been married for five years and have no children. They take expensive vacations several times a year. Both have good jobs and both save the maximum allowed in their Section 401(k) plans. The mortgage on their house is at a 6% rate. The current mortgage rate is 3.75%. Their credit card balance has been approximately $1,500 for some time, and they make minimum payments each month. The couple has a monthly net cash flow deficit of $98. What would be your recommendations to increase their monthly net cash flow?

CHAPTER 5 SUPPLEMENT

Calculations for Retirement Needs and Key West Home for the Nelsons

Retirement Needs Analysis Using Capital Needs Analysis and the Annuity Method

Step 1 Determine gross dollar needs.

We assume the Nelsons wish to maintain their current lifestyle at retirement. At retirement, the Nelsons will have eliminated Social Security taxes (FICA), Section 401(k) plan contributions, child care expenses, and disability insurance premiums. We also assume that the recommendations were implemented by the Nelsons.

Current salary	$70,000
FICA	– 5,355 (calculated at the 7.65% FICA rate)
Section 401(k) plan contributions	– 4,900
Child care expenses	– 600
Disability insurance premiums	– 2,161
	$56,984 yearly retirement need in today's dollars

Step 2 Determine net dollar needs.

We estimate David's Social Security benefits at age 67 to be $24,756 per year in today's dollars. Because David's ideal would be to retire at age 62, we estimate the Social Security benefit at that age to be $17,220 in today's dollars.

Gross retirement needs	$56,984
Social Security benefits	–17,220
	$39,764 net retirement need per year

Step 3 Calculate inflated preretirement dollar needs.

n	=	25 (62 – 37)
i	=	2.6 (inflation estimate)
PV	=	–$39,764
PMT	=	$0
FV	=	$75,539.50 (first-year need for retirement)

Step 4 Calculate capital need at retirement.

n	=	30 (92 – 62) Expect to live to age 92
i	=	5.75049 {[(1.85 ÷ 1.026) – 1] × 100} (return on investments of 8.5%)
FV	=	$0
PMT	=	–$75,539.50
PV_{AD}	=	$1,129,573.05 (total capital needed at retirement)

Step 5 Calculate yearly deposits to savings.

n	=	25 (62 – 37)
i	=	8.5 (Estimated return on investment)
FV	=	$1,129,573.05
PV	=	–$62,669 [Section 401(k) plan + stocks at end of 2018]
PMT	=	$8,235.28 needs to be saved each year to achieve goal
Required savings		$6,336.40
Current savings		–7,000.00 (includes employer contribution)
		$1,235.28 additional savings required

Key West house purchase

n	=	5
i	=	9 (estimated return on investment)
PV	=	$0
FV	=	$40,000 (20% × $200,000)
PMT	=	$6,683.70 required savings

Key West mortgage payment

P/YR	=	12
n	=	360 (30 × 12)
i/yr	=	8 (assumes 8% interest on 30-year mortgage in 5 years)
PV	=	–$160,000 ($200,000 – $40,000 down payment)
FV	=	$0
PMT	=	$1,174.02 monthly payment

SECTION 2 IN BRIEF

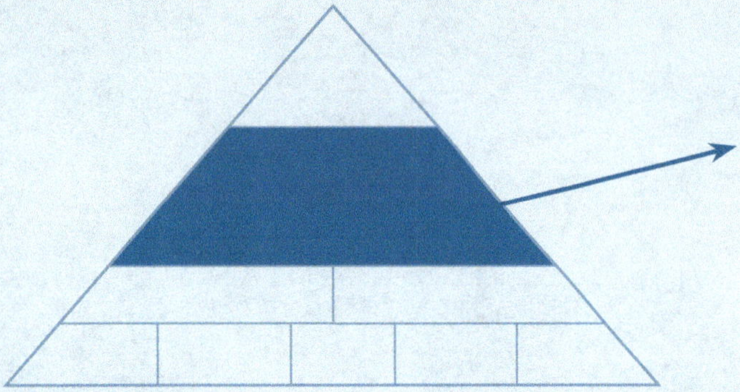

- The power of compound interest
- Basic tools for time value of money
- Future value of an ordinary annuity
- Future value of an annuity due
- Present value of a dollar
- Present value of an ordinary annuity
- Present value of an annuity due
- Financial aid programs for education
- Tax advantages related to education

- Uneven cash flows
- Internal rate of return and net present value
- Yield to maturity
- Solving for terms or yield
- Serial payments

- Discount rate selection
- Rule of 72
- Education funding
- Investments for education

SECTION

2 Basic Financial Planning Tools

CHAPTERS

Risks	Goals	Data Collection	Data Analysis
■ Misunderstanding the impact of inflation ■ Failure to understand compounding	■ Understanding the importance of time value of money to financial planning ■ Adequate resources for education of children	■ Financial aid programs ■ Financial aid information of client ■ Current cost of education ■ Inflation rate ■ Expected earnings rate ■ Tax-advantaged education programs	■ Projected cost of education ■ Education funding choices ■ Education funding analysis ■ Investment selections

CHAPTER 6

Time Value of Money

LEARNING OBJECTIVES

After learning the material in this chapter, you will be able to do the following:

- Define the time value of money (TVM) concept and explain its importance to financial planning
- Define the terms present value and future value and illustrate their roles in the calculation of compound interest
- Calculate the future value and the present value of a dollar
- List and explain the tools used in TVM analysis
- Calculate the present and future values of an ordinary annuity and an annuity due
- Explain the differences between an ordinary annuity and an annuity due
- Reconcile the difference between an ordinary annuity and an annuity due
- Prepare an amortization table for debt repayment
- Explain and apply the Rule of 72

- Understand how unequal cash flows and serial payments affect the future value of an investment
- Compare and contrast the concepts of net present value (NPV) and internal rate of return (IRR)
- Define yield to maturity and explain how it is used to determine a bond's earned interest
- Explain how solving for term given the other variables is useful in debt management
- Understand how inflation affects the real rate of return of an investment
- Define perpetuities and explain how they affect financial planning

UNDERSTANDING TIME VALUE OF MONEY

Time value of money (TVM) is one of the most useful and important concepts in finance and personal financial planning. Essentially, the concept of TVM is money received today is worth more than the same amount of money received sometime in the future. A dollar received today is worth more than a dollar received one year from today because the dollar received today can be invested and will be worth more in one year. Alternatively, a dollar to be received a year from now is worth less than a dollar today. Comparisons of funds received and paid at the same time are necessary to solve many financial planning problems and to make sound financial decisions. Thus, TVM calculations are fundamental to financial planning. The TVM calculation is a tool that allows financial planners to properly plan a client's goals and objectives.

Future value
The future dollar amount to which a sum certain today will increase compounded at a defined interest rate over a period of time

Present value
The current dollar value of a future sum discounted at a defined interest rate over a period of time

The two values used in TVM analysis are future value and present value. **Future value** is the future dollar amount to which a sum certain today will increase when compounded at a defined interest rate over a period of time. **Present value** is the current dollar value of a future sum when discounted at a defined interest rate over a period of time. Future value is calculated using a process called compounding. Present value is calculated using a process called discounting. Suppose, for example, a dollar was invested in a bank savings account paying 5% annual interest. At the end of the year, the dollar would have grown to $1.05. The initial dollar would be referred to as the present value. The 5% represents the interest rate. The term is for one year. Therefore, the $1.05 equals the future value. The interest earned (in this case, $.05) is compensation for delaying consumption for one year. We will discuss compounding and discounting later in the chapter.

There are numerous important questions in financial planning that can be answered using TVM concepts:

- If I have a certain dollar amount today, how much will it be worth at some time in the future if it is invested at a certain rate of interest?
- If I invested a certain dollar amount at regular intervals and at a constant interest rate, how much would I accumulate at some future date?
- If I wanted to save for the college education of my children, how much would I need to save starting today at regular intervals to pay for that education?

- If I wanted to pay off my home mortgage early, what amount would I need to add to each monthly payment?
- What is the present value of my expected Social Security retirement benefits?
- How much investment capital will I need to retire at a particular age in order to maintain my desired retirement lifestyle?

All of these questions and many other financial planning questions can be answered by applying TVM concepts.

FUTURE VALUE AND THE POWER OF COMPOUND INTEREST

Compound interest
Interest earned on interest

Understanding **compound interest** is essential to understanding the future value of money. Compound interest is interest earned on interest. Compounding occurs when interest earned is reinvested in the same investment and interest is then earned on both the principal and the reinvested interest. Mathematically, the growth is exponential (a power function as opposed to a linear function).

If the entire $1.05 in the previous example remained in the investment for a second year earning 5% interest annually, the future value at the end of the second year would be $1.1025:

$FV = PV\ (1 + i)$

$FV = \$1.05\ (1 + 0.05)$

$FV = \$1.1025$

The interest earned in the second year, $.0525, reflect the interest on the original dollar ($.05) and the interest on the $.05 earned in the first year ($.0025).

The mathematical expression for compounding interest at a constant rate is:

$FV = PV\ (1 + i)^n$, where n represents the number of periods (term) the investment is to be held.

Notice that i must be expressed in the same terms as n (e.g., yearly, semiannually, quarterly, or monthly). If i is expressed as an annual interest or earnings rate, n must also be expressed annually.

To illustrate the compounding of interest, assume $2,000 is invested by a 25-year-old in an individual retirement account (IRA) and left for 5 years earning 12% interest compounded annually. What would be the future value of the investment at the end of 5 years when our investor is age 30?

$FV = PV\ (1 + i)^n$

$FV = (\$2{,}000)\ (1.12)^5$

$FV = (\$2{,}000)\ (1.7623)$ [The exact mathematical factor obtained using a calculator.]

$FV = \$3{,}524.68$

Future value calculations of this type can be performed in a variety of ways using the tools available for TVM calculations. Generally, the illustrated examples in this chapter have been calculated using an HP 10bII+ calculator. (Keystrokes are the same for each calculator.) Where multiple steps were required to solve a problem, we did not round the intermediate steps. If you are attempting to calculate the problems in the chapter and are using table factors or a different calculator, or if you round intermediate steps, you may receive an answer slightly different from that calculated in the chapter. Where we used table factors, you will notice some rounding error. Where we used mathematical exponentials, you will notice differences from calculator or table results. For example, if the problem just listed had been calculated with rounded interest, the answer would be \$3,524.60 (rounding error of \$.08).

BASIC TOOLS FOR TIME VALUE OF MONEY (TVM) ANALYSIS

In addition to mathematical equations, there are a number of other tools a financial planner can use to understand TVM problems, help the client answer TVM questions, and present quantitative information to clients. Among these tools are **cash flow timelines**, TVM tables, financial calculators, cash flow computer software, and accumulation schedules. We will illustrate the various tools of TVM by calculating the future value for the previous example (\$2,000 invested for 5 years earning 12% interest compounded annually).

Cash flow timeline *TVM analysis tool that graphically depicts cash inflows (cash received) and cash outflows (cash deposited or invested) over a certain period (the term)*

Timelines

Timelines are a useful tool to visualize both inflows and outflows. Exhibit 6.1 shows a timeline based on the previous example. Notice the \$2,000 invested in time period 0 is listed with a parenthesis, indicating it is an outflow from the investor. Respectively, the future value of \$3,524.68 is presented as an inflow to the investor at time period 5.

EXHIBIT 6.1 Cash Flow Timeline

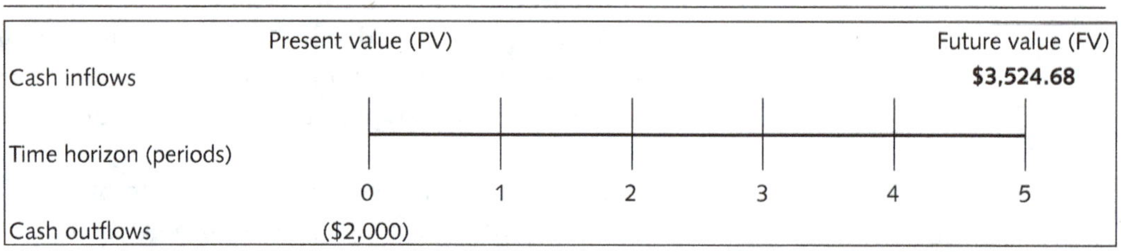

The more complex the TVM problem, the more useful a timeline can be in illustrating the positions of the cash flows.

TVM Tables

TVM tables represent the various values for combinations of i and n. These tables can be found in the Appendix (B-1 through B-6). The Future Value of a Dollar table is necessary to calculate the answer to our problem. The amounts given in the table represent the value of a dollar deposited today (to be received in the future) and compounded at a defined rate (i) for a defined period (n). The interest factor in Table 1 for 12% and 5 years is 1.7623 (rounded). This number is the equivalent of $(1.12)^5$, or (1.12)(1.12)(1.12)(1.12)(1.12) = 1.7623. Thus, when using TVM tables, the future value formula is also represented as FV = PV × (Exhibit 6.2 factor at 12% for 5 years). In our example, \$2,000 × 1.7623 = \$3,524.60.

EXHIBIT 6.2 Future Value Factor of a Dollar (Excerpt from Appendix B-2)

Period	2%	4%	6%	8%	10%	12%
1	1.0200	1.0400	1.0600	1.0800	1.1000	1.1200
2	1.0404	1.0816	1.1236	1.1664	1.2100	1.2544
3	1.0612	1.1249	1.1910	1.2597	1.3310	1.4049
4	1.0824	1.1699	1.2625	1.3605	1.4641	1.5735
5	1.1041	1.2167	1.3382	1.4693	1.6105	**1.7623**

Notice the tables have been rounded off to four decimals for presentation convenience. The rounding in the tables will cause a slight error in calculation. The amount of the error in the example just listed is $.08: $3,524.60 (1.7623 × $2,000) versus $3,524.68 (1.762341683 × $2,000).

Financial Calculators

A wide variety of useful hand-held financial calculators may be used to accurately calculate the solution to TVM problems. Financial calculators are fairly inexpensive and more accurate and flexible than the TVM tables. Calculators are also useful when the financial planner is out of the office and unable to access computer-based TVM software.

The following are among the most widely used financial calculators:

- Hewlett Packard HP 10bII and 10bII+
- Hewlett Packard HP 12C
- Hewlett Packard HP 17BII
- Texas Instruments TI BA II Plus
- Sharp EL-733A

Each of these has its own mathematical algorithm for solving TVM problems, and to master each calculator requires some practice. Regardless of which calculator you select, you should review your calculator's user manual and become familiar with the various keys. Familiarity with the following keys is essential:

- [SHIFT] [P/YR] = stores/calculates the number of compounding periods per year
- [PV] = stores/calculates the present value
- [FV] = stores/calculates the future value
- [PMT] = stores/calculates the amount of each payment
- [N] = stores/calculates the total number of payments or periods
- [I/YR] = stores/calculates the interest or discount rate

In calculating the TVM problems throughout this chapter and this text, the HP 10bII+ is used.

Illustrated below are the HP 10bII+ keystrokes used to solve the previous future value problem.

Keystroke	Display
1 [SHIFT] [P/YR]	1
2000 [+/–] [PV]	–2,000.0000
5 [N]	5.0000
12 [I/YR]	12.0000
0 [PMT]	0.0000
[FV]	3,524.6834

Computer Software

Essentially, computer software uses the same or similar mathematical algorithms as the hand-held calculators. In fact, TVM software testers usually use a hand-held calculator to ensure the computer algorithm's accuracy. TVM software and application software using TVM concepts are widely available to aid both individuals and practitioners.

Accumulation Schedules

Knowing the future value of a deposit made today is useful for investment planning for expenditures. It is also useful to know both the amount of interest earned and the balance of an investment account on a yearly or periodic basis. To determine the investment interest accumulation on a periodic basis, prepare a basic accumulation schedule similar to Exhibit 6.3.

EXHIBIT 6.3 Accumulation Schedule

Year (Col 1)	Beginning Balance (Col 2)	Interest (Col 3)	Ending Balance (Col 2) + (Col 3) = (Col 4)
1	$2,000.00	$240.00	$2,240.00
2	$2,240.00	$268.80	$2,508.80
3	$2,508.80	$301.06	$2,809.86
4	$2,809.86	$337.18	$3,147.04
5	$3,147.04	$377.64	$3,524.68
Totals	**$2,000.00**	**$1,524.68**	**$3,524.68**

Column 1 is the year in question, Column 2 is the account balance at the beginning of each year, Column 3 is the interest earned during the year (Column 2 × 12%), and Column 4 is the balance at the year end for each year (Column 2 + Column 3). The Total row shows the original amount deposited, $2,000; interest earned over the 5 years, $1,524.68, and the final balance, $3,524.68. As we will demonstrate, this type of schedule can be expanded or modified to illustrate the extinguishment of debt and is useful for a variety of other illustrative purposes.

Although TVM tables and accumulation schedules are useful for learning, professional financial planners do not generally rely on them. Rather, they rely on hand-held financial calculators or computer software. The remaining calculations in this chapter will be illustrated using the HP 10bII+ financial calculator.

FUTURE VALUE OF AN ORDINARY ANNUITY (FV_{OA})

Annuity
A series of deposits or payments of equal size deposited over a finite number of equal-interval periods

Ordinary annuity
Deposits or payments are made at the end of each period

Annuity due
Deposits or payments are made at the beginning of each period

Future value of an ordinary annuity
The future amount to which a series of deposits of equal size will equal when deposited over a finite number of equal-interval periods, based on a defined interest rate, when the deposits are made at the end of each period

Thus far we have calculated the future value of a single deposit made at the beginning of a period. Now consider, instead of a single deposit, that a series of deposits are made into an account. Instead of our previous example of the $2,000 deposited once in the IRA, our investor deposits $2,000 each year in the IRA for 5 years, earning an annual rate of return of 12%. The series of deposits of equal size is known as an **annuity** when deposited over a finite number of equal-interval periods. It will make a difference whether the deposits are made at the end of each period (known as an **ordinary annuity**) or deposited at the beginning of each period (known as an **annuity due**). The ordinary annuity is quite common in investments and debt repayment and is sometimes referred to as a payment made in arrears. An annuity due calculation is commonly used in education funding and for retirement planning.

To demonstrate the calculation of the **future value of an ordinary annuity**, assume David deposits $2,000 per year at year end for 5 years into an IRA earning 12% annually.

Your financial calculator has a feature (generally a BEG or END or a combination BEG/END key) that will allow you to switch between an ordinary annuity (use END) and an annuity due (use BEG). Calculate the future value of the ordinary annuity using the following keystrokes (using the HP 10bII+):

Keystroke	Display
1 [SHIFT] [P/YR]	1
5[N]	5.0000
12[I/YR]	12.0000
2000 [+/–] [PMT]	–2,000.0000
0[PV]	0.0000
[FV]	12,705.6947

FUTURE VALUE OF AN ANNUITY DUE (FV_{AD})

Future value of an annuity due
The future value to which a series of deposits of equal size will amount when deposited over a definite number of equal-interval periods, based on a defined interest rate, and the deposits are made at the beginning of each period

The calculation for an annuity due is exactly the same as the ordinary annuity, except the first deposit or payment for the annuity due is made at the beginning of the period rather than at the end. This is quite common for education funding calculations where the institution demands tuition payments be made in advance rather than in arrears. Making payments at the beginning of the period creates one additional compounding period when compared to payments made at the end of the period. For this reason, the **future value of an annuity due** will always be greater by one period's interest than the same deposits made for an ordinary annuity of the same term and interest rate. Other common uses of the annuity due concept are for rents and retirement income, which are both commonly paid in advance.

We can solve the problem using the HP 10bII+. Notice that the calculator should be set to BEG mode (using the BEG key or the BEG/END key, depending on the calculator used) mode to indicate an annuity due calculation.

Keystroke	Display
1 [SHIFT] [P/YR]	1
[SHIFT] [BEG/END]	0.0000 BEG
5[N]	5.0000
12[I/YR]	12.0000
2000 [+/–][PMT]	–2,000.0000
0[PV]	0.0000
[FV]	14,230.3781

The annuity due has an account balance at the end of year 5 of $14,230.38, although the ordinary annuity had an account balance of $12,705.69. The difference of $1,524.69 is equal to the total interest earned in the fifth year ($12,705.69 × .12 = $1,524.68).

PRESENT VALUE OF A DOLLAR (PV)

This calculation is used to determine the current value of a sum of money to be received in a future year based on a specific discount rate. For many financial planning decisions, such as education funding or retirement funding, it is important to determine the present value of a future amount rather than the future value of a present amount. In this section, we explain how to calculate the present value of a future investment amount. To illustrate, suppose an investor wanted to have $20,000 in 5 years and could earn an annual return of 8%. How much must be invested today to meet the goal of $20,000 in 5 years?

Keystroke	Display
1 [SHIFT] [P/YR]	1
20000 [FV]	20,000.0000
8 [I/YR]	8.0000
5[N]	5.0000
0[PMT]	0.0000
[PV]	–13,611.6639

PRESENT VALUE OF AN ORDINARY ANNUITY (PV_{OA})

Present value of an ordinary annuity *The value today of a series of equal payments made at the end of each period for a finite number of periods discounted at a defined interest rate*

An investor or a business commonly receives a series of equal payments for a finite period from debt repayment, from a life insurance settlement, from an annuity, or as a pension payment. The question usually asked is, "What is the present value of such a series of payments?" Remember the ordinary annuity assumed that each payment is made at the end of each period (arrears). For example, consider receiving $25,000 per year for the next 5 years with each payment made at year end. Also assume an interest (discount) rate of 8%. What is the present value in dollars of that income stream? The **present value of an ordinary annuity** is calculated as follows:

Keystroke	Display
1 [SHIFT] [P/YR]	1
5[N]	5.0000
8 [I/YR]	8.0000
25000[PMT]	25,000.0000
0[FV]	0.0000
[PV]	–99,817.7509

PRESENT VALUE OF AN ANNUITY DUE (PV_{AD})

Present value of an annuity due
The value today of a series of equal payments made at the beginning of each period for a finite number of periods discounted at a defined interest rate

The difference between the **present value of an annuity due** and the present value of an ordinary annuity is the annuity due's payments are made at the beginning of each period rather than at the end, as for an ordinary annuity. This makes the present value of an annuity due always larger than the present value of an ordinary annuity with the same payments over the same time period. The annuity due calculation is quite common in financial planning and is most often used for education funding and for retirement capital needs analysis. Using the previous problem as an education funding problem where the parent is to pay $25,000 each year for 5 years with payments occurring at the beginning of each year and the interest (discount) rate is 8%, we can calculate the present value of the annuity due. (For simplicity, we have assumed an inflation rate of zero.)

Keystroke	Display
1 [SHIFT] [P/YR]	1
[SHIFT] [BEG/END]	0.0000 BEG
5[N]	5.0000
8 [I/YR]	8.0000
25000[PMT]	25,000.0000
0[FV]	0.0000
[PV]	–107,803.1710

OTHER TVM CONCEPTS

Uneven cash flows
Investment returns or deposits that are neither single interval deposits nor equal payments

Net present value (NPV)
The difference between the initial cash outflow (investment) and the present value of discounted cash inflows (i.e., NPV = PV of CF – cost of investment)

Internal rate of return (IRR)
The discount rate that causes cash inflows to equal cash outflows, thus allowing comparison of rates of return on alternative investments

Now that we have a better understanding of the concepts and basic mathematics and mechanics of TVM, it is time to discuss some of the common TVM applications. Included in these applications are **uneven cash flows,** combining sum certains with annuities, **net present value (NPV), internal rate of return (IRR),** yield to maturity (YTM), solving for term, selecting the interest rate, serial payments, perpetuities, education funding, and capital needs analysis for retirement. In the next section of this chapter, we will present the basics of most of these TVM concepts. YTM will be covered more extensively in Chapter 12 Supplement A (Fixed-Income Securities). We will defer coverage of education funding until Chapter 7 (Education Funding) and capital needs analysis until Chapter 15 (Introduction to Retirement Planning).

Uneven Cash Flows

Investment returns or deposits are not always single interval deposits or equal payments. For example, assume an investor deposits $400, $500, $600, and $700 into an investment account at the end of each of four years, respectively. How much would the investment be worth if the interest rate was a constant 8% annually?

Using a financial calculator (HP 10bII+), we can easily calculate the problem by using the uneven cash flow keys. The first step in the calculation determines the present value of the uneven deposits. The second step calculates the future value. The keystrokes for the uneven cash flow problem are below:

Step 1

Keystroke	Display
0 [CFj]	0.0000
400 [+\–] [CFj]	–400.0000
500 [+\–] [CFj]	–500.0000
600 [+\–] [CFj]	–600.0000
700 [+\–] [CFj]	–700.0000
8[I/YR]	8.0000
[SHIFT] [NPV]	1,789.8600

Step 2

Keystroke	Display	
[PV]	–1,789.8600	(This step inputs the NPV from Step 1 as the PV for Step 2.)
4[N]	4.0000	
8[I/YR]	8.0000	
0[PMT]	0.0000	
[FV]	2,435.0848	

Combining Sums Certain With Annuities

For some investments, such as bonds, the investment returns are received in the form of both an annuity and a sum certain. Assume an investor purchased a 3-year $1,000 corporate bond paying $30 interest twice a year (semiannually) and then paying $1,000 (the maturity value) back to the holder at the end of the 3-year period. If the holder expected an 8% annual return, what amount should be paid for the bond at the beginning of the 3-year period? Assume the interest is paid as an ordinary annuity (arrears). The solution can be easily calculated using the following keystrokes:

Keystroke	Display
6[N]	6.0000
4 [I/YR]	4.0000
30[PMT]	30.0000
1000[FV]	1,000.0000
[PV]	–947.5786

Net Present Value Analysis

Net present value analysis (NPV) is a commonly used TVM technique employed by businesses and investors to evaluate the cash flows associated with capital projects and capital expenditures. The concept is common to capital budgeting. NPV analysis helps determine whether one should select one capital investment over another capital investment. The result of the analysis is in terms of dollars. The method discounts the future cash flows at an appropriate discount rate and allows the present value of inflows to be compared to the present value of outflows. This technique is important to financial planners in helping clients decide which investment projects to consider undertaking.

The model itself is deterministic, that is, it assumes information is known about the future (e.g., cash flows). The NPV model assumes all reinvestments of cash flows received are made at the weighted average cost of the capital of the firm or the required rate of return of the investor.

NPV equals the difference between the initial cash outflow (investment) and the present value of discounted cash inflows. For example, if the present value of a series of cash flows is $200 and the initial outflow is $150, the NPV equals $50. Businesses generally look for investments with a positive NPV.

EXAMPLE Assume you are a financial planner debating whether to purchase a copy machine. You currently pay $.12 per copy for reproducing materials and expect to make 3,000 copies per month. The copier you are considering costs $5,000 and is expected to last 5 years with a $1,000 salvage value. Your cost for reproducing on the new copier would be $.07 per copy. Assuming a 12% discount rate, what is the net present value of the copier?

To solve this problem, first convert the relevant data to monthly figures. If you purchase a copy machine, each copy would save you $.05 ($.12 – $.07 = $.05). If you made 3,000 copies per month, you would save $150 per month ($.05 × 3,000 = $150). Then calculate the present value of the cash flows discounted at 12% (1% monthly). The keystrokes for this calculation (using the HP 10bII+) are shown below:

Keystroke	Display	
12 [SHIFT] [P/YR]	12	Periods per year (monthly compounding)
5000 [+/–] [CFj]	–5,000.0000	Initial investment
150 [CFj]	150.0000	Monthly positive cash flow savings
59 [SHIFT] [Nj]	59.0000	59 months
1150 [CFj]	1,150.0000	Final monthly cash flow savings of $150 plus the salvage value of $1,000
12 [I/YR]	12.0000	Annual interest
[SHIFT] [NPV]	2,293.7054	

The positive NPV indicates the purchase of the copy machine would be recommended. The purchase will essentially save $2,293.71, in today's dollars, over the life of the machine.

Internal Rate of Return (IRR)

The internal rate of return is the discount rate that equates the discounted cash inflows and outflows of a specific investment or project. IRR calculations allow the financial planner to compare rates of return on alternative investments of unequal size and investment amounts. The NPV model and the IRR model make different assumptions regarding the reinvestment rate of cash flows received during the period of investment. Recall that NPV assumes the reinvestment rate to be the weighted average cost of capital or the required return. The IRR calculation assumes the reinvestment rate equals the IRR. NPV is considered a superior model to IRR when comparing investment projects of unequal lives because assuming reinvestment at the required return is more reasonable than at the IRR.

The formula below describes the basic present value model used for discounting cash flows.

$$PV = \frac{CF_1}{(1 + k)^1} + \frac{CF_2}{(1 + k)^2} + \cdots + \frac{CF_n}{(1 + k)^n}$$

PV = the value of the security or asset today
CF_n = the cash flow for a particular period, *n*
k = the discount rate or IRR
n = the number of cash flows to be evaluated

The formula states that the PV of a series of cash flows is equal to each cash flow divided by 1 plus the discount rate raised to a power equal to the period in which the cash flow occurs.

The internal rate of return is the exact discount rate (labeled *k* in the formula) that makes the discounted future cash inflows equal to the initial cash outflow, or investment. One of the underlying assumptions in the equation is that the cash flows received during the investment period will be reinvested at the investment's internal rate of return.

EXAMPLE Megan owns 1 share of Praha, Inc., stock. She purchased this share of stock 3 years ago for $50. The current market value of the stock is $40 per share. Since buying the stock, the following dividends have been paid:

Dividend year 1 (end)	$4.80 per share
Dividend year 2 (end)	$5.90 per share
Dividend year 3 (end)	$7.25 per share

What is the IRR that Megan has earned on her investment? Because the IRR is the rate of discount that equalizes the cash inflows and outflows, using a financial calculator is the easiest method. The financial calculator keystrokes (HP 10bII+) are shown below.

Keystroke	Display	
50[+\-] [CFj]	–50.0000	
4.8 [CFj]	4.8000	
5.9 [CFj]	5.9000	
47.25[CFj]	47.2500	($40 current market value + $7.25 dividend)
[SHIFT] [IRR]	5.5695	

Yield to Maturity

Yield to maturity (YTM) is the calculation of the rate of return that will make the discounted cash flows of a bond equal to the current price of that bond. This calculation is the application of the IRR model to bond investments. YTM is generally calculated on the basis of semiannual coupon payments (even with zero-coupon bonds). Financial planners need to understand YTM to begin understanding bonds and other debt investments.

Three adjustments must be made to calculate YTM for a bond that makes semiannual coupon payments.

- P/YR—This represents the number of compounding periods per year. When changing the number of compounding periods, the I/YR is still entered as an annual figure on the HP 10BII+ and the calculator converts it appropriately.

- *n*—The number of periods is determined by multiplying the number of years by 2 so as to reflect two coupon payments per year. For example, the *n* for a 10-year bond would be 20 to reflect 20 coupon payments.
- PMT—The coupon rate is stated as a percentage of the face value ($1,000) of the bond. Therefore, a 10% coupon bond will pay a total of $100 each year ($50 twice per year). The adjustment is to divide the $100 by 2 to reflect the two payments of $50 during the year.
- YTM—The YTM that will be calculated will be a semiannual YTM rate. Therefore, multiply the calculated YTM by 2 to determine the annual YTM.

EXAMPLE Julian is considering the purchase of a 5-year $1,000 bond selling for $1,162.22. What is the YTM for this bond if it has a 12% coupon, paid semiannually? The yield to maturity is 8% annually, or 4% per semiannual interest payment.

To calculate the yield to maturity using a financial calculator:

Keystroke	Display	
2 [SHIFT] [P/YR]	2	Number of periods per year (semi-annual compounding)
10[N]	10.0000	Term of the bond expressed for semiannual payments (5 × 2)
1162.22 [+\-][PV]	–1,162.2200	The current cost of the bond
60[PMT]	60.0000	The semiannual interest payment for a 12% annual coupon
1000 [FV]	1,000.0000	Maturity value of the bond
[I/YR]	8.0000	Yield to maturity

Solving for Term Given the Other Variables

Solving for term *n* (or on the calculator N) determines the period necessary (in days, months, quarters, or years) to save or pay at a given rate to accomplish a stated goal. This type of analysis is particularly useful in debt management, such as determining the term to:

- pay off student loans;
- pay off a mortgage;
- save for college education; and
- save for a special purchase (e.g., car, home, or vacation).

EXAMPLE Margaret bought a house using a mortgage loan of $240,000 issued for 15 years at 6.25% per year on May 1. Her first payment was June 1. Now, on January 1 of the following year, she has made 7 payments of $2,057.81 and has 173 payments remaining and a remaining mortgage balance of $234,256.20. Margaret wants to know how many more months she will have to pay if she increases her monthly payment by $500 to $2,557.81. Using a financial calculator (HP 10bII+), we calculate the term using the following keystrokes:

Keystroke	Display	
12 [SHIFT] [P/YR]	12	Periods per year
234256.20[PV]	234,256.2000	Current balance
0 [FV]	0.0000	Future value
2557.81 [+\-][PMT]	-2,557.8100	New payment
6.25 [I/YR]	6.2500	Annual interest rate
[N]	124.7745	Number of payments remaining

Margaret is thus able to reduce her remaining payments from 173 to 125 (rounded) by increasing her monthly payment by $500 to $2,557.81. Her last payment (payment 125) will be $1,982.12.

Selecting the Rate of Interest for Accumulating or Discounting

When utilizing TVM analysis, the planner must frequently decide which interest rate or earnings rate to use. The choices include the expected earnings for a particular investment, the client's **opportunity cost**, the risk-free rate, the Consumer Price Index (CPI), the specific inflation rate for particular services (education and medical), or the **real rate of return**, which accommodates both the nominal interest rate and a measure of inflation.

Opportunity cost
When faced with investment alternatives, it is the highest-valued alternative not chosen—it represents what is forgone by choosing another alternative; when discounting a future sum or series of payments back to present value, it is the composite rate of return on the client's assets with similar risk to the assets being examined

Real rate of return
The nominal rate of return adjusted for inflation

Generally, when projecting the future value of an investment, either a lump-sum investment or one made with annuity contributions, the appropriate compounding rate will be the expected rate of return for that particular investment. When discounting a future sum or series of payments back to present value, however, either the client's opportunity cost or the risk-free rate of return will be used. The client's opportunity cost is usually the composite rate of return on the client's assets with similar risk to the assets being examined. The risk-free rate is the Treasury rate for the selected period or term.

When calculating future retirement income needs, it is common to use the general Consumer Price Index (CPI) as the inflation rate, although in the case of college education, the recent and projected rate of inflation for college education should be used.

Financial planners should use an inflation-adjusted interest rate for calculating retirement capital needs or education funding because the costs in the future are generally increasing at one rate (the inflation rate) and the investments are growing at a different rate (the earnings rate). Thus, the way to make the increasing cash outflows equal is to treat them as real dollars of purchasing power and use an inflation-adjusted discount rate that takes into consideration the interest rate and inflation rate. The combination of the nominal earnings rate reduced mathematically by the inflation rate is known as the real rate of return.

The loss of purchasing power is one of the risks investors must overcome to achieve their financial goals. Real economic returns reflect the earnings from an investment above the inflation rate. However, simply subtracting the rate of inflation from the nominal interest rate will not yield the real economic rate of return. Real economic returns must be calculated by using the following formula:

$$\left(\frac{1 + R_n}{1 + I} - 1\right) \times 100$$

R_n = nominal rate of return
I = inflation rate

Assume $1,000 is invested at the beginning of the year and earns 10%, resulting in a balance at the end of the year of $1,100. Also assume that over the same period inflation has been 4%. Thus, $1,040 at the end of the year is equal to the initial investment of $1,000 at the beginning of the year, in terms of real dollars or purchasing power. The real return is equal to the difference between the earnings from interest ($100) and the increase as a result of inflation ($40), which is $60, divided by the initial investment adjusted for inflation ($1,040). This result equals a real rate of return of 5.77%.

- Conceptually, the return of 5.77% makes sense in that the absolute return was 10% and the inflation rate was 4%, with the difference being 6%:

$$\left(\frac{(1 + 0.10)}{(1 + 0.04)} - 1\right) \times 100 = 5.7692$$

- The nominal earnings from interest for this investment are $100. The real earnings are $57.69 in today's dollars ($60.00 ÷ 1.04 = $57.69).

Serial Payments

Serial payment
A payment that increases at a constant rate (usually, the rate of inflation) on an annual basis

A **serial payment** is a payment that increases at a constant rate (usually inflation) on an annual basis. There are situations when investors are more comfortable increasing payments or deposits on an annual basis because the investor is expecting increases in income with which to make those increasing payments. Examples include investment deposits, life insurance premiums, education needs, retirement needs, or any lump-sum future expenditure.

Serial payments differ from fixed annuity payments (both ordinary annuities and annuities due) because the payments are increasing at a constant rate. The result is the initial serial payment will be less than a fixed annuity payment but the last payment will be greater than the fixed annuity payment.

EXAMPLE Alex wants to start his own business in 3 years, and he needs to accumulate $100,000 (in today's dollars) to reach his goal. Alex expects a 4% inflation rate and an 8% rate of return on his investments. What serial payment should Alex make at the end of each year to attain his goal?

The serial payment is calculated by adjusting the interest rate for inflation to determine the real economic rate of return (nominal rate 8%, adjusted for inflation, 4%). This adjustment is accomplished using the following formula:

$$\left(\frac{1 + R_n}{1 + I} - 1\right) \times 100$$

$$\left(\frac{1 + 0.08}{1 + 0.04} - 1\right) \times 100 = 3.8462$$

Therefore, the real rate of return used for the calculation is 3.8462.

The serial payment calculation is as follows:

1 [SHIFT] [P/YR]
0 [PV]
100000 [FV]
3 [N]
[(1.08 ÷ 1.04) – 1] × 100 = 3.8462 [I/YR]
Solve for [PMT] –32,083.53

–32,083.53 [+/–] × 1.04 = 33,366.87 (payment at the end of year 1)
33,366.87 × 1.04 = 34,701.55 (payment made at end of year 2)
34,701.55 × 1.04 = 36,089.61 (payment made at end of year 3)

The exhibit below proves the increasing payments are correct.

EXHIBIT 6.4 Schedule of Investment

Year	Beginning Balance Needed	Deposit (Payments)	8% Interest Earned	Accumulation Ending Balance
1	$100,000.00	$33,366.87	$0.00	$33,366.87
2	$104,000.00	$34,701.55	$2,669.35	$70,737.77
3	$108,160.00	$36,089.61	$5,659.02	$112,486.40
End of Year 3	**$112,486.40**	**$104,158.03**	**$8,328.37**	**$112,486.40**

Note: Alex could have saved $34,649.58 per year. An annuity of this amount would have provided him with the same future value of $112,486.40. This payment is calculated as follows:

FV = $112,486.40
n = 3
i = 8
PMT = $34,649.58

Notice that the payment of $34,649.58 is greater than the first serial payment but less than the last one.

Perpetuities

A perpetuity is a payment cash flow stream that remains constant. An example of a common perpetuity is preferred stock, which generally pays a set dividend each year. To determine the value of this type of payment stream, simply divide the payment (PMT) by the discount rate (i):

$$PV = \frac{PMT}{i}$$

EXAMPLE Gleason Corporation always pays a $4 preferred stock dividend, and the client's required rate of return is 10%. The value of the preferred stock equals $40 as illustrated below:

$$PV = \frac{PMT}{i}$$

$$PV = \frac{\$4}{0.10}$$

$$PV = \$40$$

OTHER TVM TOOLS

Timelines, mathematics, TVM tables, accumulation schedules, financial calculators, and computer software are basic tools of TVM analysis. There are other TVM tools, including amortization tables and the Rule of 72. An understanding of each of these tools will assist the financial planner solve other complex TVM problems.

Amortization Tables

Amortization table
TVM tool used primarily to illustrate the amortization, or extinguishments, of debt. The table presents the number of years of indebtedness, the beginning balance, level payments, interest amount, principal reduction, and ending balance of indebtedness.

An **amortization table** is an extension of the accumulation schedules illustrated earlier in the chapter. Amortization tables are primarily used to illustrate the amortization, or extinguishment, of debt. Initially we create a table with the beginning balance of the debt, a level payment, the portion of the payment that is interest, the portion of the payment that is used to reduce the principal indebtedness, and the ending balance of the indebtedness for each year.

EXHIBIT 6.5 Amortization Table (Blank)

Month (Col 1)	Beginning Balance (Col 2)	Payment (Col 3)	6.25% Interest (Col 4) = 6.25% ÷ 12 × (Col 2)	Principal Reduction (Col 5) = (3) – (4)	Ending Mortgage Balance (Col 6) = (2) – (5)
—	—	—	—	—	—
—	—	—	—	—	—

The beginning balance of the indebtedness less the principal amount of reduction will equal the ending balance of the indebtedness. The remainder of the payment was interest as determined in the interest amount column. The common usage for amortization tables is for mortgages, but they can be used to illustrate any indebtedness repayment schedule.

EXAMPLE Josh secures a $240,000 mortgage with the first payment to be made in January and repaid over 15 years on a monthly basis at 6.25% annual interest.

12 [SHIFT] [P/YR]	=	12	Periods per year
PV	=	$240,000	Mortgage amount
n	=	180 months	Term in months
i	=	6.25	Annual interest rate
PMT	=	–$2,057.8166	Payment of an ordinary annuity
FV_{12}	=	$230,023.66	Balance of mortgage after 12 payments

Notice that Column 2 of Exhibit 6.6 is the beginning balance of indebtedness of $240,000. Josh then makes 12 monthly payments of $2,057.81 (total $24,693.72) during year 1 of which $14,717.44 is interest, and the remainder, $9,976.34, is used to reduce the mortgage balance so that at the end of year 1, Josh owes $230,023.66 on the mortgage (Column 6).

The amortization table can be extended for the full 15 years and illustrates exactly when the balance of the mortgage will reach any certain amount, the amount of interest for a given period, and the amount of principal reduction during a given period. The table may be presented for only one year, as above, or yearly or monthly for the entire indebtedness period. If the mortgage begins some time other than January, the table can be modified so that the mortgage interest expense for each calendar year for estimating the mortgage interest income tax deduction for federal income tax.

EXHIBIT 6.6 Mortgage Amortization Table

Month (Col 1)	Beginning Balance (Col 2)	Payment (Col 3)	6.25% Interest (Col 4) = 6.25% ÷ 12 × (Col 2)	Principal Reduction (Col 5) = (3) − (4)	Ending Mortgage Balance (Col 6) = (2) − (5)
Yr 1 Jan	$240,000.00	$2,057.81	$1,250.00	$807.81	$239,192.19
Yr 1 Feb	$239,192.19	$2,057.81	$1,245.79	$812.02	$238,380.17
Yr 1 Mar	$238,380.17	$2,057.81	$1,241.56	$816.25	$237,563.92
...	...	...	...	...	...
Yr 1 Dec	$230,878.98	$2,057.81	$1,202.49	$855.32	$230,023.66
Total Yr 1		**$24,693.72**	**$14,717.44**	**$9,976.34***	

*rounding error of $0.06

Mortgage amortization calculations may be quickly performed using a financial calculator. Using the previous example, upon calculating the mortgage payment, the financial calculator can provide the amortization details for any period of time during the amortization. To determine the amount of interest and principal paid in the first year and the remaining balance after 12 payments, the calculation is as follows using the HP 10bII+:

12 [SHIFT] [P/YR]
240000 [PV]
0 [FV]
180 [N]
6.25 [I/YR]
Solve for [PMT] –2,057.81

Without clearing, enter:

1 [INPUT] 12
[SHIFT] [AMORT] (AMORT is the shift function of the [FV] key)

The display will now show 1 – 12. Pressing the [=] key will toggle through the principle paid in months 1–12 (9,976.34), the interest paid in months 1–12 (14,717.44), and the principal balance remaining after 12 months (230,023.66). Any combination of months may be entered and the amortization details for that period will be displayed. For example, entering 13 [INPUT] 24 [SHIFT] [AMORT] will display the amortization details for year 2 of the mortgage. Provided the calculator is not cleared, it is not necessary to reenter the mortgage terms to input a different period of months.

Qualified residence interest expense may be deductible for taxpayers who itemize their deductions on their federal income tax return. The mortgage company sends the interest payer a Form 1098 (Mortgage Interest Statement) providing the payer with the amount of interest paid for the prior year. For example, Josh should have received a Form 1098 for the first year of $14,717.44 interest paid.

The Rule of 72

Frequently, professionals want to approximate rates of interest or the time needed to achieve a certain financial goal when the interest rate or the time, but not both, is known. The professional may need only an estimate rather than a mathematically precise answer or does not have access to the appropriate tool to perform precise calculations.

Rule of 72
A method of approximation that estimates the time it takes to double the value of an investment where the earnings (interest) rate is known (by dividing 72 by the interest rate); it can also estimate the earnings (interest) rate necessary to double an investment value if the time is known (by dividing 72 by the period of investment)

The **Rule of 72** is such a method of approximation. Initially used by accountants, it is now used by financial planners to estimate the time it takes to double the value of an investment when the interest rate is known. Alternatively, the Rule of 72 will estimate the interest rate necessary to double an investment value if the time is known. The Rule of 72 states if you know a rate of return, you can determine the time it takes to double the value of the investment by dividing 72 by the interest rate. For example, if the annual interest rate is 6%, then 72 ÷ 6 = 12. Therefore, if a dollar is invested at 6% for 12 years, it should be equal to $2 at the end of the 12-year term. Conversely, if the term is known to be 12 years and you need an amount to double during that term, you can divide 72 by 12 to determine the interest rate necessary (72 ÷ 12 = 6). Therefore, you would need an interest rate of 6% in order to double your investment in 12 years.

EXHIBIT 6.7 Rule of 72 Examples

Interest Rate	Period to Double (n)
4%	18.0
6%	12.0
8%	9.0
9%	8.0
10%	7.2

Although the Rule of 72 is extremely helpful as an approximator and a control on the reasonableness of an answer determined by a calculator or computer, it has a small error, especially at extremely low or high rates or terms. Consider, for example, how long it would take to double $1 if the rate of interest were 72% annually. According to the Rule of 72, 72 ÷ 72 = 1, indicating to us that we should double our money in one year, but we know that the value at the end of one year is $1.72, not $2. Many financial planners are using the Rule of 72 without considering the error factor. Exhibit 6.8 is a table of the error percentage rate for the Rule of 72 at various interest rates.

The error rate is calculated in the following using the actual value of $2 as the numerator and the actual calculated amount as the denominator to get the error percentage. The minus signs indicate that the actual value is less than the Rule of 72 estimated by the calculated percentage. The values that are not bracketed are greater than the Rule of 72 estimated by the calculated percentage indicated. For example, at 1%, the actual value of $1 at 1% for 72 periods is $2.047, or 2.4% above $2.

EXHIBIT 6.8 Error Rate Using the Rule of 72

Interest Rate	Error %
1	2.4
2	2.0
3	1.6
4	1.3
5	1.0
6	0.6
7	0.3
8	0.05
9	–0.4
10	–0.6
11	–0.9
12	–1.3
13	–1.4
14	–1.8
15	–2.1
18	–3.1
24	–4.7
40	–7.6
50	–8.5
72*	–14.0

*The error rate for a given interest rate equal to or greater than 72% will always be 14%.

As you can see from Exhibit 6.8, the error rate as a percentage of the future value can range from +2.4% to –14%. Therefore, although the Rule of 72 is a good approximation, especially at interest rates between 6% and 10%, it loses some of its precision when outside the 6–10% interest rate range.

The Rule of 72 can also be used to approximate the effects of inflation in retirement. The doubling time for an asset growing at the rate of inflation will also give the time it will take for prices to double. Prices doubling is the same thing as inflation cutting purchasing power in half. The long-term inflation rate since the establishment of the Federal Reserve is about 3% (72 ÷ 3 = 24 years). Thus, a person retiring at 65 will see prices double in the general economy by about the time he is 89. Age 89 is approximately the life expectancy of an average 65-year-old couple retiring today.

WHERE ON THE WEB

American Savings Education Council **www.asec.org**

Financial Industry Regulatory Authority (FINRA) **www.finra.org**

Investor Desktop, Financial and Insurance Calculators **www.investordesktop.com**

Kiplinger **www.kiplinger.com**

U.S. News **www.usnews.com**

DISCUSSION QUESTIONS

1. What is the time value of money (TVM) concept, and why is it so important in financial planning?
2. What are the important questions in financial planning that can be answered using TVM concepts?
3. What is meant by present value and future value, and how are these two concepts used in the calculation of compound interest?
4. What are the basic tools used in TVM analysis?
5. How are TVM tables computed?
6. What is the difference between the future value of an ordinary annuity (FV_{OA}) and the present value of an ordinary annuity (PV_{OA})?
7. What is the difference between the future value of an annuity due (FV_{AD}) and the present value of an annuity due (PV_{AD})?
8. When would you use an ordinary annuity or an annuity due in financial planning?
9. What are some TVM concepts other than annuities?
10. How do unequal cash flows affect the future value of an investment?
11. How do net present value (NPV) and internal rate of return (IRR) differ in financial planning calculations?
12. What is yield to maturity (YTM), and how is it used to determine a bond's interest rate?
13. How is the concept of solving for term given the other variables useful in debt management?
14. What alternative rate choices exist when selecting the rate of interest for accumulating or discounting?
15. How is the real return of an investment affected by the inflation rate?
16. How do serial payments affect the future value of an investment?
17. How can amortization tables and the Rule of 72 help solve present TVM problems?

EXERCISES

1. Calculate the present value of $10,000 to be received in exactly 10 years, assuming an annual interest rate of 9%.
2. Calculate the future value of $10,000 invested for 10 years, assuming an annual interest rate of 9%.
3. Calculate the present value of an ordinary annuity of $5,000 received annually for 10 years, assuming a discount rate of 9%.
4. Calculate the present value of an annuity of $5,000 received annually that begins today and continues for 10 years, assuming a discount rate of 9%.
5. Calculate the future value of an ordinary annuity of $5,000 received for 10 years, assuming an interest rate of 9%.
6. Calculate the future value of an annual annuity of $5,000 beginning today and continuing for 10 years, assuming an interest rate of 9%.
7. Mike borrows $240,000 at 8% for a mortgage for 15 years. Prepare an annual amortization table assuming the first payment is due January 30 of the current year exactly 30 days after the loan.
8. Joan invested $5,000 in an interest-bearing account earning an 8% annual rate of interest compounded monthly. How much will the account be worth at the end of 5 years, assuming all interest is reinvested at the 8% rate?
9. Callie expects to receive $50,000 in 2 years. Her opportunity cost is 10% compounded monthly. What is the sum worth to Callie today?
10. Lola purchased a zero-coupon bond 9 years ago for $600. If the bond matures today and the face value is $1,000, what is the average annual compound rate of return (calculated semiannually) that Lola realized on her investment?
11. Today Evan put all of his cash into an account earning an annual interest rate of 10%. Assuming he makes no withdrawals or additions to this account, approximately how many years must Evan wait to double his money? Use the Rule of 72 to determine the answer.
12. Anthony has been investing $1,500 at the end of each year for the past 12 years. How much has he accumulated, assuming an interest rate of 8% compounded annually?
13. Dennis has been dollar cost averaging in a mutual fund by investing $1,000 at the beginning of every quarter for the past 5 years. He has been earning an average annual compound rate of return of 11% compounded quarterly. What is the value of the fund today?
14. Casey, injured in an automobile accident, won a judgment that provides him $2,500 at the end of each 6-month period over the next 3 years. If the escrow account that holds Casey's settlement award earns an average annual rate of 10% compounded semiannually, how much was the defendant initially required to pay Casey to compensate him for his injuries?
15. Stacey wants to withdraw $3,000 at the beginning of each year for the next 5 years. She expects to earn 8% compounded annually on her investment. What lump sum should Stacey deposit today?

16. Gary wants to purchase a beach condo in 7 years for $100,000. What periodic payment should he invest at the beginning of each quarter to attain the goal, assuming an annual interest rate of 11%, compounded quarterly?

17. Ann purchased a car for $25,000. She is financing the auto at a 10% annual interest rate, compounded monthly for 4 years. What payment is required at the end of each month to finance Ann's car?

18. Josh purchased a house for $215,000 with a down payment of 20%. What is the amount of his monthly payment assuming the balance is financed at 10% over 30 years?

19. Chase purchased a house for $300,000. He put 20% down and financed the remaining amount over 30 years at 8%. How much interest will he pay over the life of the loan assuming he pays the loan as agreed? (Round to the nearest dollar.)

PROBLEMS

1. Lucy wants to give her son $80,000 on his wedding day in 4 years. How much should she invest today at an annual interest rate of 9.5% compounded annually to have $80,000 in 4 years? Alternatively, how much would she need to invest today if she could have her interest compounded monthly? Explain which interest option would be most beneficial to Lucy.

2. Rachel, who just turned 18, deposits a $15,000 gift into an interest-bearing account earning a 7.5% annual rate of interest. How much will she have in the account when she retires at age 60, assuming all interest is reinvested at the 7.5% rate? If Rachel decided she only needed $300,000 at retirement, could she retire at 59? Explain.

3. Kerri won the lottery today. She has two options. She can receive $30,000 at the end of each year for the next 15 years or take a lump-sum distribution of $200,000. Her opportunity cost is 12% compounded annually. Based on present values, which option should she choose?

4. Darrin wants to donate $8,000 to his church at the beginning of each year for the next 20 years. What lump sum should Darrin deposit today if he expects to earn 11% compounded annually on his investment? Alternatively, how much should he deposit if he wants to have $50,000 left at the end of the 20 years?

5. James deposited $800 at the end of the past 16 years to purchase his granddaughter, Kali, a car. James earned 8% interest compounded annually on his investment. If the car Kali chooses costs $22,999, would she have enough money in the account to purchase the vehicle? What would be the deficit or surplus?

6. Brenda has been investing $150 at the beginning of each month for the past 20 years. How much has she accumulated, assuming she has earned an 11% annual return compounded monthly on her investment? If instead of earning 11%, Brenda was only able to earn 10% (compounded monthly), how much would her payments need to be to have the same accumulated amount?

7. Kenneth took out a loan today to purchase a boat for $160,000. He will repay the loan over 30 years at 9% interest (with payments occurring monthly). What will be his remaining principal balance at the end of the first year?

8. Cody estimates his opportunity cost on investments at 9% compounded annually. Which of the following is the best investment opportunity?
   - To receive $100,000 today
   - To receive $400,000 at the end of 15 years
   - To receive $1,500 at the end of each month for 10 years compounded monthly
   - To receive $75,000 in 5 years and $100,000 5 years later
   - To receive $75,000 in 5 years and $175,000 10 years later

9. Patricia and Scott are ready to retire. They want to receive the equivalent of $30,000 in today's dollars at the beginning of each year for the next 20 years. They assume inflation will average 4% over the long run, and they can earn an 8% compound annual after-tax return on investments. What lump sum do Patricia and Scott need to invest today to attain their goal?

10. Margaret wants to retire in 9 years. She needs an additional $200,000 in today's dollars in 10 years to have sufficient funds to finance this objective. She assumes inflation will average 5% over the long run, and she can earn a 4% compound annual after-tax rate of return on investments. What serial payment should Margaret invest at the end of the first year to attain her objective?

11. Kristi wants to buy a house in 10 years. She estimates she will need $200,000 at that time. She currently has a zero-coupon bond with a market value of $4,600 that she will use as part of the required amount. The zero-coupon bond has a face value of $10,000 and will mature in 10 years. The bond has a semiannual effective interest rate of 4.323%. In addition to the bond, she wants to save a monthly amount to reach her goal. What is Kristi's required monthly payment made at the beginning of each month in order to accumulate the $200,000, including the zero-coupon bond, at an assumed interest rate of 11%?

CHAPTER 7

Education Funding

LEARNING OBJECTIVES

After learning the material in this chapter, you will be able to do the following:

- Discuss the various issues that parents should consider when setting goals for financing their children's education
- List the types of financial aid information that can be gathered from a college's financial aid office
- Explain the importance of the Expected Family Contribution (EFC) formula in student financial aid application
- Describe the major student financial assistance programs available through the U.S. Department of Education
- Describe the campus-based financial aid programs available to college students
- Describe the several financial aid programs available to college students
- List the benefits of qualified tuition programs (QTPs)
- Describe the various income tax-saving financial aid vehicles
- Understand how time value of money concepts are used to help calculate the cost of a child's education

INTRODUCTION

One of the most common financial planning goals of parents is to provide an education for their children. Education funding is a common area of concern for those seeking financial planning advice because paying for higher education is one of the largest financial burdens a family will face. Even clients with high income levels must take into account paying for their children's tuition and school-related expenses. Recently, education costs have dramatically outpaced inflation. Over the past 10 years, tuition at public colleges and universities throughout the country has increased at a rate approximately twice as much as the Consumer Price Index (CPI). Also, recent trends show an increase in the number of years students remain in college and increased requirements for postgraduate education. Along with the expense of a home and taxes, providing for a child's education is one of the largest expenses for families and one of the most important decisions.

EXHIBIT 7.1 Average Published Tuition and Fees in 2021 Dollars by Sector, 1991–92 to 2021–22

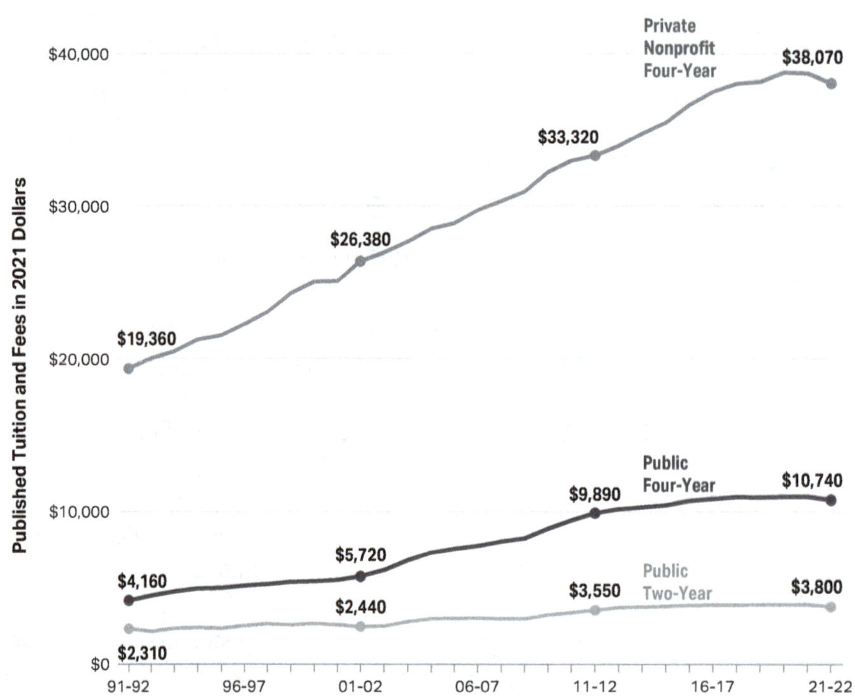

Source: Trends in College Pricing and Student Aid 2021. Copyright 2021 by College Entrance Examination Board. www.collegeboard.org

This chapter discusses how to develop a plan for funding a child's education by addressing the issues that must be raised, the information that must be gathered, and the goals that should be set, taking the family's circumstances into account. Once the goals have been set, the implementation of the plan will depend on the sources of funding available, which may include a savings campaign, financial aid, and various payment options. Once the plan is designed and the strategies have been identified, action must be taken to implement and monitor the plan.

ISSUES AND GOALS

To formulate a plan that best meets the needs of the particular family, goals must be identified and agreed upon and appropriate provisions made to achieve those goals. The key is to set feasible, realistic goals.

When formulating a plan for the education of a child, one of the most significant considerations is how much time there is before the child enters college. There are many options available for parents of very young children who are years away from entering college. Those parents with children nearing college age or currently entering college do not have as many options and savings methods. It cannot be stressed enough that, as with most areas of planning, time is crucial in planning for a child's education. Time allows consistent and persistent contributions toward savings vehicles, allowing them to grow and, hopefully, meet or surpass the cost of tuition. Meanwhile, inflation will continue to drive tuition costs higher over time. It will clearly be less stressful and easier to manage costs, however, with the benefit of 10, 15, or more years of saving versus evaluating options, one's ability to pay, and formulating a plan during the student's junior or senior year in high school. In addition to concerns about college tuition, families should decide whether they want to fund private elementary and secondary school education for their children. A family should also decide whether to provide some or all funding for graduate or professional school education.

One way for parents to ultimately defray the cost of education is paying for only a portion of the child's college expenses and leaving some of the expenses to be paid by the child. Some view this method as a way of building character for the child and educating the child in accepting responsibility, without forcing the child to assume all the financial responsibility for college-related expenses (that may burden the child with overwhelming loans and debt when beginning a career). Again, decisions such as these will depend on the preferences and desires of the parents. However, most parents do not consider that the person their child will marry will also, in all probability, bring college debt to the marriage. Combining two moderate college debts can be a major burden on a young family as they begin married life.

During the goal-setting process, some individuals struggle with the notion of sending their children to public elementary or secondary school, while investing resources to a college education fund. This decision is often based on the quality of the public education available to the child. The parents should also consider that, while private elementary and secondary education will require additional funds, there may be a return on that investment; the child may obtain a more advanced education and perhaps acceptance to prestigious colleges that may provide scholarships or less-stringent financial aid requirements. Of course, these are issues that a financial planner should discuss with the parents so they can make an informed decision based on their own circumstances. Although there are many important issues and financial decisions to be made regarding elementary and secondary education, the majority of this chapter will deal with preparation and planning for a child's college expenses.

Parents should be reminded that families are in a better position to fund college expenses over a long period because their income will likely increase in future years. In addition, with a longer investment time horizon there exists a higher probability of positive returns in funds invested for educational purposes, as well. This will motivate some parents to begin a savings regimen that does not meet all the financial requirements right away but can be increased as the years progress and provide an incentive to increase savings as college years grow nearer.

INFORMATION GATHERING

During the goal-setting process, financial planners must forecast anticipated tuition and related expenses. This forecasting can be accomplished by first determining current tuition and related expenses for the schools in the area and for the schools that the parents believe would be most appropriate for the child. This information can be found by calling the school's administrative office. Additionally, there are numerous college guides in bookstores and local libraries that provide tuition and room and board expenses at colleges and universities throughout the country.

Once these expenses are obtained, the financial planner must adjust these expenses to account for inflation until the child enters college. The planner must assume a tuition inflation rate, probably between 3% and 5% greater than CPI per year for college and related expenses, and then calculate the anticipated expenses for each year the child will attend college. The following example uses a 6% tuition inflation rate.

EXAMPLE

Assumptions:

- Child's current age—10 years
- Anticipated college age—18–22 years
- Current tuition and room and board—$13,000 per year
- Tuition inflation rate—6%

Estimated costs [future value (FV) or actual cost] of tuition and room and board:

- Freshman year—$20,720, (PV = +/–13,000, N = 8, I/YR = 6)
- Sophomore year—$21,963, (PV = +/–13,000, N = 9, I/YR = 6)
- Junior year—$23,281, (PV = +/–13,000, N = 10, I/YR = 6)
- Senior year—$24,678, (PV = +/–13,000, N = 11, I/YR = 6)

Once these expenses have been identified and adjusted for inflation, one can determine the estimated four-year cost of a college education. As will be discussed in this chapter, depending on how much money will be available when the child enters college, a formula can be used to determine how much money must be invested to meet the amount of savings necessary for college (i.e., the Expected Family Contribution). Other expenses that should be considered include books and school supplies, transportation, travel expenses, and entertainment, as shown in Exhibit 7.2—College Expenses Checklist.

Because college is a major investment, families should carefully evaluate potential schools. Some of the information families should obtain includes a copy of the documents describing the school's accreditation and licensing, current school tuition, and on-campus room and board. Also, families should ask about the school's loan default rate. The default rate is the percentage of students who attend the school, obtain federal student loans, and ultimately fail to repay the loan. This information is important because schools with high default rates may not be eligible to obtain federal aid for certain federal financial assistance programs. This may also indicate that students are poorly matched with the school.

EXHIBIT 7.2 College Expenses Checklist

These are the college expenses that most families should keep in mind when planning for payment of a child's education:

- Tuition and tuition-related expenses
- Books, school supplies, and equipment (calculator and computer)
- Lodging
- Meals
- Transportation
- Entertainment (school sporting events) and leisure (health club)
- Travel expenses
- Tutoring (if necessary)
- Extracurricular (fraternity or sorority dues)
- Clothing and attire
- Other considerations particular to the student or family

If a school advertises its job placement rates, it must also publish the most recent employment statistics, graduation statistics, and any other information that would justify its representations. Another relevant item of information is the school's refund policy. If a student enrolls but never attends classes, the student should be refunded the majority of his money. If a student begins attending classes but leaves before completing his coursework, the student may be able to receive a partial refund. Many state university systems allow for prepayment of tuition at current prices for enrollment in the future. Prepaid Tuition Plans are discussed later in this chapter.

A prospective student can obtain the following financial aid availability information from a school:

- Availability of financial assistance, including information on all federal, state, local, private, and institutional financial aid programs
- Procedures and deadlines for submitting financial aid program applications
- The school's process for determining a financial aid applicant's eligibility
- The school's method for determining a student's financial need
- The school's method for determining each type and amount of assistance in a student's financial aid package
- How and when the student will receive financial aid
- The school's method for determining whether the student is making satisfactory academic progress and the consequences if the student is not (whether the student continues to receive federal financial aid depends, in part, on whether the student makes satisfactory academic progress)
- If the student is awarded a job through the Federal Work-Study program, what type of job is involved, the amount of hours the student must work, the duties of the student in that job, the rate of pay, and how and when the student will be paid
- The availability and counseling procedures of the school's financial aid office

The client may also wish to ask the school for a copy of its equity-in-athletics report. Any coeducational school where a student can receive federal financial aid that has an interschool athletic program must prepare an equity-in-athletics report giving financial and statistical information for men's and women's sports. This information is designed to advise students of a school's commitment to providing equitable athletic opportunities for its male and female students.

The client should also be encouraged to consult with high school counselors, local employers, and the state higher education agency. These are invaluable sources of information for those exploring options of higher education.

DETERMINING FINANCIAL NEED

As mentioned earlier, most financial aid packages depend heavily on the financial need of the student. Therefore, it is important to evaluate whether a client may have the requisite financial need when estimating costs of tuition and availability of funds for college.

Free Application for Federal Student Aid (FAFSA) *An application form that must be submitted by a college student to become eligible for federal financial aid*

The financial aid process is initiated by filling out financial aid forms available from high schools, the United States Department of Education, or from the college the student will attend. This financial aid application form is called a **Free Application for Federal Student Aid (FAFSA)**. A FAFSA must be submitted by the student applicant to become eligible for federal financial aid. The student can obtain and complete a FAFSA application in one of the following ways:

- Complete and mail a paper FAFSA, which can be obtained from the student's high school, potential college, or college where attending
- Have the student's school submit the completed FAFSA electronically
- Use FAFSA on the web (**www.fafsa.ed.gov**), which is quickly becoming the most common means of application

Colleges usually appoint an agency to conduct an analysis of the financial need of the student and the student's family. The completed information on the FAFSA is sent to colleges requested by the applicant. The college may also have the applicant complete other forms to enable the college to conduct its own needs analysis of the student. Once the student is accepted to a college, the college may inform the student of any available financial aid.

Expected Family Contribution (EFC) *A formula that indicates how much of a student's family's resources ought to be available to assist in paying for the student's college education*

When applying for student financial assistance, the information reported by the applicant is used in a formula established by Congress. The formula is called the **Expected Family Contribution (EFC)** for a child's education. The EFC indicates how much of a student's family's resources ought to be available to assist in paying for the student's education. Some of the factors used in this calculation include taxable and nontaxable income, assets, and benefits, such as unemployment and Social Security.

Although low-income families are more likely to qualify for financial aid than higher-income families, higher-income families should not be discouraged from applying for aid because the EFC formula also takes into account various factors including the number of children in private school or college, the size of the family, the number of years until the parents' retirement, and large financial burdens, such as medical bills. The EFC calculation is used to determine eligibility for financial aid programs, except for unsubsidized student loans and PLUS loans, which are provided regardless of financial need. If the EFC is below a certain amount, the student may be eligible for financial aid, such as a Federal Pell Grant, assuming other eligibility requirements are met. Such eligibility requirements include the cost of attendance at the school (tuition, room and board, and related expenses); full-time, half-time, or part-time status; and academic standing.

There is no maximum EFC because the EFC used in a calculation depends on where the student attends school and the cost of attendance at that school. When the student consults with the school's financial aid administrator, the financial aid administrator will calculate the student's financial need by subtracting the student's EFC from the cost of attendance at the school. The remaining figure equals the student's financial need. The formula is as follows:

Tuition/cost of attendance	$ Amount
– Expected Family Contribution (EFC)	–$ Amount
= Financial need	$ Amount

As is evident from the above calculation, a student may have financial need at one school but not another because financial need depends on the cost of attendance, whereas the student's EFC remains constant for the year regardless of which school the student attends. If circumstances warrant it, financial aid administrators can, at their discretion, adjust the cost of attendance or adjust data in calculating a student's EFC. More information on the EFC calculation can be obtained through the Federal Student Aid Information Center at **http://studentaid.ed.gov**.

At this point, most individuals ask how they can reduce their EFC. In other words, how can a family reduce the amount of money it is expected to contribute to a child's education in order to receive more financial assistance? There are various methods that a family can use to reduce EFC. First, however, one must determine the dependency status of the student.

The income and assets of the student's family will be counted only if the student is considered dependent on the parents. If the student applying for financial aid is independent, only the student's income and assets will be considered. The reasoning behind this rule is that a student who has access to parental support should not be able to reap the benefits of student financial aid programs to the exclusion of those needy, independent students who do not have access to parental support. Some of the criteria that will result in a student being considered independent are the following:

- Born before January 1, 1999 (for the 2022–2023 academic year)
- Married
- Enrolled in a master's or doctorate program
- Has legal dependents (other than a spouse or children) who live with the student and receive more than one-half of their support from the student
- Has children who receive more than half their support from the student
- An orphan or ward of the court, or was a ward of the court until age 18
- A veteran of the U.S. Armed Forces, or currently serving on active duty
- Legally emancipated minor

Another common method for reducing a family's EFC is creating a trust for the child and diminishing the family's estate through gifts. This may create problems, however, because the child's own assets will be considered in the child's financial needs analysis. A family may also reduce its EFC by providing all information surrounding the factors that tend to diminish their EFC, such as large medical bills and more than one child in the family attending college. Finally, the school's financial aid adviser may be able to adjust a family's EFC if the circumstances so require. Here, the burden is on the family or student to communicate information to the financial aid adviser that may reduce the EFC.

FINANCIAL AID PROGRAMS

The United States Department of Education has the following major student financial assistance programs:

- Federal Pell Grant
- Stafford Loan
- PLUS Loan
- Consolidation Loan
- Federal Supplemental Educational Opportunity Grant (FSEOG)
- Federal Work-Study

These federal programs are the largest sources of student aid in the United States. According to the U.S. Department of Education, available student aid topped $234.8 billion in 2020–2021.

EXHIBIT 7.3 Undergraduate Student Aid by Source (in Billions), 2020–2021

Pell Grants	$26.0
Other Federal Grant Programs	$12.0
State Grants	$12.9
Institutional Grants	$71.1
Private and Employer Grants	$16.5
Federal Loans	$83.7
Federal Work-Study	$1.2
Education Tax Credits and Deductions	$11.4
Total	**$234.8**

Source: Trends in Student Aid 2020–2021. College Entrance Examination Board. www.collegeboard.org. (Numbers in the table are rounded)

The following subsections identify and describe these federal programs as well as some state and other programs.

Federal Pell Grants

Pell Grant
A grant from the federal government awarded to undergraduate students who have not earned bachelor's or professional degrees; the EFC calculation, which is based on one's financial need, is used to determine a student's eligibility for a Pell Grant and how much is awarded to a student

A Federal **Pell Grant** is not a loan; rather, it is a grant from the federal government that does not require repayment. The EFC calculation, which is based on one's financial need, is used to determine a student's eligibility for a Pell Grant and how much is awarded to a student. Pell Grants are awarded to undergraduate students who have not earned bachelor's or professional degrees. Graduate, professional, and postgraduate students generally are not awarded Pell Grants. Each year's awards depend on program funding for that year. A student can receive only one Pell Grant award per year. A student must be enrolled on at least a half-time basis to qualify.

Stafford Loans

Stafford Loan
The primary type of financial aid provided by the United States Department of Education; Stafford loans are either subsidized or unsubsidized

The **Stafford Loan** is the primary type of financial aid provided by the United States Department of Education. Stafford Loans are either subsidized or unsubsidized. There is no interest charged on the subsidized loan until repayment of the loan begins, which is typically six months after one of the following occurs:

- Graduation
- Leaving school
- Dropping below half-time status

Half-time status is considered half of the minimum hours to be considered full time. For instance, if a school on a semester basis has a 12-hour minimum requirement each semester for a student to be considered full-time, the student is considered half-time if he is enrolled in at least 6 credit hours each semester.

A subsidized loan is based on the financial need of the student as determined by the EFC formula. An unsubsidized Stafford Loan is a loan in which the borrower is charged interest on the principal from the moment of disbursement until the loan is paid off. Those who receive unsubsidized loans have the option of allowing the interest to be capitalized (which means that the interest accumulates and is added to the principal during the life of the loan until principal reduction payments are required) or paying the interest as it accrues. The process of capitalization costs more over the long term because the interest that accumulates is added to the principal balance, and subsequent interest is charged on the entire outstanding balance. However, some students or their families may not be in a financial position to pay the interest while the student is in school, and the capitalization method lets them postpone payment. The interest rates for the 2021–2022 academic year were 3.73% for undergraduate subsidized and unsubsidized loans. Rates of 5.28% apply for graduate or professional unsubsidized loans.

When Stafford Loans are disbursed to a student, an origination fee of 1.059% is charged. Thus, when determining the amount of funds through Stafford Loans required for a school term, the student must remember that the disbursement for a $7,000 Stafford Loan, for example, will only be $6,925.87 ($7,000 × 1.059% = $74.13, and $7,000 − $74.13 = $6,925.87).

Repayment of Stafford Loans begins after a grace period of six months following graduation, leaving school, or dropping below half-time enrollment. The subsidized Stafford Loan is attractive because no interest is charged and no principal payment is required during the six-month grace period. Essentially, the student has received a free loan during school and for six months thereafter under the subsidized loan program. Once the grace period is over, however, the subsidized loan begins to accrue interest, and principal and interest reduction payments must begin. Although interest is charged during the grace period on an unsubsidized Stafford Loan, no repayment of principal or interest is required during the grace period. If the interest is not paid on an unsubsidized loan during the grace period, it accrues and continues to be capitalized.

Students may obtain a deferment of the loan, which is a temporary postponement of payments on the loan. If the student has a subsidized loan, interest will not be charged during the period of deferment. For unsubsidized loans, the interest is capitalized during deferment unless the student chooses to pay the interest as it accrues during deferment. A deferment is allowed only after proving special circumstances to the agency, sender, or holder of the loan. The most common circumstances that may give rise to a deferment of repayment on a Stafford Loan include the following:

- At least half-time enrollment at a postsecondary school
- Economic hardship (for up to three years)
- Former student's inability to attain full-time employment (for up to three years)

Forbearance is a period when repayment of a loan is temporarily postponed for reasons that do not qualify for a deferment. Although forbearance also postpones repayment, subsidized loans accrue interest during the period of forbearance. Direct Stafford Loans can be repaid under several payment plans. Each payment plan has a different term ranging from 10 (the standard term) to 25 years.

Under certain conditions, Stafford Loans may be canceled or recipients may receive repayment assistance. One of the following conditions must be met for the loan to be canceled:

- Death of the student or borrower (i.e., parent of student)
- The borrower becomes totally and permanently disabled
- The student is a full-time teacher for five consecutive years in a designated elementary or secondary school serving students from low-income families
- The loan is discharged in bankruptcy
- The student's school closes before the student completes the program
- The school falsely certifies the loan

Repayment assistance may be available to students who serve in the military or become registered nurses and serve in eligible facilities in areas experiencing a nursing shortage.

PLUS Loans

Parent Loans for Undergraduate Students (PLUS Loans)
Loans that allow parents with good credit histories to borrow funds for a child's education expenses

Parent Loans for Undergraduate Students (PLUS Loans) allow parents with good credit histories to borrow funds for a child's education expenses. The child must be a dependent student enrolled at least half time in an eligible program at an eligible school. The parents complete a PLUS Loan application and Promissory Note with the school's financial aid office. As long as the parents do not have an adverse credit history, they may be entitled to receive a loan equal to the cost of attendance less any other available financial aid.

For instance, if the cost of attendance is $7,500 and the student has $5,000 in other financial aid, the parents may borrow up to $2,500. The interest rate on a new PLUS Loan is fixed at 6.28% (2021–2022). Interest accrues on the loan from the moment of disbursement until the loan is paid off. A fee of 4% is deducted from the funds disbursed to help defray the cost of the loan to the government. At least two disbursements of funds are made because no installment may exceed half of the loan amount.

Normally, parents must begin repaying PLUS Loans within 60 days after the final loan disbursement for the current academic year. Parents must commence repayment of both principal and interest while the student is in school. The same rules that apply to deferment or forbearance of Stafford Loans apply to PLUS Loans. However, because PLUS Loans are not subsidized, interest will continue to accrue and will thus be capitalized during the period of deferment or forbearance. PLUS Loans generally must be repaid within 10 years, although extended repayment terms of up to 25 years may be available.

Consolidation Loans

Consolidation loan
A loan that provides borrowers with a way to consolidate various types of federal student loans with separate repayment schedules into one loan

A **consolidation loan** provides borrowers with a vehicle to consolidate various types of federal student loans with separate repayment schedules into one loan. The Consolidation Loan Program benefits student and parent borrowers by extending the term of repayment, requiring only one payment per month, and in some cases providing a lower interest rate than on one or more of the loans. The interest rate is based on the weighted average of the interest rates on the loans being consolidated. The school's financial aid adviser can explain the many combinations of consolidation loan options.

Campus-Based Student Financial Aid

There are three campus-based programs that are administered directly by the financial aid office at participating schools:

- The Federal Supplemental Education Opportunity Grant (FSEOG) Program
- The Federal Work-Study Program
- The Federal Perkins Loan Program

Each program extends aid based on financial need of the student and the availability of funds at the school.

The Federal Supplemental Education Opportunity Grant Program

Federal Supplemental Education Opportunity Grant (FSEOG)
Campus-based student financial aid grant awarded to undergraduate students with low EFCs that gives priority to students who receive federal Pell Grants

An **FSEOG** is a grant, an outright gift, which does not require repayment. The FSEOG is awarded to undergraduate students with low EFCs who have not obtained a bachelor's or professional degree and gives priority to students who receive Federal Pell Grants. The difference between a Federal Pell Grant and an FSEOG is that the United States Department of Education guarantees that each eligible school will receive sufficient funds to pay Federal Pell Grants to all eligible students, whereas an FSEOG is paid to eligible students only if funds are available. Once all available FSEOG funds are used at the school, remaining eligible students will not receive an FSEOG. The FSEOG is in the range of $100 to $4,000 per academic year. The amount paid depends on the level of need, the time of application, and the school's funding level.

The Federal Work-Study Program

Federal Work-Study Program
Campus-based student financial aid program that enables undergraduate and graduate students to earn money for education expenses through jobs that pay at least current minimum wages but do not exceed the award received through the program

Federal Work-Study programs enable undergraduate and graduate students with financial need to earn money for education expenses through jobs that pay at least current minimum wages. Some jobs may pay higher hourly rates depending on the work done and skill required. The amount earned through the Federal Work-Study program cannot exceed the award received through the program. Federal Work-Study jobs may be on campus or off campus depending on the employer participating in the program.

The Federal Perkins Loan Program

Federal Perkins Loan
Campus-based, low-interest student loan program that provided financial aid to undergraduate and graduate students that had exceptional financial need

Although the Perkins loan program officially ended on September 30, 2017, it is worthy of mention because students may still have these loans. The final loans were approved for disbursement through June 30, 2018. Prior to the program end, Perkins loans were low interest rate loans funded by the federal government but administered by individual schools. These loans were available both to undergraduate and graduate students. They were need-based and were available to students who were attending on at least a half-time basis and who had an exceptional financial need.

Limits applied to the amount of funds that were borrowed. These loans featured a 5% interest rate, which was not charged during the period that the individual was a student. In addition, borrowers were not charged interest until nine months following graduation, leaving school, or dropping to less than half time, at which time repayment begins. Repayment is typically for 10 years.

For more information about federal education programs and financial aid applications, visit the United States Department of Education's website at **www.ed.gov**.

State Governmental Aid

Most states have programs that are very similar to the federal student financial aid programs previously discussed. The state programs rely heavily on the student's financial need and superior academic performance. States also require that the student be a resident of the state and attend a college or university in that state. Information on a given state's financial aid programs can be obtained from the school or the state's Department of Education.

Other Financial Aid Sources

Aid Directly from the Institution

Each school has its own method of providing aid through loans, scholarships, discounts, and campus jobs. The school's financial aid adviser should adequately explain to the student the school's available options and programs. Some schools will allow a student to pay tuition on a monthly installment plan, which may provide more flexibility to the student and parents. Other schools may offer discounts or scholarships for superior athletic or academic performance either before or after enrollment. The school has an incentive to entice superior athletes and academic students in order to increase their level of top students and to better compete with other schools, which in turn enhances the school's image.

Aid from Armed Forces

The U.S. Armed Forces have numerous programs and scholarships that may pay for tuition, fees, and books for those who enlist or enroll in the military. The student may also receive monthly payments for other expenses. Information regarding the many programs available through the U.S. Armed Forces can be obtained from the college attended or from the Administrative Office of the desired branch of military. Visit any of the following websites for Armed Forces aid:

- **www.goarmy.com/rotc**
- **www.goarmy.com/benefits/education-benefits.html**
- **www.gibill.va.gov**
- **www.marines.mil**
- **www.af.mil**
- **www.uscg.mil**
- **www.navy.mil**

Other Grants, Scholarships, and Fellowships

There are many forms of scholarships that are awarded by groups that are separate and apart from the school and state or federal government. For instance, there are numerous civic organizations, such as the American Legion, the Knights of Columbus, and the Boy Scouts of America, that award scholarships based on need, merit, and the student's or parents' affiliation with that civic organization. Of course, there are various types of scholarships available to students who have high grades and high standardized (entrance) test scores, including National Merit Scholarships. Also, scholarships can be provided through a particular church or religious organization. Although finding out about these scholarships will take some effort, it may prove to be time well spent.

In addition to scholarships, which typically do not include funds for living expenses, many organizations offer grants and fellowships. Grants and fellowships are similar to scholarships in that the funds awarded do not require repayment. Grants, however, are need-based awards, and fellowships are generally awarded to graduate students on the basis of academic merit and include living expenses as well as funds for tuition and fees.

TAX ADVANTAGES FROM EDUCATION EXPENSES AND TAX ISSUES

Although much time has been spent in this chapter discussing the costs of education and the increase in education expenses, there is some tax relief available. There are various vehicles available that allow the family or taxpayer who bears the brunt of education expenses to realize tax savings and benefits.

Qualified Tuition Programs (QTPs)
Also known as 529 plans, QTPs allow individuals to either participate in Prepaid Tuition Plans in which tuition credits are purchased for a designated beneficiary for payment or waiver of higher education expenses or participate in College Savings Plans in which contributions of money are made to an account to eventually pay for qualified higher education expenses of a designated beneficiary

Qualified Tuition Programs

One popular vehicle used to prepare for college tuition and related costs is the **Qualified Tuition Program (QTP)**. QTPs are also commonly referred to as 529 plans after IRC Section 529. The Internal Revenue Code permits the states to enact and tailor their own QTPs within the parameters established by Section 529. All 50 states have 529 plans, and tax laws have made it possible for institutions of higher education to establish their own 529 plans. In addition to state-sponsored plans and plans associated with a specific college or university, the Tuition Plan Consortium, a nonprofit consortium of independent colleges and universities, offers a national Prepaid Tuition Plan for private institutions.

The Benefits of QTPs

The benefits of QTPs are as follows:

- Growth is tax-deferred.
- Distributions from QTPs are excludable from gross income if used to pay for qualified education expenses. There is no limit on the amount of qualified educational expenses that can be withdrawn income tax-free for higher education expenses each year. Since January 1, 2018, up to $10,000 per year can be withdrawn from a 529 plan for K-12 tuition.
- The contributor can remove assets from the taxable estate.
- QTPs generally charge low commissions and have low management fees.

- Many states provide state tax deductions or tax exemptions for at least a portion of contributions.
- The contributor or owner has full control of the asset and can change the beneficiary.

Although each state's QTP legislation varies and has different features, all provide for at least one of two types of plans: Prepaid Tuition Plans and College Savings Plans. QTPs allow individuals to participate in either Prepaid Tuition Plans, whereby tuition credits are purchased for a designated beneficiary for payment or waiver of higher education expenses, or College Savings Plans, whereby contributions of money are made to an account to eventually pay for qualified K-12 or higher education expenses of a designated beneficiary.

QTPs are attractive to states because they can provide incentives to residents and nonresidents (depending on the state's individual plan) to invest in higher education and into that state's educational system. These plans are inexpensive for states to run, as many states provide turn-key contracts to financial services firms or investment companies to professionally manage the statewide plan.

Prepaid Tuition Plans

Prepaid Tuition Plans
Plans where prepayment of college tuition is allowed at current prices for enrollment in the future; in other words, a parent can lock in future tuition at current rates

Prepaid Tuition Plans allow prepayment of tuition at current rates for enrollment in the future. In other words, the parent can lock in future tuition at current rates. Participating in a school's prepayment program presupposes that the child will ultimately attend that school. The parents also assume the risk that the child may not meet the school's academic and admission requirements. Starting a tuition prepayment plan years in advance prevents the student from choosing his own college. Other risks include the possibility that the student may be the recipient of a scholarship to that or another college and the QTP would not be used for qualified expenses, negating the tax advantages. Moreover, the college chosen for tuition prepayment, although a well-respected and accredited school, could have a less-than-desirable curriculum in the student's major or area of interest. The client should weigh these risks with the benefits obtained at the particular school through tuition prepayment. Unused prepaid tuition benefits can be transferred to another family member held for possible future use. Refund and transfer options are available, but it is recommended that the family fully investigate the terms and conditions of the specific Prepaid Tuition Plan in order to understand the consequences if the student attends a different college, fails to meet academic qualifications, or does not attend college. Prepaid tuition plans are becoming less common. Whereas 18 states once offered plans, the number has recently diminished to 11.

College Savings Plans

College Savings Plan
Offered only by states, state-sponsored organizations, and eligible educational institutions. The contribution rules are the same as those for prepaid tuition plans. In this type of plan, tuition is not being prepaid, but, rather, a tax-advantaged savings plan is established from which tax-free distributions are made to pay for qualified education expenses.

College savings plans may be offered only by states, state-sponsored organizations, and eligible educational institutions. The contribution rules are the same as those for prepaid tuition plans. In this type of plan, tuition is not being prepaid, but, rather, a tax-advantaged savings plan is established from which tax-free distributions are made to pay for qualified education expenses. The investment options offered in college savings plans often include stock mutual funds, bond mutual funds, and money market mutual funds. Some plans offer age-based portfolios that automatically shift toward more conservative investments as the beneficiary gets closer to college age.

A significant advantage of the college savings plan over the prepaid tuition plan is that it does not restrict where the child beneficiary may attend college. Rather, the private savings plan permits open enrollment and is available for either out-of-state public university costs or private university costs without any loss of account value. Also, while most prepaid tuition plans are established solely for tuition and mandatory fees, the typical college savings plan may be used for qualified education expenses beyond tuition and mandatory fees. Qualified education expenses may include tuition, fees, books, or supplies required for attendance and room and board (for a student attending at least half time). However, unlike the prepaid tuition plan, funds in the college savings plan are not guaranteed by the sponsoring state, and, if the contributor is unhappy with the performance of the college savings plan, the only real alternative is to roll over the account to a different college savings plan.

The following table illustrates the major differences between a prepaid tuition plan and college savings plan.

Prepaid Tuition Plan	College Savings Plan
Inflation-based performance	Market-based performance
Suitable for risk-averse investor	Suitable for risk-tolerant investor
May offer state-guaranteed return on assets	No state-guaranteed return on assets
Usually restricted enrollment options	Open enrollment
May restrict out-of-state tuition costs and, if less than in-state, may not refund difference	Available for out-of-state tuition costs without any refund difference
Covers tuition and mandatory fees only	In addition to tuition and mandatory fees, covers books, required supplies, and room and board (students attending at least half time)

Taxes and the QTP

As discussed, a student's financial aid eligibility depends on the student's financial condition and the financial condition of her family. The existence of a QTP may affect the formula calculation for a student depending on the type of plan involved. For instance, a College Savings Plan is deemed an asset of the owner/contributor of the account.

Contributions to QTPs are deemed to qualify for the annual gift tax exclusion. A five-year averaging election for purposes of the gift tax annual exclusion may be applied to the transfer. If one's contributions exceed $16,000 (2022), the contributor is permitted to spread out one contribution over a five-year period. For example, if Walter (father-contributor) contributes $35,000 to a QTP account for Joey (beneficiary-child) in one year, Walter can elect to spread this contribution over five years—that is, $7,000 per year—and avoid a gift tax [less than the $16,000 (2022) exclusion]. The QTP thus permits the owner/contributor to shift his taxable estate to the beneficiary.

Any distribution or in-kind benefit transferred within 60 days under a QTP to the credit of a new designated beneficiary who is a family member of the old designated beneficiary will not be treated as a distribution and thus is exempt from income taxation and penalty. A change in the designated beneficiary of an interest in a QTP will not be treated as a distribution if the new beneficiary is a family member of the old beneficiary.

Except to the extent provided in the regulations, a tuition program maintained by a private institution is not treated as qualified unless it has received a ruling or determination from the IRS that the program satisfies applicable requirements. This exclusion from gross income for qualified education expenses was extended to distributions from QTPs established and maintained by an entity other than a state.

QTPs are extremely useful tools that provide significant tax savings, allow for substantial investments for a child's education, and, if used correctly, provide a tool for avoidance of gift and estate taxes. When comparing the tax savings alone from a QTP College Savings Plan versus a taxable account, the tax benefits can be substantial. If a family contributes $300 per month to a taxable account earning 10% annually for 16 years, the accumulated value of the account will be approximately $100,000 if the assumed federal and state tax rates total 34%. However, if that same $300 monthly contribution is made for 16 years into a QTP earning 10% annually, the account will be worth approximately $140,000. The difference is a tax savings of approximately $40,000.

Coverdell Education Savings Accounts (ESAs)

Coverdell Education Savings Account (Coverdell ESA)
An investment account established with cash contributions that grow tax-free within the account; money withdrawn from the account remains free from tax or penalty if the funds are used for qualified educational expenses; if not, the earnings are subject to income tax and a 10% penalty

Coverdell Education Savings Accounts (Coverdell ESAs), formerly known as Educational IRAs, were also authorized by the Taxpayer Relief Act of 1997. Coverdell ESAs are designed to offer tax benefits to individuals who wish to save money for a child or grandchild's qualified education expenses. A Coverdell is an investment account established with cash that is not tax-deductible. The contributions are made for the benefit of children under age 18. The contributions are allowed to grow tax-free within the account. Money withdrawn from the account is free from tax or penalty if the funds are used for qualified education expenses. If the funds are used for anything other than qualified education expenses, the earnings are subject to income tax and a 10% penalty.

Coverdell ESAs permit up to $2,000 in annual contributions, whereas QTPs allow larger contributions. However, if the individual family plans to contribute only $2,000 or less annually to the student/beneficiary's college fund, Coverdell ESAs might be more attractive because they offer the same tax benefits as 529 plans and the owner/contributor has the power to direct the specific investments. A person contributing funds to a Coverdell ESA may also contribute funds to a QTP in the same year for the same beneficiary.

A Coverdell can be established for any child under age 18 by a parent, grandparent, other family members or friends, or even the child, as long as the contributor who establishes the account does not have $220,000 ($110,000 for single) or more of modified family annual gross income (the 2022 phaseout is $190,000 to $220,000 for married filing jointly and $95,000 to $110,000 for single filers). If money from the Coverdell is not used for qualified education expenses by the designated beneficiary by the time the beneficiary turns 30, the beneficiary will need to take a distribution and pay both tax and a 10% penalty on the accumulated earnings or the funds may be rolled over into a Coverdell for a family member of the original beneficiary.

No contributions can be made to the account once the beneficiary turns 18. Distributions or withdrawals from Coverdell ESAs comprise of principal and earnings. The principal portion is always excluded from taxation, whereas earnings are excluded if used to pay for qualified education expenses. Although contributors may establish more than one account in a given child's name, the aggregate maximum annual contribution is $2,000. Withdrawals are tax free whether the student is enrolled full time, half time, or less than half time as long as the withdrawals do not exceed the child's qualified education expenses.

The definition of qualified education expenses (beyond undergraduate or graduate level courses) that may be paid tax-free from a Coverdell ESA include qualified elementary and secondary school expenses. These expenses include (1) tuition, fees, academic tutoring, special need services, books, supplies, and other equipment incurred in connection with the enrollment or attendance of the beneficiary at a public, private, or religious school providing elementary or secondary education (kindergarten through grade 12) as determined under state law; (2) room and board, uniforms, transportation, and supplementary items or services (including extended day programs) required or provided by such a school in connection with such enrollment or attendance of the beneficiary; and (3) the purchase of any computer technology or equipment or internet access and related services, if such technology, equipment, or services are to be used by the beneficiary and the beneficiary's family during any of the years the beneficiary is in school. The Tax Cuts and Jobs Act of 2017 broadened the definition of qualified education expenses for 529 plans to include up to $10,000 per year of K-12 tuition. This has made Coverdell ESA less important but they would still be available for clients who wished to withdraw more than $10,000 per year for K-12 expenses costs other than tuition.

Traditional IRA

Generally speaking, if a taxpayer withdraws funds from his traditional IRA before age 59½, the taxpayer is required to pay a 10% early withdrawal penalty on all or part of the amount withdrawn. However, the 10% penalty does not apply if a taxpayer withdraws funds from a traditional IRA to pay for qualified higher education expenses for the taxpayer, the taxpayer's spouse, or the child or grandchild of the taxpayer or taxpayer's spouse. Unlike a Coverdell, the taxpayer will owe federal income tax on the amount withdrawn.

Roth IRA

Roth IRA
An IRA created by the Taxpayer Relief Act of 1997; contributions to a Roth IRA are nondeductible; qualified distributions are excluded from an individual's taxable income; distributions used for qualified educational expenses can also avoid the 10% penalty

The **Roth IRA** does not provide tax deductions for contributions. However, contributions grow tax-free within the Roth IRA. Contributions are limited to $6,000 in 2022, plus an additional $1,000 for taxpayers who are age 50 or older. Contributions can be made as late as the due date of the individual's tax return for the previous tax year. Since 2022, contributions to all IRAs (both traditional and Roth IRAs) can be at any age as long as there is earned income. Even older people age 72 and beyond can contribute to an IRA if they or their spouse have earned income. This has always been true for Roth IRAs. The SECURE Act changed the law to allow contributions to traditional IRAs for people at any age. Contributions to Roth IRAs are phased out for joint filers with adjusted gross income between $204,000–$214,000 for 2022, and for single taxpayers with adjusted gross income between $129,000–$144,000 for 2022. The range for taxpayers who are married but file separately is $0–$10,000.

A distribution from a Roth IRA is not includable in the owner's gross income if it is a qualified distribution, or to the extent that it is a return of the owner's contributions to the Roth IRA. Qualified distributions are distributions that occur after a five-year holding period and for one of the following four reasons:

- Death
- Disability
- Attainment of age 59½
- First-time home purchase (limit of $10,000)

If a distribution is not a qualified distribution and it exceeds contribution (and conversions) to Roth IRAs, the distribution will be subject to income tax and may be subject to the 10% penalty. However, these excess distributions can avoid the 10% penalty if the proceeds are used for qualified higher education costs. Qualified higher education expenses are tuition, fees, and room and board. The taxpayer is always able to withdraw amounts up to his total contribution without income tax or penalty.

In short, Roth IRAs may be an even more attractive vehicle for education savings than Coverdell ESAs because the age of the student is irrelevant (vs. the 30-year-old limit) and because contribution limits are higher. In addition, funds in a Roth IRA not used for education can be used for retirement. On the other hand, distributions from a Roth IRA will raise the EFC in the future. This effect takes place after a two-academic-year delay. Thus,

Roth IRA distributions could be used to pay for the last two years of schooling and other assets, especially assets in the child's name, could be used for the first years.

The American Opportunity Tax Credit

American Opportunity Tax Credit
A tax credit available for qualified tuition, enrollment fees, books, and course materials for the first four years of post-secondary education for the taxpayer, spouse, or dependent

The **American Opportunity Tax Credit** is equal to 100% of the first $2,000 in qualified education expenses and 25% of the next $2,000, for a total of $2,500. Students are eligible during their first four years of college. In addition, books and course materials are eligible for the credit. In order to qualify for the full credit, modified adjusted gross income is limited to $80,000 for single taxpayers and $160,000 for joint filers. The American Opportunity Tax Credit is not available to married taxpayers who file separate returns. Up to 40% of the credit is refundable.

Modified AGI Phaseout for the American Opportunity Tax Credit

	2022
Married filing jointly	$160,000–$180,000
All other taxpayers	$80,000–$90,000

The Lifetime Learning Credit

Lifetime Learning Credit
A tax credit available to pay for tuition and enrollment fees for undergraduate or graduate degree programs

The **Lifetime Learning Credit** is available for tuition and enrollment fees for undergraduate or graduate degree programs or courses that help students acquire or improve job skills. The lifetime learning credit provides a tax credit for qualified college tuition and fees per family of $2,000 per year. The taxpayer must spend $10,000 annually on qualified expenses to qualify for the full credit. This credit is based on a 20% factor of the qualified expenses.

The Lifetime Learning Credit can be claimed for an unlimited number of years. If two or more children in the same household incur qualified expenses in the same year, the parents may claim a Lifetime Learning Credit or an American Opportunity Tax Credit for both children, or a Lifetime Learning Credit for one child and an American Opportunity Tax Credit for the other. However, only one credit is allowed per child per year. Also note that the maximum credit of $2,000 applies to the family, not per student as with the American Opportunity Tax Credit. For 2022, this credit is phased out when modified adjusted gross income (AGI) is between $80,000 and $90,000 for single taxpayers ($160,000–$180,000 for joint returns). No credit can be claimed if modified AGI is above $90,000 for single taxpayers or more than $180,000 for joint filers.

Taxpayers may claim an American Opportunity Tax Credit or Lifetime Learning Credit for a taxable year and exclude from gross income amounts distributed from a Coverdell ESA or QTP on behalf of the same student as long as the distribution is not used for the same expenses for which a credit was claimed.

Series EE Bonds

Series EE United States Savings Bonds (EE Bonds)
If used to pay for qualified higher education expenses at an eligible institution or state tuition plan, EE bonds bestow significant tax savings—that is, no federal income tax is due on the interest

Another vehicle that may be used to save for college is **Series EE United States Savings Bonds (EE bonds)**. EE bonds are useful tools for college tuition. The electronic (paper bonds were discontinued as of January 1, 2012) EE bonds are sold at 100% of face value in any denomination from $25 to $10,000 and are eligible to earn interest for up to 30 years. Since May 2005, the interest rate applied to EE bonds is fixed for the life of the bond (with the rate for new issues adjusted semiannually).

If used to pay for qualified higher education expenses at an eligible institution or state tuition plan, EE bonds bestow significant tax savings—that is, no federal income tax is payable on the interest. This interest exclusion is subject to phaseout based on adjusted gross incomes greater than $85,800 for single taxpayers and $128,650 for married filing jointly taxpayers for 2022. To attain tax-free status, EE bonds must be purchased in the name of one or both parents of the student/child. The parent(s) must be the owners of the bond and at least 24 years old before the first day of the month of the issue date of the bond. Also, the owners must redeem the bonds in the same year that the student/child's qualified higher education expenses are paid. In addition, Series I bonds have the same tax benefits as EE bonds for purposes of qualified higher education costs.

Uniform Gift to Minors Act

Uniform Gift to Minors Act (UGMA) *Allows parents to put cash and securities in a custodial account for a child*

The **Uniform Gift to Minors Act (UGMA)** allows parents to put cash and securities in a custodial account for a child. UGMA accounts give the child full ownership of the assets at the age of majority (age 18 or 21, depending on the state). If the child is under age 19, all income over $2,600 for 2022 earned by the assets is taxed at the parent's marginal federal income tax rates. If the child is 19 years or older, the income earned by the assets is taxed at the child's tax rate. In 2022, the kiddie tax rules apply to full-time students under age 24 at the end of the year who do not provide more than 50% of their own support. Notably, this is considered an asset of the child and is considered in determining financial aid. Therefore, the account can significantly reduce a student's eligibility for need-based financial aid.

Uniform Transfers to Minors Act

Uniform Transfers to Minors Act (UTMA) *Allows parents to put cash, securities, and real property in a custodial account for a child*

The **Uniform Transfers to Minors Act (UTMA)** is similar to the Uniform Gift to Minors Act. It provides for the transfer of assets to a custodial account for the benefit of a minor. The tax treatment of the income earned on the assets is the same as for UGMA, and an UTMA account is considered an asset of the child for financial aid purposes. There are differences between the two acts. UTMA is more flexible than UGMA. Parents may transfer real property as well as cash and securities to an UTMA account. Because both UTMAs and UGMAs are considered the child's asset when determining financial aid, these accounts should usually be the first money spent to pay for qualified higher education expenses. This will help position the student for higher need-based aid in future years.

Interest on Education Loans

Up to $2,500 of interest paid on student loans for undergraduate and graduate education may be deducted as an adjustment to the taxpayer's AGI. The loaned funds must have been spent on tuition and enrollment fees, books, supplies, equipment, room and board, transportation, or other necessary expenses. For 2022, the amount of the student loan interest deduction is phased out for joint taxpayers with modified adjusted gross incomes (AGI) of between $145,000 and $175,000. There is no deduction if modified AGI is $175,000 or more. For single taxpayers, the loan interest deduction is phased out when modified AGI is between $70,000 and $85,000. No interest deduction can be taken if modified AGI is $85,000 or more.

Employer's Educational Assistance Program

Employer's Educational Assistance Program
Under this program, an employer can pay for an employee's undergraduate tuition, enrollment fees, books, supplies, and equipment while these employer benefits are excluded from the employee's income up to $5,250

Under the **Employer's Educational Assistance Program**, an employer can pay for an employee's tuition (both graduate and undergraduate), enrollment fees, books, supplies, and equipment while these employer benefits are excluded from the employee's income up to $5,250.

Taxpayers are not eligible to claim the deduction and an American Opportunity Tax Credit or Lifetime Learning Credit in the same year for the same student. A taxpayer may not claim a deduction for amounts taken into account in determining the amount excludable resulting from a distribution (i.e., the earnings and the contribution portion of a distribution) from a Coverdell or the amount of interest excludable with respect to education savings bonds.

Equity Lines of Credit

A home equity loan or line of credit is yet another vehicle that can be used to fund college-related expenses. Because home equity loans are secured by a house, the interest rate on a home equity loan may be lower than rates for an unsecured student loan. Many state schools do not consider the value of the home when determining eligibility for financial aid, but numerous private colleges take equity in the home into account. If equity in the home is considered in the financial aid equation, a home equity loan could decrease home equity and possibly improve one's eligibility for financial aid. Furthermore, the interest on home equity loans used for college costs was deductible from the taxpayer's AGI. This ended on December 31, 2017. As a general rule, using home equity loans and lines of credit to pay for higher education expenses should be a last resort, or at least done after researching all other options, rates, and conditions for alternative funding. Borrowing too much against the home could result in foreclosure or other difficult situations.

HIGHLIGHTS OF TAX BENEFITS FOR HIGHER EDUCATION

The following exhibit provides the highlights of the various tax benefits covered in this section.

EXHIBIT 7.4 Highlights of Tax Benefits for Higher Education for 2022

	American Opportunity Tax Credit	Lifetime Learning Credit	Coverdell Education Savings Account	Traditional and Roth IRAs	Student Loan Interest	Section 529 Plans (QTPs)	Education Savings Bond Program
What is your benefit?	Credits can reduce the amount of tax you must pay		Earnings are not taxed	No 10% additional tax on early withdrawal	Above the line (for AGI) deduction of interest	Earnings are not taxed	Interest is not taxed
What is the annual limit?	Up to $2,500 per student	Up to $2,000 per family	$2,000 contribution per beneficiary	Amount of qualifying expenses	$2,500	None	Amount of qualifying expenses
What expenses qualify besides tuition and required enrollment fees?	None		Books Supplies Equipment Room and board if at least a half-time student Payments to qualified tuition program including K-12	Books Supplies Equipment Room and board if at least a half-time student	Books Supplies Equipment Room and board Transportation Other necessary expenses	Books Supplies Equipment Room and board if at least a half-time student Up to $10,000 per year for K-12 tuition	Payments to Coverdell ESAs Payments to qualified tuition programs
What education qualifies?	First 4 years of undergraduate	All undergraduate and graduate					
What are some of the other conditions that apply?	Must be enrolled at least half-time in a degree program.		Can also contribute to qualified tuition programs in the same year Cannot contribute after 18th birthday of beneficiary Must withdraw assets by age 30		Must have been at least half-time student in a degree program.	Distribution is excluded from gross income. American Opportunity Tax and Lifetime Learning Credits are permitted in the same year but not for the same expenses.	Applies only to qualified Series EE bonds issued after 1989 or Series I bonds
In what income range do benefits phase out?	MAGI Single $80,000–$90,000 MFJ $160,000–$180,000	MAGI Single $80,000–$90,000 MFJ $160,000–$180,000	MAGI Single $95,000–$110,000 MFJ $190,000–$220,000	No phaseout[1]	MAGI Single $70,000–$85,000 MFJ $145,000–$175,000	No phaseout	MAGI Single $85,800–$110,800 MFJ $128,650–$158,650

[1] Phaseouts exist at time of contribution. They are not relevant for withdrawals.

EDUCATION FUNDING/SAVINGS REGIMEN EXAMPLE

Now that all sources of education funding have been discussed and the investment vehicles and tax benefits identified, the most pressing issue is how much the parent or family needs to save now to pay for the child's college education. Calculating the cost of a child's college education through a savings plan is always a helpful exercise.

There are numerous ways to calculate the funding necessary to pay for a child's college education. In the following example, Scott plans to pay for the college education of his daughter, Hannah. As a general rule, Scott should establish a savings schedule for Hannah's college fund. This savings schedule can be created using the time value of money concepts discussed in Chapter 6.

The type of information needed to conduct this analysis includes the age of the child, the age the child will attend college, the parents' after-tax annual earnings rate, the current cost of tuition, related costs and books, and the tuition inflation rate. Scott is willing to fund Hannah's room and board either out of his own pocket when those expenses are incurred or by Hannah working to pay them.

Hannah is one day old, and Scott anticipates that Hannah will be 18 years old when she begins college. Scott expects to earn an after-tax annual rate of return over the 18-year period of 11%. The current cost of tuition, tuition-related expenses, and books and equipment at Hannah's projected category of schools is $25,000 per year. The rate of increase of tuition and tuition-related expenses is assumed to be 6%. The CPI inflation rate for this 18-year period is assumed to be 4%, which is less than the rate of increase of tuition. Therefore, to be conservative, the higher rate of 6% for tuition increases will be used instead of the CPI inflation rate. Other assumptions and necessary data for this exercise are as follows.

- Scott's annual investment, or savings payments, will commence at the end of each year from now until the day Hannah starts college (expected to be in 18 years).
- Scott will stop making savings payments once Hannah starts college so that he can pay for Hannah's monthly room and board expenses.
- Scholarship money and financial aid will not be considered in these calculations.
- Scott will postpone his decision whether to place any burden of education-related expenses on Hannah while she is in school (i.e., work or loans) until a later date.
- Scott desires to fund all college education expenses without having to borrow any funds.

This problem can be viewed in terms of a timeline (below) from year zero until year 21.

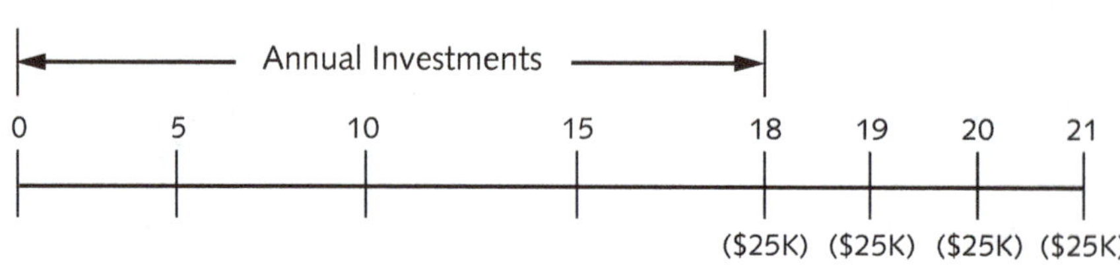

Using what is referred to as the uneven cash flow method, there are two series of cash flows that are important: 1) the cash flows invested annually into the account by Scott over an 18-year span and 2) the four annual payments out of the account starting at the beginning of year 18 and continuing through year 21 for Hannah's college education.

Step 1 Determine the Cost of College Tuition for the Four-Year Period, in Today's Dollars

The first step in this calculation is to determine the present value of the four consecutive annual payments of tuition in years 18 through 21 as of period zero, which is the present day. Using a financial calculator, enter a cash flow of zero for 18 years and a cash flow of $25,000 for the next four years. Then, discount these cash flows to the present day by an adjusted, assumed interest rate of 4.72%. The interest rate of 11% is adjusted for the annual increase in tuition of 6% as follows:

$$\left(\frac{1+\text{assumed interest rate}}{1+\text{assumed tuition increase rate}}-1\right)\times 100=\text{adjusted assumed annual rate}$$

Formula calculation pertaining to Scott and Hannah's circumstances:

Scott's annual interest rate: 1 + 0.11 = 1.11

Scott's assumed tuition inflation rate: 1 + 0.06 = 1.06

[(1.11 ÷ 1.06) –1] × 100 = 4.72%

Earnings from the interest per year are thus assumed in the calculation to be 4.72%. The net present value (NPV) of the four cash flows of $25,000 (today's dollars) at the beginning of years 18 through 21 equals $40,760.80.

This calculation is illustrated step by step on the following chart, using an HP 10bII+ calculator:

Keystroke	Display
[■][C ALL]	0.0000
0 [CFj]	0.0000
0 [CFj]	0.0000
17[■][Nj]	17.0000
25000[CFj]	25,0000.0000
4[■][Nj]	4.0000
[(1.11 [÷] 1.06) [–] 1] [x] 100 [=] 4.7170 [I/YR]	4.7170
[■][NPV]	40,760.8043

Step 2 Determine the Annual Payments Needed to Fund College Tuition Costs

The next step is to determine the annual payments from year zero through the end of year 17 that are needed to fund the outgoing cash flows for tuition at the beginning of years 18 through 21. Using a financial calculator, the required annual investment or payment is $5,292.50. This calculation is broken down step by step on the following chart, using an HP 10bII+ calculator in END mode:

Keystroke	Display
40,760.80 [PV]	40,760.8043
18 [N]	18.0000
11 [I/YR]	11.0000
0 [FV]	0.0000
[PMT]	5,292.4998

Therefore, Scott must save $5,292.50 per year, at the end of each year, beginning one year from now, the start of year zero, and continuing until the end of year 17 (a total of 18 payments) so that when Hannah attends college at the start of year 18, Scott can pay for her college education.

INVESTMENT STRATEGIES TO ACCOMPLISH EDUCATION GOALS

Financial planners should keep in mind that the investment strategies employed by the family should rely heavily on the amount of time until the child will be enrolled in school. In other words, the time horizon is probably the most important factor (besides risk tolerance) to consider in deciding what securities to invest in, how much to invest, and when to invest. The more time before the child enrolls in school, the more options and time for accumulation of principal and growth for a savings regimen will be available for the parents or family.

Using the education funding example above, if Scott wants to completely pay for his one-day-old daughter Hannah's college tuition, he has a time horizon of 18 years to invest enough money to fund four years of tuition. The funds Scott invests will have numerous years to grow and accumulate, and Scott's risk tolerance for investments will be higher than those parents who start to save for their children's college expenses years after they are born. Scott could invest in more growth- and equity-oriented funds with higher potential rates of return.

Compare Scott's situation to that of Katie, a parent with a 10-year-old daughter named April. Katie will have only eight years to save and invest money to pay for four years of college for April. Katie does not have the luxury of time. Furthermore, Katie cannot tolerate as much risk as Scott because there is less time to recover from a bear market. Therefore, Katie would probably invest substantially more conservatively than Scott.

As discussed earlier in this chapter, QTPs follow this investment principle. QTPs generally require a decrease in risk levels of investments the closer the child gets to the targeted year to begin college. This method is referred to as age-banding. Various QTP managers will generally comply with the sequence illustrated in the exhibit below.

EXHIBIT 7.5 Age-Banding Example

Student's age	Stocks	Bonds	Money market/cash
0–13	70–100%	0–30%	0
14–17	25–40%	35–50%	10–40%
18+	0–10%	20–30%	60–80%

Depending on the specifics of a state's QTP legislation, which varies from one state to another, managers of QTPs must comply with this decrease (or a similar decrease) in the percentage of investment in growth and equity funds because, as the child ages, the risk of losing principal and interest is too great considering that the prospect of attending college hangs in the balance.

Finally, after completing the analysis and a savings plan has been developed and saving has begun, the contributor must monitor and reassess the plan on a consistent, periodic basis (at least annually). This review process is necessary because the parents' financial situation may change or the goals may be changed. If a family experiences a significant increase in income or finances, an increase in the savings amount may be made in order to alleviate the risks of the assumptions made in the analysis, or to broaden the potential colleges and universities the child may consider. If a family experiences a decrease in income or finances, it may be more realistic to lower the expectations or assumptions in the analysis or determine whether the family would qualify for financial aid or assistance, such as a Pell Grant.

Other assumptions may also change over time. For instance, in our earlier example, Scott's daughter, Hannah, may prove to be an extraordinary student or athlete, and the increased likelihood of her receiving a scholarship could be factored into Scott's plan.

In conclusion, the education funding savings plan should be developed and implemented as early as possible to take advantage of time-horizon principles. Once the plan is in place, the plan should be monitored and updated because numerous assumptions and unknowns enter into the analysis. The amount necessary to fund college must be identified, but the family can attempt to minimize the contributions it must make through identifying the issues addressed previously, setting goals, gathering the necessary information regarding financial aid, school loans, scholarships and other assistance, maximizing tax benefits, choosing the best investment vehicles for themselves, and making choices that are best suited to the family's needs, expectations, and desires.

WHERE ON THE WEB

College Board (a not-for-profit education association that created and controls the SAT and PSAT/NMSQT Examinations) **www.collegeboard.org**

College Savings Plans Network (the official website for State 529 plans/QTPs; affiliated with the National Association of State Treasuries; provides links on the internet to individual state plans) **www.collegesavings.org**

Education Commission of the States **www.ecs.org**

Knowledge Center—Information for Financial Aid Professionals **ifap.ed.gov**

National Association for College Admission Counseling **www.nacacnet.org**

National Association of Student Financial Aid Administrators **www.nasfaa.org**

The SmartStudent™ Guide to Financial Aid (discusses financial aid eligibility and calculations; student loan analysis; scholarship availability) **www.finaid.org**

Information on college savings, calculators, 529 plan rankings, financial aid, scholarships, and other ways to save and pay for college **www.savingforcollege.com**

DISCUSSION QUESTIONS

1. What are the issues and goals of education funding?
2. What education funding information should students and parents collect?
3. How is financial need determined?
4. What is a Federal Pell Grant?
5. What are Stafford Loans?
6. What is the difference between a subsidized student loan and an unsubsidized student loan?
7. What are PLUS Loans?
8. What is a Consolidation Loan?
9. What campus-based student financial aid is available?
10. What are the tax advantages and issues with respect to education expenses?
11. What are the benefits of Qualified Tuition Plans, and how are they taxed?
12. What are Prepaid Tuition Plans, and how do they work?
13. How do contributions to QTPs affect gift taxes?
14. What is a Coverdell Education Savings Account?
15. How can a Roth IRA be used for education funding?
16. What is the maximum credit permitted with the American Opportunity Tax Credit?
17. What are the eligibility requirements to use a lifetime learning credit?
18. What are Series EE bonds?
19. What is the Uniform Gift to Minors Act?
20. What is the Employer's Educational Assistance Program?

EXERCISES

1. Compare and contrast grants, scholarships, and fellowships.
2. Compare and contrast subsidized and unsubsidized Stafford Loans.
3. Shawna, age 18, recently graduated from high school with a 3.6 GPA. Shawna currently lives at home and works part-time as an office assistant. She has been accepted to Texas State University. Her parents cannot afford to assist her with expenses. She wants to obtain a college education but is having trouble affording tuition and other college expenses. What financial aid programs would you recommend to Shawna and why?
4. Karen, age 20, is in her second year at the University of California. She will not be able to hold down a part-time job and complete her bachelor's degree program in four years. She will receive approximately $30,000 from a trust fund left to her by her grandmother on her 22nd birthday. What federal aid programs are available to Karen? Would you recommend that Karen borrow against the trust fund in order to support herself during the next two years? Why or why not?
5. Gordon and Rhonda want to start saving now for their two-year-old daughter's college education. Tuition and fees at a four-year public university are currently $25,000 per year, and tuition has increased approximately 7% each year. How much should Gordon and Rhonda expect to pay for college when their daughter turns 18? (Calculate the expected cost for each age and add them.)
6. Christian and Emily have two children, Bethany, age 5, and Taylor, age 7. Christian's parents would like to pay for Bethany and Taylor's college education. They are considering gifting the money to Bethany and Taylor by setting up savings accounts for them. Would you recommend this approach? Why or why not? If not, whom should the grandparents pass the money to and why?
7. Brandon and Myra are married and have an adjusted gross income of $55,000. They have two children, Beth, age 18, and Brett, age 20. Both Beth and Brett are full-time students attending the local university. Are Brandon and Myra eligible to take advantage of any education tax credits? If so, which ones, and what is the maximum credit they are allowed?
8. Leslie is in her third year of college and has received subsidized Stafford Loans to help her pay for college. She does not have to borrow any more money before she receives her degree. She wants to immediately start paying off her student loans. Given the choices for repaying student loans, what would you recommend to Leslie?
9. Brad was recently awarded financial aid through his university. Although the aid helped, he still needs more financial aid than the school offered. What would you recommend to Brad to help him pay for college?
10. Tyra plans to attend the local university next year. Her parents make too much money to qualify for federal aid programs, but Tyra still needs assistance. What financial aid, if any, is available for Tyra?
11. Julie's parents would like to assist her with the cost of college tuition. Tuition and fees are estimated at $13,000 per school year. Julie's parents apply and qualify for a PLUS Loan. How much can they borrow?

12. John and Sue, both age 30, have a child born today. They plan to save the maximum amount in their respective IRAs until their child goes to college in 18 years. Would you recommend a Roth IRA or a Coverdell ESA? Explain.

13. David intends to open a QTP Savings Plan for his daughter but wants to know whether he can direct the specific investments himself. Can David direct where and how much of the contributions are invested? Can David direct how much of the funds are used to purchase stock or bonds? Explain.

14. In the prior exercise, David was interested in placing a percentage of the QTP funds into stocks and a percentage into bonds. What is this principle called? Also, provide an example as to how it is used.

15. Robby plans to attend college but cannot afford tuition. He decides to apply for federal financial aid. Generally, how will Robby's financial aid eligibility be calculated?

16. Bob established a QTP College Savings Plan for his son Ricky at age 5. When Ricky turned 18, Ricky decided not to attend college and began working as a bartender in the Bahamas. Can Ricky withdraw funds from the QTP account, which has a value of $100,000? What can Bob do (if anything) with the account?

17. Claire established a QTP College Savings Plan for Matt, her son. While Matt was attending college, he asked Claire for money to buy a ski boat. Claire agreed, withdrew $10,000 from the QTP account, and purchased the boat for Matt in his name. Will this $10,000 withdrawal and payment be taxed, and if so, whose tax rate will be used? Would it be important to know what portion of the $10,000 represents contributions and what portion represents earnings from interest? Explain.

18. Let's take Exercise 17 one step further. Would there be any penalty assessed on the $10,000 withdrawal? Would it be important to know what portion of the $10,000 is contributed and what portion is interest?

19. What if, in Exercise 17, Matt had received a full scholarship for his remaining years in college, the semester before Claire gave him $10,000 for the boat?

PROBLEMS

1. Rena and Hunter Alesio have two children, ages 5 and 7. The Alesios want to start saving for their children's education. Each child will spend 6 years at college and will begin at age 18. College currently costs $20,000 per year and is expected to increase at 6% per year. Assuming the Alesios can earn an annual compound return of 12% and inflation is 4%, how much must the Alesios deposit at the end of each year to pay for their children's educational requirements until the younger child is out of school? Assume that education expenses are withdrawn at the beginning of each year and that the last deposit will be made at the beginning of the last year of the younger child.

2. Chelsea was recently divorced and has two children. The divorce decree requires that she pay 1/3 of the college tuition cost for her children. Tuition cost is currently $15,000 per year and has been increasing at 7% per year. Her son and daughter are 12 and 16, respectively, and will attend college for four years beginning at age 18. Assume that her after-tax rate of return will be 9% and that general inflation has been 4%. How much should she save each month, beginning today for the next 5 years, to finance both children's education?

3. Ken and Amy Charvet have two children, ages 4 and 6. The Charvets want to start saving for their children's education. Each child will spend 5 years in college and will begin at age 18. College currently costs $30,000 per year and is expected to increase at 7% per year. Assuming the Charvets can earn an annual compound investment return of 12% and inflation is 4%, how much must the Charvets deposit at the end of each year to pay for their children's educational requirements until the younger child goes to school? Assume that education expenses are withdrawn at the beginning of each year and that the last deposit will be made at the beginning of the first year of the younger child.

4. Barry and Virginia have a 5-year-old son, Daniel. They have plans for Daniel to attend a 4-year private university at age 18. Currently, tuition at the local private university is $15,000 per year and is expected to increase at 7% per year. Assuming Barry and Virginia can earn an annual compound return of 10% and inflation is 4%, how much do Barry and Virginia need to start saving per year, starting today, to be able to pay for Daniel's college education? Assume their last payment is made at the beginning of Daniel's first year in college.

SECTION 3
IN BRIEF

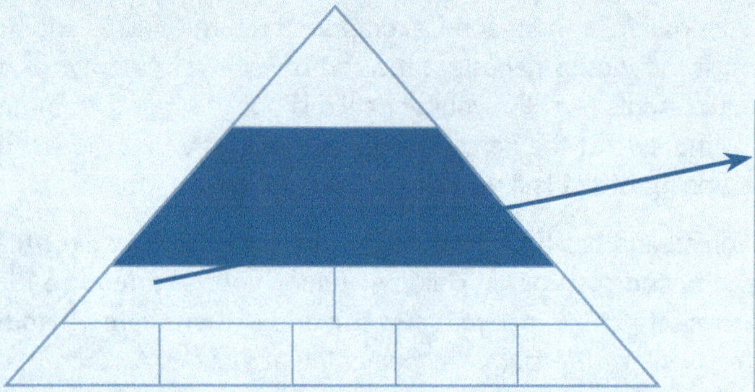

- Risk
- Perils and hazards
- Adverse selection
- Insurable losses
- Law of insurance contracts
- Insurance policy features
- Selecting an insurance company
- Risk management process

- Measuring needs related to premature death
- Characteristics of life, health and disability policies
- Annuities
- Long-term care insurance

- Automobile insurance
- Homeowners insurance
- Liability insurance
- Property insurance
- Business insurance

- Social Security insurance and benefits
- Taxation of Social Security benefits
- Medicare benefits

SECTION

3 Insurance Planning

CHAPTERS

Risks	Goals
■ Untimely death ■ Disability ■ Unemployment ■ Medical illness ■ Long-term health care ■ Damage to property ■ Tort liability	■ Appropriate insurance coverage and reasonable premiums for the risks identified to person, property, and/or liabilities of the client.

Data Collection	Data Analysis
■ Life insurance policies ■ Disability policies ■ Employer benefit summaries ■ Health plan policies ■ Long-term care policies ■ Automobile policies ■ Homeowners policies, riders, etc. ■ Personal liability umbrella policies ■ Business policies	■ Life insurance policy analysis ■ Health insurance policy analysis ■ Disability insurance policy analysis ■ Homeowners policy analysis ■ Automobile insurance analysis ■ Liability insurance analysis ■ Business insurance analysis

CHAPTER 8

An Introduction to Insurance and Risk Management

LEARNING OBJECTIVES

After learning the material in this chapter, you will be able to do the following:

- Define risk and the different types of risk, and understand how risk impacts the personal financial planning process
- Understand the insurable loss exposures faced by the typical client
- Understand the responses to pure risk and how they can be incorporated into a risk management plan
- Define insurance and understand how it is used as a risk management tool
- Distinguish between a peril and a hazard and understand how each relates to the need for insurance

- Define adverse selection and explain its impact on insurance
- Summarize the requisites for an insurable risk and understand what distinguishes insurance from gambling
- Explain the elements of a valid contract and identify the distinguishing features of an insurance contract
- Understand the reason for, and the effect of, various contractual features in an insurance contract
- Know the different types of authority given to agents to act on behalf of an insurance company
- Understand the methods of loss valuation
- Know the insurance company rating agencies and how they evaluate the financial condition of insurers
- Define risk management and explain the steps in the risk management process

INTRODUCTION

Proper insurance coverage is essential to a client's financial plan. Most people do not have the right types and amounts of insurance coverage. Financial planners must have a basic understanding of risk and insurance in order to properly assist their clients in evaluating their current insurance coverage and to determine their future insurance needs. For most clients, basic insurance needs can be covered with life insurance, health insurance, disability insurance, homeowners or renters insurance, long-term care insurance, automobile insurance, and personal liability insurance. This section of the text is designed as an introduction to the various types of insurance. Chapter 8 discusses risk, the legal foundation of insurance, and the transfer of risk using insurance contracts. Chapter 9 identifies risks to the individual, namely premature death, catastrophic illness, disability, and the need for long-term care. Chapter 10 identifies the risks associated with property and liability exposures. Chapter 11 covers the types and availability of social insurance.

UNDERSTANDING RISK

Risk
The chance of loss, possibility of loss, uncertainty, or a variation of actual from expected results

Risk is the chance of loss, possibility of loss, uncertainty, or a variation of actual from expected results. An insured homeowner knows that one will not likely experience a house fire, but the possibility of fire exists, and the consequences could be financially devastating. Thus, the homeowner transfers the risk of fire to an insurance company by paying an insurer a premium to cover the risk.

RISK CLASSIFICATION

Pure vs. Speculative Risk

Pure risk
A risk in which the results are either a loss or no loss

Speculative risk
A risk with three possible outcomes: profit, loss, or no loss

A **pure risk** is one in which the results are either loss or no loss (e.g., death). While death is a certainty, there is still risk in determining when each person will die. A **speculative risk**, on the other hand, is one where there is potential for profit as well as loss or no loss. Entrepreneurs regularly encounter speculative risk when they begin a new business or sell a new product. Speculative risks are generally undertaken voluntarily and are not insurable.

Consider the risks associated with the purchase of a home. A speculative risk is the potential fluctuation in the value of the house after purchase. The market value of the home could remain the same as the original purchase price, increase, or decline. Also, a variety of pure risks are associated with home ownership, such as the risk of a fire, flood, or theft of property. If a theft occurs, the insured will suffer a loss; however, the condition of the house remains the same. To summarize, a pure risk has two possible outcomes—loss or no loss—while a speculative risk has three: profit, loss, or no loss. Therefore, only pure risks are commercially insurable.

Dynamic vs. Static Risk

Dynamic risk
A risk that results from changes in society or the economy (e.g., inflation)

Static risk
A risk dependent on factors other than a change in society or the economy (e.g., natural disaster)

Risks that can be classified in terms of whether they are affected by society or the economy are called **dynamic risks**. For example, changes in technology can make a company's product obsolete, leading to great financial loss. Dynamic losses are difficult to predict; therefore, insurance companies are not inclined to assume this type of risk.

Static risks, on the other hand, involve losses that would occur regardless of changes in society or the economy (e.g., death of a family's breadwinner). Losses that result from static risks tend to occur with regularity and are generally predictable. For this reason, insurance companies are generally willing to accept these types of risks.

Subjective vs. Objective Risk

Subjective risk
A person's unique perception of risk; varies greatly from individual to individual

Subjective risk is a person's perception of risk and varies greatly among individuals. Consider two people, each having slept only two hours in the last two days, who need to drive home from work late at night. The first person drinks coffee habitually and considers an hour's drive no problem, thus reflecting a low level of subjective risk. The second person does not drink coffee and is tired. One should either not drive home or drive carefully because one has fallen asleep behind the wheel before under similar circumstances. The second person's perception is an example of high subjective risk. A perception of low subjective risk may result in less than prudent conduct, whereas a perception of high subjective risk is more likely to result in prudent conduct.

Objective risk
The relative variation of an actual loss to an expected loss

Objective risk does not depend on a particular person's perception, but rather, the relative variation of an actual loss to an expected loss.

For example, suppose an auto insurer has 1,000 new cars insured each year. On average, 100 cars, or 10% of the car owners, file collision claims each year. If in the first year, 110 car owners file claims, and the next year only 90 filed claims, there is a 10-car variation each year, equaling a 10% objective risk. Objective risk varies *inversely* with the number of exposures involved. As the number of exposures increases, the insurance company can more accurately predict future loss experience based on the law of large numbers (to be discussed later in the chapter).

Particular vs. Fundamental Risk

Particular risk
Personal risk that involves a possible loss for an individual or a small group

Fundamental risk
An impersonal risk that involves a possible loss for a large group

Risks can also be classified in terms of how large a population they affect. **Particular risks** are personal and involve a potential loss to an individual or a small group of individuals rather than a large segment of the population. Theft of a family's personal property is an example of particular risk. **Fundamental risks**, on the other hand, are impersonal and involve a potential loss for a large group. For example, the possibility of rising waters during a hurricane is a fundamental risk.

Financial vs. Nonfinancial Risk

Financial risk
A risk that involves a monetary loss

Nonfinancial risk
A risk that involves a non-monetary loss

Whether a risk involves financial loss is another means of classification. **Financial risks** involve monetary losses. The possibility that a family may be faced with a significant loss of income in the event of an income producer's disability is an example of a financial risk. **Nonfinancial risk** may also be associated with a breadwinner's disability, such as pain and suffering. Generally, insurance is intended for financial losses, although some liability policies will compensate for nonfinancial losses that give rise to legal liability. For example, pain and suffering caused by the insured is covered by a liability policy if it gives rise to liability for monetary damages.

Probability of Loss

Actuary
A person who manages and measures risk

Insurance companies employ highly skilled professionals, known as actuaries, who are experts in the fields of mathematics, statistics, and probability theory. The **actuary**, or team of actuaries, is typically responsible for predicting the losses for various risk pools, calculating required reserves, and producing premium rates that will cover losses while producing a profit for the insurer. The actuary must strike a delicate balance in pricing risks because the insurer's products must compete favorably in a highly competitive market. In addition, both the market and regulatory authorities demand that the insurer remain in a position of financial strength.

For an actuary to estimate how many losses will occur in a given year, one must know the chance of loss for members of a given risk pool. The chance of loss is more commonly referred to as the probability of loss and measures the long-term frequency in which an event occurs.

For example, if 700 out of 100,000 homes suffer a fire each year, the probability of a fire can be calculated as 700 ÷ 100,000, or 0.007. For each individual member of the pool, the probability of loss is a moot point. Whether the probability is 7 in 1,000 or 7 in 100, the insured's concern is that it could be one's home that burns and that such a loss would be financially devastating. Probability analysis provides useful information for the insurer, however, because it allows the insurer to determine the number of insureds who will suffer losses and, therefore, to estimate the aggregate claims. The expected total cost of claims can then be evenly distributed among the members of the pool in the form of policy premiums.

Note that probability represents the long-term chance. This implies that numerous events must occur before the probability can be calculated with reasonable accuracy. To illustrate, consider how one might determine the probability of a tossed coin landing on heads. The probability is .5 (or a 50% chance), but suppose one does not know this chance. To discover the probability of tossing a head, assume the coin is tossed 10 times. With many iterations of the same test, some will obtain 5 out of 10 heads, but others will not. One may erroneously conclude that the probability is .7 (7 out of 10) when 7 heads turn up. In order to calculate the true probability, one must toss the coin several thousand times, recording each of the results. Perhaps there were 5,021 heads, resulting in a better estimate of the true probability (5,021 ÷ 10,000 = 0.5021) than tossing the coin just 10 times.

How does probability relate to objective risk? Objective risk is the chance that predictions about losses will be wrong given certain probabilities. The more reliable the probability figures are, the more accurate the predictions will be, and thus a lower objective risk will be the result.

Law of Large Numbers

Law of large numbers
The chance that predicted results will reflect true results increases as the number of exposures increases

Probability figures must be determined over time. The previous coin toss example illustrates that the more times one repeats an experiment, the more likely the true probability will be revealed. Therefore, the larger the number of exposure units, the more likely the predictions will be accurate. A related conclusion is that the **law of large numbers** helps reduce objective risk, which depends on the variation in, or uncertainty of, possible outcomes.

For example, consider the risk faced by an insurer that has 1,000 insureds in a life insurance pool versus that of an insurer with 100,000 insureds. If the probability of death is 5 in 1,000, or .005, the insurer with the smaller pool estimates that 5 people in the pool will die this year. The larger insurer estimates that 500 people will die. Suppose 5 additional people in each pool die. For the smaller insurer, the extra deaths result in a 100% increase in claims beyond what was originally predicted. For the larger insurer, however, the 5 additional deaths result in an increase of only 1%. Because there are more observations in the larger pool, the variation in possible outcomes declines, which reduces the insurer's objective risk.

RESPONSES TO PURE RISK

Individuals and businesses may respond to pure risk exposures in one or more of the following ways:

- Risk avoidance
- Risk reduction
- Risk retention
- Risk transfer

Risk Avoidance

Risk avoidance
The avoidance of any chance of loss

Risk avoidance is simply the avoidance of any chance of loss. If the probability of loss becomes zero, there is no risk of future losses. How does one eliminate the possibility of dying in an airplane crash? Avoid air travel.

Avoidance works for some, but not all possible, loss exposures. If one risk is avoided, another risk may likely appear in its place. For example, the person who wishes to avoid dying in a plane crash can certainly avoid flying, but then how does one get from one place to another? Perhaps using a car, but many people would also prefer to avoid dying in an automobile accident. So, those persons would have to walk, which in turn involves its own inherent risks.

Certain risks can be avoided; however, some risks are potentially frequent and severe and some people will simply avoid all chance of the risks occurring. For example, some doctors have left private practice because of the fear of medical malpractice suits. They find other ways to earn a living (e.g., teaching or research), thus avoiding the risk of a malpractice suit completely.

Risk Reduction

Risk reduction
Taking measures that reduce the frequency or severity of losses

Risk reduction involves taking measures that reduce the frequency or severity of losses. A person who cannot avoid driving faces the risk of an auto accident but has several risk reduction devices at one's disposal. Taking a defensive driving class and practicing defensive driving techniques are means of reducing the probability of being involved in an accident. In much the same way, wearing a seatbelt reduces the possibility that one will sustain injuries in an automobile accident.

Risk reduction measures are undertaken only when the costs are feasible. To minimize the severity of injuries sustained in a car accident, one might decide to purchase the safest automobile on the market; however, if that automobile costs $50,000, it may be cost prohibitive.

Certain risk reduction techniques that reduce the severity of losses, such as seat belts, may give some drivers a false sense of security. These drivers may more readily exhibit risky behaviors, such as speeding, which increases the probability of loss from an accident and, thus, mitigates the reduction of risk gained by wearing a seatbelt.

Risk retention
Bearing all or part of the financial burden in the event of a loss

Risk Retention

Active risk retention
One is fully aware of the chance for loss and consciously plans to retain all or part of the risk

When a person or firm is exposed to risk and decides to bear all or part of the financial burden if a loss occurs, this is known as **risk retention**, and may occur in one of two forms, active or passive.

Active risk retention means that one is fully aware of the chance for loss and consciously plans to retain all or part of the risk. The person who has a $100,000 home may choose to retain the first $500 of any loss through a deductible, whereas the person with a $1,500 automobile may choose to retain the whole risk of automobile damage by not carrying comprehensive and collision coverage because the severity of loss is low.

Passive risk retention
Being unaware of a risk, but taking no steps to manage it properly

Passive risk retention is being unaware of a risk but taking no steps to manage it properly. When another risk management method is not chosen, retention is selected by default.

Risk transfer
Shifting the probability of loss to another party, such as an insurance company

Risk Transfer

Contractual agreements
Often include guarantees at the time of sale; often known as warranties

Hedging
A means of trying to match profit on one transaction to the expected loss of another

Incorporation
Results in limited liability for businessowners

Risk transfer involves shifting the probability of loss to another party, such as an insurance company. The purchase of insurance is often an economical method of transferring a pure risk. Three other techniques for handling risk transference include contracts, hedging, and incorporation. **Contractual agreements** may include guarantees at the time of sale, often known as warranties. **Hedging** is a means of trying to match profit on one transaction to the expected loss of another. In stock market transactions, a speculator can hedge unfavorable price fluctuations by buying and/or selling option contracts. **Incorporation** results in limited liability for businessowners. When a business is operated as a sole proprietorship or a partnership, liability is unlimited for the owner(s); however, if a business is incorporated, stockholder liability is limited and the risk of insufficient funds or assets to meet the demands of business expenses rests with the corporation or is shifted to creditors.

INSURANCE AS A RISK MANAGEMENT TOOL

Individuals and businesses can obtain protection against certain risks of financial loss through the use of insurance. While there are many ways to suffer a financial loss, insurance is designed to deal specifically with the financial consequences of pure risks. As you will recall, pure risk involves situations in which there is only the possibility of loss or no loss. The possibility of loss when owning property is an example of pure risk. A homeowner is confronted with the possibility that something may damage the home and the potential consequences are loss or no loss.

Insurance
A mechanism through which risk is transferred to an insurer, evidenced by a promise to pay, in exchange for an equitable premium

Insurance is a mechanism through which risk is transferred to an insurer, evidenced by a promise to pay, in exchange for an equitable premium. The insurer agrees to indemnify the losses incurred by the insured, to pay other financial benefits, or to provide services related to the risk. By combining a large number (pool) of similar (homogenous) exposure units (risks), the overall losses of the pool can be predicted due to the law of large numbers. The result is that the potential losses of each member (unit) are shared with the other members of the pool in the form of policy premiums. In the same manner as the overall losses of the group, premiums can be estimated only because of the law of large numbers. Insurance is, therefore, a unique device capable of transferring a large amount of individual risk at a disproportionately reduced cost.

Transfer of Losses

Insurance transfers the risk of loss to the insurer who is a financial intermediary that specializes in assuming risk. The insured pays the insurer a premium and the insurer agrees that if certain events (losses) occur, compensation will be provided to the insured to pay for the consequences of the insured's losses. In exchange, the insurer provides the insured with a legally binding contract, called the insurance policy, that defines covered losses, how those losses will be valued, and what duties are owed by each party to the contract. Almost any risk can be transferred for the right price. Of course, the greater the chance that a loss will occur, the higher the insurance premium and the lower the likelihood that an insurance company will agree to insure the potential loss.

Sharing Losses With Others

Cooperation and sharing are essential to the insurance process. Insureds facing similar risks of loss are pooled together. The insurer mathematically predicts the expected losses for the entire pool, divides the cost of those losses among each insured, and adds a charge for the insurer's operating expenses and profit margin.

Each insured contributes a fair share of money to the pool. Those who pose a greater amount of risk contribute more to the pool. Actuarial science allows insurance companies to estimate losses and, thus, to calculate premiums for each person in the pool.

For example, assume First Mutual Insurance Company has a life insurance pool of 1,000 30-year-old males. Each insured joined the pool because he was concerned about dying during the year and wanted to leave money behind to cover his financial obligations. Human life expectancy is quite predictable, so the actuary can determine with considerable certainty how many of those in this particular pool will die during the year. Suppose the actuary determines that two of the 1,000 men in the pool will die this year. If each man in the pool purchased $100,000 of life insurance coverage, this means that the actuary expects the insurer to pay $200,000 in claims for the year. If the $200,000 in claims (losses) is divided among the 1,000 people in the pool, each person's share is $200. The insurer will add a charge for expenses and profit, perhaps $50 per insured. Thus, the cost of insurance (premium) for each person in the pool for that year will be $250.

Each insured in the pool voluntarily pays $250 for the security of knowing that if he is one of the two insureds to die, his beneficiary will receive $100,000. At the same time, each insured hopes that he does not die and that his $250 will be paid as someone else's death claim.

Notice that in the second year, only 998 insureds are left in the pool if two did in fact die the preceding year. Suppose the actuary determines that, once again, only two people in the pool will die. For the $100,000 death benefit to be paid on each claim, the insurer must again collect a total of $200,000. When this amount is spread over 998 insureds, each is now responsible for $200.40. When the insurer's expenses (again, assume they are $50) are added, the total premium charged is $250.40. This premium is slightly higher than for the previous year. Note that it would be even higher had the actuary determined that three or more people in the pool would likely die the following year.

Because death rates increase as people get older, life insurance premiums rise at an increasing rate. This occurs because the number of people dropping out of the pool increases each year due to death and lapsing policies. Thus, fewer persons remain in the pool to share the expense of future death claims.

Self-Insurance

Self-insurance is essentially the retention of a known risk and, where applicable, the related administrative functions that are typically performed by an insurer. Self-insurance is most often practiced in mid- to large-sized organizations with ample cash reserves. Affluent families will also self-insure by retaining risks that would traditionally be insured. When self-insuring, one normally establishes reserves for future losses in lieu of purchasing insurance.

By self-insuring a portion of their risk, organizations seek to gain more control over their cost of risk while potentially improving loss coverage and limits. Additionally, the organization is in control of claims processing and loss control, and self-insurance may improve cash flow provided the organization experiences losses equal to or less than expected and they manage the program efficiently. However, unless certain provisions are made, the company remains highly vulnerable to unexpected catastrophic losses that could dramatically exceed the loss reserves set aside by the company.

Protected Self-Insurance Program

Under a protected self-insurance program, the business or another entity keeps and administers the manageable, predictable risk within its operations and transfers the catastrophic risk to an insurer. Insurance on the excess is placed with specific and aggregate limits so the entity can know the future cost of protection.

First, the insured organization must determine the maximum amount that it can absorb for the particular line of insurance. Second, the organization creates a loss fund limit in the amount of the losses it expects to incur in a given period. This amount is based on the organization's loss history and future inflation.

When losses exceed the self-insured retention, specific excess insurance, known as *stop-loss coverage*, finances the losses, typically at 100%, up to a specified maximum limit. Thus, the insured organization is protected from losses above the self-insured retention, up to the excess limits of the excess insurance.

Pure Self-Insurance

Large organizations having significant cash reserves on hand may choose to self-insure against both predictable and catastrophic risks. In these cases, a reserve fund is created in the amount of the losses expected to incur in a given period, assuming the probability that a catastrophic loss may occur.

CAUSES OF INSURED LOSSES

Perils

Peril
The proximate, or actual, cause of a loss

Open perils policy
A policy in which all perils or causes of loss are covered unless they are specifically listed in the exclusions section

Named perils policy
A policy that provides protection against losses caused by the perils specifically listed in the policy

Too often the concept of risk, or the chance of loss, is confused with the terms *peril* and *hazard*. A **peril** is the proximate or actual cause of a loss. Some common examples of perils are fire, windstorm, tornado, earthquake, burglary, and collision.

Insurance policies may be written in either an open-perils or named-perils format. Historically, open perils policies were called "all-risks" policies because they covered all risks of loss (perils) not specifically excluded. The name *all-risks* proved to be somewhat misleading to the typical consumer, implying that "all" risks were covered. As a result, the industry has moved toward the use of the term *open perils* to describe this type of coverage agreement. An **open perils policy** is one in which all perils or causes of loss are covered unless specifically listed in the exclusions section. A **named perils policy** provides protection against losses caused by the perils specifically listed in the policy. Because there is always a chance of loss being caused by an unknown peril, an open perils policy is preferable to a named perils policy. Consequently, the open perils policy premium is higher because it provides broader coverage.

Hazards

Hazard
A condition that creates or increases the likelihood of a loss occurring

A **hazard** is a condition that creates or increases the likelihood of a loss occurring.

Physical Hazard

Physical hazard
A tangible condition or circumstance that increases the probability of a peril occurring and/or the severity of damages that result from a peril

A **physical hazard** is a tangible condition or circumstance that increases the probability of a peril occurring and/or the severity of damages that result from a peril. Common examples of physical hazards include poor lighting, icy roads, storing gasoline in a household garage, and defective wiring.

Moral Hazard

Moral hazard
A character flaw or level of dishonesty that causes or increases the chance for loss

Moral hazard is a character flaw or level of dishonesty that causes or increases the chance for loss. In property insurance claims, a good example of a moral hazard is arson. Fraud in auto and health claims also occurs frequently. Unfortunately, these types of losses result in premium increases for all insureds. When insureds submit an inflated or intentionally caused claim, they are stealing from all insureds including themselves.

Morale Hazard

Morale hazard
Indifference to a loss based on the existence of insurance

Morale hazard is the indifference to loss based on the existence of insurance. Certain people think that because they have insurance there is no need to be concerned about protecting their property. As a direct result, the chance of loss is increased. Persons may feel that because they are insured, there is no reason to lock their homes or cars. This should not be confused with a moral hazard, which, for example, would be burning their house down or purposely damaging their own car to collect insurance.

Adverse Selection

Adverse selection
The increased tendency of higher-than-average risks (people who need insurance the most) purchasing or renewing insurance policies

Adverse selection is the increased tendency of higher-than-average risks (i.e., people who need insurance the most) to purchase or renew insurance policies. Calculating insurance premiums depends on the existence of a balance of both favorable and unfavorable risks in the pool. When higher-than-average loss levels occur among a group of insureds, meaning a greater proportion of bad versus good risks, adverse selection may be the problem.

For instance, if someone with no insurance needs surgery, lives in a flood-prone area, or has recently acquired a life-threatening disease, that person is more likely to desire insurance coverage. Adverse selection makes insurance less affordable for all insureds. One could conclude that if all people were to purchase insurance only when they knew that they would incur a financial loss, then insurance would not exist. The premiums insurers collect would be depleted before all the claims could be accounted for, thus causing insurance companies to go out of business.

The problem of adverse selection is primarily managed through effective underwriting, which is the process of selecting and classifying insureds according to their respective risk levels. Each level of risk can be thought of as a pool, and the insureds within a given pool must share similarities in expected losses so they can be charged a premium representative of their risk levels. Although a person with a terminal illness may wish to purchase life insurance (a clear example of adverse selection), the underwriting process should detect the condition and the underwriter should reject the application for insurance.

INSURABLE LOSSES

Insurance vs. Gambling

Many people view insurance and gambling as similar activities. A common statement is, "Insurance is a gamble because the insurance company and the insured are betting if and when an unfortunate event will occur." Although in insurance there are monetary transactions that take place on the basis of chance, insurance and gambling are inherently different.

Insurance allows the insured to transfer a risk to the insurer, whereas gambling creates a risk where none previously existed. In gambling, the risk of loss is created when the transaction itself occurs. For example, when a card player bets $100 on a hand against the dealer, one has immediately created a speculative risk (risk of gain or loss) for oneself. Insurance takes the consequences of a pure risk (loss, no loss) and makes them manageable for the insured.

Requisites for an Insurable Risk

Several conditions must exist before a risk is considered insurable.

- A large number of homogeneous (similar) exposure units.
- Insured losses must be accidental from the insured's standpoint.

- Insured losses must be measurable and determinable.
- Losses must not pose a catastrophic risk for the insurer.

A Large Number of Homogeneous (Similar) Exposure Units

The insurance process depends on the establishment of fair and properly priced premiums for insureds. If accurate estimates of the probability of an occurrence are to be made, a large number of cases must be considered. The law of large numbers states that in order to predict the average frequency and severity of a loss with accuracy, a sufficient number of homogeneous exposure units must be present within each class.

Homogeneous and heterogeneous groups are two distinct entities. If dissimilar exposure units are placed in the same group to be observed, predictions on their loss experience will likely be inaccurate. Imagine a pool of homeowners that consists of people from California, Texas, Montana, and Maine. Because the natural disaster perils each state faces are considerably different, the resulting expected loss predictions would be imprecise. To estimate losses for homeowners in California as one group and to make separate loss estimates for persons living in the other states as another makes more sense. The exposure units must be homogeneous, or similar in nature, to obtain an accurate measure of the underlying probability for the loss experience of an insured group.

Insured Losses Must be Accidental From the Insured's Standpoint

To be insurable, losses need to be unintentional and unexpected from the insured's perspective. If not for this requirement, moral hazards would be created and encouraged; if intentional losses were paid, premiums would skyrocket. As a direct result, fewer people would purchase insurance. This, in turn, would change the ability of companies to predict probabilities based on a large number of homogeneous units.

Insured Losses Must be Measurable and Determinable

To prevent fraud, insurance companies' policies state whether a loss is covered and how much will be paid for that loss. A loss must be both measurable and determinable as to reason, time, location, and price before accurate loss predictions can be made. Difficult risks to predict include flood, earthquake, and nuclear contamination. Losses that are difficult to measure and determine include sentimental value of property (such as the value of a family photograph) and cash losses. Although proving that a house or car existed and what each was worth is straightforward, proving how much cash one had on hand at the time a wallet is stolen is not as easy. Thus, insurers typically provide very limited coverage for losses of cash, while they readily pay for fire damage to houses and for theft of automobiles.

Losses Must Not Pose a Catastrophic Risk for the Insurer

Logically, an insurer cannot provide coverage against a loss that could cause financial insolvency. Dangerous risks for an insurer include those that are not accurately predictable and those that can cause damage to a significant portion of the insurer's pool.

Recall that insurable losses must be predictable and measurable. Otherwise, the insurer cannot accurately estimate the appropriate premium for the coverage. A war is an example of a risk that is not predictable. No statistical trend exists that can be used to determine future losses. For this reason, insurers virtually never provide coverage for war-related losses.

Another source of catastrophic risk for an insurer is any peril, such as a hurricane, that could cause loss to a significant portion of the insureds in the pool. Imagine the loss exposure faced by an insurer that sells property insurance only in Florida. With the hurricane risk faced by a large portion of that state, one massive storm could damage a significant portion of the insured's property. Compare this situation with an insurer that sells coverage in all 50 states and only a small portion of its business is in Florida. In this case, a hurricane in Florida would not be as financially devastating to the insurer.

THE LAW OF INSURANCE CONTRACTS

A contract is valid only if the legal system enforces the terms and conditions. Our legal system has established certain principles upon which insurance contracts are based and interpreted when claims or disputes arise.

Elements of a Valid Contract

The elements of a valid contract include the following:

- Offer and acceptance
- Legal competency of all parties
- Consideration
- Legal purpose

Offer and Acceptance

A valid contract exists only if based on the mutual assent, or the meeting of the minds of the contracting parties. Mutual assent consists of a valid offer made by one party and an acceptance of that offer by the other party. In most cases, an offer is made by the prospective insured to an insurer, via the agent, by filling out and signing an application that is accompanied by an initial premium. Next, the insurance company must decide whether to accept, make a counteroffer, or reject the offer. For a contract to become effective, the insurer or the agent acting on behalf of the company must accept the offer.

Legal Competency of All Parties

The law requires that both the offeror and offeree be legally competent. Most people are considered legally competent, so it is easier to explain which people are deemed legally incompetent. These may include insane persons, intoxicated persons, and minors. Those under age 18 are subject to special state provisions in order to provide a basis for competency.

Entering into a contract with someone who is incompetent is not specifically illegal; however, it may be inadvisable. This is because the contract is generally voidable at the option of the incompetent party once he becomes competent or once someone responsible for the incompetent party discovers the existence of the contract.

Suppose Joe, 16, buys a life insurance policy and pays premiums until he is 18 years old. If upon turning 18, Joe becomes legally competent, he may be able to void the contract on the grounds that he was not competent when he first entered into the contract. By voiding the contract, Joe is stating that he never wanted to be a part of it and is entitled to a refund of all premiums paid. Yet, had Joe died during the two years the policy was in force, the insurer would have been legally required to pay the death claim. Therefore, from the insurer's standpoint, entering into a contract with anyone who is not legally competent is ill-advised.

Consideration

Each party to a contract must provide something of value, known as *consideration*. Payment (or the promise of payment) of the first premium along with the statements made in the insurance application are generally consideration on the part of the insured. The insurer's consideration is the promise to pay losses covered by the policy and uphold the terms of the policy.

Legal Purpose

In a court of law, a contract deemed to have an illegal purpose, or a purpose that is against the public interest in general, is invalid. Any insurance contract that promotes actions contrary to the public interest is unenforceable. For example, an insurer will not pay the beneficiary of a life insurance policy if that beneficiary murdered the insured. To do so would encourage murder, which is illegal and against public policy. Recall that moral hazards are character flaws in persons who may intentionally create losses. They are willing to commit illegal acts to profit from insurance. If insurance policies did not eliminate coverage for illegal activities, they would encourage crime and, thus, be against public policy.

Legal Principles of Insurance Contracts

As a legally enforceable contract, a life insurance contract contains three legal principles.

The Principle of Indemnity

Insurance is a contract of indemnity, which means that a person is entitled to compensation only to the extent that a financial loss has occurred. Insurance exists only to indemnify a person's losses, not to place one in a better financial position than before the loss occurred. If an insured could profit from the perils covered by insurance policies, one would have an incentive to make sure those perils constantly occurred.

Principle of indemnity
A person is entitled to compensation only to the extent that financial loss has been suffered

In some cases, an insured will exaggerate an insurance claim violating the **principle of indemnity**. If the insured suffers a theft of a leather jacket purchased at a discount store for $100 yet tells the insurance company the jacket was a designer item that cost $1,000, and the insurer pays the claim without question, the insured has actually made a profit from the insurance, which is clearly a violation of the principle of indemnity and also an obvious moral hazard.

People fail to realize that any excessive money an insurance company pays for incurred losses will ultimately result in higher premiums being charged to everyone in the pool. As a result, even when insureds manage to violate the principle of indemnity without being caught, they are only taking money from themselves and others in the pool.

Subrogation clause
States that the insured cannot indemnify oneself from both the insurance company and a negligent third party for the same claim

One way insurers enforce the principle of indemnity is by including a subrogation clause in property and liability policies. The **subrogation clause** states that the insured cannot indemnify oneself from both the insurance company and a negligent third party for the same claim. If the insured collects against the policy, he then relinquishes the right to collect damages from the negligent party.

The Principle of Insurable Interest

Principle of insurable interest
To have an insurable interest, an insured must be subject to emotional or financial hardship resulting from damage, loss, or destruction

An insured must be subject to emotional or financial hardship resulting from damage, loss, or destruction of property in order to have an insurable interest. The **principle of insurable interest** as a legal principle is clearly congruent with the principle of indemnity. For example, if Susan is allowed to insure a building she does not own and has no financial interest in, she has every incentive to destroy the building.

In property and liability insurance, an insurable interest must be present both at the time of policy inception and at the time of loss. In the case of life insurance, an insurable interest is necessary only when the policy is issued. These rules exist in part because life insurance is a long-term contract, whereas property and liability contracts are short-term contracts, usually renewed at six-month or one-year intervals. To require a property owner to give up insurance on property one no longer owns does not impose a financial burden. On the other hand, the policyowner who insures a spouse for 20 years and then gets divorced might suffer a severe financial penalty and loss of investment if the policy were automatically terminated due to the loss of insurable interest.

The Principle of Utmost Good Faith

Principle of utmost good faith
Requires that the insured and the insurer both be forthcoming with all relevant facts about the insured risk and the coverage provided for that risk

Also known as the principle of fair dealing, the **principle of utmost good faith** requires that both the insured and the insurer be forthcoming with all relevant facts about the insured risk and the coverage provided for that risk. Recall that to have a binding contract, both a valid offer and a valid acceptance must be present, which together constitute mutual assent. Unless all pertinent facts are revealed by the insured in the application process, the insurer does not have a valid offer on which to base its acceptance. The same is true of any counteroffer the insurer might make to the insured before binding coverage.

Throughout the life of the insurance policy, it is presumed that both parties will tell each other the truth about all matters relevant to the contract. If this standard of honesty is not upheld, then the insured could commit insurance fraud (thus violating the principle of indemnity). Similarly, the insurer could refuse to pay claims for which the insured is legally entitled to receive compensation. The insurer is expected to comply with all terms of the contract and all provisions of the insurance law in the state(s) where it operates. The legal system recognizes three different areas of enforcement that apply to the insured:

1. Warranty
2. Representation
3. Concealment

Warranty
Promise made by the insured to the insurer that is part of the insurance contract to which the insurer must adhere

Warranty A **warranty** is merely a promise made by the insured to the insurer that is part of the insurance contract and, as such, must be adhered to. The promise can be that something is true when coverage is applied for (also called an affirmative warranty), or it can be a promise that the insured will or will not do something during the life of the policy (promissory warranty). Historically, any violation of a warranty was grounds for the contract being voided; however, most U.S. jurisdictions have determined that statements made on an application for insurance coverage are not affirmative warranties but are representations. The legal effects of representations are covered next.

The effect of a breach of a promissory warranty is much clearer and more severe. For example, a homeowner promises to purchase and maintain a security system for the home as part of the insurance contract. The homeowner decides to save money, so he disconnects the security service. If a burglary occurs three months later, the insurer likely will not have to pay the claim because a breach of a warranty is grounds for voiding a policy.

Representation
Statement made by the proposed insured to the insurer in the application process

Representation **Representations** are statements made by the proposed insured to the insurer in the application process. Material (relevant) misrepresentations give the insurer the right to void the policy once they are discovered. Why? Once again, mutual assent is a necessary element to any contract. If the proposed insured lied to the insurer during the application (offer) process, the insurer has not received a valid offer and mutual assent was never reached.

The misrepresentation must be material before the insurer may void the policy and ultimately deny payment of a claim. The test of materiality is simple: if the insurer had known the truth, would it have affected the insurer's underwriting decision to such an extent that the policy would not have been issued? For example, if Carmen states on her application for life insurance that she does not smoke when in fact she does, this misstatement definitely would have affected the insurer's underwriting decision. While coverage might have still been sold to Carmen, she would have been placed into a different underwriting class and, thus, charged a higher premium.

Now, suppose Carmen's life insurance application asked if she had ever been seen by a doctor for any medical condition over the past five years (which is a very vague question), and she answered, "No." In reality, she had been seen once a year for an annual check-up and was treated for the flu two years ago. If the insurer discovered the misrepresentation and wanted to void the policy, it would have to prove that knowing she had annual check-ups plus one case of the flu would have changed the underwriting decision. In reality, this type of routine medical treatment probably would not affect the underwriting decision, so the insurer would be barred from voiding the policy.

Concealment
When the insured is silent about a fact that is material to the risk

Concealment **Concealment** occurs when the insured is silent about a fact that is material to the risk. If an insured does not reveal material information that he knows and that is not specifically asked about, he has concealed that information. Contrast the notion of concealment with that of misrepresentation. A misrepresentation is an untruthful answer to a question, whereas concealment is not revealing a fact that is of importance to the insurer.

In practice, most insurers do not void coverage on the grounds of concealment because it is very difficult to prove. U.S. law requires the insurer to prove that the concealed information was important to the underwriting process and that the insured knew that it was important but intentionally kept it a secret. This is a very difficult standard of proof because the typical consumer has no way of knowing precisely what is or is not relevant to an underwriter's decision.

Legal Form

Although not required to be written, the form and content of an insurance contract are generally governed by state law. Each contract must be filed and approved by a state regulatory agency before the insurance policy may be sold in that state.

Adhesion
A characteristic of insurance that means insurance is a take-it-or-leave-it contract. The proposed insured must accept (or adhere to) the contract as written without any bargaining over the terms and conditions

Distinguishing Characteristics of Insurance Contracts

Adhesion

In most cases, two parties form a contract through the bargaining process. In insurance, however, this is not the case because insurance is a contract of **adhesion**. Adhesion means the insured must accept the contract as written without any bargaining over the terms and conditions. Most insurance companies today use standardized policy forms that may not be modified by the insurer to meet an individual need, and in the vast majority of cases, the proposed insured cannot bargain over the specific terms and conditions contained in the contract.

If the drafter of the contract (in this case, the insurer) leaves the contract ambiguous in any way, such ambiguities will be interpreted in favor of the person who was not allowed to bargain over the terms of the contract (in this case, the insured). This legal doctrine imposes a stringent burden on insurers to use very precise wording in their contractual products. The test of ambiguity is, "How would a reasonable layperson (not an insurance expert) interpret the contract?" If a court determines that a contractual provision is ambiguous to the average person, it will interpret the provision in a manner that is most favorable to the insured.

Aleatory

Aleatory
A characteristic of insurance meaning that monetary values exchanged by each party in an insurance agreement are unequal

Monetary values exchanged by each party to an insurance contract are commonly unequal. This is known as the **aleatory** feature of an insurance contract. While the insured pays a small premium, the insurer might ultimately have to pay a large dollar amount as the result of a claim. There have been a few cases, for example, when the insured died within a few days of the life insurance policy's issuance. Perhaps one $80 premium payment was made, yet the insurer had to pay a $250,000 death claim. On the other hand, an insured might pay premiums for years and never submit a claim, especially with homeowners or automobile insurance.

Unilateral

Unilateral
Only the insurer agrees to a legally enforceable promise

Insurance policies are unilateral contracts because only one party, the insurer, agrees to a legally enforceable promise to provide the coverages shown in the policy and to abide by all terms and conditions of the policy as long as the insured pays the premiums. On the other hand, the insured is not legally obligated to pay premiums. Although the insured must continue to pay premiums to keep the insurance protection in force, the insurer cannot legally force an insured to remain in the contract and to continue paying premiums.

Conditional

Conditional
Insurer is only obligated to compensate the insured if certain conditions are met

Every contract lists provisions or conditions that outline the duties of each party involved. An insurance policy is **conditional** in that the insurer is obligated to compensate the insured only if certain conditions are met. Therefore, every insured should carefully read and understand the conditions listed in a policy before the application is signed.

THE LAW OF AGENCY

Agents and Brokers

The financial planner should understand the relationship between insurers, insureds, agents, and brokers. Often clients will not be aware of potential conflicts of interest inherent in certain agent-insurer or broker-insurer relationships. The financial planner has a responsibility to make clients aware of these relationships and inform them of the various methods of obtaining recommended insurance coverage.

Agent
Legal representative of the insurer that has authority to enter into agreements on its behalf

Broker
Legal representative of the insured who can offer products from many insurers

General agent
An independent businessperson who represents only one insurer for a designated territory

Independent agent
An agent that represents multiple insurers

Surplus lines agent
An agent who is licensed to place coverage with nonadmitted insurers

An **agent** is a legal representative of the insurer and has authority to enter into agreements on its behalf. Agents are used by insurance companies as a marketing and sales tool. Types of agencies include general agencies, branch agencies, independent agencies, and surplus-lines agencies. In contrast, **brokers** are legal representatives of the insured and can offer products from many insurers. They are usually licensed to sell insurance products, which facilitates issuance of insurance policies.

A **general agent** is an independent businessperson who represents only one insurer in a designated territory. The general agent is responsible for hiring, training, and paying other agents to work under the supervision of the agency. The general agent is compensated by commissions received from the insurance company for sales produced by the agency, and the insurer may provide some financing for office expenses.

Insurance companies may also market their products via a branch office. The manager in charge of the office is an agent similar to a general agent with respect to duties and compensation, but the manager is an employee of the insurer rather than an independent contractor. The difference between the general agent and the branch manager would not be apparent to the public, and their relationship with insureds is identical.

Independent agents are insurance agents that represent multiple unrelated insurers. Conflicts of interest may arise in the independent agency system because commissions are based on the product line offered and which insurer writes the policy. Agents may have an incentive to sell products that offer higher commissions and may be under pressure to maintain a certain level of product sales offered by the insurance companies they represent in order to maintain a sales contract.

Sometimes the policy requested by a consumer is not available from any insurer that is licensed to do business in the state (an admitted insurer). In this situation, **surplus lines agents** will be employed. These agents have the authority to place business with non-admitted (out-of-state) insurers when the proper type of insurance is not available within the state.

Agency Relationships

Because brokers are representatives of the insured and not of the insurer, insurance companies are not bound by statements made by the broker to the insured. Disagreements will not involve the insurer. Instead, the broker and the insured will be the parties involved if legal controversy arises.

An agent, on the other hand, is designated by an insurance company as a legal representative. Thus, the insurer, known as the principal in the relationship, is generally responsible for statements made by the agent to the insured. The authority of an agent is derived from three sources: express authority, implied authority, and apparent authority.

Express authority
The actual authority an insurance company gives representatives (agents) via the agent's written contract

Implied authority
The authority that the public reasonably perceives the agent to possess, even without express authority

Express authority is the actual authority an insurance company gives representatives (agents) via the agent's written contract and involves powers that are explicitly given or denied to the agent by the insurer. Usually these are stated in the agency contract between the agent and the insurer. One typical power is the ability to solicit applicants for insurance products. Limits on the amount of insurance the agent can offer may be included in the contract as an additional restriction. The insurance company is responsible for the acts of its agents per express authority.

Implied authority is the authority that the public reasonably perceives the agent to possess, even without express authority. This type of authority gives the agent the power to perform any incidental act required in fulfilling the obligations of the agency agreement. For example, the agent may have an express authority to deliver policies to the insured. Accepting the first premium due under the policy would be an implied power of the agent. Under implied authority, an insurer is liable for the acts of an agent even if the agent knowingly misled the insured.

Apparent authority
The insured is led to believe that the agent has authority, either express or implied, where no such authority actually exists

Apparent authority is when the insured is led to believe that the agent has authority, either express or implied, where no such authority actually exists. The insurer may be liable for misrepresentations made by the agent even if it is unaware of such acts.

EXAMPLE An insurer may be liable for unauthorized actions of agents if the company was aware of their actions but did nothing to stop them. Apparent authority is based on this principle of estoppel. For example, an agent who has an insurer's logo on one's stationery and on the office's signage has the apparent authority to represent that insurer to the public. If the insurer withdraws the agent's authority but does not make certain the company's logo is removed from the stationery and the sign, the insurer could still be bound by the future actions of the agent.

IMPORTANT FEATURES OF INSURANCE CONTRACTS

Exclusions

Exclusions are a necessary part of every insurance contract because not every peril or property can be covered in every policy. Moreover, some items are simply uninsurable because they do not meet the requisites of an insurable risk.

The exclusions found in an insurance contract specifically outline items that will not be covered. The doctrine of concurrent causation makes it necessary for even a named perils policy to include numerous exclusions. Concurrent causation exists when a loss can be attributed to more than one peril. The law states that if at least one of the contributing perils is covered, the insurer must pay the entire loss. For example, while a named perils policy may cover fire, the insurer may not wish to cover fires that result from an earthquake. If the insurer does not specifically state that fires caused by earthquake are excluded from coverage, when an earthquake occurs and even a small fire results, the entire loss will have to be paid.

Insurers may exclude coverage for perils (e.g., war and flood), losses (the cost of a private hospital room when a semiprivate room is sufficient), or specific items of property (money over $200 and valuable papers are generally excluded from homeowners insurance coverage).

Riders and Endorsements

Riders (endorsements)
Written additions to an insurance contract that modify the original provisions

Riders and **endorsements** are two terms used interchangeably by the insurance industry to describe written additions to an insurance contract that modify the original provisions. They make it possible to slightly customize an insurance contract to fit an individual's needs by extending coverage, changing premiums, or making corrections to the policy that take precedence over any conflicting terms in the preprinted policy form.

Valuation of Insured Losses

Insurance policies must not only specify what is covered and excluded, but they must also explain how losses will be paid. Without valuation provisions in the policy, the insured and the insurer would have numerous disputes over how much a particular claim is worth.

For example, property insurance policies typically value losses in one of three ways:

1. Replacement cost
2. Actual cash value
3. Agreed-upon value

Replacement Cost

Replacement cost is the current cost of replacing property with new materials of like kind and quality. If, for example, a house were damaged by fire, the damaged carpet would be replaced with new carpet, even though the old carpet was somewhat worn and soiled. Replacement cost is often found by comparing what was once owned with what is currently on the market. Many homeowners policies have replacement cost provisions covering the dwelling and other structures.

Actual Cash Value (ACV)

Actual cash value
Calculated as replacement cost minus functional depreciation

Actual cash value is equal to replacement cost minus functional depreciation. For example, if the functional life of a roof is 20 years and it is destroyed after 5 years, the roof is assumed to be 25% depreciated at the time of the loss. The insurer would thus pay 75% of the roof's replacement cost if the policy valued losses on an ACV basis.

From the standpoint of a homeowner, ACV coverage can impose a serious financial burden if a severe loss occurs on older property. Replacement cost coverage is more often suggested, even though it is more expensive. Virtually all automobile policies use ACV, rather than replacement cost, because automobiles depreciate so rapidly. The cost of providing replacement cost coverage on autos would be too high for most consumers.

Agreed-Upon Value

Because valuing certain losses is so difficult, amounts paid for a loss are agreed upon by the insurer and the insured at the time a policy is issued. In writing this type of contract, no violation of the principle of indemnity occurs because the insurer will generally agree to a value that is reflective of the property's fair market value. Fine artwork and antiques are often insured under the valued policy principle. Life insurance is a valued policy because it is impossible to determine the precise value of a person's life objectively and/or calculate the replacement cost of a person.

Deductibles and Co-Payments

Deductible
A stated amount of money the insured is required to pay on a loss before the insurer will make any payments under the policy

Co-payments
In health insurance policies, amounts an insured must pay in addition to the deductible to receive certain covered services

A **deductible** is a stated amount of money the insured is required to pay on a loss before the insurer will make any payments under the policy. Deductibles help eliminate small claims, reduce premiums, and decrease morale hazards. Deductibles are used mainly in property, health, and automobile insurance contracts. Disability policies use an elimination period, which is a waiting period, measured in days, which must be satisfied before benefits become payable. This elimination period essentially acts as a time deductible.

Co-payments are nominal amounts an insured must pay to obtain certain covered services and are commonly used in health insurance policies. For example, an insured might have to pay a $10 co-payment for each visit to a doctor's office.

Coinsurance

Coinsurance
The percentage of financial responsibility the insured and the insurer must share under the policy

Coinsurance defines the percentage of financial responsibility that the insured and the insurer must share under the policy. As used in property insurance, coinsurance provisions encourage all insureds to cover their property for at least a stated percentage of the property's value or else suffer a financial penalty. Because the vast majority of property losses are partial, without coinsurance clauses, many insureds would attempt to save money on insurance by purchasing less insurance than the full value of their property. While underinsuring is not an illegal practice, it presents a problem for the underwriter and actuary who base expected loss estimates, and thus premiums, on the full value of the properties in the pool.

The amount paid on a property insurance claim with a coinsurance clause is determined by comparing several values. If the insured purchases coverage that meets or exceeds the coinsurance requirement (usually 80% of replacement value for homeowners insurance), payment on a claim for a loss will be the least of the face value of the policy, replacement cost, or actual expenditures (minus any deductible). However, if the insured purchases coverage that is less than the coinsurance requirement (e.g., 60% of the replacement value), then payment on a claim for a loss will be the greater of the actual cash value or the result of the following formula subject to the face value of the policy:

$$\frac{\text{Amount of coverage purchased}}{\text{Coinsurance requirement}} \times \text{Replacement cost}$$

EXAMPLE Nicholas owns a home with a replacement value of $300,000 and a depreciated actual cash value equal to 50% of the replacement value. He purchases $200,000 of insurance with a coinsurance requirement of 80%. If Nicholas experiences a $100,000 loss, the insurance company will pay the greater of:

$$\text{Actual cash value} = 50\% \times \$100{,}000 = \$50{,}000$$

or

$$\frac{\text{Amt purchased}}{\text{Coinsurance}} \times \text{Replacement cost} = \frac{\$200{,}000}{80\% \times \$300{,}000} \times \$100{,}000 = \$83{,}333$$

Because the coinsurance formula results in the greater value, Nicholas will receive $83,333 for his $100,000 loss (minus any deductible).

As used in medical insurance indemnity policies, coinsurance refers to the percentage paid by the insurer and the insured for claims after the deductible has been met and before the stop-loss limit is reached. For example, in a plan with 80/20 coinsurance, a $500 deductible, and a $1,000 stop-loss limit, the insured would pay 100% of costs until the $500 deductible was reached. After the first $500 in claims, the insured would pay 20% of costs until claims reached $5,500 ($1,000 stop-loss ÷ 20% coinsurance + $500 deductible) and then 0%. The insurance company would be responsible for 100% of all further covered claims during that policy period.

INDIVIDUAL LOSS EXPOSURES AND INSURANCE COVERAGES

Perils That Can Reduce and/or Eliminate the Ability to Earn Income

The three main types of pure risk that can interrupt one's earned income stream are dying too soon, living too long, and disability.

Dying Too Soon

The risk of a person dying before reaching full life expectancy is known as premature death. In most cases, a person who dies prematurely has a number of potential financial obligations, including a family to support, a mortgage to pay, and children to send through college. To prevent economic upheaval for surviving dependents, proper financial and estate planning using life insurance will provide for dependents in the event of the premature death of an income producer.

Living Too Long

While it may sound ridiculous to say that someone lived "too long," the risk of outliving one's financial resources (called *superannuation*) exists. Medical and technological advances have led to substantial increases in human life expectancy. Currently, the average person retiring at age 65 is expected to live another 20 years. Approximately 50% of all retirees will live beyond the average life expectancy of 20 years. How does one guarantee that savings and other assets will last until death? Various financial planning products make it possible to ensure that one does not outlive one's assets.

Disability

An unexpected accident or illness may result in high medical costs along with the inability to work and earn income. The cost of medical treatment continues to rise at a rate that exceeds general inflation. The cost of providing a lifetime of medical care, while simultaneously being unable to earn an income, can be astronomical. Long-term disability insurance can be used to mitigate this risk.

Perils That Can Destroy or Deplete Existing Assets

Along with earned income, various assets such as cash, real estate, and automobiles are acquired throughout one's lifetime. Even if the individual's ability to earn income is never hindered, financial loss could result if existing assets are destroyed or lost. The two main exposures that exist in this category are damage to property and legal liability for injuries inflicted upon others.

Damage to Property

A host of perils threaten an individual's property, including natural disasters, crimes, and careless accidents. The financial consequences of these perils and their resulting damage can be severe.

Damage to property can result in one of two types of financial losses: direct and indirect. A direct loss is an immediate result of an insured peril. The cost of repairing fire damage to one's house is a direct loss. An indirect loss occurs as a result of a direct property loss. The types of expenses that are incurred as indirect losses are numerous. If a section of a fire-damaged house is being rented out, the lost rent due to the property being uninhabitable is an example of an indirect loss. In addition, the family also has to pay for the cost of hotel accommodations until the house can be repaired, which is another indirect loss resulting from the fire damage. If the hotel does not accept pets, the family will have to pay a kennel or other boarding facility to keep the pets until the home is repaired. All of these expenses add up quickly and can easily exceed the cost of the direct property loss.

Legal Liability for Injuries Inflicted Upon Others

Under the U.S. legal system, one is held legally liable if one causes bodily injury or property damage to another. Personal savings and other assets can be seized to pay for legal liability.

Liability risk is especially dangerous from a financial standpoint because there is no upper limit on the amount of loss one can suffer. Consider the physician who treats 20 to 40 patients each day. If one of those patients is injured as a result of the doctor's malpractice, and a court finds the doctor guilty of malpractice, the injured patient might be awarded millions of dollars in damages. In addition to the damages claimed by the injured party, the insured also suffers another loss: the cost of settling or defending lawsuits. A person found to be free of causing an injury could still have enormous legal bills.

CHARACTERISTICS OF INSURANCE COMPANIES

Types of Ownership

Stock Insurance Company

Stock insurance company
Operate for-profit and owned by stockholders

A **stock insurance company** is operated for profit and is owned by stockholders who purchase shares of the insurance company. The capital received provides funding for operating expenses until premiums and investment earnings are sufficient. Stockholders receive a return on their investment through dividends and capital appreciation of the shares of the company. The board of directors, whose members are elected by the shareholders, declares dividends at its discretion.

Mutual Insurance Company

Mutual insurance company
Owned by policyholders and distributes profit in the form of policy dividends

In contrast to stock insurance companies, **mutual insurance companies** are owned by the policyholders. Most mutual insurance companies operate in the same manner as stock insurance companies and distribute profits in the form of policy dividends to policyholders.

Insurance Underwriting

Underwriters
Classify proposed insureds in a way as to adequately protect the insurance company from adverse selection

To combat the difficulty with loss prediction, especially dealing with adverse selection, insurance companies employ underwriters. **Underwriters** classify proposed insureds in a way as to adequately protect the insurance company from adverse selection. Actuaries develop rates that can be translated into insurance premiums based on particular risk characteristics. The underwriter decides which risk characteristics describe the individual or group applying for coverage. After determining relevant risk exposures, the underwriter will designate the prospect as insurable or uninsurable according to company guidelines. If the potential insured is deemed insurable, the underwriter will determine the appropriate premium to charge based on the actuarial table and level of risk associated with the insured.

Reinsurance

Reinsurance provides sharing of risk across two or more insurance providers. With reinsurance, a company can reduce the exposure to risk of catastrophic loss that could result in insolvency. One method of reinsurance is excess-loss. Under this method, the reinsurer is liable for losses that exceed a specified limit, thereby protecting the original insurer from large claims. The reinsurer will receive premiums from many policies but will likely have only a few claims. Many firms that self-insure for employer-provided health insurance reinsure using the excess-loss method.

EXAMPLE Company A is willing to expose itself to a maximum of $500,000 of risk (retention limit). Reinsurer B accepts the risk in excess of Company A's $500,000 retention limit. For acceptance of the excess risk, Reinsurer B receives a premium from Company A.

Insurance Regulation

Insurance regulation is intended to create and maintain a market that prevents insurers from placing themselves at risk of insolvency or engaging in abusive market behavior. Historically, the insurance industry has been regulated by state governments. In 1945, with the passage of the McCarran-Ferguson Act, regulation of insurance companies was explicitly given to the states.

Each state has an insurance regulator, often known as the Commissioner, or Administrator, of Insurance, who is either appointed by the governor or elected by registered voters. The Commissioner oversees the execution of state laws related to the insurance industry. Among the Commissioner's duties are licensing insurance agents and companies, approving proposed rate changes, investigating consumer complaints, reviewing insurance forms, and regularly auditing insurance companies to ensure solvency.

National Association of Insurance Commissioners (NAIC)

The National Association of Insurance Commissioners (NAIC) is a voluntary association of the insurance regulators of the 50 states, the District of Columbia, and the four U.S. territories (American Samoa, Guam, Puerto Rico, and the Virgin Islands). The purpose of the NAIC is not to serve as a regulatory body but instead to provide a common forum of interaction for matters that transcend the states. The association exists as a collaborative effort to increase the effectiveness of insurance regulation through the development of common standards, practices, and model legislation.

NAIC Criteria

The NAIC provides assistance to the states' solvency efforts in numerous ways. Among these are uniform statutory financial reporting requirements, solvency screening through financial analysis systems and peer review, and the subsequent reporting of deficiencies to regulatory officials. The NAIC examines all insurers' financial conditions on site and assists with regulatory action when an insurer's financial condition fails to meet established standards.

Risk-Based Capital Model Act The NAIC established a regulatory capital framework for insurance companies when it introduced the Risk-Based Capital Model Act. States that have adopted the act require insurance companies to file annual reports detailing the following risks:

- Risks associated with assets of the insurer
- Risks associated with adverse experience of the insurer related to liabilities and obligations (underwriting risk)
- Interest rate risk associated with the insurer's business (for life insurance products)
- Other relevant business risks as outlined in the RBC instructions

Risk-based capital model (RBCM)
Adjusts an insurer's capital base according to the amount and types of risk to which it is exposed

The **risk-based capital model (RBCM)** adjusts an insurer's capital base according to the amount and types of risk to which it is exposed. Risk-based capital ratios are measured against minimum established guidelines. If four or more of these ratios fall outside the minimum guidelines, regulatory action may be required.

Regulatory action involves either an attempted rehabilitation or declaration of the insurance company's insolvency. A state insurance department is authorized to take over, or seize, an insurance company if the state can show to the applicable state court that the insurer will be unable to meet its contractual obligations to policyholders.

SELECTING AN INSURANCE COMPANY

Several rating agencies specialize in the financial assessment of insurers. Due to recent financial crises encountered by some insurers, the evaluations of these companies have become more and more important to consumers. The ratings of these agencies reflect their opinions of the insurance companies' financial condition and their ability to meet their obligations to policyowners.

The financial stability of an insurance company is essential for all types of insurance. These ratings may be of greater significance to life insurance policy-owners due to the long-term nature of the life insurance contract. Policyowners need to be concerned with financial stability for obvious investment reasons, and, as a professional, the financial planner should be diligent when recommending insurance products.

Rating Agencies

Four major private rating agencies evaluate the financial condition of insurers and make their ratings available to the public. The examined elements of the insurance companies vary between the rating companies and include recent performance, financial statements, leverage, and management stability. External factors such as competition, diversification, and market presence may also be considered. Each organization provides a description of its analysis and defines its rating scores (see Exhibit 8.1).

A.M. Best, Inc., has been providing ratings for insurance companies since 1899. Specializing in insurance companies, it is the largest and longest-established company devoted to issuing in-depth reports and financial-strength ratings.

Fitch Investors Service, Inc., provides credit opinions for over 800 insurance companies.

Moody's Investors Service is a source for credit ratings, research, and the risk analysis of thousands of companies, including insurers. Generally, Moody's analyzes the financial condition of a company at its request, using internal and external information. The company also rates some companies with only available public information.

Standard & Poor's Corporation provides two types of ratings. Claims-paying ability ratings are issued by request of a company. There is a cost to the requesting company for this service. Qualified solvency ratings are issued using public information only and are free of charge.

When purchasing insurance products, the consumer ideally will use a company that has received a top-tier rating from the majority of the agencies. For safety's sake, any company that has received a low-tier rating from any of the agencies should be avoided.

EXHIBIT 8.1 Insurer Ratings

Rating Service	Ratings (from highest to lowest)
A.M. Best	A++ through S
Standard & Poor's	AAA through D
Moody's	Aaa through C
Fitch Ratings	AAA through D

Additional Considerations

Besides agency financial ratings, consumers should also consider the following when deciding on an insurance provider:

- Asset size and age of the company
- Track record
- Financial operating ratios
- Lapse ratio—percentage of policies that are terminated each year
- Average policy size
- Product lines offered
- Average investment returns
- Form of ownership

THE RISK MANAGEMENT PROCESS

Risk management is a systematic process for identifying, evaluating, and managing pure risk exposures faced by a firm or individual. The six steps in the risk management process include:

1. determining the objectives of the risk management program;
2. identifying the risks to which the company or individual is exposed;
3. evaluating the identified risks as to the probability of outcome and potential loss;
4. determining alternatives for managing risks and selecting the most appropriate alternative for each risk;
5. implementing a risk management plan based on the selected alternatives; and
6. periodically evaluating and reviewing the risk management program.

Determining the Objectives of the Risk Management Program

The first step in the risk management process is determining the goals of the risk management program. Unfortunately, this step in the process is one of the most ignored. Due to vague risk management objectives, many parts of a client's risk management program are not cohesive. Risk management objectives can range from obtaining the most cost-effective protection against risk to continuing income after a loss.

Identifying the Risk Exposures

The next step is to identify all possible pure risk exposures of the client. Though it is difficult to generalize risks that companies face due to differences in structure and conditions, potential exposures mirror those described for individuals. Businesses, of course, are concerned with damage to existing assets and any perils that might interrupt their ability to generate income. As most businesses generate income through the efforts of their personnel, risk managers are also concerned with the recruitment, selection, hiring, training, health, and welfare of personnel.

For a corporate risk manager to identify the risks that the company faces, one must delve into the operations of the firm. Some common methods of research are physical inspection, risk analysis questionnaires, flow process charts, review of financial statements, and reports on past losses.

For the individual consumer, identifying risks is a somewhat simpler process. Analyzing and valuing the properties owned or leased, recognizing activities that could result in injuries to others, and determining how to protect one's ability to generate an income are all reasonably straightforward activities.

Evaluating the Identified Risks

Loss frequency
Expected number of losses that will occur within a given period

Loss severity
Potential size or damage of a loss

The next logical step in the risk management process is to evaluate the potential frequency and severity of losses. **Loss frequency** is the expected number of losses that will occur within a given period. **Loss severity** refers to the potential size or damage of a loss. By identifying loss frequency and severity, a risk manager can prioritize the urgency of dealing with each specific risk.

Recall that probability is useful when applied to large numbers. Relying solely on probability-based predictions for an individual, however, is not recommended. Of greater concern to the individual is the potential severity of the losses that occur. The person who owns a $200,000 home has a maximum possible severity of loss on that asset equal to $200,000. This would be, for the vast majority of consumers, a high severity loss. On the other hand, the person who owns a car worth $1,500 has a fairly low severity loss potential. To the particular person, the $1,500 loss might lead to significant averse consequences, however, and could possibly affect income generation if he could no longer drive to work.

Determining and Selecting the Best Risk Management Alternative

Insurance is neither necessary, nor is it even available, for every risk of loss an individual faces. Choosing the appropriate risk management tool depends largely on the potential severity and frequency of encountered loss exposures. Where more than one tool is deemed appropriate, the costs and benefits of each should be examined to determine which is most economical and beneficial.

As discussed earlier, there are generally four ways to manage a risk: avoidance, reduction, retention, or transference. How does one know the best risk management technique for a particular risk? Exhibit 8.2, based on the frequency and severity of expected losses, can be used as a general guideline for selecting an appropriate risk management tool.

EXHIBIT 8.2 Risk Management Guidelines

	High Frequency	Low Frequency
High Severity	Avoidance	Insurance
Low Severity	Retention/Reduction	Retention

The first type of loss exposure is a combination of high severity and high frequency. This is perhaps the most serious type of exposure and is often handled by avoidance. Assume John applies for the position of chauffeur for Divine Limousine Company. He has previously been arrested for miscellaneous misdemeanors and convicted twice for driving while intoxicated. Clearly, John is an unsafe driver and hiring him as an employee creates potential liability for Divine Limousine. Therefore, Divine Limousine should avoid this exposure by not hiring John.

Exposures that are low in frequency and high in potential severity are best handled by insurance. The high-severity losses can leave a person in a dire financial position, yet their low frequency makes sharing the cost of losses with others economically feasible. Examples of high-severity/low-frequency loss exposures include fire damage to a house and a loss due to an automobile collision.

The remaining types of losses are both low severity in nature. Transferring low-severity losses to an insurer is not economically feasible because the insurer will have substantial expenses associated with processing numerous small claims. The risk of low-severity losses is generally retained. When low-severity losses occur with high frequency, their aggregate impact can have financially devastating effects. Thus, it is suggested that high-frequency, low-severity losses are retained and controlled in an effort to reduce frequency. For an individual, low-severity losses include dings on cars, road-damaged tires, and minor injuries and illnesses.

Implementing a Risk Management Plan Based on the Selected Alternatives

The risk management plan must reflect the chosen response to risk. If risk reduction is the appropriate response to a given risk, the proper risk reduction program must be designed and implemented. If a decision is made to retain a risk, the individual or company must determine whether a reserve fund will be used. If the response to a given risk is to transfer the risk through insurance, an assessment and selection of an insurer are usually followed by planning meetings and the purchase of appropriate insurance products.

Periodically Evaluating and Reviewing the Risk Management Program

The purpose of periodic evaluation and review is twofold. First, the risk management process does not take place independent of external influences. Circumstances change over time along with risk exposures. The risk management technique that was most suitable last year may not be the most prudent solution this year, and adjustments may have to be made to the plan. Second, errors in judgment may occur and periodic reviews allow the risk manager to discover these errors and revise the risk management plan as needed.

WHERE ON THE WEB

A.M. Best, Inc. **www.ambest.com**

Fitch Ratings Insurance Group **www.fitchratings.com**

Independent Insurance Agents and Brokers of America **www.independentagent.com**

Insurance Information Institute **www.iii.org**

Investor Desktop **www.investordesktop.com**

Moody's Investors Service **www.moodys.com**

National Association of Insurance Commissioners **www.naic.org**

Property Casualty Insurers Association of America **www.pciaa.net**

Standard & Poor's **www.standardandpoors.com**

DISCUSSION QUESTIONS

1. What is risk?
2. What are the different types of risk, and how does each impact the personal financial planning process?
3. What is the difference between subjective and objective risk?
4. Name the common responses to risk. For which of the response(s) is insurance an appropriate risk management tool?
5. How does a peril differ from a hazard, and how does each relate to the need for insurance?
6. What is adverse selection, and how does it affect the insurance contract?
7. What are the requisites for an insurable risk, and what distinguishes insurance from gambling?
8. What are the elements of a valid contract? What distinguishing features do insurance contracts possess?
9. What are the reasons for and the effects of various contractual features in insurance contracts?
10. What is the principle of indemnity?
11. What is the principle of insurable interest?
12. What is a contract of adhesion?
13. Distinguish between an agent and a broker.
14. Differentiate between a general agent, an independent agent, and a surplus lines agent.
15. Describe the various types of agent authority.
16. What are the insurable loss exposures faced by the typical individual consumer?
17. What are the various insurance company rating agencies? Describe each.
18. What are the steps in the risk management process?
19. How do frequency of loss and severity of loss affect risk management?

EXERCISES

1. Briefly explain the difference between pure and speculative risk. Give an example.
2. Name three perils that could cause a loss around a home or apartment. What are the hazards that may increase the probability of these perils?
3. Explain the difference between moral hazard and morale hazard. Give two examples of each.
4. Differentiate between gambling and insurance.
5. How would an insurer reduce or manage the risk of adverse selection in a group dental insurance program?
6. John has an insurance policy for $150,000 on a building located at 175 Pine Street. The policy expires December 31, 2022. John sold the property to Bill on October 31, 2022, for $150,000. That very night, the building burned to the ground. Can John collect on the policy? If so, how much? If not, what legal characteristics would prevent him from collecting? Will John get any money from the insurer?
7. Which of the following people have an insurable interest in Mike's life?
   A. Angel, Mike's 25-year-old daughter
   B. James, Mike's 30-year-old son
   C. Cassie, Mike's ex-wife and Angel's mother
   D. John, Mike's employer
   E. Donna, Mike's daughter-in-law
   F. Scott, Mike's business partner
   G. Rita, Mike's fiancée
8. Leon is the risk manager for ABC, Inc. He has evaluated the following risks in terms of frequency and severity and asks your opinion as to which risk management tool(s) to use:

		Probability/ Frequency	Severity per Occurrence
A.	Fire destroys factory	0.0001	$10,000,000
B.	Loss of property through employee theft	0.1	$1,000
C.	On-the-job employee disability	0.01	$1,500,000
D.	Loss due to misplaced inventory (computer)	0.1	$2,000
E.	Loss due to failure to reduce energy bill (lights off, air conditioner off on weekends)	0.02	$400
F.	Air conditioning unit failure (compressor)	0.01	$2,000

CHAPTER 9

Managing Life, Health, and Disability Risks

LEARNING OBJECTIVES

After learning the material in this chapter, you will be able to do the following:

- Identify the risks associated with premature death
- Measure the needs related to premature death
- Determine disability income and long-term care needs
- List and define the various types of term life insurance
- List and define the various types of whole life insurance
- List and define the various types of universal life insurance
- Distinguish between term, whole life, and universal life insurance, and explain their advantages and disadvantages
- List and define the various types of annuities

- Explain the differences between annuities and life insurance contracts
- Describe the important policy provisions and contractual features of life and annuity contracts
- Understand the taxation of life insurance and annuities
- Be familiar with important policy provisions and major contractual features of individual health coverage
- Discuss health savings accounts (HSAs) and high-deductible health plans (HDHPs)
- Describe the important policy provisions and contractual features of long-term care insurance
- Describe the important policy provisions and major contractual features of individual health and disability coverage
- List and describe the primary types of employer-provided group health and disability coverage
- Be familiar with the history of managed care and understand today's prevalent methods of health care delivery
- Explain how group health coverage may be continued or transferred when employment terminates
- List and describe the primary types of employer-provided health and disability coverage
- Discuss the various business uses of life insurance
- Describe the types of nonqualified benefits often provided to key employees of a company
- Be familiar with other employee benefits, such as Section 125 plans, flexible spending accounts, fringe benefits, voluntary employee benefit associations (VEBAs), and prepaid legal services

INTRODUCTION

Life, health, and disability risks include premature death, catastrophic illness, the inability to work, and the need for long-term care. Although these risks are generally low in frequency, they are potentially catastrophic in severity. Thus, the financial planner must assist the client in mitigating the impact of these risks by selecting and implementing appropriate insurance coverage. This chapter examines each of the above catastrophic risks and describes insurance products, particularly life and health insurance, that can mitigate those risks.

Life insurance is a fundamental element in a comprehensive financial plan for most clients, particularly those with dependents. The financial planner should be familiar with each type of life insurance in order to identify and meet client needs.

Health insurance is crucial for each member of the family because an uninsured illness can disrupt income security and reduce personal wealth. Therefore, the financial planner needs to be familiar with major medical insurance, disability insurance, and long-term care insurance.

IDENTIFYING RISKS ASSOCIATED WITH PREMATURE DEATH

Predicting the timing of a person's death may be impossible, but protecting the survivors against the financial distress they can suffer from the loss of an income provider is possible. The purchase of life insurance is one of the most effective methods of protecting against the financial consequences of an untimely death. Financial planners must be able to recognize and quantify two fundamental needs for the capital generated by a life insurance policy: replacing income and preserving assets.

Inadequate Financial Resources

The loss of an income producer may have a significant financial impact on the surviving dependent family members, which can be addressed by using life insurance proceeds.

Providing Income for the Readjustment Period

When a breadwinner dies, the family's income diminishes, and, as a result, the surviving family members likely experience a lower standard of living. Ultimately, the family may adjust the standard of living to fit the new income level, or other family members may be able to work to replace the lost income of the deceased. Moreover, a family usually encounters an unsettling and emotionally stressful readjustment period after the loss of a loved one. The surviving spouse and other dependents will require time to process grief and resume their lives. In some situations, a surviving spouse may have to be re-educated and trained to enter the workforce for the first time. Life insurance paid directly to the family members or heirs of one's estate can replace lost income and provide for the family's financial support during this period of readjustment.

Providing Financial Support for Dependents

When an income producer has dependents, the dependents' financial well-being is the major concern. The mother who is the sole support for her children concerns herself with how their financial needs will be met if she dies prematurely. A life insurance policy guarantees that when the insured dies, a certain amount of money will be available to support her dependents.

When considering how much money is required for this particular life insurance need, a number of questions must be addressed. First, who actually qualifies as a dependent? For income tax purposes, most people are able to claim only children as dependents. However, other people may be financially dependent on the insured, such as the insured's parents who are elderly and on a fixed income and a spouse who either does not work outside the home or does not earn enough income to survive without the insured's wages. Responsible financial planning considers the needs of all dependents, not just those of minor children.

Secondly, how much financial support should be given to the various dependents? Should dependent children be supported until they are 18 years old, or should they be supported until they complete college? What standard of living does the insured wish to guarantee for survivors? Many questions must be answered before the insured can determine how much life insurance to purchase and maintain.

Earmarking Funds for Specific Goals

In addition to providing survivors with income, insureds may also wish to provide survivors with funds to achieve specific goals, such as paying off a mortgage or providing funds for the education expenses of each child.

Estate Preservation

People work throughout their lives to accumulate wealth. A common fear shared by many people is that their assets will be depleted by the time they die. The following types of postmortem expenses that are imposed upon surviving dependents validate this concern.

Funeral Expenses

Each person has specific preferences about how one's body should be handled after death, such as cremation, burial, being placed in a mausoleum, and even having the body donated to medical science. In fact, some of the choices can be very costly. The final ceremonies or services held for the deceased person, whether they include a simple memorial service or an elaborate funeral, must also be paid. These costs vary according to the decedent's preferences and are normally much higher than expected. When determining the amount of life insurance to carry, disposal and ceremonial expenses should always be taken into consideration.

Probate Expenses

After death, a person's estate normally goes through probate court for final settlement of most financial matters. The probate process provides for the distribution of the deceased's assets that fall within the terms of the decedent's will and for payment of debts. Life insurance proceeds may be used to expedite the prompt settlement of a person's probate estate, including the payment of court costs, taxes, and outstanding debts.

Taxes

During the probate process, federal and state estate taxes, accrued property taxes, and federal and state income taxes for the current year, as well as any back taxes due, will be collected by the appropriate agencies. If cash is not available to pay these taxes, assets may have to be liquidated to satisfy the debts. Life insurance can provide the cash necessary to satisfy the tax liabilities.

Debt Retirement

Most people die with outstanding debts such as credit card balances, unpaid bills, student loans, and automobile loans. A fund may be established to retire some or all of a decedent's debts.

MEASURING NEEDS RELATED TO PREMATURE DEATH

Generally, the following three methods are used to determine the financial needs related to premature death:

1. The human life value approach
2. The financial needs approach
3. The capital retention approach

Human Life Value Approach

Human life value approach
Uses projected future earnings as the basis for measuring life insurance needs

The **human life value (HLV) approach** uses projected future earnings as the basis for measuring life insurance needs. The HLV approach projects the individual's income throughout his remaining work life expectancy. Then, using an appropriate discount rate, the present value of the future earnings is determined. Note that cash flows are adjusted downward by amounts that would have otherwise been used for personal consumption and for the payment of taxes on income. The net amount is known as the FSE (family's share of earnings).

EXAMPLE Alex, who is married and the father of four, is age 45 and expects to work to age 65. He earns $70,000 per year and expects annual salary increases of 5%. Alex expects inflation to be 4% over his working life. His personal consumption is equal to 10% of after-tax earnings, and his combined federal and state marginal tax bracket is 20%.

Step 1 Calculate the family's share of earnings (FSE).

Annual earnings	=	$70,000
Annual taxes	=	$70,000 × .20 = $14,000
Personal consumption	=	(After-tax income × consumption %)
	=	[($70,000 – $14,000) × .10)]
	=	($56,000 × .10)
	=	$5,600

FSE = Annual earnings – (annual taxes + annual personal consumption)
= $70,000 – ($14,000 + $5,600)
= $70,000 – $19,600
= **$50,400**

Step 2 Calculate work life expectancy (WLE).

WLE = Expected age of retirement – current age
= 65 – 45
= 20 years

Step 3 Calculate the future value of the family share of earnings (FSE) over Alex's work life expectancy (WLE).

PMT	=	–$50,400
i	=	5%
n	=	20
FV	=	$1,666,524

Step 4 Determine the human life value (HLV).

FV = $1,666,524
i = 4%
n = 20
PV = $760,580 = HLV

Financial needs approach
Evaluates the income replacement needs of one's survivors in the event of untimely death

Financial Needs Approach

The **financial needs approach** evaluates the income replacement and lump-sum needs of survivors in the event of an income producer's untimely death. The effect of inflation over the years is taken into consideration when using this approach.

A family that loses an income producer is likely to have the following common needs:

Lump-sum (cash) needs	Income (cash flow) needs
Final expenses and debts	Readjustment period
Mortgage liquidation or payment fund	Dependency period
Education expenses	Spousal life income (pre- and post-retirement)
Emergency expenses	

Income (Cash Flow) Needs

The deceased's survivors are accustomed to a particular lifestyle. Most breadwinners will want to make sure that their dependents will not suffer a decrease in their standard of living.

Final Expenses and Debts

Final expense fund
Fund requiring immediate access by survivors to pay for final expenses and debts of the decedent

A fund for final expenses and debts, commonly known as a **final expense fund**, is needed immediately by the survivors, to pay for a deceased's out-of-pocket medical expenses prior to death, funeral costs, and other unplanned expenditures. Estate administration expenses, federal estate taxes, state death taxes, inheritance taxes, and income taxes must also be funded from a source outside the estate, such as a loan, if no liquid assets are in the estate to cover the costs.

Mortgage Liquidation or Payment Fund

The family may choose to set aside funds to pay off an existing mortgage at the time of the breadwinner's death. If no mortgage prepayment penalty exists, this can be an effective way to reduce the cash flow needs of the surviving family members. A fund may also be established from which monthly mortgage payments are made, as it may be advantageous for the surviving spouse to utilize the annual mortgage interest deduction for income purposes. In some respects, there is an offsetting effect. If a client chooses to pay off the mortgage, life insurance proceeds will be required to cover that. However, if the mortgage is paid off, the ongoing monthly financial need is less, which will require less capital for the future. The reverse is also true. Maintaining the mortgage lowers the amount of life insurance needed earlier. However, it raises the monthly income need and thus can increase the life insurance need for ongoing monthly expenses. In all, a planner needs to help the client find a solution that matches her unique circumstances.

Education Expenses

If an education funding plan is not in place, funds may be set aside for private or secondary school and for college and postcollege education. If the survivors choose not to set aside funds, and education expenses will occur in the future, these expenses should be factored into the life income needed by the family.

Emergency Expenses

The purpose of this fund is to provide survivors with a cash reserve for unforeseen expenses that may arise as the family makes a transition to life without the deceased.

Readjustment Period Income Needs

Readjustment period
The period of time that lasts for one to two years following the death of a breadwinner

The **readjustment period** typically lasts for one to two years following the death of a breadwinner. During this period, the family should receive approximately the same amount of income it received while the deceased was alive. Families will usually have certain nonrecurring expenses as they adjust to a new lifestyle. For a family that will experience a decline in its standard of living, this period income allows the family to achieve the necessary readjustment.

Dependency Period Income Needs

Dependency period
The period of time during which others (the deceased's spouse, children and, in some cases, parents) would have been dependent on the deceased

The **dependency period** is one in which others (the deceased's spouse, children, and, in some cases, parents) would have been dependent on the deceased. In most cases, income needs are largest during this period. The length of the dependency period is determined by the number of dependents, their ages, and the deceased's contribution to the family's total income.

Spousal Lifetime Income Needs

At some point, the children will no longer be dependent upon the surviving spouse; however, the surviving spouse may still need to replace a part of the wage earner's income, especially if the spouse does not work outside the home. Surviving spouses who reenter the workforce after years at home may often find it difficult to find employment that enables them to maintain the prior standard of living. Therefore, arranging a lifetime income for the surviving spouse may be advisable.

Blackout period
The period of time beginning when Social Security benefits to the surviving spouse are discontinued (usually when the last child reaches age 16) and ending when the spouse begins to receive Social Security retirement benefits at age 60 or later

Two income periods should be considered: (1) the **blackout period** and (2) the period during which the surviving spouse receives Social Security benefits. The blackout period refers to the period of time beginning when survivor Social Security benefits to the spouse are discontinued (usually when the last child reaches age 16) and ending when the spouse begins to receive Social Security retirement benefits at age 60 or later. During the blackout period, income must be provided by employment, insurance, investments, or some other source. Once Social Security benefits resume, the amount of supplemental income may be reduced.

If both spouses earned an income prior to death, a smaller percentage of total family income must be replaced upon one of the spouse's deaths. If, however, the sole breadwinner of the family has died, the ability (or desire) of the surviving spouse to secure employment must be considered.

In most cases, the children of the deceased will be entitled to Social Security benefits (see Chapter 11, Social Security benefits). The benefits received by the spouse, as caretaker of the children and on behalf of the children, will decrease the income needs of the family during the dependency period. In addition, if parents were dependents of the deceased, any Social Security benefits received by them as a result of the death of their adult child may also decrease their income needs during the period.

EXAMPLE Assume Frank is a consultant who earns $72,000 annually. His spouse, Julie, is a homemaker, and they have one child, Betty. Frank is covered by a $200,000 life insurance policy. The couple assumes an average annual inflation rate of 3%.

Frank and Julie have set the following goals and assumptions:

Income needed—readjustment period (one year)	$ 72,000/yr
Income needed—dependency period	$ 48,000/yr
Income needed—"empty nest" period	$ 36,000/yr
Estate expenses and debts	$ 15,000
Education fund needed (in today's dollars)	$180,000
Emergency fund	$ 15,000
Investment assets (cash/cash equivalents)	$100,000
Julie's life expectancy	85 years
Discount rate	6%

Given the information provided, how much life insurance should Frank purchase?

Step 1 Calculate the family's income (cash flow) needs for each period.

	Readjustment (1 year)	Child's Age (4–16)	Child's Age (17–18)	Blackout Period (Age 46–60)	Retirement (25 years)
Annual income needed	$72,000	$48,000	$48,000	$36,000	$36,000
OASDI (Social Security)	26,400	26,400	10,800	0	18,000
Net annual income needed (PMT)	45,600	21,600	37,200	36,000	18,000
Inflation-adjusted interest rate $i = \left(\frac{1.06}{1.03} - 1\right) \times 100 =$	2.9126	2.9126	2.9126	2.9126	2.9126
Years needed	1	11	2	15	25
PV of net annual income needed (use begin mode)	$45,600	$206,677	$73,347	$445,092	$325,730
PV of total annual income needed: $1,096,446					

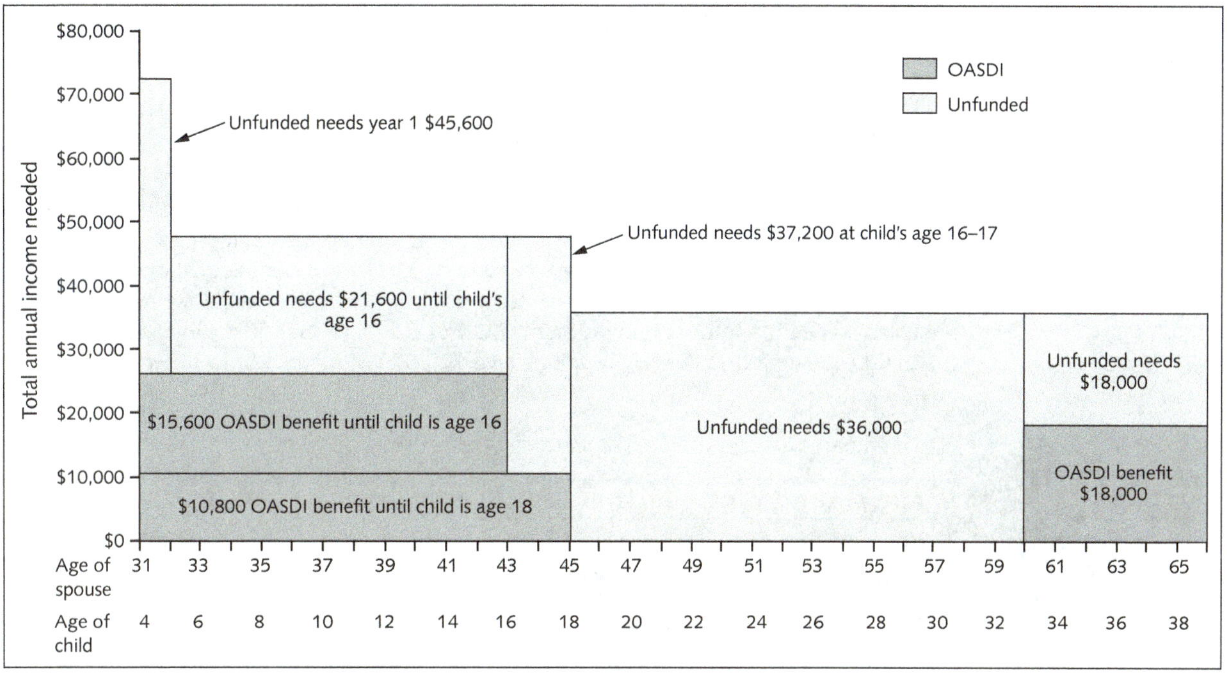

Step 2 Calculate the family's lump-sum funding needs.

Final expenses and debts	$ 15,000
Education fund needed (in today's dollars)	180,000
Emergency fund	15,000
Total lump-sum funding needs	**$ 210,000**

Step 3 Calculate the life insurance death benefit needed.

Total need	$ 1,306,446 ($1,096,446 + $210,000)
Less life insurance already in place	– 200,000
Less liquid assets	– 100,000
Net death benefit needed	**$1,006,446**

Capital Retention Approach

Capital retention approach
Provides a death benefit amount that, along with the family's other assets, is sufficient to provide a level of investment income that covers the projected needs of the family without having to invade the death benefit principal

Unlike the financial needs approach, the **capital retention approach** provides a death benefit amount that, along with the family's other assets, is sufficient to provide a level of investment income that covers the projected needs of the family without having to invade the death benefit principal. Other income-producing assets may be available, which will reduce the required death benefit. In other words, under this approach, survivor income needs are met from the earnings of the other assets. As a result, the income-producing assets remain available for distribution to the children or other heirs.

The capital retention approach involves three steps:

1. *Prepare a statement of financial position*—Prepare a list all of assets and liabilities to arrive at a projected statement of financial position at death. Assets should include any life insurance from other sources, such as existing personal policies, coverage through employers, or death benefits available through retirement plans.

2. *Calculate the capital available for income*—Subtract liabilities, cash needs, and non-income-producing capital from total assets.
3. *Determine the amount of additional capital required*—Compare the family's income objectives with other sources of income available, such as Social Security.

EXAMPLE Nicholas wants to provide his family with $60,000 of annual income in the event of his death. He wants to provide his children with an inheritance upon the death of his spouse, Kelly. He also wants to establish an emergency fund of $15,000 and an education fund of $60,000 for his children and pay off the mortgage. He assumes that, over the years, any principal used to provide income will earn a return on investment (ROI) of 6%, and that final expenses upon his death will be $15,000. Assume that the family will receive $20,000 of income from other sources each year after Nicholas's death.

1. Prepare Nicholas and Kelly's statement of financial position.

Assets (A)		**Liabilities (L)**	
House	$300,000	Mortgage	$220,000
Automobiles	30,000	Auto loans	20,000
Personal property	25,000	Credit card debt	10,000
Investments	20,000	Total liabilities	$250,000
Life insurance	200,000	Net worth (A – L)	$325,000
Total	$575,000	Total liabilities and net worth	$575,000

2. Calculate the capital available for income.

Total assets	$575,000
Less:	
Mortgage	$220,000
Other liabilities	30,000
Emergency fund	15,000
Education fund	60,000
Final expenses	15,000
Non-income-producing capital	135,000
(Equity in home, autos, personal property)	
Total deductions	$475,000
Capital available for income (CAI)	$100,000

3. Determine the amount of additional capital required.

Annual income objective for the family	$60,000
Less:	
Capital currently available for income	– 6,000
(CAI × ROI = $100,000 × 0.06)	
Annual income from other sources	– 20,000
Annual income shortfall	$ 34,000
Total additional capital required to cover shortfall	$566,667
(Shortfall/ROI – $34,000 ÷ 0.06)	

Unlike the financial needs approach, the capital retention approach has the advantages of simplicity and preservation of capital and may offer protection from inflation (rising costs). A key disadvantage, however, is the larger amount of life insurance needed so that assets may be preserved for heirs.

INDIVIDUAL LIFE INSURANCE POLICIES

Life insurance is a contractual means by which an individual transfers the risk of loss from death to an insurance company. The policyowner exchanges a stated premium for a promise to pay a stated death benefit. The insurer combines a large number of similar risks into groups or pools. Using the law of large numbers, the insurer's actuaries can predict the number of deaths that will occur during a given period with a fairly high level of accuracy. Policy premiums can then be calculated according to an underwriting class. Although it is impossible to determine which insureds will die, it is possible to know the probability of how many within the pool will die. As a result, life insurance becomes a viable mechanism for transferring a risk that would otherwise result in an economically devastating loss.

Consumers have a wide array of life insurance choices. Policies vary on the basis of the term of coverage, the flexibility of the premium or death benefit, whether the policy has cash value, and whether the underlying interest rate assumptions are fixed or variable. In addition, riders and other options, such as waiver of premium or accidental death benefit, can be added to a policy to suit the client's needs.

Life insurance policies commonly are classified in the following categories:

- Term
- Whole life
- Universal life

Term Life Insurance

Term life insurance
Provides temporary life insurance protection for a given period

Renewable
A feature whereby the policyowner may continue a term policy for an additional period without evidence of insurability at a premium based on the insured's current or attained age

Convertible
A term policy that may be exchanged for a cash value life insurance policy without evidence of insurability

Annual renewable term (ART)
Term insurance issued for one year; renewable for subsequent periods to a stated age without evidence of insurability

Term life insurance is commonly known as pure insurance because it provides nothing more than death benefit protection for a temporary or limited period, and the death benefit is paid only if the insured dies during the period. Term life insurance has no cash value, although some long-term policies build up a small reserve to cover future mortality costs and expenses. This reserve is depleted by the end of the policy term.

Most term life insurance policies are **renewable**, which gives the policyowner the right to continue coverage for an additional period without evidence of insurability at a premium based on the insured's current or attained age. The period of renewal may be the same length as the original term period. The majority of term life insurance policies are also **convertible**, which means that the term policy may be exchanged for a cash value life insurance policy without evidence of insurability. Together, the renewability and convertibility features protect the policyowner against the loss of insurability.

Types of Term Insurance Policies

There are several forms of term insurance available in the market today that vary by premium and death benefit design.

Annual Renewable Term **Annual renewable term (ART)**, also known as yearly renewal term (YRT), is coverage issued for one year, and the policyowner can renew for a subsequent period up to a maximum age without evidence of insurability. Premiums increase each year as the insured ages.

A key advantage of annual renewable term insurance is that no evidence of insurability is required at the time of renewal. One disadvantage, however, is that premiums are re-evaluated at the end of each annual term and will increase as the pool of insured ages and the death rate begins to increase. Because the rate of death rises at an increasing rate with age, the premiums for this type of policy may become prohibitively expensive as the insured gets older. Although initially less expensive than an ordinary whole life insurance policy, ART premiums will far exceed the level premium for the whole life policy as the insured ages. Exhibit 9.1 illustrates a comparison of the premium cost per $1,000 of insurance of an ART policy with an ordinary whole life policy. Notice how the exponential increase of the annual renewable term premium reflects the increased probability of mortality as age increases.

EXHIBIT 9.1 Annual Renewable Term Premium and Premium for Ordinary Whole Life

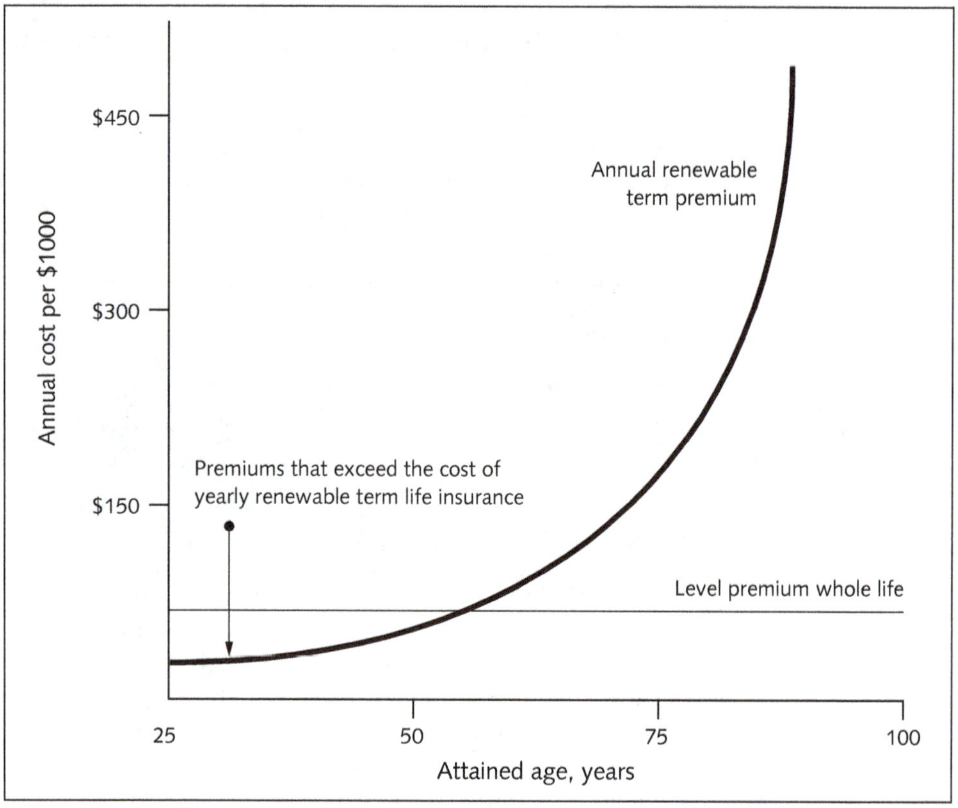

Level term
A policy with a level death benefit and a fixed level premium for a stated period

Level Term **Level term** insurance features a level death benefit and a level premium for a stated period of time. Level premium periods for this type of policy are typically 5, 10, 15, and 20 years. However, 35-year and 40-year level term policies may be available at younger ages. In most cases, premiums for the early years of the term are higher than those for an annual renewable term policy. This overpayment in early years funds the coverage for later ages when premiums for an ART policy would have been exceedingly expensive and unaffordable. Premiums for the level term period normally reflect the average of ART premiums, with discounting applied for time value of money. Therefore, the cash outlay for a fixed-period, level term policy is less than if the insured had purchased an annually renewable term policy for the same number of years. Note, however, that after the initial level term period, premiums often increase annually, unless the insured is in good health and, in some cases, provides additional evidence of insurability.

Decreasing term
Term insurance that features a level premium with a decreasing death benefit

Decreasing Term **Decreasing term** insurance features a level premium with a decreasing death benefit. In some policies, premiums discontinue a few years before the coverage ends. Decreasing term policies are most commonly used to provide a death benefit to pay off a mortgage in the event a breadwinner dies. Because mortgage balances decrease over time, a decreasing term policy may be the most appropriate type of life insurance to meet this need.

Reentry term
A policy under which the insurer may renew coverage at a lower premium rate if the insured provides satisfactory evidence of insurability

Reentry Term **Reentry term** is a life insurance policy under which the insurance company may renew coverage at a lower premium rate than would otherwise apply, provided that, at the time of renewal, the insured furnishes satisfactory evidence of insurability (e.g., medical exam). The ability to apply for lower rates may or may not be guaranteed in the contract. Rate schedules are provided in the policy, and a guaranteed maximum rate that the policyowner must pay is also provided if the insured no longer qualifies for preferred rates. Reentry term policies reward an insured who remains in good health, and they maintain the insurance coverage of those who no longer qualify as preferred risks. Some level term policies have reentry provisions at the end of each level term period.

Term Life Insurance Policy Riders

Rider
Provides additional coverage for something specifically not covered within the primary policy

A **rider** provides additional coverage for something specifically not covered within the primary policy. The rider is added to the primary policy, and the policyholder pays an extra amount to cover the cost of the rider. A discussion of common term policy riders follows.

Waiver of premium rider
Waives the premium due on a policy while the insured is disabled

Waiver of Premium The **waiver of premium rider** prevents the policy from lapsing because of nonpayment of premiums during the insured's disability. If the insured is disabled, premium payments are not required during the period of disability. In most cases, however, total disability is required. Definitions of disability can range from own occupation (i.e., unable to perform the material and substantial duties of the insured's regular occupation) to any occupation (i.e., unable to engage in any paying work).

Standard elimination (waiting) periods vary from 90 days to six months. In other words, for a 90-day elimination period, 90 days must pass before premiums are waived. Therefore, the policyowner must continue to pay premiums during the waiting period, but, in many cases, the company will return the premiums paid during the waiting period and will continue to waive the premiums until the end of the disability.

Note that premiums waived on behalf of the policyowner are not considered loans and, as such, need not be repaid. During the period in which premiums are waived, all features and benefits of the policy continue just as if the insured were paying the premiums.

Accidental death benefit rider
A policy rider that pays the beneficiary an additional death benefit if the insured dies accidentally, as defined in the rider

Accidental Death Benefit The **accidental death benefit rider** pays the beneficiary an additional death benefit if the insured dies accidentally, as defined in the rider. The definition of *accident* usually requires that death occur within 90 days of a purely unexpected event and not be related to any medical condition of the insured. The accidental death benefit rider is typically provided in the form of double indemnity, whereby the rider pays a benefit equal to the face value of the base policy. The result is double the amount of the initial death benefit.

Accelerated death benefit rider
Allows the policyowner to receive a portion of the policy's death benefit during the insured's lifetime if the insured contracts a terminal illness

Accelerated Death Benefit The **accelerated death benefit rider** allows the policyowner to receive a portion of the policy's death benefit before death, if the insured contracts a terminal illness and/or has a limited life expectancy. This rider is also known as a living benefit rider and is often provided without additional cost.

Return of premium rider
Returns the premium paid for a policy (less any administrative charges, fees, or rider premiums) to the policyowner at the end of the policy term

Return of Premium The **return of premium rider** returns the premium paid for a policy (less any administrative charges, fees, or rider premiums) to the policyowner at the end of the policy term. If the insured dies before the end of the policy term, the beneficiary will receive the death benefit and the amount of premiums paid up to death.

Spouse and child insurance riders *Provide life insurance coverage on the lives of the insured's spouse or children*

Spouse and Child Insurance **Spouse and child insurance riders** provides life insurance coverage on the lives of the insured's spouse and/or children. One child rider usually covers all children of the insured.

Advantages

Maximum Coverage per Premium Dollar Because term insurance provides pure death protection for a specified, temporary period only, term insurance is less expensive over the short term than a cash value whole life policy that provides coverage for the insured's lifetime. Term insurance premiums must cover only mortality, administrative expenses, and profit margin. Because part of the premium is not allocated for cash value accumulation, a term insurance policy is less expensive than a cash value policy.

Meets Temporary Need for Coverage Insurance protection under term insurance is temporary. The insurer provides coverage for a specified period only; therefore, term insurance is ideal for a temporary need, such as the payoff of a mortgage in the event of a breadwinner's death.

Protects Insurability A person with a current need for a large amount of coverage but with limited funds can obtain a lower cost term policy to provide protection. Later, if the policy is convertible, the term policy can be converted to a cash value, permanent policy at the same death benefit level, even if the insured develops a medical condition that renders him uninsurable.

Limitations

Cost Prohibitive at Older Ages Perhaps the most notable limitation of term insurance is the increase of premiums based on the aging of the insured, making term insurance impractical for many older people desiring coverage.

No Savings Feature A term life insurance policy does not possess the cash value feature found in an ordinary whole life policy (see next section). Term life insurance's primary function is to provide pure death protection. If one's goal is to accumulate wealth for retirement or education funding through an insurance policy, term life is inappropriate.

No Lifetime Coverage If the insured has a lifetime need for coverage, a term life insurance policy is not an appropriate option. Term life insurance is designed to provide coverage for a limited period and is priced to provide affordability during the early to mid portion of an insured's lifetime. However, term life insurance becomes increasingly uneconomical as the insured enters her later years and approaches life expectancy. Term life insurance should never be viewed as a form of lifetime protection because it generally may not be renewed after age 65 or 70. A convertibility feature provides an exception to the limited potential for lifetime protection with term life insurance. Some term life insurance policies have the ability to be converted into permanent policies without evidence of insurability. The client would have to remember to convert the term life insurance policy into a permanent policy at some point in the future based on the contract's terms and conditions.

Whole life insurance *Provides coverage during the lifetime of the insured as long as the premiums are paid according to the policy contract*

Whole Life Insurance

Whole life insurance provides coverage during the lifetime of the insured, as long as the premiums are paid according to the policy contract. Whole life insurance accumulates a cash value that is available to the policyowner through withdrawals and loans during the insured's lifetime.

A whole life policy offers permanent protection for the insured's "whole life" at a relatively moderate premium, because mortality costs and other expenses are spread over the full policy period (usually to age 100). All whole life policies involve the prepayment of future mortality costs.

Characteristics

Guaranteed Cash Value and Death Benefit In addition to the permanent coverage whole life insurance provides, the policy is often purchased for the low-risk, tax-deferred cash accumulation feature. Cash value in a traditional whole life policy increases at a steady rate, equaling the policy face amount at age 100.

A traditional whole life insurance policy generates a fairly low rate of return that is unattractive to many consumers, so traditional whole life should not be purchased solely for investment purposes. However, permanent insurance can be used as part of an overall investment and risk management plan. The insurance protection can serve as a risk management component, and the cash value can be appropriate as a low-risk, tax-deferred component of an overall investment program.

Exhibit 9.2 illustrates the cash value feature of a level premium, whole life insurance policy. Notice the original cost per thousand of $13.50 is substantially greater than the $1.95 per thousand mortality cost at the inception of the policy.

EXHIBIT 9.2 The Savings Element of a Level-Premium, Whole Life Insurance Policy

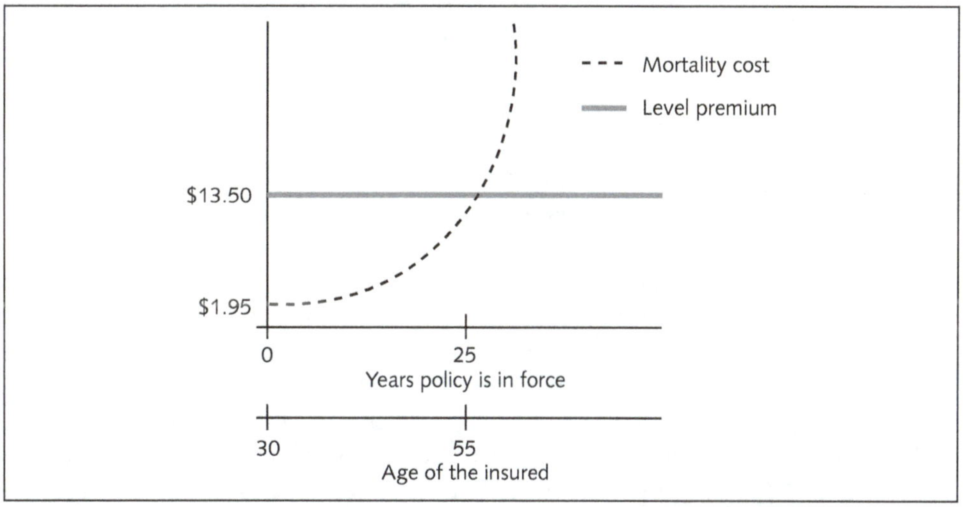

Legal reserve
A fund that is accumulated and maintained by the insurer to meet future obligations, such as administrative expenses and mortality charges

Level Premium Unlike term life insurance, for which premiums may increase with age, a whole life policy involves a level premium payable for the life of the policy. A whole life policy steadily builds cash values by prepaying premiums in the earlier years with the excess accumulating, thereby subsidizing higher mortality expenses in the later years. The excess premiums in the early years are kept in a **legal reserve**, which is a fund that is accumulated and maintained by the insurer to meet future obligations, such as administrative expenses and mortality charges.

Mortality charge
The amount of money the insurance company charges for providing a death benefit

Mortality Charge All whole life policies include a **mortality charge**, which is the amount of money the insurance company charges for providing the death benefit. Few people die at younger ages, so the mortality charge is fairly low. As the insureds age, however, the chance of death increases and so does the mortality charge.

Administrative Costs and Insurer Profit As with all types of insurance, whole life premiums cover not only mortality charges, but administrative expenses and a profit margin as well.

A whole life policy's savings element, or **cash value**, increases over the life of the policy as long as the premiums are paid according to the contract. The policy may be surrendered for the cash value (surrender charges may apply), or cash may be borrowed under a loan provision.

Cash value
Increases over the life of the policy as long as the premiums are paid according to the contract

Types of Whole Life Policies

An **ordinary (straight) life policy** is a continuous-premium policy in which premiums are paid regularly until either death or age 100. The insured may choose from various premium modes, including annual, semiannual, quarterly, or monthly. Of the types of whole life policies, the ordinary life policy provides the maximum permanent death protection for the lowest possible premium, but consumers should be aware that the premium must be paid continuously, even past retirement, until death. If the insured survives to age 100, the face amount will be paid to the policyowner as a living benefit.

Ordinary (straight) life policy
A continuous-premium whole life policy in which premiums are paid regularly until either death or age 100

Under a **limited-payment policy**, the insurance is permanent, and the insured has lifetime protection. Premiums, however, are payable for only a limited number of years, after which the policy becomes paid up for the stated face amount. A **paid-up policy** is one for which no future premium payments are due, but the policy remains in effect for life. Because the years in which premiums are paid are fewer than those of an ordinary life policy, limited-payment premiums are higher.

Limited-payment policy
Permanent life insurance for which premiums are payable for a limited number of years, after which the policy becomes paid up for its stated face amount

Paid-up policy
A policy for which no future premium payments are due; remains in effect for life

The premiums for a limited-payment policy may be fixed for any number of years (e.g., 10 years) or to a stated age. The name of the policy reflects the premium period; for example, if a premium payment is for 10 years, the policy is usually known as a 10-pay whole life policy.

Individuals who anticipate a limited number of high-income years during which they can most afford life insurance premium payments often choose limited-payment policies. Limited-payment policies are not suited for individuals with a restricted amount of financial resources and a need for a large death benefit.

Under a **modified whole life** policy, premiums are lower for the first few years (typically three to five years) and increase to a higher level premium thereafter. Modified life is traditional whole life insurance with a unique premium payment arrangement designed to accommodate a policyowner that anticipates higher income in the future.

Modified whole life
Premiums are lower for the first few years after policy issue, typically three to five years, and increase to a higher level premium thereafter

A **single premium whole life** policy requires a single lump-sum payment made at policy issue with no future premiums due. Single premium whole life may be suitable for a person with a cash windfall and a death benefit need; however, adverse income tax implications may render this type of policy inappropriate. Even though single premium whole life policies build immediate cash value, they may be classified as modified endowment contracts (MECs) and, as such, may be subject to taxation and penalties on loans or withdrawals. (Refer to the Modified Endowment Contracts section in this chapter for additional information.)

Single premium whole life
Single lump-sum payment made at policy issue with no future premiums due

A **current assumption whole life** (CAWL) policy uses new-money interest rates and current mortality assumptions to determine cash values. In essence, the insurer shares the investment experience and profits with the policyowner. Interest rates may fluctuate with the experience of the insurer, but the policy also has a stated guaranteed minimum interest rate. Mortality costs vary, as well, with maximum mortality charges stated in the policy.

Current assumption whole life
Uses new-money interest rates and current mortality assumptions to determine cash values

Variable life
A fixed-premium, whole life policy in which the death benefit and cash values fluctuate on the basis of the performance of subaccounts sometimes referred to as separate accounts

Joint life
Covers two or more lives under one policy at a cost lower than premiums for multiple separate policies

First-to-die policy
Pays the face amount upon the first death of two or more insureds

Last-to-die policy
Makes a death benefit payment upon the last death of multiple insureds

Nonparticipating
A policy that does not pay dividends

Participating
A policy that pays dividends

Variable life, a type of whole life insurance with a fixed premium, has a death benefit and cash values that fluctuate on the basis of the performance of subaccounts, which are professionally managed portfolios of debt and equity securities. The policyowner directs the investment of the policy's cash values among these subaccounts and bears all the investment risk. If the investment experience is weak, the death benefit amount may be reduced but will never fall below the original face amount.

Because variable life insurance policies are securities-based products, they are subject to regulation at both the state and federal levels. Agents and brokers who sell variable life products must be licensed to sell both life insurance and securities.

Joint life insurance covers two or more lives under one policy at a cost lower than multiple, separate policies. A **first-to-die policy** pays the face amount upon the first death of two or more insureds. Spouses may use this type of policy to provide for mortgage payments or education funding. A **last-to-die policy**, also known as a survivorship policy, pays the death benefit upon the last death of multiple insureds and is an effective estate planning tool when the unlimited marital deduction is used and estate taxes are due at the death of the surviving spouse. Premiums usually are based on the underwriting characteristics of the individual with the longest life expectancy.

Dividend Options A whole life policy that pays dividends is considered a participating policy. Policies that do not pay dividends are considered **nonparticipating**. Dividends declared by the insurer are never guaranteed because they are considered to be a refund of excess policy premiums that remain with the insurer as a result of excess earnings, expense savings, and better-than-anticipated mortality experience. Owners of **participating** whole life policies are entitled to receive policy dividends declared by the insurer. Following are the several dividend options available to policyowners.

Cash Under the cash option, a policyowner will receive a check on the policy anniversary equal to the full amount of the declared dividend. In most cases, cash dividends are payable only after the policy has been in force for a certain period.

Dividends to Reduce Premium With the dividends to reduce premium option, dividends are applied toward the payment of the premium, with the policyowner paying the difference, if any, between the total premium and the annual dividend.

Dividends to Accumulate at Interest When the dividends to accumulate at interest option is chosen, dividends are left on deposit with the insurance company and interest is earned on the dividends. The amount accumulated is added to the death benefit if the insured dies, or to the cash value if the policy is surrendered. The interest earned is taxable as ordinary income in the year earned.

Paid-Up Additions If the policyowner chooses the paid-up additions option, dividends are used to purchase additional paid-up life insurance coverage, which increases the policy's total death benefit and cash value. The additional amount is what a single premium equal to the dividends would purchase for the same whole life plan. No evidence of insurability is required.

One-Year Term Insurance Under the one-year term insurance option, dividends are used to purchase one-year term insurance. This is sometimes referred to as the fifth dividend option. In many cases, the face amount of the term insurance policy is the death benefit amount that an annual premium equal to the dividend amount will purchase as annually renewable term. Alternately, the dividends can be used to purchase a one-year term policy equal to the cash value of the original policy. Any remaining dividends are used to purchase increments of paid-up life insurance or accumulate at interest.

Nonforfeiture Options During the insured's lifetime, the nonforfeiture options apply if the policy is discontinued. Under this provision, the insured does not forfeit the cash value accumulation but chooses how the policy's cash value will be used.

Cash Surrender Value The cash surrender value option allows the policyowner who ceases premium payments and no longer has a need for the original life insurance protection to surrender the policy and receive the policy's cash surrender value (cash value less any surrender charges). Policyowners who surrender policies may incur an income tax liability on the cash value that exceeds the policy's cost basis.

Reduced Paid-Up Insurance With the reduced paid-up insurance option, the net cash value of the original life insurance policy is used as a net single premium to purchase a lesser amount of fully paid-up insurance and is suitable for the policyowner who wants to maintain some level of permanent death protection but wants no future premium outlay. The insurance purchased under this option is the same type of policy as the policy being discontinued. The face amount of the new policy depends on the cash value of the original policy, current age of the insured, and policy expenses.

Extended Term Insurance The extended term insurance option uses the net cash surrender value of the original policy as a net single premium to purchase a term insurance policy with a face amount equal to that of the original policy and is most appropriate for someone who wants to preserve death protection equal to the original policy's net face value for a limited time. The extended term coverage will require no future premium payments, but it will last only as long as the original policy's cash value will support it, on the basis of the insured's attained age.

Whole Life Insurance Policy Riders

Waiver of Premium A waiver of premium rider ensures that valuable insurance coverage is not lost if the policyholder is unable to pay premiums because of a disability. With this rider, the insurance company waives all premiums should the insured become totally disabled.

Accidental Death Benefit The accidental death benefit rider pays the beneficiary an additional death benefit if the insured dies accidentally, as defined in the rider. The definition of *accident* usually requires that death occur within 90 days of a purely unexpected event and not be related to any medical condition of the insured. An accidental death benefit is termed *double indemnity* when twice the face amount is paid for an accidental death.

Spouse and Child Insurance Spouse and child insurance riders allow the policyowner to purchase term insurance on the spouse and children of the insured.

Term insurance rider
Offers additional term life insurance on the insured

Term Insurance Rider A **term insurance rider** offers additional term life insurance on the insured. Premiums are usually guaranteed for a specified number of years; thereafter, premiums may increase annually. Often, the rider can be converted into permanent insurance on an attained age basis.

Living Benefits Rider The living benefits rider, also known as an accelerated death benefit rider, gives the policyowner access to a portion of the policy's eligible death benefit if the insured is diagnosed with a terminal illness with a life expectancy of 12 months or less. (Some states have established other life expectancy periods once terminal illness is diagnosed.)

Paid-up insurance rider
Increases the whole life death benefit protection and builds additional cash value

Paid-Up Insurance Rider The **paid-up insurance rider** is an economical way to increase the death benefit protection and build additional cash value. Premiums for this rider are used to purchase additional, paid-up whole life insurance in addition to the original whole life death benefit.

Advantages

Fixed Premiums In traditional whole life policies, premiums remain fixed for the duration of the policy.

Tax-Deferred Accumulation The policyowner pays no current income tax on the cash value accumulation of a whole life policy.

Lifetime Coverage Whole life policies provide death benefit protection over the insured's lifetime, as long as premiums are paid as stipulated in the policy.

Limitations

Inflexible Premiums Policyowners cannot modify whole life premiums in the event their financial situation changes. Therefore, much-needed death benefits may lapse if policyowners become ill, unemployed, or find themselves in unfavorable financial circumstances. In some cases, riders can protect the policyowner from several adverse situations.

Gradual Cash Value Growth Cash values can be insignificant in the early years of a whole life policy but steadily increase over the duration of the policy. Compared with other tax-deferred investments, such as IRAs or Section 401(k) plans, the internal rate of return of a whole life policy may be low.

Surrender Charges An insurer may penalize a policyowner for canceling a whole life policy, especially during the first few years of the policy, and the penalty is administered through a surrender charge, which is deducted from the cash value. Because the insurer's major expenses associated with the policy issuance are incurred up front (e.g., underwriting cost and agent's commission), the insurer imposes a surrender charge so it can recover some of the costs should the policy be terminated.

Universal Life Insurance

Universal life insurance
Gives policyowners the ability to adjust the premiums, death benefit, and cash values up or down to meet individual needs (within certain limits)

Universal life insurance allows policyholders, within certain limits, to adjust the premium, cash value, or death benefit up or down to meet individual needs. In comparison to whole life policies, which are based on the long-term return of an insurer's general account, universal life premiums are based on a current assumed interest rate that is equal to or (usually) greater than the policy's guaranteed interest rate. Therefore, some of the investment risk is shifted from the insurer to the policyowner.

The basic structure of how a universal life insurance policy operates is a bit complex. Mortality charges based on the insured's age and the policy's net amount at risk, along with the policy's administrative expenses, are deducted from the premium due. The amount left is credited to the policy's cash value, which is then credited with interest, usually at current interest rates, to result in the end-of-period cash surrender value. Exhibit 9.3 illustrates the basic structure of a universal life policy.

EXHIBIT 9.3 Structure of a Universal Life Policy

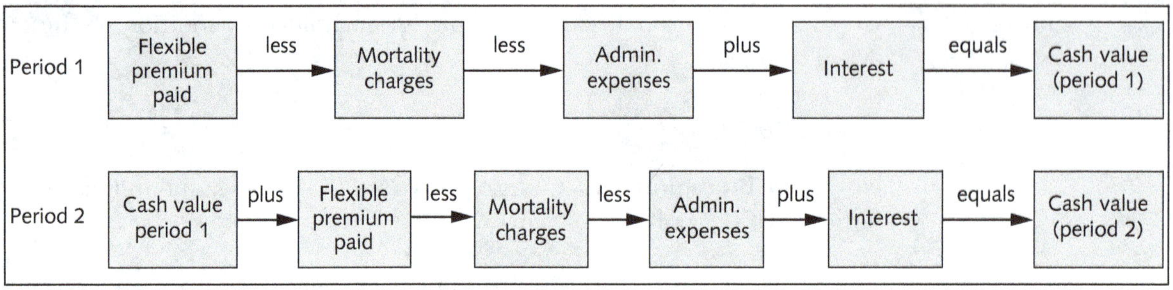

Death Benefit Options

Option A (Option 1) Option A pays a level death benefit. The net amount of risk (NAR) for a universal life policy is the difference between the cash value and the death benefit. Therefore, for an Option A policy, the NAR decreases as the cash value increases, as Exhibit 9.4 illustrates.

EXHIBIT 9.4 Death Benefit Options

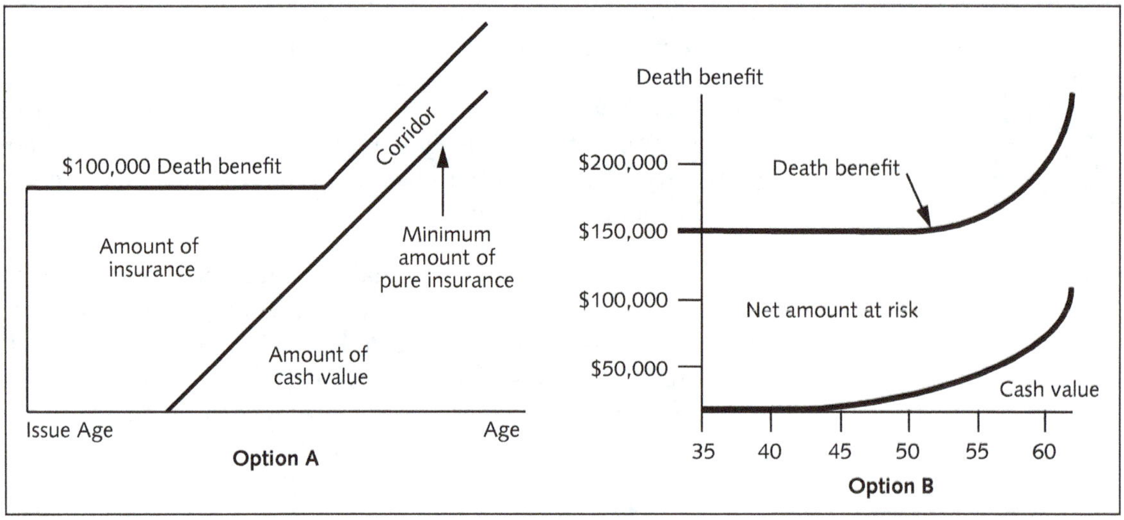

In some cases, an Option A death benefit will begin to increase in the later years, as a result of the tax law that imposes a "DEFRA corridor" of NAR if the cash value becomes too large (as defined by law) relative to the death benefit. This corridor is named after the Deficit Reduction Act of 1984, and it imposes minimum death benefits at certain NAR levels to prevent the policy from becoming more like an investment and less like a life insurance policy.

Option B (Option 2) Option B provides an increasing death benefit, which is the death benefit plus the cash value. As a result, the NAR under this option remains level throughout the policy.

Premium Payments

Universal life policyowners can choose the amount of premium they pay into their policies, subject to insurer minimums and maximums. However, this premium flexibility can be a disadvantage in cases where insufficient premiums will cause the policy to lapse. For this reason, many insurers require a target, or planned, premium for a given number of years, after which policyowners can determine the premiums paid into the policy. As long as the policy has enough cash value to cover mortality charges and administrative expenses, additional premiums may not be required.

Variable Universal Life

In the 1980s, the life insurance industry unveiled variable universal life (VUL) insurance, a type of universal life insurance policy in which one could buy insurance with the option to invest in managed portfolios called subaccounts, sometimes referred to as separate accounts. Unlike whole life policies, VUL policyholders could actually see a breakdown of the premium payments, expense charges, earnings, and policy values on periodic statements. Because securities are used as variable universal life investment options, agents and brokers who sell variable life products must be licensed to sell both life insurance and securities.

Variable universal life (VUL) insurance *Combines the investment component of variable life and the premium, death benefit, and cash value flexibility features of universal life*

Flexible Premiums and Death Benefits A **variable universal life (VUL) insurance** policy combines the investment component of variable life insurance with the premium, death benefit, and cash value flexibility features of universal life insurance. VUL policies have increasing or decreasing death benefits and flexible premium payments that mirror universal life policies.

Self-Directed Investment Accounts As with variable life, the policyowner directs the investment of the policy's cash values and bears the investment risk; the cash value is maintained in one or more subaccounts. The cash values reflect the policyowner's pro rata share of assets held in the subaccount and are subject to fluctuations similar to other securities-based products.

Variable Universal Life Policy Structure The basic structure of a VUL policy is the same as a universal life policy, with mortality charges and administrative expenses being deducted from the policy's cash value and the cash value being credited with interest and/or performance, which is dependent on the asset allocation of the cash value.

Riders and Optional Benefits

Universal life and variable universal life have riders available that are similar to those of other life policies.

Waiver of Premium The waiver of premium (or waiver of monthly deductions) rider waives mortality and expense charges if the insured becomes totally and permanently disabled before a stated age, usually age 65. The policy continues as if the policyowner were paying an amount equal to these charges. Insurers have recently developed an upgraded form of the traditional waiver of premium rider that pays the target premium of the policy, rather than paying only the mortality and expense charges. This feature allows the policy to continue in a manner similar to how it was likely being funded before an insured's disability. Most waiver of premium riders require that a waiting period be satisfied before the waiver of monthly deductions can begin.

Accidental Death Benefit Rider The accidental death benefit rider pays the beneficiary an additional death benefit if the insured dies accidentally, as defined in the rider. The definition of accident usually requires that death occur within 90 days of a purely unexpected event and not be related to any medical condition of the insured. An accidental death benefit is termed *double indemnity* when twice the face amount is paid for an accidental death.

Other insured rider
Offers level term insurance coverage on the insured's spouse or children

Living benefits rider
Gives the policyowner access to a portion of the policy's eligible death benefit if the insured is diagnosed with a terminal illness and has a life expectancy of 12 months or less

Other Insured Rider The **other insured rider** offers level term insurance coverage on the insured's spouse or children. Most often, coverage is convertible to permanent insurance at specified ages.

Living Benefits Rider The **living benefits rider**, also known as an *accelerated death benefit rider*, gives the policyowner access to a portion of the policy's eligible death benefit if the insured is diagnosed with a terminal illness and has a life expectancy of 12 months or less. (Some states have established other life expectancy periods once terminal illness is diagnosed.)

Advantages

Flexible Premium The ability to adjust the amount of premium payments is beneficial when financial circumstances change.

Flexible Death Benefit Universal life offers cost-effective increases in the death benefit without the need to purchase a separate policy; however, proof of insurability may be required. The death benefit can also be decreased if the current death benefit is no longer needed by the policyowner.

Current Assumptions Because interest rates and mortality are based on current experience, the accumulated value of a universal life policy is often higher than that of a whole life policy. In addition, the overall cost for a universal life policy may be lower than that of a whole life policy.

Limitations

Flexible Premium Policyowners may decide not to make premium payments at certain times, resulting in a significant decrease in the accumulated value or the lapse of the policy. Owners of universal life policies must be disciplined enough to make the premium payments needed to yield the desired accumulated value and keep the policy in force.

Fewer Guarantees The accumulated value of a universal life policy can drop to zero if sufficient premiums are not paid. In addition, the target premium for some policies may not keep the policy in force into later years. As a result, the premium required to keep the policy in force may actually be higher than a whole life premium.

On the other hand, a whole life policy is guaranteed to have a specified cash value and death benefit at any given time as long as premiums are paid. Although universal life policies can guarantee a minimum accumulated cash value and death benefit, the premium necessary for the guarantee may not be much less than a whole life policy.

Equity-Indexed Universal Life (EIUL)

Equity-indexed universal life (EIUL)
A universal life policy that offers an upside potential for cash value growth with limited downside risk

The **equity-indexed universal life** policy form first emerged in the late 1990s shortly after equity-indexed annuities gained popularity. EIUL appeals to clients who want upside potential for cash value growth with limited downside risk. Most policies guarantee that returns will not drop below 0%, and in return, the policies will share in the upside by placing a cap, or maximum percentage, that limits the extent to which the policyowner participates in the performance of the index. Most contracts have a fixed account to and from which policy values can be exchanged without incurring a fee; in addition, a policy may have a no-lapse guarantee rarely exceeding five years. The usual and customary riders of universal life policies also are available on most EIUL policies.

Modified Endowment Contracts (MECs)

According to the Internal Revenue Code, in order for life insurance contracts to receive favorable tax treatment, they must meet the federal tax law definition of life insurance. As a result, a net level premium is established by the Internal Revenue Code for each policy. If the cumulative premium payments exceed the net level premium for the policy during the first seven years of the contract or seven years following a material change to the contract, the policy becomes a **modified endowment contract (MEC)**. The premium is called the 7-pay premium and depends on the amount of the policy's death benefit and the age and life expectancy of the insured.

Modified endowment contract (MEC)
A life insurance policy that exceeds its net level (7-pay) premium during the first seven years or during the seven years following a material change of the policy

If the policy is or becomes a MEC, the policyholder may be subject to additional taxes and penalties on any distributions (other than the death benefit) from the policy during the life of the insured. Any distribution (including loans or withdrawals) from a MEC will be taxed on a LIFO (last-in, first-out) basis, which means that policy income or gains are taxed first at the time of distribution. The distribution is then includible in taxable income, up to the amount the account value exceeds the basis in the policy. Once all of the gain is loaned or withdrawn, subsequent distributions are considered a return of basis. In addition, a 10% penalty is assessed to any taxable amount, unless the policyowner has attained age 59½ or older.

EXHIBIT 9.5 Feature Comparison of Common Life Insurance Policies

	Term Life	Whole (Ordinary) Life	Universal Life	Variable Life	Variable Universal Life	Equity Indexed Universal Life
Premium amount	Increasing or level	Fixed; may decrease if dividends are used to reduce premiums	Adjustable at policyowner's discretion, subject to minimum and maximum limits	Fixed; may decrease if earnings used to reduce premiums	Adjustable at policyowner's discretion, subject to minimum and maximum limits; required premiums may increase or decrease based on investment performance of subaccounts	Adjustable at policyowner's discretion, subject to minimum and maximum limits; the maximum required premium is based on the minimum guaranteed return
Death benefits	Fixed or decreasing	Fixed; will increase if dividends are used to purchase paid-up additions	Option A: Level (increases at DEFRA corridor) Option B: Increases by amount of cash value	Has a guaranteed minimum but can increase if investment experience on cash value is favorable	No long-term guarantee No lapse riders can be purchased for a limited number of years Option A: Level (increases at DEFRA corridor) Option B: Increases by amount of cash value	No long-term guarantee No lapse riders can be purchased for a limited number of years Option A: Level (increases at DEFRA corridor) Option B: Increases by amount of cash value
Policyowner's control over cash value investments	N/A	None	None	Complete	Complete	None
Rate of return on cash value investment	N/A	Fixed; may also pay dividends, which vary	Minimum guaranteed rate, but may be higher depending on current interest rates	No minimum guarantee, but positive investment experience can yield lofty returns	No minimum guarantee, but positive investment experience can yield lofty returns	Minimum guarantee lower than standard universal life
Use	Limited resources, large and/or temporary need, no lifetime coverage	Maximum guarantees, minimum flexibility, lifetime coverage	No investment responsibility, maximum flexibility, lifetime coverage (requires disciplined funding)	Requires investment responsibility, minimal flexibility, lifetime coverage	Requires investment responsibility, moderate flexibility, lifetime coverage (requires discipline funding and reasonable investment performance)	Requires a certain level of risk tolerance to hold through down markets Lifetime coverage (requires disciplined funding and reasonable performance of the underlying index)

Group Life Insurance

Group life insurance covers a large group of insureds under a single master contract. The employer holds the master contract and is responsible for making premium payments to the insurer. The employer can fund premium payments in whole or in part and, in many cases, the employee pays no portion of the premium. If employees pay part of the premiums, the employer generally collects the employee contributions through payroll deductions.

Group insurance is typically less expensive than individual insurance because of the savings the insurer realizes in lower administrative expenses and underwriting costs. Individual underwriting is not required of group insurance participants, so no evidence of insurability is required and no medical examinations are necessary. The employer may set up its requirements for eligibility. Eligibility requirements for a typical plan might include that participating employees be full-time workers and satisfy a minimum probationary period.

Group Term Insurance

Group term life insurance is the most common form of group life insurance selected by employers. Group term life insurance offers the same benefits as an individual term life insurance policy. Group term premiums, like those of individual term policies, increase with age. When an employer provides group term insurance, there is no tax consequence to the employee on the premium paid by the employer if the death benefit under the policy does not exceed $50,000. The imputed cost of coverage in excess of $50,000 must be included in income using the IRS Premium Table and is subject to Social Security and Medicare taxes (IRC Section 79). The actual premiums paid by the employer for group term insurance are tax deductible by the employer as a business expense.

The amount of coverage provided by an employer through a group term plan must be determined by some formula that precludes adverse selection on the part of employees. Most employers provide employees with either a flat amount of coverage, such as $25,000, or coverage equal to a multiple of the employee's annual salary. In some cases, employees are allowed to purchase additional amounts of coverage in prespecified multiple amounts. The insurer may require proof of insurability for optional higher coverage amounts.

A covered employee typically has the right to convert a group term policy, upon termination from the company, to a regular cash value policy at a rate based on his attained age. The insurer usually grants a 31-day grace period after an employee withdraws from the group in which basic death benefits remain in effect. The conversion privilege is, in one respect, advantageous to the insured because no evidence of insurability is required upon conversion. However, adverse selection comes into play with group conversions as those who are uninsurable or are not easily insurable eagerly opt for the conversion privilege, and those who can be favorably underwritten discover much better values in the individual market.

Group Whole Life Insurance

Group whole life insurance allows the insured to obtain death benefit coverage, as well as accumulate a level of savings through the policy's cash value. Group whole life insurance is not a frequently chosen employee benefit because it does not have the tax advantages of group term life insurance. Generally, the employee must report the premiums paid by the employer for a group whole life policy as taxable income.

Group Universal Life Insurance

Some employers offer group universal life plans. Often, these policies serve as optional supplements to the more traditional group term plans. In most cases, employees pay the entire cost of the coverage; the premiums are paid through payroll deductions, resulting in some administrative cost savings for the insurer. The savings are then passed on to employees in the form of lower premiums. Most plans allow the employee to purchase coverage up to a specified maximum face value without providing evidence of insurability.

Group Variable Universal Life (GVUL) Insurance

The newest addition to many employers' optional benefits program is group variable universal life (GVUL) insurance. Major insurers are beginning to introduce GVUL policy forms designed and priced specifically for large groups; they feature very low expenses and surrender charges that range from low down to zero. The result is a readily available alternative for life insurance protection that provides a tax-favored investment, even in the early years of the policy. Because GVUL policies involve mortality and administrative expenses, they should be purchased only by those in need of the protection element.

LIFE INSURANCE POLICY SELECTION

The first step in selecting an insurance policy is to determine the type of product that best suits the needs of the prospective policyowner. Policy cost, duration of the need, amount of coverage, and risk tolerance all must be considered during the process. Term insurance policies are almost always the least expensive in the short term, especially at younger ages. Over the long term, however, they are generally the most expensive and, absent an unexpected accident or the early onset of terminal illness, rarely result in a death benefit being paid. If the need is long term and permanent insurance is required, a higher initial premium must be accounted for in the budgeting process. Universal life policies have more premium flexibility, and premiums are generally lower than traditional whole life policies. Prospective policyowners with higher risk tolerances may be inclined to opt for a variable product.

Once the most appropriate type of life insurance policy is determined, it is necessary to identify the resources for premium payments. When a premium range has been established and budgeted for, policies from various insurers should be compared. Today, this is usually done using one of three methods. First, the National Association of Insurance Commissioners (NAIC) has adopted interest-adjusted cost indices as a method of comparing life insurance policies. There are two types of interest-adjusted cost indices: the interest-adjusted surrender cost index and the interest-adjusted net payment cost index. The interest-adjusted surrender cost is a measure of the true anticipated cost of keeping a policy in force, adjusted for interest, for a specified number of years (usually 10 or 20) and then surrendering it for its cash value. The net payment cost index assumes that the policy remains in force, adjusted for interest, until the insured dies. Today, interest-adjusted cost indices are widely used for policy comparisons.

A second method of policy comparison uses a surrender cost index, which compares cash value levels and costs, assuming that at some point in the future the policy will be surrendered for its cash value. The net payment cost index compares the cost of the death benefit provided. Policyowners can compare future costs, for example, in 10 to 20 years, assuming that premiums are continuously paid and the policy's cash value remains in the policy.

LIFE INSURANCE POLICY ILLUSTRATIONS

Policy illustrations show important policy features and values, on a guaranteed and current basis, and show how a policy is structured and how it can be expected to perform.

Please note that policy illustrations are not forecasts of future performance. They project what policy values could be if the policy performed at illustrated rates, assuming insurer variables, such as investment performance, remain steady. Prospective policyowners should not confuse the policy illustration with the actual policy. Illustrations show some values that are contractually guaranteed, but they also usually show nonguaranteed values as well.

Policy illustrations reflect assumptions pertaining to interest, mortality, loading, and lapse rates. Assumed policy interest rates will probably differ from actual interest/growth rates in the future. As a result, the policy's actual performance will differ from that of the policy illustrated. Care should be taken, however, to project reasonable interest rates and show mortality rates that reflect insurer experience. Policy loads should be sufficient to cover expenses and the insurer's profit margin, so that prospective policyowners are not misled.

LIFE INSURANCE POLICY REPLACEMENT

The decision to replace one policy with another should be made with caution. The methodology for such a decision includes gathering facts, calculations, and benchmark comparisons. One such comparison uses the Belth price of protection model:

$$CPT = \frac{(P + CV_0)(1+i) - (CV_1 + D)}{(DB - CV_1)(0.001)}$$

CPT = cost per thousand

P = annual premium

CV_0 = cash value at beginning of year

i = net after-tax earning rate

CV_1 = cash value at year end

D = current dividend

DB = death benefit

Belth Benchmark Table

Age	Benchmark price of insurance per $1,000
<30	$1.50
30–34	$2.00
35–39	$3.00
40–44	$4.00
45–49	$6.50
50–54	$10.00
55–60	$15.00
60–64	$25.00
65–69	$35.00
70–74	$50.00
75–79	$80.00
80–84	$125.00

(Joseph M. Belth, author)

To use this model, the insured should calculate the cost per thousand (CPT) for one's current insurance and compare the result to the appropriate Belth benchmark per thousand. If the CPT is more than twice the benchmark price, the insured should consider replacement.

EXAMPLE Joan is 62 years old and has a whole life policy with the following features:

- Annual premium = $800
- Cash value on January 1, 2022 = $400,000
- Cash value on December 31, 2022 = $405,000
- After-tax earning rate = 4.2%
- Current dividend = $600
- Death benefit = $750,000

$$\text{CPT} = \frac{(\text{P}+\text{CV}_0)(1+\text{i})-(\text{CV}_1+\text{D})}{(\text{DB}-\text{CV}_1)(0.001)}$$

$$\text{CPT} = \frac{(\$800+\$400{,}000)(1+0.042)-(\$405{,}000+\$600)}{(\$750{,}000-\$405{,}000)(0.001)}$$

$$\text{CPT} = \$34.88$$

The Belth benchmark for a 62-year-old individual is $25. The CPT for Joan's current insurance is less than $50 (2 × $25), so she should retain her current policy.

LIFE INSURANCE POLICY PROVISIONS

Grace Period

Grace period
Amount of time following the premium due date in which the policyowner may pay the overdue premium

Life insurance policies allow for a **grace period** (typically 31 days) after the premium due date in which the policyowner may pay the overdue premium. During this grace period, the policy remains in force. In some cases, interest may be charged on the overdue premium. If the insured dies within the grace period, the insurer deducts the premium (and, in some cases, pro rata premium) from the death benefit payable to the beneficiary.

Incontestability Clause

Incontestability clause
Prevents the insurer from canceling the policy after it has been in force for two years in the event the life insurer discovers material misrepresentation or concealment

The **incontestability clause** in a life insurance policy prevents the insurer from canceling the policy after it has been in force usually for two years in the event the life insurer discovers material misrepresentation or concealment.

Entire Contract Clause

Entire contract clause
Maintains that the life insurance policy and the policyowner's application compose the complete life insurance contract

The **entire contract clause** maintains that the life insurance policy and the policyowner's application compose the complete life insurance contract. As a result, any statements made on the application are part of the contract and, if these statements are false, can be used as basis to void or alter the contract.

Misstatement of Age or Gender Provision

Misstatement of age or gender provision
If a misstatement is made, the insurer can adjust the face amount to the amount the premium would have purchased had the age or gender been correctly stated

The **misstatement of age or gender provision** provides that, if a misstatement of age or gender is discovered after the policy is issued, the life insurance company can adjust the face amount of the policy to an amount that the premium would have purchased had the insured's age or gender been correctly stated. Usually, the misstatement of age or gender is discovered after the insured dies, when the insurance company receives a death certificate showing the correct information.

EXAMPLE Suppose Abby is age 45 and she incorrectly states her age as 35 on a life insurance application for a $100,000 policy. Based on the information provided, she is charged a $100 monthly premium for her policy. The insurer, however, would have charged Abby $200 per month had it known she were 45. If she dies and the insurer discovers the misstatement of age, it will recalculate her death benefit on the basis of the premium amount she should have paid. Because she paid only half as much as she should have ($100 instead of $200), the insurer will pay only half the death benefit, or $50,000.

Policy Assignment

Absolute assignment
All life insurance policy ownership rights are transferred to a designated assignee

Collateral assignment
A life insurance policy is transferred to a creditor as security for a loan or debt

An assignment is an agreement under which the policyowner (the assignor) transfers some of the ownership rights in a policy to another party (the assignee). Two types of assignments are available, absolute and collateral.

An **absolute assignment** is an assignment of a life insurance policy under which the policyowner transfers all policy ownership rights to a designated assignee.

A **collateral assignment** is the assignment of a life insurance policy to a creditor as security for a loan or debt. The creditor is entitled to receive the proceeds or cash value of the policy only to the extent of the amount of the unpaid debt. The assignment will terminate when the debt is paid.

Suicide Clause

Suicide clause
Asserts that, if the insured commits suicide within a specified period of time, the policy will be voided and premiums will be refunded to the beneficiary

To mitigate the risk that a person will purchase a life insurance policy in contemplation of suicide, a life insurance policy includes a **suicide clause**. The clause asserts that, if the insured commits suicide within a specified period, the policy will be voided and premiums will be refunded to the beneficiary. Most suicide clauses have a specified time limit of two years.

Reinstatement Clause

Reinstatement clause
Outlines the conditions under which a lapsed policy may be reinstated

A life insurance policy will lapse if the premium payments are not paid by the insured as stated in the policy. The **reinstatement clause** in a policy outlines the conditions under which a lapsed policy may be reinstated. In most cases, evidence of insurability is not needed if the reinstatement takes place within 31 days of grace period expiration. Thereafter, the policy may be reinstated during the reinstatement period (up to five years) with submission of unpaid premiums plus interest and satisfactory evidence of insurability.

Policy Loan Provision

Policy loan provision
Allows the policyowner to borrow (with interest) against the cash surrender value of a permanent insurance policy

A **policy loan provision** allows the policyowner to borrow (with interest) against the cash value of a permanent insurance policy. Any loans and interest payments outstanding at the time of the insured's death will be deducted from the death benefit.

Automatic Premium Loan

Automatic premium loan
Directs the insurance company to pay an overdue premium by making a loan against the policy's cash value if the overdue premium remains unpaid upon the expiration of the grace period

Some whole life policies include a provision for an **automatic premium loan** (APL), which directs the insurance company to pay an overdue premium by making a loan against the policy's cash value if the overdue premium remains unpaid upon the expiration of the grace period. The policyowner must specifically request the provision either on the initial coverage application or in writing at a later date. As with the policy loan provision, any outstanding loans and interest payments at the insured's death will be withheld from the death benefit paid to the beneficiary.

Beneficiary Designations

Revocable beneficiary
Can be changed by the policyowner (who may or may not be the insured) at any time

Irrevocable beneficiary
Cannot be changed without the beneficiary's consent

The proceeds of a life insurance policy are distributed upon death to a beneficiary selected by the policyowner. A life insurance beneficiary can be an individual, a group of individuals, the insured's estate, or an entity, such as a charity or business.

The two types of beneficiary designations are revocable and irrevocable. A **revocable beneficiary** can be changed by the policyowner at any time. An irrevocable beneficiary cannot be changed without the beneficiary's consent. An **irrevocable beneficiary** must give consent before the policyowner can change the beneficiary designation and is often used in divorce settlements to guarantee one parent with a death benefit in the event the other parent dies.

The **primary beneficiary** of a life insurance policy is the party designated by the policyowner to receive the death benefit. A **contingent beneficiary** is an individual, group, or entity designated to receive the policy proceeds if the primary beneficiary dies before the insured. A contingent beneficiary can be secondary (receives a benefit if primary beneficiary predeceases the insured) or tertiary (receives a benefit when both the primary and secondary beneficiaries predecease the insured).

Primary beneficiary *The party designated by the policyowner to receive death benefits*

Contingent beneficiary *An individual, group, or entity designated to receive the policy proceeds if the primary beneficiary predeceases the insured*

If the primary beneficiary is deceased, and all contingent beneficiaries are deceased or simply not named in the policy, the death benefit proceeds will be paid to the policyowner or to the policyowner's estate if the deceased insured was also the policyowner. In this event, the proceeds will be included in the probate estate and therefore subject to additional costs and delays.

Aviation Exclusion

Although no longer a common exclusion in policies issued today, the aviation exclusion denies coverage for those who die in noncommercial flights, such as private pilots, passengers, and military pilots. The death benefit is not paid; however, premiums are usually returned to the beneficiary.

War Exclusion

War exclusion *Allows the insurer to deny a death claim if the insured's death is related to war or military service*

The **war exclusion** allows the insurer to deny a death claim if the insured's death is related to war or military service. In lieu of paying the death benefit, premiums are usually returned to the beneficiary with interest.

Survivorship Clause

Survivorship clause *Requires that a beneficiary survive the insured by a specified period (usually 30 to 60 days) in order to receive the death benefit proceeds*

The **survivorship clause**, also known as the common disaster clause, in a life insurance policy requires that a beneficiary survive the insured by a specified period (usually 30 or 60 days) in order to receive the death benefit proceeds. Otherwise, the policy proceeds will be paid as though the beneficiary had predeceased the insured.

Simultaneous Death Provision

A situation may arise in which the insured and the beneficiary both die within a short time of each other in an accident and it is not readily determinable who died first. Patterned after the Uniform Simultaneous Death Act, which has been adopted by most states, the simultaneous death provision establishes that the proceeds of the life insurance policy will be distributed as though the insured survived the beneficiary. If more than one beneficiary has been named on the policy, the next in the line of succession shall receive the proceeds. If no other beneficiaries are designated, the proceeds will be paid to the policyowner or the policyowner's estate if the deceased insured was also the policyowner.

LIFE INSURANCE SETTLEMENT OPTIONS

Settlement options
Allow the policyowner or beneficiary to choose either cash or one of several alternatives to how the death benefit proceeds will be paid

Most life insurance policies provide **settlement options** to a beneficiary as an alternative to receiving a lump sum check at the death of an insured. Moreover, these available alternatives may protect a beneficiary who is unable to manage a large lump sum of cash.

Interest Only

Interest-only option
The insurance company retains the death benefit and pays the primary beneficiary interest on that sum

Under the **interest-only option**, the insurance company retains the death benefit and pays the primary beneficiary interest on that sum. In some cases, the primary beneficiary may be given the right to withdraw some or all of the proceeds in a lump sum. The policyowner or primary beneficiary may name a contingent beneficiary to receive the balance of the proceeds at the primary beneficiary's death.

Fixed Amount

Fixed-amount option
Specifies that a designated amount of income will be provided to the beneficiary on a regular basis until the proceeds and accumulated interest are depleted

The **fixed-amount option** specifies that a designated amount of income will be provided to the beneficiary on a regular basis until the proceeds and accumulated interest are depleted. If the beneficiary dies with a balance of unpaid proceeds and accumulated interest, the balance is paid to a contingent beneficiary or included in the deceased beneficiary's estate.

Fixed Period

Fixed-period option
The beneficiary will receive the maximum periodic payments that the death benefit proceeds will purchase for a specified period

If the **fixed-period option** is chosen, the beneficiary will receive the maximum periodic payments that the death benefit proceeds will purchase for a specified period. If the beneficiary dies within the payment period, the balance is paid to a contingent beneficiary or included in the estate of the deceased beneficiary.

Life Income

Life income option
Allows the beneficiary to receive a specified periodic payment, usually for life

The **life income option** allows the beneficiary to receive a specified periodic payment, usually for life. The amount of the proceeds and the life expectancy of the beneficiary at the time of the insured's death are used to determine the amount of life income payable.

Life Income With Period Certain

Life income with period certain option
Provides an income to the beneficiary for life or a specified period, if longer

The **life income with period certain option** provides an income to the beneficiary for life or a specified period, if longer. The balance of the payments will be made to a contingent beneficiary if the primary beneficiary dies during the certain period. For example, a life income with 20 years certain option will provide a specified amount for at least 20 years (either to the primary beneficiary, if living, or to a contingent beneficiary, if the primary dies) or longer if the primary beneficiary outlives the 20-year period.

Life Income With Refund

Life income with refund option
The life insurance company agrees that if the primary beneficiary dies before the total amount paid under the option equals the proceeds of the policy, the company will pay the difference to a contingent beneficiary

Under the **life income with refund option**, the life insurance company agrees that if the primary beneficiary dies before the total amount paid under the option equals the proceeds of the policy, the life insurance company will pay the difference to a contingent beneficiary either in a lump sum or installments.

Joint and last survivor income option
Provides joint beneficiaries a stated amount of income during their lives, and a continuation of the original or reduced amount for the remaining beneficiaries' lives

Joint and Last Survivor

The **joint and last survivor income option** provides joint beneficiaries a stated amount of income during their lives, and a continuation of the original or reduced amount for the remaining beneficiaries' lives. A period certain may also be stipulated as part of this option.

ANNUITY CONTRACTS

An annuity is a contract designed to provide payments to the holder at specified intervals, usually for a fixed period, for the annuitant's life, or for the lives of two or more joint annuitants. Sold by insurance companies, annuities are commonly used to supplement retirement benefits. Similar to life insurance benefits, annuity payments are based on the pooling of the risk and life expectancy of a group.

Annuities may be classified in a number of ways, but generally they are categorized according to the time when the benefit payments begin (immediate or deferred annuity), by the method of premium payment (flexible or single premium annuity), or by the form of annuity payment (fixed or variable).

Types of Annuities

Immediate vs. Deferred

The insured has the option of having annuity payments made monthly, quarterly, semiannually, or annually. In addition, the insured may also specify whether the annuity payments should be immediate or deferred.

Immediate annuity
One in which the first annuity payment is made one payment interval from the purchase date

Immediate Annuities An **immediate annuity** is one in which the first annuity payment is made one payment interval from the purchase date. Immediate annuities are purchased with a single lump-sum premium.

Deferred annuity
Provides income at some date in the future

Deferred Annuities A **deferred annuity** provides income at some date in the future. The most popular form of a deferred annuity is a retirement annuity in which monetary value accumulates for a number of years and is paid in installments when the insured reaches retirement. A deferred annuity is purchased with either a single premium or periodic level premiums.

Flexible Premium vs. Single Premium

Flexible premium annuity
Allows the insured the option to vary premium deposits

Flexible Premium Annuities A **flexible premium annuity** allows the insured the option to vary premium deposits. The amount of retirement income will relate directly to the accumulated sum in the annuity when it becomes due and payable. Under a flexible premium plan, the insured spreads payments over a designated period by making periodic premium payments.

Single premium annuity
An annuity purchased with a single lump sum

Single Premium Annuities An annuity purchased with a single lump sum is known as a **single premium annuity**. Proceeds from life insurance policies may be used to purchase single premium annuities at special rates under a life income settlement option. Single premium annuities can be either immediate or deferred.

Fixed, Variable, and Equity Indexed Annuities

Fixed annuity
Insurer agrees to credit a specified interest rate over a stated period

Variable annuity
Does not guarantee specific payments but has a potential for greater returns

Subaccounts
Portfolios of stocks and/or bonds that are professionally managed according to a specific investment objective

Accumulation units
Units of measurement that, when combined, equal the total account value of a variable annuity

Equity indexed annuities (EIAs)
Based on the simple concept of returns that are equal to a percentage, or participation rate, of a popular market index (e.g., S&P 500)

Deferred income annuities (DIA)
Guarantee income for life or a certain period of time, however, the future income start dates are chosen at contract issuance

Fixed Annuities **Fixed annuities** are those in which the insurer agrees to credit a specified interest rate over a stated period. In addition, the insurance company can guarantee a certain annuity payment amount upon annuitization. A fixed annuity provides more security of principal than a variable annuity, but it has limited upside potential.

Variable Annuities Variable annuities do not guarantee specific annuity payments; however, they have potential for greater returns. In a **variable annuity**, the annuity owner chooses to allocate funds among one or more **subaccounts**. Subaccounts, sometimes referred to as separate accounts, are portfolios of stocks and/or bonds that are professionally managed according to specific investment objectives. Gains and losses are credited and debited to the annuity using what are known as **accumulation units**. Accumulation units are the units of measurement that, when combined, equal the total account value of a variable annuity.

The owner of a variable annuity accepts more short-term volatility because the value of the annuity fluctuates with the stock and bond markets, which is simply the trade-off between risk and return.

Equity Indexed Annuities (EIAs) **Equity indexed annuities (EIAs)** are based on the simple concept of returns that are equal to a percentage, or participation rate, of a popular market index (e.g., S&P 500). The credited rate is capped at a percentage of the increase in the index, which limits the upside. The insurer buys bonds to mature at a value sufficient to make good on its guarantee of the principal amount, and uses the remainder to invest in options, which, if in the money, can be exercised; thus, profits are available to share with the annuitant according to the participation rate.

An owner of an EIA enjoys features and benefits of both fixed and variable annuities. Although the upside of the index can work in one's favor, a guaranteed return of principal (not a guaranteed return) provides some downside protection for an individual who cannot afford to place any of the retirement funds at risk.

EIAs are a good fit for an individual who cannot afford to risk the principal investment but desires a potentially higher rate of return than one would receive from a fixed annuity, such as a person nearing retirement but wanting to (partially) participate in marketlike returns.

The EIA provides the annuitant with downside protection during the accumulation phase. Similarly, it provides protection against reduced income payments due to market decline. However, the participant will often be subject to surrender charges, sometimes for a substantial period of time. Also, money withdrawn before the completion of the contract may change the manner in which the return on that money was calculated.

Deferred income annuities (DIA), also known as longevity annuities, guarantee income for life or a certain period of time. One unique characteristic of these types of annuities is that the future income start dates are chosen at contract issuance. Generally, for most deferred annuity contracts, the contract owner would make that decision at some point in the future.

The elected income start date may be any time after the first contract year and generally up to age 85. Premium payments may be single premium or flexible premium. The income start date for annuity benefits will be the same regardless of when the premium payments were made into the contract.

DIA annuity purchase rates (annuitization rates) are established at the time of the initial premium payment or subsequent premium payments. The annuity purchase rates will vary depending on when the premiums are paid. This differs from a typical deferred annuity. With a deferred annuity, if the contract owner decides to annuitize, the annuity purchase rates are determined at the time of annuitization, not when the premium payments are made into the contract.

On July 1, 2014, the U.S. Department of the Treasury and the Internal Revenue Service (IRS) issued final rules regarding **qualified longevity annuity contracts (QLACs)**, an insurance option that ensures retirees have a stream of regular income throughout their advanced years. QLACs are a type of deferred income annuity (DIA). QLACs provide an income stream that begins at an advanced age and continues throughout the individual's life. The final rules made longevity annuities accessible to 401(k) plans and other employer-sponsored individual account plans and IRAs by amending the required minimum distribution (RMD) regulations so that longevity annuity payments will not need to begin prematurely in order to comply with RMD regulations.

Qualified longevity annuity contracts (QLACs)
An insurance option that ensures retirees have a stream of regular income throughout their advanced years

The following are key provisions of the final regulations covering QLACs purchased on or after July 2, 2014:

- *Maximum age at commencement of income.* The QLAC contract must provide that distributions under the contract commence not later than a specified annuity starting date stated in the contract. The specified annuity starting date must be no later than the first day of the month following the employee's attainment of age 85.
- *Maximum allowed investment.* A 401(k) or similar plan, or IRA, may allow plan participants to use up to 25% of their account balance or $125,000, whichever is less, to buy a QLAC without concern about noncompliance with the age 70½ minimum distribution requirements.
- *Allowing return of premium (ROP) death benefit.* A longevity annuity in a plan or IRA can now provide that, if buying retirees die before or after the age when the annuity begins making payments (i.e., annuitization), the premiums they paid but have not yet received as annuity payments will be returned to their accounts and can be paid to their beneficiaries.
- *Protecting persons against unintentional payment of excess longevity annuity premiums.* Individuals who inadvertently exceed the 25% or $125,000 limits on premium payments are allowed to correct the excess without disqualifying the purchase.
- *Allowing more flexibility in issuing QLACs.* When the contract is issued, the contract (or a rider or endorsement with respect to that contract) must state that the contract is intended to be a QLAC.

Annuitization

Annuitization
An irrevocable exchange of a lump-sum amount for a periodic income stream

Annuitization refers to the irrevocable exchange of a lump-sum amount for a periodic income stream. Annuitization is the same process that occurs with various life insurance settlement options, because the beneficiary is exchanging a lump-sum death benefit for one of several common forms of periodic annuity payments, the timing of which and the guarantees, if any, will vary among the numerous options and income streams.

Straight Life Annuity

Straight life annuity
Provides a lifetime income to the annuitant regardless of how long the annuitant lives

Often referred to as a pure life annuity, a **straight life annuity** provides a lifetime income to the annuitant regardless of how long the annuitant lives. After the annuitant dies, no further annuity payments are made by the insurer. For a given purchase price, the highest amount of lifetime income per dollar spent is earned through the pure life annuity.

A straight life annuity provides no guaranteed minimum number of payments the insurer must make, and the dependents of the annuitant receive nothing from the contract once the annuitant has died. Therefore, the pure life annuity is ideal for the person who needs maximum income over his lifetime and has no living dependents to whom to leave the assets.

Life annuity with period certain
Guarantees the greater of a life income to the annuitant or a minimum number of payments to the annuitant's beneficiary

Life Annuity With Period Certain

A **life annuity with period certain** guarantees the greater of a life income to the annuitant or a minimum number of payments to the annuitant's beneficiary. Two common guarantee options are the 10-year period certain and the 20-year period certain. If the annuitant dies before the guarantee period expires, a named beneficiary receives the remaining guaranteed payments. If the annuitant outlives the guarantee period, payments continue until the annuitant's death.

Installment refund annuity
The insurer promises to continue periodic payments after the annuitant has died until the sum of all annuity payments equals the purchase price of the annuity

Installment Refund Annuity

The **installment refund annuity** continues periodic payments after the annuitant has died until the sum of all annuity payments equals the purchase price of the annuity.

Cash refund annuity
Provides that, upon the death of an annuitant before payments totaling the purchase price have been made, the excess of the amount paid by the purchaser over the total annuity payments received will be paid in one sum to designated beneficiaries

Cash Refund Annuity

In cases where an annuitant dies before periodic payments equal or exceed the price paid for the annuity, the insurer pays a lump sum equal to the difference between the price paid and the total payments received by the annuitant to the beneficiary of the annuity.

Joint and survivor annuity
Based on the lives of two or more annuitants

Joint and Survivor Annuity

A **joint and survivor annuity** is based on the lives of two or more annuitants, most often husband and wife. Annuity payments are made until the death of the last annuitant. A joint and 100% survivor annuity pays the full monthly payment to both parties and continues the same payment to the survivor. Some persons, however, choose a joint and survivor annuity that pays the survivor only a portion of the payment that was paid on both lives. For example, a joint and 75% survivor annuity would pay the survivor 75% of the payment received during both annuitants' lifetimes. Joint and last survivor is the most popular form of multilife (2+ annuitants) annuities.

TAXATION OF LIFE INSURANCE AND ANNUITIES

Tax Treatment of Life Insurance

A life insurance contract receives favorable tax treatment in a number of ways. First, death proceeds paid to beneficiaries are generally excluded from taxable income. Second, earnings on the cash value are not taxable until withdrawn. If the insured dies without surrendering the policy or withdrawing the cash value, the cash value accumulated will never be subject to income tax. Third, excluding modified endowment contracts (MECs), loans against a life insurance policy are tax-free. Fourth, under Section 1035 of the Internal Revenue Code, exchanges of one life insurance policy for another or for an annuity or qualified long-term care policy will not result in any recognition of gain. The owner's cost basis for the original life insurance policy will transfer to the new policy or contract.

Taxation of Lifetime Benefits

Dividends

Generally, dividends distributed are not taxable; instead, they are considered a return of a portion of premium payments that reduce the policyowner's basis. If dividends distributed exceed total premiums paid, the excess dividends are taxed to the owner as ordinary income in the year earned.

Withdrawals

Withdrawals from a life insurance policy receive FIFO (first-in, first-out) treatment. In other words, withdrawals of principal are tax-free until the accumulated premiums (less any prior withdrawals or loans) have been paid out (IRC §72(e)).

Modified endowment contracts (MECs) will be subject to LIFO (last-in, first-out) treatment for the life of the policy and a 10% penalty on taxable gains withdrawn before age 59½. (See the Modified Endowment Contracts section in this chapter.)

Cash Surrenders

When the owner of a policy surrenders a life insurance contract, the insurer is no longer obligated to pay the death benefit to the beneficiary. The policyowner will receive the cash surrender value of the policy by one of three methods: lump-sum payment, interest payments, or installment payments. Under the **lump-sum payment method**, the total cash value of the life insurance policy is paid to the policyowner. The gain at surrender equals the cash surrender value minus the investment in the contract (basis), taxed as ordinary income. The investment in the contract equals the premiums paid minus any dividends received minus any outstanding loans or withdrawals.

Lump-sum payment method
The total cash value of the life insurance policy is paid to the policyowner

Upon cash surrender of the policy, the owner may choose to leave the cash value proceeds with the insurer and receive only interest payments on the cash value. Known as the interest only option, the interest is taxable as ordinary income when received or credited to the payee.

Under the **installment payment method**, the policyowner receives the cash value and accrued interest over a period, usually in fixed amounts. This payment method is similar to an annuity, and each payment will include a return of basis and interest. The basis portion is excludable from taxable income and is calculated by using the exclusion ratio, or the ratio of the basis to the total expected payments.

Installment payment method
The policyowner receives the cash value and accrued interest over a period, usually in fixed amounts

For example, Brigette selected the installment payment option on a policy with a cash value of $150,000. She will receive $1,000 per month for the remainder of her life, which according to life expectancy tables will be 20 more years.

Total expected payments = $1,000 × 12 × 20 = $240,000

Brigette's tax basis = $150,000

Exclusion ratio = $150,000 ÷ $240,000 = 0.625

Thus, 62.5%, or $625, of each payment is excludable from gross income.

If the beneficiary who chose the installment method for receipt of death benefits survives beyond her life expectancy, the annuity payments will retain the original exclusion ratio for income tax purposes. If the beneficiary dies before the projected life expectancy, no basis can be recovered and annuity payments will end.

Section 1035 exchange
Provides for the replacement of an existing insurance-based contract for a newer insurance-based contract without having to pay taxes on any gain in the original contract

Section 1035 Exchanges

Internal Revenue Code Section 1035 provides for an exchange of an existing insurance-based contract for a newer insurance-based contract without having to pay taxes on any gain in the original contract. A **Section 1035 exchange** can provide new opportunities for flexibility and tax-deferred accumulation without paying taxes on the cash value growth. Note that the tax on the contract's gain is merely deferred, not eliminated.

IRC Section 1035 provides the postponement of taxes resulting from an exchange of:

- two life insurance contracts;
- a life insurance contract for an endowment insurance contract, an annuity contract, or a qualified long-term care insurance policy;
- two annuity contracts;
- an annuity contract for a qualified long-term care insurance policy;
- an endowment insurance contract for an annuity contract or a qualified long-term care insurance policy;
- two endowment insurance contracts, if the new contract provides for regular payments beginning on a date no later than the date payments would have begun under the contract that was exchanged; or
- two qualified long-term care insurance policies.

The basis for the new contract is the same as the basis in the original contract, plus any premiums paid into the new contract, less any dividends received for the new policy. New sales and surrender charges may be imposed on the new contract.

An exchange of an annuity contract for a life insurance policy cannot be accomplished tax-free. This is because the life insurance policy is taxed more favorably (notably, the income-tax-free nature of the policy's death benefit) than the annuity (that does not have a tax-free death benefit).

Transfer for Value

If an existing policy is transferred for valuable consideration, the insurance proceeds are includable in the gross income of the transferee to the extent the proceeds exceed the basis. Thus, the usual income tax exclusion for life insurance proceeds is lost. Instances in which the transfer of a policy does not result in inclusion of proceeds in the income of the transferee are:

- a transfer to the insured;
- a transfer to a business partner of the insured;
- a transfer to a partnership of which the insured is a partner;
- a transfer to a corporation of which the insured is an officer or shareholder; and
- a transfer that results in the transferee's basis being determined by reference to the transferor's basis, such as a gift.

Premiums

Generally, premium payments for individual life insurance policies are not tax-deductible. Life insurance premiums that are considered alimony, however, are tax-deductible to the payor and taxable as income to the recipient for pre-2019 divorce decrees.

Taxation of Benefits Received After Death

The beneficiary of a life insurance policy generally has the same options for payment as the policyowner does when surrendering a contract. However, the taxation of proceeds may be different. A lump-sum death benefit received as a result of the insured's death is excludable from gross income and is tax-exempt for income tax purposes. Under the interest-only payment option, the insurer pays interest earned on the death benefit to the beneficiary. Because these distributions are 100% interest and 0% death benefit, they are fully includable in the gross income of the beneficiary. Installment payments generally will be made in the form of an annuity, and each payment will include a return of basis and interest. The return of basis component is equal to the ratio of the face value of the policy to the total amount of expected payments to be received.

For example, Benjamin selected the installment payment option on a policy with a face value of $300,000. He will receive $1,750 per month for the remainder of his life, which according to life expectancy tables will be 25 more years.

Total expected payments = $1,750 × 12 × 25 = $525,000

Benjamin's tax basis = $300,000

Exclusion ratio = $300,000 ÷ $525,000 = 0.5714

Thus, 57.14%, or approximately $1,000, of each payment is excluded from gross income.

Viatical Agreements

Viatical agreement
The owner of a policy covering a terminally ill insured sells a life insurance policy to a third party without the proceeds being subject to income tax

Terminal Illness When the insured of a life insurance policy owns a policy and becomes terminally ill (defined as having a life expectancy of 24 months or less), the policyowner may sell the policy to a third party without the proceeds being subject to income tax. This type of settlement, known as a **viatical agreement**, occurs when a third-party purchaser will receive the death benefit of the policy upon the death of the insured and will incur an income tax liability for proceeds that exceed the purchase price and any subsequent premiums paid.

Chronic Illness Another type of viatical agreement with the same tax advantages for the insured is the sale of a life insurance policy whereby the proceeds are used to pay for long-term care for the insured. In this case, the insured must be chronically ill or suffer from substantial cognitive impairment, or be unable to perform at least two of six activities of daily living (ADLs). ADLs are discussed in the Long-Term Care section of this chapter.

Annuities

Each payment from a fixed annuity is considered a partially tax-free return of basis and partially taxable income, using the exclusion ratio. In general, the numerator for the exclusion ratio is the total investment in the annuity. The denominator is the total expected return from the annuity. Unlike an annuity resulting from a life insurance settlement, an annuity payment from a purchased annuity that occurs beyond the original life expectancy is fully taxable as ordinary income to the annuitant. If the annuitant dies before full recovery of basis, the unrecovered basis may be deducted on the decedent's final IRS 1040 form.

Part of each fixed annuity payment an annuitant receives is considered to be a return of principal, which is not taxed; however, the remaining portion of the payment is taxable because it consists of earnings. The exclusion ratio determines the nontaxable portion of each payment indicated by the following formula:

$$\frac{\text{Investment in the contract}}{\text{Expected return}}$$

The exclusion ratio is no longer used once the principal in the contract has been fully paid out to the annuitant. In other words, when the entire amount of principal has been exhausted, the entire annuity payment will be taxable as ordinary income.

INDIVIDUAL HEALTH INSURANCE

Prudent financial planning includes preparation for the financial impact of a serious injury or illness. Not only may medical bills be incurred, but a loss of income might also occur if the ill or injured person is unable to continue working. The probability of needing medical attention during one's life is very high. However, the severity of the illness and the ultimate cost of treatment are unknown. For example, treating the flu is generally affordable for most people, but obtaining a heart or liver transplant is not.

Purpose

Individual health insurance coverage allows individuals to customize their own insurance package. Health insurers typically allow an insured to choose from a wide array of coverage to meet individual needs. A direct relationship exists between the amount of coverage desired and the price of the premium, which means that as more coverage is chosen, the premium increases.

Cost Concerns

Most people who have health insurance coverage today obtain it through either a group plan or a social insurance program. Individual health coverage is not as popular as group coverage. With individual health coverage, the insured may have to pay the full cost of the coverage, and individual health coverage may not be as comprehensive or generous as that offered through group plans.

Major medical insurance
Health insurance that provides broad coverage of all reasonable and necessary expenses associated with an illness or injury, whether incurred at a doctor's office, a hospital, or the insured's home

Major Medical Insurance

Characteristics

Major medical insurance is designed to provide broad coverage of all reasonable and necessary expenses associated with an illness or injury, whether incurred at a doctor's office, a hospital, or the insured's home. Some major medical policies are stand-alone coverage that pays for a wide range of medical services. Others are written in conjunction with a basic medical plan to provide coverage in excess of that provided by the basic coverage. Many consumers are attracted to major medical insurance because it generally covers a wide range of expenses, including hospitalization charges, physician and surgeon's fees, physical therapy, prescription drugs, wheelchairs, and other medical supplies.

Major medical policies have a few exclusions. Self-inflicted injuries, injuries sustained in war, and elective cosmetic procedures are typically not covered.

Usual and customary expenses *Health care costs that are consistent with the average rate or charge for identical or similar services in a particular geographic area*

Coinsurance *The cost sharing of covered health care expenses between the insured and the insurer*

Stop-loss limit *A dollar amount of covered benefits to which the coinsurance provision is applied, but it does not include the deductible; once the stop-loss limit is reached, the insurer pays 100% of all covered expenses*

Most major medical policies have a deductible ranging from $500 to as high as $10,000. The deductible normally applies per person per year, with a maximum number of aggregate deductibles per family. After the deductible has been met, the insurer typically pays the majority of the remaining usual and customary expenses, subject to a coinsurance amount. **Usual and customary expenses** are health care costs that are consistent with the average rate or charge for identical or similar services in a particular geographical area. **Coinsurance** is the cost sharing of health care expenses between the insured and the insurer, with common amounts ranging from 60%/40% to 80%/20%. In these examples, the insurer would pay either 60% or 80% of covered medical expenses above the deductible, and the insured would be responsible for the remainder. A **stop-loss limit** is the dollar amount of covered benefits to which the coinsurance provision is applied, but it does not include the deductible. Once the stop-loss limit is reached, the insurer pays 100% of all covered expenses for the rest of the year.

For example, Ryan and Sherri have a major medical policy with a $1,000 deductible, 70%/30% coinsurance, and a stop-loss limit of $20,000. Last summer, Ryan suffered from gallstones that resulted in surgery. The medical bills covered by Ryan and Sherri's plan totaled $45,000. No other claims were incurred during the year. Ryan and Sherri's major medical policy would pay as follows:

	Insurer	Ryan and Sherri
Total bills	$45,000	
Less deductible		$1,000
Balance	$44,000	
Coinsurance (of $20,000)	$14,000	$6,000
Ryan and Sherri maximum out-of-pocket		$7,000 ($1,000 deductible + $6,000 coinsurance payment)

Note: Ryan's medical expenses exceeded the policy's $20,000 stop-loss limit. The maximum out-of-pocket for this policy is $7,000 per year. The insurance company is responsible for the remaining $38,000 ($14,000 coinsurance plus $24,000 remaining balance).

2010 Health Care Reform Legislation

The Patient Protection and Affordable Care Act of 2010 and the Health Care and Education Reconciliation Act of 2010 made sweeping changes to the American health care system. For example, most people who are not eligible for Medicare, Medicaid, or other government-provided health care must maintain certain minimum levels of health care coverage. However, the penalty for individuals not having qualified health care coverage was reduced zero for months after December 31, 2018. Refundable tax credits help make health care coverage more affordable for low-income earners.

The legislation provides that plans covering dependents must allow coverage for adult children until age 26, prohibit lifetime coverage limits for essential health benefits, and require plans to provide preventive services without charging deductibles, copayments, or coinsurance. Insurers cannot cancel coverage after an insured gets sick unless there was fraud in the application.

The Affordable Care Act defines essential health benefits to include the following:

- Ambulatory patient services, emergency services, and hospitalization
- Maternity and newborn care and pediatric services, including oral and vision care
- Mental health and substance use disorder services, including behavioral health treatment
- Prescription drugs and laboratory services
- Rehabilitative services and devices
- Preventive and wellness services and chronic disease management

In addition, insurers may no longer impose pre-existing conditions or exclusions or deny coverage based on pre-existing conditions for children under age 19 (not applicable to grandfathered plans). Most plans are prohibited from imposing pre-existing condition exclusions and denials of coverage based on pre-existing conditions for any insured. Insurers cannot impose higher deductibles, copayments, or coinsurance for emergency services provided by an out-of-network provider. Plans are required to provide women with direct access to in-network OBs and GYNs and children with in-network pediatricians (i.e., no preauthorization or referral from primary care physician is necessary). Employer-provided health plans are also prohibited from establishing eligibility rules that discriminate in favor of higher-paid employees.

Medical Expense Insurance

Basic Medical Insurance Coverage

Traditionally, there have been three basic coverages an insured could purchase to provide for a specific type of medical expense: hospital expense insurance, surgical expense insurance, and physician's expense insurance.

Hospital expense insurance
Provides payment for expenses incurred by the insured while in the hospital

Hospital expense insurance provides payment for expenses incurred by the insured while in the hospital. Coverage under hospital expense insurance includes a daily hospital benefit and a miscellaneous expense benefit. The daily hospital benefit pays a specified amount for room and board charges incurred during each day the insured is hospitalized and may be paid on a reimbursement basis, subject to a maximum daily limit, or it may be a flat amount per day. Also, some plans have a maximum number of days covered, such as 90 or 180 days.

A lump-sum benefit may be paid if the patient incurs miscellaneous expenses for items, such as x-rays, medications, surgical supplies, and use of an operating room. The miscellaneous expense benefit may be subject to a maximum dollar amount. This expense would be subject to the 2010 health care reform legislation.

Caution must be exercised in purchasing this type of coverage because many expensive procedures are now performed outside of a hospital. Also, physician's and surgeon's fees are billed separately from hospital services, so hospital expense coverage does not provide for payment of those fees. Purchasing only hospital expense coverage is not sufficient to meet the needs of most individuals.

Surgical expense insurance
May be added to a hospital expense insurance policy to provide payment of surgeon's fees, even when procedures are not performed in a hospital

Surgical expense insurance may be added to a hospital expense insurance policy to provide for the payment of the surgeon's fees, even when surgery is not performed in a hospital. Insurers typically base maximum benefits payable on a generic list of surgical procedures and their estimated costs, but some other benefit determination formula may be used. This expense would also be subject to the limitations imposed by the 2010 health care reform legislation.

Physician's expense insurance
Pays for fees charged by physicians that provide nonsurgical care

Physician's expense insurance pays for fees charged by physicians who provide the insured with nonsurgical care. Treatment can be administered in the doctor's office, the patient's home, or the hospital. Once again, this expense would also be subject to the 2010 health care reform legislation limits.

Limitations

Basic medical coverage, sometimes referred to as indemnity coverage, sets rigid limits on the amount payable for any one event. The maximum benefit provided for any single illness or injury may not be enough to pay the actual expenses incurred. Although having this coverage is better than having no coverage at all, insureds must be aware that benefit levels are restricted.

HEALTH SAVINGS ACCOUNTS (HSAs)

Health savings account (HSA)
Special account that is used to pay for current and future medical expenses in conjunction with a high-deductible health plan (HDHP)

Health savings accounts (HSAs) are special accounts used to pay for current and future medical expenses in conjunction with a high-deductible health plan (HDHP). Although HSAs are commonly offered through an employer, they are not employer-owned accounts; rather, they are individually owned accounts. Therefore, it is the individual who makes decisions regarding participation, contributions, usage, and distributions. The individual also chooses the trustee, or custodian, as well as how funds within the account will be invested.

Eligibility

To be eligible for an HSA, an individual must be covered by an HDHP, cannot be covered by other health insurance or enrolled in Medicare, and cannot be claimed as a dependent on another's tax return. Children are not eligible to establish their own HSAs. However, spouses can establish their own HSAs, provided the spouse meets the normal eligibility requirements. Neither income limits restricting contributions exist, nor are there any earned income requirements that must be met before one can establish an HSA.

High-deductible health plan (HDHP)
A health plan, often used in conjunction with a health savings account (HSA); the HSA is used to pay for expenses up to the deductible amount

High-Deductible Health Plan (HDHP) Except for preventive care, HDHPs do not cover first-dollar medical expenses and are the responsibility of the individual HSA owner. The individual has the option to use his HSA to pay for these expenses.

As long as certain requirements are met, the HDHP can be an HMO, PPO, or indemnity plan. The HDHP must meet the following requirements to be used in conjunction with an HSA.

The minimum deductibles for 2022 are:

- $1,400 for self-only coverage; and
- $2,800 for family coverage.

In 2022, the maximum annual out-of-pocket, including deductibles and co-payments are:

- $7,050 for self-only coverage; and
- $14,100 for family coverage

Note that the minimum HSA deductibles and maximum annual out-of-pocket amounts are indexed annually for inflation.

Contribution Rules Contributions to HSAs can be made by the employer, the individual, or both. Employer contributions are not taxable to the employee (excluded from income and wages). Individual contributions are treated as an above-the-line deduction.

Individuals can make a one-time transfer from their IRA to an HSA, subject to the contribution limits applicable for the year of the transfer.

In 2022, the maximum contributions to an HSA from all sources are:

- $3,650 for self-only coverage; and
- $7,300 for family coverage.

These amounts are indexed annually.

For individuals age 55 and older, an additional catch-up contribution of $1,000 is allowed.

Contributions must stop once an individual is eligible for Medicare.

Employees can make contributions to their HSAs through a salary reduction arrangement within a cafeteria plan (Section 125 plan). These elections can change on a monthly basis (unlike salary reduction contributions to an FSA). Contributions to HSAs through a cafeteria plan are pretax and not subject to individual or employment taxes.

The HSA owner's employer can make cafeteria plan contributions on the individual's behalf unless the individual elects to not have such contributions made (negative elections).

Employer contributions are always excluded from an employee's income (pretax) and must be comparable for all employees participating in the HSA. Self-employed, partnership members and S corporation shareholders are normally not considered employees and therefore are ineligible to receive employer contributions; however, they can make deductible HSA contributions on their own behalf.

Distributions An employer cannot place restrictions on an individual's use of HSA distributions. However, reasonable limitations as to frequency and size of distributions can be placed on the individual by the HSA's custodian or trustee.

The individual has the option to save HSA funds for the future by using alternative resources to pay for current medical expenses. If an individual makes withdrawals from an HSA for purposes other than a qualifying medical expense, the withdrawals will be subject to income tax and a 20% penalty. The 20% penalty does not apply to withdrawals made after the individual reaches age 65, dies, or becomes disabled. Over-the-counter medicines and drugs (other than insulin) do not qualify without a doctor's prescription.

Individual account holders must file Form 8889 on their annual federal tax returns and report the amount of their distributions used for qualified medical expenses.

Tax-free distributions can be taken for qualified medical expenses of a person covered by an HDHP, the spouse of the individual (even if not covered by the HDHP), and any dependent of the individual (even if not covered by the HDHP).

Transfers and Rollovers Rollovers from HSAs are permitted once per year. A rollover to a new HSA must be completed within 60 days; direct trustee-to-trustee transfers of HSA amounts are not subject to the rollover restriction. Therefore, multiple trustee-to-trustee transfers are allowed in a single year. Direct rollovers from Section 401(k), 403(b), and 457 plans are not permitted.

Treatment of HSAs upon Death If the spouse is the beneficiary, the spouse inheriting the HSA is treated as the owner. To the extent the spouse is not the beneficiary, the account will no longer be treated as an HSA upon the death of the individual. Instead, the account will become taxable to the decedent in the decedent's final tax return if the estate is the beneficiary, or it will be taxable to the recipient.

The taxable amount will be reduced by any qualified medical expenses incurred by the deceased individual before death and paid by the recipient of the HSA and further reduced by the amount of estate tax paid because of inclusion of the HSA in the deceased individual's estate.

Trustees and Custodians Banks, credit unions, insurance companies, and previously approved IRA or Archer MSA trustees or custodians are eligible to serve as trustees. The HSA trustee must report all distributions annually to the individual on Form 1099 SA. Trustees are not required to determine whether distributions are used for medical purposes; this is the individual's responsibility. Trustee or custodian fees can be paid from the assets in the HSA account without being subject to taxes or penalties. They can also be paid directly by the beneficiary without being counted toward the HSA contribution limits.

Advantages The HSA has many advantages. Among these are no "use it or lose it rules" such as those that apply to flexible spending arrangements (FSAs). All amounts in the HSA are fully vested, and unspent balances in accounts remain in the accounts until spent. The HSA encourages the account holder to be a more conscientious consumer of medical care and to shop around for the best value for health care. Furthermore, the owner's funds can be left to grow through investment earnings, in much the same way and with the same investment options as IRAs.

Disadvantages The primary disadvantage of an HSA lies in the fact that many have enrolled in HSA programs, but many have not actually established an HSA. Among those who have established an HSA, the majority are not funding them adequately. Rather, they have purchased an HDHP, and without funding the HSA, large numbers of Americans lack the resources to fund the first-dollar expenses associated with an HDHP, and many of them are at risk of not receiving the health coverage the HSA was designed to provide.

LONG-TERM CARE INSURANCE

Long-term care insurance
Provides coverage for nursing home stays and other types of routine care that are not covered by other health insurance

Skilled nursing care
Daily nursing care and rehabilitation services ordered and monitored by a physician

Intermediate nursing care
Occasional nursing and rehabilitative care ordered and monitored by a physician

An elderly person might be able to live alone but may need assistance each day with dressing and bathing. Medical expense policies (including Medicare) neither cover these types of expenses, nor do they pay for stays in extended care facilities, such as nursing homes. **Long-term care insurance** provides coverage for nursing home stays and other types of assistance with activities of daily living that are not covered by other health insurance. The premium charged for long-term care coverage depends on the insured's age, the insured's health condition, and the level of benefits chosen.

There are seven types of coverage:

1. **Skilled nursing care** is the highest level of medical care and is provided by traditional nursing homes. Daily nursing care is provided, along with rehabilitation services, and the patient's care is ordered and monitored by a physician.
2. **Intermediate nursing care** is similar to skilled nursing care, except that care is provided occasionally rather than on a daily basis. Again, a physician must order and monitor this type of treatment.

Custodial care
Provides assistance with the regular tasks of daily life, such as eating, dressing, bathing, and taking medications

Home health care
Part-time skilled nursing care and rehabilitative therapy provided at the patient's home

Assisted living facilities
Apartment-style housing combined with support services and basic health care

Adult day care
Basic assistance and supervision provided outside the home usually during the primary caregiver's working hours

Hospice care
Care that provides dignity and comfort to terminally ill patients

3. **Custodial care** provides assistance with the regular tasks of daily life, such as eating, dressing, bathing, and taking medications. These services normally can be provided by nonmedical personnel and do not have to be ordered or supervised by a physician.
4. **Home health care** allows the patient to remain at home and receive part-time skilled nursing care, rehabilitative therapy, and other necessary assistance. Depending on the level of treatment needed, services may be provided by skilled professionals or nonmedical personnel.
5. **Assisted living facilities** (ALFs) provide apartment-style housing, support services, and basic health care for individuals who need help with the tasks of daily life. Some assisted living facilities are connected with skilled nursing facilities and allow patients to transfer back and forth as required by their health status.
6. **Adult day care** is provided for persons who need assistance and supervision during times when a spouse or other family caregiver must work. The purpose of adult day care is quite similar to that of infant and child day care—to allow family members living with a person who cannot take care of oneself to maintain their careers.
7. **Hospice care** is care for the terminally ill and can take place at the patient's home, a hospice care center, a hospital, or a nursing facility. Unlike most health care services, hospice care does not seek to cure the patient of an ailment. Rather, the goals of hospice care are providing pain management, emotional and spiritual support, and treatment that provides the patient with dignity and comfort.

The need for long-term care insurance is often overlooked in the financial planning process. When an individual requires long-term care that other health insurance will not cover, assets may be quickly depleted paying for such care. In extreme cases, some people ultimately liquidate all assets so they can qualify for long-term care benefits through the Medicaid (welfare) program. As many long-term care facilities are not Medicaid providers, the insured's choice of care facilities may be severely restricted.

Benefits

Defined-period approach
Long-term care coverage provided for a specified period following an elimination period

Pool-of-money concept
Long-term care coverage provided up to a specific dollar amount, regardless of time

Long-term care insurance is a recent innovation prompted by the extension of life provided by today's technology. The two benefit approaches used are the defined-period approach and the pool-of-money approach. The **defined-period approach** is the more popular method and provides coverage for a defined period following an elimination period generally ranging from 30 to 365 days. Benefits may be provided for a specified period or until death. Under the **pool-of-money concept**, the insured is covered up to a specific dollar amount regardless of the period.

Most of the features of other health insurance policies are also found in long-term care insurance policies, including an elimination period and waiver of premium. When determining the appropriateness and desirable characteristics of long-term care insurance, financial planners should consider the benefits available under Medicare, Medicaid, the client's assets, and family health history.

Tax-qualified long-term care insurance
Policies that meet standards established with the passage of the Health Insurance Portability and Accountability Act of 1996 (HIPAA)

Tax-Qualified Long-Term Care Insurance A class of long-term care insurance policies called **tax-qualified long-term care insurance** was established with the passage of the Health Insurance Portability and Accountability Act of 1996 (HIPAA). Policies that meet standards set forth in this act state on their cover and in marketing materials that the policy is intended to be a qualified plan. The word *intend* or *intended* is used because the federal government does not have a mechanism for certifying that policies are qualified. However, a policy that clearly does not meet the standards cannot state that it is intended to be a qualified plan.

A tax-qualified (TQ) long-term care insurance policy is any contract that provides only coverage of qualified long-term care services and meets the following additional requirements.

- The contract must not provide for a cash surrender value or other money that can be paid, assigned, borrowed, or pledged.
- Refunds under the contract (other than refunds paid upon the death of the insured or complete surrender or cancellation of the contract) and dividends may be used only to reduce future premiums or to increase future benefits.
- The contract must meet certain consumer protection standards (see Exhibit 9.6).
- The contract must coordinate benefits with Medicare (unless Medicare is a secondary payor) unless the contract is an indemnity or per diem contract.

EXHIBIT 9.6 Consumer Protection Standards

To qualify for favorable tax treatment under HIPAA, a long-term care policy must have certain consumer protection features. These protections include the following:

- All contracts must be guaranteed renewable.
- Pre-existing conditions can be excluded up to a maximum of six months after issue. (If a new contract replaces another contract, the new contract must recognize the previous contract's satisfaction of the insured's six-month pre-existing condition.)
- Contracts cannot require prior hospitalization before paying nursing home benefits or require prior institutionalization before paying home care benefits.
- Contracts cannot exclude any specific illnesses (such as Alzheimer's disease).
- Contracts must provide protection against unintentional lapses because of a physical or cognitive impairment.
- Companies cannot utilize postclaims underwriting.
- Contracts providing home care benefits cannot restrict allowable care to only skilled care and must provide coverage for a meaningful length of time.
- Contracts must offer inflation protection.
- Companies must offer a nonforfeiture option.

Qualified long-term care services
As defined by HIPAA, include necessary diagnostic, preventative, therapeutic, caring, treating, rehabilitative services, and maintenance or personal care services required by a chronically ill or cognitively impaired person and provided by a plan prescribed by a licensed health care practitioner

Chronically ill individual
A person who has an illness or injury resulting in the inability to perform, without substantial assistance, at least two of the six activities of daily living for a period expected to last at least 90 days

Activities of daily living (ADLs)
Eating, bathing, dressing, transferring from bed to chair, toileting, and continence

Qualified long-term care services include necessary diagnostic, preventative, therapeutic, caring, treating, rehabilitative services, as well as maintenance or personal care services that are required by a chronically ill or cognitively impaired person. These services are provided in accordance with a plan of care prescribed by a licensed health care practitioner.

A **chronically ill individual** is any person certified within the previous 12 months by a licensed health practitioner as (1) being unable to perform at least two **activities of daily living (ADLs)** for a period expected to last at least 90 days owing to a loss of functional capacity, (2) requiring substantial supervision to protect the person from threats to health and safety because of severe cognitive impairment, or (3) having a similar level of disability as designated by some future regulation.

Under the ADL trigger, the policy must take into account at least five of the following ADLs in determining whether an individual is chronically ill: eating, toileting, transferring, bathing, dressing, and continence.

Plans that do not meet these requirements are considered non-tax-qualified (NTQ) long-term care insurance, and the plans are identified by one or more of the following characteristics:

1. The physical impairment does not need to be expected to last at least 90 days.
2. The physical impairment requirement can be met with just one ADL impairment.
3. The physical impairment requirement can be met with an impairment with two or more of any ADLs.
4. Fewer than five ADLs can be assessed in determining whether an individual is chronically ill.
5. The physical impairment requirement can be met with an impairment of instrumental activities of daily living (IADLs) only.
6. The physical impairment requirement can be met without reference to the need for substantial assistance.
7. The insured can qualify for benefits:
   - because of a medical necessity;
   - without a severe cognitive impairment; and
   - without a plan of care submitted to the insurance company.
8. The benefits reimburse for actual charges but do not coordinate with Medicare.
9. The plan pays benefits for services received from unskilled providers or family members.*
10. The plan pays benefits for services not related to caring for the insured.
11. The plan pays for capital improvements to a home.
12. The plan includes a cash payment return of premium at lapse that pays in excess of the premiums paid for the policy.

*A tax-qualified (TQ) long-term care insurance plan can also pay benefits for unskilled providers or family members and does not have to coordinate benefits with Medicare if the benefits are paid without regard to actual cost and are referred to as *indemnity plans*. In contrast, plans that are concerned with actual cost are referred to as *reimbursement plans*.

HIPAA allows favorable tax treatment for premiums paid to and benefits received from qualified plans. Premiums paid by the individual are deductible as medical expenses for itemized deduction purposes, depending on the individual's age. Exhibit 9.7 outlines the maximum annual premium allowed to be deducted for 2022 income tax purposes. If an employer pays for long-term care insurance, the premiums are tax-deductible to the employer and are not taxable income to the employee. Long-term care benefits cannot be included in a cafeteria plan or a flexible spending account on a tax-advantaged basis. In other words, if the premiums are deducted from the employee's pay, they must be deducted on an after-tax basis. Regardless of who makes the premium payments, benefits received from qualified long-term plans are excluded from income.

EXHIBIT 9.7 Maximum Allowable Federal Income Tax Deduction for Long-Term Care Premiums (2022)

Age of insured	2022 Maximum deduction
40 or younger	$450
41–50	$850
51–60	$1,690
61–70	$4,520
Older than 70	$5,640

Long-Term Care Needs

Many people overlook the need to protect against the expenses associated with the special nonmedical care created by prolonged illness or old age. Serious health problems, cognitive impairment, and lack of mobility can have a devastating impact on a family's financial security. Statistics show that over 70% of people over the age of 65 will encounter a long-term care need during their lifetime.

Long-term care insurance can help cover the costs associated with providing assistance with the activities of daily living that individuals cannot perform on their own. Long-term care insurance pays for the costs of caring for a person who requires daily assistance from someone else. Long-term care insurance can help protect against the financial hardship due to a lengthy illness commonly occurring from old age.

Exhibit 9.8 lists some questions to consider when determining long-term care insurance needs.

EXHIBIT 9.8 Long-Term Care—Things to Consider

- What is your family medical history?
- Does this history show a predisposition for long life and a need for residency in a nursing home?
- Does this history show that medical assistance was needed during old age? If so, what general type?
- Do you have assets (e.g., investments) that will provide income during your old age?
- Do you anticipate any other income during your old age?
- What is the current daily/monthly rate for nursing homes in your area?
- What is the projected future daily/monthly rate for nursing homes in your area?
- Other considerations:

____

____

____

____

DISABILITY INCOME INSURANCE

Overview

Disability income insurance
A type of insurance that provides a replacement income while the insured is unable to work because of illness or injury

Disability income insurance provides replacement income while the insured is unable to work because of illness or injury. Premiums for this coverage are a function of the insured's health, occupation, gender, age, and the level of income benefits provided by the policy. Most insureds purchase either a flat dollar amount of coverage, such as $2,000 per month, or coverage that replaces some portion of predisability earnings (such as 60%–80%).

To qualify for disability income, one must become disabled, as defined by the policy, while the policy is in force and remain so until the elimination (waiting) period has ended. Once these qualifications are met, monthly indemnity will be made payable at the end of each month of disability. Premiums for disability insurance are based partially on **morbidity** rates for the benefit term. The morbidity rate is the probability of a person becoming disabled.

Morbidity
Relates to the probability of becoming disabled

Disability insurance may cover injuries only or injuries and illness. Coverage for injury and illness is preferred but will result in a higher premium. Injury is defined in the policy as either accidental bodily injury or bodily injury by accidental means. **Accidental bodily injury** requires only that the injury incurred be accidental. **Bodily injury by accidental means** requires accidental injury by accidental means.

Accidental bodily injury
Only the injury incurred is accidental

Bodily injury by accidental means
Requires accidental injury by accidental means

Thus, if Max's co-worker intentionally drops a computer monitor on Max's foot, Max's disability insurance would provide coverage if it provides for accidental bodily injuries. Max would not be covered, however, if his policy defined injury as bodily injury by accidental means, because the co-worker intentionally dropped the monitor. The definition of *illness* usually precludes pre-existing conditions and may require a probationary period.

Disability Income Needs

During an individual's income-earning years, the probability of becoming disabled is greater than the probability of death. As a result, a client should make sure that he is protected against loss of income due to a disability.

Disability Needs Analysis Questionnaire

Exhibit 9.9 is a disability needs analysis questionnaire that addresses an individual's income needs should a disability occur. The questionnaire can help determine how much disability income insurance is required to maintain the current lifestyle of the breadwinner and family. Please note that some costs, such as medical expenses, may actually increase during periods of disability and should be taken into consideration when calculating income needs.

EXHIBIT 9.9 Disability Needs Analysis Questionnaire

Monthly Expenses		
Mortgage or Rent	$__________	
Food	$__________	
Clothing	$__________	
Utilities	$__________	
Medical/Dental	$__________	
Personal Care	$__________	
Automobile Expenses	$__________	
Tuition	$__________	
Insurance Premiums	$__________	
Loans/Credit Card Payments	$__________	
Other: ____________________	$__________	
Other: ____________________	$__________	
Other: ____________________	$__________	
Other: ____________________	$__________	
Other: ____________________	$__________	
Other: ____________________	$__________	
Total		$__________
Monthly Gross Earned Income		
Insured	$__________	
Spouse	$__________	
Total		$__________
Income from Other Sources (use after-tax amounts)		
Group Disability Insurance	$__________	
Mortgage Insurance	$__________	
Creditor Insurance	$__________	
Disability Pension Benefits	$__________	
Investment Income	$__________	
Total		$__________

After calculating total expenses, subtract any income that will continue during disability, including spousal income and income from other sources.

Total monthly expenses	$__________
Total monthly income	$__________
Maximum amount of monthly disability income	$__________

Characteristics

Definitions of Disability

A key feature of disability income insurance is the definition of *disability*, which specifies what constitutes a disability for the purposes of receiving policy benefits. Unless the insured's condition complies with the disability definition in the policy, the insurer does not pay income benefits. Different types of disability definitions exist, including any occupation, own occupation, and a combination of the two, known as the *split definition*.

Any occupation
Definition of disability in which an insured is considered totally disabled if the duties of any occupation cannot be performed

Any Occupation A person insured under the **any occupation** definition is considered totally disabled if she cannot perform the duties of any occupation. The courts have interpreted this clause to mean any occupation for which the insured is suited by education, experience, and training. Thus, a disabled brain surgeon can draw benefits from the policy even if she is still able to work at a fast food restaurant. But, if the surgeon is able to teach, lecture, or do research related to her field of expertise, then the insurer would likely not consider her to be disabled.

Own occupation
Definition of disability in which an insured is considered totally disabled if the insured cannot perform the substantial and major duties of the insured's own occupation

Own Occupation The **own occupation** definition is much more accommodating than the any occupation definition, because it states that the insured must be able to perform the substantial and major duties of his own occupation or he is considered disabled. This means that a surgeon who cannot perform surgery because of a broken hand is considered totally disabled even if he moves to a hospital administration position.

Split Definition Many disability income insurance policies today include a combination of the any and own occupation definitions. Typically, the own occupation definition of disability applies only during the first one to five years after an illness or injury occurs; after that, the any occupation definition applies.

Social Security
Definition of disability for Social Security in which an insured is considered totally disabled if the insured cannot perform any gainful employment

Social Security Disability Definition The law defines disability as the inability to do any substantial gainful activity by reason of any medically determinable physical or mental impairment that can be expected to result in death or has lasted or can be expected to last for a continuous period of not less than 12 months. To meet this definition, you must have a severe impairment(s) that makes you unable to do your past relevant work or any other substantial gainful work that exists in the national economy.

Features

Elimination period
The amount of time that must pass before benefits are paid

Elimination Period Short-term disability benefits normally begin to pay within several days of the date of disability. However, long-term policies require the insured to satisfy an **elimination**, or waiting, **period**, ranging in length from of one month to one year, in an effort to reduce small claims and to help reduce the level of moral hazard associated with fraudulent claims. As one might expect, the premium increases as the elimination period gets shorter.

Short-term disability
Provides coverage for up to two years

Long-term disability
Provides coverage for specified term greater than two years, until specified age, or until death

Benefit Period Disability insurance distinguishes between short-term and long-term coverage. **Short-term disability** typically provides coverage for up to two years. Many employers offer group short-term disability insurance that provides employees with a percentage of their salary while disabled. **Long-term disability** typically provides coverage until normal retirement age, until death, or for a specified term longer than two years. Some employers offer group long-term disability insurance with premiums generally paid for by the employee. Employer-sponsored plans are usually not portable and terminate when the employee leaves the firm, unless the reason for leaving employment is directly related to the disability.

Waiver of Premium The waiver of premium removes the requirement for the policyowner to make premium payments after the insured has satisfied the elimination period. In most cases, premiums paid during the elimination period are refunded upon commencement of benefits and do not resume until the insured is deemed no longer disabled.

Riders

Partial disability rider
The insured cannot perform all of the substantial and material duties of the job

Partial Disability Rider Many policies include automatically, or by adding a policy rider, coverage for partial disability, which is defined as a disability that prevents the insured from performing some, but not all, of the substantial and material duties of the job, with exact definitions varying among policies. The **partial disability rider** provides payments that are less than those paid for total disability, but these benefits usually last for only a short time (such as six months). By covering a partial disability in this manner, the insurer gives the insured some incentive to return to work sooner rather than later.

Cost-of-living adjustment (COLA) rider
Increases benefits being received by the policyowner each year; based on an index, such as the CPI

Cost-of-Living Adjustment (COLA) Rider Disability insurance claims often result in benefit payments that last for a number of years. A cost-of-living adjustment is made to the benefit each year to protect benefits from the effects of inflation for as long as the insured remains disabled. The increases are normally based on either the Consumer Price Index (CPI) with a cap or a fixed-percentage rate that is elected at the time of application by the policyowner, usually ranging from 2%–5% and computed on either a simple or compounded basis. Please note that this benefit does not increase the monthly benefit from the date of policy issue but provides for an increase in benefits that are actually being paid.

Future Increase Option Rider The future increase option protects future earnings by allowing the policyowner to increase the potential monthly benefit as the insured gets older and earns more, regardless of any health changes. The rider guarantees insurability for a certain period of time (normally to age 55) for an additional premium. Please note that this option affects the monthly benefit; in other words, the potential benefit paid in the event a disability occurs is increased.

Automatic Increase Rider The automatic increase rider raises the total monthly benefit coverage each year for a specified number of years (a common increase is 5% per year for five years). Premiums will increase as the monthly coverage increases, and the rider is often used to have the monthly benefit coverage keep pace with inflation.

Residual benefits provision
Policyowner receives a percentage of the disability benefit on the basis of the percentage of income loss due to sickness or injury

Residual Benefits Under the **residual benefits provision,** or rider, the policyowner receives a percentage of the disability benefit on the basis of the percentage of income loss due to sickness or injury. The benefit payable is equal to a proportionate amount of the monthly benefit.

EXAMPLE Assume Dr. Turner earns $10,000 per month as a practicing physician. She becomes disabled and returns to work as a consultant earning $6,000 per month, resulting in a drop in income of 40%. Dr. Turner had a disability income policy with a residual benefits provision and a monthly benefit of $5,000. Under the residual benefit provision of the policy, she would receive a benefit of $2,000 (40% of the $5,000) per month.

Taxation of Benefits

Individual disability income insurance premiums are generally not tax-deductible by the insured. As a result, benefit payments received during a period of disability are not subject to income taxation.

Integration of Benefits

Financial planners should realize that Social Security may provide disability benefits to a disabled person; however, the Social Security definition of disability is much more restrictive than most definitions used in private disability income insurance. In addition, the Social Security program requires the disabled person to wait five months before receiving benefits and prove that he cannot engage in any gainful employment and that the disability is expected to last at least 12 months or result in death.

A disability income policy may integrate with Social Security disability coverage. A policy that integrates with Social Security reduces benefits payable by the amount of

Social Security benefits the disabled person is eligible to receive. This type of coverage is less expensive than a similar policy that does not integrate with Social Security because the insurer expects to pay out lower benefits if the insured is disabled for a long time.

The insured may have a $2,000 monthly disability benefit provided by the policy, but if one is also eligible for a $1,200 monthly Social Security disability benefit, the individual policy might pay only $800 per month. When shopping for an individual disability income policy, the insured should be aware that some policies contain such integration provisions.

Termination of Benefits

Benefit payments cease at either the end of the benefit period or the date when the insured is no longer disabled, whichever occurs first.

EXHIBIT 9.10 Long-Term Disability Insurance Checklist

Feature	Desirable coverage
Amount of benefit	60%–70% of gross pay
Benefit term	Work life expectancy
Covered conditions	Injury and illness
Elimination period	Based on client's liquid assets and emergency fund
Definition of disability	Own occupation or split definition
Integration	To reduce premiums, integration with Social Security or workers' compensation may be desirable

Health and Disability Insurance Policy Provisions

Pre-Existing Conditions

Pre-existing condition
A medical condition that required treatment during a specified period before the insured's effective date

Preexisting conditions clause
Excludes coverage for pre-existing conditions for a specified period, such as 12 months, after the effective date of coverage

A **pre-existing condition** is a medical condition that required treatment during a specified period (e.g., six months) before the insured's effective date of coverage under a health insurance plan. In some policies, the definition of *pre-existing condition* includes medical conditions known to the insured, even though no medical care was provided for the condition during the specified period. A **pre-existing conditions clause** excludes coverage for pre-existing conditions for a specified period, such as 12 months, after the effective date of coverage and is used to control adverse selection. As noted earlier, the use of pre-existing conditions clauses in health insurance plans has been restricted by the 2010 health care reform legislation.

Grace Period

The grace period is the time (usually 31 days) beyond the premium due date during which an insurance premium payment may be made without cancellation of the coverage. During the grace period, the policy remains in force.

Reinstatement

Included in every health insurance policy is a procedure for policy reinstatement if coverage lapses because of nonpayment of premium. The reinstatement clause specifies a time limit within which the insured may reinstate the policy and indicates whether proof of insurability is required. Reinstated policies usually have pre-existing clauses that exclude coverage for illnesses incurred during a given period.

Time Limit on Certain Defenses

The time limit on certain defenses is an optional provision that may be used in noncancelable or guaranteed renewable health insurance contracts. Similar to an incontestability clause in a life insurance policy, it states that the insurer may not contest the validity of the contract, except in cases of fraud, after it has been in force for a certain period (typically two years).

Rights of Renewability

Noncancelable

Noncancelable
Insurer guarantees the renewal of the policy for a given period or to a stated age without an increase in premium

A health or disability insurance policy that is **noncancelable** provides the greatest amount of security for the insured. The insurance company guarantees the renewal of the policy for a given period or to a stated age. In addition, the insurer may not make changes to the policy, including increases in premiums.

Guaranteed Renewable

Guaranteed renewable
The insurer is required to renew the policy for a specified period, regardless of changes in the insured's health (premiums may be increased) by class of insureds

If a health or disability insurance policy is **guaranteed renewable**, the insurance company is required to renew a policy for a specified period (e.g., to age 65), regardless of changes in the health of the insured. Under this agreement, premiums must be paid when due, and renewal of the policy is at the sole discretion of the insured. The insurance company, however, reserves the right to increase premiums as deemed necessary, as long as the premium increase is for an entire class of insureds.

Conditionally Renewable

Conditionally renewable
Cannot be canceled by the insurer during the policy term, but insurer may refuse to renew the contract for another term if certain conditions exist

A policy that is **conditionally renewable** cannot be canceled by the insurance company during the policy term (usually one year), but it may refuse to renew the contract for another term if certain conditions exist as stipulated in the policy.

Optionally Renewable

Optionally renewable
The insurer may not cancel the policy during the term, but the insurer may decline to renew the policy for a subsequent term

Under a policy that is **optionally renewable**, the insurance company may not cancel the policy during the term (usually one year), but it may decline to renew the policy for a subsequent term. Hence, very little security to the insured is provided.

GROUP HEALTH INSURANCE

Most medical expense insurance coverage sold today is in the form of a group policy. Pooling together a large number of employees lowers the administrative costs of providing coverage, and adverse selection is usually reduced. As a result, more features and benefits are usually provided through a group health insurance plan.

Eligibility

To be eligible for group health care coverage, one must be a member of a group that has come together for some purpose other than to purchase insurance. Some examples of eligible groups are debtor-creditor groups, labor union groups, multiple-employer trusts, trade and professional associations, and any single employer group. Most eligible groups require participants to:

- be a full-time employee (or a qualifying member) of the group;
- satisfy a probationary period; and
- be actively at work the day coverage begins.

Characteristics

Group underwriting procedures are different from those for individual health coverages. Instead of looking at each insured on an individual basis, the underwriter looks at the overall composition of the group. All employees in the group are automatically eligible for coverage under a group contract.

The employer holds the master contract, and employees are given individual coverage certificates. The employer generally pays most, or all, of the premium, which further prevents adverse selection. The employer is responsible for enrolling new employees and collecting any premiums due from employees. The insurer thus saves a great deal on administrative expenses, and those savings are passed on to the employer or employees in the form of lower premiums.

Group supplemental plans
Often attached to basic medical expense coverage, these policies allow the employer to use more than one provider for coverage, offer first-dollar coverage, or use different contribution rates for basic and supplemental coverage

Basic and Major Medical

Group basic medical insurance provides coverage for hospital, surgical, and physician's expenses that are similar to those discussed previously under Individual Health Coverage. Basic medical plans have low maximum limits on coverage and are often used in conjunction with major medical plans.

Group major medical expense coverage is also very similar to individual major medical coverage. The two main types of group major medical plans are supplemental and comprehensive. **Group supplemental plans**, often attached to basic medical expense coverage, allow the employer to use more than one provider for coverage, offer first-dollar coverage, or use different contribution rates for basic and supplemental coverage.

Comprehensive major medical
Stand-alone coverage that provides a broad range of medical services and high limits of coverage

Comprehensive major medical is a stand-alone coverage that provides a broad range of medical services and high limits of coverage. Deductibles are usually low, and employees pay some percentage of all medical expenses above the deductible, subject to some maximum out-of-pocket dollar limit. As with individual plans, these group major medical plans cover all necessary medical expenses unless they are specifically excluded in the contract. Coverage under these plans has expanded to pay for items, such as extended care facilities, home health care centers, hospice care, ambulatory care, birthing centers, diagnostic x-ray and laboratory services, radiation therapy, supplemental accident benefits, prescription drugs, and vision care.

EXAMPLE Assume that Alexander's employer offers him comprehensive group major medical coverage. The policy has a $250 per person annual deductible and after that pays 80% of all covered charges. The policy further limits Alexander's out-of-pocket expenses to $1,000 per year (including the deductible). After Alexander has spent $1,000 of his own money, the insurer will pay 100% of covered medical expenses.

If Alexander is involved in a boating accident and incurs $1,250 of medical expenses, he must pay the first $250 of the covered expenses as his deductible. Then, the insurer will pay 80% of the remaining $1,000, or $800, and Alexander will pay 20%, or $200. If two months later, Alexander suffers another injury, he does not have to pay the $250 deductible again because he has a "per person per year" deductible. He only has to pay 20% of his medical expenses. Once he has paid $1,000 out of his pocket for the entire year (including the deductible), his insurer will begin paying 100% of all covered expenses.

Health Care Reimbursement Arrangements (HCRAs)

Health care reimbursement arrangements (HCRAs) are employer-sponsored health-spending accounts that allow employees to accumulate funds for health expenses. Under these plans, an employer sets up an HCRA on behalf of a covered employee and deposits a certain amount of money into the plan each year. Funds that accumulate in the HCRA tax-free are used to reimburse the employee for qualified medical expenses, such as medical bills, prescription drugs, health insurance deductibles, and health insurance premiums. HCRAs differ from health savings accounts (HSAs) because all of the contributions into an HCRA are made by the employer.

Employers that sponsor HCRAs frequently provide high-deductible health plans as well. Once the funds in the HCRA are depleted, the employee's health expenses are covered by the high-deductible health plan, after any co-payment, coinsurance, or deductible requirements are met. If funds remain in the HCRA at the end of the year, they can be rolled over to the following year and used for future health expenses.

Offering an HCRA in conjunction with a high-deductible health plan can be much less expensive for employers. Employees may benefit, too, from having more control over their health care. HCRAs are becoming increasingly popular as employers look for ways to cut health care costs without sacrificing flexible health benefits.

Dental and Vision

Many medical health insurance plans do not provide coverage for dental or vision care. However, most companies today offer supplemental plans for vision and dental coverage to their employees. Preventive care is usually encouraged, so routine checkups are often covered. As a result, they are quite popular with employees, even when the employees must pay 100% of the cost of coverage.

GROUP DISABILITY INCOME INSURANCE

Group disability income insurance is structured in much the same fashion as individual disability income coverage. Under a group disability income plan, however, payments are based on the disability being either long term or short term. Generally, short-term disability payments are made from either the first day of injury resulting from an accident or the eighth day of disability resulting from sickness. Benefits are payable on a weekly basis for a specified benefit period. Long-term disability coverage will pay when short-term benefits expire or when the insured has satisfied the required long-term elimination period. Long-term disability benefits under a group plan are usually paid until the disability ends or until the insured reaches age 65, whichever occurs first; however, the employee should check the term of benefits because they may not be as long as the employee's remaining work life expectancy.

Health Insurance and Managed Care

Various forms of health insurance and discount plans are available on the market. The most prevalent plans today are preferred provider organizations (PPOs), point of service (POS), consumer-driven health plans (CDHPs), and either a health care savings account (individual) or a health care reimbursement account (group) is used in combination with a high-deductible health plan (HDHP). Although traditional major medical and health maintenance organizations are still available, they are rarely seen today.

Health Maintenance Organizations (HMOs) HMOs share the common goals of comprehensive care, delivery of services, and cost control. An HMO assumes the responsibility and risk of providing a broad range of services to members, including preventive medical services, such as checkups and mammograms, in exchange for a fixed monthly or annual enrollment fee. HMOs usually allow their members very little choice of service providers. The patient must generally use a contract provider, or no benefits will be paid. A copayment usually must be paid by the insured for each office visit.

Primary care doctors are either salaried employees of the HMO, or they are in private practice and receive a monthly fee (capitation payment) for each patient they agree to treat, whether or not the patient receives care. Specialists may also be salaried employees or they may be in private practice and receive fees for only the services they provide.

HMO enrollments have declined sharply, particularly in the private sector. Many believe this is primarily a result of the highly restrictive utilization requirements that were placed on members and an overall public dissatisfaction with the care provided. The traditional HMO plan has virtually disappeared, thereby spawning myriad of managed care models that address many of the shortcomings of the traditional HMO.

Preferred provider organization (PPO)
A contractual arrangement between the insured, the insurer, and the health care provider that allows the insurer to receive discounted rates from service providers

Preferred Provider Organizations (PPOs) A **preferred provider organization (PPO)** is merely a contractual arrangement between the insured, the insurer, and the health care provider that allows the insurer to receive discounted rates from service providers. PPOs are structured in much the same way as HMOs with two main exceptions: (1) members are allowed to use non-PPO providers, although they pay higher deductibles and coinsurance than required when they use PPO doctors, and (2) primary care doctors (as well as specialists) are paid on a fee-for-service basis rather than as employees under the traditional HMO.

PPOs offer insureds a greater choice of health care providers than most HMOs. Many find the HMO concept objectionable because benefits are not provided if the covered person uses a doctor outside of the HMO's network of providers (in other than an emergency). Although the insured pays more out-of-pocket by going outside the network of preferred providers offered by a PPO, medical benefits are still payable but at a reduced level.

Advantages and Disadvantages Managed health care companies are highly competitive and often improve services or reduce costs to gain market share. Most managed health care plans are service-oriented and focus on assisting the patient to receive the most appropriate care for the money. To maintain quality of care, managed care plans provide coordination and continuity in the process of delivering care that is deemed medically necessary.

The primary disadvantage of managed care is reduced choice for the patient. Although many managed care plans allow the insured to go outside the network of preferred providers, most plans do not allow physicians to perform certain procedures without prior approval from the plan, which reduces the patient's options for care. Furthermore, some managed care organizations put gag clauses in their contracts with providers that require the provider to remain silent about treatment options for the patient if the managed care plan excludes coverage for those procedures, such as experimental bone marrow transplants. Much criticism focuses on the fact that nonmedical personnel are controlling the medical options offered to patients by their doctors. As a result of this criticism, several states have passed laws restricting or prohibiting the use of gag clauses in managed care plans.

Coverage for Retirees

Historically, many companies continued group health insurance coverage for their retired employees, although Medicare was the primary payor of benefits and the group plan served to fill coverage gaps in the Medicare program. The employer would pay some or all of the premiums on the retiree's coverage. In 1993, however, the Financial Accounting Standards Board (FASB) began requiring employers to recognize (on the balance sheet) the present value of the cost of providing retiree coverage during the employee's active working years. This ruling had a very negative effect on the earnings of employers, so many employers have stopped offering paid benefits to retirees.

Another problem employers face when they offer paid health benefits to retirees is the tendency of U.S. courts to prohibit a reduction in benefits after retirement. If an employer offers a retiree benefits, it may have to continue those benefits as long as the retiree chooses, potentially creating a rather lengthy commitment for the employer that could prove financially burdensome during periods of reduced sales or profits.

Coverage for Elderly Employees

Employees who are 65 and older and who are also eligible for Medicare benefits still must be eligible for the employer's group health coverage. The group plan is the primary payor of benefits, and Medicare is the secondary payor.

Coordination of Benefits

Because of the rising number of dual-income families across America today, insurers have taken measures to prevent insureds from receiving benefits twice for the same ailment. One such measure is known as the **coordination of benefits (COB) clause**. The goal of this measure is to avoid duplicate payments for a single service. COB is used in all group health insurance plans to prevent the insured who is covered by both his own employer's plan and his spouse's plan from receiving more than 100% of the actual cost of health care received.

Coordination of benefits (COB) clause
Prevents an insured from receiving greater than 100% of the cost of health care received when covered by multiple insurance policies

Termination of Benefits

Upon permanent termination of employment with a company, one may still maintain group health insurance benefits for 31 days in order to have adequate time to replace the group insurance with individual insurance. If new employment provides health insurance for the terminated employee, the previous employer's coverage automatically expires, even if the 31-day period has not elapsed.

Consolidated Omnibus Budget Reconciliation Act (COBRA)

Consolidated Omnibus Budget Reconciliation Act (COBRA)
Requires certain employers to provide previously covered persons with the same coverage received before discontinuation of coverage

Employees and dependents previously covered under a group health insurance may have that group coverage extended under a federal law known as the **Consolidated Omnibus Budget Reconciliation Act (COBRA)**. COBRA requires certain employers to provide the previously covered persons (including dependents and spouses) with the same coverage received before unemployment or another event affecting health care coverage. The benefit recipient must pay the full cost of the coverage, however, which may be prohibitively expensive if the recipient is unemployed. The employer is also allowed to charge up to 2% of the premium to cover administrative expenses, but under no circumstances may the employee be charged more than 102% of the total cost of the plan during the period of coverage.

To continue health insurance coverage through COBRA, the group coverage must terminate because of a qualifying event, including:

- voluntary or involuntary termination of the employee (except for gross misconduct);
- death of the covered employee;
- reduction of employee's hours from full time to part time;
- divorce or legal separation of covered employee from spouse;
- employee becomes eligible for Medicare; and
- a dependent child is no longer eligible for coverage under the employee's plan, as would be the case when the child was no longer a student, reached a certain age, or got married.

COBRA applies only to employees who offer a group health plan and have at least 20 employees. Affected employers must offer coverage for a specified period, depending on the type of qualifying event:

- Termination or part-time status, 18 months
- Death of covered employee, 36 months
- Divorce or legal separation, 36 months
- Loss of dependent status, 36 months
- Medicare eligibility, 36 months
- Up to 29 months if employee meets Social Security definition of disabled, or up to 36 months if the beneficiary experiences, during a period of COBRA coverage, a second COBRA qualifying event

Taxation of Group Health Benefits

Currently, employer-provided medical expense coverage is not taxable as income to the employee, and the premiums paid by the employer are tax-deductible as a business expense. Employer-paid premiums for disability income coverage are not taxed as current income to the employee, but if a disability occurs, the benefits paid by the plan are taxable as income to the employee. If the employee pays the entire cost of disability income coverage, the premiums are not tax-deductible for the employee. However, any disability benefits received from an employee-paid policy are not subject to income tax. If the employer and employee share the cost of disability income coverage, disability benefits that are attributable to employer contributions are taxable as income to the employee.

BUSINESS USES OF LIFE INSURANCE AND OTHER EMPLOYEE BENEFITS

Buy-Sell Agreements

Owners of closely held businesses are concerned about what might occur if one of the owners dies. Surviving owners want to make certain that the economic value of the corporate interest is preserved, and this may not be the case if the interest passes to the deceased owner's family members. The surviving owners also would like to avoid interference from the deceased shareholder's family. If surviving owners want to meet these objectives by purchasing the deceased owner's interest, they most often want to be certain that they will have the economic resources to do so. A **buy-sell agreement** funded with life insurance will often meet the concerns of the owners.

Buy-sell agreement
An arrangement in which a deceased owner's share of a business is purchased by using the life insurance proceeds from a policy on the deceased owner's life

Types of Buy-Sell Agreements

The three basic types of buy-sell agreements are a cross-purchase arrangement, an entity purchase agreement, and a wait-and-see agreement. The arrangements differ in terms of policy ownership, ease of administration, disparity of premiums, and whether the remaining shareholders receive a step-up in basis at the deceased shareholder's death.

Cross-Purchase Agreements

Cross-purchase agreement
Each owner of the corporation purchases an insurance policy on the other shareholders; the death proceeds are used to purchase a deceased owner's shares

With a **cross-purchase agreement**, each owner of the corporation purchases an insurance policy on the other shareholders. The purchaser is both owner and beneficiary of the policies. Upon the death of a shareholder, the other shareholders are able to use the life insurance proceeds to purchase the deceased owner's shares.

There are several advantages to the cross-purchase form of the buy-sell agreement. Under the traditional stepped-up basis rules, the family of the deceased owner will have a tax basis equal to the fair market value of the decedent's stock at the date of death, thus avoiding any income tax consequences resulting from the sale. The fair market value of the shares should be defined by the buy-sell agreement.

The life insurance proceeds received by the surviving owners are not subject to income taxation. For newly purchased shares, the corporate shareholders will be entitled to a tax basis equal to the purchase price. The stepped-up basis should reduce future income taxes if the surviving shareholders later sell their interests. The insurance proceeds are not subject to the claims of corporate creditors. The creditor protection exists because the proceeds are paid directly to the individual shareholders.

However, the cross-purchase form of the buy-sell agreement has several disadvantages. The plan is difficult to administer if numerous shareholders are required to purchase a policy on all of the other shareholders. For example, for five owners to cross-purchase life insurance would require 20 policies (five owners purchasing four policies on the other owners). The number of policies can multiply even further if disability coverage is also part of the buy-sell agreement.

Another disadvantage of the cross-purchase agreement is that the age or the insurable status of the partners can create a disparity in premiums. Younger or healthier owners may incur higher premiums to cover older and less healthy owners. A possible solution to this problem is to have the corporation raise salaries to cover the premium (and any tax payable on the additional salary) paid by each owner.

Entity Purchase Agreements

Entity purchase agreement
The corporation owns policies on the lives of the shareholders; at the death of a shareholder, the corporation buys the deceased shareholder's interest in the company with the insurance proceeds

With an **entity purchase agreement**, the corporation owns policies on the lives of the shareholders. When a shareholder dies, the corporation buys the deceased shareholder's interest in the company with the insurance proceeds. A major advantage of the entity purchase agreement is that it is easier to administer for multiple shareholders. An additional advantage to an entity purchase buy-sell is that the corporation bears the premium differences associated with age disparities among shareholders.

The corporation will not recognize income for tax purposes when it receives the insurance proceeds. The corporation must, however, show the effect of the entire transaction (proceeds received and redemption of the deceased's stock) on the earnings and profits of the corporation. The earnings and profits increase with the life insurance proceeds received and decrease as a result of the stock redemption. Therefore, the corporation must pay attention to the overall net effect on earnings and profits and consider how that might affect the dividend policy to shareholders.

A key disadvantage of the entity purchase agreement is that the remaining shareholders do not get the benefit of a stepped-up basis when the corporation purchases the deceased shareholder's interest. In other words, the continuing shareholders retain their original cost basis in the company. Compared with the cross-purchase agreement, the entity purchase agreement creates greater capital gains upon the ultimate disposition of shares if made before death of the surviving owners. After the stock redemption is completed, however, the corporate assets should be relatively unchanged (the insurance proceeds have been used to purchase the deceased's interest), but each owner now enjoys a greater percentage of ownership.

Wait-and-See Agreements

The respective advantages and disadvantages of cross-purchase and entity-purchase buy-sell agreements may make it difficult for businessowners to decide which type of agreement better meets their needs. Even if the owners initially select a plan, their circumstances or the business's circumstances may later change and their initial choice of plan may no longer be suitable.

Wait-and-see agreement
A hybrid version of the cross-purchase and entity-purchase buy-sell agreement that allows the businessowners to wait until an owner dies or retires before deciding whether the surviving owners or the business entity will purchase the deceased or retired owner's share

The **wait-and-see agreement** is a hybrid version of the cross-purchase and entity-purchase buy-sell agreement that allows the businessowners to wait until an owner dies or retires before deciding whether the surviving owners or the business entity will purchase the deceased or retired owner's share. With a wait-and-see agreement, the ultimate purchaser of a deceased or retired owner's interest might be the business itself, the other businessowners, or some combination of the business and the other owners.

To implement a wait-and-see agreement, each businessowner buys and names himself the beneficiary of a life insurance policy on the life of every other owner. This is the same as with a cross-purchase plan; unlike a cross-purchase plan, a wait-and-see plan typically gives the business entity the right of first refusal to purchase all or part of the interest of an owner who dies. If the business doesn't purchase the interest or purchases only part of it, the other owners then have the right to purchase any remaining portion of the interest. If the other owners fail to purchase the entire remaining interest, the business entity must purchase it. This assures there will be a buyer for the deceased owner's entire interest.

As with a cross-purchase plan, the life insurance proceeds are received by the other owners rather than the business entity. If the business entity elects to purchase the interest of a deceased owner, the other owners must either loan the policy proceeds to the business or use the proceeds as a contribution to capital. The surviving owners get an increase in basis if they use the proceeds to purchase the interest directly from the estate of the deceased owner or if they use the proceeds as a contribution to capital so the business entity can make the purchase.

A wait-and-see agreement has some of the same potential disadvantages as a cross-purchase agreement. For example, the number of policies required may become cumbersome if there are numerous owners, and there may be inequities in the premium payments if there are considerable age differences between the owners. The major advantage of a wait-and-see approach is the flexibility it provides in determining who will purchase a deceased or retired owner's interest in the business.

Disability Buy-Sell Arrangements

Owners of closely held corporations should also consider ownership transfer in the event of an owner's disability for the same reasons they would consider a buy-sell agreement that takes effect at death.

Disability buy-sell policies pay benefits when an owner is totally disabled, and usually after at least a one-year elimination period. The policies pay benefits in the form of a lump sum or payments over several years, and in some cases, a combination of the two. In most cases, insurers will provide a benefit up to 80% of the value of the business.

Estate Tax Treatment of Buy-Sell Arrangements

With a cross-purchase agreement, the proceeds from the life insurance are not included in the deceased shareholder's estate. Because the deceased is not the owner of the policy, the insurance proceeds payable at death are not included in the estate.

With an entity purchase buy-sell, however, the estate tax consequences can become more significant when the deceased shareholder has a controlling interest. Under IRC Section 267, a shareholder who owns more than a 50% interest either directly or indirectly is deemed to control a corporation. In this case, the shareholder has an ownership interest in the life insurance policy because of the shareholder's ability to designate a beneficiary, as well as other ownership interests. The fact that the majority shareholder controls interest in the policy results in the proceeds being includable in the deceased's estate. Thus, the after-tax returns on life insurance policies can be substantially reduced if estate taxes are owed as a result of the life insurance proceeds being included in the estate.

Nonqualified Plans

Nonqualified plans are usually used to supplement qualified plans for key employees beyond the qualified plan 415 limit. These plans are not subject to the same ERISA rules as qualified plans and, as a result, they do not benefit from the same tax advantages as qualified plans or other tax-advantaged plans.

Nonqualified deferred compensation (NQDC) plans are a common type of nonqualified plan. Under these plans, part of the employee's compensation is deferred and not paid until some time in the future, such as after the employee retires. If the plan is structured properly, the employee does not pay income taxes on the deferred compensation until the year it is actually received. The employer can deduct the deferred compensation in the same year the employee reports it as income.

Nonqualified plans normally involve no more than a promise to pay from the employer, which is where life insurance often becomes involved. Because there is a substantial risk of loss to the executive, one must accept the promise to pay as the only guarantee of receiving the compensation that could have been paid presently. Corporate-owned life insurance (COLI) provides an excellent means of matching promised benefits with a tax-efficient funding vehicle that provides added security and peace of mind for the executive.

Executive Bonus Plans

Executive bonus plan
A discriminatory fringe benefit that provides life insurance to key employees with tax-deductible dollars

An **executive bonus plan** is a discriminatory fringe benefit that provides life insurance to key employees with tax-deductible dollars. In this arrangement, the employee purchases a personal life insurance plan and names a beneficiary. The business pays the policy premium to the insurer and can deduct the premiums as long as the total payments on behalf of the employee are considered reasonable compensation. The employee pays income taxes on the premium; however, the business can bonus both the premium and tax liability amounts. This is known as a gross-up bonus plan, and total payments must be considered reasonable compensation in this case as well.

The business has several benefits with an executive bonus plan. Premium payments are deductible, the plan is easy to administer, no IRS reporting is required, the plan can be discriminatory, and the plan can be terminated at any time.

There are also advantages to the key employee:

- The business pays most or all of the employee's costs
- The employee's beneficiary receives an income-tax-free death benefit
- The employee owns and controls the policy and the cash values
- The policy is portable; an employee can take it when she leaves the company

Split-Dollar Plans

Split-dollar plan
An agreement between an employer and employee who share the costs and benefits associated with a life insurance policy

Under a **split-dollar plan**, a business provides permanent life insurance on the life of its executives, using corporate funds. Unlike other nonqualified benefit plans, split-dollar plans usually provide that the business will recover the cost of the plan. In split-dollar plans, the agreements are most often between an employer and an employee who share (or split) the costs and the benefits associated with a life insurance policy. The objective of the arrangement is to assist the employee (again, usually an executive) with his life insurance needs by using the financial resources of the employer. When the insured employee dies, the corporation recovers its premium outlay, with the balance of the policy proceeds being paid to the employee's designated beneficiary or beneficiaries. The arrangement is best suited for an executive in the early stage of his employment career because the split-dollar plan requires a reasonable length of time to build up adequate cash value for the employer. There are two basic policy ownership methods by which the split-dollar arrangement may be established: the collateral assignment method and the endorsement method.

Collateral assignment split dollar
An arrangement in which an employer is obligated to make interest-free loans to the employee in the amount of the policy premium; the employee then makes a collateral assignment of the policy to the employer for the amount of premium paid by the employer

Collateral Assignment Method Under the **collateral assignment split dollar** method, the employee-insured is the policyowner. The employer is obligated to make interest-free loans to the employee in the amount of the premium that the employee has agreed to pay. The employee then makes a collateral assignment of the policy to the employer for the amount of premium paid by the employer.

At the insured employee's death, the employer, as collateral assignee, recovers the loan amount from the death proceeds. The remainder of the death benefit is then paid to the employee's designated beneficiary.

Endorsement split dollar
An arrangement in which the employer owns the policy and is responsible for making all premium payments; when the insured employee dies, the employer receives a portion of the death benefit equal to its premium outlay, with the remainder of the death proceeds payable to the employee's designated beneficiary

Endorsement Method Under the **endorsement split dollar** method, the employer owns the policy and is responsible for making all premium payments. When the insured employee dies, the split beneficiary designation provides for the employer to receive a portion of the death benefit equal to its premium outlay, with the remainder of the death proceeds payable to the employee's designated beneficiary. The method gets the name from the employee's rights that are protected by endorsing the policy over to the employer, thus giving the employee the right to name the residual beneficiary. A significant advantage of the endorsement method is that the employer owns the excess cash values in the insurance policy (whereas in the collateral assignment method, this excess is owned by the employee). As a result, the endorsement method is typically used for an employee who is not a shareholder in the corporation.

Methods Compared

Attribute	Collateral Assignment	Endorsement
Owner of policy	Employee	Employer
Tax treatment of policy premiums	Nondeductible	Nondeductible
Employer's portion of death proceeds	Employer is refunded loan equal to premiums paid	Equal to amount of cash value
Employee's portion of death proceeds	Remainder to employee's beneficiary	Remainder to employee's beneficiary

Disadvantage of Either Form A significant disadvantage of either split-dollar ownership form is that the employee must pay income taxes each year on the economic benefit derived from the arrangement. The economic benefit is usually measured by the Table 2001 cost to the employee. In addition, any payment made by an employer under a split-dollar arrangement must be accounted for either as a loan (collateral assignment method) or as compensation (endorsement method) to the employee.

Key Person Life Insurance

Key person life insurance
After the death of a key employee, used to recruit and train a replacement and compensate the company for lost business

Key person life insurance protects a business upon the loss of a key employee. The tax-free proceeds from the policy can be used to recruit and train a replacement and compensate the company for lost business during the transition.

For small businesses, key employees have a more direct effect on the bottom line. If the key employee's departure is planned, as in the case of retirement, a businessowner can prepare for the loss and take steps to minimize the impact. However, if the employee dies, the loss is unpredictable and leaves the business exposed to financial risks. The income-tax-free death benefit from a key person life insurance policy can greatly reduce the financial risks associated with the loss of a key person.

Key person life insurance is often required to obtain funding for the business. Investors want an assurance that they can recover their investment in the business in the event a key employee dies.

Business Overhead Expense Insurance

Business overhead expense insurance
Helps a business meet its liabilities in the event a significant income producer becomes disabled

Some employees are essential to the success of the business. This is often the case when the business relies on the knowledge and expertise of professionals, such as physicians, attorneys, and accountants. **Business overhead expense insurance** helps the business meet its liabilities in the event a significant income producer becomes disabled and can be structured to meet the needs of an individual business. Elimination periods vary, and policies may require total or partial disability. Benefit periods generally extend up to two years. In most cases, benefits are paid whether the disability is expected to be temporary or permanent. Expenses covered by business overhead expense insurance are outlined in the policy and may include rent or mortgage payments, utilities, administrative salaries, the salary of a replacement employee, property taxes, and other fixed expenses. However, the owner's salary is not covered under this policy, but instead, it is covered by an individual disability insurance policy.

Other Employee Benefits

Section 125 Plans

Section 125 (cafeteria plan)
A plan in which employers offer their employees a choice between cash and a variety of nontaxable qualified benefits that are excludable from the employee's income

Employers can offer their employees a choice between cash and a variety of nontaxable qualified benefits under IRC Section 125. Also known as **cafeteria plans, Section 125 plans** provide qualified benefits, including health care, dental and vision care, accident and health insurance, group term life insurance, and adoption assistance. These benefits are excludable from the employee's gross income, and the employee is not deemed to be in constructive receipt of the benefits.

Cafeteria plans must not discriminate in favor of highly compensated employees in terms of contribution amounts and benefits provided. In addition, all employees must be covered under the plan at the beginning of the year following their third anniversary of employment. If a plan is found to be discriminatory, highly compensated employees are taxed on the benefits.

Flexible Spending Accounts (FSAs)

Flexible spending account (FSA)
An account typically funded by employee salary reductions that allows employees the benefit of paying for their health-care-related expenses with pretax income

Employers also may offer **flexible spending accounts** to employees under a cafeteria plan that provides coverage under which specified, incurred expenses may be reimbursed. FSAs are typically funded by employee salary reductions and allow employees the benefit of paying for their health-care related expenses with pretax income. FSAs include health and dental accounts for expenses not reimbursed by any other health or dental plan, and dependent care assistance programs. If both types of expenses are reimbursed under the FSA, separate accounts are maintained for each type of expense. Note that if the FSA account balance is not used by 2½ months after the close of the contribution year, the account balance is forfeited.

Fringe Benefits

Meals and lodging furnished for the employer's convenience. These benefits are excludable from the employee's gross income and, in many cases, can be provided on a discriminatory basis. Meals must be furnished on the employer's premises; lodging, which must be provided on the employer's premises, must be a condition of the employee's employment. In addition, both meals and lodging must be received by the employee solely for the convenience of the employer.

Qualified adoption assistance plans. These expenses include court costs, attorney's fees, and any adoption expenses directly related to the legal adoption of a "qualified child." Costs for a qualified child do not include expenses associated with surrogate parenting or the adoption of a spouse's child. The maximum excludable amount for all years is $14,890 per child (2022). In 2022, the exclusion phases out for taxpayers with adjusted gross income above $223,410 and will be completely phased out at $263,410.

Education assistance programs. These plans offer income-tax-free reimbursement for education expenses incurred by an employee when acquiring knowledge to perform his job or improve job skills. Covered expenses include tuition, fees, books, and other necessary supplies. Currently, the maximum amount of reimbursement is $5,250 annually.

Dependent care assistance plans. Under these plans, employers can reimburse employees for child care expenses, or they can actually provide day care for employees' dependents. Employees receive benefits income tax-free, and expenses paid by employers are tax-deductible as Section 162 compensation. Qualified dependent care expenses must be for dependent care, not education. These expenses include the cost of a sitter, preschool and kindergarten expenses, after-school care for children under age 13, and summer camp for children under age 13. Benefits must be made available on a nondiscriminatory basis.

Other fringe benefits. FICA and FUTA are not paid on the benefit amounts for the following fringe benefits, which are excludable from gross income:

- Qualified employee discounts that are made on a nondiscriminatory basis
- "No additional cost" services that are offered to employees free or at a bargain price; the employer cannot incur any significant additional cost to provide the benefits, which include vacant hotel rooms, airline tickets, and cable TV services, and the benefits must be nondiscriminatory
- De minimis fringe benefits, such as personal use of an employer's fax machine or copier, or meals before, during, or after an employee's work shift if the employer provides food service
- Qualified moving expense reimbursement was repealed for the years 2018–2025 for all people except active duty members of the armed forces and their families
- Working-condition fringes provided to an employee that would otherwise be deductible by the employee as an employee business expense, had the employee paid for the services; nondiscrimination rules do not apply (examples of working-condition fringes include payment of industry journal subscriptions and the use of a company vehicle)
- Qualified tuition reduction provided by an educational organization for education up to, but not including, the graduate level

Voluntary Employees' Benefit Associations (VEBAs)

Voluntary Employee Benefit Association (VEBA)
A tax-exempt trust authorized by IRC Section 501(c)(9); in a VEBA, an employer makes tax-free deposits to the plan on an employee's behalf

A VEBA is a tax-exempt trust authorized by IRC Section 501(c)(9). In a VEBA, an employer makes tax-free deposits on an employee's behalf to the plan. The employee's account is credited with tax-free investment earnings, and an employee may obtain tax-free reimbursements for medical expenses and insurance premiums payments from the account.

Generally, VEBAs are managed by the membership or trustees/fiduciaries chosen by the employee membership. VEBAs do not pay taxes on net earnings if arranged as a tax-exempt trust or nonprofit organization.

Prepaid Legal Services

Prepaid legal services
Under this arrangement, law firms, in exchange for a monthly payment, provide specific legal services at no or greatly reduced cost

Under this arrangement, law firms, in exchange for a monthly payment, provide specific legal services at no or greatly reduced cost. Employers can deduct the cost of such a plan and, if the plan is a qualified group legal services plan under Section 120 of the Internal Revenue Code, any services provided under the plan are income tax-free when received by the employees.

Services often include the drafting of wills and other legal documents, conferences with attorneys, and domestic legal work. Representation in civil and criminal matters may be available but is usually limited in scope.

WHERE ON THE WEB

A.M. Best Company **www.ambest.com**

American Council of Life Insurers **www.acli.com**

Centers for Medicare and Medicaid Services **www.cms.gov**

Fitch Ratings **www.fitchratings.com**

America's Health Insurance Plans **www.ahip.org**

Insure.com (S & P ratings)
www.insure.com/interactive-tools/sandp/newtool1.jsp

Long-Term Care **longtermcare.acl.gov/**

Medicare **www.medicare.gov**

Moody's Investors Service **www.moodys.com**

National Hospice and Palliative Care Organization **www.nhpco.org**

Standard & Poor's Index Services **us.spindices.com**

TIAA Life Insurance Information **www.tiaa.org**

U.S. Government's Agency for Healthcare Research & Quality
www.ahrq.gov

DISCUSSION QUESTIONS

1. What are some of the potential losses associated with the risk of premature death? How can life insurance reduce (or eliminate) the effect of these losses?
2. What are the three recognized methods for measuring the needs related to premature death?
3. What is used as the basis for risk measurement under the human value life approach to identifying life insurance needs?
4. What specific needs make up the financial needs approach to the amount of life insurance needed?
5. How do term, whole life, and universal life insurance differ? What are the advantages and disadvantages of each policy?
6. Identify the various types of term life insurance.
7. Identify the various types of whole life insurance.
8. Identify and discuss the death benefit options offered in a universal life insurance policy.
9. What differentiates variable life insurance from variable universal life insurance?
10. At what threshold is an employee taxed on group term life insurance provided by an employer?
11. How do annuities differ from life insurance contracts?
12. What are the various types of annuities?
13. What are the tax implications of life insurance and annuities?
14. What are the various contractual provisions and options that pertain to life and annuity contracts?
15. What are the major types of individual health coverage?
16. What are the important policy provisions and major contractual features of individual health coverage?
17. What are the major types of employer-provided group health insurance coverage?
18. What are the important policy provisions and major contractual features of group health coverage?
19. What is the purpose of disability income insurance? What are some of the various definitions of disability?
20. What are the major types of disability coverage?
21. What are the important policy provisions and major contractual features of disability income insurance?
22. What is the tax treatment of health and disability insurance coverage?
23. How do indemnity plans and managed care plans differ?
24. How can group health coverage be continued or transferred when employment terminates?

EXERCISES

1. Comment on each of the following statements concerning the methods of providing life insurance protection.
   - An insurance company can use three approaches to provide life insurance protection: term insurance, which is temporary; whole life insurance, which is permanent protection that builds up a reserve or savings component; and universal life, which is protection that accrues cash value at interest rates usually higher than the guaranteed interest rate.
   - Term insurance is a form of life insurance in which the death proceeds are payable in the event of the insured's death during a specified period, and nothing is paid if the insured survives past the end of the period.
   - The net premium for term insurance is determined by the morbidity rate for the attained age of the individual.
   - Because death rates rise at an increasing rate as ages increase, the net premium for term insurance also rises at an increasing rate.
   - Universal life insurance offers the policyowner more flexibility than traditional whole life insurance.
2. Identify circumstances for which the following types of life insurance would be most appropriate:
   - Term insurance
   - Whole life insurance
   - Variable life insurance
   - Universal life insurance
   - Variable universal life insurance
3. Compare the primary functions of life insurance and annuities.
4. Discuss the following types of annuities:
   - Immediate versus deferred
   - Flexible premium versus single premium
   - Fixed versus variable
5. Identify and describe the features of a major medical plan.
6. Identify and describe the features of a long-term disability insurance policy.
7. Comment on the need for long-term care insurance.
8. Frank, age 45, is married to Julie. Frank makes $120,000 per year. He has two children, ages 9 and 10. He pays income taxes of $26,000 per year and FICA taxes of $5,000 per year. Frank consumes $20,000 per year of the family's expenses. He expects raises of 4% annually and plans to retire at age 65. He expects inflation to be 3%. Using the human life value approach, calculate the required amount of life insurance.
9. Describe the distinguishing features of whole life, universal life, variable life, and variable universal life in terms of premium amount, death benefit, the policyowner's control over investment, and the expected rate of return from the cash value invested.

10. Calculate the amount of money a major medical insurance policy will pay if:
    - the surgeon's charge is $12,500;
    - there is an 80/20 coinsurance clause;
    - the deductible is $500; and
    - the usual and customary charge for this surgery is $10,000.
11. Briefly explain the purpose of an elimination period in a long-term disability policy.
12. Differentiate between an HMO and a PPO.
13. What are the qualifying events that allow for COBRA benefits? What is the maximum benefit period for each qualifying event?

PROBLEMS

Problem 1

Julian, age 27, has two children, ages 4 and 3, from his first marriage. He is now married to Margaret. The children live with their mother, Alice. Julian and Margaret each make $26,000 per year and have recently bought a house for $100,000, with a $95,000 mortgage. They have the following life, health, and disability insurance coverage:

Life Insurance

	Policy A	Policy B	Policy C
Insured	Julian	Julian	Margaret
Face amount	$250,000	$78,000	$20,000
Type	20-year level term	Group term	Group term
Annual premium	$250	$156	$50
Premium payor	Trustee	Employer	Employer
Beneficiary	Trustee*	Alice	Julian
Policyowner	Trust	Julian	Margaret

*Children are beneficiaries of the trust required by divorce decree.

Health Insurance Julian and Margaret are covered under Julian's employer plan, which is a PPO plan with a $500 in-network deductible per person per year and a $1,500 out-of-network deductible per person per year, an in-network 80/20 coinsurance clause with a family annual out-of-pocket maximum of $2,500, and an out-of-network 60/40 coinsurance clause with a family maximum out-of-pocket of $4,500.

Long-Term Disability Insurance Julian is covered by an own occupation policy, with premiums paid by his employer. The benefit equals 60% of his gross pay after a 180-day elimination period. The policy covers both sickness and accidents. The benefit period is five years (60 months). Margaret is not covered by disability insurance.

1. Assume that Julian dies. Who would receive the proceeds of the insurance policies?
2. Does Julian have adequate life insurance?
3. Is Julian's health and disability coverage adequate? If not, why not?
4. Should Margaret have disability insurance? Why or why not?
5. Are any of the premiums or benefits received from the life, health, or disability insurance taxable to Julian and Margaret?

Problem 2

Richard graduated from a state university with a Bachelor of Science degree in accounting. He has been employed at Knoth & Cartez, a small local accounting firm (50 employees) for almost seven years. He makes $62,000 per year. Richard has been married to Marianne for six years. She graduated from a private university with a Bachelor of Science degree in elementary education. She is employed as a fourth-grade teacher at Riverside Preparatory School. She makes $35,000 per year. Richard and Marianne have three children: Carlos, age four; and twin girls, Maria and Anna, age two.

The Richards have the following insurance:

Health Insurance Health insurance is provided for the entire family by Knoth & Cartez. The family is covered by an HMO. Doctor's visits are $10 per visit, prescriptions are $5 for generic brands and $10 for other brands, and there is no co-payment for hospitalization in semiprivate accommodations. Private rooms are provided when medically necessary. For emergency treatment, a $50 copayment is required.

Life Insurance Richard has a $50,000 group term life insurance policy through Knoth & Cartez. Marianne has a $20,000 group term policy through Riverside Preparatory School. The owners of the policies are Richard and Marianne, respectively, with each other as the respective beneficiary.

Disability Insurance Richard has disability insurance through the accounting firm. Short-term disability benefits begin for any absence due to accident or illness over six days and will continue for up to six months at 80% of his salary. Long-term disability benefits are available if disability continues over six months. If Richard is unable to perform the duties of his own current position, the benefits provide him with 60% of his gross salary while disabled until recovery, death, retirement, or age 65 (whichever occurs first). All disability premiums are paid by Knoth & Cartez. Marianne currently has no disability insurance.

1. What happens to the family's health insurance if Richard is terminated from his job? What are the alternatives?
2. Does Richard have adequate life insurance?
3. Does either of the group term policies cause taxable income to Richard and Marianne?
4. Should Marianne have disability insurance?

CASE SCENARIO

Use the information provided to answer the following questions regarding the Nelson family.

NELSON FAMILY CASE SCENARIO
DANA AND DAVID NELSON
As of 12/31/2022

Personal Background and Information

David Nelson (age 37) is a bank vice president. He has been employed there for 12 years and has an annual salary of $70,000. Dana Nelson (age 37) is a full-time homemaker. David and Dana have been married for eight years. They have two children, John (age 6) and Gabrielle (age 3), and are expecting their third child in two weeks. They have always lived in this community and expect to remain indefinitely in their current residence.

General Goals (Not Prioritized)

- Save for college education
- Reduce debt
- Save for retirement
- Estate planning
- Invest wisely

Insurance Information

Health Insurance

The entire family is insured under David's employer's health plan (PPO). For covered expenses, a $1,000 in-network deductible and a $2,000 out-of-network deductible apply, after which 80%/20% coinsurance applies in network and 60%/40% applies out of network. There is a stop-loss limit of $20,000 annually in network and $30,000 annually out of network. The entire monthly premium of $1,123.54 is paid by David's employer.

Life Insurance

David's employer provides group term life insurance equal to two times David's current salary. The premium is paid entirely by his employer, and Dana is the primary beneficiary. No contingent beneficiary is named.

Disability Insurance

David's employer also offers a contributory group long-term disability insurance program toward which the employer contributes 60% of the $158.54 monthly premium. David is a participant in the program, which provides a monthly disability income benefit equal to 70% of his current salary, payable to his Social Security normal retirement age, provided that he remains disabled per the policy's "own occupation" definition of disability. David must satisfy a 90-day elimination period before he is eligible to begin receiving benefits.

David's employer doesn't offer dental or vision coverages and the Nelsons have not obtained any private form of individual dental or vision insurance benefits.

Homeowners Insurance

The Nelsons have an HO-3 policy with replacement cost on contents. There is a $250 deductible. The annual premium is $950.

Automobile Insurance

The Nelsons have automobile liability and bodily injury coverage of $100,000/$300,000/$100,000. They have both comprehensive coverage and collision. The deductibles are $250 (comprehensive) and $500 (collision). The annual premium is $900.

Relevant External Environmental Information

- Mortgage rates are 5.0% for 30 years and 4.5% for 15 years, fixed.
- Gross domestic product is expected to grow at less than 3%.
- Inflation is expected to be 2.6%.
- Expected return on investment is 8% for common stocks, 9% for small company stocks, and 1.1% for U.S. Treasury bills.
- College education costs are $15,000 per year.

Investment Information

The bank offers a Section 401(k) plan in which David is an active participant. The bank matches contributions dollar for dollar up to 3% of David's salary. David currently contributes 5.43% of his salary. His employer's plan allows for employee contributions of up to 16% of salary. In the Section 401(k) plan, the Nelsons have the opportunity to invest in a money market fund, a bond fund, a growth and income fund, and a small-cap fund. The Nelsons consider themselves to have a moderate investment risk tolerance. David's assets within the plan are currently earning 8.5%, based on his investment choices within the plan.

Income Tax Information

David and Dana tell you that they are in the 12% federal income tax bracket. They pay $820 annually in state and local income taxes.

Education Information

John is 6 years old and currently attending first grade at a private school. Gabrielle is 3 years old. She will attend private school from pre-kindergarten through high school. The current balance of the college fund is $14,000. They expect to contribute $1,000 at the end of each year to this fund.

Gifts, Estates, Trusts, and Will Information

David has made Dana his primary beneficiary on his Section 401(k) plan, and the children are the contingent beneficiaries. Because most of their assets are owned jointly, David doesn't see the need for a will. Dana also does not have a will.

Dana and David Nelson
Statement of Financial Position
12/31/2021

ASSETS			**LIABILITIES AND NET WORTH**		
Cash/cash equivalents			**Current liabilities**		
JT	Checking account	$1,425	JT	Credit cards	$4,000
JT	Savings account	$950	JT	Mortgage on principal residence	$1,234
			David	Boat loan	$1,493
Total cash/cash equivalents		$2,375	**Total current liabilities**		$6,727
Invested assets			**Long-term liabilities**		
Dana	ABC stock	$12,500	JT	Mortgage on principal residence	$196,654
JT	Education fund	$14,000	David	Boat loan	$12,065
David	Section 401(k) plan	$32,197			
Total invested assets		$58,697	**Total long-term liabilities**		$208,719
Personal-use assets			**Total liabilities**		$215,446
JT	Principal residence	$245,000			
JT	Automobile	$18,000			
David	Boat	$25,000	**Net worth**		$207,626
Dana	Jewelry	$13,000			
JT	Furniture/household	$61,000			
Total personal-use assets		$362,000			
Total assets		$423,072	**Total liabilities and net worth**		$423,072

Dana and David Nelson
Statement of Financial Position
12/31/2022

ASSETS			LIABILITIES AND NET WORTH		
Cash/cash equivalents			**Current liabilities**		
JT	Checking account	$1,268	JT	Credit cards	$3,655
JT	Savings account	$950	JT	Mortgage on principal residence	$1,370
	Total cash/cash equivalents	$2,218	David	Boat loan	$1,048
				Total current liabilities	$6,073
Invested assets				**Long-term liabilities**	
Dana	ABC stock	$14,050	JT	Mortgage on principal residence	$195,284
JT	Education fund	$15,560	David	Boat loan	$16,017
David	Section 401(k) plan	$38,619		**Total long-term liabilities**	$211,301
David	XYZ stock	$10,000			
	Total invested assets	$78,229			
Personal use assets				**Total liabilities**	$217,374
JT	Principal residence	$250,000			
JT	Automobile	$15,000			
David	Personal watercraft	$10,000		**Net worth**	$241,573
David	Boat	$30,000			
Dana	Jewelry	$13,500			
JT	Furniture/household	$60,000			
	Total personal-use assets	$378,500			
Total assets		$458,947		**Total liabilities and net worth**	$458,947

Notes to financial statements:

- Assets are stated at fair market value.
- The ABC stock was inherited from Dana's aunt on November 15, 2021. Her aunt originally paid $20,000 for it on October 31, 2012. The fair market value at the aunt's death was $12,000.
- Liabilities are stated at principal only.
- JT = joint tenancy; client name = separate property

Dana and David Nelson
Personal Statement of Cash Flows
For 2022

INFLOWS		
Salary—David		$70,000
Investment income		
Interest income	$ 900	
Dividend income	$ 150	$ 1,050
Total inflow		**$71,050**
Savings		
Reinvestment (interest/dividends)	$ 1,050	
Section 401(k) plan deferrals	$ 3,803	
Education fund	$ 1,000	
Total savings		**$ 5,853**
Available for outflows		**$65,197**
OUTFLOWS		
Ordinary living expenses		
Food	$ 6,000	
Clothing	$ 3,600	
Child care	$ 600	
Entertainment	$ 1,814	
Utilities	$ 3,600	
Auto maintenance	$ 2,000	
Church	$ 3,500	
Total ordinary living expenses		**$21,114**
Debt payments		
Credit card payments principal	$ 345	
Credit card payments interest	$ 615	
Mortgage payment principal	$ 1,234	
Mortgage payment interest	$20,720	
Boat loan principal	$ 1,493	
Boat loan interest	$ 1,547	
Total debt payments		**$25,954**
Insurance premiums		
Automobile insurance premiums	$ 900	
Disability insurance premiums	$ 761	
Homeowners insurance premiums	$ 950	
Total insurance premiums		**$ 2,611**
Tuition and education expenses		**$ 1,000**
Taxes		
FICA and federal income tax (W/H)	$12,855	
State (and city) income tax	$ 820	
Property tax (principal residence)	$ 1,000	
Total taxes		**$14,675**
Total outflows		**$65,354**
Net cash flow (deficit)		**($157)**

1. The Nelsons wish to evaluate and update their life insurance coverage. David would like to have enough insurance to provide the family with 60% of his current salary. ABC stock and XYZ stock have average annual returns of 9%. The education fund is invested 100% in U.S. Treasuries. David's Section 401(k) plan is invested 50% in a diversified common stock fund and 50% in a small company stock fund. Using the capital retention approach, an interest rate of 8%, and ignoring Social Security benefits, how much additional life insurance do the Nelsons need? Evaluate David's group term life insurance from an income tax perspective as well.
2. Evaluate the Nelsons' disability insurance coverage, and determine what portion of the policy premium is taxable and what portion of the benefit would be income taxable if received.
3. Assume that the Nelsons incurred medical expenses of $30,000 in 2022.

All covered services were received in network. What was the total cost to the Nelsons for these services?

CHAPTER 10

Personal Property and Liability Insurance

LEARNING OBJECTIVES

After learning the material in this chapter, you will be able to do the following:

- Identify the need for homeowners, auto, and liability umbrella insurance coverages
- List and define the basic coverages provided by a homeowners policy
- Be aware of the various homeowners forms that are available
- Understand and explain the various contractual options and provisions in homeowners insurance
- List and define the basic coverages provided by a personal automobile insurance policy
- Understand and explain the various contractual options and provisions in a personal automobile insurance policy

- Identify the need for a personal umbrella liability policy and explain its distinguishing characteristics
- Identify the coverages available to businesses and businessowners

INTRODUCTION

Often a home is the largest investment a family will make. Although the frequency of perils causing financial loss to the home is small, the severity of loss is potentially large. Therefore, it is important that this valuable asset be protected against damage and destruction. The professional financial planner should be knowledgeable about the property risks as well as the liability risks associated with a client's property. Although property insurance protects the assets the client already owns, liability insurance protects the client against financial loss from legal action. Therefore, coverage for both property and liability risks is an essential part of a client's financial plan.

Automobiles are major assets owned by numerous individuals. The personal automobile policy (PAP) mitigates the risk of loss to the automobile and those involved in an automobile accident. For a client, automobile insurance may be among the most expensive aspects of owning a car. Another type of insurance, a personal umbrella liability policy, provides coverage in excess of the liability coverage provided in the homeowners and automobile policies.

Various types of insurance coverage, such as the commercial package policy, the businessowners policy, and professional liability insurance, provide protection for businessowners and self-employed professionals.

This chapter introduces each of these types of insurance to help the planner understand and evaluate the client's property and liability needs and recommend appropriate coverage.

PERSONAL PROPERTY AND LIABILITY INSURANCE

The U.S. legal system holds individuals responsible for the bodily injuries and property damage they cause to others due to their negligence. When one is legally liable for injuries to another, the law requires that payment be made for those injuries along with the possibility of punitive damages being assessed to punish the defendant. Where money is not available to make the necessary restitution, future wages along with other assets may be seized, potentially jeopardizing an individual's future standard of living. Liability insurance provides the insured with financial protection against lawsuits and other claims for damages that result from the insured's actions.

This chapter discusses the three policies most commonly used to protect against personal property and liability risks: homeowners insurance, automobile insurance, and liability umbrella insurance. Homeowners and automobile insurance are package policies that provide both property and liability coverage in one contract. The personal liability umbrella policy provides a layer of personal liability protection above the coverage provided under the homeowners and automobile policies, in the unfortunate event that those policies do not provide adequate compensation to the injured parties.

Each of the following discussions is based on the standard policy forms drafted by the Insurance Services Office (ISO). Because insurance is regulated at the state level, each state may require certain modifications to the standard ISO form. Thus, the ensuing discussions are general in nature. Absolute statements cannot be made about a particular policy without reading the policy thoroughly.

Homeowners (HO) Insurance: Basic Coverage

Homeowners insurance
A package insurance policy that provides both property and liability coverage for the insured dwelling, other structures, personal property, and loss of use

Homeowners (HO) insurance is a package insurance policy that provides both property and liability coverage for the insured dwelling, other structures, personal property, and loss of use. Each homeowners insurance form consists of two sections: Section I provides property coverage, and Section II provides liability coverage.

Levels of Coverage

A **peril**, as defined in a homeowners insurance policy, is a cause of financial loss. The level of coverage afforded by a homeowners insurance policy is determined by the perils it covers.

Named-perils coverage
Protects from perils that are specifically listed in the policy

Named-perils coverage. **Named-perils coverage** protects from perils that are specifically listed in the policy.

EXHIBIT 10.1 List of Covered Perils

Basic Named Perils

1. Fire	7. Vehicles
2. Lightning	8. Smoke
3. Windstorm	9. Vandalism or malicious mischief
4. Hail	10. Explosion
5. Riot or civil commotion	11. Theft
6. Aircraft	12. Volcanic eruption

Broad Named Perils: Basic Named Perils 1–12, plus 13–18:

13. Falling objects
14. Weight of ice, snow, and sleet
15. Accidental discharge or overflow of water or steam
16. Sudden and accidental tearing apart, cracking, burning, or bulging of a steam, hot water, air conditioning, or automatic fire protective sprinkler system, or from within a household appliance
17. Freezing of a plumbing, heating, air conditioning, or automatic fire sprinkler system, or of a household appliance
18. Sudden and accidental damage from artificially generated electrical current

Open-perils coverage
Coverage designed to protect against all perils except those specifically excluded from coverage

Open-perils coverage. **Open-perils coverage** is designed to protect against all perils except those specifically excluded from coverage. This increased coverage results in a higher premium for the insured.

Perils Generally Excluded

The following perils are excluded from most homeowners policies.

Movement of the ground. Property damage arising from earth movement is excluded. This includes damage from an earthquake, volcanic eruption, or landslide.

Ordinance or law. A loss due to an ordinance or law that regulates the construction, repair, or demolition of a building or structure is excluded.

Damage from water. Property damage from the following are specifically excluded from coverage under the homeowners policy:

- Floods, surface water, waves, tidal water, and overflow or spray of a body of water

- Water below the surface of the ground that exerts pressure on or seeps through a building, sidewalk, driveway, foundation, swimming pool, or other structure
- Water backing through sewers or drains

Coverage for naturally occurring floods is available through the National Flood Insurance Program (NFIP) offered by the federal government. Residential flood insurance provides coverage for physical loss from a flood. Loss settlement is on an actual cash value basis, but replacement cost is available for a one- to four-family dwelling that is occupied by the owner at least 80% of the year. Coverage is subject to the standard exclusions and a deductible. A flood policy is enforceable immediately during the first 30 days that coverage is available in a community. After the 30th day, there is a 30-day waiting period for coverage to be effective. There are some private insurance companies that may also offer flood insurance in certain locations. Coverage for sewer backup is available in some areas as an endorsement to the HO policy.

War or nuclear hazard. Property damage from war or nuclear hazard, including radiation, or radioactive contamination is excluded. If a radiation leak from a nuclear power plant near an insured's home contaminates the property, there is no coverage for the loss.

Power failure. Losses due to power failure caused by an uninsured peril, such as a freezer thawing out and its contents spoiling because of local power plant malfunctions, are not covered. If, however, a covered peril, such as fire or lightning on the premises causes the power failure, the resulting damage is covered.

Intentional act. If a loss is discovered to be an intentional act on the part of any insured, it is not covered. For example, one cannot intentionally burn the house down and recover insurance benefits.

Neglect. If an insured fails to use all reasonable and necessary means to save and preserve the property during or after the loss, or when the property is endangered by an insured peril, the loss is not covered.

Section I Coverage

Section I, which protects property and belongings, helps the policyowner repair, rebuild, or completely replace a house, furniture, and belongings in the event of a casualty. Section I provides the types of coverage listed below:

- Coverage A: Dwelling
- Coverage B: Other structures
- Coverage C: Personal property
- Coverage D: Loss of use
- Additional coverage: Debris removal, damage to trees, credit card loss

Coverage A: Dwelling

Dwelling
Residential structure covered under a homeowners policy

Coverage A provides coverage for repair or replacement of damage to a **dwelling**, a residential structure covered under a homeowners policy. This section also covers attached structures and building materials on the premises. The homeowner typically buys an amount of coverage equal to the replacement cost of the dwelling and, in some cases, will be required to carry even more if the property is mortgaged. A mortgage lender usually demands an amount of coverage on the dwelling at least equal to the total amount of the mortgage.

Replacement cost
The amount necessary to purchase, repair, or replace the dwelling with materials of the same or similar quality at current prices

Actual cash value (ACV)
The depreciated value of the insured property

Covered losses to the dwelling and other structures are paid on the basis of replacement cost with no deduction for depreciation. **Replacement cost** is the amount necessary to purchase, repair, or replace the dwelling with materials of the same or similar quality at current prices. If the insured does not carry insurance of at least 80% of the replacement cost (coinsurance) at the time of a partial loss, the insured will receive the larger of the following:

- **Actual cash value (ACV)** for the part of the dwelling that is damaged
- [Insurance carried ÷ (coinsurance % × replacement value)] × amount of loss

EXAMPLE Amanda owns a home with a replacement value of $280,000 and a depreciated actual value equal to 50% of the replacement value. She purchases $200,000 of insurance with a coinsurance requirement of 80%. If Amanda experiences a $100,000 loss, the insurance company will pay the greater of:

$$\text{Actual cash value} = 50\% \times \$100{,}000 = \$50{,}000 \text{ or}$$

$$\frac{\text{Insurance Purchased}}{\text{Coinsurance}} \times \text{Amount of Loss} =$$

$$\frac{\$200{,}000}{80\% \times \$280{,}000} \times \$100{,}000 = \$89{,}286, \text{less any deductible}$$

Because the coinsurance formula results in the greater value, Amanda will receive $89,286, less any applicable deductible. It is important to remember that the homeowners insurance policy will only cover up to the policy limit. Even if a policyholder has the required 80% multiplied by the replacement cost of the dwelling in coverage, the policy will not pay out more than its limit or face amount.

Certain properties attached to the dwelling or considered an integral part of the dwelling are covered only on an actual cash value basis. These properties include awnings, household appliances, outdoor antennas, outdoor appliances, and nonbuilding structures.

Coverage B: Other Structures

Other structures
Structures not attached to a dwelling, such as detached garages, small greenhouses, storage buildings, and gazebos

Coverage B provides coverage for small, detached structures on the dwelling property. These **other structures** include detached garages, small greenhouses, storage buildings, and gazebos. The limit of insurance in Coverage B is typically 10% of the Coverage A (dwelling) limit. Like the dwelling coverage, this coverage pays on a replacement cost basis.

Note that detached structures used for business purposes are not covered under Section B of a personal homeowners policy. Additionally, Section B does not apply to any structure rented to someone who is not a tenant of the dwelling, unless the structure is used solely as a private garage.

Coverage C: Personal Property

Under Coverage C, personal property refers to the belongings possessed by the policyowner and personal property of any resident family members. This property includes furniture, clothing, electronics, and other personally owned possessions, regardless of where the property is located at the time of loss. The limit of insurance for Coverage C is typically 50% of the Coverage A (dwelling) limit.

Note that the standard HO form provides only actual cash value (ACV) coverage on personal property. An optional endorsement is available to increase coverage up to the replacement cost, and this option is recommended for most homeowners. Because the contents of a home depreciate rapidly, a homeowner could suffer a serious financial loss if replacement cost coverage were not provided.

Consider the price of a man's suit, which is about $300. Assume that after a short time, a homeowner's suits depreciate to a value of $150 each and the homeowner loses five suits in a fire. Under the ACV option, the insurer will only pay the depreciated value of the suits at the time of loss, in this case a total of $750. If the homeowner has an optional replacement cost endorsement, the insurance company will pay the entire replacement cost of the suits.

Certain kinds of personal property have maximum dollar limits on the amount that will be paid for any loss. A typical HO policy contains the following limits of liability:

- $200—cash and currency, bank notes, bullion, coin collections, and medals
- $500—loss of business use property not on premises
- $1,500—securities, manuscripts, stamp collections, valuable papers, and airline tickets
- $1,500—theft of jewelry, watches, gems, precious metals, and real furs
- $1,500—watercraft (including motor and trailer), trailers (not boat affiliated), and equipment
- $1,500—loss of electronic apparatus
- $2,500—theft of firearms
- $2,500—theft of silverware, goldware, pewterware, and similar property
- $2,500—loss of business use property on premises

Property with considerable value, such as jewelry, furs, or stamp collections, may be protected by additional amounts of insurance beyond the limits listed above. These items may be covered under a **scheduled personal property endorsement**. This endorsement provides open-peril coverage under the same terms as if separate contracts were purchased for each type of property. Types of property that may be covered under this type of endorsement may include jewelry, musical instruments, silverware, fine art, cameras, furs, coin collections, and stamp collections. In most cases, the amount for which an item is insured is considered the value of the item if a loss occurs.

Scheduled personal property endorsement
Provides open-peril coverage under the same terms as if separate contracts were purchased for each type of property; the amount for which an item is insured is considered the value of the item if a loss occurs

Certain items of personal property are excluded from coverage because they are either uninsurable or outside the normal range of property owned by the typical homeowner. Because there is an unusual risk exposure for these types of property, the homeowner must request special coverage outside the homeowners coverage. The following types of personal property are specifically excluded from coverage under a homeowners policy:

- Animals, birds, and fish
- Articles separately described and specifically insured
- Motorized land vehicles used off premises
- Property of roomers or boarders not related to the insured
- Aircraft and parts
- Furnishings on property rented out to others
- Property held as samples, held for sale, or sold but not delivered
- Business data, credit cards, and funds transfer cards
- Business property held away from the residence premises

Coverage D: Loss of Use

Loss of use
Coverage that provides reimbursement to an insured homeowner for additional living expenses or loss of fair rental value

Additional living expenses
The difference between the cost of living in temporary arrangements and the normal costs that would have been incurred had there been no loss

Loss of fair rental value
The gross rental value less charges and expenses that do not continue during the period in which the property is uninhabitable

Loss of use coverage may provide reimbursement to an insured homeowner for additional living expenses or loss of fair rental value.

Additional living expenses. Loss of use coverage provides repayment of any extra living expenses incurred as the result of having to live elsewhere while the home is being restored following a Coverage A loss. **Additional living expenses** are defined as the difference between the cost of living in temporary arrangements and the normal costs that would have been incurred had there been no loss. Typically, coverage is limited to a maximum of 20% of the Coverage A (dwelling) limit.

Assume that Betsy cannot live in her house for several weeks because of severe damage that is covered by her homeowners policy. She incurs hotel charges of $4,000, pays $1,500 for meals, and has $150 in laundry costs while living away from home. Had there been no loss, her expenses for her home, meals, and laundry would have been $3,250. Loss of use protection would provide $2,400 in additional living expenses to compensate her for the extra costs associated with being temporarily displaced from her home while it is being repaired ($4,000 + $1,500 + $150 – $3,250 = $2,400).

Loss of fair rental value. Under Coverage D, an insured lessor may recover the loss of fair rental value on property held for rental purposes. Benefits for **loss of fair rental value** are paid on the basis of the gross rental value less charges and expenses that do not continue during the period in which the property is uninhabitable. In this case, coverage is usually limited to a maximum of 20% of the Coverage A (dwelling) limit.

Suppose Janice owns a house in which she rents a section to a university student for $300 per month. The house is deemed uninhabitable for two months after a fire. Each month, she has maintenance expenses for this section of the house totaling $50, which she does not incur during the repair of the house. Janice can recover $500 [($300 – $50) × 2] for the loss of rent during the restoration of the house.

If a civil authority prevents an insured from using the premises because of damage by a covered peril to a neighborhood, loss of use coverage typically will be provided for up to two weeks. This is a unique feature of the HO form, considering that the insured need not directly experience any damage to the property to collect for loss of use. Consider the various forest fire episodes in California. If a civil authority orders a homeowner to vacate the premises because of the spread of fire in the area, loss of use coverage can provide reimbursement of additional living expenses incurred as a result of the evacuation.

Preferred Provisions

Exhibit 10.2 summarizes the preferred provisions of homeowners insurance.

EXHIBIT 10.2 Homeowners Checklist

Part A – Dwelling	■ Replacement cost ■ Open perils
Part B – Other Structures	■ Replacement cost ■ Open perils
Part C – Personal Property	■ Replacement cost* ■ Open perils* ■ Scheduled items
Part D – Loss of Use	■ Additional living expenses ■ Loss of fair rental value
Riders	■ Extra coverage for valuable personal property ■ Aircraft ■ Watercraft ■ Furnishings on property rented out to others ■ Business property ■ Earthquake insurance ■ Sewer backup coverage

*An endorsement is required for HO-3 policies.

Section II Coverage

Coverage E: Personal Liability

Coverage E protects the insured homeowner and all resident family members against liability for bodily injury and property damage that may occur on or off the insured's premises due to negligence. The basic limit for liability is $100,000 per occurrence, although this limit may be increased. An **occurrence** is an accident, including exposure to conditions, that results in bodily injury or property damage during the policy period. For example, covered occurrences may include a guest to an insured's home falling on a patch of ice on the walkway, or a dog biting a mail carrier on or off the insured's premises. Coverage E only applies if the insured is found to be legally liable.

Occurrence
An accident, including exposure to conditions, which results in bodily injury or property damage during the policy period

As part of the coverage, the insurer pays all defense and settlement costs associated with a claim for damages made by an injured party. Personal liability coverage does not, however, cover the homeowner for liability arising from the operation of a business in the home.

EXAMPLE Mr. Smith owns a home in Central Florida, which he has insured with a standard homeowners policy. He has an adventurous dog that tends to wander around the neighborhood. If Mr. Smith's dog bites a pedestrian on or off his property, his standard homeowners policy's liability coverage (Coverage E: Personal Liability) will cover him up to the policy limits for any damage or negligence as a result of his dog (dog bite lawsuit) for which he is found legally liable. Coverage F: Medical Payments to Others may also be applied for any medical bills, typically up to $1,000 for coverage of an occurrence on or off the insured property.

EXAMPLE Mr. Smith is on vacation in California. While golfing with friends, he slices his drive into an adjacent fairway and hits another golfer, causing several thousand dollars' worth of medical bills. This is an additional case or occurrence that Mr. Smith's liability coverage within his homeowner's policy (Coverage E: Personal Liability) would protect him against litigation up to the policy limit because he is legally liable for his negligent drive of his golf ball. Coverage F: Medical Payments to Others may also be applied for any medical bills, typically up to $1,000.

EXAMPLE Mr. Smith decided to have a backyard party that included a campfire for his guests to roast marshmallows. The wind picks up and blows the flames from the campfire onto his neighbor's house, causing several thousand dollars in damages. This would be an additional occurrence, and Mr. Smith would be covered for up to the liability limits of his homeowners insurance policy.

Coverage F: Medical Payments to Others

This coverage pays necessary medical expenses of others that result from bodily injury. Bodily injuries must arise out of the insured's activities, premises, or animal(s) on or off the insured's property. Medical expenses must be incurred within three years of the accident; however, this coverage will not pay for medical expenses incurred by the insured or any regular resident of the household, except a residence employee (e.g., a maid or butler).

On the surface, this coverage may seem to duplicate the coverage provided in Coverage E; however, there is an important difference between the two. Coverage F is a no-fault coverage that will automatically pay for bodily injuries, whereas Coverage E pays for both bodily injuries and property damage for which the insured is legally liable. Generally, Coverage F will pay up to $1,000 per person per occurrence. For example, if five people become ill from the food at Marie's dinner party, each person may receive up to $1,000 to cover any necessary medical expenses.

EXAMPLE Suppose Vada hosts a party at her house and invites Katie. While dancing on the coffee table, Katie slips, falls, and is injured. Vada rushes Katie to the hospital. Coverage F will pay up to the policy limit for Katie's medical expenses incurred by the incident, even though her injuries are her own fault, because they occurred on Vada's premises. If, on the following day, Katie files a lawsuit against Vada, asking her for $1 million for pain and suffering damages, Vada's homeowners policy will defend Vada, but if a court determines that Katie's injuries were her own fault, it may deny payment to Katie under the theory that Vada is not legally liable.

Medical Payment Exclusions to Coverage E and Coverage F

Neither Coverage E nor Coverage F will pay for the following injuries or damages:

- That are expected or intended by the insured
- Resulting from the insured's business or professional activities
- Resulting from the rental of premises; however, coverage will be provided when (1) part of an insured location is rented on an occasional basis or solely as a residence to no more than two roomers or boarders and (2) part of an insured location is rented out as an office, school, studio, or private garage
- Arising out of premises the insured owns, rents, or leases to others that have not been declared an insured location
- Arising out of the ownership or use of watercraft, motorized vehicles, and aircraft (however, certain vehicles and watercraft are covered for liability):
  - Trailers that are not connected to a motorized land conveyance
  - A vehicle designed primarily for use off public roads that the insured does not own or that the insured does own but that are on an insured location

- Motorized golf carts while being used on a golf course
- Vehicles not subject to motor vehicle registration that include lawnmowers, motorized wheelchairs, and vehicles in dead storage on the insured location
- Nonmotorized watercraft (e.g., canoes and rowboats)
- Low-powered boats the insured owns or rents and small (less than 26 feet long) sailboats
- Model and hobby aircraft that are not designed to carry people or cargo
- Note that the exclusions of watercraft liability are very detailed; any time the insured plans to purchase, rent, or use a watercraft, the HO policy should be consulted to determine whether coverage exists

- Caused by war or nuclear weapons of any kind
- Caused by the transmission of a communicable disease
- Arising out of sexual molestation, corporal punishment, or physical or mental abuse
- Resulting from the use, sale, manufacture, delivery, transfer, or possession of a controlled substance (other than legally obtained prescription drugs)
- Note that liability for injuries to a residence employee (e.g., a maid or butler) is generally covered; this type of liability coverage is provided to protect the homeowner who needs to hire domestic help but who is not required to purchase workers' compensation coverage for such employees

Exclusions to Coverage E Only

Certain exclusions pertain only to Coverage E of the policy, including the following:

- Damage to property of any insured (should be covered under Section I)
- Damage to premises the insured is renting or has control of, unless caused by fire, smoke, or explosion
- Contractual liability; however, two types of contractual liability are covered: (1) where the insured has entered into a contract that directly relates to the ownership, maintenance, or use of an insured location, and (2) where the liability of others is assumed by the insured in a contract prior to an occurrence
- Liability for loss assessments charged against the insured as a member of an association or organization of property owners (e.g., a condominium association charges individual unit owners for damage to community property)
- Liability for injuries to employees that falls under a workers' compensation or other disability law
- Liability for bodily injury or property damage for which the insured is also covered by a nuclear energy liability policy

Exclusions to Coverage F Only

Coverage F will not provide coverage for the following bodily injuries:

- Sustained by the insured or any family member
- Sustained by a regular resident of an insured location

- Sustained by a residence employee of the insured that occur outside of the scope of employment
- Sustained by anyone eligible to receive benefits for their injuries under a workers' compensation or similar disability law
- Resulting from nuclear reaction radiation, regardless of cause

EXHIBIT 10.3 Summary of Liability Exclusions Applicable to Coverage E and F

Exclusion	Coverage E: Personal Liability	Coverage F: Medical Payments
Intentional injury	✓	✓
Business and professional activities	✓	✓
Rental of property	✓	✓
Professional liability	✓	✓
Uninsured premises	✓	✓
Motor vehicles	✓	✓
Watercraft	✓	✓
Aircraft	✓	✓
War	✓	✓
Communicable disease	✓	✓
Sexual molestation or abuse	✓	✓
Nuclear exclusion	✓	✓
Workers' compensation	✓	✓
Controlled substance	✓	✓
Contractual liability	✓	—
Property owned by or in custody of insured	✓	—
Residence employee away from premises	—	✓
Persons residing on premises	—	✓

HOMEOWNERS (HO) INSURANCE: BASIC FORMS

The basic homeowners (HO) insurance forms available are as follows:

- HO-2: Broad Form (named perils)
- HO-3: Special Form (open perils)
- HO-4: Tenants or Renters
- HO-5: Comprehensive Form (open perils, coverages A, B, C, and D)
- HO-6: Condominium Owners
- HO-8: Modified Form for Special Risks

HO-2: Broad Form

The HO-2 policy provides broad coverage for the dwelling and personal property. In addition, this form broadens certain perils and adds other perils.

HO-3: Special Form

This is the most popular and widely purchased of the basic homeowners policies, accounting for nearly 80% of all homeowners policies sold today. Under an HO-3 policy, real property is covered on an open-perils basis, unless the peril is specifically excluded by the policy. Personal property is covered on a named-perils basis.

An HO-3 policy covers all of the perils listed in an HO-2 policy and any other peril not excluded. The value of the HO-3 is that this form will cover certain unusual losses not specifically named as perils in the HO-2. For example, suppose an insured homeowner with an HO-2 policy, who lives in a rural area, owns a shed that is damaged when a neighbor's livestock gets loose. Because none of the named perils addresses this particular situation, the loss will not be covered. However, had the shed been insured under an HO-3 policy, the damage would have been covered because an HO-3 policy generally has no such exclusions.

HO-4: Tenants or Renters

HO-4 is designed for tenants who do not own their dwelling. In such cases, the tenant has a need only for personal liability coverage, plus coverage for contents and loss of use. The HO-4 policy does not protect the actual building or dwelling (Coverage A or Coverage B), which should be covered by the landlord's policy.

Tenants or Renters provides protection against losses caused by the 18 perils listed in an HO-2 policy. The minimum amount of coverage sold under the HO-4 is $4,000 of personal property coverage (Coverage C). Coverage D (Loss of Use) limit is commonly equal to 30% of the Coverage C limit.

HO-5: Comprehensive Form

The HO-5 is similar to the HO-3 except that Coverage C (personal property) for an HO-5 policy is written on an open-perils basis. The HO-5 was withdrawn from use in 1984 but was reintroduced by the ISO in 2000. In the interim, an HO-15 endorsement was added to an HO-3 policy to provide coverage similar to that of an HO-5 policy.

HO-6: Condominium Owners

The insurance needs of condominium owners differ from those of single-family residence owners because the condo property's common areas (e.g., elevators, hallways, lobbies, and laundry rooms) are covered by insurance policies owned by the condo association. An HO-6 policy provides coverage for the condo owner's personal belongings and any owned structural part of the building. In most cases, the minimum amount of insurance that must be purchased for Coverage C (personal property) under an HO-6 is $6,000. Loss of use coverage is limited to 40% of Coverage C. The HO-6 policy does provide liability protection.

HO-8: Modified Form for Special Risks

The HO-8 policy provides coverage for those who live in an older home whose replacement cost exceeds its market value. The HO-8 policy uses a functional replacement cost provision for loss. Under the functional replacement cost, the insurance company agrees to pay the amount necessary to repair damage, but the coverage cannot be more than the materials and labor that make the dwelling functionally equivalent to its original style. The HO-8 policy covers basic perils only. Liability and medical payments coverage are also part of the policy.

EXHIBIT 10.4 Summary of Covered Perils

	HO-2	HO-3	HO-4	HO-5	HO-6	HO-8
Coverage A: Dwelling	Broad	Open	N/A	Open	Limited	Basic
Coverage B: Other Structures	Broad	Open	N/A	Open	N/A	Basic
Coverage C: Personal Property	Broad	Broad*	Broad	Open	Broad	Basic
Coverage D: Loss of Use	Broad	Open	Broad	Open	Broad	Basic

*Can be endorsed with HO-15 endorsement to provide coverage for personal property on an open-perils basis and can be endorsed to provide loss settlement for personal property on a replacement cost basis

HOMEOWNERS (HO) INSURANCE: ADDITIONAL COVERAGES

Additional coverage is available under homeowners insurance policies. Most of these may be included in an HO-3 policy without additional cost, and not all additional coverage features are available on all policies:

- All-risk coverage for property while it is being moved from one place to another and for an additional 30 days thereafter
- Removal of debris from covered property damaged by an insured peril
- A fire department service charge up to $1,000 for loss by an insured peril; however, a fire department call for rescuing a cat from a tree or people in a home being threatened by a flood is not covered
- The cost of reasonable repairs to protect the property from further damage after a covered loss occurs
- Damage to trees, shrubs, plants, and lawns from all covered perils except for wind (often limited to 5% of the dwelling coverage but not more than $1,000 for any one tree or plant)
- Up to $1,000 per loss for assessments against an insured by a group of property owners arising from loss or damage to property jointly owned by all of the members collectively (e.g., condominium owners)
- Costs resulting from damage to property arising from the collapse of a building caused by an insured peril in addition to several circumstances per the insurance contract
- Damage caused by breakage of glass or safety glazing material that is part of the building, storm doors, or storm windows
- Up to $2,500 for damage to landlord's furnishings in an apartment on the insured's dwelling premises
- Up to $500 for loss due to unauthorized use of credit cards, fund transfer cards, forgery of checks, acceptance of counterfeit money, and any incurred court costs or attorney fees may be available

- Theft coverage for property of students while away at school
- Damage caused by the accidental discharge of water from a waterbed

HOMEOWNERS (HO) INSURANCE: ENDORSEMENTS

Several endorsements are available for homeowners policies at an additional cost, including the following:

Replacement Cost for Personal Property

All of the forms previously discussed provide personal property coverage on the basis of actual cash value (ACV) of the personal property. With this endorsement, covered losses are paid on the basis of what it costs to replace the property without a deduction for depreciation.

Inflation Protection

An inflation protection endorsement provides for an annual pro rata increase in the limits of liability under Coverages A, B, C, and D. The insured specifies the percentage increase, for example 6%, when the endorsement is purchased.

Assume the homeowner chooses an inflation protection endorsement with an annual pro rata increase of 6%. The homeowner's house, originally insured for $200,000, would have coverage of $212,000 at the end of the year.

Because it is uncommon for a home to increase in value at precisely the same rate of inflation, the inflation protection endorsement is not a comprehensive form of protection against inflation and should not be a substitute for regular and careful review of adequate insurance coverage.

Earthquake Endorsement

An earthquake endorsement can be added to Section I of a homeowners policy to provide coverage for earthquakes, landslides, and earth movement. A minimum deductible of $250 applies to any one loss and up to a 10% deductible of the total amount of applicable insurance may apply to the loss.

Water Backup Coverage

This endorsement to Section I of a homeowners policy provides coverage for loss to property as a result of water that backs up through a sewer or drain. An overflow from a sump is also covered, even if the overflow is the result of a mechanical failure of the sump.

Building Law and Ordinance Coverage

Coverage under this endorsement arises from a homeowner's legal responsibility to abide by building laws, ordinances, and codes. If a homeowner is legally required to demolish a partially destroyed house, or if the building codes require more-costly construction methods or materials in the replacement or restoration of a structure, this endorsement provides coverage on the basis of the extra costs.

Personal Injury

Section II of the standard HO policy protects the insured only against liability for bodily injury and property damage. An insured may be liable for personal injury or damage to someone's reputation as well. The HO policies can be endorsed to provide limited personal injury protection to the insured. This endorsement adds coverage for the following unintentional offenses (remember that if the loss is intentionally caused, the policy will not provide coverage):

- False arrest, detention or imprisonment, or malicious prosecution
- Libel, slander, defamation of character, or violation of the right of privacy
- Invasion of right of private occupation, wrongful eviction, or wrongful entry

Open Perils

An endorsement may be purchased to change coverage to open perils from broad perils.

HOMEOWNERS (HO) INSURANCE: CONTRACTUAL CONDITIONS

Section I Conditions

Loss Settlement

This condition specifies how certain property items will be valued (e.g., ACV basis or replacement cost basis). The coinsurance provision of the policy is also contained in this clause.

Duties After a Loss

The insured is required to fulfill a number of obligations before the loss can be settled. Immediately after the loss, the insured must perform the following duties:

- Give notice to the insurance company or agent
- Protect the property against any further damage
- Prepare an inventory of loss to the building and personal property
- File written proof of the loss with the insurance company, within the company's time constraints; the insurer must provide a state-approved form for the proof of loss

Appraisal

This clause gives the insured the right to dispute the amount of settlement offered by the insurer. If the insured and the insurer disagree on the amount of loss, either party may demand an appraisal by a competent appraiser. Both the insurer and the insured hire their own appraisers. If the two appraisers cannot reach an agreement on the loss amount, an umpire mediates their differences. Each party pays for its own appraiser, and both the insured and the insurer equally share the expense of hiring the umpire.

Settlement at Insurer's Option

The insurer retains the right to repair or replace any part of damaged property with similar property, as long as it notifies the insured of this right within 30 days after receiving the insured's sworn proof of loss.

Mortgage Clause

Because many homes are mortgaged property, the insurer includes this clause to protect the mortgagee's (lender's) interest in the insured home. This clause gives the mortgagee important rights. The mortgagee has the right to receive payment for valid claims on the property to the extent of its interest, even if the insurer has denied the insured's claim (which would happen in the case of misrepresentation by the insured or an intentionally caused loss). The mortgagee also has the right to receive notice of policy cancellation or nonrenewal at least 10 days before the coverage on the property ends.

This clause also imposes certain obligations on the mortgagee. The mortgagee is responsible for notifying the insurer if there is a change in ownership or occupancy of the mortgaged property. The mortgagee must also pay any homeowner premiums that are due but that the insured has neglected to pay and file proof of loss statements if the insured fails to do so.

Abandonment of Property

The insurance company does not have to accept property abandoned by an insured. A homeowner who suffers fire damage, for example, might try to force the insurer to take control of the house and be responsible for cleanup, repairs, and even mortgage payments.

Recovered Property

When the insured or the insurer recovers property for which the insurer has already paid a claim (as might be the case following a theft), each must notify the other party of the recovery. The insured then has the option to return the recovered property to the insurer or keep the recovered property. If the insured keeps the property, the loss payment must be adjusted accordingly.

Loss to a Pair or a Set

When there has been a loss to a pair or a set (such as a partial loss of a set of china or the theft of only one earring), the insurer may either repair or replace the damaged or lost items or pay the difference between the value of the property as a set (before the loss) and the value after the loss.

Other Insurance

When a loss covered under one policy is also covered by another policy, the insured cannot collect from each policy in full. To do so would place the insured in a better position after the loss than before the loss, thus violating the principle of indemnity. The Other Insurance clause states that when more than one policy covers a loss, each insurer will pay only a proportion of the loss based on the limits of coverage provided in the policy.

Suppose Erin has two homeowners policies. One provides a limit of $50,000; the other provides a limit of $100,000. Erin's house is worth only $100,000; after a fire destroys it, she will collect a proportion of the loss from each insurer. Because the first insurer provides one-third of all coverage provided ($50,000 ÷ $150,000), it will pay one-third of the loss, or $33,333. The second insurer will pay two-thirds of the loss, or $66,667.

Suit Against the Insurance Company

This clause gives the insured the right to sue the insurer only after complying with all the policy provisions and requires that the suit be brought within one year of the date of the loss.

Loss Payment

After an agreement is reached regarding the amount of loss to provide, the insurer has 60 days to pay the insured.

No Benefit to Bailee

Bailee
A party that holds the property of another

A **bailee** is a party that holds the property of another. If the insured has left property with a bailee, such as a moving company or dry cleaner, the insurer will not pay for loss or damaged property on behalf of the bailee. This clause does not say that claims by the insured will not be paid; it merely states that the coverage will not protect or benefit the bailee. If, for example, a fire on the premises of a dry cleaner destroyed the insured's personal property, the insurer would pay the insured's claim; however, the insurer would then subrogate against, or seek restitution from, the dry cleaner.

Volcanic Eruption Period

All volcanic eruptions occurring within a 72-hour period are considered one occurrence. Because volcanoes tend to erupt gradually over a period of days, this clause protects the insured from having to pay a new deductible for each eruption.

Section II Conditions

Limit of Liability

The insurer will not pay more than the policy's coverage limit for each occurrence, regardless of the number of suits or claims filed against the insured for any one event.

Duties After a Loss

The insured is expected to give notice of any accident or occurrence to the insurer or its agent. The insured must also promptly forward to the insurer all summons and demand letters. The insured must cooperate and assist the insurer in the investigation and settlement of any claims. Finally, the insured must not voluntarily make payments for anything other than first aid at the time a bodily injury is sustained.

Duties of an Injured Person—Coverage F

An injured person or a representative must give the insurer written proof of a claim as soon as practical after a loss and give the insurer permission to obtain medical records of the injured person. The injured person must also submit to a physical exam by the insurer's doctor if instructed to do so by the insurer.

Payment of Claim—Coverage F

This clause states that paying any claim under Coverage F is in no way an admission of liability by the insurer or the insured.

Bankruptcy of Insurance Company

The bankruptcy or insolvency of any insurer does not terminate coverage or relieve the insurer of its obligations under the policy.

Sections I and II Conditions

Concealment or Fraud

Dishonesty either before or after a loss may void the policy. Examples of dishonesty that will void the policy include intentionally concealing or misrepresenting material facts and intentionally causing losses.

Cancellation and Nonrenewal

State laws regarding the insurer's right of cancellation and nonrenewal vary, so it is important to examine the specific policy to understand the law. Generally, however, the insured may cancel the policy at any time by notifying the insurer, whereas the insurer may cancel the policy only for nonpayment of premium, material misrepresentation of fact, or a substantial change in the risk. In most cases, the insurer must provide a 10-day notice of cancellation only when it is canceling a newly issued policy or when it is canceling for nonpayment of premium. Other cancellations and nonrenewals usually require a 30-day notice. Cancellations generally result in a pro rata refund of unused premium.

Assignment

For a homeowners policy, the insured may not assign rights under the policy without the insurer's written consent.

Subrogation

The insurer may require the insured to assign rights of recovery for payments made by the insurer. This allows the insurer to take over the insured's subrogation rights against negligent third parties. The insurer does not, however, subrogate for claims made under Coverage F of the policy.

EXHIBIT 10.5 Summary of Common Homeowners Insurance Policies

	HO-2 (Broad Form)	HO-3 (Special Form)	HO-8 (For Older Homes)	HO-4 (Renter's Contents Broad Form)	HO-6 (For Condominium Owners)
Perils covered	Perils 1–18	All perils except those specifically excluded from buildings; perils 1–18 on personal property	Perils 1–12	Perils 1–18	Perils 1–18
Section 1: Property coverages/limits					
House and any other attachments	Amount based on replacement cost, minimum $15,000	Amount based on replacement cost, minimum $20,000	Amount based on actual cash value of the home, minimum $15,000	Improvements and betterments coverage up to 10% of the amount of personal property coverage	$1,000 on owner's additions and alterations to the unit
Detached buildings	10% of insurance on the home	10% of insurance on the home	10% of insurance on the home	Not covered	Included in Dwelling Coverage
Trees, shrubs, plants, etc.	5% of insurance on the home, $500 maximum per item	5% of insurance on the home, $500 maximum per item	5% of insurance on the home, $250 maximum per item	10% of personal property insurance, $500 maximum per item	10% of personal property insurance, $500 maximum per item
Personal property (contents)	50% of insurance on the home	50% of insurance on the home Covers same as Broad Form	50% of insurance on the home	Chosen by the tenant to reflect the value of the items, minimum $6,000	Chosen by home owner to reflect the value of the items, minimum $6,000
Loss of use and/or add'l living expense	20% of insurance on the home	20% of insurance on the home	10% of insurance on the home	30% of personal property insurance	40% of personal property insurance
Credit card, forgery, counterfeit money	$500	$500	$500	$500	$500
Section 2: Liability coverage/limits					
Comprehensive personal liability	$100,000	$100,000	$100,000	$100,000	$100,000
Damage to property of others	$250–$500	$250–$500	$250–$500	$250–$500	$250–$500
Medical payments	$1,000	$1,000	$1,000	$1,000	$1,000

*Special limits apply on a per-occurrence basis (e.g., per fire or theft): money, coins, bank notes, precious metals (e.g., gold and silver), $200; securities, deeds, stocks, bonds, tickets, and stamps, $1,500; watercraft and trailers, including furnishings, equipment, and outboard motors trailers other than for watercraft, $1,500; trailers other than for watercraft, $1,500; jewelry, watches, and furs, $1,500; silverware and goldware, $2,500; guns, $2,500.

AUTOMOBILE INSURANCE

Automobile insurance is required in every state, although to varying degrees. Mandatory automobile insurance laws expressly require the purchase of liability insurance before owning or operating a motor vehicle. Some states require the purchase of no-fault coverage that pays for bodily injuries on a first-party basis. Each state implicitly requires automobile insurance by compelling motorists to be financially responsible for a minimum amount of bodily injury and property damage.

In addition to these statutory requirements, many people purchase automobile insurance because their automobiles are financed and the lender requires the borrower to carry coverage for direct physical damage to the auto. Many people purchase increased amounts of automobile insurance because they recognize that the financial burden associated with an automobile accident could be devastating. One at-fault accident could result in thousands of dollars of damage, and the insured would be responsible for those damages. In addition, with most new cars costing into the tens of thousands of dollars, the damage to the insured's vehicle could be very costly to repair.

The owner and operator of an automobile should be concerned about the following losses:

- Damage to or loss of the insured's vehicle
- Injury to the insured or family members
- Legal liability for injuries and damages done to other persons or property

PERSONAL AUTO POLICY (PAP) COVERAGES

Personal automobile policy (PAP)
Provides physical damage insurance, medical payments, liability coverage, and uninsured motorist protection

No-fault insurance
Used in states that require drivers to carry insurance for their own protection; places limits on the insured's ability to sue other drivers for damages

The **personal automobile policy (PAP)** is an insurance package policy that can protect against the three major losses listed above. A PAP may be used to provide physical damage insurance, medical payments, liability coverage, and uninsured motorist protection. These policies may also provide no-fault benefits in states that require this type of protection. **No-fault insurance** is used in states that require drivers to carry insurance for their own protection and also places limits on the insured's ability to sue other drivers for damages. Under this type of insurance, each insurance company pays only for its insured driver's damages, up to policy limits, regardless of who was at fault for the accident. Most insurers use the Insurance Services Office (ISO) Program; however, various state laws may result in different policy provisions and coverage. Therefore, policyowners should carefully read each policy.

Policy Overview

Eligible Vehicles

The PAP may be used to insure four-wheel passenger automobiles, pickup trucks, and vans that are owned by individuals or leased by individuals for at least six months. The vehicle must be owned by an individual or by a married couple who are residents of the same household. Pickups and vans must have a gross vehicle weight of less than 10,000 pounds and not be used primarily for business purposes (other than farming, ranching, or the installation, maintenance, or repair of equipment or furnishings). The policy may be used to insure one vehicle or all the vehicles owned in a household (usually subject to a maximum of four vehicles on one policy). To save premium dollars, all the vehicles in one household should be insured on the same policy rather than insuring each vehicle with a separate policy.

The PAP may be used to insure vehicles that are used for pleasure and recreation (e.g., motorcycles, recreational vehicles, or golf carts). An endorsement is used to provide coverage when it is used for these types of vehicles.

Policy Design

Throughout the personal automobile policy, "you" and "your" refer to the named insured and spouse. "We," "us," and "our" refer to the insurance company. Policy language is usually simplified as much as possible while maintaining the required legal form.

The PAP is arranged into six parts listed as follows:

- Part A: Liability Coverage
- Part B: Medical Payments Coverage
- Part C: Uninsured Motorists Coverage
- Part D: Coverage for Damage to Your Auto
- Part E: Duties After an Accident or Loss
- Part F: General Provisions

Parts A through D are four separate types of coverage that may be included in a PAP. Each part has its own insuring agreement, insured persons covered, and exclusions. Each type of coverage is effective by declaration in the policy and payment of premium for the coverage.

Part A: Liability Coverage

In the PAP's Liability Coverage section, the insurance company agrees to pay damages caused by an accident, up to the policy limit, for which the insured is legally responsible. The insurer retains the right to defend or settle any claim or suit, and settlement and defense costs are paid in addition to the policy limits.

Covered Persons and Autos

Definition of "Insured." An insured is defined in Part A as the following:

- You or any family member, for the ownership, maintenance, or use of any auto or trailer (this includes the use of borrowed autos and even rental cars)
- Any person using your covered auto with permission or belief of right to use
- Any organization that is responsible for the conduct of someone driving your covered auto (e.g., an employer or charitable organization)
- Any organization that is responsible for your conduct or the conduct of a family member while you are driving a nonowned automobile (e.g., an employer that might be responsible for your actions when you are using a coworker's car for business purposes)

Primarily, coverage is provided for the insured or spouse residing in the same household (referred to as "you" in the policy) or any family member for the use of any auto or trailer. "Family member" refers to a person related to the named insured by blood, marriage, adoption, or a foster child residing with the insured. The insured and family members are covered when operating any auto, which includes both the covered auto and rented or borrowed vehicles.

Individuals other than the named insured and family members are covered while using the covered auto. The person using the vehicle, however, must have a reasonable belief that he has the right to do so.

Coverage under a PAP extends to an individual or organization held vicariously liable for damage or injury. Vicarious liability exists when one party is liable for the negligent actions of another, even though the first party was not directly responsible for the injury. The following parties would be covered under a PAP:

EXAMPLE Those who are vicariously liable for the operation of the insured automobile. Assume Erin is the insured under a PAP policy, which covers her 2014 Mustang. She uses this automobile to run an errand for her employer, Bobby. While running the errand, Erin collides with Don's vehicle and injures him. Don not only brings suit against Erin for damages, he also sues Bobby as Erin's employer. Under the PAP, Bobby is covered in addition to Erin because, as Erin's employer, Bobby is vicariously liable for the injuries she causes.

EXAMPLE Those held vicariously liable for the operation of a nonowned vehicle by the named insured or family member. Assume Jenni is insured under a PAP policy. Jenni borrows Reggie's 2012 Hummer to call on a client of Eddie, her employer. Jenni rear ends Peggy's vehicle. Peggy is injured and files suit against both Jenni and Eddie as Jenni's employer. Jenni's PAP policy will provide coverage for Eddie's vicarious liability. However, it will not cover Reggie should he be sued as owner of the Hummer. Reggie would, however, be covered under his own PAP.

"Covered Auto" Defined. "Your covered auto" is defined as any of the following:

- Any vehicle shown in the policy declarations
- Any new vehicle in addition to those shown in the declarations, but only for a specified period (policies vary, most often for a 14- or 30-day period) or until the new vehicle is reported to the insurer; the insurer will charge a premium from the date the vehicle was acquired, and the new vehicle will have the broadest coverage provided on any declared vehicle for the specified period
- Any new vehicle that replaces a vehicle shown in the declarations; the new vehicle will have the same coverage as the vehicle it replaced, and the insured must report the new vehicle within 30 days only if coverage for damage to your auto is desired
- Any trailer the insured owns
- Any auto or trailer that the insured does not own but that is used as a temporary substitute while a covered vehicle is unavailable because of loss, breakdown, repair, service, or destruction

Exclusions

PAP liability coverage is quite broad in nature. However, it excludes coverage for the following persons and situations.

- *Vehicle used by auto dealer*—No coverage is provided for any auto dealer or other person in the automobile business who is driving your car. A person in the automobile business should have coverage under his own policy.
- *Bodily injury to an employee*—No coverage is provided for injuries to an employee; such injuries are most often covered by workers' compensation. One exception is that the insured will be covered for liability for injuries to a domestic employee.
- *Insured's owned property*—Liability insurance is designed to pay for damages caused by the insured to third parties. By definition, liability insurance does not pay for damages to the insured's owned property. Therefore, in an auto accident, damages to the insured's car and its contents are not paid by the liability coverage Part A. Damage to the car would be covered by the PAP's Part D–Damage to Your Auto, and damage to contents of the vehicle may be covered by homeowners coverage.

- *Property in the insured's care, custody, and control*—Along the same lines as the previous exclusion, this one prohibits the insured from recovering under his own liability insurance for items that are not true liability losses. When property, such as a rental car is damaged in an automobile accident, the PAP treats it as if it were the insured's owned auto. The insured may not use the liability coverage to pay for damages to the rental car.
- *Intentional acts*—Any person who intentionally causes an auto accident is not covered for liability by the policy.
- *Public livery*—Coverage is not provided for any person or vehicle while transporting people or property for a fee. A share-the-expense car pool is not considered a for-fee activity and is, thus, covered. This can be an issue for drivers of rideshare companies (e.g., Uber or Lyft). While the rideshare company will usually provide some coverage, there often are gaps in coverage. Some insurance companies have riders to add coverage back for this type of exposure.
- *Commercial vehicles used in business*—This exclusion eliminates coverage for business use of automobiles but then gives back coverage for business use of any private passenger auto, owned pickup or van, or temporary or substitute pickup or van. The intent is to limit business coverage on autos to either private passenger autos or owned pickups and vans.
- *Using auto without permission*—No coverage is provided for any person who uses an automobile without having a reasonable belief that he has permission to do so.
- *Regular use of nonowned or nondeclared auto*—Coverage is not provided when the insured has the regular use of an automobile that is not shown on the declarations page, either because the employer provides a company car or because the insured owns a nondeclared vehicle. If the insured has a company vehicle, the employer should provide coverage or the insured should declare the vehicle as a nonowned vehicle and purchase coverage for the vehicle. Recall that the named insured is covered while using any auto. If this exclusion were not in the policy, the insured could own 10 vehicles and buy coverage on only one but have coverage on all 10. This exclusion makes it clear that the insurer will only cover owned vehicles that have been declared and for which a premium has been paid.
- *Autos with fewer than four wheels*—Motorcycles and recreational vehicles having fewer than four wheels must be specifically insured under a different policy. No coverage is provided for these types of vehicles, whether they are owned or borrowed.

Coverage Limits

The limits of coverage for Part A are shown on the declarations page, and in most cases, represent three separate liability coverage limits—two for bodily injury, and one for property damage. These **split limits** are often written as 50/100/25 and are expressed in thousands. All limits are on a per-occurrence basis. The first number represents a per person bodily injury limit. A per person limit of $50,000 indicates that any one injured person may not receive more than $50,000 for bodily injuries. The second number represents a per-occurrence bodily injury limit for all bodily injuries. If this limit were $100,000, the insurer would pay up to $100,000 for all the bodily injuries sustained in one accident, regardless of the number of persons injured. The third number represents the property damage limit and specifies the most the insurer will pay for all property damage caused by one accident.

Split limits
Lists the per-person bodily injury limit, the per occurrence bodily injury limit for all bodily injuries, and the property damage limit

EXAMPLE Alan carried 50/100/25 coverage and had a major accident deemed to be his fault. The following claims were filed by injured parties in the other vehicle: Stephen sustained $75,000 in bodily injuries, Scott sustained $22,000 in bodily injuries, and Cheryl sustained $53,000 in bodily injuries. Alan, the driver, incurred $17,000 in automobile repair and rental car costs. Barbara, a nearby homeowner on whose lawn the two cars ultimately landed, sustained $9,000 in lawn and shrubbery damage. All claims are settled in the order mentioned previously.

First, address the bodily injury claims. Stephen is allowed to collect only $50,000 because that is the per-person limit. Note that Stephen will likely sue for the $25,000 deficiency. Scott may collect the full $22,000. Cheryl will collect only $28,000 because, at that point, the $100,000 per occurrence limit has been reached. Claims are paid in the order that they are settled, not on a pro rata basis, so it is important that claimants begin the settlement process as soon as possible.

Next, consider the property damage claims. The policy provides a total of $25,000 of coverage, yet there is a total of $26,000 in property damage claims. Thus, the insurer will pay all of Alan's damages ($17,000), and Barbara will receive only $8,000.

Increased Limits in Another State

As mentioned, all states require some minimum level of financial responsibility or automobile liability insurance. When the insured in one state drives to another state and has an accident, the insured must generally have sufficient limits to meet the requirements of the state in which the accident occurred. In most cases, PAPs providing at least minimum coverage in the home state will provide additional coverage up to the minimum requirements of a visited state.

EXAMPLE A driver from Arizona who has only the minimum required limits of 25/50/25 who drives to Texas, where the minimum limits are 30/60/30, would be expected to have those coverage limits if an accident occurred in Texas. The PAP automatically provides the increased limits required by state law. Therefore, the Arizona driver's policy would pay up to 30/60/30 if an accident occurred while in Texas.

Please note that this policy provision never reduces the limits of liability the insured has purchased. If a Texas driver with the 30/60/30 coverage limits drives to Arizona, his policy will pay up to those limits for any accident. The policy will not reduce the amount of coverage provided to 25/50/25.

Loss Sharing With Other Coverage

When more than one auto policy covers a loss, the general rule is that insurance on the automobile is primary, while insurance on the driver is excess.

EXAMPLE If Caitlin borrows Joshua's car and has an accident while driving his car, Joshua's PAP coverage will pay first. When Joshua's limits of coverage have been exhausted, Caitlin's policy will pay on an excess basis. If more than one policy is primary (e.g., if an automobile is declared and covered by two separate policies), the policies share losses on a proportionate basis (similar to homeowners insurance).

Part B: Medical Payments

Medical payments
A no-fault, first-party insurance coverage designed to pay for bodily injuries sustained in an auto accident

Medical payments are optional no-fault, first-party coverage designed to pay for bodily injuries sustained in an auto accident. Expenses must be incurred within three years of the auto accident. Limits of insurance are provided on a per-person, per-occurrence basis. A typical limit of coverage is $5,000 per person per occurrence. This means that if four covered persons are injured in an auto accident, each may collect up to $5,000 for reasonable and necessary medical and funeral expenses.

Who Is Covered?

An insured in this coverage is defined as any of the following:

- You or any family member while occupying a motor vehicle
- You or any family member as a pedestrian when struck by a motor vehicle
- Any other person while occupying your covered auto

Exclusions

Medical payment coverage excludes the following.

- *Public livery*—No coverage is provided while the vehicle is used to carry persons or property for a fee.
- *Auto used as a residence*—Although trailers are included as covered autos, this exclusion prevents someone from having medical payments coverage on a house trailer. This type of nonstandard risk must be specifically insured.
- *Injury while working*—Any benefits that are payable under workers' compensation or other disability benefit laws preclude coverage under this policy.
- *Using auto without permission*—No coverage is provided for any person who uses an automobile without having a reasonable belief that he has permission to do so.
- *Regular use of nonowned or nondeclared auto*—When the insured has the regular use of an automobile that is not shown on the declarations page, either because the employer provides a company car or because the insured owns a nondeclared vehicle, coverage is not provided.
- *Autos with fewer than four wheels*—Motorcycles and recreational vehicles with fewer than four wheels must be specifically insured under a different policy. No coverage is provided for these types of vehicles, regardless of whether they are owned or borrowed.
- *Auto used in insured's business*—The same exclusion that was discussed in Part A applies here. Coverage is provided for private passenger autos used in business and for owned pickups and vans used in business.
- *War and nuclear hazard injuries*—Consistent with other policies, this coverage does not apply to any injuries sustained because of acts of war or because of nuclear contamination or radioactive hazards.
- *Racing*—No coverage is provided when the vehicle is located inside a racing facility or when the vehicle is practicing for, preparing for, or competing in any type of racing or speed contest.

Part C: Uninsured Motorists

Purpose

Because so many drivers do not obey financial responsibility and compulsory automobile insurance laws, the PAP offers insureds the option of purchasing uninsured motorist coverage that covers damages caused by an uninsured or underinsured motorist.

What Is Covered?

Part C will pay for bodily injuries and, in many states, property damages that are sustained by an insured because of an uninsured or underinsured motorist. In other words, this coverage will pay what the uninsured, at-fault motorist's liability insurance should have paid had it been in place.

Who Is Covered?

An insured for this coverage is defined as follows:

- You or any family member
- Any other person occupying your covered auto
- Any person who might also be entitled to damages (e.g., a spouse or child) for the injuries sustained by a person described above

Definitions of an Uninsured/Underinsured Motorist

Uninsured/underinsured motorist
Motorist without liability coverage or whose insurer cannot or will not pay the claim, hit-and-run driver, or motorist with insufficient liability coverage according to state law

An **uninsured or underinsured motorist** is one who has no liability coverage, has limits of liability coverage less than those required by the insured's home state law, is an unidentified hit-and-run driver, or has liability insurance but whose insurer cannot or will not pay the claim. For the insured to collect from this coverage, the uninsured or underinsured driver must be at fault in the accident.

Exclusions and Limitations

Many of the exclusions contained in Part B are repeated in this coverage:

- Public livery
- Regular use of nonowned auto
- Injury while working
- Regular use of nondeclared auto
- Using auto without permission
- Auto used in insured's business

In addition, the insurer will not pay for any bodily injuries when the insured or legal representatives settle a bodily injury claim without the insurer's consent. Furthermore, this coverage will not pay for punitive damages.

Part D: Coverage for Damage to Your Auto

Coverage D provides direct damage coverage on your covered auto, plus any nonowned auto. A nonowned auto is any private passenger auto, pickup, van, or trailer not owned by or furnished for the use of a family member that is in your (or a family member's) custody. This would include a borrowed car, a rental car, and a temporary substitute auto.

Two Coverages Available

Part D provides the insured with two different direct damage coverages: collision and comprehensive. The insured may purchase one, both, or neither of these coverages. Automobile lenders will generally require the insured to carry both coverages.

Collision
Auto insurance coverage that protects the insured against upset and collision damages

Comprehensive (other-than-collision)
Auto insurance coverage that protects the insured's auto against perils out of the insured's control, such as missiles or falling objects, fire, theft, earthquake, hail, flood, and vandalism

Collision is defined under Part D as "the upset of your covered auto or its impact with another vehicle or object." Therefore, this provision covers damages incurred in an accident involving other vehicles or those sustained when an automobile runs off the road and into a tree.

Comprehensive, or **other-than-collision,** coverage protects the insured against the following perils: missiles or falling objects, fire, theft, explosion, earthquake, windstorm, hail, water or flood, malicious mischief or vandalism, riot or civil commotion, contact with a bird or animal, and breakage of glass. These perils are typically viewed as accidental and out of the insured's control. Thus, the premium for this coverage is lower than that for collision coverage.

Dispute Resolution (Appraisal Clause)

If the insured and the insurer do not agree on the amount of a loss, the insured may demand an appraisal process similar to that provided for in a homeowners policy.

Loss Payment

The insurer retains the sole option either to pay for repairs or to declare the vehicle a total loss and pay the actual cash value of the vehicle, less any deductible. The collision coverage deductible is typically twice as high as the other-than-collision (comprehensive) deductible. In most cases, insureds should carry a minimum $250 other-than-collision deductible and $500 collision deductible. Higher (and lower) deductibles are also available; however, higher deductibles generally reduce premiums.

Loss Sharing With Other Policies

When more than one auto policy covers a loss, the general rule is that insurance on the automobile is primary, while insurance on the driver is excess.

EXAMPLE If Ben borrows Justin's car and has an accident, Justin's collision damage coverage will be primary. Ben's policy will pay on an excess basis but will not pay more than the loss and will still require Ben to pay his own deductible.

If more than one policy is primary (e.g., if an automobile is declared and covered by two separate policies), the policies share losses on a proportionate basis (similar to homeowners insurance).

Exclusions

Many of the exclusions described in other coverages also apply here:

- Public livery
- Custom furnishings on a pickup or van
- Using auto without permission
- Radar detectors
- Racing

- Most electronic equipment, except permanently installed sound reproducing equipment [this generally includes global positioning systems (GPSs), scanning and television monitor receivers, and personal computers]
- War
- Nuclear damages

As with most direct property coverages, the PAP excludes coverage for normal wear and tear and ordinary maintenance losses, such as road damage to tires. Loss caused by destruction or confiscation by governmental authorities, as could occur if the insured vehicle were involved in a crime, is also excluded. Losses to nonowned autos are not covered when the auto is used or maintained by anyone in the automobile business.

Finally, no coverage is provided for a rental vehicle if the insured has purchased a loss damage waiver from the rental car company. Loss damage waivers relieve the insured of liability for damage to the rented vehicle, so the insurer will not provide coverage.

Part E: Duties After an Accident or Loss

After a loss, the insured should notify the insurer, file proof of loss, and cooperate with the insurer in the investigation and settlement of any claim. In addition, the insured must file a police report to have theft coverage for a stolen vehicle or to have uninsured motorist coverage for a hit-and-run incident.

Part F: General Provisions

There are several general provisions and conditions of the auto policy that are similar to those contained in the HO policies. One, however, deserves special attention: the PAP coverage territory.

The PAP provides coverage only in the United States, Puerto Rico and other U.S. territories and possessions, and Canada. When the insured travels to Mexico (where auto accidents are automatically criminal offenses) or to any other country outside the coverage territory, the PAP is not effective. If the insured intends to drive in such a locale, the appropriate local coverages must be arranged.

LEGAL LIABILITY

Intentional interference
Intentional act committed against another that causes injury

Slander
Verbal statement that causes harm to another

Libel
Written statement that causes harm to another

A client may be exposed to three types of risk: torts (civil wrongs), breach of contract, and crimes (public wrongs). Liability insurance will cover certain classes of torts but not breaches of contract or criminal offenses. If a court decides that an individual is liable for a civil wrong that causes injury to another, the individual will be required to make restitution, usually in the form of monetary compensation.

The three general types of torts related to liability are intentional interference, strict and absolute liability, and negligence. **Intentional interference** is an intentional act committed against another that causes injury. Many of the actions that fall under intentional interference are also criminal acts and would not be covered under liability insurance. Slander and libel, however, are usually covered under personal liability insurance policies. **Slander** is defamation or harm caused by a verbal statement, and **libel** is defamation caused by a written statement.

Strict and absolute liability
Liability resulting from law; strict liability allows for defense, and absolute liability does not

Under **strict and absolute liability**, one party is held legally liable regardless of who is responsible for the injury. Workers' compensation laws are examples of absolute liability. Under workers' compensation laws, the employer is liable for any injury to an employee engaged in business activities. Even if the employee causes injury to himself, the employer will be liable unless the employer can prove the injury was due to intoxication or failure to follow orders. If workers' compensation laws provided for absolute liability, the employer would be liable even if the employee were intoxicated. Under strict liability, responsible parties have few options for defense, but under absolute liability, the responsible party has no options for defense.

Negligence
Tort caused by acting without reasonable care

Direct negligence
Involves acts or omissions directly attributable to an individual

Vicarious acts
Negligent acts performed by someone else but for which the individual is held at least partially responsible

If an individual causes harm to another by failing to act with appropriate care, he will be subject to liability due to **negligence**. In determining whether an individual has used appropriate care, the courts use the prudent person standard. The standard is met if a reasonable person confronted with the same circumstances would have performed the same acts. **Direct negligence** refers to acts or omissions directly attributable to an individual. An individual may also be liable for **vicarious acts**, which are negligent acts performed by someone else but for which the individual is held at least partially responsible. For example, in many states bartenders are vicariously liable for the negligent acts of intoxicated patrons. Liability insurance generally covers both types of negligence.

PERSONAL UMBRELLA LIABILITY POLICY

Purpose

Personal umbrella liability policy
Coverage designed to provide a catastrophic layer of liability coverage on top of the individual's homeowners and automobile insurance policies

The **personal umbrella liability policy** is designed to provide a catastrophic layer of liability coverage on top of the individual's homeowners and automobile insurance policies. The standard amount of coverage is \$1 million, although higher limits may be purchased. The need for this policy is largely dictated by the insured's personal wealth. The more the insured stands to lose, the more likely it is that an umbrella policy is a suitable purchase. While each individual is different, it is often considered a significant financial planning weakness to not have a personal umbrella liability policy.

Characteristics

Most insurers will require the insured to maintain certain underlying limits of coverage through an HO and a PAP; if the insured also has other liability exposures to insure, such as watercraft liability, minimum limits of coverage will be required for those policies as well.

In most cases, the policy provides the insured with a large amount of coverage at an affordable price. The coverage provided is generally quite broad and may even provide coverages in addition to those provided by the underlying policies. For example, the policy might provide personal injury coverage (e.g., for defamation of character or false arrest) even though the underlying HO policy does not cover this type of incident. Where these additional coverages are provided, the insured is usually required to pay a **self-insured retention** (SIR) for each loss. The SIR is similar to a deductible.

Self-insured retention
A payment similar to a deductible that an insured is usually required to pay for each loss under a personal liability umbrella policy (PLUP)

Where both an umbrella and underlying policy cover a loss, the umbrella does not pay any claims until the underlying coverage has been exhausted. From there, the umbrella picks up with no SIR imposed on the insured.

EXAMPLE If Carol has an HO policy with a Coverage E (Personal Liability) limit of $200,000 and a $1 million umbrella policy and is held liable for bodily injuries totaling $700,000, her HO policy will pay the first $200,000 of the claims, and then the umbrella policy will pay the remaining $500,000.

Exclusions

Umbrella liability forms are nonstandard, so it is difficult to generalize about what exclusions will be included in each policy. Certain exclusions almost universally found in these policies include damage to the insured's property, injuries sustained by the insured or a family member, injuries that were intentionally inflicted or caused by the insured, injuries to another party that should be paid under a workers' compensation law, and business and professional liability incidents.

BUSINESS AND PROFESSIONAL USE OF PROPERTY AND LIABILITY INSURANCE

Some of the policies used by businesses to cover property and liability include the commercial package policy, inland marine policies, the businessowners policy, business liability insurance, workers' compensation, business automobile, business liability umbrella policies, professional insurance, and errors and omissions.

The ISO has developed a commercial insurance program including a package policy (two or more coverages).

The Commercial Package Policy (CPP)

Commercial package policy (CPP)
Property and liability coverage combined into a single policy used by businesses

Used by businesses, a **commercial package policy (CPP)** is property and liability coverage combined into a single policy. The advantages of such a policy include lower premiums and fewer gaps in overall coverage. Workers' compensation coverage and surety coverages are not part of a CPP. A CPP policy format includes (1) a declarations page, (2) a policy conditions page, and (3) two or more coverage parts or forms (property, general liability, crime, boiler and machinery, inland marine, commercial auto, or farm). Each part or form of a CPP will specify covered property, additional coverages, extension of coverages, other provisions, deductibles, coinsurance, valuation provisions, optional coverages, and a cause-of-loss form. Coverages for causes of loss are basic, broad, special, or earthquake form. These forms are similar to the parallel homeowners forms. Business interruption insurance may be added. Also, a builders-risk-coverage form can be added to a CPP for buildings under construction.

Inland Marine Policies

Inland marine policies cover domestic goods in transit, property held by bailees, mobile equipment and property, property of certain dealers, and means of transportation and communication. They may also be used to increase coverage limits on nonmovables, such as furs and jewelry.

The Businessowners Policy (BOP)

The businessowners policy is specifically designed for the needs of small to medium-size businesses, covers buildings and business personal property, and is available in two forms: basic and special. The basic form covers listed perils, as distinguished from the special form, which covers all perils not excluded. The policy has a standard $500 deductible and covers business liability for bodily injury and property damage.

Business Liability Insurance

General liability is the legal liability arising out of business activities not related to autos, motorized vehicles, aircraft, and employee (workers' compensation) injuries. Liability issues, not including the exceptions mentioned, are covered by commercial general liability (CGL) policies. CGL can be written either as a stand-alone policy or as a part of a commercial package policy (CPP). The usual coverage, Coverage A, is for bodily injury, property damage, and legal defense, but has significant exclusions. Coverage B is for personal and advertising injury liability, and Coverage C covers medical payments.

Workers' Compensation

Most businesses are required to carry insurance providing workers' compensation insurance, employer liability insurance, and other state insurance. Part One, workers' compensation insurance, covers benefits provided by the insurer (state). Part Two covers lawsuits by employees injured in the course of employment but not covered by state workers' compensation law. Part Three provides coverage for other listed states (e.g., business trips).

Business Auto

The business auto coverage form is used to insure the private passenger and commercial auto exposures of all businesses other than garages, truckers, and motor carriers. Because of the specialized nature of these businesses and their unique coverage needs, separate forms were designed to cover these risks. This form includes coverage for liability and physical damage. Uninsured Motorists, Medical Payments, and Underinsured Motorists coverage can be added by endorsement.

Business Umbrella Liability

Businesses may use commercial umbrella liability policies for excess coverage on liability beyond the coverage provided by a firm's basic liability policy.

Malpractice Insurance

Most people understand **malpractice insurance** as liability insurance for health service providers, especially physicians and surgeons. Malpractice insurance, however, is available for all professional service providers and generally covers intentional as well as unintentional negligent acts committed by the insured. A typical policy will have a maximum per-incident limit and an aggregate limit. The insurer is usually allowed to settle claims out of court without obtaining consent from the insured.

Malpractice insurance
Used where the deficient conduct of the insured provider of professional services may result in damages

Errors and Omissions

Errors and omissions insurance
Provides protection against loss from negligent acts, errors, and omissions by the insured

Errors and omissions insurance provides protection against loss from negligent acts, errors, and omissions by the insured. Many professionals (e.g., real estate agents, insurance agents, accountants, stockbrokers, attorneys, and engineers) need errors and omissions coverage for negligent acts, omissions, or failure to act within their own profession that may cause legal liability. Policies usually have large deductibles ($1,000 or more).

A special type of errors and omissions coverage, called Directors and Officers Errors and Omissions insurance, is available for business executives. Directors and officers insurance provides protection against liability due to mismanagement. Policies usually have high deductibles and require that the insured be financially responsible for a percentage of any claims.

Product Liability

Businesses that manufacture products are subject to liability with respect to those products. Acts that can expose a company to product liability include the following:

- Manufacturing a harmful product
- Selling a defective product
- Packaging the product inappropriately
- Providing insufficient directions or warnings for use

EXHIBIT 10.6 Summary of Insurance for Businesses and Professionals

	Businesses	Professionals
Property Insurance—Buildings	CPP	CPP
Property Insurance—Personalty	CPP	CPP
General Liability Insurance	As needed	As needed
Inland Marine Coverage	If transporting goods	If transporting goods
Business Interruption Coverage	As needed	As needed
Builders' Risk Insurance	If construction	If construction
Workers' Compensation	If employees	If employees
Commercial Auto Insurance	If autos	If autos
Commercial Umbrella Policy	Excess liability coverage	Excess liability coverage
Malpractice	N/A	Yes
Errors and Omissions	N/A	Yes
Product Liability	If manufacturer	N/A

WHERE ON THE WEB

Federal Emergency Management Agency **www.fema.gov**

Independent Insurance Agents and Brokers of America **www.independentagent.com**

Insurance Information Institute **www.iii.org**

Instant Insurance Quotes **www.insure.com/index.html**

DISCUSSION QUESTIONS

1. Describe the need for homeowners, auto, and liability umbrella insurance coverages.
2. List and define the basic coverages provided by a homeowners policy.
3. List the various homeowners forms.
4. Explain the contractual options and provisions in homeowners insurance.
5. List and define the basic coverages provided by the personal automobile policy (PAP).
6. Explain the various contractual options and provisions in a personal automobile policy (PAP).
7. Explain the distinguishing characteristics of a personal umbrella liability policy.
8. What type of coverage does Section 1 of a homeowners policy provide?
9. What type of coverage does Section 2 of a homeowners policy provide?
10. Are intentional acts usually covered by insurance?

EXERCISES

1. What are the three types of property and liability loss exposures facing families and businesses?
2. What is a named-perils policy?
3. Why is it that property insurance policies only pay for the policyowner's insurable interest in a loss?
4. How do property insurance policies determine how losses will be valued?
5. List some examples of the types of property with limited coverage under a typical homeowners policy.
6. List four major exclusions found in homeowners insurance policies pertaining to real property.
7. List the 18 perils that constitute broad coverage.
8. If Joe is injured in an automobile accident, will his own auto policy pay for his medical injuries?
9. Differentiate between the HO-2 and the HO-3 form of homeowners insurance.
10. Jan rents an apartment and has $40,000 of contents coverage. If she is unable to occupy her apartment due to a negligent fire, for how many months could she rent a $700 per month apartment if her damaged apartment rented for $600 per month?
11. Patrice lives in Nebraska, where she carries the state-mandated minimum liability insurance on her car (25/50/25) through her personal automobile policy (PAP). She is driving through Texas and has a wreck. Texas requires minimum liability insurance of 30/60/30. She injures Sherri in an amount equal to $30,000 and Sherri's vehicle in an amount of $35,000. How much will Sherri collect from Patrice's PAP?

12. Pat and Matt are fraternity brothers who frequently drive each other's cars. Their automobiles are insured as follows:

Insured	Insurance Company	Amount
Pat	XYZ Co.	25/50/10
Matt	All Auto	100/300/25

Pat is negligent while driving Matt's car and has an accident, and the bodily injury loss to the other party involved in the accident is $30,000. Which insurer will pay, and how much will be paid?

PROBLEMS

1. Jimmy and Mary Sue, ages 28 and 27, respectively, are married and have a net worth of $100,000. They both work, Jimmy has a 2014 Chevy truck, and Mary Sue has a 2016 Toyota Corolla. They also own a 1966 Indian motorcycle. They rent an apartment and have the following automobile and renter's insurance policies:

Renters Insurance:

- HO-4 renter's policy without endorsements
- Content Coverage: $25,000; Liability: $100,000

Automobile Insurance:

- Both Car and Truck

Type	PAP
Bodily Injury	$25,000/$50,000
Property Damage	$10,000
Medical Payments	$5,000 per person
Physical Damage	Actual Cash Value
Uninsured Motorist	$25,000/$50,000
Comprehensive Deductible	$500
Collision Deductible	$500
Premium (annual)	$2,500

- What risk exposures are not covered by the HO-4 policy?
- Comment on the efficiency and effectiveness of the PAP.
- Is the motorcycle covered under the PAP?
- Do they have adequate liability coverage? If not, what would you suggest?

2. The Nicholsons recently purchased a new stereo system (FMV $10,000). They asked and received permission to alter their apartment to build speakers into every room. The agreement with the landlord requires them to leave the speakers if they move because they are permanently installed and affixed to the property. The replacement value of the installed speakers is $4,500, and the noninstalled components are valued at $5,500. The cost of the entire system was $10,000. The Nicholsons have an HO-4 policy with $25,000 of content coverage and $100,000 of liability coverage.

   - If the Nicholsons were burglarized and had their movable stereo system components stolen, would the burglary be covered under the HO-4 policy, and, if so, for what amount?
   - If there was a fire in the Nicholsons' apartment building and their in-wall speaker system was destroyed, would they be covered under the HO-4 policy, and, if so, to what extent?
   - If a fire forces the Nicholsons to move out of their apartment for a month and rent elsewhere at a higher cost, would the HO-4 policy provide any coverage?

3. Ken and Mary Claire Powell, both age 40, own their own home, with the land valued at $80,000 and the dwelling with a replacement value of $150,000. They have a total net worth of $550,000. They have the following property/liability insurance coverages:

   Homeowners Insurance

   The Powells currently have an HO-3 policy with a replacement value endorsement on contents. The policy provides open-perils coverage. The deductible is $250, and the premium is $533.60 per year.

   The dwelling coverage is $100,000, contents $50,000, and liability $100,000.

   Automobile Insurance

   The Powells have full coverage on both cars, including:

   - $100,000 bodily injury for one person
   - $300,000 bodily injury for all persons
   - $50,000 property damage
   - $100,000 uninsured motorist

   Deductibles

   - $500 comprehensive
   - $1,000 collision

   This insurance includes medical payments, car rentals, and towing.

   The cost of the auto insurance is $2,123.50 per year because of the number of speeding tickets Mary Claire has received.

   - The Powells suffer a burglary and lose personal property items purchased for $20,000 and having a replacement value of $27,000. How much will the insurance company pay?
   - If a fire destroys two-thirds of their house and the loss is $100,000, how much will the insurance company pay?
   - Do the Powells have adequate liability coverage?

- What would you recommend regarding their liability coverage?
- While Mary Claire's car was parked in a parking lot next to a school playground, a young student missed a ball being thrown and it dented the hood of Mary Claire's car. The damage was estimated to cost $1,840 to repair. How much will the insurer pay?

CASES

The Bannisters

Derek Bannister, age 26, has been employed for five years at a computer store as a salesperson and trainer. He earns $30,000 per year. His wife, Olga Bannister, age 26, is a German citizen and is employed as a floral designer for a local florist. She earns $28,000 per year. Derek and Olga have been married for two years and have one child, Prissy, age 1.

Insurance Information:

	Life Insurance
Insured	Derek
Owner	Derek
Beneficiary	Olga
Face amount	$50,000
Cash value	0
Type of policy	Term
Settlement option	Lump sum
Premium	Employer-provided

	Health Insurance
Premium	Employer-provided for Derek; Olga and Prissy are dependents under Derek's policy
Coverage	Major medical
	Dental coverage is not provided
Deductible	$250 per person (3-person maximum)
Family out-of-pocket limit	$2,500

	Disability Insurance
Neither Derek nor Olga has disability insurance	

	Automobile Insurance
Premium	$1,000 total annual premium for both vehicles
Bodily Injury and Property Damage	$10,000/$25,000/$5,000 for each vehicle
Comprehensive	$250 deductible
Collision	$500 deductible

	Renter's Insurance
Type	HO-4
Contents Coverage	$35,000
Premium	$600 annually
Deductible	$250
Liability	$100,000
Medical Payments	$1,000 per person

Homeowners 04 Policy Declaration Page

Policy Number: **H04-123-ZA-996**
Policy Period: **12:01 a.m. Central Time at the residence premises**
From: **January 1, 2022** To: **December 31, 2022**

Name insured and mailing address:
Derek and Olga Bannister
123 Raleigh Way, Apartment 8
Anytown, State 00001

The residence premises covered by this policy is located at the above address unless otherwise indicated.
Same as above.

Coverage is provided where a premium or limit of liability is shown for the coverage.

Section I Coverages	Limit of Liability	Premium
A. Dwelling	**N/A**	**N/A**
B. Other Structures	**N/A**	**N/A**
C. Personal property	**$35,000**	**$475**
D. Loss of use	**N/A**	**N/A**
Section II Coverages		
A. Personal liability: each occurrence	**$100,000**	**$100**
B. Medical payments to others: each occurrence	**$1,000**	**$ 25**
Total premium for endorsements listed below		
	Policy Total	**$600**

Forms and endorsements made part of this policy:

Number	Edition	Date	Title	Premium
Not applicable.				

DEDUCTIBLE - Section I: **$250**
In case of a loss under Section I, we cover only that part of the loss over the deductible stated.
Section II: Other insured locations: **Not applicable.**

[Mortgagee/Lienholder (Name and address)]
Not applicable.

Countersignature of agent/date Signature/title - company officer

While on a vacation in Colorado, the Bannisters experienced several unfortunate incidents.

- A deer collided with their car, causing $800 damage.
- Derek rented a motorcycle. While riding the motorcycle, his wallet was stolen, but Derek thought he had lost the wallet on the mountain during a fall, so he did not report the loss to the credit card company until he returned home.
- Derek, not experienced driving in the mountains, collided with another motorcycle on the road causing damage to both motorcycles and injuring Derek. The driver of the other motorcycle, Oscar, suffered a broken arm.
- Upon returning home, the Bannisters discovered that their apartment building had been destroyed by fire.

1. How much will the insurance company pay to have the front of the car repaired from the collision with the deer?
2. The fire that destroyed the apartment building also destroyed all of their personal property. Although the depreciated or actual cash value of all their property is $8,000, it would cost the Bannisters about $37,000 to replace all of their lost items. How much will the insurance company pay for this loss?
3. Derek's collision with the motorcycle caused $2,000 of damage to Oscar's motorcycle. Will the HO-4 liability policy cover the loss?
4. Oscar, the motorcycle owner, suffered $350 in emergency medical expenses to reset his broken arm caused by the incident. Will the HO-4 cover the loss?
5. In the motorcycle accident, Derek suffered medical expenses of $1,850. Is Derek covered by the HO-4 for this loss?
6. What deficiencies do you think are in the Bannisters' overall insurance program?

CASE SCENARIO

Use the information provided to answer the following questions regarding the Nelson family.

NELSON FAMILY CASE SCENARIO
DANA AND DAVID NELSON
As of 12/31/2022

Personal Background and Information

David Nelson (age 37) is a bank vice president. He has been employed there for 12 years and has an annual salary of $70,000. Dana Nelson (age 37) is a full-time homemaker. David and Dana have been married for eight years. They have two children, John (age 6) and Gabrielle (age 3), and are expecting their third child in two weeks. They have always lived in this community and expect to remain indefinitely in their current residence.

General Goals (Not Prioritized)

- Save for college education
- Reduce debt
- Save for retirement
- Estate planning
- Invest wisely

Insurance Information

Health Insurance

The entire family is insured under David's employer's health plan (PPO). For covered expenses, a $1,000 in-network deductible and a $2,000 out-of-network deductible apply, after which 80%/20% coinsurance applies in network and 60%/40% applies out of network. There is a stop-loss limit of $20,000 annually in network and $30,000 annually out of network. The entire monthly premium of $1,123.54 is paid by David's employer.

Life Insurance

David's employer provides group term life insurance equal to two times David's current salary. The premium is paid entirely by his employer, and Dana is the primary beneficiary. No contingent beneficiary is named.

Disability Insurance

David's employer also offers a contributory group long-term disability insurance program toward which the employer contributes 60% of the $158.54 monthly premium. David is a participant in the program, which provides a monthly disability income benefit equal to 70% of his current salary, payable to his Social Security normal retirement age, provided that he remains disabled per the policy's "own occupation" definition of disability. David must satisfy a 90-day elimination period before he is eligible to begin receiving benefits.

David's employer doesn't offer dental or vision coverages and the Nelsons have not obtained any private form of individual dental or vision insurance benefits.

Homeowners Insurance

The Nelsons have an HO-3 policy with replacement cost on contents. There is a $250 deductible. The annual premium is $950.

Automobile Insurance

The Nelsons have automobile liability and bodily injury coverage of $100,000/$300,000/$100,000. They have both comprehensive coverage and collision. The deductibles are $250 (comprehensive) and $500 (collision). The annual premium is $900.

Relevant External Environmental Information

- Mortgage rates are 5.0% for 30 years and 4.5% for 15 years, fixed.
- Gross domestic product is expected to grow at less than 3%.
- Inflation is expected to be 2.6%.
- Expected return on investment is 8% for common stocks, 9% for small company stocks, and 1.1% for U.S. Treasury bills.
- College education costs are $15,000 per year.

Investment Information

The bank offers a Section 401(k) plan in which David is an active participant. The bank matches contributions dollar for dollar up to 3% of David's salary. David currently contributes 5.43% of his salary. His employer's plan allows for employee contributions of up to 16% of salary. In the Section 401(k) plan, the Nelsons have the opportunity to invest in a money market fund, a bond fund, a growth and income fund, and a small-cap fund. The Nelsons consider themselves to have a moderate investment risk tolerance. David's assets within the plan are currently earning 8.5%, based on his investment choices within the plan.

Income Tax Information

David and Dana tell you that they are in the 12% federal income tax bracket. They pay $820 annually in state and local income taxes.

Education Information

John is 6 years old and currently attending first grade at a private school. Gabrielle is 3 years old. She will attend private school from pre-kindergarten through high school. The current balance of the college fund is $14,000. They expect to contribute $1,000 at the end of each year to this fund.

Gifts, Estates, Trusts, and Will Information

David has made Dana his primary beneficiary on his Section 401(k) plan, and the children are the contingent beneficiaries. Because most of their assets are owned jointly, David doesn't see the need for a will. Dana also does not have a will.

Dana and David Nelson
Statement of Financial Position
12/31/2022

ASSETS			**LIABILITIES AND NET WORTH**		
Cash/cash equivalents			**Current liabilities**		
JT	Checking account	$1,425	JT	Credit cards	$4,000
JT	Savings account	$950	JT	Mortgage on principal residence	$1,234
			David	Boat loan	$1,493
Total cash/cash equivalents		$2,375	**Total current liabilities**		$6,727
Invested assets			**Long-term liabilities**		
Dana	ABC stock	$12,500	JT	Mortgage on principal residence	$196,654
JT	Education fund	$14,000	David	Boat loan	$12,065
David	Section 401(k) plan	$32,197			
Total invested assets		$58,697	**Total long-term liabilities**		$208,719
Personal-use assets			**Total liabilities**		$215,446
JT	Principal residence	$245,000			
JT	Automobile	$18,000			
David	Boat	$25,000	**Net worth**		$207,626
Dana	Jewelry	$13,000			
JT	Furniture/household	$61,000			
Total personal-use assets		$362,000			
Total assets		$423,072	**Total liabilities and net worth**		$423,072

Dana and David Nelson
Statement of Financial Position
12/31/2022

ASSETS		
Cash/cash equivalents		
JT	Checking account	$1,268
JT	Savings account	$950
	Total cash/cash equivalents	$2,218
Invested assets		
Dana	ABC stock	$14,050
JT	Education fund	$15,560
David	Section 401(k) plan	$38,619
David	XYZ stock	$10,000
	Total invested assets	$78,229
Personal-use assets		
JT	Principal residence	$250,000
JT	Automobile	$15,000
David	Personal watercraft	$10,000
David	Boat B	$30,000
Dana	Jewelry	$13,500
JT	Furniture/household	$60,000
	Total personal-use assets	$378,500
Total assets		**$458,947**

LIABILITIES AND NET WORTH		
Current liabilities		
JT	Credit cards	$3,655
JT	Mortgage on principal residence	$1,370
David	Boat loan	$1,048
	Total current liabilities	$6,073
Long-term liabilities		
JT	Mortgage on principal residence	$195,284
David	Boat loan	$16,017
	Total long-term liabilities	$211,301
Total liabilities		**$217,374**
Net worth		**$241,573**
Total liabilities and net worth		**$458,947**

Notes to financial statements:

- Assets are stated at fair market value.
- The ABC stock was inherited from Dana's aunt on November 15, 2022. Her aunt originally paid $20,000 for it on October 31, 2013. The fair market value at the aunt's death was $12,000.
- Liabilities are stated at principal only.
- JT = joint tenancy; client name = separate property.

Dana and David Nelson
Personal Statement of Cash Flows
For 2022

INFLOWS		
Salary—David		$70,000
Investment income		
Interest income	$ 900	
Dividend income	$ 150	$ 1,050
Total inflow		**$71,050**
Savings		
Reinvestment (interest/dividends)	$ 1,050	
Section 401(k) plan deferrals	$ 3,803	
Education fund	$ 1,000	
Total savings		**$ 5,853**
Available for outflows		**$65,197**
OUTFLOWS		
Ordinary living expenses		
Food	$ 6,000	
Clothing	$ 3,600	
Child care	$ 600	
Entertainment	$ 1,814	
Utilities	$ 3,600	
Auto maintenance	$ 2,000	
Church	$ 3,500	
Total ordinary living expenses		**$21,114**
Debt payments		
Credit card payments principal	$ 345	
Credit card payments interest	$ 615	
Mortgage payment principal	$ 1,234	
Mortgage payment interest	$20,720	
Boat loan principal	$ 1,493	
Boat loan interest	$ 1,547	
Total debt payments		**$25,954**
Insurance premiums		
Automobile insurance premiums	$ 900	
Disability insurance premiums	$ 761	
Homeowners insurance premiums	$ 950	
Total insurance premiums		**$ 2,611**
Tuition and education expenses		**$ 1,000**
Taxes		
FICA and federal income tax (W/H)	$12,855	
State (and city) income tax	$ 820	
Property tax (principal residence)	$ 1,000	
Total taxes		**$14,675**
Total outflows		**$65,354**
Net cash flow (deficit)		**($157)**

1. Evaluate the Nelsons' personal property and liability insurance coverage.
2. What business and professional insurance coverage(s) may be relevant to the Nelsons?
3. The Nelsons' homeowners insurance provides dwelling coverage for $180,000 with an 80% coinsurance requirement. On March 31, 2022, a stampeding herd of cattle ran through their house, causing $100,000 of damage to the home and $40,000 of damage to furniture and other personal property. How much of the $140,000 of damage will be paid for by their insurance? Assume the replacement value for the home is $240,000.
4. A deer ran into the Nelsons' car while they were on a trip to the supermarket. The damage to the car was $3,000, and Dana, the driver, required $1,200 of medical care in the emergency room (she was not admitted to the hospital). What portion of the accident expenses will be Dana and David's responsibility to pay, if any?

CHAPTER 11

Social Security and Other Social Insurance

LEARNING OBJECTIVES

After learning the material in this chapter, you will be able to do the following:

- Identify the major categories of benefits administered by the Social Security Administration
- Understand how the Social Security program works
- List the eligibility requirements that must be satisfied for a person to qualify as a Social Security beneficiary
- Calculate a worker's average indexed monthly earnings (AIME) and primary insurance amount (PIA)
- Discuss how "bend points" affect a worker's Social Security benefit
- Understand how early and late retirement options affect a worker's Social Security benefit

- List the ways that a worker's Social Security benefit might be reduced
- Explain how modified adjusted gross income affects the taxation of Social Security benefits
- Understand how Medicare is structured and the benefits it offers

OVERVIEW OF THE U.S. SOCIAL SECURITY SYSTEM

Social Security benefits were never intended to provide total financial support upon retirement. Social Security was created to supplement one's pension, savings, investments, and assets. Typically, individuals who retire need 70–80% of their preretirement income to maintain their same preretirement standard of living.

Although Social Security can supplement other sources of retirement income, it generally replaces only a portion of a worker's preretirement income. Workers earning more than the maximum Social Security wage base ($147,000 in 2022) receive a lower percentage of their preretirement income than lower earning workers because the maximum retirement benefit is based on the Social Security wage base.

Retirement benefit
The most familiar Social Security benefit, full retirement benefits are payable at full retirement age, with reduced benefits as early as age 62, to anyone who has obtained at least a minimum amount of Social Security credits

From a financial planning standpoint, professionals should understand Social Security and the various benefits that are available. This chapter provides a basic overview of the Social Security system and its benefits. Six major categories of benefits are administered by the Social Security Administration: (1) retirement benefits, (2) disability benefits, (3) family benefits, (4) survivors benefits, (5) Medicare, and (6) Supplemental Security Income (SSI) benefits. SSI benefits are not funded by Social Security taxes but are funded by the general Treasury.

Disability benefit
Social Security benefit available to recipients who have a severe physical or mental impairment that is expected to prevent them from performing substantial work for at least one year or result in death, and who have the sufficient amount of Social Security credits

The **retirement benefit** is the most familiar Social Security benefit. Full retirement benefits are payable at full retirement age, with reduced benefits available as early as age 62, to anyone who has obtained at least a minimum amount of Social Security credits. Based on a change in Social Security law in 1983, the age when full retirement benefits are paid began to rise in 2000 from age 65 and increases to age 67 for people born in 1962 and later. Those workers who delay retirement beyond the full retirement age will receive a special increase in their retirement benefits when they ultimately retire.

The **disability benefit** is payable at any age to workers who have sufficient credits under the Social Security system. Recipients must have a severe physical or mental impairment that is expected to prevent them from performing any substantial work for at least one year or result in death. According to Social Security guidelines, earnings of $1,350 or more per month (in 2022) are considered substantial for someone who is not blind. The disability insurance program has built-in incentives to smooth the transition back to the workforce, including continuation of benefits and health care coverage.

Family benefit
Social Security benefit available to certain family members of workers eligible for retirement or disability benefits

Survivors benefit
Social Security benefit available to surviving family members of a deceased, eligible worker

The **family benefit** is provided to certain family members of workers eligible for retirement or disability benefits. Such family members include spouses age 62 or older, spouses under age 62 but caring for a child under age 16, unmarried children under 18, unmarried children under age 19 and full-time students in secondary schools, and unmarried children of any age who were disabled before age 22. The **survivors benefit** applies to certain members of the worker's family if the worker earned sufficient Social Security credits. Family members entitled to survivors benefits include those listed for family benefits, and may also include the worker's parents if the worker was their primary means of support. A special one-time payment of $255 may be made to the spouse or minor children upon the death of a Social Security covered worker.

Medicare
A federal health insurance plan for those who have attained full retirement age or have been disabled whether retired or still working

Supplemental Security Income (SSI)
Program administered by the Social Security Administration and funded by the general Treasury that is available to those at full retirement age or disabled who have a low income and few assets

The next benefit, **Medicare**, provides hospital and medical insurance. People who are 65 and older, have received disability benefits for at least two years, or are on kidney dialysis treatment and in end-stage renal failure automatically qualify for Medicare.

Finally, **Supplemental Security Income (SSI)** (funded by general tax revenues, not by Social Security taxes) is another benefit of monthly payments to those disabled or at full retirement age who have a low income and few assets. Generally, those who receive SSI will also qualify for Medicaid, food stamps, and other public assistance.

THE HISTORY OF SOCIAL SECURITY BENEFITS

Ever-changing social and economic conditions have dictated the social welfare structure of the United States. During its infancy, the country's economy was predominantly agricultural. As late as 1870, over half of the nation's adult workers were farmers. Then, the country transformed. With the advent of the Industrial Revolution, the country began to specialize. One of the consequences of this industrialization and specialization was more dependence on wages and income to maintain and provide for the family.

Federal, state, and local governmental bodies throughout the country recognized the inherent risks in an industrialized and ever-specializing economy. The perception was that such risks could best be handled through an approach dominated by a philosophy of social insurance. Social insurance is the act of contributing financing over time to social programs to provide protection as a matter of right to everyone without regard to need. Social insurance has its roots in workers' compensation laws dating back to as early as 1908. Various social and other retirement programs were developed and implemented in piecemeal fashion. In addition, the federal government began programs to provide benefits to those who served in the military.

The Depression of the 1930s compelled action by the federal government. State and local governmental entities could not shoulder the immense needs of so many Americans. The federal government extended loans and grants to the states to provide relief and created special programs. By 1935, however, President Franklin D. Roosevelt proposed that Congress enact economic security legislation, resulting in the passage of the Social Security Act signed into law August 14, 1935.

The Social Security Act established two national social insurance programs: old-age benefits and unemployment benefits. The old-age benefits were intended for retired workers employed in industry and commerce, and unemployment benefits were for breadwinners faced with limited employment opportunities. Congress added benefits for dependents of retired and deceased workers in 1939.

By 1950, the Social Security program was expanded to cover a number of jobs that had previously been excluded. The range of the program was further broadened by the inclusion, in 1956, of disability insurance for severely disabled workers aged 50 or older and for adult disabled children of deceased or retired workers. The requirement of attaining age 50 was removed in 1960, and disability benefits were available to widows and widowers by 1967. An annual **cost-of-living adjustment (COLA)** based on the Consumer Price Index was implemented through legislation in 1972, as was the delayed retirement credit that increased benefits for workers retiring after the full retirement age.

COLA
Cost-of-living adjustment provided for Social Security benefits

Medicaid
Provides medical assistance for persons with low incomes and resources

The Medicare program was established through the 1965 amendments to the Social Security Act. The program provided for medical coverage for those age 65 or older, regardless of income. Legislation passed in 1965 also created **Medicaid**, which provides medical assistance for persons with low incomes and resources. Medicare and Medicaid have been subject to numerous legislative changes since 1965. In 1972, the state-administered assistance programs for the aged, blind, and disabled were replaced by the essentially federally administered SSI program.

The 1983 amendments made coverage compulsory for federal civilian employees and for employees of nonprofit organizations; in addition, state and local governments were prohibited from opting out of the system. Gradual increases in the age of eligibility for full retirement benefits from age 65 to age 67 were implemented for those retiring in 2000 or later. Benefits also became subject to income tax for those with higher incomes.

SOCIAL SECURITY TAXES AND CONTRIBUTIONS

Although the Social Security retirement benefits program is thought by many to be one of the most complicated and confusing programs created, the basic concept is quite simple. The basic theory is that employees, employers, and self-employed individuals pay Social Security taxes (FICA) during their working years. These payments are pooled in special trust funds. Contributing workers become covered workers, meaning that they will fall under the Social Security umbrella of benefits after contributing for approximately 10 years, and they will receive retirement benefits based on those contributions.

FICA (Federal Insurance Contributions Act)
The law allowing Social Security taxes, including Medicare, to be deducted from paychecks

FICA stands for the **Federal Insurance Contributions Act**, the law allowing paycheck deductions for Social Security and Medicare taxes that are used to pay for Social Security benefits. A portion of these FICA taxes pays part of the Medicare coverage. Separate and apart from Social Security taxes, general tax revenues are used to finance Supplemental Security Income, commonly referred to as SSI. Administered by the Social Security Administration, the SSI program pays benefits to persons who have limited income and assets.

OASDI
Old Age, Survivors, and Disability Insurance, commonly referred to as Social Security

Both employers and employees pay the taxes for Social Security and Medicare. An employer and employee each pay 6.2% of the employee's gross salary up to a limit of $147,000 (2022) for **Old Age, Survivors, and Disability Insurance (OASDI)**. The salary limit may rise annually on the basis of annual increases in average wages. Self-employed workers pay 12.4% (6.2% × 2) of their taxable income up to the same salary limit. The Medicare portion of the Social Security tax is 1.45% for employers and employees each and 2.9% for self-employed workers. For example, if an employee earns a salary of $160,000 in 2022, the first $147,000 of the employee's salary will be taxed at a rate of 7.65% (6.2% + 1.45%), and the remaining $13,000 will be subject to a tax of only 1.45%. The employer pays the same amount as the employee. A Medicare surtax of 0.9% applies to wages, compensation, and self-employment income in excess of certain thresholds. These thresholds include $250,000 for married couples filing joint returns and $200,000 for single individuals. Exhibit 11.1 shows the complete listing of Medicare surtax filing status thresholds.

EXHIBIT 11.1 Medicare Surtax Filing Status Thresholds

Filing Status	Threshold Amount
Married filing jointly	$250,000
Married filing separate	$125,000
Single	$200,000
Head of household (with qualifying person)	$200,000
Qualifying widow(er) with dependent child	$200,000

Source: Internal Revenue Service (www.irs.gov)

EXAMPLE Mr. and Mrs. Jones, a married couple filing jointly, have a combined salary of $300,000. The first $250,000 will be taxed at the rate of 1.45%, and the next $50,000 will be taxed at the rate of 2.35% (1.45% + 0.9%).

The 0.9% Medicare surtax is paid only by the employee or self-employed person, and there is no employer share.

An additional Medicare surtax of 3.8% applies to the net investment income of taxpayers whose modified adjusted gross income (MAGI) exceeds certain thresholds. These thresholds are $250,000 for married couples filing jointly and $200,000 for single individuals. The 3.8% surtax applies to net investment income, which generally includes total gross income from interest, dividends, annuities, royalties, and rents, as well as net taxable gain from the disposition of property. The surtax does not apply to distributions from most retirement plans and IRAs or the excludible gain from the sale of a taxpayer's personal residence.

EXAMPLE Sue has MAGI of $240,000 and a filing status of single. She has net investment income of $50,000. Of that $50,000, $40,000 is subject to the Medicare 3.8% surtax (the lesser of her net investment income or the amount by which her MAGI exceeds $200,000).

THE SOCIAL SECURITY TRUST FUNDS AND THEIR RELATIVE SOLVENCY

The U.S. Social Security system operates on a pay-as-you-go basis. Social Security taxes are collected and divided among several trust funds. The federal Old Age, Survivors, and Disability Insurance (OASDI) Trust Fund pays retirement and survivors benefits and receives 5.3% of the FICA tax. The federal Disability Insurance (DI) Trust Fund pays benefits to workers with disabilities and their families and receives 0.9% of the FICA tax. OASI and DI are the two trust funds used for payment of Social Security benefits.

The two Medicare trust funds are the federal Hospital Insurance (HI) Trust Fund, which pays for services covered under the hospital insurance provisions of Medicare (Part A), and the federal Supplementary Medical Insurance (SMI) Trust Fund, which pays for services covered under the medical insurance provisions of Medicare, known as Part B. The SMI Trust Fund is partially funded by the general fund of the Treasury, with the remainder funding coming from monthly premiums paid by the individuals enrolled in Part B.

EXHIBIT 11.2 Sources of Funding to Social Security Trust Funds

OASI Trust Fund	5.3% (limited to the maximum taxable earnings)
DI Trust Fund	0.9% (limited to the maximum taxable earnings)
HI Trust Fund	1.45% (all earnings taxed) (In 1993, the Omnibus Budget Reconciliation Act of 1993 abolished the ceiling on taxable earnings for Medicare.)
SMI Trust Fund	-0- (no FICA taxes used; funded by general federal tax revenues and monthly premiums paid by enrollees)

Tax revenues are deposited into the trust funds daily. Social Security benefits are paid from these funds. Money that is not needed to pay benefits is invested daily in U.S. government bonds. This method of investing leftover funds into U.S. government bonds is called the "partial reserve" method of funding, which has been used since 1983. The goal is to receive more revenue than that which is paid out so as to accumulate large reserve funds to aid in paying benefits to the increasing number of retired workers. The increase in retired workers represents a society that is living longer as a result of medical improvements, better health information, and less stressful lifestyles. The number of retired workers will continue to rise because of the baby boom generation (born from 1946 to 1964) that has begun to retire in the past few years.

The trust funds are governed by The Board of Trustees of the Social Security and Medicare Trust Funds, whose members are the Secretary of the Treasury, Secretary of Labor, Secretary of Health and Human Services, Commissioner of Social Security, and two public trustees with four-year terms. By law, the trust funds can be used only to pay Social Security benefits and for administrative costs of the program. However, legislation has been adopted to help control future HI program costs and to extend the retirement age to receive retirement benefits. These and other measures may help extend the useful life of the trust funds.

SOCIAL SECURITY BENEFITS—ELIGIBILITY AND CALCULATIONS

Covered Workers and Insured Status

To qualify for retirement benefits, a worker must be "fully insured," which means that a worker has earned a certain number of credits of coverage under the Social Security system. Since 1978, credits of coverage have been determined on the basis of annual earnings. In other words, earning a designated amount of money, regardless of when it was earned during the year, will credit the worker with one credit of coverage for that year. In 2021, the designated amount for one credit of coverage was $1,470, while in 2022, the amount is $1,510. Thus, workers who earned at least $5,880 were credited with four credits of coverage for 2021, and workers who earn at least $6,040 are credited with four credits of coverage for 2022. No worker may earn more than four credits in one year, regardless of earnings. Exhibit 11.3 lists the designated amounts for a credit of coverage, dating back to 1991.

EXHIBIT 11.3 Designated Amounts of Earnings Needed for One Credit of Social Security Coverage

Year	Amount of Earnings Needed to Receive a Credit for One Quarter	Year	Amount of Earnings Needed to Receive a Credit for One Quarter
1991	$540	2007	$1,000
1992	$570	2008	$1,050
1993	$590	2009	$1,090
1994	$620	2010	$1,120
1995	$630	2011	$1,120
1996	$640	2012	$1,130
1997	$670	2013	$1,160
1998	$700	2014	$1,200
1999	$740	2015	$1,220
2000	$780	2016	$1,260
2001	$830	2017	$1,300
2002	$870	2018	$1,320
2003	$890	2019	$1,360
2004	$900	2020	$1,410
2005	$920	2021	$1,470
2006	$970	2022	$1,510

Source: Social Security Administration (www.ssa.gov)

For most persons, 40 credits of coverage (10 years of work in employment covered by Social Security) or one credit of coverage earned per year beginning the calendar year after the insured attains age 21 with a minimum of six credits. Fully insured workers are entitled to the benefits under the Social Security system, although some benefits, such as survivors benefits, are available to "currently" (although not necessarily fully) insured individuals. Currently insured workers are those individuals who have at least six credits of coverage out of the previous 13 quarters.

Social Security Beneficiaries

As indicated, Social Security benefits are paid upon retirement, disability, or death, if the eligibility requirements are satisfied. The worker's spouse and children also may be eligible to receive benefits when the worker satisfies eligibility requirements. Generally, monthly Social Security benefits can be paid to the following persons:

- A disabled insured worker under full retirement age
- A retired insured worker at age 62
- The spouse of a retired or disabled worker entitled to benefits who
  - is at least 62 years old; or
  - is caring for a child under age 16 or disabled
- The divorced spouse of a retired or disabled worker entitled to benefits if age 62 and married to the worker for at least 10 years and not remarried by age 60
- The divorced spouse of a fully insured worker who has not yet filed a claim for benefits if both are at least age 62, were married for at least 10 years, and have been finally divorced for at least 2 continuous years

- The dependent, unmarried child of a retired or disabled worker entitled to benefits, or of a deceased insured worker if the child is
  - under age 18,
  - under age 19 and a full-time elementary or secondary school student, or
  - age 18 or over but under a disability that began before age 22
- The surviving spouse (including a surviving divorced spouse) of a deceased insured worker if the widow(er) is age 60
- The disabled surviving spouse (including a surviving divorced spouse in some cases) of a deceased insured worker if the widow(er) is age 50
- The surviving spouse (including a surviving divorced spouse) of a deceased insured worker, regardless of age, if caring for an entitled child of the deceased who is either under age 16 or disabled before age 22
- The dependent parents of a deceased insured worker at age 62

In addition to monthly survivor benefits, a lump-sum death payment of $255 is payable upon the death of an insured worker. Exhibit 11.10 provides a summary of those eligible for OASDI benefits and the percentages of the worker's primary insurance amount (PIA) that each beneficiary will receive. The PIA is the retirement benefit that the worker will receive if he retires at full retirement age.

Social Security Retirement Benefits—A Closer Look

The most commonly known Social Security benefit is the retirement benefit. Until 2000, full retirement age, the age at which full retirement benefits are available to the retiree, was 65 years old. The age at which full benefits are paid began to rise in the year 2000. Exhibit 11.4 shows the phase-in, which raises the full retirement age with full benefits to age 67.

EXHIBIT 11.4 Age Full Retirement Benefits Begin

Full Retirement Age with Full Benefits	Year Born
65 years	Before 1938
65 years, 2 months	1938
65 years, 4 months	1939
65 years, 6 months	1940
65 years, 8 months	1941
65 years, 10 months	1942
66 years	1943–1954
66 years, 2 months	1955
66 years, 4 months	1956
66 years, 6 months	1957
66 years, 8 months	1958
66 years, 10 months	1959
67 years	1960–present

People who delay retirement beyond full retirement age receive an increase in their benefit when they do retire (up to age 70). People who take early retirement, currently as early as age 62, receive an actuarially reduced monthly benefit. (Early and late retirement options are discussed later in this chapter.)

When engaging in financial planning for an individual, it may be appropriate to calculate the individual's expected Social Security retirement benefit or ask the client to request a Social Security statement and consider the benefit in that individual's retirement plan. Some financial planners, however, choose not to consider the estimated retirement benefit in order to be conservative in developing a financial plan. Others justify exclusion of Social Security retirement benefits from financial planning based on fear of drastic changes to the Social Security system through legislative action or through economically driven forces. The exclusion of estimated Social Security benefits would greatly increase the amount of retirement savings needed to prepare for retirement.

The Social Security Statement

Social Security Statement, Form SSA-7005
A written report, mailed by the Social Security Administration to all workers age 25 and over who are not yet receiving Social Security benefits; provides an estimate of the worker's eventual Social Security benefits and instructions on how to qualify for those benefits

The Social Security Administration automatically mails a **Social Security Statement, Form SSA-7005**, to all workers age 25 and over who are not yet receiving Social Security benefits. The Social Security Statement should prove to be a valuable tool in the process of personal financial planning for the worker and her family. The statement provides an estimate of the worker's eventual Social Security benefits and instructions on how to qualify for those benefits.

The Social Security Statement (1) includes the worker's lifetime earnings history, as reported to the Social Security Administration; (2) estimates the amount of Social Security taxes (FICA) and Medicare taxes (FICA-Med) that the worker and employer (if applicable) have paid; (3) and forecasts the ultimate benefits to be paid to the worker and family through retirement, disability, and/or survivorship. It is important to review the lifetime earnings history because mistakes in the earnings history can lower a worker's monthly benefits.

The mail-out campaign is designed to keep the worker informed as to his earnings history and to ensure the accuracy and completeness of the Social Security Administration's records. If any earnings are incorrect or incomplete, the worker can notify the Social Security Administration of the problem well in advance of the time of the worker's retirement age. The statement also serves as a quick and reliable reference to the worker for use in financial planning and forecasting, whether done by the individual worker or by a financial planner. The statement will be mailed to the individual worker roughly three months prior to her birthday and will continue to be mailed at or near that time every year until the worker begins to receive Social Security benefits.

Workers can request a Social Security Statement at any time from the Social Security Administration. A statement can be requested by the worker from the Social Security Administration by filling out and mailing a Request for a Social Security Statement, SSA Form 7004 or by requesting it online at **www.ssa.gov**. Applicants can also obtain the request form by calling Social Security at 1-800-772-1213 and asking for Form SSA-7004. The Social Security Administration will also answer questions and set up appointments with representatives at local Social Security offices through the toll-free number.

The Retirement Benefit Calculation

Average indexed monthly earnings (AIME)
Dollar amount used to calculate Social Security benefits. Actual earnings are adjusted (or indexed for inflation) to calculate the AIME.

Determining a worker's retirement benefit requires specific, detailed information pertaining to age, earnings history, and the worker's retirement date. Social Security benefits are based on earnings averaged over most of a worker's lifetime. Actual earnings are first adjusted or indexed to current dollars to account for changes in average wages since the year the earnings were received. Then, the Social Security Administration calculates the **average indexed monthly earnings (AIME)** (pronounced either "Amy" or "A-I-M-E") during the 35 years in which the applicant had the most earnings and applies a formula to these earnings to arrive at a basic benefit, which is referred to as the **primary insurance amount (PIA).** The Social Security retirement benefit is based on the worker's PIA. The PIA determines the amount the applicant will receive at his full retirement age. The PIA is indexed to the Consumer Price Index (CPI) annually.

Primary Insurance Amount (PIA)
Amount on which a worker's retirement benefit is based. The PIA determines the amount the applicant will receive at full retirement age. The PIA is indexed to the Consumer Price Index (CPI) annually.

Calculating the Worker's Average Indexed Monthly Earnings (AIME)

To determine a worker's AIME, the worker's annual earnings from the calendar year after the worker attains age 21 to age 62 must be converted into current dollars by multiplying the worker's total annual earnings for each year by an indexing factor. The indexing factor is the result of dividing the national average wage for the year in which the worker attains age 60 by the national average wage for the actual year being indexed. For instance, to calculate the indexing factor for 1982 for a worker born in 1954, the indexing factor for 1982 is determined by dividing the national average wage for 2014 (when the worker attained age 60), which was $46,481.52, by the national average wage for 1982 (the year being indexed), which was $14,531.34, yielding a factor of 3.19871. Exhibit 11.5 provides national average wages from 1966 to 2020.

EXHIBIT 11.5 National Average Wage Indexing Series, 1966–2020

Year	Amount	Year	Amount	Year	Amount
1966	$4,938.36	1984	$16,135.07	2002	$33,252.09
1967	$5,213.44	1985	$16,822.51	2003	$34,064.95
1968	$5,571.16	1986	$17,321.82	2004	$35,648.55
1969	$5,893.76	1987	$18,426.51	2005	$36,952.94
1970	$6,186.24	1988	$19,334.04	2006	$38,651.41
1971	$6,497.08	1989	$20,099.55	2007	$40,405.48
1972	$7,133.80	1990	$21,027.98	2008	$41,334.97
1973	$7,580.16	1991	$21,811.60	2009	$40,711.61
1974	$8,030.76	1992	$22,935.42	2010	$41,673.83
1975	$8,630.92	1993	$23,132.67	2011	$42,979.61
1976	$9,226.48	1994	$23,753.53	2012	$44,321.67
1977	$9,779.44	1995	$24,705.66	2013	$44,888.16
1978	$10,556.03	1996	$25,913.90	2014	$46,481.52
1979	$11,479.46	1997	$27,426.00	2015	$48,098.63
1980	$12,513.46	1998	$28,861.44	2016	$48,642.15
1981	$13,773.10	1999	$30,469.84	2017	$50,321.89
1982	$14,531.34	2000	$32,154.82	2018	$52,145.80
1983	$15,239.24	2001	$32,921.92	2019	$54,099.99
				2020	$55,628.60

Source: Social Security Administration (www.ssa.gov)

Next, each year's annual earnings must be multiplied by the corresponding indexing factor to arrive at the indexed earnings for the years from age 22 to 60. Note that the indexing factor will always equal 1 for the years in which the worker is 60 or older. After all annual earnings are indexed or converted to current dollar amounts, the highest 35 years of indexed earnings are added together for a total. The sum of the highest 35 years is then divided by 420 (which represents 35 years multiplied by 12 months per year). This yields the average amount of monthly earnings for all indexed years; hence, the name average indexed monthly earnings, or AIME. Once the worker's AIME is determined, the next step in determining the worker's retirement benefit is to calculate the primary insurance amount, or PIA.

Calculating the Worker's Primary Insurance Amount (PIA)

Generally, the PIA is the actual Social Security retirement benefit for the retiree who retires at full retirement age. For those who retire early or late and for family or surviving beneficiaries, the PIA is not the actual amount of the benefit, but the PIA is used to determine their actual benefit.

The PIA is a figure derived from the worker's AIME. The PIA is calculated by applying a benefit formula to AIME. This benefit formula changes from year to year and depends on the worker's first year of eligibility, that is, when the worker turns 62, becomes disabled, or dies.

Bend points
The three separate percentages of portions of the AIME that are summed to arrive at the PIA

The PIA is the sum of three separate percentages of portions of the AIME known as the **bend points**. For 2022, these portions are the first $1,024 of AIME, the amount of AIME between $1,024 and $6,172, and the AIME over $5,785. For individuals who first become eligible for retirement benefits or disability insurance benefits in 2022 or who die in 2022 before becoming eligible for benefits, their PIA will be the sum of:

90% of the first $1,024 of their AIME *plus*
32% of their AIME over $1,024 up to $6,172 *plus*
15% of their AIME that exceeds $6,172.

The sum of these three calculations is rounded down to the next lower multiple of $.10 (if it is not already a multiple of $.10). For calculations in subsequent years, it is useful to know how to determine a given year's bend points. Exhibit 11.6 shows the established bend points from 1985 through 2022.

EXHIBIT 11.6 Bend Point Table

Dollar Amounts (bend points) in PIA Formula		
Year	First	Second
1985	$280	$1,691
1986	$297	$1,790
1987	$310	$1,866
1988	$319	$1,922
1989	$339	$2,044
1990	$356	$2,145
1991	$370	$2,230
1992	$387	$2,333
1993	$401	$2,420
1994	$422	$2,545
1995	$426	$2,567
1996	$437	$2,635
1997	$455	$2,741
1998	$477	$2,875
1999	$505	$3,043
2000	$531	$3,202
2001	$561	$3,381
2002	$592	$3,567
2003	$606	$3,653
2004	$612	$3,689
2005	$627	$3,779
2006	$656	$3,955
2007	$680	$4,100
2008	$711	$4,288
2009	$744	$4,483
2010	$761	$4,586
2011	$749	$4,517
2012	$767	$4,624
2013	$791	$4,768
2014	$816	$4,917
2015	$826	$4,980
2016	$856	$5,157
2017	$885	$5,336
2018	$895	$5,397
2019	$926	$5,583
2020	$960	$5,785
2021	$996	$6,002
2022	$1,024	$6,172

Source: Social Security Administration (www.ssa.gov)

Figures for the PIA rise each year based on a cost-of-living adjustment (COLA) that is applied to reflect changes in the cost of living. Recent COLAs, which are based on inflation, are shown in Exhibit 11.7.

EXHIBIT 11.7 Cost of Living Adjustment (COLA) Per Year

Year	COLA	Year	COLA
1996	2.9%	2009	0.0%
1997	2.1%	2010	0.0%
1998	1.3%	2011	3.6%
1999	2.5%	2012	1.7%
2000	3.5%	2013	1.5%
2001	2.6%	2014	1.7%
2002	1.4%	2015	0.0%
2003	2.1%	2016	0.3%
2004	2.7%	2017	2.0%
2005	4.1%	2018	2.8%
2006	3.3%	2019	1.6%
2007	2.3%	2020	1.3%
2008	5.8%	2021	5.9%

Annual COLA increases are determined by October of each year and go into effect for monthly benefit checks received in January of the following year.

Early and Late Retirement Options

Workers entitled to retirement benefits can currently take early retirement benefits as early as age 62. The worker will receive a reduced benefit because he will receive more monthly benefit payments than if the worker had waited and retired at full retirement age. The reduction to one's monthly benefit for early retirement is permanent. Conversely, a delayed or postponed retirement will permanently increase the monthly retirement benefit for a worker.

For each month of early retirement, a worker will receive a reduction in her monthly retirement benefit of 0.5555%, or 1/180, for each month of early retirement taken up to the first 36 months. For subsequent months of early retirement, the permanent reduction percentage is 0.4167%, or 1/240, per month.

EXAMPLE Vada, a fully insured worker begins receiving retirement benefits 11 months before her full retirement age. Her monthly retirement benefit will be reduced by 11/180ths (approximately 6.11%). If Vada's monthly retirement benefit at full retirement age (FRA) were $1,000, she would receive $938.80 per month for the remainder of her life, subject to COLA adjustments.

Although the FRA will increase to age 67, workers will still have the option of taking early retirement at age 62. However, the reduction percentage that is applied to the monthly retirement benefit will increase until 2027. Before 2000, those who retired at age 62 received 80% of their retirement benefit, but the increase in full retirement age has increased the number of months from 62 until FRA. For instance, in 2022, covered workers who retire at age 62 were born in 1958. That means their FRA is 66 years and 8 months. Thus, retiring at 62 is 4 years and 8 months early or 56 months early. The first 36 months are penalized $\frac{5}{9}$ of a percent per month (0.5555% per month), which is a total of 20%. The remaining 20 months are penalized $\frac{5}{12}$ of a percent per month (0.4167% per month) for an additional reduction of 8.33%. Thus, the total reduction would be 28.33% less than their full retirement benefit. By 2022, a covered worker retiring at age 62 (FRA would be 67) will receive only 70% of his monthly retirement benefit. Exhibit 11.8, which was compiled by the Social

Security Administration, shows the phasein of the Social Security full retirement age and accompanying reductions for early retirement at age 62.

EXHIBIT 11.8 Social Security Full Retirement and Reductions* by Age

Year of Birth	Full Retirement Age	Age 62 Reduction Months	Monthly Percentage Reduction	Total Percentage Reduction
1937 or earlier	65	36	0.555	20.00
1938	65 and 2 months	38	0.548	20.83
1939	65 and 4 months	40	0.541	21.67
1940	65 and 6 months	42	0.535	22.50
1941	65 and 8 months	44	0.530	23.33
1942	65 and 10 months	46	0.525	24.17
1943-1954	66	48	0.520	25.00
1955	66 and 2 months	50	0.516	25.84
1956	66 and 4 months	52	0.512	26.66
1957	66 and 6 months	54	0.509	27.50
1958	66 and 8 months	56	0.505	28.33
1959	66 and 10 months	58	0.502	29.17
1960 and later	67	60	0.500	30.00

*Percentage monthly and total reductions are approximate because of rounding. The actual reductions are 0.555%, or five-ninths of 1%, per month for the first 36 months and 0.416%, or five-twelfths of 1%, for subsequent months.

Source: Social Security Administration (www.ssa.gov)

No matter what a worker's full retirement age is, she may start receiving benefits as early as age 62. She also can retire at any time between age 62 and full retirement age; however, if she starts at one of these early ages, her benefits are reduced a fraction of a percent for each month before her full retirement age.

EXAMPLE Assume Betty, a worker born in 1958, decided to retire on her 62nd birthday. Assume that her full retirement benefit would have been $1,429.20 at age 66 and eight months, her full retirement age. If she retires at age 62, what will her monthly retirement benefit be?

The answer is $1,025.00 (decreased to the next lower multiple of 10 cents). As shown in Exhibit 11.8, Betty is retiring 56 months early, and her total percentage reduction is 28.28% ($1,429.20 × 71.72% = $1,025.02).

EXAMPLE What if Betty retires at age 64 and 10 months? What will be her permanent monthly retirement benefit (subject to COLA increases)?

In this case, Betty is retiring 22 months early. Therefore, her total percentage reduction is 12% (22 months × 0.5555% per month = 12%, rounded off). Her permanent monthly retirement benefit (subject to COLA increases) will be $1,258 (rounded).

For those covered individuals who postpone retirement, that is, take late retirement, the monthly retirement benefit and the benefit paid to the surviving spouse will increase, as shown in Exhibit 11.9.

EXHIBIT 11.9 Percentage Increases For Delayed Retirement

Increase for Year Born	Annual Percentage Each Year of Late Retirement (Up to Age 70)	After Age
1939	7.0%	65 and 4 months
1940	7.0%	65 and 6 months
1941	7.5%	65 and 8 months
1942	7.5%	65 and 10 months
1943 and later	8.0%	66

Source: Social Security Administration (www.ssa.gov)

Those taking delayed retirement receive a permanent increase to their monthly retirement benefit.

Although the calculations explained above can provide estimates of what benefits a retiring worker may receive, a financial planner should have the client obtain his entire earnings history up to the moment of retirement from the Social Security Administration to get the most accurate benefit estimate.

Reduction of Social Security Benefits

Retirement earnings limitations test
One of the ways in which Social Security benefits are reduced on the basis of earnings

Besides early retirement, there are two other ways beneficiaries' benefits can be reduced. The first method is through reduction of benefits on the basis of earnings, referred to as the **retirement earnings limitations test**. The other method is through taxation of Social Security benefits. Both of these measures reduce beneficiaries' net benefits.

A person can continue to work even though he is receiving Social Security retirement benefits. The earnings received by the beneficiary cannot exceed certain limitations without triggering a reduction in Social Security benefits. Beneficiaries can earn up to the limitation and receive all of their benefits, but if those earnings exceed the designated limit for the calendar year, then some or all benefits will be withheld. The law provides an annual earnings limitation of $19,560 for those under the full retirement age for 2022. The Social Security Administration deducts $1 in benefits for each $2 earned by those beneficiaries above annual earnings limitation. In the year that the retiree reaches full retirement age, $1 in benefits will be deducted for each $3 earned above the given year's limit, but only for earnings before the month the retiree reaches full retirement age. For 2022, the limit for earnings in the year the retiree reaches full retirement age is $51,960. The earnings limitation increases every year as median earnings nationwide increase.

If a beneficiary's earnings exceed the limitation, that beneficiary's benefits will be reduced, depending on her age. The beneficiary must file an annual report of her earnings to the Social Security Administration by April 15 of the year following the year worked and must provide the exact earnings for that year and an estimate for the current year. The filing of a federal tax return with the IRS does not satisfy the filing requirement with the Social Security Administration. Also, wages count toward the earnings limitation when they are earned, not when paid, whereas income for the self-employed normally counts when paid, not earned. If other family members receive benefits based on the beneficiary's Social Security record, then the total family benefits may be affected by the beneficiary's earnings that exceed the earnings limitation. In such a case, the Social Security Administration will withhold not only the worker's benefits but also those benefits payable to family members.

EXAMPLE George is 64 years old and, despite being retired from his occupation as an attorney, earned $25,000 in 2022 while working as a golf instructor at a local golf course. George's monthly retirement benefit from Social Security is normally $2,500, which totals $30,000 for the entire year. Because George exceeded the retirement earnings limitation, how much money will be deducted from George's retirement benefit for 2022?

George's total earnings in 2022	$25,000
Earnings limitation	($19,560)
Remainder excess	$ 5,440
One-half deduction	÷ 2
	$ 2,720

The Social Security Administration will thus deduct $2,720 from George's benefits for the year. George will receive $27,280 in retirement benefits ($30,000 annual retirement benefit less $2,720 reduction). George's total income for 2022 would be $52,280, instead of $55,000.

Another commonly asked question is this: What income counts toward the retirement earnings limitation? Generally, only wages and net self-employment income count; income from savings, investments, and insurance does not. The following is a nonexclusive list of income sources that DO NOT count toward the earnings limitation:

- Pension or retirement pay
- Section 401(k) plan and IRA withdrawals
- Dividends and interest from investments
- Capital gains
- Rental income
- Workers' compensation benefits
- Unemployment benefits
- Court-awarded judgments, less components of award that include lost wages
- Contest winnings

TAXATION OF SOCIAL SECURITY BENEFITS

Modified adjusted gross income
On the 1040 federal tax return, modified adjusted gross income is the sum of adjusted gross income, nontaxable interest, and foreign-earned income

Separate and apart from the earnings limitations, some beneficiaries may be required to pay taxes on their Social Security benefits. For persons with substantial income in addition to Social Security benefits, up to 85% of their annual benefits may be subject to federal income tax. The Social Security Administration is concerned with beneficiaries' **modified adjusted gross income**. On the 1040 Federal tax return, modified adjusted gross income is the sum of adjusted gross income, nontaxable interest, and foreign-earned income.

Generally, up to 50% of Social Security benefits are subject to federal income taxes for beneficiaries who file a federal tax return as an individual and have a modified adjusted gross income between $25,000 and $34,000. For those with a modified adjusted gross income over $34,000, up to 85% of their Social Security benefits will be subject to federal income taxation. For those beneficiaries that file a joint federal tax return and have a modified adjusted gross income with their spouse between $32,000 and $44,000, up to 50% of their Social Security benefits will be subject to federal income taxes. Finally, if beneficiaries filing a joint tax return have a modified adjusted gross income that exceeds

$44,000, up to 85% of their Social Security benefits will be subject to federal income taxation.

To summarize, for persons with substantial income in addition to their Social Security benefits, up to 85% of their annual benefits may be subject to federal income tax. The amount of benefits subject to federal income tax for taxpayers with modified adjusted gross income under $34,000 ($44,000 if married filing jointly) is the smaller of the following:

- One-half of their benefits
- One-half of the amount by which their adjusted gross income, plus tax-exempt interest, plus foreign-earned income, plus one-half of their Social Security, exceeds
  - $25,000 if single,
  - $25,000 if married and not filing a joint return and did not live with a spouse at any time during the year,
  - $32,000 if married and filing a joint return, and
  - $0 if married and not filing a joint return and did live with a spouse at any time during the year.

OTHER SOCIAL SECURITY BENEFITS

Disability Benefits and Disability Insured

Benefits are payable at any age to people who have enough Social Security credits and who have a severe physical or mental impairment that is expected to prevent them from doing substantial work for one year or more, or who have a condition that is expected to result in death. Essentially, workers are insured for disability if they are fully insured and, except for persons who are blind or disabled before age 31, have a total of at least 20 credits of coverage during the 40-quarter period ending with the quarter in which the worker became disabled. Workers who are disabled before age 31 must have total credits of coverage equal to one-half the calendar quarters that have elapsed since the worker reached age 21, ending in the quarter in which the worker became disabled. However, a minimum of six credits is required.

Earnings of $1,350 or more per month for 2022 are considered substantial for someone who is not blind. The disability program includes incentives to smooth the transition back into the workforce, including continuation of benefits and health care coverage. Disability under the Social Security system is defined as an inability to engage in substantial gainful activity by reason of a physical or mental impairment expected to last at least 12 months or to result in death. The impairment must be of such severity that the applicant is not only unable to do his previous work but cannot, considering age, education, and work experience, engage in any other kind of substantial gainful work that exists in the national economy.

Family Benefits

If an individual is eligible for retirement or disability benefits, other members of the individual's family might receive benefits as well. Family members who may receive benefits include the following:

- A spouse caring for a child under age 16, or caring for a child who was disabled before age 22
- A child, if the child is unmarried and under age 18, under age 19 but still in secondary school, or age 18 or older but disabled before age 22

For those workers who are entitled to retirement or disability benefits, an ex-spouse could also be eligible for benefits on the worker's record.

The child's benefit stops the month before the child reaches 18, unless the child is unmarried and is either disabled or is a full-time elementary or secondary school student. Approximately five months before the child's 18th birthday, the person receiving the child's benefits will get a form explaining how benefits can continue. A child whose benefits stop at 18 can have them start again if the child becomes disabled before reaching 22 or becomes a full-time elementary or secondary school student before reaching 19. If the child continues to receive benefits after age 18 due to a disability, the child also may qualify for SSI disability benefits. When a student's 19th birthday occurs during a school term, benefits can be continued up to two months to allow completion of the school term.

Survivors Benefits

If a worker earned enough Social Security credits during his or her lifetime, certain members of the worker's family may be eligible for benefits when the worker dies. The family members of a deceased worker who may be entitled to survivors benefits include:

- a widow or widower age 60, age 50 if disabled, or any age if caring for a child under age 16 or a disabled child,
- a child of the deceased worker, if the child is unmarried and under age 18, under age 19 but still in school, or age 18 or older but disabled, and
- parents of the deceased worker, if the deceased worker was their primary means of support, and dependent parent(s) is(are) age 62 or older.

A special one-time payment of $255 may be made to a deceased worker's spouse or minor children upon death. If a spouse was living with the beneficiary at the time of death, the spouse will receive a one-time payment of $255. The payment may be made to a spouse who was not living with the beneficiary at the time of death or an ex-spouse if the spouse or ex-spouse was receiving Social Security benefits based on the deceased's earnings record. If there is no surviving spouse, a child (or children) eligible for benefits on the deceased's work record in the month of death may claim the payment.

EXHIBIT 11.10 Summary of Social Security OASDI Benefits

	Assuming Full Retirement Age of the Worker			
	Retirement	Survivorship		Disability
	Fully Insured (2)	Fully Insured (2)	Currently Insured (3)	(4)
Participant	100%	Deceased	Deceased	100%
Child under 18 (6)	50%	75%	75%	50%
Spouse with child under 16 (7)	50%	75%	75%	50%
Spouse, full retirement age (1)	50%	100%	0%	50%
Spouse, age 62 (1)	32.5%–35%	(8)	0%	35%
Spouse, age 60 (1)	N/A	71.5%	0%	N/A
Dependent parent, age 62	0%	75%/82.5% (5)	0%	0%

(1) Includes divorced spouse if married at least 10 years (unless they have remarried). Survivors benefits are also available to divorced spouse if remarried after age 60.

(2) Fully insured is 40 credits of coverage or 1 credit for each year after age 21 but before age 62.

(3) Currently insured is at least 6 credits of coverage in the last 13 quarters.

(4) Disability insured is based on age as follows:

- Before age 24—must have 6 credits of coverage in the last 12 quarters
- Age 24 through 30—must be covered for half of the available credits after age 21
- Age 31 or older—must be fully insured and have 20 credits of coverage in the last 40 quarters

(5) Parent benefit is 82.5% for one parent and 75% for each parent if two parents.

(6) Child under age 19 and a full-time student in secondary school or of any age and disabled before age 22 also qualifies.

(7) Spouse with child disabled before age 22 also qualifies.

(8) Benefit is prorated for months between age 60 and full retirement age.

THE MAXIMUM FAMILY BENEFIT

When a person dies, her survivors receive a percentage of the worker's Social Security benefits ranging from 75% to 100% each. There is a limit on the amount of monthly Social Security benefits that may be paid to a family called the **maximum family benefit**, which is determined through a formula based on the worker's PIA. Although the limit varies, it is equal to roughly 150–180% of the deceased worker's PIA. If the sum of the family members' benefits exceeds the limit, the family members' benefits are proportionately reduced. For old-age and survivor family benefits, the formula computes the sum of four separate percentages of portions of the worker's PIA.

Maximum family benefit
The limit on the amount of monthly Social Security benefits that may be paid to a family

The following are the bend points for the maximum family benefit formula for 2022, with percentage calculations:

150% of the first $1,308 of the worker's PIA, plus
272% of the worker's PIA over $1,308 through $1,889, plus
134% of the worker's PIA over $1,889 through $2,463, plus
175% of the worker's PIA over $2,463.

MEDICARE BENEFITS

Medicare is a federal health insurance plan for people who are 65 and over, whether retired or still working. People who are disabled or have permanent kidney failure can get Medicare at any age. The Health Care Financing Administration, part of the U.S. Department of Health and Human Services, administers Medicare. Medicare is the nation's largest health insurance program, covering over 61.2 million individuals. There are four parts to Medicare: Hospital Insurance (Part A), Medical Insurance (Part B), Medicare Advantage (Part C), and Prescription Drug Coverage (Part D).

Generally, individuals who are age 65 and over qualify for Medicare. Also, individuals who have received Social Security disability benefits for at least two years automatically qualify for Medicare. All other individuals must file an application for Medicare.

Medicare Part A: Hospital Insurance is paid for by a portion of the Social Security tax. Part A helps pay for necessary medical care and services furnished by Medicare-certified hospitals, inpatient hospital care, skilled nursing care, home health care, hospice care, and other services. The number of days that Medicare covers care in hospitals and skilled nursing facilities is measured by the **benefit period**. A benefit period begins on the first day a patient receives services as a patient in a hospital or skilled nursing facility and ends after the patient has been released for 60 consecutive days. There is no limit to the number of benefit periods a beneficiary may have in a single year.

Benefit period
The number of days that Medicare covers care in hospitals and skilled nursing facilities

The benefit period is identified because deductibles, coinsurance, and premiums relate to the benefit period instead of the calendar year. For instance, for coverage under Medicare Part A in 2022, a deductible of $1,556 applies per benefit period. For the 61st through the 90th day of each benefit period, the insured individual must pay $389 per day in the form of coinsurance. Any days over 90 in a benefit period are considered lifetime reserve days. There are 60 lifetime reserve days available with a coinsurance amount of $778 per day. Lifetime reserve days do not renew with each new benefit period. It is important, therefore, to determine the number of days used in each benefit period.

EXHIBIT 11.11 Medicare Deductible, Coinsurance, and Premium Amounts for 2022

Hospital Insurance (Part A)

- **Deductible**—$1,556 per benefit period
- **Coinsurance**—$389 per day for days 61–90, per benefit period; $778 per day for days 91–150 for each lifetime reserve day (total of 60 lifetime reserve days—nonrenewable)
- **Skilled nursing facility coinsurance**—$194.50 per day for days 21–100, per benefit period
- **Hospital insurance premium**—$499 per month (paid only by individuals who are not otherwise eligible for premium-free hospital insurance and have fewer than 30 credits of Medicare covered employment)
- **Reduced hospital insurance premium**—$259 for individuals with 30 to 39 quarters of coverage

Medical Insurance (Part B)

- **Deductible**—$233 per year
- **Monthly premium**—$170.10*

*Premium is higher for high-income enrollees
Source: Social Security Administration (www.ssa.gov)

Medicare Part A helps pay for up to 90 days of inpatient hospital care during each benefit period. Covered services for inpatient hospital care include semiprivate room and meals, operating and recovery room costs, intensive care, drugs, laboratory tests, x-rays, general nursing services, and any other necessary medical services and supplies. Convenience items such as television and telephones provided by hospitals in private rooms (unless medically necessary) are generally not covered. Medicare will not pay for custodial services for activities of daily living such as eating, bathing, and getting dressed. However, Medicare will pay for skilled nursing facility care for rehabilitation, such as recovery time after a hospital discharge. Part A may pay for up to 100 days in a participating skilled nursing facility in each benefit period. Medicare pays all approved charges for the first 20 days relating to skilled nursing facility care, and then the patient pays a coinsurance amount for days 21 through 100. Medicare may also pay the full, approved cost of covered home health care services, which includes part-time or intermittent skilled nursing services prescribed by a physician for treatment or rehabilitation of homebound patients. Normally, the only cost to the insured for home health care is a 20% coinsurance charge for durable medical equipment such as wheelchairs and walkers.

Medicare Part B pays for 80% of approved charges for most covered services. Unless an individual declines Part B medical insurance protection, the premium will automatically be deducted from her Social Security check. Medicare Part B usually does not cover charges for routine physical examinations or services unrelated to the treatment of injury or illness. Dental care, dentures, cosmetic surgery, hearing aids, and eye examinations are not covered by Part B. Part B covers a limited number of outpatient prescription drugs that are not typically self-administered and that are provided in a hospital outpatient department or doctor's office.

Prescription drug coverage under Medicare Part D is available to everyone who is covered under Medicare. Enrollees pay a monthly premium. There is also an annual deductible and a co-payment requirement. Various plans are available with differing premiums and benefit levels.

2022 Outpatient Prescription Coverage (Part D)

Medicare Part D pays for prescription drugs using four stages. First, there is the Part D deductible of $480 in 2022. Next comes the initial coverage using copayments and coinsurance. This lasts until the patient and the plan have paid $4,430 in 2022 in this stage of coverage. The third stage is called the "coverage gap" or the "donut hole." Initially, there was no help from Part D for these expenses. Over time, Part D has covered more and more of the expenses in this range, but it does not cover all expenses. In 2022, the "donut hole" is considered closed because Medicare Part D is now involved in paying some portion of all expenses in this category. The maximum a person pays in this category is 25%. Once the person has spent $7,050 out-of-pocket in 2022, the patient is out of the coverage gap and into the "catastrophic coverage" stage. Most of the remaining expenses are paid by Medicare Part D, but there are still some copayments and coinsurance costs borne by the person.

Source: Centers for Medicare & Medicaid Services
(See www.cms.hhs.gov or www.medicare.gov for updates)

Various plans under Medicare are available to insureds. The original Medicare Plan is the means by which most individuals get their Medicare Part A and Part B benefits. This is the traditional payment-per-service arrangement whereby the individual insured may go to any doctor, specialist, or hospital that accepts Medicare, and Medicare pays its share after services are rendered. Medicare carriers and fiscal intermediaries are private insurance organizations that handle claims under the original Medicare Plan. Carriers handle Part B claims, and fiscal intermediaries handle Part A plans. The Social Security Administration does not handle claims for Medicare payments.

Medicare Advantage
A managed care plan that uses a network of doctors, hospitals, and health care providers approved by Medicare

Medical savings account (MSA)
Used to pay the out-of-pocket medical expenses of an insured enrolled in a high-deductible insurance plan

Furthermore, an individual may opt to enroll in a Medicare managed care plan called **Medicare Advantage** (Medicare Part C). These plans are offered by private Medicare-approved companies and are networks of doctors, hospitals, and other health care providers that agree to give care in return for a set monthly payment from Medicare. Individuals are eligible to enroll in Medicare Advantage if they are enrolled in Medicare Parts A and B, pay the Part B premium, do not have end-stage renal disease, and live in the plan's service area.

Another option under Medicare Advantage is a high-deductible insurance plan and a **medical savings account (MSA)**. Funds from the MSA can be used to pay the out-of-pocket medical expenses of an insured enrolled in a high-deductible insurance plan. Medicare will pay the premium and make contributions to the MSA. These contributions are equal to the amount Medicare would pay to a Medicare Advantage plan in the individual's area less the premium for the high-deductible insurance plan.

Many private insurance companies sell Medicare supplemental insurance policies, Medigap and Medicare SELECT. These supplemental policies help bridge the coverage gaps in the original Medicare plan. These supplemental policies also help pay Medicare's coinsurance amounts and deductibles, as well as other out-of-pocket expenses for health care.

When a worker is first enrolled in Part B at age 65, there is a six-month open enrollment period for Medigap plans. During the time of open enrollment, the health status of the applicant cannot be used as a reason to refuse a Medigap policy or charge more than other open enrollment applicants. However, the insurer may require a six-month waiting period for coverage of pre-existing conditions. If, however, the open enrollment period has expired, the applicant may be denied a policy on the basis of health status or may be charged higher rates.

Other Medicare Health Plan Choices

Medicare offers alternative methods of obtaining Medicare benefits through other health plan choices. Choices that vary by area include coordinated care or Medicare managed care plans, such as health maintenance organizations (HMOs), HMOs with a point of service option, provider sponsored organizations (PSOs), and preferred provider organizations (PPOs). These plans involve specific groups of doctors, hospitals, and other providers who furnish care to an insured member of the plan, such as many employer-sponsored plans throughout the country. Medicare managed care plans not only provide the same services covered by Part A and Part B, but most Medicare managed plans also offer a variety of additional benefits such as preventative care, prescription drugs, dental care, eyeglasses, and other items not covered by the original Medicare Plan. The cost of these extra benefits varies among the plans.

Other Medicare health plan choices beyond the original Medicare plan and Medicare managed care plans include Private Fee-for-Service Plans, Medicare medical savings account plans (MSAs), and religious fraternal benefits plans. These plans provide all services covered by both Part A and Part B, as well as a variety of additional benefits. MSAs are funded through a lump-sum payment from traditional Medicare to obtain a high deductible insurance policy. Any remaining balance can be used by the beneficiary for payment of medical expenses not covered by traditional Medicare or for other use. This amount could be subject to taxation if not used for medically related purposes. For information about these various health plan choices, visit the official internet site of Medicare at **www.medicare.gov**, which is very helpful and provides many links to other informative sources.

Applying for Medicare Benefits and Coverage

If a worker applies for retirement or survivor benefits before her 65th birthday, there is no need to file a separate application for Medicare. The worker will receive information in the mail before she turns 65, explaining what needs to be done. Coverage starts automatically at age 65, even without receiving a Medicare card in the mail.

Those who are not receiving Social Security benefits must file an application for Medicare benefits. Spouses can qualify for Medicare Part A at age 65 on the basis of the other spouse's work record if the other spouse is eligible for monthly Social Security benefits or if the other spouse is receiving Social Security disability benefits. Applications should be submitted three months before the applicant's 65th birthday. If the worker does not enroll and delays taking Part B for one year, that worker's monthly premiums for Part B will increase. For every 12 months the worker could have used Part B but does not take it, the monthly premium increases by 10%. If the worker decides to delay opting into Part B because of the worker's current group health plan coverage (if applicable), the worker may be able to avoid the increased monthly premium by applying for Part B either while participating in the group coverage or within eight months after the employment ends or group health coverage ends, whichever occurs first.

Even if an individual continues to work after turning 65, she should sign up for Part A of Medicare. Part A may help defray some costs not otherwise covered by group health plans. Applying for Part B may or may not be advantageous if the worker has health insurance through an employer. The worker would be required to pay the monthly Part B premium, yet Part B benefits may be of limited value because the employer plan will be the primary source of payment of medical bills.

SUPPLEMENTAL SECURITY INCOME BENEFITS

SSI makes monthly payments to individuals with low incomes and few assets. In order to obtain SSI benefits, an individual must be age 65, disabled, or blind. The definition of disability is satisfied when the individual is unable to engage in any substantial gainful activity because of a physical or mental problem expected to last at least one year or result in death. Children as well as adults can qualify for SSI disability payments. As its name implies, Supplemental Security Income supplements the beneficiary's income up to various levels, depending on where the beneficiary lives. If an otherwise eligible SSI applicant lives in another's household and receives support from that person, the federal SSI benefit is reduced by one-third.

The federal government pays a basic rate, which is $840 (2022) per month for one person and $1,261 (2022) per month for married couples. Some states supply additional funds to qualified individuals. To ascertain the SSI benefit rates in a certain state, the financial planner or client can contact a local Social Security office in that state, or visit the Social Security Administration's website. Generally, individuals who receive SSI benefits also qualify for Medicaid, food stamps, and other public assistance.

FILING FOR SOCIAL SECURITY BENEFITS

The Social Security Administration reports that many people fail to file claims with the Social Security Administration or fail to do so in a timely fashion. Individuals should file for Social Security or SSI disability benefits as soon they become too disabled to work or for survivors benefits when a family breadwinner dies. Social Security benefits do not start automatically. Social Security will not begin payment of benefits until the beneficiary files an application. When filing for benefits, applicants must submit documents that show eligibility, such as a birth certificate for each family member applying for benefits, a marriage certificate if a spouse is applying, and the most recent W-2 forms or tax returns.

To file for benefits, obtain information, or to speak to a Social Security representative, individuals must call the Social Security Administration's toll-free number, 1-800-772-1213, or visit the Social Security Administration's website. The toll-free number can be used to schedule an appointment at a local Social Security office. The Social Security Administration treats all calls confidentially. Periodically, a second Social Security representative will monitor incoming and outgoing telephone calls to ensure accurate and courteous service.

SOCIAL SECURITY CHANGES FOR 2021–2022

Each year, the Social Security Commissioner issues a Fact Sheet summarizing the changes in Social Security. Exhibit 11.12 contains the Commissioner's Fact Sheet for 2021 and 2022.

EXHIBIT 11.12 Social Security Changes for 2021–2022

Fact Sheet

SOCIAL SECURITY

2022 SOCIAL SECURITY CHANGES

Cost-of-Living Adjustment (COLA):

Based on the increase in the Consumer Price Index (CPI-W) from the third quarter of 2020 through the third quarter of 2021, Social Security and Supplemental Security Income (SSI) beneficiaries will receive a 5.9 percent COLA for 2022. Other important 2022 Social Security information is as follows:

Tax Rate	2021	2022
Employee	7.65%	7.65%
Self-Employed	15.30%	15.30%

NOTE: The 7.65% tax rate is the combined rate for Social Security and Medicare. The Social Security portion (OASDI) is 6.20% on earnings up to the applicable taxable maximum amount (see below). The Medicare portion (HI) is 1.45% on all earnings. Also, as of January 2013, individuals with earned income of more than $200,000 ($250,000 for married couples filing jointly) pay an additional 0.9 percent in Medicare taxes. The tax rates shown above do not include the 0.9 percent.

	2021	2022
Maximum Taxable Earnings		
Social Security (OASDI only)	$142,800	$147,000
Medicare (HI only)	No Limit	
Quarter of Coverage		
	$1,470	$1,510
Retirement Earnings Test Exempt Amounts		
Under full retirement age	$18,960/yr. ($1,580/mo.)	$19,560/yr. ($1,630/mo.)
NOTE: One dollar in benefits will be withheld for every $2 in earnings above the limit.		
The year an individual reaches full	$50,520/yr.	$51,960/yr.

Social Security National Press Office Baltimore, MD

EXHIBIT 11.12 Social Security Changes for 2021–2022 (continued)

retirement age	($4,210/mo.)	($4,330/mo.)
NOTE: Applies only to earnings for months prior to attaining full retirement age. One dollar in benefits will be withheld for every $3 in earnings above the limit.		
Beginning the month an individual attains full retirement age	None	

	2021	2022
Social Security Disability Thresholds		
Substantial Gainful Activity (SGA)		
Non-Blind	$1,310/mo.	$1,350/mo.
Blind	$2,190/mo.	$2,260/mo.
Trial Work Period (TWP)	$ 940/mo.	$ 970/mo.
Maximum Social Security Benefit: Worker Retiring at Full Retirement Age		
	$3,148/mo.	$3,345/mo.
SSI Federal Payment Standard		
Individual	$ 794/mo.	$ 841/mo.
Couple	$1,191/mo.	$1,261/mo.
SSI Resource Limits		
Individual	$2,000	$2,000
Couple	$3,000	$3,000
SSI Student Exclusion		
Monthly limit	$1,930	$2,040
Annual limit	$7,770	$8,230
Estimated Average Monthly Social Security Benefits Payable in January 2022		
	Before 5.9% COLA	**After 5.9% COLA**
All Retired Workers	$1,565	$1,657
Aged Couple, Both Receiving Benefits	$2,599	$2,753
Widowed Mother and Two Children	$3,009	$3,187
Aged Widow(er) Alone	$1,467	$1,553
Disabled Worker, Spouse and One or More Children	$2,250	$2,383
All Disabled Workers	$1,282	$1,358

This press release was produced and disseminated at U.S. taxpayer expense.

OTHER ISSUES

Effect of Marriage or Divorce on Benefits

Marriage or divorce may affect one's Social Security benefits, depending on the kind of benefits received. If a worker receives retirement benefits on the basis of his own earnings record, the worker's retirement benefits will continue whether he is married or divorced. If an individual receives benefits on the basis of his spouse's record, the individual's benefits will cease upon divorce, unless the individual is age 62 or older and was married at least 10 years. Widows and widowers, whether divorced or not, will continue to receive survivors benefits upon remarriage if the widow or widower is age 60 or older. Disabled widows and widowers, whether divorced or not, will continue to receive survivors benefits upon remarriage if the disabled widow or widower is age 50 or older.

For all other forms of Social Security benefits, benefits will cease upon remarriage, except in special circumstances. When a person marries, it is presumed that at least one person in the marriage can provide adequate support. Likewise, Social Security benefits may recommence based on the previous spouse's benefits if the marriage ends.

Change of Name

If an individual changes her name because of marriage, divorce, or a court order, that individual must notify the Social Security Administration of the name change so that the Social Security Administration will be able to show the new name in its records and properly credit that individual for earnings. This will ensure that the individual's work history will be accurately recorded and maintained.

Leaving the United States

Beneficiaries who are U.S. citizens may travel or live in most foreign countries without affecting their eligibility for Social Security benefits. However, there are a few countries where Social Security checks cannot be sent. These countries currently include Cuba and North Korea. In general, the Social Security Administration will not send payments to persons in Azerbaijan, Belarus, Kazakhstan, Kyrgyzstan, Moldova, Tajikistan, Turkmenistan, Ukraine, and Uzbekistan. Exceptions may be made for certain eligible recipients in these countries.

Beneficiaries should inform the Social Security Administration of their plans to go outside the United States for a trip that lasts 30 days or more. By providing the name of the country or countries to be visited and the expected departure and return dates, the Social Security Administration will send special reporting instructions to the beneficiaries and arrange for delivery of checks while abroad.

WHERE ON THE WEB

Centers for Medicare and Medicaid Services **www.cms.gov**

Medicare Rights Center **www.medicarerights.org**

National Organization of Social Security Claimants' Representatives **www.nosscr.org**

Social Security Online (official website of the U.S. Social Security Administration) **www.ssa.gov**

Social Security Disability **www.ssa.gov/disability**

Social Security Forms **www.ssa.gov/forms**

U.S. Government website for Medicare **www.medicare.gov**

DISCUSSION QUESTIONS

1. For purposes of Social Security and disability benefits, what is the meaning of substantial work in 2022?
2. When was Social Security legislation passed?
3. When was Social Security legislation passed to include a cost-of-living adjustment (COLA)?
4. How are Social Security benefits financed?
5. Is there a maximum payroll amount to which Social Security taxes apply?
6. To qualify for OASDI disability benefits, what definition of disability must be met?
7. Describe the six major benefits under the Social Security program.
8. Identify and describe the benefits available to those covered under OASDI.
9. How would a person who is entitled to Social Security benefits become ineligible for benefits?
10. What are the coverages that make up the Medicare program?
11. Define and explain the meaning of fully insured, currently insured, and disability insured under the OASDI program.
12. What are the requirements to be fully insured under OASDI?
13. What Social Security benefits are available to the dependents of a deceased worker who was only currently insured?
14. What Social Security benefits would a fully insured worker have that a currently insured worker would not have until achieving fully insured status?
15. What requirements must a person satisfy to collect Social Security (OASDI) disability income benefits?
16. How is Social Security funded?
17. To qualify for Social Security OASDI benefits, how many credits of coverage does one need? How is a credit determined?
18. How is OASDI insured status determined, and why is it important?
19. How are monthly payments under OASDI determined?
20. What is normal retirement age for OASDI benefits for someone born in 1959?
21. Is a recipient of Social Security benefits subject to purchasing-power risk?
22. What are the four benefits payable under the OASDI program?

EXERCISES

1. Michael was 33 and had two dependent children, ages 4 and 6, who are cared for by their mother when he died this year. He had accumulated 20 credits of coverage under Social Security at the time of his death. To what benefits are his survivors entitled under Social Security?

2. In 2022, James earned $6,500 from employment subject to Social Security between January 1 and March 31. He was then unemployed for the remainder of the year. How many credits of coverage did he earn for Social Security for 2022?

3. Charles, age 38, has just died. He was credited with the last 30 consecutive credits of coverage since he left school. He did not work before leaving school. Which of the following persons are eligible to receive Social Security survivor benefits as a result of Charles's death?
   A. Bill, Charles's 16-year-old son
   B. Dawn, Charles' 18-year-old daughter
   C. Margaret, Charles's 38-year-old widow
   D. Betty, Charles's 60-year-old dependent mother

4. Under Social Security (OASDI), what benefits are available to the survivors of a deceased who was currently insured?

5. Which of the following persons are eligible to receive immediate survivor income benefits on the basis of a deceased worker's primary insurance amount (PIA) under OASDI (Social Security)?
   1. A surviving spouse caring for an under-16-year-old child
   2. Unmarried children under age 18 who are dependents
   3. Unmarried disabled children who became disabled before age 22
   4. Any surviving divorced spouse over 50, with no children who was married to decedent for over 10 years and who is disabled

6. How is a worker's insured status determined under Social Security?

7. Philip began his professional corporation single practitioner CPA firm 38 years ago at age 25. He worked profitably as a sole practitioner for the full 38 years and is now age 63 and 2 months. He retired December 31, 2021. On January 1, 2022, he sold his practice for $400,000 to be received in four equal annual installments beginning on January 1, 2022. Is Philip eligible for Social Security retirement benefits during 2022? Why or why not? What would be the ramifications if Philip started his Social Security benefits now?

PROBLEMS

1. Larry was married at the following ages and to the following wives. Larry is fully insured and is 62 and married to Dawn.

	Wife	Current Age	Larry's Age at Marriage	Current Marital Status	Length of Marriage
1	Alice	62	20	Single	10 years, 1 month
2	Betty	63	31	Single	10 years, 1 month
3	Claire	64	42	Single	9 years
4	Dawn	65	53	Married	9 years

Who among the former wives/wives may be eligible to receive Social Security retirement benefits on the basis of Larry's earnings if Larry is 1) retired, or 2) not retired?

2. Rob earned $62,000 in 2022. Calculate his FICA contribution for the year. How much did his employer pay toward FICA?

3. Last year, Michelle, filing single, received $10,400 in Social Security benefits. For the entire year, she had adjusted gross income of $28,000. How much, if any, of her Social Security benefit is taxable?

4. Mike is 68 years old in 2022. He has a full-time job working as a masseur. This year he anticipates earning $32,000 from his job. How much, in dollars, will Mike's Social Security benefits be reduced?

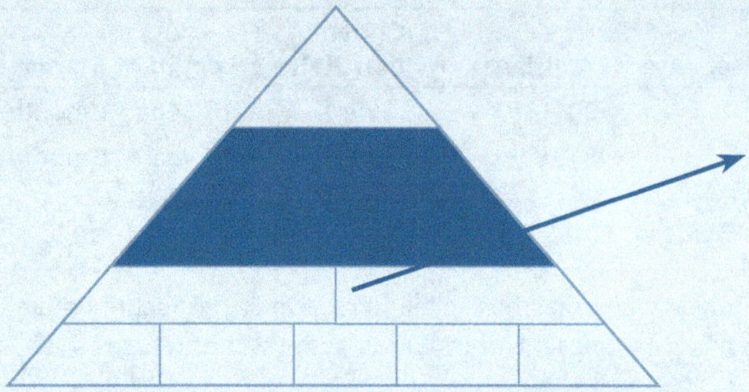

SECTION 4 IN BRIEF

- Risk and return of asset classes
- Types of investment vehicles

- The Internal Revenue Service and Administration
- Income tax liability, audits, interest, and penalties
- Selecting the proper business form

- Retirement income needs analysis
- Qualified and other tax-advantaged retirement savings plans
- Nonqualified retirement plans and deferred compensation

- Estate planning goals and documents
- Probate process
- Gift and estate taxation
- Use of trusts

SECTION

4 Investment, Income Tax, Business, Retirement, and Estate Planning

CHAPTERS

Risks

- Unrealized financial planning goals
- Investment losses
- Systematic and unsystematic risk
- Excessive tax liability (income, estate, gift)
- Excessive general liability exposure
- Outliving one's assets
- Failure to provide for survivors
- Inefficient distribution of estate assets
- Failure to meet assisted living and end-of-life care needs

Goals

- Minimize tax liability
- Match business goals with entity formation
- Ensure inflation-protected retirement income
- Efficient transfer of assets

Data Collection

- Business entity characteristics
- Financial statements
- Family health history
- Projected inflation rate
- Investment history
- Risk tolerance
- Tax returns and information forms
- Current investment and asset allocation
- Life insurance policies and property titles
- Retirement plan and deferred compensation information
- Estate planning documents and trust information

Data Analysis

- Liquidity needs
- Investment portfolio risks and returns bench-mark comparison
- Tax efficiency of investments
- Tax-saving strategies
- Retirement needs analysis
- Adequacy of life insurance and other wealth transfer techniques

CHAPTER 12

Introduction to Investment Concepts

LEARNING OBJECTIVES

After learning the material in this chapter, you will be able to do the following:

- Describe the steps involved in the investment planning process
- List the most common investment goals and how to achieve them
- Explain the difference between direct investing and indirect investing
- Differentiate between systematic risk and unsystematic risk
- Define lending investments and ownership investments
- Identify attributes of an investment in tangible assets (collectibles) or natural resources (oil and gas wells)
- Describe the two common measures of risk: beta and standard deviation
- Understand how to calculate several measures of investment return

- Define the efficient frontier, and explain its role in modern portfolio theory
- Describe the capital asset pricing model (CAPM), the capital market line (CML), and the security market line (SML)
- Describe the efficient market hypothesis
- Describe the basic principles of behavioral finance

INTRODUCTION TO INVESTING

As this text's opening chapters point out, the professional financial planner's purpose is to assist clients in achieving their financial goals and objectives, while simultaneously helping them manage personal and financial risks. Investment planning and portfolio evaluation are key elements in achieving many financial planning goals, such as saving for retirement, saving for children's education, and the accumulation and preservation of wealth. This chapter will provide the financial planner with the background and reference information necessary to develop a solid foundation of investment planning—an essential ingredient in the financial planning process.

Investing is based on the concept that forgoing immediate consumption provides for greater future consumption. Investing provides an opportunity for discretionary funds to grow and accumulate over time. Therefore, the first step in developing a sound financial plan is to save rather than spend. This current sacrifice implies an expectation that funds saved today will provide for greater expenditures in the future.

Without the ability to invest and grow through savings, interest income, dividend payments, rental income, and capital appreciation, investors would have difficulty achieving their financial goals. However, financial growth is only one element to consider in achieving financial goals. Taxes, inflation, and other risks stand in the way.

THE INVESTMENT PLANNING PROCESS

This process begins with a client establishing a clear set of goals and developing and implementing an investment strategy that is in agreement with the goals. The formal steps in the investment planning process include determining whether the client has the means to invest, establishing the time horizon for investment based on the client's financial objectives, and ascertaining the appropriate level of risk and return for the investment portfolio based on the investor's risk tolerance and required rate of return. Investment planning requires a thorough review of the client's current financial situation. The investment professional needs to assist the client in making the proper financial choices to help the client meet the goals. In order to provide effective investment counseling, the advisor should examine and review the client's financial goals, risk tolerance, tax situation, liquidity needs, and financial statements.

ESTABLISHING FINANCIAL GOALS

Financial or investment goals are the objectives that a client wishes to accomplish through the investing process. Ultimately the investment choices that a client will make is dictated by their investment goals.

The time horizon for goals can be short, intermediate, or long. Short-term goals are commonly fulfilled within two years, and include saving for small purchases or for a down payment on an automobile. Intermediate goals are often accomplished within 2 to 10 years, and include funding a child's college education or saving for a down payment on a home. Long-term goals generally take over 10 years to achieve, and include saving for retirement.

Investment Policy Statement

Investment policy statement
A written document that sets forth a client's objectives, as well as limitations on the investment manager

An **investment policy statement** (IPS) is a written document that sets forth a client's objectives, as well as limitations on the investment manager. This document also gives guidance to the investment manager and provides a means for evaluating investment performance. Specifically, the objectives portion of the statement should include the desired portfolio return as well as the client's risk tolerance. To determine the client's risk tolerance, many advisors use a questionnaire. In addition, advisors use the following constraints as part of an IPS:

- Investment time horizon
- Liquidity needs of the investor during the investment period
- Tax status of the investor's portfolio
- Laws and regulations that may affect the investor's portfolio
- Any unique circumstances and/or investor preferences (e.g., a pending inheritance)

Typical Financial Planning Goals

Purchasing a home is likely one of the largest financial commitments clients will make during their lifetimes. Most people begin the process by saving for a few years to accumulate a down payment. If the price of an average home is $150,000, many people attempt to make a down payment of approximately $30,000, or 20%. Generally, the average time to save for a down payment is between two and five years. This short period offers minimal opportunity for growth and deters the client from incurring a significant amount of investment risk. Therefore, the appropriate types of securities or investments for this situation are relatively conservative.

One typical goal for parents is funding their children's college education. The cost of tuition and fees ranges from a few thousand dollars to over $75,000 per school year. In some cases, parents will pay the entire cost of education from their current income. However, with tuition costs increasing at a rate of approximately 5–7% per year, parents are finding it increasingly difficult to pay for a child's college education. As a result, many parents are beginning to plan and save for college as soon as their child is born, giving themselves an investment time horizon of approximately 18 years. Other parents with young children may not have the resources to begin planning for college until the child is beginning high school. In their case, the time horizon for saving and investing is closer to four or five years. Clearly, the 18-year time horizon presents a longer compounding period of growth and a greater amount of risk tolerance than does the shorter time horizon.

Even individuals and couples without children or those whose children choose not to attend college still need to plan for retirement. Today's Social Security system may not provide enough income for most individuals to maintain their current standard of living during retirement. Consequently, the burden of funding retirement falls mainly upon the individual. As people become more knowledgeable about financial planning, they are beginning to save earlier for retirement. Someone who is 25 years old has approximately 40 years to save for retirement, assuming retirement begins around age 65. Others will not begin to save until much later but will still have a long-term investment time horizon because the average person may spend 10 to 20 years or longer in retirement. Therefore, the total investment period may still last for 40 or more years.

In each of these cases, accomplishing the specific financial planning goal requires that the individual save and invest funds for a certain period. However, because the time horizon of each goal is different, the ability to tolerate fluctuation in the value of the invested assets varies. For example, investors can tolerate more fluctuation when planning for retirement than when saving for a down payment on a home.

Budgeting

The purpose of budgeting is to manage the amount of income and expenses on a monthly basis. For most people, income is reasonably fixed in the short term, while expenses may vary widely throughout the year. For example, some items are paid monthly, such as utilities, mortgage payments, and phone bills, but other items are paid semiannually, such as automobile insurance. In addition, certain expenses are necessities, or nondiscretionary, such as mortgage payments, groceries, and utilities—while other expenses are discretionary, such as dining out or purchasing new clothes. By identifying necessary and discretionary monthly expenses, one can then begin to find ways to reduce expenses and increase savings. For those who live on a relatively fixed income or salary, the only way to increase savings is to reduce expenditures.

Methods of Increasing Savings

Reducing expenditures, especially discretionary expenditures, is an excellent way to increase cash flow for investment. One way to accomplish this is a savings method called "pay yourself first." Paying yourself first means that the first bill paid every pay period is a deposit to his savings. This method of savings is particularly effective for people without savings discipline because it can be accomplished automatically. For instance, a mutual fund account can be set up to automatically draft a certain amount of investment dollars from a checking account every month or each pay period. Paying yourself first ensures saving on a regular basis and promotes living within a budget.

Another method to increase savings over time is to allocate a portion of future raises and other increases in household income to savings. As increases in salary occur, increases in savings should occur simultaneously. If a person was able to live on $4,000 last month and received a 5% raise, the person should be able to live on less than $4,200 next month and can allocate up to $200 of the raise to savings.

Elective savings programs, such as Section 401(k) plans (cash or deferred arrangements), are another method of increasing personal savings and net worth. These plans facilitate automatic savings in the form of a payroll deduction on a pretax basis. Employee salary deferrals are usually accompanied by employer-matching contributions, which are like free money, and individuals should take full advantage of these contributions. A Section 401(k) plan can facilitate both the "pay yourself first" and the allocating raises methods of increasing savings.

EXAMPLE One of the most important steps in achieving financial goals is to begin sooner rather than later. Time is a great asset in achieving financial planning objectives. For example, a 25-year-old saving $2,000 per year for 10 years will accumulate more by age 65 than a 35-year-old saving $2,000 for 30 years. Although the younger investor invested only one-third of the amount of the older investor, the younger investor has more assets at age 65. How can this be? The simple answer is time. Exhibit 12.1 demonstrates this concept using three different earnings rates.

EXHIBIT 12.1 Time/Savings Example (Accumulation at Age 65)

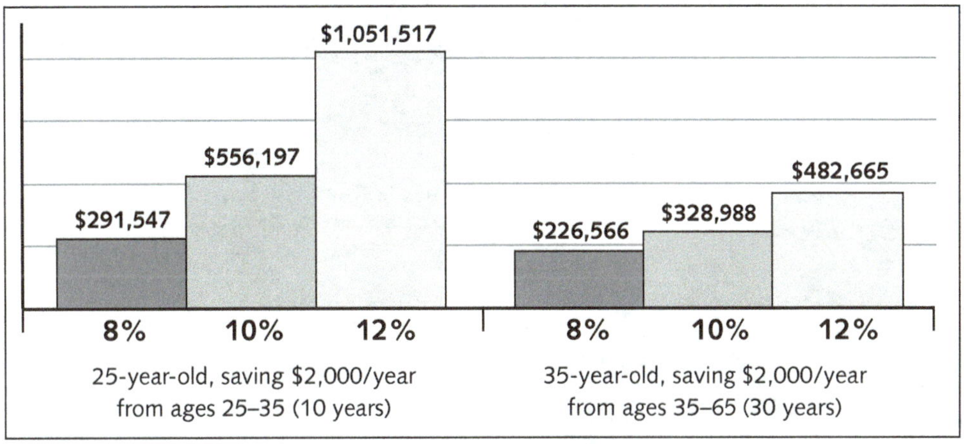

Direct vs. Indirect Investing

Direct investing
A process of investing where investors purchase actual securities

Indirect investing
A process of investing where investors invest in companies that invest directly in securities

Investing in bonds or stocks can be accomplished by purchasing the actual securities or by investing in companies that purchase the actual securities. **Direct investing** occurs when investors purchase actual securities. For example, an investor who purchased an IBM corporate bond or Microsoft's common stock would be investing directly. Direct investing can be accomplished by investing through a brokerage account.

Indirect investing is a process of investing in securities (e.g., mutual funds)that invest directly. Mutual funds are companies that invest in stocks, bonds, and other various securities. Over the last 40 years, indirect investing has gained in popularity. In fact, there are currently more investment companies (mutual funds) than there are listed securities.

INVESTMENT RISKS

Individuals, corporations, and institutions all invest to accumulate wealth. The investor's returns, however, are indeterminable at the inception of the investment because of uncertainty. This uncertainty is a risk that is perceived and managed differently by individual investors. Risk can be thought of as the uncertainty of future outcomes or defined as the probability of an adverse result. In either case, investors expect higher returns when they accept higher levels of uncertainty or risk. The two most important investment strategies that assist investors in managing investment risk are portfolio diversification and asset allocation. They both facilitate the achievement of a fundamental investment goal: obtaining the highest possible return while assuming the lowest amount of risk.

EXHIBIT 12.2 The Risk Pyramid

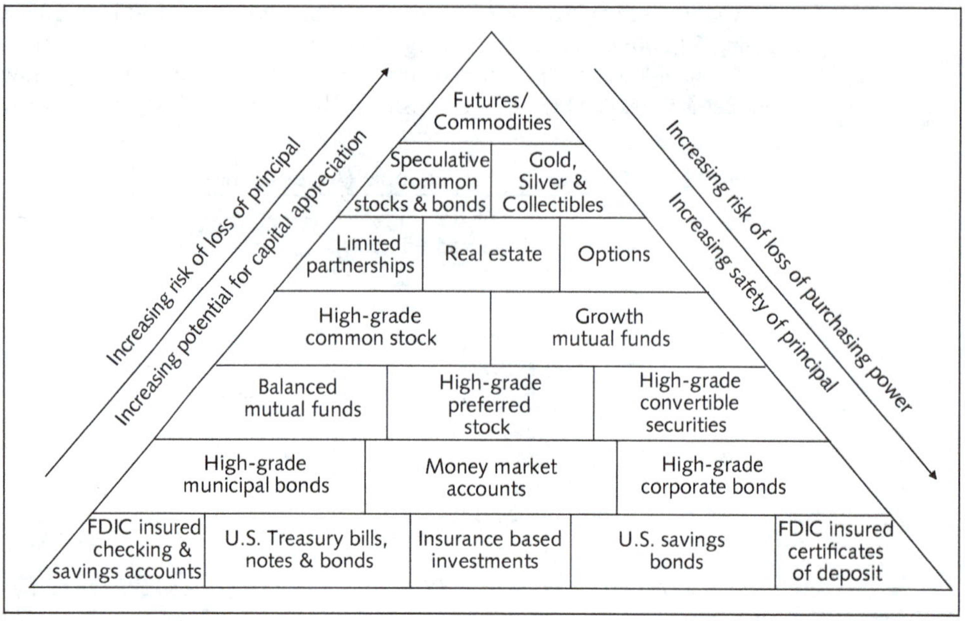

Investors must accept a certain level of risk. Some investors think they can avoid all risks; however, certain risks influence all securities, such as the risk of inflation and fluctuations in interest rates. Even the most conservative investors, invested in the least risky fixed-income securities, are subject to purchasing power risk (inflation) and interest rate risk (changes in interest rates). Other types of risk may only affect a single security, industry, or country. On the basis of these differences, there are two broad categories of risk: systematic risks and unsystematic risks. Exhibit 12.3 summarizes the types of risks under each category.

EXHIBIT 12.3 Systematic and Unsystematic Risks

Systematic Risks	Unsystematic Risks
Purchasing power risk	Business risk
Reinvestment rate risk	Financial risk
Interest rate risk	Default risk
Market risk	Country risk
Exchange rate risk	Liquidity risk
	Marketability risk
	Tax risk

Systematic Risks

Systematic risks
Investment risks impacted by broad macroeconomic factors that influence all securities

Systematic risks are investment risks impacted by broad macroeconomic factors that influence all securities. These risks include purchasing power risk, reinvestment rate risk, interest rate risk, market risk, and exchange rate risk. Diversification cannot eliminate all systematic risk because at least one of these factors affects every security. To recall the components of systematic risk, use the mnemonic *PRIME*, which uses the first letter of each risk source.

Purchasing Power Risk

Purchasing power risk
A systematic risk in which inflation erodes the real value of the investor's assets

The risk that inflation will erode the real value of the investor's assets is referred to as **purchasing power risk**. As the price of goods increases, the purchasing power of assets decreases. The objective of investment planning is to generate returns in excess of inflation to ensure that the real value of assets does not erode. Unanticipated inflation is the main cause of purchasing power risk. Bonds held to maturity are likely to suffer from purchasing power risk because maturity values and coupon payments remain constant regardless of price changes.

Reinvestment Rate Risk

Reinvestment rate risk
A systematic risk in which earnings (cash flows) distributed from current investments cannot be reinvested at a rate of return equal to the expected yield of the current investments

Reinvestment rate risk is the risk that earnings (cash flows) distributed from current investments cannot be reinvested at a rate of return equal to the expected yield of the current investments. For example, if a bond purchased today yields 4% and market rates subsequently decline, interest payments from the bond cannot be reinvested at 4%; thus, the overall realized return will decline. Zero-coupon bonds (bonds that do not make regular periodic interest payments), are not subject to reinvestment rate risk during the term of the bond because payments are not made to the investor until maturity.

Interest Rate Risk

Interest rate risk
A systematic risk in which changes in interest rates affect the value of securities

The risk that changes in interest rates will affect the value of securities is known as **interest rate risk**. An inverse relationship exists between the value of fixed investments and changes in interest rates: as interest rates increase, the value of bonds decreases. Rising interest rates generally have a negative effect on stocks as well. Reasons for this negative pressure include the increased discount rate used for valuation of cash flows, increased borrowing costs for corporations (thus, an expectancy of lower earnings), and increased yields on alternative investments, such as bonds.

Market Risk

Market risk
A systematic risk describing the tendency of stocks to move in concert with the market

The tendency for securities to move in concert with the market is **market risk**. When the market is rising, stocks have a tendency to increase in value. Conversely, most stocks tend to fall with declines in the overall market. Often, a move in the market is prefaced by some change in the economic environment.

In addition, certain events, such as wars and economic collapse, could have a large impact on a client's portfolio. Forecasting and planning for these types of events may be difficult, but communicating their possibility over a long-term investment horizon is important for financial planners. If a sudden disruption in the market occurs, the financial planner should recommend that the client remain focused on the long term and avoid implementing financial decisions based solely on emotion.

Exchange Rate Risk (Foreign Currency Risk)

Exchange rate risk
A systematic risk due to the potential change in the relationship between the value of the dollar (or investor's currency) and the value of the foreign currency during the period of investment; also known as foreign currency risk

Exchange rate risk is the risk that a change in the relationship between the value of the dollar (or investor's currency) and the value of the foreign currency will occur during the period of investment. This risk affects investments in foreign stocks and bonds as well as domestic corporations that export products or import factors of production.

EXAMPLE John invests $1 million in the Orval Corporation based in Mexico. If the conversion rate for pesos to dollars is 10:1, John must invest 10 million pesos in Orval Corporation. Orval Corporation does extremely well, and John is able to sell his interest for 15 million pesos. If John attempts to convert the pesos into dollars when the exchange rate has changed to 12:1, he will receive $1,250,000 (15,000,000 ÷ 12).

This gain comprises a 50% (5,000,000 pesos) gain on the investment and a loss of 16.67% [(10 pesos per dollar ÷ 12 pesos per dollar) – 1], or $250,000, from the change in the currency rate. The net result is a 25% gain on the original investment; however, it is only half of the gain generated from the appreciation of Orval Corporation.

Unsystematic Risks

Unsystematic risks
Types of investment risks unique to a single company, industry, or country that can be eliminated by portfolio diversification

Unsystematic risks are unique to a single security, company, industry, or country and include default risk, business risk, financial risk, and country risk. Unlike systematic risk, these risks can be eliminated through diversification. Several studies have found that unsystematic risk declines significantly with a portfolio consisting of as few as 10 randomly chosen stocks. As more stocks are added to a portfolio, the losses of one company in the portfolio will have less impact on the total performance of the portfolio.

EXHIBIT 12.4 Total Portfolio Risk

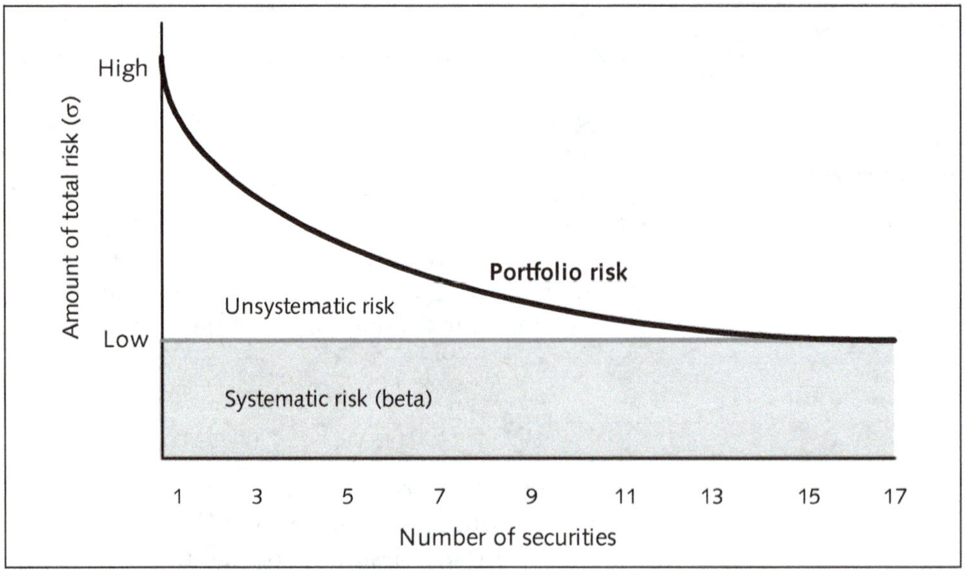

Exhibit 12.4 illustrates the concept of diversification. As more securities are added to the portfolio, the overall risk of the portfolio declines. There are several other points of interest. First, unsystematic risk can be reduced and effectively eliminated. This is not the case for systematic risk. Systematic risk cannot be eliminated because it represents the risk to all securities. Systematic risk is generally measured by beta, whereas total risk (systematic risk + unsystematic risk) is measured by standard deviation. For portfolios that have significantly reduced unsystematic risk, beta is a good measure of total risk. Conversely, when unsystematic risk is not reduced, beta does a poor job of estimating total risk.

Business Risk

Business risk
An unsystematic risk based on predictability of operating income for a specific business; dependent upon management and industry characteristics

Business risk, or the level of risk associated with the specific business, includes the speculative nature of the business, the management of the business, and the philosophy of the business. Different types of businesses will have different levels of risk. For instance, searching for oil is generally riskier than operating a grocery store; however, each has unique risks. Business risk is also related to the uncertainty of operating income. Utility companies have relatively stable and predictable income streams and, therefore, have lower business risk. Because cyclical companies, such as auto manufacturers, have unsteady or fluctuating operating income levels, they have higher business risk.

Financial Risk

Financial risk
An unsystematic risk based on the inclusion of debt in the capital structure of a firm, which affects the return on equity (ROE) for a company

Financial risk is based on the inclusion of debt in the capital structure of a firm. The decision to finance some of the firm's assets with debt creates additional risk which is absorbed by shareholders. Specifically, the use of debt magnifies the return on equity (ROE) and makes gains and losses more volatile.

EXAMPLE For example, a firm that is financed with 75% debt (25% equity) will have an ROE four times larger than a similar firm with the same net income and financed 100% with equity. This financial leverage occurs because the return is based on a smaller amount of equity. In this example, the equity of the leveraged company is one-fourth that of the nonleveraged firm, so that returns and losses for the leveraged firm will be four times larger on a percentage basis. Financial risk is associated with the liability side of the firm's balance sheet.

	Company A	Company B
Net income	$50,000	$50,000
Debt	$0	$300,000
Equity	$400,000	$100,000
ROE	12.5%	50%

Default Risk

Default risk
An unsystematic risk associated with the inability of a business to service its debt

The risk that a business will be unable to service its debt is **default risk**. Bonds issued by both corporations and municipalities are subject to default risk. Rating agencies, such as Moody's and Standard & Poor's, rate bonds issued by corporations and municipalities from the highest grade to default. Obligations of the U.S. government are considered free from default risk. In addition, equity investments are not subject to default risk.

Country Risk

Country risk
An unsystematic risk associated with the potential adverse effect of changes in a country's laws or political situation

International investments are subject to **country risk**, which is the unique risk associated with a particular country and the potential adverse effect of changes in a country's laws or its political situation. These risks include political and economic risks. The United States is generally thought to have the lowest country risk because its political and economic systems are the most stable. An investor is able to minimize country risk by investing in several countries in various parts of the world.

Liquidity and Marketability Risk

Liquidity
The ability to sell an investment quickly and at a competitive price, with no loss of principal and minimal price concession

Liquidity is the ability to sell an investment quickly and at a competitive price, with no loss of principal and minimal price concession. If the security markets do not have sufficient liquidity to absorb a trade, the trader may find that a price concession is necessary to execute the trade. **Marketability** refers to the ability of an investor to find a ready

Marketability
The ability of an investor to find a ready market where the investor may sell an investment to a willing buyer

market where the investor may sell an investment to a willing buyer. Real estate is marketable but may not be liquid. Treasury bills are both liquid and marketable. Liquidity and marketability may be realized as points along a continuum, with cash and cash equivalents being the most liquid and most marketable.

Tax Risk

Tax risk
The uncertainty associated with the tax laws that may impact the ownership and/or disposition of investment assets

Tax risk is the risk that taxation of investment gains or losses will adversely affect an investor's investment return. An investor must take into consideration how a country's tax laws may potentially affect the after-tax return of an investment.

Risk and Return

An investment's risk and expected return have a direct relationship. As the level of risk increases, the expected return increases. Meanwhile, as the level of risk declines, the expected return declines. Thus, to achieve higher returns, an investor must accept the trade-off of greater risk and typically more volatile returns.

Risk Tolerance

Risk tolerance
An estimate of the level of risk an investor is willing to accept within a portfolio

Risk tolerance is an estimate of the level of risk that an investor is willing to accept in a portfolio. Certain investors are unwilling to accept any risk, whereas others invest in only the riskiest securities. A planner estimates a client's tolerance for risk using two common methods. The first method is to develop a clear understanding of the client's investment preferences and investment history. This information provides a basis for determining how comfortable a client is with investments in equities, fixed-income securities, and other risky securities. The second method is to use a questionnaire designed to elicit the client's feelings about risky assets and their overall comfort level given certain changes in the portfolio. When combined, these two methods can guide the planner toward accurately assessing a client's risk tolerance.

INVESTMENT CHOICES

The level of risk and the specific risks investors must face greatly influence their choice of investments. Investors today have a wide variety of investment options, ranging from interest-bearing checking accounts to sophisticated derivatives. Although investments can be extremely complicated and risky, as in the case of derivatives, investments generally fall within one of two categories: lending investments or ownership investments.

Lending Investments

Savings accounts and bonds are examples of lending investments. When cash is deposited into a savings account, the owner has loaned money to the bank and will receive interest payments. The bank will then lend money to others in the form of mortgages or other debt instruments. Interest may be based on a fixed rate, or it may vary based on a variable-rate benchmark, such as the 90-day Treasury bill rate.

Bonds are more structured investments than savings accounts. Bonds have specific maturity dates, stated face values, and defined interest (coupon) payments. Although a savings account is, in effect, an indefinite loan, bonds have a specific maturity date. This date is the time at which the borrower (bond issuer) must repay the loan to the lender (bondholder).

Bonds generally have a par value (face value) of $1,000. Bond issuers compensate the bondholder by making specified interest payments. These interest payments, generally paid semiannually, are based on an interest rate called the coupon rate. A bond with a stated coupon rate of 4% will pay interest of $20 ($1,000 × 4% ÷ 2) twice per year for a total of $40 per year. These coupon payments continue for the life of the bond. Therefore, a 30-year bond will generally make 60 coupon payments. At the time the bond matures, the investor will receive the par value of the bond.

Bonds provide investors with a certain level of security because they generally make regular, specified payments to the bondholders. Many investors, especially retired individuals, rely on these coupon payments as a source of income.

Ownership Investments in Business (Common and Preferred Stock)

Ownership investments take the form of common or preferred stock. Common stockholders accept the risks inherent in owning a company. Although bondholders have a right to be repaid funds that were loaned, common stockholders have invested in the potential future profitability of the business. If the company is successful, the value of the common stock will increase. If the company is unsuccessful, then the value of the common stock will decline. Investors in common stock are rewarded for accepting risk in two ways. The first is through appreciation in the value of the stock. The second is from earnings that are paid to the shareholders in the form of dividends. A dividend is a payment made by the corporation to the shareholders as their share of the profits of the corporation.

Common stockholders assume more risk than bondholders because, in the event of bankruptcy, bondholders are paid before stockholders. Investors require higher returns for common stock to compensate for the increased risks associated with owning equity securities. In addition, equities tend to have more price volatility than bonds.

Preferred stock has the characteristics of both bonds and common stock. Similar to bonds, preferred stock generally pays a fixed payment, called a preferred stock dividend, which is determined as a percentage of the par value of the preferred stock. Preferred stock is valued similarly to bonds and is subject to many of the same risks as bonds. Some preferred stocks have mandatory redemption dates that occur 30 years or more after issuance; however, most bonds typically mature within 30 years. Some preferred stocks have no redemption features, similar to common stocks, and continue for the life of the company unless retired.

Ownership Investments in Real Estate

Real estate is another type of ownership asset that is valuable to investors. Stocks, bonds, money market securities, and derivatives are all intangible financial assets, whereas real estate is a tangible asset. Investments in real estate are characterized by the following attributes:

- Each parcel of land or real estate is unique in its location and composition
- Real estate is immovable
- Land is virtually indestructible
- Limited supply

An investor can choose from a variety of real estate investments, including residential real estate, commercial real estate, partnerships and limited partnerships, developed land, undeveloped land, and **real estate investment trusts** (REITs). REITs invest in real estate, short-term construction loans, and mortgages. Like closed-end companies, some REITs are publicly traded on the exchanges and can sell at premiums or discounts to net asset value. As a result, the REIT investor achieves diversification and marketability that is generally lacking with a real estate limited partnership. The advantages of investing in real estate include the generation of cash flow, depreciation deductions, and low correlation to other asset classes.

Real estate investment trust (REIT)
A form of indirect ownership of real estate that invests in real estate, short-term construction loans, and mortgages

Derivatives

Derivatives
Securities whose value is based on the value of some other security

Derivatives are securities whose value is based on the value of some other security. For example, an ABC option contract will derive its value from the value of ABC stock. Changes in the value of ABC stock will cause the associated option contract to also change in value.

Options

Options
Derivatives that give the holder, or buyer, the right to sell or purchase the underlying asset

Call option
A derivative that gives the holder the right to purchase the underlying asset, generally a stock, at a specified price within a specified period

Put option
A derivative that gives the holder the right to sell the underlying asset, generally a stock, at a specified price within a specified period

Options are derivatives that give the holder, or buyer, the right to sell or purchase the underlying asset. **Call options** give the holder the right to purchase the underlying asset, generally a stock, at a specified price within a specified period.

Put options give the holder the right to sell the underlying asset, generally a stock, at a specified price within a specified period. Options can be either bought or sold (also referred to as "written"). Therefore, there are four unique positions that an investor can take with an option: to buy a call option, to sell (write) a call option, to buy a put option, or to sell (write) a put option. However, investors will often combine multiple option positions or combine an option position with a stock position to create different risk-return characteristics.

Exercise price
The price at which an underlying stock may be sold (put) or purchased (call) by the holder of an option

Premium
The cost of an option contract

The **exercise price** of an option contract is the price at which the underlying stock may be sold (put) or purchased (call) by the holder of the option. The **premium** for any option is simply the cost of the option contract. The premium is generally impacted by the following factors: the price of the underlying security, the exercise price of the underlying security, the time until the option expires, the volatility of the underlying security, and the risk-free rate of return. Each option contract represents 100 shares of the underlying stock.

What are the reasons that an investor might enter into an option contract? As with most derivatives, options can be used for specific purposes or simply as a leveraged investment. Investors who believe that the underlying security is going to appreciate may purchase call options. Investors will generally sell call options when they believe that the underlying security is going to remain flat or decline in value. Often, when an investor is holding a long position in a stock that has appreciated rapidly within a short period of time, the investor will sell (write) a call option to generate the premium for additional income.

Put options are often purchased to establish a floor or to protect against a decline in the value of a long position in a stock. For example, an investor might own ABC stock and be concerned that it is overvalued. In this case, the investor might purchase a put option at a level slightly below the current market price. In the event that the stock decreased in value, the investor could sell the stock at the exercise price. In other words, a put option provides downside protection by establishing the minimum price at which the investor will be able to sell the ABC stock.

Put options can be sold by an investor to generate an option premium for a stock that the investor believes will increase in price and that he may own or wish to own. If the investor is correct and the stock does increase, the investor will receive the option premium as income. In the event that the stock goes down and someone puts the stock to the investor (forces the investor to purchase the stock), the investor probably will still believe that the stock was a good stock to own. A summary of the maximum economic gain and loss, with respect to basic option positions, is shown in Exhibit 12.5.

EXHIBIT 12.5 Options: Maximum Gain or Loss

Option Position	Maximum Gain	Maximum Loss
Buy Call	Unlimited	Amount of premium paid
Write Call	Amount of premium received	Unlimited (if naked)
Buy Put	Exercise price less amount of premium paid	Amount of premium paid
Write Put	Amount of premium received	Exercise price less amount of premium received

LEAPS

Long-term Equity Anticipation Securities (LEAPS)
Long-term options that generally have expiration dates of up to three years

Long-term Equity Anticipation Securities (LEAPS) are long-term options that allow investors to establish positions that can be maintained for up to three years. LEAPS provide investors with a longer term view of the market as a whole or on an individual stock. LEAPS can be purchased on a limited number of individual stocks and indexes. Equity LEAPS can provide long-term stock market investors an opportunity to benefit from the growth of large capitalization companies without having to directly purchase the stock.

Warrants

Warrants
A long-term, customized call option to purchase the stock of a given corporation within a specified period of time

Similar to a call option, a **warrant** is essentially a long-term call option giving the owner the right to purchase the stock of the issuing corporation. Warrants give the owner the right to purchase a specified number of common stock shares for a specified period of time at a specified price. A warrant has the following characteristics which differentiate it from a call option:

- A warrant is issued by a corporation, whereas a call is written by an investor
- A warrant is customized to fit the needs of the issuing corporation and owner, whereas a call includes standardized terms
- A warrant typically has a maturity date of at least several years, whereas a call generally has an expiry date of no more than nine months

If corporations issue warrants, they usually do so in conjunction with a new bond issue or preferred stock issue. These warrants give the bond or stock purchaser a sweetener or equity kicker, making the particular issue more attractive to buyers. As a result, issuing the bond or preferred stock with a warrant will typically permit the issuer to lower the coupon or dividend rate on the offering.

Futures

Futures contract
An agreement between two parties to make or take delivery of a specified amount of a commodity or financial asset at a future time, place, and unit price

Unlike options, which give the holder a right to purchase or sell a specific security, a **futures contract** is an agreement to transact something in the future. Generally, purchasing (selling) a futures contract obligates the buyer (seller) to take delivery (make delivery) of a specific commodity at a specific time in the future. Because a futures contract is an agreement to make or take delivery in the future, the investor will be required to put up a good faith deposit, known as an initial margin, until the agreement is fulfilled.

Over time, the futures contract, which is required to be marked to the market on a daily basis, will generate gains and losses. Each of these daily gains and losses will either add to or reduce the initial margin. If the initial amount put up is reduced to a level below the maintenance margin, the investor will be required to restore the initial margin. Both the initial margin percentage and the maintenance margin amount are set at the inception of the contract.

Speculators and hedgers use futures contracts for different reasons. Speculators use futures contracts as a leveraged investment. Government studies have suggested that approximately 90% of individual investors who speculate in futures lose money. The majority of these investors invest in futures contracts only once. Unlike speculators, hedgers use futures contracts to reduce or offset certain risks.

For example, farmers who sell commodities, such as cotton, are concerned about decreasing commodity prices. To offset this risk, farmers can sell futures contracts to ensure that the cotton produced sells at a specific price. This type of hedge, referred to as a short hedge, protects against decreasing prices.

Other investors who hedge using futures contracts include manufacturers who use commodities as raw material. For example, if a furniture manufacturer is concerned about rising lumber prices, the manufacturer might purchase lumber futures contracts to lock in the price at which he will buy lumber in the future. This type of hedge, referred to as a long hedge, protects against rising prices. The following table summarizes the two types of hedge positions.

Hedger	Cash Position	Hedge Needed	Action
Grower	Long	Short	Sell futures contracts
Manufacturer	Short	Long	Buy futures contracts

In general, derivatives provide investors with a variety of speculative and hedging strategies that would not be available using traditional investment alternatives and allow for a more complete market.

Tangible Assets

These investments take the form of either collectibles or, sometimes, precious metals (e.g., gold or silver). Collectibles (e.g., baseball cards) may provide the dual benefits of maintaining a collection and possible capital appreciation. However, the collectibles market is inefficient and is characterized by an inherent lack of liquidity. Alternatively, precious metals derive their value from factors that are external to the financial markets (e.g., with the purchase of gold, an investor's fear of inflation). As a result, the price of precious metals often moves inversely (i.e., has a negative correlation) with the prices of stocks. Therefore, investing in gold bullion or silver may be used as a hedge against a declining, or bearish, stock market.

Natural Resources

An investment in natural resources includes an investment in oil and gas properties or timber lands. There are three ways to invest in natural resources:

- Direct investing in the properties or lands via (typically) a limited partnership
- Investing in the stock of companies who develop the natural resources
- Investing in mutual funds that specialize in natural resources

A major advantage of investing in natural resources is the pass-through of certain tax benefits, such as deductions for depletion and/or intangible drilling costs. Natural resources also have historically exhibited some negative correlation with that of financial assets (stocks and bonds). However, a major disadvantage of such an investment is the higher degree of risk, particularly if the activity involves exploratory drilling for oil wells.

MEASURES OF RISK

We defined risk earlier in the chapter as the probability of an adverse result. In the field of investments and financial planning, risk is generally measured in terms of volatility.

Beta

Beta
A commonly used measure of systematic risk that is derived from regression analysis

Beta is a commonly used measure of risk derived from comparing the return variability of the market to the return variability of an investment. Beta measures systematic risk and provides an indication of the volatility of a portfolio compared to the market. The market is defined as having a beta of 1.0. Portfolios with a beta greater than 1.0 are more volatile than the market, whereas portfolios with a beta less than 1.0 are less volatile than the market. A portfolio with a beta of 1.5 is considered to be 50% more volatile than the market. Similarly, a portfolio with a beta of 0.7 is considered to be 30% less volatile than the market.

Because beta only measures systematic risk, it is a good measure of risk for fully diversified portfolios. Diversified portfolios have minimal unsystematic risk, which means that beta is capturing the majority of the risk of the portfolio. However, when the diversification of the portfolio is low and the portfolio has a substantial amount of unsystematic risk, beta does not capture all of the volatility within the portfolio. Beta is more appropriate for portfolios and mutual funds that are well-diversified and, therefore, highly correlated to the market.

Standard Deviation

Standard deviation
Measures both total volatility and total risk (systematic and unsystematic risk) of the portfolio

Unlike beta, **standard deviation** measures a portfolio's total risk (volatility). Standard deviation is a statistical measure of how far actual returns deviate from the mean (average) return.

Normal Probability Distribution

A normal probability distribution is characterized by a single peak in the center, which is the location of the arithmetic mean of the series of observations. The series of observations, normally referred to as a bell curve, implies a 50% chance that an observation selected at random will fall to the right of the mean and a 50% chance that it will fall to the left of the mean. A bell curve is illustrated in Exhibit 12.6.

EXHIBIT 12.6 Normal Probability Distribution

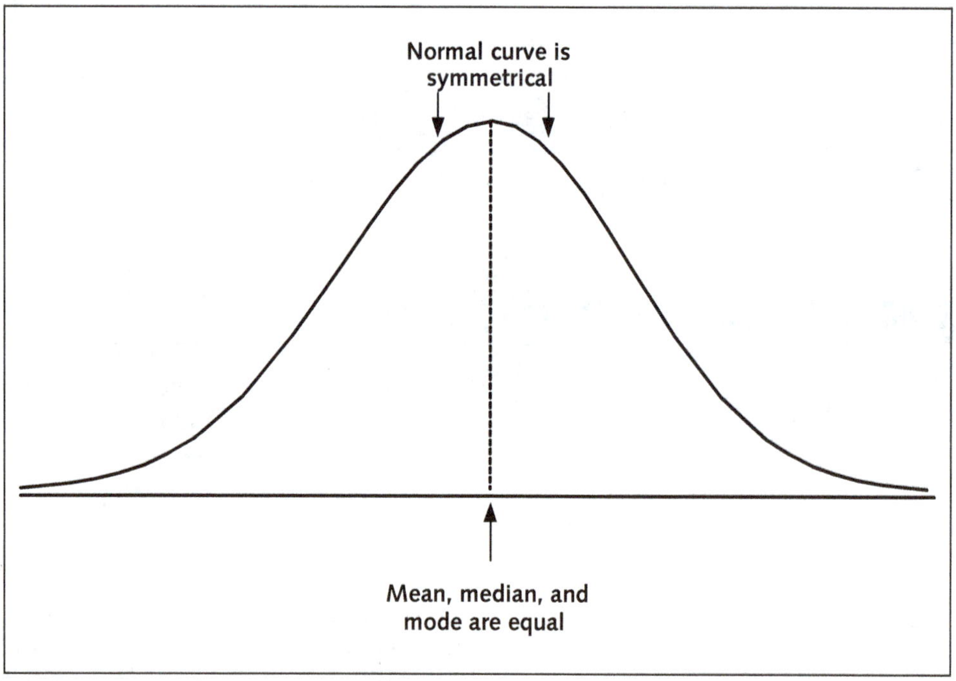

EXHIBIT 12.7 Area Under the Curve

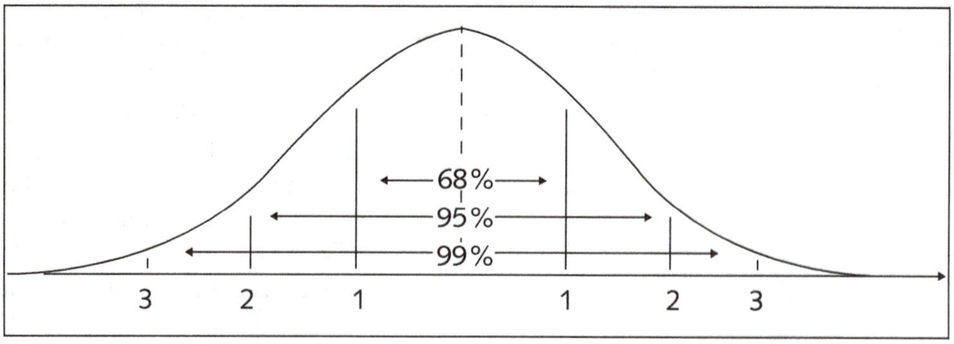

When interpreting standard deviation, a return (observation) will occur 68% of the time within one standard deviation of the mean, 95% of the time within two standard deviations of the mean, and 99% of the time within three standard deviations of the mean as shown in Exhibit 12.7. Returns falling outside of three standard deviations are considered outliers.

Semivariance
Measures the variability of returns that fall below the average or expected return

Semivariance

Semivariance is another statistical measure of risk. In contrast to standard deviation, semivariance only considers the downside risk of an investment. Specifically, semivariance measures the variability of returns that fall below the average or expected return.

Critics of standard deviation state that investors do not complain, nor are they concerned, about volatility above the average return. Rather, investors are only concerned about volatility below the average return. Therefore, a portfolio manager with a large standard deviation may be punished for having superior positive returns. Semivariance attempts to correct for this perceived flaw by only considering returns and volatility below the expected or average return.

MEASURES OF RETURN

Financial advisors and planners use a variety of measures of return, including, but not limited to, holding period return, arithmetic mean, geometric mean, internal rate of return, and real rate of return. Each of these calculations of return has certain advantages and disadvantages.

Simple rate of return
Calculated by dividing the total return by the number of years invested

Simple Rate of Return

A **simple rate of return** for an investment is calculated by dividing its total return (income earned plus capital appreciation divided by the original investment) by the number of years that the investor has held the asset. This computation results in an annualized noncompounded rate of return.

EXAMPLE Eugene owned an investment that generated a total return of 25% over the past five years. His simple rate of return is 5% (25% ÷ 5).

Compound rate of return
Assumes the interim proceeds are reinvested over the holding period and is usually calculated by using a financial calculator.

Compound Rate of Return

The **compound rate of return** computation for an investment assumes that all interim proceeds, such as interest and repayment of principal, are reinvested (thereby generating additional return) over the holding period. This return is easily calculated with a financial calculator using the time-value-of-money keys or the uneven-cash-flow and net-present-value keys.

EXAMPLE Allison deposits $1,000 in a one-year CD that pays an annual interest rate of 3% compounded monthly. She will have a total of $1,030.42 ($1,000 +/–PV; 1 × 12 N; 3 I/YR; solve for FV) in her account at the end of the year. Therefore, Allison's compound rate of return is 3.04% ($1,000 +/–PV; $1,030.42 FV; 1 N; solve for I/YR).

Annual percentage rate
The yearly cost of funds expressed as a percentage.

Annual Percentage Rate and Effective Annual Rate

The nominal **annual percentage rate (APR)** is the yearly cost of funds expressed as a percentage. However, the nominal APR does not take compounding into consideration. If a lender advertises a 1.25% monthly rate, the APR is 15% (1.25% × 12).

The **effective annual rate (EAR)** is the annual percentage rate taking into consideration the impact of compounding. This calculation provides the annual rate of interest of an investment or debt when compounding occurs more than once per year.

$$EAR = [1 + (i \div n)]^n - 1$$

i = annual interest rate
n = number of periods

If an investor has a certificate of deposit paying monthly interest based on annual rate of 1.75%, the effective annual rate will be more than 1.75% due to the effect of compounding. This is a result of a greater principal onto which the interest is calculated each month. The resulting effective annual rate is 1.77%.

EXAMPLE Janine carries a balance on her credit card. The nominal APR is 14.99% compounded daily. The effective annual rate is actually 16.17%, calculated as follows:

$$EAR = [1 + (.1499 \div 365)]^{365} - 1 = .1617, \text{ or } \mathbf{16.17\%}$$

Holding Period Return

Holding period return
Measures the total return an investor receives over a specific time period

The **holding period return** (HPR) measures the total return an investor receives from an investment over a specific time period.

$$HPR = \frac{\text{ending value of investment} - \text{beginning value of investment} +/- \text{cash flows}}{\text{beginning value of investment}}$$

EXAMPLE Glen purchased a stock for $50 per share. Later, he sells the stock for $75 per share. During his period of ownership, the stock paid dividends of $10. The holding period return equals 70% as follows:

$$HPR = \frac{\$75 - \$50 + \$10}{\$50} = 70\%$$

Is 70% an acceptable return? At first, you might think that a 70% return is great. However, we have no idea how long the investment was held. Therefore, there is no way to compare an HPR to other alternative investments, such as the risk-free rate of return. Because the HPR ignores the time value of money, it is not commonly used as a return measure.

Arithmetic Mean

Arithmetic mean
A measure of investment return that is the result of averaging periodic returns

The **arithmetic mean** is a measure of investment return that is the result of averaging periodic returns.

EXAMPLE Assume a client had the following returns for four consecutive years:

Year	Return
1	12%
2	3%
3	10%
4	15%

The arithmetic mean equals 10%, calculated as follows:

$$AM = \frac{12\% + 3\% + 10\% + 15\%}{4} = 10\%$$

Geometric Mean

Geometric mean
A method of calculating the internal rate of return based on periodic rates of return

The **geometric mean** is a method of calculating the internal rate of return based on periodic rates of return.

EXAMPLE Assume a client had the following returns for four consecutive years (same example as above):

Year	Return
1	12%
2	3%
3	10%
4	15%

The geometric mean equals 9.91%, calculated as follows:

PV = –1

FV = (1 + .12)(1 + .03)(1 + .10)(1 + .15) = 1.4593

n = 4

Solve for i = 9.91%

Using the same series of returns (12%, 3%, 10%, and 15%) has resulted in a different outcome for the arithmetic mean and the geometric mean. This difference is a result of the geometric mean taking into consideration the compounding of the investment returns over time.

In this case, the geometric mean is less than the arithmetic mean. Will this always be the case? No, but the geometric mean will always be less than or equal to the arithmetic mean. They will be equal only when the periodic returns are identical. The difference between the two measures will increase as the volatility in returns increases.

EXAMPLE John invests $100 at the beginning of the year. At the end of the year, his investment is worth $200. At the end of the following year, his investment is worth $100. The returns for the two years are as follows:

Year	Beginning of the Year	End of the Year	Rate of Return
1	$100	$200	100%
2	$200	$100	–50%

The arithmetic mean equals 25%, calculated as follows:

$$AM = \frac{100\% - 50\%}{2} = 25\%$$

The geometric mean equals 0.00%, calculated as follows:

PV = –$100
FV = $100
n = 2
i = 0%

Obviously, a big difference exists between a 25% return and a 0% return. Therefore, the arithmetic mean is not as practical for evaluating investment returns as the geometric mean.

Internal Rate of Return

Internal rate of return
A measure of return that equates discounted future cash flows to the present value of an asset

Internal rate of return (IRR) is one of the most common measures of return. This measure equates discounted future cash flows to the present value of an asset. Consider the basic present value model:

$$PV = \frac{CF_1}{(1+r)^1} + \frac{CF_2}{(1+r)^2} + \cdots + \frac{CF_n}{(1+r)^n}$$

PV = Present value of future cash flows

CF_n = Cash flows for period n

n = Number of cash flows in the analysis

r = Internal rate of return

An important assumption of this model is that any cash flows that occur before the end of the investment will be reinvested at the IRR. If these cash flows are not reinvested at the IRR, the actual return received will be different than expected.

EXAMPLE A bond selling at par ($1,000) with an annual coupon rate of 10% (coupon payments of $100) will have an IRR of 10%. If the annual coupon payments of $100 are reinvested at a rate of return of 10%, the actual return received by the investor will be 10%. However, if the coupon payments are invested at a rate of return less (or greater) than 10%, the actual return the investor receives will be less (or greater) than 10%. This is an example of reinvestment rate risk.

Real Rate of Return

Nominal return
The stated return from an investment

Real rate of return
The nominal rate of return adjusted for inflation

As discussed earlier in the chapter, inflation erodes returns and the purchasing power of assets. Therefore, financial planners should understand both nominal returns and real returns. The **nominal return** is the stated return from the investment. The **real rate of return**, sometimes referred to as the inflation-adjusted rate of return, is the nominal return adjusted for inflation.

$$\text{Real return} = \left[\frac{(1+R_n)}{(1+I)} - 1\right] \times 100$$

R_n = nominal rate of return

I = rate of inflation

EXAMPLE Renee owns a corporate bond with a coupon rate of 6.00%. If the annual inflation rate is 3.5%, her real rate of return on the bond is 2.42%, calculated as follows:

$$\left[\frac{(1+0.06)}{(1+0.035)}-1\right]\times 100=(1.0242-1)\times 100=2.4155 \text{ (rounded to 2.42)}$$

MODERN PORTFOLIO THEORY

The familiar adage, "Don't put all your eggs in one basket" reminds us that it is safer to spread your risk around than to concentrate in one area. This simple truth is especially applicable to investing. Investors diversify risk by investing in more than one security and more than one asset class. Through diversification, investors are able to reduce the risk of their investment portfolios. Diversification involves the acquisition of assets that have different risk characteristics in order to mitigate portfolio risk.

Modern portfolio theory (MPT)
A theory created by Harry Markowitz that describes portfolio diversification gained by combining securities with varying characteristics

The reason diversification works is that unsystematic risks can be minimized by adding additional securities to the portfolio. Similarly, adding additional asset classes to a portfolio can minimize or reduce the unique risks associated with a specific asset class.

Modern portfolio theory (MPT) is based on this diversification process. Harry Markowitz, considered the father of MPT, developed this theory using the following assumptions:

- Investors consider each investment opportunity as being represented by a probability distribution of expected returns over a specified holding period
- Investors estimate the risk of the portfolio on the basis of the variability of returns
- Investors base decisions solely on expected return and risk; therefore, their indifference curves are a function of expected return and the expected variance of returns only
- Investors base their indifference to alternative investments on the maximization of wealth over a specified period, and this indifference diminishes as they get beyond this period
- For a given level of risk, investors prefer higher returns to lower returns

Efficient Frontier

Efficient frontier
Consists of investment portfolios with the highest expected return for a given level of risk

Markowitz found that by combining different asset classes and varying the weightings of each asset class, he could create portfolios that had higher returns with less volatility (risk). Markowitz used standard deviation (σ) as a measure of risk. The portfolios that had the highest expected return [E(r)] for the given level of risk referred to as efficient portfolios. By combining these efficient portfolios, he created the **efficient frontier**.

EXHIBIT 12.8 The Efficient Frontier

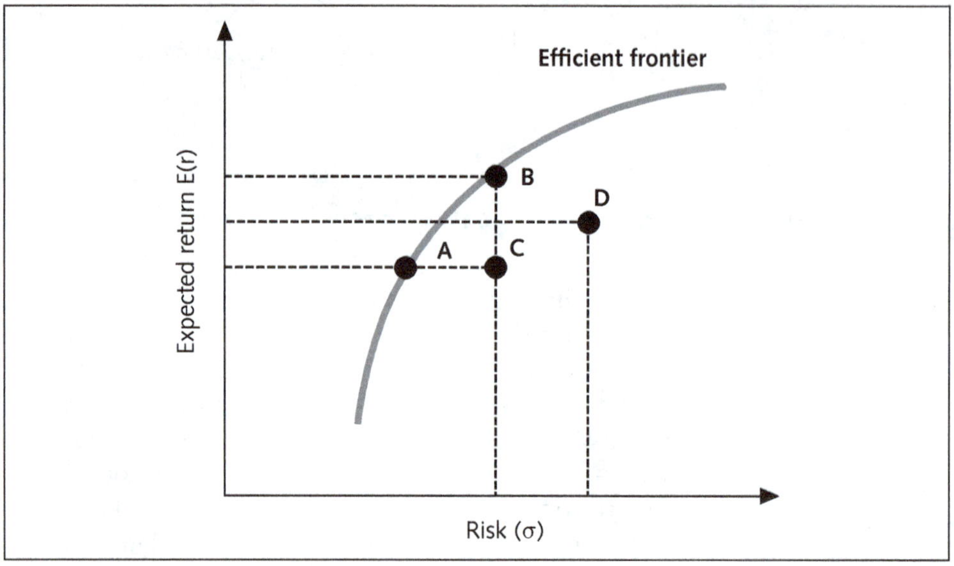

The efficient frontier consists of portfolios with the highest expected return for a given level of risk. Notice in Exhibit 12.8 above that only portfolios A and B are efficient portfolios. Portfolio A is more efficient than Portfolio C because it has the same expected return with less risk. Portfolio B is more efficient than Portfolio C because it has a much higher expected return for the same level of risk. Portfolio B is also more efficient than Portfolio D because B has a higher expected return and less risk. Markowitz came up with the following three rules for choosing efficient portfolios:

- For any two portfolios with the same expected return, choose the one with the lower risk
- For any two portfolios with the same risk, choose the one with the higher expected return
- Choose any portfolio that has a higher expected return and lower risk

Portfolios C and D are inefficient because they have not maximized the return for a given level of risk. Portfolios do not exist above the efficient frontier because the efficient frontier consists of the most efficient portfolios (portfolios of assets with the highest expected return for a given level of risk).

Each risk-averse investor (a fundamental assumption of modern portfolio theory) will choose to establish a portfolio lying somewhere on this efficient frontier by implementing her own set of indifference curves. **Indifference curves**, which graphically represent the risk-reward trade-off that the investor is willing to make, will cross the efficient frontier in two locations, lie tangent to the efficient frontier, or not intersect the efficient frontier at all. The portfolio that lies at the point of tangency is the optimal portfolio for the investor. The efficient frontier, investor's indifference curves, and an optimal portfolio are illustrated in Exhibit 12.9.

Indifference curves
A graphical representation of the risk-reward trade-off that an investor is willing to make

EXHIBIT 12.9 Indifference Curves

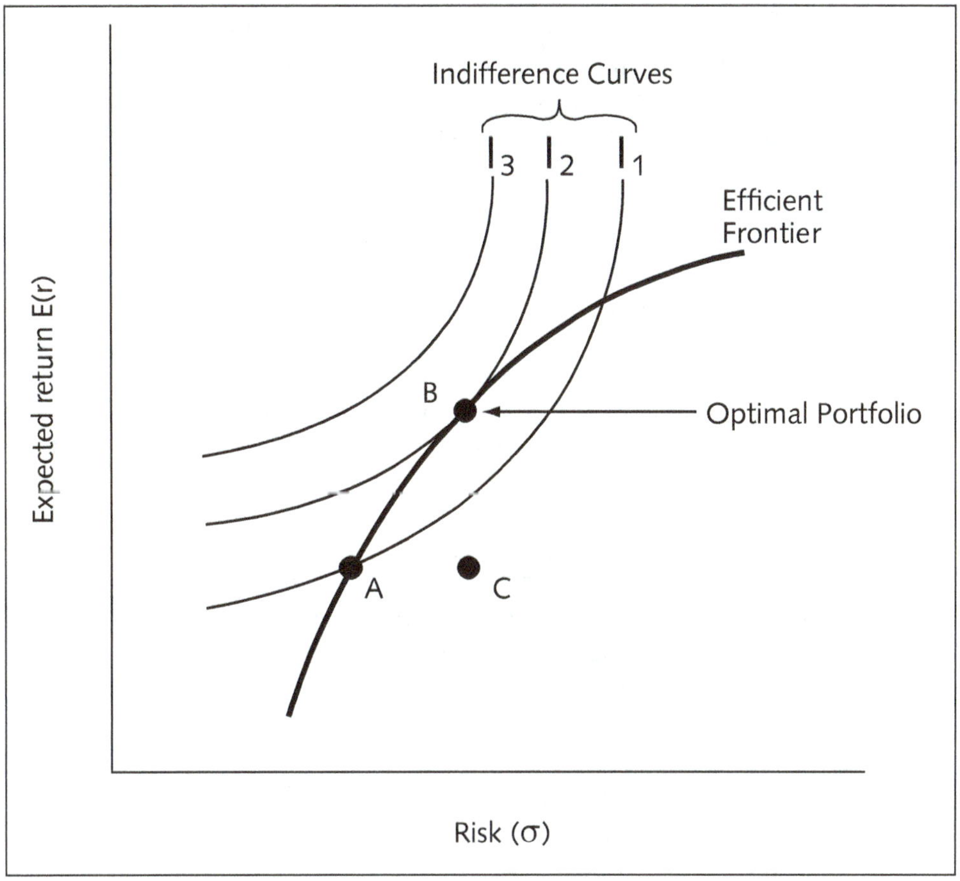

Markowitz developed a model to estimate the efficient frontier by using security standard deviations, correlation coefficients, and expected returns in calculating the standard deviation of a multiasset portfolio and the expected return of a portfolio.

These calculations are the foundation for most of the asset allocation software packages used by financial planners. The purpose of these software packages is to build an investment portfolio capable of accomplishing the goals of the client, while matching the level of risk in the portfolio to the investor's risk tolerance. Most financial planners who provide investment counseling use some type of mean-variance optimization software to determine an optimum portfolio or asset allocation based on a client's goals, risk tolerance, time horizon, tax situation, and economic forecasts.

The goal in using these software packages is to build an efficient portfolio for the client. Remember that an efficient portfolio is one that has the highest level of return (in practice, the return should be an after-tax return) for the given level of risk.

Capital Asset Pricing Model

Capital asset pricing model (CAPM)
An asset pricing model that developed from Markowitz's efficient frontier and from the introduction of a risk-free asset

The **capital asset pricing model** (CAPM) is an asset pricing model that was developed from Markowitz's efficient frontier and from the introduction of a risk-free asset.

$$r_i = r_f + (r_m - r_f)\beta_i$$

r_i = expected return for a stock
r_m = market rate of return
r_f = risk-free rate of return
β_i = beta, measures systematic risk of a particular stock

This model is actually made up of two separate components. One component is known as the *stock risk premium* and is the part of the model reflected by the following formula: $(r_m - r_f)\beta_i$, where r_m is the market return, r_f is the risk-free return, and β_i is the beta coefficient of the stock. The other component is the *market risk premium* and is the part of the model reflected by the following formula: $r_m - r_f$, where r_m is the market return and r_f is the risk-free return. The stock risk premium may compel the individual to invest in a particular stock, whereas the market risk premium provides incentive to invest in the securities market in general. The CAPM accounts for the impact of systematic risk only and does not take into consideration unsystematic risk, which is assumed to have been diversified away.

Finally, as a part of MPT, the major contribution of the CAPM to investment theory was the creation of a quantitative investment risk measure and a statistical association with the investment's rate of return. Specifically, the CAPM allows analysts to compute the required rate of return for an investment and compare it to the expected rate of return for that investment. For example, if the CAPM required rate of return is higher than the investment's expected rate of return, all other investment considerations being equal, the investment should not be made. Conversely, if the CAPM required rate of return is lower than the investment's expected rate of return, a decision to invest is warranted.

As you recall from the discussion of Markowitz, any portfolio that lies on the efficient frontier is considered an efficient portfolio, and thus, it has the highest level of return for the given level of risk. However, by introducing a risk-free asset (r_f), a new set of portfolios can be created that is more efficient than the Markowitz efficient frontier. Exhibit 12.10 illustrates this concept.

EXHIBIT 12.10 Capital Market Line

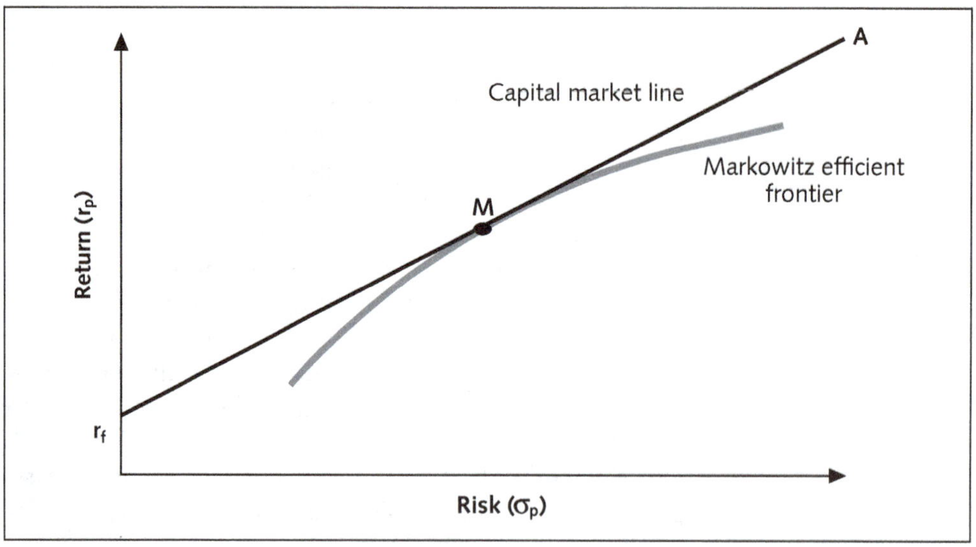

The capital market line (CML) is the new efficient frontier. However, instead of providing a maximum return, as did the efficient frontier of Markowitz, the CML provides an expected return based on the level of risk. The equation for the CML is written as follows:

$$r_p = r_f + \sigma_p \left[\frac{r_m - r_f}{\sigma_m} \right]$$

r_p = expected return of the portfolio
r_f = risk-free rate of return
r_m = market rate of return
σ_m = standard deviation of the market
σ_p = standard deviation of the portfolio

The CML provides an expected return for a portfolio based on the expected return of the market, the risk-free rate of return, and the standard deviation of the portfolio in relation to the standard deviation of the market. The CML is generally used to evaluate diversified portfolios. The security market line (SML), which is derived from the CML and is the same as the CAPM, allows us to evaluate individual securities for use in a diversified portfolio.

The SML is written as follows:

$$r_i = r_f + (r_m - r_f)\beta_i$$

r_i = expected return for asset *i*
r_f = risk-free rate of return
r_m = market rate of return
β_i = beta of asset *i*

The security market line determines the expected return for an asset (r_i) on the basis of its beta and the expectations about the market and the risk-free rate.

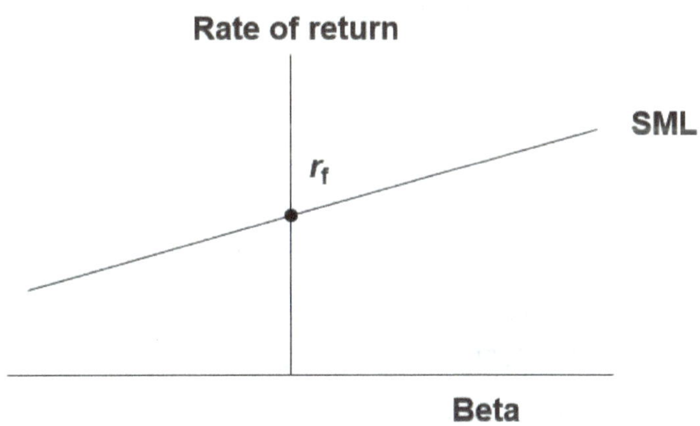

EXAMPLE If the beta of ABC Company is 1.2 and the market return is expected to be 13% with a risk-free return of 3%, then the expected return of ABC is 15%, as follows:

$r_i = r_f + (r_m - r_f)\beta_i$

$r_i = 0.03 + 1.2\ (0.13 - 0.03) = 0.15$, or 15%

Therefore, on the basis of the level of systematic risk of ABC Company, the stock should earn a return of 15%. The SML helps identify how the characteristics of a portfolio will be impacted when a security is added to the portfolio.

Asset Allocation

Asset allocation
The distribution of investments in a portfolio by asset class

The primary purpose of a modern portfolio theory approach is to determine an efficient allocation for an investor's portfolio based on the goals of the client and tolerance for risk. An **asset allocation** is the specific distribution of investment asset classes within a portfolio. By including a target asset allocation in an Investment Policy Statement (IPS), the financial planner presents an investor with a guide as to how much of the portfolio should be invested in each asset class. Exhibit 12.11 illustrates three possible asset allocations: one for a conservative investor, one for a moderate investor, and one for an aggressive investor.

EXHIBIT 12.11 Sample Asset Allocations

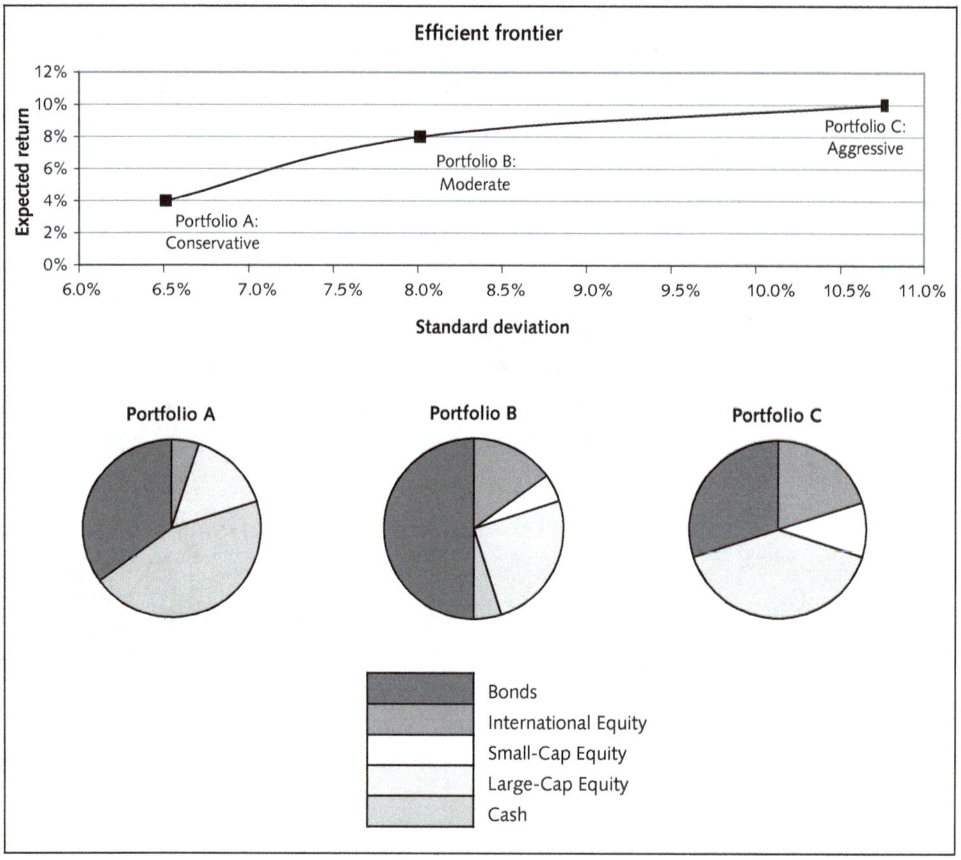

Strategic Asset Allocation

The purpose of strategic asset allocation is to determine an appropriate allocation based on the long-term financial goals of the client. Accordingly, the risk tolerance of the client is assessed in conjunction with the current phase of the client's life cycle. When implementing a strategic asset allocation, once the allocation is determined, it remains constant until (typically) some life-changing event occurs. Because the investment performance of the selected asset classes is different, rebalancing must take place to bring the portfolio in line with the strategic mix. However, changing market conditions play a small role in determining the appropriate asset mix.

Tactical Asset Allocation

In contrast to the strategic approach, tactical asset allocation (TAA) continuously adjusts the asset allocation and class mix in an attempt to take advantage of changing market conditions and overall investor sentiment. When implementing a TAA, portfolio adjustments are driven solely by perceived changes in the market values of the asset classes, and little consideration is given to the long-term financial goals of the client. In essence, TAA is a market timing portfolio management approach that is intended to take advantage of perceived market inefficiencies (and opportunities for investor profit).

Selection of a Type of Asset Allocation

The type of asset allocation to use likely depends on the investor's or manager's portfolio management style. Certainly, an investor or manager who believes in active portfolio management (and that the market is inherently inefficient) will tend towards tactical asset allocation. Alternatively, an investor or manager who adopts more of a long-term buy-and-hold strategy (passive management style) will find strategic asset allocation to be preferable. Above all, a thoughtful analysis of these asset allocation techniques, that accounts for both one's time horizon and investment preferences, serves as a key factor impacting long-term portfolio performance and, therefore, is of the highest importance to financial planners, managers, and investors.

Asset Allocation Using Mutual Funds

Research (by Brinson, Hood, Beebower, 1986, and Vanguard, 2003) has shown that asset allocation is the most important factor in determining long-term variability of (risk) portfolio returns. According to their studies, asset allocation may account for more than 90% of such variation. Obviously, asset allocation is an important facet of the investment planning process. How, then, can mutual funds be used in implementing such an asset allocation strategy?

Early in the investment planning process, the financial planner, together with the client, identifies the client's goals, objectives, and risk tolerance. Once these have been determined, the planner will often help the client select an appropriate asset allocation. In other words, the planner assists the client in determining what portion of the client's assets should be invested in cash, fixed-income investments, equity investments, real estate, international investments, and so on. The asset allocation decision usually involves a narrowing process, in which the allocation to fixed-income investments is separated into municipal (tax-free) versus taxable and an appropriate average duration is chosen. Similarly, the equity portion of the portfolio will be subdivided into core, value, and growth investment styles and then separated into large, mid, and small capitalization equities. International investments are generally separated into large capitalization or emerging markets and could be divided into different regions or countries around the world.

EXAMPLE James and Stacey, ages 40 and 37, respectively, would like to develop an investment plan for their retirement. Assume that after evaluating the timing of their goal and through discussions with them, their financial planner classifies them as moderately aggressive investors. Also, assume that an appropriate asset allocation for them is a portfolio that is 80% equity (60% domestic equities and 20% foreign equities) and 20% fixed-income investments, with no allocation to cash or money markets. The allocation might be further divided as shown in the following table.

Equities		Fixed Income	
Large-cap value	10%	Taxable fixed income	8%
Large-cap core	20%	Municipal fixed income	8%
Large-cap growth	10%	Foreign fixed income	4%
Mid-cap growth	10%		
Small-cap growth	10%		
Large-cap foreign	20%		
Total equity allocation	80%	Total fixed-income allocation	20%

The above asset allocation provides James and Stacey with an investment portfolio that is heavily weighted toward equity investments. This equity allocation is divided between domestic and foreign and between large, mid, and small capitalization securities. The fixed-income allocation is also divided between domestic and foreign, as well as taxable and municipal (nontaxable).

Once the asset allocation decision has been made, mutual funds can be used as the vehicle to implement the investment plan. Planners and investors should select mutual funds that are consistent with the concepts and underlying assumptions of the asset allocation process. Specifically, an asset allocation for a client's portfolio should be derived through a **mean-variance optimization model** to determine the highest level of return (based on combinations of asset classes and different weightings of asset classes) for a specified level of risk. This level of risk is generally the client's risk level or risk tolerance.

Mean-variance optimization model *Used to determine the highest level of return (based on combinations of asset classes and different weightings of asset classes) for a specified level of risk tolerance*

A mean-variance optimization model generally uses all of the following inputs for each asset class represented in the model:

- Historical return or expected return for each asset class
- Standard deviation of each asset class (historical or expected)
- Correlation coefficients (historical or expected) for each asset class compared to all other asset classes

Most of the time, these inputs for the asset classes are derived from indexes that represent the asset class. For example, the large-cap equity asset class is usually represented by the S&P 500 Index. Small-cap equities are often represented by the Russell 2000® Index, and fixed-income securities may be represented by one of the J.P. Morgan Indices.

Because the assumptions used in the model are derived from indexes, selected funds should have characteristics consistent with the index they are representing. This means that if there is an allocation to the large-cap growth-asset class, then the fund selected to represent this asset class should have risk and return characteristics consistent with that index. However, this does not mean that index funds are the only choice for implementing an asset allocation strategy because all highly correlated funds deserve investment consideration.

As with all facets of financial planning, the investment planning process is not complete at implementation. The portfolio selections and allocations must be monitored on a continual basis to ensure that the quality of the investments has not changed and that the allocations and risk tolerance of the client have not significantly changed. This monitoring process generally includes quarterly, semiannual, or annual performance measurement reports and subsequent client meetings.

An investment performance report should include sufficient information to determine whether the investment portfolio has performed as intended and what, if any, changes should be made to the investment portfolio. The report should indicate the return for the overall portfolio, as well as the return for each asset class. These returns should be reported for the recent quarter and the past year, three-year, and five-year periods (if available). Each of these returns should be compared to an appropriate benchmark to determine the performance of the fund or investment.

In addition to return information, performance reports should provide the investor with information about the risk characteristics of the overall portfolio. This includes measures for standard deviation and, possibly, beta.

DIVERSIFICATION

As previously discussed, the goal of diversification is to reduce unsystematic risk within a portfolio. Diversification is achieved by structuring an individual's investment portfolio with an appropriate combination of aggressive, moderate, and conservative investments.

Covariance

Covariance
A measure of the extent to which two variables move in a predictable manner to one another, either positively or negatively

Covariance, which is a nonstandardized version of the correlation coefficient, measures the extent to which two variables move in a predictable manner to one another, either positively or negatively. If two assets move together simultaneously, either up or down, they have perfect positive covariance. Conversely, if the assets move exactly opposite one another, they exhibit perfect negative covariance. Finally, if the assets move in completely independent directions, their covariance is zero. The range for covariance is negative infinity to positive infinity. A drawback of covariance is that there are no boundaries within which to measure the relationship between two stocks. The concept of covariance is the key to minimizing the standard deviation of an overall portfolio and, therefore, managing risk.

Correlation Coefficient

Correlation coefficient (R)
A statistical measure of the direction and strength of the relationship between two sets of data

The **correlation coefficient**, generally denoted by the symbol **R**, is a statistical measure generated from a regression analysis that provides insight into the relationship between two securities, two portfolios, or two indexes. The correlation coefficient indicates the direction of the relationship between the two indexes or securities and the strength between the two items. The correlation coefficient ranges between +1.0 and –1.0. At +1.0, there is perfect positive correlation between the two items. In other words, the two items will move together over time. At –1.0, there is perfect negative correlation between the two items. The two items will move in opposite directions over time. At a correlation of zero, there is no relationship between the two items and they will move independent of each other. Exhibit 12.12 depicts these relationships.

The correlation coefficient is key to the concept of asset allocation. When the correlation coefficient between two asset classes is less than 1.0, combining the asset classes will reduce the overall risk of the investment portfolio. The lower the correlation, the lower the standard deviation of the combined portfolio and, therefore, the lower the risk.

EXHIBIT 12.12 Correlation Coefficient

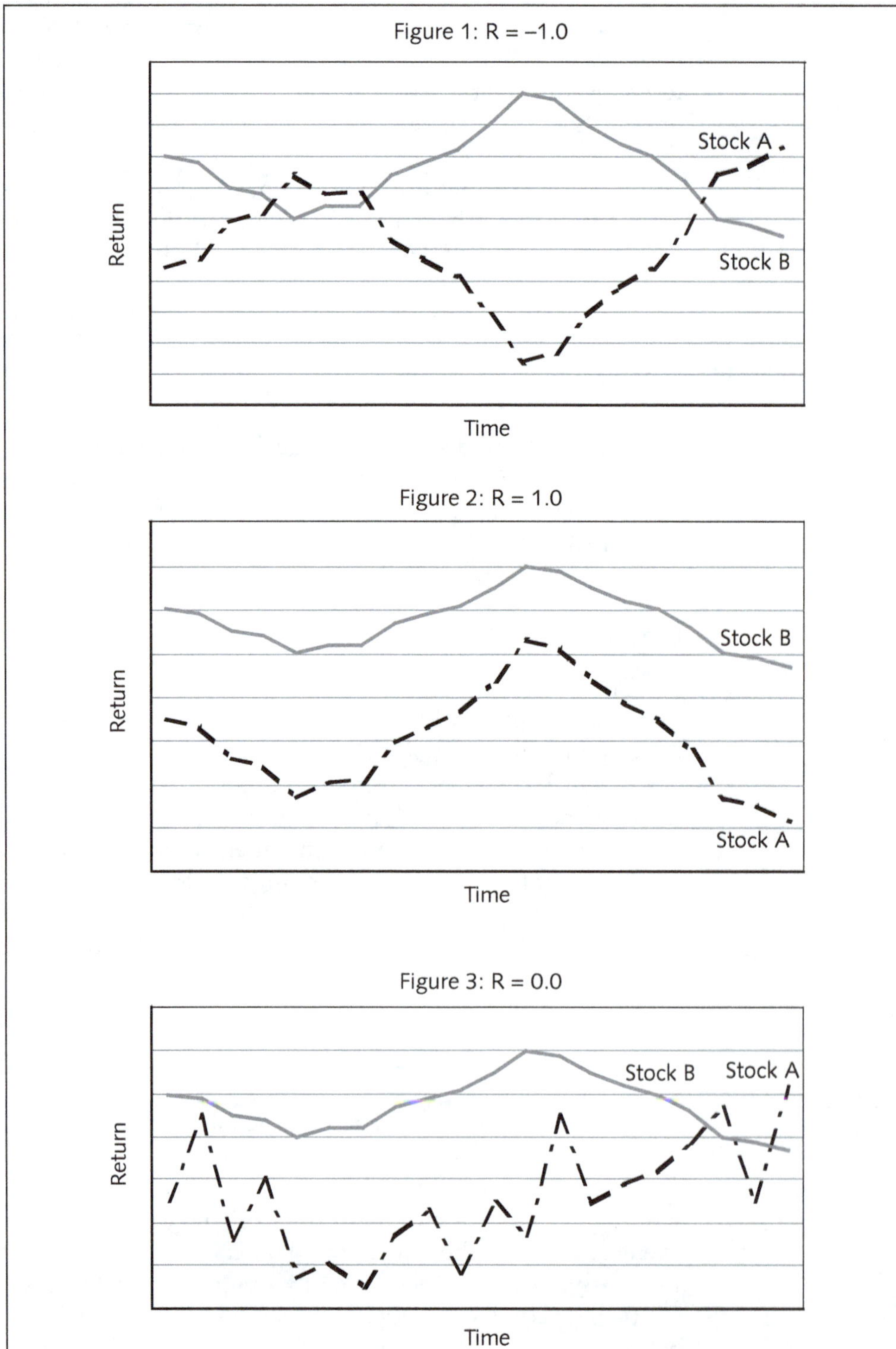

Coefficient of Determination

Coefficient of determination (R^2)
A modern portfolio theory statistic that indicates the percentage change in a portfolio or mutual fund that can be explained by changes in the market

The **coefficient of determination (R^2)** is calculated by squaring the correlation coefficient. The coefficient of determination describes the percentage of variability of returns of an asset that can be explained by changes in the returns of another asset. For example, assume that the correlation coefficient between portfolio X and the S&P 500 index is .95. The coefficient of determination would be $(.95)^2 = .9025$. This means that approximately 90% of the variability of portfolio X is explained by changes in the index. The remaining 10% of the movement of portfolio X is caused by other variables. If we consider the S&P 500 index as a measure of the market, the 10% would be considered unsystematic risk.

INVESTMENT STRATEGIES AND THEORIES

Efficient Market Hypothesis

Efficient market hypothesis
A theory that suggests that securities are priced fairly and efficiently by the market, and investors are unable to consistently outperform the market on a risk-adjusted basis

Random walk
An unpredictable pattern that describes the movement of security prices over time

The **efficient market hypothesis** (EMH) is a theory that suggests that the market prices securities fairly and efficiently and investors are unable to consistently outperform the market on a risk-adjusted basis. In fact, the EMH states that securities prices reflect all historical information. Therefore, analyzing historical information using technical or fundamental analysis will not provide an advantage in investing. The only information that will affect the price of a security will be new, unknown information. As new information affecting a security is released, the price of the security will increase if the information is positive and decrease if the information is negative. Because new information is by its very nature unknown, it is random, or unpredictable. Thus, security prices should follow a **random walk**, or an unpredictable pattern.

The efficient market hypothesis is often evaluated under three forms: the weak, semistrong, and strong. The level of information thought to be efficiently incorporated into a security's price differs between the three EMH forms.

The weak form asserts that a security's price reflects information related to its trading data including price information, volume information, and short-interest information. Under this form, analyzing trends in the price of a security is irrelevant because the price of a security should already fully reflect this information.

The semistrong form states that a security's price not only reflects its trading data but also all publicly available information related to the security. This public information includes analysis of the company's products, management, fixed and variable cost structure, earnings, and cash flow and analysis of the industry in which the company is included.

The strong form goes even farther than the other forms. This form asserts that all public and private information is included in the price of a security. Therefore, even corporate inside information will not allow investors to outperform the market on a consistent basis.

The types of market information considered relevant in attaining above-market rates of return for each form of the EMH are summarized in Exhibit 12.13.

EXHIBIT 12.13 Efficient Market Hypothesis: Three Forms

Form of EMH	Relevant Information
Weak	Insider information and credible fundamental analysis
Semistrong	Insider information
Strong	Nothing

Is the efficient market hypothesis correct? Are markets so efficient that investors are unable to consistently outperform on a risk-adjusted basis? These questions have been plaguing the investment community for decades without a definitive answer. For our purposes, it is fair to say many of the aspects of the EMH are correct. Stock prices will generally move because of new information. Investors may find it difficult to outperform the market on a consistent basis, as evidenced by the thousands of mutual funds that do not outperform the market each year (especially after adjusting for transaction costs and expenses).

Anomalies
Occurrences in the stock market that are not supported by the concept of the efficient market hypothesis

However, there are counterarguments to the validity of the EMH. **Anomalies** are occurrences in the stock market that are not supported by the concept of an efficient market. For example, if a method of trading results in superior returns, the trading method implies that the market is not perfectly efficient. Numerous anomalies have been studied at great length throughout the years. Some of these anomalies end up supporting the EMH based on the extended research, whereas others remain unexplained by the EMH principles. The most common anomalies are listed below:

- The *price-to-earnings (P/E) ratio effect* suggests that higher returns may be attainable with portfolios comprised of securities with low P/E ratios. This effect is also a fundamental premise of value investing, which is the practice of mega-investors such as Warren Buffett.
- The *small or neglected firm effect* relates to the number of security analysts who follow smaller companies. When fewer analysts follow a stock, the security may not be as efficiently priced and may result in undervalued stocks.
- The *January effect* suggests that stocks have a tendency to decline during the month of December and move up significantly in early January. This anomaly likely is the result of tax selling and buying, which are most prevalent during the months when the anomaly is observed.
- The *Value Line® enigma* relates to stocks that are rated 1 on Value Line's scale of 1–5 ratings (with 1 being the highest rating and a recommended buy). Historically, these stocks have had a tendency to outperform lower rated stocks by Value Line, a noted source of investment research.

Finally, it is fair to say that the markets are efficient, without defining the level of efficiency, and that it is difficult for professional portfolio managers to outperform the market. In addition, certain markets are more efficient than others. For example, the U.S. large-cap equity market is more efficient than the international emerging equity market. This is due to the fact that the U.S. large-cap market has fewer barriers to entry, and the financial statements of large publicly traded U.S. companies are readily available and reviewed by analysts. The degree to which one subscribes to a given level of market efficiency directly influences his decision to implement an active or passive investment strategy.

Active vs. Passive Investing

Active and passive investment strategies are commonly used approaches to investing. Active management is an attempt to outperform the returns that are available to investors who use a passive approach. To secure higher returns, active managers attempt to find undervalued or mispriced securities. Active management often requires more research and support than passive strategies. Therefore, the expenses associated with active management are generally higher than for passively managed approaches.

A passive approach to investment management does not rely on the discovery of undervalued securities. Instead, this approach assumes that investors will be unable to consistently outperform the market over the long term. As a result, managers will not employ active strategies and will maintain a well-diversified portfolio, often based on an asset allocation strategy. Over time, the portfolio may have to be rebalanced because of different rates of return for different asset classes within the portfolio. One commonly employed method of passive investing is the use of index funds.

Indexing

Investors often ask, "How did my portfolio perform compared to the market?" The market is generally represented by an index, or benchmark, such as Standard & Poor's 500 Index. These indexes provide investors with a baseline for performance comparison within different segments of the market.

Indexing is the concept of investing in the same securities and in the same proportions represented by an index. For instance, an investor might purchase the same securities that make up the S&P 500 Index. However, purchasing 500 stocks and purchasing them in the correct proportions requires a substantial investment. Therefore, investors will often invest in index mutual funds. These funds provide an inexpensive method for investors to receive the performance of an index without the hassle of having to mimic the structure of the index.

Indexing has proven to be an effective investment strategy. Historical return results indicate that the majority of active managers do not produce returns in excess of returns earned by indexes or index mutual funds.

Market Timing

Market timing is a strategy whereby investors attempt to be fully invested in periods of upward movements in the market and to be out of the market when prices are declining. This type of strategy can be applied to equities, fixed-income securities, or portfolios. Knowing when to buy and when to sell is the inherent difficulty with this strategy. Although there are a vast number of methods to time the market, many of which can be found on the internet, the majority of academic studies indicate that outperforming the market by attempting to time its rise and fall is neither reliable nor repeatable.

Buy and Hold

The buy-and-hold strategy is the conceptual opposite of market timing. This strategy, in its purest form, means that no purchases for or sales from an investor's existing portfolio will be transacted over a long period (i.e., investment time horizon). Buy and hold is a passive management strategy and is supported by the efficient market hypothesis.

The buy-and-hold strategy features three advantages:

- The investor can minimize the transaction costs in the acquisition and trading of securities.
- The investor's income tax obligations (particularly income tax liabilities or tax due) may be managed more effectively.
- The strategy ensures that the investor will not be out of the market during an upturn in prices or its most profitable trading days.

Behavioral Finance

Behavioral finance
A branch of personal finance that proposes psychology-based theories to explain investor behavior and stock market anomalies

Behavioral finance is a branch of personal finance that proposes psychology-based theories to explain investor behavior and stock market anomalies. Behavioral finance argues that investors are not nearly as rational as believed by traditional finance theorists. Critics of behavioral finance contend that the theory is merely a collection of market anomalies that are not correlated to irrational investor behavior and that these anomalies eventually will be priced out of the market. To advance the understanding of personal decisions in financial matters, prominent behavioral finance researchers have proposed the following theories:

- People's decisions are often affected by how the problem or opportunity is framed.
- Investors usually fear losses much more than they value gains. Accordingly, they will most often choose the smaller of two potential gains if it avoids a sure loss. This behavior is also known as prospect theory.
- People tend to look for information that supports their previously established decision, even if that decision was imprudent. This helps explain why investors tend to hold onto losing stock far too long before selling. This behavior is also known as confirmation bias.
- An investor's personal experiences and gender can play a significant role in investment planning.

WHERE ON THE WEB

CME Group (Futures & Options Trading) **www.cmegroup.com**

Commodity Futures Trading Commission **www.cftc.gov**

MSN Money **www.moneycentral.msn.com/investor**

Investor Guide **www.investorguide.com**

Investor's Clearinghouse **www.investoreducation.org**

National Futures Association **www.nfa.futures.org**

North American Securities Administrators Association **www.nasaa.org**

Securities and Exchange Commission—Investor Education and Assistance **www.sec.gov/investor/teachers.shtml**

DISCUSSION QUESTIONS

1. How does investment planning fit into the overall framework of financial planning?
2. What investment goals are common to most investors, and how are these goals achieved?
3. What are two methods of increasing the savings rate for an investor?
4. How are systematic risk and unsystematic risk different?
5. Compare lending investments and ownership investments.
6. What are the benefits of owning real estate in an investment portfolio?
7. What are two types of derivatives?
8. What are the differences in the obligations and rights with regard to option and futures contracts?
9. What is the difference between direct and indirect investing?
10. Describe the basic theoretical assumption of behavioral finance.
11. How are the two common measures of risk—beta and standard deviation—different?
12. What are the differences between strategic and tactical asset allocation?
13. How are the nominal rate of return and real rate of return different?
14. What is the efficient frontier and what is its role in modern portfolio theory?
15. What type of information is conveyed by the correlation coefficient?
16. What is the efficient market hypothesis (EMH)?
17. What makes market timing such a difficult investment strategy?
18. What are anomalies and how do they provide a counterargument to the validity of the EMH?
19. What is indexing and how is it used in investment planning?
20. What is the difference between active and passive portfolio management?

EXERCISES

1. List five systematic risks and explain each.
2. List five unsystematic risks and explain each.
3. Compare and contrast common and preferred stock.
4. ABC stock has recently had a market correction. If Bill likes the long-term prospects of the stock, what option position(s) might he choose and why?
5. Harry bought XYZ Company stock 15 years ago. The stock has greatly appreciated, and he is concerned about a correction. List two alternatives that he could implement to minimize losses in the event of a correction.
6. The efficient market hypothesis is often evaluated under three forms. Identify each form and explain how each incorporates information into a security's price.
7. Discuss the two major components of the capital asset pricing model (CAPM).

PROBLEMS

1. Michael invests $10,000 in Bonsai, Inc., which is based in Japan. The conversion rate at the time of the investment is 100 yen to $1. Michael sells his interest six months later for 1,750,000 yen. However, the exchange rate now is 125 yen to $1. What is Michael's return on the investment (before yen to dollars), return due to exchange rate risk, and net result on the original investment?

2. Kyle purchases 100 shares of Superstock for $6,500. One year later, he sells the lot when the stock is trading for $79 per share. Superstock does not pay dividends. What is Kyle's holding period return?

3. Based on the following chart, calculate the arithmetic mean and geometric mean for the 5-year period.

Year	Return
1	10%
2	–5%
3	18%
4	6%
5	1%

4. Eric recently purchased furniture for his family room on his credit card. If the nominal APR is 5.95% (compounded monthly), what is the effective annual rate?

5. Janet has a portfolio that has a correlation with the market of 0.8 and a standard deviation of 20%. Determine how much unsystematic risk is within Janet's portfolio.

6. JEM stock has a beta coefficient of 1.35, and the market has a rate of return of 8.50%. The risk-free rate of return is 1.75%. Calculate the expected rate of return for this stock.

7. Sandra expects to earn a long-term after-tax rate of return of 10%. If inflation is expected to continue at 3%, what is Sandra's real rate of return?

8. If portfolio A has a coefficient of determination of 0.81 when compared to the S&P 500 Index, what portion of the portfolio's risk is considered unsystematic risk?

9. Lucas invested $15,000 into a 5-year CD that pays an annual interest rate of 3.5% compounded quarterly. What will be his annual compound rate of return after the 5 years?

CHAPTER 12

Supplement A: Fixed-Income Securities

LEARNING OBJECTIVES

This supplement provides information on fixed-income securities. The following topics are covered:

- Bond concepts
- Valuation
- Measures of return
- Types, risks, and volatility of fixed-income securities
- Term structure of interest rates
- Duration and immunization

BASIC CONCEPTS OF LENDING SECURITIES

Fixed-income securities
Securities with specified payment dates and amounts, primarily bonds

Lending securities
Securities wherein the investor lends funds to the issuer in exchange for a promise of a stream of periodic interest payments and a repayment of the loaned principal at maturity

Coupon payments
Interest payments paid to the bondholder on a semiannual basis and based on a percentage of the par value of the bond

Maturity
The period through which the issuer has control over the bond proceeds and the period it must continue to pay coupon payments

As described in this chapter, **fixed-income securities**, including bonds, are known as **lending securities**. A bond investor lends funds to the issuer in exchange for a promised stream of periodic interest payments and a repayment of the loaned principal at maturity. These interest payments are called coupon payments and are often paid on a semiannual basis, or twice per year. **Coupon payments** are based on a percentage of the par value, or face value, of the bond, which is typically $1,000. For example, a bond that contains a 5% coupon will pay $50 per year (generally, $25 twice per year) for the life of the bond.

Bonds provide investors with an alternative to other types of securities and can be used for the purpose of diversifying portfolios or providing income to individuals who need a stream of cash flows. Although bonds generally have lower returns than equity investments, they are less risky than equities and provide higher returns than bank certificates of deposit and savings accounts.

A variety of entities issue bonds, including domestic and foreign governments and domestic and foreign companies; however, the U.S. federal government, agencies, municipalities, and domestic corporations issue the majority of the fixed-income securities. Bonds may be issued in public markets or private offerings and each offer different characteristics.

One of the key features of a bond is the length of its term, or **maturity**. The maturity of the bond indicates the period through which the issuer has control over the bond proceeds and must continue to pay coupon payments. The maturity of a bond also affects the yield that is received by the investor. Usually, the yield that is received by the investor will be higher for longer maturity bonds. However, as we will see later, this potential for higher yields depends on the shape of the yield curve. The maturity also affects the volatility of the bond and can affect other types of risk associated with the bond.

VALUATION OF FIXED-INCOME SECURITIES

As with most financial securities, the value of a bond is equal to the present value of the expected future cash flows. Conceptually, the cash flows of a bond are straightforward: fixed-coupon payments on a periodic basis and a return of principal at maturity. To determine the present value of a bond, these expected cash flows are discounted at an appropriate discount rate, which depends on the market yields being offered on comparable fixed-income securities. The value of a bond is determined in the same manner as the value of an annuity, by using time value of money concepts.

Basic Calculation Example

EXAMPLE Assume a three-year junk bond (face value of $1,000) is issued by XYZ Company that pays an 8% coupon semiannually ($40 twice each year). What is the value of the bond if comparable bonds are yielding 10%?

$$V = \frac{CF_1}{(1+y)^1} + \frac{CF_2}{(1+y)^2} + \frac{CF_3}{(1+y)^3} + \frac{CF_4}{(1+y)^4} + \frac{CF_5}{(1+y)^5} + \frac{CF_6}{(1+y)^6}$$

$$V = \frac{40}{(1.05)^1} + \frac{40}{(1.05)^2} + \frac{40}{(1.05)^3} + \frac{40}{(1.05)^4} + \frac{40}{(1.05)^5} + \frac{1{,}040}{(1.05)^6}$$

$$V = 38.10 + 36.28 + 34.55 + 32.91 + 31.34 + 776.06$$

$$V = \$949.24 \text{ (The bond should sell for \$949.24)}$$

Each cash flow is discounted by first raising the sum of 1 plus the periodic discount rate to the power in which the cash flow occurs and then dividing the cash flow by this amount. For example, the present value of the first cash flow is equal to $40 divided by 1.05 [1 + (10% ÷ 2)] resulting in a discounted value of $38.10. We used 5%, because it is half of the 10% yield, to reflect the semiannual coupon payments.

The value of a bond can also be calculated using a financial calculator. Using the previous example, a bond's value would be calculated using the following inputs:

Present Value of a Bond			
n	=	6	Semiannual periods
i	=	10	Discount rate or YTM
PMT	=	$40 ($80 ÷ 2)	Semiannual coupon
FV	=	$1,000	Maturity value
PV	=	($949.24)	Present value

MEASURES OF RETURN

One of the important issues relating to bonds is the determination of various measures of return. Investors in fixed-income securities will be rewarded with interest or coupon payments, capital appreciation (or loss), and the reinvestment of coupon payments. Each of the following types of returns takes into consideration some or all of these factors.

Current Yield

Current yield
A bond's annual coupon payment divided by the current market price

The **current yield** (CY) of a bond is an indication of the income or cash flow an investor will receive on the basis of the coupon payment (in dollars) and the current market price. The formula for calculating the current yield is:

$$\text{Current yield} = \frac{\text{Annual coupon payment}}{\text{Current market price}}$$

EXAMPLE For example, a 10-year bond that has a 4.5% coupon rate and is currently selling for $850 will have a current yield of 5.29%, calculated as follows:

$$\text{CY} = \frac{\$1{,}000 \times 4.5\%}{\$850}$$

$$\text{CY} = \frac{\$45}{\$850}$$

$$\text{CY} = 5.29\%$$

This type of measure is useful for determining the income or cash flow that can be earned on the purchase of a bond. For example, a person living on a fixed income might choose to invest in fixed-income securities if the yield is sufficiently high enough to cover living and other expenses. Notice that the calculation does not consider appreciation of the bond or reinvestment of the coupon payments.

Yield to Maturity

Yield to maturity (YTM)
The compounded rate of return on a bond purchased at the current market price and held to maturity

In the previous section, we illustrated the method for determining the price of a bond, which is based on its cash flows and the discount rate. The discount rate used in the calculation is generally the **yield to maturity (YTM)** and is determined by solving for the earnings rate that equates the current market price of the bond to the discounted cash flows from the bond. In calculating the yield to maturity, you would solve for the *y* that equates the present value of the bond to the discounted cash flows from the bond.

$$PV = \frac{CF_1}{(1+y)^1} + \frac{CF_2}{(1+y)^2} + \frac{CF_3}{(1+y)^3} + \frac{CF_4}{(1+y)^4} + \frac{CF_5}{(1+y)^5} + \ldots + \frac{CF_n}{(1+y)^n}$$

PV = present value
CF_n = cash flow for period *n*
y = yield to maturity
n = number of periods

EXAMPLE Calculating yield to maturity using this formula is a long and arduous process. Instead, a financial calculator is recommended to calculate the yield to maturity, using the present value of the bond, term of the bond, coupon payments, and par value. For example, a 30-year bond that pays a coupon payment of 5% semiannually and is selling for $1,149.45 has a yield to maturity of 4.12%, calculated as follows:

Present Value of a Bond			
PV	=	($1,149.45)	Current market price
n	=	60 (30 years × 2)	Semiannual periods
PMT	=	$25 ($50 ÷ 2)	Semiannual coupon
FV	=	$1,000	Maturity value
i	=	2.06 × 2 = 4.12%	Yield to maturity

The calculation of the yield to maturity is based on certain important assumptions. First, the calculation assumes that the investor will hold the bond until it matures and the calculation accounts for the timing of the cash flows. Second, this calculation also assumes that any cash flows that occur during the life of the bond will be reinvested at the calculated yield to maturity rate of return. This is an important limitation of the model. If the reinvestment rate differs from the yield to maturity, then the actual yield received on the bond will be different from the expected yield calculated at inception. Specifically, if the reinvestment rate is less than the yield to maturity, then the actual yield earned on the bond will be less than the calculated yield to maturity. If the reinvestment rate is greater than the yield to maturity, then the actual yield earned on the bond will be greater than the calculated yield to maturity.

As stated, the calculation assumes that the bond is held until it matures. If the investor sells the bond before maturity and the bond is sold at either a premium or discount, the actual yield will differ from the calculated yield to maturity, because of the capital gain or loss. A premium occurs when the bond sells for a price greater than par, while a discount occurs when the price of a bond is less than par. Note the following relationships among the price of a bond, the coupon rate, the current yield, and the yield to maturity.

Bond Selling At	Relationship				
Par	Coupon rate	=	Current yield	=	Yield to maturity
Discount	Coupon rate	<	Current yield	<	Yield to maturity
Premium	Coupon rate	>	Current yield	>	Yield to maturity

Yield to Call (YTC)

Yield to call (YTC)
The expected return on a bond from the purchase date to the first date that the bond may be called

Yield to call (YTC) is the rate of return that equates the present value of the bond (purchase price) to the expected cash flows, adjusted for the call feature. Calculating yield to call is performed using the same method as that used to calculate yield to maturity, with two adjustments. A bond containing a call feature generally allows the issuer the right to call the bond before maturity, but usually at a premium above par value. Therefore, in the calculation of yield to call, the number of periods needs to be adjusted to reflect the shorter term of the bond resulting from the call feature and the future value must be adjusted to reflect the premium paid by the issuer.

For example, assume a 30-year bond ($1,000) that pays a coupon rate of 5% semiannually is selling for $1,149.45, has a yield to maturity of 4.12%, and has a call provision. If the call provision provides that the bond may be called in five years at 103 (meaning 103% of the par value), then the yield to call equals 2.38%, calculated as follows:

Present Value of a Bond			
PV	=	($1,149.45)	Current market price
n	=	10 (5 years × 2)	Semiannual periods
PMT	=	$25 ($50 ÷ 2)	Semiannual coupon payments
FV	=	$1,030 (103% × $1,000)	Par value plus call premium
i	=	1.19 × 2 = 2.38%	Yield to call

Note that the yield to call is different from the yield to maturity. Investors who are considering the purchase of a callable bond should calculate both the YTM and the YTC in case the issuer decides to call the bond. The lesser of the YTM or YTC is the more conservative estimate of the actual yield.

Comparing Corporate Returns and Municipals Returns

The taxable bond market and the tax-exempt bond market make up the U.S. bond market. The taxable bond market consists of U.S. Treasury bonds, U.S. government agency bonds, and corporate bonds. The tax-exempt bond market consists of bonds issued by municipalities, which includes states, counties, cities, and parishes. The exemption from federal income tax is the reason municipal bonds are referred to as tax exempt. Interest from bonds issued by municipalities is exempt from federal income tax and, in some cases, exempt from state income tax. Interest from U.S. Treasury securities is subject to federal income tax, but not subject to state income tax. Corporate bond interest and interest derived from U.S. agency bonds are subject to federal and state income tax. Because various types of bonds have different tax treatment, planners must compare yields for different bonds on a consistent basis. This comparison can be performed on an after-tax basis or a pretax basis.

Taxable equivalent yield
A method for investors to compare the yield on municipal bonds with the yield on taxable (e.g., corporate) bonds

An investor can convert a municipal bond yield to a taxable equivalent yield (TEY) using the following formula:

$$\text{TEY} = \frac{\text{tax-exempt yield}}{1 - \text{marginal tax rate}}$$

EXAMPLE For example, Tom, who is in the 35% marginal income tax bracket, is considering the purchase of a Big State municipal bond that is offering a 3% yield, while comparable, credit-worthy corporate bonds are offering a yield of 4.5%. To determine which bond is preferred, on the basis of yield, Tom could determine the taxable equivalent yield for the municipal bond, as illustrated:

$$\text{TEY} = \frac{0.03}{1-0.35} = 0.04615 = 4.62\%$$

Because the taxable equivalent yield equals 4.62%, the municipal bond yield of 3% is preferable to the corporate bond yield of 4.5%. The comparison can also be made on an after-tax basis by multiplying the taxable yield of the corporate bond by the difference between 1 and the marginal tax rate, as follows:

$$\text{After-tax yield} = 0.045 \times (1 - 0.35) = 0.02925 = 2.93\%$$

Because the 3% tax-free municipal yield is greater than the 2.93% after-tax corporate bond yield, the municipal bond appears to be the better choice, on the basis of yield.

Generally, a tax-exempt entity should never purchase a municipal bond over a taxable bond because pretax yields on taxable instruments are generally higher than yields for tax-exempt securities of similar risk. Similarly, municipal bonds should not be used in tax-deferred accounts, such as IRAs and Section 401(k) plans.

TYPES OF FIXED-INCOME SECURITIES

Money market
Consists of debt securities that have the following characteristics: short-term maturity, low credit risk, and high liquidity

The Money Market

The **money market** consists of debt securities that have the following characteristics: short-term maturity, low credit risk, and high liquidity. These securities include U.S. Treasury bills, commercial paper, certificates of deposit, banker's acceptances, repurchase agreements, and Eurodollars.

Treasury Bills (T-bills)

The U.S. Treasury issues 4-week, 8-week, 13-week, 26-week, and 52-week bills in $100 denominations. The Treasury auctions these bills on a weekly basis. In addition to being purchased directly from the Treasury, these securities may be purchased and sold in the secondary market.

Treasury bills are issued at a discount or percentage of face value. If an investor paid $997.27 for a $1,000 bill, the bill will mature at its face value of $1,000, providing the investor with income of $2.73. Because T-bills have a maturity date of no more than one year, they are not subject to the original issue discount taxation rules that apply to other bonds. Interest income from the bill, which is not taxable until the bill matures, is taxed at ordinary federal income tax rates but is not subject to state income tax.

Commercial Paper

Commercial paper consists of a private sector company's issue of short-term, unsecured promissory notes. This type of debt is issued in denominations of $100,000 or more and serves as a substitute for short-term bank financing. Maturities for commercial paper are 270 days or less and are often backed by lines of credit from banks. In comparison to Treasury bills, these instruments have a slightly higher default risk and are slightly less liquid. Therefore, commercial paper has slightly higher yields than T-bills of similar term structures.

Certificates of Deposit

Negotiable certificates of deposit (also known as jumbo CDs) are deposits of $100,000 or more placed with commercial banks at a specific stated rate of interest. These short-term securities can be bought and sold in the open market. These instruments usually yield slightly higher returns than T-bills because they are less marketable.

Banker's Acceptances

Banker's acceptances are securities that act as a line of credit issued from a bank. Companies that are too small to issue commercial paper will use banker's acceptances to fund short-term debt needs. When using a banker's acceptance, the bank usually acts as an intermediary between the American company and the foreign company. For example, an American importer may request acceptance financing from its bank when the foreign company will not provide credit. As a result, the importer's bank agrees to pay the foreign supplier on behalf of the importer. The importer is then contractually obligated to repay the bank within three to six months. In turn, the importer's bank may sell the obligation at a discount to obtain immediate cash. These securities usually have slightly higher interest rates than commercial paper, reflecting greater default risk and less liquidity.

Repurchase Agreements

Securities dealers use repurchase agreements (known as "repos") to finance large inventories of marketable securities from one to a few days. The issuer or seller both sells and agrees to repurchase the underlying security at a specified price and date. The repurchase price is higher than the selling price, creating the required return to compensate the holder for participating in the repurchase agreement. The opposite of the repo is the reverse repurchase agreement (or reverse repo). In a reverse repo, the dealer buys government securities from another dealer and then sells them back later at a higher price.

Eurodollars

Eurodollars are U.S. dollar-denominated deposits at banks outside the United States. The average deposit is in the millions and has a maturity of less than six months. Therefore, the market for this investment is generally only the largest financial institutions and the only way for individuals to invest is indirectly through a money market mutual fund. A variation on the Eurodollar time deposit is the Eurodollar CD (or euro CD). This type of CD shares the same characteristics as its domestic counterpart except that the obligation is the liability of a non-U.S. bank. Accordingly, euro CDs are less liquid and, therefore, offer a slightly higher yield than domestic CDs. Generally, only the largest financial institutions invest in the Eurodollar market. Similar to Eurodollars, individual investors may participate in the Eurodollar market indirectly through the use of money market mutual funds.

Government Debt Securities

U.S. Treasury Notes and Bonds

U.S. Treasury notes and bonds have virtually the same characteristics with the exception of maturity. Specifically, U.S. Treasury notes are issued with a maturity date of no more than 10 years, whereas U.S. Treasury bonds have a maturity of 30 years. The minimum purchase amount for both types of securities is $100. Treasury notes and bonds pay interest on a semiannual basis. As with Treasury bills, pricing for notes and bonds is done through the auction process. Treasury notes and bonds are considered default risk-free and are exempt from income taxation at both the state and local levels. For federal income tax purposes, all interest from either obligation is taxable at ordinary income tax rates in the year earned.

Treasury Inflation-Protected Securities (TIPS)

Treasury inflation-protected securities (TIPS)
Marketable securities whose principal is adjusted by changes in the Consumer Price Index (CPI)

In 1997, the Treasury began issuing notes and bonds that are indexed with the Consumer Price Index (CPI) referred to as **Treasury inflation-protected securities (TIPS)**. These securities have the same basic characteristics as non-inflation-adjusted Treasury notes and bonds, except for the inflation-adjustment feature.

The interest rate paid on these securities is determined through the auction process, just as the other Treasury obligations; however, the principal value of the bond is adjusted for changes in the CPI. Thus, the semiannual interest payments received by the investor are determined by multiplying the inflation-adjusted principal value by one-half of the stated coupon payment.

One of the primary risks to which fixed-income securities are subject is changes in interest rates, both from devaluation in principal and from loss of purchasing power. The indexed Treasuries provide protection from both of these risks, making them an attractive security for investors concerned about rising inflation and devaluation due to loss of purchasing power.

Treasury STRIPS

Treasury STRIPS
Acronym for Separate Trading of Registered Interest and Principal of Securities, a program that permits investors to hold and trade the individual interest and principal components of eligible Treasury notes and bonds as separate securities

The **Treasury STRIPS** (Separate Trading of Registered Interest and Principal of Securities) program permits investors to hold and trade the individual interest and principal components of eligible Treasury notes and bonds as separate securities. The Treasury does not issue or sell STRIPS directly to investors. STRIPS can be purchased and held only through financial institutions and government securities brokers/dealers who are the parties that separate the original security into its components.

When a Treasury fixed-principal or inflation-indexed note or bond is stripped, each interest payment becomes a separate zero-coupon security, as does the principal payment. Each component has its own identifying number and can be held or traded separately. For example, a Treasury note with 10 years remaining to maturity consists of a single principal payment at maturity and 20 interest payments, one every six months for 10 years. When this note is converted to STRIPS form, each of the 20 interest (coupon) payments and the principal payment become a separate (zero-coupon) security. STRIPS are also called zero-coupon securities because the only time investors receive a payment during the life of STRIPS is when they mature.

U.S. Savings Bonds

Savings bonds, a part of the federal government debt structure, include Series E, EE, H, HH, and I bonds. Historically purchased for patriotic reasons, these bonds may be purchased and used for funding education costs and gifting.

Series EE Savings Bonds

The Treasury issued the new Series EE savings bond beginning July 1, 1980, in order to replace the older Series E bond. The interest rate earned on Series EE savings bonds is a fixed rate determined by the U.S. Treasury Department, with a new rate announced each May and November. The electronic (paper bonds were discontinued as of January 1, 2012) EE savings bond is sold at 100% of face value. Series EE bonds reach original maturity 20 years after the date of issue and continue to earn interest until they reach final maturity 30 years after the date of issue. Bonds may be redeemed at any time, subject to the following restrictions and penalties: (1) bonds must be held for at least 12 months, and (2) if a bond that is less than five years old is redeemed, the penalty is the forfeiture of the last three months of interest.

One of the attractions of Series EE bonds is the special tax treatment of the income attributable to these securities. Interest earned from bonds that are issued at a discount, such as zero-coupon bonds and STRIPS, must be reported as taxable income on an annual basis even though cash may not be received during the year. Because of the special tax treatment afforded Series EE bonds, however, the interest accrued on these securities is generally not taxed on an annual basis, but rather upon redemption. However, taxpayers are permitted to make an election to include for tax purposes the income from these securities on an annual basis. This elected tax treatment can be beneficial under certain circumstances, such as for a child with income under the standard deduction. In such a case, basis can be established without incurring tax.

Another tax benefit of Series EE bonds is that the interest earned on these securities can be completely excluded from taxable income if the proceeds from the bonds are used for qualified higher education costs of the taxpayer, spouse, or dependents. These costs include books, tuition, and fees for these family members.

Series HH Savings Bonds

Unlike Series EE bonds that are sold for cash, Series HH savings bonds could be only acquired through an exchange of Series E or EE bonds or with redemption proceeds of another H bond (and savings notes issued prior to 1970). Series HH bonds were issued at 100% of the face amount until September 1, 2004, when they were discontinued. Series HH bonds pay interest semiannually at a fixed rate set on the date of issuance and adjusted on the 10th anniversary. The interest payments are required to be included in income for federal income tax purposes.

Series HH bonds have an original maturity period of 10 years and have been granted one 10-year extension of maturity with interest, bringing their final maturity to 20 years. Series HH bonds were issued only in registered physical form and are not transferable. In other words, Series HH bonds are not marketable securities.

Series I Savings Bonds

The Treasury offers Series I savings bonds in an attempt to provide individuals a way to accrue income and protect the purchasing power of their investment. Series I bonds are issued at 100% of the face value. The bonds have an interest-paying life of 30 years after issue and cease to increase in value on that date. Like EE and HH bonds, Series I bonds are not transferable or marketable.

The Series I bond earnings rate is a combination of two separate rates: a fixed rate of return and a semiannual inflation rate. Each May and November, the Treasury announces a fixed rate of return that applies to all Series I bonds issued during the six-month period beginning with the effective date of the announcement, May 1 or November 1. The fixed rate for any given Series I bond remains the same for the life of the bond.

In addition, every May and November, the Treasury announces a semiannual inflation rate based on changes in the Consumer Price Index for all urban consumers (CPI-U). The semiannual inflation rate announced in May is a measure of inflation from the previous October through March; the rate announced in November is a measure of inflation from the previous April through September. The CPI-U is published monthly by the Department of Labor's Bureau of Labor Statistics. The semiannual inflation rate is then combined with the fixed rate of the Series I bond to determine the bond's earnings rate for the next six months. In the rare event that the CPI-U is negative during a period of deflation and the decline in the CPI-U is greater than the fixed rate, the redemption value of Series I bonds remains the same until the earnings rate becomes greater than zero.

Series I bonds receive special income tax treatment. The interest from Series I bonds is not subject to state and local income tax. Interest is accrued for Series I bonds and is not taxable until redeemed. In addition, the interest can be completely excluded from taxable income if the proceeds are used for qualified higher education expenses of the taxpayer, spouse, or dependents.

Series I bonds can be redeemed at any time 12 months after the issue date. The owner will receive the original investment plus the earnings; however, Series I bonds are meant to be long-term investments. So, if a Series I bond is redeemed within the first five years, there is a three-month earnings penalty. Exhibit 12A.1 illustrates the differences among the three types of savings bonds.

EXHIBIT 12A.1 Summary of U.S. Savings Bonds

	Series EE	Series HH	Series I
Range of denominations	$25 to $10,000	No longer issued	$25 to $10,000
Purchased	With cash (electronically)	By exchanging E or EE bonds	With cash (electronically)
Maturity date	20 years (30-year interest earning period)	20 years	30 years
Interest rate	Fixed rate	1.5% fixed rate	Combination of fixed and variable rates
Interest payments	Accrues	Paid semiannually	Accrues
Taxation of interest	Deferred	Taxed annually	Deferred
Interest can be completely excluded for qualified higher education costs	Yes (if not above phase-out)	Not eligible	Yes (if not above phaseout)

Municipal Bonds

Municipal bonds
Debt instruments issued by municipalities (states, counties, parishes, cities, or towns)

Municipalities include states, counties, parishes, cities, and towns. These government agencies issue debt instruments, referred to as **municipal bonds**. The unique characteristic of municipal bonds is their income tax treatment. The interest from municipal bonds is not subject to federal income tax and, in some cases, is not subject to state income tax. Although the yields on municipals are generally lower than those of Treasuries, their special tax treatment makes them the choice for higher income investors because of their higher after-tax yields. Two common types of municipal bonds are general obligation bonds and revenue bonds.

General obligation bonds
A municipal bond backed by the full faith, credit, and taxing power of the municipality

General obligation bonds are backed by the full faith and credit of the government issuing the debt and are repaid through taxes collected by the governmental body. Because these bonds are backed by the taxing authority of the municipality, they are only subject to minimal default risk.

Revenue bonds
A municipal bond backed by a specific source of revenue

Revenue bonds are issued by government bodies to raise funds to finance specific revenue-producing projects. Examples of revenue bonds include airport revenue bonds, college and university revenue bonds, hospital revenue bonds, sewer revenue bonds, toll road revenue bonds, and water revenue bonds. These bonds are not backed by the full faith and credit of the issuing body. Instead, the interest and principal are repaid from revenue generated from the project that was financed with the bond proceeds. Because the revenue generated from the project may differ from what is expected, these bonds are riskier than general obligation bonds and, thus, require higher yields for similar maturities.

There are other differences between municipal bonds besides sources of repayment. For example, municipal bonds may be either term bonds or serial bonds. The principal for term bonds is repaid in full upon maturity, whereas serial bonds require that the municipality retire a certain amount of the bond issue each year.

Corporate Bonds

Corporations raise funds by issuing both equity and debt obligations. Debt obligations provide corporations with a method of raising needed capital funds without diluting the ownership of the entity; however, excessive amounts of debt can strain the financial health of the company by using precious resources for debt service. In general, debt increases the leverage of a company, and specifically, it impacts the return on equity. Excessive use of debt can cause increased fluctuations in the share price of the common stock.

The corporate bond market is typically classified by the type of issuer. The five broad categories of corporate bonds are banks and finance companies, industrials, public utilities, transportations, and international. Each of these categories can be further subdivided. For example, transportation can be divided into airlines, railroads, and trucking. Along with bond ratings, these subcategory classifications can assist investors in analyzing and comparing various debt issues.

Bond indenture agreement
The legal document that sets forth the repayment schedules, restrictions, and promises between the issuer of a corporate bond and the borrower

The **bond indenture agreement** is the legal document that sets forth the repayment schedules, restrictions, and promises between the issuer and the borrower. Information that may be found in the indenture agreement includes call provisions, sinking fund provisions, collateral provisions, and conversion options.

Call Provisions

Call provision
Right to redeem the bond issue before maturity

A **call provision** provides the issuer of the debt instrument the right to redeem the bond issue prior to maturity. Generally, a call provision will require the issuer to pay a premium if the bond issue is redeemed before maturity. When interest rates decline, call provisions allow the issuer to redeem the outstanding debt and reissue it at a lower interest rate. By refinancing the debt, companies can save significant amounts of interest payments that would have been paid to the creditors.

Sinking Fund Provisions

Sinking funds
Funds usually held by trustee to ensure repayment of borrowed principal

Sinking funds may be established and funded by the bond issuer each year and may accumulate to pay off debt upon maturity. These funds are usually held by a trustee to ensure the repayment of the borrowed principal. Such a fund is included to reduce the default risk associated with some bond issues.

Collateral Provisions

Mortgage bond
Bond secured by real property

Bonds may be unsecured or secured. A secured bond has a claim on specific assets of the issuing company in the event of liquidation. A **mortgage bond** is secured by real property, such as real estate holdings. Generally, a mortgage bond will have a lien on the specified property, but it could have a lien on all assets of the firm. A mortgage bond may be open ended, limited open ended, or closed ended, which indicates the degree to which additional debt may be issued against the same property.

Collateral trust bonds
Bonds secured by securities issued by other companies

Collateral trust bonds are usually secured by stocks and bonds of other companies held in trust. For companies with insufficient real property, providing a lien on securities held by the company is a method of providing security to creditors. The investments that are pledged act as collateral for the loan.

Companies are willing to provide security for bond issues to reduce and minimize interest payments and expense. The market interest rate required for secured bonds will be less than that of unsecured bonds.

Debentures
Unsecured corporate bonds whose holders have no claim to specific assets of the issuing corporation

Unsecured bonds are called **debentures**. Investors who hold debentures do not have a claim to specific assets of the corporation. However, if liquidation occurs, debenture holders, who are general creditors of the issuing corporation, will be paid only after secured creditors have been repaid. Subordinated debentures have an even lower claim on assets than general creditors, such as debenture holders.

Zero-Coupon Bonds

Zero-coupon bond
A bond that does not pay periodic coupon or interest payments

A **zero-coupon bond** is a bond that does not pay periodic coupon or interest payments; therefore, this bond will always sell at a deep discount from (less than) par. As a result, the only cash flow that occurs and needs to be considered in the valuation of a zero-coupon bond is the maturity value or principal value. Although coupon payments are not actually paid, the number of periods that are used when valuing a zero is the same as if the coupon payments were being paid. In other words, the number of periods will equal the number of years until maturity of the bond multiplied by 2. Therefore, the valuation methodology of a zero-coupon bond will be consistent with, and comparable to, the valuation methodology of a coupon-paying bond.

Corporations may favor zero-coupon bonds because they have an extended period to use the borrowed money without the obligation of making periodic interest payments. Thus, these bonds can be an effective cash management tool. Investors favor zero-coupon bonds because the heavily discounted bond price means they can purchase more bonds with the same amount of investment dollars and can time the maturity of the bonds to coincide with future financial needs and expenses.

Convertible Bonds

Convertible bonds
Hybrid securities that permit the holder to acquire shares of common stock from the issuing company by exchanging the currently held debt security for a specific number of common stock shares

Corporate bonds may contain provisions permitting the conversion of the fixed-income security into equity securities. **Convertible bonds** are hybrid securities that permit the holder to acquire shares of common stock from the issuing company by exchanging the currently held debt security according to a specific formula. Similar to an option contract, the holder's ability to convert the current security into common stock is a right, not an obligation. The conversion decision hinges on the value of the stock upon conversion. If the value of the stock after conversion would be less than the value of the bond, then the investor should hold on to the fixed-income security.

Convertible securities allow the issuer to reduce the cost of interest for a bond issue by paying a lower yield. The lower yield is a result of the buyer purchasing not only a steady stream of cash flows, but also an option to convert the bond to common stock.

Convertible securities provide investors with several advantages over nonconvertible securities. They provide the holder with a steady stream of income and the ability to participate in the growth of the underlying company. Convertible bonds have a relatively low correlation to other bonds and only a moderate correlation to stocks, providing investors the opportunity to diversify a portfolio. Convertible securities are senior securities in terms of liquidation and are highly marketable.

Asset-backed securities
Bundled securities issued against some type of asset-linked debts, such as mortgages

Asset-Backed Securities

Asset-backed securities, such as mortgage-backed securities and collateralized mortgage obligations, contain more uncertainty with regard to their cash flows. First, coupon payments and repayment of principal are based on payments made by the mortgagors, who often have the right to prepay principal. Prepayments cause the schedule of cash flows to change, which adjusts the value of the bond. The second issue related to asset-backed securities is the potential for defaults. Clearly, in a large pool of mortgages, some of the mortgages may result in default. In such a case, the cash flows are affected, causing the value of the bond to change. Each of these issues can be incorporated into the projection of the expected cash flows and, therefore, incorporated into the valuation of the asset-backed securities.

Mortgage-backed securities (MBSs)
Ownership claims on a pool of mortgages

Securitization
The process of transforming nonnegotiable securities into negotiable securities

Mortgage-Backed Securities

Mortgage-backed securities (MBSs) are ownership claims against a pool of mortgages. The originating mortgage lender will sell loans to investors in the secondary market. These investors pool mortgages together and sell interests in the pool to other investors. This process of transforming nonpublicly traded securities into marketable assets is known as **securitization**.

Mortgage-backed securities are often referred to as pass-through securities because the monthly mortgage payments are passed along to the holders of the MBSs, less a small servicing fee. These monthly mortgage payments consist of scheduled interest and principal payments, as well as unscheduled principal prepayments. These unscheduled principal prepayments result from borrowers making additional principal payments on their loans or paying off loans, such as in the case of refinancing.

Because MBSs are backed by mortgages (all of which are secured by real property, with many backed by the government), they have little credit risk. However, MBSs are subject to other risks. Similar to other fixed-income obligations, these securities are subject to fluctuations in interest rates. As interest rates increase, the value of the MBS decreases; as interest rates decrease, the value of the MBS increases.

Because MBSs pass through payments on a monthly basis, the investor must reinvest these cash flows in some other investment. This reinvestment rate risk impacts MBSs in the same manner as other fixed-income securities that have cash flows occurring during the life of the security.

Prepayment risk
The risk that homeowners will pay off their loans before the scheduled loan maturity date

Unlike other fixed-income obligations, MBSs are subject to **prepayment risk**, which is the risk that homeowners will pay off their loans before the scheduled loan maturity date. Because the value of these securities is based on the schedule of cash flows, any mortgage prepayments will impact the return an investor receives. In addition to creating uncertainty as to the timing of the cash flows, these prepayments present a situation in which the investor must reinvest the additional principal payments, possibly at a lower interest rate. Ultimately, this propagates the reinvestment rate risk.

Mortgage-backed securities also have "extension risk." This is the risk that the MBS will not be paid off as projected. MBSs are generally projected to last about 12 years (for a 30-year pool). Typically homeowners don't have their mortgage for 30 years. If rates rise and/or real estate sales slow, mortgages are repaid at a slower-than-expected rate, resulting in an extension of the time required to recoup all principal.

The majority of the mortgage-backed securities have been issued by three agencies: the Federal National Mortgage Association (FNMA or Fannie Mae), the Government National Mortgage Association (GNMA or Ginnie Mae), and the Federal Home Loan Mortgage Corporation (FHLMC or Freddie Mac).

Collateralized Mortgage Obligations (CMOs)

Collateralized mortgage obligations (CMOs)
Mortgage-backed securities that are divided into tranches

Due to the popularity of the mortgage-backed securities, private investment firms have created their own pass-through securities, known as **collateralized mortgage obligations (CMOs)**. Collateralized mortgage obligations are similar to MBSs in that they are backed by mortgages. However, they differ from MBSs in that the cash flow associated with the pool of mortgages is divided into repayment periods called tranches. In the traditional MBS, the cash flow an investor will receive each month includes a pro rata share of principal and interest.

The principal repayment method for collateralized mortgage obligations is different from the method for MBSs. As described, tranches, or repayment periods, are established to dictate when an investor will receive principal repayments. Each of the tranches will receive regular interest payments, with the investors of the first tranche receiving all principal payments until they are completely repaid their principal. Once the obligations of the first tranche are satisfied, all principal payments are made to the second tranche and so on, until all of the tranches are repaid. The holders of the CMOs of the first tranche have less interest rate risk than the holders of the CMOs of the last tranche because the maturity is longer for these securities.

Promissory Notes

A promissory note is a private transaction between a lender and a borrower commonly used to finance business operations or expansion. The structure of a promissory note is similar to that of a bond (i.e., it generally involves a fixed amount and time of payment), and many of the same investment considerations that apply to a bond are also relevant to a promissory note. The present value of a promissory note is found using time value of money principles and discounting back future cash flows from the note at a specified discount rate over the stipulated time period of the note.

Rating Agencies

Rating agencies are responsible for assisting investors in evaluating the default risk of fixed-income securities. Bond rating agencies analyze the financial information of thousands of companies attempting to determine a credit rating for the various debt issues in the market. The two largest and most popular rating agencies are Standard & Poor's and Moody's. Their credit rating systems are listed in Exhibit 12A.2.

EXHIBIT 12A.2 Standard Credit Rating Systems

Bonds	Standard & Poor's	Moody's
Investment grade		
■ High grade	AAA–AA	Aaa–Aa
■ Medium grade	A–BBB-	A–Baa
Noninvestment grade		
■ Speculative	BB+–B	Ba–B
■ Default	CCC–D	Caa–C
Overall range	AAA–D	Aaa–C

Investment grade bonds have a high probability of timely payment of both interest and repayment of principal, and noninvestment grade bonds are those in which a significant risk exists surrounding interest or principal payments.

The rating agencies generally provide the same rating for a specific debt issue. In some cases, there may be a slight difference between the ratings of a specific issue by the different agencies; this difference is referred to as a split rating.

RISKS OF FIXED-INCOME SECURITIES

Fixed-income securities can provide substantial returns to investors; however, there are a variety of risks to which investors of fixed-income securities are subject, including the following:

Systematic Risks	Unsystematic Risks
Interest rate risk	Default risk
Reinvestment rate risk	Call risk
Purchasing power risk	

Interest Rate Risk

Interest rate risk is the risk that fluctuations in interest rates will adversely impact the value of a security. This risk is generally the greatest risk for a bond investor. There is an inverse relationship between changes in interest rates and bond prices. As interest rates fall, bond prices increase. Conversely, as interest rates rise, the value of bonds declines.

Planners should understand that a decline in the value of a bond, which is attributable to an increase in interest rates, is of little relevance to an investor holding the bond to maturity. In such a case, the decline in value of the bond is simply a reflection of the change in market interest rates. The investor will still receive the scheduled coupon payments and the par value upon maturity. For an investor who sells before maturity, an increase in interest rates means that the investor will incur a capital loss. Interest rate risk impacts bonds, bond portfolios, and bond mutual funds.

Default Risk

As discussed previously, investing in a fixed-income obligation is a process of lending money. The bond issuer is effectively borrowing money from the investor in return for a promise to make periodic interest (coupon) payments and repay the principal at the maturity of the bond. However, because bonds are often issued with maturities exceeding 10, 20, and 30 years, there is a risk that the financial well-being of the bond issuer will change over this long period. In some cases, the financial health of a company will be in such turmoil that the company cannot uphold its promise to repay the borrowed proceeds. The risk that this might occur is referred to as default, or credit, risk. Rating agencies, such as Standard & Poor's and Moody's, provide investors with analysis of the financial stability of companies and their ability to service their debt.

Another issue of default risk is the impact that a change in a company's financial well-being will have on the value of a bond issue. When a company's financial health diminishes, it increases the probability of default. Because of this increased likelihood of default, as small as it may be, the market value of the bond will decline relative to other bonds with similar characteristics. Therefore, it is not simply a matter of default, but also how changes in the general financial health of the bond issuer impact the price of a fixed-income security.

Reinvestment Rate Risk

Simply put, reinvestment rate risk is the risk that cash flows received during the holding period of an investment will not be able to be invested at a rate that is at least as great as the expected internal rate of return or yield to maturity of the original investment.

Purchasing Power Risk

Purchasing power risk, also referred to as inflation risk, is the risk that inflation will erode the purchasing power of the investor's assets. Bondholders can especially be impacted by purchasing power risk. For example, if an investor owns a bond with a coupon rate of 3% when inflation is 4%, the investor is losing purchasing power at a rate of 0.96% $[(1.03 / 1.04) - 1 \times 100 = -0.96\%]$ per year. As discussed, there are certain inflation-adjusted bonds, such as those issued by the U.S. Treasury, that can help minimize the adverse impact of inflation.

Call Risk

For bonds that have a call feature, there is a risk that the bond will be called from the investor prior to maturity. Bond issuers will generally call a bond when interest rates decline low enough to justify the cost of calling and refinancing the bonds (i.e., if the yield to call is lower than the yield to maturity), which means that the investor will have to reinvest the proceeds in an environment of lower interest rates.

VOLATILITY OF FIXED-INCOME SECURITIES

Volatility is defined as the magnitude and frequency of changes in the price of a security, such as bonds, within a given time period. The two key factors that influence volatility are the coupon rate and maturity.

Coupon Rate

The volatility in a bond's price is inversely related to the bond's coupon payment when interest rates change. A bond with a higher coupon rate is more stable with regard to interest rate changes than is a bond with a lower coupon rate. A zero-coupon bond's value will generally be more volatile than a bond with a 5% coupon.

Maturity

A bond with a longer term is subject to more volatility in an environment of changing interest rates than is a bond with a shorter term. A 30-year Treasury bond will be more volatile than a five-year Treasury note when interest rates change. This is illustrated in Exhibit 12A.3.

EXAMPLE Bond A is a five-year high-yield bond with a 10% coupon rate. Bond B is a 30-year high-yield bond, also with a 10% coupon rate. Because Bond B has a longer maturity, it will experience more volatility when interest rates change.

EXHIBIT 12A.3 Impact of Maturity on Bond Volatility

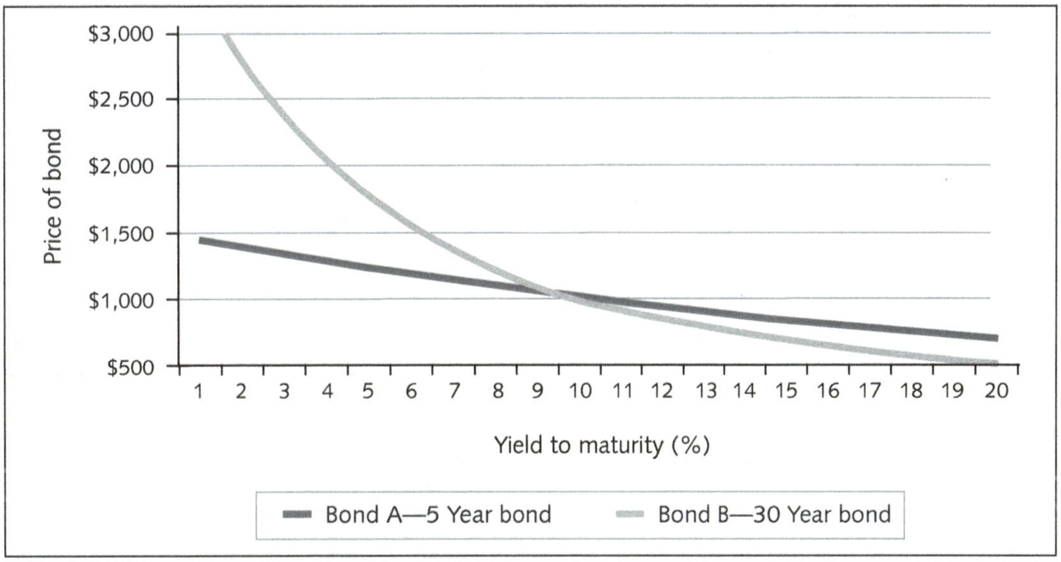

Notice that Bond B's slope is steeper than Bond A's. At a YTM of 10%, the price of both bonds is equal at $1,000. When interest rates decrease, the price of Bond B increases more than Bond A. When interest rates increase, the price of Bond B decreases more than Bond A.

TERM STRUCTURE OF INTEREST RATES

Yield Curves

Yield curves
Graphical representations that reflect current market interest rates for various bond maturities

Traditionally, interest rates for bonds have been reflected in graphical representations called **yield curves.** These yield curves reflect current market interest rates for various bond maturities. The most popular of these yield curves is the Treasury yield curve, which depicts current yields for Treasury securities. The yield curve is generally upward sloping, indicating that yields on longer-term bonds are higher than yields on shorter-term bonds.

However, there have been times when the structure of interest rates has caused the yield curve to be shaped differently. The yield curve is generally described as upward sloping (normal), flat, or downward sloping (inverted) as shown in Exhibit 12A.4.

EXHIBIT 12A.4 Yield Curves

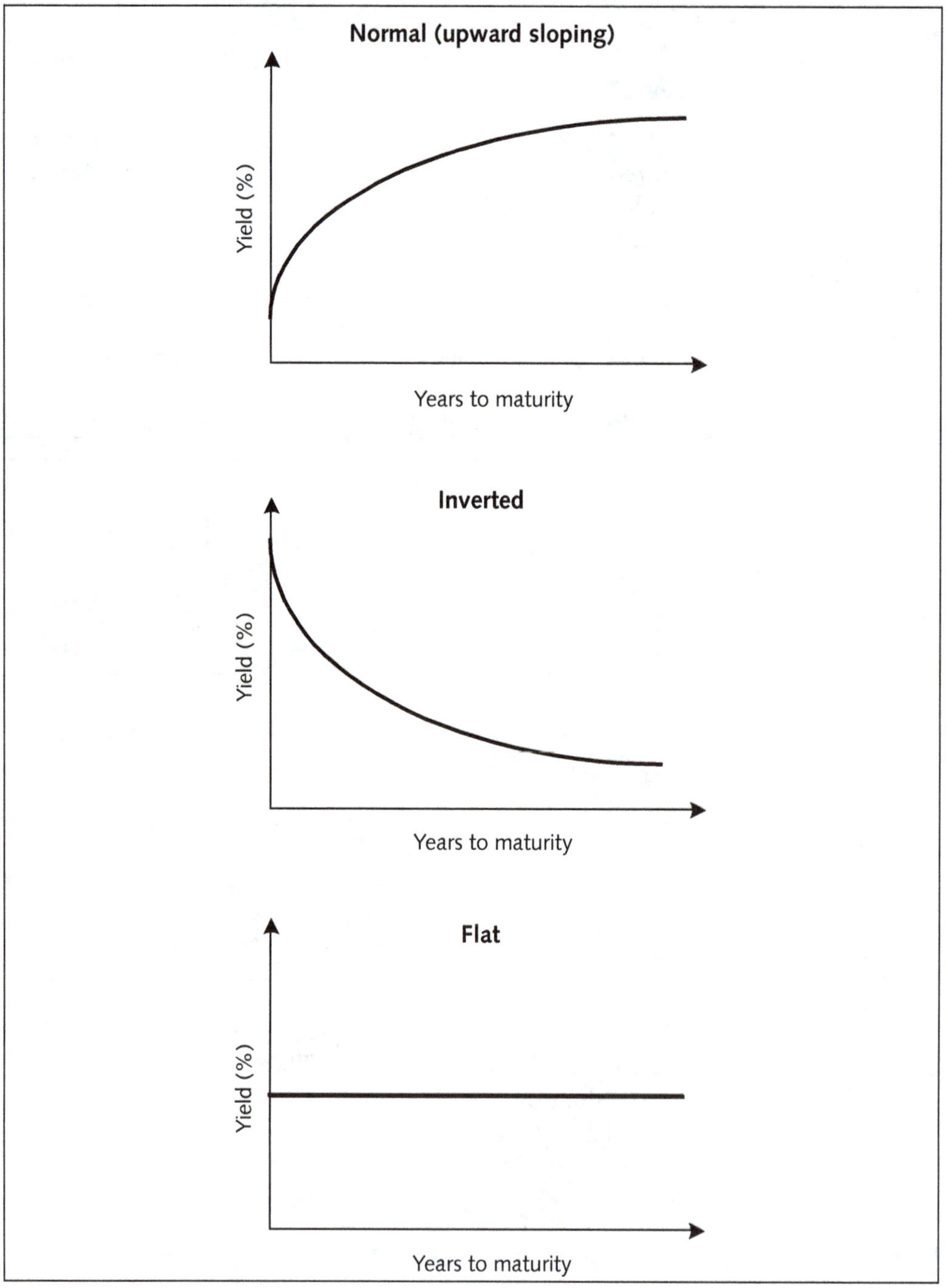

The most important point regarding yield curves is that their shape varies according to changes in the economic cycle; therefore, they may be used to make predictions about the future state of the economy.

- A normal or positive yield curve occurs during periods of economic expansion and generally predicts that market interest rates will rise in the future.
- An inverted yield curve occurs when the Federal Reserve has tightened credit in an inflationary economy. This type of curve predicts interest rates will fall and, sometimes, can signal an upcoming economic recession.
- A flat yield curve occurs when the economy is peaking and, therefore, no change in future interest rates (particularly down) is expected.

The Treasury yield curve is often used as a benchmark for other fixed-income securities. The Treasury yield curve is an effective benchmark for pricing bonds and determining yields of bonds in other sectors because it is not impacted by credit risk or liquidity risk. Treasuries are backed by the full faith and credit of the U.S. government and, as a result, are not subject to credit risk. The Treasury market is extremely liquid because it is the largest and most actively traded bond market.

The traditional method for valuing or pricing non-Treasury bonds has been to use the yield on the Treasury yield curve for the appropriate maturity, plus a premium for additional risk.

An alternative way to conceptualize the valuation of bonds is to consider them as a series of individual cash flow, each one an independent zero-coupon bond. For example, a 10-year, 3% coupon Treasury note could be viewed as 20 separate and distinct zero-coupon bonds. These individual cash flows can then be valued on the basis of market yields for zero-coupon Treasuries with similar maturities.

Yield Curve Theories

Several theories attempt to explain the reason for the shape of the yield curve. These include the expectations theory, the liquidity theory, the preferred habitat theory, and the market segmentation theory.

The Expectations Theory

Expectations theory
Yield curve theory asserting long-term interest rates are based on expectations about future short-term interest rates

The **expectations theory** asserts that long-term rates are based on expected future short-term rates. In other words, forward rates should indicate the market's perception of which direction rates will be moving. For example, an upward-sloping yield curve would indicate that future short-term rates would be increasing; a flat yield curve indicates that future short-term rates will remain constant; and a downward, or inverted, yield curve represents the expectation that short-term rates will be declining. One shortcoming of this theory is that it does not reflect the inherent increased risk or uncertainty in longer-term bonds.

The Liquidity Preference Theory

Liquidity preference theory
Yield curve theory asserting long-term bonds have greater yields to compensate investors for increased interest rate risk

According to the **liquidity preference theory**, investors prefer certainty and expect to be compensated for uncertainty. This theory incorporates a liquidity premium into the expectations theory model. Under this theory, investors require a premium for the increased exposure to interest rate risk inherent in long-term bonds. Yield curves generally will be upward sloping, reflecting a higher premium for longer term bonds.

The Preferred Habitat Theory

Preferred habitat theory
Yield curve theory asserting financial institutions prefer to match asset maturities to liability maturities

The **preferred habitat theory** is similar to the market segmentation theory (described in the next paragraph), and it states that institutions (generally financial institutions) prefer to match the maturity of their assets to that of their liabilities. In other words, institutions generally try to match the maturity or duration of their assets and liabilities. Under this theory, institutions have an incentive to shift their maturities or duration if the premium for the switch is significant enough. Therefore, it is possible to have any shape yield curve under this theory.

Market Segmentation Theory

Market segmentation theory
Yield curve theory asserting yields are determined by the laws of supply and demand for specific bond maturities

According to the **market segmentation theory**, interest rates for varying maturities are determined by supply and demand. Institutions may have liabilities that are short term, intermediate term, or long term and will generally want to match the maturity of their assets with the maturity of their liabilities. As a result, there are certain types of institutions that lend and borrow using different categories of maturities. This results in a separate market for short-term borrowings, intermediate-term borrowings, and long-term borrowings. Each maturity market has its own balance between supply and demand, creating the possibility of a yield curve of almost any shape.

DURATION AND IMMUNIZATION

Duration
Provides a time-weighted measure of a security's cash flows in terms of payback

The concept of **duration**, developed by Frederick Macaulay in 1938, provides a time-weighted measure of a security's cash flows in terms of payback. Duration is defined as the average time it takes a bondholder to receive the interest and principal from a bond in present value dollars. This number can be used by bond investors to measure a bond's price volatility compared with those issues of equal coupon rates and different maturity dates.

Duration can be used for the following:

- Measuring of a bond's volatility
- Estimating the change in the price of a bond on the basis of changes in interest rates
- Immunizing a bond or bond portfolio against interest rate risk

Calculating Duration

EXAMPLE Consider a three-year corporate bond selling for $973.27, paying interest annually, with a face value of $1,000, a coupon rate of 5%, and a YTM of 6%.

Year	Cash Flow	PV of CF	PV × Year
1	$50.00	$47.17	$47.17
2	$50.00	$44.50	$89.00
3	$1,050.00	$881.60	$2,644.80
Total		**$973.27**	**$2,780.97**

Duration is then determined by dividing $2,780.97 by the current market price of the bond ($973.27). Calculating duration for a bond requires the following steps.

1. List the years
2. List the cash flows
3. Determine the present value of the cash flows using the year and the YTM for the bond, 6%
4. Multiply the year number by the present value (e.g., 2 × 44.50 = 89.00)
5. Sum the last column and divide by the current market price

The duration of this bond is determined by dividing the sum in the last column by the current market price of the bond, yielding 2.8573 years ($2,780.97 ÷ $973.27).

Duration as a Measure of a Bond's Volatility

Duration provides investors with a method to easily compare a bond's volatility to the volatility of other bonds. Simply, bonds with higher durations are more volatile when interest rates change than bonds with lower durations. Therefore, the volatility of bonds increases as the duration increases. The main factors that impact a bond's duration are coupon rate, maturity, and yield to maturity.

Coupon Rate

The coupon rate of a bond and its duration have an inverse relationship. The duration of a bond cannot exceed the maturity of a bond. Generally, the duration of a bond is less than its term to maturity. A bond's duration will equal its maturity only if the bond is a zero-coupon bond.

When the coupon rate is increased, the investor is receiving cash flows more quickly, decreasing the time the investor must wait to be paid back the initial investment. A quicker payback means a shorter duration.

Term to Maturity

The term to maturity of a bond and its duration have a direct relationship. Bonds with greater maturities have longer durations. However, the increase in duration is at a diminishing rate. Exhibit 12A.5 illustrates this point. This graph shows the duration for a bond with a 10% coupon and a 10% YTM, calculated for maturities ranging between 1 year and 30 years.

EXHIBIT 12A.5 Duration at Various Maturities for a 10% Coupon Bond with 10% YTM

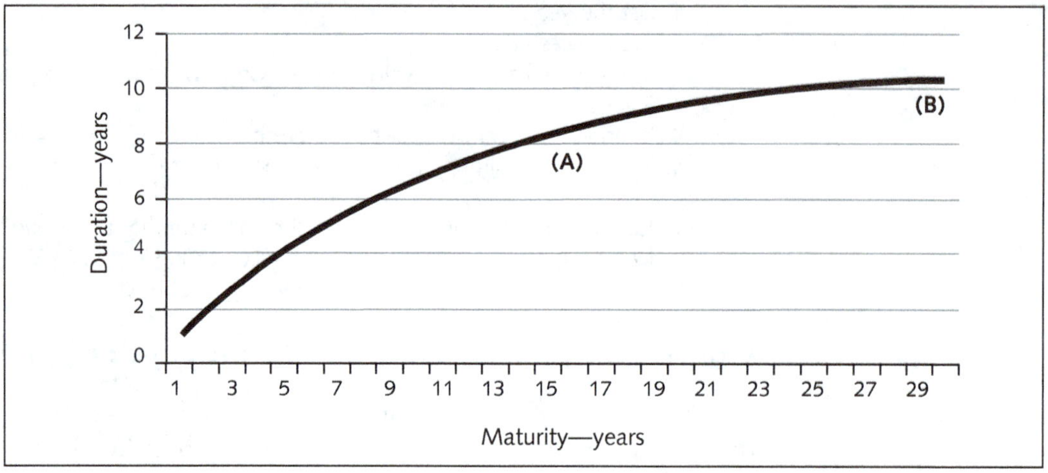

As shown, duration is directly impacted by maturity, however, at a decreasing rate. In this graph, the duration for a maturity of 15 years is approximately 8.4 years (A), and the duration for a maturity of 30 years is only 10.4 years (B). Although the actual maturity doubled, the duration of the bond increased by only two years.

Yield to Maturity

As with the coupon rate of a bond, the market interest rate, or current yield to maturity, is inversely related to duration. As the level of interest rates increases, the durations of bonds decrease, and, if interest rates decrease, durations will increase. A reduction in market interest rates results in a lower reinvestment rate for coupon payments, which extends the payback period for the bond.

Bond Price Changes

Another important application of duration is its use in determining the price change in a bond or bond portfolio on the basis of changes in interest rates. As interest rates change, bond prices are impacted. Exposure to interest rate risk is a significant variable to fixed-income investors. What is the percentage of change in the bond or bond portfolio, given a specific change in interest rates? The answer to this question can be determined by understanding the relationship between a bond's price and its duration. As we discussed, coupon, maturity, and YTM all impact duration. These same factors also determine the price of a bond. Therefore, duration can assist us in determining the estimated change in the price of a bond on the basis of changes in interest rates. The following formula provides an estimate, based on the duration and the change in market interest rates, of the percentage change in the price of a bond:

$$\frac{\Delta P}{P} = -D\left[\frac{\Delta y}{1+y}\right]$$

$\Delta P/P$ = percentage change in the price of a bond
D = duration of the bond
y = yield to maturity for the bond
Δy = change in YTM as a decimal

As the formula describes, the estimated change in the price of a bond equals the duration of a bond divided by one plus the YTM and multiplied by the change in interest rates.

EXAMPLE How much will the price of a bond with a price of $974.22 and a duration of 2.8 years increase if its YTM changed from 8% to 7.5%? (Assume a 7% coupon rate)

$$\frac{\Delta P}{P} = -2.8\left[\frac{-.005}{1+0.08}\right]$$

$$\frac{\Delta P}{P} = 0.01296$$

The price of the bond should increase by 0.01296, or 1.3%, resulting in a new price of $986.88 (1.013 × $974.22).

Using Duration to Immunize Bond Portfolios

As noted in the previous section, interest rate risk is one of the major concerns of fixed-income investors, and managers of fixed-income portfolios. When interest rates increase, the price of bonds will decline. However, an offsetting position must be considered. As interest rates increase, the reinvested coupon payments can be invested at higher rates, offsetting the decline in the value of the bond. This offsetting of price and reinvested coupon payments is illustrated in the following table.

Interest Rates Move	Value of Bond (Inverse to Interest Rates)	Value of Reinvested Coupon Payments (Direct to Interest Rates)
↑	↓	↑
↓	↑	↓

As demonstrated previously, when interest rates increase, the value of bonds declines, but the value of reinvested coupon payments increases. Similarly, as interest rates decline, bond prices increase and the value of reinvested coupon payments decreases. This offsetting is the basis for immunizing a bond or bond portfolio against interest rate risk.

Immunization
Minimizing the impact of changes in interest rates on the value of investments

Immunization is the concept of minimizing the impact of changes in interest rates on the value of investments. The goal of immunization is to protect the bond portfolio against interest rate fluctuations and reinvestment rate risk. The purpose of immunization is to provide a stable compound rate of return that equals the calculated YTM at the purchase of the bond, despite interest rate fluctuations. The portfolio is considered immunized if the realized rate of return is at least as great as the computed YTM calculated at inception. Another way to think of immunization is that a bond portfolio is immunized when the actual future value is at least as great as had been expected at inception.

A bond portfolio is initially immunized at the point of duration. Therefore, if an investor were to match the duration of a bond portfolio to the time horizon of his goal, his portfolio would be initially immunized. This can be easily accomplished with a zero-coupon bond. An investor who had a cash need in 10 years could simply purchase a 10-year, zero-coupon bond and hold it to maturity. This will eliminate all reinvestment rate risk and interest rate risk. However, purchasing a zero-coupon bond with the desired maturity may not always be feasible. Although not as ideal as a zero-coupon bond, an ordinary coupon bond can effectively immunize a portfolio.

Matching the duration to the investor's cash need immunizes the portfolio against initial changes in interest rates. As time passes, however, the bond portfolio will need to be rebalanced so that the duration and remaining time continue to match. Rebalancing should be done once or twice per year. If rebalancing is performed more frequently than twice per year, transaction costs will minimize any benefits derived through the strategy.

Traditional Methods of Immunizing Bond Portfolios

Traditional strategies for immunizing bond portfolios from interest rate risk include the ladder strategy, the barbell strategy, and the bullet strategy.

The Ladder Strategy

Ladder strategy
Portfolio immunization strategy that uses a portfolio of bonds with staggered maturities

The **ladder strategy** is accomplished by establishing a portfolio of bonds with staggered maturities. For example, ten $20,000 bonds could be purchased with maturities ranging from one to ten years for a total portfolio value of $200,000. The shorter maturity bonds would be less subject to price fluctuation than the longer term bonds, and they would combine to provide the desired duration. This approach provides two advantages. First, because there is a combination of long- and short-term bonds in the portfolio, the laddered portfolio will provide higher yields than a portfolio consisting entirely of short-term bonds. Second, because one bond matures each year, cash is regularly available to the investor.

The Barbell Strategy

Barbell strategy
Portfolio immunization strategy that uses a portfolio of short- and long-term bonds

When using the **barbell strategy**, one-half of the portfolio is invested in short-term bonds, and the other half is invested in long-term bonds. The long-term end of the barbell allows the investor to lock in attractive long-term interest rates, whereas the short-term end ensures that the investor will have the opportunity to invest in other assets if the bond market declines in value. For example, a $200,000 fixed-income portfolio might be invested as $100,000 in five-year bonds and $100,000 in 15-year bonds.

The Bullet Strategy

Bullet strategy
Portfolio immunization strategy that uses a portfolio of bonds with similar maturities

When investors purchase a series of bonds with similar maturities, focused around a single point in time, they are utilizing a **bullet strategy**. Like the previous two strategies, the portfolio is created to achieve the desired duration. For example, assume that an investor wants all of the bonds to mature in 10 years. Therefore, using the bullet strategy, the investor buys two bonds immediately, two bonds two years from now, and two more bonds four years from now. As a result, the bonds purchased immediately have a maturity date of 10 years, the bonds purchased two years later have maturity dates of eight years, and the bonds purchased four years later have maturity dates of six years.

WHERE ON THE WEB

Bloomberg **www.bloomberg.com**

Bureau of the Fiscal Service **www.publicdebt.treas.gov**

CNN Money **money.cnn.com**

Ginnie Mae (GNMA) **www.ginniemae.gov**

Marketwatch from Dow Jones **www.marketwatch.com**

Moody's Investors Service **www.moodys.com**

MSN Money **www.msn.com/en-us/money**

Securities Industry and Financial Markets Association (formerly the Bond Market) **www.sifma.org**

Standard & Poor's **www.standardandpoors.com**

Treasury Direct (U.S. Savings Bonds) **www.savingsbonds.gov**

CHAPTER 12

Supplement B: Equity Securities

LEARNING OBJECTIVES

This supplement provides information on equity securities. The following topics are covered:

- Characteristics of equities
- Types of common stock
- Preferred stock
- Foreign securities
- Risks associated with equities
- Measures of return
- Equity markets
- Market indexes and averages

- Market positions
- Margin accounts
- Trading securities
- Methods of security analysis
- Valuation models

BASIC CONCEPTS OF OWNERSHIP INVESTMENTS

What Ownership Means

Ownership securities are securities that represent some form of ownership interest in a corporation. Corporations are artificial, legal entities whose creation and operation are controlled by state statutes. To become a corporation, a business must incorporate within a state. As part of the incorporation process, and as one method of raising additional capital, a corporation may issue shares of common stock. Holders of these shares have certain rights and benefits, including the right to receive dividends, the right to vote on corporate issues, the right to limited liability, and, finally, the right to ultimate distribution of assets in the event of liquidation.

Numerous risks are inherent in owning common stock. The primary reason that investors are willing to accept these risks is that equities have earned significantly higher returns than other types of investments over long periods. Common stock returns consist of two primary sources, dividends and capital appreciation.

Dividends
Distributions of cash or additional shares of stock paid to the shareholders of a corporation

Declaration date
Date on which a corporation's board of directors declares a dividend payment creating an obligation on the company to make a dividend payment to shareholders

Record date
The date at which an owner of the common stock of a corporation is entitled to receive the dividend payment

Ex-dividend date
The date on which the market reflects the dividend payment

Payable date
The date that the dividend will actually be paid

Dividends

Companies have positive net income when their earnings are greater than their expenses. A company's excess earnings may be reinvested into the business in the form of new or existing projects or paid to the shareholders of the corporation in the form of **dividends**.

Four dates are important when discussing payment of a dividend: the **declaration date**, the **record date**, the **ex-dividend date**, and the **payable date**. The board of directors declares a dividend payment, which creates an obligation for the company to make a dividend payment to shareholders. The record date represents the date on which an investor needs to be an owner of the common stock to be entitled to receive the dividend payment. The ex-dividend date is one business day before the date of record. Because most trades settle two business days after the trade date, a customer must purchase the stock two business days before the date of record to qualify for the dividend.

Finally, the payable date is simply the date on which the dividend will actually be paid to the shareholders of record. Therefore, someone who sells shares after the record date, but before the payable date, will receive the dividend payment.

Dividend reinvestment plans (DRIPs)
Dividends are automatically reinvested into the company's stock without the use of a broker

Many companies allow investors to automatically reinvest dividends rather than receive them in cash. These **dividend reinvestment plans (DRIPs)** allow investors to accumulate wealth over time by reinvesting cash dividends back into their equity holdings. DRIPs have traditionally been programs established by corporations to allow their shareholders to purchase additional shares without a broker and to automatically reinvest dividend payments. These programs can provide cost-efficient investing for the average investor.

Capital Appreciation

Capital appreciation
The form of return the investor receives when a company chooses to retain the earnings and invest in additional projects; appreciation of the stock

A company may choose to retain the earnings it has generated and invest in additional projects. In this case, the owner or investor receives the return in the form of appreciation of the stock, which is referred to as **capital appreciation**. Capital appreciation is simply an increase in the market price of the common stock.

Voting

Statutory voting
One vote per share of common stock

Cumulative voting
A shareholder casts votes equal to the number of vacant positions on the board of directors multiplied by the number of shares owned, allocated in any way the shareholder wishes

Proxy voting
Authorizing an agent to cast the votes for the shareholder

In addition to the returns from dividend income and capital appreciation, owners of common stock have voting rights. These voting rights include the right to vote for the board of directors and the right to vote on corporate issues such as certain mergers and acquisitions.

Voting can take the form of statutory voting or cumulative voting. **Statutory voting** authorizes one vote per share of common stock for each item on the ballot, such as seats on the board of directors. **Cumulative voting** may be advantageous for small/minority shareholders by giving them a greater opportunity to offset the votes of large shareholders. With cumulative voting, a shareholder casts votes equal to the number of vacant positions on the board of directors multiplied by the number of shares owned, allocated in any way the shareholder wishes. In addition, voting can be done in person or by proxy. **Proxy voting** involves sending a written authorization to an agent to cast the votes for the shareholder.

Maintaining Ownership Percentage

Preemptive right
Allows shareholders to maintain ownership percentage by requiring new issues of stock to be offered first to current shareholders

Some companies permit owners to maintain their ownership percentage in the event of any new offering of company stock. For example, an investor who owns 10% of a company might be given the opportunity to purchase 10% of any new stock offering. This right, known as a **preemptive right**, allows the investor to maintain the current ownership percentage. A rights offering allows stockholders to purchase common stock below the current market price during the subscription period. Stockholders may exercise their rights, sell them, or let them expire.

Liability

Because corporations are separate legal entities, they are generally responsible for all debts and claims arising from all sources. As a result, shareholders are protected from personal liability.

TYPES OF EQUITY SECURITIES

Common Stock

Common stock
Ownership interest in a company

Common stock represents an ownership interest in a firm. If the company succeeds, the investor will receive returns from the investment. However, if the company does not perform well, then the value of the stock will decline. Because there are thousands of companies, various classification systems have been developed to categorize equity securities. One classification system is based on the type of stock. This classification system includes defensive stocks, cyclical stocks, blue-chip stocks, growth stocks, income stocks, interest-sensitive stocks, value stocks, and technology stocks.

Defensive Stocks

Defensive stocks
Stock of companies that are relatively unaffected by general fluctuations in the economy

Stocks that are relatively unaffected by general fluctuations in the economy are considered **defensive stocks**. These companies tend to have steady (although slow) growth, become popular during economic recessions, and lose popularity during economic booms. Many of these companies provide products that are necessary for everyday life. Thus, the demand for these products will not be adversely affected by changing economic cycles. Defensive stocks are usually found in the following industries:

- Utilities
- Soft drinks
- Groceries
- Candy
- Drugs/pharmaceuticals
- Tobacco

Another way to think of defensive stocks is that they have low systematic risk because they are not greatly affected by changes in the economy and the market. Therefore, these securities will typically have low betas relative to the overall market.

Cyclical Stocks

Cyclical stocks
Stock of companies that tend to prosper in expanding economies and perform poorly during down business cycles

Cyclical stocks tend to prosper during economic expansion and perform poorly during a downturn in the business cycle. When the economy is growing, demand strengthens, and these companies are able to make large profits. When the economy is in a downturn, these companies are hurt by declines in demand and are less profitable. In recessions, they employ cost-cutting measures to improve the bottom line (earnings) and, as a result, these companies end up in a healthy financial position for the next economic upturn. The companies regarded as cyclicals usually have large investments in plant and equipment and, therefore, high fixed costs. These stocks come from industries that include the following:

- Automobiles
- Cement
- Paper
- Airlines
- Railroads

- Machinery
- Steel

Because these stocks typically perform well when the economy is booming and perform poorly when the economy is in recession, cyclical stocks are highly correlated with the overall stock market. In addition, these stocks will typically have higher betas relative to the overall market.

Blue-Chip Stocks

Blue-chip stocks
Stock issued by older, well-established companies that maintain the ability to pay dividends both in years the company has income and in years the company has losses

Stocks issued by highly regarded investment quality companies are called **blue-chip stocks**. These older, well-established companies tend to maintain their ability to pay dividends both in years the company has income and in years the company has losses. These companies are often leaders in their respective industries. They tend to offer investors quality investments with steady dividend streams and relatively consistent growth.

Growth Stocks

Growth stocks
Stock issued by companies whose sales, earnings, and market share are growing at higher rates than the average or the general economy

Growth stocks are stocks issued by companies that have sales, earnings, and market share growing at higher rates than the average or the general economy. Many blue-chip stocks can also be classified as growth stocks. Because these companies are growing and expanding, they typically do not pay large dividends. Most of the earnings generated from these companies are reinvested in the company to support future growth. These companies are expected to grow and appreciate more rapidly than other companies.

Price appreciation is appealing to investors because it remains untaxed until the appreciation is recognized (i.e., there is no taxable gain until the stock is sold and the gain is recognized for tax purposes). This growth acts as an income tax deferral and allows for higher compounding returns. Because investors trying to accumulate wealth do not usually need current income, these stocks match their financial needs better than other investments due to smaller dividends and tax deferred appreciation.

Emerging growth stocks are a subset of growth stocks, comprised of smaller and younger companies. These companies have survived the early years and are beginning to grow and expand. Emerging growth stocks have great potential for investment but are also subject to tremendous risk.

Income Stocks

Income stock
Stock issued by companies in the maturity phase of the industry life cycle and that pay out the majority of their earnings in the form of dividends

As discussed earlier, dividends are one of the two ways investors benefit from investing in common stock. Some stocks are attractive because they make large divided payments relative to other firms. Often these companies are in the maturity phase of the industry life cycle and pay out the majority of their earnings in the form of dividends. Utilities are a good example of an **income stock**.

Interest-Sensitive Stocks

Interest-sensitive stock
Stock issued by companies whose performance is largely affected by changes in interest rates

Because the performance of some companies is largely affected by changes in interest rates, their stock is considered **interest-sensitive stock**. For example, the housing industry is more productive and has more demand when interest rates are low because it is cheaper for consumers to purchase homes. When interest rates rise, the cost of purchasing of a home goes up, causing the demand for a new home to decline. These trends also affect lumber, plumbing, furnishing, and household equipment companies. Rising interest rates cause the cost of debt to increase; therefore, companies that have large amounts of debt may have increasing interest expense. These companies, like consumers, have the opportunity to refinance their debt during periods of low interest rates.

Companies heavily affected by interest rates include insurance companies and commercial banks.

Value Stocks

Value stocks
Stock trading at prices that are low given the stock's historical earnings and current asset value

Stocks trading at prices that are low given their historical earnings and current asset value are referred to as **value stocks**. These securities tend to have low price-to-earnings ratios and tend to be out of favor in the market. Value investment managers attempt to find these high-quality companies that are temporarily undervalued by the market in hopes that the market will recognize their true value and their price will increase.

Technology Stocks

Technology stocks
Stocks of companies involved in high-technology fields categorized by above-average earnings potential and high risk

Technology stocks are part of the broader technology sector that encompasses the research, development, and distribution of technology based products. These stocks include companies that are involved in electronics, data storage, computer software, robotics, and life science companies. Companies in this sector sell and service tech-based equipment, networking systems, and online services to businesses, governmental agencies, and home users. Tech stocks offer the investor large potential gains coupled with high risk because of business uncertainty and fierce competition. Therefore, the typical tech stock investor must have a high risk tolerance, and be prepared to assume a high level of risk.

Preferred Stock

Preferred stock
A type of stock that has characteristics of both fixed-income investments and of common stock in that dividend payments must be paid each year before paying a dividend to the common shareholders

Cumulative preferred stock
Preferred stock that requires receipt of previously unpaid preferred dividends before common shareholders receive dividend payments

Participating preferred stock
Preferred stock that receives dividend based on the performance of the firm in addition to the specified preferred dividend

Preferred stock has characteristics of both fixed-income investments and of common stock. Shareholders of preferred stock generally receive dividends each year equal to a stated percentage of the par value of the stock if declared by the company. For example, a $100 par, 5.5% issue of preferred stock pays a dividend of $5.50 each year for each share owned. The corporation must satisfy these dividend payments before paying a dividend to the common shareholders. If the corporation is required to pay any unpaid preferred dividends from prior years before paying a dividend to the common stockholders, the stock is referred to as **cumulative preferred stock**.

Preferred stock also may be participating, which means that preferred shareholders share in the profits of the corporation. With **participating preferred stock**, the preferred shareholders generally receive dividend payments. Then, holders of common stock receive dividends equal to the amount paid to the preferred shareholders. Additional funds for dividends are then allocated between the participating preferred and common shareholders, according to stock agreements.

Preferred stock has a preferential right over common shareholders to the assets of the corporation. This right must be satisfied before the common shareholders receive any assets upon liquidation. However, secured and unsecured creditors will be compensated before preferred shareholders receive any assets of the corporation.

Convertible preferred stock
Preferred stock that includes the right to convert preferred stock into a specific number of common shares at the option of the stockholder

Convertible preferred stock has a conversion right that allows holders to redeem or trade in the preferred stock for a specified number of common stock shares. Convertible preferred stock provides the safety of a fixed-income security with the growth potential associated with common stock.

Foreign Securities

Foreign securities
Securities issued by non-U.S. firms

Foreign securities may provide significant benefits to U.S. investors. First, securities issued outside the United States have substantial return potential. Many of the countries outside the United States are less developed and, therefore, provide opportunities for significant growth. Second, foreign markets are generally not as efficient as the U.S. market and, consequently, provide opportunities to find undervalued securities. Third, foreign securities provide diversification benefits. The returns and movements in the equity markets of most foreign countries are not highly correlated with that of the U.S. market. Therefore, adding foreign asset classes to a portfolio may increase the efficiency of the portfolio.

Foreign securities are generally classified as being from developed countries or emerging markets. Developed countries include Canada, Japan, England, and France. Emerging markets include those countries with significant growth potential that are currently underdeveloped. Examples of emerging markets are Argentina, Brazil, and Chile.

American Depositary Receipts (ADRs)

American depositary receipts (ADRs)
Certificates issued by U.S. banks representing ownership in shares of stock of a foreign company that are held on deposit in a bank in the firm's home country

American depositary receipts (ADRs) are one of the easiest methods of acquiring individual foreign securities. They are certificates issued by U.S. banks representing ownership in shares of stock of a foreign company that are held on deposit in a bank in the firm's home country. ADRs are denominated in U.S. dollars and pay dividends in U.S. dollars. Although they are denominated in U.S. currency, they do not protect holders from exchange rate risk. Changes in currency rates between the firm's currency and the U.S. dollar will be reflected by a change in the value of the ADR.

ADRs are considered cross-listed because the foreign shares are listed on the U.S. stock exchange as well as the foreign exchange. One of the benefits of ADRs is that the foreign company must satisfy the requirements of U.S. exchanges, including compliance with U.S. Generally Accepted Accounting Principles (GAAP) and certain disclosure and reporting requirements.

Purchasing Foreign Shares on Foreign Stock Exchanges

Direct purchases of foreign securities on foreign exchanges are more difficult than indirect purchases. However, with the advance of technology, the process has simplified. Establishing a brokerage account in a foreign country or using a foreign branch of a U.S. broker can accomplish the purchase of foreign shares on foreign exchanges. The foreign transactions require completion in the local currency. Monitoring direct foreign investments is certainly more difficult than monitoring a mutual fund.

RISKS OF EQUITY SECURITIES

As with all securities and investments, certain inherent risks (both systematic and unsystematic) associated with equity investments must be considered. Some of the investment risks that we will discuss include market risk, interest rate risk, business risk, financial risk, exchange rate risk, and country risk.

Market Risk

Market risk represents the tendency for changes in the market to influence the prices of equities. When the market is on the rise, most stocks increase in value. Conversely, stocks tend to fall with declines in the market. Often, a move in the market is prefaced by some change in the broad economic environment.

Interest Rate Risk

Interest rate risk is one of the major risks affecting fixed-income securities and bond portfolios. Equity securities also are affected by changes in interest rates. When interest rates rise, there is negative pressure on the value of common stocks and when interest rates fall, stocks tend to increase in value. The three primary reasons for this relationship are increased borrowing costs, attractiveness of alternative investments, and the valuation of securities.

Increased Borrowing Costs Most companies use debt to finance capital expansion and acquire assets. The cost of debt is interest payments. When interest rates rise, the cost of future borrowing will increase. This increased borrowing cost can cause earnings to decline. When earnings decrease, the value of the company is reduced. Therefore, changes in interest rates have a direct impact on the cost of borrowing and, thus, on the earnings of a firm.

Attractiveness of Alternative Investments When interest rates rise, so do the corresponding yields on fixed-income securities. As yields increase, bonds become more attractive. Investors become unwilling to assume the additional risk inherent in equities when the spread between the expected return on bonds and stocks is small. Therefore, as investors decrease investments in equities so that they can take advantage of the fixed-income yields, there is downward pressure on the equity market, causing it to decline.

The Value of Equities The value of a security today is the sum of the discounted future cash flows expected from the investment. As interest rates rise, the discount rate used to value a security must also increase. Because an increase in the discount rate results in a lower valuation, stocks generally decline when interest rates rise.

Business Risk

Business risk is a risk associated with a specific business, which includes the speculative nature of the business, the management of the business, and the philosophy of the business. Different types of businesses will have different levels of risk. For instance, we generally consider technology securities to be more risky than defensive stocks.

Business risk can also be thought of as the uncertainty of operating income. Utility companies have relatively stable and steady operating income streams and, therefore, have lower business risk. Because they have unsteady or fluctuating operating income levels, cyclical companies (such as auto manufacturers) have higher business risk.

Financial Risk

The method by which firms acquire their assets is directly related to financial risk or financial leverage. With regard to their capital structure, companies may use debt through the issuance of bonds, or they may issue equity securities. When companies choose debt to finance the purchase of additional assets, the level of financial risk increases. This increased leverage is the same as for individuals when they use margin to purchase securities.

EXAMPLE Consider two firms that each earn $50,000 of net income. Both firms are in the same business, and each has $400,000 of assets. Company A has not issued debt and has financed all of its assets with equity. Company B has issued $300,000 of debt and $100,000 of equity.

	Company A	Company B
Net income	$50,000	$50,000
Debt	$0	$300,000
Equity	$400,000	$100,000
ROE (return on equity)	12.5%	50%

Notice that while each company's earnings and assets are the same, the return on equity is quite different. This disparity results from the different capital structure of each firm. Because Company B has chosen to use debt as a method of financing, it has increased the leverage of the firm. However, Company B's returns are likely to be more volatile over time than Company A's returns.

Exchange Rate Risk

The uncertainty of returns in foreign investments due to changes in the value of a foreign currency relative to the valuation of the investor's domestic currency is referred to as exchange rate risk. A foreign investment is subject not only to the inherent risk of the investment, but also to the risk that the foreign currency will weaken relative to the domestic currency, decreasing the gains (or increasing the losses) from the investment.

Country Risk

International investments are subject to country risk, which is the unique risk associated with a particular country. These risks include both political and economic risks. The United States is generally thought to have the lowest country risk because its political and economic systems are considered the most stable.

MEASURES OF RETURN

The primary purpose of investing is to earn a positive return. Investors seek investments that are consistent with their risk and return preferences in an attempt to achieve financial goals. Therefore, investors should understand and be able to calculate the returns from equity securities. There are several methods of calculating returns from equity securities, each with distinct advantages and disadvantages.

Time-weighted returns
A method of determining an internal rate of return by evaluating the performance of portfolio managers without the influence of additional investor deposits or withdrawals to or from the portfolio

Dollar-weighted returns
A method of determining the internal rate of return that an individual investor earned on the basis of the investor's particular cash flow into and out of the portfolio

Time-Weighted and Dollar-Weighted Returns

Although time-weighted returns and dollar-weighted returns are both methods of determining an internal rate of return, they have very different purposes. **Time-weighted returns** are used to evaluate the performance of portfolio managers separate from the influence of additional investor deposits or withdrawals. **Dollar-weighted returns** are used to determine the rate of return an individual investor earned on the basis of the investor's particular cash flows into and out of a portfolio. The example comparing Portfolios A and B illustrates the difference between dollar-weighted returns and time-weighted returns.

Assume we are comparing two portfolios, A and B. Over a four-year period, they each earn exactly the same return per period. However, each portfolio has a different set of investor deposits and withdrawals.

Portfolio A

Period	Investor Cash Flows	Beginning of Period Value	End of Period Value	Periodic Rate of Return
0	($1,000)	$1,000	$1,200	20.00%
1	$400	$800	$700	–12.50%
2	($300)	$1,000	$1,400	40.00%
3	$200	$1,200	$1,000	–16.67%
4	$1,000	—	—	—
DWR =	8.2311%		TWR =	5.2034%

Portfolio B

Period	Investor Cash Flows	Beginning of Period Value	End of Period Value	Periodic Rate of Return
0	($1,000)	$1,000	$1,200	20.00%
1	($400)	$1,600	$1,400	–12.50%
2	$400	$1,000	$1,400	40.00%
3	($400)	$1,800	$1,500	–16.67%
4	$1,500	—	—	—
DWR =	2.0245%		TWR =	5.2034%

Note: Negative cash flows are deposits and positive cash flows are withdrawals.

Using the uneven cash flow keys of a financial calculator, we have calculated the dollar-weighted return (DWR) for Portfolio A to be 8.23% and the DWR for Portfolio B to be 2.02%. Is it reasonable to use a methodology that results in drastically different returns when each portfolio produced the same periodic rates of return? The answer depends on our goal. To evaluate the overall return for the portfolio, we want to use DWR. This provides investors with their actual return. For portfolio managers, DWR is generally not used. This is because managers do not control the timing of additional investments into the portfolio or withdrawals from the portfolio. A more accurate measure of the portfolio manager's ability is the time-weighted return (TWR).

The TWR for Portfolios A and B is calculated as follows (r = return for given period; n = number of periods):

$$\text{TWR} = [(1 + r_1)(1 + r_2)(1 + r_3)\ldots(1 + r_n)^{1/n} - 1] \times 100$$

$$(1 + .20)(1 - .1250)(1 + .40)(1 - .1667)^{1/4} - 1 = .0520338 \times 100 = 5.2034\%$$

Total Return

Total return
The sum of the capital appreciation/depreciation on an investment plus any income or earnings generated by the investment

Total return may be thought of as the sum of:

- the capital appreciation/depreciation on the underlying principal of the investment; and
- any income or earnings generated from that investment.

For example, a typical annual dividend paid (income or earnings) on a stock is 2%. If, in addition, the market value of the stock increases 6% from the beginning of the year to year end, the investor would have a total return on the stock of 8% (2% income + 6% capital appreciation). Whether an investor values the income or capital growth component of total return more highly (or both are valued equally) depends on both tax status and cash flow needs.

Dividend Yield

Dividend yield
The measure of a security's annual dividend payment as a percentage of the current market price

The measure used to compare the dividend payments from one company to another is called the **dividend yield** and is calculated as follows:

$$DY = \frac{\text{annual dividend per share}}{\text{current market price}}$$

If XYZ Company is paying an annual dividend of \$4 per share and the current market price of the stock is \$50, then the dividend yield of XYZ equals 8% (\$4 ÷ \$50). The dividend yield measure is useful for selecting stocks for inclusion in a portfolio of an investor who needs income derived from the portfolio.

EQUITY MARKETS AND BENCHMARKS

Primary Market

Primary market
The market where new issues of securities are first offered to the public

Initial public offering (IPO)
First offering of equity securities to the general public

The **primary market** is the place where securities are initially offered to the public. These security offerings are in the form of **initial public offerings**, commonly referred to as IPOs. IPOs allow businesses and entrepreneurs access to the capital markets. Business owners may issue additional shares to the public to raise capital for the expansion and growth of their business. Although an IPO will dilute the ownership of the existing shareholders, it can provide the capital and resources necessary to dramatically expand the business.

Underwriting

Underwriting
The process by which investment bankers purchase an issue of securities from a firm and resell it to the public

To issue shares to the public, companies enlist the assistance of investment bankers to underwrite the stock issue. In the process of **underwriting** an IPO, the investment banker may assume some of the risk associated with selling the securities to the public. For example, an investment banker might agree to purchase an issue for \$12 per share and then resell the issue to the public for \$13 per share. This \$1 profit is referred to as an underwriter's spread. In addition, underwriters often help the issuing firm determine its financial needs and the best investment vehicle to achieve the desired capital target.

Firm commitment
Equity underwriting in which the underwriter purchases the entire issue at a specific price from the firm and resells it on the open market

Standby underwriting
Equity underwriting in which the underwriter purchases any securities remaining after an initial offering

Best efforts agreement
Equity underwriting in which the firm agrees to repurchase any securities remaining after the initial offering is made by the underwriter

Private placement
A corporation selling a new issue of securities to a small group of institutions or sophisticated individual investors

Underwriting can take one of four forms: firm commitment, standby underwriting, best efforts, and private placement.

Firm Commitment With a **firm commitment**, the underwriter purchases the entire issue of securities at a specific price, then attempts to sell it at a higher price. This arrangement shifts all risk to the underwriter. If the issue cannot be resold at a price above the purchase price, the underwriter will lose money on the transaction. Often, a syndicate of underwriters will be set up to spread the potential risk.

Standby Underwriting When the underwriter purchases the remaining securities at a predetermined price after an initial offering (usually to existing shareholders/owners), the form of underwriting is called **standby underwriting**. This type of underwriting may reduce the issuer's risk, but it will increase the underwriter's risk.

Best Efforts Under a **best efforts agreement**, the underwriter sells as much of the issue as possible, and the remainder is returned to the issuing company. No risk is shifted to the underwriter. This arrangement occurs when the issuing company is confident that the issue will be sold or the underwriter is concerned about the financial stability of the company.

Private Placement The main attraction of a **private placement** is the lack of registration requirements associated with an IPO, resulting in less expense and less time. Generally, the issue can be placed quickly and at a low cost. Bonds have been the most common privately placed issues. A private placement cannot be sold to more than 35 unaccredited investors. An unaccredited investor is one who does not fit into one of the following categories:

- Net worth of more than $1 million
- Gross income in excess of $200,000 for each of the past two years, with the anticipation of the same level of income ($300,000 if the investor is a married couple)

In addition to reduced costs, private placements avoid the registration requirements of the SEC and the public's access to information that occurs when conforming to SEC requirements. Although private placements are limited to 35 unaccredited investors, there is no limit to the number of accredited investors.

Secondary Market

Secondary market
The market where investors can buy and sell securities with other investors

The **secondary market** is where investors buy and sell securities that have been issued previously in the primary markets. The secondary market provides liquidity to the capital markets and allows for the efficient trade of public securities.

- The first market is the exchange (auction) market where listed securities trade and includes the New York Stock Exchange (NYSE) and the over-the-counter (OTC) market.
- The second market provides a method of trading unlisted securities (OTC and Nasdaq).

Third market
Over-the-counter trading of equity shares that are listed on an exchange

Fourth market
Composed of institutional traders who trade without the help of brokers

- The **third market** consists of stocks traded both on the organized exchanges and on the OTC market. This market is especially important when the exchange is not trading a security or when trading occurs outside the normal operating hours of the exchange.
- The **fourth market** is commonly used by institutions (e.g., pension funds) that trade in very large volumes among themselves without the help of brokers (INSTINET).

EXHIBIT 12B.1 Secondary Market

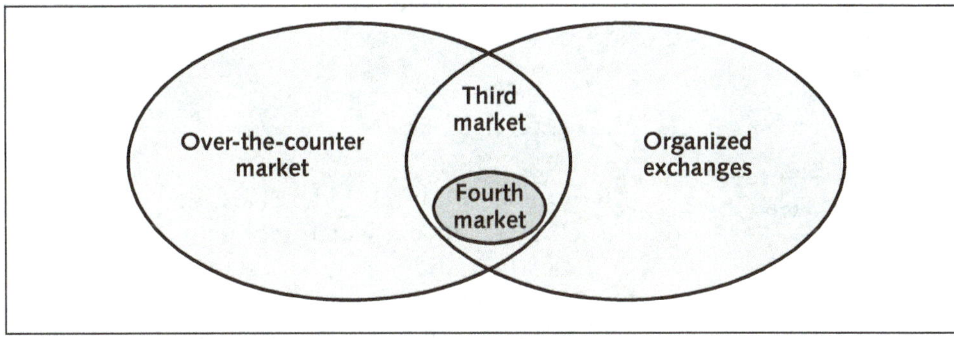

Market Indexes and Averages

The purpose of a market index or average is to provide information to investors and advisers concerning the overall movement and performance of the securities markets. Most securities are positively correlated with their respective index; the securities tend to increase when their index is increasing and decrease when their index is decreasing.

Dow Jones Industrial Average

Dow Jones Industrial Average (DJIA)
A financial index that is a price-weighted average of 30 leading industrial stocks used to measure the status of the equity market

The **Dow Jones Industrial Average** (DJIA), probably the best-known financial index in the United States, is a price-weighted average of 30 leading industrial stocks used to measure the status of the equity market.

The DJIA consists of stocks that are considered blue-chip stocks. Although these companies are often leaders in their industry, the composition of the average does change over time. However, the DJIA does have fundamental shortcomings as it fails to reflect payment of cash dividends, ignores stock dividends of less than 10%, fails to account for the number of shares outstanding, and consists of a biased sample of stocks. Even with these shortcomings, the DJIA is highly correlated with other broader market indexes, such as the S&P 500. The correlation coefficient between the DJIA and the S&P 500 is greater than 95%. A high correlation indicates that the DJIA is an adequate representation of the market in spite of its fundamental weaknesses.

Standard & Poor's 500 Index

Standard & Poor's Index (S&P 500)
A financial index of 500 U.S. equities chosen for market size, liquidity, and industry group representation

Market capitalization
The product of the number of outstanding common stock shares and current stock price

The **Standard & Poor's Index** (S&P 500) traditionally has been the measure of the U.S. large capitalization market used by academics and financial service professionals. The index consists of 500 U.S. equities chosen for market size, liquidity, and industry group representation.

The S&P 500 is a market capitalization-weighted index. This means that a company's **market capitalization** (outstanding shares multiplied by the current stock price) is represented in the index. Market capitalization indexes typically provide a better measure of the market than averages such as the DJIA. (However, the DJIA is highly correlated with the S&P 500.)

Russell Indexes

Russell 2000® Index
A well-known index used to benchmark small capitalization companies

All of the U.S. Russell indexes are market capitalization weighted and are subsets of the Russell 3000® Index, which represents 99% of the U.S. equity market. The **Russell 2000® Index** is an index that is used to benchmark small capitalization companies. The Russell 1000® Index represents the thousand largest companies in the Russell 3000® Index. Russell also maintains numerous value and growth indexes that allow for comparisons with various portfolio manager styles.

Wilshire 5000 Index

Wilshire 5000 Index
A financial index consisting of over 5,000 U.S.-based companies; often used as a measure of the overall market within the United States

The **Wilshire 5000 Index** is another well-known index that is used as a measure of the U.S. broad market. This index consists of over 5,000 U.S.-based companies and is often used as a measure of the overall market within the United States.

MSCI EAFE Index

MSCI EAFE Index
An index measuring the international securities markets

The **MSCI EAFE** (Morgan Stanley Capital International Europe, Australasia, and Far East) **Index** is a measure of the international securities markets. This index provides an indication of how a portfolio consisting of companies outside the United States might perform over time and is probably the best known measure of international markets.

Benchmarks

The indexes just discussed can be used to compare portfolio results and evaluate an investment manager's performance. Although many investors use comparisons with other managers as a measure of performance, benchmarks should also be examined for comparative purposes. A good benchmark includes the following characteristics:

- Unambiguous—the composition and weighting of the components of the benchmark must be clearly delineated
- Investable—the option to invest in the benchmark is available

- Measurable—the benchmark's return should be calculated on a relatively frequent basis
- Appropriate—the benchmark must be consistent with the manager's investment philosophy and style
- Reflective of current investment opinions—the manager has current investment knowledge of the securities that make up the benchmark
- Specified in advance—the benchmark should be constructed before the beginning of the evaluation period

These six properties improve the usefulness of a benchmark as an investment management tool and allow for a better measure of a portfolio manager's performance.

PURCHASING EQUITY SECURITIES

Long Positions

Long position
The purchase of a stock in hopes that it will appreciate over time

The most prevalent type of position investors take is a long position. A **long position** is the purchase of a stock in hopes that it will appreciate over time. If a stock is purchased for $45 and is sold for $100, then the stock has increased in price, resulting in a gain of $55.

Short Positions

Short position
A type of position investors take by selling borrowed shares in hopes that the stock price will decline over time

Investors also may benefit when they find securities that are believed to be overvalued. A short sale allows the investor to profit from the decline in the value of the security. A short sale is selling shares that are not owned by the investor. This transaction is accomplished by borrowing shares of a stock from a broker. Once the shares are sold in the market, the investor is credited with the proceeds. However, the investor must, at some point, replace the borrowed shares. This is known as covering the **short position** and is accomplished by purchasing the shares in the market and replacing the shares that were borrowed.

The short seller will profit if the shares can be purchased at a price less than the price at which the shares were sold. If the stock appreciates after the shares are sold short, the investor will lose money.

Two technical issues must be discussed regarding short selling. The first concerns dividend payments that occur before closing the short position. A short sale involves borrowing stock and selling it in the market. At the time of a short sale, two investors believe that they own the stock and are entitled to receive any dividend payment that is declared and paid. However, the company declaring the dividend will only recognize one owner (the third party who purchased the shares in the market) and will only make one dividend payment. Therefore, the short seller has the responsibility to make up the other dividend payment to the party from whom the stock was originally borrowed.

The second issue is that a short seller is required to have a margin account and post margin as if the investor were acquiring stock. If the stock increases, then the short seller may be required to restore the margin.

EXAMPLE Allison sells short 100 shares of ALC stock currently trading at $35 per share. The initial margin requirement is 50%. If the price of ALC stock declines to $25 and Allison covers her short position by repurchasing the stock, what is her gain in both dollars and as a percentage?

Allison's investment		$1,750 (100 shares × 0.5 × $35)
Short sale proceeds		$3,500
Cost to repurchase	–	$2,500
Dollar gain	=	**$1,000**
Percentage gain	=	**57.14%** ($1,000 ÷ $1,750)

Margin Accounts

Cash accounts
A type of brokerage account that requires all securities purchased by the investor to be paid for in full without any indebtedness

Margin accounts
A type of brokerage account that allows the investor to borrow funds from the broker to purchase additional securities without adding cash to the account

An investor opens a brokerage account as either a cash account or a margin account. **Cash accounts** require that all securities purchased by the investor be paid for in full without any indebtedness. If a cash account is fully invested in securities, then the only way to purchase additional securities is to add cash to the account or sell some of the current securities to generate cash. In contrast, **margin accounts** allow the investor to borrow funds from the broker to purchase additional securities without adding cash to the account. Margin accounts give investors flexibility and the ability to use leverage.

Margin accounts require that the account owner pay for a certain percentage of the cost of an investment. The margin percentage that must be established for the purchase of a security is referred to as the initial margin. The Federal Reserve Board sets the minimum initial margin percentage, which is currently 50%. Therefore, the initial purchase of a security requires the investor to put up at least 50% of the initial purchase.

In addition to the amount that initially must be put up by the investor, the investor must maintain an equity position in the account that equals or exceeds the maintenance margin. The maintenance margin is typically 35%, which means that the equity in the account must equal or exceed 35%. However, some securities may require a higher maintenance requirement. If the equity in the account drops below the maintenance margin, then the account holder receives a margin call from the broker. A margin call is a request for funds in order to restore the account equity to the maintenance margin.

Determining the Price for a Margin Call

Account equity is defined as the market value of the securities in the account less any outstanding debt. The equity percentage equals the account equity divided by the market value of the securities. The price at which a margin call is received occurs when the equity percentage drops below the maintenance margin.

EXAMPLE Lauren purchases 100 shares of Solvent Company for $104 per share. Lauren uses a margin account with a 50% initial margin for the purchase and is concerned about receiving a margin call. If the maintenance margin equals 35%, then Lauren will receive a margin call if the stock falls below $80 per share, as illustrated:

$$\text{Margin call} = \frac{\text{debit balance}}{1 - \text{maintenance margin}}$$

$$\text{Margin call} = \frac{\$52}{1 - 0.35} = \$80$$

(Note: The debit balance is 50% of the cost per share of $104.)

Determining How Much to Deposit to Restore Account Equity

If the stock or account drops below the price at which there is a margin call, then the account owner must deposit sufficient funds to restore the account equity to the maintenance margin. This amount can be determined by asking two questions. How much equity does the broker require? How much equity does the investor currently have?

Using the above example, assume that the stock drops in value to $70. In this case, Lauren would be required to deposit $6.50 per share ($24.50 – $18.00).

Required Equity		Current Equity Position	
Current value of stock	$70.00	Current value of stock	$70.00
Equity %	35%	Loan amount	(52.00)
Required equity	$24.50	Current equity	$18.00

The investor must maintain an equity position of 35%, which is the given maintenance margin. Because the price of the stock is currently $70, Lauren must have $24.50 ($70 × 35%) of equity in her account. To determine Lauren's current equity position, subtract the outstanding debt from the value of the stock. Because her current equity position equals $18, and she must have $24.50 of equity, Lauren must fund the account with the difference of $6.50 per share for a total of $650 (100 shares × $6.50).

Trading Securities

Investors should be aware of the different types of orders that can be used to acquire shares of common stock. The four standard types of orders include market orders, limit orders, stop loss orders, and stop limit orders. All orders are considered day orders unless otherwise specified. If an order is not filled within the trading day, it will expire. Orders can be good for a specific time, or they can be good-til-canceled. Time limits are often used with limit and stop orders because they are not as likely as market orders to be filled during the day.

Market Order

Market order
Type of securities order that requires the trade be made at the best current market price

Most orders are **market orders.** In fact, 75–80% of all orders have traditionally been market orders and these orders have the highest priority. A market order is an order to buy or sell a security at the best current market price. These orders must be filled before the other types of orders are considered. Although these are the fastest orders, they do not have limits or a specific price and, therefore, are subject to the fluctuations and time lines of the market.

Limit Order

Limit order
Type of securities order that requires the trade be made at a specified price or better

The objective of a **limit order** is to acquire or sell a security at a specific price—that is, one that is better than the market at the time the order is placed. The price acts as a ceiling for purchases and a floor for sales, and the order will be held until filled or canceled. Limit orders are maintained in chronological order. Higher priced purchase limit orders take priority over lower priced purchase limit orders. Even if the price for the stock is below (or above) the limit order, there is no guarantee that it will be filled.

EXAMPLE David, a seasoned investor, has reviewed all the relevant financial information and has determined that the Ashbey Corporation is worth $45 per share. While the stock is trading between $48 and $50, he places a limit order at $45. This will ensure that if the order is filled to purchase shares of Ashbey Corporation, David's price will be no higher than $45. If Ashbey continues to trade above $45, David's order will not be filled.

Stop Loss Order

Stop loss order
A type of securities order that becomes a market order when the security's price reaches a specific level

Stop loss orders are used to protect investors against large losses. If the market price reaches a certain point, the stop order will turn into a market order. For instance, an investor who is long in a security might place a stop order 10 points below the current market price to protect the appreciation of the stock against serious declines in market price. Likewise, these orders can be used to limit losses in connection with short sales.

EXAMPLE Steve purchased Roland, Inc. for $29 per share. The stock is now trading at $73 per share. He has an unrecognized gain of $44. If Steve is concerned about the price of the stock declining, he can place a stop order at $70. If the stock price drops to $70, a market order is placed immediately. However, the order may be filled at $69 or $68. The stop order protects his profit position.

Stop Limit Order

Stop limit order
A type of securities order that becomes a limit order when the security's price reaches a specific level

Stop limit orders are similar to stop loss orders except they turn into limit orders when triggered. The stop order price and the limit order price are both specified. Stop limit orders are the least used type of order.

EXAMPLE If Dina owns 5,000 shares of Prez's Pretzels, which is selling for $35 per share, and she is concerned about the price dropping, she may want to place a stop limit order. If she places the order "sell 5,000 shares at $32 stop, $30 limit," and the price drops to $32, the broker will attempt to sell the stock for $32 but will not sell below the $30 limit order.

Good-Til-Canceled Order

Good-til-canceled order
An order to buy or sell a security at a specific or limit price that lasts until the order is completed or canceled

A **good-til-canceled (GTC) order** is an order to buy or sell a security at a specific or limit price that lasts until the order is completed or canceled. A GTC order will not be executed until the limit price has been reached, regardless of the time frame. Investors often use GTC orders to set a limit price that is far away from the current market price. Some brokerage firms may limit the time a GTC order can remain in effect and may charge more for executing this type of order.

METHODS OF ANALYSIS

The two primary forms of analysis used by security analysts to determine whether a particular security should be purchased or, if already owned, should be sold are technical analysis and fundamental analysis.

Technical Analysis

Technical analysis
The search for identifiable and recurring stock price patterns

Technical analysis is an attempt to determine the demand side of the supply/demand equation for a particular stock or set of stocks. This method is based on the belief that studying the history of security trades will help predict future movements. Technical analysts (or chartists, due to their reliance on charts) believe that the history of the stock price will tell the whole story of the security and that there is no need to be concerned with earnings, financial leverage, product mix, and management philosophy. Recall that technical analysis is in direct contradiction to the efficient market hypothesis that, at all levels, states that the current price already reflects all historical price data. Technical analysts believe that basic economic assumptions support the theory of technical analysis.

- The interaction between supply and demand is the foundation for the value of all goods and services.
- Both rational and irrational factors control supply and demand. The market weighs each of these factors.
- The market and individual securities tend to move in similar trends that endure for substantial lengths of time.
- Variations in the relationship between supply and demand can change prevailing trends.
- Shifts or variations in supply and demand can be detected in the movement of the market.

Technical analysts use a variety of techniques to predict the trend of the market, such as moving averages, relative strength analysis, contrary opinion rules, and breadth of the market indicators. One of the most significant stock price and volume techniques is called the Dow theory.

The Dow theory, developed initially by Charles H. Dow and later expanded by William Hamilton, is the basis for many of the theories of technical analysis. The Dow theory suggests three types of price movements. Primary moves are the first type of movement and represent large trends that last anywhere from one to four years. These moves are considered to be bull or bear markets for up or down moves, respectively. The second type of movement is called an intermediate move that is a temporary change in movement called a technical correction. The time frame for these corrections is generally less than two months. The final type of movement is referred to as a ripple that occurs during both primary and secondary movements and represents a small change in comparison to the first two movements. The belief is that all three of these movements are occurring at the same time.

The Dow theory uses the Dow Jones Industrial Average (DJIA) and the Dow Jones Transportation Average (DJTA) as indicators of the market. This theory is based on the concept that measures of stock prices, such as averages and indexes, should move coincidentally. Thus, if the DJIA is moving upward, the DJTA should also be increasing. Support from both market indicators would suggest a strong bull market. Likewise, if both averages are declining, there is considerable support for a strong bear market.

When the averages are moving in opposite directions, the future direction of stock prices is unclear.

Fundamental Analysis

Fundamental analysis
The analysis of a stock's value using basic, publicly available data, such as the stock's earnings, sales, risk, and industry analysis

Fundamental analysis is the process of determining the intrinsic value of a security. This intrinsic value is generally thought of as the present value of future cash flows (often the dividend stream of an equity security). Through fundamental analysis, investors attempt to determine what the company is worth. Once the value is determined, it is compared to the market value of the security. If the market value of the security is less than the intrinsic value, then the investor will purchase the security. If the market value of the security is greater than the intrinsic value, the investor should sell shares currently held or delay the purchase of shares.

The process of determining the value of a security encompasses many aspects. The fundamental analyst incorporates broad macroeconomic trends, industry analysis, and company analysis into an estimate of a security's value. The analysis of broad economic trends includes analyzing growth of the economy, analyzing monetary and fiscal policy, interest rates, unemployment, consumer spending, and inflation. Analysts look at industry data to determine market competitiveness, strengths and weaknesses, and other factors that impact the value of a security within the context of its industry. At the company level, fundamental analysts use financial statement analysis, valuation models, and ratio analysis to assist in determining the company's worth. Once forecasts about future cash flows are developed, a fundamental analyst uses valuation models to determine the value of the company.

Fundamental analysts may be further differentiated according to where they begin (and finish) their analysis. A top-down fundamental analyst begins with researching the overall economy and current state of the secondary market. Specifically, such an analyst then selects an industry (or industry sector) that he believes will perform best over an upcoming time frame. Finally, the analyst then screens a database of securities within that industry to find acceptable companies (and acceptable stocks) in which to recommend investment.

The other type of fundamental analyst, the bottom-up fundamental analyst, begins with an examination of the company's fundamentals and then considers the financial prospects for the industry in which the company operates. Indeed, because of emphasis first and foremost on the security itself, the bottom-up analyst is sometimes known as a stock-picker. Finally, this type of analyst then considers the prospects for the overall economy.

VALUATION MODELS

One of the components of selecting a stock in which to invest is determining its intrinsic value using one of the following valuation models.

Valuing Preferred Stock

Because preferred stock generally pays a fixed dividend and often has no maturity, it is considered a perpetuity. In other words, the dividend continues indefinitely. Therefore, we can use the no-growth (perpetuity) dividend discount model to value a preferred stock.

$$V = \frac{D}{r}$$

The value of a preferred stock equals the dividend (*D*) divided by the required rate of return of the investor (*r*). For example, if a preferred stock is paying a dividend of $6 and the investor's required rate of return equals 12%, the intrinsic value of the preferred stock should equal $50, as follows:

$$V = \frac{\$6}{0.12} = \$50$$

If the current market price of the security were greater than $50, the investor should not purchase the preferred stock as an investment. However, if the stock was trading at a price of $50 or less, the purchase of the security would be a wise decision.

Constant Growth Dividend Discount Model

Common stock dividends typically do not remain steady over time. Generally, the dividend grows over time. Assuming a constant rate of growth for the dividend, we can expand the above model to accommodate the growth component of the dividend stream. The following formula is used to value a common stock with a constant growing dividend:

$$V = \frac{D_1}{r - g}$$

The value of a common stock equals the dividend one period from today (D_1) divided by the difference between the investor's required rate of return (*r*) and the expected growth rate of the dividend (*g*).

EXAMPLE JEM stock is paying a current annual dividend of $6, which is growing at a constant rate of 4% per year. If the investor's required rate of return equals 12%, then the intrinsic value of the common stock equals $78:

$$V = \frac{\$6 \times (1.04)}{0.12 - 0.04} = \$78$$

D_1 must be determined by multiplying the current dividend (D_0) by one plus the growth rate (1 + *g*). The model is based on a constant growing dividend and on the required return of the investor. Notice that the model will be meaningless if the growth rate (*g*) equals or exceeds the required rate of return of the investor (*r*). This model is most appropriate for mature companies.

Multistage Growth Dividend Discount Model

The multistage (variable) growth dividend discount model assumes that the growth rate of the stock's dividend is not constant but rather changes (either up or down). This model is most appropriately used for a company in the growth phase. To determine the intrinsic value of a stock using this model, follow a three-step process.

1. Compute the value of each future dividend until the growth rate stabilizes.
2. Use the constant growth dividend discount model to compute the remaining intrinsic value of the stock at the beginning of the year when the dividend growth rate stabilizes.
3. Use the uneven cash flow method to solve for the net present (intrinsic) value of the stock.

EXAMPLE Consider CPM stock with a current dividend of $1 per share and a current market price of $25.56 per share. The current dividend is expected to grow for three years at a rate of 3% annually and then 2% annually thereafter. Assume an investor's required rate of return is 6%.

1. Compute the value of each future dividend until the growth rate stabilizes (Years 1–3).
   D_1 = $1.00 × 1.03 = **$1.03**
   D_2 = $1.03 × 1.03 = **$1.06**
   D_3 = $1.06 × 1.03 = **$1.09**
2. Use the constant growth dividend discount model to compute the remaining intrinsic value of the stock at the beginning of the year when the dividend growth rate stabilizes (Year 4).
   D_4 = $1.09 × 1.02 = $1.11
   V = $1.11 ÷ (0.06 – 0.02) = **$27.75**
3. Use the uneven cash flow method to solve for the net present (intrinsic) value of the stock.
   CF_0 = $0
   CF_1 = $1.03
   CF_2 = $1.06
   CF_3 = $1.09 + $27.75 = $28.84
   I/YR = 6%
   Solve for NPV = $26.13

In this example, the intrinsic value of the stock is **$26.13**.

Price-to-Earnings (P/E) Ratio

P/E ratio
A measure of how much the market is willing to pay for each dollar of earnings of a company

The **P/E ratio** is a measure of how much the market is willing to pay for each dollar of earnings of a company. The ratio is determined by dividing the current market price of the security by the earnings per share (EPS) for the company:

$$P/E = \frac{\text{current market price}}{\text{earnings per share}}$$

EXAMPLE If XYZ stock is trading at $50 per share and has earnings per share of $4, its P/E ratio equals 12.5.

The P/E ratio may be used to compare companies within an industry. Better quality companies generally have higher P/E ratios than lower quality companies. Investors are willing to pay more for each dollar of earnings from a high-quality company.

Valuing the Company vs. Valuing the Stock

Up to this point, we have limited our valuation methodology to those stocks that pay dividends. With preferred stock, we use the valuation of a perpetuity to determine its price. Similarly, we valued common stock with a constant growing dividend. What about those companies that do not regularly pay dividends? Our focus simply needs to shift from the valuation of the stock to the valuation of the company. Instead of looking at the cash flows from the security, we need to address the cash flows that are generated by the company.

By using the models developed for finding the present value of a stream of cash flows, we can obtain the value of the company. The inputs in the model are the relevant cash flows and the discount rate.

Free cash flow to equity
Term that describes the available cash after meeting all of the firm's operating and financial needs; used to calculate the value a company

The term **free cash flow to equity** describes the available cash after meeting all of the firm's operating and financial needs and is generally calculated as follows:

	Revenue
–	Operating expenses
=	**Earnings before interest, taxes, and depreciation (EBITDA)**
–	Depreciation
–	Amortization
=	**Earnings before interest and taxes (EBIT)**
–	Interest
–	Taxes
=	Net income
+	Depreciation
+	Amortization
=	**Cash flow from operations**
–	Preferred dividends
–	Capital expenditures
–	Working capital needs
–	Principal repayments (loan)
+	Proceeds from new debt issues
=	**Free cash flow to equity**

Once the cash flow is forecasted, then it can be used to value the company. The discount rate that is used can be derived from reviewing comparable companies in the market or by using models such as the capital asset pricing model.

Once the value of the company is established, then the value of the stock can be derived from the company's valuation. However, valuing the share price of the stock is not as simple as dividing the value of the company by the outstanding shares of common stock. The value of the company reflects an inherent control premium. This premium reflects the ability to change the board of directors, change the dividend policy, and influence the business opportunities that are undertaken. The concept of the control premium can be seen in the market any time a company acquires another company. The acquiring company is willing to pay more than the current market price of the stock because it is acquiring control. Therefore, the value of a share of stock as listed on an exchange has been discounted from the proportionate value of the company because the stock represents a minority interest.

WHERE ON THE WEB

American Association of Individual Investors **www.aaii.com**

American Stock Exchange **www.amex.com**

Barron's Online **www.barrons.com**

Bloomberg.com **www.bloomberg.com**

MSN Money **www.msn.com/en-us/money**

CNN Money **www.money.cnn.com**

S&P Dow Jones Indices **us.spindices.com**

Kiplinger **www.kiplinger.com**

Nasdaq **www.nasdaq.com**

NYSE Euronext (NYSE Group, Inc. and Euronext, N.V. combined) **www.nyse.com**

TD Ameritrade **www.tdameritrade.com**

U.S. Securities and Exchange Commission **www.sec.gov**

Yahoo Finance **finance.yahoo.com**

CHAPTER 12

Supplement C: Mutual Funds

LEARNING OBJECTIVES

This supplement provides additional information on mutual funds. The following topics are covered:

- Types of investment companies
  - Unit investment trusts
  - Exchange-traded funds
  - Closed-end investment companies
  - Open-end investment companies (mutual funds)
  - Hedge funds
- Mutual fund fees
- Mutual fund classification
- Advantages of mutual funds
- Types and objectives of mutual funds
- Mutual fund selection

- Performance measures
- Mutual fund selection issues

TYPES OF INVESTMENT COMPANIES

Investment companies
Financial services companies that sell shares of stock to the public and use the proceeds to invest in a portfolio of securities

Investment companies are financial services companies that sell shares of stock to the public and use the proceeds to invest in a portfolio of securities. Although each investor or shareholder may have a relatively small investment in total, the funds of all shareholders pooled together allow the investment company to create a widely diversified portfolio with certain economies of scale. The four types of investment companies are unit investment trusts, exchange-traded funds, closed-end funds, and open-end investment companies (mutual funds).

Investment companies are generally nontaxable entities. These companies do not pay federal or state income tax. Instead, investment companies act as flow-through entities or conduits whereby interest income, dividends, and capital gains all flow through from the investment company to the shareholders and are reported on the investor's individual tax return. The income that flows through retains its character as to ordinary income or capital gain and is allocated to each shareholder based on the number of shares owned. The tax treatment of investment companies is similar in concept to the tax treatment of partnerships and S corporations.

In addition to meeting specific requirements of the Internal Revenue Code, investment companies are also regulated by the Securities and Exchange Commission (SEC) under the Investment Company Act of 1940. Investment companies are also regulated under the Securities Act of 1933, the Securities Exchange Act of 1934, and the Investment Advisors Act of 1940. For more information on these acts, see Appendix C at the end of the text.

Unit Investment Trusts

Unit investment trust (UIT)
A registered investment company that is passively managed and may invest in stocks, bonds, or other securities

A **unit investment trust** (UIT) is a registered investment company that is passively managed and may invest in stocks, bonds, or other securities. Investors generally purchase units, which are sold at net asset value plus a commission, with the idea that they will hold the units until they mature. As income is earned and securities mature, investors receive both income (interest and/or dividends) and principal from the trust.

In the case of a UIT that invests in stocks, the trust will have a defined maturity date, at which time the investor will have the option of rolling over the proceeds, receiving a pro rata distribution of the UIT's underlying securities, or receiving cash from the investment.

UITs are known as unmanaged, or passively managed, funds because professional managers initially select securities to be included in the portfolio, and those securities are generally held until they mature. For example, a UIT investing in municipal bond securities may have a portfolio of municipal bonds with staggered maturities. These bonds will generally be held until they mature. As coupon payments are received from the bond issuer, they are passed along to the unit holders. When a bond matures, the face value will be passed through to the unit holders. Although the holdings of UITs are monitored, the securities within the fund generally remain the same throughout the life of the fund.

The traditional UIT invested in fixed-income securities. Today, however, there are a variety of UITs available to meet the objectives and risk tolerances of investors. UITs invest in a wide array of securities, including municipal bonds, corporate bonds, U.S. government bonds, international bonds, and mortgage-backed securities.

Exchange-Traded Funds (ETFs)

Exchange-traded fund (ETF)
A type of investment company whose investment objective is to achieve the same return as a particular market index

Exchange-traded funds (ETFs) are portfolios or baskets of stocks that are traded on an exchange. ETFs are index-based equity instruments that represent ownership in either a fund or a unit investment trust and give investors the opportunity to buy and sell shares of an entire stock portfolio as a single security. Common examples include QQQ (Nasdaq-100 Index) and SPDRs (Standard & Poor's Depositary Receipts, tracking the S&P 500 index or sectors of the index). Unlike mutual funds, ETFs can be purchased and sold throughout the day. In addition, they can be bought on margin and sold short. ETFs typically have lower annual expenses than mutual funds.

Exchange-traded funds are often passively managed (however, some are now actively managed) and attempt to track a specific index or sector within the index. Although ETFs are traded on exchanges, investors may be able to buy or redeem shares from the fund family, generally in 50,000-share blocks. The price of ETF shares is based on the value of the underlying securities; however, it may not be equal to NAV because of supply and demand for the shares. Although the price of ETF shares may trade at a discount or premium, the difference should be minimal.

In most cases, the annual expense ratio for ETF shares is lower than for the majority of index mutual funds. However, ETF shares that are purchased using a broker require a commission to be paid. Depending on the commission and the size of the investment, one alternative may be better than the other. ETFs have low turnover and, therefore, lower taxable distributions than most mutual funds. When there is a substantial amount of mutual fund share redemptions, the manager is forced to liquidate some of the underlying securities to generate enough cash for redemptions. This does not occur in ETFs because shares are either sold or redeemed in-kind.

Most mutual funds have cash that is not invested, which is a result of new contributions into the fund or cash that is maintained for redemptions. ETFs do not have this cash management problem and may have better performance than mutual funds.

International Exchange-Traded Funds (ETFs)

International ETFs are passively managed foreign index funds designed after Standard & Poor's Depositary Receipts (SPDRs), which track the S&P 500 index. They are similar to open-end investment companies (mutual funds) in that they are open ended and the shares trade at or near net asset value (NAV). However, as with closed-end funds, international ETFs trade in the secondary market.

International ETFs, along with the other methods of foreign investing, provide investors with numerous advantages over investing solely in domestic equities. When foreign investment is combined with domestic investment, advantages include higher potential returns, lower levels of risk, and greater portfolio efficiency.

Closed-End Investment Companies

Closed-end fund
A type of investment company whose shares trade in the same manner that publicly traded stocks trade in the secondary market

A **closed-end fund** is a type of investment company whose shares trade in the same manner that publicly traded stocks trade in the secondary market. Shares of closed-end funds are listed on a stock exchange or trade in the over-the-counter market. Because shares trade in the same manner as other stocks, their prices are subject to the fluctuations in the supply and demand for the shares in the market. Although the value of securities held within the fund is relatively easy to determine, the share price for the fund will rarely be directly equal to the value of the underlying securities. The shares will generally sell at a premium or discount relative to the net asset value of the fund.

After the initial public offering, a closed-end fund will generally not issue additional shares. Unlike an open-end fund, a closed-end fund's capitalization is considered fixed, because it generally does not add assets to the fund after initial capitalization.

Because the pool of assets to be invested for a closed-end fund is fixed and shares are not redeemed, the manager of a closed-end fund has a great deal of flexibility in managing the assets within the fund. For example, the closed-end fund manager does not have to plan for cash redemptions as with a mutual fund (open-end investment company). This characteristic of closed-end funds allows the manager to invest in less liquid securities that may have higher expected returns than more liquid securities.

Closed-end funds invest in a wide array of securities, including municipal bonds, corporate bonds, U.S. government bonds, international bonds, mortgage-backed securities, convertible securities, domestic equities, and foreign equities. A particularly interesting closed-end fund is known as an equity dual-purpose fund. This type of fund invests primarily in securities of U.S. companies but has two classes of shares. The first class of shares consists of income shares that receive all dividend income, but no capital appreciation. The second class of shares consists of capital shares that receive all capital appreciation, but no dividend income. An investor interested in income only, such as a retiree, might purchase the first class of shares.

One likely reason that closed-end funds have not been as popular as open-end funds is that the fees generated by the fund managers and operators of closed-end funds are not as high as those of open-ended funds. Good performance in an open-end fund attracts significant increases in fund assets, resulting in a larger base of assets upon which to charge the management fee. A closed-end fund that has great performance may have shares selling at a premium, but additional funds are generally not forthcoming. Therefore, increasing the management fees through an open-end mutual fund is easier than a closed-end fund.

Another reason that closed-end funds may not be as popular as open-end funds is the requirement of a broker to buy or sell shares for a closed-end fund. With an open-end fund, an investor must simply call the fund to request the shares be redeemed. The process of purchasing mutual fund shares directly from a fund family is easier than setting up a brokerage account and purchasing closed-end fund shares. In addition, open-end funds are easier for investors to comprehend because their share price is based solely on the price of the underlying securities.

Open-End Investment Companies (Mutual Funds)

Mutual funds
Open-end investment companies that sell shares of stock to the public and use the proceeds to invest in a portfolio of securities on behalf of their shareholders

Mutual funds are investment vehicles that provide individual investors and institutional investors easy access to capital markets. They are a type of investment company that sells shares of stock to the public and uses the proceeds to invest in a portfolio of securities on behalf of its shareholders. The many benefits to investing in mutual funds will be discussed in this section.

Over the past few decades, mutual funds have become the predominant method for small investors to gain access to equity and fixed-income investments. The growing popularity of mutual funds is evidenced by the increasing number of mutual funds available to investors as well as the amount of assets invested in mutual funds. In the United

Open-end investment company
An investment company whose capitalization constantly changes as new shares are sold and outstanding shares are redeemed

States, there are more than 7,500 mutual funds, which means that there are more mutual funds than there are listed equity securities. Assets invested in mutual funds increased to almost $24 trillion at the end of 2020.

Open-end investment companies are referred to as open-end because they are not limited in the number of shares that can be sold. The total capitalization of these funds is constantly changing. Some investors are purchasing shares while others are redeeming their shares. All shares are sold by the mutual fund family and redeemed by the mutual fund family. Investors must be provided with specific information when purchasing mutual funds. The prospectus contains information regarding the fund's investment policies, objectives, sales charge, performance, and management expenses.

Net asset value (NAV)
The price at which shares of an open-end investment company are sold. The NAV of a fund is determined by subtracting total liabilities from total assets of the fund and dividing the difference by the outstanding shares.

The price at which shares are sold is referred to as **net asset value** (NAV). Subtracting total liabilities from total assets (cash + current value of securities) of the fund and dividing the difference by the outstanding shares determines the net asset value of the fund. Each day, as the prices of the underlying securities change in value, so will the NAV for the fund. All shares will be purchased for and redeemed at NAV. However, commissions and other sales charges may be charged against the purchase or redemption of shares.

Mutual fund shares are either purchased directly from the fund family or purchased through a broker. Purchases made directly with the fund family are processed by mail, telephone, internet, or by visiting office locations. Shares purchased through a broker or other financial services person will ordinarily be charged a commission or a sales charge. These fees compensate the broker as an investment adviser.

EXHIBIT 12C.1 The Structure of a Mutual Fund

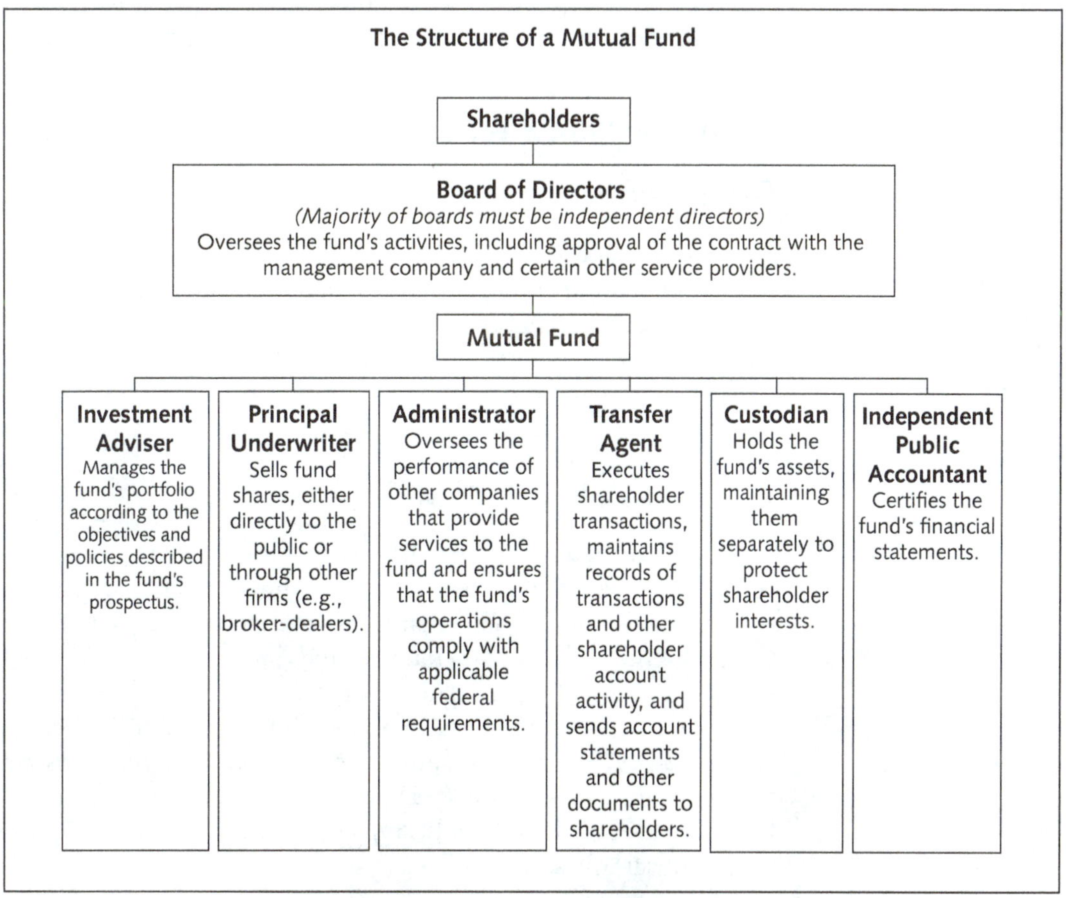

Source: *A Guide to Understanding Mutual Funds*, Investment Company Institute, Washington, DC, 2007

Hedge Funds

Hedge funds
An unregistered, privately offered, managed pool of capital for wealthy, financially sophisticated investors

A **hedge fund** is an unregistered, privately offered, managed pool of capital for wealthy, financially sophisticated investors. The fund typically implements a wide array of trading strategies, including, but not limited to, heavy borrowing and selling short, in an attempt to achieve a superior return for investors. A hedge fund strives to capture market inefficiencies and uses active management techniques. Unlike mutual fund managers, whose compensation solely depends on the amount of assets under management, hedge fund managers are paid on the basis of fund performance sometimes taking up to 20% of the profits, plus a base fee of up to 2% of the assets under management.

An investor of considerable means who is most interested in managing the risk of possible loss from an investment is the most likely type of investor in a hedge fund. In addition, an investor who is very concerned about the skill and expertise of the portfolio manager should strongly consider contributing to a hedge fund. Conversely, such a fund is usually beyond the financial means of the smaller investor who is looking for capital growth or current income, the two primary investment objectives of mutual fund shareholders.

MUTUAL FUND FEES

Just like other service providers, investment professionals charge fees for the management of an investor's assets. Fees are charged by the mutual fund company and by financial service professionals who sell mutual funds to their clients. These fees are generally categorized into loads or sales charges and operating expenses.

Loads or Sales Charges

Front-End Load

Front-end load
A sales charge based on the initial investment into a mutual fund

Front-end load is simply a term to describe a sales charge based on the value of the initial investment into the mutual fund. This load is incurred when an investor purchases shares of a mutual fund from a commission-based financial adviser. The sales charge is used to compensate the investment professional (usually someone unrelated to the fund itself) for advice related to the selection of the mutual fund.

Back-End Load

Back-end load
A sales charge incurred upon the sale or redemption of mutual fund shares rather than at the time of purchase

Back-end load is a term also used to describe a contingent deferred sales charge (CDSC) or redemption fee. However, the sales charge is incurred upon the sale or redemption of mutual fund shares rather than at the time of purchase. Today, many of the back-end loads found in mutual funds are in the form of a declining redemption fee, such that the percentage sales charge declines each year that the fund is held. For example, a fund might charge a 5% declining redemption fee. In such a case, an investor would pay 5% of the amount invested into the fund for redemption within the first year, 4% within the second year, and so on. After five years, no redemption fee would be charged. A back-end load is typically assessed on the lesser of the redemption value or the initial investment value.

Other Mutual Fund Fees

12b-1 Fees

12b-1 fee
A fee that pays for the services of brokers who sell mutual funds and who maintain the client relationship

Under the Investment Company Act of 1940, Section 12b-1, fees are permitted to pay for marketing and distribution expenses directly from a fund's asset base. The so-called **12b-1 fee** charged by the mutual fund company is used to pay for the services of brokers who sell the mutual funds and who maintain the client relationships. This fee is often paid in the form of trailing commissions, where commissions are paid to the broker over a period of years. The maximum 12b-1 fee that can be charged is 75 basis points per year. However, a separate 25 basis points can be charged as a "service fee," which effectively raises the total annual fee to 100 basis points or 1% of assets.

Management Fee

Management fee
A fee charged by an investment adviser for the management of a mutual fund's assets

The **management fee**, which is typically a predetermined annual percentage of the portfolio's asset value, is the fee charged by the investment adviser for the management of the fund assets. This fee is generally the single largest expense of a mutual fund and is included in the expense ratio.

Expense Ratio

Expense ratio
An indication of the annual fund expenses, stated as a percentage of total assets

The **expense ratio** is disclosed by all mutual funds in the fund prospectus and is an indication of the annual fund expenses, stated as a percentage of total assets. Included in this figure are the management fee, the 12b-1 fee, and other operating expenses related to running and operating the fund. The expense ratio does not include any applicable sales charges and is calculated by dividing a fund's expenses by its net average assets.

An investor should realize that reducing the expense ratio by a percentage point is essentially the same as increasing the rate of return by a percentage point. Therefore, managing the expenses paid for the management of mutual fund assets is an important element of the investment planning process.

MUTUAL FUND CLASSIFICATION

Mutual funds may be classified as either no-load funds or load funds. No-load funds are sold directly by the fund to the investor and do not charge front- or back-end loads.

Load funds
Mutual funds that charge either a front-end load or back-end load

Load vs. No-Load Funds

No-load funds
Mutual funds purchased directly through the mutual fund family without the assistance of a broker

Mutual funds that charge either a front-end load or a back-end load are considered **load funds**. As stated previously, sales charges are used to compensate the brokers or sales force for their sales efforts. Note that funds without a typical front-end or back-end load that have a 12b-1 fee exceeding 25 basis points (.25% or .0025) are also considered load funds. Only if the 12b-1 fee is 25 basis points or less can the fund be called a no-load fund. Generally, **no-load funds** are purchased directly through the mutual fund family without the assistance of a broker.

Classes of Load Fund Shares

Many fund families that offer load funds have different classes of shares that contain various sets of loads and expenses. Although there are no legal requirements as to the classification of shares of a load fund, most of the industry follows a similar classification system. Shares are generally categorized into three classes, known as class A shares, class B shares, and class C shares:

- Class A shares—these shares usually charge a front-end load with a lower 12b-1 fee.
- Class B shares—these shares usually charge a deferred redemption fee plus a higher 12b-1 fee. In addition, many of the class B shares will have a conversion feature that automatically converts the class B shares to class A shares after a period of years. The advantage of the conversion feature is that the investor will save expenses because the 12b-1 fee is lower for class A shares than for class B shares. However, the trend over the past several years has been for mutual funds to eliminate this share class.
- Class C shares—these shares often have a level deferred sales charge (often 1%), plus a higher 12b-1 fee. However, these shares do not convert to class A shares.

Many fund families have additional classes of shares that have a variety of features and fees. As a result, investors should carefully review the prospectus of each fund to determine the actual fees charged to shareholders.

Expense Ratios for Different Types of Funds

High-quality funds may have high or low expense ratios. However, as a general rule, the higher the expenses of the mutual fund, the more the fund manager will have to overcome to achieve strong return performance.

What expense ratio is appropriate for a mutual fund? The answer to this question depends on the objectives of the mutual fund. For example, actively managed funds (those that frequently buy and sell securities) require more research and support than passively managed index funds. Therefore, most actively managed funds will have higher expense ratios than passively managed funds. Similarly, it is more costly to manage international equities than domestic equities (usually 1–1.5%) because there are many more companies internationally than within the United States. In addition, the availability of accounting and financial information outside the United States is not as robust, making research more difficult and more costly. Therefore, international equity funds tend to have higher expense ratios relative to domestic equity funds.

ADVANTAGES OF MUTUAL FUNDS

Mutual funds provide many benefits to investors including access to a diversified portfolio with professional management and other benefits that are not found in other securities including low initial investment amounts, tax efficiency, liquidity, transaction cost efficiency, and shareholder services.

Overall, the dramatic growth of mutual funds has provided a great opportunity to the small investor. This growth has allowed an increasing number of individuals access to professional money managers, in both Section 401(k) plans and taxable investment accounts. When considering mutual fund investments, however, investors must be careful to understand the risks inherent in investing in the underlying securities when selecting a particular mutual fund.

Low Initial Investment

Most mutual funds have very low minimum investment requirements, allowing smaller investors access to many choices of mutual funds. In fact, most mutual funds have minimums of $1,000 or less. These low minimum investment requirements allow individuals, who would otherwise be precluded from such investments, access to the equity and fixed-income markets.

Diversification

Mutual funds provide an easy way to diversify a portfolio at a low cost. Some mutual funds have thousands of different securities in a single portfolio. This broad diversification, coupled with a low minimum investment requirement, achieves investor portfolio diversification at a very low outlay.

Ease of Access

Investors can purchase mutual funds easily. Mutual funds can be purchased directly from the mutual fund family or through a broker, bank, or other financial institution. To invest in a mutual fund directly through the fund family, an investor must call the fund family for an account application and prospectus, complete the application, and return the application to the fund family with a check for the amount of the initial investment. Investing in a mutual fund through a broker is as easy as calling the broker and requesting the purchase of the mutual fund. Usually, a brokerage account must be established before the purchase of the mutual fund can be made.

Professional Management

The same benefits that institutional investors find with professional portfolio managers can be found in mutual funds. The manager is constantly evaluating the holdings of the funds and alternative investment choices. Managers either have research departments or access to research that assists them in attempting to achieve above-average returns. Individual investors may find it difficult to match the performance of professional managers over time and through different markets. Therefore, mutual funds provide access to professional management without subjecting investors to the same restrictions on minimum account size.

Liquidity

Investors of mutual funds are always able to redeem their shares because mutual funds are required to redeem shares when requested by investors. These shares will be redeemed at the next available net asset value minus any applicable sales charge.

Transaction Cost Efficiency

Because mutual funds typically have billions of dollars under management, they enjoy economies of scale with regard to transaction costs. Many of their investment trades can be executed for pennies per share or less. These transaction costs are significantly less on a per share and dollar basis than most individuals could achieve on their own.

Variety of Mutual Funds

With more than 7,600 mutual funds available today, an investor has a plethora of choices in which to invest. There are mutual funds that can meet almost any investor's objectives, whether a growth fund, a sector fund, or a **socially responsible fund**.

Socially Responsible Fund
A fund that invests in environmental, social, or governance focused companies

Shareholder Services

Mutual funds provide investors with a variety of services that they would not have with an individual portfolio of securities. Basic services such as reporting may include monthly or quarterly statements that provide investors with a variety of information about their investments. This information generally includes the number of shares owned, net asset value of those shares, and total value of the mutual fund investment. In addition, statements will often provide information on investors' rate of return and tax basis in the fund.

Other services that are extremely helpful in accomplishing certain financial goals include automatic investing into the fund, often called **dollar cost averaging**. Investors can set up a mutual fund account such that an automatic electronic transfer of a certain dollar amount from the investor's checking or savings account is invested into the fund on a certain day each month regardless of market conditions or market prices. This allows an investor to automatically invest on a periodic basis, similar to payroll reduction with a Section 401(k) plan. The effect of this technique is to increase the number of shares gradually over a long period of time.

Dollar cost averaging
The process of purchasing securities over time by investing a predetermined amount at regular intervals

Like automatic investing, automatic (or systematic) withdrawals or sales services may also be provided. Individuals who need a certain sum of money every month can set up a directive to the mutual fund to automatically sell a certain number of shares to provide for this income need. The proceeds from the sale are then transferred into the investor's checking or savings account.

Other services that are common to mutual funds include automatic reinvestment of dividends and capital gain distributions, check-writing privileges, maintaining the shareholder adjusted tax basis, and telephone and wire redemptions.

TYPES AND OBJECTIVES OF MUTUAL FUNDS

Although the classification system for mutual funds is not completely standardized or precise, there are certainly specific types and objectives of mutual funds that can be discussed. Mutual funds can be categorized into equity funds, bond funds, hybrid funds, or money market funds. As Exhibit 12C.2 shows, at the end of 2018, there were 4,753 equity funds, 2,174 bond funds, 783 hybrid funds, and 368 money market funds.

EXHIBIT 12C.2 Number of Mutual Funds (Year-End 2018)

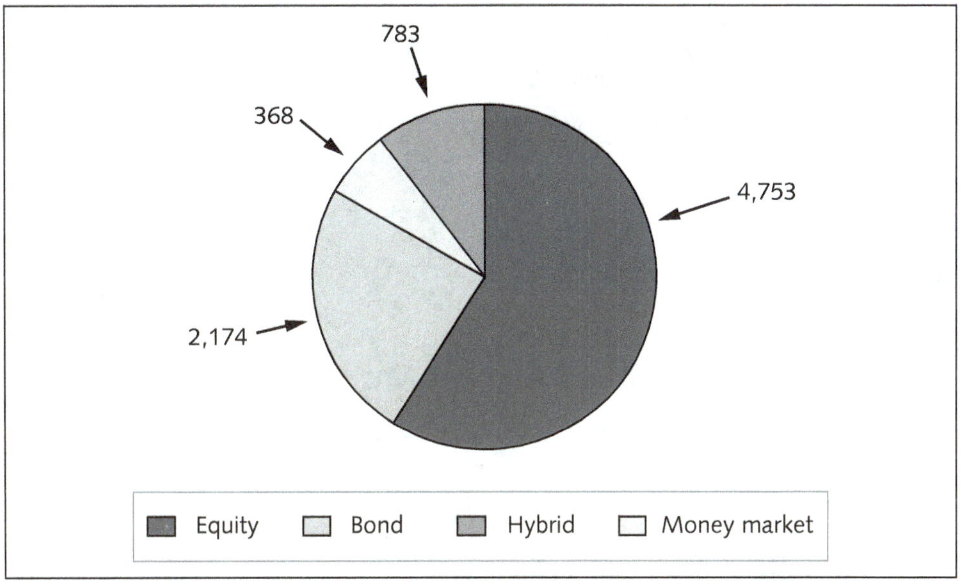

Source: *2019 Investment Company Fact Book*, Investment Company Institute, Washington, DC

EXHIBIT 12C.3 Types of Mutual Funds

Stock Funds

- *Growth*: Invested in stocks of companies that are growing rapidly, these funds are focused on stocks that generate capital gains rather than income and are oftentimes further categorized as large cap; mid cap, or aggressive; or small cap, or growth (*cap* stands for capitalization and references the market size of the company's outstanding stock issues).
- *Income*: An income fund emphasizes current income over growth. The fund's objectives are accomplished by investing in the stocks of companies with long histories of dividend payments, such as utility companies or blue-chip stocks.
- *Growth and income*: These funds invest in securities offering potentially increasing value. They are primarily interested in so-called *value stocks*, or stocks that are underpriced relative to a stock that exhibits similar risk and return characteristics.
- *Index*: These funds invest in securities designed to mirror a selected market index, such as the Standard & Poor's 500 Index. They track the selected index's performance and buy and sell securities in a manner that mirrors its composition.
- *Sector*: A fund that restricts its investments to a particular sector of the market, such as energy or health care. Such fund tends to be more volatile than a more diversified fund and/or portfolio.

Bond Funds

- *Corporate bond funds*: These funds seek a high level of income by investing two-thirds or more of their portfolios in corporate bonds and have no explicit restrictions on average maturity.
- *U.S. government bond funds*: These funds purchase securities issued by the U.S. Treasury or an agency of the U.S. government. Investors in these funds seek current income and maximum safety.

EXHIBIT 12C.3 Types of Mutual Funds (continued)

Hybrid Funds

- *Asset allocation funds:* These funds focus on providing a diversified portfolio by investing across various asset classes, including equities, bonds, and money markets.
- *Balanced funds:* These funds invest in fixed percentages of equity, bond, and money market securities.

Foreign Funds

- *International mutual funds:* Invest in debt and equity securities of governments and companies that are located outside the United States.
- *Global mutual funds:* Invest in securities that are traded worldwide, including U.S. issues.

Money Market Mutual Funds

Money market mutual funds
A mutual fund that invests in money market instruments, such as Treasury bills and negotiable CDs

Money market mutual funds provide investors the opportunity to earn money market returns with the added benefits of ease of access and liquidity. Investors who have a portion of their portfolio invested in cash, or those who create cash by selling other long-term securities, can use money market mutual funds as an appropriate, competitive money market investment or as a temporary holding place for cash. In addition, an investor can choose to invest in either taxable or tax-exempt money market mutual funds, depending on the investor's tax situation.

With such short maturities, these funds have minimal interest rate risk, and because of the quality and diversity of the investments, these funds have little or no credit risk. However, they are subject to reinvestment rate risk and purchasing power risk.

Money market mutual funds have a target net asset value set at $1 per share. However, the NAV may fall below $1 if the investments perform poorly. Interest for these funds is earned and credited on a daily basis. Most of these funds allow investors check-writing privileges as long as a minimum balance is maintained. This check-writing feature allows competitive short-term returns with the flexibility of a checking account.

Unlike some fixed-income and equity mutual funds, money market mutual funds do not charge front-end loads or redemption fees. However, a fee is charged for the management of the assets within the fund.

Fixed-Income Mutual Funds

Fixed-income (or bond) mutual funds
A mutual fund that invests in fixed-income securities ranging in maturity of several months to 30 years or longer. Bond funds invest in numerous bond issues to diversify the investment portfolio from default risk.

Fixed-income, or **bond, mutual funds** invest primarily in fixed-income securities ranging in maturity from several months to 30 years or longer. Like money market mutual funds, bond funds invest in numerous bond issues to diversify the investment portfolio from default risk. Fixed-income funds provide investors with current income, making them ideal for retired investors who need continuing income generated by their investments for retirement expenditures. In addition, bond funds are appropriate for investors wishing to allocate a certain portion of their portfolio to fixed-income securities.

The risks investors accept when using bond funds are the same risks that any investor faces with fixed-income securities. Because mutual fund portfolios are well diversified, there is minimum default risk associated with bond mutual funds. As with other fixed-income securities, purchasing power risk is a relevant factor to consider when investing in bond mutual funds. However, the most significant risk associated with bond mutual funds is interest rate risk. Just as the value of an individual bond will decline when interest rates increase, so will the value of a bond mutual fund. Conversely, as interest rates decrease, the value of bond mutual funds will increase.

Bond mutual funds may have a variety of fees, costs, and expenses, including management fees, sales charges (both front-end and deferred), and 12b-1 fees. Regarding management fees, some of the objectives require higher management fees than others. For example, a fund that matches the Barclays Capital U.S. Aggregate Bond Index will require less cost and time than a fund that is actively managed, because no research is required to determine which securities to select. Most bond funds have an expense ratio of 1% or below, with higher expenses for actively managed and international bond funds.

Equity Mutual Funds

Equity mutual funds *A mutual fund that invests primarily in equity or ownership type securities, such as preferred stock and common stock*

Equity mutual funds invest primarily in equity (ownership interest) securities, such as common stocks, and have a variety of objectives (as shown in Exhibit 12C.3). These funds have become tremendously popular over the last few decades and, in fact, make up the highest percentage of total assets invested in mutual funds (see Exhibit 12C.4).

EXHIBIT 12C.4 How Mutual Fund Assets are Invested (Year-End 2018)

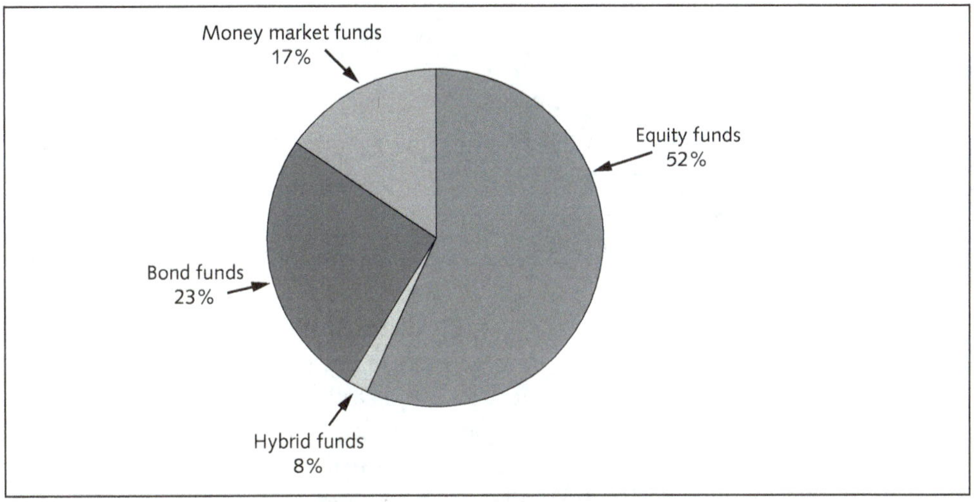

Source: *2019 Investment Company Fact Book*, Investment Company Institute, Washington, DC

As we previously discussed, equities have had higher returns than have fixed-income securities, and equity mutual funds provide investors easy access to common stock securities in an efficient method. The public's increased awareness of higher potential returns is a major contributing factor to the popularity of equity mutual funds.

Just as bond mutual funds have a variety of risks, so do equity mutual funds. One of the most important risks that an equity mutual fund investor must consider is market risk. Recall that market risk is the risk that movements in the market will have a detrimental effect on the value of an investment. There is a strong tendency for equities and equity mutual funds to fluctuate in the same direction and at a similar rate as the entire market. If the market has a sudden decline, most equity funds will also decline in value.

For those investors who invest similar amounts on a monthly basis into an equity mutual fund, temporary declines in the market and equity funds provide the opportunity to invest at lower prices. Equity funds are, however, usually more volatile than bond funds but historically have earned higher returns over a long-term time horizon.

Hybrid (or Balanced) Funds

Hybrid (or balanced) mutual funds
A mutual fund that invests in a combination of cash, fixed-income securities, and equity securities

Hybrid, or **balanced, mutual funds** are mutual funds that cannot be categorized into any of the three types of fund classifications discussed previously (money market, bond, or equity). These funds generally have an objective of investing in a balanced fashion, such that a portion of the portfolio is invested in cash, fixed-income securities, and equity securities.

Investors can build appropriate asset allocation portfolios by investing in a combination of selected money market funds, bond funds, and equity funds. Alternatively, investors can simply select a hybrid fund, such as an asset allocation fund, that meets their asset allocation objective and use it as their only or primary investment vehicle.

Foreign Funds

Foreign funds
Securities that provide investors with the easiest method of investing in foreign markets in the context of a diversified portfolio

Today, numerous mutual funds have the objective of investing internationally. These **foreign funds** provide investors with an easy method of investing in foreign markets within a diversified portfolio. Foreign funds have a variety of objectives, ranging from regions of the world to size of the market.

HOW DO PROFESSIONAL INVESTMENT ADVISERS SELECT MUTUAL FUNDS?

With the thousands of mutual funds available to investors, how does an investor or a professional investment adviser select a mutual fund for inclusion in a portfolio? In other words, what distinguishes an appropriate mutual fund from an inappropriate mutual fund? In general, an appropriate fund is one that meets the client's objectives and has the best risk-adjusted historical performance compared with similar funds. In addition, investment advisers should review information regarding the fund's performance, costs, taxation, portfolio turnover, and services offered.

Professionals use databases of mutual fund information, such as Morningstar, to help narrow the thousands of mutual funds down to a few that meet the objectives of the investor. These databases contain a substantial amount of information about each mutual fund and allow advisers to establish specific criteria and search through voluminous information quickly to select appropriate funds for clients. Much of this information comes from the mutual fund prospectus; the remainder comes from the database company's analysis of the funds.

PERFORMANCE MEASURES

As described in Chapter 12, the concepts of modern portfolio theory have been widely accepted among financial practitioners. These MPT statistics provide insight into the fund's risk-return characteristics.

The three most common performance measures used with mutual funds include Jensen's alpha, Sharpe ratio, and Treynor ratio. In addition, we will examine the information ratio which is a relatively new risk-adjusted measure for portfolio evaluation.

These performance measures provide a method of quantifying the risk-adjusted performance of investments, including mutual funds.

Jensen's Alpha

Jensen's alpha
An absolute measure of performance indicating how the actual performance of an investment compares with the expected performance

Jensen's alpha is an absolute measure of performance indicating how the actual performance of the investment compares with the expected performance. Specifically, alpha is measured as the portfolio's actual or realized return in excess of (or deficient to) the return predicted by the capital asset pricing model. A positive alpha means that the portfolio manager has added value on an absolute basis compared with the required return based on the level of investment risk undertaken. A negative alpha means that the manager has underperformed.

$$\alpha_p = \bar{r}_p - \left[\bar{r}_f + \left(\bar{r}_m - \bar{r}_f\right)\beta_p\right]$$

α_p = alpha

r_p = actual return of the portfolio

r_f = risk-free rate of return

β_p = beta of the portfolio

r_m = market rate of return

EXAMPLE A higher alpha indicates that the actual return of the investment is better than what was expected, based on the level of risk of the investment. For instance, if the actual return of a portfolio is 12% and the expected return was 7%, then the alpha equals 5%. In other words, the portfolio performed five percentage points better than expected on a risk-adjusted basis. Similarly, a negative alpha implies that the return of the investment was less than expected based on the level of risk. An alpha of zero means that the investment performed as expected.

Sharpe Ratio

Sharpe ratio
A measure of risk-adjusted portfolio performance that uses standard deviation as the risk measure

The **Sharpe ratio** is also a measure of risk-adjusted performance. However, like the Treynor ratio, it is a relative measure of performance, meaning that the ratio by itself has little or no meaning. The ratio is meaningful only when compared to alternative investments. Unlike Treynor and Jensen, which use beta as the risk measure, Sharpe uses standard deviation. Because Sharpe uses standard deviation, this ratio incorporates total risk (both systematic and unsystematic risk) into the calculation.

$$S_p = \frac{\bar{r}_p - \bar{r}_f}{\sigma_p}$$

S_p = Sharpe ratio

r_p = actual return of the portfolio

r_f = risk-free rate of return

σ_p = standard deviation of the portfolio

EXAMPLE If ABC growth mutual fund returned 12%, while the risk-free rate was 3% and the standard deviation was 20%, then the Sharpe ratio would equal 0.45. Again, the ratio of 0.45 has no meaning in and of itself; however, when compared with alternative investments, it becomes meaningful. Consider, for instance, the Sharpe ratios for the following mutual funds.

Fund name	Sharpe ratio
High Growth Mutual Fund	1.20
S&P 500 Index Mutual Fund	0.95
ABC Growth Mutual Fund	0.45
XYZ Growth Mutual Fund	0.30

Clearly, on a risk-adjusted basis, XYZ Growth Mutual Fund (0.30 Sharpe ratio) and ABC Growth Mutual Fund (0.45 Sharpe ratio) are mediocre performing funds. Two better alternatives appear to be the High Growth Mutual Fund (1.20 Sharpe ratio) and the S&P 500 Index Mutual Fund (.95 Sharpe ratio).

Treynor Ratio

Treynor ratio
A measure of risk-adjusted portfolio performance that uses beta as the risk measure

The **Treynor ratio** is a similar relative performance measure to the Sharpe ratio except for its measure of risk. Treynor uses beta as its measure of risk. Therefore, the same issues with regard to the use of beta in the calculation of alpha also apply to the calculation of the Treynor ratio.

$$T_p = \frac{\overline{r}_p - \overline{r}_f}{\beta_p}$$

T_p = Treynor ratio
r_p = actual return of the portfolio
r_f = risk-free rate of return
β_p = beta of the portfolio

The Treynor ratio also evaluates the incremental return above the risk-free rate of return. Alternative investments should be ranked in order from the highest to the lowest ratio. The investment with the highest Treynor ratio is the one that has the highest risk-adjusted return.

If all of the performance measures provide a quantification of the risk-adjusted return of investments, should the rankings, from highest to lowest, for each of the three measures be the same? The answer to this question is that "it depends." Specifically, it depends on the value of R^2 (coefficient of determination). If R^2 is high (at least 0.70), then the three performance measures will provide similar rankings. However, if R^2 is not high, then the three performance measures may not provide similar rankings. This inconsistency occurs because of the use of beta instead of standard deviation as the measure of risk in two of the performance measures.

Information ratio
A ratio of expected return to risk as measured by standard deviation that seeks to quantify the amount of incremental risk undertaken by a portfolio manager to achieve an excess return

Information Ratio

The **information ratio** is the ratio of expected return to risk as measured by standard deviation that seeks to quantify the amount of incremental risk undertaken by a portfolio manager to achieve an excess return.

$$IR = \frac{R_P - R_B}{\sigma_A}$$

IR = information ratio

R_P = average rate of return for a given time period

R_B = average rate of return on the benchmark portfolio; CAPM's required rate of return may be used

σ_A = standard deviation of portfolio returns

This ratio reduces to the Sharpe ratio when the benchmark portfolio is a constant-return, risk-free asset and is extremely difficult to interpret when the alpha for the subject portfolio is negative. Therefore, the information ratio should be used only when the alpha is positive (i.e., the portfolio manager has added value) and the beta is meaningful. Because the information ratio measures return and risk only relative to a benchmark, using the right benchmark is crucial to getting an accurate measure.

Coefficient of Variation

Coefficient of variation
A relative measure of total risk per unit of expected return

The **coefficient of variation (CV)** is a relative measure of total risk per unit of expected return and is used to compare investments with varying rates of return and standard deviations. The CV is computed by dividing the standard deviation of an asset by its average or mean return. When using this ratio to compare two alternatives, the one with the lower CV is usually the preferable choice.

EXAMPLE ABC stock has a mean return of 10.75% and a standard deviation of 7.18%. XYZ stock has a mean return of 20% and a standard deviation of 12%. Therefore, if an investor is solely basing an investment decision on the amount of total risk, the choice would most likely be ABC stock because this stock has a lower standard deviation. However, in determining the CV for each stock, ABC stock has a CV of 0.6679, whereas XYZ stock has a CV of only 0.60. This means that ABC stock has more total risk per unit of expected return; thus, the investor may instead choose to invest in XYZ stock.

ISSUES TO LOOK FOR WHEN MANAGING PORTFOLIOS OF MUTUAL FUNDS

Once an investment strategy, including one that involves mutual funds, has been implemented, the portfolio must be monitored. Certain aspects of mutual funds should be monitored to be certain that the fund is performing as anticipated. The issues to consider include changing asset size, style drift, manager changes, built-in gains, and portfolio turnover.

Changing Asset Size

When mutual funds have good performance for several consecutive years, new money flows to these funds, making their asset base much larger. This asset accumulation can result in a change in the basic dynamics of the fund (this is especially true for funds that invest in small-cap and mid-cap asset classes). Therefore, when a small-cap mutual fund dramatically increases its asset base, the fund may no longer be able to invest the additional assets as efficiently or effectively as it had in the past. If this occurs, returns could suffer and assets may begin to leave the fund. To prevent this problem, some funds will close temporarily to new investors, thus limiting the asset base of the fund to protect the dynamics of the fund.

Style Drift

As part of the asset allocation process, the large-cap equity allocation is often segregated into value, growth, and core styles. The purpose of this segregation is to have one growth fund, one value fund, and one core fund, for example. What happens, though, if the value fund begins adopting more of a growth style? Suddenly, the diversified portfolio becomes more heavily weighted toward growth, which results in style drift. Even though the portfolio has potential for strong performance with the new allocation, it is likely that when the growth style goes out of favor, the portfolio may decline significantly. Therefore, the fund's style should remain consistent with the stated objective.

Manager Changes

The reason mutual fund managers are well compensated is that they make the buy-and-sell decisions, which cause the fund to have good or poor performance. Because the manager is responsible for the performance of the fund, it is important to watch for changes in the management structure. In most cases, one person manages the fund; in other cases, a team manages the fund. A change in investment management means that there is increased risk that the fund will not be managed as before and, therefore, historical returns may be less significant in predicting future returns.

Built-In Gains

Mutual funds normally have appreciated securities within their portfolio. This appreciation is considered a built-in gain inside the mutual fund. Selling these appreciated securities by the mutual fund causes income to be recognized for income tax purposes by the fund, which is passed through to the investor. Investors who purchase shares of mutual funds having these built-in gains may subject themselves to potential taxable income without any associated economic gain. The built-in gain on mutual funds can range widely and depends on past performance of the fund. Investors should be cautious when purchasing mutual funds with large amounts of unrecognized appreciation.

Portfolio Turnover

The costs of buying and selling securities within a mutual fund are reflected in the portfolio turnover ratio. In many instances, aggressive growth funds may contain an annual turnover rate of 100% or more. A 100% turnover rate means the fund replaces the entire portfolio annually. If the fund achieves superior returns, the strategy of buying and selling is working; if not, the strategy is possibly subjecting investors to undue costs.

The portfolio turnover rate reflects a fund's holding period. If a fund has a turnover rate of 100% or more, the fund generally is holding its securities for less than one year. Therefore, all capital gain distributions are likely to be short-term and subject to the maximum tax rate.

WHERE ON THE WEB

American Association of Individual Investors **www.aaii.com**

American Stock Exchange **www.amex.com**

Bloomberg **www.bloomberg.com**

Closed-End Fund Association **www.cefa.com**

MSN Money **www.msn.com/en-us/money**

CNN Money **www.money.cnn.com**

Investment Company Institute **www.ici.org**

Kiplinger **www.kiplinger.com**

Morningstar **www.morningstar.com**

Mutual Fund Investor's Center **www.mfea.com**

Statista **www.statista.com**

Trustnet (Unit Investment Trust Info) **www.trustnet.com**

CHAPTER 13

Individual Income Tax and Tax Planning

LEARNING OBJECTIVES

After learning the material in this chapter, you will be able to do the following:

- List the objectives of the federal income tax law and give examples of each
- Name three different tax rate structures under which income can be taxed and discuss how those rate structures differ
- Perform the calculation to determine a client's income tax liability
- Describe the types of IRS rulings issued as guidance to taxpayers and IRS agents
- List the various civil penalties imposed on taxpayers who violate the tax law
- Understand the IRS audit selection and screening process

- Identify the various payroll taxes imposed on individuals through the Federal Insurance Contributions Act (FICA) and the Federal Unemployment Tax Act (FUTA)
- Discuss the difference between tax avoidance and tax evasion
- Discuss the various tax-advantaged investment options available to taxpayers

INCOME TAX PLANNING

One of the most important areas of financial planning is income tax planning. Income taxes have an impact on almost every business and investment decision as well as many personal decisions. The objective of tax planning is to pay the lowest tax legally permissible consistent with overall financial planning objectives. The financial planner must not only consider the tax ramifications of a proposed action or transaction but must also develop an appropriate tax planning strategy consistent with the client's goals and objectives.

Effective tax planning has been complicated over the years by constant changes to the tax law. The federal income tax system in the United States is among the most complex tax systems in the world. Changes have been made frequently to the Internal Revenue Code (IRC) in an attempt to raise revenues for the federal government or accomplish other social goals.

History

Under the U.S. Constitution, any direct tax imposed by Congress was required to be apportioned among the individual states based on that state's relative population. In 1913, the Sixteenth Amendment to the U.S. Constitution was ratified, which allowed Congress to levy taxes on all income without apportionment among the states.

The Sixteenth Amendment states, "The Congress shall have the power to lay and collect taxes on incomes, from whatever source derived, without apportionment among the several states, and without regard to any census or enumeration."

After 1913, Congress exercised its taxing authority with the passage of several revenue acts, adding to the complexity of the income tax system. In an attempt to resolve confusion, Congress combined the separate sources of the tax law in 1939. This legislation, named the Internal Revenue Code of 1939, systematically arranged all previous legislation and provided the basis for a standardized income tax law.

The 1939 Code was revised in 1954 and again in 1986. The governing federal income tax law today is the Internal Revenue Code of 1986, as amended.

Objectives of the Federal Income Tax Law

There are several objectives of the federal income tax law. These objectives can be classified as revenue raising, economic, and/or social in nature.

The revenue-raising objective is the most important. The primary goal of taxation is to provide the resources necessary to fund governmental expenditures. Individual income taxes provide just over 50% of the annual revenues of the federal government.

The federal income tax system also addresses certain economic goals. Taxation is a major tool used by the government to achieve the goals of economic growth and full employment. During periods of recession, taxes can be lowered, thereby increasing the disposable income in the hands of taxpayers. This can allow individuals to spend more money, which can increase demand, resulting in economic growth.

Social objectives are also accomplished through effective income tax legislation. The Internal Revenue Code (the Code) contains many economic incentives designed to encourage certain social behavior. For example, contributions to charitable organizations are socially desirable. Therefore, to encourage contributions, the Code permits limited deductions for contributions of money or property to qualified charitable organizations. In addition, the Code provides various tax benefits for homeowners and those saving for retirement.

INDIVIDUAL INCOME TAX RATES

Tax rates are applied to an individual's taxable income to determine the amount of tax due. Currently, income can be taxed under three different rate structures: ordinary tax rates, capital gain tax rates, and alternative minimum tax (AMT) rates.

Ordinary Rates

Once taxable income has been calculated, the income must be separately classified as ordinary or capital, because different tax rates may apply to capital gains.

Ordinary income
Any income that arises from services or from property that is not classified as a capital asset

Ordinary income includes any income that arises from services or from property that is not classified as a capital asset. Salaries, interest, dividends, rents, and income earned from a sole proprietorship, partnership, S corporation, or LLC/LLP are all considered ordinary income.

If the taxpayer's income is classified as ordinary income, the tax on this income is calculated on the basis of one of four rate tables. The appropriate tax rate table is chosen on the basis of the individual's filing status, which is one of the following:

- Married individuals filing joint returns (includes qualifying widow/widower)
- Married individuals filing separate returns
- **Head of household**
- Single

Head of household
The filing status that identifies a taxpayer as an unmarried individual who maintains a household for another and satisfies certain conditions set forth in the Internal Revenue Code

The income tax rate tables are graduated, meaning that the rates increase as taxable income increases. The ordinary income tax rates are the same for each filing status; however, the taxable income thresholds for which these rates apply vary between the tables. Ordinary income tax rates are 10%, 12%, 22%, 24%, 32%, 35%, and 37%. These tax tables are contained in the Annual Limits provided in Appendix 13.2.

Capital Gain Rates

Taxpayers may be eligible to use lower tax rates when they incur a gain upon the disposition of certain types of assets, known as capital assets. Several factors must be present for a gain to be afforded preferential treatment. In general, the asset must be:

- a capital asset;
- sold or exchanged; or
- held long term.

Capital Asset

Capital asset
Broadly speaking, all assets are capital except those specifically excluded by the Internal Revenue Code; excluded assets include property held for resale in the normal course of business (inventory), trade accounts and notes receivable, and depreciable property and real estate used in a trade or business

The Internal Revenue Code defines a **capital asset** by listing the types of assets that are not considered capital. All other assets disposed of are presumably capital assets. The following types of assets are not considered capital assets:

- Accounts or notes receivable arising in the ordinary course of a trade or business
- Copyrights or creative works held by the creator
- Inventory or property held for sale to customers in the ordinary course of the taxpayer's trade or business
- Depreciable real or personal property used in a trade or business
- A U.S. government publication held by a taxpayer who received it other than by purchase

Assets that are not capital assets can be remembered most easily by using the mnemonic ACID, which is the first letter of the first four types of assets listed.

Therefore, property held for personal use is a capital asset, as is property used for the production of income. Examples of capital assets include securities held for investment, a personal residence, and a personal automobile.

Sale or Exchange

Sale
Transfer of property for an amount of money or money equivalent that is fixed or determinable

Exchange
Transfer of property for property other than money

Gains or losses from the disposition of property will not qualify as a capital gain or loss unless the property is disposed of by a sale or exchange. A **sale** is a transfer of property for an amount of money or money equivalent that is fixed or determinable. An **exchange** is a transfer of property for property other than money.

It is generally not difficult to determine whether a sale or exchange has occurred. However, the Internal Revenue Code has provided for several situations in which capital gain treatment is afforded even though a sale or exchange has not occurred. For example, capital loss treatment is allowed for a security that becomes worthless during the year, even though no sale or exchange has occurred.

Long-Term Holding Period

Once it has been determined that the asset is a capital asset that has been sold or exchanged, the taxpayer may qualify for lower capital gain tax rates if the property is held long term. In general, a capital asset is held long term if the taxpayer owned the asset for more than one year (i.e., a year and one day). The date the asset is disposed of is part of the holding period. For example, if property is acquired on March 3, 2022, the property will need to be sold on or after March 4, 2023, to be considered long-term.

Tax Treatment of Long-Term Capital Gains If the taxpayer recognizes a **long-term capital gain**, which is a gain from a sale of a capital asset that has been held for more than one year, the gain may be taxed at a lower rate than the individual's ordinary income tax rate. Following are the long-term capital gains (LTCG) tax rates for 2022.

Long-Term Capital Gains Rate	Single Taxpayer	Married Filing Jointly	Head of Household	Married Filing Separately
0%	Up to $41,675	Up to $83,350	Up to $55,800	Up to $41,675
15%	$41,676–$459,750	$83,351–$517,200	$55,801–$488,500	$41,676–$258,600
20%	Over $459,750	Over $517,200	Over $488,500	Over $258,600

If the asset is a collectible, such as a work of art, or if the asset is small business stock (as defined in Section 1202), the recognized gain is taxed at a maximum capital gain rate of 28%. In addition, capital gains on sales of depreciable real estate are taxed at a maximum rate of 25%, to the extent of any unrecaptured straight-line depreciation on the property. The following table summarizes the different capital gain rates for 2022.

EXHIBIT 13.1 Capital Gain Rates

Type of Capital Asset	Minimum Holding Period	2022 Maximum Rate
Collectibles (antiques, etc.) or Section 1202 stock	Greater than 1 year	28%
Depreciable real estate	Greater than 1 year	25%
Other capital assets	Greater than 1 year	Depends on taxpayer's AGI

Short-term capital gain
A gain from a sale or exchange of a capital asset that has been held for one year or less

Tax Treatment of Short-Term Capital Gains A **short-term capital gain** is a gain from a sale or exchange of a capital asset that has been held one year or less. It receives no special treatment and is taxed as ordinary income.

Qualified dividends
Dividends received from domestic corporations and foreign corporations incorporated in a U.S. possession, such as Puerto Rico

Tax Treatment of Qualified Dividends **Qualified dividends** are dividends received from domestic corporations and foreign corporations incorporated in a U.S. possession, such as Puerto Rico. Taxpayers may elect to use the long-term capital gain tax rates for qualified dividends.

Capital loss
A loss from the sale or exchange of a capital asset

Tax Treatment of Capital Losses A **capital loss** is a loss from the sale or exchange of a capital asset. An individual taxpayer may deduct capital losses only to the extent of capital gains plus the lesser of $3,000 ($1,500 for the taxpayer filing as married filing separately) or the net capital loss. The net capital loss is the excess of capital losses for the year over capital gains for the year.

EXAMPLE For example, if an individual not filing as married filing separately has a short-term capital loss of $200 and a long-term capital loss of $3,700, the taxpayer is permitted to deduct $3,000 from ordinary income. The remaining loss of $900 ($200 + $3,700 – $3,000) can be carried forward to later years indefinitely until it is absorbed. The short-term loss is utilized first, so the carryover is $900 of long-term capital loss.

Net investment tax
A Medicare tax on investment income for taxpayers whose modified gross income (MAGI) exceeds certain thresholds

Net Investment Income Tax

A 3.8% tax is levied on net investment income of tax payers with MAGI exceeding applicable thresholds listed below.

Filing Status	Threshold Amount
Married filing jointly	$250,000
Married filing separately	$125,000
Single	$200,000
Head of household (with qualifying person)	$200,000
Qualifying widow(er) with dependent child	$250,000

Long-term capital gain
A gain from a sale or exchange of a capital asset that has been held for more than one year

The tax is 3.8% of the lesser of net investment income or the excess of modified adjusted gross income over the threshold amount. This tax is in addition to any other taxes on the investment income (ordinary or capital gain).

For an estate or trust, the tax is 3.8% of the lesser of (1) undistributed net investment income or (2) the excess of AGI over the dollar amount at which the highest income tax bracket applicable to an estate or trust begins. The tax does not apply to nonresident aliens and certain charitable trusts.

Net investment income is gross investment income reduced by deductions allowed against the income tax that are properly allocated to such items.

Net investment income includes (but is not limited to) interest, dividends, capital gains, rental and royalty income, nonqualified annuities, income from businesses involved in the trading of financial instruments or commodities, and businesses that are passive activities to the taxpayer. In addition to these types of income, net investment income includes gains such as those from the sale of stocks, bonds, and mutual funds, capital gain distributions from mutual funds, gain from the sale of investment real estate, and gains from the sale of partnership or S corporation interests.

The gain that is excludable from a taxpayer's gross income under Section 121 on the sale of a personal residence is not subject to the tax, but all or a portion of any excess is taxable if the taxpayer's MAGI exceeds the threshold for their filing status. Another exception is a distribution from most retirement plans and IRAs. While the distribution is not subject to the tax, its inclusion in the taxpayer's MAGI may force the taxpayer over the threshold and make net investment income taxable. Tax-exempt bond interest is also exempt from the tax.

EXAMPLE Jane has MAGI of $220,000 and has a filing status of single. She has net investment income of $25,000. Of that, $20,000 will be subject to the net investment income tax of 3.8% (the lesser of the amount her MAGI exceeds the threshold or the net investment income).

EXAMPLE Paul and Cindy sold their home this year and had a gain of $650,000 on the sale. Their MAGI is $175,000 in the year of the sale (before including the capital gain on the home sale), and they had net investment income of $10,000. Because the couple's MAGI is now $325,000, the net investment income tax of 3.8% will apply to $75,000 ($325,000 – $250,000) of their total net investment income.

Alternative Minimum Tax Rates

Alternative minimum tax (AMT)
System designed to ensure that individuals with large deductions and other tax benefits pay at least a minimum amount of tax

The **alternative minimum tax (AMT)** is a separate tax system that parallels the regular tax system. The AMT system was designed to ensure that individuals with large deductions and other tax benefits pay at least a minimum amount of tax.

The AMT calculation begins with the individual's taxable income, which is adjusted to arrive at alternative minimum taxable income (AMTI). AMT tax rates are then applied to AMTI, resulting in the tentative minimum tax. If the tentative minimum tax exceeds the individual's regular tax liability, the excess amount is the alternative minimum tax. The AMT calculation is summarized in the table below.

EXHIBIT 13.2 Alternative Minimum Tax Calculation

	Taxable income
+	Positive AMT adjustments
–	Negative AMT adjustments
=	Taxable income after AMT adjustments
+	Tax preferences (always positive)
=	**Alternative minimum taxable income (AMTI)**
–	AMT exemption
=	Minimum tax base
×	AMT rate
=	**Tentative AMT**
–	Regular income tax on taxable income
=	**AMT**

A taxpayer may incur an AMT liability if he has one or more of the following items of deduction or income, which are added back to the taxpayer's taxable income to determine AMTI:

- State and local income taxes
- Real property taxes
- Interest income on certain private activity bonds purchased before January 1, 2009 and after December 31, 2010
- Exercise of incentive stock options
- Gain on sale of certain small business stock (as defined in Section 1202)

Adjustments made to taxable income in the basic individual AMT formula (see previous page) may be either positive or negative; most adjustments relate to timing differences because of the regular income tax and AMT rules. A positive adjustment is made when the deduction allowed for regular income tax purposes exceeds the deduction allowed for AMT purposes. A negative adjustment is made when the deduction allowed for AMT purposes exceeds that for regular income tax purposes.

EXHIBIT 13.3 Adjustments to Taxable Income (2022)

Adjustment	Regular Tax	Individual AMT	Positive/Negative
Standard deduction amount	Allowed	Disallowed	Positive
Itemized deduction—income and property taxes	Allowed	Disallowed	Positive

A taxpayer may have to pay the AMT if the taxpayer's taxable income for regular income tax purposes, combined with any AMT tax adjustments and preference items, exceeds (2022):

- $75,900 if the filing status is that of a single taxpayer;
- $59,050 for a filing status of married filing separately (MFS); or
- $118,100 for a married taxpayer filing jointly (MFJ).

These exemption amounts begin to be phased out in 2022 on a one-for-four basis when the MFJ taxpayers' AGI exceeds $1,079,800, and for all other taxpayers (except estates and trusts) when AGI exceeds $539,900.

The tentative minimum tax is applied at 26% of AMTI up to $206,100 ($103,050 for MFS). AMTI exceeding $206,100 ($103,050 for MFS) is taxed at 28%.

DETERMINING INCOME TAX LIABILITY

Of all the sources providing revenues to the federal government, individual income tax is the largest. Calculating an individual's income tax liability can be very complicated. The tax liability itself is a product of the taxpayer's taxable income, which is summarized in the following formula:

EXHIBIT 13.4 Taxable Income

Total income (from whatever source derived)	$xx,xxx
Less: exclusions from gross income	(x,xxx)
Gross income	$xx,xxx
Less: deductions for adjusted gross income	(x,xxx)
Adjusted gross income (AGI)	$xx,xxx
Less: the larger of:	
standard deduction or itemized deductions	(x,xxx)
Taxable income	$xx,xxx

Total Income and Gross Income

Gross income
The Internal Revenue Code Section 61(a) defines gross income as "all income from whatever source derived"

Exclusion
Income exempt from tax and not included in a taxpayer's gross income

The tax computation begins with the determination of the taxpayer's total income. The Internal Revenue Code Section 61(a) defines **gross income** as "all income from whatever source derived." In general, all income is taxable unless Congress has specifically exempted the income from taxation. In tax terminology, this exemption is called an **exclusion** and is income exempt from tax and not included in a taxpayer's gross income.

In determining gross income, the taxpayer may exclude many different types of income received. Some of the more common types of income that may be excluded are as follows:

- Most retirement plan salary deferrals
- Accident insurance proceeds
- Bequests received
- Child support payments received
- Certain employee fringe benefits
- Gain on the sale of a personal residence (limited)
- Gifts received
- Group term life insurance premiums paid by an employer (limited)
- Interest received from municipal bonds
- Life insurance proceeds received (unless the policy is subject to transfer for value rules)
- Meals and lodging (furnished for the convenience of the employer on the employer's premises)
- Scholarship grants (for tuition and books of a degree candidate)
- Workers' compensation

The amount of income remaining after removing the exclusions is termed the taxpayer's gross income. Gross income is generally the starting point for the federal individual income tax return (Form 1040).

EXAMPLE During this year, Joe received salary of $60,000, dividends of $2,000, tax-exempt interest of $500, and a gift of $20,000 from his parents. Joe has total income for this year of $82,500, because total income is based on income from all sources. However, Joe's gross income reported on his tax return is $62,000, the sum of the $60,000 salary and the $2,000 taxable dividend income. The remaining $500 of tax-exempt interest income and $20,000 gift is excluded from gross income.

Adjusted Gross Income (AGI)

Above-the-line deduction (deduction for AGI)
An above-the-line deduction that reduces gross income directly

Adjusted gross income
A determination peculiar to individual taxpayers that represents gross income less business expenses, expenses attributable to the production of rent or royalty income, the allowed capital loss deduction, and certain personal expenses (deductions for AGI)

The gross income can be reduced further by allowed deductions. Deductions that reduce gross income directly are referred to as **above-the-line deductions (deductions for AGI)**. The line referred to in this phrase is **adjusted gross income (AGI).** A determination peculiar to individual taxpayers that represents gross income less business expenses, expenses attributable to the production of rent or royalty income, the allowed capital loss deduction, and certain personal expenses (deductions for AGI).

AGI is a very important concept for individual income taxation. It represents the basis for calculating percentage limitations on certain itemized deductions such as the charitable and medical itemized deductions. AGI also serves as a benchmark for passive rental real estate losses.

In determining adjusted gross income, the taxpayer may reduce gross income by the following, as well as certain other, less common items:

- Ordinary and necessary expenses incurred in a trade or business
- Net capital losses (limited)
- Deductible employer share of self-employment tax paid
- Alimony paid to an ex-spouse (This applies only if the divorce was finalized before 1/1/19. For divorce decrees finalized or amended on or after 1/1/19 alimony paid is not deductible.)
- Certain payments to a Keogh, SIMPLE, or SEP retirement plan
- Contributions to a traditional IRA (limited)
- Forfeited interest penalty for premature withdrawal of time deposits
- Self-employed health insurance premiums and qualified long-term care premiums
- Interest paid on qualifying education loans (limited)

Deductions for AGI are more favorable than itemized deductions because they are generally subject to fewer limits than itemized deductions, and they do not require the taxpayer to itemize to receive a benefit from the deduction. They also reduce AGI, which reduces calculated hurdles for itemized deductions, and can reduce phased-out items.

Itemized Deductions and the Standard Deduction

Below-the-line deduction (deduction from AGI)
Deduction that is allowed to reduce adjusted gross income

Basic standard deduction
The amount allowed all taxpayers who do not itemize their deductions

Several deductions are allowed to reduce adjusted gross income. This type of deduction is often referred to as a **below-the-line deduction (deduction from AGI)**.

The **basic standard deduction** is the amount allowed all taxpayers who do not itemize their deductions. It represents the government's estimate of tax-deductible expenses a taxpayer might have. The allowed standard deduction is based on the tax year and the taxpayer's filing status. The allowed basic standard deductions for 2022 are summarized in the table below.

EXHIBIT 13.5 Allowed Basic Standard Deduction

Filing Status	Basic Standard Deduction 2022
Single	$12,950
Married, filing jointly/SS*	$25,900
Head of household	$19,400
Married, filing separately	$12,950

*SS—Surviving spouse

Itemized deductions
Deductions in excess of the standard deduction that are used in lieu of the standard deduction

Taxpayers who have deductible expenses in excess of the standard deduction may choose to itemize and deduct these itemized expenses instead of taking the standard deduction. These expenses, referred to as **itemized deductions**, are generally personal expenses. In addition, some of the itemized deductions have separate AGI limitations that may reduce their deductibility.

EXAMPLE For example, medical expenses are only deductible to the extent they exceed 7.5% of the taxpayer's AGI. If an itemizing taxpayer's AGI is $100,000 and he incurs unreimbursed medical expenses during the year of $10,500, only $3,000, or $10,500 – ($100,000 × 7.5%), of the medical expenses is deductible.

The following is a brief list of some of the more common itemized deductions. Note that some of the deductions listed below are subject to AGI or income limitations.

- Medical expenses*
- State and local income taxes, real estate taxes, and personal property taxes (Note that the deduction for taxes is capped at $10,000, in the aggregate.)
- Mortgage interest
- Investment interest*
- Charitable contributions*
- Casualty losses from a federally declared disaster*

  * AGI or income limited

EXAMPLE Mary is a single taxpayer, age 45. In 2022, she paid mortgage interest of $3,500, real estate taxes of $1,500, and state income taxes of $2,000 and incurred medical expenses of $600. Assuming Mary's AGI is $50,000, her itemized deductions would total $7,000 ($3,500 + $1,500 + $2,000). The medical expenses are not deductible as itemized deductions because they do not exceed 7.5% of Mary's AGI. Because Mary is a single taxpayer, her standard deduction would be $12,950, for 2022, and therefore it would be beneficial for Mary to use the standard deduction.

Not everyone is entitled to the standard deduction. No standard deduction is allowed for the following individuals:

- A married person filing a separate return if his spouse itemizes deductions
- A nonresident alien
- An individual filing a tax return for a period of less than 12 months

The basic standard deduction is reduced under the Tax Code for an individual who may be claimed as a dependent of another taxpayer for a taxable year beginning in the calendar year in which the individual's taxable year begins. The basic standard deduction is limited to the greater of $1,150 (2022) or the sum of $400 and the individual's earned income, limited to $12,950 (2022).

In addition to the basic standard deduction, a taxpayer will be entitled to an additional standard deduction if the taxpayer is blind or turns 65 by the end of the tax year.

EXHIBIT 13.6 Additional Standard Deduction

Filing Status	2022 Additional Standard Deduction
Single	$1,750
Married, filing jointly/SS	$1,400
Head of household	$1,750
Married, filing separately	$1,400

Determining Who Is a Dependent

Dependent
An individual who meets the definition of a qualifying child or a qualifying relative and who can be listed by a taxpayer on an income tax return

Qualifying child
A taxpayer may claim an individual as a dependent if the individual satisfies all of the following requirements: relationship, abode, age, support, citizenship, and joint return

Qualifying relative
A taxpayer may claim an individual as a dependent if the individual satisfies all of the following requirements: relationship, support, gross income, citizenship, and joint return

To use either the qualifying widow(er)/surviving spouse status after the year of a spouse's death or the head of household filing status, the taxpayer must have a qualifying child or qualifying relative as a dependent. The qualifying person on the taxpayer's return also applies to whether or not a taxpayer may use the child tax credit or the child and dependent care credit. In all cases, the dependent's Social Security number or taxpayer identification number must be on the return.

Per tax code, a dependent can be claimed if an individual is either a **qualifying child** or **qualifying relative** of the taxpayer. In order to claim an individual as a dependent, the individual must either be a qualifying child or a qualifying relative of the taxpayer. Certain tests must be met before an individual will satisfy either definition.

Requirement	Qualifying Child	Qualifying Relative
Relationship test	Must be taxpayer's: child, stepchild, foster child, brother, stepbrother, sister, stepsister, or a descendent of any of the previously listed	Not a qualifying child as identified in column 2; either bears a specified relationship to the taxpayer, including parent, in-law, niece, nephew, aunt, or uncle; or is unrelated to the taxpayer, but the individual resided in the taxpayer's principal home during the tax year
Income test	N/A	Gross income must be less than the standard deduction amount for a single person; nontaxable income, such as Social Security benefits, when used as support by the individual, counts toward the threshold
Residence test	Must have lived with the taxpayer more than half of the taxable year	A parent does not have to reside in the same household with the taxpayer
Age test	The individual must pass an age test (meet one of the following): under age 19 at the close of the tax year; is a full-time student and under age 24 at the close of the tax year; or, is totally and permanently disabled at any time during the tax year	N/A
Support test	Dependent must not have provided more than 50% of own support (scholarships do not count)	Taxpayer must have provided more than 50% of support
Dependents test	Individual cannot claim any other individual as a dependent	Individual cannot claim any other individual as a dependent
Filing	The individual may not file a joint return for the tax year (unless the only reason a return was filed was to obtain a refund of tax withheld)	The individual may not file a joint return for the tax year (unless the only reason a return was filed was to obtain a refund of tax withheld)
Citizenship	The individual generally must also be a U.S. citizen, U.S. national, or resident of the United States, Canada, or Mexico	The individual generally must also be a U.S. citizen, U.S. national, or resident of the United States, Canada, or Mexico

NOTE: **Relatives who do not have to live with you.** A person related to you in any of the following ways does not have to live with you all year as a member of your household to meet the "Member of Household or Relationship Test" (IRS Pub 501).

- Your child, stepchild, foster child, or a descendant of any of them (e.g., your grandchild). (A legally adopted child is considered your child.)
- Your brother, sister, half brother, half sister, stepbrother, or stepsister.
- Your father, mother, grandparent, or other direct ancestor, but not foster parent.
- Your stepfather or stepmother.
- A son or daughter of your brother or sister.
- A son or daughter of your half brother or half sister.
- A brother or sister of your father or mother.
- Your son-in-law, daughter-in-law, father-in-law, mother-in-law, brother-in-law, or sister-in-law.

Any of these relationships that were established by marriage are not ended by death or divorce.

As long as all the tests are met, an individual can be identified as a dependent for a person who dies during the year, without a reduction.

Taxable Income and Tax Rates

Taxable income is calculated by reducing the adjusted gross income by the standard or itemized deduction. Taxable income is the tax base upon which the tax rates are applied to determine the taxpayer's tax liability before credits.

The tax rate schedule is based on the current tax year and the individual's filing status. The 2022 tax rates for all filing statuses are included in the Annual Limits provided in Appendix 13.2.

Tax Credits

Once the individual's tax liability is determined, it may be reduced further by any allowable tax credits. Tax credits result in a direct, dollar-for-dollar reduction in tax liability. A credit may be refundable or nonrefundable. Most credits are nonrefundable, meaning that the credit can reduce an individual's tax liability to zero but not below zero. Common tax credits include the foreign tax credit, the child and dependent care credit, the child tax credit, the American Opportunity Tax Credit, and the Lifetime Learning Credit.

IRS GUIDANCE

Letter Ruling
A written statement issued by the National Office of the IRS that gives guidance on the way the IRS will treat a prospective or contemplated transaction for tax purposes

Determination Letter
A written statement issued by an IRS district director that applies the principles and precedents announced by the National Office to a given set of facts

Due to the complexity of the federal tax law, the IRS often issues guidance as to how it will treat certain transactions for tax purposes. This guidance is often given using Letter Rulings, Determination Letters, Revenue Rulings, Revenue Procedures, and Technical Advice Memoranda.

A **Letter Ruling** is essentially a statement by the IRS of the way it will treat a prospective or contemplated transaction for tax purposes. In response to a written request from a taxpayer, the National Office prepares the Letter Ruling. A ruling is generally honored only with respect to the specific taxpayer to whom the ruling was issued. Other taxpayers cannot assume that the IRS will apply the Letter Ruling to them, even if they engage in the same transaction set out in the Letter Ruling. It does, however, give other taxpayers an idea of the IRS's application of the law.

A **Determination Letter** is a written statement issued by a District Director of the IRS. The letter applies the principles and precedents announced by the National Office to a given set of facts. Determination letters are issued only if the issue can be resolved on the basis of clearly established rules. They are typically used when establishing a qualified retirement plan, such as a pension or profit-sharing plan.

Revenue Rulings
Official interpretation on how the law should be applied to a specific set of facts

Private Letter Rulings
Statements issued for a fee upon a taxpayer's request that describe how the IRS will treat proposed transactions for tax purposes

Revenue Procedures
Statements reflecting the internal management practices of the IRS that affects the rights and duties of taxpayers

Internal Revenue Bulletin (IRB)
Announces official rulings and procedures of the IRS and publishes Treasury Decisions, Executive Orders, Tax Conventions, legislation, court decisions, and other items of general interest

Technical Advice Memoranda
Advice or guidance in memorandum form furnished by the National Office of the IRS to IRS agents who request such advice or guidance during an audit

The National Office of the IRS issues **Revenue Rulings**. They provide an official interpretation on how the law should be applied to a specific set of facts. They are typically issued because of many requests for **Private Letter Rulings** with respect to an area of the tax law. Private Letter Rulings are statements issued for a fee upon a taxpayer's request that describe how the IRS will treat proposed transactions for tax purposes. Taxpayers may rely on Revenue Rulings in determining the tax consequences of their transactions; however, taxpayers must determine whether their facts closely resemble the facts presented in the ruling.

Revenue Procedures are statements reflecting the internal management practices of the IRS that affect the rights and duties of taxpayers.

The **Internal Revenue Bulletin (IRB)** announces official rulings and procedures of the IRS and publishes Treasury Decisions, Executive Orders, Tax Conventions, legislation, court decisions, and other items of general interest. Rulings and procedures reported in the IRB do not have the force and effect of Treasury tax regulations, but they may be used as precedents. In contrast, any documents not published in the IRB cannot be relied on, used, or cited as precedents in the disposition of other cases.

Technical Advice Memoranda give advice or guidance in memorandum form and are furnished by the National Office of the IRS. An IRS agent typically requests the memorandum during an audit. The purpose of technical advice is to help IRS personnel close cases and maintain consistent holdings throughout the IRS.

PENALTIES AND INTEREST

Various civil penalties are imposed on taxpayers and tax return preparers who violate the tax law. Included in the civil penalties are failure-to-file penalties, failure-to-pay-tax penalties, accuracy-related penalties, and fraud penalties.

Failure-to-File-Tax-Return Penalty

Failure-to-file penalty
A civil penalty imposed on taxpayers and tax return preparers who fail to file tax returns according to the requirements of tax law

The **failure-to-file penalty** was enacted to ensure the timely filing of tax returns. Generally, a return is considered filed on the date it is delivered to the IRS.

The penalty is 5% of the amount of tax required to be shown on the return for each month or fraction of a month that the failure continues, up to a maximum penalty of 25% of the unpaid tax. If the return is filed more than 60 days after the due date or the extended due date, the minimum penalty is the lesser of $435 or 100% of the unpaid tax. If a taxpayer can show that there was reasonable cause for the failure to file the return, the IRS will not assess the penalty. The penalty period runs from the due date of the tax return, including extensions, to the date the IRS actually receives the return.

The failure-to-file penalty is reduced by any failure-to-pay penalty.

Failure-to-Pay-Tax Penalty

Failure-to-pay-tax penalty
A civil penalty imposed on taxpayers who, without reasonable cause, fail to pay the tax shown on their return

The **failure-to-pay-tax penalty** is imposed on taxpayers who, without reasonable cause, fail to pay the tax shown on a return. The penalty is one-half of 1% of the tax shown for each month or fraction of a month that it is not paid, up to a maximum penalty of 25%.

EXAMPLE Jim files his tax return 40 days after the due date. He remits a check for $7,000 that represents the balance of the tax due. Jim's failure-to-file and failure-to-pay penalties total $700, calculated as follows:

Failure-to-pay ($7,000 × .5% × 2 months)		$70
Failure-to-file ($7,000 × 5% × 2 months)		$700
Less: failure-to-pay penalty	(70)	$630
Total penalty		$700

Interest is generally payable whenever any tax or civil penalty is not paid when due, even if the taxpayer has been granted an extension of time to pay the tax. Interest on unpaid tax liabilities runs from the last day prescribed by the Tax Code for payment to the date paid.

Accuracy-Related Penalties

Accuracy-related penalty
A penalty of 20% of the portion of the tax underpayment attributable to negligence, substantial understatement of tax, or substantial valuation misstatement without intent to defraud

The **accuracy-related penalty** is a penalty of 20% of the portion of the tax underpayment attributable to negligence, substantial understatement of tax, or substantial valuation misstatement without intent to defraud.

Negligence includes any failure to make a reasonable attempt to comply with the tax laws, exercise reasonable care in return preparation, and keep proper books and records or properly substantiate items. If the IRS has evidence that the taxpayer was negligent, the taxpayer must establish that he was not negligent by a preponderance of the evidence.

A substantial understatement of income tax occurs when an individual fails to report on his income tax return the appropriate amount of tax that should be imposed, and this understatement exceeds the larger of (1) 10% of the correct tax or (2) $5,000.

Substantial valuation misstatement occurs when a taxpayer undervalues or overvalues property or services, resulting in the understatement of income tax liability. The valuation misstatement is considered substantial if the value claimed on the return is 200% or more of the correct value. However, the penalty does not apply unless the understatement of tax liability exceeds $5,000.

EXAMPLE Scott, who is in the 32% marginal tax rate, contributes artwork to a charitable organization and claims a deduction of $40,000. Assuming the actual fair market value of the art is $18,000, Scott would be subject to the 20% accuracy-related penalty because the overstatement of the asset's value was more than 200% of the correct value and the understatement of tax liability is more than $5,000.

The accuracy-related penalty does not apply with respect to any portion of an underpayment if the taxpayer has a reasonable cause for the position taken on the return. The determination of whether a taxpayer acted with reasonable cause and in good faith is made on a case-by-case basis, taking into account all pertinent facts and circumstances.

Fraud Penalties

The fraud penalty is 75% of the portion of the tax underpayment attributable to the fraud. The IRS must prove that there was an underpayment and that the underpayment was attributable to fraud.

Fraud penalty
A penalty levied against a taxpayer by the IRS after it has proven an underpayment of tax by the taxpayer and proven that the underpayment was attributable to a willful attempt to evade tax

For the **fraud penalty** to apply, there must be a willful attempt to evade tax. The taxpayer must have intended to mislead the IRS or conceal information to prevent the collection of taxes. Civil fraud has not been clearly defined, but courts have inferred fraudulent intent from factors, such as understatement of income, failure to file tax returns, and failure to cooperate with tax authorities.

The fraud penalty does not apply with respect to any portion of an underpayment if the taxpayer has a reasonable cause for the position taken on the return. In addition, the imposition of the fraud penalty precludes the imposition of the accuracy-related penalty on the same underpayment.

AUDIT PROCESS

Audit
When the IRS examines a tax return "to determine if income, expenses, and credits are being reported accurately" (Publication 556)

A goal of the IRS is to promote the highest degree of compliance with the Internal Revenue Code. Tax compliance is a voluntary process. Without some sort of audit process, the IRS would have no means by which to ensure compliance with the law. In an **audit**, the IRS examines a tax return "to determine if income, expenses, and credits are being reported accurately" (Publication 556). Before conducting an audit, the IRS must use a screening process to determine which taxpayers will be subject to audit, who will perform the audit, and what type of audit will be conducted.

The percentage of returns audited each year varies depending on the IRS's available staff. Returns on which all or most of the income is subject to withholding and where taxpayers did not itemize their deductions are the returns least likely to be audited.

Discriminant Index Function (DIF) system
A mathematical technique used to classify tax returns as to their examination potential

Selection and Screening Process

The IRS employs various methods and procedures for identifying and selecting individual returns for examination.

One selection method employed by the IRS is the **Discriminant Index Function (DIF) system.** The DIF system is a mathematical technique used to classify tax returns as to their examination potential. Under this system, returns are divided into different audit classes. Weights are then assigned to certain return characteristics according to a formula that varies with each audit class. These weights are added to arrive at the total DIF score for the return. Returns with the highest DIF scores are made available to the examination division of the IRS for manual screening.

Although DIF scores indicate examination potential, tax examiners must manually screen returns to identify issues in need of examination and to eliminate returns that do not warrant an audit. Depending on the complexity of the issues involved and the degree of auditing skills required to perform the examination, either revenue agents or tax auditors manually screen individual returns.

If an audit examination is to be conducted, a classification check sheet is prepared and attached to the return. The check sheet lists significant items to be considered and identifies whether a correspondence audit, an office audit, or a field audit will be performed. Which type of audit to conduct is determined on the basis of the complexity of the return and which type of audit is most conducive to effective and efficient tax administration.

Correspondence audit
An audit conducted almost entirely by written correspondence and telephone contact with the taxpayer and typically involves simple issues

Office audit
The audit is conducted at the IRS office near the taxpayer's home and usually involve issues too complicated to be resolved by mail, such as travel and entertainment expenses, income from rents, and large itemized deductions

Field audit
An audit conducted for complex individual returns with business or other financial activities. IRS revenue agents handle field audits, as opposed to office audits, which are conducted by less-experienced tax auditors and are typically conducted at the taxpayer's business or wherever the taxpayer's books are maintained.

Types of Audits

A **correspondence audit** is conducted almost entirely by written correspondence and telephone contact with the taxpayer. These audits typically involve simple issues, such as itemized deductions, IRA contribution limits, and self-employment tax.

Office audits usually involve issues too complicated to be resolved by mail, such as travel and entertainment expenses, income from rents, and large itemized deductions. In most cases, the audit is conducted at the IRS office near the taxpayer's home. The taxpayer is informed that his tax return is being audited and is usually requested to furnish certain information.

Field audits are conducted for complex individual returns with business or other financial activities. IRS revenue agents handle field audits, as opposed to office audits, which are conducted by less-experienced tax auditors. These audits are typically conducted at the taxpayer's business or wherever the taxpayer's books are maintained. Before the field audit begins, the examiner makes a precontact analysis of the return to determine which items should be examined.

Outcomes of Audits

Once the audit is complete, there are four possible outcomes to determinations made by the examiner:

- No change to the return—the examiner proposes no change in the taxpayer's tax liability.
- Taxpayer agrees with examiner's findings—if the taxpayer agrees with the examiner's proposed changes, the taxpayer signs an agreement form and pays any additional taxes and interest owed. The taxpayer may even receive a refund because of the audit.
- Taxpayer does not agree with examiner's findings—if the taxpayer does not agree with the examiner's proposed changes, the taxpayer has the right to appeal. The IRS will send the taxpayer a *30-day letter* notifying the taxpayer of his right to appeal the proposed changes within 30 days. If the taxpayer does not respond within 30 days, the IRS will send a *90-day letter*, which is a notice of deficiency.
  - The notice of deficiency officially informs the taxpayer that the IRS has determined that a tax deficiency exists and details the basis for and the amount of the deficiency. Once an individual has received a 90-day letter, he may pay the deficiency, file a Tax Court petition, or take no action.
- Taxpayer partially agrees with examiner's findings—the taxpayer agrees with some, but not all, of the examiner's proposed changes.

If a taxpayer has exhausted all of his administrative remedies, he may litigate a case in court. The following chart details the court system as it applies to tax litigation.

EXHIBIT 13.7 Income Tax Appeal Procedure

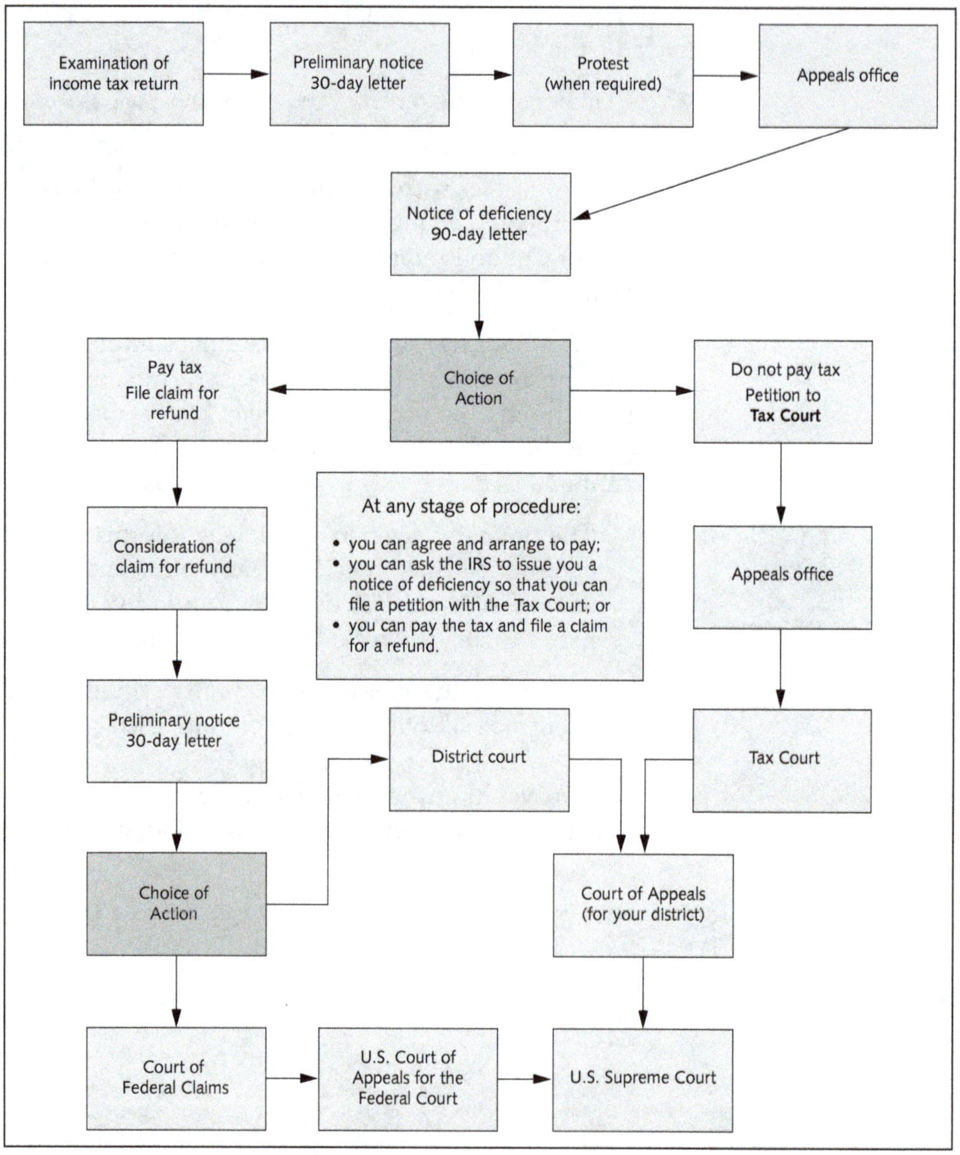

The litigation begins in a court of original jurisdiction, or trial court. The U.S. Tax Court, U.S. District Court, and U.S. Court of Federal Claims are all trial courts that may hear tax cases.

- The U.S. Tax Court tries only tax cases. The taxpayer does not pay the alleged deficiency but files suit against the IRS Commissioner to stop the collection of tax. The court consists of 19 judges, and a jury trial is not available. The Small Case Division may try the case if the deficiency is equal to or less than $50,000.

- The U.S. District Court tries tax cases as well as many other types of civil and criminal cases. The taxpayer pays the alleged deficiency and files suit against the U.S. government for a refund. There are approximately 90 district courts, and a jury trial is available. If the taxpayer has filed for bankruptcy, the Federal Bankruptcy Division may try the case.
- The U.S. Court of Federal Claims tries tax cases as well as other cases against the federal government. The taxpayer pays the alleged deficiency and files suit against the U.S. government for a refund. The court consists of 16 judges, and a jury trial is not available.

The appropriate appellate court depends on which trial court hears the case. If the case is tried in the Tax Court or District Court, the appeals are taken to the U.S. Court of Appeals. Appeals from the Claims Court are taken to the U.S. Court of Appeals for the Federal Circuit.

PAYROLL TAXES

The federal government, through the Federal Insurance Contributions Act (FICA), imposes employment taxes on employers, employees, and self-employed individuals. These taxes provide for a federal system of old age, survivors, disability, and hospital insurance.

The Federal Unemployment Tax Act (FUTA) provides for payments of unemployment compensation to workers who have lost their jobs.

FICA Taxes for Employers and Employees

The Federal Insurance Contributions Act (FICA) created several different programs designed to prevent people from becoming poverty stricken. The two most important and well-recognized programs created by FICA are Old Age, Survivors, and Disability Insurance (OASDI), better known as Social Security, and the Hospital Insurance (HI) program, better known as Medicare Part A. These taxes have different tax rates, and only the OASDI tax has a wage base limit.

Contributions to these programs are made by salary reductions for employees and by direct payments to the government by employers and self-employed individuals. FICA taxes are imposed on employees at a combined rate of 7.65%. This rate represents the total of the 6.2% rate for the OASDI portion and the 1.45% rate for the HI portion. The OASDI rate is applied to the employee's total wages for the year, up to the taxable wage base ($147,000 in 2022) for the Social Security portion of the tax. The employer is required to make a matching contribution for each employee. There is no wage ceiling on the Medicare (hospital insurance) portion of the tax.

EXAMPLE If Tom earns a salary of $150,000 in 2022 for ABC Company, he will have $10,712 withheld from his paycheck for FICA taxes, computed as follows:

Social Security portion (6.2% × $147,000)	$9,114
Medicare portion (1.45% × $150,000)	$2,175
Total FICA taxes	$11,289

In 2022, Tom would have had 6.2% deducted as the Social Security portion from his check ($9,114). ABC Company will be required to pay the amount withheld from Tom's paycheck, plus the company's own contribution. ABC's contribution would be 6.2% up to the taxable wage base for the Social Security portion ($147,000 in 2022) and 1.45% for the Medicare portion. ABC Company will also receive a deduction for its share of the FICA taxes paid.

Additional Medicare Tax

Additional Medicare tax
A Medicare tax of 0.9% paid by taxpayers above certain income thresholds that is in addition to the 2.9% Medicare tax

The **Additional Medicare Tax** has a tax rate of 0.9%. An individual is liable for the Additional Medicare Tax if the individual taxpayer's wages, other compensation, or self-employment income (combined with a spouse if filing as married filing jointly) exceeds the thresholds listed below for the taxpayer's filing status.

Filing Status	Threshold Amount
Married filing jointly	$250,000
Married filing separately	$125,000
Single	$200,000
Head of household (with qualifying person)	$200,000
Qualifying widow(er) with dependent child	$200,000

Unlike the 2.9% Medicare tax, which is divided between an employer and an employee share, only the employee pays the full 0.9% tax. This tax is in addition to the 1.45% employee share regular Medicare tax. The tax is applied to the amount of income that is in excess of the threshold for the taxpayer's filing status.

Employers are required to begin collecting the Additional Medicare Tax from employees in the first payroll period the employee's compensation from the employer exceeds $200,000. Only the amount in excess of $200,000 is subject to the payroll tax deduction. The employer does not match the employee contribution of the Additional Medicare Tax.

If an employee who files as MFJ does not have income exceeding $250,000 when the spouses combine their income and file their income tax return, or when the spousal incomes are combined and the amount of Additional Medicare Tax that should have been paid is less than what was deducted, any excess payments can be refunded to the taxpayer when the income tax return is filed.

Additionally, if a taxpayer expects to have income above the threshold for the taxpayer's filing status when combined with a spouse's income, and/or any self-employment income, the taxpayers may ask for additional federal income tax withheld by the employers, even though neither taxpayer's compensation will reach the $200,000 threshold. A self-employed taxpayer may make additional estimated tax payments to cover this contingency as well.

It must be emphasized that this is in addition to the 2.9% that is assessed on all compensation and net self-employment income.

Self-employment tax
Tax paid by self-employed individuals that is based on net earnings, not on the individual's wages. Because the self-employed must bear the burden of both the employer and employee portion of FICA, the self-employment tax rate is 15.3% (up to the taxable wage base)—double the employee's rate of 7.65%. Net SE income exceeding the TWB is taxed at the 2.9% Medicare tax rate, which has no income ceiling, and is added to the SE tax calculated for the SE income up to the TWB.

Self-Employment Tax

Self-employed individuals must bear the burden of both the employer and employee portion of FICA taxes. Therefore, the **self-employment tax** rate is 15.3%, double the employee's rate of 7.65% [subject to the taxable wage base (TWB) limit]. If the net earnings exceed the taxable wage base, the Medicare tax of 2.9% is levied on the amounts that exceed the TWB. This tax is calculated on Schedule SE, which is attached to the individual's Form 1040.

Self-employment tax is calculated in the same fashion as FICA tax; however, the tax is based on net earnings from self-employment, not on the individual's wages. The net earnings from self-employment is the gross income from the trade or business, less any allowable deductions. Before applying the income tax rates, net earnings may be reduced by 7.65%, which represents the deductible employer share of the FICA tax.

EXAMPLE If Andrea owns her own business and during 2022 her income after allowed deductions is $200,000, she will incur $23,584.30 in self-employment tax, calculated as follows:

Net earnings from self-employment	$200,000
Less: 7.65% of net earnings	(15,300)
Amount subject to self-employment tax	$184,700

Social Security portion (12.4% × $147,000)	$18,228
Medicare portion (2.9% × $184,700)	$5,356.30
Total self-employment taxes	$23,584.30

Andrea will report the self-employment tax on her income tax return and receive a deduction of $11,792 the employer deductible share of the self-employment tax in 2022. This amount will be deducted in arriving at adjusted gross income (above-the-line deduction).

Federal Unemployment Tax Act

The Federal Unemployment Tax Act (FUTA) provides for payments of unemployment compensation to workers who have lost their jobs. Most employers pay both a federal and state unemployment tax. The employee is not responsible for paying unemployment tax.

Federal unemployment taxes are imposed on employers who pay wages of $1,500 or more during any calendar quarter during the year or who employ at least one individual for at least a part of a day in any 20 or more different weeks during the current or previous year. There are different limits for an employer of farm workers. For many years the FUTA rate has been 6.2%, and it was applied to the first $7,000 the employer pays each employee as wages during the year. Therefore, the maximum FUTA payment required for a covered employee was $434 ($7,000 × 6.2%). In most cases, where an employer has paid state unemployment taxes, a credit of up to a maximum of 5.4% could be taken to reduce the amount of FUTA due. The effective tax rate then became 0.6%.

TAX AVOIDANCE VS. TAX EVASION

Tax avoidance
The legal minimization of taxes, which is accomplished by applying knowledge of the IRC and the Treasury regulations to an individual's income tax situation

The goal of most income tax planning is to reduce and minimize the amount of tax a person must pay to the government. **Tax avoidance** is the legal minimization of taxes. This avoidance is accomplished by applying knowledge of the Internal Revenue Code (also referred to as the Tax Code) and the Treasury regulations to an individual's income tax situation. Every individual has the right to reduce his tax burden within the scope of the law.

The taxpayers' legal right to minimize or reduce personal income taxes has been upheld by the courts. In the case of *Commissioner v. Newman*, Judge Learned Hand wrote:

> Over and over again courts have said that there is nothing sinister in so arranging one's affairs so as to keep taxes as low as possible. Everybody does so, rich or poor, and all do right, for nobody owes any public duty to pay more than the law demands; taxes are enforced extractions, not voluntary contributions. To demand more in the name of morals is mere cant.

Tax planning and tax avoidance involve only legal actions. Tax planning is the process of arranging one's actions in light of their tax consequences. In many cases, tax planning can be accomplished simply by changing the form of a transaction. For example, if an individual is invested in tax-exempt bonds, the individual is not required to pay tax on the interest income earned by the bonds, and therefore his tax liability is less than if he invested in taxable bonds.

Tax evasion
Any of the various fraudulent methods by which a taxpayer may pay less than his proper tax liability

Whereas tax avoidance is the term applied to the legal interpretation of the tax laws to minimize *tax liabilities*, **tax evasion** is the term generally applied to any of the various fraudulent methods by which a taxpayer may pay less than his proper tax liability.

For example, if an individual works part time at home babysitting the neighbors' children or mowing lawns for others, the income received must be reported as income on the individual's income tax return. Because the babysitting income may not be reported to the government by the individual's neighbors, the individual may decide illegally to exclude the income from the tax return.

This example of tax evasion may lead to additional tax liability, as well as interest and penalties, if the tax return is audited. The amount of interest and penalties depends on the amount of understatement. Criminal tax evasion can even lead to fines and an occasional jail sentence.

TAX-ADVANTAGED INVESTMENTS

One goal shared by most financial planners and their clients is the minimization of all current and future taxes. Because taxes are often an individual's highest expenditure each year, effective reduction of taxes is of extreme importance.

Although Congress has significantly reduced the opportunities available to minimize income taxes, there are still a few opportunities available for investors interested in or already involved in tax-advantaged investments. Included in these opportunities are investments in tax-exempt securities, investment in tax shelters and vacation homes, use of tax-advantaged employee benefits, use of acceleration/deferral techniques, and awareness of other tax-reduction opportunities.

Investment in Tax-Exempt Securities

As a rule, interest income is taxable regardless of its source. However, interest income from certain state and local bonds and interest on educational savings bonds is excluded from income for federal income tax purposes.

Interest on obligations of a state, territory, U.S. possession (such as Puerto Rico), or any of their political subdivisions is nontaxable. If an individual has money to invest, one may wish to invest in state bonds if income tax reduction is an important goal. It should be noted, however, that state governments typically offer lower interest rates on these bonds than the rate offered on taxable investments. Therefore, to determine whether an investment in a tax-exempt security is a wise choice, one can calculate an interest rate that a tax-exempt investment must earn to break even with the higher rate offered by a taxable investment. The formula to determine the break-even interest rate is:

$$\text{Taxable interest rate} \times (1 - \text{marginal tax rate}) = \text{tax-free rate}$$

EXAMPLE Joe has a 35% marginal income tax rate, and he would like to invest in State of Kentucky bonds. If similar taxable investments yield 10%, Joe must earn a rate of return on the State of Kentucky bonds of at least 6.5%, or 10% x (1 – 35%), to make this a worthwhile investment.

In addition to state bonds, interest on U.S. savings bonds such as Series EE bonds may be either tax deferred or tax exempt. The interest earned on the bond can be tax deferred until the year the bond matures or is redeemed by the individual. The taxpayer can also elect to recognize the interest income as it is earned instead of deferring the recognition until redemption or maturity. The interest income from a Series EE bond is completely tax-free if the bond was issued after 1989 and if the accrued interest and principal amount of the bond are used to pay for qualified education expenses of the taxpayer, spouse, or dependents, subject to AGI limitations.

Tax Shelters and Passive Activities

Under prior law, an individual could reduce or eliminate her tax liability by investing in tax shelters that produced losses that could be used to offset other income. These shelters often created paper losses in excess of the amount of capital the investor provided, causing the tax shelter business to grow into a thriving industry.

Typically, tax shelters took the form of limited partnerships, thus allowing losses to flow through to the individual partners. In the first few years of the partnerships' operation, losses were generally high due to low revenues and high expenses, such as interest, taxes, and accelerated depreciation.

The Tax Reform Act of 1986 significantly curtailed the benefits available to investors in tax shelters by the introduction of the passive activity loss limits. Passive activities include all rental operations and all other businesses in which the taxpayer does not materially participate. An individual meets the material participation test only if he is involved in the operation of the activity on a regular, continuous, and substantial basis.

Although there are many exceptions, a taxpayer will be considered a material participant if she spends more than 500 hours in the activity during the year or if she spends more than 100 hours in the activity and no other individual spends more time on the activity. If the investor is not a material participant, the activity is considered passive. Investors have two rules that govern deductibility of a loss from a passive activity. Under the **at-risk rule**, a taxpayer can deduct losses only to the extent of the amount the taxpayer has at risk in the investment (amount invested). Losses in amounts in excess of the amount at risk in the investment are suspended until the taxpayer increases the amount invested in the passive activity, either by additional investment or by a profit from the activity. Under the **passive loss rule**, passive losses may only offset income from the same or another passive activity. If the passive activity is a publicly traded partnership (master limited partnership), losses from that activity may only be offset by income from the same publicly traded partnership. Investors may not use passive activity losses to offset ordinary taxable income, such as salary, interest, and dividends. If a loss is disallowed (suspended) under the passive loss rule, it can subsequently be utilized when the taxpayer disposes of the activity.

At-risk rule
A taxpayer can deduct losses only to the extent of the amount the taxpayer has at risk in the investment (amount invested). Losses in amounts in excess of the amount at risk in the investment are suspended until the taxpayer increases the amount invested in the passive activity, either by additional investment or by a profit from the activity.

Passive loss rule
Passive losses may only offset income from another passive activity. If the passive activity is a publicly traded partnership (master limited partnership), losses from that activity may only be offset by income from the same publicly traded partnership.

Even though deductions for passive losses are generally disallowed, there are situations in which a taxpayer would benefit by investing in a tax shelter. For example, if the taxpayer has an investment in a passive activity that is generating income, any passive losses could be used to offset the passive income. In addition, a taxpayer may deduct a limited amount of loss against active income when the taxpayer invests in rental real estate.

A taxpayer who actively participates in a rental real estate activity may deduct up to $25,000 ($12,500 for taxpayers married but filing separately) of losses annually. A taxpayer is considered an active participant if he participates in management decisions such as approving new tenants and owns at least a 10% interest in the activity. The allowance is reduced by 50% of the excess of the individual's MAGI over $100,000 ($50,000 for MFS) and is therefore completely phased out when the taxpayer's MAGI reaches $150,000 ($75,000 for MFS).

Acceleration of Deductions

In addition to pursuing tax-advantaged investments, the taxpayer may take advantage of opportunities to accelerate income tax deductions or defer income tax gains. This also referred to as *deduction clustering*. However, this must be looked at in concert with the alternative minimum tax (AMT) implications. Some of these deductions are added back to regular taxable income to arrive at alternative minimum taxable income (AMTI), exposing the taxpayer to a possible AMT liability. This liability is the difference between the tax due on regular taxable income and the tax due on AMTI.

The Internal Revenue Code allows individual taxpayers to claim deductions for various personal, investment, and business expenses. The deduction can generally be claimed in the year in which the expenses are paid; therefore, individuals have some flexibility with respect to the timing of deductions. A taxpayer wishing to reduce or eliminate a potential tax liability can accelerate deductions by prepaying the expense. For example, state income taxes can be paid during the current tax year rather than waiting until the following year when the tax is due. Taxpayers can also make additional contributions to charity before the close of the tax year, resulting in an income tax deduction in the current year.

Deferral of Tax Gains

When a taxpayer disposes of property, any resulting gain is usually reported, or recognized, on the individual's income tax return in the year of disposition. However, there are several situations where a taxpayer can dispose of property and defer recognition of the gain until a later date.

Section 1031 of the Tax Code allows a taxpayer to exchange certain types of domestic (U.S.) real estate property without recognizing a gain. These like-kind exchanges are afforded beneficial tax treatment. If property other than like-kind property, commonly called **boot**, is received in the exchange, gain may be recognized.

Boot
Property (other than like-kind property) that qualifies as a tax gain when received in a property exchange

If a taxpayer is not required to recognize gain from a real estate like-kind exchange, the basis of the property received by the taxpayer must be reduced by the unrecognized (deferred) gain, resulting in recognition of the deferred gain when the acquired property is subsequently sold.

EXAMPLE Jack received vacant land worth $60,000 in exchange for vacant land with a tax basis to Jack of $35,000. Assuming the vacant land qualifies as like-kind property, Jack's realized gain of $25,000 ($60,000 – $35,000) will not be reported on his income tax return. Jack's basis in the land received will be $35,000 ($60,000 – $25,000 deferred gain).

Taxpayers do not always dispose of their property intentionally. Occasionally, property is lost due to theft or to a casualty, such as a fire or storm. When this occurs, the taxpayer may receive some sort of compensation, such as insurance proceeds. The proceeds received may even exceed the taxpayer's basis in the property, resulting in a gain. Absent special provisions, the gain would be fully taxable in the year of the conversion, resulting in a potential financial hardship for the taxpayer.

Section 1033 of the Internal Revenue Code allows a taxpayer (even a related one) who undergoes an involuntary conversion to postpone recognition of the gain. If the amount reinvested in the replacement property equals or exceeds the amount realized, the realized gain is not recognized. If the amount reinvested in the replacement property is less than the amount realized, the gain is recognized to the extent the proceeds are not reinvested.

Normally, the taxpayer has a two-year time period from the end of the taxable year in which any gain is realized from an involuntary conversion (e.g., fire) to replace the property. However, if a condemnation of real property by a governmental authority is the reason for the conversion, this time period is extended to three years from the end of the taxable year in which any gain is realized. The general requirement to apply

Section 1033 is that the replacement property must be similar in service or use to the involuntarily converted property.

SUMMARY OF VALUATION RULES FOR SECTIONS 1031 AND 1033

	Section 1031 Real Estate Exchanges	Section 1033 Involuntary Conversions
Realized gain =	FMV of all property received – adjusted basis of all property given up	amount realized – adjusted basis of old property

Recognized gain occurs if boot received =	Recognized gain* occurs if boot received
	■ LESSER of:
	  ■ Boot received
	  ■ Realized gain
	*Recognized gain also occurs if appreciated boot is given up	

Recognized gain =		amount realized but not reinvested in new property (limited to realized gain)
Deferred gain =	realized gain – recognized gain	realized gain – recognized gain
Basis in like-kind property received =	FMV of property received in exchange – deferred gain	
Basis in new property =		FMV of property at acquisition – deferred gain

Exemption Opportunities

The Tax Code has traditionally provided tax breaks for homeowners, including the allowance of deductions for mortgage interest and property taxes. The tax law also provides for the exclusion of some or all of the gain on the sale of a residence. The provision applies to residence sales as frequently as every two years, to gains in amounts up to $250,000 for single taxpayers and $500,000 for married taxpayers.

The exclusion is applicable to the sale of a residence owned by the taxpayer and used as a principal residence for two of the five years preceding the sale. If the taxpayer fails the use or ownership test, a partial exclusion may be available if the home is sold due to a change in employment, health, or other unforeseen circumstances. The allowed exclusion is based on a ratio of the number of qualifying months to 24 months.

Under the Mortgage Forgiveness Debt Relief Act of 2007, the gain exclusion has been expanded for surviving spouses. Because the $500,000 exclusion required filing of a joint income tax return, surviving spouses could only take advantage of the full $500,000 gain exclusion in the year of a spouse's death. Effective for sales and exchanges occurring after December 31, 2007, surviving single spouses qualify for the up-to-$500,000 exclusion amount (all other rules apply) for sales occurring up to two years from the date of death of the other spouse. It is important to understand that the two years expires with the second anniversary of the actual date of death and not just occurring in the second tax year after death. For example, if a spouse dies February 15, 2022, and the surviving spouse sells the residence February 1, 2024, the rule applies. If the residence is sold March 1, 2024, the surviving spouse is treated as single and only qualifies for up to $250,000 of gain exclusion.

EXAMPLE Mary, a single taxpayer, owned and used her home as a principal residence for 18 months. She then sold her home because of a new job in another city, realizing a gain on the sale of $300,000. Mary would be entitled to an exclusion of $187,500 ($250,000 × 18/24), resulting in a reportable capital gain of $112,500 ($300,000 – $187,500).

If a married couple filing jointly does not meet the conditions for claiming the full $500,000 exclusion, the excludible gain will be the sum of the exclusion that each spouse would be entitled to if both were single. For this purpose, each spouse is treated as owning the home for the period that either spouse owned the home.

EXAMPLE When Al and Susan were married, Susan moved into the home Al had owned and had been using as his principal residence for over 20 years. They used the home as their principal residence for six months, then sold the home (gain of $600,000) because of a new job. The couple can exclude $312,500 of the gain because Al will receive the full $250,000 exclusion and Susan will be entitled to a partial exclusion of $62,500 ($250,000 × 6/24).

Another exemption opportunity exists for taxpayers owning vacation homes. If the home is rented to others for 14 days or less during the year, any rental income from the home is excludible from the taxpayer's gross income, no matter how much rent is charged.

CONCLUSION

The federal tax system in the United States is among the most complex tax systems in the world. A financial planner must realize the importance of gaining a comprehensive understanding of the tax law because income taxes are often the largest single expenditure of a client in a given year.

Although changes to the law have made income tax avoidance much more difficult over the last few years, many tax planning opportunities still exist. It is the financial planner's duty to a client to be aware of these opportunities to prevent the client from paying more tax than he is obligated to pay.

WHERE ON THE WEB

American Bar Association **www.abanet.org**

American Institute of Certified Public Accountants (CPA/PFS) **www.aicpa.org**

Certified Financial Planner Board of Standards, Inc. **www.cfp.net**

Financial Planning Association **www.fpanet.org**

Internal Revenue Service **www.irs.gov**

National Association of Personal Financial Advisors **www.napfa.org**

National Association of State Boards of Accountancy **www.nasba.org**

National Association of Tax Professionals **www.natptax.com**

RIA (Research Institute of America) Thomson Tax and Accounting **www.riathomson.com**

Society of Financial Service Professionals **www.financialpro.org**

DISCUSSION QUESTIONS

1. What are the objectives of federal income tax law?
2. What is the alternative minimum tax?
3. What is a capital asset?
4. What is the formula for determining a client's income tax liability?
5. What are some of the types of government rulings issued as guidance to taxpayers and IRS agents?
6. When taxpayers violate the tax laws, what civil penalties might they expect to incur?
7. What payroll taxes did the Federal Insurance Contributions Act and the Federal Unemployment Tax Act create?
8. What tax-advantaged investment options are available to taxpayers?

EXERCISES

1. Joe, a self-employed individual, earns $150,000 in self-employment income. How much self-employment tax will Joe owe for 2022?
2. Kay sold the following investments during the current year:

Property	Date Sold*	Date Acquired*	Sales Price	Adjusted Basis
ABC stock	2/3/CY	1/2/PY	$3,300	$1,300
Bond	2/5/CY	2/5/PY	$1,200	$1,400
Land	4/5/CY	5/4/PY	$4,300	$3,400

* CY = current year; PY = prior year

What is the amount of net long-term gain and net short-term gain on the sale of the investments?

3. Cindy sold 300 shares of XYZ stock for $5,200. She had paid $3,000 for the stock. Commissions of $300 on the sale and $180 on the purchase were paid.

What is Cindy's amount realized and her gain realized, respectively, on this sale?

4. Don, age 61, incurred $28,000 of medical expenses in the current year. His insurance company reimbursed him $6,000. Assuming his AGI is $100,000, what is the amount of medical expense deduction Don can claim for the year?

5. The Durrs are a married couple with two school-age children they fully support. Use the following information about their 2022 finances to answer the following question.

Gross income	$91,350
Deductions for AGI	$6,000
Itemized deductions	$14,800

Assuming the Durrs file a joint income tax return, what is their taxable income for 2022?

6. Susan, a single taxpayer, sold her home because she has a new job in another city. On the sale date, she had owned the home and used it as a personal residence for 18 months. What is the maximum gain that Susan can exclude on the sale of the residence?

7. During the current year, Scott had long-term capital losses of $2,000 and short-term capital losses of $1,500. If this is the first year he has experienced capital gains or losses, what amount of these losses may Scott deduct this year? Assume Scott files as single for federal income tax.

8. Pablo, a single individual, purchased a new personal residence for $375,000. Pablo sold the property 12 months later for $550,000 so he could take a new job that involved a promotion. How much gain must Pablo recognize?

9. David exchanged an apartment complex that he had owned for 8 years for farmland. The farmland was worth $1,050,000, and David's basis in the apartment complex was $475,000. David received $100,000 cash in the transaction. How much is David's gain realized and gain recognized because of this exchange?

10. Doug and Susan, ages 45 and 40, are married and file a joint return for 2022. The following pertains to their return for the year:

Adjusted gross income	$61,600
Itemized deductions	$26,000

What is their taxable income and tax liability for 2022?

11. Joe is a single taxpayer who has taxable income of $175,000, including the capital gain. During the current year, he sold the following assets:

Investment	Gain
ABC Company stock	$4,500
XYZ Company stock	$1,000
Baseball card collection	$2,000
Corporate bonds	$6,000
Antiques	$8,000

All of the assets were held longer than one year. How will Joe be taxed on the capital gains?

12. Susan filed her tax return 70 days after the due date. She remitted a check for $8,000 that represented the balance of the tax due. Calculate her total failure-to-file and failure-to-pay penalties.

13. Jim is in the 32% marginal income tax rate, and he would like to invest in State of Louisiana bonds. If similar taxable investments yield 9%, how much must Jim earn to make this a worthwhile investment?

14. Allison is age 12 and has the following income:

Investment income	$1,800
Income from a summer job	$2,200

Assuming her parents list Allison as a dependent on their income tax return, what is her taxable income for 2022?

15. Billy sold the following investments during the year:

Description	Holding Period	Gain/(Loss)
ABC Stock	Short-term	$30,000
XYZ Stock	Long-term	$45,000
Bonds	Short-term	($20,000)
Real estate	Long-term	($60,000)

As a taxpayer who files with his spouse as married, filing jointly, what is the net short-term or long-term gain or loss, and how much must Billy include or deduct in the current year?

PROBLEMS

1. David and Sue are married and file a joint return. They have two children, Billy and Suzy, ages 8 and 6, respectively.

David is a self-employed real estate appraiser, and the results for his business for the current year are as follows (he paid self-employment tax of $4,705):

Gross receipts	$50,000
Expenses:	
Advertising	$900
Insurance	$1,000
Interest	$500
Dues	$700
Depreciation	$1,200
Office rent	$12,000

Sue, who is employed by a marketing company, earned a salary of $40,000 for the current year. She participates in the company Section 401(k) plan and made contributions to the plan of $6,000 for the current year (the company does not provide any matching contributions).

David and Sue also received the following income during the year:

Interest:

Second National Bank, Dallas	$1,100
State of Louisiana Municipal Bonds	$500

Qualified dividends:

ABC Company cash dividend	$350
XYZ Company cash dividend	$400

They sold their principal residence after owning and living in the home for five years. The following information relates to the sale of the residence:

■ Sales price	$700,000
■ Original cost	$150,000

David and Sue incurred the following expenses during the current year:

■ Real estate taxes	$10,000
■ Mortgage interest	$4,500
■ Sales taxes	$800

Assuming David paid $5,000 in alimony to his ex-wife, calculate the couple's taxable income for 2022.

2. Scott and Laura are married and file a joint income tax return. They have taxable income for the current year of $65,000. In arriving at taxable income, they took the following deductions:

Mortgage interest	$8,000
Real estate taxes	$10,000
State income taxes	$8,000
Charitable contributions	$300

In addition, Scott and Laura received the following tax-exempt interest:

Municipal bonds	$600
Private activity bonds issued in 2005	$3,000

Laura also exercised incentive stock options (ISOs) during the year. The option entitled her to purchase 500 shares at $50 per share. The stock was worth $110 per share at the time of exercise.

Calculate the couple's AMTI before considering the AMT exemption amount.

3. Steve and Elaine exchange real estate investments. Steve gives up property with an adjusted basis of $250,000 (FMV $400,000). In return for this property, Steve receives property with a FMV of $300,000 (adjusted basis $200,000) and cash of $100,000.

What are Steve and Elaine's realized, recognized, and deferred gains because of the exchange?

4. Anne, a CPA employed by a CPA firm, is an unmarried taxpayer. She earned a salary of $100,000 for the current year (2022) and did not participate in the firm's Section 401(k) plan.

   Anne also received the following income and incurred the following expenses during the year:

Income:		
	Interest	$2,000
	Ordinary dividends	$900
Expenses:		
	Medical (unreimbursed)	$1,500
	Real estate taxes	$7,000
	Mortgage interest	$5,000
	Interest on auto loan	$2,500

   Ignoring any credits, how much lower would Anne's tax liability have been had she made a deductible employee contribution ($12,000) to the Section 401(k) plan?

CASE SCENARIO

Use the information provided to answer the following questions regarding the Nelson family.

NELSON FAMILY CASE SCENARIO
DANA AND DAVID NELSON
As of January 1, 2022

Personal Background and Information

David Nelson (age 37) is a bank vice president. He has been employed there for 12 years and has an annual salary of $70,000. Dana Nelson (age 37) is a full-time homemaker. David and Dana have been married for eight years. They have two children, John (age 6) and Gabrielle (age 3), and are expecting their third child in two weeks. They have always lived in this community and expect to remain indefinitely in their current residence.

General Goals (Not Prioritized)

- Save for college education
- Reduce debt

- Save for retirement
- Estate planning
- Invest wisely

Insurance Information

Health Insurance

The entire family is insured under David's employer's health plan (PPO). For covered expenses, a $1,000 in-network deductible and a $2,000 out-of-network deductible apply, after which 80%/20% coinsurance applies in-network and 60%/40% applies out-of-network. There is a stop-loss limit of $20,000 annually in-network and $30,000 out-of-network annually. The entire monthly premium of $1,123.54 is paid by David's employer.

Life Insurance

David's employer provides group term life insurance equal to two times his current salary. The premium is paid entirely by his employer, and Dana is the primary beneficiary. No contingent beneficiary is named.

Disability Insurance

David's employer also offers a contributory group long-term disability insurance program toward which the employer contributes 60% of the $158.54 monthly premium. David is a participant in the program, which provides a monthly disability income benefit equal to 70% of his current salary, payable to his Social Security normal retirement age, provided that he remains disabled per the policy's "own occupation" definition of disability. David must satisfy a 90-day elimination period before he is eligible to begin receiving benefits.

David's employer doesn't offer dental or vision coverage, and the Nelsons have not obtained any private form of individual dental or vision insurance benefits.

Homeowners Insurance

The Nelsons have an HO-3 policy with replacement cost on contents. There is a $250 deductible. The annual premium is $950.

Automobile Insurance

The Nelsons have automobile liability and bodily injury coverage of $100,000/$300,000/$100,000. They have both comprehensive coverage and collision. The deductibles are $250 (comprehensive) and $500 (collision). The annual premium is $900.

Relevant External Environmental Information

- Mortgage rates are 5.0% for 30 years and 4.5% for 15 years, fixed.
- Gross domestic product is expected to grow at less than 3%.
- Inflation is expected to be 2.6%.
- Expected return on investment is 8% for common stocks, 9% for small company stocks, and 1.1% for U.S. Treasury bills.
- College education costs are $15,000 per year.

Investment Information

The bank offers a Section 401(k) plan in which David is an active participant. The bank matches contributions dollar for dollar up to 3% of David's salary. David currently contributes 5.43% of his salary. His employer's plan allows for employee contributions of up to 16% of salary. In the Section 401(k) plan, the Nelsons have the opportunity to invest in a money market fund, a bond fund, a growth and income fund, and a small-cap stock fund. The Nelsons consider themselves to have a moderate investment risk tolerance. David's assets within the retirement plan are currently earning 8.5%, based on his investment choices within the plan.

Income Tax Information

David and Dana tell you that they are in the 12% federal income tax bracket. They pay $820 annually in state and local income taxes.

Education Information

John is 6 years old and currently attending first grade at a private school. Gabrielle is 3 years old. She will attend private school from pre-kindergarten through high school. The current balance of the college fund is $14,000. They expect to contribute $1,000 at the end of each year to this fund.

Gifts, Estates, Trusts, and Will Information

David has made Dana his primary beneficiary on his Section 401(k) plan, and the children are the contingent beneficiaries. Because most of their assets are owned jointly, David doesn't see the need for a will. Dana also does not have a will.

Dana and David Nelson
Statement of Financial Position
12/31/2021

ASSETS			LIABILITIES AND NET WORTH		
Cash/cash equivalents			**Current liabilities**		
JT	Checking account	$1,425	JT	Credit cards	$4,000
JT	Savings account	$950	JT	Mortgage on principal residence	$1,234
			David	Boat loan	$1,493
Total cash/cash equivalents		$2,375	**Total current liabilities**		$6,727
Invested assets			**Long-term liabilities**		
Dana	ABC stock	$12,500	JT	Mortgage on principal residence	$196,654
JT	Education fund	$14,000	David	Boat loan	$12,065
David	Section 401(k) plan	$32,197			
Total invested assets		$58,697	**Total long-term liabilities**		$208,719
Personal-use assets			**Total liabilities**		$215,446
JT	Principal residence	$245,000			
JT	Automobile	$18,000			
David	Boat	$25,000	**Net worth**		$207,626
Dana	Jewelry	$13,000			
JT	Furniture/household	$61,000			
Total personal-use assets		$362,000			
Total assets		$423,072	**Total liabilities and net worth**		$423,072

Dana and David Nelson
Statement of Financial Position
12/31/2022

ASSETS			LIABILITIES AND NET WORTH		
Cash/cash equivalents			**Current liabilities**		
JT	Checking account	$1,268	JT	Credit cards	$3,655
JT	Savings account	$950	JT	Mortgage on principal residence	$1,370
Total cash/cash equivalents		$2,218	David	Boat loan	$1,048
			Total current liabilities		$6,073
Invested assets			**Long-term liabilities**		
Dana	ABC stock	$14,050	JT	Mortgage on principal residence	$195,284
JT	Education fund	$15,560	David	Boat loan	$16,017
David	Section 401(k) plan	$38,619	**Total long-term liabilities**		$211,301
David	XYZ stock	$10,000			
Total invested assets		$78,229			
Personal-use assets			**Total liabilities**		$217,374
JT	Principal residence	$250,000			
JT	Automobile	$15,000			
David	Personal watercraft	$10,000	**Net worth**		$241,573
David	Boat B	$30,000			
Dana	Jewelry	$13,500			
JT	Furniture/household	$60,000			
Total personal-use assets		$378,500			
Total assets		$458,947	**Total liabilities and net worth**		$458,947

Notes to financial statements:

- Assets are stated at fair market value.
- The ABC stock was inherited from Dana's aunt on November 15, 2021. Her aunt originally paid $20,000 for it on October 31, 2012. The fair market value at the aunt's death was $12,000.
- Liabilities are stated at principal only.
- JT = joint tenancy; client name = separate property.

Dana and David Nelson
Personal Statement of Cash Flows
For 2022

INFLOWS		
Salary—David		$70,000
Investment income		
Interest income	$900	
Qualified dividends	$150	$1,050
Total inflow		**$71,050**
Savings		
Reinvestment (interest/dividends)	$1,050	
Section 401(k) plan deferrals	$3,803	
Education fund	$1,000	
Total savings		**$5,853**
Available for outflows		**$65,197**
OUTFLOWS		
Ordinary living expenses		
Food	$6,000	
Clothing	$3,600	
Child care	$600	
Entertainment	$1,814	
Utilities	$3,600	
Auto maintenance	$2,000	
Church	$3,500	
Total ordinary living expenses		**$21,114**
Debt payments		
Credit card payments principal	$345	
Credit card payments interest	$615	
Mortgage payment principal	$1,234	
Mortgage payment interest	$20,720	
Boat loan principal	$1,493	
Boat loan interest	$1,547	
Total debt payments		**$25,954**
Insurance premiums		
Automobile insurance premiums	$900	
Disability insurance premiums	$761	
Homeowners insurance premiums	$950	
Total insurance premiums		**$2,611**
Tuition and education expenses		**$1,000**
Taxes		
FICA and federal income tax (W/H)	$12,855	
State (and city) income tax	$820	
Property tax (principal residence)	$1,000	
Total taxes		**$14,675**
Total outflows		**$65,354**
Net cash flow (deficit)		**($157)**

1. Calculate the Nelsons' taxable income and tax liability for 2022 (ignoring any credits).
2. The Nelsons exchanged their boat (Boat A) plus $5,000 for Boat B on December 31, 2022. David had paid $22,000 for Boat A a few years ago. What are the realized gain and recognized gain from this transaction?
3. If David increased his contributions to maximize his employer's match to his Section 401(k) plan, what would be the reduction in the Nelsons' tax liability in 2022?

APPENDIX 13.1 2022 Form 1040

Form **1040** Department of the Treasury—Internal Revenue Service (99)
U.S. Individual Income Tax Return **2021** OMB No. 1545-0074 IRS Use Only—Do not write or staple in this space.

Filing Status Check only one box.
☐ Single ☐ Married filing jointly ☐ Married filing separately (MFS) ☐ Head of household (HOH) ☐ Qualifying widow(er) (QW)
If you checked the MFS box, enter the name of your spouse. If you checked the HOH or QW box, enter the child's name if the qualifying person is a child but not your dependent ▶

Your first name and middle initial	Last name		**Your social security number**
If joint return, spouse's first name and middle initial	Last name		**Spouse's social security number**
Home address (number and street). If you have a P.O. box, see instructions.		Apt. no.	**Presidential Election Campaign** Check here if you, or your spouse if filing jointly, want $3 to go to this fund. Checking a box below will not change your tax or refund. ☐ **You** ☐ **Spouse**
City, town, or post office. If you have a foreign address, also complete spaces below.	State	ZIP code	
Foreign country name	Foreign province/state/county	Foreign postal code	

At any time during 2021, did you receive, sell, exchange, or otherwise dispose of any financial interest in any virtual currency? ☐ **Yes** ☐ **No**

Standard Deduction **Someone can claim:** ☐ You as a dependent ☐ Your spouse as a dependent
☐ Spouse itemizes on a separate return or you were a dual-status alien

Age/Blindness **You:** ☐ Were born before January 2, 1957 ☐ Are blind **Spouse:** ☐ Was born before January 2, 1957 ☐ Is blind

Dependents (see instructions):
If more than four dependents, see instructions and check here ▶ ☐

(1) First name	Last name	(2) Social security number	(3) Relationship to you	(4) ✔ if qualifies for (see instructions): Child tax credit	Credit for other dependents
				☐	☐
				☐	☐
				☐	☐
				☐	☐

Attach Sch. B if required.

Standard Deduction for—
• Single or Married filing separately, $12,550
• Married filing jointly or Qualifying widow(er), $25,100
• Head of household, $18,800
• If you checked any box under *Standard Deduction*, see instructions.

1	Wages, salaries, tips, etc. Attach Form(s) W-2				1	
2a	Tax-exempt interest	2a		b Taxable interest	2b	
3a	Qualified dividends	3a		b Ordinary dividends	3b	
4a	IRA distributions	4a		b Taxable amount	4b	
5a	Pensions and annuities	5a		b Taxable amount	5b	
6a	Social security benefits	6a		b Taxable amount	6b	
7	Capital gain or (loss). Attach Schedule D if required. If not required, check here ▶ ☐				7	
8	Other income from Schedule 1, line 10				8	
9	Add lines 1, 2b, 3b, 4b, 5b, 6b, 7, and 8. This is your **total income** ▶				9	
10	Adjustments to income from Schedule 1, line 26				10	
11	Subtract line 10 from line 9. This is your **adjusted gross income** ▶				11	
12a	**Standard deduction or itemized deductions** (from Schedule A)	12a				
b	Charitable contributions if you take the standard deduction (see instructions)	12b				
c	Add lines 12a and 12b				12c	
13	Qualified business income deduction from Form 8995 or Form 8995-A				13	
14	Add lines 12c and 13				14	
15	**Taxable income.** Subtract line 14 from line 11. If zero or less, enter -0-				15	

For Disclosure, Privacy Act, and Paperwork Reduction Act Notice, see separate instructions. Cat. No. 11320B Form **1040** (2021)

APPENDIX 13.1 2022 Form 1040 (continued)

Form 1040 (2021) Page 2

Line	Description	Box	Amount	Line	Amount
16	**Tax** (see instructions). Check if any from Form(s): 1 ☐ 8814 2 ☐ 4972 3 ☐ ______			16	
17	Amount from Schedule 2, line 3			17	
18	Add lines 16 and 17			18	
19	Nonrefundable child tax credit or credit for other dependents from Schedule 8812			19	
20	Amount from Schedule 3, line 8			20	
21	Add lines 19 and 20			21	
22	Subtract line 21 from line 18. If zero or less, enter -0-			22	
23	Other taxes, including self-employment tax, from Schedule 2, line 21			23	
24	Add lines 22 and 23. This is your **total tax** ▶			24	
25	Federal income tax withheld from:				
a	Form(s) W-2	25a			
b	Form(s) 1099	25b			
c	Other forms (see instructions)	25c			
d	Add lines 25a through 25c			25d	
26	2021 estimated tax payments and amount applied from 2020 return			26	
27a	Earned income credit (EIC)	27a			
	Check here if you were born after January 1, 1998, and before January 2, 2004, and you satisfy all the other requirements for taxpayers who are at least age 18, to claim the EIC. See instructions ▶ ☐				
b	Nontaxable combat pay election — 27b				
c	Prior year (2019) earned income — 27c				
28	Refundable child tax credit or additional child tax credit from Schedule 8812	28			
29	American opportunity credit from Form 8863, line 8	29			
30	Recovery rebate credit. See instructions	30			
31	Amount from Schedule 3, line 15	31			
32	Add lines 27a and 28 through 31. These are your **total other payments and refundable credits** ▶			32	
33	Add lines 25d, 26, and 32. These are your **total payments** ▶			33	

If you have a qualifying child, attach Sch. EIC.

Refund

Line	Description	Box	Amount	Line	Amount
34	If line 33 is more than line 24, subtract line 24 from line 33. This is the amount you **overpaid**			34	
35a	Amount of line 34 you want **refunded to you.** If Form 8888 is attached, check here ▶ ☐			35a	
▶ b	Routing number ▶ c Type: ☐ Checking ☐ Savings				
▶ d	Account number				
36	Amount of line 34 you want **applied to your 2022 estimated tax** ▶	36			

Direct deposit? See instructions.

Amount You Owe

Line	Description	Box	Amount	Line	Amount
37	**Amount you owe.** Subtract line 33 from line 24. For details on how to pay, see instructions ▶			37	
38	Estimated tax penalty (see instructions) ▶	38			

Third Party Designee

Do you want to allow another person to discuss this return with the IRS? See instructions ▶ ☐ **Yes.** Complete below. ☐ **No**

Designee's name ▶ Phone no. ▶ Personal identification number (PIN) ▶

Sign Here

Under penalties of perjury, I declare that I have examined this return and accompanying schedules and statements, and to the best of my knowledge and belief, they are true, correct, and complete. Declaration of preparer (other than taxpayer) is based on all information of which preparer has any knowledge.

Your signature	Date	Your occupation	If the IRS sent you an Identity Protection PIN, enter it here (see inst.) ▶
Spouse's signature. If a joint return, **both** must sign.	Date	Spouse's occupation	If the IRS sent your spouse an Identity Protection PIN, enter it here (see inst.) ▶
Phone no.	Email address		

Joint return? See instructions. Keep a copy for your records.

Paid Preparer Use Only

Preparer's name	Preparer's signature	Date	PTIN	Check if: ☐ Self-employed
Firm's name ▶			Phone no.	
Firm's address ▶			Firm's EIN ▶	

Go to *www.irs.gov/Form1040* for instructions and the latest information. Form **1040** (2021)

APPENDIX 13.1 2022 Form 1040 (continued)

SCHEDULE 1 (Form 1040) Department of the Treasury Internal Revenue Service	**Additional Income and Adjustments to Income** ▶Attach to Form 1040, 1040-SR, or 1040-NR. ▶Go to *www.irs.gov/Form1040* for instructions and the latest information.	OMB No. 1545-0074 2021 Attachment Sequence No. 01
Name(s) shown on Form 1040, 1040-SR, or 1040-NR		Your social security number

Part I Additional Income

1	Taxable refunds, credits, or offsets of state and local income taxes			1	
2a	Alimony received			2a	
b	Date of original divorce or separation agreement (see instructions) ▶ ______				
3	Business income or (loss). Attach Schedule C			3	
4	Other gains or (losses). Attach Form 4797			4	
5	Rental real estate, royalties, partnerships, S corporations, trusts, etc. Attach Schedule E			5	
6	Farm income or (loss). Attach Schedule F			6	
7	Unemployment compensation			7	
8	Other income:				
a	Net operating loss	8a	( )		
b	Gambling income	8b			
c	Cancellation of debt	8c			
d	Foreign earned income exclusion from Form 2555	8d	( )		
e	Taxable Health Savings Account distribution	8e			
f	Alaska Permanent Fund dividends	8f			
g	Jury duty pay	8g			
h	Prizes and awards	8h			
i	Activity not engaged in for profit income	8i			
j	Stock options	8j			
k	Income from the rental of personal property if you engaged in the rental for profit but were not in the business of renting such property	8k			
l	Olympic and Paralympic medals and USOC prize money (see instructions)	8l			
m	Section 951(a) inclusion (see instructions)	8m			
n	Section 951A(a) inclusion (see instructions)	8n			
o	Section 461(l) excess business loss adjustment	8o			
p	Taxable distributions from an ABLE account (see instructions)	8p			
z	Other income. List type and amount ▶ ______	8z			
9	Total other income. Add lines 8a through 8z			9	
10	Combine lines 1 through 7 and 9. Enter here and on Form 1040, 1040-SR, or 1040-NR, line 8			10	

For Paperwork Reduction Act Notice, see your tax return instructions. Cat. No. 71479F **Schedule 1 (Form 1040) 2021**

APPENDIX 13.1 2022 Form 1040 (continued)

Schedule 1 (Form 1040) 2021 | Page 2

Part II Adjustments to Income

11	Educator expenses	11	
12	Certain business expenses of reservists, performing artists, and fee-basis government officials. Attach Form 2106	12	
13	Health savings account deduction. Attach Form 8889	13	
14	Moving expenses for members of the Armed Forces. Attach Form 3903	14	
15	Deductible part of self-employment tax. Attach Schedule SE	15	
16	Self-employed SEP, SIMPLE, and qualified plans	16	
17	Self-employed health insurance deduction	17	
18	Penalty on early withdrawal of savings	18	
19a	Alimony paid	19a	
b	Recipient's SSN ▶		
c	Date of original divorce or separation agreement (see instructions) ▶		
20	IRA deduction	20	
21	Student loan interest deduction	21	
22	Reserved for future use	22	
23	Archer MSA deduction	23	
24	Other adjustments:		
a	Jury duty pay (see instructions) — 24a		
b	Deductible expenses related to income reported on line 8k from the rental of personal property engaged in for profit — 24b		
c	Nontaxable amount of the value of Olympic and Paralympic medals and USOC prize money reported on line 8l — 24c		
d	Reforestation amortization and expenses — 24d		
e	Repayment of supplemental unemployment benefits under the Trade Act of 1974 — 24e		
f	Contributions to section 501(c)(18)(D) pension plans — 24f		
g	Contributions by certain chaplains to section 403(b) plans — 24g		
h	Attorney fees and court costs for actions involving certain unlawful discrimination claims (see instructions) — 24h		
i	Attorney fees and court costs you paid in connection with an award from the IRS for information you provided that helped the IRS detect tax law violations — 24i		
j	Housing deduction from Form 2555 — 24j		
k	Excess deductions of section 67(e) expenses from Schedule K-1 (Form 1041) — 24k		
z	Other adjustments. List type and amount ▶ — 24z		
25	Total other adjustments. Add lines 24a through 24z	25	
26	Add lines 11 through 23 and 25. These are your **adjustments to income.** Enter here and on Form 1040 or 1040-SR, line 10, or Form 1040-NR, line 10a	26	

Schedule 1 (Form 1040) 2021

APPENDIX 13.2 2022 Annual Limits Relating to Financial Planning

COLLEGE FOR FINANCIAL PLANNING®
A KAPLAN COMPANY

2022 ANNUAL LIMITS RELATING TO FINANCIAL PLANNING

Compiled by the faculty of the College for Financial Planning

RETIREMENT PLANS	
Elective deferrals 401(k), 403(b), 457, and SARSEPs	$20,500
Catch-up contribution	$6,500
Defined contribution (§415(c)(1)(A))	$61,000
Defined benefit (§415(b)(1)(A))	$245,000
SIMPLE plan	$14,000
SIMPLE catch-up contribution	$3,000
Maximum includible compensation	$305,000
Highly compensated employee	
Lookback to 2021	$130,000
Lookback to 2022	$135,000
Key employee (top-heavy plan)	>$200,000
SEP participation limit	$650
IRA or Roth IRA contribution limit	$6,000
IRA or Roth IRA catch-up	$1,000
IRA deduction phaseout for active participants	
Single	$68,000-$78,000
Married filing jointly	$109,000-$129,000
Married filing separately	$0-$10,000
Non-active participant married to active participant	$204,000-$214,000
Roth IRA phaseout	
Single	$129,000-$144,000
Married filing jointly	$204,000-$214,000

SOCIAL SECURITY	
SS wage base	$147,000
FICA tax rate—employee [3]	7.65%
SECA tax rate—self-employed	15.3%
Earnings limitation:	
Below FRA ($1 for $2)	$19,560
Persons reaching FRA ($1 for $3)	$51,960
(Applies only to earnings for months prior to attaining FRA)	
Social Security cost-of-living adjustment	5.9%
Quarter of coverage	$1,510
Maximum benefit: worker retiring at FRA	$3,345
Estimated average monthly benefit	$1,657

SOCIAL SECURITY FRA

Year of Birth	Social Security FRA	Year of Birth	Social Security FRA
1943–54	66	1958	66 and 8 months
1955	66 and 2 months	1959	66 and 10 months
1956	66 and 4 months	1960 and later	67
1957	66 and 6 months		

ESTATE AND GIFT TAX	
Annual gift tax exclusion	$16,000
Estate and gift tax basic exclusion	$12,060,000
Applicable credit amount	$4,769,800
Generation skipping exemption	$12,060,000
Maximum estate tax rate [4]	40%

MEDICARE	
Monthly premium:	
Part A [1]	$499
Part B [2]	$170.10
Part A:	
First 60 days—patient pays a deductible	$1,556
Next 30 days—patient pays per day	$389
Next 60 days (lifetime reserve days) patient pays per day	$778
Skilled nursing benefits	
First 20 days—patient pays per day	-0-
Next 80 days—patient pays per day	$194.50
Over 100 days—patient pays per day	All costs
Part B:	
Deductible	$233
Coinsurance	20%
Part D (Prescription Standard Benefit Model):	
Deductible	$480
25% coinsurance on next	$4,430
Out-of-pocket (OOP) threshold	$7,050
Beneficiary then pays coinsurance amount for additional covered expenses.	

2022 MEDICARE PART B PREMIUM RATES:

YOU PAY		If your 2020 income was:	
Premium	PART D Surcharge	SINGLE	MARRIED COUPLE
$170.10 not Hold Harmless		$91,000 or less	$182,000 or less
$238.10	$12.40	$91,001–$114,000	$182,001–$228,000
$340.20	$32.10	$114,001–$142,000	$228,001–$284,000
$442.30	$51.70	$142,001–$170,000	$284,001–$340,000
$544.30	$71.30	$170,001–$500,000	$340,001–$750,000
$578.30	$77.90	Above $500,000	Above $750,000

YOU PAY	PART D Surcharge	If you are married filing separately and your 2020 income was:
$170.10		$91,000 or less
$544.30	$71.30	$91,001–$409,000
$578.30	$77.90	Above $409,000

FIGURE - 1

1. The Part A premium of $499 per month applies to persons who have fewer than 30 quarters of coverage under Social Security. For those having 30-39 quarters, the Part A Premium is $259 per month.
2. Beneficiaries not subject to the "hold harmless" provision includes persons not receiving Social Security, those who enroll in Part B for the first time in 2022, dual eligible beneficiaries who have their premiums paid by Medicaid, and beneficiaries who pay an additional income-related premium. See Premium rates (Figure 1)
3. The FICA tax rate is comprised of two separate payroll taxes: Employer portion—6.20% for Old-Age, Survivors, and Disability Insurance (OASDI), and 1.45% for Hospital Insurance (HI); Employee portion—6.20% for Old-Age, Survivors, and Disability Insurance (OASDI), and 1.45% for Hospital Insurance (HI). For self-employeds, the SECA is 12.40% for OASDI and 2.90% for HI.
4. A deceased spouse's unused credit amount is portable to a surviving spouse.

APPENDIX 13.2 2022 Annual Limits Relating to Financial Planning (continued)

STANDARD MILEAGE RATES	
Business use	58.5¢ per mile
Charitable use (not indexed)	14¢ per mile
Medical use	18¢ per mile

MISCELLANEOUS ITEMS	
PBGC maximum monthly benefit (at age 65)	$6,205
LTC per diem limit	$390
LTC premium as medical expense limitation	
Age 40 or under	$450
Age 41-50	$850
Age 51-60	$1,690
Age 61-70	$4,510
Age 71 or older	$5,640
Qualified Transportation Fringes (monthly)	
Commuter highway vehicle/transit pass	$280
Qualified parking	$280
Qualified Longevity Annuity Contract	Max $145,000
Health Care Flexible Spending Account	Max $2,850
Health Care FSA Carryover Amount	Max $570

LTCG RATES BASED ON TAXABLE INCOME			
Filing Status	0% rate	15% rate	20% rate
Single	up to $41,675	$41,676-$459,750	over $459,750
Head of household	up to $55,800	$55,801-$488,500	over $488,500
Married filing jointly	up to $83,350	$83,351-$517,200	over $517,200
Married filing separately	up to $41,675	$41,676-$258,600	over $258,600
Estates and trusts	up to $2,800	$2,801-$13,700	over $13,700

2022 TAX RATE SCHEDULES				
If Taxable Income Is		Then the Gross Tax Payable Is:		
Over	But Not Over	Amount	Plus (percent)	Of the Amount Over
SINGLE TAXPAYERS (other than surviving spouses and heads of households)				
$0	$10,275	10% of taxable income		
10,275	41,775	$1,027.50	12%	$10,275
41,775	89,075	4,807.50	22%	41,775
89,075	170,050	15,213.50	24%	89,075
170,050	215,950	34,647.50	32%	170,050
215,950	539,900	49,335.50	35%	215,950
539,900	--	162,718	37%	539,900
HEADS OF HOUSEHOLDS				
$0	$14,650	10% of taxable income		
14,650	55,900	$1,465	12%	$14,650
55,900	89,050	6,415	22%	55,900
89,050	170,050	13,708	24%	89,050
170,050	215,950	33,148	32%	170,050
215,950	539,900	47,836	35%	215,950
539,900	--	161,218.50	37%	539,900
MARRIED INDIVIDUALS (and surviving spouses) FILING JOINT RETURNS				
$0	$20,550	10% of taxable income		
20,550	83,550	$2,055	12%	$20,550
83,550	178,150	9,615	22%	83,550
178,150	340,100	30,427	24%	178,150
340,100	431,900	69,295	32%	340,100
431,900	647,850	98,671	35%	431,900
647,850	--	174,253.50	37%	647,850
MARRIED INDIVIDUALS FILING SEPARATE RETURNS				
$0	$10,275	10% of taxable income		
10,275	41,775	$1,027.50	12%	$10,275
41,775	89,075	4,807.50	22%	41,775
89,075	170,050	15,213.50	24%	89,075
170,050	215,950	34,647.50	32%	170,050
215,950	323,925	49,335.50	35%	215,950
323,925	--	87,126.75	37%	323,925
FIDUCIARY (estates and trusts) TAXPAYERS				
$0	$2,750	10% of taxable income		
2,750	9,850	$275	24%	$2,750
9,850	13,450	1,979	35%	9,850
13,450	--	3,239	37%	13,450

HEALTH SAVINGS ACCOUNT	
Minimum Deductible Amount	
Single	$1,400
Family	$2,800
Maximum Out-of-Pocket Amount	
Single	$7,050
Family	$14,100
HSA Statutory Contribution Maximum	
Single	$3,650
Family	$7,300
Catch-up contributions (age 55 or older)	$1,000

EDUCATION	
EE bonds for education—exclusion phaseout	
Single	$85,800-$100,800
Married filing jointly	$128,650-$158,650
Coverdell Education Savings Account ($2,000 limit) phaseout	
Single	$95,000-$110,000
Married filing jointly	$190,000-$220,000
Lifetime Learning Credit—20% of qualified expenses up to $10,000	
Single	$80,000-$90,000
Married filing jointly	$160,000-$180,000
American Opportunity tax credit—maximum of $2,500	
100% up to $2,000 of qualified expenses	
25% on next $2,000—phaseout:	
Single	$80,000-$90,000
Married filing jointly	$160,000-$180,000
Education loan deduction ($2,500) phaseout	
Unmarried	$70,000-$85,000
Married filing jointly	$145,000-$175,000

INCOME TAX	
Standard deduction	
Single	$12,950
Married filing jointly	$25,900
Head of household	$19,400
Married filing separately	$12,950
Kiddie tax limited standard deduction	$1,150
Individual eligible to be claimed as dependent—greater of $1,150 or earned income plus $400, not to exceed full standard deduction of $12,950.	
Elderly or blind additional deduction	
Single	$1,750
Married	$1,400
Section 179	
Maximum election	$1,080,000
Phaseout begins	$2,700,000
Adoption credit (nonrefundable)	
Maximum	$14,890
Phaseout	$223,410-$263,410
Medicare Contribution tax and additional Medicare tax	
Single	$200,000
Head of household	$200,000
Married filing jointly	$250,000
Child tax credit	
Dependent under age 17	$2,000
Other dependents	$500
Phaseout ($50 for every $1,000 over)	
Single	$200,000
Married filing jointly	$400,000

ALTERNATIVE MINIMUM TAX (AMT)	Exemption	Phaseout
Single	$75,900	$539,900
Married filing jointly	$118,100	$1,079,800
Married filing separately	$59,050	$539,900
Trusts and estates	$26,500	$88,300

AMT RATES
26% up to $206,100 of AMT base
28% over $206,100 of AMT base

COLLEGE FOR FINANCIAL PLANNING® A KAPLAN COMPANY

CALL – 800.237.9990 | CLICK – WWW.CFFP.EDU

For updates, please visit https://www.kaplanfinancial.com/resources/industry-updates/annual-limits.

CHAPTER 14

Business Entities

LEARNING OBJECTIVES

After learning the material in this chapter, you will be able to do the following:

- Identify the different types of business entities that a businessowner may choose as a legal form of business
- Characterize each type of business entity listed below with regard to formation requirements, operation, ownership restrictions, tax treatment, legal liability risk, and management operations:
  - Sole proprietorship
  - Partnership
  - Limited liability partnership
  - Corporation
  - S corporation
  - Limited liability company
- List the basic factors that a businessowner should consider when selecting a legal form of business

- Explain how each type of business entity is different with regard to simplicity of formation and operation, ownership restrictions, limited liability, management operations, and tax characteristics
- Discuss family limited partnerships and how FLPs are used in estate planning
- Discuss taxation and legal liabilities of partnerships, corporations, and S corporations
- Discuss the components of the financial statements used by business entities

BUSINESS ENTITIES

One of the major decisions confronting a businessowner from a tax and legal perspective concerns selecting the form in which the business will operate. The businessowner can choose from several different business forms, each with its own advantages and disadvantages.

Businessowners may choose to run their business as a sole proprietorship, a partnership, a limited liability partnership (LLP), a corporation, or a limited liability company (LLC). Each of these business forms has different formation requirements, tax rules, legal liability risk, and type of management.

Once a business entity has been created, the next step is operating the business. The type of entity chosen will help determine which individuals will be responsible for making the day-to-day business decisions.

Another consideration in the selection of a legal form of business entity is the legal liability of the owners. A major concern of businessowners is the preservation and growth of personal assets, especially in today's litigious society. Therefore, it is critical to select a form of business entity that not only provides the desired asset protection but also allows the appropriate level of freedom to run the company.

Income tax considerations play an important role in the selection of a business entity. Although many of the entities are taxed in a similar fashion, each entity is subject to a set of rules that provides the businessowner with tax consequences that are either advantageous or detrimental. The following sections detail the different tax consequences of the formation and operation of sole proprietorships, partnerships, limited liability partnerships (LLPs), corporations, and limited liability companies (LLCs). Beginning in 2018, there is a deduction for pass-through income of 20% allowed to a noncorporate taxpayer, including a trust or estate, who has qualified business income (QBI) from a partnership, S corporation, or sole proprietorship. The calculation is complex and will not be covered in this book. The student should only be aware that it exists.

The creator of a new business can choose from several legal business forms. The owner must carefully analyze the available options to determine which type of business entity is most appropriate. As a personal financial planner, it is important to understand the different types of business forms available. The most common forms and their basic characteristics are discussed in this chapter.

SOLE PROPRIETORSHIP

Sole proprietorship
A business owned and controlled by one person who is personally liable for all debts and claims against the business

Proprietor
The owner of a sole proprietorship

A **sole proprietorship** is a business owned and controlled by one person who is personally liable for all debts and claims against the business. Separate financial records are regularly maintained. However, for tax purposes, the sole proprietorship is not treated as a separate taxable entity. Rather, the income and deductions of the business are reported directly on the individual owner's federal income tax return (Schedule C of Form 1040).

Advantages of a sole proprietorship include its ease of formation and its simplicity of operation and taxation. **Proprietors** own all business property and need not consult partners or other managers before making business decisions. In addition, this form of business entity may provide some state and federal tax advantages over other entities. For example, if the proprietorship incurs a loss for the year, the loss will be reported on the individual's income tax return, where it may provide immediate tax relief because the loss may be deductible against other taxable income.

Management Operation and Decision Making of a Proprietorship

The proprietor is responsible for the day-to-day operation of the business and is responsible for making all of the business decisions. This allows for great flexibility in the operation of the business. For example, the owner may choose to add a new line of business or discontinue an existing line of business without the approval of others.

Legal Liability of a Proprietorship

The major disadvantage of the sole proprietorship is that the proprietor has unlimited personal liability for the indebtedness of the sole proprietorship. Business liabilities may be satisfied from the owner's personal assets, and any personal liabilities may be satisfied from the business assets. The owner may purchase business liability insurance. This insurance does not exempt the owner from creditor's claims, but it does provide protection against lawsuits.

Taxation of a Proprietorship

Although separate financial records are maintained for tax purposes, the sole proprietorship is not treated as a separate taxable entity.

Tax Ramifications of Formation of a Proprietorship

The formation of a sole proprietorship is very straightforward. No formal transfer of assets to the business is required to enable a proprietorship to engage in business activities. Also, the owner generally is not required to file documents with local authorities (except perhaps for a business license), unless the owner is planning to operate the business under an assumed name. When a sole proprietorship is established, there are no federal income tax ramifications.

Tax Ramifications of Business Operation of a Proprietorship

When the proprietorship generates income and incurs losses, it is not required to file a separate federal income tax return. Instead, the income or loss from the business is reported directly on Schedule C of the proprietor's individual income tax return, Form 1040. When reported, the income or loss is combined with the proprietor's other income to determine the taxpayer's adjusted gross income (AGI). The income from the business is taxed at ordinary income tax rates applicable to individual taxpayers and is generally subject to self-employment taxes.

Schedule C of Form 1040 is used to report the name of the proprietor, as well as the name, address, and accounting method of the proprietorship. This form also contains separate sections to report income earned by the business, such as gross receipts, and expenses incurred by the business, such as advertising, supplies, and wages paid. A sole proprietorship generally may deduct ordinary and necessary business expenses as incurred. A self-employed businessowner is allowed an above-the-line (for AGI) deduction for appropriate contributions to retirement plans, and, in amounts not to exceed net earnings from self-employment, 100% of health insurance premiums and qualified long-term care premiums paid.

The net profit or loss from Schedule C is reflected on the individual income tax return Form 1040. If Schedule C reflects a net profit for the year, this profit is subject to self-employment tax. Self-employment tax is calculated in the same fashion as FICA tax; however, the tax is based on net earnings from the sole proprietorship instead of wages. Before applying the tax rates, net earnings are reduced by 7.65%, which is the deductible share of the self-employment tax rate.

EXHIBIT 14.1 Schedule 1 of Form 1040

Part I Additional Income

1	Taxable refunds, credits, or offsets of state and local income taxes	1	
2a	Alimony received	2a	
b	Date of original divorce or separation agreement (see instructions) ▶		
3	Business income or (loss). Attach Schedule C	3	
4	Other gains or (losses). Attach Form 4797	4	
5	Rental real estate, royalties, partnerships, S corporations, trusts, etc. Attach Schedule E	5	
6	Farm income or (loss). Attach Schedule F	6	

To terminate a sole proprietorship, the taxpayer need only cease operations, pay off all vendors, and report final income or loss on Schedule C of Form 1040 in the tax year the business is terminated.

EXAMPLE If Stan owns his own proprietorship business, and during 2022 his business income after allowed deductions is $300,000, he would incur $22,728.45 in self-employment tax, calculated as follows:

Net earnings from sole proprietorship	$300,000
Less 7.65% of net earnings	($22,950)
Amount subject to self-employment tax	$277,050

Social Security portion (12.4% × $147,000)	$18,228.00
Medicare portion (2.9% × $277,050)	8,034.45
Total self-employment taxes	$26,262.45

The self-employment tax is calculated on Schedule SE, which is attached to the proprietor's Form 1040. The proprietor is allowed a deduction for deductible share (employer share) of the self-employment tax paid, or $13,131.23, in the example. This amount will be deducted in arriving at adjusted gross income (above-the-line deduction). In addition, Stan would be subject to the 0.9% Additional Medicare tax in excess of his applicable threshold. The tax is not a deductible expense. The amount would depend on Stan's filing status.

PARTNERSHIP

Partnership
An association of two or more entities or individuals that operate as co-owners of a business for the purpose of making a profit

Partner
An individual, corporation, trust, estate, or other partnership that has an ownership interest in a partnership

A **partnership** is an association of two or more entities or individuals that operate as co-owners of a business for the purpose of making a profit. Generally, forming a partnership is a simple process because formality is ordinarily unnecessary. The partnership form of business is very flexible because there are no limitations on the number of **partners**, and partners can be individuals, corporations, trusts, estates, and even other partnerships. There are two types of partnerships—general and limited. These differ primarily in the nature of the rights and obligations of the partners. General partnerships are owned entirely by general partners. Each partner can act on behalf of the partnership. A limited partnership is a partnership formed under the limited partnership laws of a state. This partnership must have at least one general partner and at least one limited partner.

Management Operation and Decision Making of a Partnership

Ordinarily, when a partnership is formed, a partnership agreement is drafted outlining the identity of the partners, the division of profits and losses, and the duties of each partner in the management of the partnership business.

General partnership
A type of business entity owned entirely by general partners, each of whom can act on behalf of the partnership

General Partnership

In a **general partnership**, the general partners participate in the management of the partnership and are directly responsible for the day-to-day operation of the business. With management and ownership consolidated among the same individuals, partners are relatively free to change operating policy. Thus, the partnership can change its operational direction at any time.

Limited Partnership

Limited partnership
In a limited partnership, limited partners are not allowed to participate in the management of operations but generally are allowed to vote on major changes affecting the structure of the partnership

In a **limited partnership**, limited partners are not allowed to participate in the management of the partnership affairs. If the limited partners do participate in management, they will become general partners and lose their limited liability status. It should be noted that even though limited partners are not allowed to participate in management, they generally are entitled to vote on major changes affecting the structure of the partnership, such as a change in the type of investments purchased.

Legal Liability of a Partnership

General Partnership

General partnerships are owned entirely by general partners. While the partnership form of business has many advantages, it also has several disadvantages. The most significant disadvantage is the unlimited personal liability of the partners.

A general partner has unlimited liability for the acts of the partnership, the other partners, and obligations made by any partner or the partnership in the performance of partnership duties. If the partnership assets are insufficient to satisfy the liabilities of the partnership, the partnership's creditors can collect against the personal assets of the general partners. The creditors have the right to make any one partner, or several partners, satisfy the entire amount of the partnership's obligations. As a result, one partner may have to make good on the partnership's obligations and then may not be able to recover these amounts from the other partners.

Limited Partnership

A limited partner is liable for partnership indebtedness only to the extent of the capital the partner has contributed or agreed to contribute. In this respect, the limited partner is treated as an investor, liable only for the amount of his investment. Although the status of a limited partner generally provides the individual with limited liability, the limited liability status may disappear, and the partner would be liable as a general partner under any of the following circumstances.

- The surname of the limited partner is included in the partnership name. This does not apply if there is a general partner with the same surname.
- The limited partner acts as a general partner by participating in the management of the business operations.
- The limited partner learns that the firm is defectively formed and fails to withdraw from the partnership.

Taxation of a Partnership

For federal income tax purposes, each general partner's share of partnership trade or business income is considered self-employment income, subject to self-employment taxes. A limited partner, however, is not allowed to participate in the management and control of the business and, therefore, is not subject to self-employment taxes on partnership earnings. A limited partner's income and losses are generally considered passive and subject to the passive activity rules, and a general partner's income and losses are ordinary.

A partnership is similar to a sole proprietorship in that both entities are **flow-through or conduit entities** for federal income tax purposes. In other words, the results of business operations for both entities are reported directly on the owner's income tax return. For federal income tax purposes, partners must take into account their distributive share of partnership taxable income and any additional items the partnership is required to report separately, such as interest and dividend income. Consequently, the partnership is not, as an entity, subject to federal income tax. The partnership items of income and expense are completely taxable to the partners at their own personal income tax rates but are reported initially on the partnership tax return (Form 1065) and then reported to each partner (Form K-1).

Flow-through or conduit entity
A type of business entity in which the results of business operations are reported directly on the owner's income tax return

Tax Ramifications of Formation of a Partnership

Partners may form a partnership by contributing cash, property, or services to the partnership in exchange for an ownership interest. When a partner contributes cash or property to the partnership, no gain or loss is recognized and the partner's basis in the partnership is equal to the value of the cash contributed or the adjusted basis of the property contributed. If a partner contributes personal or professional services to the partnership, the partner must recognize ordinary compensation income for the value of the services. The amount of income recognized becomes the partner's basis in the partnership interest.

EXAMPLE Assume Tom contributes the following to the ABC partnership in exchange for a 50% general partnership interest in the partnership:

Contribution	Fair market value
Cash	$10,000
Land (Tom's basis is $40,000)	$50,000
Services	$ 5,000

Tom would recognize ordinary income of $5,000, the value of the services he contributed to the partnership. His basis in the partnership interest would be $55,000 ($10,000 + 40,000 + 5,000).

Tax Ramifications of Business Operation of a Partnership

Once the partnership has been created, it is treated for federal income tax purposes as an aggregate of the separate partners, rather than as a separate taxable entity. The partnership itself is not required to pay any income tax, but must file an information return, Form 1065, detailing the items of income and expense that will be reported on the partner's individual income tax return.

Partners must take into account their distributive share of partnership taxable income and any separately stated items in computing their individual taxable incomes. Generally, a partner's interest in the partnership's capital and profits determines the partner's share of income, gain, loss, deduction, or credit. The partners may change the traditional allocation of tax items through the partnership agreement. This special allocation of an item or items must have a substantial economic effect to be valid. In many cases, special allocations allow the benefits of deductions to pass to those partners who have a greater use for such deductions.

Each partner's distributive share of items is reported on Form 1065 Schedule K-1, which is furnished by the partnership to both the Internal Revenue Service (IRS) and to each partner. Schedule K-1 details the partner's share of partnership ordinary income, which is the net profit or loss resulting from the partnership's trade or business. If the partner is a general partner, this allocation of ordinary income will be subject not only to ordinary income tax but also to self-employment tax, similar to a proprietorship.

Form 1065 Schedule K-1 also reflects various items that must be reported separately from ordinary income. These separately stated items—dividend income, interest income, and capital gains—are reported also on the partner's individual income tax return.

The partner's adjusted taxable basis in the partnership interest must be adjusted each year to reflect the allocated items of income and expense. Adjusted taxable basis is increased by a partner's distributive share of both taxable and nontaxable partnership income and is decreased by the partner's share of partnership losses, nondeductible expenses, and distributions.

Continuing with the example of ABC, if the partnership reported earnings of $40,000 for the first year, Tom, a 50% partner, would report $20,000 of ordinary income on his federal income tax return even if no cash was actually distributed. His basis in the partnership after the first year would be adjusted to $75,000 ($55,000 original basis + $20,000 of allocated income). Because Tom is a general partner, the $20,000 distributable share of partnership earnings would also be subject to self-employment tax.

Tax Ramifications of Withdrawals or Distributions from a Partnership

Partners may withdraw cash or property from the partnership to meet their needs or as advance payments of their share of partnership income. Regardless of the reason for the withdrawal, the recipient partner generally recognizes no gain on the distribution. Instead, the withdrawal is treated as a return of capital that reduces the partner's adjusted taxable basis in the partnership. For example, if Tom, the ABC partner, withdrew the $20,000 earned, his adjusted taxable basis would return to $55,000. Once the partner's basis has been reduced to zero, any additional withdrawals taken from the partnership result in a capital gain to the partner.

The dissolution or termination of a general or limited partnership, family limited partnership (FLP), and a limited liability partnership (LLP) is more complex. The events that can trigger a termination of a partnership are varied, and the requirements to dissolve a partnership are not encompassed by this textbook.

FAMILY LIMITED PARTNERSHIP

Family limited partnership (FLP)
A limited partnership of family members that is used to generate valuation discounts for estate and gift tax purposes on the transfer of the limited interest in the partnership

A **family limited partnership (FLP)** is an estate planning technique utilizing a limited partnership of family members. The arrangement is generally structured so that a senior family member transfers appreciating, capital-intensive property, such as real estate, to a limited partnership in return for a minimal general partnership interest (typically 1%) and a significant limited partnership interest (typically 99%). Over the senior family member's lifetime, the limited partnership interests are transferred to junior family members by gift or sale.

One of the primary objectives of the family limited partnership arrangement is to generate valuation discounts for estate and gift tax purposes on the transfer of the limited interest in the partnership. The estate and gift tax value of a limited partnership interest in a properly structured family limited partnership typically is determined by applying minority interest and lack of marketability discounts.

- *Minority interest discount*—A reduction in value of an asset transferred is often allowed if the asset transferred represents a minority interest in a business. A minority interest is any interest that, in terms of voting, is not a controlling interest. Because minority owners cannot control the business or compel its sale or liquidation, outside buyers would not be willing to pay the same amount for a minority interest as they would for a majority or controlling interest.
- *Lack of marketability discount*—A reduction in value of an asset transferred is often allowed if the asset transferred has an inherent lack of marketability. Limited partnership interests in a family limited partnership are more difficult to sell than

interests in other assets such as publicly traded stock. Therefore, a discount is often allowed for the lack of marketability.

The family limited partnership has many advantages. One of the major advantages is that the senior family member can retain control of the business because the senior family member is the only family member with a general partnership interest. (Limited partners are not allowed to participate in the management of the business.) Additional advantages of this technique include creditor protection and the ability to place restrictions on transfers of limited partnership interests by junior family members. Also, it can allow income shifting from higher to lower tax bracket family members.

Management Operation and Decision Making of a Family Limited Partnership

The management of a family limited partnership is the same as that of a limited partnership. The general partner manages the partnership and is directly responsible for the day-to-day operation of the business. Thus, the partnership can change its operational direction at any time.

Legal Liability of a Family Limited Partnership

The general partner (senior family member) has unlimited liability for the acts of the partnership, the other partners, and obligations made by any partner or the partnership in the performance of partnership duties. The limited partners (junior family members) are treated as investors, liable only for the amount of each of their investments, and their respective shares of profits and losses are subject to the passive activity rules.

Taxation of a Family Limited Partnership

The partnership agreement governs how partnership income is divided among the partners. Generally, both general and limited partners share income and cash flow on the basis of their percentage interest in the partnership. The taxable income of the FLP is reported annually and allocated to each partner on the basis of that partner's percentage interest. The allocation is noted on Form K-1 issued to each partner. Usually, the general partner annually distributes at least enough cash to pay the income tax liability attributable to each partner. Distributions from the partnership are not taxable to the extent the partner has basis in the partnership interest. Distributions to the extent of basis are return of capital. The partnership itself (unlike a corporation) is not subject to tax because it passes through all items of income and deduction to the partners.

LIMITED LIABILITY PARTNERSHIP

A **limited liability partnership (LLP)** is similar to a general partnership, except an LLP provides additional liability protection to the partners. Only certain professionals (such as attorneys and accountants) are eligible for LLPs.

Limited liability partnership (LLP)
A form of business entity similar to a general partnership, except that an LLP provides additional liability protection to the partners

Management Operation and Decision Making of a Limited Liability Partnership

The management of an LLP is the same as that of a general partnership. The partners participate in the management of the partnership and are directly responsible for the day-to-day operation of the business. With management and ownership consolidated among the same individuals, partners are relatively free to change operating policy. Thus, the partnership can change its operational direction at any time.

Legal Liability of a Limited Liability Partnership

In an LLP, partners are personally liable for their own acts of wrongdoing, but their personal assets (those outside the partnership entity) are protected from claims arising from the wrongful acts of other partners. This liability protection in many states extends only to tort (e.g., malpractice) law, not contract law.

Taxation of Limited Liability Partnerships

For federal income tax purposes, an LLP is treated in the same fashion as a partnership. The LLP is considered a conduit, or flow-through entity, which is not subject to federal income tax. Partners must take into account their distributive share of partnership taxable income and any additional items the partnership is required to report separately.

CORPORATION

C corporation
A business entity created by state law that is separate and distinct from its shareholders

Shareholders
The owners of a corporation who elect the corporation's board of directors

A corporation (regular **C corporation**) is an entity created by state law that is separate and distinct from its **shareholders** (owners). A corporation can be closely held if owned by a few shareholders, or publicly held if owned by many shareholders.

The shareholders enjoy limited liability—they can lose only the amount they have invested in the corporation. They do not represent the corporation but vote for a board of directors, which determines corporate policy and appoints officers. The officers manage the corporation.

Management Operation and Decision Making of a Corporation

Directors
Individuals who, acting as a group known as the board of directors, manage the business affairs of a corporation

Board of directors
The governing body of a corporation whose members are elected by shareholders

Corporations have management advantages over other business forms. With a corporation, there is a separation of management from ownership so that the mere ownership of corporate stock does not give the owner the right to participate in management. The management is centralized, with the directors and officers handling management of corporate affairs.

Directors are the individuals who, acting as a group known as the **board of directors**, manage the business affairs of a corporation. Elected by the shareholders, the board of directors is the governing body of a corporation. Directors may be shareholders or individuals with no financial interest in the corporation. The directors are responsible for selecting the officers and for the supervision and general control of the corporation.

Officers
Individuals appointed by a corporation's board of directors to carry out the board's policies and make day-to-day operating decisions

Officers of a corporation are individuals appointed by the board of directors. Like directors, officers may be shareholders or individuals with no financial interest in the corporation. The officers are responsible for carrying out the board's policies and for making day-to-day operating decisions.

The decisions made by the officers and directors are based in part on the corporation's bylaws. Bylaws are the regulations of a corporation that, subject to statutory law and the articles of incorporation, provide the basic rules for the conduct of the corporation's business affairs.

Legal Liability of a Corporation

The shareholders' liability for the acts, omissions, debts, and other obligations of the corporation generally is limited to the shareholders' capital contributions. There are several situations, however, in which the shareholders will be held personally liable for the debts of the corporation.

- A lender to a closely held corporation requires that the primary shareholders guarantee the loan to the corporation. If this is the case, the shareholders are liable to the extent of their guarantees, in addition to their capital contributions.
- A court may ignore the legal fiction of the corporation as an entity (pierce the corporate veil) when the corporation has been used to perpetuate fraud, circumvent law, accomplish an illegal purpose, or otherwise evade law.
- The courts may disregard the corporate form of business entity if the corporation is not maintained as a separate entity from its shareholders. This arises occasionally in the case of closely held corporations.

Taxation of a Corporation

A corporation is an entity created under state law that is separate and distinct from its owners. It may be formed only through compliance with state incorporation statutes. For federal income tax purposes, the corporation is treated as a separate taxable entity, not as a flow-through or conduit entity.

Tax Ramifications of Formation of a Corporation

When a corporation is formed, cash or property is generally transferred to the corporation in exchange for shares of stock. When cash is transferred to the corporation, the transferor will recognize no gain or loss for federal income tax purposes. The transferor will have a basis in the shares received equal to the cash transferred.

In the case of property transfers, no gain or loss will be recognized if the transfer meets the requirements of Section 351. Section 351 provides that gain or loss is not recognized if property is transferred to a corporation in exchange for stock in the corporation, and, if immediately after the transfer, the transferors are in control of the corporation.

Tax Ramifications of Business Operation of a Corporation

A corporation is treated as a separate entity for federal income tax purposes. Computing a corporation's income tax liability can be complicated. The tax liability itself is a product of the corporation's taxable income, which is summarized in the formula shown in Exhibit 14.2.

EXHIBIT 14.2 Corporate Taxable Income Formula

Total income (from whatever source derived)	$xx,xxx
Less exclusions from gross income	(x,xxx)
Gross income	$xx,xxx
Less deductions	(x,xxx)
Taxable income	$xx,xxx

Total income and gross income—The tax computation begins with the determination of the corporation's total income, from whatever source derived. In general, all income is taxable unless Congress has specifically exempted the income from taxation. In tax terminology, income exempt from tax and not included in a taxpayer's gross income is referred to as an exclusion. The amount of income remaining after removing the exclusions is the corporation's gross income, which is generally the starting point for the corporate income tax return (Form 1120).

Deductions—Several deductions are allowed to reduce gross income in arriving at corporate taxable income. Fewer restrictions are placed on corporate deductions than are placed on individual deductions because all activities of a corporation are considered business activities. For example, casualty losses incurred in a federally declared disaster area are fully deductible by a corporation but are subject to a $100 floor and a 10% of AGI limitation for individuals.

Some deductions are allowed only for corporations. For example, corporations are allowed a deduction for dividends received from other corporations. The amount of the **dividends-received deduction (DRD)** is based on the percentage owned by the corporation receiving the dividend. If the dividend-receiving corporation owns less than 20% of the dividend-paying corporation, the dividends-received deduction will be 50% of the dividend actually received. Exhibit 14.3 summarizes the dividend-received deduction for different ownership levels.

Dividends-received deduction (DRD)
A deduction for dividends received by one corporation from another corporation. The amount of the DRD is based on the percentage owned by the corporation receiving the dividend.

EXHIBIT 14.3 Dividend-Received Deduction Based on Corporate Ownership Level

Ownership %	DRD
Less than 20%	50%
At least 20% and less than 80%	65%
At least 80% (affiliated corporations)	100%

EXAMPLE If ABC Company owns 15% of XYZ Company, and XYZ pays a $10,000 dividend during the year to ABC Company, ABC will include the $10,000 of dividend income in its gross income. However, ABC will be entitled to a dividends-received deduction of $5,000 ($10,000 × 50%).

Taxable income and tax—The corporate taxable income is calculated by subtracting allowed deductions from the corporation's gross income. The tax on this income is generally taxed at the 21% rate for all corporations. However, the investment income of a personal holding company will generally still be taxed at the 20% rate.

If a corporation incurs a net operating loss (NOL) for the year, the loss may be carried forward indefinitely. When the NOL is used in a future year, it may only offset 80% of the income for that year.

Personal service corporation (PSC)
A C corporation in which substantially all of the activities involve the performance of services in the fields of health, law, engineering, architecture, accounting, actuarial science, or consulting

Personal service corporation—A **personal service corporation (PSC)** is defined as a C corporation in which substantially all of the activities involve the performance of services in the fields of health, law, engineering, architecture, accounting, actuarial science, or consulting, and substantially all of the stock is owned by employees. The taxable income of a personal service corporation is taxed at the regular corporate income tax rate of 21%. Prior to the TCJA, PSCs were potentially subject to corporate tax rates as high as 35%. However, corporate tax rates were permanently reduced to 21%. Thus, PSCs may in some cases be an attractive business entity option for tax sensitive, self-employed professionals.

Tax Ramifications of Withdrawals or Distributions From a Corporation

Double taxation of dividends
The taxation of income at the corporate level and the subsequent taxation of dividend distributions at the individual shareholder's level

One of the major tax disadvantages of the corporate legal form of business entity is the **double taxation of dividends** paid by the corporation to its shareholders. Double taxation refers to the taxation of income at the corporate level and the subsequent taxation of dividend distributions at the individual shareholder's level. However, this impact is lessened because qualified dividends are taxed at the relatively low long-term capital gains rates. There is no deduction from the taxable income of a corporation for dividends distributed to shareholders.

EXAMPLE If a corporation has taxable income of $1,000 that is taxed at the 21% rate, there will only be $790 remaining to distribute to shareholders. If the shareholders are in the 32% tax bracket, the $790 dividend received will result in an additional tax of $119 (15% capital gains rate for qualified dividends), leaving the shareholder with only $671 in cash.

S CORPORATION

S corporation
A special type of corporation formed under state law like a regular corporation; however, for income tax purposes, is treated similar to a partnership

An **S corporation** is a special type of corporation for federal income tax purposes. The corporation is formed like a regular corporation (with limited liability as a separate entity) under state law; however, it is treated similarly to a partnership for income tax purposes. Therefore, all items of corporation income and deduction are passed through to the shareholders and reported on their personal income tax returns. The entity itself files an informational tax return (Form 1120S).

These corporations are called S corporations because they must satisfy the requirements of Subchapter S of the Internal Revenue Code to receive this special tax treatment. The essential elements of an S corporation include that the corporation must be a domestic corporation and may not have more than 100 shareholders. In addition, nonresident aliens, C corporations, partnerships, and certain trusts are not allowed to hold stock in an S corporation.

Management Operation and Decision Making of an S Corporation

S corporations are identical to regular corporations in terms of their management characteristics. However, closely held S corporations are often managed in a similar fashion to partnerships.

Legal Liability of an S Corporation

As with regular corporations, one of the major advantages of the S corporation is the limited liability enjoyed by shareholders.

The shareholders' liability for the acts, omissions, debts, and other obligations of the corporation generally is limited to the shareholders' capital contributions. There are several situations, however, in which the S corporation's shareholders are personally liable for the debts of the corporation.

- A lender to a closely held corporation requires that the primary shareholders guarantee the loan to the corporation. If this is the case, the shareholders are liable to the extent of their guarantees, in addition to their capital contributions.
- A court may ignore the legal fiction of the corporation as an entity (pierce the corporate veil) when the corporation has been used to perpetuate fraud, circumvent law, accomplish an illegal purpose, or otherwise evade law.
- The courts may disregard the corporate form of entity if the corporation is not maintained as a separate entity from its shareholders. This arises occasionally in the case of closely held corporations.

Taxation of an S Corporation

Even though an S corporation is similar to a regular, or C corporation, in that it is an entity created under state law that is separate and distinct from its owners, the federal income tax treatment of an S corporation is similar to the treatment of a partnership.

In order for a corporation to be taxed according to the rules of Subchapter S, an election must be filed on Form 2553 within 2 months and 15 days after the corporation's taxable year begins. A corporation must meet all of the following requirements at all times for the S election to be initially and continually valid.

- *Maximum of 100 shareholders*—An S corporation cannot have more than 100 eligible shareholders. Members of a family who own stock are treated as a single taxpayer (attribution rules).
- *Eligible shareholders*—Ownership of S corporation stock is restricted to individuals who are U.S. citizens or residents, estates, certain trusts, and charitable organizations. Nonresident aliens, C corporations, and partnerships are prohibited from holding stock in an S corporation.
- *Domestic corporation*—The corporation must be an eligible corporation created under the laws of the United States or of any state.

- *Eligible corporation*—Insurance companies, domestic international sales corporation (DISCs), and certain financial institutions are not eligible for S corporation status.
- *One class of stock*—The corporation is allowed only one class of outstanding stock. The shares generally must provide identical rights to all shareholders. However, an S corporation may have two classes of stock if the only difference is that one class has voting rights and the other class does not.

Tax Ramifications of Formation of an S Corporation

An S corporation is formed in the same manner as a C corporation, with the rules of Section 351 applying to transfers of property to the corporation. Therefore, under qualifying circumstances, property can be transferred to the corporation without gain or loss recognition by the transferors receiving stock.

Conceptually, the computation of a shareholder's basis in S corporation stock is similar to that for partners in a partnership. Both calculations are designed to ensure that there is neither a double taxation of income nor double deduction of expenses.

Tax Ramifications of Business Operation of an S Corporation

Once the S corporation election has been made, the corporation is treated for federal income tax purposes in a similar fashion to that of a partnership. The S corporation itself is generally not required to pay any income tax but must file an information return, Form 1120S, detailing the items of income and expense that will be reported on the shareholder's individual income tax return.

Shareholders must take into account their distributive share of corporate taxable income and any separately stated items in computing their taxable incomes. A shareholder's weighted-average ownership in the stock of the company determines the share of income, gain, loss, deduction, or credit. Special allocations are not allowed with S corporations. All items of income must be allocated on the basis of pro rata ownership.

Each shareholder's distributive share of items is reported on Schedule K-1, which is furnished by the S corporation to both the IRS and the shareholder. The K-1 for an S corporation is similar to that of a partnership, except the K-1 for an S corporation does not include a reconciliation of capital accounts or a line for guaranteed payments.

The S corporation K-1 details the shareholder's share of partnership ordinary income, which is the net profit or loss resulting from the corporation's trade or business. Ordinary income allocated to a shareholder from an S corporation is not subject to self-employment tax. The Schedule K-1 also reflects various items that must be reported separately from ordinary income. These separately stated items, which include dividend income, interest income, and capital gains, are afforded special treatment on the shareholder's individual income tax return.

LIMITED LIABILITY COMPANY

Limited liability company (LLC)
A relatively new and versatile form of business entity created under state law by filing articles of organization

Members
The owners of an LLC who can be individuals, partnerships, trusts, corporations, or other LLCs

A **limited liability company** (LLC) is a relatively new type of business entity and is one of the most versatile. An LLC is created under state law by filing articles of organization. Its owners, referred to as **members**, can be individuals, partnerships, trusts, corporations, or other LLCs. A limited liability company is a business entity that is generally able to provide the limited personal liability of corporations and the flow-through or conduit taxation of partnerships or S corporations.

One reason for the versatility of LLCs is that they can be taxed as a sole proprietorship, partnership, C corporation, or S corporation. Generally, however, LLCs are treated as general partnerships for federal income tax purposes. If the LLC is taxed as a partnership or sole proprietorship, all items of LLC income and expense are reported on the individual member's income tax return. Unlike a general partnership or sole proprietorship, however, members are not personally liable for the obligations of the LLC. This protection from personal liability for members, coupled with the favorable flow-through federal income tax treatment, has made the LLC a popular choice as a business entity.

Management Operation and Decision Making of a Limited Liability Company

Articles of organization
Document filed in compliance with state law to create a limited liability company (LLC)

Managers
Individuals who are responsible for the maintenance, administration, and management of the affairs of a limited liability company

When an LLC is formed through the filing of **articles of organization**, the LLC is registered with the state. When drafting the articles of organization, the members of the LLC must determine whether the LLC will be managed directly by all of its members, or if the administration of the LLC will be delegated to one or more managers.

Managers are individuals who are responsible for the maintenance, administration, and management of the affairs of the LLC. In most states, the managers serve a particular term and report to and serve at the discretion of the members. Specific duties of the managers may be detailed in the articles of organization or the operating agreement of the LLC. In some states, the members of an LLC may also serve as the managers.

Legal Liability of a Limited Liability Company

A member of an LLC has no personal liability for the debts or obligations of the LLC. This limited liability applies to members who participate in management and those who do not. The ability to participate in management and still have limited liability is one of the most attractive features of LLCs. A member who participates in management is similar to a general partner in a partnership, except the member of the LLC has limited liability.

Taxation of a Limited Liability Company

An LLC with two or more owners is generally treated as a partnership for federal income tax purposes, unless it elects to be treated as a corporation. The election to be treated as a corporation is made by checking a box on IRS Form 8832, the Entity Classification Election form. If the LLC has only one member, it may be treated as a sole proprietorship, unless the LLC elects to be taxed as an S corporation in those states that permit one-member LLCs. In some states, the LLCs that elect to be treated as a corporation for federal income tax purposes are also permitted to elect small business treatment, causing the LLC to be taxed as an S corporation. The election of S corporation treatment for an LLC is accomplished in the same manner as a regular C corporation, by the filing of Form 2553.

A major advantage of an LLC is the limited liability of its members. The protection of owners from personal liability for obligations of the entity, coupled with the flow-through federal income tax treatment, has spurred the enactment of LLC legislation in most states.

Tax Ramifications of Formation of a Limited Liability Company

Generally, limited liability companies are classified as partnerships for federal income tax purposes. As such, the income tax consequences applicable to the formation of an LLC are identical to those applicable to a partnership. When a member contributes cash or property to the LLC, no gain or loss is recognized, and the member's basis in the LLC interest is equal to the value of the cash contributed or the basis of the property contributed. If a member instead contributes services to the LLC, the member must recognize ordinary income for the value of the services contributed.

Tax Ramifications of Business Operation of a Limited Liability Company

An LLC with two or more members can be taxed as a partnership or a corporation. If the LLC is classified as a partnership for income tax purposes, the LLC must file an information return, Form 1065, detailing the items of income and expense that will be reported on the member's individual income tax return. The members receive a Schedule K-1 detailing their allocable amounts of income, loss, deduction, and credit. If the LLC is classified as a corporation, the LLC must file Form 1120 and is responsible for any tax on business income.

If the LLC is composed of only one member, all results from the business will be reported directly on Schedule C of the member's individual income tax return, unless the LLC makes a timely election to be treated as an S corporation. Therefore, the income from the business is taxed at the member's individual income tax rate.

SELECTING THE PROPER BUSINESS LEGAL FORM

The selection of an appropriate business legal form has probably never been as challenging as it is today. Each business entity has its own characteristics that make it more suitable or attractive in a particular situation. The basic factors that should be considered in selecting a business entity include simplicity of formation and operation, ownership restrictions, limited liability, management operations, and tax characteristics. Exhibit 14.4 summarizes some of the more critical legal liability and tax considerations for various business entities.

EXHIBIT 14.4 Summary of Legal Liability and Tax Considerations for Various Business Entities

	Sole Proprietor	Partnership*	LLP	LLC**	S Corp	Corporation
What type of liability do the owners have?	Unlimited	General partnership—unlimited; Limited partnership—limited	Limited	Limited	Limited	Limited
What federal tax form is required to be filed for the organization?	Form 1040, Schedule C	Form 1065	Form 1065	Form 1040, Schedule C, Form 1065, Form 1120, or Form 1120S	Form 1120S	Form 1120
Under what concept is the organization taxed?	Individual level	Flow-through/ conduit	Flow-through/ conduit	LLCs can be taxed as sole proprietorships, partnerships, C corporations, or S corporations	Flow-through/ conduit	Entity level
On what tax form is the owner's compensation reported?	Form 1040, Schedule C	Schedule K-1	Schedule K-1	Form 1040, Schedule C, or Schedule K-1; or Form W-2 and Schedule K-1; or Form W-2	Form W-2 and Schedule K-1	Form W-2 (dividends are reported on Form 1099-DIV)
What is the nature of the owner's income from the organization?	Self-employment income	Self-employment income for general partners; ordinary income for limited partners	Self-employment income	Self-employment income; or W-2 income and ordinary income; W-2 income	W-2 income and ordinary income	W-2 income and dividend income

Flow-through/conduit: all items of income flow from the entity to the individual partner's/owner's/member's return while retaining the character of the income at the entity level.

* Limited partners will generally not have self-employment income.
**The LLC will have the same tax characteristics and attributes as the type of entity it has elected for taxation.

Simplicity of Formation and Operation

If the main factor in the determination of a business legal form is simplicity of formation, either the sole proprietorship or the general partnership is the business form of choice. No special documents need to be prepared for a sole proprietorship or general partnership to begin activities. However, it is customary for a general partnership to draft a written partnership agreement, and the partnership must file a separate income (informational) tax return each year.

The formation of a limited partnership requires the filing of a certificate of limited partnership with the Secretary of State in the state where the partnership is being organized. Otherwise, the operation of the limited partnership is similar to the general partnership in that income and losses are allocated to the partners, and the limited partnership is required to file a separate informational tax return each year.

A corporation is often the most expensive form of entity to organize and operate. If the corporate form is selected, the businessowners must prepare a certificate of incorporation, articles of incorporation, and bylaws, and must pay filing fees. Corporations must file annual reports with the state and must file annual federal income tax returns and state franchise tax returns. An S corporation also must make an initial election to be treated as an S corporation for tax purposes.

A limited liability company is formed by filing articles of organization with the state in which the entity is to be registered. This process is similar to filing articles of incorporation for a corporation. Limited liability companies are generally classified as partnerships for federal income tax purposes. As such, the income tax consequences applicable to an LLC are almost identical to those applicable to a partnership.

Ownership Restrictions

Some business forms place restrictions on the number and types of owners. The ownership structure of the business must be considered before selecting a type of business entity.

C corporations are extremely flexible in the number and types of owners allowed. A regular C corporation can have an unlimited number of shareholders, and the shareholders are not limited to individuals. However, ownership of an S corporation is limited to 100 eligible shareholders. Eligible shareholders are individuals who are U.S. citizens or residents, estates, certain trusts, and charitable organizations. Nonresident aliens, C corporations, and partnerships are prohibited from holding stock in an S corporation.

No limit is placed on the number of members of an LLC. In addition, almost any type of entity may be a member. This flexibility in the number and types of owners makes an LLC more attractive than an S corporation in many situations.

A sole proprietorship can have only one owner. Therefore, this type of business form is unacceptable for joint owners of a business. No limit is placed on the number of partners in a general or limited partnership; however, a limited partnership must have at least one general partner and at least one limited partner.

Limited Liability

A major concern of most businessowners is the risk of personal liability. As a result, the limited liability company, although relatively new, has become a very popular business form. Members of an LLC have no personal liability for the debts or obligations of the LLC. The ability to participate in management without assuming personal liability for debt is one of the most attractive features of an LLC. Limited liability status also applies to C corporations and S corporations.

A general partner has unlimited liability for the acts of the partnership, the other partners, and obligations made by any partner or the partnership in the performance of partnership duties. If the partnership assets are insufficient to satisfy the liabilities of the partnership, the partnership's creditors can collect against the personal assets of the general partners. Therefore, if legal liability is a major concern for the business, a general partnership is a poor choice of business form.

Management Operations

Another consideration in the selection of a business legal form is the structure and flexibility provided to management.

The management of sole proprietorships and partnerships is straightforward. With a sole proprietorship, the proprietor is responsible for the day-to-day operation of the business and for making all of the business decisions. This allows for great flexibility in the operation of the business. With partnerships, the general partners participate directly in the management of the partnership and are directly responsible for the day-to-day operation of the business. Limited partners are not allowed to participate in management.

Corporations have management advantages and disadvantages over other business forms. One advantage is that there is a separation of management from ownership so that the mere ownership of corporate stock does not give the owner the right to participate in the management. The management is centralized, with the directors and officers handling management of corporate affairs. A disadvantage, however, is that the decision process may become time consuming and expensive because of the formalities involved.

In the case of an LLC, the members of the LLC must determine initially whether the LLC will be managed directly by all of its members, similar to a partnership, or if the administration of the LLC will be delegated to one or more managers, similar to a corporation.

Tax Characteristics

Startup Losses

A business that expects losses in the first few years of operation will typically opt for a different type of business legal form than that of a business expecting immediate profits. If the business expects losses, a flow-through entity, such as a partnership, S corporation, or limited liability corporation is generally the entity of choice. Losses will flow through to the owners of the entity and can generally be used immediately to offset other income at the individual level.

In contrast, losses incurred by a C corporation can only benefit the corporation. Therefore, several years may pass before the loss can be utilized against corporate profits.

Double Taxation of Dividends

As discussed previously in this chapter, one of the major tax disadvantages of the corporate form is the double taxation of dividends paid by the corporation to its shareholders. Double taxation refers to the taxation of income at the corporate level and the subsequent taxation of dividend distributions at the individual shareholder's level. There is no deduction from the taxable income of a corporation for dividends distributed to shareholders. This double taxation may be an incentive to discourage the use of the regular C corporation form.

BUSINESS ENTITY FINANCIAL STATEMENTS

We discussed several types of financial statements used by individuals in Chapter 4. Business entities also use financial statements to report their financial condition.

Balance Sheet

In a business context, the functional equivalent of the personal statement of financial position is the balance sheet. Like the personal statement of financial position, the business **balance sheet** is a snapshot of the company's financial standing at an instant in time. The balance sheet reports the company's assets, liabilities, and net worth, which is often referred to as stockholder's equity or retained capital in the business context. As with an individual, a company's net worth equals its assets minus its liabilities.

Balance sheet
A financial statement that reports a business's assets, liabilities, and net worth on a given date

A balance sheet shows several types of assets and liabilities that are unique to businesses and that do not appear on an individual's statement of financial position. Examples of these business assets include the following:

- Accounts receivable
- Inventory
- Land and buildings
- Machinery and equipment
- Certain intangible assets, such as copyrights, patents, and business goodwill

Examples of business liabilities include:

- Accounts payable
- Accrued expenses
- Certain contingent liabilities, such as lawsuits, warranties, and company guarantees of loan repayment

Income Statement

The functional equivalent of the personal statement of cash flows in a business context is the **income statement**. Also known as the profit and loss statement (or simply, P&L statement), the income statement shows all the income and expenses of the business over a given period. That is, it shows how profitable (or not profitable) the business actually is. As noted earlier, whether these profits are reported at the business entity level or are reported by the businessowner(s) individually depends on whether the business is organized as a regular, or C, form of corporation or as a sole proprietorship, partnership, or some other form of pass-through entity.

Income statement
A financial statement that reports a business's income and expenses over a given period

A **pro forma income statement** is similar to the business income statement except that it projects for the future rather than reporting the past. Pro forma income statements are an important tool for planning future business operations. If the projections accurately predict a decline in business profitability, the businessowner can make operational changes, such as increasing prices or decreasing costs, before these events actually occur. The pro forma statement is created first by estimating gross profit and total expenses for the coming year or years and then accounting for any taxes that will be due on the net profit.

Pro forma income statement
A financial statement that projects a business's income and expenses for the future rather than reporting the past

Statement of cash flows
A financial statement that reflects the cash inflows and outflows of a business and reconciles the net changes in cash between two balance sheets

Cash flows from operations
Cash inflows or outflows that are generated by a company's actual business activities as opposed to incidental activities such as investing or borrowing

Cash flows from investing
Cash inflows or outflows resulting from a business's buying and selling of investments

Cash flows from financing
Cash inflows from a business's issuance of additional debt (bonds) or equity (stocks) and cash outflows for the repayment of debt (principal)

Statement of Cash Flows

One statement that is typically used only in businesses is the **statement of cash flows**. The statement of cash flows assists in the reconciliation of the business income statement to changes between two balance sheets. For a given period, the statement of cash flows reflects the inflows and outflows of the business and the net changes in cash between two balance sheets. It also identifies the changes in some of the accounts from one balance sheet to the next. Typically, there are three components of the statement of cash flows.

- **Cash flows from operations** are the cash inflows or outflows that were generated by the company's actual business activities, as opposed to incidental activities such as investing or borrowing. These cash flows are important to investors and lenders because they indicate whether the business is successful in generating cash from its core business activities.
- **Cash flows from investing** include the cash outflows used to acquire investments and the cash inflows from the sale of investments. Investments may include not only intangible assets such as stocks and bonds but also physical assets such as the company's plants and equipment.
- **Cash flows from financing** include cash inflows from the issuance of additional debt (bonds), or equity (stocks), and cash outflows for the repayment of debt (principal). Increases in cash flows are created, for example, when the business increases long-term indebtedness (i.e., obtains a loan) and receives cash at the inception of the transaction.

Note that the statement of cash flows used by businesses is not the same statement as the personal statement of cash flows, which we discussed in Chapter 4 in the context of individuals. The personal statement of cash flows is more analogous to the income statement in the business context.

WHERE ON THE WEB

Bureau of National Affairs (Search for BNA Portfolios) **www.bna.com**

Cornell Law School **www.law.cornell.edu**

Internal Revenue Service **www.irs.gov**

LSU Libraries Federal Agencies Directory **www.lib.lsu.edu/gov/index.html**

National Association of Tax Professionals **www.natptax.com**

RIA (Research Institute of America) Thomson Tax and Accounting **www.ria.thomson.com**

Small Business Center **www.quicken.com/small_business**

Small Business Taxes and Management **www.smbiz.com**

Tax and Accounting Sites Directory **www.taxsites.com**

U.S. Small Business Administration **www.sba.gov**

DISCUSSION QUESTIONS

1. What are the different types of business entities that a businessowner may choose as a legal form of business?
2. How is a limited liability partnership (LLP) taxed?
3. What are the differences between general and limited partners?
4. How does each type of business entity differ regarding the personal liability of owners?
5. What are the tax ramifications of withdrawals or distributions from a C corporation?
6. What type of business entity should owners choose if they expect the business to produce losses in the first few years?
7. What is the tax treatment of a limited liability company?
8. What type of business entity should an owner choose if simplicity of formation and operation is a major priority?
9. What are the components of a financial statement for a business entity?

EXERCISES

1. A bookkeeper performed services for ABC Partnership and, in lieu of her normal fee, accepted a 20% unrestricted capital interest in the partnership with a fair market value of $7,500. How much income from this arrangement should the bookkeeper report on her income tax return?
2. An S corporation has the following information for its taxable year:

Net income before the items below	$60,000
Salary to employee	(18,000)
Rental income	22,000
Rental expenses	(29,000)
Net income	$35,000

   John is a 40% owner of the S corporation, and he performs services for the business. What is John's self-employment income from the corporation, subject to self-employment tax?

3. During the year, Susan purchased 5 shares of an S corporation's 100 shares of common stock outstanding. She held the shares for 146 days during the taxable year. If the S corporation reported taxable income of $200,000, how much must Susan include on her personal income tax return?
4. Alpha Company (a C corporation) owns 25% of Zeta Company. During the year, Zeta Company paid a $30,000 dividend to Alpha Company. For tax purposes, how will Alpha Company treat the dividend received?

5. Mark received a 70% capital interest in a general partnership by contributing the following:

Item transferred	Mark's basis	FMV
Land	$60,000	$100,000
Debt (on land)	N/A	(50,000)
Inventory	$10,000	$8,000
Services	N/A	$2,500

What is Mark's basis in the partnership after the contribution?

6. Brooke Industries, Inc. (a C corporation) had the following income and loss items during the year:

Gross receipts	$200,000
Cost of goods sold	(50,000)
Dividend income from ABC Corp. (Brooke owns 15% of ABC)	$ 20,000
Operating expenses	(40,000)
Net operating loss carryforward	(12,000)

What is Brooke Industries' taxable income for the year?

7. In its first year of business, Sanifone Corp (a C corporation) had gross income of $160,000 and deductions of $40,000. The company also paid a qualified dividend of $20,000 to its only shareholder, Joe, who files as single for income tax reporting and has compensation of $475,000 before considering his Sanifone dividend. What are the tax implications to Sanifone and Joe?

8. Tommy is a general partner in RichTech, a general partnership. Tommy received a K-1 from the partnership, which contained the following items:

Partnership taxable income	$200,000
Dividend income	$2,500
Long-term capital gain (on investments)	$6,000

How much self-employment tax will Tommy have to pay in 2022?

9. What is the management structure of a C corporation?

10. What are the requirements for an S Corporation?

11. What are the components of a balance sheet?

PROBLEMS

1. Hugh is a single taxpayer with no children. He is a self-employed real estate appraiser, and the results for his business for the current year are as follows:

Gross receipts	$150,000
Expenses:	
Advertising	$ 2,000
Insurance	$ 1,000
Dues	$ 1,500
Office rent	$12,000
Meals and entertainment	$ 800

Hugh also received the following income during the year:

Interest	$1,100
Dividends	$1,400

Hugh incurred the following expenses during the year:

Real estate taxes	$9,000
Mortgage interest	$5,000

Assuming Hugh was divorced in 2018 and paid $10,000 in alimony to his ex-wife in 2022, calculate his taxable income and self-employment tax for tax year 2022.

2. Pete is a single taxpayer with no dependents. During the year, he invested $40,000 in an S corporation. He received the following information on the K-1 from the S corporation:

Net income before salary	$60,000
Salary to Pete (S corporation)	$18,000
Interest income	$ 2,000
Qualified dividend income	$ 1,000
Long-term capital gain	$ 4,500
Charitable contributions	$ 2,000

Pete also received a distribution of $5,500 from the S corporation, and earned a salary of $50,000 at his full-time job. Calculate Pete's taxable income in 2022.

3. Doug, a single taxpayer, will be starting a new business in 2022. He is not sure whether to operate the business as a C corporation or S corporation. Given the following estimates of income and expenses, determine the total tax that would be due under either scenario.

Gross profit	$150,000
Operating expenses (excluding salary)	(60,000)
Salary paid to Doug	$50,000
Cash distribution to Doug	$10,000

APPENDIX 14.1 Schedule C of Form 1040

SCHEDULE C (Form 1040)
Department of the Treasury
Internal Revenue Service (99)

Profit or Loss From Business

(Sole Proprietorship)

▸ Go to *www.irs.gov/ScheduleC* for instructions and the latest information.
▸ Attach to Form 1040, 1040-SR, 1040-NR, or 1041; partnerships must generally file Form 1065.

OMB No. 1545-0074
2021
Attachment Sequence No. **09**

Name of proprietor | **Social security number (SSN)**

A Principal business or profession, including product or service (see instructions) | **B Enter code from instructions** ▸

C Business name. If no separate business name, leave blank. | **D Employer ID number (EIN)** (see instr.)

E Business address (including suite or room no.) ▸
City, town or post office, state, and ZIP code

F Accounting method: **(1)** ☐ Cash **(2)** ☐ Accrual **(3)** ☐ Other (specify) ▸

G Did you "materially participate" in the operation of this business during 2021? If "No," see instructions for limit on losses . ☐ Yes ☐ No

H If you started or acquired this business during 2021, check here ▸ ☐

I Did you make any payments in 2021 that would require you to file Form(s) 1099? See instructions ☐ Yes ☐ No

J If "Yes," did you or will you file required Form(s) 1099? ☐ Yes ☐ No

Part I Income

1	Gross receipts or sales. See instructions for line 1 and check the box if this income was reported to you on Form W-2 and the "Statutory employee" box on that form was checked ▸ ☐	1	
2	Returns and allowances	2	
3	Subtract line 2 from line 1	3	
4	Cost of goods sold (from line 42)	4	
5	**Gross profit.** Subtract line 4 from line 3	5	
6	Other income, including federal and state gasoline or fuel tax credit or refund (see instructions)	6	
7	**Gross income.** Add lines 5 and 6 ▸	7	

Part II Expenses. Enter expenses for business use of your home **only** on line 30.

8	Advertising	8		18	Office expense (see instructions)	18	
9	Car and truck expenses (see instructions)	9		19	Pension and profit-sharing plans	19	
				20	Rent or lease (see instructions):		
10	Commissions and fees	10		a	Vehicles, machinery, and equipment	20a	
11	Contract labor (see instructions)	11		b	Other business property	20b	
12	Depletion	12		21	Repairs and maintenance	21	
13	Depreciation and section 179 expense deduction (not included in Part III) (see instructions)	13		22	Supplies (not included in Part III)	22	
				23	Taxes and licenses	23	
				24	Travel and meals:		
14	Employee benefit programs (other than on line 19)	14		a	Travel	24a	
15	Insurance (other than health)	15		b	Deductible meals (see instructions)	24b	
16	Interest (see instructions):			25	Utilities	25	
a	Mortgage (paid to banks, etc.)	16a		26	Wages (less employment credits)	26	
b	Other	16b		27a	Other expenses (from line 48)	27a	
17	Legal and professional services	17		b	**Reserved for future use**	27b	

28	**Total expenses** before expenses for business use of home. Add lines 8 through 27a ▸	28	
29	Tentative profit or (loss). Subtract line 28 from line 7	29	
30	Expenses for business use of your home. Do not report these expenses elsewhere. Attach Form 8829 unless using the simplified method. See instructions. **Simplified method filers only:** Enter the total square footage of (a) your home: ______ and (b) the part of your home used for business: ______ Use the Simplified Method Worksheet in the instructions to figure the amount to enter on line 30	30	
31	**Net profit or (loss).** Subtract line 30 from line 29. • If a profit, enter on both **Schedule 1 (Form 1040), line 3,** and on **Schedule SE, line 2.** (If you checked the box on line 1, see instructions). Estates and trusts, enter on **Form 1041, line 3.** • If a loss, you **must** go to line 32.	31	

32 If you have a loss, check the box that describes your investment in this activity. See instructions.

• If you checked 32a, enter the loss on both **Schedule 1 (Form 1040), line 3,** and on **Schedule SE, line 2.** (If you checked the box on line 1, see the line 31 instructions.) Estates and trusts, enter on **Form 1041, line 3.**
• If you checked 32b, you **must** attach **Form 6198.** Your loss may be limited.

32a ☐ All investment is at risk.
32b ☐ Some investment is not at risk.

For Paperwork Reduction Act Notice, see the separate instructions. Cat. No. 11334P **Schedule C (Form 1040) 2021**

APPENDIX 14.1 Schedule C of Form 1040 (continued)

Schedule C (Form 1040) 2021 Page **2**

Part III **Cost of Goods Sold** (see instructions)

33	Method(s) used to value closing inventory: **a** ☐ Cost **b** ☐ Lower of cost or market **c** ☐ Other (attach explanation)		
34	Was there any change in determining quantities, costs, or valuations between opening and closing inventory? If "Yes," attach explanation . . . ☐ **Yes** ☐ **No**		
35	Inventory at beginning of year. If different from last year's closing inventory, attach explanation . . .	35	
36	Purchases less cost of items withdrawn for personal use . . .	36	
37	Cost of labor. Do not include any amounts paid to yourself . . .	37	
38	Materials and supplies . . .	38	
39	Other costs . . .	39	
40	Add lines 35 through 39 . . .	40	
41	Inventory at end of year . . .	41	
42	**Cost of goods sold.** Subtract line 41 from line 40. Enter the result here and on line 4 . . .	42	

Part IV **Information on Your Vehicle.** Complete this part **only** if you are claiming car or truck expenses on line 9 and are not required to file Form 4562 for this business. See the instructions for line 13 to find out if you must file Form 4562.

43 When did you place your vehicle in service for business purposes? (month/day/year) ▶ ____ / ____ / ____

44 Of the total number of miles you drove your vehicle during 2021, enter the number of miles you used your vehicle for:

a Business ____________ **b** Commuting (see instructions) ____________ **c** Other ____________

45 Was your vehicle available for personal use during off-duty hours? . . . ☐ **Yes** ☐ **No**

46 Do you (or your spouse) have another vehicle available for personal use? . . . ☐ **Yes** ☐ **No**

47a Do you have evidence to support your deduction? . . . ☐ **Yes** ☐ **No**

b If "Yes," is the evidence written? . . . ☐ **Yes** ☐ **No**

Part V **Other Expenses.** List below business expenses not included on lines 8–26 or line 30.

48 **Total other expenses.** Enter here and on line 27a . . .	48	

Schedule C (Form 1040) 2021

APPENDIX 14.2 Schedule SE

SCHEDULE SE (Form 1040)

Department of the Treasury Internal Revenue Service (99)

Self-Employment Tax

▶ Go to *www.irs.gov/ScheduleSE* for instructions and the latest information.
▶ Attach to Form 1040, 1040-SR, or 1040-NR.

OMB No. 1545-0074 | 2021 | Attachment Sequence No. **17**

Name of person with self-employment income (as shown on Form 1040, 1040-SR, or 1040-NR) | Social security number of person with **self-employment** income ▶

Part I Self-Employment Tax

Note: If your only income subject to self-employment tax is **church employee income,** see instructions for how to report your income and the definition of church employee income.

A If you are a minister, member of a religious order, or Christian Science practitioner **and** you filed Form 4361, but you had $400 or more of **other** net earnings from self-employment, check here and continue with Part I . . . . ▶ ☐

Skip lines 1a and 1b if you use the farm optional method in Part II. See instructions.

1a	Net farm profit or (loss) from Schedule F, line 34, and farm partnerships, Schedule K-1 (Form 1065), box 14, code A			1a	
b	If you received social security retirement or disability benefits, enter the amount of Conservation Reserve Program payments included on Schedule F, line 4b, or listed on Schedule K-1 (Form 1065), box 20, code AH			1b	( )
	Skip line 2 if you use the nonfarm optional method in Part II. See instructions.				
2	Net profit or (loss) from Schedule C, line 31; and Schedule K-1 (Form 1065), box 14, code A (other than farming). See instructions for other income to report or if you are a minister or member of a religious order			2	
3	Combine lines 1a, 1b, and 2			3	
4a	If line 3 is more than zero, multiply line 3 by 92.35% (0.9235). Otherwise, enter amount from line 3			4a	
	Note: If line 4a is less than $400 due to Conservation Reserve Program payments on line 1b, see instructions.				
b	If you elect one or both of the optional methods, enter the total of lines 15 and 17 here			4b	
c	Combine lines 4a and 4b. If less than $400, **stop;** you don't owe self-employment tax. **Exception:** If less than $400 and you had **church employee income,** enter -0- and continue ▶			4c	
5a	Enter your **church employee income** from Form W-2. See instructions for definition of church employee income	5a			
b	Multiply line 5a by 92.35% (0.9235). If less than $100, enter -0-			5b	
6	Add lines 4c and 5b			6	
7	Maximum amount of combined wages and self-employment earnings subject to social security tax or the 6.2% portion of the 7.65% railroad retirement (tier 1) tax for 2021			7	142,800
8a	Total social security wages and tips (total of boxes 3 and 7 on Form(s) W-2) and railroad retirement (tier 1) compensation. If $142,800 or more, skip lines 8b through 10, and go to line 11	8a			
b	Unreported tips subject to social security tax from Form 4137, line 10	8b			
c	Wages subject to social security tax from Form 8919, line 10	8c			
d	Add lines 8a, 8b, and 8c			8d	
9	Subtract line 8d from line 7. If zero or less, enter -0- here and on line 10 and go to line 11 ▶			9	
10	Multiply the **smaller** of line 6 or line 9 by 12.4% (0.124)			10	
11	Multiply line 6 by 2.9% (0.029)			11	
12	**Self-employment tax.** Add lines 10 and 11. Enter here and on **Schedule 2 (Form 1040), line 4**			12	
13	**Deduction for one-half of self-employment tax.** Multiply line 12 by 50% (0.50). Enter here and on **Schedule 1 (Form 1040), line 15**	13			

Part II Optional Methods To Figure Net Earnings (see instructions)

Farm Optional Method. You may use this method **only** if **(a)** your gross farm income[1] wasn't more than $8,820, **or (b)** your net farm profits[2] were less than $6,367.

14	Maximum income for optional methods	14	5,880
15	Enter the **smaller** of: two-thirds (2/3) of gross farm income[1] (not less than zero) **or** $5,880. Also, include this amount on line 4b above	15	

Nonfarm Optional Method. You may use this method **only** if **(a)** your net nonfarm profits[3] were less than $6,367 and also less than 72.189% of your gross nonfarm income,[4] **and (b)** you had net earnings from self-employment of at least $400 in 2 of the prior 3 years. **Caution:** You may use this method no more than five times.

16	Subtract line 15 from line 14	16	
17	Enter the **smaller** of: two-thirds (2/3) of gross nonfarm income[4] (not less than zero) **or** the amount on line 16. Also, include this amount on line 4b above	17	

[1] From Sch. F, line 9; and Sch. K-1 (Form 1065), box 14, code B.
[2] From Sch. F, line 34; and Sch. K-1 (Form 1065), box 14, code A—minus the amount you would have entered on line 1b had you not used the optional method.
[3] From Sch. C, line 31; and Sch. K-1 (Form 1065), box 14, code A.
[4] From Sch. C, line 7; and Sch. K-1 (Form 1065), box 14, code C.

For Paperwork Reduction Act Notice, see your tax return instructions. Cat. No. 11358Z **Schedule SE (Form 1040) 2021**

APPENDIX 14.3 Form 1065—Schedule K-1

651121

☐ Final K-1 ☐ Amended K-1 OMB No. 1545-0123

Schedule K-1 (Form 1065) **2021**
Department of the Treasury
Internal Revenue Service

For calendar year 2021, or tax year

beginning / / 2021 ending / /

Partner's Share of Income, Deductions, Credits, etc. ▶ See back of form and separate instructions.

Part I Information About the Partnership

A Partnership's employer identification number

B Partnership's name, address, city, state, and ZIP code

C IRS center where partnership filed return ▶

D ☐ Check if this is a publicly traded partnership (PTP)

Part II Information About the Partner

E Partner's SSN or TIN (Do not use TIN of a disregarded entity. See instructions.)

F Name, address, city, state, and ZIP code for partner entered in E. See instructions.

G ☐ General partner or LLC member-manager ☐ Limited partner or other LLC member

H1 ☐ Domestic partner ☐ Foreign partner

H2 ☐ If the partner is a disregarded entity (DE), enter the partner's:

TIN ______ Name ______

I1 What type of entity is this partner? ______

I2 If this partner is a retirement plan (IRA/SEP/Keogh/etc.), check here ▶ ☐

J Partner's share of profit, loss, and capital (see instructions):

	Beginning	Ending
Profit	%	%
Loss	%	%
Capital	%	%

Check if decrease is due to sale or exchange of partnership interest . ▶ ☐

K Partner's share of liabilities:

	Beginning	Ending
Nonrecourse . .	$	$
Qualified nonrecourse financing	$	$
Recourse	$	$

Check this box if Item K includes liability amounts from lower tier partnerships ▶ ☐

L **Partner's Capital Account Analysis**

Beginning capital account . . . $ ______
Capital contributed during the year . . $ ______
Current year net income (loss) . . . $ ______
Other increase (decrease) (attach explanation) $ ______
Withdrawals and distributions . . . $ (______)
Ending capital account . . . . $ ______

M Did the partner contribute property with a built-in gain (loss)?
☐ **Yes** ☐ **No** If "Yes," attach statement. See instructions.

N **Partner's Share of Net Unrecognized Section 704(c) Gain or (Loss)**
Beginning . . . . $ ______
Ending . . . . $ ______

Part III Partner's Share of Current Year Income, Deductions, Credits, and Other Items

1	Ordinary business income (loss)	14	Self-employment earnings (loss)
2	Net rental real estate income (loss)		
3	Other net rental income (loss)	15	Credits
4a	Guaranteed payments for services		
4b	Guaranteed payments for capital	16	Schedule K-3 is attached if checked . . . . ▶ ☐
4c	Total guaranteed payments	17	Alternative minimum tax (AMT) items
5	Interest income		
6a	Ordinary dividends		
6b	Qualified dividends	18	Tax-exempt income and nondeductible expenses
6c	Dividend equivalents		
7	Royalties		
8	Net short-term capital gain (loss)	19	Distributions
9a	Net long-term capital gain (loss)		
9b	Collectibles (28%) gain (loss)	20	Other information
9c	Unrecaptured section 1250 gain		
10	Net section 1231 gain (loss)		
11	Other income (loss)		
12	Section 179 deduction	21	Foreign taxes paid or accrued
13	Other deductions		

22 ☐ More than one activity for at-risk purposes*
23 ☐ More than one activity for passive activity purposes*
*See attached statement for additional information.

For IRS Use Only

For Paperwork Reduction Act Notice, see the Instructions for Form 1065. www.irs.gov/Form1065 Cat. No. 11394R Schedule K-1 (Form 1065) 2021

APPENDIX 14.4 Corporation Form 1120-S

Form **1120-S**

Department of the Treasury
Internal Revenue Service

U.S. Income Tax Return for an S Corporation

▶ Do not file this form unless the corporation has filed or is attaching Form 2553 to elect to be an S corporation.
▶ Go to *www.irs.gov/Form1120S* for instructions and the latest information.

OMB No. 1545-0123

2021

For calendar year 2021 or tax year beginning , 2021, ending , 20

	TYPE OR PRINT	
A S election effective date	Name	D Employer identification number
B Business activity code number (see instructions)	Number, street, and room or suite no. If a P.O. box, see instructions.	E Date incorporated
C Check if Sch. M-3 attached ☐	City or town, state or province, country, and ZIP or foreign postal code	F Total assets (see instructions) $

G Is the corporation electing to be an S corporation beginning with this tax year? See instructions. ☐ Yes ☐ No
H Check if: (1) ☐ Final return (2) ☐ Name change (3) ☐ Address change (4) ☐ Amended return (5) ☐ S election termination
I Enter the number of shareholders who were shareholders during any part of the tax year . . . . ▶
J Check if corporation: (1) ☐ Aggregated activities for section 465 at-risk purposes (2) ☐ Grouped activities for section 469 passive activity purposes

Caution: Include **only** trade or business income and expenses on lines 1a through 21. See the instructions for more information.

Income	1a	Gross receipts or sales	1a		
	b	Returns and allowances	1b		
	c	Balance. Subtract line 1b from line 1a		1c	
	2	Cost of goods sold (attach Form 1125-A)		2	
	3	Gross profit. Subtract line 2 from line 1c		3	
	4	Net gain (loss) from Form 4797, line 17 (attach Form 4797)		4	
	5	Other income (loss) (see instructions—attach statement)		5	
	6	**Total income (loss).** Add lines 3 through 5 ▶		6	
Deductions (see instructions for limitations)	7	Compensation of officers (see instructions—attach Form 1125-E)		7	
	8	Salaries and wages (less employment credits)		8	
	9	Repairs and maintenance		9	
	10	Bad debts		10	
	11	Rents		11	
	12	Taxes and licenses		12	
	13	Interest (see instructions)		13	
	14	Depreciation not claimed on Form 1125-A or elsewhere on return (attach Form 4562)		14	
	15	Depletion **(Do not deduct oil and gas depletion.)**		15	
	16	Advertising		16	
	17	Pension, profit-sharing, etc., plans		17	
	18	Employee benefit programs		18	
	19	Other deductions (attach statement)		19	
	20	**Total deductions.** Add lines 7 through 19 ▶		20	
	21	**Ordinary business income (loss).** Subtract line 20 from line 6		21	
Tax and Payments	22a	Excess net passive income or LIFO recapture tax (see instructions)	22a		
	b	Tax from Schedule D (Form 1120-S)	22b		
	c	Add lines 22a and 22b (see instructions for additional taxes)		22c	
	23a	2021 estimated tax payments and 2020 overpayment credited to 2021	23a		
	b	Tax deposited with Form 7004	23b		
	c	Credit for federal tax paid on fuels (attach Form 4136)	23c		
	d	Add lines 23a through 23c		23d	
	24	Estimated tax penalty (see instructions). Check if Form 2220 is attached ▶ ☐		24	
	25	**Amount owed.** If line 23d is smaller than the total of lines 22c and 24, enter amount owed		25	
	26	**Overpayment.** If line 23d is larger than the total of lines 22c and 24, enter amount overpaid		26	
	27	Enter amount from line 26: **Credited to 2022 estimated tax** ▶ **Refunded** ▶		27	

Sign Here

Under penalties of perjury, I declare that I have examined this return, including accompanying schedules and statements, and to the best of my knowledge and belief, it is true, correct, and complete. Declaration of preparer (other than taxpayer) is based on all information of which preparer has any knowledge.

▶ Signature of officer | Date | ▶ Title

May the IRS discuss this return with the preparer shown below? See instructions. ☐ Yes ☐ No

Paid Preparer Use Only				
Print/Type preparer's name	Preparer's signature	Date	Check ☐ if self-employed	PTIN
Firm's name ▶			Firm's EIN ▶	
Firm's address ▶			Phone no.	

For Paperwork Reduction Act Notice, see separate instructions. Cat. No. 11510H Form **1120-S** (2021)

APPENDIX 14.4 Corporation Form 1120-S (continued)

Form 1120-S (2021) Page **2**

Schedule B **Other Information** (see instructions)

		Yes	No
1	Check accounting method: a ☐ Cash b ☐ Accrual c ☐ Other (specify) ▶		
2	See the instructions and enter the: a Business activity ▶ b Product or service ▶		
3	At any time during the tax year, was any shareholder of the corporation a disregarded entity, a trust, an estate, or a nominee or similar person? If "Yes," attach Schedule B-1, Information on Certain Shareholders of an S Corporation . .		
4	At the end of the tax year, did the corporation:		
a	Own directly 20% or more, or own, directly or indirectly, 50% or more of the total stock issued and outstanding of any foreign or domestic corporation? For rules of constructive ownership, see instructions. If "Yes," complete (i) through (v) below		

(i) Name of Corporation	(ii) Employer Identification Number (if any)	(iii) Country of Incorporation	(iv) Percentage of Stock Owned	(v) If Percentage in (iv) Is 100%, Enter the Date (if applicable) a Qualified Subchapter S Subsidiary Election Was Made

		Yes	No
b	Own directly an interest of 20% or more, or own, directly or indirectly, an interest of 50% or more in the profit, loss, or capital in any foreign or domestic partnership (including an entity treated as a partnership) or in the beneficial interest of a trust? For rules of constructive ownership, see instructions. If "Yes," complete (i) through (v) below		

(i) Name of Entity	(ii) Employer Identification Number (if any)	(iii) Type of Entity	(iv) Country of Organization	(v) Maximum Percentage Owned in Profit, Loss, or Capital

		Yes	No
5a	At the end of the tax year, did the corporation have any outstanding shares of restricted stock? . . . . If "Yes," complete lines (i) and (ii) below. (i) Total shares of restricted stock . . . . ▶ (ii) Total shares of non-restricted stock . . . . ▶		
b	At the end of the tax year, did the corporation have any outstanding stock options, warrants, or similar instruments? . If "Yes," complete lines (i) and (ii) below. (i) Total shares of stock outstanding at the end of the tax year . ▶ (ii) Total shares of stock outstanding if all instruments were executed ▶		
6	Has this corporation filed, or is it required to file, **Form 8918,** Material Advisor Disclosure Statement, to provide information on any reportable transaction?		
7	Check this box if the corporation issued publicly offered debt instruments with original issue discount . . . . . ▶ ☐ If checked, the corporation may have to file **Form 8281,** Information Return for Publicly Offered Original Issue Discount Instruments.		
8	If the corporation **(a)** was a C corporation before it elected to be an S corporation **or** the corporation acquired an asset with a basis determined by reference to the basis of the asset (or the basis of any other property) in the hands of a C corporation, **and (b)** has net unrealized built-in gain in excess of the net recognized built-in gain from prior years, enter the net unrealized built-in gain reduced by net recognized built-in gain from prior years. See instructions . . . . ▶ $		
9	Did the corporation have an election under section 163(j) for any real property trade or business or any farming business in effect during the tax year? See instructions		
10	Does the corporation satisfy one or more of the following? See instructions		
a	The corporation owns a pass-through entity with current, or prior year carryover, excess business interest expense.		
b	The corporation's aggregate average annual gross receipts (determined under section 448(c)) for the 3 tax years preceding the current tax year are more than $26 million and the corporation has business interest expense.		
c	The corporation is a tax shelter and the corporation has business interest expense. If "Yes," complete and attach Form 8990.		
11	Does the corporation satisfy **both** of the following conditions?		
a	The corporation's total receipts (see instructions) for the tax year were less than $250,000.		
b	The corporation's total assets at the end of the tax year were less than $250,000. If "Yes," the corporation is not required to complete Schedules L and M-1.		

Form **1120-S** (2021)

APPENDIX 14.4 Corporation Form 1120-S (continued)

Form 1120-S (2021) Page **3**

Schedule B	**Other Information** (see instructions) *(continued)*	Yes	No
12	During the tax year, did the corporation have any non-shareholder debt that was canceled, was forgiven, or had the terms modified so as to reduce the principal amount of the debt?		
	If "Yes," enter the amount of principal reduction ▶ $		
13	During the tax year, was a qualified subchapter S subsidiary election terminated or revoked? If "Yes," see instructions		
14a	Did the corporation make any payments in 2021 that would require it to file Form(s) 1099?		
b	If "Yes," did the corporation file or will it file required Form(s) 1099?		
15	Is the corporation attaching Form 8996 to certify as a Qualified Opportunity Fund?		
	If "Yes," enter the amount from Form 8996, line 15 ▶ $		

Schedule K		**Shareholders' Pro Rata Share Items**			**Total amount**
Income (Loss)	1	Ordinary business income (loss) (page 1, line 21)		1	
	2	Net rental real estate income (loss) (attach Form 8825)		2	
	3a	Other gross rental income (loss)	3a		
	b	Expenses from other rental activities (attach statement)	3b		
	c	Other net rental income (loss). Subtract line 3b from line 3a		3c	
	4	Interest income		4	
	5	Dividends: **a** Ordinary dividends		5a	
		b Qualified dividends	5b		
	6	Royalties		6	
	7	Net short-term capital gain (loss) (attach Schedule D (Form 1120-S))		7	
	8a	Net long-term capital gain (loss) (attach Schedule D (Form 1120-S))		8a	
	b	Collectibles (28%) gain (loss)	8b		
	c	Unrecaptured section 1250 gain (attach statement)	8c		
	9	Net section 1231 gain (loss) (attach Form 4797)		9	
	10	Other income (loss) (see instructions) Type ▶		10	
Deductions	11	Section 179 deduction (attach Form 4562)		11	
	12a	Charitable contributions		12a	
	b	Investment interest expense		12b	
	c	Section 59(e)(2) expenditures Type ▶		12c	
	d	Other deductions (see instructions) Type ▶		12d	
Credits	13a	Low-income housing credit (section 42(j)(5))		13a	
	b	Low-income housing credit (other)		13b	
	c	Qualified rehabilitation expenditures (rental real estate) (attach Form 3468, if applicable)		13c	
	d	Other rental real estate credits (see instructions) Type ▶		13d	
	e	Other rental credits (see instructions) Type ▶		13e	
	f	Biofuel producer credit (attach Form 6478)		13f	
	g	Other credits (see instructions) Type ▶		13g	
International Transactions	14	Attach Schedule K-2 (Form 1120-S), Shareholders' Pro Rata Share Items—International, and check this box to indicate you are reporting items of international tax relevance ▶ ☐			
Alternative Minimum Tax (AMT) Items	15a	Post-1986 depreciation adjustment		15a	
	b	Adjusted gain or loss		15b	
	c	Depletion (other than oil and gas)		15c	
	d	Oil, gas, and geothermal properties—gross income		15d	
	e	Oil, gas, and geothermal properties—deductions		15e	
	f	Other AMT items (attach statement)		15f	
Items Affecting Shareholder Basis	16a	Tax-exempt interest income		16a	
	b	Other tax-exempt income		16b	
	c	Nondeductible expenses		16c	
	d	Distributions (attach statement if required) (see instructions)		16d	
	e	Repayment of loans from shareholders		16e	
	f	Foreign taxes paid or accrued		16f	

Form **1120-S** (2021)

APPENDIX 14.4 Corporation Form 1120-S (continued)

Form 1120-S (2021) Page 4

Schedule K **Shareholders' Pro Rata Share Items** *(continued)*

				Total amount
Other Information	17a	Investment income	17a	
	b	Investment expenses	17b	
	c	Dividend distributions paid from accumulated earnings and profits	17c	
	d	Other items and amounts (attach statement)		
Recon-ciliation	18	**Income (loss) reconciliation.** Combine the amounts on lines 1 through 10 in the far right column. From the result, subtract the sum of the amounts on lines 11 through 12d and 16f	18	

Schedule L **Balance Sheets per Books**

		Beginning of tax year		End of tax year	
	Assets	(a)	(b)	(c)	(d)
1	Cash				
2a	Trade notes and accounts receivable				
b	Less allowance for bad debts	( )		( )	
3	Inventories				
4	U.S. government obligations				
5	Tax-exempt securities (see instructions)				
6	Other current assets (attach statement)				
7	Loans to shareholders				
8	Mortgage and real estate loans				
9	Other investments (attach statement)				
10a	Buildings and other depreciable assets				
b	Less accumulated depreciation	( )		( )	
11a	Depletable assets				
b	Less accumulated depletion	( )		( )	
12	Land (net of any amortization)				
13a	Intangible assets (amortizable only)				
b	Less accumulated amortization	( )		( )	
14	Other assets (attach statement)				
15	Total assets				
	Liabilities and Shareholders' Equity				
16	Accounts payable				
17	Mortgages, notes, bonds payable in less than 1 year				
18	Other current liabilities (attach statement)				
19	Loans from shareholders				
20	Mortgages, notes, bonds payable in 1 year or more				
21	Other liabilities (attach statement)				
22	Capital stock				
23	Additional paid-in capital				
24	Retained earnings				
25	Adjustments to shareholders' equity (attach statement)				
26	Less cost of treasury stock		( )		( )
27	Total liabilities and shareholders' equity				

Form **1120-S** (2021)

APPENDIX 14.4 Corporation Form 1120-S (continued)

Form 1120-S (2021) Page 5

Schedule M-1 **Reconciliation of Income (Loss) per Books With Income (Loss) per Return**

Note: The corporation may be required to file Schedule M-3. See instructions.

1	Net income (loss) per books		5	Income recorded on books this year not included on Schedule K, lines 1 through 10 (itemize):	
2	Income included on Schedule K, lines 1, 2, 3c, 4, 5a, 6, 7, 8a, 9, and 10, not recorded on books this year (itemize)		a	Tax-exempt interest $	
3	Expenses recorded on books this year not included on Schedule K, lines 1 through 12 and 16f (itemize):		6	Deductions included on Schedule K, lines 1 through 12 and 16f, not charged against book income this year (itemize):	
a	Depreciation $		a	Depreciation $	
b	Travel and entertainment $		7	Add lines 5 and 6	
4	Add lines 1 through 3		8	Income (loss) (Schedule K, line 18). Subtract line 7 from line 4	

Schedule M-2 **Analysis of Accumulated Adjustments Account, Shareholders' Undistributed Taxable Income Previously Taxed, Accumulated Earnings and Profits, and Other Adjustments Account** (see instructions)

		(a) Accumulated adjustments account	(b) Shareholders' undistributed taxable income previously taxed	(c) Accumulated earnings and profits	(d) Other adjustments account
1	Balance at beginning of tax year				
2	Ordinary income from page 1, line 21				
3	Other additions				
4	Loss from page 1, line 21	( )			
5	Other reductions	( )			( )
6	Combine lines 1 through 5				
7	Distributions				
8	Balance at end of tax year. Subtract line 7 from line 6				

Form **1120-S** (2021)

APPENDIX 14.5 Form 8832

Form **8832**
(Rev. December 2013)
Department of the Treasury
Internal Revenue Service

Entity Classification Election

▶ **Information about Form 8832 and its instructions is at *www.irs.gov/form8832*.**

OMB No. 1545-1516

Type or Print	Name of eligible entity making election	**Employer identification number**
	Number, street, and room or suite no. If a P.O. box, see instructions.	
	City or town, state, and ZIP code. If a foreign address, enter city, province or state, postal code and country. Follow the country's practice for entering the postal code.	

▶ Check if: ☐ Address change ☐ Late classification relief sought under Revenue Procedure 2009-41
☐ Relief for a late change of entity classification election sought under Revenue Procedure 2010-32

Part I **Election Information**

1 **Type of election** (see instructions):

a ☐ Initial classification by a newly-formed entity. Skip lines 2a and 2b and go to line 3.
b ☐ Change in current classification. Go to line 2a.

2a Has the eligible entity previously filed an entity election that had an effective date within the last 60 months?

☐ **Yes.** Go to line 2b.
☐ **No.** Skip line 2b and go to line 3.

2b Was the eligible entity's prior election an initial classification election by a newly formed entity that was effective on the date of formation?

☐ **Yes.** Go to line 3.
☐ **No.** Stop here. You generally are not currently eligible to make the election (see instructions).

3 Does the eligible entity have more than one owner?

☐ **Yes.** You can elect to be classified as a partnership or an association taxable as a corporation. Skip line 4 and go to line 5.
☐ **No.** You can elect to be classified as an association taxable as a corporation or to be disregarded as a separate entity. Go to line 4.

4 If the eligible entity has only one owner, provide the following information:

a Name of owner ▶ ____________
b Identifying number of owner ▶ ____________

5 If the eligible entity is owned by one or more affiliated corporations that file a consolidated return, provide the name and employer identification number of the parent corporation:

a Name of parent corporation ▶ ____________
b Employer identification number ▶ ____________

For Paperwork Reduction Act Notice, see instructions. Cat. No. 22598R Form **8832** (Rev. 12-2013)

APPENDIX 14.5 Form 8832 (continued)

Form 8832 (Rev. 12-2013) Page 2

Part I Election Information (Continued)

6 **Type of entity** (see instructions):

a ☐ A domestic eligible entity electing to be classified as an association taxable as a corporation.
b ☐ A domestic eligible entity electing to be classified as a partnership.
c ☐ A domestic eligible entity with a single owner electing to be disregarded as a separate entity.
d ☐ A foreign eligible entity electing to be classified as an association taxable as a corporation.
e ☐ A foreign eligible entity electing to be classified as a partnership.
f ☐ A foreign eligible entity with a single owner electing to be disregarded as a separate entity.

7 If the eligible entity is created or organized in a foreign jurisdiction, provide the foreign country of organization ▶ ______________

8 Election is to be effective beginning (month, day, year) (see instructions) . . . . ▶ ______________

9 Name and title of contact person whom the IRS may call for more information | **10** Contact person's telephone number

Consent Statement and Signature(s) (see instructions)

Under penalties of perjury, I (we) declare that I (we) consent to the election of the above-named entity to be classified as indicated above, and that I (we) have examined this election and consent statement, and to the best of my (our) knowledge and belief, this election and consent statement are true, correct, and complete. If I am an officer, manager, or member signing for the entity, I further declare under penalties of perjury that I am authorized to make the election on its behalf.

Signature(s)	Date	Title

Form **8832** (Rev. 12-2013)

APPENDIX 14.5 Form 8832 (continued)

Form 8832 (Rev. 12-2013) Page 3

Part II Late Election Relief

11 Provide the explanation as to why the entity classification election was not filed on time (see instructions).

Under penalties of perjury, I (we) declare that I (we) have examined this election, including accompanying documents, and, to the best of my (our) knowledge and belief, the election contains all the relevant facts relating to the election, and such facts are true, correct, and complete. I (we) further declare that I (we) have personal knowledge of the facts and circumstances related to the election. I (we) further declare that the elements required for relief in Section 4.01 of Revenue Procedure 2009-41 have been satisfied.

Signature(s)	Date	Title

Form **8832** (Rev. 12-2013)

APPENDIX 14.5 Form 8832 (continued)

Form 8832 (Rev. 12-2013) Page **4**

General Instructions

Section references are to the Internal Revenue Code unless otherwise noted.

Future Developments

For the latest information about developments related to Form 8832 and its instructions, such as legislation enacted after they were published, go to *www.irs.gov/form8832*.

What's New

For entities formed on or after July 1, 2013, the Croatian Dionicko Drustvo will always be treated as a corporation. See Notice 2013-44, 2013-29, I.R.B. 62 for more information.

Purpose of Form

An eligible entity uses Form 8832 to elect how it will be classified for federal tax purposes, as a corporation, a partnership, or an entity disregarded as separate from its owner. An eligible entity is classified for federal tax purposes under the default rules described below unless it files Form 8832 or Form 2553, Election by a Small Business Corporation. See *Who Must File* below.

The IRS will use the information entered on this form to establish the entity's filing and reporting requirements for federal tax purposes.

Note. An entity must file Form 2553 if making an election under section 1362(a) to be an S corporation

TIP *A new eligible entity should not file Form 8832 if it will be using its default classification (see* Default Rules *below).*

Eligible entity. An eligible entity is a business entity that is not included in items 1, or 3 through 9, under the definition of **corporation** provided under *Definitions*. Eligible entities include limited liability companies (LLCs) and partnerships.

Generally, corporations are not eligible entities. However, the following types of corporations are treated as eligible entities:

1. An eligible entity that previously elected to be an association taxable as a corporation by filing Form 8832. An entity that elects to be classified as a corporation by filing Form 8832 can make another election to change its classification (see the *60-month limitation rule* discussed below in the instructions for lines 2a and 2b).

2. A foreign eligible entity that became an association taxable as a corporation under the foreign default rule described below.

Default Rules

Existing entity default rule. Certain domestic and foreign entities that were in existence before January 1, 1997, and have an established federal tax classification generally do not need to make an election to continue that classification. If an existing entity decides to change its classification, it may do so subject to the 60-month limitation rule. See the instructions for lines 2a and 2b. See Regulations sections 301.7701-3(b)(3) and 301.7701-3(h)(2) for more details.

Domestic default rule. Unless an election is made on Form 8832, a domestic eligible entity is:

1. A partnership if it has two or more members.

2. Disregarded as an entity separate from its owner if it has a single owner.

A change in the number of members of an eligible entity classified as an **association** (defined below) does not affect the entity's classification. However, an eligible entity classified as a partnership will become a disregarded entity when the entity's membership is reduced to one member and a disregarded entity will be classified as a partnership when the entity has more than one member.

Foreign default rule. Unless an election is made on Form 8832, a foreign eligible entity is:

1. A partnership if it has two or more members and at least one member does not have limited liability.

2. An association taxable as a corporation if all members have limited liability.

3. Disregarded as an entity separate from its owner if it has a single owner that does not have limited liability.

However, if a qualified foreign entity (as defined in section 3.02 of Rev. Proc. 2010-32) files a valid election to be classified as a partnership based on the reasonable assumption that it had two or more owners as of the effective date of the election, and the qualified entity is later determined to have a single owner, the IRS will deem the election to be an election to be classified as a disregarded entity provided:

1. The qualified entity's owner and purported owners file amended returns that are consistent with the treatment of the entity as a disregarded entity;

2. The amended returns are filed before the close of the period of limitations on assessments under section 6501(a) for the relevant tax year; and

3. The corrected Form 8832, with the box checked entitled: Relief for a late change of entity classification election sought under Revenue Procedure 2010-32, is filed and attached to the amended tax return.

Also, if the qualified foreign entity (as defined in section 3.02 of Rev. Proc. 2010-32) files a valid election to be classified as a disregarded entity based on the reasonable assumption that it had a single owner as of the effective date of the election, and the qualified entity is later determined to have two or more owners, the IRS will deem the election to be an election to be classified as a partnership provided:

1. The qualified entity files information returns and the actual owners file original or amended returns consistent with the treatment of the entity as a partnership;

2. The amended returns are filed before the close of the period of limitations on assessments under section 6501(a) for the relevant tax year; and

3. The corrected Form 8832, with the box checked entitled: Relief for a late change of entity classification election sought under Revenue Procedure 2010-32, is filed and attached to the amended tax returns. See Rev. Proc. 2010-32, 2010-36 I.R.B. 320 for details.

Definitions

Association. For purposes of this form, an association is an eligible entity taxable as a corporation by election or, for foreign eligible entities, under the default rules (see Regulations section 301.7701-3).

Business entity. A business entity is any entity recognized for federal tax purposes that is not properly classified as a trust under Regulations section 301.7701-4 or otherwise subject to special treatment under the Code regarding the entity's classification. See Regulations section 301.7701-2(a).

Corporation. For federal tax purposes, a corporation is any of the following:

1. A business entity organized under a federal or state statute, or under a statute of a federally recognized Indian tribe, if the statute describes or refers to the entity as incorporated or as a corporation, body corporate, or body politic.

2. An association (as determined under Regulations section 301.7701-3).

3. A business entity organized under a state statute, if the statute describes or refers to the entity as a joint-stock company or joint-stock association.

4. An insurance company.

5. A state-chartered business entity conducting banking activities, if any of its deposits are insured under the Federal Deposit Insurance Act, as amended, 12 U.S. C. 1811 et seq., or a similar federal statute.

6. A business entity wholly owned by a state or any political subdivision thereof, or a business entity wholly owned by a foreign government or any other entity described in Regulations section 1.892-2T.

7. A business entity that is taxable as a corporation under a provision of the Code other than section 7701(a)(3).

8. A foreign business entity listed on page 7. See Regulations section 301.7701-2(b)(8) for any exceptions and inclusions to items on this list and for any revisions made to this list since these instructions were printed.

9. An entity created or organized under the laws of more than one jurisdiction (business entities with multiple charters) if the entity is treated as a corporation with respect to any one of the jurisdictions. See Regulations section 301.7701-2(b)(9) for examples.

Disregarded entity. A disregarded entity is an eligible entity that is treated as an entity not separate from its single owner for income tax purposes. A "disregarded entity" is treated as separate from its owner for:

- Employment tax purposes, effective for wages paid on or after January 1, 2009; and
- Excise taxes reported on Forms 720, 730, 2290, 11-C, or 8849, effective for excise taxes reported and paid after December 31, 2007.

APPENDIX 14.5 Form 8832 (continued)

Form 8832 (Rev. 12-2013) Page **5**

See the employment tax and excise tax return instructions for more information.

Limited liability. A member of a foreign eligible entity has limited liability if the member has no personal liability for any debts of or claims against the entity by reason of being a member. This determination is based solely on the statute or law under which the entity is organized (and, if relevant, the entity's organizational documents). A member has personal liability if the creditors of the entity may seek satisfaction of all or any part of the debts or claims against the entity from the member as such. A member has personal liability even if the member makes an agreement under which another person (whether or not a member of the entity) assumes that liability or agrees to indemnify that member for that liability.

Partnership. A partnership is a business entity that has at least two members and is not a corporation as defined above under *Corporation.*

Who Must File

File this form for an eligible entity that is one of the following:

- A domestic entity electing to be classified as an association taxable as a corporation.
- A domestic entity electing to change its current classification (even if it is currently classified under the default rule).
- A foreign entity that has more than one owner, all owners having limited liability, electing to be classified as a partnership.
- A foreign entity that has at least one owner that does not have limited liability, electing to be classified as an association taxable as a corporation.
- A foreign entity with a single owner having limited liability, electing to be an entity disregarded as an entity separate from its owner.
- A foreign entity electing to change its current classification (even if it is currently classified under the default rule).

Do not file this form for an eligible entity that is:

- Tax-exempt under section 501(a);
- A real estate investment trust (REIT), as defined in section 856; or
- Electing to be classified as an S corporation. An eligible entity that timely files Form 2553 to elect classification as an S corporation and meets all other requirements to qualify as an S corporation is deemed to have made an election under Regulations section 301.7701-3(c)(v) to be classified as an association taxable as a corporation.

All three of these entities are deemed to have made an election to be classified as an association.

Effect of Election

The federal tax treatment of elective changes in classification as described in Regulations section 301.7701-3(g)(1) is summarized as follows:

- If an eligible entity classified as a partnership elects to be classified as an association, it is deemed that the partnership contributes all of its assets and liabilities to the association in exchange for stock in the association, and immediately thereafter, the partnership liquidates by distributing the stock of the association to its partners.
- If an eligible entity classified as an association elects to be classified as a partnership, it is deemed that the association distributes all of its assets and liabilities to its shareholders in liquidation of the association, and immediately thereafter, the shareholders contribute all of the distributed assets and liabilities to a newly formed partnership.
- If an eligible entity classified as an association elects to be disregarded as an entity separate from its owner, it is deemed that the association distributes all of its assets and liabilities to its single owner in liquidation of the association.
- If an eligible entity that is disregarded as an entity separate from its owner elects to be classified as an association, the owner of the eligible entity is deemed to have contributed all of the assets and liabilities of the entity to the association in exchange for the stock of the association.

Note. For information on the federal tax consequences of elective changes in classification, see Regulations section 301.7701-3(g).

When To File

Generally, an election specifying an eligible entity's classification cannot take effect more than 75 days prior to the date the election is filed, nor can it take effect later than 12 months after the date the election is filed. An eligible entity may be eligible for late election relief in certain circumstances. For more information, see *Late Election Relief*, later.

Where To File

File Form 8832 with the Internal Revenue Service Center for your state listed later.

In addition, attach a copy of Form 8832 to the entity's federal tax or information return for the tax year of the election. If the entity is not required to file a return for that year, a copy of its Form 8832 must be attached to the federal tax returns of all direct or indirect owners of the entity for the tax year of the owner that includes the date on which the election took effect. An indirect owner of the electing entity does not have to attach a copy of the Form 8832 to its tax return if an entity in which it has an interest is already filing a copy of the Form 8832 with its return. Failure to attach a copy of Form 8832 will not invalidate an otherwise valid election, but penalties may be assessed against persons who are required to, but do not, attach Form 8832.

Each member of the entity is required to file the member's return consistent with the entity election. Penalties apply to returns filed inconsistent with the entity's election.

If the entity's principal business, office, or agency is located in:	Use the following Internal Revenue Service Center address:
Connecticut, Delaware, District of Columbia, Florida, Illinois, Indiana, Kentucky, Maine, Maryland, Massachusetts, Michigan, New Hampshire, New Jersey, New York, North Carolina, Ohio, Pennsylvania, Rhode Island, South Carolina, Vermont, Virginia, West Virginia, Wisconsin	Cincinnati, OH 45999

If the entity's principal business, office, or agency is located in:	Use the following Internal Revenue Service Center address:
Alabama, Alaska, Arizona, Arkansas, California, Colorado, Georgia, Hawaii, Idaho, Iowa, Kansas, Louisiana, Minnesota, Mississippi, Missouri, Montana, Nebraska, Nevada, New Mexico, North Dakota, Oklahoma, Oregon, South Dakota, Tennessee, Texas, Utah, Washington, Wyoming	Ogden, UT 84201
A foreign country or U.S. possession	Ogden, UT 84201-0023

Note. Also attach a copy to the entity's federal income tax return for the tax year of the election.

Acceptance or Nonacceptance of Election

The service center will notify the eligible entity at the address listed on Form 8832 if its election is accepted or not accepted. The entity should generally receive a determination on its election within 60 days after it has filed Form 8832.

Care should be exercised to ensure that the IRS receives the election. If the entity is not notified of acceptance or nonacceptance of its election within 60 days of the date of filing, take follow-up action by calling 1-800-829-0115, or by sending a letter to the service center to inquire about its status. Send any such letter by certified or registered mail via the U.S. Postal Service, or equivalent type of delivery by a designated private delivery service (see Notice 2004-83, 2004-52 I.R.B. 1030 (or its successor)).

If the IRS questions whether Form 8832 was filed, an acceptable proof of filing is:

- A certified or registered mail receipt (timely postmarked) from the U.S. Postal Service, or its equivalent from a designated private delivery service;
- Form 8832 with an accepted stamp;
- Form 8832 with a stamped IRS received date; or
- An IRS letter stating that Form 8832 has been accepted.

APPENDIX 14.5 Form 8832 (continued)

Form 8832 (Rev. 12-2013) Page 6

Specific Instructions

Name. Enter the name of the eligible entity electing to be classified.

Employer identification number (EIN). Show the EIN of the eligible entity electing to be classified.

Do not put "Applied For" on this line.

Note. Any entity that has an EIN will retain that EIN even if its federal tax classification changes under Regulations section 301.7701-3.

If a disregarded entity's classification changes so that it becomes recognized as a partnership or association for federal tax purposes, and that entity had an EIN, then the entity must continue to use that EIN. If the entity did not already have its own EIN, then the entity must apply for an EIN and not use the identifying number of the single owner.

A foreign entity that makes an election under Regulations section 301.7701-3(c) and (d) must also use its own taxpayer identifying number. See sections 6721 through 6724 for penalties that may apply for failure to supply taxpayer identifying numbers.

If the entity electing to be classified using Form 8832 does not have an EIN, it must apply for one on Form SS-4, Application for Employer Identification Number. The entity must have received an EIN by the time Form 8832 is filed in order for the form to be processed. An election will not be accepted if the eligible entity does not provide an EIN.

Do not apply for a new EIN for an existing entity that is changing its classification if the entity already has an EIN.

Address. Enter the address of the entity electing a classification. All correspondence regarding the acceptance or nonacceptance of the election will be sent to this address. Include the suite, room, or other unit number after the street address. If the Post Office does not deliver mail to the street address and the entity has a P.O. box, show the box number instead of the street address. If the electing entity receives its mail in care of a third party (such as an accountant or an attorney), enter on the street address line "C/O" followed by the third party's name and street address or P.O. box.

Address change. If the eligible entity has changed its address since filing Form SS-4 or the entity's most recently-filed return (including a change to an "in care of" address), check the box for an address change.

Late-classification relief sought under Revenue Procedure 2009-41. Check the box if the entity is seeking relief under Rev. Proc. 2009-41, 2009-39 I.R.B. 439, for a late classification election. For more information, see *Late Election Relief*, later.

Relief for a late change of entity classification election sought under Revenue Procedure 2010-32. Check the box if the entity is seeking relief under Rev. Proc. 2010-32, 2010-36 I.R.B. 320. For more information, see *Foreign default rule,* earlier.

Part I. Election Information

Complete Part I whether or not the entity is seeking relief under Rev. Proc. 2009-41 or Rev. Proc. 2010-32.

Line 1. Check box 1a if the entity is choosing a classification for the first time (i.e., the entity does not want to be classified under the applicable default classification). Do not file this form if the entity wants to be classified under the default rules.

Check box 1b if the entity is changing its current classification.

Lines 2a and 2b. 60-month limitation rule. Once an eligible entity makes an election to *change* its classification, the entity generally cannot change its classification by election again during the 60 months after the effective date of the election. However, the IRS may (by private letter ruling) permit the entity to change its classification by election within the 60-month period if more than 50% of the ownership interests in the entity, as of the effective date of the election, are owned by persons that did not own any interests in the entity on the effective date or the filing date of the entity's prior election.

Note. The 60-month limitation does not apply if the previous election was made by a newly formed eligible entity and was effective on the date of formation.

Line 4. If an eligible entity has only one owner, provide the name of its owner on line 4a and the owner's identifying number (social security number, or individual taxpayer identification number, or EIN) on line 4b. If the electing eligible entity is owned by an entity that is a disregarded entity or by an entity that is a member of a series of tiered disregarded entities, identify the first entity (the entity closest to the electing eligible entity) that is not a disregarded entity. For example, if the electing eligible entity is owned by disregarded entity A, which is owned by another disregarded entity B, and disregarded entity B is owned by partnership C, provide the name and EIN of partnership C as the owner of the electing eligible entity. If the owner is a foreign person or entity and does not have a U.S. identifying number, enter "none" on line 4b.

Line 5. If the eligible entity is owned by one or more members of an affiliated group of corporations that file a consolidated return, provide the name and EIN of the parent corporation.

Line 6. Check the appropriate box if you are changing a current classification (no matter how achieved), or are electing out of a default classification. Do not file this form if you fall within a default classification that is the desired classification for the new entity.

Line 7. If the entity making the election is created or organized in a foreign jurisdiction, enter the name of the foreign country in which it is organized. This information must be provided even if the entity is also organized under domestic law.

Line 8. Generally, the election will take effect on the date you enter on line 8 of this form, or on the date filed if no date is entered on line 8. An election specifying an entity's classification for federal tax purposes can take effect no more than 75 days prior to the date the election is filed, nor can it take effect later than 12 months after the date on which the election is filed. If line 8 shows a date more than 75 days prior to the date on which the election is filed, the election will default to 75 days before the date it is filed. If line 8 shows an effective date more than 12 months from the filing date, the election will take effect 12 months after the date the election is filed.

Consent statement and signature(s). Form 8832 must be signed by:

1. Each member of the electing entity who is an owner at the time the election is filed; or

2. Any officer, manager, or member of the electing entity who is authorized (under local law or the organizational documents) to make the election. The elector represents to having such authorization under penalties of perjury.

If an election is to be effective for any period prior to the time it is filed, each person who was an owner between the date the election is to be effective and the date the election is filed, and who is not an owner at the time the election is filed, must sign.

If you need a continuation sheet or use a separate consent statement, attach it to Form 8832. The separate consent statement must contain the same information as shown on Form 8832.

Note. Do not sign the copy that is attached to your tax return.

Part II. Late Election Relief

Complete Part II only if the entity is requesting late election relief under Rev. Proc. 2009-41.

An eligible entity may be eligible for late election relief under Rev. Proc. 2009-41, 2009-39 I.R.B. 439, if **each** of the following requirements is met.

1. The entity failed to obtain its requested classification as of the date of its formation (or upon the entity's classification becoming relevant) or failed to obtain its requested change in classification solely because Form 8832 was not filed timely.

2. Either:

a. The entity has not filed a federal tax or information return for the first year in which the election was intended because the due date has not passed for that year's federal tax or information return; or

b. The entity has timely filed all required federal tax returns and information returns (or if not timely, within 6 months after its due date, excluding extensions) consistent with its requested classification for all of the years the entity intended the requested election to be effective and no inconsistent tax or information returns have been filed by or with respect to the entity during any of the tax years. If the eligible entity is not required to file a federal tax return or information return, each affected person who is required to file a federal tax return or information return must have timely filed all such returns (or if not timely, within 6 months after its due date, excluding extensions) consistent with the

APPENDIX 14.5 Form 8832 (continued)

entity's requested classification for all of the years the entity intended the requested election to be effective and no inconsistent tax or information returns have been filed during any of the tax years.

3. The entity has reasonable cause for its failure to timely make the entity classification election.

4. Three years and 75 days from the requested effective date of the eligible entity's classification election have not passed.

Affected person. An affected person is either:

• with respect to the effective date of the eligible entity's classification election, a person who would have been required to attach a copy of the Form 8832 for the eligible entity to its federal tax or information return for the tax year of the person which includes that date; or

• with respect to any subsequent date after the entity's requested effective date of the classification election, a person who would have been required to attach a copy of the Form 8832 for the eligible entity to its federal tax or information return for the person's tax year that includes that subsequent date had the election first become effective on that subsequent date.

For details on the requirement to attach a copy of Form 8832, see Rev. Proc. 2009-41 and the instructions under *Where To File.*

To obtain relief, file Form 8832 with the applicable IRS service center listed in *Where To File,* earlier, within 3 years and 75 days from the requested effective date of the eligible entity's classification election.

If Rev. Proc. 2009-41 does not apply, an entity may seek relief for a late entity election by requesting a private letter ruling and paying a user fee in accordance with Rev. Proc. 2013-1, 2013-1 I.R.B. 1 (or its successor).

Line 11. Explain the reason for the failure to file a timely entity classification election.

Signatures. Part II of Form 8832 must be signed by an authorized representative of the eligible entity and each affected person. See *Affected Persons,* earlier. The individual or individuals who sign the declaration must have personal knowledge of the facts and circumstances related to the election.

Foreign Entities Classified as Corporations for Federal Tax Purposes:

American Samoa—Corporation
Argentina—Sociedad Anonima
Australia—Public Limited Company
Austria—Aktiengesellschaft
Barbados—Limited Company
Belgium—Societe Anonyme
Belize—Public Limited Company
Bolivia—Sociedad Anonima
Brazil—Sociedade Anonima
Bulgaria—Aktsionerno Druzhestvo
Canada—Corporation and Company
Chile—Sociedad Anonima
People's Republic of China—Gufen Youxian Gongsi
Republic of China (Taiwan)—Ku-fen Yu-hsien Kung-szu
Colombia—Sociedad Anonima
Costa Rica—Sociedad Anonima
Croatia—Dionicko Drustvo
Cyprus—Public Limited Company
Czech Republic—Akciova Spolecnost
Denmark—Aktieselskab
Ecuador—Sociedad Anonima or Compania Anonima
Egypt—Sharikat Al-Mossahamah
El Salvador—Sociedad Anonima
Estonia—Aktsiaselts
European Economic Area/European Union—Societas Europaea
Finland—Julkinen Osakeyhtio/Publikt Aktiebolag
France—Societe Anonyme
Germany—Aktiengesellschaft
Greece—Anonymos Etairia
Guam—Corporation
Guatemala—Sociedad Anonima
Guyana—Public Limited Company
Honduras—Sociedad Anonima
Hong Kong—Public Limited Company
Hungary—Reszvenytarsasag
Iceland—Hlutafelag
India—Public Limited Company
Indonesia—Perseroan Terbuka
Ireland—Public Limited Company
Israel—Public Limited Company
Italy—Societa per Azioni
Jamaica—Public Limited Company
Japan—Kabushiki Kaisha
Kazakstan—Ashyk Aktsionerlik Kogham
Republic of Korea—Chusik Hoesa
Latvia—Akciju Sabiedriba
Liberia—Corporation
Liechtenstein—Aktiengesellschaft
Lithuania—Akcine Bendroves
Luxembourg—Societe Anonyme
Malaysia—Berhad
Malta—Public Limited Company
Mexico—Sociedad Anonima
Morocco—Societe Anonyme
Netherlands—Naamloze Vennootschap
New Zealand—Limited Company
Nicaragua—Compania Anonima
Nigeria—Public Limited Company
Northern Mariana Islands—Corporation
Norway—Allment Aksjeselskap
Pakistan—Public Limited Company
Panama—Sociedad Anonima
Paraguay—Sociedad Anonima
Peru—Sociedad Anonima
Philippines—Stock Corporation
Poland—Spolka Akcyjna
Portugal—Sociedade Anonima
Puerto Rico—Corporation
Romania—Societe pe Actiuni
Russia—Otkrytoye Aktsionernoy Obshchestvo
Saudi Arabia—Sharikat Al-Mossahamah
Singapore—Public Limited Company
Slovak Republic—Akciova Spolocnost
Slovenia—Delniska Druzba
South Africa—Public Limited Company
Spain—Sociedad Anonima
Surinam—Naamloze Vennootschap
Sweden—Publika Aktiebolag
Switzerland— Aktiengesellschaft
Thailand—Borisat Chamkad (Mahachon)
Trinidad and Tobago—Limited Company
Tunisia—Societe Anonyme
Turkey—Anonim Sirket
Ukraine—Aktsionerne Tovaristvo Vidkritogo Tipu
United Kingdom—Public Limited Company
United States Virgin Islands—Corporation
Uruguay—Sociedad Anonima
Venezuela—Sociedad Anonima or Compania Anonima

CAUTION *See Regulations section 301.7701-2(b)(8) for any exceptions and inclusions to items on this list and for any revisions made to this list since these instructions were printed.*

Paperwork Reduction Act Notice

We ask for the information on this form to carry out the Internal Revenue laws of the United States. You are required to give us the information. We need it to ensure that you are complying with these laws and to allow us to figure and collect the right amount of tax.

You are not required to provide the information requested on a form that is subject to the Paperwork Reduction Act unless the form displays a valid OMB control number. Books or records relating to a form or its instructions must be retained as long as their contents may become material in the administration of any Internal Revenue law. Generally, tax returns and return information are confidential, as required by section 6103.

The time needed to complete and file this form will vary depending on individual circumstances. The estimated average time is:

Recordkeeping	2 hr., 46 min.
Learning about the law or the form	3 hr., 48 min.
Preparing and sending the form to the IRS	36 min.

If you have comments concerning the accuracy of these time estimates or suggestions for making this form simpler, we would be happy to hear from you. You can write to the Internal Revenue Service, Tax Forms and Publications, SE:W:CAR:MP:TFP, 1111 Constitution Ave. NW, IR-6526, Washington, DC 20224. Do not send the form to this address. Instead, see *Where To File* above.

CHAPTER 15

Introduction to Retirement Planning

LEARNING OBJECTIVES

After learning the material in this chapter, you will be able to do the following:

- Define financial security
- Identify and understand the major factors that affect retirement planning
- Understand the work life expectancy/retirement life expectancy dilemma
- Explain the impact that timeliness of savings has on savings accumulation
- Discuss the balance that must be achieved between increasing and decreasing retirement income needs
- Define the wage replacement ratio and explain how it is used to estimate retirement income needs
- Differentiate between the top-down approach and the budgeting approach to calculating the wage replacement ratio
- Discuss the qualitative factors that affect retirement planning

- Differentiate among the three capital needs analysis calculations: the pure annuity model; the capital preservation (CP) model; and the purchasing power preservation (PPP) model
- Determine capital needs for various clients
- Make projections to prepare a capital needs analysis presentation

INTRODUCTION

One of the main financial planning goals for many people is long-term financial security and independence. This goal is realized when individuals are financially secure enough to live at their desired comfort level without the need for employment income. Financial security at retirement requires individuals to plan carefully. Unfortunately, the majority of American workers have no idea how much money they will need to fund their retirement. When coupled with changes in Social Security, tax laws, the economy, and the value structure of our society, retirement planning becomes a necessary but difficult and time-consuming process. Because of the complex nature of retirement planning, financial planners often are enlisted to provide direction and guidance. This chapter discusses the fundamental concepts that financial planners must know to effectively plan for a client's retirement. Chapter 16 discusses the characteristics of actual retirement plans.

BASIC FACTORS AFFECTING RETIREMENT PLANNING

Several basic factors affect retirement planning. The following areas must be considered: the remaining work life expectancy (WLE), the retirement life expectancy (RLE), basic savings concepts, the annual income needed (needs), the wage replacement ratio (WRR), the sources of retirement income, inflation, investment returns, and other qualitative factors.

REMAINING WORK LIFE EXPECTANCY (RWLE)

Work life expectancy (WLE)
The number of years a person spends in the workforce, generally 30–40 years

Remaining work life expectancy (RWLE)
The work period remaining at a certain point in time prior to retirement

Work life expectancy (WLE) is the period of time a person is in the work force, generally 30–40 years. There has been a substantial decline in the overall WLE because of increased education, which causes later entry into the workforce and earlier than normal retirement.

Remaining work life expectancy (RWLE) is the work period that remains at a certain point in time before retirement. For example, a 50-year-old client who expects to retire at age 62 has a RWLE of 12 years. Determining the remaining work life expectancy is important for the financial planner because this figure tells the planner the remaining number of years the client has to save for retirement. In the past, normal retirement age was most often age 65 because this age was the retirement age historically set forth by the Social Security Administration. Today, however, the average retirement age is several years less than age 65, with age 62 being a common retirement age, especially when one spouse earns less than the other spouse.

Exhibit 15.1 presents a skewed distribution of all retirees' retirement ages. Notice that the area identified as A represents 93% of the area of the curve, illustrating that approximately 93% of all individuals retire between ages 62 and 65 (inclusive).

EXHIBIT 15.1 Average Retirement Age (United States)

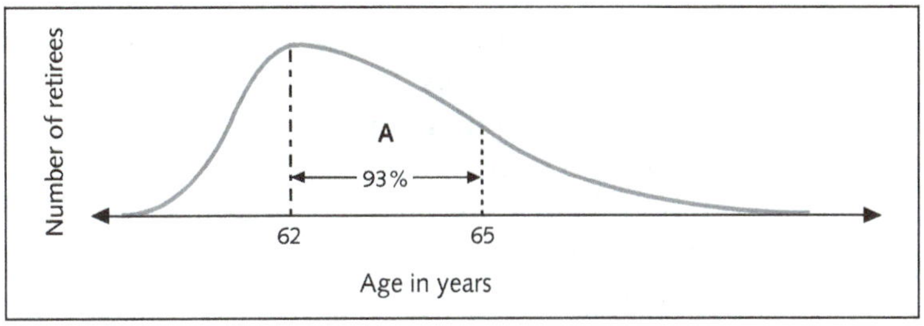

RETIREMENT LIFE EXPECTANCY (RLE)

Retirement life expectancy (RLE)
The time period beginning at retirement and extending until death; the period of retirement that must be funded

Retirement life expectancy (RLE) is the time period beginning at retirement and extending until death. Although the average RLE for a group of 65-year-olds is approximately 20 years, many clients may live beyond this statistical average. In 1900, the average life expectancy for a newborn was 47 years. The average life expectancy in the United States has risen to 79.05 years for those born in 2022. This increase in life expectancy, and the corresponding increase in RLE, is a direct result of a decline in the death rate, especially the birth mortality rate. The overall death rate has declined because of medical and technological advances in disease diagnoses, cures, and prevention. With each new medical advancement, life expectancy will, no doubt, increase. However, even these numbers do not tell the real life expectancy story. First, *life expectancy* is defined as the time until half the defined population has expired. Thus, by definition, everyone who is reasonably healthy has at least a 50% probability of living longer than their "life expectancy." Second, for retirees and those approaching retirement, the important numbers are not life expectancy at birth, but remaining life expectancy in retirement. Third, the life expectancy of more educated and more wealthy individuals is longer than those who are struggling to get by.

The WLE-RLE Relationship

A financial planner needs to understand the relationship between WLE and RLE. If either period changes, the other period is affected. Exhibit 15.2 presents the work life expectancy/retirement life expectancy dilemma.

EXHIBIT 15.2 The WLE/RLE Dilemma

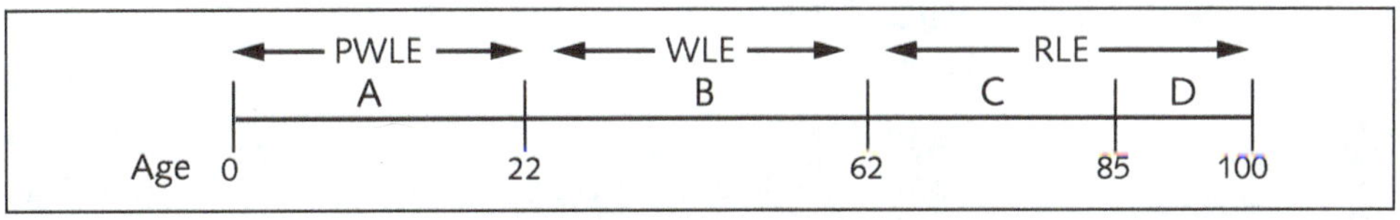

Area A represents the prework life expectancy (PWLE) and lasts until the person enters the workforce on a full-time basis. Generally, the PWLE ends between ages 18 and 26, with the average age being 22. Area B, the WLE, represents the period of working years before retirement. This period begins at the end of the PWLE and ends at the beginning of C, the RLE, usually around age 62. The RLE (Area C) generally lasts to age 85, but may continue beyond age 100. With a longer RLE period to finance and a shortened WLE in which to save and accumulate assets, careful planning is needed to meet the funding requirements for a financially secure retirement.

SAVINGS CONCEPTS

The savings amount, the savings rate, the timing of savings, and investment decisions are important concepts in retirement planning. If our society were adequately saving for retirement beginning at an early age, people would be saving about 10% of their gross annual income and investing in a broad portfolio of growth investments over their entire work life. They would be ever mindful of investment returns and inflation to ensure sufficient savings. Unfortunately, workers save at a much lower rate than is necessary, are not investment savvy, and are, generally, insensitive to the impact of inflation.

Savings Amount

In general, persons who begin the financial security planning process at an early age (25–30) should save 10–15% of their gross annual pay. If individuals do not begin at an early age, then they must save a greater amount of their gross pay to compensate for the missed years of contributions and compounding. Exhibit 15.3 shows how much individuals must save if they choose to wait until later years to begin saving for retirement.

EXHIBIT 15.3 Required Savings Rate for Retirement

Age Beginning Regular and Recurring Savings*	Savings (As Percentage of Gross Pay) Rate Required to Create Appropriate Capital*
25–35	10–13%
35–45	15–18%
45–55	20–25%
55–65	30–35%

*Assumes appropriate asset allocation for reasonable-risk investor through accumulation year; also assumes normal salary increases and an 80% wage replacement ratio at Social Security normal retirement age.

Exhibit 15.3 illustrates a major problem with delaying retirement savings. Namely, many individuals find it difficult to begin saving such large amounts even if they are accustomed to saving. Saving requires foregoing current consumption, and most individuals find it difficult to decrease consumption by 20–30%, especially when they have been accustomed to maintaining a certain standard of living for long periods.

Savings Rate

The savings rate is an important concern in financial planning. Overall savings rates had declined over the past decade until the United States fell into a period of recession a few years ago. Facing uncertain economic times, Americans began to cut expenses and increased savings. The U.S. personal savings rate, as reported by the Federal Reserve Bank of St. Louis, was 6.8% in 2016, 7.9% in 2019, and down to 6.3% in February 2022.

Timing of Savings

The earlier a person begins to save, the greater the number of future compounding periods available before retirement. A greater number of compounding periods leads to a lower required savings rate and a larger accumulation of capital at retirement. When saving is delayed, the power of compounding is lost, and individuals must compensate by saving a greater percentage of their disposable income.

EXAMPLE Ann saves $3,000 a year from age 25 to 34 inclusively and invests in an account earning 8% annually. Ann stops investing at age 34 but does not withdraw the accumulation until age 65. Ann's accumulation at age 65 is $472,300 even though she only deposited $30,000. In contrast, Bob saves $3,000 a year from age 35 to 65 inclusively and invests in an account similar to Ann's, earning 8% annually. Even though Bob saved $93,000 more than Ann, he will have accumulated $102,300 less than Ann at age 65. The deposits and balances for Ann and Bob at age 65 are presented in Exhibit 15.4.

EXHIBIT 15.4 Time/Savings Example (Accumulation at Age 65)

	Ann	Bob
Total Invested (OA)	$30,000	$93,000
Balance at 65	$472,300	$370,000
Earnings Rate	8%	8%

Even though Bob invested more than three times as much as Ann, Ann has 28% more than Bob at age 65. This result demonstrates the power of compound earnings over the longer period of 41 years versus 31 years. Exhibit 15.5 shows this phenomenon graphically.

EXHIBIT 15.5 Accumulation Example

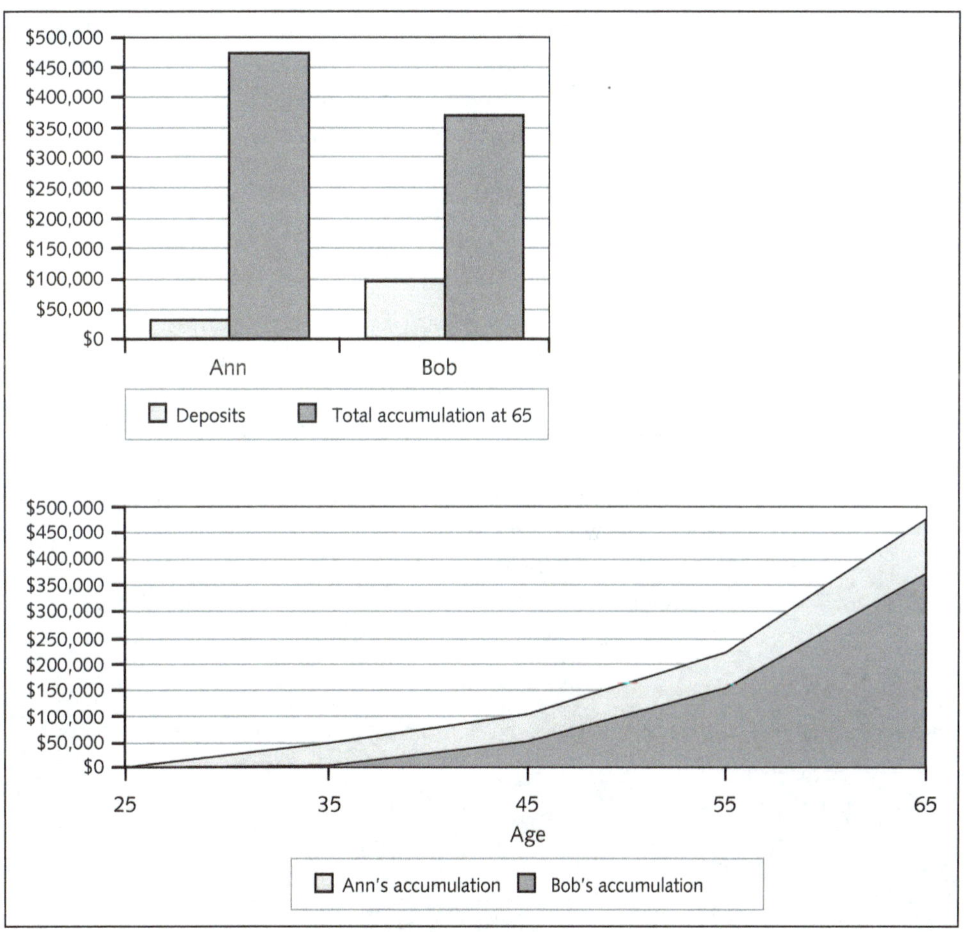

This example highlights the importance of starting early and not withdrawing money early. However, while Ann's results are clearly superior to Bob's, why would she want to stop saving for her future? If she would have simply continued to invest the same amount each year, her balance at 65 would have been $839,400 instead of $472,300. Also, if inflation averaged 3% per year, her balance at retirement of $472,300 would only be worth around $98,400 in her age 25 dollars (present value). If she would have continued to save at the same pace, her $839,400 would have been worth approximately $175,000 in age 25 dollars (present value). No matter how much better Ann did than Bob, retiring today with a nest egg of $98,400 is worse than retiring with $175,000. Actually, a retirement nest egg of $175,000 today is clearly inadequate to maintain even a middle-class lifestyle during a retirement period that could last 30 years.

INVESTMENT DECISIONS

A fundamental understanding of investment decisions and their consequences is essential to retirement planning. In this chapter, we will briefly identify some of the relationships between investments and retirement planning. More in-depth investment information is provided in Chapter 12 of this book.

All assets do not have the same historical investment returns. When planning for retirement, it is important to have an historical perspective of investment returns for various investment alternatives. One would expect that when investors are young, their investment portfolios would be dominated by common stocks because they generally can afford the risk. As investors near retirement, their asset allocation generally shifts to lower risk alternatives while still maintaining some growth component to mitigate the risk of inflation.

Inflation

Inflation
An increase in the price level of goods and services

Inflation causes a loss of purchasing power. If a retiree has a fixed retirement income beginning at age 65 and inflation is 2% (the approximate average rate for the past 20 years), the retiree would experience a loss in purchasing power of 18% in 10 years, 33% in 20 years, and 45% in 30 years. If inflation were to increase to an average annual rate of 3%, which is the 100-year average in the U.S., the retiree would experience a loss in purchasing power of 26% in 10 years, 46% in 20 years, and 60% in 30 years. Although Social Security retirement benefits are inflation adjusted, many private pension plans are not. Accordingly, the financial planner must account for inflation when projecting retirement needs and advise clients to save accordingly. Exhibit 15.6 illustrates the decline in purchasing power that a 2% inflation rate can cause over a 50-year span.

EXHIBIT 15.6 Impact of Inflation

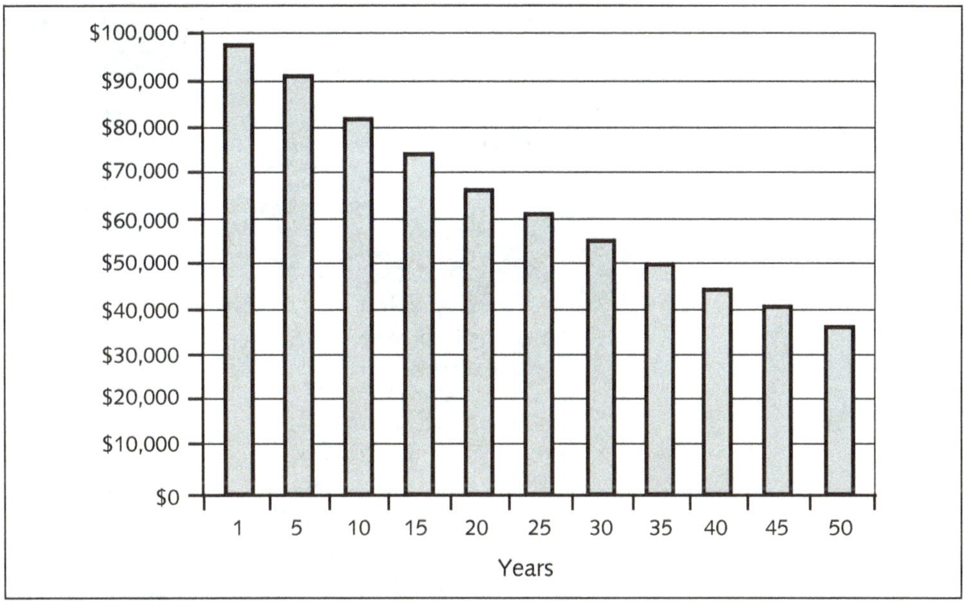

DEFINING RETIREMENT GOALS (NEEDS)

How much income does a person need to be financially independent? Most individuals entering retirement intend to maintain at least the same lifestyle they had before retirement. Clients generally do not radically reduce their expenses downward unless it is necessary. When a retirement budget is prepared, it should include amounts similar to the preretirement budget, with a few adjustments. Some costs in retirement will decrease, while others will increase. The reduced costs in retirement may include: (1) the elimination of costs associated with employment (e.g., certain clothing costs, parking, some meal costs); (2) the elimination of mortgage costs if the mortgage debt is scheduled to be repaid by retirement; (3) the elimination of costs associated with raising children (e.g., tuition and clothes); (4) the elimination of payroll costs (FICA); and (5) the elimination of savings, because the plan will require the use of accumulated savings. For some individuals, retirement can bring increased spending on travel and other lifestyle changes. Often, retirees are at risk for increases in health care costs. Exhibit 15.7 presents lists of potential decreasing and increasing costs when entering retirement.

EXHIBIT 15.7 Balancing Increasing and Decreasing Retirement Income Needs

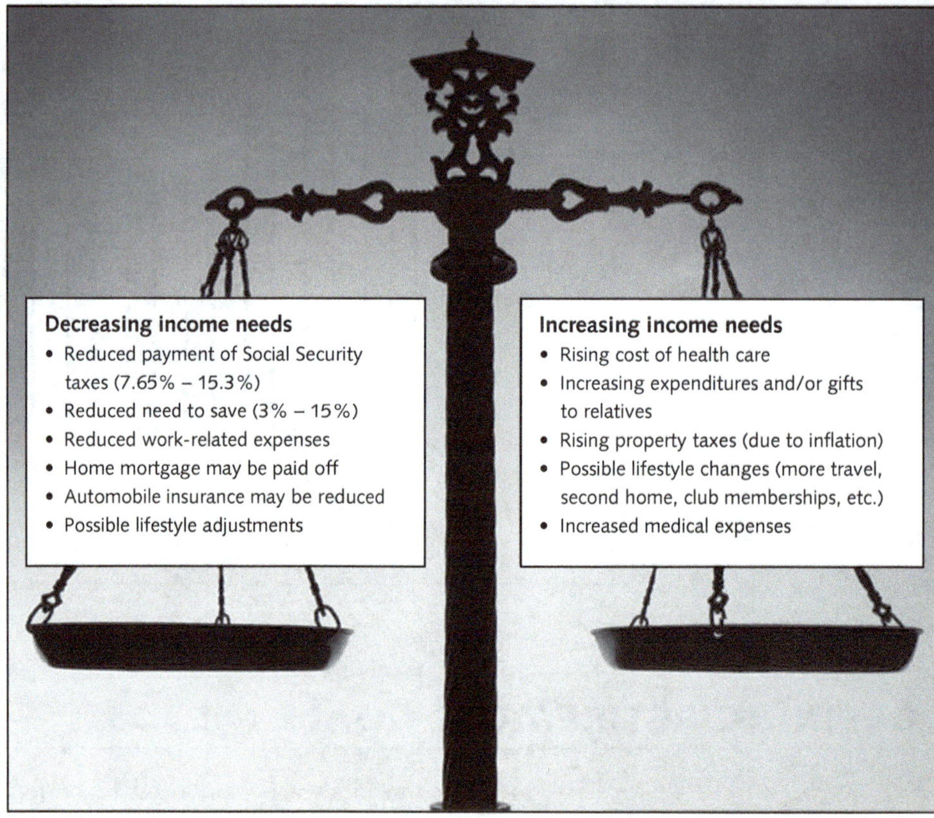

Planning for Retirement—Pretax or After Tax

Retirement needs may either be planned for on a pretax basis or an after-tax basis. Many financial planners calculate needs in pretax dollars believing that pretax is what their clients best understand. The pretax assumption is that clients are more likely to know their gross income than to know their net after-tax cash flow. Therefore, planners sometimes create retirement plans on a pretax basis, and the clients simply pay whatever income taxes for which they are liable out of their gross retirement income, similar to what clients do during preretirement years. Many CPAs think in terms of after-tax dollars and plan for retirement on an after-tax basis. After-tax planning assumes that income taxes are paid before other retirement needs. Planning can be effective either way as long as the client understands the difference between pretax and after-tax planning.

WAGE REPLACEMENT RATIO (WRR)

Wage replacement ratio (WRR)
An estimate of the percentage of income needed at retirement compared to earnings prior to retirement

The **wage replacement ratio (WRR)** is an estimate of the percentage of annual income needed during retirement compared to income earned prior to retirement. The wage replacement ratio or percentage is calculated by dividing the amount of money needed on an annual basis in retirement by the preretirement income. For example, if a client in the last year of work (prior to retirement) earns $100,000, and that client needs $80,000 in the first retirement year to maintain the same preretirement lifestyle, the wage replacement ratio (WRR) is 80% (80,000 ÷ 100,000).

Calculating the Wage Replacement Ratio

There are two methods to calculate the wage replacement ratio: the top-down approach and the budgeting approach (or bottom-up approach).

Top-Down Approach

The top-down approach is commonly used with younger clients where expenditure patterns are likely to change dramatically over time. As clients approach retirement age, a more precise wage replacement ratio should be calculated using a budgeting approach. This approach estimates the wage replacement ratio using common sense and percentages.

EXAMPLE To illustrate, assume a 40-year-old client earns $50,000 a year, pays 7.65% of his gross pay in Social Security payroll taxes, and saves 10% of his gross income annually. If we assume that any work-related savings resulting from retirement are expected to be completely offset by additional spending adjustments during retirement, and that the client wants to maintain his exact preretirement lifestyle, we would expect that the client would need a wage replacement ratio of 82.35% (100% – 7.65% – 10%).

$50,000	=	100.00%	of salary
(5,000)	=	(10.00%)	current savings
(3,825)	=	(7.65%)	payroll taxes
$41,175	=	82.35%	wage replacement ratio

Notice that the client is currently living on 82.35% of his gross pay. The remaining 17.65% is allocated to FICA taxes and savings. Therefore, the 82.35% is a reasonable estimate, or proxy, of the amount necessary, as a percentage of current income, to maintain the preretirement lifestyle.

Budgeting Approach

The second method used to calculate the wage replacement ratio is called the budgeting approach. This approach used with older clients because, as a person nears retirement, it is possible to examine the actual expenditure patterns of the individual. In cooperation with the client, the planner can determine which costs in the current (preretirement) budget will change (plus or minus) in the retirement budget and thus determine, with greater precision than the top-down approach, an estimate of actual retirement needs.

EXAMPLE Clients A and B each earn $100,000 in preretirement income. Client A has arranged her financial affairs so she will have no mortgage payment or car payment during retirement. Client B, on the other hand, expects to continue to have both a mortgage payment and a car payment throughout the majority of his retirement years. Exhibit 15.8 illustrates that Client A will need a 59.1% WRR, and Client B will need a 79.6% WRR. The difference is due to Client B's $15,000 mortgage payment and $5,500 car payment.

EXHIBIT 15.8 Budgeting Approach to Wage Replacement Ratio

	Clients A & B Budget	Client A Retirement Budget	Client B Retirement Budget
Annual income (current) budget	$100,000	$100,000	$100,000
Expenses:	Current	Retirement	Retirement
Income and payroll taxes	$27,650	$20,000	$20,000
Food	4,800	4,800	4,800
Utilities/phone	2,400	2,400	2,400
Mortgage	15,000	0	15,000
Health insurance	1,000	1,000	1,000
Auto insurance	1,000	1,000	1,000
Entertainment	5,000	5,000	5,000
Clothing	2,000	1,500	1,500
Auto maintenance/operation	1,000	750	750
Auto payment	5,500	0	5,500
Charity	4,800	4,800	4,800
Savings	12,000	0	0
Miscellaneous	17,850	17,850	17,850
Total expenses	$100,000	$59,100	$79,600
Wage replacement percentage needed		**59.1%**	**79.6%**

Does a person really need the same wage replacement percentage throughout the entire retirement period? There are clear indications that consumption slows dramatically as people age. The 70–80% wage replacement ratio is probably most appropriate from the beginning of retirement, regardless of age, until one's late 70s. A person's consumption beyond age 80 declines primarily as a result of limited mobility. Although this may be correct for society at large, certain individuals will incur dramatic medical costs during the latter part of their retirement period. Therefore, although most who study retirement expenditures would suggest a consumption function similar to the one provided in Exhibit 15.9, such a model may not apply to a particular individual.

EXHIBIT 15.9 Real Consumption by Age

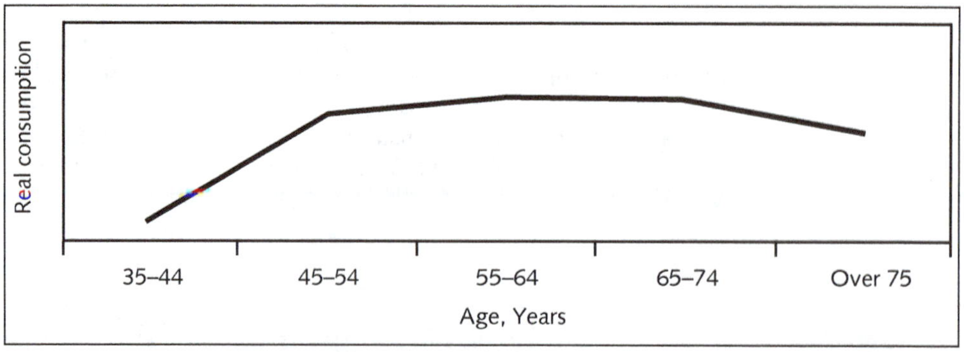

Exhibit 15.10 presents the adjustments from preretirement to retirement in terms of estimated percentages. Notice that many of the adjustments in Exhibit 15.10 will be client-specific.

EXHIBIT 15.10 Adjustments from Preretirement to Retirement

Adjustments to Expenditures Needed From Preretirement Income to Retirement Income	
Adjustments that decrease income needs:	
■ No longer pay Social Security taxes	Savings of 7.65–15.3%
■ No longer need to save for retirement	Savings of 3–15%
■ May no longer pay home mortgage	May decrease income needs
■ No longer pay work-related expenses	*
■ Auto insurance may be reduced	*
■ Possible lifestyle adjustments	*
Adjustments that may increase income needs:	
■ Increasing cost of health care	*
■ Lifestyle changes	*
■ Increase in travel	*
■ Second home	*
■ Clubs and activities	*
■ Expenditures on family/gifts/grandchildren	*
■ Increased property taxes	*
■ Need to continue saving for vehicle replacements/ maintenance and major home repairs/maintenance	*

* Amounts must be estimated for each individual.

Many financial planners conclude that most clients need at least 70–80% of their preretirement current income to retire and maintain their preretirement lifestyle. Although many clients would fall into this range, there are also those particularly frugal clients who may need as little as 40% of preretirement income and others who need substantially more than the 80% wage replacement ratio.

THE SOURCES OF RETIREMENT INCOME

Historically, retirees generally relied on three sources of income for retirement: Social Security, private pension plans, and personal savings. Today, the reality for many retirees is a fourth leg: working during retirement, either on a full- or part-time basis. Why the fourth leg? For some retirees who haven't saved enough for retirement, work is an economic necessity to help make ends meet. For other retirees, work is an optional activity that gives them something productive to do with their time. Surveys of baby boomers often show an expectation or willingness to work long past the traditional retirement ages of 62, 65, or even 70. Whatever their reasons, many retirees will include work during retirement as a part of their retirement plan. All four of these sources complement each other to provide adequate retirement income. Exhibit 15.11 shows the average amount of income for the average retiree from each of these four sources.

EXHIBIT 15.11 Retirement Income Sources

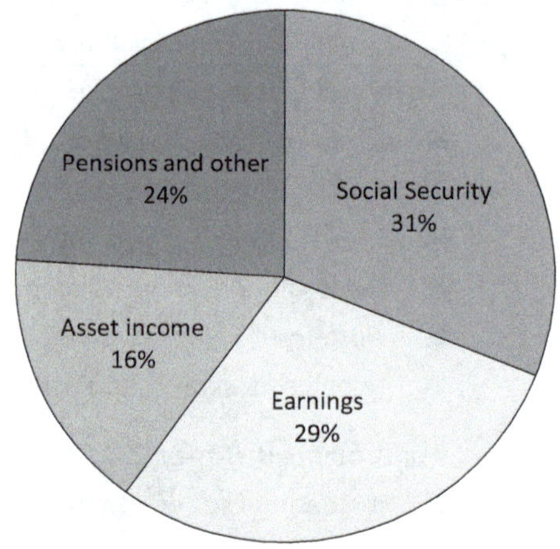

Source: Social Security Administration, *Fast Facts and Figures about Social Security*, 2015 (the latest update as of May, 2020)

Social Security

Social Security provides the foundation of retirement earnings. Social Security covers almost all occupational groups (except 25% of state and local government employees) with retirement benefits adjusting for inflation. It is considered the safety net of a secure income, but for most income levels it will not be a sufficient source of income replacement during retirement. As illustrated in Exhibit 15.12, Social Security may be an adequate wage replacement for lower-wage earners to maintain their lifestyle, but it is clearly inadequate to provide sufficient replacement income for middle- to upper-wage earners. (Social Security and Social Security benefits are covered in detail in Chapter 11.)

EXHIBIT 15.12 Social Security Retirement Benefits as a Percentage of Earnings

Base Year's Average Earnings	Annual Retirement Benefit	Percentage of Earnings Replaced
$20,000	$11,100	55.55%
$40,000	$15,228	29.36%
$80,000	$23,484	27.61%
$100,000	$27,612	27.61%
$200,000	$37,536	18.77%

Source: Social Security Administration Quick Benefit Calculator (www.ssa.gov)
Assumptions: Client was born in 1956 and retires in 2022.

Private Pension and Company-Sponsored Retirement Plans

Private pension plans are the second source of retirement income. Private pension plans provided by employers are covered in Chapter 16. As you will see, private pension plans have dramatically changed over the last few years from employer-sponsored and funded plans to employee self-reliance plans, putting more and more emphasis on personal savings as the primary source of retirement income for middle- to upper-wage workers.

Personal Savings

Personal savings is the third source of retirement income and the one most influenced by the individual. The more personal savings put aside for retirement, the larger the accumulation at retirement and the larger the retirement income for the individual.

Whenever a retiree has income from invested assets, it can mean a substantially higher overall retirement income. The median income of those retirees with asset income is more than twice as large as the income of retirees with no asset income. As Exhibit 15.13 illustrates, retirees without asset income are concentrated in the lowest income categories.

EXHIBIT 15.13 Income Categories of Retirees

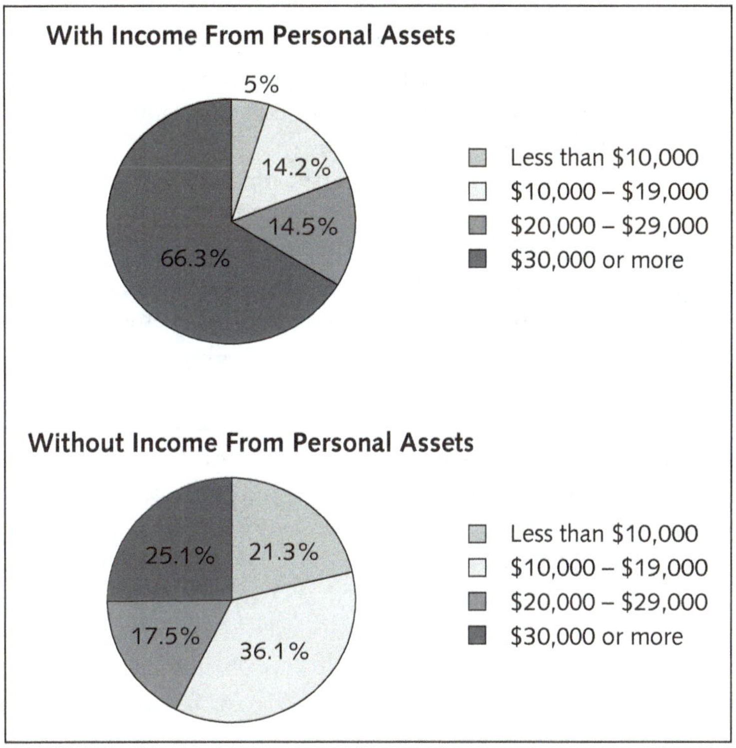

Source: Social Security Administration, *Income of the Aged Chartbook*

WORK

According to the U.S. Bureau of Labor Statistics, over 40% of Americans age 55 and older were employed in 2017. Though many preretirees expect to work during their traditional retirement years, the unfortunate reality is that unpredictable events such as layoffs, downsizing, illness, and family obligations often curtail their plans.

QUALITATIVE FACTORS IN RETIREMENT—ADVISING CLIENTS

Qualitative factors associated with retirement are no less important than the financial or quantitative factors. Qualitative factors include involuntary versus voluntary retirement, emotional and psychological factors such as loss of self-esteem and boredom, and the decision to relocate.

The best overall advice financial planners can give their clients is to know themselves and their support systems, have a well-planned qualitative plan for retirement, and have a system in place to maintain their egos and self-esteem. Many individuals in our culture define themselves by what they do. The mere act of going to work may be a ritual or a habit that provides that person with a sense of self-worth and a purpose in life. A trusted colleague at the workplace may be a source of support and personal gratification. Voluntary retirement, even when well planned, means change—and change is often difficult.

Involuntary retirement, if perceived as undesirable, can have as devastating an impact on an individual as the death of a loved one or a bitter divorce. The client may follow the same psychological pattern of grief: shock, anger, denial, and acceptance. Financial planning professionals need to be aware of the emotional affect retirement can have on clients and realize that when an individual is emotionally troubled, major decisions—financial or otherwise—are sometimes best delayed. Rather than abruptly making important financial decisions, it may be better to do minimal financial maneuvering during a grieving period. Such grieving may last for a period of a year or longer. Trying to optimize the financial situation when the client is emotionally unable to determine her goals or priorities is probably counterproductive and may add stress to the situation.

A client's decision to change physical locations after retirement (for example, move to another state) should be carefully considered over a long period of planning. Some retirees do not realize that when they move, they will have a completely new environment to adjust to, as well as a substantial loss of their former support system of friends and family. An individual who is considering moving should conduct a trial transition over a number of years, spending increasingly longer periods at the desired location. This gradual adjustment will help determine whether what the retiree believes will actually enhance retirement will, in fact, be true. Persons considering retiring abroad will encounter even more of a challenge, thereby necessitating more detailed planning.

SUMMARY OF FACTORS AFFECTING RETIREMENT PLANNING

Financial planners may encounter clients who subjectively "feel" they are financially secure because they have a good job and/or a good net worth. If a good job is lost through premature death, disability, layoff, termination, unexpected illness, or other events, or if the net worth decreases dramatically, the client's financial security is suddenly lost. In most instances, the client's actual determination of financial security is subjective rather than objective. Therefore, the financial planner must be the intermediary between the client's subjective feelings and the overall objective of financial security.

Other factors that complicate the retirement planning process include at least two societal issues. Society has become more mobile with the traditional family unit deteriorating. Having lost the close connection to family, older individuals may not be able to depend on family members to provide retirement assistance. Thus, there is a greater need for financial independence for each individual. In addition, because society seems to place more value on youth than on age and wisdom in the workplace, retirees have less chance of being hired for part-time employment, which could supplement retirement income.

Many people begin planning for retirement too late in life and save too little to effectively meet retirement capital accumulation needs. Some people do not even consider retirement funding until they are in their 40s. Even when people do save, many of them make poor investment choices and, therefore, have poor investment returns.

In addition, inflation erodes purchasing power. For recipients of fixed incomes, inflation is like a progressive tax causing declining purchasing power. Exhibit 15.14 lists the factors that challenge effective retirement planning and the negative impact associated with each factor.

EXHIBIT 15.14 Factors that Negatively Affect Retirement Planning and their Impact on the Planning Process

Factor	Impact
Reduced WLE	Insufficient savings period
Increased RLE	Increased capital needs
Reduced family reliance	Fewer alternatives in retirement
Reduced ability to work	Fewer alternatives in retirement
Planned too late	Fewer compounding periods
Low savings rate	Unable to meet capital requirements
Inflation	Reduced purchasing power
Poor earnings rate and asset allocation	Unable to meet capital requirements

Long-term financial security does not happen automatically. It requires careful planning, a clear understanding of quantified goals, and identification and management of the risks involved. Retirement planning requires the collection, analysis, and projection of data and must be conducted meticulously and conservatively.

RISKS TO FINANCIAL INDEPENDENCE

There are many risks to achieving financial independence. Selected risks are identified in Exhibit 15.15. People should begin saving at an early age, save a sufficient amount, invest wisely, and not underestimate retirement needs or the impact of inflation. The risks identified in Part B of Exhibit 15.15 are more thoroughly discussed in the chapters on risk management and insurance.

EXHIBIT 15.15 Summary of Factors Affecting Retirement Planning

Factor	Risk	Mitigator
	Part A: Risks Discussed in this Chapter	
Work Life Expectancy (WLE)	Shortened because of untimely death, disability, health, unemployment	Life insurance, disability insurance, health insurance, education, training, experience, diet, exercise
Retirement Life Expectancy (RLE)	Lengthened	Adequate capital accumulation, possible immediate annuity
Savings rate, amount, and timing	Too low and too late	Save more; start early; asset allocation
Inflation	Greater than expected	Realistically project inflation rate and income needs
Retirement income needs	Underestimated	Use wage replacement estimators
Investment returns	Inadequate to amass needed retirement capital	Knowledge of investments; broad portfolio of diversified investments and proper asset allocation
Sources of retirement income	Overestimation of Social Security benefits, private pension plans, work or personal income (or adverse changes in taxation of such income)	Conservatively estimate and plan for such income; monitor income projections and tax policy
	Part B: Risks Discussed in Risk Management and Insurance Chapters	
Qualitative factors including changes in lifestyle, employment, and major assets	Unexpected cost increases due to changes in personal situation; losses due to perils	Plan conservatively to provide for the unexpected; property and liability insurance

CAPITAL NEEDS ANALYSIS

Capital needs analysis
The process of calculating the amount of investment capital needed at retirement to maintain the desired lifestyle and mitigate the impact of inflation during the retirement years

Capital needs analysis is the process of calculating the amount of investment capital needed at retirement to maintain the desired lifestyle and mitigate the impact of inflation during the retirement years. There are three commonly used models for analyzing capital needs: the pure annuity model, the capital preservation model, and the purchasing power preservation model.

Basic Planning—Pure Annuity Model

The following steps are used to determine the capital necessary at the beginning of retirement to fund the retirement period:

Step 1 Calculate WRR. Determine the wage replacement ratio (WRR) today using one of the two methods identified earlier (top-down or budgeting).

Step 2 Determine gross dollar needs. Determine the wage replacement amount in today's dollars from Step 1.

Step 3 Determine net dollar needs. Reduce the result from Step 2 by any expected Social Security benefits in today's dollars or other benefits that are indexed to inflation.

Step 4 Calculate preretirement dollar needs adjusted for inflation. Inflate the result from Step 3 to the retirement age at the CPI rate to determine the first annual retirement payment.

Step 5 Calculate capital needed at retirement age. Calculate the present value at retirement of an annuity due (BEGin mode) for an annual payment equal to the result from Step 4 over the full retirement life expectancy (estimate life expectancy conservatively at 90–95) and use the inflation-adjusted earnings rate.

Step 6 Determine the amount to save during the work life expectancy. Discount the capital needed at retirement using the savings rate and investment earnings rate, being mindful as to whether the client is expected to save annually or more frequently, and whether the client is expected to save under an annuity due or an ordinary annuity scheme.

EXAMPLE Mary Jones, age 41, currently earns $80,000. Her wage replacement ratio is determined to be 80%. She expects that inflation will average 3% for her entire life expectancy. She expects to earn 10% on her investments and retire at age 62, living possibly to age 90. She has sent for and received her Social Security benefit statement, which indicated that her Social Security retirement benefit in today's dollars adjusted for early retirement is $12,000 per year.

1. Calculate Mary's capital needed at retirement at age 62.
2. Calculate the amount she must save monthly, at month end, assuming she has no current savings to accumulate the capital needed for retirement at age 62.
3. Calculate the amount she must save monthly, at month end, assuming that she has $50,000 in current retirement savings.

Calculate her capital needed at retirement at age 62.

Step 1	80% WRR		
Step 2	($80,000 × 0.80)	=	$64,000 Total needs in today's dollars
Step 3			−12,000 Less Social Security in today's dollars
			$52,000 Annual amount needed in today's dollars
Step 4	*n*	=	21 (62 − 41)
	i	=	3 (inflation rate)
	PV	=	$52,000 (Step 3)
	PMT	=	0
	FV	=	$96,735.32 (Step 4) First-year needs for retirement
Step 5	*n*	=	28 (90 − 62)
	i	=	6.7961 {[(1 + earnings rate) ÷ (1 + inflation rate)] − 1} × 100 [(1.10 ÷ 1.03) − 1] × 100
	FV	=	0
	PMT_{AD}	=	$96,735.32 (from Step 4)
	$PV_{AD@62}$	=	$1,278,954.46 (Step 5 – amount needed at age 62)

Calculate the amount she must save monthly, at month end, assuming she has no current savings to accumulate the capital needed for retirement at age 62.

$FV_{@62}$	=	$1,278,954.46 (from Step 5)
n	=	252 (21 years × 12 months)
i	=	0.8333 (10 ÷ 12) I/YR is 10%
PV	=	0
PMT_{OA}	=	$1,502.09 (monthly savings necessary)

Calculate the amount she must save monthly, at month end, assuming she has $50,000 in current retirement savings.

$FV_{@62}$	= $1,278,954.46
n	= 252
i	= 0.8333
PV	= −$50,000
PMT_{OA}	= $1,026.70 (monthly savings necessary)

Accurate Assumptions Are Essential

Assumptions are made for the wage replacement ratio, the work life expectancy, the retirement life expectancy, inflation, investment earnings, Social Security, and any other benefits. If these assumptions are inaccurate, the projection using those assumptions will be flawed. The wage replacement ratio should be carefully calculated, especially for a client near retirement. Estimating life expectancy usually begins with the IRS tables and is conservatively estimated at 90–95, owing to the risk of outliving retirement money. Where family history indicates a particularly long life expectancy, that age could be increased. The estimate of the work life expectancy is critical, as one less year of work means one less year of retirement savings and account growth. It also means one more year of retirement withdrawals. Conversely, working one additional year or so may make an otherwise unworkable retirement plan work quite nicely because of the additional year of savings, the additional year of earnings accumulation, and one less year of consumption.

The assumptions regarding inflation and earnings rates are obviously essential ingredients in capital needs analysis. Historical data are available for inflation; however, inflation is difficult to predict. Perhaps the best estimate is the inflation rate from the most recent three to five years. Investment earnings rates are dependent on the client's asset allocation and the markets but can be estimated for a well-diversified portfolio over a long period. Conservatively estimating inflation (increase it a bit) and earnings (decrease a bit) is wise in retirement planning. Such estimation provides a little conservatism in case one or more of the assumptions are not realized. Social Security benefits and pension benefits that are inflation protected should be carefully determined and documented. The retirement plan and capital needs analysis can be adjusted on an annual basis as information becomes more certain.

As one might expect, small changes in earnings, life expectancy, and needs may have a dramatic impact on the retirement plan. The uncertainty of these assumptions can be accommodated in some of the latest retirement planning software packages that incorporate Monte Carlo analysis (MCA). MCA uses a random-number generator for data input into a software package that will provide an output with specific probabilities of outcomes. MCA provides insight into the most likely outcome, but with other possible outcomes. This analysis provides the financial planner with a best-case scenario and a worst-case scenario with which to make decisions.

Advanced Planning—Capital Preservation (CP) Model

Pure annuity model
The basic capital needs analysis approach that is generally prepared on a pretax basis

The basic capital needs analysis is a **pure annuity model**, generally prepared on a pretax basis. The annuity concept means that if all of the assumptions occur exactly as expected, the person will die exactly at the assumed life expectancy with a retirement account balance of zero. There is a substantial risk that many clients could outlive their assets using this annuity approach. Therefore, they will actually need more money at retirement. Two models used to mitigate the risk of outliving money are the capital pres-

Capital preservation (CP) model
This model maintains the original balance needed at retirement under the pure annuity model for the entire retirement life expectancy.

ervation model and the purchasing power preservation model. The **capital preservation model** maintains the original balance needed at retirement under the pure annuity model for the entire retirement life expectancy. The purchasing power preservation model maintains the purchasing power of the original pure annuity capital balance at retirement for the entire retirement life expectancy. In spite of any conservatism that we may have built into the annuity model with our assumptions, it is always possible that one or more of our assumptions will be unrealized. To mitigate the risk of the assumptions being overly optimistic, we can make use of a capital preservation model or a purchasing power preservation model rather than a simple annuity model to determine capital needs. These two additional models help to overcome the risks of the pure annuity model (primarily, the risk of running out of money, or superannuation).

Recall that the capital amount needed under the pure annuity model for Mary Jones at age 62 calculated was $1,278,954.46. If we discount that amount at the expected earnings rate of 10%, we can then determine the additional amount of capital necessary to leave an estate of $1,278,954.46 at the projected life expectancy.

$n = 28$

$i = 10$

$FV_{@90}$ = $1,278,954.46 (amount at life expectancy)

$PV_{@62}$ = $88,686.99

1,367,641.45 = 88,686.99 + 1,278,954.46 (amount needed for capital preservation model)

Thus, the capital preservation model will require $88,686.99 more at retirement than the pure annuity model, but it will reduce the risk of superannuation. Such an increase in capital will also require that savings be increased in Exhibit 15.16 that presents parts B and C of the Mary Jones example.

EXHIBIT 15.16 Comparison of the Capital Preservation Model with the Annuity Model (Mary Jones)

	CP Model		Annuity Model	
	No savings B	Savings C	No savings B	Savings C
$FV_{@62}$	$1,367,641.45	$1,367,641.45	$1,278,954.46	$1,278,954.46
n	252	252	252	252
i	0.8333	0.8333	0.8333	0.8333
PV	0	–$50,000	0	–$50,000
PMT_{OA}	$1,606.25	$1,130.86	$1,502.09	$1,026.70

Even though the capital preservation model would increase the savings need of Mary Jones by about $100 per month, it would diminish many of the risks in the traditional capital needs annuity approach.

Advanced Planning—Purchasing Power Preservation (PPP) Model

Purchasing power preservation (PPP) model
A capital needs analysis method that assumes the client will have a capital balance of equal purchasing power at life expectancy as he did at retirement

An even more conservative approach to capital needs analysis is the **purchasing power preservation model.**

The calculation steps under the purchasing power preservation model are essentially the same as the steps in the capital preservation model, with the exception that an inflation-adjusted interest rate is used.

$n = 28$

$i = 6.7961$

FV = 1,278,954.46

PMT = \$96,735.32 (amount needed the first year of retirement)

$PV_{AD@62}$ = \$1,481,866.64 (capital needed for purchasing power preservation model)

The additional accumulation at retirement using a purchasing power model is \$202,912.18 greater than the pure annuity approach.

The amounts in B and C in the exhibit would change.

EXHIBIT 15.17 Comparison of the Purchasing Power Preservation Model with the Annuity Model (Mary Jones)

	PPP model		Annuity model	
	No savings	Savings	No savings	Savings
	B	C	B	C
$FV_{@62}$	\$1,481,866.64	\$1,481,866.64	\$1,278,954.46	\$1,278,954.46
n	252	252	252	252
i	0.8333	0.8333	0.8333	0.8333
PV	0	−\$50,000	0	−\$50,000
PMT_{OA}	\$1,740.41	\$1,265.02	\$1,502.09	\$1,026.70

EXHIBIT 15.18 Capital Needs Analysis Summary for Mary Jones

	Annuity model	CP model	PPP model
Capital needed at retirement (A)	\$1,278,954.46	\$1,367,641.45	\$1,481,866.64
Monthly savings with no initial balance (B)	\$1,502.09	\$1,606.25	\$1,740.41
Monthly savings with \$50,000 initial balance (C)	\$1,026.70	\$1,130.86	\$1,265.02

There are other methods of alleviating risk in projections, including sensitivity analysis, that are beyond the scope of this text, most of which would be covered in a full semester course on retirement planning.

WHERE ON THE WEB

AARP (formerly American Association of Retired Persons) **www.aarp.org**

American Society on Aging **www.asaging.org**

International Foundation for Retirement Education **www.infre.org**

MSN.money: Retirement and Wills
www.moneycentral.msn.com/retire/home.asp

National Council on Aging **www.ncoa.org**

Senior Law Homepage **www.seniorlaw.com**

Social Security Online **www.ssa.gov**

The Retire Early Homepage **www.retireearlyhomepage.com**

U.S. Administration on Aging **www.aoa.gov**

U.S. Census Bureau **www.census.gov**

DISCUSSION QUESTIONS

1. What is the U.S. savings rate?
2. List the steps necessary to calculate capital needs analysis.
3. What is the difference between capital needs analysis prepared on an annuity basis and capital needs analysis prepared using a capital preservation model? A purchasing power preservation model?
4. What are the four sources of retirement income?
5. What are the two methods for determining the wage replacement ratio?
6. Which method for determining the wage replacement ratio is appropriate for a client who is 50 years old? Why?
7. How is financial security defined?
8. List the financial factors that affect retirement planning.
9. Should retirement planning (capital needs analysis) be prepared on a pretax basis or an after-tax basis? Why?
10. What percentage of retirement income is provided by Social Security for the average retiree?
11. Does Social Security favor lower-wage or higher-wage individuals in terms of retirement benefits and wage replacement? How and why?
12. What is one of the main goals for many individuals regarding personal financial planning?
13. When is financial security realized?
14. What is the WLE?
15. What is the RWLE?
16. How has life expectancy changed over the past century?
17. How and why does the timing of savings affect the ultimate amount of accumulation?
18. How does inflation affect retirement planning?
19. What adjustments are normally made to the preretirement budget to arrive at the retirement budget?
20. What is the wage replacement ratio?
21. Does the wage replacement ratio remain constant over the retirement life expectancy?
22. What wage replacement ratio does Social Security provide for a worker with $20,000 income?
23. What is capital needs analysis?
24. What advanced models are used to perform capital needs analysis?

EXERCISES

1. Donna, age 45, is self-employed and earns $70,000 annually. She is fairly settled in her lifestyle. She currently saves 15% of her gross income. Her mortgage payment (principal and interest) is fixed at $1,166.67 per month. She has scheduled her mortgage payments to cease at retirement. On the basis of the information given, what do you expect Donna's wage replacement ratio to be?

2. Kim, age 30, begins saving $2,500 per year at year-end, continues for 8 years, and then stops saving. Joy, age 40, begins saving $2,500 per year at year-end and saves continuously until age 65. Assume that both Kim and Joy earn a 12% return compounded annually. Calculate the total amount of savings and the accumulated balance for Kim and Joy, respectively, at age 65. Explain the difference.

Use the following information for Exercises 3–10:

Mike, age 48, has $60,000 saved for retirement. He is currently saving 10% of his annual income of $50,000 on a monthly basis. His employer matches his savings contributions with $1,500 annually, paid on a monthly basis. Mike projects that inflation will be 3.5%, and he can earn 9.5% before and during retirement. Mike needs a wage replacement ratio of 75% of his preretirement income. He plans to retire at age 62 with Social Security benefits of $10,000 in today's dollars. His life expectancy is age 90.

3. How much will Mike's salary be at age 62, assuming his income increases yearly equal to the inflation rate?

4. How much are the Social Security benefits expected to be at age 62?

5. What will be Mike's retirement income need in the first year of retirement, taking into consideration his anticipated Social Security income?

6. How much capital will Mike need at age 62 to fund his retirement?

7. How much will Mike have at age 62, assuming he continues his current savings and investment program?

8. How much additional monthly savings would be required for Mike to retire at age 62?

9. After reflection, Mike wants to know at what age he can retire, assuming he continues to follow his current savings plan. Make a schedule for years 62, 64, and 66 so Mike can make some informed decisions.

10. You remind Mike that if he waits until age 66 to retire, he will receive $14,344 in Social Security benefits in today's dollars rather than the reduced benefit of $10,000 he would receive at age 62. Would this additional cash flow suggest that he could retire at age 66, or perhaps earlier?

11. Marion, age 65, is a pensioner who receives a fixed pension of $17,500 for life from her employer's pension plan. Marion also receives $12,000 currently from Social Security. Marion is concerned about how inflation will affect her rent, food, and other expenses. She estimates that inflation will be 3% per year for the next 10 years. What loss of purchasing power will she have in today's dollars in 10 years?

12. George, a financial planner, has determined that Dennis, his client, needs $2 million at age 66 to retire by using an annuity model based on a retirement income of $150,337.75 per year for 24 years to age 90. If the earnings rate was 10% and the inflation rate was 3%, what additional amount would be needed at age 66 to provide a capital preservation model solution?

13. Referring to Exercise 12, what additional amount would Dennis need at age 66 to fund a purchasing power presentation model?

PROBLEMS

Bill, age 45, wants to retire at age 60. He currently earns $60,000 per year. His goal is to replace 80% of his preretirement income. He wants the retirement income to be adjusted for inflation. Bill has an investment portfolio valued at $150,000, which is currently earning 10% average annual returns. Bill expects inflation to average 3% and, based on his family health, predicts he will live to age 90. Bill is currently saving 7% of his gross income at each year-end and expects to continue this level of savings. Bill wants to ignore any Social Security benefits for purposes of retirement planning.

1. What will Bill's annual income needs be at age 60?
2. Will the need be for an ordinary annuity or an annuity due?
3. How much total capital will Bill need at age 60?
4. How much capital will Bill have at age 60?
5. Will Bill have enough income at retirement?
6. What is the earliest age that Bill could retire utilizing the current savings and investment plan?
7. How much would Bill need to increase his savings on an annual basis to meet his goal of retiring at age 60?
8. Even assuming that Bill increases his savings to an appropriate amount, what are the risks that may affect the success of the plan?
9. How could the capital needs analysis be modified to reduce the risks identified above?

CHAPTER 16

Basic Retirement Plans

LEARNING OBJECTIVES

After learning the material in this chapter, you will be able to do the following:

- Describe a qualified retirement plan
- Identify and articulate the characteristics of qualified retirement plans
- Describe some disadvantages of qualified retirement plans
- Define vesting and list two accepted vesting schedules
- Identify the reasons for the creation of qualified retirement plans
- Calculate and determine the benefits of tax deferral in a qualified retirement plan
- Identify the various types of qualified retirement plans
- Distinguish between pension and profit-sharing plans
- Distinguish between defined benefit plans and defined contribution plans
- Distinguish between noncontributory and contributory plans
- Describe the operations and benefits of a Section 401(k) plan

- Distinguish between Keogh and corporate plans
- Identify other tax-advantaged retirement plans
- Describe IRAs, SEPs, SIMPLEs, and Section 403(b) plans
- Describe distributions from qualified retirement plans and other tax-advantaged retirement plans
- Describe and identify nonqualified plans
- Clarify why nonqualified plans are useful to employers

RETIREMENT PLANS

In the previous retirement chapter, we discussed the four general sources of funding used to provide retirement income: Social Security, private retirement plans, personal savings, and earned income from employment. We determined that the retirement benefits from Social Security alone provided a poor wage replacement ratio during retirement except for those beneficiaries who are the lowest wage earners. This chapter provides an introduction to private retirement plans, including qualified retirement plans, other tax-advantaged retirement plans, and nonqualified plans. Exhibit 16.1 illustrates the various types of retirement plans.

EXHIBIT 16.1 Retirement Plans

Qualified Plans		Tax-Advantaged Plans	Nonqualified Plans
Pension Plans	**Profit-Sharing Plans**		
Traditional defined benefit pension	Profit-sharing plans	SEPs	Nonqualified deferred compensation plans
Cash balance pension plans	Stock bonus plans	IRAs (including Roth)	Nonqualified stock option plans
Money purchase pension plans	ESOPs	Section 403(b) plans (including Roth)	Incentive stock option plans
Target benefit pension plans	Section 401(k) plans	SIMPLE (IRA)	Phantom stock plans
DB(k) plans	Thrift plans	SIMPLE 401(k)	Restricted stock
	SIMPLE 401(k)	Roth 401(k)	Employee stock purchase plans (ESPP)
	Age-based, profit-sharing plans		Junior class shares
			Stock appreciation rights (SARs)
			Section 457 plans

QUALIFIED RETIREMENT PLANS

Qualified retirement plans are sponsored by either a self-employed individual or another employer. The word qualified means the plan meets Internal Revenue Service requirements. To encourage retirement savings, Congress has created or approved various types of qualified plans that provide tax advantages for the employer who sponsors the plan and the employees who participate in the plan.

Exhibit 16.2 summarizes the advantages and disadvantages of qualified plans.

EXHIBIT 16.2 Advantages and Disadvantages of Qualified Retirement Plans

Advantages/Rules	Disadvantages	Limits
Employer contributions are deductible	Costs	***Covered Compensation***
Employer contributions are not subject to payroll taxes	Limits	$305,000 (2022)
	Min. participation reqs.	***Defined Benefit***
Employee contributions are pretax (except Roth and thrift)		$245,000 (2022)
	Min. vesting reqs.	***Defined Contribution***
Earnings are tax deferred	Top-heavy rules	Lesser of 100% comp. or $61,000 (2022)
10-year forward averaging or pre-1974 capital gains treatment	Minimum contribution rules	***Salary Deferral****
ERISA protection	Reporting reqs.	$20,500 (2022)
Net unrealized appreciation	Disclosure reqs.	Sections 401(k), 403(b), 457, and SARSEP
	Nondiscrimination reqs.	
	Highly compensated limits	*Before catch-up contribution
	Minimum coverage reqs.	
	Testing reqs.	**Testing**
	Key employee limits	50/40 Coverage Test—DB Plans
	Employee contributions and salary deferrals are subject to payroll taxes	Ratio % Test
		Average Benefit % Test
		Section 401(k) ACP
		Section 401(k) ADP

Characteristics of Qualified Retirement Plans

Employer Contributions Are NOT Subject to Federal Income Tax

Unlike most business transactions that result in an income tax deduction for one party and taxable income for another party, contributions made to qualified retirement plans result in a mismatch of income and deductions. Employer contributions to a qualified plan are deductible by the employer for income tax purposes for the year in which they were made, but they are not included in current employee taxable income until distributed to the employee. This favorable tax treatment is a major advantage for both employers and employees. Employers receive a current deduction for the contribution, whereas employees receive deferral of income. Because of this favorable tax treatment, however, qualified retirement plans must satisfy numerous nondiscrimination requirements to ensure a certain percentage of the nonhighly compensated employees are benefiting from the plan.

Employer Contributions Are NOT Subject to Payroll Tax

Another major advantage of contributions to qualified retirement plans is that employer contributions are not subject to payroll tax. This means compensation in the form of qualified retirement plan contributions will avoid the expense for the Federal Insurance Contributions Act (FICA). Such avoidance benefits both the employer and the employee because both parties are required to pay this tax. If the same amount of money contributed to a qualified retirement plan is paid as employee compensation, then both the employer and the employee would be required to pay FICA taxes.

Employee Pretax Contributions Are NOT Subject to Federal Income Tax

Similar to employer contributions, employee contributions to qualified retirement plans generally are not includable in the employee's current taxable income. Therefore, employees can save a portion of their income on a pretax basis. Income contributed to a qualified retirement plan will avoid federal and, in most cases, state income taxes at the time of deferral to a qualified retirement plan. An example of a qualified retirement plan that allows these pretax employee contributions is the Section 401(k) plan. There are certain other qualified retirement plans that provide for employee after-tax contributions, such as thrift plans, Roth 401(k) plans, and certain defined benefit plans.

Employee Contributions ARE Subject to Payroll Tax

Unlike the payroll tax treatment of employer contributions, employee contributions to qualified retirement plans generally are subject to payroll tax. Therefore, contributions made by employees will be subject to FICA taxes for both the employer and the employee. This is why an employee's Form W-2 may have different income amounts for federal income tax and Social Security purposes.

EXHIBIT 16.3 Form W-2

22222	a Employee's social security number	OMB No. 1545-0008	
b Employer identification number (EIN)		1 Wages, tips, other compensation	2 Federal income tax withheld
c Employer's name, address, and ZIP code		3 Social security wages	4 Social security tax withheld
		5 Medicare wages and tips	6 Medicare tax withheld
		7 Social security tips	8 Allocated tips
d Control number		9	10 Dependent care benefits
e Employee's first name and initial Last name Suff.		11 Nonqualified plans	12a Code
		13 Statutory employee / Retirement plan / Third-party sick pay	12b Code
		14 Other	12c Code
f Employee's address and ZIP code			12d Code

15 State Employer's state ID number	16 State wages, tips, etc.	17 State income tax	18 Local wages, tips, etc.	19 Local income tax	20 Locality name

Form **W-2** **Wage and Tax Statement** 2022 Department of the Treasury—Internal Revenue Service

Copy 1—For State, City, or Local Tax Department

Tax-Deferred Growth

Assets that are contributed to a qualified retirement plan are held in trust for the benefit of the participants or their beneficiaries. Qualified retirement plan trusts are tax-exempt entities; therefore, the earnings accruing from contributions from both employers and employees grow income tax deferred until distributed. The tax-deferred growth of both contributions and earnings is a significant benefit provided by qualified retirement plans.

Special Income Tax Averaging

There is a provision for special 10-year-forward income tax averaging on lump-sum distributions made from qualified retirement plans. This provision may reduce the federal income tax liability for taxpayers taking a full and complete distribution from a qualified retirement plan. Only those taxpayers who were born before January 2, 1936, however, are eligible for this special provision.

In addition to receiving special income tax averaging, taxpayers born before January 2, 1936, may also be eligible to receive capital gains treatment on a portion of their lump-sum distribution. The portion of a distribution that may receive capital gains treatment is that which is attributable to participation in the qualified plan before 1974. Because of this qualifying date, fewer clients will qualify for this special tax treatment each year.

Net Unrealized Appreciation

In general, distributions from qualified retirement plans are made in cash and are taxable as ordinary income. There is an exception, however, for lump-sum distributions of employer securities (generally stock) that have appreciated while being held in a qualified retirement plan. When such securities are distributed (typically in the form of a lump-sum distribution) from a qualified retirement plan, the appreciation above the cost basis, called net unrealized appreciation (NUA), is not subject to income tax upon distribution. In addition, the net unrealized appreciation will be taxed as a capital gain (not as ordinary income), when the securities are subsequently sold. With the large disparity between ordinary income tax rates and capital gains tax rates, this exception provides significant benefits to taxpayers who receive qualifying distributions of employer securities. However, this special treatment is not available for distributions from individual retirement accounts (IRAs). Therefore, a rollover of otherwise qualifying securities from a qualified retirement plan to an IRA will eliminate this potential benefit. It is important to note, however, that the cost basis in these shares (the value of the shares at the time of contribution to the plan) is taxed as ordinary income at the time of the lump-sum distribution.

ERISA Protection

Assets held in a qualified retirement plan are protected from creditors by the Employee Retirement Income Security Act (ERISA). ERISA prohibits the alienation of benefits, which means that the benefits of the qualified retirement plan may be used only by the participant or by the participant's family members. Therefore, even those unfortunate individuals who are forced into bankruptcy have protection for their qualified retirement plan assets. In 2005, the Bankruptcy Abuse Prevention and Consumer Protection Act (BAPCPA) created protection for up to $1 million (indexed) for contributory IRAs and unlimited protection for eligible IRA rollovers.

Small Business Tax Credit

America has a huge problem. About 40% of American workers are employed by firms that do not offer a retirement plan for their workers. To help alleviate this problem, the law offers an income tax credit to small employers to encourage them to start offering a retirement plan. The previous law was updated in 2022 by the SECURE Act. Now the employer's tax credit for retirement plan start-up costs is the lesser of 50% of the qualified plan start-up costs or the greater of $500 or $250 times the number of nonhighly compensated employees eligible to participate in the plan.

Retirement Plans as Part of a Compensation Package

From the perspective of the employees in the labor market, many qualified retirement plans essentially have become part of their overall compensation package. The employee recognizes the need for retirement savings and typically accepts an overall compensation package as salary, retirement plan, and other employee fringe benefits, rather than just salary.

This does not suggest that the employee chooses the qualified retirement plan. The employer chooses the type of qualified retirement plan, and it usually becomes part of an overall compensation package offered to current and future employees. The employees then evaluate the complete compensation package, given their personal goals and opportunity costs, to make appropriate employment decisions. Today, employees are aware of the benefits of using a qualified retirement plan's taxable income deferral as an alternative to receiving additional current compensation, which would be currently subject to income tax.

In the late 1990s, many employees chose to work for companies that provided minimal salaries but offered employee stock options. Employees recognized these high-tech companies as having tremendous growth potential. Employees were willing to sacrifice current income in hopes that their employer's stock would appreciate significantly enough to compensate them for their current sacrifice of higher salaries elsewhere.

Microsoft is a good example of this phenomenon. Base salaries were small, but the right to participate in the ownership of the company was tremendously enticing to potential employees. As it turns out, many of these employees became quite wealthy because of their stock options and other fringe benefits.

Disadvantages of Qualified Retirement Plans

Qualified retirement plans were created by Congress to provide incentives for employers to sponsor and promote retirement savings. Congress has known for some time that Social Security would not provide an adequate wage replacement for many workers. However, whenever Congress creates a plan that proffers income tax relief or tax advantage, there are usually costs, limitations, or disadvantages to the successful implementation of such a plan. Some of these disadvantages are discussed next.

Costs to Qualify the Plan

To establish a qualified retirement plan, employers must have a legal plan document drafted by a pension attorney or one preapproved by the IRS (a prototype plan). The plan document sets forth the rules for administration of the plan, provides for how benefits are earned and allocated to employees, and names the classes of employees that will benefit under the plan. Generally, there are attorney costs to having a plan document drafted. A determination letter is often obtained from the Internal Revenue Service (IRS) to ensure that the plan meets the requirements of Internal Revenue Code (IRC) Section 401(a).

The determination letter assures the plan sponsor that the plan meets the requirements to be a qualified retirement plan. EGTRRA 2001 allows some small employers to receive determination letters without paying a fee.

Many financial institutions have prototype plans available to their clients. Prototype plans are qualified retirement plan documents that have already been approved by the IRS as meeting the requirements of IRC Section 401(a). These prototype plans usually allow only a few options for the client to select regarding the plan's operation. These options are selected by the client on an adoption agreement. The remainder of the document is a standard form. Prototype plans are inexpensive to establish and are preapproved by the IRS.

Costs to Fund the Plan

To meet qualification requirements, qualified retirement plans must be funded on a regular basis. Pension plans must be funded at least annually, whereas contributions to profit-sharing plans must be only substantial and recurring and are not mandatory each year. Employer-deductible plan contributions may be as much as 25% of covered payroll for defined contribution plans and even higher for defined benefit plans. During years of poor earnings, funding a qualified plan can be a substantial drain on a company's cash flow.

Costs of Administering the Plan

Qualified retirement plans require ongoing administration and maintenance. Information compliance tax returns (such as IRS Form 5500) must be filed with the IRS annually. Allocation of contributions to employees' accounts, or determination of accrued benefits, also must be completed at least annually for most plans. Other administrative duties include annual testing to comply with IRS regulations and amending the plan document for tax law changes. In addition to performing administrative duties, the plan sponsor must retain and supervise an investment adviser to ensure that plan assets are managed for the sole benefit of participants and their beneficiaries. Defined benefit plans require the services of an actuary each year. The plan sponsor may outsource each of these tasks to a third-party administrator or other provider.

Annual Compensation Limit

The Internal Revenue Code limits the amount of compensation that can be considered for purposes of funding qualified retirement plans. This compensation limit, although indexed, was an attempt to limit the contribution to highly compensated employees and increase the contributions to nonhighly compensated employees. Exhibit 16.4 illustrates the annual compensation limits for the years from 1993 to 2022.

EXHIBIT 16.4 Annual Compensation Limit (1993–2022)

Year	Compensation Limit	Year	Compensation Limit
1993	$235,850	2008	$230,000
1994	$150,000	2009	$245,000
1995	$150,000	2010	$245,000
1996	$150,000	2011	$245,000
1997	$160,000	2012	$250,000
1998	$160,000	2013	$255,000
1999	$160,000	2014	$260,000
2000	$170,000	2015	$265,000
2001	$170,000	2016	$265,000
2002	$200,000	2017	$270,000
2003	$200,000	2018	$275,000
2004	$205,000	2019	$280,000
2005	$210,000	2020	$285,000
2006	$220,000	2021	$290,000
2007	$225,000	2022	$305,000

For 2022, up to $305,000 of compensation can be considered for purposes of funding a qualified plan on behalf of a participant. Any income earned above this limit is disregarded. The compensation limit is indexed annually to the CPI in $5,000 increments. When an employer wants to provide benefits on earnings above the annual limit, it is generally done in the form of deferred compensation, which does not have the same tax benefits as qualified plans.

Eligibility Requirements

Minimal standards need to be met by an employee in order to be eligible to participate in a qualified retirement plan provided by an employer. Generally, all employees who are at least age 21 and have one year of service (defined as 1,000 hours within a 12-month period) are considered eligible for the plan. As the number of eligible employees for the plan increases, so does the number that must benefit under the plan for the plan to remain qualified. Obviously, an increase in the number of employees under the plan increases the cost of the plan. Union employees, who are covered by a separate collective bargaining agreement, are not required to be covered by their employer's qualified retirement plan. The reason for the exception of union employees is that these individuals generally have retirement benefits provided by the union, and employers generally are required to contribute to these union plans.

Coverage Requirements for Employees

A qualified retirement plan must benefit a broad range of employees, not just the highly compensated. Although there are exceptions, in general, employers are required to cover 70% of the eligible nonhighly compensated employees. For defined benefit plans only, the employer also must cover 50 employees or 40% of those eligible, whichever is less. Coverage under the plan means that the employee is somehow benefiting, either from employer contributions or from the ability to defer employee taxable income in the plan [such as a Section 401(k) plan]. Highly compensated employees are defined as those employees who owned more than 5% of the company stock or had income above a certain limit in the previous year ($135,000 in 2022). An election also is available that allows only the top 20% of wage earners to be considered highly compensated. Nonhighly compensated employees are those employees who are not classified as highly compensated.

As long as the qualified retirement plan meets the coverage requirement, it is permitted to exclude certain groups of eligible employees from participating in the plan. For example, salaried employees or commissioned employees might be excluded from the plan as a class. These types of class exclusions may reduce the employer's contribution to the plan and reduce the overall cost of the plan. The plan must meet the basic coverage rules, however, and the class exclusions should be considered in the overall context of employee compensation and as a business decision.

Vesting Requirements

Vesting
An employee's nonforfeitable right to receive a present or future pension benefit

Vesting is the process by which employees accrue benefits in the form of ownership provided by an employer's contribution. In the context of qualified retirement plans, an employee is vested when he has ownership rights to the contributions (or benefits) provided by the employer. In general, employees vest over a specific period.

The two standard vesting schedules preapproved by the IRS are referred to as cliff and graduated vesting. The cliff vesting schedule requires an employee to complete a certain number of years of service such as three or five; the number depends on whether a defined benefit or defined contribution plan is being considered. In a defined benefit plan, for instance, after five years of service (one year of service defined as 1,000 hours within a 12-month period), the employee is fully or 100% vested, meaning that the employee has ownership rights to all previous employer contributions and any contributions made on his behalf in the future. Graduated vesting allows employees to become partially vested over a period of years. In the case of three-to-seven-year graduated vesting for defined benefit plans, employees accrue ownership rights as shown in Exhibit 16.5.

EXHIBIT 16.5 Defined Benefit Vesting Schedules

Vesting Schedule (5-Year Cliff)		Vesting Schedule (3–7 Year Graduated)	
Years of Service	Portion Vested	Years of Service	Portion Vested
1	0%	1	0%
2	0%	2	0%
3	0%	3	20%
4	0%	4	40%
5	100%	5	60%
		6	80%
		7	100%

Graduated vesting allows those employees who worked for four years, for example, to leave the company with some benefit; whereas, under the five-year-cliff vesting schedule, such employees would receive nothing from the contributions made by the employer and nothing from the earnings on employer contributions. Contributions and the earnings on contributions made by the employee [such as with a Section 401(k) plan], however, are always 100% vested and remain the property of the employee.

The vesting schedule an employer selects could be more liberal than the prescribed vesting schedules under the Internal Revenue Code. For instance, instead of choosing a five-year-cliff vesting schedule, an employer may elect to have employees' accounts vest over four years at 25% each year. However, the employer may not select a vesting schedule that is more restrictive than the five-year-cliff or three-to-seven-year graduated methods for defined benefit plans.

Defined contribution plans, employer-matching contributions, and top-heavy defined benefit plans are required to vest at least as quickly as a three-year-cliff or two-to-six-year graduated vesting schedule (see Exhibit 16.6).

EXHIBIT 16.6 Vesting for Defined Contribution Plans, Matching Contributions, and Top-Heavy Defined Benefit Plans

Vesting Schedule (3-Year Cliff)		Vesting Schedule (2–6 Year Graduated)	
Years of Service	Portion Vested	Years of Service	Portion Vested
1	0%	1	0%
2	0%	2	20%
3	100%	3	40%
4	100%	4	60%
5	100%	5	80%
6	100%	6	100%

Top-Heavy Plans

Under IRC Section 416(g), defined benefit retirement plans are considered top heavy if more than 60% of the benefits are attributable to a group of owners and officers called key employees. If a plan is top heavy, there are two consequences. First, the standard vesting schedules are required to be shortened (cliff vesting to three years and graduated using a two-to-six-year schedule) such that benefits vest more quickly for the nonkey employee group. Second, there are certain minimum contributions that must be provided to the nonkey employees on the basis of the benefits accrued or contributions made for the key employees. The top-heavy rules ensure that a defined benefit retirement plan actually benefits the rank-and-file employees of the company, not just owners and officers. The Pension Protection Act of 2006 requires that all employer contributions to a defined contribution plan vest at least as quickly as one of the two accelerated vesting schedules. Again, an employer may use a schedule that vests more quickly than the accelerated schedules.

Disclosure Requirements

The employer is required to provide a summary of the details of the qualified retirement plan to employees, participants, and beneficiaries under pay status. The employer also is required to provide to the plan participants notices of any plan amendments or changes. These documents help to inform the employee of his rights under ERISA and of the rights of the qualified retirement plan.

Annual Testing of Qualified Retirement Plans

As described previously, many recurring requirements must be met to maintain a qualified retirement plan. Therefore, annual testing is necessary to ensure that the plan continues to meet each of these requirements.

BENEFITS OF TAX DEFERRAL

For an employee who participates in a qualified retirement plan, tax deferral is perhaps the biggest benefit. Neither the contributions to the plan nor the earnings on these contributions are currently subject to income tax. The expectation is that in retirement, when distributions begin, the plan participant will be in a lower income tax bracket than during the working years.

EXAMPLE A client's employer will either pay the client $1,000 that is subject to payroll and income tax (see A), or contribute $1,000 to a qualified retirement plan (see B) on his behalf. The client would save the net received from A and earn 12% per year for 40 years. The contribution made to the qualified retirement plan (B) is made by the employer.

	A		B	
	Not Tax-Advantaged		Qualified Plan	
Deposit	$1,000.00		$1,000.00	
Less	76.50	Payroll tax	0.00	Payroll tax
Less	240.00	24% assumed income tax rate	0.00	Tax rate
Net deposited	$ 683.50		$1,000.00	
PV	$ 683.50		$1,000.00	
i	9.12%	(12% × 0.76) (24% income tax rate)	12%	
n	40 years		40 years	
FV	$22,243.31		$93,050.97	
Net of tax	$22,243.31		$70,718.74	(24% tax bracket)

The above example (A) assumes that the 12% earnings is subject to income tax each year, thus the use of the 9.12 earnings rate (1 − tax rate)(ER) = [(1 − 0.24) × 12] = 9.12%. However, even if we assumed a portfolio of non-dividend-paying stocks that were only subject to capital gains rates of 15% at the end of 40 years, the advantage would still be to the qualified retirement plan.

	A	B
	Not Tax-Advantaged	Qualified Plan
Deposit	$683.50	$1,000.00
PV	$683.50	$1,000.00
n	40	40
i	12%	12%
FV	$63,600.34	$93,050.97
Tax rate	15% on capital gains ($63,600.34 − $683.50)	24% on ordinary income
Net after tax	$63,600.34 ($63,600.34 − $9,437.53 capital gains tax)	$70,718.74 [FV × (1 − 0.24)]

The difference between A and B in both examples is partially due to the payroll tax, which was not applicable to the qualified retirement plan, and partially due to the current income tax on the non-tax-advantaged fund (A).

TYPES OF QUALIFIED RETIREMENT PLANS

Qualified retirement plans may be classified as:

- pension or profit-sharing plans;
- defined benefit plans, defined contribution plans, target/age-weighted (hybrid) plans;
- contributory or noncontributory plans; and
- corporate or Keogh plans.

Exhibit 16.7 identifies 11 common types of qualified retirement plans.

EXHIBIT 16.7 Qualified Retirement Plans

Type	Pension Plans	Profit-Sharing Plans
Defined benefit plans	(1) Traditional defined benefit pension plan (2) Cash balance pension plan	None
Defined contribution plans	(1) Target benefit pension plan (2) Money purchase pension plan	(1) Profit-sharing plan (2) Section 401(k) plan (3) Thrift plan (4) Stock bonus plan (5) Employee stock ownership plan (6) Age-based profit-sharing plan (7) New comparability plan

Pension Plans

Pension plan
A qualified plan structured to provide a regularly paid, fixed sum at retirement

The legal requirement or "promise" of a **pension plan** is to either regularly pay a fixed sum of money at retirement (defined benefit pension plans) or to make a stated contribution to the pension plan (defined contribution pension plans). Because of this promise, pension plans have certain requirements and characteristics. Pension plans require mandatory funding. In general, this means that pension plans must be funded on an annual basis, regardless of whether the company has sufficient cash flow. The reason for annual funding is to ensure that sufficient assets will be available to fulfill the promise of a pension during retirement.

Pension plans are permitted to allow in-service withdrawals only to participants still employed with the company who are age 62 or over. An in-service withdrawal is an employee distribution while the employee is still in the active service of the employer. However, loans are not considered in-service withdrawals.

Pension plans are limited to investing no more than 10% of the qualified retirement plan assets in employer securities. To be consistent with the underlying promise of the pension plan, the investments of the qualified retirement plan should be reasonably diversified to limit the amount of risk undertaken by the portfolio.

There is a limit on contributions to defined contribution pension plans. An employer can contribute up to, and in some cases exceed, 25% of aggregate covered compensation. Contributions to defined benefit pension plans may exceed 25% of covered compensation if a higher amount is actuarially determined to assure the promised benefits. The term *covered compensation* describes the portion of payroll that may be considered for qualified retirement plan purposes. These high contribution limits provide ample opportunity for the employer to fulfill the promise of pension benefits.

There are four types of pension plans, as indicated in Exhibit 16.7. Each type of plan differs from the others in complexity and costs. The traditional defined benefit pension plan is the most complex and costly, requiring the annual services of an actuary. The money purchase pension plan is the least complex and least costly. A prototype plan for a money purchase pension plan is available from almost any financial institution. A target benefit pension plan is a special type of money purchase plan. Each pension plan has particular applications that make it a better choice than the others depending on the employer-sponsor's goals; the number of participants; and the census of participants, including length of service, age, and compensation levels. Cash balance pension plans are a special type of defined benefit pension plan and are beyond the scope of this text.

Small businesses tend to avoid pension plans because of the strict mandatory funding requirement. Small businesses prefer profit-sharing plans or other tax-advantaged retirement plans that permit more discretion over the funding of contributions.

Profit-Sharing Plans

Profit-sharing plan
A qualified defined contribution plan featuring a flexible (discretionary) employer-contribution provision. Profit-sharing plans are structured to offer employees participation in company profits that they may use for retirement purposes

Stock bonus plan
A defined contribution profit-sharing plan in which all employer contributions are in the form of employer stock. Distributions to participants can be made in the form of employer stock.

Section 401(k) profit-sharing plan
A defined contribution profit-sharing plan that gives participants the option of reducing their taxable salary and contributing the salary reduction on a tax-deferred basis to an individual account for retirement purposes

A **profit-sharing plan** is a qualified defined contribution plan featuring a flexible (discretionary) employer contribution provision. The funding discretion is allowed regardless of cash flows or profits. An employer is permitted to fund a profit-sharing plan (including stock bonus plans) in any amount up to 25% of aggregate covered employee compensation.

The legal promise of a profit-sharing plan is to defer taxes rather than provide retirement benefits. There is no particular time requirement for the deferral of taxes. The deferral period could be until retirement, or the plan may be designed to allow in-service withdrawals as early as after two years of participation. The plan document (the plan legal description) will dictate what is, or is not, permitted.

Unlike the restriction of pension plans, profit-sharing plans do not have restrictions on the amount of employer securities that can be purchased within the plan. Profit-sharing plans are permitted to invest 100% of the qualified retirement plan assets in employer securities. **Stock bonus plans** and employee stock ownership plans (ESOPs) are examples of profit-sharing type plans that often invest entirely in employer securities.

There are seven different profit-sharing plans, as shown in Exhibit 16.7. Each one has a particular application depending on costs; complexity; sponsor goals; and the census of employees, including age, length of service, and compensation levels.

The most common type of profit-sharing plan is the **Section 401(k) profit-sharing plan**. This plan is the most popular self-reliant qualified retirement plan and gets its name after Section 401(k) of the Internal Revenue Code. The Section 401(k) plan permits an employee to save, on a pretax basis, $21,500 (indexed to inflation in $500 increments) in 2022, or a certain percentage of income per year. In some cases, that savings is matched, or partially matched, by the employer. Employer-matching contributions typically range from $0.50 to $1.00 per dollar contributed by the participant, often with an overall limit as to the maximum matching contribution by the employer. For example, the employer may match dollar for dollar on the first 6% of compensation deferred by the participant.

The advantage of this kind of plan to the employer is that the funding is heavily employee dependent and self-reliant. Advantages to the employee are the size of the pretax savings, any employer match, and the prospects for a substantial accumulation over the work life expectancy.

EXAMPLE Assume Joe, age 25, participates in a Section 401(k) plan, and his annual salary is $50,000. Joe contributes 6% annually to his Section 401(k) plan, and the contribution is matched $0.50 per dollar by his employer. Joe intends to contribute the same amount each month for the next 40 years. Assume that Joe can earn 10% annually, compounded monthly, on his and his employer's contributions and balances. How much will Joe accumulate at age 65 assuming no increase in salary or in the amount of the monthly contribution?

PV	= 0
n	= 480 (40 × 12) months
i	= 0.8333 (10 ÷ 12)
PMT_{OA}	= $375.00 [(50,000 × 6%) + (50,000 × 3%)] ÷ 12
$FV_{@65}$	= $2,371,529.84

The accumulation is substantial. Joe and his employer deposited only $180,000 ($375 × 12 × 40), and at age 65, Joe has accumulated $2,371,530. The assumed rate of return is excellent in the example, but Joe started saving early and reaped the benefits of a long period of compounding. In actual practice, we would hope and expect that as Joe's salary increased, he would maintain at least a 6% savings rate, as opposed to the $375 per month, thus increasing his contributions with each raise. Joe's contribution, as well as the employer match, would increase with each increase in salary, thus increasing the deposits and the accumulation at age 65.

The Section 401(k) plan has become one of the most popular and widely used qualified retirement plans. The plan is self-reliant and easily understood by employees and is popular with employers because it is relatively inexpensive, as employees provide most of the funding.

Section 401(k) plans [and Section 403(b) plans] may allow a participant to elect to have all or a portion of the participant's elective deferrals under the plan treated as Roth contributions. As with contributions to Roth IRAs, these participant-elective deferrals would be subject to current taxation (not tax deferred) but would be exempt from taxation when distributed if certain requirements were met. These after-tax contributions can accumulate in the Roth account on a tax-deferred basis. This addition to Section 401(k) plans may be one of the most beneficial enhancements of qualified plans that has been seen in many years.

Legislation created plans known as solo Section 401(k) plans or individual Section 401(k) plans. These plans cover only one participant (a businessowner) or only a businessowner and spouse.

Employee elective deferrals do not count against the plan limit for employer contributions. Also, plans allowing elective deferrals may allow for additional catch-up contributions for employees age 50 and older. In 2022, the maximum catch-up contribution is $6,500.

Exhibit 16.8 summarizes the major differences between pension plans and profit-sharing plans.

EXHIBIT 16.8 Major Differences Between Pension and Profit-Sharing Plans

Plan Features	Pension Plans	Profit-Sharing Plans
In-service withdrawals	Permitted for employees age 62 or older	Permitted after 2 years
Mandatory funding	Yes	No
Percentage of employer stock permitted in the plan	10%	100%
Employer contribution limit	25% of aggregate covered compensation (defined contribution plans)	25% of aggregate covered compensation

Defined Benefit and Defined Contribution Plans

Qualified retirement plans are characterized as either defined benefit or defined contribution plans. In a defined benefit plan, the contributions are actuarially determined to produce a certain future retirement benefit under a formula. The annual funding for a defined benefit plan depends on six factors: (1) the life expectancies of the participants, (2) the mortality experience in the employee group, (3) the earnings rate and expected earnings rate on plan assets, (4) the expected wage increases of employees, (5) the expected inflation rate associated with plan costs, and (6) the expected turnover rate of employees. An actuary makes an annual analysis of the six variables to determine the annual funding. Obviously, defined benefit plans are both costly and complex. There are two defined benefit plans, the traditional **defined benefit pension plan** and the cash-balance pension plan, as well as a hybrid plan called a DB(k), which combines a defined benefit plan with a Section 401(k) provision. Generally, large corporations use these where the costs of administration, including actuarial costs, can be spread over a large number of employee participants. Small businesses will occasionally make use of defined benefit plans, though typically in very limited situations. For instance, a highly paid older professional (such as a doctor or lawyer) with a few young, lower-income staff employees might be an excellent candidate for a defined benefit plan.

Defined benefit pension plan
A retirement plan that specifies the benefits that each employee receives at retirement. Defined benefit plans actuarially determine the benefit to be paid at normal retirement age.

Defined benefit plan assets are invested and managed by the employer, as trustee, or by an outside trustee. Actuaries for defined benefit plans determine the annual funding necessary to assure payment of the future promised benefit to be paid at normal retirement age (frequently age 65). Contributions to defined benefit plans generally are provided by the employer only. Because the employer is responsible for meeting the benefit obligations, it bears the investment risk for the funding. If the performance of the fund assets is better than expected, contributions can be reduced. If investment returns are less than expected, however, the employer is required to make higher contributions than anticipated.

The benefits payable under a defined benefit plan commonly are paid as a lifetime annuity, although some plans provide a cash-out option at retirement. The older a person is when entering into the plan, the greater the funding requirements; therefore, defined benefit plans are said to favor older-age entrants and long-term employees.

There is some risk that the employer will be unable to sustain the payment of retirement benefits from a defined benefit plan, so sponsors of these plans generally are required to participate in the Pension Benefit Guarantee Corporation (PBGC) termination insurance program. The PBGC is a federal corporation created under ERISA that guarantees benefits to participants of defined benefit plans. Plan sponsors make premium payments to the PBGC based on the number of plan participants and the level of plan funding. The PBGC does not guarantee the full amount of benefits but only a set amount as limited by law ($74,454 in 2022). The PBGC does not guarantee benefits of defined contribution plans.

Defined contribution plan
A retirement plan that specifies the annual employer current contribution. The amount of benefit received by an employee depends on the account balance at retirement.

Defined contribution plans specify the annual employer current contribution (as opposed to an ultimate future benefit). The investment risk in a defined contribution plan is borne by the participant; therefore, the final benefit is not guaranteed and will be dependent on the participant's account balance.

There are two defined contribution pension plans and seven defined contribution profit-sharing plans. Usually, defined contribution plan funding is borne solely by the employer [except for the Section 401(k) plan and thrift plan], but the assets are maintained in each participant's individual account. The investment risk is borne by the participants, and the investment of the plan assets is often self-directed, meaning the plan participant chooses which investment option(s) to invest the participant's plan contributions (deferrals and employer contributions) from a menu of investment options offered by the plan. Defined contribution plans favor younger participants who have a longer compounding and accumulation period. Unlike defined benefit plans, defined contribution profit-sharing plans have no annual mandatory funding requirement. Thus, accumulations in these accounts are dependent on the contributions made and the earnings performance.

Exhibit 16.9 summarizes the characteristics and differences between defined benefit and defined contribution plans.

EXHIBIT 16.9 Characteristics of Selected Retirement Plan

	Defined Benefit	Defined Contribution
Plan typically benefits older, long-term employees	Yes	No
Requires PBGC insurance	Yes	No
Benefits insured by PBGC	Yes	No
Actuarial costs	Yes	No
Can encourage early retirement	Yes	Possibly
Can provide benefits based on prior service	Yes	No
Maximum annual benefit $245,000 (2022)	Yes	No
Higher plan costs and complexity	Yes	No
Individual accounts	No	Yes
Contribution is percentage of compensation	No	Yes
Investment risk	Employer	Employee
Annual additions limited to lesser of 100% of comp. or $61,000 (2022)	No	Yes
Forfeitures reduce plan costs	Yes	Possibly
Assets in plan	Commingled funds	Separate accounts

Target/Age-Weighted Plans

Target benefit pension plan
An age-weighted money purchase pension plan; a hybrid between a defined contribution plan and a defined benefit plan

Age-based profit-sharing plan
A profit-sharing plan with an age-weighted factor in the allocation formula

Target benefit pension plans and age-weighted profit-sharing plans allow for higher contributions for older plan participants.

A traditional **target benefit pension plan** is a hybrid between a defined contribution pension plan and a traditional defined benefit plan. The traditional target benefit pension plan is an age-weighted money purchase pension plan.

The **age-based profit-sharing plan** is a profit-sharing plan with an age-weighted factor in the allocation formula. Because the plan allocations are age weighted, older plan participants are favored.

New comparability plan
A defined contribution plan that maximizes the age-weighted discrepancy permitted under the cross-testing provisions of proposed nondiscrimination regulations

The **new comparability plan** represents an attempt to push age weighting to its maximum limit under the cross-testing provisions of nondiscrimination regulations.

Contributory vs. Noncontributory Plans

Qualified retirement plans may be distinguished as either contributory (employee makes some contribution) or noncontributory (employer pays all). Most pension and profit-sharing plans are noncontributory. The common exceptions are the Section 401(k) plan and the thrift plan (an after-tax savings plan).

Corporate vs. Keogh (Self-Employed) Plans

Qualified retirement plans are either corporate sponsored (regular C corporations and S corporations) or Keogh (self-employed, partnerships, LLCs filing as partnerships) plans. Corporations can adopt any of the qualified retirement plans, pension plans, or profit-sharing plans discussed previously, as well as other tax-advantaged plans that are not qualified. Self-employed persons can adopt the majority of qualified retirement plans (except stock bonus and ESOP plans) as well as other tax-advantaged plans.

Keogh plan
A qualified plan for unincorporated businesses

The intent of Congressional legislation regarding self-employed individuals was to put **Keogh plans** in parity with corporate plans. There are two important differences, however, between corporate plans and Keogh plans. The first is the calculation of the maximum contribution allowed by the self-employed person; the second is the availability of loans from the Keogh plan to these self-employed individuals. Any type of qualified plan may be adopted as a Keogh plan (except stock bonus and ESOP plans).

Self-Employed Maximum Contribution Calculation

Forfeitures
Employer contributions that are not fully vested and thus revert to the employer in the event that an employee terminates service

Traditional employees receive a Form W-2 that reflects their earnings for the current year. Maximum annual contributions, referred to as annual additions, to defined contribution plans cannot exceed the lesser of 100% of an employee's compensation or $61,000 in 2022. Annual additions include employer contributions, employee contributions, and **forfeitures** reallocated to plan participants. For example, an employee with compensation of $100,000 in 2022 would be limited to $61,000 in annual additions for a single year.

Unfortunately for self-employed individuals, their maximum contribution calculation is more complicated. These individuals are limited in their contributions to the lesser of 25% of earned income from self-employment or $61,000 for 2022. Earned income from self-employment is different from compensation and is defined as self-employment income reduced by one-half of self-employment tax paid (net self-employment income) and reduced by the retirement plan contribution. Reducing the income that can be used as the base for the retirement plan contribution by the retirement plan contribution creates what is known as a circular equation. To resolve this circular equation, the retirement plan contribution percentage is divided by the sum of one plus the retirement plan contribution percentage. This factor is then multiplied by the difference between self-employment income and one-half self-employment tax paid.

EXAMPLE Bob has self-employment income of $105,000 and self-employment tax of $14,836 in 2022. His contribution for the tax year is limited to a maximum of $19,516 (see the following calculation).

Keogh Plan Contribution Calculation

1.	Self-employment income	$105,000	
2.	Less ½ self-employment tax	7,418	½ × $14,836
3.	Equals net self-employment income	97,582	
4.	Less Keogh plan contribution	(19,516)	$97,582 × (0.25 ÷ 1.25)
5.	Equals earned income	78,066	
6.	Times Keogh contribution percentage	× 25%	
7.	Equals Keogh plan contribution	$19,516	

Notice that the contribution of $19,516 is calculated by multiplying $97,582 by 20%, which equals earned income (line 5 above) multiplied by 25%. Therefore, it is not necessary to extend the analysis through steps 5 to 7. Determining the contribution is usually calculated by dividing the plan percentage by the sum of one plus the plan percentage and multiplying the result by the difference between self-employment earnings and the deductible share of self-employment tax. The following table displays the percentage often used for Keogh calculations, depending on the plan contribution percentage limit.

Plan Percentage	Keogh Limit	Plan Percentage	Keogh Limit
1%	0.9901%	14%	12.2807%
2%	1.9608%	15%	13.0435%
3%	2.9126%	16%	13.7931%
4%	3.8462%	17%	14.5299%
5%	4.7619%	18%	15.2542%
6%	5.6604%	19%	15.9664%
7%	6.5421%	20%	16.6667%
8%	7.4074%	21%	17.3554%
9%	8.2569%	22%	18.0328%
10%	9.0909%	23%	18.6992%
11%	9.9099%	24%	19.3548%
12%	10.7143%	25%	20.0000%
13%	11.5044%		

OTHER TAX-ADVANTAGED PLANS

Other than qualified retirement plans, there are individually-sponsored and employer-sponsored retirement plans that are tax advantaged but are not technically qualified plans. Generally, these plans appeal to individuals or small employers because they are less costly to maintain. Tax-advantaged plans typically have lower contribution limits but function much like qualified plans, offering tax deferred earnings; some plans allow tax deductible contributions. Exhibit 16.10 lists these plans.

EXHIBIT 16.10 Other Tax-Advantaged Plans

- Individual retirement account or annuity (IRA)
  - Deductible
  - Nondeductible
- Roth IRA
- Simplified employee pension (SEP) plan
- Savings incentive match plan for employees (SIMPLE)
- Section 403(b) plans (tax-sheltered annuities)

Individual Retirement Accounts (IRAs) or IRA Annuities

In general, the IRA is a tax-deferred investment and savings account that serves as a personal retirement fund for persons with earned income.

An individual worker with earned income at any age in 2022 and afterward can contribute to an IRA. Annual IRA contributions are limited to the lesser of $6,000 or earned income for 2022. If a married person has a nonworking spouse, the annual contribution limit is increased to $12,000 for 2022. IRA contribution limits are periodically adjusted for inflation in $500 increments.

Deductibility Rules

The deductibility of an IRA contribution is affected by the taxpayer's status as an active participant in an employer-sponsored retirement plan and by the taxpayer's modified adjusted gross income (MAGI). For taxpayers who are not active participants in a qualified plan, SEP, SARSEP, SIMPLE, or Section 403(b) plan, contributions to a traditional IRA are fully deductible, regardless of the taxpayer's MAGI. For taxpayers who are active participants in a qualified plan, SEP, SARSEP, SIMPLE, or Section 403(b) plan, the deduction for traditional IRA contributions is limited (or eliminated) when a taxpayer's adjusted income reaches certain levels. These phaseout levels are listed in Exhibit 16.11.

EXHIBIT 16.11 IRA Current Phaseout Limits

	Phaseout Range, by Taxpayer Filing Status	
Tax Year	Single	Married Filing Jointly
2022	$68,000–$78,000	$109,000–$129,000

An individual will not be considered an active participant in an employer-sponsored retirement plan solely because her spouse is an active participant. However, when only one spouse is an active participant, the nonparticipant spouse will have his deduction phased out at AGI levels between $204,000 and $214,000 in 2022.

Catch-up contributions are available for individuals over 50 years old. Any individual who attains 50 by the end of the taxable year can make additional contributions of $1,000.

Thus, a taxpayer age 50 or older in 2022 could contribute a total of $7,000 to an IRA. This contribution consists of the annual limit plus the catch-up contribution.

Roth IRA
An individual retirement account in which contributions are made on an after-tax basis and qualifying distributions are made tax free

Roth IRA

The **Roth IRA** is a special type of IRA. Contributions to a Roth IRA are made on an after-tax basis. Earnings are not subject to current taxation, and distributions of earnings are generally tax-exempt if certain qualifying conditions are met. Taxpayers can contribute to Roth IRAs with no age restriction and are not forced to receive minimum distributions at age 72 as they are with traditional IRAs. Only taxpayers with incomes less than those listed below qualify to make a contribution to a Roth IRA in 2022.

Taxpayer status	2022 Phaseout MAGI
Single	$129,000–$144,000
Married filing jointly	$204,000–$214,000
Married filing separately	$0–$10,000

Simplified Employee Pensions (SEPs)

Simplified employee pension (SEP)
A tax-deferred, noncontributory retirement plan that uses an individual retirement account (IRA) as the receptacle for contributions

A **simplified employee pension (SEP)** plan is a tax-deferred noncontributory retirement plan that is employer sponsored and similar to a qualified profit-sharing plan with regard to funding requirements and contribution limits. In contrast to qualified profit-sharing plans, SEPs are much easier to implement, are less costly to administer, and are not subject to the same extensive filing requirements. SEPs are funded through employer contributions to an IRA in the name of the employee. All contributions are immediately 100% vested. The funding is discretionary on the part of the employer up to 25% of covered employee compensation to a maximum of $305,000 in 2022, not to exceed $61,000 in 2022. The advantage of a SEP versus an IRA is the significantly higher potential amount of funding.

The plan is uncomplicated and inexpensive, compared with qualified retirement plans. Generally, the individual participant has the responsibility and risk for investment returns. SEPs may not be appropriate for small businesses with permanent part-time employees because part-time employees must be covered under the plan. A major advantage of a SEP is that it can be established and funded as late as the due date of the employer's federal income tax return, including extensions. Qualified plans, on the other hand, must be established by the end of the tax year for which contributions are being made.

SIMPLE IRAs

A savings incentive match plan for employees (SIMPLE) is a tax-deferred, employer-sponsored retirement plan that more closely resembles an IRA. Like the SEP, it has minimal filing requirements. The SIMPLE IRA allows employees to make elective contributions to an IRA up to the lesser of 100% of compensation or $14,000 in 2022.

Catch-up provisions are available for individuals age 50 and above. Any individual who attains age 50 by the end of the tax year may be eligible to make an additional contribution of $3,000 (2022).

The employer is required to provide one of the following two types of benefits to the participants in the plan: (1) provide a dollar-for-dollar match up to 3% of the participant's compensation, or (2) make a contribution of 2% of compensation for each eligible employee without regard to the employee's contribution. All contributions are immediately 100% vested. The benefits are portable; however, withdrawals made within two years of participation are subject to a 25% premature-distribution penalty tax.

The advantage of the SIMPLE IRA over the traditional IRA is the larger amount of contribution allowed. The advantage of the SIMPLE IRA over the SEP is that the SIMPLE IRA is funded mostly through employee contributions, and there is no percentage limit for contributions to a SIMPLE IRA.

To sponsor a SIMPLE IRA, the employer must have fewer than 100 employees. SIMPLE IRAs are essentially governed by the same rules as IRAs. Individual accounts are created, and employees choose the investments from those offered by the plan.

One big disadvantage of a SIMPLE IRA is that no other types of qualified retirement plans are permitted to be simultaneously maintained by the employer. Therefore, if the employer wanted to sponsor a pension or profit-sharing plan, the SIMPLE IRA would have to be terminated. However, the employer, if eligible, can maintain a Section 457 plan for the benefit of its employees.

SIMPLE 401(k)

A Section 401(k) plan may also be structured as a SIMPLE for eligible employers. Employers with 100 or fewer employees earning $5,000 (or more) during the preceding year may adopt a SIMPLE 401(k). The employer may not maintain any other qualified or employer-sponsored plan. However, the employer, if eligible, can maintain a Section 457 plan for the benefit of its employees. The SIMPLE 401(k) is exempt from the special nondiscrimination testing that applies to the traditional Section 401(k).

Participants in a SIMPLE 401(k) may make elective deferrals (similar to the traditional Section 401(k) plan). Deferral limits are less than traditional Section 401(k) plans, $14,000 for 2022, with an additional $3,000 catch-up allowance for participants age 50 and above. The employer-sponsor of the plan must either match those elective deferral amounts, up to 3% of employee compensation, or, alternatively, make a flat (nonelective) contribution of 2% of compensation for all eligible employees. SIMPLE 401(k)s are not subject to the 25% penalty on withdrawals within the first two years of participation. Rather, the penalty for an early withdrawal is the same as for all other plans, 10%. Unlike traditional Section 401(k) employer contributions (where vesting schedules are permissible), the employee is always 100% vested in the contributions made to a SIMPLE 401(k) by the employer.

Historically, the major advantage for employer implementation of the SIMPLE 401(k) option (rather than the SIMPLE IRA) was, as a qualified plan, creditor protection of the assets within the plan. The Bankruptcy Act of 2005 minimized this advantage in part. Specifically, subsequent to October 2005, the first $1 million of assets included in initially established IRAs of any type (including the SIMPLE IRA) are protected from creditor claims. This amount is unlimited for a rollover IRA. Thus, it is anticipated that the use of the SIMPLE 401(k) may recede even further from its admittedly narrow market under law.

Section 403(b) Plans

Section 403(b) plan
A retirement plan similar to a 401(k) plan that is available to certain tax-exempt organizations and to public schools

Congress established Section 403(b) plans to encourage workers in certain tax-exempt organizations to establish retirement savings programs. The name, like that of Section 401(k) plans, refers to the relevant section of the Internal Revenue Code. A **Section 403(b) plan** is a tax-deferred savings and retirement plan that, while not a qualified plan, provides many of the same benefits and is governed by many of the same rules that govern qualified retirement plans. The plan is essentially the Section 401(k) of the not-for-profit industry. Participants contractually reduce their salaries, and elective deferrals are subject to the same limits as the Section 401(k). Contributions are made on a before-tax basis, and the only allowable funding vehicles are mutual funds and tax-sheltered annuities. The contributions and earnings grow tax deferred until distribution, and the benefit received is equal to the account balance at the accumulation date (usually retirement). Similar to the Section 401(k) and other defined contribution plans, the responsibility and risk of investment returns is on the individual participant.

Nonrefundable Credit for Elective Deferrals

A special nonrefundable tax credit is available to low-income and moderate-income savers for elective deferrals or contributions made to a Section 401(k) plan, Section 403(b) plan, eligible deferred-compensation arrangement of a state or local government (a Section 457 plan), SIMPLE, SEP, or IRA.

The maximum annual contribution eligible for the credit is $2,000. The credit rates are based on AGI (adjusted for inflation).

The credit is in addition to any deduction or exclusion that would otherwise apply with respect to the contribution. The credit offsets alternative minimum tax liability as well as regular tax liability. The credit is available to individuals who are age 18 or older, but not individuals who are full-time students or claimed as a dependent on another taxpayer's return.

When figuring this credit, the taxpayer generally must subtract the amount of distributions received from retirement plans from the contributions made. This rule applies for distributions starting two years before the year the credit is claimed and ending with the filing deadline for that tax return. In the case of a distribution from a Roth IRA, this rule applies to any such distributions, whether taxable or not.

DISTRIBUTIONS FROM QUALIFIED AND OTHER TAX-ADVANTAGED PLANS

Distributions from qualified retirement plans and other tax-advantaged plans generally are subject to the following income tax treatment: If the contributions were made pretax, then both contributions and earnings are treated as ordinary income equal to the distribution and thus receive ordinary income tax treatment. If the contributions were made after tax, the contributions are treated as a return of capital, and the earnings are treated as ordinary income.

In general, distributions from qualified retirement plans and other tax-advantaged retirement plans made before age 59½ (except for death or disability, for instance) are penalized by a premature penalty tax of 10%. Annual distributions from qualified retirement plans and other tax-advantaged retirement plans typically must begin no later than the year when the participant attains age 72, although the first distribution may be delayed until April 1 of the following year.

EXHIBIT 16.12 Taxation of Distributions

Contributions	Distribution	Earnings on Contributions
Pretax	Taxable as ordinary income	Ordinary income
After-tax	Nontaxable return of capital	Ordinary income

The two common exceptions to the general income tax treatment of distributions from tax-advantaged retirement accounts are Roth IRA distributions and lump-sum distributions consisting of employer securities. A Roth IRA has nondeductible contributions but generally provides for tax-exempt distributions and is not subject to the rules on minimum distributions at age 72.

As previously discussed, distributions from qualified plans that consist of employer securities may be eligible to receive deferred recognition treatment of the net unrealized appreciation in the securities, with the gains taxable at capital gains rates instead of ordinary income tax rates.

NONQUALIFIED PLANS

Nonqualified plan
A retirement plan that can discriminate in favor of executives but is not eligible for all of the special tax benefits available for qualified or other tax-advantaged retirement plans

A **nonqualified plan** is any retirement plan, savings plan, or deferred-compensation plan or agreement that does not meet the qualified retirement plan tax requirements of the Internal Revenue Code. All qualified retirement plans and other tax-advantaged plans are in some way a form of deferred compensation but with some form of current income tax deduction and/or deferral of taxation on earnings. Most nonqualified retirement plans offer deferral of taxation on earnings but do not allow an immediate tax deduction to the employer. The employer receives a deduction for contributions only when the participant recognizes the distribution as income for income tax purposes. If the nonqualified plan agreement delays receipt of taxable income by the participant, then the employer/sponsor's income tax deduction also is delayed.

Employers use nonqualified plans to provide additional financial benefits that are not, or cannot be, provided in qualified retirement plans. Nonqualified plans can reward employees (usually key executives) on a more selective basis than qualified retirement plans that require broad participation, coverage, and nondiscrimination. An example of one benefit that can be provided by a nonqualified plan is a deferred-compensation plan to provide retirement benefits to a key employee in excess of the limits that may be provided under a qualified retirement plan. Recall that the limit for covered compensation that can be considered for purposes of qualified retirement plans is $305,000 for 2022. Employees who earn exactly $305,000 for 2022 have a much higher wage replacement ratio than those who make $1 million under the same qualified retirement plan. Even though the person is earning $1 million, her qualified retirement plan acts as if she is making only $305,000 for 2022. The deferred-compensation, nonqualified plan is used to mitigate this wage replacement ratio inequity.

Nonqualified plans generally have some risk as to whether the employee/participant will receive the benefits. (A substantial risk of forfeiture or a lack of funding is essential for the plan to defer taxation to the employee/participant.) If there is no substantial risk of forfeiture and the benefit is funded, there is constructive receipt of the funds, and the benefits are currently taxable rather than being deferred. In addition, nonqualified plans are not protected from creditors under ERISA's nonalienation of benefits rules.

A number of nonqualified plans may be used to attract, compensate, and retain key personnel on a discriminatory or selective basis and include deferred-compensation plans, split-dollar life insurance plans, and employee stock option plans.

Deferred Compensation Plans

Deferred compensation plan
A nonqualified plan that is a contractual agreement between the employer and selected employees; takes the form of either salary reduction or salary continuation. Compensation is deferred until retirement, disability, death, or termination of employment, but usually only at normal retirement age.

Nonqualified deferred compensation agreements are contractual arrangements between the employer and selected employees. **Deferred compensation plans** take the form of salary reduction or, more commonly, salary continuation. Either way, compensation is deferred generally until retirement, disability, death, or termination of employment, but usually only at normal retirement age.

The employer does not receive any tax deduction unless and until the employee recognizes taxable income. The presumption is that the executive employee may be in a lower income tax bracket during retirement than during the maximum earnings years of employment. Another reason for using nonqualified plans is to delay the receipt of taxable cash flow to the executive until it is actually needed.

Employee Stock Option Plan

In employee stock option plans, the employer grants to the employee a right (option) to purchase a fixed number of shares of the employer's stock for a set price (exercise price) during a specified period. The purpose of granting such stock options to employees is to align more closely executive compensation to stock performance. These options may be nonqualified stock options (NQSOs) or incentive stock options (ISOs). The NQSO is taxable to the recipient at the time of exercise to the extent of the difference between the fair market value of the stock and the exercise price as ordinary Form W-2 income. The exercise of ISOs does not currently create taxable income for regular income tax purposes, as with NQSOs. There is income, however, for alternative minimum tax purposes created upon the exercise of the ISO. The alternative minimum tax (AMT) may apply when employees exercise ISOs. In addition, the shares acquired through the ISO exercise cannot be sold before one year from the date of exercise or two years from the date of grant. If this holding period is satisfied, the gain upon the sale of the ISO shares will be a long-term capital gain; otherwise, the income will be ordinary. Therefore, ISOs provide some important advantages to the employees but also have certain restrictions on the number that can be granted and when the shares can be sold.

Section 457 Plans

A Section 457 plan is a deferred compensation plan of governmental units, governmental agencies, and non-church-controlled, tax-exempt organizations. In 2022, the amount deferred annually by an employee under a Section 457 plan cannot exceed the lesser of $20,500 or 100% of the employee's compensation currently includable in gross income. In addition, individuals who have attained age 50 may make catch-up contributions. The additional catch-up amount is $6,500 for 2022.

The contribution limit is doubled in the three years before an individual's retirement. During this three-year period (before retirement), the catch-up rule does not apply.

Plan distributions cannot be made before any of the following:

- The calendar year in which the participant attains age 70½ (Note that the SECURE Act did not change this age to 72)
- Separation from service
- An unforeseeable emergency as defined in regulations

Distributions must begin no later than April 1 of the calendar year after the year in which the plan participant attains age 72.

THE FINANCIAL PLANNER'S ROLE IN RETIREMENT PLANNING

The financial planner's role in retirement planning is to assist clients in the accomplishment of their retirement goals. Retirement plans have many tax advantages, business benefits, and other advantages. Financial planners must be able to identify the objectives of the client and assist the client in choosing a retirement plan that meets those objectives.

WHERE ON THE WEB

American Benefits Council **www.appwp.org**

American Society of Pension Professionals and Actuaries **www.asppa.org**

Benefits Link **www.benefitslink.com**

The ESOP Association **www.esopassociation.org**

Employee Benefit Research Institute **www.ebri.org**

Employee Benefits Security Administration **www.dol.gov/ebsa**

Internal Revenue Service **www.irs.gov**

International Foundation of Employee Benefit Plans **www.ifebp.org**

National Institute of Pension Administrators **www.nipa.org**

National Tax Sheltered Accounts Association (403(b) and 457 plans) **www.ntsaa.org**

Pension Benefit Guaranty Corporation (PBGC) **www.pbgc.gov**

Profit Sharing/401(k) Council of America **www.psca.org**

DISCUSSION QUESTIONS

1. What is a qualified retirement plan?
2. What are the advantages of a qualified retirement plan, and what are its disadvantages?
3. What is vesting?
4. What are the standard vesting schedules for defined benefit plans and defined contribution plans?
5. Why were qualified retirement plans created?
6. What are the benefits of tax deferral in a qualified retirement plan and how can they be calculated?
7. What are the different types of qualified retirement plans?
8. How do pension plans and profit-sharing plans differ?
9. How do defined benefit plans and defined contribution plans differ?
10. How do noncontributory plans and contributory plans differ?
11. What is a Section 401(k) plan, and how does it operate?
12. How do Keogh (self-employed) plans and corporate plans differ?
13. What are some examples of tax-advantaged retirement plans?
14. What are IRAs, SEPs, SIMPLEs, and Section 403(b) plans?
15. How are distributions from qualified retirement plans and other tax-advantaged retirement plans the same, and how do they differ?
16. What is a nonqualified plan, and what are some examples of this type of plan?
17. Why are nonqualified plans useful to employers?
18. Which qualified retirement plans permit in-service withdrawals?
19. Which qualified retirement plans require immediate vesting of employer contributions?

EXERCISES

1. Shawna, a 73-year-old single taxpayer, retired two years ago and is receiving a pension of $700 per month from her previous employer's qualified pension plan. She recently started a new job with a discount retail outlet that has no pension plan. She will receive $12,000 in compensation from her current job, as well as the $8,400 from her pension. How much can she contribute to a deductible IRA in 2022?

2. What deductible contribution amount may the following individuals make to an IRA in 2022? Assume none of the persons listed or their spouses participate in an employer-sponsored pension plan, and none are age 50 or over.

Person	Marital Status	AGI
Larry	Single	$ 32,000
Mark	Married	$ 87,000
Lee Anne	Single	$ 56,000
Dennis	Married	$120,000

3. Tom and Denise, both age 45, are married and filed a joint income tax return for the tax year. Tom earned a salary of $70,000 in 2022. Tom and Denise earned interest of $5,000 in 2022 on their joint savings account. Denise is not employed, and the couple had no other income. What amount could Tom and Denise contribute to IRAs to take advantage of their maximum allowable IRA deduction on their 2022 tax return?

4. Evan and Jody, both age 52, are married and filed a joint income tax return for the year 2022. Their 2022 adjusted gross income was $100,000. The couple had no other income, and neither spouse was covered by an employer-sponsored plan. What amount could Evan and Jody contribute to IRAs to take advantage of their maximum allowable IRA deduction on their 2022 tax return?

5. Darlene and Rick are married and file a joint income tax return. They are both covered by a qualified retirement plan. Their 2022 adjusted gross income was $85,000. The couple had no other income. Assuming the couple is under age 50, what amount could Darlene and Rick contribute to a Roth IRA this year?

6. In January of the current year, Phil (age 47) took a $500,000 premature distribution from a rollover IRA, leaving a balance in his IRA of $1 million. On October 31 of the current year, Phil died with the IRA account balance of $1.2 million. Which penalty or penalties will apply to Phil as a result of these facts?

7. What is the maximum deductible contribution to a defined contribution qualified pension plan on behalf of Ann, a self-employed individual whose income from self-employment is $25,000 and whose Social Security taxes are $3,532 in 2022?

8. Refer back to the previous exercise concerning Ann, the self-employed person. What is the maximum Ann could contribute to a profit-sharing plan?

9. Robbins, Inc., a regular C corporation, is considering the adoption of a qualified retirement plan. The company has had fluctuating cash flows in the recent past, and such fluctuations are expected to continue. The average age of nonowner employees is 24, and the average number of years of service is 3 with the high being 4 and the low, 1. Approximately 25% of the 12-person labor force turns over each year. The two owners receive about two-thirds of the total covered compensation. Which is the most appropriate vesting schedule for Robbins, Inc.?

10. What is the minimum number of employees that must be covered in a defined benefit plan to conform to ERISA requirements for a company having 100 eligible employees?

PROBLEMS

1. XYZ Company has two employees: John, who earns $300,000 annually, and his assistant Kim, age 26, who has worked for John for 4 years. Kim earns $20,000. XYZ has a contributory pension plan using graduated vesting. Kim's account balance reflects the following:

Contributions		Earnings From Contributions		Kim's Total Balance
Employee	Employer	Employee	Employer	
$1,500	$2,000	$800	$1,200	$5,500

Reviewing the account and assuming that Kim terminated employment when the account balance was as above after 4 years of employment, how much could she take with her, plan permitting?

2. The following table contains qualified plan information for Yarbrough, Inc., as of 12/31/2022. Yarbrough, Inc., maintains a noncontributory qualified profit-sharing plan with 3-year cliff vesting.

Employee	Compensation	Ownership Interest	Years of Service*	Plan Account Balance*
A	$320,000	5%	2	$20,000
B	$180,000	8%	10	$300,000
C	$130,000	6%	8	$180,000
D	$60,000	1%	3	$27,000
E	$40,000	0%	2	$7,500

* As of 12/31/2022

Please answer all of the following questions:

A. What is the total covered compensation for 2022?
B. What is the maximum profit-sharing contribution Yarbrough can make for 2022?
C. Which of the employees is highly compensated?
D. Is the plan top-heavy?
E. If employees D and E quit in January 2023, what are their respective vested balances in the plan?

CHAPTER 17

Introduction to Estate Planning

LEARNING OBJECTIVES

After learning the material in this chapter, you will be able to do the following:

- Define estate planning and describe the estate planning process
- Discuss the objectives of and the benefits derived from planning an estate
- Explain the risks of failing to plan for estate transfer
- Identify the steps in the estate planning process
- List the types of client information necessary to begin and complete the estate planning process
- Identify the most common estate transfer objectives
- Discuss the types of property ownership interests and how each interest is transferred at death
- Identify and describe the basic essential estate planning documents

- Describe the probate process and list its advantages and disadvantages
- Understand why a unified gift and estate tax system exists
- Define the annual exclusion and explain its tax ramifications
- Explain the concept of gift splitting
- Identify the basic strategies for transferring wealth through the process of making gifts
- Define and explain the purpose of the federal estate tax
- Describe the gross estate, what assets are included in the gross estate, and the expenses and deductions that reduce the gross estate
- Describe how charitable planning impacts estate planning
- Define the marital deduction and explain how it affects estate planning
- Define the generation-skipping transfer tax and explain how it affects estate planning
- List the various estate planning techniques available to reduce the estate tax

BASICS OF ESTATE PLANNING

This chapter presents the goals of efficient and effective wealth transfer, during life or at death, and the risks associated with such transfers. When a personal financial planner begins the estate planning process for a client, certain personal and financial data are collected from the client and analyses of that data are performed. Client interest in the estate planning process generally begins at or near the beginning of the distribution/gifting phase of the client's personal lifecycle. However, all clients need to have at least basic documents (e.g., will, durable power of attorney, and advanced medical directives) and provisions in the will for the care of minor children.

Estate Planning Defined

Estate planning may be broadly defined as the process of accumulation, management, conservation, and transfer of wealth considering legal, tax, and personal objectives. It is financial planning for our inevitable death. The goal of estate planning is the effective and efficient transfer of assets. An effective transfer occurs when the client's assets are transferred to the person or institution intended by the client. An efficient transfer occurs when wealth transfer costs are minimized consistent with the greatest assurance of effectiveness.

The Objectives of Estate Planning

Common objectives of estate planning include transferring (distributing) property to particular persons or entities consistent with client wishes; minimizing all taxes (income, gift, estate, state inheritance, and generation-skipping taxes); minimizing the transaction costs associated with the transfer (costs of documents, lawyers, and the legal probate process); and providing liquidity to the estate to pay for costs which commonly arise, such as taxes, funeral expenses, and final medical costs.

EXHIBIT 17.1 Estate Planning Objectives

- Fulfill client's property transfer wishes
- Minimize taxes
- Minimize costs
- Provide needed liquidity

Everyone needs a basic estate plan to provide for health care and property decisions and for transferring property according to the individual's wishes. An important estate planning objective is to ensure that the decedent's property is received by the person, persons, or entities that the client desires.

Heir
One who inherits; beneficiary

Risks associated with failing to plan for estate transfer include the transfer of property contrary to the client's wishes, insufficient financial provision for the client's family, and liquidity problems at the time of death. Any of these risks could be catastrophic to the decedent's **heirs** and family. For example, a decedent's assets could be tied up in probate court for an indefinite period if that person has no will or has competing and conflicting heirs. Another consideration in estate planning is the high transfer tax rates. In 2022, for example, the maximum gift tax, estate tax, and generation-skipping transfer tax rate is 40%. These tax rates have been higher than 55% in the past, and it is possible that higher rates will be imposed again in the future.

EXHIBIT 17.2 Risks in Failing to Plan an Estate

- Client's property transfer wishes go unfulfilled.
- Taxes are excessive.
- Transfer costs are excessive.
- Client's family is not properly provided for.
- There is insufficient liquidity to cover client's debts.

The Estate Planning Team

The estate planning team consists of the attorney, accountant, life insurance consultant, trust officer, and financial planner. The role of the professional financial planner is to help integrate the work of the estate planning team in developing the overall estate plan.

The estate planning process is complex and can be somewhat confusing. A CPA is usually involved as a member of the estate planning team because the process requires the identification of assets, calculation of the related adjusted tax basis, and other tax issues. An insurance specialist, such as a CLU or ChFC, is usually involved to help ensure liquidity at death and protection for the client from the risks of untimely death. A licensed attorney is almost always a part of the team because the process requires drafting numerous legal documents. The financial planner may serve as the team captain and assist in data collection, analysis, and investment decisions. Although each member of the planning team may individually be an estate expert, each specialty brings with it a particular and unique perspective, the combination of which is more likely to produce a better result for the client. The financial planner, unless a licensed attorney, should be careful not to engage in any act that could be found to be the unauthorized practice of law.

The Estate Planning Process

There are eight basic steps to the estate planning process.

1. Gather client information, including the client's current financial statements.
2. Establish the client's transfer objectives, including family and charitable objectives.
3. Define any problem areas, such as the disposition of assets, liquidity issues, excessive taxes or costs, and other situational needs, such as disability of an identified heir.
4. Determine the estate liquidity needs now and at five-year intervals for the life expectancy of the transferor, including estate transfer costs.
5. Establish priorities for all client objectives.
6. Develop a comprehensive plan of transfer consistent with all information and objectives.
7. Implement the estate plan.
8. Review the estate plan periodically, and update the plan when necessary (especially for changes in family situations).

Steps 1 and 2 are briefly discussed below. An estate planning course would cover steps 3 through 8.

Collecting Client Information and Defining Transfer Objectives

The collection of information is essential to gain a complete financial and family picture of the client and to assist the client in identifying financial risks. Information about prospective heirs and legatees needs to be collected to properly arrange for any transfer that the client wants to make.

To begin the estate planning process, the planner should collect the following:

- Current financial statements
- Family information (i.e., parents, children, any other dependents, their ages, and health status)
- A detailed list of assets and liabilities, including the fair market value, adjusted tax basis, and expected growth rate for all assets, how title is held, and the date acquired
- Copies of medical and disability insurance policies
- Copies of all life insurance policies in force identifying the ownership of each policy, the named insured, and the designated beneficiaries
- Copies of annuity contracts
- Copies of wills and trusts
- Identification of powers of attorney and general powers of appointment
- Copies of all previously filed income tax and gift tax returns (as available)
- Identification of assets previously gifted
- Other pertinent information

Once client and family information is collected, the process of determining the transfer objectives can be completed. Usually, the most important objective of the client is to transfer assets as the client wishes. Secondarily, the client generally wishes to avoid the shrinkage of the estate resulting from costs associated with the transfer. Exhibit 17.3 provides a list of common transfer objectives.

EXHIBIT 17.3 Common Transfer Objectives

- Minimize estate and transfer taxes to maximize the assets received by heirs.
- Avoid probate.
- Use lifetime transfers (gifts).
- Meet liquidity needs at death.
- Plan for children.
- Plan for the incapacity of the transferor.
- Provide for the needs of the surviving spouse.
- Fulfill charitable intentions of the transferor.

BASIC DOCUMENTS INCLUDED IN AN ESTATE PLAN

The basic documents used in estate planning include wills, living wills or medical directives, durable powers of attorney for health care or property, and side letters.

Will
A legal document used in estate planning that provides the testator, or will maker, the opportunity to control the distribution of property and avoid the state's intestacy law distribution scheme

Testamentary capacity
Having the mental capability to make a will to transfer assets; being of sound mind

Wills

A **will** is a legal document that provides the testator, or will maker, the opportunity to control the distribution of property and avoid the state's intestacy law distribution scheme. In general, a will is valid when the will maker is at least 18 years old or an emancipated minor and is "of sound mind," that is, possessing **testamentary capacity**. The "sound mind" rules are not as rigorous as the rules that are required to form contracts. In other words, a person who may not have the legal capacity to form a contract may have sufficient legal capacity to make a will.

Intestate
To die without a valid will

Intestacy laws
State laws that direct how a decedent's property will be distributed when the decedent dies without a will

Intestacy

To die **intestate** is to die without a valid will. In such a case, the state directs how the decedent's property will be distributed by creating a hypothetical will according to the state's **intestacy laws**. One size does not fit all, and the intestacy laws are not likely to distribute property the way every person would wish had he written his own will. There are possible adverse consequences of intestacy. In certain states, a spouse's share of the decedent's estate will be equal to a child's. For example, the surviving spouse's share with one child might be one-half, but with nine children it will be one-tenth. Certain states provide that a spouse's share is only a life estate with the true owner being the children. When there are no children, the surviving spouse may be forced to share with the deceased spouse's parents or brothers and sisters. Although each child's needs may be quite different, children may be treated equally and, therefore, not necessarily equitably. A person who has a will can appoint an executor in the will and, in many states, can specify that the executor serve without posting a bond. Intestacy may require the probate

Administrator
In the event a decedent dies intestate (without a valid will) or where an executor cannot be appointed by the probate court, the court appoints an administrator with powers called letters of administration, which enable the administrator to perform duties set down in the laws of intestacy

court to appoint an **administrator**, who will usually have to furnish a surety bond, thereby raising the costs of administration. The court, not the decedent, will select any administrator of the estate.

Types of Wills

Holographic will
Handwritten will dated and signed by the testator

Nuncupative (oral) will
Dying declarations made before sufficient witnesses

Statutory (formal) will
Generally drawn by an attorney and signed in the presence of witnesses, complying with the statutes for wills of the domiciliary state

Codicil
A document that amends or revises a prior will

There are three types of wills: holographic, nuncupative (oral), and statutory.

- **Holographic wills** are handwritten. The material provisions of the will are in the testator's handwriting. The will is dated and signed by the testator and does not need to be witnessed. Holographic wills are valid in most states.
- **Nuncupative (oral) wills** are dying declarations made before sufficient witnesses. In some states, nuncupative wills may be able to pass personal property only, not real property. The use of nuncupative wills is fairly restricted and is not permitted in all states.
- **Statutory (formal) wills** are generally drawn by an attorney, complying with the statutes for wills of the domiciliary state. They are usually signed in the presence of two witnesses. A person who is a beneficiary under the will usually cannot be a valid witness.

A document that amends or revises a prior will is known as a **codicil**.

Common Clauses

Although all wills are different, there are certain clauses that appear in almost all wills. Common clauses that are generally found in even the simplest will include the following:

- An introductory clause to identify the testator
- The establishment of the testator's domicile and residence
- A declaration that this is the last will and testament of the testator
- A revocation of all prior wills and codicils by the testator
- The identification and selection by the testator of the executor and successor executor
- A directive for the payment of debts clause
- A directive for the payment of taxes clause
- A disposition of tangible personal property clause
- A disposition of real estate clause (i.e., the residence and other real estate)
- Clauses regarding specific bequests of intangibles and cash
- A **residuary clause**—the transfer of the balance of any other assets to someone or to some institution (note that the failure to have a residuary clause means that the state intestacy laws will determine the distribution of any assets that are not specifically addressed in the will; also, taxes will be paid from the residuary unless specifically directed otherwise)
- An appointment and powers clause, naming fiduciaries, guardians, trustees, and so forth

Residuary clause
A general provision in a will that provides for the transfer of the balance of any assets not specifically mentioned in the will to someone or to some institution named by the testator

- A testator's signature clause
- An attestation clause, or witness clause
- A self-proving clause, which allows the probate court to find that the will was executed properly without the witnesses having to testify in court

Simultaneous death clause
In the event that both spouses die simultaneously, this clause provides a presumption that one spouse (predetermined) predeceased the other spouse

Survivorship clause
Provides that the beneficiary must survive the decedent for a specified period in order to receive the inheritance or bequest

Disclaimer clause
A common clause in a decedent's will that allows property to pass from one party to another without gift tax consequences

Other Clauses

More sophisticated wills often have additional clauses that dictate specific wishes regarding the handling of the estate. Additional clauses may include the following.

- A **simultaneous death clause**—In the event that both spouses die simultaneously, this clause provides a presumption of which spouse dies first.
- A **survivorship clause**—This clause provides that the beneficiary must survive the decedent for a specified period in order to receive the inheritance or bequest. This clause prevents property from being included in two different estates in rapid succession. For transfers to qualify for the estate tax marital deduction, the survival period included in a survivorship clause for a spouse can be no longer than six months.
- A **disclaimer clause**—A disclaimer clause simply reminds the heir that disclaiming inheritances may be an effective tool in estate planning. A disclaimer allows property to pass from one party to another without gift tax consequences.
- A no-contest clause—This clause discourages heirs from contesting the will by substantially decreasing or eliminating their bequest if they file a formal contest to the will.
- A spendthrift clause—This clause bars transfer of a beneficiary interest to a third party and stipulates that the interest is not subject to claims of the beneficiary's creditors. This clause is usually ineffective in a will.

Attorney-in-fact
The person designated by the principal in a power of attorney to act in place of the principal on the principal's behalf

Principal
In a power of attorney document, the person (power giver) who designates another person or persons to act as his attorney-in-fact

Power of Attorney

People frequently need another trusted person to make decisions for them regarding property or to make health care decisions for them under certain circumstances. A power of attorney is the legal document that allows the trusted person to act in one's place. It gives the right to one person, the **attorney-in-fact**(the power holder), to act in the place of the other person, the **principal** (power giver). A power of attorney may be very broad or very specific. For example, a power of attorney might limit the attorney-in-fact's authority to paying the principal's bills or be broad enough to allow the attorney-in-fact to handle all of the principal's financial affairs. All powers are revocable by the giver and cease at the death of giver. A durability feature should be included if the giver intends that the power survive the incapacity or disability of the giver. The principal (the power giver) must be at least 18 years old and legally competent.

Durable power of attorney issued either for health care or for property
A written document enabling the principal to designate another person or persons to act as the principal's attorney-in-fact

Durable feature
The power survives incapacity and disability of the principal

Durable Power of Attorney for Health Care or Property

A specific form of power of attorney is a **durable power of attorney issued either for health care or for property**. These powers are frequently issued to separate persons or, in the case of property, a financial institution. The power of attorney for health care or property eliminates the necessity to petition a local court to appoint a guardian ad litem or conservator to make health care or property decisions for a person who is incapacitated. It provides for continuity in the management of affairs in the event of disability and/or incapacity. The power may be springing or immediately effective (nonspringing). Generally, if the power is springing, the document must indicate that the power springs upon disability or incapacity and is not affected by subsequent disability or incapacity. The power is revocable by the principal. Durable powers of attorney are generally less expensive to set up and administer than a living trust or conservatorship. Durable powers of attorney can be abused, so the principal should give serious consideration to choosing the person to hold such power. The **durable feature** means the power survives incapacity and disability of the principal.

Note: A person possessing a durable power of attorney, in most cases, is not permitted to make gifts to himself or other family members (usually in conjunction with estate planning). If the power to gift to charitable or noncharitable donees is a desirable feature of the power of attorney, it should be separately and explicitly stated.

Living Wills and Advance Medical Directives

A living will (also known as an advance medical directive) is not a will at all but rather the maker's last wishes regarding sustaining life. It establishes the medical situations and circumstances in which the maker of the document no longer wants life-sustaining treatment. Such a document, though authorized in all states, must generally meet the formal requirements specified by state statute. A living will, or advance medical directive, only covers a narrow range of situations and usually applies only to terminally ill patients. Generally, a durable power of attorney issued for health care is insufficient to make decisions regarding the termination of life-sustaining procedures.

Side Instruction Letter or Personal Instruction Letter

Side instruction letter
Also known as a personal instruction letter, separate from a will; details the testator's wishes regarding the disposition of tangible possessions (household goods), the disposition of the decedent's body, and funeral arrangements

A **side instruction letter**, or personal instruction letter, details the testator's wishes regarding the disposition of tangible possessions (household goods), the disposition of the decedent's body, and funeral arrangements. Because the side instruction letter exists separately from the will itself, it avoids cluttering the will with small details that may cause conflict among heirs. The letter is given to the executor. The letter may contain information regarding the location of important personal documents, safe deposit boxes, outstanding loans, and other personal and financial information that is invaluable to the executor. Although in most cases, the letter has no legal standing, the executor will generally perform the wishes of the decedent.

THE PROBATE PROCESS DEFINED

The **probate process** proves the validity of any will, supervises the orderly distribution of assets to the heirs, and protects creditors by ensuring that valid debts of the estate are paid. In addition, when a person dies, there must be some legal way for the surviving heirs to obtain legal title to the property inherited. Probate is the legal process that performs the function of changing title to properties that do not change title any other way (e.g., by operation of law or by contract).

Probate process
Proves the validity of any will, supervises the orderly distribution of assets to the heirs, and protects creditors by ensuring that valid debts of the estate are paid. Probate is also the legal process that performs the function of changing property title from a decedent's name to an heir's name.

Exhibit 17.4 identifies the primary duties of an executor or administrator in the probate process. When an executor is named in a valid will, the probate court usually accepts that person and provides the executor with powers called letters testamentary. In the event of intestacy, or where an executor named in a will cannot be appointed by the probate court, the court will appoint an administrator (generally, a family member of the decedent). The court provides any appointed administrator with powers called letters of administration. The main differences between an executor and an administrator are that the decedent chooses the executor, the probate court names the administrator, and the administrator (but not always the executor) must post a bond.

EXHIBIT 17.4 Duties of Executor and/or Administrator

When the Decedent Dies Testate (with a Will)	When the Decedent Dies Intestate (without a Will)
■ The executor: — Locates and proves the will. — Locates witnesses to the will. — Receives letters testamentary from court.	■ The administrator: — May petition court for his own appointment. — Receives letters of administration. — Posts the required bond.

Duties of the Executor or Administrator

- Locates and assembles property
- Safeguards, manages, and invests property
- Advertises in legal newspapers that person has died and creditors and other interested parties are on notice
- Locates and communicates with potential beneficiaries
- Pays the expenses of the decedent's estate
- Pays the debts of the decedent
- Files federal and state tax returns, such as Forms 1040, 1041, and 706, and makes tax payments
- Distributes assets to beneficiaries according to the will or the laws of intestacy

Property Passing Through Probate

Property passing through probate includes property disposed of by a will. Also included in probate is property that does not pass by operation of law or by contract, or that is not covered by the will, such as intestate property resulting from the failure to provide a residuary clause. Exhibit 17.5 illustrates various assets that pass through and around probate.

EXHIBIT 17.5 Assets Passing Through and Around the Probate Process

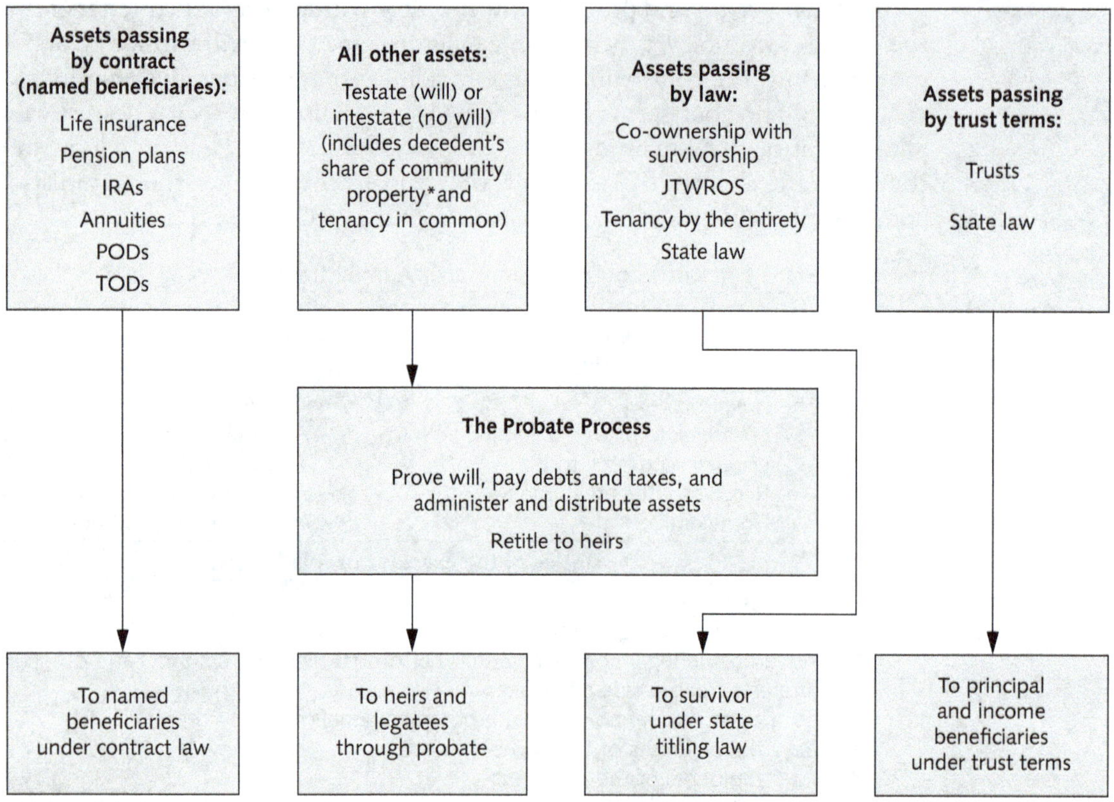

*Note that community property states vary on their probate treatment of community property passed to spouses.

Property Passing Outside of the Probate Process

Property that passes outside of the probate process includes property passing by contract and property passing by operation of law. Property passing by contract includes life insurance proceeds with a named beneficiary, pension plans and IRAs with named beneficiaries, annuities with named joint annuitants, and pay-on-death/transfer-on-death accounts. Property passing by operation of law includes property held as joint tenants with rights of survivorship (JTWROS or tenants by the entirety). Trust property passes outside of probate according to trust terms under state trust laws.

Advantages of the Probate Process

Probate has many advantages. It protects creditors by ensuring that the debts of the estate are paid before distribution to heirs. It implements the disposition objectives of the testator of the valid will. It provides clean title to heirs or legatees. It increases the chances that all parties in interest have notice of the proceedings and, therefore, a right to be heard. Finally, it provides for an orderly administration of the decedent's assets. The probate process requires the executor or administrator to advertise the upcoming probate for a certain period in legal newspapers to give interested parties notice to enter into the process.

Disadvantages of the Probate Process

Probate also has disadvantages. Probate can be both costly and complex. The legal notice requirement, attorney fees, and court costs create some of the costs. Delays are frequently caused by identification of property, valuation, identification of creditors and heirs, court delays, conflicts, and filing of taxes, to name a few. Real property located in a state outside the testator's domicile will require a separate ancillary probate in that state. One of the biggest disadvantages is loss of privacy because probate is open to public scrutiny.

OWNERSHIP AND TRANSFER OF PROPERTY

Property may be described as real property (land and buildings), tangible personal property (moveable property that may be touched and is not affixed to the land), or intangible personal property (stocks, bonds, patents, and copyrights). Some property is specifically titled to a named person or persons. Examples include real estate, automobiles (assuming the state has a motor vehicle title law), stocks, bonds, bank accounts, and retirement accounts. Other property may not have a specific title (e.g., household goods). The law of the state in which a person is domiciled determines the ways in which personal property can be transferred from one person to another, either during life or at death. For real estate, these matters are determined by the law of the state in which the property is located (the "situs"). Not all states have every alternative type or form of property interest. The forms have developed over time for the convenience of the citizens of the states that have adopted these forms.

The financial planning professional needs a working knowledge of the various forms of property interest and how each is transferred. Clients will need to be advised as to the initial ownership form depending on the client's objectives and the process the client will have to go through to transfer the property during life or at death.

Probate and Property Interests (Title and Ownership)

Property interests take several different legal forms and include fee simple, tenancy in common, joint tenancy, tenancy by the entirety, community property, pay-on-death accounts, and transfer-on-death accounts. In addition, there are property ownerships that are less than complete, including life estates, and interests for term.

Fee Simple

Fee simple
The complete individual ownership of property with all rights associated with outright ownership, such as the right to use, sell, gift, alienate, or convey

Fee simple is the complete individual ownership of property with all rights associated with outright ownership, such as the right to use, sell, gift, alienate, or convey. This type of property ownership interest is also known as fee simple absolute.

Tenancy in Common

Tenancy in common
Two or more persons hold an undivided interest in a whole property

Tenancy in common is where two or more persons hold an undivided interest in the whole property. The percentage owned by each party may differ. The property interest is treated as if it were owned outright, and the owner's interest can be used, sold, donated, willed, or passed with or without a will. When one of the owners dies, the other owner does not receive the decedent's interest by right of survivorship. The property passes through the probate process for retitling purposes and will pass under the owner's will or according to the state intestacy laws if the owner does not have a valid will. There is a right of partition, called the right to sever, in the event the owning parties cannot agree.

Joint Tenancy with Right of Survivorship (JTWROS)—Nonspouses or Spouses

Joint tenancy
Two or more persons, called equal owners, hold the same fractional interest in a property

Joint tenancy is where two or more persons, called equal owners, hold the same fractional interest in a property. The persons may be nonspouses or spouses. The right of survivorship (JTWROS) is normally implied. Joint tenants have the right to sever their interest in property without the consent of the other joint tenant, thereby destroying the survivorship right for that portion of the property. For example, if there are two joint tenants and one tenant severs his interest, the joint tenancy is destroyed. If there are three or more joint tenants and one tenant severs his interest, only that portion of the property is now held as tenants in common with the other two tenants. The joint tenancy between the remaining tenants is unaffected and will survive until altered by death or further severed by any of the other joint tenants. Property held JTWROS at the time of death of a tenant passes to the surviving tenant(s) outside of the probate process according to state law regarding survivorship rights.

Tenancy by the Entirety: JTWROS Between Spouses Only

Tenancy by the entirety
Joint tenancy with right of survivorship (JTWROS) that can only occur between a married couple

Tenancy by the entirety is a JTWROS that can only occur between a married couple. Generally, neither tenant is able to sever his interest without the consent of the other tenant spouse. At the death of the first tenant, the property is passed to the surviving spouse according to the state law regarding tenancy by the entirety. Because the state law provides for retitling upon presentation of a legal death certificate, there is no need for this property to go through the probate process.

Community Property

Community property
A regime where married individuals own an equal undivided interest in all wealth accumulated during marriage

Community property is a regime recognized in some states where married individuals own an equal undivided interest in all wealth accumulated during the marriage. Spouses may also own separate property that was acquired before marriage, or that was inherited or received by gift during marriage. It is possible to create separate property out of a community property by donating a spouse's interest to the other spouse. Community property does not have a survivorship feature, and thus the decedent's half will generally require the probate process for retitling. If a spouse passes away, one-half of the community property is included in the gross estate of the decedent spouse for estate tax purposes. There is also a step-up to fair market value for both halves of the community property at the death of the first spouse. This is in contrast to property titled as JTWROS or tenancy by the entirety, where only the decedent's one-half interest receives a step-up to fair market value. Community property may be dissolved by death, divorce, or agreement between the spouses.

Pay-on-Death (POD) and Transfer-on-Death (TOD) Accounts

Pay-on-death bank accounts are fairly new devices. Most states have adopted these devices for bank accounts (PODs) and/or investment accounts (TODs). Essentially, they provide that if the owner of the account has a named beneficiary for the account, that account will legally transfer to the named beneficiary without going through the probate process. Such transfers reduce transfer transaction costs and may improve liquidity for the named heirs, thereby providing estate liquidity. A similar transfer mechanism has existed for a long time with regard to IRAs and other retirement accounts, annuities, and life insurance where a named person is the beneficiary of the accounts or policy. These beneficiary transfer mechanisms are easy and efficient and avoid the probate process.

Less Than Complete Ownership Interests

Property law also provides for the creation of, or transfer of, less than the full and complete ownership of property. Two of the most common types of less than full ownership are the life estate and the interest for term.

Life Estate

Life estate
An interest in property that ceases upon the death of the owner of the life interest or estate

A **life estate** is an interest in property that ceases upon the death of the owner of the life interest or estate. A life estate provides a right to income, a right to use, or both. It may be thought of as a right for a life term. Generally at the date of death of the party having the life estate, the property is transferred to the person who has the remainder interest. An example of a life estate is where one person leaves the use of his beach house to someone for life and then to a charitable or noncharitable beneficiary when that person dies.

Interest for Term

An interest for term is another example of less than full ownership, but instead of a life interest, the interest is for a definite term. An interest for term could involve an income, a use interest, or both. At the end of the interest for term, the property is either transferred to the remainderman or reverts back to the original owner, such as with a lease.

Methods of Transfer

In general, property ownership can be transferred during life or at death using one of the following three methods: outright, legal, or beneficial. In an outright transfer, the transferee receives both the legal title and beneficial (equitable) interest, or economic, ownership. In a legal transfer, the transferee, such as a trust officer, receives only the legal title but not the beneficial (equitable) interest or economic ownership. In a beneficial transfer, the transferee receives beneficial (equitable) interest or economic ownership, as with a trust beneficiary, but not the legal title.

Transfers During Life (Inter Vivos)

Property ownership transfers during life include transfer by sale, by gift, and by partial gift or sale. Transfer by sale is a transfer for the full value and full consideration (i.e., straight sale or installment sale). Transfer by completed gift is a transfer for less than full fair market value. The concept of a completed gift is where the donor no longer has any control over the property that constituted the gift. When the value received by the transferor in a sale is less than the fair market value of the property, the transfer is called a bargain sale. This type of transaction may be treated as a completed sale for state property law but will be treated by the IRS as a transfer without full and adequate consideration and so will be part gift and part sale of the property.

Transfers at Death (Testamentary)

Transfers at death include transfers by will, by laws of intestacy, by other laws such as jointly held property with a survivorship feature (i.e., JTWROS or tenancy by the entirety), by contract, and by trust. Transfers at death by contract with a named beneficiary include insurance policies, IRAs, retirement plan assets such as Section 401(k) plans, marriage contracts, and annuities. Transfers at death by trust instrument may also include revocable trusts and irrevocable trusts. All revocable trusts become irrevocable at death.

Transfers at death require retitling of the property from the decedent to the new owner. There are various retitling mechanisms, including state laws, which automatically retitle jointly held property where a survivorship feature exists. There are also legal contracts, which call for immediate retitling, such as life insurance and annuities, retirement accounts, and PODs/TODs with named beneficiaries. Where property is not automatically retitled under one of these other mechanisms, it will go through the probate process and either pass under the decedent's will (testate) or following the state laws of intestacy for retitling to the heirs.

Consequences of Property Transfers

The consequences of transfers of property depend on the method of transfer. If the transfer is for less than full consideration, the transfer is by gift. Gift taxes may be due for inter vivos (during life) transfers and are usually paid by the donor-transferor. If the transfer is by sale, there is a loss of the sold asset and the possibility of capital gain taxes; however, the consideration received replaces the asset sold. If the transfer is at death, there are the issues of costs, federal and state estate taxes, delays, and publicity.

INTRODUCTION TO TRUSTS

Trust
A legal arrangement, usually provided for under state law, in which property is transferred by a grantor to a trustee for the management and conservation of the property for the benefit of the named beneficiaries

A **trust** is a legal arrangement (usually provided for under state law) in which property is transferred by a grantor to a trustee for the management and conservation of the property for the benefit of the named beneficiaries. The trustee could be either an individual or a financial institution (i.e., a bank). There are usually three parties to a trust: the grantor, the trustee, and the beneficiary. The grantor, or creator, transfers property to a trustee, who takes legal title to those assets for the benefit of all trust beneficiaries. The trustee must adhere to the trust provisions regarding investments, distributions of income and corpus, and eventual termination of the trust. The trust earns income on the trust assets and may distribute that income to those entitled to it, called income beneficiaries. Usually, the grantor has created two types of beneficiaries: the income beneficiary and the remainder beneficiary. The remainder beneficiary receives the trust corpus upon termination of the trust. The income beneficiary and remainder beneficiary may be the same person, which we refer to as a single beneficiary trust. Exhibit 17.6 illustrates the basic structure of a trust.

EXHIBIT 17.6 Structure of a Trust

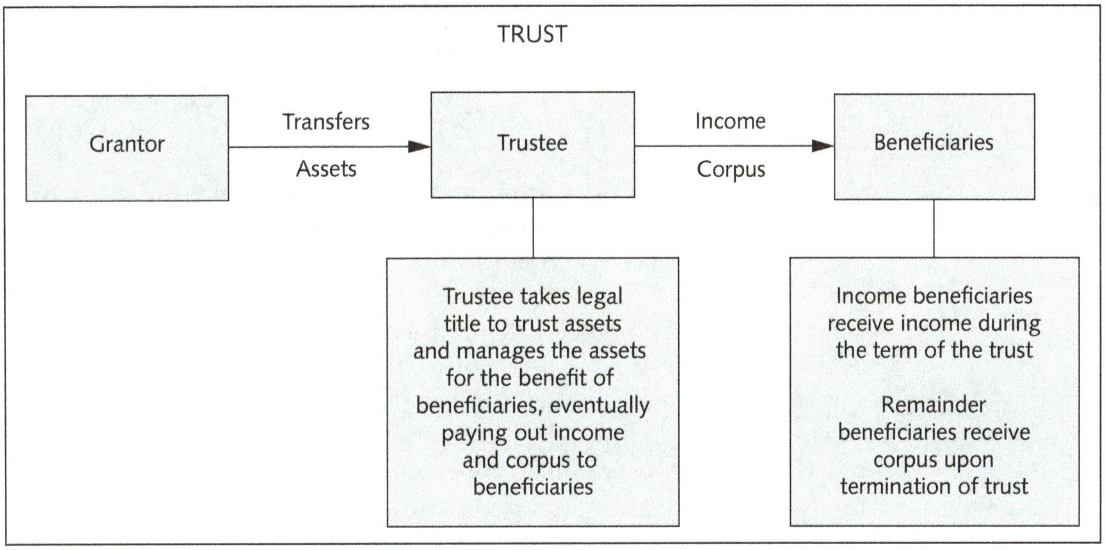

Trusts are created for a variety of purposes, including the avoidance of probate, transfer tax reduction, and the management of the trust assets. Exhibit 17.7 lists some types of trusts and their uses.

EXHIBIT 17.7 Types and Uses of Trusts

Type of Trust	Use of Trust
Living trust (revocable)	Used to manage assets. Protects in emergencies, such as medical. Avoids publicity and costs of probate. Property is included in the gross estate of the grantor (a type of grantor trust).
Irrevocable trusts (inter vivos)	Used to make gifts. Grantor has loss of control. Assets not included in gross estate of grantor unless grantor has reserved an interest (e.g., right to income) in the trust.
Testamentary trusts	Created by the will. Property is included in the gross estate and does not avoid probate. Generally used to manage assets of heirs.
Trust for minors	Manages assets for minors. May shift income tax burden to lower-bracket taxpayer.
Irrevocable life insurance trust (ILIT)	An irrevocable trust, usually created during life, used to hold an insurance policy and thus remove the proceeds from the insured's gross estate. The ILIT usually provides income to the spouse and the remainder interest to children or grandchildren.

Whether a trust is selected depends somewhat on the transfer goals of the grantor, the size of the estate, the nature of the relationship with and the financial competence of the spouse, any income needs of the spouse, the nature of the relationship with and financial security and competence of any adult children, any minor children, and any charitable intentions of the grantor. Where there is a split interest in assets (an income interest to one party and the remainder interest to a different party), a trust is used to reduce the risk that the income party will use all of the assets, leaving nothing for the remaindermen.

Common split interest trusts include the irrevocable life insurance trust, the credit equivalency trust, and QTIP trust, all of which may call for income to the decedent's spouse and the remainder to children or grandchildren. Trusts are also created to provide income to a noncharitable beneficiary (grantor/grantor spouse) with the remainder to a charity.

Trusts are either revocable or irrevocable and are either created during life (inter vivos) or at death (testamentary). If the trust is revocable, the property will be included in the gross estate of the grantor. A revocable trust will avoid the costs and process of probate but will not reduce federal estate taxes because the trust assets will be included in the grantor's gross estate. If the trust is irrevocable, the property will generally not be included in the gross estate of the grantor unless the grantor has reserved an interest, such as the right to receive income, in the trust assets. Irrevocable lifetime trusts are used to reduce estate taxes and to avoid probate. One example is the irrevocable life insurance trust (ILIT).

The inter vivos trust is created during the life of the grantor and may be revocable or irrevocable by the grantor. The property in an inter vivos trust avoids the probate process because the trust property is titled to the trust and not to the decedent. Alternatively, the property used to fund trusts created testamentary (by the will) first goes through the probate process before being retitled to the trust.

Although testamentary trusts neither reduce the estate tax nor avoid the costs and process of probate, they are useful in estate planning to protect the interests of minors, incompetents, or spendthrifts. Testamentary trusts are also useful when there is a split interest (income to one person and the remainder to someone else) such that the grantor did not want either party to be dependent on the other party for interest.

EXHIBIT 17.8 Trusts Summary Box

Established During Life	Probate	Gross Estate	Income Tax	Gift Tax
Revocable	Avoid	Included	To grantor	None at creation
Irrevocable	Avoid	Generally excluded	To trust or beneficiary	May be subject to
Established by Will				
Testamentary	Does not avoid	Included	To trust or beneficiary	Not applicable

Living Trusts

A living trust is one in which the grantor creates an inter vivos trust that is funded with part or all of the grantor's property. The advantage of a living trust is that the property does not pass through probate at death, but rather passes according to the trust provisions and with a minimum of publicity, expense, and delays.

A revocable living trust is revocable during the grantor's life and becomes irrevocable at the grantor's death. The fair market value of the assets in a revocable trust is included in the gross estate of the grantor. The grantor incurs no gift tax at the time of creation of a revocable trust because there is no completed gift.

For an irrevocable trust created during life, the grantor places property into a trust that he cannot rescind or amend. Transfers of property to an irrevocable trust constitute completed gifts, and any gift tax applies at the time the trust is created and funded. Assuming the grantor of the trust has no retained ownership interest in the irrevocable trust assets at death, such assets are generally not included in the grantor's gross estate, thereby providing both income tax and estate tax benefits to the grantor.

Grantor Trusts

A grantor trust is a trust in which the grantor transfers property into a trust but retains some right of enjoyment of the property, usually an income right. The Internal Revenue Code provides that if a grantor has control over the trust, a completed gift has not been made and the trust is not a separate taxable entity. Consequently, all the income, deductions, and credits of the trust pass through to the grantor for income tax purposes.

Later in this chapter, we identify some other trusts that are useful in certain situations and are used to reduce transfer taxes. These application trusts are listed in Exhibit 17.9.

EXHIBIT 17.9 Application Trusts and Their Uses

Application trusts	Trust uses
Credit equivalency trust (B trust—B stands for "bypassing the spouse's estate")	A B trust is usually created by the will (testamentary) and provides an amount equal to any credit equivalency (allowed by the federal estate tax laws) to be placed in trust with the spouse, the usual income beneficiary, and the children or grandchildren, or remaindermen. The principal of the trust is not included in the gross estate of the surviving spouse.
Power of appointment (POA or A) trust	A power of appointment trust is usually created by will (testamentary) providing all income annually to the spouse and with the spouse having a power to invade the principal. The assets in this trust qualify for the unlimited marital deduction at the death of the first spouse. The assets will be included in the gross estate of the surviving spouse to the extent they are not consumed during the surviving spouse's life.
Qualified terminable interest property (QTIP) trust	A testamentary trust whereby the executor elects QTIP status. The assets selected for this trust qualify for the unlimited marital deduction. The surviving spouse must receive all the trust income, paid at least annually. The remaindermen are chosen by the decedent. The assets remaining at the death of the surviving spouse are included in the gross estate of the surviving spouse.
Charitable remainder trusts (CRTs)	Charitable remainder trusts are irrevocable and may be created during life or testamentary. They are created to provide income to noncharitable beneficiaries (sometimes the grantor and/or spouse) with the remainder interest going to a charity at the end of the trust term.

REDUCING THE GROSS ESTATE

Generally speaking, if the amount of the gross estate is small, the amount of the estate tax liability will also be small. Appropriate use of qualified transfers (qualifying transfers directly to medical or educational institutions), gifts less than the annual exclusion amount, and the lifetime use of the exemption equivalency will all reduce the size of the gross estate at death. Obviously, personal consumption and lifetime transfers to charities will also reduce the gross estate. Removing the value of the proceeds of life insurance from the gross estate can dramatically reduce the size of the gross estate. There is generally little value in a decedent having an ownership interest in a life insurance policy where the decedent is the insured. The insured generally does not benefit from the proceeds during life and is usually attempting to benefit heirs at the time of the decedent's death. Why not let heirs (beneficiaries) or an ILIT own the insurance policy on the life of the insured? These are the two preferred financial and estate planning methods of owning life insurance. However, like everything else in financial planning, there are no absolutes, and careful consideration should be given as to who should own any insurance policy for a particular insured.

It is relatively easy to have a zero estate tax liability: either leave the entire taxable estate to a charity or leave the estate to the decedent's spouse in a way that qualifies for the marital deduction. However, the decedent may not have any charitable intentions or may not have a spouse to whom the decedent wants to leave the balance of the estate.

If a decedent first spouse leaves everything in a qualifying way to the surviving spouse, that will cause the deferral of estate tax until the death of the second spouse, which may (and many times does) occur shortly after the first death. In addition, because qualified transfers to a surviving spouse are added to the surviving spouse's personally owned assets to determine the gross estate of the surviving spouse, such transfers could increase the combined federal estate tax rate and amount of tax for the surviving spouse.

There are a wide variety of techniques for reducing the estate tax, all of which would be thoroughly covered in an estate planning course but are beyond the scope of this text. However, consider that only qualified transfers to a spouse qualify for the marital deduction. Is it possible to have a spouse benefit from assets without those assets qualifying for the unlimited marital deduction? The answer is yes, and as a result, the first decedent can transfer an amount equal to the estate tax exemption to nonspouse beneficiaries, simultaneously providing the spouse with a life income interest from that same transfer. Because this type of transfer is a so-called split interest (an income interest to the spouse and a remainder interest to someone else), the arrangement calls for a trust.

The Use of Life Insurance in Estate Planning

The federal estate tax return (Form 706) must be filed and the tax must generally be paid within nine months of the decedent's death. Thus, estate liquidity planning is essential and may require the purchase of life insurance because the life insurance proceeds are quickly available from the insurer upon presentation of a proper death certificate.

There is usually a need for liquid assets when someone dies. The hospital wants to be paid, the funeral home and cemetery must be paid, and creditors want to be paid. Even the costs associated with getting a death certificate from the coroner must be paid. Often the need for liquidity at death is satisfied with life insurance proceeds because life insurance is one of the quickest sources of liquidity. The beneficiary needs only to send a certified copy of the death certificate to the insurer, and the proceeds are generally paid immediately. Although insurance is an effective tool to provide liquidity at death, the proceeds of such insurance will be included in the decedent's gross estate if the insured (decedent) has any incidents of ownership in the life insurance policy at death, if the proceeds are payable to the decedent's estate, or if the decedent gifted the policy within three years of death. Therefore, it is wise for either the beneficiary of the insurance policy or an irrevocable life insurance trust to own the life insurance on the insured. Either of these arrangements will avoid including the life insurance proceeds in the insured's (decedent's) gross estate. The beneficiary-owner can then loan to the estate the cash needed for liquidity, keeping the policy proceeds from inclusion in the decedent-insured's gross estate.

COMMON ESTATE PLANNING MISTAKES

Invalid, Out-of-Date, or Poorly Drafted Wills

Having an invalid, out-of-date, or poorly drafted will can be detrimental to estate planning. No one wants to spend time developing an estate plan only to have it fall apart due to an inadequate will. An invalid will subjects the estate to intestacy laws that may distribute property contrary to the decedent's wishes. A will may be deemed invalid because it does not meet statutory requirements or because the decedent has moved to another state or domicile and has not reflected the new state's laws in the will. An outdated will often fails to minimize estate taxes because it does not contemplate changes in the tax law. Poorly drafted wills generally lack residuary clauses or other common drafting specificities, which can leave estate issues unresolved.

Simple Wills ("Sweetheart" or "I Love You" Wills)

A simple will leaves everything to the decedent's spouse. Leaving everything to a spouse can cause an overqualification of the estate because it fails to take advantage of the credit equivalency for the first spouse who dies. The second spouse to die may pay estate taxes that could have been avoided with a credit equivalency trust or bequest. There is also the risk of mismanagement of assets. Assets may be put in the hands of a spouse who does not have the education, experience, training, or desire to manage them efficiently and effectively.

Improperly Arranged or Inadequate Life Insurance

Improperly arranged or inadequate life insurance can defeat successful estate planning. If an insurance policy is arranged improperly, the proceeds will be included in the decedent's gross estate. Inclusion will occur when the policy is owned by the decedent, the proceeds are made payable to the estate, or the decedent has any incidents of ownership. Inclusion will also occur if the decedent gifted the policy to someone else within the last three years of the decedent's life.

An insurance policy is also improperly arranged when the beneficiary is ill equipped (emotionally, in legal capacity, or because of young age) to receive and manage those assets. A trust may provide the necessary management of the insurance needs.

Another way an insurance policy can be improperly arranged is when the decedent fails to name a contingent beneficiary. If the original beneficiary predeceases the decedent and there is no contingent beneficiary, the proceeds may be placed back in the estate, where the proceeds may be subject to creditor claims, state inheritance laws, federal estate taxes, or all three.

Another improper arrangement of life insurance that should be avoided is when the policy is owned by the spouse on the insured's life, and the spouse then names a child the beneficiary. At the death of the insured, the spouse has made a gift to the child.

An insurance policy is generally inadequate when it does not cover the needs of the insured, including survivor needs and estate liquidity needs. Survivor needs are generally calculated as the present value of the lost income (net of taxes and the decedent's consumption) over the remaining work life expectancy. An industry rule is to use 10 times salary to offset inflation. However, this may not provide sufficient estate liquidity where the majority of the other assets in the estate are both large in value and illiquid (real estate or a closely held business).

Possible Adverse Consequences of Jointly Held Property

Although having jointly held property with rights of survivorship offers some benefits, it can also pose several problems. One problem is that the decedent may not be able to direct the property to the person or entity he wishes because the survivor obtains complete ownership of the property. Another problem is that creating jointly held property might result in a completed gift. The consequence of this may be a federal and state gift tax liability as well as an estate tax liability.

Estate Liquidity Problems

Insufficient cash assets and inadequate planning are two estate liquidity problems that should be avoided. When there are insufficient cash assets and estate planning has been inadequate, the estate may be forced to liquidate assets when they are not fully valued or have not reached their potential value. The result is that assets may have to be sold at less than full value.

Wrong Executor/Trustee/Manager

Having the wrong executor/trustee/manager can cause several problems in the estate plan. When the named executor/trustee is incapable of administering the estate efficiently and effectively, it can make costs increase as a result of poor estate management. It can also cause potential conflicts of interest when there are proximity problems or family conflicts.

THE UNIFIED GIFT AND ESTATE TRANSFER TAX SYSTEM

The federal estate tax is a method of raising revenue for the federal government. It is also a method of social reallocation of wealth. The estate tax system prevents large masses of wealth from being transferred from one generation to subsequent generations. When a taxpayer with a large estate dies, a large portion of the estate will be paid to the federal government in the form of estate tax and thus will be reallocated to other members of society.

The unified estate and gift transfer tax system exists to prevent individuals (donors) from freely transferring property to others (donees) in an attempt to minimize income and estate tax. Congress, ever mindful of the resolve and ingenuity with which some taxpayers try to avoid federal taxes, established an excise tax for gifts during life. The excise tax is applied to the transfer of property gratuitously during life. In 1976, Congress unified the gift and estate tax schedules to prevent taxpayers from manipulating transfers during life and death.

The general theory behind the **unified gift and estate transfer tax system** is that at the time of transfer of property, either during life (gifts) or at death (bequests), the transferor will pay the same tax rate or amount for the transfer. Later in the chapter, we will point out major differences between transfers made during life and those made at death. Observe in Exhibit 17.10 that the maximum gift and estate tax rate in 2022 is 40%. As with many other types of taxes, there are ways to arrange one's financial affairs to reduce or eliminate the transfer tax, thus preserving a greater portion of the estate for heirs.

Unified gift and estate transfer tax system
Unified tax transfer system created by Congress to ensure that at the time of transfer of property, either during life (gifts) or at death (bequests), the transferor will pay the same tax rate or amount for the transfer

EXHIBIT 17.10 Unified Tax Rate Schedule for Gifts and Estates for 2022

More than $0 but not over $10,000	**18%** of such amount
More than $10,000 but not more than $20,000	$1,800 plus **20%** of any amount over $10,000
More than $20,000 but not more than $40,000	$3,800 plus **22%** of any amount over $20,000
More than $40,000 but not more than $60,000	$8,200 plus **24%** of any amount over $40,000
More than $60,000 but not more than $80,000	$13,000 plus **26%** of any amount over $60,000
More than $80,000 but not more than $100,000	$18,200 plus **28%** of any amount over $80,000
More than $100,000 but not more than $150,000	$23,800 plus **30%** of any amount over $100,000
More than $150,000 but not more than $250,000	$38,800 plus **32%** of any amount over $150,000
More than $250,000 but not more than $500,000	$70,800 plus **34%** of any amount over $250,000
More than $500,000 but not more than $750,000	$155,800 plus **37%** of any amount over $500,000
More than $750,000 but not more than $1,000,000	$248,300 plus 39% of any amount over $750,000
More than $1,000,000	$345,800 plus 40% of any amount over $1,000,000

The estate and gift tax rates and credit exemption amount for 2022 are as shown in Exhibit 17.11.

EXHIBIT 17.11 Estate and Gift Tax Rates and Credit Exemption Amount for 2022

Calendar Year	Estate, Gift, and GST Tax Exemption	Highest Estate and Gift Tax Rates
2022	$12,060,000	40%

Most property inherited from a decedent receives a stepped-up basis equal to its fair market value on the date of death or on the alternate valuation date (AVD) if the decedent's estate elected to use the AVD on the federal estate tax return. Property inherited from a decedent is always considered to be long-term property for purposes of the capital gains tax.

THE FEDERAL GIFT TAX SYSTEM

Purpose and Definition

Gift
In estate planning, a direct transfer of property or cash made during life

Recall that one of the estate planning objectives mentioned earlier in this chapter was the effective and efficient transfer of property. What could be more effective or efficient than a direct **gift** from the client during life to a loved one? First, because the client is still living, the transferor can ensure the completion of the gift. Second, the direct gift generally has little transaction cost except perhaps the cost to change the title to the asset (such as when retitling a car in the name of the donee). Third, the client (transferor) is able to see the beneficial effect of his transfer and the joy the gift brings to the donee while also enjoying the pleasure of making the gift. Unfortunately, whenever a gift is made, the client loses control of the asset given and loses income from the asset, which may be needed currently or at some point in the future. The creation of a joint bank account is not a gift until the joint tenant removes the money for his own benefit. Also, the client has financially empowered the donee (transferee), which may turn out to be ill advised. The transferee may not use the property wisely, as the transferor intended, or may no longer behave in a way in which the transferor desired. Even with these noted disadvantages, lifetime gifts remain a cornerstone of estate planning for the reasons stated here and for the reasons discussed next.

If the overall objective of the client is estate reduction, it may be wise to transfer the property with the greatest potential for future appreciation rather than cash or property that has already appreciated. A gift of property will be valued for gift tax purposes at the fair market value as of the date of the gift or transfer. Therefore, any future appreciation on the transferred property will be to the transferee (donee) and, thus, out of the transferor's gross estate. Property that commonly has substantial future appreciation includes (1) business interests, (2) real estate, (3) art or other collections, (4) investment securities (stocks and bonds), and (5) other intangible rights (patents, copyrights, and royalties). Thus, the selection of property for gifting requires careful financial and estate planning consideration.

Annual Exclusion

Annual exclusion
A result of a de minimis rule by Congress to eliminate the need for taxpayers to keep an account of, or report, small gifts. All individuals are allowed to gift, tax-free, up to $16,000 (for 2022) per donee per year.

All individuals are allowed to gift, tax free, up to $16,000 (for 2022) per donee per year. This **annual exclusion** is a result of a de minimis rule by Congress to help reduce reporting requirements of taxpayers for small gifts. However, to qualify for the annual exclusion, the gift must be of a present interest, which means that the donee can currently benefit from the gift. If the gift is of a future interest, such as a gift of a remainder interest in a trust, the gift does not qualify for the annual exclusion. The annual exclusion amount is indexed to the CPI.

Split gift
A joint gift made by spouses that has the effect of doubling the annual exclusion of gifts to the donee. A split gift requires the consent of the spouse and spouse's signature on Form 709.

If a person (transferor) is married and joins with his spouse to use both annual exclusions for a particular donee, the exclusion is effectively increased to $32,000 per donee per year. When one donor makes the gift but the donor's spouse consents and agrees to use their annual exclusion for that donee, then the joint gift is called a **split gift**. A gift tax return (Form 709) is required for all split gifts, and both spouses are required to sign the gift tax return. In addition, if an election to split gifts is made, it applies to all gifts made from both spouses during the year while the spouses were married. Only gifts made while the donors are married qualify for split gift treatment.

Not all joint gifts are subject to gift splitting. Gifts of community property, for example, do not require gift splitting because each spouse is deemed to own one-half of any community property. Therefore, any gift of community property is a joint gift not subject to gift splitting. Gift splitting was enacted to equalize community and noncommunity property states. Because gifts of community property are not considered gift splits, a return is not required unless the gifts constitute taxable gifts (i.e., exceed $32,000 to an individual recipient).

EXAMPLE Gift Splitting

Kelly made the following gifts in the current year:

Gift		Donee	Value
Cash		Nephew	$16,000
6-month CD		Niece	8,000
Antique rifle		Friend	21,000
Bonds in trust—Life estate to		Father	61,000
	Remainder to:	Niece	18,000
		Total	$124,000

Kelly's total taxable gifts for the current year equal $68,000 as described below:

Donee	FMV	Less Annual Exclusion	Total Taxable Gifts
Nephew	$16,000	$16,000	0
Niece	8,000	8,000	0
Friend	21,000	16,000	5,000
Father	61,000	16,000	45,000
Niece	18,000	Not available	18,000
Total gifts	$124,000	$56,000	$68,000

All of Kelly's gifts qualified for the annual exclusion except the gift to her niece consisting of the remainder interest in a trust. Because her niece is unable to currently use the gift, it is not a gift of a present interest and, therefore, does not qualify for the annual exclusion. All of the other gifts qualify because they are of a present interest.

EXAMPLE Gift Splitting Comparison

John and Mary made the following gifts during the current year:

	From John	From Mary	Total
To son, Paul	$40,000	$16,000	$56,000
To daughter, Virginia	40,000	6,000	46,000
To granddaughter, Terry	20,000	4,000	24,000
	$100,000	$26,000	$126,000

A comparison of gift splitting and not using gift splitting is provided for John and Mary's taxable gifts below.

If Gift Splitting Is Elected (the Parties Must Split All Gifts Made During Year)

	From John	From Mary	Total
To Paul	$28,000	$28,000	$56,000
To Virginia	23,000	23,000	46,000
To Terry	12,000	12,000	24,000
Total gross gifts	$63,000	$63,000	$126,000
Less annual exclusions			
For Paul	$16,000	$16,000	$32,000
For Virginia	16,000	16,000	32,000
For Terry	12,000	12,000	24,000
Total exclusions	$44,000	$44,000	$88,000
Current taxable gifts	$19,000	$19,000	$38,000

If Gift Splitting Is Not Elected

	From John	From Mary	Total
To Paul	$40,000	$16,000	$56,000
To Virginia	40,000	6,000	46,000
To Terry	20,000	4,000	24,000
Total gross gifts	$100,000	$26,000	$126,000
Less annual exclusions			
For Paul	$16,000	$16,000	$32,000
For Virginia	16,000	6,000	22,000
For Terry	16,000	4,000	20,000
Total exclusions	$48,000	$26,000	$74,000
Current taxable gifts	$52,000	$0	$52,000

An election to the split gifts in the above example results in a decrease in the total taxable gifts from $52,000 to $38,000. The $14,000 difference is a result of the couple not making full use of their annual exclusions when they don't use gift splitting ($52,000 – $38,000 = $14,000).

Applicable Credit Amount; Lifetime Exemption

In addition to the annual exclusion, a lifetime gift and estate tax credit is used to offset the gift and estate tax on inter vivos and testamentary transfers. This credit allows taxpayers to transfer during life assets totaling $12,060,000 (for 2022) without incurring any transfer tax. This amount is known as the applicable exclusion amount or the lifetime exemption amount.

EXHIBIT 17.12 Applicable Exclusion (Lifetime Exemption) Amount and Applicable Credit Amount

	2022
Applicable exclusion (lifetime exemption) amount	$12,060,000
Applicable credit amount	$4,769,800

The $12,060,000 exemption amount is a cumulative lifetime total and applies to all taxable gifts made during life. Any portion of the exemption amount that remains unused at death is applied toward the estate tax.

Portability Between Spouses

The $12,060,000 lifetime exemption amount is portable between spouses. Portability means that a surviving spouse may use any portion of a predeceased spouse's exemption amount that remained unused when the predeceased spouse died. For example, if the predeceased spouse used none of her exemption during life or at death, the surviving spouse could potentially have a $24,120,000 exemption. The surviving spouse may apply the predeceased spouse's unused exemption amount both to lifetime transfers and to transfers at death.

The restrictions on portability are as follows.

- The predeceased spouse must have died after December 31, 2010.
- The predeceased spouse's estate must have filed a timely estate tax return and made an election to permit the surviving spouse to use the deceased spouse's unused exemption amount.
- If a surviving spouse has more than one predeceased spouse, only the unused exemption amount of the last predeceased spouse is available.

EXAMPLE James and Margaret are married. James made no taxable gifts during his life. When he died in 2022, his taxable estate was $3 million. Because James used only $3 million of his $12,060,000 exemption amount when he died, Margaret can add his $9,060,000 unused exemption to her own $12,060,000 exemption amount for a total of $21,120,000. Margaret can apply the $21,120,000 exemption amount to lifetime taxable gifts and when she dies, her estate can apply any remaining amount against her estate tax.

Qualified Transfers

Qualified transfer
A payment made directly to an educational institution for tuition and fees or to a medical provider for medical expenses for the benefit of someone else

Certain transfers, called qualified transfers, are not subject to gift tax. A **qualified transfer** is a payment made directly to an educational institution for tuition and fees or directly to a medical provider for medical expenses for the benefit of someone else. These qualified transfers allow taxpayers to effectively transfer wealth to others without being subject to gift tax. However, to qualify for this treatment, the payments must be paid directly to the specific institution.

EXAMPLE Jennifer, who is single, gave an outright gift of $60,000 to her friend, Tiffany, who needed the money to pay her medical expenses. Because the gift was made to Tiffany instead of being paid directly to the medical institution, it cannot be considered a qualified transfer. However, the gift is of a present interest and, therefore, qualifies for the $16,000 annual exclusion. Therefore, Jennifer has made a taxable gift of $44,000 and must file a gift tax return to report the gift. If Jennifer had paid the medical expenses directly to the medical institution for Tiffany, the entire $60,000 received for Tiffany would have escaped gift taxes. In addition, Jennifer would have been able to give Tiffany another $16,000 that would qualify for the annual exclusion.

Because qualified transfers are not subject to gift tax and there is no limitation on the amount of the qualified transfer, it allows family members to provide assistance to other family members without worrying about transfer taxes. In addition, families can make use of the rules to minimize gift tax within the family by allowing, for example, grandparents to pay for college education for their grandchildren instead of making taxable gifts to the parents, who would, in turn, pay for the college expenses. Although qualified transfers are often used in family situations, the gift tax exclusion for qualified transfers is not limited to family members; it is available even if the donor is unrelated to the person who benefits from the transfer.

Gifts to Spouses

Marital deduction
unlimited deduction for transfers of property to a spouse during life (gifts) or at death (bequests)

The law provides an unlimited marital deduction for gifts and bequests to a spouse, including a same-sex spouse. To be eligible for the gift tax **marital deduction**, however, the donee spouse must be a citizen of the United States. When the donee spouse is a non-citizen, there is a special annual exclusion that shelters allows gifts of up to $164,000 per year to the non-citizen spouse (in 2022).

The estate tax marital deduction for non-citizen spouses is discussed later in this chapter.

Payments for Support

Payments for legal support
transfers to children that are essentially legal support obligations; exempt from gift tax rules

Payments for legal support are transfers to children that are essentially legal support obligations. Payments of support are exempt from the gift tax rules.

Reporting and Paying Taxes

Taxable gifts are reported on the federal gift tax return, Form 709. The gift tax return is due April 15 but may be extended until October 15, as with individual income tax returns. However, the gift tax is not extended as a result of the extension of time to file and is therefore due on April 15, similar to individual income tax. The donor is liable for any gift tax due. The gift tax return is also used to report transfers that are subject to generation-skipping transfer tax, which is discussed later in the chapter.

EXHIBIT 17.13 Basic Strategies for Transferring Wealth Through Gifting

Generally, if the objective of the transferor is to reduce the size of his gross estate, he can use the following lifetime gifting techniques to achieve a lower gross estate at death:

- Make optimal use of qualified educational transfers (pay tuition for children and grandchildren from private school through professional education).
- Pay medical costs for children, grandchildren, and heirs directly to provider institutions.
- Make optimal use of the $16,000 annual gift exclusion ($32,000 if the gift is made jointly with the spouse). Example: John is married to Joan and has 3 adult children who all have stable marriages, and there are 7 grandchildren. John and Joan can gift $416,000 per year without incurring any gift tax: $32,000 × 13 transferees (3 children, 3 spouses, 7 grandchildren)
- A spouse may make unlimited lifetime gifts to a spouse who is a U.S. citizen.
- If the above four strategies are completely exhausted, the transferor can begin using his applicable exclusion amount ($12,060,000) while still paying no gift tax until the summation of lifetime taxable gifts exceeds the lifetime credit equivalency amount.
- Any gift tax paid on gifts prior to three years of death is also excluded from the gross estate of the transferor. This is discussed later in this chapter.

EXHIBIT 17.14 Form 709

Form **709**

Department of the Treasury
Internal Revenue Service

United States Gift (and Generation-Skipping Transfer) Tax Return

▶ Go to *www.irs.gov/Form709* for instructions and the latest information.
(For gifts made during calendar year 2021)
▶ See instructions.

OMB No. 1545-0020

2021

Part 1—General Information

1 Donor's first name and middle initial	2 Donor's last name	3 Donor's social security number
4 Address (number, street, and apartment number)		5 Legal residence (domicile)
6 City or town, state or province, country, and ZIP or foreign postal code		7 Citizenship (see instructions)

		Yes	No
8	If the donor died during the year, check here ▶ ☐ and enter date of death ____________, ______.		
9	If you extended the time to file this Form 709, check here ▶ ☐		
10	Enter the total number of donees listed on Schedule A. Count each person only once ▶		
11a	Have you (the donor) previously filed a Form 709 (or 709-A) for any other year? If "No," skip line 11b		
b	Has your address changed since you last filed Form 709 (or 709-A)?		
12	**Gifts by husband or wife to third parties.** Do you consent to have the gifts (including generation-skipping transfers) made by you and by your spouse to third parties during the calendar year considered as made one-half by each of you? (See instructions.) (If the answer is "Yes," the following information must be furnished and your spouse must sign the consent shown below. **If the answer is "No," skip lines 13–18.**)		
13	Name of consenting spouse — 14 SSN		
15	Were you married to one another during the entire calendar year? See instructions		
16	If line 15 is "No," check whether ☐ married ☐ divorced or ☐ widowed/deceased, and give date. See instructions ▶		
17	Will a gift tax return for this year be filed by your spouse? If "Yes," mail both returns in the same envelope		
18	**Consent of Spouse.** I consent to have the gifts (and generation-skipping transfers) made by me and by my spouse to third parties during the calendar year considered as made one-half by each of us. We are both aware of the joint and several liability for tax created by the execution of this consent.		
	Consenting spouse's signature ▶ **Date ▶**		
19	Have you applied a DSUE amount received from a predeceased spouse to a gift or gifts reported on this or a previous Form 709? If "Yes," complete Schedule C		

Part 2—Tax Computation

1	Enter the amount from Schedule A, Part 4, line 11	1	
2	Enter the amount from Schedule B, line 3	2	
3	Total taxable gifts. Add lines 1 and 2	3	
4	Tax computed on amount on line 3 (see *Table for Computing Gift Tax* in instructions)	4	
5	Tax computed on amount on line 2 (see *Table for Computing Gift Tax* in instructions)	5	
6	Balance. Subtract line 5 from line 4	6	
7	Applicable credit amount. If donor has DSUE amount from predeceased spouse(s) or Restored Exclusion Amount, enter amount from Schedule C, line 5; otherwise, see instructions	7	
8	Enter the applicable credit against tax allowable for all prior periods (from Sch. B, line 1, col. C)	8	
9	Balance. Subtract line 8 from line 7. Do not enter less than zero	9	
10	Enter 20% (0.20) of the amount allowed as a specific exemption for gifts made after September 8, 1976, and before January 1, 1977. See instructions	10	
11	Balance. Subtract line 10 from line 9. Do not enter less than zero	11	
12	Applicable credit. Enter the smaller of line 6 or line 11	12	
13	Credit for foreign gift taxes (see instructions)	13	
14	Total credits. Add lines 12 and 13	14	
15	Balance. Subtract line 14 from line 6. Do not enter less than zero	15	
16	Generation-skipping transfer taxes (from Schedule D, Part 3, col. G, total)	16	
17	Total tax. Add lines 15 and 16	17	
18	Gift and generation-skipping transfer taxes prepaid with extension of time to file	18	
19	If line 18 is less than line 17, enter **balance due.** See instructions	19	
20	If line 18 is greater than line 17, enter **amount to be refunded**	20	

Attach check or money order here.

Sign Here

Under penalties of perjury, I declare that I have examined this return, including any accompanying schedules and statements, and to the best of my knowledge and belief, it is true, correct, and complete. Declaration of preparer (other than donor) is based on all information of which preparer has any knowledge.

May the IRS discuss this return with the preparer shown below? See instructions. ☐ **Yes** ☐ **No**

▶ Signature of donor | Date

Paid Preparer Use Only

Print/Type preparer's name	Preparer's signature	Date	Check ☐ if self-employed	PTIN
Firm's name ▶			Firm's EIN ▶	
Firm's address ▶			Phone no.	

For Disclosure, Privacy Act, and Paperwork Reduction Act Notice, see the instructions for this form. Cat. No. 16783M Form **709** (2021)

EXHIBIT 17.14 Form 709 (continued)

Form 709 (2021) Page 2

SCHEDULE A Computation of Taxable Gifts (Including transfers in trust) (see instructions)

A Does the value of any item listed on Schedule A reflect any valuation discount? If "Yes," attach explanation . . . . Yes ☐ No ☐

B ☐ ◄ Check here if you elect under section 529(c)(2)(B) to treat any contributions made this year to a qualified tuition program as made ratably over a 5-year period beginning this year. See instructions. Attach explanation.

Part 1—Gifts Subject Only to Gift Tax. Gifts less political organization, medical, and educational exclusions. See instructions.

A Item number	B • Donee's name and address • Relationship to donor (if any) • Description of gift • If the gift was of securities, give CUSIP no. • If closely held entity, give EIN	C	D Donor's adjusted basis of gift	E Date of gift	F Value at date of gift	G For split gifts, enter 1/2 of column F	H Net transfer (subtract col. G from col. F)
1							
Gifts made by spouse—*complete **only** if you are splitting gifts with your spouse and he/she also made gifts.*							
Total of Part 1. Add amounts from Part 1, column H . . . . . ►							

Part 2—Direct Skips. Gifts that are direct skips and are subject to both gift tax and generation-skipping transfer tax. You must list the gifts in chronological order.

A Item number	B • Donee's name and address • Relationship to donor (if any) • Description of gift • If the gift was of securities, give CUSIP no. • If closely held entity, give EIN	C 2632(b) election out	D Donor's adjusted basis of gift	E Date of gift	F Value at date of gift	G For split gifts, enter 1/2 of column F	H Net transfer (subtract col. G from col. F)
1							
Gifts made by spouse—*complete **only** if you are splitting gifts with your spouse and he/she also made gifts.*							
Total of Part 2. Add amounts from Part 2, column H . . . . . ►							

Part 3—Indirect Skips and Other Transfers in Trust. Gifts to trusts that are indirect skips as defined under section 2632(c) or to trusts that are currently subject to gift tax and may later be subject to generation-skipping transfer tax. You must list these gifts in chronological order.

A Item number	B • Donee's name and address • Relationship to donor (if any) • Description of gift • If the gift was of securities, give CUSIP no. • If closely held entity, give EIN	C 2632(c) election	D Donor's adjusted basis of gift	E Date of gift	F Value at date of gift	G For split gifts, enter 1/2 of column F	H Net transfer (subtract col. G from col. F)
1							
Gifts made by spouse—*complete **only** if you are splitting gifts with your spouse and he/she also made gifts.*							
Total of Part 3. Add amounts from Part 3, column H . . . . . ►							

(If more space is needed, attach additional statements.) Form **709** (2021)

EXHIBIT 17.14 Form 709 (continued)

Form 709 (2021) Page **3**

Part 4—Taxable Gift Reconciliation

1	Total value of gifts of donor. Add totals from column H of Parts 1, 2, and 3			1	
2	Total annual exclusions for gifts listed on line 1 (see instructions)			2	
3	Total included amount of gifts. Subtract line 2 from line 1			3	
Deductions (see instructions)					
4	Gifts of interests to spouse for which a marital deduction will be claimed, based on item numbers ______ of Schedule A	4			
5	Exclusions attributable to gifts on line 4	5			
6	Marital deduction. Subtract line 5 from line 4	6			
7	Charitable deduction, based on item numbers ______ less exclusions	7			
8	Total deductions. Add lines 6 and 7			8	
9	Subtract line 8 from line 3			9	
10	Generation-skipping transfer taxes payable with this Form 709 (from Schedule D, Part 3, col. G, total)			10	
11	**Taxable gifts.** Add lines 9 and 10. Enter here and on page 1, Part 2—Tax Computation, line 1			11	

Terminable Interest (QTIP) Marital Deduction. (See instructions for Schedule A, Part 4, line 4.)

If a trust (or other property) meets the requirements of qualified terminable interest property under section 2523(f), and:

a. The trust (or other property) is listed on Schedule A; and

b. The value of the trust (or other property) is entered in whole or in part as a deduction on Schedule A, Part 4, line 4, then the donor shall be deemed to have made an election to have such trust (or other property) treated as qualified terminable interest property under section 2523(f).

If less than the entire value of the trust (or other property) that the donor has included in Parts 1 and 3 of Schedule A is entered as a deduction on line 4, the donor shall be considered to have made an election only as to a fraction of the trust (or other property). The numerator of this fraction is equal to the amount of the trust (or other property) deducted on Schedule A, Part 4, line 6. The denominator is equal to the total value of the trust (or other property) listed in Parts 1 and 3 of Schedule A.

If you make the QTIP election, the terminable interest property involved will be included in your spouse's gross estate upon his or her death (section 2044). See instructions for line 4 of Schedule A. If your spouse disposes (by gift or otherwise) of all or part of the qualifying life income interest, he or she will be considered to have made a transfer of the entire property that is subject to the gift tax. See *Transfer of Certain Life Estates Received From Spouse* in the instructions.

12 Election Out of QTIP Treatment of Annuities

☐ ◀ Check here if you elect under section 2523(f)(6) **not** to treat as qualified terminable interest property any joint and survivor annuities that are reported on Schedule A and would otherwise be treated as qualified terminable interest property under section 2523(f). See instructions. Enter the item numbers from Schedule A for the annuities for which you are making this election ▶

SCHEDULE B Gifts From Prior Periods

If you answered "Yes" on line 11a of page 1, Part 1, see the instructions for completing Schedule B. If you answered "No," skip to the Tax Computation on page 1 (or Schedule C or D, if applicable). Complete Schedule A before beginning Schedule B. See instructions for recalculation of the column C amounts. Attach calculations.

A Calendar year or calendar quarter (see instructions)	B Internal Revenue office where prior return was filed	C Amount of applicable credit (unified credit) against gift tax for periods after December 31, 1976	D Amount of specific exemption for prior periods ending before January 1, 1977	E Amount of taxable gifts
1 Totals for prior periods	1			

2	Amount, if any, by which total specific exemption, line 1, column D, is more than $30,000	2	
3	Total amount of taxable gifts for prior periods. Add amount on line 1, column E, and amount, if any, on line 2. Enter here and on page 1, Part 2—Tax Computation, line 2	3	

(If more space is needed, attach additional statements.) Form **709** (2021)

EXHIBIT 17.14 Form 709 (continued)

Form 709 (2021) Page **4**

SCHEDULE C Deceased Spousal Unused Exclusion (DSUE) Amount and Restored Exclusion

Provide the following information to determine the DSUE amount and applicable credit received from prior spouses. Complete Schedule A before beginning Schedule C.

A Name of deceased spouse (dates of death after December 31, 2010, only)	B Date of death	C Portability election made?		D If "Yes," DSUE amount received from spouse	E DSUE amount applied by donor to lifetime gifts (list current and prior gifts)	F Date of gift(s) (enter as mm/dd/yy for Part 1 and as yyyy for Part 2)
		Yes	No			
Part 1—DSUE RECEIVED FROM LAST DECEASED SPOUSE						
Part 2—DSUE RECEIVED FROM PREDECEASED SPOUSE(S)						
TOTAL (for all DSUE amounts applied from column E for Part 1 and Part 2) . . . . ▶						

1	Donor's basic exclusion amount (see instructions)	1	
2	Total from column E, Parts 1 and 2	2	
3	Restored Exclusion Amount (see instructions)	3	
4	Add lines 1, 2, and 3	4	
5	Applicable credit on amount in line 4 (see *Table for Computing Gift Tax* in the instructions). Enter here and on line 7, Part 2—Tax Computation	5	

SCHEDULE D Computation of Generation-Skipping Transfer Tax

Note: Inter vivos direct skips that are completely excluded by the GST exemption must still be fully reported (including value and exemptions claimed) on Schedule D.

Part 1—Generation-Skipping Transfers. List items from Schedule A first, then items to be reported on Schedule D, including any transfers subject to an Estate Tax Inclusion Period (ETIP).

A Item number (from Schedule A, Part 2, col. A, then ETIP transfers, if any)	B Description (only for ETIP transfers)	C Value (from Schedule A, Part 2, col. H, or close of ETIP described in col. B)	D Nontaxable portion of transfer	E Net transfer (subtract col. D from col. C)
1				
Gifts made by spouse (for gift splitting only)				

(If more space is needed, attach additional statements.) Form **709** (2021)

EXHIBIT 17.14 Form 709 (continued)

Form 709 (2021) Page **5**

Part 2—GST Exemption Reconciliation (Section 2631) and Section 2652(a)(3) Election

Check here ▶ ☐ if you are making a section 2652(a)(3) (special QTIP) election. See instructions.

Enter the item numbers from Schedule A of the gifts for which you are making this election ▶ ________________

1	Maximum allowable exemption (see instructions)	1	
2	Total exemption used for periods before filing this return	2	
3	Exemption available for this return. Subtract line 2 from line 1	3	
4	Exemption claimed on this return from Part 3, column C, total below	4	
5	Automatic allocation of exemption to transfers reported on Schedule A, Part 3. To opt out of the automatic allocation rules, you must attach an "**Election Out**" statement. See instructions	5	
6	Exemption allocated to transfers not shown on line 4 or line 5 above. **You must attach a "Notice of Allocation."** See instructions	6	
7	Add lines 4, 5, and 6	7	
8	Exemption available for future transfers. Subtract line 7 from line 3	8	

Part 3—Tax Computation

A Item number (from Schedule D, Part 1)	B Net transfer (from Schedule D, Part 1, col. E)	C GST exemption allocated	D Divide col. C by col. B	E Inclusion ratio (Subtract col. D from 1.000)	F Applicable rate (multiply col. E by 40% (0.40))	G Generation-skipping transfer tax (multiply col. B by col. F)
1						
Gifts made by spouse (for gift splitting only)						
Total exemption claimed. Enter here and on Part 2, line 4, above. May not exceed Part 2, line 3, above			**Total generation-skipping transfer tax.** Enter here; on page 3, Schedule A, Part 4, line 10; and on page 1, Part 2—Tax Computation, line 16			

(If more space is needed, attach additional statements.) Form **709** (2021)

THE FEDERAL ESTATE TAX SYSTEM

Purpose and Definition

Federal estate tax
An excise tax on the right to transfer assets by a decedent

The **federal estate tax** is an excise tax on the right to transfer assets by a decedent. To properly determine the estate tax liability, the executor must first determine what assets are included in the gross estate. Generally, the gross estate includes all property that the decedent owned at death at the fair market value of the decedent's interest.

The gross estate (Exhibit 17.15, line 1) less the enumerated deductible expenses (lines 2–6) equals the adjusted gross estate (line 8). From the adjusted gross estate (line 7) are three deductions: (1) the value of property left to a qualified charity and (2) the value of qualified property left to the decedent's spouse and (3) state death taxes paid. The net result of the adjusted gross estate (line 7) less any state death taxes paid (line 10), any marital deduction (line 9) and any charitable deduction (line 8) equals the taxable estate (line 11).

Following the determination of the taxable estate, any taxable gifts (transfers that did not qualify for the annual exclusion) made after 1976 are added to determine the tentative tax base (line 11 + line 12 = line 13). The tentative tax (line 14) is calculated using the Unified Estate and Gift Tax Schedule. From the tentative tax are subtracted any credits, such as previous gift tax paid (line 15) and the applicable credit amount (line 16), to determine the federal estate tax liability (line 17).

EXHIBIT 17.15 The Estate Tax Formula

(1)	Gross estate (GE)		$ ________	Gross estate
	Less deductions:			
(2)	Last medical	$ ________		
(3)	Administrative costs	$ ________		
(4)	Funeral	$ ________		
(5)	Debts	$ ________		
(6)	Losses during estate administration	$ ________	$ ________	Deductions
(7)	Equals: adjusted gross estate (AGE)		$ ________	Adjusted gross estate
(8)	Less: charitable deduction	$ ________		
(9)	Less: marital deduction	$ ________		
(10)	Less: state death tax paid	$ ________	$ ________	
(11)	Equals: taxable estate (TE)		$ ________	Taxable estate
(12)	Add: previous taxable gifts (post-1976)		$ ________	Post-1976 gifts
(13)	Equals: tentative tax base (TTB)		$ ________	Tentative tax base
(14)	Tentative tax (TT)		$ ________	Tentative tax
	Less: credits			
(15)	Previous gift tax deemed paid	$ ________		
(16)	Applicable credit amount	$ ________		
(17)	Equals: federal estate tax liability (FETL)		$ ________	Federal estate tax liability

Reporting and Paying Taxes

Federal estate tax is reported on the federal estate tax return (Form 706). The federal estate tax return is due nine months from the date of death but may be extended six months. However, an extension of time for filing does not extend the time for paying the estate tax. Therefore, unless permitted by one of the statutory exceptions, estate tax is payable nine months after the date of death.

The Gross Estate

The financial planner must have a clear understanding of the size of the client's **gross estate** in order to develop a meaningful estate plan. The size and types of assets included in the gross estate will directly determine which planning techniques should be implemented. Exhibit 17.16 illustrates most of the asset types that may be included in the gross estate as covered in Section 2033 (the relevant code section) of the Internal Revenue Code.

Gross estate
All assets included in a decedent's estate, including but not limited to cash, stocks, bonds, annuities, retirement accounts, notes receivable, personal residences, automobiles, art collections, life insurance proceeds, and income tax refunds due

EXHIBIT 17.16 Assets Included in the Gross Estate

Cash
Stocks and bonds
Annuities
Retirement accounts
Notes receivable
Personal residence
Other real estate
Household goods
Automobiles
Business interests
Proceeds of life insurance
Collections (art, wine, jewelry)
Vested future rights
Outstanding loans due decedent from others
Income tax refunds due
Patents/copyrights
Damages owed decedent
Dividends declared and payable
Income in respect of decedent
Decedent's share of property held with others
Other tangible personal property

*List may not be all inclusive.

Note that the gross estate includes the decedent's interest in any jointly held property and the proceeds of life insurance on the decedents life where (1) the decedent had any incidents of ownership in the policy at the time of death, (2) the decedent had assigned (gifted) the insurance to someone else within three years of the decedent's death, or (3) the proceeds are payable to the decedent's estate. The valuation of property included in the gross estate is either the fair market value at the date of death or, if properly elected, the value for the alternate valuation date (six months from the date of death or date of sale if it occurs between the date of death and the alternate valuation date). The alternate valuation date is provided to give relief to a decedent who happened to die on a date when the gross estate was valued very highly as a result of the temporary market conditions. Certain requirements must be met in order to elect the alternate valuation date.

Deductions From the Gross Estate

Adjusted gross estate
Gross estate less deductions provided for by law in recognition that the entire value of the gross estate will not be transferred to the heirs due to costs, debts, and certain other deductions

Once the assets are identified and the value of the gross estate is determined, the next step is to determine the allowed deductions to arrive at the **adjusted gross estate** (see Exhibit 17.15). The deductions are provided in recognition that the entire value of the gross estate will not be transferred to the heirs because of costs, debts, and certain other deductions.

The adjusted gross estate is determined by deducting the following:

- Funeral expenses
- Last medical costs
- Administration expenses
- Debts
- Losses during estate administration

Funeral Costs

Reasonable expenditures related to the funeral, such as interment costs, burial plot, grave marker, and transportation of the body to the place of burial, are deductible for estate tax purposes.

Last Medical Costs

Medical costs related to the decedent's last illness are deductible from the gross estate as long as they are not deducted on the decedent's final federal income tax return.

Administrative Expenses

Any expenses related to the administration of the estate are deductible from either the estate tax return (Form 706) or the estate's income tax return (Form 1041). These expenses generally include attorney and accountant fees for preparing the estate tax return, the final Form 1040, and the estate income tax return and expenses related to the retitling of assets through the probate process. These costs may also include appraisal and valuation fees necessary to determine values of assets included in the gross estate for estate tax purposes.

Debts

All debts of the decedent are deductible from the gross estate. These debts include any amounts the decedent was obligated to pay while alive, plus interest accrued to the date of death. Debts generally include such items as outstanding mortgages, income tax due, credit card balances, and other miscellaneous outstanding debts.

Losses During Estate Administration

Any losses to the estate during the period of administration, including casualty and theft losses, are deductible expenses to the extent they exceed insurance reimbursements.

State Death Taxes

There is also a deduction for death taxes actually paid to any state. The deduction for the state death taxes paid is not deducted to arrive at the adjusted gross estate; instead, the state death taxes are deducted from the adjusted gross estate at the same time both the charitable and marital deductions are made to arrive at the taxable estate. (See Exhibit 17.15, line 10).

THE CHARITABLE DEDUCTION

Definition

Charitable deduction
A charitable contribution made as a gift to a qualified organization

Internal Revenue Code 170(c) defines a charitable contribution as a gift made to a qualified organization. To qualify for a **charitable deduction**, a contribution must be made to one of the following organizations:

- A state or possession of the United States or any subdivision thereof
- A corporation, trust, or community chest, fund, or foundation that is situated in the United States and is organized exclusively for religious, charitable, scientific, literary, or educational purposes or for the prevention of cruelty to children or animals
- A veteran's organization
- A fraternal organization operating under the lodge system
- A cemetery company

The IRS publishes a list (Publication 78) of organizations that have applied for and received tax-exempt status under section 501 of the Internal Revenue Code.

Types of Charitable Bequests

Direct Charitable Bequests

A direct charitable bequest of any property to a qualifying organization is fully deductible from the gross estate in arriving at the taxable estate.

Charitable remainder trust (CRT)
A split-interest trust; if created during life, the income goes to one or more parties, usually the grantor, or grantor and spouse for life, and upon the income beneficiary's death, the principal (remainder) is transferred to a charity; if the CRT is created testamentary, the usual income beneficiary is the spouse for life

Charitable Trusts

A **charitable remainder trust (CRT)** is an estate planning vehicle used to reduce the impact of income and estate taxes. A CRT is created by transferring property to a charitable trust. Although the property transferred to the trust may be cash, it generally consists of appreciated property. Because it is a nontaxable entity, the CRT can dispose of property without incurring taxable income upon the disposition. The trust is established so that an income interest, which may be in the form of an annuity or a unitrust payment, is paid to either the donor or a family member of the donor. At the termination of the income interest, which generally occurs at the death of the income beneficiary, the remaining assets in the CRT are transferred to the charity named in the trust document. Because there are two beneficiaries—the income beneficiary or annuitant and the named charity of a CRT—the CRT is considered a split-interest trust.

Charitable remainder trusts can be established during life or at the death of the donor. CRTs that are established during life provide several benefits. First, the donor will receive an income tax deduction equal to the value of the property transferred to the trust less the value of the income stream that is expected to be received by the income beneficiary. Second, although all or part of the trust assets will be included in the donor's gross estate if the donor reserved the right to income from the CRT during his life, the donor's estate is entitled to a charitable deduction for the value of the remainder interest that passes to charity. Third, the CRT provides an income stream to the donor or the donor's family member. Finally, if the property transferred to the trust was highly appreciated, the trust is able to dispose of the property without current income taxation. CRTs that are established at death are primarily used to reduce the estate tax and to provide an income stream to one of the donor's heirs.

Charitable lead trust (CLT)
A split-interest trust where a charity is the income beneficiary, and there is a noncharitable remainderman

In some cases, the income beneficiary is the charity with the remaining property being passed to one of the donor's heirs. This type of arrangement is called a **charitable lead trust (CLT)**. A CLT is generally used to transfer property to heirs in the future while paying gift tax at the current valuation of the property. Any appreciation in the value of the property will escape transfer tax.

THE MARITAL DEDUCTION

Definition

A marital deduction occurs when the decedent's estate claims as a deduction from the adjusted gross estate an unlimited qualifying bequest or transfer of property to a surviving spouse. This treatment parallels the unlimited marital deduction for gifts and for gift tax purposes. If the surviving spouse is not a U.S. citizen, a bequest to the spouse does not qualify for the marital deduction unless a qualified domestic trust (QDOT) is used, as discussed later in this chapter.

Qualifications for the Marital Deduction

Terminable interest
An interest that ends upon an event or contingency

To qualify for the marital deduction, the property must be included in the decedent's gross estate and passed to the decedent's spouse. This includes a spouse in a same-sex marriage. The interest in the property must not be a terminable interest. A **terminable interest** is an interest that ends upon an event or contingency. In other words, if the spouse initially gets the interest in the property and then later this interest terminates upon some event (usually death) and the interest passes to someone else, it is a terminable interest. Terminable interests do not qualify for the unlimited marital deduction unless they meet one of the exceptions to the terminable interest rule.

The following are some exceptions to the terminable interest rule.

- When the only condition of a bequest is that the survivor spouse lives for a period not exceeding six months, the marital deduction is allowed if the surviving spouse actually lives for the period specified.
- When there is a right to the income from the property for life coupled with a general power of appointment.

- When there is a bequest to a spouse of income from a charitable remainder annuity trust or a charitable remainder unitrust and the spouse is the only noncharitable beneficiary.
- Certain marital trusts are exceptions to the terminable interest rule (i.e., qualified terminable interest property, or QTIP).

Direct bequest (to a spouse)
The first spouse who dies leaves everything outright to the surviving spouse

Direct Bequests to a Spouse

In a **direct bequest**, the first spouse who dies leaves everything outright to the surviving spouse. The estate of the decedent spouse gets a 100% marital deduction equal to the adjusted gross estate. Any property that is not consumed by the surviving spouse during life will be included in the gross estate of the surviving spouse. The advantages of direct bequests are that they are simple and inexpensive. The surviving spouse gets unfettered control over all of the assets of the decedent. One disadvantage of this approach is that a direct bequest may overqualify the estate because the first spouse to die does not take advantage of the decedent's available applicable credit amount or its equivalency. Overqualification means that the decedent failed to make use of his applicable exclusion opportunity to pass his exemption equivalency amount ($12,060,000 for 2022) to someone other than the spouse and still pay no estate tax. If an estate is overqualified, the total estate tax on the death of the second spouse may be greater than it would have been had they arranged their affairs differently. Another disadvantage is that the first spouse is unable to retain control over the ultimate disposition of the assets.

Qualified terminable interest property (QTIP) trust
Allows a terminable interest to be passed to a surviving spouse and the property to still qualify for the unlimited marital deduction; the election is made by the executor on IRS Form 706

Qualified Terminable Interest Property (QTIP) Trust

If a direct bequest to a spouse is determined to be inappropriate and the decedent wishes no transfer tax at the first death, the alternatives are a QTIP or a power of appointment trust. A **qualified terminable interest property trust**, sometimes called a C trust or a Q trust, allows a terminable interest to be passed to a surviving spouse and the property to still qualify for the unlimited marital deduction. The election is made by the executor on IRS Form 706. There are certain rules associated with QTIPs that must be followed to qualify the transfer for the unlimited marital deduction.

Any income from the trust must be payable to the surviving spouse at least annually and for life. The trust income cannot be payable to anyone other than the surviving spouse. The trust assets will be included in the gross estate of the surviving spouse at death to the extent they are not consumed during the surviving spouse's lifetime. The first spouse to die determines the ultimate disposition of the property from the trust (names the remainder beneficiaries) in the trust provisions. This is an especially useful device when the surviving spouse is not the parent of the children of the decedent spouse.

Power of appointment trust
Allows a terminable interest to be passed to a surviving spouse and the property to still qualify for the marital deduction; unlike a QTIP trust, no election is required

Power of Appointment Trust

A **power of appointment trust**, sometimes called an A trust, allows a terminable interest to be passed to a surviving spouse and the property to still qualify for the marital deduction. Unlike a QTIP trust, no election is required. The rules require that income from the trust be payable to the surviving spouse at least annually for life. Any assets in the trust when the surviving spouse dies will be included in the gross estate of the surviving spouse. The surviving spouse is given a general power of appointment (the power to appoint the assets to anyone, including himself) over the property during life or at death.

The first spouse to die does not control the ultimate disposition of the property because the surviving spouse has a general power of appointment over the trust assets.

OPTIMIZING THE MARITAL DEDUCTION

If the objective of the married decedent is to have a zero-tax-liability estate, he can simply leave all assets in a qualifying way to the surviving spouse. The problem with such a strategy is that it fails to utilize the decedent's right to leave the applicable exclusion amount ($12,060,000 for 2022) to someone other than the spouse. Therefore, all assets, less the applicable exclusion amount, can be left to the spouse in a qualifying way and still have a zero estate tax liability for the estate of the first spouse to die. Although the $12,060,000 is left to another heir, the decedent may provide that income from the property is to be paid exclusively to the surviving spouse while the spouse is alive. The common method of leaving the applicable exclusion amount where the spouse has a need for the income from such assets is called a bypass trust. In the event a spouse has no need for the income or assets from the credit equivalency amount, the spouse can disclaim, as discussed next. Keep in mind, however, that bequests to surviving spouses who are not U.S. citizens must meet special requirements to qualify for the marital deduction, as described later in this section.

The Bypass Trust (Credit Equivalency)

Bypass trust (B trust)
Avoids inclusion in, or bypasses, the surviving spouse's gross estate; the assets transfer to a future generation free of estate taxes; the purpose of a bypass trust is to take advantage of the applicable credit amount

A **bypass trust** avoids inclusion in, or bypasses, the surviving spouse's gross estate. The assets transfer to a future generation free of estate taxes. The purpose of a bypass trust (B trust) is to take advantage of the applicable credit amount. The property does not qualify for the unlimited marital deduction when the first spouse dies, but it escapes taxation because it is covered by the estate tax applicable exclusion amount. A common scenario is for the first spouse to leave everything to the surviving spouse except for the credit equivalent amount, which goes into a bypass trust. The surviving spouse may be the income beneficiary of the bypass trust and may also be able to invade the trust for health, education, maintenance, or support (HEMS). When the surviving spouse dies, the bypass trust assets are not included in that spouse's gross estate but rather pass to children or other heirs.

A bypass trust can be used instead of an outright bequest to heirs who are not sophisticated or mature enough to handle property. In addition, the bypass trust is used where the surviving spouse needs the income from the trust but wants to avoid inclusion of the assets in the surviving spouse's gross estate. In this case, the choice of the trust over the simple bequest may give the transferor some peace of mind. Often, highly appreciating assets are placed into the bypass trust. This freezes the value for estate tax purposes for the spouses at the death of the first spouse. A bypass trust may also be called a credit equivalency trust, a credit shelter trust, a family trust, or a B trust.

The Mechanics of the Bypass Trust (Credit Equivalency)

Recall that the property that qualified for the marital deduction reduced the taxable estate of the decedent and that the amount of such transfer is unlimited. Also recall that each individual has a lifetime exemption (Exhibit 17.12) and that this exemption would be lost to the first spouse were he to transfer to the surviving spouse all of his property in a way that qualifies for the marital deduction. A credit equivalency (bypass) trust can be used to avoid these problems. Usually testamentary, a credit equivalency trust is provided for in the will with a provision to fund the trust with an amount equal to the current (at the time of death) applicable exclusion amount with the spouse having a lifetime interest in the income and the remaindermen being someone else, usually children. Such a transfer does not qualify for the marital deduction, and those assets will not be included in the gross estate of the surviving spouse when he dies. The assets are included in the taxable estate of the grantor but will not result in any federal estate tax liability as demonstrated in the following example.

EXAMPLE Sherri and Gary are married with two children. They each have property worth $15 million. Each spouse has a will bequeathing all property to the surviving spouse.

Calculation of the total estate tax paid, assuming Gary died first on January 3, 2022 (assume the applicable credit amount and estate tax rates remain the same when Sherri dies but that she is not eligible for the portability provision):

	Gary	Sherri	
Assets	$15,000,000	$15,000,000	
Inheritance		$15,000,000	
Gross estate	$15,000,000	$30,000,000	
Marital deduction	(15,000,000)	-0-	
Taxable estate	-0-	$30,000,000	
Tentative tax	-0-	11,945,800	
Applicable credit	-0-	(4,769,800)	(2022)
Estate tax	$-0-	$7,176,000	
Total estate tax paid by family	$7,176,000		

Calculation of the total estate tax paid assuming Gary died on January 3, 2022, using a maximized credit equivalency trust with the children as beneficiaries (assume the applicable credit amount and estate tax rates remain the same when Sherri dies):

	Gary	Sherri	
Assets	$15,000,000	$15,000,000	
Inheritance	-0-	$2,940,000	
Gross estate	$15,000,000	$17,940,000	
Marital deduction	(2,940,000)	-0-	
Taxable estate	$12,060,000	$17,940,000	
Tentative tax	$4,769,800	$7,121,800	
Applicable credit	(4,769,800)	(4,769,800)	(2022)
Estate tax	$ -0-	$2,352,000	
Total estate tax paid by family	$2,352,000		

Conclusion: By using the credit equivalency trust, the family saved $4,824,000 ($7,176,000 without shelter – $2,352,000 with shelter = $4,824,000 savings) in estate tax. This savings is a result of the couple taking full advantage of the applicable credit amount by placing the applicable exclusion amount of funds at the first death in a credit equivalency trust for the children. Sherri can receive income from the trust for the remainder of her life and have the right to withdraw limited amounts of principal. The credit equivalency trust assets will pass untaxed to the children at Sherri's death.

Effect of Portability

As discussed earlier, current tax law allows for the portability of the $12,060,000 (in 2022) applicable exclusion amount between spouses. The portability feature reduces the need for bypass planning because with portability, the predeceased spouse's applicable exclusion amount is not necessarily wasted if the predeceased spouse does not utilize it in his estate. If certain requirements are met, the unused applicable exclusion amount may be available to the surviving spouse. For example, a married couple with total assets of $24,120,000 in assets might elect to use no applicable exclusion amount in the estate of the first spouse to die and instead use the entire $24,120,000 exclusion when the second spouse dies.

There are some restrictions on the use of the portability feature, however. For example, under the portability provision, only the unused exemption amount of the last predeceased spouse is available to a surviving spouse. If a surviving spouse remarries and the second spouse also predeceases the surviving spouse, the unused exemption amount of the first predeceased spouse is no longer available. A second example is that a timely estate tax return must be filed for the first spouse to die, and the executor for the first spouse to die must elect on the Form 706 Estate Tax Return to allow the surviving spouse to use portability. Many people neglect to file the estate tax return if no estate tax will be due and thus forfeit the benefits of portability.

Use of Disclaimers

Disclaimer
The refusal of the receipt of an estate; the use of disclaimers allows an individual to disclaim or renounce receiving any part of an estate

A **disclaimer** allows a spouse or anyone else to disclaim or renounce receiving any part of a bequest. A specific direction to disclaim is not necessary in the will or trust device. If the spouse disclaims property, his interest in and control over the property is extinguished. Because disclaimers must be made within nine months of the decedent's death, the surviving spouse may find it difficult to give up property at a time when he may not be feeling emotionally or financially secure. When a person disclaims, he is not making a gift but rather is simply bypassed.

Alien Surviving Spouses

Qualified domestic trust (QDOT)
For a noncitizen spouse who was a U.S. resident at the time of the decedent's death, the marital deduction is allowed if the property is placed in a QDOT that passes to the noncitizen surviving spouse

Section 2056(d) disallows the unlimited marital deduction if the surviving spouse is not a U.S. citizen. If a noncitizen spouse becomes a U.S. citizen before the federal estate tax return is filed (Form 706 within nine months), Section 2056(d) does not apply. For a noncitizen spouse who was a U.S. resident at the time of the decedent's death, the marital deduction is allowed if the property is placed in a **qualified domestic trust (QDOT)** that passes to a noncitizen surviving spouse. The trust document for a QDOT requires at least one trustee to be a U.S. citizen or a U.S. corporation. The trustee must have a right to withhold estate tax on distribution of assets or income and must meet requirements of the U.S. Treasury. The executor must make an irrevocable election to establish a QDOT.

GENERATION-SKIPPING TRANSFER TAX (GSTT)

Generation-skipping transfer tax (GSTT)
A tax in addition to the unified gift and estate tax designed to tax large transfers that skip a generation (i.e., from grandparent to grandchild)

The **generation-skipping transfer tax (GSTT)** is in addition to the unified gift and estate tax and is designed to tax large transfers that skip a generation (i.e., from grandparent to grandchild). The purpose of the tax is to collect potentially lost tax dollars from the skipped generation. Were it not for the generation-skipping tax, one could leave all of one's assets to a grandchild and avoid the unified gift and estate tax on the middle generation. The current unified tax scheme would tax from the first to the second generation and from the second to the third generation. For a transfer made from the first generation directly to the third generation, some unified gift and estate tax is avoided. The generation-skipping transfer tax attempts to make up for that loss of tax.

The GSTT rate is the highest marginal rate for the unified gift and estate tax rates (40% in 2022). There are several exceptions to this tax. First, the annual exclusion also applies to a generation-skipping transfer ($16,000 in 2022). Second, there is a lifetime exemption per donor ($12,060,000 in 2022). Unlike the gift tax and estate tax exemption, the GSTT lifetime exemption is not portable between spouses. There is also an exception for transfers to a person of a skipped generation where a parent has predeceased the transferee prior to the transfer. For example, if a parent died, the grandparent may donate or devise to the grandchild without the grandchild being considered a skip person. In effect, the grandchild steps into the shoes of the deceased parent. An unrelated person 37½ years younger than the donor-transferor is considered a skip person. A spouse of a person in a nonskip generation is not a skip person because they are assigned to their spouse's generation. For example, a brother's wife who is 40 years younger than the donor is not a skip person. Finally, qualified transfers, such as medical costs and tuition paid directly to the provider, are also excluded from GSTT. Gift splitting is available for the annual exclusion exceptions as long as both spouses elect to split gifts.

THE ROLE OF THE FINANCIAL PLANNER IN ESTATE PLANNING

Estate planning is very personal and requires the financial planner to seek out the particulars that characterize each client's individual situation and goals. Financial planners must be able to ascertain the objectives of the client while forecasting the long-range ramifications of the plan.

Reducing the estate tax is a matter of taking full advantage of various planning opportunities (summarized in Exhibit 17.17). Initially, getting the life insurance out of the gross estate is generally a wise idea. The next step for most clients is to make full use of the qualified transfers to educational and medical institutions. Then, the client should be encouraged to make optimal use of the annual exclusion ($16,000 or $32,000 if split) on a yearly basis. At some time, either during life or at death, the client should make effective use of the applicable exclusion amount ($12,060,000 at death for 2022) by transferring these assets so as to avoid inclusion in the surviving spouse's gross estate. Then the spouse who has accomplished all of the above can leave the balance of the gross estate to his spouse in a qualifying way and, thus, have an estate tax liability of zero. Charitable contributions during life will reduce his gross estate, and the income on those transferred assets will not be taxed to the transferor. Charitable transfers at death are deductible from the adjusted gross estate and thus are not taxable.

EXHIBIT 17.17 Estate Tax Reduction Techniques

There are several techniques to reduce estate tax:

- Do not overqualify the estate. Use the applicable exclusion amount.
- Do not underqualify the estate. Use an appropriate amount for the marital deduction, generally to reduce estate tax to zero.
- Generally, remove life insurance from the estate of the client.
- Change the ownership of life insurance or use irrevocable life insurance trust (must remove all incidents of ownership).
- Use lifetime gifts. Make use of annual exclusions with gift splitting.
- Use basic trusts.
- Use charitable contributions, transfers, and trusts

Estate planning calls for a broad range of sophisticated talents. An attorney and CPA may need to be called into the estate team at this point, if not before, to cover the legal and tax aspects.

CONCLUDING COMMENTS ON THE UNIFICATION SCHEME OF GIFTS AND ESTATES

Although it may appear that the unification scheme (the unified tax table) for gifts and estates provides equality or parity for transfers during life or at death, there are at least four important distinctions.

First, the annual exclusion of $16,000 per donee per year that is provided for gifts is essentially lost if the transfer does not occur until death. Thus, the annual exclusion is a perishable right, the total value of which declines with each passing year. A married couple with four children and two grandchildren can transfer $192,000 ($32,000 to each descendent) per year total during life to the six donees without any gift tax consequences. If this money is not transferred by gift or consumed by the decedent, it will be included in the gross estate at the decedent's death and may be subject to estate tax.

The second, and perhaps the most important, advantage of making lifetime gifts is that any future appreciation of any asset transferred is not included in the gross estate of the transferor at death. For example, suppose William gave his son, James, some XYZ.com stock, with a fair market value of $16,000. William (donor) pays no gift tax on the transfer because it is equal to the annual exclusion amount of $16,000 in 2022. Now assume that James holds the stock for 10 years; at the end of the 10-year period, the stock is worth $300,000, and William dies. No part of the value of the stock is included in William's gross estate. If William had retained the stock, he would have had to include the entire $300,000 in his gross estate. Thus, for assets that appreciate, transfers during life are more advantageous than transfers at death in reducing the gross estate.

Third, if any gift tax is paid on gifts made, that gift tax is also not included in the gross estate of the donor unless such gift tax is paid on gifts made within three years of death.

DISCUSSION QUESTIONS

1. What is estate planning, and what are its objectives?
2. What risks are associated with failing to plan for an estate transfer?
3. Which professionals make up the estate planning team?
4. What steps make up the estate planning process?
5. What client information needs to be gathered to begin a successful estate transfer?
6. What are some common estate transfer objectives?
7. What are the basic documents used in estate planning?
8. What is the probate process, and what are its advantages and disadvantages?
9. Why is having a will important?
10. What are the three types of wills, and how do they differ?
11. What are some provisions typically found in wills?
12. What is a power of attorney?
13. What is a durable power of attorney for health care?
14. What are the definitions of the terms community property, separate property, and tenancy by the entirety?
15. What are the types of property ownership interests, and how are they transferred at death?
16. What are the duties of the executor/administrator of a will?
17. What is a living trust?
18. What is a grantor trust?
19. How can the gross estate be reduced?
20. What are the common estate planning mistakes?
21. What is the applicable credit amount, and how does it affect an individual's federal estate tax liability?
22. How can the annual gift tax exclusion be used as an estate planning tool?
23. What is gift splitting?
24. What are qualified transfers?
25. When is the gift tax return due?
26. What are the advantages and disadvantages of the unlimited marital deduction?
27. What are the steps in calculating the estate tax?
28. What are at least three estate planning techniques available to reduce gift and estate taxes?
29. When is the estate tax return due?

30. What are the applicable credit amounts against federal gift and estate taxes for 2022?

31. On which IRS form do you deduct funeral expenses?

32. What is a trust, and what are the benefits of creating one?

33. What are different types of trusts that can be created?

34. What is the generation-skipping transfer tax?

EXERCISES

1. Which of the following people need estate planning?
    1. Steve, who has a wife, 1 small child, and a net worth of $350,000.
    2. Earl, married with 9 children, 6 grandchildren, and a net worth of $4,000,000.
    3. Ellen, divorced, whose only son is severely mentally challenged.
    4. Mary, who is single, has a net worth of $150,000, and has 2 cats she considers her children.

2. Place the following estate planning steps in their proper order.
    1. Establish priorities for estate objectives.
    2. Prepare a written plan.
    3. Define problem areas including liquidity, taxes, etc.
    4. Gather client information and establish objectives.

3. Which arrangements are plausible when dealing with unanticipated incapacity.

4. Describe why each of the following would be considered potential problems of an estate plan.
    1. Ancillary probate
    2. A will that includes funeral instructions
    3. A will that attempts to disinherit a spouse and/or minor children

5. Describe each of the following common provisions in a well-drafted will.
    1. Establishment of the domicile of testator
    2. An appointment and powers clause
    3. A survivorship clause
    4. A residuary clause

6. Which of the following statements is(are) NOT correct?
    1. A durable power of attorney for health care is always a direct substitute for a living will.
    2. A living will only covers a narrow range of situations.
    3. A living will must generally meet the requirements specified by state statute.
    4. Many well-intentioned living wills have failed because of vagueness and/or ambiguities.

7. Marleen has a general power of appointment over the assets in a trust established by her mother. Which of the following statements regarding the power is(are) CORRECT?
    1. Marleen can appoint the trust assets to pay for the needs of her mother.
    2. Marleen can appoint money to Marleen's creditors.
    3. Marleen must only appoint money using an ascertainable standard (health, education, maintenance, and support).
    4. If Marleen were to die, Marleen's gross estate would include the trust assets, although they were not previously appointed to Marleen.

8. Describe each of the following property ownership arrangements.
    1. Tenancy in common
    2. Joint tenancy with right of survivorship
    3. Tenancy by the entirety
    4. Community property

9. Which of the following statements regarding joint tenancy is(are) CORRECT?
    1. Under a joint tenancy, each tenant has an undivided interest in the property.
    2. Joint tenancies may only be established between spouses.
    3. Community property is the same as joint tenancy and has been adopted in many states.
    4. Assuming a spousal joint tenancy, the full value of the property will be included in the gross estate of the first spouse to die without regard to the contribution of each spouse.

10. Generally speaking, which of the following property is included in the probate estate?
    1. Property owned outright in one's own name at the time of death.
    2. An interest in property held as a tenant in common with others.
    3. Life insurance, and other death proceeds, payable to one's estate at death.
    4. The decedent's half of any community property.

11. Describe at least 3 advantages and 3 disadvantages of the probate process.

12. Identify alternatives to probate regarding disposition of property.

13. John and Mary are married and are both 36 years old with one child, Patrick, age 6. What documents does the couple need for estate planning?

14. Given Mark's assets below, which will go through the probate process if Mark dies?

Life insurance	Face	$100,000	Beneficiary is Mary
IRA	Balance	$200,000	Beneficiary is Mary
Personal residence	Value	$280,000	Titled JTWROS with Mary
Automobile	Value	$4,000	Owned by Mark

15. Ann is married to Roy. They have no children. Given that Ann has the following assets, what could she do to reduce her gross estate?

Life insurance	Face	$2,000,000	Owner is Ann
Cash	Amount	$4,000,000	Owner is Ann

16. During 2022, Bob gave $100,000 to his son and $100,000 to his daughter. Bob's wife, Lori, also gave $5,000 to their son. No other gifts were made during the year. Bob and Lori elected to split the gifts on their gift tax returns. What is the amount of taxable gifts made by Bob and Lori?

17. Which of the following situations would not constitute a taxable transfer under the gift tax statutes?
    1. Frank creates an irrevocable trust under the terms of which his son is to receive income for life and his grandson the remainder at his son's death.
    2. Frank, with personal funds, purchases real property and has the title conveyed to himself and his brother as joint tenants with right of survivorship.
    3. Frank creates a trust giving income for life to his wife providing that, at her death, the corpus is to be distributed to their daughter. Frank reserves the right to revoke the trust at any time.

18. Stephen created a joint bank account for himself and his friend, Anna. When is there a gift to Anna?

19. During 2022, Mark and Lydia made joint gifts of the following items to their son:
    1. A bond with an adjusted basis of $13,000 and a fair market value of $40,000
    2. Stock with an adjusted basis of $22,000 and a fair market value of $33,000
    3. An auto with an adjusted basis of $13,000 and a fair market value of $15,000
    4. An interest-free loan of $6,000 for a computer (for the son's personal use) on January 1 that was paid by their son on December 31 (assume the applicable federal rate was 2% per annum)

    What is the gross amount of gifts includable in Mark and Lydia's gift tax returns for this year?

20. Tamara, who is single, gave an outright gift of $50,000 to a friend, Heather, who needed the money to pay her medical expenses. In filing the gift tax return, how much is Tamara entitled to exclude?

21. Which of the following represent(s) taxable gifts?
    1. The transfer of wealth by a parent to a dependent child that represents legal support.
    2. Payment of a child's tuition to Loyola Law School by a parent.
    3. Payment of $20,000 from a grandparent to a grandchild for educational purposes.
    4. Payment of $15,000 of medical bills for a friend paid directly to the medical institution.

22. Victor wants to begin a program of lifetime giving to his 3 grandchildren and 5 great-grandchildren. He wants to control the amount of annual gifts to avoid the imposition of federal gift tax, and he does not desire to use any of his or his wife Veronica's applicable credit amount. Veronica is willing to split each gift over a period of 10 years. What is the total amount of gifts, including gift splitting, that Victor can give over the 10-year period? (Assume the annual exclusion for all years is the same as for 2022.)

23. Rodney and his wife, Lois, have 4 children, each over the age of majority, 2 grandchildren over age 21, and 6 minor grandchildren. Rodney and Lois want to make gifts to their children and grandchildren sufficient to make maximum use of the tax provisions providing for annual exclusions from federal gift tax. Considering that desire only, what is the total amount of gifting that Rodney and Lois can make during 2022?

24. Kurt died on July 31. His assets and their fair market value at the time of his death were:

Cash	$150,000
Personal residence	$7,500,000
Life insurance on Kurt's life	$3,500,000
Series EE bonds	$200,000

    Kurt had a balance on his residence mortgage of $150,000. What is the total of Kurt's gross estate?

25. Evelyn died on August 1 this year. What is her gross estate?
    - Two years ago, Evelyn gave cash of $30,000 to her friend. No gift tax was paid on the gift.
    - Evelyn held property jointly with her brother. Each paid $2 million of the total purchase price of $4 million. Fair market value of the property at date of death was $7 million.
    - In 2012, Evelyn purchased a life insurance policy on her own life and gave it as a gift to her sister. Evelyn retained the right to change the beneficiary. Upon Evelyn's death, her sister received $5 million under the policy.
    - In 2004, Evelyn gave her son a summer home (fair market value in 2004, $1 million). Evelyn continued to use it until her death pursuant to an understanding with her son. The fair market value at the date of death was $2 million.

26. Jane died on May 2, 2022, leaving an adjusted gross estate of $18 million at the date of death. Under the terms of the will, $3,750,000 was bequeathed outright to her husband. The remainder of the estate was left to her mother. No taxable gifts were made during her lifetime. In computing the taxable estate, how much should the executor claim as a marital deduction?

27. Joshua died in 2022 with a taxable estate of $18 million. He had made no previous taxable gifts during his lifetime. How much is his federal estate tax?

28. Identify at least 3 alternative methods of limiting, reducing, or avoiding federal estate taxes.

29. Which of the following transfers qualify for the unlimited marital deduction?
    1. Outright bequest to resident alien spouse
    2. Property passing to citizen spouse in QTIP
    3. Income beneficiary of CRT is a nonresident alien spouse (trust is not a QDOT)
    4. Outright bequest to resident spouse who, prior to the decedent's death, was not a citizen but who, after the decedent's death and before the estate return was filed, became a U.S. citizen

30. Who among the following would be skip persons for purposes of the GSTT? Matt, the transferor, is 82 years old.
    - Tim, the grandson of Matt, whose mother, Bonnie, is living but whose father, Ben, son of Matt, is deceased.
    - Mindy is the great-grandchild of Matt. Both Mindy's parents and grandparents are living.
    - Sharon is the 21-year-old wife of Matt's second son, Alan, age 65.

31. Rosalie, who is single, is diagnosed with a serious disease and expects to be completely incapacitated in three years. Rosalie has two daughters and two grandchildren. She has $500,000 in net worth including her principal residence. Which of the following estate planning tools would you recommend for Rosalie?
    1. Set up a durable power of attorney.
    2. Immediately gift annual exclusion amounts to children and grandchildren.
    3. Set up a revocable living trust.
    4. Set up an irrevocable living trust.
    5. Set up a QTIP trust.

32. On April 30 Dennis transfers property to a trust which he retains the right to revoke. The trust is to pay Kim 5% of the trust assets valued annually for her life, with the remainder to be paid to a qualified charity. On August 31, Dennis dies and the trust becomes irrevocable. Identify the type of trust.

PROBLEMS

1. Kristi and Patrick are married, and both are 35 years old with 2 children, Christopher (age 4) and Andrew (age 2). The couple has simple wills that leave everything to each other. They have asked you to help them update their wills. What would you recommend?

2. Tomas is a wealthy golfer who would prefer that his assets not be subject to public scrutiny when he dies. What tools can he use to accomplish his goal?

3. George owns the following property:
   1. Boat (fee simple)
   2. Condominium on the beach (tenancy in common with his brother and sister)
   3. House and two cars with his wife, Ann (tenancy by the entirety)
   4. Checking account with his son, Bill (POD)
   5. Karate business (JTWROS with his partner, Eric)

   Which items will go through probate? Which property could he sell without the consent of a co-owner?

4. Neal is a widower with a taxable estate of $15 million. He had made no taxable lifetime gifts. What is his federal estate tax due before the applicable credit if he dies in 2022? What is the amount of the applicable credit?

5. Denise and Barry are married and own total assets with a fair market value of $16 million, all of which are in Barry's name alone. Barry leaves his entire estate to Denise, and Denise leaves her entire estate to their children. Assume Barry dies in January 2022 and Denise dies in November 2022. What is the total amount of federal estate tax that will be paid on the two estates? (Assume the fair market value of the estate is unchanged when Denise dies and Denise is not entitled to take advantage of the portability provision.)

6. In 2022, Georgia gave a $10,000 cash gift to her friend, Mary. How much is the taxable gift?

7. For each of the past 10 years, Jessica has given $16,000 to each of her 6 grandchildren and $26,000 each to her son and daughter. What is the total amount of taxable gifts? (Assume the annual exclusion for all 10 years is the same as 2022.)

8. Ken and Libby have the following assets:
   - $800,000 house in Ken's name
   - $1,100,000 investment account in Libby's name
   - $26,000,000 in rental property jointly owned as JTWROS
   - $300,000 beach condo that Libby co-owns with her sister as tenants in common

   They have 2 adult children and have made no previous taxable gifts. How much can they transfer to the children free of all transfer tax in a lifetime transfer in 2022?

9. Charles is an 85-year-old widower with 2 sons and a daughter, 3 grandchildren, and a 27-year-old girlfriend. He has an estate currently worth $650,000, including a house worth $300,000. His estate also includes a life insurance policy on his life with a face value of $120,000, and the primary beneficiaries are his children. Charles was recently diagnosed with Alzheimer's disease. The doctors predict a rapid progression and recommend that Charles go into a nursing home soon. He currently has a will that leaves all of his assets equally to his children. He has not taken advantage of any other estate planning techniques. Which of the following would you recommend to Charles while he still has all his mental faculties, and why?
   1. Create a living will, a general power of attorney, and a power of attorney for health care.
   2. Transfer ownership of his residence to his children so that it will not be counted as a resource when he goes into the nursing home.
   3. Create an irrevocable trust containing all of his assets and naming his children as beneficiaries.
   4. Create a revocable trust containing all of his assets and naming his children as beneficiaries.
   5. Create a QTIP trust naming his girlfriend as the income beneficiary and his children as the remaindermen beneficiaries.

CASE SCENARIO

Use the information provided to answer the following questions regarding the Nelson family.

NELSON FAMILY CASE SCENARIO
DANA AND DAVID NELSON
As of 1/1/2022

Personal Background and Information

David Nelson (age 37) is a bank vice president. He has been employed there for 12 years and has an annual salary of $70,000. Dana Nelson (age 37) is a full-time homemaker. David and Dana have been married for eight years. They have two children, John (age 6) and Gabrielle (age 3), and are expecting their third child in two weeks. They have always lived in this community and expect to remain indefinitely in their current residence.

General Goals (Not Prioritized)

- Save for college education
- Reduce debt
- Save for retirement
- Estate planning
- Invest wisely

Insurance Information

Health Insurance

The entire family is insured under David's employer's health plan (PPO). For covered expenses, a $1,000 in-network deductible and a $2,000 out-of-network deductible apply, after which 80%/20% coinsurance applies in network and 60%/40% applies out of network. There is a stop-loss limit of $20,000 annually in network and $30,000 annually out of network. The entire monthly premium of $1,123.54 is paid by David's employer.

Life Insurance

David's employer provides group term life insurance equal to two times David's current salary. The premium is paid entirely by his employer, and Dana is the primary beneficiary. No contingent beneficiary is named.

Disability Insurance

David's employer also offers a contributory group long-term disability insurance program toward which the employer contributes 60% of the $158.54 monthly premium. David is a participant in the program, which provides a monthly disability income benefit equal to 70% of his current salary, payable to his Social Security normal retirement age, provided that he remains disabled per the policy's "own occupation" definition of disability. David must satisfy a 90-day elimination period before he is eligible to begin receiving benefits.

David's employer doesn't offer dental or vision coverages and the Nelsons have not obtained any private form of individual dental or vision insurance benefits.

Homeowners Insurance

The Nelsons have an HO-3 policy with replacement cost on contents. There is a $250 deductible. The annual premium is $950.

Automobile Insurance

The Nelsons have automobile liability and bodily injury coverage of $100,000/$300,000/$100,000. They have both comprehensive coverage and collision. The deductibles are $250 (comprehensive) and $500 (collision). The annual premium is $900.

Relevant External Environmental Information

- Mortgage rates are 5.0% for 30 years and 4.5% for 15 years, fixed.
- Gross domestic product is expected to grow at less than 3%.
- Inflation is expected to be 2.6%.
- Expected return on investment is 8% for common stocks, 9% for small company stocks, and 1.1% for U.S. Treasury bills.
- College education costs are $15,000 per year.

Investment Information

The bank offers a Section 401(k) plan in which David is an active participant. The bank matches contributions dollar for dollar up to 3% of David's salary. David currently contributes 5.43% of his salary. His employer's plan allows for employee contributions of up to 16% of salary. In the Section 401(k) plan, the Nelsons have the opportunity to invest in a money market fund, a bond fund, a growth and income fund, and a small-cap fund. The Nelsons consider themselves to have a moderate investment risk tolerance. David's assets within the plan are currently earning 8.5%, based on his investment choices within the plan.

Income Tax Information

David and Dana tell you that they are in the 12% federal income tax bracket. They pay $820 annually in state and local income taxes.

Education Information

John is 6 years old and currently attending first grade at a private school. Gabrielle is 3 years old. She will attend private school from pre-kindergarten through high school. The current balance of the college fund is $14,000. They expect to contribute $1,000 at the end of each year to this fund.

Gifts, Estates, Trusts, and Will Information

David has made Dana his primary beneficiary on his Section 401(k) plan, and the children are the contingent beneficiaries. Because most of their assets are owned jointly, David doesn't see the need for a will. Dana also does not have a will.

Dana and David Nelson
Statement of Financial Position
12/31/2021

ASSETS			LIABILITIES AND NET WORTH		
Cash/cash equivalents			**Current liabilities**		
JT	Checking account	$1,425	JT	Credit cards	$4,000
JT	Savings account	$950	JT	Mortgage on principal residence	$1,234
			David	Boat loan	$1,493
Total cash/cash equivalents		$2,375	**Total current liabilities**		$6,727
Invested assets			**Long-term liabilities**		
Dana	ABC stock	$12,500	JT	Mortgage on principal residence	$196,654
JT	Education fund	$14,000	David	Boat loan	$12,065
David	Section 401(k) plan	$32,197			
Total invested assets		$58,697	**Total long-term liabilities**		$208,719
Personal-use assets			**Total liabilities**		$215,446
JT	Principal residence	$245,000			
JT	Automobile	$18,000			
David	Boat	$25,000	**Net worth**		$207,626
Dana	Jewelry	$13,000			
JT	Furniture/household	$61,000			
Total personal-use assets		$362,000			
Total assets		$423,072	**Total liabilities and net worth**		$423,072

Dana and David Nelson
Statement of Financial Position
12/31/2022

ASSETS			LIABILITIES AND NET WORTH		
Cash/cash equivalents			**Current liabilities**		
JT	Checking account	$1,268	JT	Credit cards	$3,655
JT	Savings account	$950	JT	Mortgage on principal residence	$1,370
	Total cash/cash equivalents	$2,218	David	Boat loan	$1,048
				Total current liabilities	$6,073
Invested assets			**Long-term liabilities**		
Dana	ABC stock	$14,050	JT	Mortgage on principal residence	$195,284
JT	Education fund	$15,560	David	Boat loan	$16,017
David	Section 401(k) plan	$38,619		**Total long-term liabilities**	$211,301
David	XYZ stock	$10,000			
	Total invested assets	$78,229			
Personal-use assets			**Total liabilities**		**$217,374**
JT	Principal residence	$250,000			
JT	Automobile	$15,000			
David	Personal watercraft	$10,000	**Net worth**		**$241,573**
David	Boat B	$30,000			
Dana	Jewelry	$13,500			
JT	Furniture/household	$60,000			
	Total personal-use assets	$378,500			
Total assets		**$458,947**	**Total liabilities and net worth**		**$458,947**

Notes to financial statements:

- Assets are stated at fair market value.
- The ABC stock was inherited from Dana's aunt on November 15, 2021. Her aunt originally paid $20,000 for it on October 31, 2012. The fair market value at the aunt's death was $12,000.
- Liabilities are stated at principal only.
- JT = joint tenancy; client name = separate property.

Dana and David Nelson
Personal Statement of Cash Flows
For 2022

INFLOWS		
Salary—David		$70,000
Investment income		
Interest income	$ 900	
Dividend income	$ 150	$ 1,050
Total inflow		**$71,050**
Savings		
Reinvestment (interest/dividends)	$ 1,050	
Section 401(k) plan deferrals	$ 3,803	
Education fund	$ 1,000	
Total savings		**$ 5,853**
Available for outflows		**$65,197**
OUTFLOWS		
Ordinary living expenses		
Food	$ 6,000	
Clothing	$ 3,600	
Child care	$ 600	
Entertainment	$ 1,814	
Utilities	$ 3,600	
Auto maintenance	$ 2,000	
Church	$ 3,500	
Total ordinary living expenses		**$21,114**
Debt payments		
Credit card payments principal	$ 345	
Credit card payments interest	$ 615	
Mortgage payment principal	$ 1,234	
Mortgage payment interest	$20,720	
Boat loan principal	$ 1,493	
Boat loan interest	$ 1,547	
Total debt payments		**$25,954**
Insurance premiums		
Automobile insurance premiums	$ 900	
Disability insurance premiums	$ 761	
Homeowners insurance premiums	$ 950	
Total insurance premiums		**$ 2,611**
Tuition and education expenses		**$ 1,000**
Taxes		
FICA and federal income tax (W/H)	$12,855	
State (and city) income tax	$ 820	
Property tax (principal residence)	$ 1,000	
Total taxes		**$14,675**
Total outflows		**$65,354**
Net cash flow (deficit)		**($157)**

1. Given David's current attitudes about the necessity for a will for himself and Dana, what problems has David created should he or Dana die today?
2. What provisions should David probably have in his will?
3. What provisions should Dana probably have in her will?
4. Assume that David and Dana have implemented recommendations for debt repayment to increase their discretionary cash available and increase life insurance coverage on David to a total of $450,000. The disability coverage has been changed to add coverage for illness as well as accident. As their financial planner, what other insurance coverages should you recommend to the Nelsons?

APPENDIX 17.1 JFK, Jr.'s Last Will and Testament

The Last Will and Testament of John F. Kennedy, Jr.

John F. Kennedy, Jr., planned to leave the bulk of his holdings to his wife, Carolyn Bessette-Kennedy, or their children. But John and Carolyn died together in a plane crash in July of 1999 without leaving any issue (children). Therefore, his property will go to the children of his sister, Caroline Kennedy Schlossberg. The bulk of his estate is left to the beneficiaries of a trust he established in 1983. Kennedy also left the scrimshaw set, or carved whale ivory set, once owned by his father to nephew John B.K. Schlossberg. Kennedy's cousin, Timothy P. Shriver was named executor of the will. Kennedy's estate is reportedly worth $100 million.

I, JOHN F. KENNEDY, JR., of New York, New York, make this my last will, hereby revoking all earlier wills and codicils. I do not by this will exercise any power of appointment.

FIRST: I give all my tangible property (as distinguished from money, securities and the like), wherever located, other than my scrimshaw set previously owned by my father, to my wife, Carolyn Bessette-Kennedy, if she is living on the thirtieth day after my death, or if not, by right of representation to my then living issue, or if none, by right of representation to the then living issue of my sister, Caroline Kennedy Schlossberg, or if none, to my said sister, Caroline, if she is then living. If I am survived by issue, I leave this scrimshaw set to said wife, Carolyn, if she is then living, or if not, by right of representation, to my then living issue. If I am not survived by issue, I give said scrimshaw set to my nephew John B.K. Schlossberg, if he is then living, or if not, by right of representation to the then-living issue of my said sister, Caroline, or if none, to my said sister Caroline, if she is then living. I hope that whoever receives my tangible personal property will dispose of certain items of it in accordance with my wishes, however made unknown, but I impose no trust, condition or enforceable obligation of any kind in this regard.

SECOND: I give and devise all my interest in my cooperative apartment located at 20-26 Moore Street, Apartment 9E, in said New York, including all my shares therein and any proprietary leases with respect thereto, to my said wife, Carolyn, if she is living on the thirtieth day after my death.

THIRD: If no issue of mine survive me, I give and devise all my interests in real estate, wherever located, that I own as tenants in common with my said sister, Caroline, or as tenants in common with any of her issue, by right of representation to Caroline's issue who are living on the thirtieth day after my death, or if none, to my said sister Caroline, if she is then living. References in this Article THIRD to "real estate" include shares in cooperative apartments and proprietary leases with respect thereto.

FOURTH: I give and devise the residue of all the property, of whatever kind and wherever located, that I own at my death to the then trustees of the John F. Kennedy Jr. 1983 Trust established October 13, 1983 by me, as Donor, of which John T. Fallon, of Weston, Massachusetts, and I are currently the trustees (the "1983 Trust"), to be added to the principal of the 1983 Trust and administered in accordance with the provisions thereof, as amended by a First Amendment dated April 9, 1987 and by a Second Amendment and Complete Restatement dated earlier this day, and as from time to hereafter further amended whether before or after my death. I have provided in the 1983 Trust for my children and more remote issue and for the method of paying all federal and state taxes in the nature of estate, inheritance, succession and like taxes occasioned by my death.

FIFTH: I appoint my wife, Carolyn Bessette-Kennedy, as guardian of each child of our marriage during minority. No guardian appointed in this will or a codicil need furnish any surety on any official bond.

APPENDIX 17.1 JFK, Jr.'s Last Will and Testament (continued)

SIXTH: I name my cousin Anthony Stanislaus Radziwill as my executor; and if for any reason, he fails to qualify or ceases to serve in that capacity, I name my cousin Timothy P. Shriver as my executor in his place. References in this will or a codicil to my "executor" mean the one or more executors (or administrators with this will annexed) for the time being in office. No executor or a codicil need furnish any surety on any official bond. In any proceeding for the allowance of an account of my executor, I request the Court to dispense with the appointment of a guardian ad litem to represent any person or interest. I direct that in any proceeding relating to my estate, service of process upon any person under a disability shall not made when another person not under a disability is a party to the proceeding and has the same interest as the person under the disability.

SEVENTH: In addition to other powers, my executor shall have power from time to time at discretion and without license of court: To retain, and to invest and reinvest in, any kind or amount of property; to vote and exercise other rights of security holders; to make such elections for federal and state estate, gift, income and generation-skipping transfer tax purposes as my executor may deem advisable; to compromise or admit to arbitration any matters in dispute; to borrow money, and to sell, mortgage, pledge, exchange, lease and contract with respect to any real or personal property, all without notice to any beneficiary and in such manner, for such consideration and on such terms as to credit or otherwise as my executor may deem advisable, whether or not the effect thereof extends beyond the period settling my estate; and in distributing my estate, to allot property, whether real or personal, at then current values, in lieu of cash.

APPENDIX 17.2 Marilyn Monroe's Last Will and Testament

The Will of Marilyn Monroe

The legendary icon, who tragically committed suicide in 1962, left most of her fortune to her friends and family.

I, MARILYN MONROE, do make, publish and declare this to be my Last Will and Testament.

FIRST: I hereby revoke all former Wills and Codicils by me made.

SECOND: I direct my Executor, hereinafter named, to pay all of my just debts, funeral expenses and testamentary charges as soon after my death as can conveniently be done.

THIRD: I direct that all succession, estate or inheritance taxes which may be levied against my estate and/or against any legacies and/or devises hereinafter set forth shall be paid out of my residuary estate.

FOURTH: (a) I give and bequeath to BERNICE MIRACLE, should she survive me, the sum of $10,000.00.
(b) I give and bequeath to MAY REIS, should she survive me, the sum of $10,000.00.
(c) I give and bequeath to NORMAN and HEDDA ROSTEN, or to the survivor of them, or if they should both predecease me, then to their daughter, PATRICIA ROSTEN, the sum of $5,000.00, it being my wish that such sum be used for the education of PATRICIA ROSTEN.
(d) I give and bequeath all of my personal effects and clothing to LEE STRASBERG, or if he should predecease me, then to my Executor hereinafter named, it being my desire that he distribute these, in his sole discretion, among my friends, colleagues and those to whom I am devoted.

FIFTH: I give and bequeath to my Trustee, hereinafter named, the sum of $100,000.00, in Trust, for the following uses and purposes:

(a) To hold, manage, invest and reinvest the said property and to receive and collect the income therefrom.
(b) To pay the net income therefrom, together with such amounts of principal as shall be necessary to provide $5,000.00 per annum, in equal quarterly installments, for the maintenance and support of my mother, GLADYS BAKER, during her lifetime.
(c) To pay the net income therefrom, together with such amounts of principal as shall be necessary to provide $2,500.00 per annum, in equal quarterly installments, for the maintenance and support of MRS. MICHAEL CHEKHOV during her lifetime.
(d) Upon the death of the survivor between my mother, GLADYS BAKER, and MRS. MICHAEL CHEKHOV to pay over the principal remaining in the Trust, together with any accumulated income, to DR. MARIANNE KRIS to be used by her for the furtherance of the work of such psychiatric institutions or groups as she shall elect.

SIXTH: All the rest, residue and remainder of my estate, both real and personal, of whatsoever nature and wheresoever situate, of which I shall die seized or possessed or to which I shall be in any way entitled, or over which I shall possess any power of appointment by Will at the time of my death, including any lapsed legacies, I give, devise and bequeath as follows:
(a) to MAY REIS the sum of $40,000.00 or 25% of the total remainder of my estate, whichever shall be the lesser,
(b) To DR. MARIANNE KRIS 25% of the balance thereof, to be used by her as set forth in ARTICLE FIFTH (d) of this my Last Will and Testament.
(c) To LEE STRASBERG the entire remaining balance.

SEVENTH: I nominate, constitute and appoint AARON R. FROSCH Executor of this my Last Will and Testament. In the event that he should die or fail to qualify, or resign or for any other reason be unable to act, I nominate, constitute and appoint L. ARNOLD WEISSBERGER in his place and stead.

EIGHTH: I nominate, constitute and appoint AARON R. FROSCH Trustee under this my Last Will and Testament. In the event he should die or fail to qualify, or resign or for any other reason be unable to act, I nominate, constitute and appoint L. Arnold Weissberger in his place and stead.

Marilyn Monroe (L.S.)

SIGNED, SEALED, PUBLISHED and DECLARED by MARILYN MONROE, the Testatrix above named, as and for her Last Will and Testament, in our presence and we, at her request and in her presence and in the presence of each other, have hereunto subscribed our names as witnesses this 14th day of January, One Thousand Nine Hundred Sixty-One

APPENDIX 17.3 Power of Attorney

United States of America
State of Louisiana
Parish of Jefferson

Be it known, that on this ______day of _________, in the year _________:

1. Before me, the undersigned authority, a Notary Public duly commissioned and qualified in and for the State and Parish set forth above, therein residing, and in the presence of the undersigned competent witnesses, personally came and appeared: ___________________ a person of the full age of majority and domiciled in St. Rose, Louisiana (the "Principal"), who declared that the Principal appoints his children,________(the "Agent," whether one or more, with either authorized to act alone), as the Principal's true and lawful agent and attorney-in-fact, general and special, granting unto the Agent full power and authority for the Principal and in the Principal's name and behalf, and to the Principal's use, to conduct, manage and transact all of the Principal's affairs, business, concerns and matters of whatever nature or kind, without any reservation whatsoever, except as hereinafter specifically set forth and subject to the following effective date. The Power of Attorney shall not become effective unless and until a personal physician of the Principal certifies in writing that the Principal is mentally or physically incapable of administering her affairs. In furtherance of this general grant of authority to the Agent, but not in limitation thereof, the Principal specifically authorizes the Agent to perform all of the following acts and exercise all of the following powers for the Principal and in the Principal's name.
2. To open all letters or correspondence addressed to the Principal and answer them.
3. To open accounts with any bank, brokerage or other entity; to deposit funds (whether represented by cash, checks or otherwise) in any account maintained by or for the Principal with any bank or other entity; to endorse all checks, bills of exchange and other instruments; to withdraw funds from any account maintained by the Principal with any bank or other person; to sign checks, bills or exchange and other instruments; to deposit any obligation with any bank or other entity for collection.
4. To represent the Principal in the Principal's capacity as a creditor or obligee of any person; to collect any funds or things owed the Principal by any person; and to attend any meeting of creditors in which the Principal may be interested and to vote in the Principal's name on all matters that may be submitted to the meeting.
5. To represent the Principal in the Principal's capacity as a stockholder of any corporation, partner in any partnership, beneficiary of any trust or member of any association or entity or as a security holder thereof. This authority shall include (but is not limited to) the authority to execute consent agreements and to attend any meetings of stockholders, partners, members, or beneficiaries or security holders of any corporation, partnership, association, trust or entity and to agree or vote (or execute proxies in favor of others to agree or vote) in the name of the Principal on all questions, including merger, sale, consolidation, any type of reorganization or matters.
6. To borrow any amounts of money for the Principal and in the Principal's name upon such terms and conditions as the Agent may in the Agent's sole discretion deem appropriate.
7. To sell, exchange, donate, transfer, or convey any property, whether immovable (real), movable (personal), tangible or intangible or corporeal or incorporeal, including stocks, bonds, notes, bills or any other security, belonging to the Principal or any interest therein and to receive the price or other consideration thereof.
8. To make gifts or other gratuitous transfers of any property belonging to the Principal either outright or in trust (including the forgiveness of debt), to any of the Principal's descendants or to the agent.
9. To purchase, acquire by exchange or otherwise acquire any property for and in the name of the Principal and to make payment therefore out of the Principal's funds or assets.
10. To create servitudes, building restrictions, other real rights, easements and covenants of any kind that burden, benefit or otherwise affect any property of the Principal.
11. To accept donations.
12. To lease, rent, let or hire (as lessor) any property belonging to the Principal.
13. To lease, rent, hire or let (as lessee) any property.

APPENDIX 17.3 Power of Attorney (continued)

14. To encumber, mortgage, pledge, pawn or otherwise grant any security interest in any property of the Principal, whether to secure obligations of the Principal or any other person or entity.
15. To grant or convey oil, gas, and other mineral leases, net profits interests, production payments, royalty interests, mineral servitudes and other interests in oil, gas and any other minerals on or under any property of the Principal; to sign division orders and transfer orders; to grant rights-of-way and easements; and otherwise to execute documents incident to the exploration for oil, gas or other minerals on or underlying property of the Principal.
16. To enter into transactions pursuant to which the Principal is lessee, grantee or vendee under or of any oil, gas or mineral lease, net profits interest, production payment, royalty deed, mineral servitude or any other interest in oil, gas or other minerals.
17. To undertake any obligations for the Principal, to act for the Principal in agreeing to guarantee any obligations of others or agreeing to defend and indemnify any person or entity against any claims, obligations or liabilities.
18. To act for the Principal and be the Principal's substitute in all cases in which the Principal may be appointed the agent or attorney of others.
19. To refer matters to arbitration and to initiate, prosecute, defend and otherwise represent the Principal in any judicial or arbitration proceeding (whether as plaintiff or defendant) and to settle and compromise any claim, dispute or proceeding; to apply for and obtain any attachments, sequestrations, injunctions, and appeals, give the requisite security, and sign the necessary bonds.
20. To represent the Principal in connection with any succession or estate in which the Principal may be or become interested (whether as heir, legatee, creditor, executor, administrator or otherwise), including the execution of any acceptance or renunciation thereof on the Principal's behalf; to apply for the administration thereof, and to demand, obtain and execute all orders and decrees as the Agent may deem proper; to settle, compromise, and liquidate the Principal's interest therein; and to receive and receipt for all property to which Principal may be entitled in respect of successions or estates.
21. To acknowledge any debt of the Principal.
22. To settle and compromise any dispute or matter involving the Principal.
23. To file any United States, State or other tax returns (including but not limited to income tax returns); to apply for extensions of time to file tax returns; and to represent the Principal in connection with any matter or dispute relating to United States, State or other taxes.
24. The Principal further authorizes and empowers the Agent to take any other action concerning the affairs, business or assets of the Principal as fully, completely and effectively and for all intents and purposes with the same validity as though the action had been expressly provided for herein and as though the Principal had taken the action in person.
25. The transactions entered into by the Agent for the Principal shall be on such terms and conditions as to payment and otherwise as the Agent may in the Agent's sole discretion determine.
26. The Agent is authorized to make, sign and execute in the name of the Principal all agreements, contracts, and instruments that may be necessary or convenient in the Agent's sole discretion to carry out transactions entered into by the Agent for the Principal or to enable the Agent fully to exercise the powers granted herein and to include therein any terms, conditions and provisions that the Agent shall deem appropriate and to bind the Principal thereby as fully as though each instrument had been signed by the Principal in person.
27. The agency created by this Power of Attorney shall be "durable" as provided by Louisiana Civil Code article 3027(B) and shall not be deemed revoked by the Principal's disability or incapacity.
28. The Principal agrees to ratify and confirm all actions that the Agent shall take pursuant to this Power of Attorney.
29. References herein to one gender shall be deemed to include the other whenever appropriate.
30. The term "property" means all kinds of property, whether movable, immovable, real, personal, mixed, corporeal, incorporeal, tangible or intangible. The term "entity" includes natural persons, corporations, partnerships, trusts, associations and any other form of legal entity and governmental and political organizations.

APPENDIX 17.3 Power of Attorney (continued)

31. THUS DONE AND PASSED in multiple originals on the date first above written in the presence of the undersigned competent witnesses, who sign their names with the Principal and me, Notary, after reading of the whole.

WITNESSES:

____

____

Print Name: ______________________

Principal ______________________________

Print Name: ______________________

____

Notary Public

APPENDIX 17.4 Medical Power of Attorney

Medical Power of Attorney

1. BE IT KNOWN, that on this _____ day of __________, in the year 20xx:

2. BEFORE ME, the undersigned authority, a Notary Public duly commissioned and qualified in and for the State and Parish set forth above, therein residing, and in the presence of the undersigned competent witnesses, personally came and appeared: (The "Principal"), who after being duly sworn, declared that the Principal appoints his children, ____________________ (the "Agent", whether one or more, with either authorized to act alone), as the Principal's true and lawful agent and attorney-in-fact, granting unto the Agent full power and authority regarding the matters set forth below.

3. Durability. This agency is "durable" and shall not be deemed revoked by the Principal's disability or incapacity.

HEALTH CARE

4. The Principal grants unto the Agent full power and authority regarding the following health care matters that the Principal could exercise on the Principal's own behalf, if capable of doing so. The Principal specifically authorizes the Agent to:

   4.1 Medical Records. Have access to any medical information in any form regarding the Principal's physical condition, and to execute such consents as may be necessary to obtain such medical information.

   4.2 Professionals. Retain, compensate and discharge any health care professionals the Agent deems necessary to examine, evaluate or treat the Principal, whether for emergency, elective, recuperative, convalescent or other care.

   4.3 Institutionalization. Admit the Principal to any health care facility recommended by a qualified health care professional, whether for physical or mental care or treatment, and remove the Principal from such institution at any time, even if contrary to medical advice.

   4.4 Treatment. Consent on the Principal's behalf to tests, treatment, medication, surgery, organ transplant or other procedures, and to revoke that consent, even if contrary to medical advice.

   4.5 Chemical Dependency. Consent on the Principal's behalf to a course of treatment for chemical dependency, whether suspected or diagnosed, and to revoke such consent.

   4.6 Pain Relief. Consent on the Principal's behalf to pain relief procedures, even if they are unconventional or experimental, even if they risk addiction, injury or foreshortening the Principal's life.

   4.7 Releases. Release from liability any health care professional or institution that acts on the Principal's behalf in reliance on the Agent.

PERSONAL CARE

5. The Principal grants unto the Agent full power and authority regarding the following personal care matters that the Principal could act on the Principal's own behalf, if capable of doing so. The Principal specifically authorizes the Agent to:

   5.1 Home Care. Provide for the Principal's continued maintenance and support. As nearly as possible, the Principal expressly authorizes the Agent to maintain the Principal's accustomed standard of living. The Agent shall provide the Principal with a suitable place to live by maintaining the Principal in the Principal's family residence or apartment (home), paying principal, interest, taxes, insurance and repairs as necessary. The Agent may retain or discharge domestic servants, attendants, companions, nurses, sitters or other persons who provide care to the Principal and the Principal's home. The Agent may authorize purchases of food, clothing, medical care and customary luxuries on the Principal's behalf.

   5.2 Institutional Care. Arrange and contract for institutional health care (hospital, retirement facility, nursing home, hospice or other) on the Principal's behalf if recommended by the Principal's physician. If reasonably advised that the Principal's return home is unlikely because of the Principal's condition, the Agent may sell, exchange, lease, sublease or dispose of the Principal's home and such of its contents as are no longer useful to the Principal and are not specifically bequeathed in the Principal's will, all on such terms as to price, payment and security as the Agent deems reasonable.

   5.3 Religious Needs. Continue the Principal's affiliation with the Principal's church, keeping the Principal accessible to the Principal's clergy, members and other representatives, continuing and renewing any pledge made by the

APPENDIX 17.4 Medical Power of Attorney (continued)

Principal whether for capital, operations or other purposes, and generally to assist the Principal in maintaining the Principal's church relationships to the extent the Principal's health permits.

5.4 Companions and Recreation. Hire, discharge, direct and compensate such companions as may be necessary for the Principal's health, recreation, travel, and general well-being.

5.5 Funeral Arrangements. Arrange and contract for the Principal's funeral including appropriate arrangements and instruction for the Principal's funeral service or memorial service, including purchase of a burial plot or other appropriate disposition of the Principal's body. The Agent shall comply with any known written instructions as the Principal may have or leave.

5.6 Curator or Guardian. Nominate on the Principal's behalf any person the Agent deems qualified, including the Agent, as the Principal's curator, undercurator, curator ad hoc, guardian, or conservator or any other fiduciary office the Principal has a right to nominate or designate, to waive any bond on the Principal's behalf and to grant to that fiduciary or representative any powers that the Principal might extend on the Principal's own behalf.

REFUSAL OF MEDICAL TREATMENT

6. The Principal declares that the Principal does not wish the Principal's dying to be prolonged artificially through extraordinary or heroic means if the Principal's condition is terminal. Even over the objection of members of the Principal's family, the Principal authorizes the Agent to:

6.1 Withdraw or Withhold Life Support. Sign on behalf of the Principal any documents, waivers or releases necessary to withdraw, withhold or cease any procedure calculated only to prolong the Principal's life, including the use of a respirator, cardiopulmonary resuscitation, surgery, dialysis, blood transfusion, antibiotics, antiarrhythmic and pressor drugs or transplants if two licensed physicians, one of whom is the Principal's attending physician, have personally examined the Principal and the Principal's attending physician has noted in the Principal's medical records that the Principal's condition is terminal and irreversible.

6.2 Nourishment. Refuse or discontinue intravenous or parenteral feeding, hydration, misting and endotracheal or nasogastric tubes, if advised that no undue pain will be caused to the Principal.

DECLARATION

7. Contemplating that the Principal's medical care may be rendered in Louisiana, or that state law might apply, the Principal has executed a Declaration Concerning Life-Sustaining Procedures ("Declaration") pursuant to State Revised Statutes 40:1299.58.1 and following as amended, a copy of which is attached. The Principal declares that by executing that Declaration the Principal does not intend to limit or reduce the powers over the Principal's person elsewhere granted to the Agent in this agency, but rather to convey to the Agent any additional powers as are necessary to make or carry out the terms of that Declaration.

8. THUS DONE AND PASSED in multiple originals on the date first above written in the presence of the undersigned competent witnesses, who signed their names with the Principal and me Notary, after reading of the whole.

WITNESSES:

____

____

Print Name:____________________ Principal

____

Print Name:____________________

____

Notary Public

APPENDIX 17.5 Living Will

Living Will Declaration

This Declaration is made on the _______ day of ______________, 20xx, pursuant to the Louisiana Natural Death Act, La. R.S. 40:1299.58.1 *et seq.*

I,________________________, being of sound mind, willfully and voluntarily make known my desire that my dying shall not be artificially prolonged under the circumstances set forth below and do hereby declare:

If at any time I should have an incurable injury, disease or illness certified to be a terminal and irreversible condition or a continual profound comatose state with no reasonable chance of recovery by two physicians who have personally examined me, one of whom shall be my attending physician, and the physicians have determined that my death will occur whether or not life-sustaining procedures are utilized and where the application of life-sustaining procedures would only serve to prolong artificially the dying process, I direct that such procedures (including but not limited to artificial means of respiration, hydration and/or nutrition) be withheld or withdrawn and that I be permitted to die naturally with only the administration of medication or the performance of any medical procedure deemed necessary to provide me with comfort care.

In the absence of my ability to give direction regarding the use of such life-sustaining procedures, it is my intention that this Declaration shall be honored by my family and physician(s) as the final expression of my legal right to refuse medical or surgical treatment and accept the consequences from such refusal.

I understand the full import of this Declaration, and I am emotionally and mentally competent to make this Declaration. Terms used in this Declaration shall have the meanings prescribed in the Louisiana Natural Death Act, La. R.S. 40:1299.58 *et seq.*, as amended now or hereafter.

____

Declarant

Metairie, Jefferson Parish, Louisiana

The declarant has been personally known to me, and I believe the declarant to be of sound mind. Both witnesses are competent adults who are not entitled to any portion of the estate of the declarant upon declarant's decease. The declarant signed this Declaration in our presence on the date set forth above.

____

Witnesses

____

Witnesses

SECTION 5
IN BRIEF

- Financial planning institutions
- Financial planning professionals
- The Code of Ethics and Standards of Conduct
- State laws
- Civil liability

- Developing a financial planning practice
- Maintaining competence
- Developing clients

- Practicing competently, ethically, and legally
- Procedures regarding discipline
- Civil liability

SECTION

5 The Financial Planning Profession

CHAPTERS

Risks	Goals	Data Collection	Data Analysis
■ Incompetence of planner ■ Improper practice ■ Unethical practice ■ Illegal practice ■ Professional discipline ■ Civil liability	■ The competent, legal, and ethical practice of financial planning	■ Financial planning institutions ■ Financial planning professionals ■ The Code of Ethics ■ Standards of Conduct ■ Malpractice laws ■ Disciplinary rules ■ Civil liability	■ Maintaining professional competence ■ Continuing education ■ Practicing lawfully and ethically ■ Building a practice

CHAPTER 18

The Practice of Financial Planning

LEARNING OBJECTIVES

After learning the material in this chapter, you will be able to do the following:

- Describe various types of financial planning institutions
- Identify the types of services that are provided by the various types of financial planning institutions
- List the common credentials associated with the financial planning industry
- Discuss common compensation methods for professional financial planners
- Identify essential aspects of building a financial planning practice and maintaining clients
- Discuss the importance of continuing education for financial planners

INTRODUCTION

The professional financial planner understands that the overall purpose of personal financial planning is to assist clients in achieving their goals and objectives. While most of those goals are financial, many are more qualitative than quantitative. The planner realizes that personal financial planning is about the adaptation of the individual client's strengths and weaknesses in an environment characterized by opportunities and risks.

The planner must possess a wide variety of skills and knowledge with which to assess the client's current financial situation, help the client establish realistic financial goals, and develop a plan or strategy for accomplishing those goals.

To be successful, the financial planning professional should have a working knowledge of the concepts within the financial planner's pyramid of knowledge.

EXHIBIT 18.1 Financial Planner's Pyramid of Knowledge

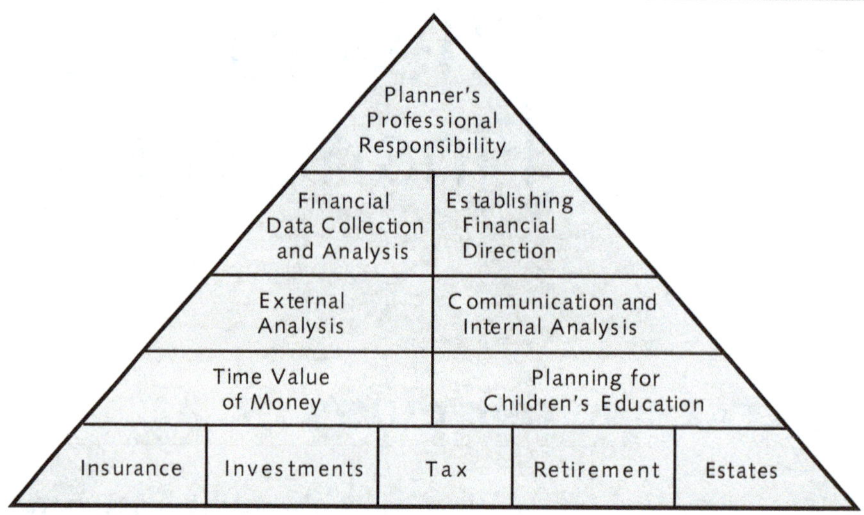

THE FINANCIAL PLANNING PROFESSION

The financial planning profession is comprised of a diverse group of individuals and institutions. Certain practitioners maintain individual private practices. Other financial planners work for accounting firms, law firms, insurance companies, personal financial planning firms, brokerage houses, mutual funds, banks, and other financial institutions that provide financial planning-related services.

Financial Planning Institutions

Accounting Firms

Accounting firms provide accounting, tax, and auditing-related services. Traditionally, these services were limited to preparing tax returns, preparing financial statements, business consulting, and business and individual tax planning. Today, accounting firms are providing even more services related to financial planning. These services include assistance in investment planning, retirement planning, and estate planning.

The American Institute of Certified Public Accountants (AICPA) has been actively assisting Certified Public Accountants (CPAs) in the development of financial planning practices in recent years. They provide training for members at national conferences and have instituted the Personal Financial Specialist (PFS) designation which is devoted solely to financial planning. The AICPA has also established relationships with other financial services firms that allow CPAs to deliver more financial planning services to their new and existing clients.

Law Firms

Attorneys have always been an integral part of developing and implementing financial and estate plans. Because attorneys draft legal documents, they are in a good position to provide additional services to their clients. Law firms have commonly drafted wills, powers of attorney, trusts, qualified plan documents, and partnership agreements. Their traditional services include tax planning, estate planning, and retirement and benefit planning.

Insurance Companies

Insurance companies primarily sell life, health, and/or property and casualty insurance products. Many insurance companies are expanding their services to include other areas of financial planning, particularly estate planning and retirement planning. Some have their own proprietary mutual funds.

Personal Financial Planning (PFP) Firms

These firms are generally small and specialize in a particular market niche. Some PFP firms manage assets and others provide comprehensive financial planning or sell products.

Brokerage Houses

Many brokerage houses provide global financial management and advisory services, including financial planning, securities underwriting, and trading and brokering. Some brokerage firms provide research, banking and insurance services, and investment banking. Brokerage houses are currently changing the nature of their businesses from transaction oriented to more service and planning related. These new services include retirement and estate planning.

Mutual Funds

Numerous mutual fund companies now provide financial planning assistance to better serve their clients and differentiate from their competition. To achieve this, mutual fund companies have established personal counselors for their large customers, while providing generic planning on the internet for all customers.

Banks

Banks offer a wide range of financial planning services. Core product offerings include checking and savings accounts, mortgages, loans, and other credit products. In addition, banks now offer comprehensive brokerage services such as stocks, bonds, mutual funds, investments, and retirement planning. They may also offer estate planning services through their trust departments.

EXHIBIT 18.2 Summary of Financial Planning Institutions

Common Practice Areas	Accounting Firms	Law Firms	Insurance Companies	PFP Firms	Brokerage Houses	Mutual Funds	Banks
Insurance			✓	✓	✓		✓
Investments	✓		✓	✓	✓	✓	✓
Tax	✓	✓		✓			
Retirement	✓	✓	✓	✓	✓	✓	✓
Estate Planning	✓	✓	✓	✓	✓		✓

In an effort to attract clients and increase assets under management, firms and individual practices are expanding services to include all elements of financial planning. This newfound diversification provides clients with one-stop shopping. Firms have accomplished changes and expansion by maintaining their traditional expertise, such as tax planning for accounting firms and investment advice for brokerage houses, and hiring specialists in the other areas. Thus, the institutions continue to dominate service and training in one specific area but have the capacity, through company experts, to cover all aspects of financial planning. In addition, the institutions themselves continue to expand as the competition increases, in order to spread the costs of experts and additional services over the greatest number of clients and the amount of assets under management.

The consolidation of the various practice areas will provide an opportunity for lower-to-middle-income clients to have access to better financial planning services. Those services may become less personal, however, with planning services offered over the internet and within financial apps. Meanwhile, the wealthiest clients will likely continue to seek the services of a team of professionals, generally from more than one institution. Individuals with large investments generally seek independent, objective advice, which may be difficult to obtain from a single institution.

Financial Planning Professionals

The public perceives, and has a reasonable expectation, that those who practice financial planning are competent and ethical. Many financial professionals are licensed at the state and federal levels in specific areas such as insurance and/or securities. They are not specifically regulated, however, for their financial planning activities, with the exception of the CERTIFIED FINANCIAL PLANNER™, who is certified by Certified Financial Planner Board of Standards, Inc. (CFP Board). Individuals who have only an elementary understanding of one or two functional areas are not prepared to assist clients faced with complex choices in a changing environment. Although there are many competent, highly trained and highly credentialed individuals practicing financial planning, there are many more holding themselves out as financial planners who are not trained, competent, or credentialed. Unfortunately, the practice of financial planning lacks uniform educational standards, professional competence standards, and commitment to one profession with a self-regulating set of ethical standards.

Many financial planning professionals attempt to distinguish themselves by earning financial planning designations. The following three sections briefly describe some of the more common credentials for individuals who work in the financial planning area.

Financial Planning Designations

Certified Financial Planner™ (CFP®) CFP® certification, perhaps the most recognized and respected financial planning certification, is awarded by CFP Board. CFP® certificants are individuals who have met CFP Board's education, examination, experience, and ethics requirements. These individuals are committed to high standards of ethical conduct and must complete biennial continuing education requirements. Additional information about CFP Board and its Code of Ethics and Standards of Conduct is provided in the following chapter.

Chartered Financial Consultant® (ChFC®) The ChFC® credential is a financial planning designation awarded by The American College of Financial Services to individuals who complete the required education program, meet the experience requirements, and agree to adhere to a code of ethics.

Personal Financial Specialist™ (PFS™) The PFS™ designation is granted exclusively to CPAs who wish to specialize in personal financial planning. The PFS™ credential is a financial planning designation awarded by the AICPA to candidates who have met the CPA education requirements, have the minimum hours of financial planning experience, and successfully complete an exam.

EXHIBIT 18.3 Summary of Financial Planning Designations

	Education/Experience	Exam	Ethics	Continuing Education	Designating Organization
CFP®	Bachelor's degree and three years of financial planning-related experience (or two years of apprenticeship experience meeting additional requirements)	6 hours (two 3-hour sessions in one day)	Yes	30 hours every two years; includes 2 hours for ethics	CFP Board
ChFC®	Nine-course financial planning curriculum from The American College of Financial Services and three years of business experience	Two-hour exam for each of the nine courses	Adherence to The American College's Code of Ethics	30 hours every two years (mandatory for certain designees who matriculated after 06/30/1989; voluntary for others)	The American College of Financial Services
PFS™	Candidates must be CPAs and practice in the area of financial planning for a minimum number of hours per year	Comprehensive seven and one-quarter hour exam covering six financial planning topic areas	Adherence to the AICPA's Code of Professional Conduct	60 hours of CPE every three years; earned through classes, research, and work experience	AICPA, only to members who meet the requirements

Other Designations Held by Financial Services Professionals

Chartered Life Underwriter® (CLU®) The CLU® designation is awarded by The American College of Financial Services to insurance and financial services professionals who have met the College's three-year business experience requirement, passed eight college-level education courses (five required, three electives), and agreed to abide by the Code of Ethics.

Chartered Financial Analyst® (CFA®) This designation is awarded by CFA Institute to experienced financial analysts who pass three examinations covering economics, financial accounting, portfolio management, securities analysis, and ethics, and complete four years of relevant work experience.

Certified Public Accountant (CPA) The CPA designation is awarded by the American Institute of Certified Public Accountants (AICPA) to accountants who pass the AICPA's Uniform CPA Examination and satisfy the work experience and statutory and licensing requirements of the state(s) in which they practice.

Other Licenses Held by Financial Services Professionals

Attorney (JD) As mentioned in the previous section, some attorneys provide financial planning services. Generally, those who provide these services specialize in estate or tax planning. The attorney is typically part of a financial planning team and may provide specific legal advice to a client, prepare legal documents, and consult on estate and tax planning issues.

Insurance Agent Insurance agents are licensed by a state or states to sell or give advice on insurance products, including life, health, disability, property, and casualty insurance. Financial planning services will vary based on the type of agent. Independent insurance agents sell products for more than one insurance company, whereas exclusive insurance agents represent only one company.

Securities Analyst These professionals are usually employed by investment brokers, banks, mutual fund managers, or other investment institutions to conduct investment research and analyze the value of securities, financial condition of a company, group of companies, or industry sector. Based on their analysis, securities analysts will make specific investment recommendations.

Registered Investment Adviser (RIA), Investment Adviser Representatives (IAR) and Registered Representatives. Registered investment advisers are firms providing securities advice for compensation. They must be registered with the Securities and Exchange Commission (SEC) or appropriate state securities agencies. Financial planning services provided by RIAs include recommendations of stocks, bonds, mutual funds, and other investments.

The Dodd-Frank Wall Street Reform and Consumer Protection Act, which changed the original Investment Advisers Act of 1940 thresholds for registration with the SEC, was signed into law on July 21, 2010. As of July 2011, advisers with assets under management of $100 million or more will continue to register as investment advisers with the SEC (unless an exemption applies). Advisers with assets under management of less than $100 million may be required to register with the SEC or with the state in which they maintain clients.

It's important to note that individuals who work for registered investment advisers must register as investment adviser representatives (IAR). This is in contrast to registered representatives, who are generally employed and sponsored by FINRA member firms. Additionally, confusion arises because one can be a dually registered adviser, who is both an investment adviser and a registered representative.

Real Estate Broker Real estate brokers are licensed by the state or states in which they practice. These individuals arrange for the purchase or sale of property in return for a commission. Financial planning services provided by real estate brokers are limited and may include helping customers finance a real estate purchase through their contacts with banks, savings and loans, and mortgage bankers.

Compensation Methods

The methods of compensation for professional financial planners are as diverse as the planners themselves and include fee-only planners, fee-based planners, commission-based planners, and those receiving fees for assets under management. In recent years, there has been a move toward fee-only and fee-based planners due to the public's perception of a conflict of interest for commission-based planners.

Fee-Only Planners

Fee-only planners typically charge an hourly rate for advice or a fixed fee for a defined engagement. These planners do not receive commissions, and, therefore, their compensation is not contingent on the purchase or sale of a product. Many attorneys, CPAs, and CFP® certificants are compensated as fee-only financial planners.

Fee-Based Planners

Fee-based planners are compensated by both fees and commissions that are contingent on the purchase or sale of financial products.

Commission-Based Planners

Commission-based planners are compensated by commissions that are contingent on the purchase or sale of financial products. These products are used in the implementation of a financial plan.

Fees for Assets Under Management

Some planners are fee-only for advice and, if they take investment assets under management, will charge a monthly, quarterly, or annual fee of some percentage of the overall portfolio value. Fees charged for the management of assets are predominantly based on a percentage of assets. The percentage charged will generally be lower as the size of the client's portfolio increases.

Compliance Issues

There are few regulations by state and federal agencies regarding financial planners as a group. However, most financial planners render some sort of advice in areas that are regulated by the federal and/or state government. Planners selling stocks and bonds, insurance products, or real estate or providing legal or tax advice are required to have licenses for the specific services they provide. In addition, most planners providing investment advice must register with their state as well as the SEC in accordance with the Investment Advisers Act of 1940. In the absence of government regulation of financial planners, those planners who are CFP® certificants have voluntarily chosen to be regulated by a professional regulatory organization, CFP Board.

Financial planners who work in the securities industry may need to register with the Financial Industry Regulatory Authority (FINRA). FINRA is a self-regulatory agency overseen by the SEC that enforces standards of practice upon its members for the protection of investors. Member firms of FINRA are entitled to participate in investment banking and securities sales sponsored by FINRA members. Employees of member firms who engage in securities transactions must register with FINRA as registered representatives, which includes passing a qualification examination that tests the employees' understanding of securities products and laws.

SECURITIES INDUSTRY ESSENTIALS (SIE) EXAM

The SIE exam is FINRA's new general industry knowledge exam testing basic information such as products, risks, the structure and function of the securities industry and its regulatory agencies, and knowledge of regulated and prohibited practices. Although ideal for university students and career changers, anyone can sit for the exam without prior association with a firm. The range of topics covered on the SIE exam includes:

- Knowledge of Capital Markets
- Understanding Products and their Risks
- Understanding Trading, Customer Accounts, and Prohibited Activities
- Overview of the Regulatory Framework

In an effort to make it easier to start a financial services career or to simply prove mastery of basic industry knowledge, FINRA does not require sponsorship with a firm to sit for the SIE exam. However, to become registered with FINRA and seek a representative level role with an employer, candidates must also pass a revised, specialized knowledge qualification exam (or "top-off"), applicable to their job function with the firm.

With a low exam fee and no firm sponsorship requirement, the SIE exam is ideal for university students looking to get a head start on a financial services career and, most importantly, stand out to potential employers by proving mastery of basic industry knowledge and the ability to pass a high-stakes examination.

The SIE exam consists of 75 multiple-choice questions, plus 10 additional experimental questions. The breakdown is as follows:

Sections	% of Exam	# of Exam Questions
Knowledge of Capital Markets	16%	12
Understanding Products and their Risks	44%	33
Understanding Trading, Customer Accounts and Prohibited Activities	31%	23
Overview of Regulatory Framework	9%	7
TOTAL	100%	75

After passing the SIE exam, a candidate has up to four years to pass the representative-level "top-off" exam for registration with FINRA and association with a firm.

The SIE exam will act as a prerequisite exam—to become registered with FINRA and seek a representative level role with an employer, candidates must also pass a revised, specialized knowledge qualification exam (or "top-off") applicable to their job function with the firm.

EXHIBIT 18.4 Required FINRA Exams

Securities Transaction	Qualification Exam Required
Mutual funds (open-end)	Series 6
Variable annuities[1]	
Variable life insurance[1]	
Unit investment trusts	
Municipal fund securities (e.g., Section 529 plans, Coverdells)	
Corporate securities	Series 7
Mutual funds	
Money market funds	
REITs	
Asset-backed securities	
Mortgage-backed securities	
Options	
Government securities	
Venture capital	
Direct participation programs	Series 22
Municipal securities	Series 52
Equity traders	Series 55
Corporate securities	Series 62
Closed-end funds	
Money market funds	
REITs	
Venture capital	
Unsolicited securities orders from firm's clients (excludes municipal securities and limited partnerships)	Series 11
Government securities	Series 72
Government agency securities	
Mortgage-backed securities	
Investment advice	Series 65/66

[1]Individuals must also be state insurance licensed.

Many financial planners are investment advisers under the SEC definition and are required to register as such. According to SEC regulations, an investment adviser is a person who:

- provides advice or issues reports or analyses regarding securities;
- is in the business of providing such services; and
- provides such services for compensation.

Exceptions include the following:

- Banks and bank holding companies
- Lawyers, accountants, engineers, or teachers, if their advisory services are solely incidental to their professions
- Brokers or dealers, if their advisory services are solely incidental to their business as brokers or dealers
- Publishers of newspapers, newsmagazines, or business or financial publications of general and regular circulation
- Persons whose advice is related only to securities that are direct obligations of or guaranteed by the United States

The SEC prohibits misstatements or misleading omissions in connection with purchases or sales of securities or investment advice. An investment adviser owes his clients undivided loyalty and may not engage in activity that creates any conflict of interest.

DEVELOPING A PROFESSIONAL PRACTICE

Building a Practice

Like any other service-oriented professional practice, a personal financial planning practice will grow and develop slowly. The professional developing a practice generally begins by writing a business or strategic plan that identifies the specific market niche of clients to be targeted and establishes goals and objectives for the practice. The planner assesses the competition for that market niche, the external environment, and internal strengths and weaknesses. The planner should implement an appropriate business strategy selected from a number of alternatives. Finally, the planner must monitor and adjust the practice on a continuing basis.

Choosing a market niche is perhaps the most important strategic decision a professional can make to develop a long-lasting, viable practice. An individual planner cannot be all things to all clients. Therefore, a professional planner must direct attention to the areas of specialization that he can penetrate and that will allow him to prosper. An appropriate approach to developing a practice is to scan the environment for a market niche that is not being well served or for a newly developing market need that is underserved or will soon be underserved.

Once a market niche is selected, the planner must effectively promote the professional services that are relevant to that particular niche. Finding the best form of promotion depends on the market demographics, the external environment, and the professional's strengths and weaknesses.

Some clients may feel insecure, skeptical, and vulnerable when engaging professional services. Therefore, clients must not only have confidence in the planner's technical abilities but must also feel that they can trust the planner. After all, they are entering into a relationship in which they must divulge personal financial information to the planner. With that in mind, a successful marketing plan might begin with promoting to an already existing client base. Such client-centered marketing is a good start because planners and their clients have already developed a relationship. In addition, planners are already familiar with their clients' concerns and needs. If planners are developing new practices, an alternative option may be to partner with other professionals who do not provide the services the planner expects to provide.

The pursuit of new clients is more of a challenge, as the ability to win the client's trust and confidence is a substantial obstacle in the sale of professional services. Clients of less than competent practitioners do not leave those practitioners just because a more competent professional becomes available. Many clients lack the ability to assess a practitioner's competence and, even if they can, they may fear and resist changing practitioners. Thus, many clients stay with poor practitioners simply because the relationship is familiar. An understanding of this phenomenon should lead the developing professional to understand that he must be creative and patient when developing a practice. Marketing to new clients may take the form of referrals, networking, educational and professional seminars, teaching financial planning courses, and direct advertising. The development of a successful practice will require a variety of promotional tools used in combination, consistent with an overall marketing and development plan.

Maintaining Clients

As mentioned, a high level of interpersonal trust is the key to long-term planner-client relationships. Regular contact, honesty, sincerity, and effective communication help develop the personal relationships that are essential to maintaining clients. Regular written communications, telephone conversations, lunch meetings, and other social activities help develop these personal relationships.

Although regular contact is important, perhaps the most essential key to a good planner-client relationship is the ability of the planner to truly listen. Clients should feel that the planner listens to their concerns, cares about their futures, and respects them. According to researchers at the University of Minnesota, on average, people spend nearly half of their communication time listening. Good listening is an active process that requires knowledge of a few basic skills and a great deal of practice. Many professionals are in such a habit of selling that they do not stop to listen. Suggestions regarding successful listening include taking notes during client meetings, restating what the client has just said and obtaining client acknowledgement, and requesting clarification when an issue is unclear. Active listening improves interpersonal skills, human relations, and personal selling opportunities. Nurturing client relationships takes time but will greatly benefit the planner in the long run and may result in additional business referrals.

Education and Continuing Education

The professional financial planner must obtain an initial education followed by a lifetime of continuing professional monitoring and education. The economy and financial environment are complex and constantly changing, as are some of the functional areas of financial planning. The risks to life, health, working ability, property, and liability change. The tax laws are complex and change so frequently that the average client may not be able to keep up or understand them. While investment information is readily available today, discerning relevant and useful facts requires more than an elementary understanding. Competent financial planning professionals make staying up to date with these changes a major priority throughout their professional careers.

Technology

A substantial part of the financial planning profession involves data collection and analysis. Fortunately, with the computer software available today, planners can harness vast amounts of financial and economic data. Financial planners who are setting up practices or upgrading their software and network systems should consider the following:

- Planning software for creating financial statements
- Software for evaluating recommendations and alternatives
- Monte Carlo simulation software to evaluate effects of various economic conditions on financial goals
- Data management tools for collecting, storing, and protecting client data
- Data mining/sorting tools to identify clients affected by legal, tax, or economic changes

WHERE ON THE WEB

American Bar Association **www.americanbar.org**

American Institute of Certified Public Accountants (CPA/PFS) **www.aicpa.org**

Certified Financial Planner Board of Standards, Inc. **www.cfp.net**

CFA Institute (CFA designation) **www.cfainstitute.org**

Financial Industry Regulatory Authority (FINRA) (NASD and NYSE consolidation) **www.finra.org**

Financial Planning Association **www.onefpa.org**

Financial Planning Magazine **www.financial-planning.com**

National Association of Insurance Commissioners **www.naic.org**

National Association of Personal Financial Advisors **www.napfa.org**

National Association of State Boards of Accountancy **www.nasba.org**

North American Securities Administrators Association **www.nasaa.org**

Securities and Exchange Commission **www.sec.gov**

Small Business Administration **www.sba.gov**

Society of Financial Service Professionals **national.societyoffsp.org**

U.S. Chamber of Commerce **www.uschamber.com**

DISCUSSION QUESTIONS

1. What are the primary differences in services provided by accounting firms and law firms?
2. Generally, which types of financial planning firms specialize in investment planning?
3. Generally, which types of financial planning firms specialize in estate planning?
4. How is the internet changing the financial planning industry?
5. What is the most recognized and respected financial planning certification?
6. What are the differences between CFP® certification and the CFA® charter?
7. Describe the fee-only compensation method.
8. What is one of the most important strategic decisions that must be made when developing a financial planning practice?
9. What can a planner do to improve the planner-client relationship?

CHAPTER 19

Ethical Responsibilities

LEARNING OBJECTIVES

After learning the material in this chapter, you will be able to do the following:

- Compare and contrast ethics, law, and code of ethics
- Define Certified Financial Planner Board of Standards, Inc. (CFP Board)
- Describe CFP Board's Code of Ethics and Standards of Conduct
- Describe the structure of CFP Board's Code of Ethics and Standards of Conduct and provide the role of each part
- List the six principles of the Code of Ethics
- Explain how the commingling of funds is regulated under the Standards of Conduct
- Discuss the requirements of the Standards of Conduct
- Explain the provisions of the Practice Standards

- Discuss the Fitness Standards for Candidates and Professionals Eligible for Reinstatement
- Compare the three distinct standards or burdens of proof to illustrate the different treatment of a CFP® certificant at various stages of disciplinary proceedings
- Differentiate among the four forms of discipline that can be applied by the Disciplinary and Ethics Commission

INTRODUCTION

CFP Board's Code of Ethics and Standards of Conduct
The set of principles of conduct that regulates behavior of CFP® certificants

Certified Financial Planner Board of Standards, Inc.
An independent professional regulatory organization that regulates financial planners

This chapter identifies, describes, and explains ethical principles for those involved in the financial planning industry through an analysis of the **CFP Board's Code of Ethics and Standards of Conduct** established by **Certified Financial Planner Board of Standards, Inc.** (CFP Board). The CFP Board occasionally updates its Code of Ethics and Standards of Conduct. While the changes have always been incremental, the key changes were adopted March 29, 2018, and made effective as of October 1, 2019. The basis for this material is to broaden the fiduciary standard to all financial advice and financial planning. Previously, the fiduciary standard only applied when doing financial planning or material elements of financial planning.

This chapter provides an overview of several important provisions of the Code of Ethics and Standards of Conduct. The full text provided in Appendix F for review. The most current version of the Code and Standards can also be downloaded at *https://www.cfp.net/for-cfp-professionals/professional-standards-enforcement/code-and-standards*.

ETHICS, LAW, AND CODES OF ETHICS

Ethics
The discipline of dealing with the moral principles or values that guide an individual

Law
Rules of conduct established by a government or other authority that command and encourage behavior considered right and prohibit behavior considered wrong

Analyzing the Code of Ethics and Standards of Conduct as it pertains to CFP® certificants proves to be an excellent guide for all of those involved in the financial planning field. First, however, it is important to distinguish among ethics, law, and codes of ethics.

Ethics is the discipline of dealing with the moral principles or values that guide an individual. When a decision must be made about a certain act, ethics aid an individual in determining what is right and wrong. In other words, ethical behavior is doing or not doing what one feels is right from within. Morals relate to one's conscience, character, and social relations. Morals form one's behavior and dictate whether one engages in conduct that is considered to be right or wrong. Thus, each individual's set of morals and values forms the ethics or ethical behavior of that individual.

Law is defined as rules of conduct established by a government or other authority that command and encourage behavior considered right and prohibit behavior considered wrong. Law and ethics differ in that laws apply to everyone, under certain authority, and compliance with laws is mandatory for those individuals. If the law is broken, that person is subject to punishment by government authorities. A violation of or deviation from one's ethics, on the other hand, does not necessarily subject that person to punishment.

Code of ethics
A set of principles of conduct that governs a group of individuals and usually requires conformity to professional standards of conduct

A **code of ethics** is a set of principles of conduct that governs a group of individuals and usually requires conformity to professional standards of conduct. Although the Code of Ethics and Standards of Conduct provides rules for ethical behavior, they are more closely aligned with law. For example, the same rule applies to attorneys concerning state bar ethics codes. The Code of Ethics and Standards of Conduct is considered the set of rules for CFP® certificants because compliance is mandatory, and failure to abide by these rules may result in disciplinary action, such as revocation or suspension of the CFP® certification.

Many professions have codes of ethics or laws of conduct created to promote ethical behavior. No finite set of ethical rules, however, can anticipate all situations or future developments in an industry. To truly satisfy the goal of an ethics code, applicable professionals must do more than merely fulfill the code's minimum requirements. To reach the ideals of a code, there must be a conscientious, good faith commitment by the professionals to the spirit of the standards of the code under all circumstances.

Ethical behavior, which conforms to moral principles, is the aim of CFP Board's Code of Ethics and Standards of Conduct. If financial planners abide by the highest standards of ethical behavior, the financial services industry will maintain or gain public trust. A need exists for a common, accepted set of ethical principles to ensure fair representation and full disclosure in financial planning services. The Standards of Conduct seek to regulate behavior of CFP® certificants with the intent to provide fairness to clients, maintain and increase public trust, and foster accountability. Public trust in the profession is crucial because opportunities for unethical behavior arise frequently in the financial planning profession. If the public loses trust in the advice of CFP® certificants, they will consult other professionals or not seek financial planning services. So compliance with the code of ethics is vital to the profession.

CFP BOARD AND THE CODE OF ETHICS AND STANDARDS OF CONDUCT

CFP Board's Disciplinary and Ethics Commission
A subsidiary board of CFP Board that interprets and applies the Code

CFP Board's Board of Directors
The governing board for the certified financial planning profession

CFP Board is an independent professional regulatory organization that owns the federally registered CFP® and Certified Financial Planner™ marks (the marks) in the United States. CFP Board regulates financial planners through trademark law by licensing individuals who meet CFP Board's certification requirements to use these federally registered marks. **CFP Board's Disciplinary and Ethics Commission** investigates, reviews, and takes appropriate action in connection with alleged violations of the Standards of Conduct.

CFP Board's Board of Directors requires compliance with the Code of Ethics and Standards of Conduct by all those who have been recognized and certified to use the CFP® marks, as well as those who seek certification. Violations may result in a letter of admonition, private censure, suspension, or revocation of the right to use the CFP® marks. Forms of discipline and an explanation of the disciplinary process are established in the Disciplinary Rules and Procedures (the Procedures). The Procedures also explain the disciplinary process. The final authority in all disciplinary matters rests solely with CFP Board and the Disciplinary and Ethics Commission.

CFP Board has several governing documents, rules, and procedures, including the following:

- Code of Ethics, which states the six Principles constituting the basis for the ethical rules stated in all the other sections
- Standards of Conduct

- Financial Planning Practice Standards
- Disciplinary Rules and Procedures
- Appeal Rules and Procedures
- Fitness Standards for Candidates and Professionals Eligible for Reinstatement

CFP® certificant
An individual who is currently certified by CFP Board

Professional eligible for reinstatement (PER)
An individual who is not currently certified by CFP Board but who was certified in the past and has an entitlement to potentially use the CFP® marks

Generally, the Code of Ethics and Standards of Conduct applies to CFP® professionals currently certified (CFP® certificants) and professionals eligible for reinstatement (PERs). A **CFP® certificant** is an individual who is currently certified by CFP Board. A **professional eligible for reinstatement** (PER) is an individual who is not currently certified but who was certified by CFP Board in the past and has an entitlement to potentially use the CFP® marks. This includes individuals who have relinquished their certification and who are eligible for reinstatement without being required to pass the current CFP® Certification Examination. For the sake of simplicity, the discussion in this chapter will reference the ethical obligations required by the Code of Ethics and Standards of Conduct in terms of their application to certificants.

NOTE ON CIVIL LIABILITY

The Code of Ethics and Standards of Conduct does not define the conduct expected of CFP® certificants for purposes of civil liability. Nonetheless, there are various areas in which a violation of the Code of Ethics and Standards of Conduct could likely result in civil liability for malpractice or professional negligence if the client sustains damages resulting from the CFP® certificant's action or inaction. For example, a certificant who violates Standard A.3 (Competence), which requires that services be provided competently may be susceptible to a lawsuit for professional negligence or malpractice if a client sustains damages resulting from the incompetence. Likewise, a certificant who violates Standard A.1 (Fiduciary Duty), which requires certificants to select financial products that are consistent with the client's needs could also be liable for the client's damages in a malpractice suit.

CODE OF ETHICS AND PROFESSIONAL RESPONSIBILITY

Principles
Aspirational statements expressing the ethical and professional ideals CFP® certificants are expected to display in their professional activities

The Code of Ethics provides six **Principles**, which express the ethical and professional ideals certificants are expected to display in their professional activities. They are aspirational in character and provide certificants with a source of guidance. The Principles contained in the Code of Ethics form the basis of the Standards of Conduct, Financial Planning Practice Standards, and Disciplinary Rules and Procedures.

Principle 1: Act with honesty, integrity, competence, and diligence. The duty of integrity means honesty in all aspects of the planner's relationship with the client. There can be no deceit or fraud in any statement or omission with a client. Honesty and candor must be more important than the planner's personal benefit. Allowance can be made for innocent error and legitimate differences of opinion, but integrity cannot coexist with deceit or subordination of one's principles. Competence involves both knowledge and skill. If the planner does not have the required knowledge or skill, she can acquire the skill, recommend someone else to provide these aspects of the plan, or limit the planning engagement to only areas in which the planer is competent. Diligence involves a thoroughness in preparation and execution.

Principle 2: Act in the client's best interest. The foundation of the CFP Board Code of Ethics and Standards of Conduct is that a CFP® certificant is held to a fiduciary standard in all financial advice. Formerly, the fiduciary standard was only applied when providing financial planning or material elements of financial planning. CFP Board defines a *fiduciary* as one who acts in the utmost good faith, in a manner he reasonably believes to be in the best interests of the client.

Principle 3: Exercise due care.

Principle 4: Avoid or disclose and manage conflicts of interest.

Principle 5: Maintain the confidentiality and protect the privacy of client information.

Principle 6: Act in a manner that reflects positively on the financial planning profession and the CFP® certification.

STANDARDS OF CONDUCT

Standards of Conduct *Rules established by CFP Board that establish the high standards expected of CFP® certificants, the violation of which may subject a certificant to discipline*

The **Standards of Conduct** establish the high standards expected of certificants. They are binding on all certificants who have the right to use the CFP® marks, regardless of their title, type of employment or method of compensation, and regardless of whether they use actually use the CFP® marks. Violations may subject a certificant to discipline.

Certificants engage in a wide range of activities, and some certificants may not perform all of the typical services provided by financial planning professionals. As a result, some of the Standards may not apply to a certificant's specific activity. In addition, when the Standards require a specific action, a certificant is considered to be in compliance with the Standards if the certificant's employer performed the action.

The Standards of Conduct are divided into duties owed to clients, the application of practice standards for the financial planning process, duties to firms and subordinates, and the prohibition on circumvention. Summaries of some of the important Standards of Conduct are discussed in the sections that follow.

Duties Owed to Clients

Fiduciary Duty

A CFP® professional always owes a fiduciary duty to the client when providing financial advice. This means always acting in the best interests of the client by fulfilling three duties: the duty of loyalty, the duty of care, and the duty to follow clients' instructions.

The duty of loyalty has two aspects:

- Placing the interests of the client above the interests of the CFP® certificant and the firm for which he or she professional works
- Avoiding conflicts of interest or fully disclosing material conflicts or interest and obtaining the client's informed consent

The duty of care means acting with skill, care, prudence, and thoroughness in light of the client's goals, risk tolerance, and circumstances.

The duty to follow client instructions means implementing the client's objectives, restrictions, and policies in accordance with the terms of the engagement.

Integrity

The duty of integrity means honesty in all aspects of the planner's relationship with the client. There can be no deceit or fraud in any statement or omission with a client.

If the services include financial planning, the certificant or the certificant's employer must enter into a written agreement governing the financial planning services with the client. The agreement must specify the services to be provided, the duration of the agreement, and procedures for terminating the agreement.

Competence

Besides the fiduciary duty and integrity in all aspects of the relationship, a CFP® certificant is required to be competent. This means certificants must offer advice only in areas in which they are competent to do so and maintain competence in any areas in which they are engaged to provide professional services. Keep in mind that financial planning is broad, and a CFP Board designee may be knowledgeable in many areas but deficient in others. This is particularly true today because financial services are quite complicated. Because of the vast diversity and scope of financial services, few people can be experts in all areas.

By virtue of having earned CFP® certification, a certificant is deemed to be qualified to practice and knowledgeable in the field of financial planning. However, it is neither sufficient simply to assimilate and absorb the common body of knowledge required to obtain CFP® certification, nor is it sufficient simply to acquire the necessary experience. Rather, a certificant must make a continuing commitment to learn and improve. As will be discussed later, CFP Board thus requires certificants to satisfy minimum continuing education requirements.

Generally, the requirement of competence involves certificant-client relationships—the Standards specifically refer to clients in defining the requirements relating to competence. The driving force behind this is that financial planning clients must be protected from incompetence. In certificant-client relationships, a certificant's incompetence can result in damage or loss to the client, not simply a disappointment or disciplinary action for the individual certificant. In addition, incompetence may reflect poorly upon the financial planning profession in general.

Certificants must exercise reasonable and prudent professional judgment when providing professional services to a client. They may only make or implement recommendations that are in the best interests of the client. This depends on the facts and circumstances of the client's situation. In addition, certificants must provide reasonable professional supervision to any subordinate or third party to whom they assign responsibility for any client services. This is yet another safeguard that ultimately benefits the client and strengthens the public's trust in the profession. All of these duties follow from the fiduciary relationship that exists between certificants and their clients.

Certificants must be in compliance with any applicable regulatory requirements governing the professional services they provide to clients. They must also advise their current clients of any suspension or revocation of their CFP® certification.

If the planner is not competent in an aspect of the relationship, the planner must obtain the competence; the engagement must be limited or terminated as necessary; or a competent professional must be found. A CFP® certificant must inform the client of any professional services that were requested by the client that will not be undertaken by the planner.

Diligence

Diligence involves giving a matter to the degree of effort expected in the client-planner relationship, including responding to the client in a timely and sufficiently thorough manner.

Disclose and Manage Conflicts of Interest

This duty involves the provision of financial advice, in particular the disclosure and management of all material conflicts of interest. This gives the client the ability to give informed consent or to reject the unacceptable aspects of the relationship.

Conflict of interest
Exists when a certificant's financial, business, property, and/or personal interests, relationships, or circumstances impair the certificant's ability to offer objective advice, recommendations, or services

A **conflict of interest** exists when a certificant's financial, business, property, or personal interests, relationships, or circumstances impair the certificant's ability to offer objective advice, recommendations, or services. Professional financial planners should recognize the inherent conflicts of interests that may arise in certificant-client relationships. The main reason for providing financial services as a financial planning practitioner is to give the client personalized financial advice that will maximize the client's financial well-being. On the other hand, the certificant is engaged in the financial services industry to earn a living and be compensated for the service. This compensation comes from the client—the same client who has engaged the certificant to improve the client's financial status. Theoretically speaking, this may be a conflict of interest in and of itself. For example, many certificants sell stocks, bonds, mutual funds, life insurance, or annuities and earn commissions from the sale of these products to their clients. This potentially creates an incentive for certificants to recommend products that may provide higher commissions or to refrain from recommending another course of action that may be in the client's best interest but would not provide any commissions. Even if the certificant is not in fact swayed in this scenario, there is an appearance that the interests of the certificant and the client are in conflict. When the appearance of such a conflict exists, it would be impractical for the certificant to disqualify himself from the relationship with the client, because then there would be no circumstance in which a certificant could earn a commission for selling a product to a client. Instead of disqualification or disengagement, the Standards require that a certificant disclose all potential conflicts of interests to the client in writing. The assumption is that, if the certificant discloses the information to the client, the client will feel as if the certificant has nothing to hide, and at the same time, the certificant is reminding himself to remain objective.

CFP Board holds that a CFP® certificant sincerely believing he is acting in the client's best interest is not sufficient to meet the duty to disclose and manage conflicts of interest. When investigating, the CFP Board will look for evidence that a reasonable client would have understood the disclosure and management aspects of the relationship in order for the client to give informed consent. The closer a planner conforms to commonly accepted business practices, the more likely the CFP Board will conclude that proper disclosure was made. Any unclear provisions in the disclosure will be interpreted in the client's favor.

Sound and Objective Professional Judgment

Under this duty, a planner's judgment may not be clouded by the interests of the planner. A CFP® certificant may not solicit or receive any gifts, noncash compensation, or other inducements that can reasonably be perceived to compromise the planner's objectivity or professional judgment.

Professionalism

The duty of professionalism involves showing clients, prospects, and other professionals respect, dignity, and courtesy.

Comply With the Law

The duty of compliance with all laws and regulations is also owed to the client. Besides the planner complying with all laws, rules, and regulations, a CFP® certificant may not intentionally assist in someone else's failure to obey all laws, rules, and regulations.

Confidentiality and Privacy

In general, a CFP® certificant may not disclose nonpublic information for any client, former client, or prospective client without consent. This is true even if the person is not harmed by the disclosure. However, client information may be shared within the purview of normal business relations when necessary. Additionally, a client's information can be shared with an authorized representative working for the client. Client information may also be shared in regard to a legal or enforcement action by a duly authorized representative of the law enforcement community or other applicable regulatory body or to defend against a legal matter brought against the planner on behalf of the client. Finally, all CFP® certificants must take reasonable steps to protect client data in both physical and electronic form.

Provide Information to the Client

A CFP® professional must provide the required information to the client at or before the start of the client engagement. The required information is dependent upon the nature of the engagement. There are two categories—when providing financial advice that does not rise to the level of financial planning according to the Practice Standards and when financial planning is occurring.

When only providing financial advice, the following information is required to be given to the client:

1. A description of the services and products involved
2. How the client pays for the services and products, including any additional charges that might be incurred
3. How the CFP® certificant and the firm are compensated
4. Any websites of governing authorities, self-regulating organizations, or professional organizations that contain the CFP® professional's public disciplinary history or any personal bankruptcy or business bankruptcy in which the planner was materially involved
5. Any other material information about the planner or firm regarding the client's decision to engage or continue to engage in the planning relationship

When providing financial planning, all the information required for financial advice is required, plus the following:

1. The terms of the engagement, including the scope of the engagement, time period, and any limits to the engagement
2. The client's responsibilities—unless excluded in the terms of the agreement, the CFP® certificant is responsible for implementing, updating. and monitoring the recommendations
3. A written disclosure of conflicts of interest and how they will be managed
4. The policies for protecting, handling, and sharing nonpublic information
5. The planner's duties when communicating with the client

Finally, for duties to provide information to the client, a CFP® professional has an obligation to give the client any material updates to the information given to the client previously. Specifically, any material updates to the CFP® professional's disciplinary history or bankruptcy information must be provided to the client within 90 days. The planner is also required to give the client the web pages that pertain to these changes.

Communicating With a Client

There is also a duty to provide accurate information and responses to questions in a timely manner in accordance with the terms of the engagement. All responses must be in a format a client would be reasonably expected to understand.

Certificants may not communicate to clients any false or misleading information related to their professional qualifications or services and may not mislead clients about the potential benefits of their services. Certificants may not fail to disclose or omit facts when disclosure is necessary to avoid misleading clients.

Certificants must disclose the following information to clients and prospective clients:

- An accurate and understandable description of the compensation arrangements being offered
- A general summary of likely conflicts of interest between the client and the certificant, the certificant's employer, or any affiliates or third parties
- Contact information for the certificant and the certificant's employer

If the certificant's services include financial planning, these disclosures must be in writing. The certificant must also make a timely disclosure to the client if any of this information materially changes.

Representing Compensation Method

There are three categories of compensation: fee-only, fee-based, and sales-related compensation. To be fee-only, neither the planner nor any part of the planner's business can receive any sales-related compensation in connection to the services provided to clients.

Fee-based compensation means the planner or the planner's firm receives both fees and sales-related compensation. The CFP Board calls this compensation *fee and commission*.

Sales-related compensation includes any compensation relating to the buying or selling of a client's financial assets other than for providing financial advice. It also includes compensation for referral of a client to an outside professional. It includes all types of commissions, 12b-1 fees, spreads, and revenue sharing arrangements. There are certain exceptions to sales-related compensation listed by the CFP Board.

A CFP® professional's duty to the client when the CFP® certificant's firm misrepresents compensation methods depends on if the CFP® professional controls the firm or not. If the CFP® professional controls the firm, then he may not allow the firm to misrepresent its compensation methods. If the CFP® certificant does not control the firm, then he must correct the firm's misrepresentations when dealing with the client.

Recommending, Engaging, and Working With Additional Persons

A duty a CFP® professional owes to clients involves the manner in which she deals with additional people in the relationship, such as attorneys and accountants. First, the CFP® professional must have a reasonable basis for recommending the additional person to a client. Second, either when the recommendation occurs or before the engagement with the client, the CFP® professional must disclose any economic benefits the planner or the firm will receive for the recommendation.

When dealing with the additional person on behalf of the client, the CFP® certificant must inform the additional person about the scope of the services and the division of responsibilities. The CFP® certificant has a responsibility to inform the client in a timely manner if the additional person is not performing adequately within the scope of the engagement.

Selecting, Using, and Recommending Technology

This duty involves the CFP® certificant only using or recommending technology in which he has an adequate understanding of the assumptions used and which he reasonably believes will produce reliable, objective, and appropriate results.

Refrain From Borrowing or Lending and Commingling Assets

A final duty owed to a client is to refrain from borrowing, lending, or commingling financial assets with the client. The only exceptions from the prohibition on CFP® certificants borrowing from or lending to a client are when the client is a family member or when the client is a money-lending institution. Finally, the CFP® professional and the firm are always prohibited from commingling financial assets with a client. Commingling is the act of mixing property (usually funds) belonging to one party with property belong to someone else; commingling occurs when a planner deposits client funds into his personal bank account. Commingling a client's property with other clients' property is prohibited unless doing so is authorized by law or the certificant has written authorization from each client and sufficient recordkeeping to accurately track the assets. Note that this rule restricts the situations when a certificant may commingle funds, even when the certificant has no negative intent. Even when a certificant has no negative intent, commingling client funds with personal funds may give rise to an appearance of impropriety.

Duties Owed to Firms and Subordinates

A certificant who is an employee or agent must perform professional services with dedication to the lawful objectives of the employer or principal and in accordance with the Code of Ethics. Certificants must also advise their current employers of any renovation or suspension of their CFP® certification.

A CFP® certificant is to provide reasonable care in the supervision of all associates acting for the CFP® certificant. The primary duty of supervision is to follow all rules, regulations, laws, and the CFP® Code of Ethics and Standards of Conduct. If a planner suspects another member of the firm with illegal or unethical behavior, she must promptly disclose it to management. The second duty is to comply with the lawful objectives of the employer. The planner will be subject to discipline by CFP Board for violations of the Code of Ethics and Standards of Conduct that do not conflict with the policies and procedures of the CFP®'s firm.

Duties Owed to CFP Board

One of the most basic of these obligations is that a certificant must meet all CFP® requirements, including continuing education requirements, to retain the right to use the CFP® marks. CFP Board requires 30 hours of continuing education biannually; of these 30 hours, at least 2 hours must cover ethics.

A certificant must notify CFP Board in writing of any conviction of a crime, other than minor traffic violations, or of any professional suspension or bar within 30 calendar days.

Finally, a certificant must not engage in any conduct that adversely reflects on (1) his integrity or fitness as a certificant, (2) upon the CFP® marks, or (3) upon the profession. The scope of this rule is broader than the other rules pertaining to professionalism, because it applies to any conduct that has an adverse effect on the certificant or the profession. There is some overlap between this requirement and the principle of integrity.

Actions Reflecting Upon the Profession

In the case of *Ibanez v. Florida Department of Business and Professional Regulation, Board of Accountancy*, 512 U.S. 136, 114 S. Ct. 2084, 129 L. Ed. 2d 118 (1994), Ibanez, an attorney, licensed CPA, and CFP® certificant, was reprimanded by the Florida Board of Accountancy for engaging in "false, deceptive, and misleading" advertising. Ibanez referred to her credentials as an attorney, a CPA, and CFP® certificant in her advertising and other communications with the public, placing CPA and CFP® certificant next to her name in her yellow pages listing and in her business cards and law office stationery.

The Florida Board of Accountancy argued that the term *certified* in the phrase *Certified Financial Planner* was misleading to the public because it implied state approval and recognition, when in fact the CFP Board certification is not given by the state. The U.S. Supreme Court rejected this argument and ruled that Ibanez had a constitutional right to promote herself as an attorney/CPA who was also a CFP® certificant. The Court then approvingly stated:

> Noteworthy in this connection, "Certified Financial Planner" and "CFP®" are well-established, protected federal trademarks that have been described as the most recognized designation(s) in the planning field. [Several thousand] persons have qualified for the designation nationwide. Over 50 accredited universities and colleges have established courses of study in financial planning approved by the CFP Board of Standards, Inc., and standards for licensure include satisfaction of certain core educational requirements, a passing score on a certification examination similar in concept to the Bar or CPA examinations, completion of a planning-related work experience requirement, agreement to abide by the CFP Board's *Code of Ethics and Professional Responsibility*, and an annual continuing education requirement.

The Court concluded that Ibanez could use all three credentials in her advertising because doing so was not misleading or false and because she had a constitutional right to commercial speech. The case also casts the CFP® marks in a favorable light, recognizing the credibility that accompanies them. Thus, Ibanez's actions did not mislead the public and did not adversely affect the profession.

THE PRACTICE STANDARDS

Practice Standards
The set of standards that (1) establish the level of professional practice that is expected of certificants engaged in personal financial planning, (2) advance professionalism in the practice of financial planning, and (3) enhance the value of the personal financial planning process

CFP Board established the Board of Practice Standards to draft the **Practice Standards** to ensure that the financial planning practice by certificants is based on agreed-upon norms of practice. The Practice Standards are also in place to advance professionalism in the practice of financial planning and to enhance the value of the personal financial planning process. A Practice Standard establishes the level of professional practice that is expected of certificants engaged in personal financial planning. The facts and circumstances of each particular situation determine the services to be provided.

Practice Standard 1

Understanding the Client's Personal and Financial Circumstances. The formal start of any engagement involves gathering the client's data and documenting it in writing. This includes the obligation of the CFP® certificant to act in the best interests of the client and to inform the client of the firm's policies and procedures. The planner must communicate to the client the need for both quantitative and qualitative data to fulfill the scope of the engagement and to collaborate with the client in obtaining the information. This data is analyzed to determine the client's personal and financial condition. If a planner cannot obtain sufficient data to fulfill the scope of the engagement, the scope of the engagement must be limited to what the data supports or the engagement must be terminated.

The scope of the engagement must be mutually defined by the financial planning practitioner and the client prior to providing any financial planning service. The process of *mutually defining* is accomplished by identifying the services to be provided, disclosing the practitioner's material conflicts of interest and compensation arrangements, determining the client's and practitioner's responsibilities, and establishing the duration of the engagement.

Practice Standard 2

Identifying and Selecting Goals. After discussing the planner's assessment of the client's personal and financial circumstances, the next issue is the client's goals. A client's personal financial goals, needs, and priorities that are relevant to the scope of the engagement and the service(s) being provided must be mutually defined by the financial planning practitioner and the client prior to making and/or implementing any recommendation. One portion of the goal-setting process is understanding that accomplishing one goal may impact other goals. When setting goals, a planner may use reasonable assumptions and estimates of items such as investment returns, inflation rates, tax rates, and other material items. Finally, the planner must inform the client of any goals the client finally selects which are not realistic in the planner's estimation.

Practice Standard 3

Analyzing the Client's Current Course of Action and Potential Alternative Course(s) of Action. A financial planning practitioner must analyze the client's present course of action and evaluate the major advantages and disadvantages of staying the course in the attempt to maximize the potential to meet the goals of the client. The CFP® certificant should also analyze the potential of alternative courses of action along with their major advantages and disadvantages in concert with the client's other goals, facts, and circumstances. This Practice Standard is intended to increase the probability of the practitioner helping the client to achieve the goals and objectives of the financial plan.

Practice Standard 4

Developing the Financial Planning Recommendation(s). The financial planning practitioner shall consider sufficient and relevant alternatives to the client's current course of action in an effort to reasonably meet the client's goals, needs, and priorities. This evaluation, which is done prior to any recommendations, may involve multiple reasonable assumptions, research, or consultation with other competent professionals. This process may result in one alternative, no alternatives, multiple alternatives, or various combinations in relation to the client's current course of action.

The financial planning practitioner must develop recommendations based on the selected alternatives and the current course of action in order to reasonably achieve the client's goals, needs, and priorities. A recommendation may be an independent action, continuation of the current course of action, inaction, or a combination of actions that may need to be implemented collectively. collectively. Each recommendation must consider the following:

1. The assumptions and estimates used to develop the recommendation
2. The basis for the recommendation including how it attempts to maximize the chance of meeting the goal and affecting the client's personal and financial situation
3. The timing and priority of the recommendation and whether the recommendation stands alone or must be implemented in coordination with another recommendation

Practice Standard 5

Presenting the Financial Planning Recommendation(s). A financial planning practitioner must communicate the recommendations to the client and the information that was required to be considered in developing the recommendations in a manner and to an extent reasonably necessary to assist the client in making an informed decision. The practitioner is charged with the responsibility of assisting the client in understanding (1) the client's current situation, (2) the recommendation itself, and (3) the impact of the recommendation on the ability to achieve the client's goals, needs, and priorities. If the client possesses an understanding of the items, the client then can make an informed decision. Presenting recommendations also provides the practitioner the opportunity to further assess whether the recommendations meet the client's expectations, the client's willingness to act on the recommendations, and whether modifications are needed.

Practice Standard 6

Implementing the Financial Planning Recommendation(s). The client and the financial planning practitioner must mutually agree on the implementation responsibilities consistent with the scope of the engagement. The client is responsible for accepting or rejecting recommendations and for retaining or delegating implementation responsibilities. The responsibilities of the financial planning practitioner may include (1) communicating with the client the recommendations being implemented, (2) identifying activities necessary for implementation, (3) determining division of activities between the client and practitioner, (4) handling referrals to and/or coordination with other professionals, (5) sharing of information as authorized, (6) selecting and securing products or services after considering the advantages and disadvantages of the action, product, or services relative to the reasonably available alternatives, and (7) discussing with the client the basis for selecting the products or services recommended and any conflicts of interest. Finally, the CFP® professional must discuss with the client any client selection that deviates from the recommendations.

The financial planning practitioner has the duty to use her judgment in investigating products or services that reasonably address the client's needs and are in the best interests of the client. The planner must discuss with the client any client selection that differs from the actions, products, and services that the planner recommended. Professional judgment incorporates information that is both qualitative and quantitative and, of course, may differ from those of other practitioners or advisers. Over time, implementing recommendations using proper products and services for the client increases the credibility of the profession in the eyes of the public.

Practice Standard 7

Monitoring Progress and Updating—Defining Monitoring Responsibilities. The financial planning practitioner and client must mutually define monitoring responsibilities. This Practice Standard clarifies the role, if any, of the practitioner so that the client's expectations are more likely to be in alignment with the level of monitoring services that the practitioner intends to provide. When monitoring services are engaged, the financial planning practitioner must make a reasonable effort to define and communicate to the client those monitoring activities that the practitioner is able and willing to provide, including an explanation of what is to be monitored, how the actions, products, and services will be monitored, the frequency of monitoring, and the communication method.

A portion of monitoring includes analyzing and updating the client's progress toward goals and reviewing the results with the client. Both quantitative and qualitative data is analyzed during the review process, including any material changes reported by the client.

FITNESS STANDARDS FOR CANDIDATES AND PROFESSIONALS ELIGIBLE FOR REINSTATEMENT

The Disciplinary and Ethics Commission (DEC), a group within CFP Board, has determined specific character and fitness standards for candidates for certification to ensure an individual's conduct does not reflect adversely upon the profession as a whole or upon the CFP® certification marks. These standards are referred to as the Fitness Standards for Candidates and Professionals Eligible for Reinstatement (PERs). CFP Board determined that such standards would benefit individuals interested in attaining CFP® certification. The following conduct (referred to as *Conduct Deemed Unacceptable*) is unacceptable and will *always* bar an individual from becoming certified:

- Felony conviction for theft, embezzlement, or other financially based crimes
- Felony conviction for tax fraud or other tax-related crimes
- Revocation of a financial (registered securities representative, broker-dealer, insurance, accountant, investment advisor, financial planner) professional license, unless the revocation is administrative in nature (i.e., the result of the individual determining not to renew the license by not paying the required fees)

- Felony conviction for any degree of murder or rape
- Felony conviction for any other violent crime within the last five years

The following conduct (referred to as *Conduct Deemed a Presumptive Bar*) is *presumed* to be unacceptable and will bar an individual from becoming certified unless the individual petitions the Disciplinary and Ethics Commission (the "Commission") for consideration, and the Commission grants the petition:

- Two or more personal or business bankruptcies
- Revocation or suspension of a nonfinancial professional (e.g., real estate agent, attorney) license, unless the revocation is administrative in nature (i.e., the result of the individual determining not to renew the license by not paying the required fees)
- Suspension of a financial professional (e.g., registered securities representative, broker-dealer, insurance agent, accountant, investment adviser, financial planner) license, unless the suspension is administrative in nature (i.e., the result of the individual determining not to renew the license by not paying the required fees)
- Felony conviction for nonviolent crimes (including perjury) within the last five years
- Felony conviction for violent crimes other than murder or rape that occurred more than five years ago

Under the procedures outlined in CFP Board's *Disciplinary Rules and Procedures*, the Commission will review other matters that may reflect adversely upon the profession or the CFP® certification marks once the candidate for CFP® certification has successfully completed the education, examination, and experience requirements for certification. These matters include, but are not limited to:

- consumer complaints;
- arbitrations and other civil proceedings;
- felony convictions for nonviolent crimes that occurred over five years ago;
- misdemeanor convictions; and
- employer investigations and terminations.

Candidates for CFP® certification and PERs are required by CFP Board to disclose certain matters on the ethics section of the initial certification application.

Individuals who have conduct that is listed in the *Conduct Deemed a Presumptive Bar* list (discussed previously) or may reflect adversely upon the profession or the CFP® certification marks may petition the Commission for consideration and a determination whether their conduct will bar certification. The basic process for these reviews will be as follows.

- When CFP Board learns that an individual's conduct falls within the *Conduct Deemed Unacceptable* list (previously discussed), CFP Board notifies the individual that he/she is permanently barred from becoming certified.
- The individual submits a written petition for consideration to the CFP Board's Professional Standards Department.
- The individual signs a form agreeing to CFP Board's jurisdiction to review the matter.

- CFP Board reviews the request to confirm that the conduct either falls within the *Conduct Deemed a Presumptive Bar* list or is conduct that may reflect adversely upon the profession or the CFP® certification marks.
- Once confirmed, CFP Board requests all relevant documentation from the individual, and a fee is paid by the individual submitting the petition for consideration.

Once the Disciplinary and Ethics Commission has reviewed the petition, it will make one of the following decisions.

- Grant the petition after determining that the conduct does not reflect adversely on the individual's fitness as a candidate for CFP® certification or upon the profession or the CFP® certification marks, and certification will be issued to the individual.
- Deny the petition but allow the individual to reapply for CFP® certification after a period not to exceed five years. The individual will be required to meet the education, examination, experience, and ethics requirements of CFP® certification at the time of reapplication.
- Deny the petition after determining that the conduct reflects adversely on the individual's fitness as a candidate for CFP® certification or upon the profession or the CFP® certification marks, and certification will be permanently barred.

Disciplinary Rules and Procedures
The rules and regulations for disciplinary proceedings against CFP Board certificants

The Commission's decision regarding a petition for reconsideration may be appealed to the Appeals Committee of the Board of Directors.

DISCIPLINARY RULES AND PROCEDURES

The Standards of Conduct also provide the rules and regulations for disciplinary proceedings against CFP Board designees. The enforcement of the Standards is accomplished through CFP Board's **Disciplinary Rules and Procedures** (the Procedures).

Notes on Burdens of Proof

Professional financial planners should understand the various standards of proof that are involved with litigation in general and in disciplinary procedures. A standard of proof, or **burden of proof,** is the requirement of proving facts to a certain degree of probability. There are three distinct burdens of proof: (1) preponderance of the evidence, (2) clear and convincing evidence, and (3) evidence beyond a reasonable doubt. A comparison of the burdens of proof illustrates that different burdens apply at various stages of disciplinary proceedings. Note that burden of proof in disciplinary proceedings is upon CFP Board. The certificant is presumed to be free from ethical violations until proven otherwise.

Burden of proof
The requirement of proving facts to a certain degree of probability. With regard to disciplinary rules and procedures, there are three distinct burdens of proof: (1) preponderance of the evidence, (2) clear and convincing evidence, and (3) evidence beyond a reasonable doubt.

The Preponderance of the Evidence Standard

Preponderance of the evidence
A measure or degree of proof. With regard to disciplinary rules and procedures, preponderance of the evidence means the evidence as a whole shows what it was intended to prove with a probability of 51% or more.

Preponderance of the evidence means that the evidence as a whole shows what it was intended to prove with a probability of 51% or more. To say it another way, the evidence tends to prove that the existence of a fact is more likely than not. For example, proof of misconduct by a certificant must be "*established by a preponderance of the evidence*." In other words, it must be shown that a certificant more than likely violated the Code. In professional negligence or malpractice cases, the standard of proof is generally by a preponderance of the evidence.

The Clear and Convincing Evidence Standard

Clear and convincing evidence
A measure or degree of proof; with regard to disciplinary rules and procedures, clear and convincing evidence means the evidence as a whole shows what it was intended to prove with a probability of 75% or more

"*Clear and convincing evidence*" requires more proof or more certainty in the eyes of the fact finder than a preponderance of the evidence. **Clear and convincing evidence** is the measure or degree of proof that will produce in the mind of the fact finder a firm belief or conviction as to allegations sought to be established and has been loosely described as a 75% certainty that a fact has been proven. Under the Procedures, a certificant who has been suspended for over a year must petition the Disciplinary and Ethics Commission for reinstatement and prove by clear and convincing evidence that he has been rehabilitated, has met continuing education requirements, and is fit to use the marks. In other words, the certificant must clearly and convincingly prove that he is worthy of reinstatement, with more certainty than by a preponderance of the evidence but less than that beyond a reasonable doubt.

In litigation involving fraud, usually the party alleging fraud must prove fraud by clear and convincing evidence.

The Beyond a Reasonable Doubt Standard

Beyond a reasonable doubt
A measure or degree of proof; with regard to disciplinary rules and procedures, beyond a reasonable doubt means the evidence as a whole shows what it was intended to prove with a probability of 99% or more

Beyond a reasonable doubt in evidence means that the fact finder is fully satisfied, entirely convinced, and satisfied to a moral certainty that a fact has been established. The fact finder can have no doubt as to the existence of a fact unless that doubt is unreasonable or irrational. Some define the term as a 99% certainty that the evidence shows as a whole the fact sought to be proven. In criminal proceedings, the burden of proof is beyond a reasonable doubt.

Grounds for and Forms of Discipline

The grounds for discipline under the Procedures are as follows:

- Any act that violates the Standards of Conduct
- Any act that fails to comply with the Practice Standards
- Any act that violates any criminal laws, whether the certificant is convicted or acquitted
- Any act that is the proper basis for professional suspension
- Any act that violates the Disciplinary Rules and Procedures or an order of discipline
- Failure to respond to a request of CFP Board without good cause, or obstruction of CFP Board or staff in the performance of one's duties
- Any false or misleading statement made to CFP Board

Private censure
An unpublished written reproach that is mailed to the censured CFP® certificant by the Disciplinary and Ethics Commission

Public letter of admonition
Written reproach of the CFP® certificant's behavior that will normally be published in a press release or other form of publicity selected by the Disciplinary and Ethics Commission

Suspension
May be ordered by the Disciplinary and Ethics Commission for a specified period of time, not to exceed five years, for individuals it deems can be rehabilitated

Revocation
The Disciplinary and Ethics Commission may order permanent revocation of a certificant's right to use the marks and to publish the revocation in a press release or other form of publicity

If grounds for discipline are established, the Disciplinary and Ethics Commission has discretion to use any of the following forms of discipline:

- **Private censure**—an unpublished written reproach that is mailed to the censured certificant by the Disciplinary and Ethics Commission
- **Public letter of admonition**—a publishable written reproach of the certificant's behavior that will normally be published in a press release or other form of publicity selected by the Disciplinary and Ethics Commission
- **Suspension**—may be ordered by the Disciplinary and Ethics Commission for a specified period, not to exceed five years, for individuals it deems can be rehabilitated; the suspension will normally be published in a press release or other form of publicity, unless extreme mitigating circumstances exist; certificants who are suspended may qualify for reinstatement
- **Revocation**—the Disciplinary and Ethics Commission may order permanent revocation of a certificant's right to use the marks and publish the revocation in a press release or other form of publicity; all revocations are permanent

In all cases, the Disciplinary and Ethics Commission can require certificants to complete additional continuing education or other remedial work.

Disciplinary proceedings under the Procedures are commenced upon a written request by any person. After commencement, the matter is referred to the Disciplinary and Ethics Commission. If the Disciplinary and Ethics Commission in its discretion determines to proceed with the investigation, CFP Board provides written notice to the certificant of the investigation and the allegations made, and the certificant has 30 calendar days from the date of service of notice of the investigation to file a written response to the allegations. If a timely response is received, CFP Board staff counsel shall compile all documents and materials and commerce probable cause determination procedures as soon thereafter as is reasonably practicable.

CFP Board staff counsel determines if there is probable cause for disciplinary action and then does one of the following: (1) dismisses the allegations as not warranting further investigation, (2) dismisses the allegations with a letter of caution—recommending remedial action and/or entering appropriate orders, or (3) issues a formal complaint, stating the grounds for discipline and the alleged wrongful conduct of the certificant. Within 20 days, the certificant must respond to all allegations and set forth any defenses or mitigating circumstances. If the certificant fails to file an answer within 20 days of service, the certificant will be in default and the allegations of the complaints will be deemed admitted. CFP Board staff counsel must serve the certificant with an Order of Revocation, stating clearly and with reasonable particularity the grounds for revocation of the certificant's right to use the CFP® marks.

Hearing panel
Panel that establishes the rules of procedures and evidence to be observed at a complaint hearing seeking disciplinary action against a certificant

All hearings on complaints seeking disciplinary action against a certificant are required to be conducted by a **hearing panel**. The hearing panel must establish the rules of procedures and evidence to be observed at the hearing. Proof of misconduct is established by a preponderance of the evidence. All testimony at hearings before the hearing panel must be transcribed.

Report, Findings of Fact, and Recommendation

After the hearing, the hearing panel records its findings of fact and recommendations and submits them to the Disciplinary and Ethics Commission for consideration. The report must recommend that the complaint be dismissed as not proven or refer the matter to the Disciplinary and Ethics Commission with the recommendation of discipline, stating which form of discipline the hearing panel deems appropriate. The hearing panel may also recommend that the Disciplinary and Ethics Commission enter other appropriate orders.

The Disciplinary and Ethics Commission has the power to review any determination made during disciplinary proceedings and to enter any order concerning that determination, including an order directing that further proceedings be conducted. Within 45 days of the hearing, the Disciplinary and Ethics Commission must mail the certificant a final order containing the Commission's findings of fact and, if appropriate, any sanction imposed. Any appeal must be submitted to the Appeals Committee within 30 days after notice of the order is sent to the certificant. Otherwise, the order becomes final.

Conviction of a Crime or Professional Suspension

Conviction of a crime or an order of professional suspension is conclusive evidence and proof of the commission of the act for purposes of disciplinary proceedings. The certificant has a duty to report a conviction or professional suspension to CFP Board within 30 days after the date on which the certificant is notified of the conviction or suspension. After receiving notice that a certificant has been convicted of a crime, other than minor traffic offenses, or has been the subject of professional discipline, CFP Board staff counsel will determine whether an investigation is warranted. If a certificant is convicted of a serious crime or is the subject of a professional suspension, CFP Board shall obtain the record of the conviction or suspension and, if appropriate, file a complaint against the certificant.

Settlement Procedure

Offer of Settlement
A certificant may tender an Offer of Settlement in lieu of a disciplinary hearing

A certificant may tender an **Offer of Settlement** in lieu of a disciplinary hearing. The Offer of Settlement may be made where the public interest and CFP Board permit. A certificant is allowed only one Offer of Settlement during the course of a disciplinary proceeding. If the Offer of Settlement is rejected by the hearing panel, the Offer is deemed void, and the matter will be set for hearing. The certificant will not be prejudiced in any way by the prior Offer, and this Offer will not be given consideration in determination of the issues involved in the pending or any other proceeding. The hearing panel may also make a Counter Settlement Offer to the certificant, subject to the same rules as to an Offer of Settlement.

Required Action After Revocation or Suspension

When an order of revocation or suspension becomes final, the certificant "*shall promptly terminate*" any use of the CFP® marks. Revocation is permanent, and no opportunity for reinstatement is available.

A certificant who has been suspended for less than one year shall be reinstated automatically after expiration of the suspension, provided that the certificant files a request for reinstatement within 30 days after the expiration of the period of suspension. A certificant who has been suspended over one year must petition the Disciplinary and Ethics Commission for reinstatement within six months of the end of the suspension, or reinstatement is relinquished or waived. If the certificant petitions the Disciplinary and Ethics Commission within six months of possible reinstatement, the certificant has the burden of proving by "*clear and convincing evidence*" that the certificant has been rehabilitated, has complied with all applicable disciplinary procedures, and is fit to use the marks.

If the certificant petitions for reinstatement, CFP Board staff counsel will initiate an investigation. The certificant must cooperate with the investigation, and CFP Board staff counsel shall submit a report of the investigation detailing the certificant's past disciplinary record and any recommendation regarding reinstatement. If the certificant is denied reinstatement, the certificant must wait two years to petition again for reinstatement. The second petition for reinstatement must be received by CFP Board within six months of the expiration of the two-year period. If the second petition is not submitted in a timely fashion or is denied, the certificant's right to use the marks is administratively relinquished. If no petition for reinstatement is sought within six months of the expiration of the two-year period for reinstatement, the failure of the individual to file the petition for reinstatement within this six-month time period will result in the individual's right to use the marks being administratively relinquished.

All proceedings and records conducted in accordance with the Procedures are confidential and will not be made public, unless otherwise provided for in the Procedures. The Procedures allow disclosure of disciplinary proceedings if the proceeding is based on criminal conviction or professional suspension, the certificant has waived confidentiality, or disclosure is required by legal process. In proceedings involving a consumer, CFP Board staff may contact the consumer or the certificant's employer to request relevant documents.

THE IMPORTANCE OF ETHICS

While understanding the fundamentals of financial planning is vital to those who aspire to work and interact in the business and financial environments, equally important is recognizing and being able to handle ethical issues that accompany interaction in the finance services industry and that accompany the provision of financial services. The negative effects of unethical practices and actions of a few not only damage the individual engaging in unethical behavior and the victim of such behavior but also damage the image and productivity of the entire industry. Ethics codes and practice standards can significantly help in reducing the incidence of unethical and damaging conduct, as well as providing much needed counsel, tutelage, guidance, and direction to the individual professional.

DISCUSSION QUESTIONS

1. Compare and contrast ethics, law, and an ethics code.
2. What is Certified Financial Planner Board of Standards, Inc.?
3. What is the role of CFP Board's Code of Ethics and Standards of Conduct?
4. What is the role of the Standards of Conduct in relation to CFP Board's Code of Ethics and Standards of Conduct?
5. What are a CFP® certificant's responsibilities with respect to client property?
6. What is the role of the Disciplinary Rules and Procedures in relation to the Code of Ethics and Standards of Conduct?
7. What restrictions apply to loans between CFP® certificants and their clients?
8. What are the six principles provided by the Code of Ethics?
9. Explain the term *commingling* and the restrictions on commingling that apply to CFP® certificants.
10. How do the three distinct standards or burdens of proof affect the treatment of a CFP® certificant at various stages of disciplinary proceedings?
11. What four forms of discipline can be applied by the Disciplinary and Ethics Commission?
12. What are the Fitness Standards for Candidates and Professionals Eligible for Reinstatement (PERs)? List the conduct that will always bar an individual from becoming certified.
13. Describe the process of an individual petitioning CFP Board for reconsideration under the Fitness Standards for Candidates and Professionals Eligible for Reinstatement (PERs). What decisions might the Disciplinary and Ethics Commission make regarding a petition for reconsideration?

SECTION

6 Appendices

APPENDICES

APPENDIX

A

Comprehensive Financial Planning Case

Today is January 1, 2023. Mark and Ava Lane have come to you, a financial planner, for help in developing a plan to accomplish their financial goals. From your initial meeting together, you have gathered the following information.

PERSONAL BACKGROUND AND INFORMATION

Mark Lane (age 30)

Mark is an assistant in the marketing department for Gas & Electric, Inc. His annual salary is $52,000.

Ava Lane (age 30)

Ava is a legal research assistant with the law firm of Sabrio, Johnson & Williams, LLC. Her annual salary is $40,000.

The Children

Mark and Ava have no children from this marriage. Mark has two children, Shawn (age 4) and Ronald (age 3), from a former marriage. Shawn and Ronald live with their mother, Kimberly.

The Lanes

Mark and Ava have been married for two years.

Mark must pay $500 per month in child support until both Shawn and Ronald are age 18. The divorce decree also requires Mark to create an irrevocable life insurance trust for the benefit of the children and contribute $350 per month for payment of life insurance premiums to the trustee, Kimberly's father. There are no withdrawal powers on the part of the beneficiaries. The trust is to be used for the education and/or maintenance of the children in the event of Mark's death. The trustee has the power to invade any trust principal for the beneficiaries at the earlier of Mark's death or when Ronald becomes age 18.

ECONOMIC INFORMATION

- Inflation is expected to be 4% annually.
- Their salaries should increase by 5% for the next 5 to 10 years.
- There is no state income tax.
- The economy is growing slowly; stocks are expected to grow at 9.5%.

Bank Lending Rates

- The 15-year mortgage rate is 3.6%.
- The 30-year mortgage rate is 4.2%.
- The rate for a secured personal loan is 10%.

INSURANCE INFORMATION

Life Insurance

	Policy A	Policy B	Policy C
Insured	Mark	Mark	Ava
Face amount	$300,000	$78,000[1]	$20,000
Type	Whole life	Group term	Group term
Cash value	$2,000	$0	$0
Annual premium	$2,100	$178	$50
Who pays premium	Trustee	Employer	Employer
Beneficiary	Trustee[2]	Kimberly	Mark
Policy owner	Trust	Mark	Ava
Settlement options clause selected	None	None	None

[1]This was increased from $50,000 to $78,000 January 1, 2021.
[2]Shawn and Ronald are beneficiaries of the trust.

Health Insurance

- Mark and Ava are covered under Mark's employer plan, which is an indemnity plan with a $200 deductible per person per year and an 80/20 major medical coinsurance clause with a family annual stop-loss limit of $10,000.

Long-Term Disability Insurance

- Mark is covered by an own occupation policy with premiums paid by his employer. The benefits equal 60% of his gross pay after an elimination period of 180 days. The policy covers both sickness and accidents and is guaranteed renewable.
- Ava is not covered by disability insurance.

Renters' Insurance

- The Lanes have an HO-4 renters' policy without endorsements.
- Content coverage is $25,000; liability coverage is $100,000.

Automobile Insurance

- Both the car and truck are covered.
- The Lanes do not have any additional insurance on Mark's motorcycle.

Type	Personal auto policy
Bodily injury	$25,000/$50,000
Property damage	$10,000
Medical payments	$5,000 per person
Physical damage	Actual cash value
Uninsured motorist	$25,000/$50,000
Comprehensive deductible	$250
Collision deductible	$500
Premium (annual)	$3,300

INVESTMENT INFORMATION

The Lanes think they need six months' cash flow net of all taxes, savings, vacation, and discretionary cash flow in an emergency fund. They are willing to include in the emergency fund the savings account and Mark's 401(k) plan balance because it has borrowing provisions.

The Amazing.com stock was a gift to Mark from his uncle Bill. At the date of the gift (July 1, 2020), the fair market value of the stock was $3,500. Bill's tax basis was $2,500, and Bill paid gift tax of $1,400 on the gift. Bill had already used up both his lifetime applicable exclusion amount and that year's annual exclusion to Mark.

The K&B stock was a gift to Ava of 100 shares from her uncle Mike. At the date of the gift (December 25, 2020), the fair market value was $8,000 and Mike had paid $10,000 for the stock in 2005 (his tax basis).

The Growth Mutual Fund (currently valued at $13,900) was acquired by Mark over the years 2017 through 2022 with deposits of $1,000, $1,000, $2,000, $2,000, $2,500, and $3,000. The earnings were all reinvested, and Mark received 1099 forms for the income and capital gains during the years of earnings ($0 in 2017, $200 in 2018, $400 in 2019, $400 in 2020, $650 in 2021, and $750 in 2022).

INCOME TAX INFORMATION

The Lanes' federal income tax filing status is married filing jointly. Both children (Shawn and Ronald) are claimed as dependents on the Lanes' tax return as part of Mark's divorce agreement. The Lanes live in a state that does not have state income tax.

Section 79 Cost from Uniform Premium Table:
Age 30 and under, $.06 per month/per $1,000

RETIREMENT INFORMATION

Mark currently contributes 3% of his salary to his Section 401(k) plan. The employer matches each $1 contributed with $.50 up to a total employer contribution of 3% of salary.

GIFTS, ESTATES, TRUSTS, AND WILL INFORMATION

- Mark has a will leaving all of his probate estate to his children.
- Ava does not have a will.
- The Lanes live in a common law state that has adopted the Uniform Probate Code.

PERSONAL STATEMENT OF CASH FLOWS

Mark and Ava Lane Personal Statement of Cash Flows (Expected to be Similar in 2023) January 1, 2022–December 31, 2022		
CASH INFLOWS		
Salaries*		
Mark	$52,000	
Ava	40,000	
Investment income**	1,090	
Total inflows		$93,090
CASH OUTFLOWS–SAVINGS AND INVESTMENTS		
Savings—house down payment	$ 2,400	
Reinvestment of investment income	1,090	
Section 401(k) plan contribution	1,560	
Total savings		$ 5,050
FIXED OUTFLOWS		
Child support	$ 7,800	
Life insurance payment (to trustee)	4,200	
Rent	19,200	
Renters' insurance	960	
Utilities	2,880	
Telephone	1,200	
Auto down payment 12/31/22***	7,400	
Auto insurance	6,600	
Gas, oil, maintenance	4,800	
Student loans	6,000	
Credit card debt	3,600	
Loan for furniture	2,400	
Total fixed outflows		$30,261
VARIABLE OUTFLOWS		
Taxes—FICA and withholding both spouses	$12,225	
Food	6,000	
Clothing	2,400	
Entertainment/vacation	3,000	
Total variable outflows		$13,935
Total outflows		$47,266
Net cash flows (deficit)		$ (176)
TOTAL OUTFLOWS		$47,090

*Mark's W-2 will reflect the Section 79 costs of $28,000 in excess group term life insurance, but this is not a cash inflow.

**$340 from dividends and $750 from other investment sources.

***P&I next year will total $3,600.

STATEMENT OF FINANCIAL POSITION

Mark and Ava Lane
Statement of Financial Position
As of January 1, 2023

ASSETS[1]		LIABILITIES[2] & NET WORTH	
Cash and equivalents		**Current liabilities**	
Cash	$ 500	Credit card balance VISA	$ 9,000
Savings account	1,000	Student loan—Mark[3]	3,240
Total cash and equivalents	**$ 1,500**	Auto loan—Ava	2,508
Invested assets		Furniture loan	1,115
Amazing.com stock (100 shares)[4]	$ 5,000	**Total current liabilities**	**$15,863**
K&B stock (100 shares)	7,200		
Growth Mutual Fund	13,900	**Long-term liabilities**	
Section 401(k) plan	1,500	Student loan—Mark	$41,821
Total invested assets	**$27,600**	Auto loan—Ava	12,288
Use assets		Furniture loan	418
Auto—Ava	$18,494	**Total long-term liabilities**	**$54,527**
Truck—Mark	4,000		
Motorcycle—Mark	1,000	**Total liabilities**	**$70,390**
Personal property & furniture	17,750	**Net worth**	**(46)**
Total use assets	**$41,244**		
Total assets	**$70,344**	**Total liabilities & net worth**	**$70,344**

Notes to financial statements:

1. Assets are stated at fair market value.
2. Liabilities are stated at principal only as of January 1, 2023, before January payments.
3. Mark's parents took out the student loans, but he is repaying his parents at a rate of $300 per month. The P & I are from his parents' records.
4. Amazing.com's current dividend is $3.40.

INFORMATION REGARDING ASSETS AND LIABILITIES

Home Furnishings

The furniture was purchased with 20% down and 18% interest over 36 months. The monthly payment is $108.46.

Automobile

The automobile was purchased December 31, 2022, for $37,000 with 20% down and 80% financed over 48 months with payments of $695.16 per month.

Student Loan

The student loans were made in Mark's parents' names and consist of a combination of home equity and PLUS loans. The interest rates vary and Mark pays his parents directly each month.

Stereo System

The Lanes have a sophisticated stereo system (FMV $10,000). They asked and received permission to alter the apartment to build speakers into every room. The agreement with the landlord requires the Lanes to leave the speakers if they move because the speakers are permanently installed and affixed to the property. The replacement value of the installed speakers is $4,500, and the noninstalled components are valued at $5,500. The cost of the system was $10,000, and it was purchased in late 2016.

REQUIREMENTS

1. Complete an engagement letter to the Lanes to advise them on financial planning.
2. Complete a client/planner worksheet.
3. Calculate the Lanes' financial ratios.
   a. Comment on any of the above ratios that you think are important.
   b. Describe the Lanes' current financial condition.
4. Identify the Lanes' financial strengths and weaknesses.
5. After reading the case, what additional information would you request from the Lanes to complete your data-gathering phase?
6. Identify the Lanes' likely appropriate mission, goals, and objectives.
7. Make recommendations based on the Lanes' goals and risks in all areas of their financial situation.

APPENDIX B

Time Value of Money Tables

APPENDIX B-1 Present Value of a Dollar

Present Value of $1

$$\left[\frac{1}{(1+i)^n}\right]$$

Period	1%	2%	3%	4%	5%	6%	7%	8%	9%	10%	11%	12%	13%
1	0.9901	0.9804	0.9709	0.9615	0.9524	0.9434	0.9346	0.9259	0.9174	0.9091	0.9009	0.8929	0.8850
2	0.9803	0.9612	0.9426	0.9246	0.9070	0.8900	0.8734	0.8573	0.8417	0.8264	0.8116	0.7972	0.7831
3	0.9706	0.9423	0.9151	0.8890	0.8638	0.8396	0.8163	0.7938	0.7722	0.7513	0.7312	0.7118	0.6931
4	0.9610	0.9238	0.8885	0.8548	0.8227	0.7921	0.7629	0.7350	0.7084	0.6830	0.6587	0.6355	0.6133
5	0.9515	0.9057	0.8626	0.8219	0.7835	0.7473	0.7130	0.6806	0.6499	0.6209	0.5935	0.5674	0.5428
6	0.9420	0.8880	0.8375	0.7903	0.7462	0.7050	0.6663	0.6302	0.5963	0.5645	0.5346	0.5066	0.4803
7	0.9327	0.8706	0.8131	0.7599	0.7107	0.6651	0.6227	0.5835	0.5470	0.5132	0.4817	0.4523	0.4251
8	0.9235	0.8535	0.7894	0.7307	0.6768	0.6274	0.5820	0.5403	0.5019	0.4665	0.4339	0.4039	0.3762
9	0.9143	0.8368	0.7664	0.7026	0.6446	0.5919	0.5439	0.5002	0.4604	0.4241	0.3909	0.3606	0.3329
10	0.9053	0.8203	0.7441	0.6756	0.6139	0.5584	0.5083	0.4632	0.4224	0.3855	0.3522	0.3220	0.2946
11	0.8963	0.8043	0.7224	0.6496	0.5847	0.5268	0.4751	0.4289	0.3875	0.3505	0.3173	0.2875	0.2607
12	0.8874	0.7885	0.7014	0.6246	0.5568	0.4970	0.4440	0.3971	0.3555	0.3186	0.2858	0.2567	0.2307
13	0.8787	0.7730	0.6810	0.6006	0.5303	0.4688	0.4150	0.3677	0.3262	0.2897	0.2575	0.2292	0.2042
14	0.8700	0.7579	0.6611	0.5775	0.5051	0.4423	0.3878	0.3405	0.2992	0.2633	0.2320	0.2046	0.1807
15	0.8613	0.7430	0.6419	0.5553	0.4810	0.4173	0.3624	0.3152	0.2745	0.2394	0.2090	0.1827	0.1599
16	0.8528	0.7284	0.6232	0.5339	0.4581	0.3936	0.3387	0.2919	0.2519	0.2176	0.1883	0.1631	0.1415
17	0.8444	0.7142	0.6050	0.5134	0.4363	0.3714	0.3166	0.2703	0.2311	0.1978	0.1696	0.1456	0.1252
18	0.8360	0.7002	0.5874	0.4936	0.4155	0.3503	0.2959	0.2502	0.2120	0.1799	0.1528	0.1300	0.1108
19	0.8277	0.6864	0.5703	0.4746	0.3957	0.3305	0.2765	0.2317	0.1945	0.1635	0.1377	0.1161	0.0981
20	0.8195	0.6730	0.5537	0.4564	0.3769	0.3118	0.2584	0.2145	0.1784	0.1486	0.1240	0.1037	0.0868
25	0.7798	0.6095	0.4776	0.3751	0.2953	0.2330	0.1842	0.1460	0.1160	0.0923	0.0736	0.0588	0.0471
30	0.7419	0.5521	0.4120	0.3083	0.2314	0.1741	0.1314	0.0994	0.0754	0.0573	0.0437	0.0334	0.0256
35	0.7059	0.5000	0.3554	0.2534	0.1813	0.1301	0.0937	0.0676	0.0490	0.0356	0.0259	0.0189	0.0139
40	0.6717	0.4529	0.3066	0.2083	0.1420	0.0972	0.0668	0.0460	0.0318	0.0221	0.0154	0.0107	0.0075
45	0.6391	0.4102	0.2644	0.1712	0.1113	0.0727	0.0476	0.0313	0.0207	0.0137	0.0091	0.0061	0.0041
50	0.6080	0.3715	0.2281	0.1407	0.0872	0.0543	0.0339	0.0213	0.0134	0.0085	0.0054	0.0035	0.0022

APPENDIX B-1 Present Value of a Dollar (continued)

Present Value of $1

$$\left[\frac{1}{(1+i)^n}\right]$$

Period	14%	15%	16%	17%	18%	19%	20%	25%	30%	35%	40%	45%	50%
1	0.8772	0.8696	0.8621	0.8547	0.8475	0.8403	0.8333	0.8000	0.7692	0.7407	0.7143	0.6897	0.6667
2	0.7695	0.7561	0.7432	0.7305	0.7182	0.7062	0.6944	0.6400	0.5917	0.5487	0.5102	0.4756	0.4444
3	0.6750	0.6575	0.6407	0.6244	0.6086	0.5934	0.5787	0.5120	0.4552	0.4064	0.3644	0.3280	0.2963
4	0.5921	0.5718	0.5523	0.5337	0.5158	0.4987	0.4823	0.4096	0.3501	0.3011	0.2603	0.2262	0.1975
5	0.5194	0.4972	0.4761	0.4561	0.4371	0.4190	0.4019	0.3277	0.2693	0.2230	0.1859	0.1560	0.1317
6	0.4556	0.4323	0.4104	0.3898	0.3704	0.3521	0.3349	0.2621	0.2072	0.1652	0.1328	0.1076	0.0878
7	0.3996	0.3759	0.3538	0.3332	0.3139	0.2959	0.2791	0.2097	0.1594	0.1224	0.0949	0.0742	0.0585
8	0.3506	0.3269	0.3050	0.2848	0.2660	0.2487	0.2326	0.1678	0.1226	0.0906	0.0678	0.0512	0.0390
9	0.3075	0.2843	0.2630	0.2434	0.2255	0.2090	0.1938	0.1342	0.0943	0.0671	0.0484	0.0353	0.0260
10	0.2697	0.2472	0.2267	0.2080	0.1911	0.1756	0.1615	0.1074	0.0725	0.0497	0.0346	0.0243	0.0173
11	0.2366	0.2149	0.1954	0.1778	0.1619	0.1476	0.1346	0.0859	0.0558	0.0368	0.0247	0.0168	0.0116
12	0.2076	0.1869	0.1685	0.1520	0.1372	0.1240	0.1122	0.0687	0.0429	0.0273	0.0176	0.0116	0.0077
13	0.1821	0.1625	0.1452	0.1299	0.1163	0.1042	0.0935	0.0550	0.0330	0.0202	0.0126	0.0080	0.0051
14	0.1597	0.1413	0.1252	0.1110	0.0985	0.0876	0.0779	0.0440	0.0254	0.0150	0.0090	0.0055	0.0034
15	0.1401	0.1229	0.1079	0.0949	0.0835	0.0736	0.0649	0.0352	0.0195	0.0111	0.0064	0.0038	0.0023
16	0.1229	0.1069	0.0930	0.0811	0.0708	0.0618	0.0541	0.0281	0.0150	0.0082	0.0046	0.0026	0.0015
17	0.1078	0.0929	0.0802	0.0693	0.0600	0.0520	0.0451	0.0225	0.0116	0.0061	0.0033	0.0018	0.0010
18	0.0946	0.0808	0.0691	0.0592	0.0508	0.0437	0.0376	0.0180	0.0089	0.0045	0.0023	0.0012	0.0007
19	0.0829	0.0703	0.0596	0.0506	0.0431	0.0367	0.0313	0.0144	0.0068	0.0033	0.0017	0.0009	0.0005
20	0.0728	0.0611	0.0514	0.0433	0.0365	0.0308	0.0261	0.0115	0.0053	0.0025	0.0012	0.0006	0.0003
25	0.0378	0.0304	0.0245	0.0197	0.0160	0.0129	0.0105	0.0038	0.0014	0.0006	0.0002	0.0001	0.0000
30	0.0196	0.0151	0.0116	0.0090	0.0070	0.0054	0.0042	0.0012	0.0004	0.0001	0.0000	0.0000	0.0000
35	0.0102	0.0075	0.0055	0.0041	0.0030	0.0023	0.0017	0.0004	0.0001	0.0000	0.0000	0.0000	0.0000
40	0.0053	0.0037	0.0026	0.0019	0.0013	0.0010	0.0007	0.0001	0.0000	0.0000	0.0000	0.0000	0.0000
45	0.0027	0.0019	0.0013	0.0009	0.0006	0.0004	0.0003	0.0000	0.0000	0.0000	0.0000	0.0000	0.0000
50	0.0014	0.0009	0.0006	0.0004	0.0003	0.0002	0.0001	0.0000	0.0000	0.0000	0.0000	0.0000	0.0000

APPENDIX B-2 Future Value of a Dollar

Future Value of $1

$(1+i)^n$

Period	1%	2%	3%	4%	5%	6%	7%	8%	9%	10%	11%	12%	13%
1	1.0100	1.0200	1.0300	1.0400	1.0500	1.0600	1.0700	1.0800	1.0900	1.1000	1.1100	1.1200	1.1300
2	1.0201	1.0404	1.0609	1.0816	1.1025	1.1236	1.1449	1.1664	1.1881	1.2100	1.2321	1.2544	1.2769
3	1.0303	1.0612	1.0927	1.1249	1.1576	1.1910	1.2250	1.2597	1.2950	1.3310	1.3676	1.4049	1.4429
4	1.0406	1.0824	1.1255	1.1699	1.2155	1.2625	1.3108	1.3605	1.4116	1.4641	1.5181	1.5735	1.6305
5	1.0510	1.1041	1.1593	1.2167	1.2763	1.3382	1.4026	1.4693	1.5386	1.6105	1.6851	1.7623	1.8424
6	1.0615	1.1262	1.1941	1.2653	1.3401	1.4185	1.5007	1.5869	1.6771	1.7716	1.8704	1.9738	2.0820
7	1.0721	1.1487	1.2299	1.3159	1.4071	1.5036	1.6058	1.7138	1.8280	1.9487	2.0762	2.2107	2.3526
8	1.0829	1.1717	1.2668	1.3686	1.4775	1.5938	1.7182	1.8509	1.9926	2.1436	2.3045	2.4760	2.6584
9	1.0937	1.1951	1.3048	1.4233	1.5513	1.6895	1.8385	1.9990	2.1719	2.3579	2.5580	2.7731	3.0040
10	1.1046	1.2190	1.3439	1.4802	1.6289	1.7908	1.9672	2.1589	2.3674	2.5937	2.8394	3.1058	3.3946
11	1.1157	1.2434	1.3842	1.5395	1.7103	1.8983	2.1049	2.3316	2.5804	2.8531	3.1518	3.4785	3.8359
12	1.1268	1.2682	1.4258	1.6010	1.7959	2.0122	2.2522	2.5182	2.8127	3.1384	3.4985	3.8960	4.3345
13	1.1381	1.2936	1.4685	1.6651	1.8856	2.1329	2.4098	2.7196	3.0658	3.4523	3.8833	4.3635	4.8980
14	1.1495	1.3195	1.5126	1.7317	1.9799	2.2609	2.5785	2.9372	3.3417	3.7975	4.3104	4.8871	5.5348
15	1.1610	1.3459	1.5580	1.8009	2.0789	2.3966	2.7590	3.1722	3.6425	4.1772	4.7846	5.4736	6.2543
16	1.1726	1.3728	1.6047	1.8730	2.1829	2.5404	2.9522	3.4259	3.9703	4.5950	5.3109	6.1304	7.0673
17	1.1843	1.4002	1.6528	1.9479	2.2920	2.6928	3.1588	3.7000	4.3276	5.0545	5.8951	6.8660	7.9861
18	1.1961	1.4282	1.7024	2.0258	2.4066	2.8543	3.3799	3.9960	4.7171	5.5599	6.5436	7.6900	9.0243
19	1.2081	1.4568	1.7535	2.1068	2.5270	3.0256	3.6165	4.3157	5.1417	6.1159	7.2633	8.6128	10.1974
20	1.2202	1.4859	1.8061	2.1911	2.6533	3.2071	3.8697	4.6610	5.6044	6.7275	8.0623	9.6463	11.5231
25	1.2824	1.6406	2.0938	2.6658	3.3864	4.2919	5.4274	6.8485	8.6231	10.8347	13.5855	17.0001	21.2305
30	1.3478	1.8114	2.4273	3.2434	4.3219	5.7435	7.6123	10.0627	13.2677	17.4494	22.8923	29.9599	39.1159
35	1.4166	1.9999	2.8139	3.9461	5.5160	7.6861	10.6766	14.7853	20.4140	28.1024	38.5749	52.7996	72.0685
40	1.4889	2.2080	3.2620	4.8010	7.0400	10.2857	14.9745	21.7245	31.4094	45.2593	65.0009	93.0510	132.7816
45	1.5648	2.4379	3.7816	5.8412	8.9850	13.7646	21.0025	31.9204	48.3273	72.8905	109.5302	163.9876	244.6414
50	1.6446	2.6916	4.3839	7.1067	11.4674	18.4202	29.4570	46.9016	74.3575	117.3909	184.5648	289.0022	450.7359

APPENDIX B-2 Future Value of a Dollar (continued)

Future Value of $1

$(1+i)^n$

Period	14%	15%	16%	17%	18%	19%	20%	25%	30%	35%	40%	45%	50%
1	1.1400	1.1500	1.1600	1.1700	1.1800	1.1900	1.2000	1.2500	1.3000	1.3500	1.4000	1.4500	1.5000
2	1.2996	1.3225	1.3456	1.3689	1.3924	1.4161	1.4400	1.5625	1.6900	1.8225	1.9600	2.1025	2.2500
3	1.4815	1.5209	1.5609	1.6016	1.6430	1.6852	1.7280	1.9531	2.1970	2.4604	2.7440	3.0486	3.3750
4	1.6890	1.7490	1.8106	1.8739	1.9388	2.0053	2.0736	2.4414	2.8561	3.3215	3.8416	4.4205	5.0625
5	1.9254	2.0114	2.1003	2.1924	2.2878	2.3864	2.4883	3.0518	3.7129	4.4840	5.3782	6.4097	7.5938
6	2.1950	2.3131	2.4364	2.5652	2.6996	2.8398	2.9860	3.8147	4.8268	6.0534	7.5295	9.2941	11.3906
7	2.5023	2.6600	2.8262	3.0012	3.1855	3.3793	3.5832	4.7684	6.2749	8.1722	10.5414	13.4765	17.0859
8	2.8526	3.0590	3.2784	3.5115	3.7589	4.0214	4.2998	5.9605	8.1573	11.0324	14.7579	19.5409	25.6289
9	3.2519	3.5179	3.8030	4.1084	4.4355	4.7854	5.1598	7.4506	10.6045	14.8937	20.6610	28.3343	38.4434
10	3.7072	4.0456	4.4114	4.8068	5.2338	5.6947	61917	9.3132	13.7858	20.1066	28.9255	41.0847	57.6650
11	4.2262	4.6524	5.1173	5.6240	6.1759	6.7767	74301	11.6415	17.9216	27.1439	40.4957	59.5728	86.4976
12	4.8179	5.3503	5.9360	6.5801	7.2876	8.0642	8.9161	14.5519	23.2981	36.6442	56.6939	86.3806	129.7463
13	5.4924	6.1528	6.8858	7.6987	8.5994	9.5964	10.6993	18.1899	30.2875	49.4697	79.3715	125.2518	194.6195
14	6.2613	7.0757	7.9875	9.0075	10.1472	11.4198	12.8392	22.7374	39.3738	66.7841	111.1201	181.6151	291.9293
15	7.1379	8.1371	9.2655	10.5387	11.9737	13.5895	15.4070	28.4217	51.1859	90.1585	155.5681	263.3419	437.8939
16	8.1372	9.3576	10.7480	12.3303	14.1290	16.1715	18.4884	35.5271	66.5417	121.7139	217.7953	381.8458	656.8408
17	9.2765	10.7613	12.4677	14.4265	16.6722	19.2441	22.1861	44.4089	86.5042	164.3138	304.9135	553.6764	985.2613
18	10.5752	12.3755	14.4625	16.8790	19.6733	22.9005	26.6233	55.5112	112.4554	221.8236	426.8789	802.8308	1477.892
19	12.0557	14.2318	16.7765	19.7484	23.2144	27.2516	31.9480	69.3889	146.1920	299.4619	597.6304	1164.105	2216.838
20	13.7435	16.3665	19.4608	23.1056	27.3930	32.4294	38.3376	86.7362	190.0496	404.2736	836.6826	1687.952	3325.257
25	26.4619	32.9190	40.8742	50.6578	62.6686	77.3881	95.3962	264.6978	705.6410	1812.776	4499.880	10819.32	25251.17
30	50.9502	66.2118	85.8499	111.0647	143.3706	184.6753	237.3763	807.7936	2619.996	8128.550	24201.43	69348.98	191751.1
35	98.1002	133.1755	180.3141	243.5035	327.9973	440.7006	590.6682	2465.190	9727.860	36448.69	130161.1	444509	1456110
40	188.8835	267.8635	378.7212	533.8687	750.3783	1051.668	1469.772	7523.164	36118.86	163437.1	700037.7	2849181	11057332
45	363.6791	538.7693	795.4438	1170.479	1716.684	2509.651	3657.262	22958.87	134106.8	732857.6	3764971	18262495	83966617
50	700.2330	1083.657	1670.704	2566.215	3927.357	5988.914	9100.438	70064.92	497929.2	3286158	20248916	117057734	637621500

APPENDIX B-3 Present Value of an Ordinary Annuity

Present Value of Ordinary Annuity

$$\left[\frac{1-\frac{1}{(1+i)^n}}{i}\right]$$

Period	1%	2%	3%	4%	5%	6%	7%	8%	9%	10%	11%	12%	13%
1	0.9901	0.9804	0.9709	0.9615	0.9524	0.9434	0.9346	0.9259	0.9174	0.9091	0.9009	0.8929	0.8850
2	1.9704	1.9416	1.9135	1.8861	1.8594	1.8334	1.8080	1.7833	1.7591	1.7355	1.7125	1.6901	1.6681
3	2.9410	2.8839	2.8286	2.7751	2.7232	2.6730	2.6243	2.5771	2.5313	2.4869	2.4437	2.4018	2.3612
4	3.9020	3.8077	3.7171	3.6299	3.5460	3.4651	3.3872	3.3121	3.2397	3.1699	3.1024	3.0373	2.9745
5	4.8534	4.7135	4.5797	4.4518	4.3295	4.2124	4.1002	3.9927	3.8897	3.7908	3.6959	3.6048	3.5172
6	5.7955	5.6014	5.4172	5.2421	5.0757	4.9173	4.7665	4.6229	4.4859	4.3553	4.2305	4.1114	3.9975
7	6.7282	6.4720	6.2303	6.0021	5.7864	5.5824	5.3893	5.2064	5.0330	4.8684	4.7122	4.5638	4.4226
8	7.6517	7.3255	7.0197	6.7327	6.4632	6.2098	5.9713	5.7466	5.5348	5.3349	5.1461	4.9676	4.7988
9	8.5660	8.1622	7.7861	7.4353	7.1078	6.8017	6.5152	6.2469	5.9952	5.7590	5.5370	5.3282	5.1317
10	9.4713	8.9826	8.5302	8.1109	7.7217	7.3601	7.0236	6.7101	6.4177	6.1446	5.8892	5.6502	5.4262
11	10.3676	9.7868	9.2526	8.7605	8.3064	7.8869	7.4987	7.1390	6.8052	6.4951	6.2065	5.9377	5.6869
12	11.2551	10.5753	9.9540	9.3851	8.8633	8.3838	7.9427	7.5361	7.1607	6.8137	6.4924	6.1944	5.9176
13	12.1337	11.3484	10.6350	9.9856	9.3936	8.8527	8.3577	7.9038	7.4869	7.1034	6.7499	6.4235	6.1218
14	13.0037	12.1062	11.2961	10.5631	9.8986	9.2950	8.7455	8.2442	7.7862	7.3667	6.9819	6.6282	6.3025
15	13.8651	12.8493	11.9379	11.1184	10.3797	9.7122	9.1079	8.5595	8.0607	7.6061	7.1909	6.8109	6.4624
16	14.7179	13.5777	12.5611	11.6523	10.8378	10.1059	9.4466	8.8514	8.3126	7.8237	7.3792	6.9740	6.6039
17	15.5623	14.2919	13.1661	12.1657	11.2741	10.4773	9.7632	9.1216	8.5436	8.0216	7.5488	7.1196	6.7291
18	16.3983	14.9920	13.7535	12.6593	11.6896	10.8276	10.0591	9.3719	8.7556	8.2014	7.7016	7.2497	6.8399
19	17.2260	15.6785	14.3238	13.1339	12.0853	11.1581	10.3356	9.6036	8.9501	8.3649	7.8393	7.3658	6.9380
20	18.0456	16.3514	14.8775	13.5903	12.4622	11.4699	10.5940	9.8181	9.1285	8.5136	7.9633	7.4694	7.0248
25	22.0232	19.5235	17.4131	15.6221	14.0939	12.7834	11.6536	10.6748	9.8226	9.0770	8.4217	7.8431	7.3300
30	25.8077	22.3965	19.6004	17.2920	15.3725	13.7648	12.4090	11.2578	10.2737	9.4269	8.6938	8.0552	7.4957
35	29.4086	24.9986	21.4872	18.6646	16.3742	14.4982	12.9477	11.6546	10.5668	9.6442	8.8552	8.1755	7.5856
40	32.8347	27.3555	23.1148	19.7928	17.1591	15.0463	13.3317	11.9246	10.7574	9.7791	8.9511	8.2438	7.6344
45	36.0945	29.4902	24.5187	20.7200	17.7741	15.4558	13.6055	12.1084	10.8812	9.8628	9.0079	8.2825	7.6609
50	39.1961	31.4236	25.7298	21.4822	18.2559	15.7619	13.8007	12.2335	10.9617	9.9148	9.0417	8.3045	7.6752

APPENDIX B-3 Present Value of an Ordinary Annuity (continued)

Present Value of Ordinary Annuity

$$\left[\frac{1-\frac{1}{(1+i)^n}}{i}\right]$$

Period	14%	15%	16%	17%	18%	19%	20%	25%	30%	35%	40%	45%	50%
1	0.8772	0.8696	0.8621	0.8547	0.8475	0.8403	0.8333	0.8000	0.7692	0.7407	0.7143	0.6897	0.6667
2	1.6467	1.6257	1.6052	1.5852	1.5656	1.5465	1.5278	1.4400	1.3609	1.2894	1.2245	1.1653	1.1111
3	2.3216	2.2832	2.2459	2.2096	2.1743	2.1399	2.1065	1.9520	1.8161	1.6959	1.5889	1.4933	1.4074
4	2.9137	2.8550	2.7982	2.7432	2.6901	2.6386	2.5887	2.3616	2.1662	1.9969	1.8492	1.7195	1.6049
5	3.4331	3.3522	3.2743	3.1993	3.1272	3.0576	2.9906	2.6893	2.4356	2.2200	2.0352	1.8755	1.7366
6	3.8887	3.7845	3.6847	3.5892	3.4976	3.4098	3.3255	2.9514	2.6427	2.3852	2.1680	1.9831	1.8244
7	4.2883	4.1604	4.0386	3.9224	3.8115	3.7057	3.6046	3.1611	2.8021	2.5075	2.2628	2.0573	1.8829
8	4.6389	4.4873	4.3436	4.2072	4.0776	3.9544	3.8372	3.3289	2.9247	2.5982	2.3306	2.1085	1.9220
9	4.9464	4.7716	4.6065	4.4506	4.3030	4.1633	4.0310	3.4631	3.0190	2.6653	2.3790	2.1438	1.9480
10	5.2161	5.0188	4.8332	4.6586	4.4941	4.3389	4.1925	3.5705	3.0915	2.7150	2.4136	2.1681	1.9653
11	5.4527	5.2337	5.0286	4.8364	4.6560	4.4865	4.3271	3.6564	3.1473	2.7519	2.4383	2.1849	1.9769
12	5.6603	5.4206	5.1971	4.9884	4.7932	4.6105	4.4392	3.7251	3.1903	2.7792	2.4559	2.1965	1.9846
13	5.8424	5.5831	5.3423	5.1183	4.9095	4.7147	4.5327	3.7801	3.2233	2.7994	2.4685	2.2045	1.9897
14	6.0021	5.7245	5.4675	5.2293	5.0081	4.8023	4.6106	3.8241	3.2487	2.8144	2.4775	2.2100	1.9931
15	6.1422	5.8474	5.5755	5.3242	5.0916	4.8759	4.6755	3.8593	3.2682	2.8255	2.4839	2.2138	1.9954
16	6.2651	5.9542	5.6685	5.4053	5.1624	4.9377	4.7296	3.8874	3.2832	2.8337	2.4885	2.2164	1.9970
17	6.3729	6.0472	5.7487	5.4746	5.2223	4.9897	4.7746	3.9099	3.2948	2.8398	2.4918	2.2182	1.9980
18	6.4674	6.1280	5.8178	5.5339	5.2732	5.0333	4.8122	3.9279	3.3037	2.8443	2.4941	2.2195	1.9986
19	6.5504	6.1982	5.8775	5.5845	5.3162	5.0700	4.8435	3.9424	3.3105	2.8476	2.4958	2.2203	1.9991
20	6.6231	6.2593	5.9288	5.6278	5.3527	5.1009	4.8696	3.9539	3.3158	2.8501	2.4970	2.2209	1.9994
25	6.8729	6.4641	6.0971	5.7662	5.4669	5.1951	4.9476	3.9849	3.3286	2.8556	2.4994	2.2220	1.9999
30	7.0027	6.5660	6.1772	5.8294	5.5168	5.2347	4.9789	3.9950	3.3321	2.8568	2.4999	2.2222	2.0000
35	7.0700	6.6166	6.2153	5.8582	5.5386	5.2512	4.9915	3.9984	3.3330	2.8571	2.5000	2.2222	2.0000
40	7.1050	6.6418	6.2335	5.8713	5.5482	5.2582	4.9966	3.9995	3.3332	2.8571	2.5000	2.2222	2.0000
45	7.1232	6.6543	6.2421	5.8773	5.5523	5.2611	4.9986	3.9998	3.3333	2.8571	2.5000	2.2222	2.0000
50	7.1327	6.6605	6.2463	5.8801	5.5541	5.2623	4.9995	3.9999	3.3333	2.8571	2.5000	2.2222	2.0000

APPENDIX B-4 Future Value of an Ordinary Annuity

Future Value of Ordinary Annuity

$$\left[\frac{(1+i)^n-1}{i}\right]$$

Period	1%	2%	3%	4%	5%	6%	7%	8%	9%	10%	11%	12%	13%
1	1.0000	1.0000	1.0000	1.0000	1.0000	1.0000	1.0000	1.0000	1.0000	1.0000	1.0000	1.0000	1.0000
2	2.0100	2.0200	2.0300	2.0400	2.0500	2.0600	2.0700	2.0800	2.0900	2.1000	2.1100	2.1200	2.1300
3	3.0301	3.0604	3.0909	3.1216	3.1525	3.1836	3.2149	3.2464	3.2781	3.3100	3.3421	3.3744	3.4069
4	4.0604	4.1216	4.1836	4.2465	4.3101	4.3746	4.4399	4.5061	4.5731	4.6410	4.7097	4.7793	4.8498
5	5.1010	5.2040	5.3091	5.4163	5.5256	5.6371	5.7507	5.8666	5.9847	6.1051	6.2278	6.3528	6.4803
6	6.1520	6.3081	6.4684	6.6330	6.8019	6.9753	7.1533	7.3359	7.5233	7.7156	7.9129	8.1152	8.3227
7	7.2135	7.4343	7.6625	7.8983	8.1420	8.3938	8.6540	8.9228	9.2004	9.4872	9.7833	10.0890	10.4047
8	8.2857	8.5830	8.8923	9.2142	9.5491	9.8975	10.2598	10.6366	11.0285	11.4359	11.8594	12.2997	12.7573
9	9.3685	9.7546	10.1591	10.5828	11.0266	11.4913	11.9780	12.4876	13.0210	13.5795	14.1640	14.7757	15.4157
10	10.4622	10.9497	11.4639	12.0061	12.5779	13.1808	13.8164	14.4866	15.1929	15.9374	16.7220	17.5487	18.4197
11	11.5668	12.1687	12.8078	13.4864	14.2068	14.9716	15.7836	16.6455	17.5603	18.5312	19.5614	20.6546	21.8143
12	12.6825	13.4121	14.1920	15.0258	15.9171	16.8699	17.8885	18.9771	20.1407	21.3843	22.7132	24.1331	25.6502
13	13.8093	14.6803	15.6178	16.6268	17.7130	18.8821	20.1406	21.4953	22.9534	24.5227	26.2116	28.0291	29.9847
14	14.9474	15.9739	17.0863	18.2919	19.5986	21.0151	22.5505	24.2149	26.0192	27.9750	30.0949	32.3926	34.8827
15	16.0969	17.2934	18.5989	20.0236	21.5786	23.2760	25.1290	27.1521	29.3609	31.7725	34.4054	37.2797	40.4175
16	17.2579	18.6393	20.1569	21.8245	23.6575	25.6725	27.8881	30.3243	33.0034	35.9497	39.1899	42.7533	46.6717
17	18.4304	20.0121	21.7616	23.6975	25.8404	28.2129	30.8402	33.7502	36.9737	40.5447	44.5008	48.8837	53.7391
18	19.6147	21.4123	23.4144	25.6454	28.1324	30.9057	33.9990	37.4502	41.3013	45.5992	50.3959	55.7497	61.7251
19	20.8109	22.8406	25.1169	27.6712	30.5390	33.7600	37.3790	41.4463	46.0185	51.1591	56.9395	63.4397	70.7494
20	22.0190	24.2974	26.8704	29.7781	33.0660	36.7856	40.9955	45.7620	51.1601	57.2750	64.2028	72.0524	80.9468
25	28.2432	32.0303	36.4593	41.6459	47.7271	54.8645	63.2490	73.1059	84.7009	98.3471	114.4133	133.3339	155.6196
30	34.7849	40.5681	47.5754	56.0849	66.4388	79.0582	94.4608	113.2832	136.3075	164.4940	199.0209	241.3327	293.1992
35	41.6603	49.9945	60.4621	73.6522	90.3203	111.4348	138.2369	172.3168	215.7108	271.0244	341.5896	431.6635	546.6808
40	48.8864	60.4020	75.4013	95.0255	120.7998	154.7620	199.6351	259.0565	337.8824	442.5926	581.8261	767.0914	1013.704
45	56.4811	71.8927	92.7199	121.0294	159.7002	212.7435	285.7493	386.5056	525.8587	718.9048	986.6386	1358.230	1874.165
50	64.4632	84.5794	112.7969	152.6671	209.3480	290.3359	406.5289	573.7702	815.0836	1163.909	1668.771	2400.018	3459.507

APPENDIX B-4 Future Value of an Ordinary Annuity (continued)

Future Value of Ordinary Annuity

$$\left[\frac{(1+i)^n - 1}{i}\right]$$

Period	14%	15%	16%	17%	18%	19%	20%	25%	30%	35%	40%	45%	50%
1	1.0000	1.0000	1.0000	1.0000	1.0000	1.0000	1.0000	1.0000	1.0000	1.0000	1.0000	1.0000	1.0000
2	2.1400	2.1500	2.1600	2.1700	2.1800	2.1900	2.2000	2.2500	2.3000	2.3500	2.4000	2.4500	2.5000
3	3.4396	3.4725	3.5056	3.5389	3.5724	3.6061	3.6400	3.8125	3.9900	4.1725	4.3600	4.5525	4.7500
4	4.9211	4.9934	5.0665	5.1405	5.2154	5.2913	5.3680	5.7656	6.1870	6.6329	7.1040	7.6011	8.1250
5	6.6101	6.7424	6.8771	7.0144	7.1542	7.2966	7.4416	8.2070	9.0431	9.9544	10.9456	12.0216	13.1875
6	8.5355	8.7537	8.9775	9.2068	9.4420	9.6830	9.9299	11.2588	12.7560	14.4384	16.3238	18.4314	20.7813
7	10.7305	11.0668	11.4139	11.7720	12.1415	12.5227	12.9159	15.0735	17.5828	20.4919	23.8534	27.7255	32.1719
8	13.2328	13.7268	14.2401	14.7733	15.3270	15.9020	16.4991	19.8419	23.8577	28.6640	34.3947	41.2019	49.2578
9	16.0853	16.7858	17.5185	18.2847	19.0859	19.9234	20.7989	25.8023	32.0150	39.6964	49.1526	60.7428	74.8867
10	19.3373	20.3037	21.3215	22.3931	23.5213	24.7089	25.9587	33.2529	42.6195	54.5902	69.8137	89.0771	113.3301
11	23.0445	24.3493	25.7329	27.1999	28.7551	30.4035	32.1504	42.5661	56.4053	74.6967	98.7391	130.1618	170.9951
12	27.2707	29.0017	30.8502	32.8239	34.9311	37.1802	39.5805	54.2077	74.3270	101.8406	139.2348	189.7346	257.4927
13	32.0887	34.3519	36.7862	39.4040	42.2187	45.2445	48.4966	68.7596	97.6250	138.4848	195.9287	276.1151	387.2390
14	37.5811	40.5047	43.6720	47.1027	50.8180	54.8409	59.1959	86.9495	127.9125	187.9544	275.3002	401.3670	581.8585
15	43.8424	47.5804	51.6595	56.1101	60.9653	66.2607	72.0351	109.6868	167.2863	254.7385	386.4202	582.9821	873.7878
16	50.9804	55.7175	60.9250	66.6488	72.9390	79.8502	87.4421	138.1085	218.4722	344.8970	541.9883	846.3240	1311.682
17	59.1176	65.0751	71.6730	78.9792	87.0680	96.0218	105.9306	173.6357	285.0139	466.6109	759.7837	1228.170	1968.523
18	68.3941	75.8364	84.1407	93.4056	103.7403	115.2659	128.1167	218.0446	371.5180	630.9247	1064.697	1781.846	2953.784
19	78.9692	88.2118	98.6032	110.2846	123.4135	138.1664	154.7400	273.5558	483.9734	852.7483	1491.576	2584.677	4431.676
20	91.0249	102.4436	115.3797	130.0329	146.6280	165.4180	186.6880	342.9447	630.1655	1152.210	2089.206	3748.782	6648.513
25	181.8708	212.7930	249.2140	292.1049	342.6035	402.0425	471.9811	1054.791	2348.803	5176.504	11247.20	24040.72	50500.34
30	356.7868	434.7451	530.3117	647.4391	790.9480	966.7122	1181.882	3227.174	8729.985	23221.57	60501.08	154106.6	383500.1
35	693.5727	881.1702	1120.713	1426.491	1816.652	2314.214	2948.341	9856.761	32422.87	104136.3	325400.3	987794.5	2912217
40	1342.025	1779.090	2360.757	3134.522	4163.213	5529.829	7343.858	30088.66	120392.9	466960.4	1750092	6331512	22114663
45	2590.565	3585.128	4965.274	6879.291	9531.577	13203.42	18281.31	91831.50	447019.4	2093876	9412424	40583319	167933233
50	4994.521	7217.716	10435.65	15089.50	21813.09	31515.34	45497.19	280255.7	1659761	9389020	50622288	260128295	1275242998

APPENDIX B-5 Present Value of an Annuity Due

Present Value of Annuity Due

$$\left[\frac{1-\frac{1}{(1+i)^{n-1}}}{i}+1\right]$$

Period	1%	2%	3%	4%	5%	6%	7%	8%	9%	10%	11%	12%	13%
1	1.0000	1.0000	1.0000	1.0000	1.0000	1.0000	1.0000	1.0000	1.0000	1.0000	1.0000	1.0000	1.0000
2	1.9901	1.9804	1.9709	1.9615	1.9524	1.9434	1.9346	1.9259	1.9174	1.9091	1.9009	1.8929	1.8850
3	2.9704	2.9416	2.9135	2.8861	2.8594	2.8334	2.8080	2.7833	2.7591	2.7355	2.7125	2.6901	2.6681
4	3.9410	3.8839	3.8286	3.7751	3.7232	3.6730	3.6243	3.5771	3.5313	3.4869	3.4437	3.4018	3.3612
5	4.9020	4.8077	4.7171	4.6299	4.5460	4.4651	4.3872	4.3121	4.2397	4.1699	4.1024	4.0373	3.9745
6	5.8534	5.7135	5.5797	5.4518	5.3295	5.2124	5.1002	4.9927	4.8897	4.7908	4.6959	4.6048	4.5172
7	6.7955	6.6014	6.4172	6.2421	6.0757	5.9173	5.7665	5.6229	5.4859	5.3553	5.2305	5.1114	4.9975
8	7.7282	7.4720	7.2303	7.0021	6.7864	6.5824	6.3893	6.2064	6.0330	5.8684	5.7122	5.5638	5.4226
9	8.6517	8.3255	8.0197	7.7327	7.4632	7.2098	6.9713	6.7466	6.5348	6.3349	6.1461	5.9676	5.7988
10	9.5660	9.1622	8.7861	8.4353	8.1078	7.8017	7.5152	7.2469	6.9952	6.7590	6.5370	6.3282	6.1317
11	10.4713	9.9826	9.5302	9.1109	8.7217	8.3601	8.0236	7.7101	7.4177	7.1446	6.8892	6.6502	6.4262
12	11.3676	10.7868	10.2526	9.7605	9.3064	8.8869	8.4987	8.1390	7.8052	7.4951	7.2065	6.9377	6.6869
13	12.2551	11.5753	10.9540	10.3851	9.8633	9.3838	8.9427	8.5361	8.1607	7.8137	7.4924	7.1944	6.9176
14	13.1337	12.3484	11.6350	10.9856	10.3936	9.8527	9.3577	8.9038	8.4869	8.1034	7.7499	7.4235	7.1218
15	14.0037	13.1062	12.2961	11.5631	10.8986	10.2950	9.7455	9.2442	8.7862	8.3667	7.9819	7.6282	7.3025
16	14.8651	13.8493	12.9379	12.1184	11.3797	10.7122	10.1079	9.5595	9.0607	8.6061	8.1909	7.8109	7.4624
17	15.7179	14.5777	13.5611	12.6523	11.8378	11.1059	10.4466	9.8514	9.3126	8.8237	8.3792	7.9740	7.6039
18	16.5623	15.2919	14.1661	13.1657	12.2741	11.4773	10.7632	10.1216	9.5436	9.0216	8.5488	8.1196	7.7291
19	17.3983	15.9920	14.7535	13.6593	12.6896	11.8276	11.0591	10.3719	9.7556	9.2014	8.7016	8.2497	7.8399
20	18.2260	16.6785	15.3238	14.1339	13.0853	12.1581	11.3356	10.6036	9.9501	9.3649	8.8393	8.3658	7.9380
25	22.2434	19.9139	17.9355	16.2470	14.7986	13.5504	12.4693	11.5288	10.7066	9.9847	9.3481	8.7843	8.2829
30	26.0658	22.8444	20.1885	17.9837	16.1411	14.5907	13.2777	12.1584	11.1983	10.3696	9.6501	9.0218	8.4701
35	29.7027	25.4986	22.1318	19.4112	17.1929	15.3681	13.8540	12.5869	11.5178	10.6086	9.8293	9.1566	8.5717
40	33.1630	27.9026	23.8082	20.5845	18.0170	15.9491	14.2649	12.8786	11.7255	10.7570	9.9357	9.2330	8.6268
45	36.4555	30.0800	25.2543	21.5488	18.6628	16.3832	14.5579	13.0771	11.8605	10.8491	9.9988	9.2764	8.6568
50	39.5881	32.0521	26.5017	22.3415	19.1687	16.7076	14.7668	13.2122	11.9482	10.9063	10.0362	9.3010	8.6730

APPENDIX B-5 Present Value of an Annuity Due (continued)

Present Value of Annuity Due

$$\left[\frac{1-\frac{1}{(1+i)^{n-1}}}{i}+1\right]$$

Period	14%	15%	16%	17%	18%	19%	20%	25%	30%	35%	40%	45%	50%
1	1.0000	1.0000	1.0000	1.0000	1.0000	1.0000	1.0000	1.0000	1.0000	1.0000	1.0000	1.0000	1.0000
2	1.8772	1.8696	1.8621	1.8547	1.8475	1.8403	1.8333	1.8000	1.7692	1.7407	1.7143	1.6897	1.6667
3	2.6467	2.6257	2.6052	2.5852	2.5656	2.5465	2.5278	2.4400	2.3609	2.2894	2.2245	2.1653	2.1111
4	3.3216	3.2832	3.2459	3.2096	3.1743	3.1399	3.1065	2.9520	2.8161	2.6959	2.5889	2.4933	2.4074
5	3.9137	3.8550	3.7982	3.7432	3.6901	3.6386	3.5887	3.3616	3.1662	2.9969	2.8492	2.7195	2.6049
6	4.4331	4.3522	4.2743	4.1993	4.1272	4.0576	3.9906	3.6893	3.4356	3.2200	3.0352	2.8755	2.7366
7	4.8887	4.7845	4.6847	4.5892	4.4976	4.4098	4.3255	3.9514	3.6427	3.3852	3.1680	2.9831	2.8244
8	5.2883	5.1604	5.0386	4.9224	4.8115	4.7057	4.6046	4.1611	3.8021	3.5075	3.2628	3.0573	2.8829
9	5.6389	5.4873	5.3436	5.2072	5.0776	4.9544	4.8372	4.3289	3.9247	3.5982	3.3306	3.1085	2.9220
10	5.9464	5.7716	5.6065	5.4506	5.3030	5.1633	5.0310	4.4631	4.0190	3.6653	3.3790	3.1438	2.9480
11	6.2161	6.0188	5.8332	5.6586	5.4941	5.3389	5.1925	4.5705	4.0915	3.7150	3.4136	3.1681	2.9653
12	6.4527	6.2337	6.0286	5.8364	5.6560	5.4865	5.3271	4.6564	4.1473	3.7519	3.4383	3.1849	2.9769
13	6.6603	6.4206	6.1971	5.9884	5.7932	5.6105	5.4392	4.7251	4.1903	3.7792	3.4559	3.1965	2.9846
14	6.8424	6.5831	6.3423	6.1183	5.9095	5.7147	5.5327	4.7801	4.2233	3.7994	3.4685	3.2045	2.9897
15	7.0021	6.7245	6.4675	6.2293	6.0081	5.8023	5.6106	4.8241	4.2487	3.8144	3.4775	3.2100	2.9931
16	7.1422	6.8474	6.5755	6.3242	6.0916	5.8759	5.6755	4.8593	4.2682	3.8255	3.4839	3.2138	2.9954
17	7.2651	6.9542	6.6685	6.4053	6.1624	5.9377	5.7296	4.8874	4.2832	3.8337	3.4885	3.2164	2.9970
18	7.3729	7.0472	6.7487	6.4746	6.2223	5.9897	5.7746	4.9099	4.2948	3.8398	3.4918	3.2182	2.9980
19	7.4674	7.1280	6.8178	6.5339	6.2732	6.0333	5.8122	4.9279	4.3037	3.8443	3.4941	3.2195	2.9986
20	7.5504	7.1982	6.8775	6.5845	6.3162	6.0700	5.8435	4.9424	4.3105	3.8476	3.4958	3.2203	2.9991
25	7.8351	7.4338	7.0726	6.7465	6.4509	6.1822	5.9371	4.9811	4.3272	3.8550	3.4992	3.2219	2.9999
30	7.9830	7.5509	7.1656	6.8204	6.5098	6.2292	5.9747	4.9938	4.3317	3.8567	3.4999	3.2222	3.0000
35	8.0599	7.6091	7.2098	6.8541	6.5356	6.2489	5.9898	4.9980	4.3329	3.8570	3.5000	3.2222	3.0000
40	8.0997	7.6380	7.2309	6.8695	6.5468	6.2572	5.9959	4.9993	4.3332	3.8571	3.5000	3.2222	3.0000
45	8.1205	7.6524	7.2409	6.8765	6.5517	6.2607	5.9984	4.9998	4.3333	3.8571	3.5000	3.2222	3.0000
50	8.1312	7.6596	7.2457	6.8797	6.5539	6.2621	5.9993	4.9999	4.3333	3.8571	3.5000	3.2222	3.0000

APPENDIX B-6 Future Value of an Annuity Due

Future Value of Annuity Due

$$\left[\frac{(1+i)^n - 1}{i}\right] \times [1+i]$$

Period	1%	2%	3%	4%	5%	6%	7%	8%	9%	10%	11%	12%	13%
1	1.0100	1.0200	1.0300	1.0400	1.0500	1.0600	1.0700	1.0800	1.0900	1.1000	1.1100	1.1200	1.1300
2	2.0301	2.0604	2.0909	2.1216	2.1525	2.1836	2.2149	2.2464	2.2781	2.3100	2.3421	2.3744	2.4069
3	3.0604	3.1216	3.1836	3.2465	3.3101	3.3746	3.4399	3.5061	3.5731	3.6410	3.7097	3.7793	3.8498
4	4.1010	4.2040	4.3091	4.4163	4.5256	4.6371	4.7507	4.8666	4.9847	5.1051	5.2278	5.3528	5.4803
5	5.1520	5.3081	5.4684	5.6330	5.8019	5.9753	6.1533	6.3359	6.5233	6.7156	6.9129	7.1152	7.3227
6	6.2135	6.4343	6.6625	6.8983	7.1420	7.3938	7.6540	7.9228	8.2004	8.4872	8.7833	9.0890	9.4047
7	7.2857	7.5830	7.8923	8.2142	8.5491	8.8975	9.2598	9.6366	10.0285	10.4359	10.8594	11.2997	11.7573
8	8.3685	8.7546	9.1591	9.5828	10.0266	10.4913	10.9780	11.4876	12.0210	12.5795	13.1640	13.7757	14.4157
9	9.4622	9.9497	10.4639	11.0061	11.5779	12.1808	12.8164	13.4866	14.1929	14.9374	15.7220	16.5487	17.4197
10	10.5668	11.1687	11.8078	12.4864	13.2068	13.9716	14.7836	15.6455	16.5603	17.5312	18.5614	19.6546	20.8143
11	11.6825	12.4121	13.1920	14.0258	14.9171	15.8699	16.8885	17.9771	19.1407	20.3843	21.7132	23.1331	24.6502
12	12.8093	13.6803	14.6178	15.6268	16.7130	17.8821	19.1406	20.4953	21.9534	23.5227	25.2116	27.0291	28.9847
13	13.9474	14.9739	16.0863	17.2919	18.5986	20.0151	21.5505	23.2149	25.0192	26.9750	29.0949	31.3926	33.8827
14	15.0969	16.2934	17.5989	19.0236	20.5786	22.2760	24.1290	26.1521	28.3609	30.7725	33.4054	36.2797	39.4175
15	16.2579	17.6393	19.1569	20.8245	22.6575	24.6725	26.8881	29.3243	32.0034	34.9497	38.1899	41.7533	45.6717
16	17.4304	19.0121	20.7616	22.6975	24.8404	27.2129	29.8402	32.7502	35.9737	39.5447	43.5008	47.8837	52.7391
17	18.6147	20.4123	22.4144	24.6454	27.1324	29.9057	32.9990	36.4502	40.3013	44.5992	49.3959	54.7497	60.7251
18	19.8109	21.8406	24.1169	26.6712	29.5390	32.7600	36.3790	40.4463	45.0185	50.1591	55.9395	62.4397	69.7494
19	21.0190	23.2974	25.8704	28.7781	32.0660	35.7856	39.9955	44.7620	50.1601	56.2750	63.2028	71.0524	79.9468
20	22.2392	24.7833	27.6765	30.9692	34.7193	38.9927	43.8652	49.4229	55.7645	63.0025	71.2651	80.6987	91.4699
25	28.5256	32.6709	37.5530	43.3117	50.1135	58.1564	67.6765	78.9544	92.3240	108.1818	126.9988	149.3339	175.8501
30	35.1327	41.3794	49.0027	58.3283	69.7608	83.8017	101.0730	122.3459	148.5752	180.9434	220.9132	270.2926	331.3151
35	42.0769	50.9944	62.2759	76.5983	94.8363	118.1209	147.9135	186.1021	235.1247	298.1268	379.1644	483.4631	617.7493
40	49.3752	61.6100	77.6633	98.8265	126.8398	164.0477	213.6096	279.7810	368.2919	486.8518	645.8269	859.1424	1145.486
45	57.0459	73.3306	95.5015	125.8706	167.6852	225.5081	305.7518	417.4261	573.1860	790.7953	1095.169	1521.218	2117.806
50	65.1078	86.2710	116.1808	158.7738	219.8154	307.7561	434.9860	619.6718	888.4411	1280.299	1852.336	2688.020	3909.243

APPENDIX B-6 Future Value of an Annuity Due (continued)

Future Value of Annuity Due

$$\left[\frac{(1+i)^n-1}{i}\right]\times[1+i]$$

Period	14%	15%	16%	17%	18%	19%	20%	25%	30%	35%	40%	45%	50%
1	1.1400	1.1500	1.1600	1.1700	1.1800	1.1900	1.2000	1.2500	1.3000	1.3500	1.4000	1.4500	1.5000
2	2.4396	2.4725	2.5056	2.5389	2.5724	2.6061	2.6400	2.8125	2.9900	3.1725	3.3600	3.5525	3.7500
3	3.9211	3.9934	4.0665	4.1405	4.2154	4.2913	4.3680	4.7656	5.1870	5.6329	6.1040	6.6011	7.1250
4	5.6101	5.7424	5.8771	6.0144	6.1542	6.2966	6.4416	7.2070	8.0431	8.9544	9.9456	11.0216	12.1875
5	7.5355	7.7537	7.9775	8.2068	8.4420	8.6830	8.9299	10.2588	11.7560	13.4384	15.3238	17.4314	19.7813
6	9.7305	10.0668	10.4139	10.7720	11.1415	11.5227	11.9159	14.0735	16.5828	19.4919	22.8534	26.7255	31.1719
7	12.2328	12.7268	13.2401	13.7733	14.3270	14.9020	15.4991	18.8419	22.8577	27.6640	33.3947	40.2019	48.2578
8	15.0853	15.7858	16.5185	17.2847	18.0859	18.9234	19.7989	24.8023	31.0150	38.6964	48.1526	59.7428	73.8867
9	18.3373	19.3037	20.3215	21.3931	22.5213	23.7089	24.9587	32.2529	41.6195	53.5902	68.8137	88.0771	112.3301
10	22.0445	23.3493	24.7329	26.1999	27.7551	29.4035	31.1504	41.5661	55.4053	73.6967	97.7391	129.1618	169.9951
11	26.2707	28.0017	29.8502	31.8239	33.9311	36.1802	38.5805	53.2077	73.3270	100.8406	138.2348	188.7346	256.4927
12	31.0887	33.3519	35.7862	38.4040	41.2187	44.2445	47.4966	67.7596	96.6250	137.4848	194.9287	275.1151	386.2390
13	36.5811	39.5047	42.6720	46.1027	49.8180	53.8409	58.1959	85.9495	126.9125	186.9544	274.3002	400.3670	580.8585
14	42.8424	46.5804	50.6595	55.1101	59.9653	65.2607	71.0351	108.6868	166.2863	253.7385	385.4202	581.9821	872.7878
15	49.9804	54.7175	59.9250	65.6488	71.9390	78.8502	86.4421	137.1085	217.4722	343.8970	540.9883	845.3240	1310.6817
16	58.1176	64.0751	70.6730	77.9792	86.0680	95.0218	104.9306	172.6357	284.0139	465.6109	758.7837	1227.1699	1967.5225
17	67.3941	74.8364	83.1407	92.4056	102.7403	114.2659	127.1167	217.0446	370.5180	629.9247	1063.697	1780.8463	2952.7838
18	77.9692	87.2118	97.6032	109.2846	122.4135	137.1664	153.7400	272.5558	482.9734	851.7483	1490.576	2583.6771	4430.6756
19	90.0249	101.4436	114.3797	129.0329	145.6280	164.4180	185.6880	341.9447	629.1655	1151.210	2088.206	3747.7818	6647.5135
20	103.7684	117.8101	133.8405	152.1385	173.0210	196.8474	224.0256	428.6809	819.2151	1555.484	2924.889	5435.7336	9972.7702
25	207.3327	244.7120	289.0883	341.7627	404.2721	478.4306	566.3773	1318.489	3053.444	6988.280	15746.08	34859.038	75750.5049
30	406.7370	499.9569	615.1616	757.5038	933.3186	1150.387	1418.258	4033.968	11348.98	31349.12	84701.51	223454.60	575250.178
35	790.6729	1013.346	1300.027	1668.994	2143.649	2753.914	3538.009	12320.95	42149.73	140583.9	455560.4	1432302.0	4368325.82
40	1529.909	2045.954	2738.478	3667.391	4912.591	6580.496	8812.629	37610.82	156510.7	630396.5	2450128	9180692.2	33171994.0
45	2953.244	4122.898	5759.718	8048.770	11247.26	15712.07	21937.57	114789.4	581125.2	2826733	13177394	58845813	251899849
50	5693.75	8300.37	12105.35	17654.72	25739.45	37503.25	54596.63	350319.6	2157689	12675177	70871203	377186028	1912864498

APPENDIX C

Regulatory Requirements

REGULATORY REQUIREMENTS—FEDERAL SECURITIES REGULATION

Introduction

The issuance and sale of corporate securities are extensively regulated by the Securities and Exchange Commission (SEC), a federal agency that administers the Securities Act of 1933, the Securities Exchange Act of 1934, and other federal statutes. A major objective of securities regulation is to protect the investing public by requiring full and correct disclosure of relevant information. Both the federal and state governments require a substantial amount of regulation; however, most is from the federal government because the majority of trading is done across state borders.

The Securities Act of 1933

This securities act is primarily concerned with new issues of securities or issues in the primary market. The term *investment security* is broadly defined as:

> Any note, stock, treasury stock, bond, debenture, evidence of indebtedness, certificate of interest or participation in any profit sharing agreement . . . investment contract . . . or, in general, any interest or instrument commonly known as a "security" or any certificate of interest or participation in . . . receipt for . . . or right to subscribe to or purchase, any of the foregoing.
>
> Securities Act of 1933, Section 2, Subsection (a)(1)

Any transaction in which a person invests money or property in a common enterprise or venture, or an investor who reasonably expects to make a profit primarily or substantially as a result of the managerial efforts of others is regulated by this act.

The 1933 Act requires full disclosure of material information that is relevant to investment decisions and prohibits fraud and misstatements when securities are offered to the public through the mail and/or interstate commerce. Registration statements, including financial statements, must be filed with the Securities and Exchange Commission (SEC) before investment securities can be offered for sale by an issuer. A registration statement, which is filed with the SEC, contains a thorough description of the securities, financial structure, condition, and management personnel of the issuing corporation. It also contains a description of material pending litigation against the issuing corporation. The 1933 Act also requires that a prospectus, based on the information in the registration statement, be given to any prospective investor or purchaser.

Securities that are exempt from registration requirements include:

- intrastate offerings where all offerees and issuers are residents of the state in which issuer performs substantially all of its operations;
- securities issued by a governmental body or nonprofit organization;
- securities issued by a bank, savings institution, common carrier, or farmers' cooperative and subject to other regulatory legislation;
- commercial paper with a maturity date of less than nine months (270 days);
- stock dividends, stock splits, and securities issued in connection with corporate reorganizations; and
- insurance, endowment, and annuity contracts.

Regulation A requires less demanding disclosures and registration for small issues of less than $1.5 million. Regulation D lists these transactions as exempt from registration requirements:

- Private, noninvestment company sales of less than $500,000 worth of securities in a 12-month period to investors who will not resell the securities within two years
- Private, noninvestment company sales of less than $5 million worth of securities in a 12-month period to:
  - accredited investors—natural persons with annual income of more than $200,000 (or $300,000 jointly with a spouse) or whose net worth exceeds $1 million;
  - investors who are furnished with purchaser representatives who are knowledgeable and experienced regarding finance and business; or
  - up to 35 unaccredited investors that have financial and business knowledge and experience, who are furnished with the same information as would be contained in a full registration statement prospectus.
- Sales of any amount of securities to accredited investors or those furnished with independent purchaser representatives (private placement)

The Securities Exchange Act of 1934 (SEA)

Although the Securities Act of 1933 was limited to new issues, the 1934 Securities Act extended the regulation to securities sold in the secondary markets. The act provides the following.

- Establishment of the SEC—the SEC's primary function is to regulate the securities markets.
- Disclosure requirements for the secondary market—annual reports and other financial reports are required to be filed with the SEC prior to listing on the organized exchanges. These reports include the annual 10K Report, which must be audited, and the quarterly 10Q Report, which is not required to be audited.
- Registration of organized exchanges—all organized exchanges must register with the SEC and provide copies of their rules and bylaws.
- Credit regulation—Congress gave the Federal Reserve Board the power to set margin requirements for credit purchases of securities. Securities dealers' indebtedness was also limited to 20 times their owners' equity capital by this act.
- Proxy solicitation—specific rules governing solicitation of proxies were established.
- Exemptions—securities of federal, state, and local governments, securities that are not traded across state lines, and any other securities specified by the SEC are exempt from registering with the SEC.
- Insider activities—a public report, called an insider report, must be filed with the SEC in every month that a change in the holding of a firm's securities occurs for an officer, director, or 10% or more shareholder. The 1934 SEA forbids insiders profiting from securities held less than six months and requires these profits be returned to the organization. In addition, short sales are not permitted by individuals considered to be insiders.
- Price manipulation—the SEA of 1934 forbids price manipulation schemes, such as wash sales, pools, circulation of manipulative information, and false and misleading statements about securities.

Liability Under the Securities Exchange Act of 1934

The Securities Exchange Act of 1934 relates to the purchase and sale of investment securities in the market (i.e., being public). Section 18 states that a financial planner is liable for false and/or misleading statements of material facts that are made in applications, reports, documents, and registration statements, which are prepared by the financial planner and filed with the SEC. Liability is imposed upon those (including financial planners) who, because of their inside positions, have access to material information (which is not available to the public and which may affect the value of securities) and trade in the securities without making a disclosure.

A financial planner may be liable to a person who purchased or sold securities when it can be established that:

- the statement or omission was material;
- the financial planner intended to deceive or defraud others; and
- as a result of his reasonable reliance upon the misrepresentation, the purchaser or seller incurred a loss.

Criminal liability for willful conduct is imposed by the Securities Act of 1933, the Securities Exchange Act of 1934, the Internal Revenue Act, and other federal statutes, as well as state criminal codes.

The Investment Advisers Act of 1940

An investment adviser is defined as any person who, for compensation and as part of a regular business, engages in the business of advising others on the value of securities or on the advisability of investing in or selling them. The advice can be delivered in person, through publications or writings, or through research reports concerning securities.

To be an investment adviser under both state and federal securities law, a person must meet the following three tests:

- Provides advice, or issues reports or analyses, regarding securities
- Is in the business of providing such services
- Provides such services for compensation (compensation is "the receipt of any economic benefit" including commissions on the sale of products)

Certain organizations and individuals are excluded from the definition of investment adviser:

- Banks and bank holding companies (except as amended by the Gramm-Leach-Bliley Act of 1999)
- Lawyers, accountants, engineers, or teachers, if their performance of advisory services is solely incidental to their professions
- Brokers or dealers, if their performance of advisory services is solely incidental to the conduct of their business as brokers or dealers, and they do not receive any special compensation for their advisory services
- Publishers of bona fide newspapers, news magazines, or business or financial publications of general and regular circulation
- Federally covered investment advisers registered with the SEC
- Any other person the Administrator specifies
- Incidental practice exception is not available to individuals who hold themselves out to the public as providing financial planning, pension consulting, or other financial advisory services

The act generally requires investment advisers entering into an advisory contract with a client to deliver a written disclosure statement on their background and business practices. Form ADV Part II must be given to a client under Rule 204-3, known as the brochure rule. The 1940 Advisers Act and the SEC's rules require that advisers maintain and preserve specified books and records and make them available for inspection.

In accordance with the Investment Adviser Brochure Rule, an investment adviser must furnish each advisory client and prospective client with a written disclosure statement, which may be a copy of Part II of Form ADV, or written documents containing at least the information required by Part II of Form ADV, or such other information as the administrator may require.

Antifraud provisions—Section 206 of the Investment Advisers Act, Section 17 of the Securities Act of 1933, Section 10(b) of the Securities Exchange Act of 1934, and Rule 10b-5 prohibit misstatements or misleading omissions of material facts, fraudulent acts, and practices in connection with the purchase or sale of securities or the conduct of an investment advisory business. An investment adviser is a fiduciary and owes clients undivided loyalty and may not engage in activity that conflicts with a client's interest.

Registration of Investment Advisers

Small Advisers—Those with less than $25 million of assets under management (AUM) are regulated by one or more states unless the state in which the adviser has its principal office and place of business has not enacted a statute regulating advisers.

Mid-Sized Advisers—Those with between $25 million and $100 million of AUM are regulated by one or more state if (i) the adviser is registered with the state where it has its principal office and place of business, and (ii) the adviser is "subject to examination" by that state authority.

Large Advisers—Those with more than $100 million of AUM must register with the SEC (unless an exemption is available), and state adviser laws are preempted for these advisers.

Investment Adviser Registration Depository

The Investment Adviser Registration Depository (IARD) is an electronic filing system for Investment Advisers sponsored by the Securities and Exchange Commission (SEC or Commission) and North American Securities Administrators Association (NASAA), with FINRA serving as the developer and operator of the system. The IARD system collects and maintains the registration and disclosure information for Investment Advisers and their associated persons. The IARD system supports electronic filing of the revised Forms ADV and ADV-W, centralized fee and form processing, regulatory review, the annual registration renewal process, and public disclosure of Investment Adviser information.

FINRA does not have regulatory authority over Investment Advisers; however, it was chosen to develop, operate, and maintain the system because of its regulatory business and technical expertise and the success of its web-based licensing and regulation system, Web CRDSM, deployed in 1999. Web CRD is a state-of-the-art web application for the registration of broker-dealers and their representatives. IARD provides regulators with the ability to monitor and process Investment Adviser information via a single, centralized system.

The SEC mandated its Investment Adviser registrants use the system to make all filings with the Commission (effective January 1, 2001). The IARD system satisfies the requirements of the National Securities Markets Improvement Act (NSMIA, 1996), which authorized electronic system registration of Investment Advisers.

IARD provides a mechanism that allows federally regulated Investment Advisers to satisfy the SEC mandate for electronic filing and related public disclosure. The system also offers states similar benefits by facilitating "Notice Filing" requirements for federal filers and registration requirements of state-regulated Investment Advisers. The IARD Program also provides for the registration of Investment Adviser Representatives (RAs) using the Individual Form Filing Functionality in Web CRD.

The IARD Program is composed of four critical components: IA Firm Registration, IA Firm Public Disclosure, IA Representative Registration, and IA Representative Public Disclosure. The Firm Registration component was released into production on January 1, 2001. This allows Investment Adviser firms to file a Form ADV and/or Form ADV-W electronically with the SEC and states. The IA Representative Registration component was implemented in Web CRD March 18, 2002. Release 4.0 in Web CRD enables firms to register their IA representatives online via the Web CRD system. In conjunction with the Release, the Uniform Forms U-4 and U-5 were revised to include the RA registration position code for IA representatives. Both the IA Firm Registration component and the IA Representative Registration component provides the ability to view the information contained on the filings, collect and disburse fees associated with these filings, request reports, and allow joint firms that are both broker-dealers and Investment Advisers, to share filing information between Web CRD and IARD.

Source: Financial Industry Regulatory Authority, Inc., *What is IARD?*, 2009, http://www.iard.com/WhatIsIARD.asp

Due Diligence

Due diligence is the process investment advisors use to make suitable investment recommendations to their clients. The advisor should gather all information necessary to establish proper suitability. This information includes, but is not limited to, the client's age, net worth, risk tolerance, and financial knowledge. Based on the client's objectives, the advisor should conduct due diligence on the various investment choices with the goal to provide investment recommendations that are in the client's best interest.

Investment Company Act of 1940

The Investment Company Act of 1940 requires registration with the SEC and restricts activities of investment companies (including mutual funds). The Investment Company Act of 1940 governs the management of investment companies. This act requires that investment companies register with the SEC, provide prospectuses to investors prior to the sale of shares, disclose the investment goals of the company, have outside members on the board of directors, use uniform accounting practices, and gain approval by shareholders for changes in management.

REFORM OF PREVIOUS ACTS

The Glass-Steagall Act (1933) prohibited commercial banks from acting as investment bankers, established the Federal Deposit Insurance Corporation (FDIC), and prohibited commercial banks from paying interest on demand deposits. This was one of the first of many securities regulation laws that impacted the investment markets. However, the Gramm-Leach-Bliley Act, passed by Congress in November 1999, eliminated many of the restrictions against affiliations among banks, securities firms, and insurance companies.

The act repealed the affiliation sections of the Glass-Steagall Act that prohibited a bank holding company and a securities firm that underwrites and deals in ineligible securities from owning and controlling each other.

It also amended the Bank Holding Company Act (1956) to permit cross-ownership and control among bank holding companies, securities firms, and insurance companies, provided that such cross-ownership and control is effected through a financial holding company that engages in activities that conform to the act.

A bank must register as an investment adviser if it provides investment advice to a registered investment company, provided that, if the bank provides such advice through a "separately identified department or division," that department or division must be deemed to be the investment adviser.

FINRA

The Financial Industry Regulatory Authority (FINRA), is the largest non-governmental regulator for all securities firms doing business in the United States. All told, FINRA oversees nearly 4,850 brokerage firms, about 173,000 branch offices and more than 647,000 registered securities representatives.

Created in July 2007 through the consolidation of National Association of Securities Dealers (NASD) and the member regulation, enforcement and arbitration functions of the New York Stock Exchange, FINRA is dedicated to investor protection and market integrity through effective and efficient regulation and complementary compliance and technology-based services.

FINRA touches virtually every aspect of the securities business—from registering and educating industry participants to examining securities firms; writing rules; enforcing those rules and the federal securities laws; informing and educating the investing public; providing trade reporting and other industry utilities; and administering the largest dispute resolution forum for investors and registered firms. It also performs market regulation under contract for The NASDAQ Stock Market, the American Stock Exchange, the International Securities Exchange and the Chicago Climate Exchange.

Source: Financial Industry Regulatory Authority, Inc., *About the Financial Industry Regulatory Authority*, 2009, http://www.finra.org/AboutFINRA/

APPENDIX D

CFP® Certification Examination Principal Topics

2021 PRINCIPAL KNOWLEDGE TOPICS (70)

The following Principal Knowledge Topics are based on the results of CFP Board's 2021 Practice Analysis Study.

The Principal Knowledge Domains will serve as the blueprint for the March 2022 CFP® Certification Examination and subsequent administrations of the exam. Each exam question will be linked to one of the following Principal Knowledge Topics, in the approximate percentages indicated following the domain headings.

The Principal Knowledge Topics also serve as a curricular framework for CFP Board's education coursework requirement and the topics CFP Board accepts for continuing education credit.

EIGHT PRINCIPAL KNOWLEDGE DOMAINS

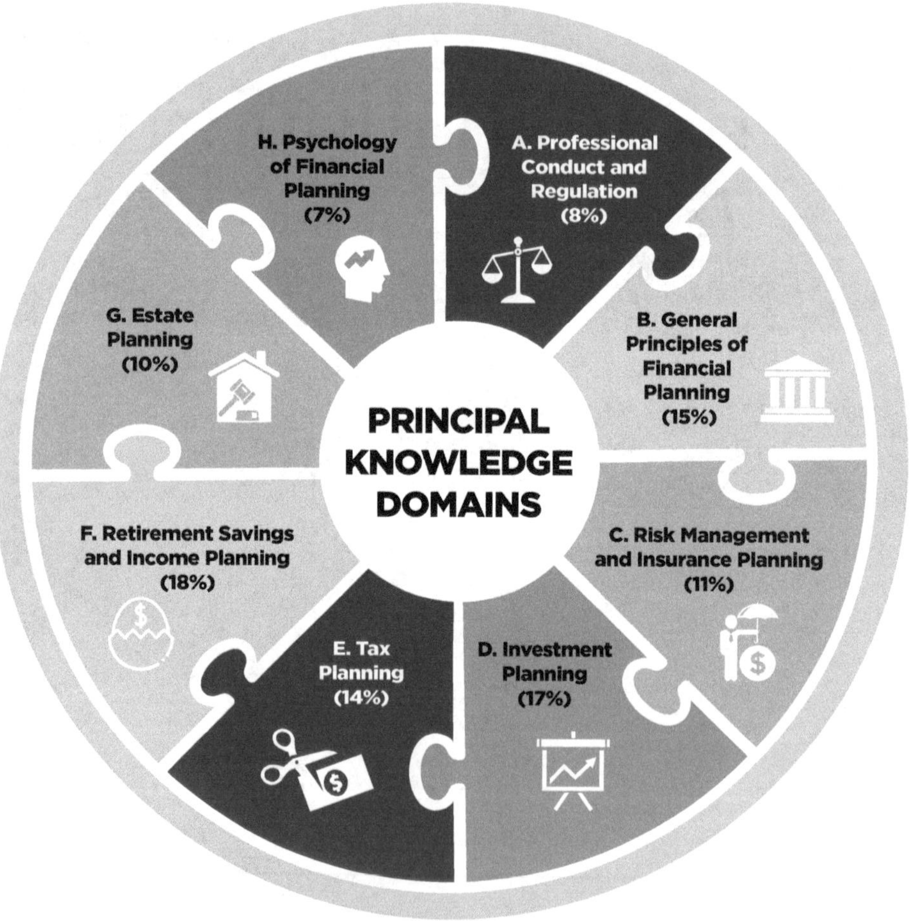

2021 PRINCIPAL KNOWLEDGE TOPICS

A. PROFESSIONAL CONDUCT AND REGULATION

A.1 CFP Board's Code of Ethics and Standards of Conduct

A.2 CFP Board's Procedural Rules

A.3 Function, purpose, and general structure of financial institutions

A.4 Financial services regulations and requirements

A.5 Consumer protection laws

A.6 Fiduciary standard and application

B. GENERAL PRINCIPLES OF FINANCIAL PLANNING

B.7 Financial planning process

B.8 Financial statements

B.9 Cash flow management

B.10 Financing strategies and debt management

B.11 Economic concepts

B.12 Time value of money concepts and calculations

B.13 Education needs analysis

B.14 Education savings vehicles

B.15 Education funding

B.16 Gift/income tax strategies

C. RISK MANAGEMENT AND INSURANCE PLANNING

C.17 Principles of risk and insurance

C.18 Analysis and evaluation of risk exposures

C.19 Health insurance and health care cost management (individual and group)

C.20 Disability income insurance (individual and group)

C.21 Long-term care insurance and long-term case planning (individual and group)

C.22 Qualified and Non-Qualified Annuities

C.23 Life insurance (individual and group)

C.24 Business owner insurance solutions

C.25 Insurance needs analysis

C.26 Insurance policy and company selection

D. INVESTMENT PLANNING

D.27 Characteristics, uses and taxation of investment vehicles

D.28 Types of investment risk

D.29 Market cycles

D.30 Quantitative investment concepts and measures of investment returns

D.31 Asset allocation and portfolio diversification

D.32 Bond and stock valuation concepts

D.33 Portfolio development and analysis

D.34 Investment strategies

D.35 Alternative investments and liquidity risk

E. TAX PLANNING

E.36 Fundamental and current tax law

E.37 Income tax fundamentals and calculations

E.38 Characteristics and income taxation of business entities

E.39 Income taxation of trusts and estates

E.40 Tax reduction/management techniques

E.41 Tax consequences of property transactions

E.42 Tax implications of special circumstances

E.43 Charitable/philanthropic contributions and deductions

F. RETIREMENT SAVINGS AND INCOME PLANNING

F.44 Retirement needs analysis

F.45 Social Security and Medicare planning

F.46 Eldercare and special needs planning

F.47 Types of retirement plans

F.48 Qualified plan rules and options

F.49 Non-qualified plan rules and options

F.50 Key factors affecting plan selection for businesses

F.51 Distribution rules and taxation

F.52 Retirement income and distribution strategies

F.53 Business succession planning

G. ESTATE PLANNING

G.54 Property titling and beneficiary designations

G.55 Strategies to transfer property

G.56 Estate and incapacity planning documents

G.57 Gift, estate, and GST tax compliance and calculation

G.58 Sources for estate liquidity

G.59 Types, features, and taxation of trusts

G.60 Marital deduction

G.61 Intra-family and other business transfer techniques

G.62 Postmortem estate planning techniques

G.63 Planning for divorce, unmarried couples and other special circumstances

G.64 Planning for special needs and circumstances

H. PSYCHOLOGY OF FINANCIAL PLANNING

H.65 Client and planner attitudes, values, biases

H.66 Behavioral finance

H.67 Sources of money conflict

H.68 Principles of counseling

H.69 General principles of effective communication

H.70 Crisis events with severe consequences

APPENDIX E

Code of Ethics and Standards of Conduct

CFP BOARD

CODE OF ETHICS AND STANDARDS OF CONDUCT

EFFECTIVE DATE: OCTOBER 1, 2019

March 2018, as revised in November 2018

PREAMBLE

CFP Board's *Code of Ethics and Standards of Conduct* reflects the commitment that all CFP® professionals make to high standards of competency and ethics. CFP Board's *Code and Standards* benefits and protects the public, provides standards for delivering financial planning, and advances financial planning as a distinct and valuable profession. Compliance with the *Code and Standards* is a requirement of CFP® certification that is critical to the integrity of the CFP® marks. Violations of the *Code and Standards* may subject a CFP® professional to discipline.

CODE OF ETHICS

A CFP® professional must:

1. Act with honesty, integrity, competence, and diligence.
2. Act in the client's best interests.
3. Exercise due care.
4. Avoid or disclose and manage conflicts of interest.
5. Maintain the confidentiality and protect the privacy of client information.
6. Act in a manner that reflects positively on the financial planning profession and CFP® certification.

STANDARDS OF CONDUCT

A. DUTIES OWED TO CLIENTS

1. FIDUCIARY DUTY

At all times when providing Financial Advice to a Client, a CFP® professional must act as a fiduciary, and therefore, act in the best interests of the Client. The following duties must be fulfilled:

a. **Duty of Loyalty.** A CFP® professional must:

   i. Place the interests of the Client above the interests of the CFP® professional and the CFP® Professional's Firm;

   ii. Avoid Conflicts of Interest, or fully disclose Material Conflicts of Interest to the Client, obtain the Client's informed consent, and properly manage the conflict; and

   iii. Act without regard to the financial or other interests of the CFP® professional, the CFP® Professional's Firm, or any individual or entity other than the Client, which means that a CFP® professional acting under a Conflict of Interest continues to have a duty to act in the best interests of the Client and place the Client's interests above the CFP® professional's.

b. **Duty of Care.** A CFP® professional must act with the care, skill, prudence, and diligence that a prudent professional would exercise in light of the Client's goals, risk tolerance, objectives, and financial and personal circumstances.

c. **Duty to Follow Client Instructions.** A CFP® professional must comply with all objectives, policies, restrictions, and other terms of the Engagement and all reasonable and lawful directions of the Client.

2. INTEGRITY

a. A CFP® professional must perform Professional Services with integrity. Integrity demands honesty and candor, which may not be subordinated to personal gain or advantage. Allowance may be made for innocent error and legitimate differences of opinion, but integrity cannot co-exist with deceit or subordination of principle.

b. A CFP® professional may not, directly or indirectly, in the conduct of Professional Services:

   i. Employ any device, scheme, or artifice to defraud;

   ii. Make any untrue statement of a material fact or omit to state a material fact necessary in order to make the statements made, in the light of the circumstances under which they were made, not misleading; or

   iii. Engage in any act, practice, or course of business which operates or would operate as a fraud or deceit upon any person.

3. COMPETENCE

A CFP® professional must provide Professional Services with competence, which means with relevant knowledge and skill to apply that knowledge. When the CFP® professional is not sufficiently competent in a particular area to provide the Professional Services required under the Engagement, the CFP® professional must gain competence, obtain the assistance of a competent professional, limit or terminate the Engagement, and/or refer the Client to a competent professional. The CFP® professional shall describe to the Client any requested Professional Services that the CFP® professional will not be providing.

4. DILIGENCE

A CFP® professional must provide Professional Services, including responding to reasonable Client inquiries, in a timely and thorough manner.

5. DISCLOSE AND MANAGE CONFLICTS OF INTEREST

a. **Disclose Conflicts.** When providing Financial Advice, a CFP® professional must make full disclosure of all Material Conflicts of Interest with the CFP® professional's Client that could affect the professional relationship. This obligation requires the CFP® professional to provide the Client with sufficiently specific facts so that a reasonable Client would be able to understand the CFP® professional's Material Conflicts of Interest and the business practices that give rise to the conflicts, and give informed consent to such conflicts or reject them. A sincere belief by a CFP® professional with a Material Conflict of Interest that he or she is acting in the best interests of the Client is insufficient to excuse failure to make full disclosure.

   i. A CFP® professional must make full disclosure and obtain the consent of the Client before providing any Financial Advice regarding which the CFP® professional has a Material Conflict of Interest.

   ii. In determining whether the disclosure about a Material Conflict of Interest provided to the Client was sufficient to infer that a Client has consented to a Material Conflict of Interest, CFP Board will evaluate whether a reasonable Client receiving the disclosure would have understood the conflict and how it could affect the advice the Client will receive from the CFP® professional. The greater the potential harm the conflict presents to the Client, and the more significantly a business practice that gives rise to the conflict departs from commonly accepted practices among CFP® professionals, the less likely it is that CFP Board will infer informed consent absent clear evidence of informed consent. Ambiguity in the disclosure provided to the Client will be interpreted in favor of the Client.

   iii. Evidence of oral disclosure of a conflict will be given such weight as CFP Board in its judgment deems appropriate. Written consent to a conflict is not required.

b. **Manage Conflicts.** A CFP® professional must adopt and follow business practices reasonably designed to prevent Material Conflicts of Interest from compromising the CFP® professional's ability to act in the Client's best interests.

6. SOUND AND OBJECTIVE PROFESSIONAL JUDGMENT

A CFP® professional must exercise professional judgment on behalf of the Client that is not subordinated to the interest of the CFP® professional or others. A CFP® professional may not solicit or accept any gift, gratuity, entertainment, non-cash compensation, or other consideration that reasonably could be expected to compromise the CFP® professional's objectivity.

7. PROFESSIONALISM

A CFP® professional must treat Clients, prospective Clients, fellow professionals, and others with dignity, courtesy, and respect.

8. COMPLY WITH THE LAW

a. A CFP® professional must comply with the laws, rules, and regulations governing Professional Services.

b. A CFP® professional may not intentionally or recklessly participate or assist in another person's violation of these *Standards* or the laws, rules, or regulations governing Professional Services.

9. CONFIDENTIALITY AND PRIVACY

a. A CFP® professional must keep confidential and may not disclose any non-public personal information about any prospective, current, or former Client ("client"), except that the CFP® professional may disclose information:

   i. For ordinary business purposes:

      a) With the client's consent, so long as the client has not withdrawn the consent;

      b) To a CFP® Professional's Firm or other persons with whom the CFP® professional is providing services to or for the client, when necessary to perform those services;

      c) As necessary to provide information to the CFP® professional's attorneys, accountants, and auditors; and

      d) To a person acting in a representative capacity on behalf of the client;

   ii. For legal and enforcement purposes:

      a) To law enforcement authorities concerning suspected unlawful activities, to the extent permitted by the law;

      b) As required to comply with federal, state, or local law;

      c) As required to comply with a properly authorized civil, criminal, or regulatory investigation or examination, or subpoena or summons, by a governmental authority;

      d) As necessary to defend against allegations of wrongdoing made by a governmental authority;

      e) As necessary to present a civil claim against, or defend against a civil claim raised by, a client;

      f) As required to comply with a request from CFP Board concerning an investigation or adjudication; and

      g) As necessary to provide information to professional organizations that are assessing the CFP® professional's compliance with professional standards.

b. A CFP® professional may not use any non-public personal information about a client for his or her direct or indirect personal benefit, whether or not it causes detriment to the client, unless the client consents.

c. A CFP® professional, either directly or through the CFP® Professional's Firm, must take reasonable steps to protect the security of non-public personal information about any client, including the security of information stored physically or electronically, from unauthorized access that could result in harm or inconvenience to the client.

d. A CFP® professional, either directly or through the CFP® Professional's Firm, must adopt and implement policies regarding the protection, handling, and sharing of a client's non-public personal information and must provide a client with written notice of those policies at the time of the Engagement and thereafter not less than annually (at least once in any 12-month period) unless (i) the CFP® professional's policies have not changed since the last notice sent to a client; and (ii) the CFP® professional does not disclose non-public personal information other than as permitted without a client's consent.

e. A CFP® professional shall be deemed to comply with this Section if the CFP® Professional's Firm is subject to, and the CFP® professional complies with, Regulation S-P under the federal securities laws or substantially equivalent federal or state laws or rules.

10. PROVIDE INFORMATION TO A CLIENT

a. **When Providing Financial Advice.** When providing or agreeing to provide Financial Advice that does not require Financial Planning in accordance with the Practice Standards, a CFP® professional must provide the following information to the Client, prior to or at the time of the Engagement, and document that the information has been provided to the Client:

i. A description of the services and products to be provided;

ii. How the Client pays for the products and services, and a description of the additional types of costs that the Client may incur, including product management fees, surrender charges, and sales loads;

iii. How the CFP® professional, the CFP® Professional's Firm, and any Related Party are compensated for providing the products and services;

iv. The existence of any public discipline or bankruptcy, and the location(s), if any, of the webpages of all relevant public websites of any governmental authority, self-regulatory organization, or professional organization that sets forth the CFP® professional's public disciplinary history or any personal bankruptcy or business bankruptcy where the CFP® professional was a Control Person;

v. The information required under Section A.5.a. (Conflict of Interest Disclosure);

vi. The information required under Section A.9.d. (Written Notice Regarding Non-Public Personal Information);

vii. The information required under Section A.13.a.ii. (Disclosure of Economic Benefit for Referral or Engagement of Additional Persons); and

viii. Any other information about the CFP® professional or the CFP® Professional's Firm that is Material to a Client's decision to engage or continue to engage the CFP® professional or the CFP® Professional's Firm.

b. **When Providing Financial Planning.** When providing or required to provide Financial Planning in accordance with the Practice Standards, a CFP® professional must provide the following information to the Client, prior to or at the time of the Engagement, in one or more written documents:

i. The information required to be provided in Sections A.10.a.i.-iv. and vi.-viii.; and

ii. The terms of the Engagement between the Client and the CFP® professional or the CFP® Professional's Firm, including the Scope of Engagement and any limitations, the period(s) during which the services will be provided, and the Client's responsibilities. A CFP® professional is responsible for implementing, monitoring, and updating the Financial Planning recommendation(s) unless specifically excluded from the Scope of Engagement.

c. **Updating Information.** A CFP® professional has an ongoing obligation to provide to the Client any information that is a Material change or update to the information required to be provided to the Client. Material changes and updates to public disciplinary history or bankruptcy information must be disclosed to the Client within ninety (90) days, together with the location(s) of the relevant webpages.

11. DUTIES WHEN COMMUNICATING WITH A CLIENT

A CFP® professional must provide a Client with accurate information, in accordance with the Engagement, and in response to reasonable Client requests, in a manner and format that a Client reasonably may be expected to understand.

12. DUTIES WHEN REPRESENTING COMPENSATION METHOD

A CFP® professional may not make false or misleading representations regarding the CFP® professional's or the CFP® Professional's Firm's method(s) of compensation.

a. **Specific Representations**

i. **Fee-Only.** A CFP® professional may represent his or her or the CFP® Professional's Firm's compensation method as "fee-only" only if:

a) The CFP® professional and the CFP® Professional's Firm receive no Sales-Related Compensation; and

b) Related Parties receive no Sales-Related Compensation in connection with any Professional Services the CFP® professional or the CFP® Professional's Firm provides to Clients.

ii. **Fee-Based.** CFP Board uses the term "fee and commission" to describe the compensation method of those who receive both fees and Sales-Related Compensation. A CFP® professional who represents that his or her or the CFP® Professional's Firm's compensation method is "fee-based" or any other similar term that is not fee-only:

a) May not use the term in a manner that suggests the CFP® professional or the CFP® Professional's Firm is fee-only; and

b) Must clearly state that either the CFP® professional or the CFP® Professional's Firm earns fees and commissions, or that the CFP® professional or the CFP® Professional's Firm are not fee-only.

b. **Sales-Related Compensation.** Sales-Related Compensation is more than a *de minimis* economic benefit, including any bonus or portion of compensation, resulting from a Client purchasing or selling Financial Assets, from a Client holding Financial Assets for purposes other than receiving Financial Advice, or from the referral of a Client to any person or entity other than the CFP® Professional's Firm. Sales-Related Compensation includes, for example, commissions, trailing commissions, 12b-1 fees, spreads, transaction fees, revenue sharing, referral or solicitor fees, or similar consideration. Sales-Related Compensation does not include:

i. Soft dollars (any research or other benefits received in connection with Client brokerage that qualifies for the "safe harbor" of Section 28(e) of the Securities Exchange Act of 1934);

ii. Reasonable and customary fees for custodial or similar administrative services if the fee or amount of the fee is not determined based on the amount or value of Client transactions;

iii. Non-monetary benefits provided by another service provider, including a custodian, that benefit the CFP® professional's Clients by improving the CFP® professional's delivery of Professional Services, and that are not determined based on the amount or value of Client transactions;

iv. Reasonable and customary fees for Professional Services, other than for solicitations and referrals, the CFP® professional or CFP® Professional's Firm provides to a Client that are collected and distributed by another service provider, including under a Turnkey Asset Management Platform; or

v. A fee the Related Party solicitor receives for soliciting clients for the CFP® professional or the CFP® Professional's Firm.

c. **Related Party.** A person or business entity (including a trust) whose receipt of Sales-Related Compensation a reasonable CFP® professional would view as directly or indirectly benefiting the CFP® professional or the CFP® Professional's Firm, including, for example, as a result of the CFP® professional's ownership stake in the business entity. There is a rebuttable presumption that a Related Party includes:

i. Family Members. A member of the CFP® professional's Family and any business entity that the Family or members of the Family Control; and

ii. Business Entities. A business entity that the CFP® professional or the CFP® Professional's Firm Controls, or that is Controlled by or is under common Control with, the CFP® Professional's Firm.

d. **In Connection with any Professional Services.** Sales-Related Compensation received by a Related Party is "in connection with any Professional Services" if it results, directly or indirectly, from Client transactions referred or facilitated by the CFP® professional or the CFP® Professional's Firm.

e. **Safe Harbor for Related Parties.** Sales-Related Compensation received by a Related Party is not "in connection with any Professional Services" if the CFP® professional or the CFP® Professional's Firm adopts and implements policies and procedures reasonably designed to prevent the CFP® professional or the CFP® Professional's Firm from recommending that any Client purchase Financial Assets from or through, or refer any Clients to, the Related Party.

f. **Misrepresentations by a CFP® Professional's Firm.** A CFP® professional who Controls the CFP® Professional's Firm may not allow the CFP® Professional's Firm to make a representation of compensation method that would be false or misleading if made by the CFP® professional. A CFP® professional who does not Control the CFP® Professional's Firm must correct a CFP® Professional's Firm's misrepresentations of compensation method by accurately representing the CFP® professional's compensation method to the CFP® professional's Clients.

13. DUTIES WHEN RECOMMENDING, ENGAGING, AND WORKING WITH ADDITIONAL PERSONS

a. When engaging or recommending the selection or retention of additional persons to provide financial or Professional Services for a Client, a CFP® professional must:

   i. Have a reasonable basis for the recommendation or Engagement based on the person's reputation, experience, and qualifications;

   ii. Disclose to the Client, at the time of the recommendation or prior to the Engagement, any arrangement by which someone who is not the Client will compensate or provide some other material economic benefit to the CFP® professional, the CFP® Professional's Firm, or a Related Party for the recommendation or Engagement; and

   iii. When engaging a person to provide services for a Client, exercise reasonable care to protect the Client's interests.

b. When working with another financial or Professional Services provider on behalf of a Client, a CFP® professional must:

   i. Communicate with the other provider about the scope of their respective services and the allocation of responsibility between them; and

   ii. Inform the Client in a timely manner if the CFP® professional has a reasonable belief that the other provider's services were not performed in accordance with the scope of services to be provided and the allocation of responsibilities.

14. DUTIES WHEN SELECTING, USING, AND RECOMMENDING TECHNOLOGY

a. A CFP® professional must exercise reasonable care and judgment when selecting, using, or recommending any software, digital advice tool, or other technology while providing Professional Services to a Client.

b. A CFP® professional must have a reasonable level of understanding of the assumptions and outcomes of the technology employed.

c. A CFP® professional must have a reasonable basis for believing that the technology produces reliable, objective, and appropriate outcomes.

15. REFRAIN FROM BORROWING OR LENDING MONEY AND COMMINGLING FINANCIAL ASSETS

a. A CFP® professional may not, directly or indirectly, borrow money from or lend money to a Client unless:

   i. The Client is a member of the CFP® professional's Family; or

   ii. The lender is a business organization or legal entity in the business of lending money.

b. A CFP® professional may not commingle a Client's Financial Assets with the Financial Assets of the CFP® professional or the CFP® Professional's Firm.

B. FINANCIAL PLANNING AND APPLICATION OF THE PRACTICE STANDARDS FOR THE FINANCIAL PLANNING PROCESS

1. **Financial Planning Definition.** Financial Planning is a collaborative process that helps maximize a Client's potential for meeting life goals through Financial Advice that integrates relevant elements of the Client's personal and financial circumstances.

2. **Examples of Relevant Elements of the Client's Personal and Financial Circumstances.** Relevant elements of personal and financial circumstances vary from Client to Client, and may include the Client's need for or desire to: develop goals, manage assets and liabilities, manage cash flow, identify and manage risks, identify and manage the financial effect of health considerations, provide for educational needs, achieve financial security, preserve or increase wealth, identify tax considerations, prepare for retirement, pursue philanthropic interests, and address estate and legacy matters.

3. **Application of Practice Standards.** The Practice Standards set forth the Financial Planning Process. A CFP® professional must comply with the Practice Standards when:

   a. The CFP® professional agrees to provide or provides:

      i. Financial Planning; or

      ii. Financial Advice that requires integration of relevant elements of the Client's personal and/or financial circumstances in order to act in the Client's best interests ("Financial Advice that Requires Financial Planning"); or

   b. The Client has a reasonable basis to believe the CFP® professional will provide or has provided Financial Planning.

4. **Integration Factors.** Among the factors that CFP Board will weigh in determining whether a CFP® professional has agreed to provide or provided Financial Advice that Requires Financial Planning are:

   a. The number of relevant elements of the Client's personal and financial circumstances that the Financial Advice may affect;

   b. The portion and amount of the Client's Financial Assets that the Financial Advice may affect;

   c. The length of time the Client's personal and financial circumstances may be affected by the Financial Advice;

   d. The effect on the Client's overall exposure to risk if the Client implements the Financial Advice; and

   e. The barriers to modifying the actions taken to implement the Financial Advice.

5. **CFP Board Evaluation.** In a disciplinary proceeding in which a CFP® professional denies CFP Board's allegation that the CFP® professional was required to comply with the Practice Standards, the CFP® professional must demonstrate that compliance with the Practice Standards was not required.

6. **No Client Agreement to Engage for Financial Planning.** If a CFP® professional otherwise must comply with the Practice Standards, but the Client does not agree to engage the CFP® professional to provide Financial Planning, the CFP® professional must either:

   a. Not enter into the Engagement;

   b. Limit the Scope of Engagement to services that do not require application of the Practice Standards, and describe to the Client the services the Client requests that the CFP® professional will not be performing;

   c. Provide the requested services after informing the Client how Financial Planning would benefit the Client and how the decision not to engage the CFP® professional to provide Financial Planning may limit the CFP® professional's Financial Advice, in which case the CFP® professional is not required to comply with the Practice Standards; or

   d. Terminate the Engagement.

C. PRACTICE STANDARDS FOR THE FINANCIAL PLANNING PROCESS

In complying with the Practice Standards, a CFP® professional must act prudently in documenting information, as the facts and circumstances require, taking into account the significance of the information, the need to preserve the information in writing, the obligation to act in the Client's best interests, and the CFP® Professional's Firm's policies and procedures.

1. **Understanding the Client's Personal and Financial Circumstances**
   a. **Obtaining Qualitative and Quantitative Information.** A CFP® professional must describe to the Client the qualitative and quantitative information concerning the Client's personal and financial circumstances needed to fulfill the Scope of Engagement and collaborate with the Client to obtain the information.
      i. Examples of qualitative or subjective information include the Client's health, life expectancy, family circumstances, values, attitudes, expectations, earnings potential, risk tolerance, goals, needs, priorities, and current course of action.
      ii. Examples of quantitative or objective information include the Client's age, dependents, other professional advisors, income, expenses, cash flow, savings, assets, liabilities, available resources, liquidity, taxes, employee benefits, government benefits, insurance coverage, estate plans, education and retirement accounts and benefits, and capacity for risk.

   b. **Analyzing Information.** A CFP® professional must analyze the qualitative and quantitative information to assess the Client's personal and financial circumstances.

   c. **Addressing Incomplete Information.** If unable to obtain information necessary to fulfill the Scope of Engagement, the CFP® professional must either limit the Scope of Engagement to those services the CFP® professional is able to provide or terminate the Engagement.

2. **Identifying and Selecting Goals**
   a. **Identifying Potential Goals.** A CFP® professional must discuss with the Client the CFP® professional's assessment of the Client's financial and personal circumstances, and help the Client identify goals, noting the effect that selecting a particular goal may have on other goals. In helping the Client identify goals, the CFP® professional must discuss with the Client, and apply, reasonable assumptions and estimates. These may include life expectancy, inflation rates, tax rates, investment returns, and other Material assumptions and estimates.

   b. **Selecting and Prioritizing Goals.** A CFP® professional must help the Client select and prioritize goals. The CFP® professional must discuss with the Client any goals the Client has selected that the CFP® professional believes are not realistic.

3. **Analyzing the Client's Current Course of Action and Potential Alternative Course(s) of Action**
   a. **Analyzing Current Course of Action.** A CFP® professional must analyze the Client's current course of action, including the material advantages and disadvantages of the current course and whether the current course maximizes the potential for meeting the Client's goals.

   b. **Analyzing Potential Alternative Courses of Action.** Where appropriate, a CFP® professional must consider and analyze one or more potential alternative courses of action, including the material advantages and disadvantages of each alternative, whether each alternative helps maximize the potential for meeting the Client's goals, and how each alternative integrates the relevant elements of the Client's personal and financial circumstances.

4. **Developing the Financial Planning Recommendation(s)**

   From the potential courses of action, a CFP® professional must select one or more recommendations designed to maximize the potential for meeting the Client's goals. The recommendation may be to continue the Client's current course of action. For each recommendation selected, the CFP® professional must consider the following information:

   a. The assumptions and estimates used to develop the recommendation,

b. The basis for making the recommendation, including how the recommendation is designed to maximize the potential to meet the Client's goals, the anticipated material effects of the recommendation on the Client's financial and personal circumstances, and how the recommendation integrates relevant elements of the Client's personal and financial circumstances;

c. The timing and priority of the recommendation; and

d. Whether the recommendation is independent or must be implemented with another recommendation.

5. **Presenting the Financial Planning Recommendation(s)**

A CFP® professional must present to the Client the selected recommendations and the information that was required to be considered when developing the recommendation(s).

6. **Implementing the Financial Planning Recommendation(s)**

   a. **Addressing Implementation Responsibilities.** A CFP® professional must establish with the Client whether the CFP® professional has implementation responsibilities. When the CFP® professional has implementation responsibilities, the CFP® professional must communicate to the Client the recommendation(s) being implemented and the responsibilities of the CFP® professional, the Client, and any third party with respect to implementation.

   b. **Identifying, Analyzing, and Selecting Actions, Products, and Services.** A CFP® professional who has implementation responsibilities must identify and analyze actions, products, and services designed to implement the recommendations. The CFP® professional must consider the basis for each selection, which must include:

      i. How the action, product, or service is designed to implement the CFP® professional's recommendation; and

      ii. The advantages and disadvantages of the action, product, or service relative to reasonably available alternatives.

   c. **Recommending Actions, Products, and Services for Implementation.** A CFP® professional who has implementation responsibilities must recommend one or more actions, products and services to the Client. The CFP® professional must discuss with the Client the basis for selecting an action, product, or service, the timing and priority of implementing the action, product, or service, and disclose and manage any Material Conflicts of Interest concerning the action, product, or service.

   d. **Selecting and Implementing Actions, Products, or Services.** A CFP® professional who has implementation responsibilities must help the Client select and implement the actions, products, or services. The CFP® professional must discuss with the Client any Client selection that deviates from the actions, products, and services the CFP® professional recommended.

7. **Monitoring Progress and Updating**

   a. **Monitoring and Updating Responsibilities.** A CFP® professional must establish with the Client whether the CFP® professional has monitoring and updating responsibilities. When the CFP® professional has responsibilities for monitoring and updating, the CFP® professional must communicate to the Client:

      i. Which actions, products, and services are and are not subject to the CFP® professional's monitoring responsibility;

      ii. How and when the CFP® professional will monitor the actions, products, and services;

      iii. The Client's responsibility to inform the CFP® professional of any Material changes to the Client's qualitative and quantitative information;

      iv. The CFP® professional's responsibility to update the Financial Planning recommendations; and

      v. How and when the CFP® professional will update the Financial Planning recommendations.

b. **Monitoring the Client's Progress.** A CFP® professional who has monitoring responsibilities must analyze, at appropriate intervals, the progress toward achieving the Client's goals. The CFP® professional must review with the Client the results of the CFP® professional's analysis.

c. **Obtaining Current Qualitative and Quantitative Information.** A CFP® professional who has monitoring responsibility must collaborate with the Client in an attempt to obtain current qualitative and quantitative information concerning the Client's personal and financial circumstances.

d. **Updating Goals, Recommendations, or Implementation Decisions.** Where a CFP® professional has updating responsibility, and circumstances warrant changes to the Client's goals, recommendations, or selections of actions, products or services, the CFP® professional must update as appropriate in accordance with these Practice Standards.

D. DUTIES OWED TO FIRMS AND SUBORDINATES

1. **Use Reasonable Care When Supervising**

   A CFP® professional must exercise reasonable care when supervising persons acting under the CFP® professional's direction, including employees and other persons over whom the CFP® professional has responsibility, with a view toward preventing violations of applicable laws, rules, regulations, and these Standards.

2. **Comply with Lawful Objectives of CFP® Professional's Firm**

   A CFP® professional:

   a. Will be subject to discipline by CFP Board for violating policies and procedures of the CFP® Professional's Firm that do not conflict with these Standards.

   b. Will not be subject to discipline by CFP Board for violating policies and procedures of the CFP® Professional's Firm that conflict with these Standards.

3. **Provide Notice of Public Discipline**

   A CFP® professional must promptly advise the CFP® Professional's Firm, in writing, of any public discipline imposed by CFP Board.

E. DUTIES OWED TO CFP BOARD

1. **Definitions.** The following definitions apply:

   a. **Felony.** A felony offense, or for jurisdictions that do not differentiate between a felony and a misdemeanor, an offense punishable by a sentence of at least one-year imprisonment or a fine of at least $1,000.

   b. **Relevant Misdemeanor.** A criminal offense, that is not a Felony, for conduct involving fraud, theft, misrepresentation, other dishonest conduct, crimes of moral turpitude, violence, or a second (or more) alcohol and/or drug-related offense.

   c. **Regulatory Investigation.** An investigation initiated by a federal, state, local, or foreign governmental agency, self-regulatory organization, or other regulatory authority. A Regulatory Investigation does not include preliminary or routine regulatory inquiries or requests for information, deficiency letters, "blue sheet" requests or other trading questionnaires, or examinations.

   d. **Regulatory Action.** An action initiated by a federal, state, local, or foreign governmental agency, self-regulatory organization, or other regulatory authority.

   e. **Civil Action.** A lawsuit or arbitration.

   f. **Finding.** A finding includes an adverse final action and a consent decree in which the finding is neither admitted nor denied, but does not include a deficiency letter, examination report, memorandum of understanding, or similar informal resolution of a matter.

g. **Minor Rule Violation.** A violation of a self-regulatory organization rule designated as a minor rule violation under a plan approved by the U.S. Securities and Exchange Commission. A rule violation may be designated as "minor" under a plan if the sanction imposed consists of a fine of $2,500 or less, and if the sanctioned person does not contest the fine.

2. **Refrain from Adverse Conduct.** A CFP® professional may not engage in conduct that reflects adversely on his or her integrity or fitness as a CFP® professional, upon the CFP® marks, or upon the profession. Such conduct includes, but is not limited to, conduct that results in:

   a. A Felony or Relevant Misdemeanor conviction, or admission into a program that defers or withholds the entry of a judgment of conviction for a Felony or Relevant Misdemeanor;

   b. A Finding in a Regulatory Action or a Civil Action that the CFP® professional engaged in fraud, theft, misrepresentation, or other dishonest conduct;

   c. A personal bankruptcy or business bankruptcy filing or adjudication where the CFP® professional was a Control Person of the business, unless the CFP® professional can rebut the presumption that the bankruptcy demonstrates an inability to manage responsibly the CFP® professional's or the business's financial affairs;

   d. A federal tax lien on property owned by the CFP® professional, unless the CFP® professional can rebut the presumption that the federal tax lien demonstrates an inability to manage responsibly the CFP® professional's financial affairs; or

   e. A non-federal tax lien, judgment lien, or civil judgment that has not been satisfied within a reasonable amount of time unless the CFP® professional can rebut the presumption that the non-federal tax lien, judgment lien, or civil judgment demonstrates an inability to manage responsibly the CFP® professional's financial affairs.

3. **Reporting.** A CFP® professional must provide written notice to CFP Board within thirty (30) calendar days after the CFP® professional, or an entity over which the CFP® professional was a Control Person, has:

   a. Been charged with, convicted of, or admitted into a program that defers or withholds the entry of a judgment or conviction for, a Felony or Relevant Misdemeanor;

   b. Been named as a subject of, or whose conduct is mentioned adversely in, a Regulatory Investigation or Regulatory Action alleging failure to comply with the laws, rules, or regulations governing Professional Services;

   c. Had conduct mentioned adversely in a Finding in a Regulatory Action involving failure to comply with the laws, rules, or regulations governing Professional Services (except a Regulatory Action involving a Minor Rule Violation in a Regulatory Action brought by a self-regulatory organization);

   d. Had conduct mentioned adversely in a Civil Action alleging failure to comply with the laws, rules, or regulations governing Professional Services;

   e. Become aware of an adverse arbitration award or civil judgment, or a settlement agreement, in a Civil Action alleging failure to comply with the laws, rules, or regulations governing Professional Services, where the conduct of the CFP® professional, or an entity over which the CFP® professional was a Control Person, was mentioned adversely, other than a settlement for an amount less than $15,000;

   f. Had conduct mentioned adversely in a Civil Action alleging fraud, theft, misrepresentation, or other dishonest conduct;

   g. Been the subject of a Finding of fraud, theft, misrepresentation, or other dishonest conduct in a Regulatory Action or Civil Action;

   h. Become aware of an adverse arbitration award or civil judgment, or a settlement agreement in a Civil Action alleging fraud, theft, misrepresentation, or other dishonest conduct, where the conduct of the CFP® professional, or an entity over which the CFP® professional was a Control Person, was mentioned adversely;

i. Had a professional license, certification, or membership suspended, revoked, or materially restricted because of a violation of rules or standards of conduct;

j. Been terminated for cause from employment or permitted to resign in lieu of termination when the cause of the termination or resignation involved allegations of dishonesty, unethical conduct, or compliance failures;

k. Been named as the subject of, or been identified as the broker/adviser of record in, any written, customer-initiated complaint that alleged the CFP® professional was involved in:

   i. Forgery, theft, misappropriation, or conversion of Financial Assets;

   ii. Sales practice violations and contained a claim for compensation of $5,000 or more; or

   iii. Sales practice violations and settled for an amount of $15,000 or more.

l. Filed for or been the subject of a personal bankruptcy or business bankruptcy where the CFP® professional was a Control Person;

m. Received notice of a federal tax lien on property owned by the CFP® professional; or

n. Failed to satisfy a non-federal tax lien, judgment lien, or civil judgment within one year of its date of entry, unless payment arrangements have been agreed upon by all parties.

4. **Provide Narrative Statement.** The written notice must include a narrative statement that accurately and completely describes the Material facts and the outcome or status of the reportable matter.
5. **Cooperation.** A CFP® professional may not make false or misleading representations to CFP Board or obstruct CFP Board in the performance of its duties. A CFP® professional must satisfy the cooperation requirements set forth in CFP Board's *Procedural Rules*, including by cooperating fully with CFP Board's requests, investigations, disciplinary proceedings, and disciplinary decisions.
6. **Compliance with *Terms and Conditions of Certification and Trademark License.*** A CFP® professional must comply with the *Terms and Conditions of Certification and Trademark License*.

F. PROHIBITION ON CIRCUMVENTION

A CFP® professional may not do indirectly, or through or by another person or entity, any act or thing that the *Code and Standards* prohibit the CFP® professional from doing directly.

GLOSSARY

CFP® Professional's Firm(s). Any entity on behalf of which a CFP® professional provides Professional Services to a Client, and that has the authority to exercise control over the CFP® professional's activities, including the CFP® professional's employer, broker-dealer, registered investment adviser, insurance company, and insurance agency.

Client. Any person, including a natural person, business organization, or legal entity, to whom the CFP® professional provides or agrees to provide Professional Services pursuant to an Engagement.

Conflict of Interest.

a. When a CFP® professional's interests (including the interests of the CFP® Professional's Firm) are adverse to the CFP® professional's duties to a Client, or

b. When a CFP® professional has duties to one Client that are adverse to another Client.

Control. The power, directly or indirectly, to direct the management or policies of the entity at the relevant time, through ownership, by contract, or otherwise.

Control Person. A person who has Control.

Engagement. An oral or written agreement, arrangement, or understanding.

Family. Grandparent, parent, stepparent, father-in-law/mother-in-law, uncle/aunt, spouse, former spouse, spousal equivalent, domestic partner, brother/sister, stepsibling, brother-in-law/sister-in-law, cousin, son/daughter, stepchild, son-in-law/daughter-in law, nephew/niece, grandchild, and any other person the CFP® professional, directly or indirectly, supports financially to a material extent.

Financial Advice.

a. A communication that, based on its content, context, and presentation, would reasonably be viewed as a recommendation that the Client take or refrain from taking a particular course of action with respect to:

   i. The development or implementation of a financial plan;

   ii. The value of or the advisability of investing in, purchasing, holding, gifting, or selling Financial Assets;

   iii. Investment policies or strategies, portfolio composition, the management of Financial Assets, or other financial matters; or

   iv. The selection and retention of other persons to provide financial or Professional Services to the Client; or

b. The exercise of discretionary authority over the Financial Assets of a Client.

The determination of whether Financial Advice has been provided is an objective rather than subjective inquiry. The more individually tailored the communication is to the Client, the more likely the communication will be viewed as Financial Advice. The provision of services or the furnishing or making available of marketing materials, general financial education materials, or general financial communications that a reasonable CFP® professional would not view as Financial Advice, does not constitute Financial Advice.

Financial Assets. Securities, insurance products, real estate, bank instruments, commodities contracts, derivative contracts, collectibles, or other financial products.

Financial Planning. A collaborative process that helps maximize a Client's potential for meeting life goals through Financial Advice that integrates relevant elements of the Client's personal and financial circumstances.

Material. Information is material when a reasonable Client or prospective Client would consider the information important in making a decision.

Professional Services. Financial Advice and related activities and services that are offered or provided, including, but not limited to, Financial Planning, legal, accounting, or business planning services.

Related Party. A person or business entity (including a trust) whose receipt of Sales-Related Compensation a reasonable CFP® professional would view as benefiting the CFP® professional or the CFP® Professional's Firm, including, for example, as a result of the CFP® professional's ownership stake in the business entity. There is a rebuttable presumption that a Related Party includes:

a. **Family Members.** A member of the CFP® professional's Family and any business entity that the Family or members of the Family Control; and

b. **Business Entities.** A business entity that the CFP® professional or the CFP® Professional's Firm Controls, or that is Controlled by or is under common Control with, the CFP® Professional's Firm.

Scope of Engagement. The Professional Services to be provided pursuant to an Engagement.

Glossary

12b-1 fee *A fee that pays for the services of brokers who sell mutual funds and who maintain the client relationship*

Above-the-line deduction (deduction for AGI) *An above-the-line deduction that reduces gross income directly*

Absolute assignment *All life insurance policy ownership rights are transferred to a designated assignee*

Abstract thinking *The third phase of a client's thinking process in establishing financial direction, in which a client becomes aware of the consequences of financial actions and understands how day-to-day savings and consumption decisions impact a financial plan*

Accelerated death benefit rider *Allows the policyowner to receive a portion of the policy's death benefit during the insured's lifetime if the insured contracts a terminal illness*

Accidental bodily injury *Only the injury incurred is accidental*

Accidental death benefit rider *A policy rider that pays the beneficiary an additional death benefit if the insured dies accidentally, as defined in the rider*

Accumulation units *Units of measurement that, when combined, equal the total account value of a variable annuity*

Accuracy-related penalty *A penalty of 20% of the portion of the tax underpayment attributable to negligence, substantial understatement of tax, or substantial valuation misstatement without intent to defraud*

Active listening *Paying full attention to what clients are saying and responding by paraphrasing their comments, thus gaining a full understanding of what clients are attempting to communicate*

Active risk retention *One is fully aware of the chance for loss and consciously plans to retain all or part of the risk*

Activities of daily living (ADLs) *Eating, bathing, dressing, transferring from bed to chair, toileting, and continence*

Actual cash value (ACV) *The depreciated value of the insured property*

Actual cash value *Calculated as replacement cost minus functional depreciation*

Actuary *An expert in the fields of mathematics, statistics, and probability theory; responsible for predicting losses for various risk pools, calculating required reserves, and producing premium rates*

Additional living expenses *The difference between the cost of living in temporary arrangements and the normal costs that would have been incurred had there been no loss*

Additional Medicare tax *A Medicare tax of 0.9% paid by taxpayers above certain income thresholds that is in addition to the 2.9% Medicare tax*

Adhesion *A characteristic of insurance that means insurance is a take-it-or-leave-it contract. The proposed insured must accept (or adhere to) the contract as written without any bargaining over the terms and conditions*

Adjusted gross estate *Gross estate less deductions provided for by law in recognition that the entire value of the gross estate will not be transferred to the heirs due to costs, debts, and certain other deductions*

Adjusted gross income *A determination peculiar to individual taxpayers that represents gross income less business expenses, expenses attributable to the production of rent or royalty income, the allowed capital loss deduction, and certain personal expenses (deductions for AGI)*

Administrator *In the event a decedent dies intestate (without a valid will) or where an executor cannot be appointed by the probate court, the court appoints an administrator with powers called letters of administration, which enable the administrator to perform duties set down in the laws of intestacy*

Adult day care *Basic assistance and supervision provided outside the home usually during the primary caregiver's working hours*

Adverse selection *The increased tendency of higher-than-average risks (people who need insurance the most) purchasing or renewing insurance policies*

Age-based profit-sharing plan *A profit-sharing plan with an age-weighted factor in the allocation formula*

Agent *Legal representative of the insurer that has authority to enter into agreements on its behalf*

Aleatory *A characteristic of insurance meaning that monetary values exchanged by each party in an insurance agreement are unequal*

Alternative minimum tax (AMT) *System designed to ensure that individuals with large deductions and other tax benefits pay at least a minimum amount of tax*

American depositary receipts (ADRs) *Certificates issued by U.S. banks representing ownership in shares of stock of a foreign company that are held on deposit in a bank in the firm's home country*

American Opportunity Tax Credit *A tax credit available for qualified tuition, enrollment fees, books, and course materials for the first four years of post-secondary education for the taxpayer, spouse, or dependent*

Amortization table *TVM tool used primarily to illustrate the amortization, or extinguishments, of debt. The table presents the number of years of indebtedness, the beginning balance, level payments, interest amount, principal reduction, and ending balance of indebtedness.*

Annual exclusion *A result of a de minimis rule by Congress to eliminate the need for taxpayers to keep an account of, or report, small gifts. All individuals are allowed to gift, tax-free, up to $14,000 (for 2016) per donee per year.*

Annual Renewable Term (ART) *Term insurance issued for one year; renewable for subsequent periods to a stated age without evidence of insurability*

Annuitization *An irrevocable exchange of a lump-sum amount for a periodic income stream*

Annuity due *Deposits or payments are made at the beginning of each period*

Annuity *A series of deposits or payments of equal size deposited over a finite number of equal-interval periods*

Anomalies *Occurrences in the stock market that are not supported by the concept of the efficient market hypothesis*

Antitrust legislation *Laws passed to protect consumers from monopolistic price practices and to protect investors by promoting fair competition*

Any occupation *Definition of disability in which an insured is considered totally disabled if the duties of any occupation cannot be performed*

Apparent authority *The insured is led to believe that the agent has authority, either express or implied, where no such authority actually exists*

Arithmetic mean *A measure of investment return that is the result of averaging periodic returns*

Articles of organization *Document filed in compliance with state law to create a limited liability company (LLC)*

Asset allocation *The distribution of investments in a portfolio by asset class*

Asset-accumulation phase *Life cycle phase through which clients pass; usually begins between the ages of 20 and 25 and lasts until about age 50, characterized by limited excess funds for investing, high degree of debt, and low net worth*

Asset-backed securities *Bundled-together securities issued against some type of asset-linked debts, such as mortgages*

Assets *Property owned completely or partially by the client*

Assisted living facilities *Apartment-style housing combined with support services and basic health care*

At-risk rule *A taxpayer can deduct losses only to the extent of the amount the taxpayer has at risk in the investment (amount invested). Losses in amounts in excess of the amount at risk in the investment are suspended until the taxpayer increases the amount invested in the passive activity, either by additional investment or by a profit from the activity.*

Attorney-in-fact *The person designated by the principal in a power of attorney to act in place of the principal on the principal's behalf*

Audit *When the IRS examines a tax return "to determine if income, expenses, and credits are being reported accurately" (Publication 556)*

Automatic premium loan *Directs the insurance company to pay an overdue premium by making a loan against the policy's cash value if the overdue premium remains unpaid upon the expiration of the grace period*

Average indexed monthly earnings (AIME) *Dollar amount used to calculate Social Security benefits. Actual earnings are adjusted (or indexed) to calculate AIME.*

Back-end load *A sales charge incurred upon the sale or redemption of mutual fund shares rather than at the time of purchase*

Bailee *A party that holds the property of another*

Bait-and-switch promotion *Deceptive sales practice in which a business advertises a low price for an item in order to engage customers and then advise them that the advertised item is no longer available or is of substandard quality, attempting to entice the customers to purchase a more expensive product*

Balance sheet *A financial statement that reports a business's assets, liabilities, and net worth on a given date*

Bankruptcy *The financial condition when a debtor is determined by the court to be unable to pay creditors*

Barbell strategy *Portfolio immunization strategy that uses a portfolio of short- and long-term bonds*

Basic standard deduction *The amount allowed all taxpayers who do not itemize their deductions*

Behavioral finance *A branch of personal finance that proposes psychology-based theories to explain investor behavior and stock market anomalies*

Below-the-line deduction (deduction from AGI) *Deduction that is allowed to reduce adjusted gross income*

Bend points *The three separate percentages of portions of the AIME that are summed to arrive at the PIA*

Benefit period *The number of days that Medicare covers care in hospitals and skilled nursing facilities*

Benefits of personal financial planning

- *Creates a framework for feedback, evaluation, and control*
- *Develops an improved awareness of financial choices*
- *Establishes measurable goals and expectations*
- *Goals identified are more likely to be achieved*
- *Helps to clearly identify risk exposures*
- *Is proactive rather than reactive*
- *Provides an opportunity for an increased commitment to financial goals*

Best efforts agreement *Equity underwriting in which the firm agrees to repurchase any securities remaining after the initial offering is made by the underwriter*

Beta *A commonly used measure of systematic risk that is derived from regression analysis*

Beyond a reasonable doubt *A measure or degree of proof; with regard to disciplinary rules and procedures, beyond a reasonable doubt means the evidence as a whole shows what it was intended to prove with a probability of 99% or more*

Blackout period *The period of time beginning when Social Security benefits to the surviving spouse are discontinued (usually when the last child reaches age 16) and ending when the spouse begins to receive Social Security retirement benefits at age 60 or later*

Blue-chip stocks *Stock issued by older, well-established companies that maintain the ability to pay dividends both in years the company has income and in years the company has losses*

Board of directors *The governing body of a corporation whose members are elected by shareholders*

Bodily injury by accidental means *Requires accidental injury by accidental means*

Bond indenture agreement *The legal document that sets forth the repayment schedules, restrictions, and promises between the issuer of a corporate bond and the borrower*

Boot *Property (other than like-kind property) that qualifies as a tax gain when received in a property exchange*

Broker *Legal representative of the insured who can offer products from many insurers*

Budgeting *A process of projecting, monitoring, adjusting, and controlling future income and expenditures*

Bullet strategy *Portfolio immunization strategy that uses a portfolio of bonds with similar maturities*

Burden of proof *The requirement of proving facts to a certain degree of probability. With regard to disciplinary rules and procedures, there are three distinct burdens of proof: (1) preponderance of the evidence, (2) clear and convincing evidence, and (3) evidence beyond a reasonable doubt.*

Business cycles *Swings in total national output, income, and employment marked by widespread expansion or contraction in many sectors of the economy*

Business overhead expense insurance *Helps a business meet its liabilities in the event a significant income producer becomes disabled*

Business risk *An unsystematic risk based on predictability of operating income for a specific business; dependent upon management and industry characteristics*

Buy-sell agreement *An arrangement in which a deceased owner's share of a business is purchased by using the life insurance proceeds from a policy on the deceased owner's life*

Bypass trust (B trust) *Avoids inclusion in, or bypasses, the surviving spouse's gross estate; the assets transfer to a future generation free of estate taxes; the purpose of a bypass trust is to take advantage of the applicable credit amount*

C corporation *A business entity created by state law that is separate and distinct from its shareholders*

Call option *A derivative that gives the holder the right to purchase the underlying asset, generally a stock, at a specified price within a specified period*

Call provision *Right to redeem the bond issue before maturity*

Capital appreciation *The form of return the investor receives when a company chooses to retain the earnings and invest in additional projects; appreciation of the stock*

Capital asset pricing model (CAPM) *An asset pricing model that developed from Markowitz's efficient frontier and from the introduction of a risk-free asset*

Capital asset *Broadly speaking, all assets are capital except those specifically excluded by the Internal Revenue Code; excluded assets include property held for resale in the normal course of business (inventory), trade accounts and notes receivable, and depreciable property and real estate used in a trade or business*

Capital formation *Production of buildings, machinery, tools, and other equipment that will help economic participants produce in the future*

Capital loss *A loss from the sale or exchange of a capital asset*

Capital needs analysis *The process of calculating the amount of investment capital needed at retirement to maintain the desired lifestyle and mitigate the impact of inflation during the retirement years*

Capital preservation (CP) model *A capital needs analysis method that assumes that at life expectancy, the client has exactly the same account balance as the client did at retirement*

Capital retention approach *Provides a death benefit amount that, along with the family's other assets, is sufficient to provide a level of investment income that covers the projected needs of the family without having to invade the death benefit principal*

Cash accounts *A type of brokerage account that requires all securities purchased by the investor to be paid for in full without any indebtedness*

Cash flow timeline *TVM analysis tool that graphically depicts cash inflows (cash received) and cash outflows (cash deposited or invested) over a certain period (the term)*

Cash flows from financing *Cash inflows from a business's issuance of additional debt (bonds) or equity (stocks) and cash outflows for the repayment of debt (principal)*

Cash flows from investing *Cash inflows or outflows resulting from a business's buying and selling of investments*

Cash flows from operations *Cash inflows or outflows that are generated by a company's actual business activities as opposed to incidental activities such as investing or borrowing*

Cash refund annuity *When an annuitant dies before periodic payments equal or exceed the price paid for the annuity, the insurer pays a lump sum equal to the difference between the price paid and the total payments received by the annuitant*

Cash value *Increases over the life of the policy as long as the premiums are paid according to the contract*

Certified Financial Planner Board of Standards, Inc. *An independent professional regulatory organization that regulates financial planners*

CFP Board's Board of Directors *The governing board for the certified financial planning profession*

CFP Board's Disciplinary and Ethics Commission *A subsidiary board of CFP Board that interprets and applies the Code*

CFP Board's Standards of Professional Conduct *The set of principles of conduct that regulates behavior of CFP® certificants*

CFP® certificant *An individual who is currently certified by CFP Board*

Change in demand *This occurs when the entire curve shifts to the right or left as the quantity demanded at each price level changes*

Changes in quantity demanded *The movements along the demand curve in response to a change in price*

Charitable deduction *A charitable contribution made as a gift to a qualified organization*

Charitable lead trust (CLT) *A split-interest trust where a charity is the income beneficiary, and there is a noncharitable remainderman*

Charitable remainder trust (CRT) *A split-interest trust; if created during life, the income goes to one or more parties, usually the grantor, or grantor and spouse for life, and upon the income beneficiary's death, the principal (remainder) is transferred to a charity; if the CRT is created testamentary, the usual income beneficiary is the spouse for life*

Chronically ill individual *A person who has an illness or injury resulting in the inability to perform, without substantial assistance, at least two of the six activities of daily living for a period expected to last at least 90 days*

Clear and convincing evidence *A measure or degree of proof; with regard to disciplinary rules and procedures, clear and convincing evidence means the evidence as a whole shows what it was intended to prove with a probability of 75% or more*

Client data collection questionnaire *A survey used by financial planners to gather internal data from clients, such as their tolerance for risk and their personal perception of their financial situation, as well as tax-related data, Social Security numbers, information relating to their dependents, and so on*

Closed-end fund *A type of investment company whose shares trade in the same manner that publicly traded stocks trade in the secondary market*

Code of ethics *A set of principles of conduct that governs a group of individuals and usually requires conformity to professional standards of conduct*

Codicil *A document that amends or revises a prior will*

Coefficient of determination (R2) *A modern portfolio theory statistic that indicates the percentage change in a portfolio or mutual fund that can be explained by changes in the market*

Coefficient of variation *A relative measure of total risk per unit of expected return*

Coinsurance *The cost sharing of covered health care expenses between the insured and the insurer*

Coinsurance *The percentage of financial responsibility the insured and the insurer must share under the policy*

COLA *Cost-of-living adjustment provided for Social Security benefits*

Collateral assignment split dollar *An arrangement in which an employer is obligated to make interest-free loans to the employee in the amount of the policy premium; the employee then makes a collateral assignment of the policy to the employer for the amount of premium paid by the employer*

Collateral assignment *A life insurance policy is transferred to a creditor as security for a loan or debt*

Collateral source rule *Damages assessed against a negligent party should not be reduced simply because the injured party has other sources of recovery available*

Collateral trust bonds *Bonds secured by securities issued by other companies*

Collateralized mortgage obligations (CMOs) *Mortgage-backed securities that are divided into tranches*

College Savings Plan *A type of QTP similar to Coverdell Education Savings Accounts (Coverdell ESAs) where the owner of the account (the parent or grandparent of the student) contributes cash to the account so that the contributions can grow tax-deferred and, hopefully, realize a higher return on the investment than could be achieved outside of the plan*

Collision *Auto insurance coverage that protects the insured against upset and collision damages*

Commercial package policy (CPP) *Property and liability coverage combined into a single policy used by businesses*

Commingling *The act of mixing property (usually funds) belonging to one party with property belong to another party*

Common law liability *Liability based on breach of contract, tort, or fraud*

Common stock *Ownership interest in a company*

Community property *A regime where married individuals own an equal undivided interest in all wealth accumulated during marriage*

Complements *Products that are usually consumed jointly; an increase in the price of one will likely decrease the demand for the other*

Compound interest *Interest earned on interest*

Comprehensive (other-than-collision) *Auto insurance coverage that protects the insured's auto against perils out of the insured's control, such as missiles or falling objects, fire, theft, earthquake, hail, flood, and vandalism*

Comprehensive major medical *Stand-alone coverage that provides a broad range of medical services and high limits of coverage*

Concealment *When the insured is silent about a fact that is material to the risk*

Conditional *Insurer is only obligated to compensate the insured if certain conditions are met*

Conditionally renewable *Cannot be canceled by the insurer during the policy term, but insurer may refuse to renew the contract for another term if certain conditions exist*

Conflict of interest *Exists when a certificant's financial, business, property, and/or personal interests, relationships, or circumstances impair the certificant's ability to offer objective advice, recommendations, or services*

Conservation/protection phase *Life cycle phase through which clients pass characterized by an increase in cash flow, assets, and net worth, with some decrease in the proportional use of debt*

Consolidated Omnibus Budget Reconciliation Act (COBRA) *Requires certain employers to provide previously covered persons with the same coverage received before discontinuation of coverage*

Consolidation loan *A loan that provides borrowers with a way to consolidate various types of federal student loans with separate repayment schedules into one loan*

Consumer Price Index (CPI) *A price index that measures the cost of a market basket of consumer goods and services purchased for day-to-day living*

Consumption movements *Economic variables that fluctuate during the business cycle; describe changes in consumer purchases*

Contingent beneficiary *An individual, group, or entity designated to receive the policy proceeds if the primary beneficiary predeceases the insured*

Contraction phase *One of the two general business cycle phases characterized by a fall in business sales, decreased growth of the gross domestic product, and increased unemployment*

Contractual agreements *Often include guarantees at the time of sale; often known as warranties*

Convertible bonds *Hybrid securities that permit the holder to acquire shares of common stock from the issuing company by exchanging the currently held debt security for a specific number of common stock shares*

Convertible preferred stock *Preferred stock that includes the right to convert preferred stock into a specific number of common shares at the option of the stockholder*

Convertible *A term policy that may be exchanged for a cash value life insurance policy without evidence of insurability*

Coordination of benefits (COB) clause *Prevents an insured from receiving greater than 100% of the cost of health care received when covered by multiple insurance policies*

Co-payments *In health insurance policies, amounts an insured must pay in addition to the deductible to receive certain covered services*

Correlation coefficient (R) *A statistical measure of the direction and strength of the relationship between two sets of data*

Correspondence audit *An audit conducted almost entirely by written correspondence and telephone contact with the taxpayer and typically involves simple issues*

Cost-of-living adjustment (COLA) rider *Increases benefits being received by the policyowner each year; based on an index, such as the CPI*

Country risk *An unsystematic risk associated with the potential adverse effect of changes in a country's laws or political situation*

Coupon payments *Interest payments paid to the bondholder on a semiannual basis and based on a percentage of the par value of the bond*

Covariance *A measure of the extent to which two variables move in a predictable manner to one another, either positively or negatively*

Coverdell Education Savings Account (Coverdell ESA) *An investment account established with cash contributions that grow tax-free within the account; money withdrawn from the account remains free from tax or penalty if the funds are used for higher education expenses; if not, the earnings are subject to income tax and a 10% penalty*

Cross-purchase agreement *Each owner of the corporation purchases an insurance policy on the other shareholders; the death proceeds are used to purchase a deceased owner's shares*

Cumulative preferred stock *Preferred stock that requires receipt of previously unpaid preferred dividends before common shareholders receive dividend payments*

Cumulative voting *A shareholder casts votes equal to the number of vacant positions on the board of directors multiplied by the number of shares owned, allocated in any way the shareholder wishes*

Current assets *Assets expected to be converted to cash within one year*

Current assumption whole life *Uses new-money interest rates and current mortality assumptions to determine cash values*

Current liability *Debt owed by the client that is expected to be paid off within the year (current ≤ 12 months)*

Current yield *A bond's annual coupon payment divided by the current market price*

Custodial care *Provides assistance with the regular tasks of daily life, such as eating, dressing, bathing, and taking medications*

Cyclical stocks *Stock of companies that tend to prosper in expanding economies and do poorly during down business cycles*

Debentures *Unsecured corporate bonds whose holders have no claim to specific assets of the issuing corporation*

Declaration date *Date on which a corporation's board of directors declares a dividend payment creating an obligation on the company to make a dividend payment to shareholders*

Decreasing term *Term insurance that features a level premium with a decreasing death benefit*

Deductible *A stated amount of money the insured is required to pay on a loss before the insurer will make any payments under the policy*

Default risk *An unsystematic risk associated with the inability of a business to service its debt*

Defensive stocks *Stock of companies that are relatively unaffected by general fluctuations in the economy*

Deferred annuity *Provides income at some date in the future*

Deferred compensation plan *A nonqualified plan that is a contractual agreement between the employer and selected employees; takes the form of either salary reduction or salary continuation. Compensation is deferred until retirement, disability, death, or termination of employment, but usually only at normal retirement age.*

Deferred income annuities (DIA) *Guarantee income for life or a certain period of time, however, the future income start dates are chosen at contract issuance*

Deficit spending *Occurs when governmental expenditures exceed the government's tax collections*

Defined benefit pension plan *A retirement plan that specifies the benefits that each employee receives at retirement. Defined benefit plans actuarially determine the benefit to be paid at normal retirement age.*

Defined contribution plan *A retirement plan that specifies the annual employer current contribution. The amount of benefit received by an employee depends on the account balance at retirement.*

Defined-period approach *Long-term care coverage provided for a specified period following an elimination period*

Deflation *The opposite of inflation; it occurs when the general level of prices is falling*

Demand curve *The graphic depiction that illustrates the relationship between a particular good's price and the quantity demanded*

Demand *The quantity of a particular good that people are willing to buy; heavily dependent on price*

Dependency period *The period of time during which others (the deceased's spouse, children and, in some cases, parents) would have been dependent on the deceased*

Dependent *An individual who meets the definition of a qualifying child or a qualifying relative and who can be claimed by a taxpayer for an exemption on an income tax return*

Depression *A persistent recession that brings a severe decline in economic activity*

Derivatives *Securities whose value is based on the value of some other security*

Determination Letter *A written statement issued by an IRS district director that applies the principles and precedents announced by the National Office to a given set of facts*

Direct bequest (to a spouse) *The first spouse who dies leaves everything outright to the surviving spouse*

Direct investing *A process of investing where investors purchase actual securities*

Direct negligence *Involves acts or omissions directly attributable to an individual*

Directors *Individuals who, acting as a group known as the board of directors, manage the business affairs of a corporation*

Disability benefit *Social Security benefit available to recipients who have a severe physical or mental impairment that is expected to prevent them from performing substantial work for at least one year or result in death, and who have the sufficient amount of Social Security credits*

Disability income insurance *A type of insurance that provides a replacement income while the insured is unable to work because of illness or injury*

Disciplinary Rules and Procedures *The rules and regulations for disciplinary proceedings against CFP Board certificants*

Disclaimer clause *A common clause in a decedent's will that allows property to pass from one party to another without gift tax consequences*

Disclaimer *The refusal of the receipt of an estate; the use of disclaimers allows an individual to disclaim or renounce receiving any part of an estate*

Discount rate *Interest rate charged by the Federal Reserve on a loan made to a member bank*

Discretionary expenses *Luxuries or expenses over which the client has complete control*

Discriminant Index Function (DIF) system *A mathematical technique used to classify tax returns as to their examination potential*

Disinflation *A decline in the rate of inflation*

Distribution/gifting phase *Life cycle phase through which clients pass characterized by excess relative cash flows, low debt, and high relative net worth*

Dividend reinvestment plans (DRIPs) *Dividends are automatically reinvested into the company's stock without the use of a broker*

Dividend yield *The measure of a security's annual dividend payment as a percentage of the current market price*

Dividends *Distributions of cash or additional shares of stock paid to the shareholders of a corporation*

Dividends-received deduction (DRD) *A deduction for dividends received by one corporation from another corporation. The amount of the DRD is based on the percentage owned by the corporation receiving the dividend.*

Dollar cost averaging *The process of purchasing securities over time by investing a predetermined amount at regular intervals*

Dollar-weighted returns *A method of determining the internal rate of return that an individual investor earned on the basis of the investor's particular cash flow into and out of the portfolio*

Double taxation of dividends *The taxation of income at the corporate level and the subsequent taxation of dividend distributions at the individual shareholder's level*

Dow Jones Industrial Average (DJIA) *A financial index that is a price-weighted average of 30 leading industrial stocks used to measure the status of the equity market*

Durable feature *The power survives incapacity and disability of the principal*

Durable goods *Products that are not consumed or quickly disposed of and can be used for several years, such as automobiles, furniture, and computers*

Durable power of attorney issued either for health care or for property *A written document enabling the principal to designate another person or persons to act as the principal's attorney-in-fact*

Duration *Provides a time-weighted measure of a security's cash flows in terms of payback*

Dwelling *Residential structure covered under a homeowners policy*

Dynamic risk *A risk that results from changes in society or the economy (e.g., inflation)*

Efficient frontier *Consists of investment portfolios with the highest expected return for a given level of risk*

Efficient market hypothesis *A theory that suggests that securities are priced fairly and efficiently by the market, and investors are unable to consistently outperform the market on a risk-adjusted basis*

Elimination period *The amount of time that must pass before benefits are paid*

Emotional intelligence *The ability to recognize and assess emotional expressions in themselves and their clients*

Employer's Educational Assistance Program *Under this program, an employer can pay for an employee's undergraduate tuition, enrollment fees, books, supplies, and equipment while these employer benefits are excluded from the employee's income up to $5,250*

Endorsement split dollar *An arrangement in which the employer owns the policy and is responsible for making all premium payments; when the insured employee dies, the employer receives a portion of the death benefit equal to its premium outlay, with the remainder of the death proceeds payable to the employee's designated beneficiary*

Engagement letter *A tool of communication between client and financial planner that sets down in writing the information about any agreements or understandings obtained at client/planner meetings, including the plan of action for developing a financial plan, the expected outcome of the engagement, and the method of compensation*

Entire contract clause *Maintains that the life insurance policy and the policyowner's application compose the complete life insurance contract*

Entity purchase agreement *The corporation owns policies on the lives of the shareholders; at the death of a shareholder, the corporation buys the deceased shareholder's interest in the company with the insurance proceeds*

Equilibrium *The state of the market where quantity demanded equals quantity supplied*

Equity indexed annuities (EIAs) *Based on the simple concept of returns that are equal to a percentage, or participation rate, of a popular market index (e.g., S&P 500)*

Equity mutual funds *A mutual fund that invests primarily in equity or ownership type securities, such as preferred stock and common stock*

Equity-indexed universal life (EIUL) *A universal life policy that offers an upside potential for cash value growth with limited downside risk*

Errors and omissions insurance *Provides protection against loss from negligent acts, errors, and omissions by the insured*

Ethics *The discipline of dealing with the moral principles or values that guide an individual*

Exchange rate risk *A systematic risk due to the potential change in the relationship between the value of the dollar (or investor's currency) and the value of the foreign currency during the period of investment; also known as foreign currency risk*

Exchange *Transfer of property for property other than money*

Exchange-traded fund (ETF) *A type of investment company whose investment objective is to achieve the same return as a particular market index*

Exclusion *Income exempt from tax and not included in a taxpayer's gross income*

Ex-dividend date *The date on which the market reflects the dividend payment*

Executive bonus plan *A discriminatory fringe benefit that provides life insurance to key employees with tax-deductible dollars*

Exercise price *The price at which an underlying stock may be sold (put) or purchased (call) by the holder of an option*

Expansion phase *One of the two general business cycle phases characterized by a rise in business sales, growth of the gross domestic product, and a decline in unemployment*

Expected Family Contribution (EFC) *A formula that indicates how much of a student's family's resources ought to be available to assist in paying for the student's college education*

Expense ratio *An indication of the annual fund expenses, stated as a percentage of total assets*

Express authority *The actual authority an insurance company gives representatives (agents) via the agent's written contract*

External environment *The whole complex of factors independent of the client that influence the financial planning process, including economic, legal, social, technological, political, and taxation factors*

External environmental analysis *The process of identifying and monitoring the environment in which a client lives and the opportunities and threats that are present*

Failure-to-file penalty *A civil penalty imposed on taxpayers and tax return preparers who fail to file tax returns according to the requirements of tax law*

Failure-to-pay-tax penalty *A civil penalty imposed on taxpayers who, without reasonable cause, fail to pay the tax shown on their return*

Fair market value (FMV) *The price at which an exchange will take place between a willing buyer and a willing seller, both informed and neither under duress to exchange*

Family benefit *Social Security benefit available to certain family members of workers eligible for retirement or disability benefits*

Family limited partnership (FLP) *A limited partnership of family members that is used to generate valuation discounts for estate and gift tax purposes on the transfer of the limited interest in the partnership*

Federal estate tax *An excise tax on the right to transfer assets by a decedent*

Federal Perkins Loan *Campus-based, low-interest student loan provided to undergraduate and graduate students that have exceptional financial need—that is, very low EFCs*

Federal Reserve (Fed) *The banking and financial system developed under the Federal Reserve Act of 1913; it makes the basic policy decisions that regulate the country's money and banking systems*

Federal Reserve discount rate *The rate at which Federal Reserve member banks can borrow funds to meet reserve requirements; the Fed will lower the discount rate when it wants to increase the money supply*

Federal Supplemental Education Opportunity Grant (FSEOG) *Campus-based student financial aid grant awarded to undergraduate students with low EFCs that gives priority to students who receive federal Pell Grants*

Federal Trade Commission (FTC) *The federal organization created in 1914 to keep competition free and fair and to protect U.S. consumers*

Federal Work-Study Program *Campus-based student financial aid program that enables undergraduate and graduate students to earn money for education expenses through jobs that pay at least current minimum wages but do not exceed the award received through the program*

Fee simple *The complete individual ownership of property with all rights associated with outright ownership, such as the right to use, sell, gift, alienate, or convey*

FICA (Federal Insurance Contributions Act) *The law allowing Social Security taxes, including Medicare, to be deducted from paychecks*

Fiduciary *Someone who acts in utmost good faith, in a manner he believes is in the best interest of the client*

Field audit *An audit conducted for complex individual returns with business or other financial activities. IRS revenue agents handle field audits, as opposed to office audits, which are conducted by less-experienced tax auditors and are typically conducted at the taxpayer's business or wherever the taxpayer's books are maintained.*

Final expense fund *Fund requiring immediate access by survivors to pay for final expenses and debts of the decedent*

Financial Accounting Standards Board (FASB) *Nongovernmental board that sets the standards for financial statements and generally accepted accounting principles (GAAP)*

Financial goals *High-level statements of financial desires that may be for the short or the long term*

Financial mission *A broad and enduring statement that identifies the client's long-term purpose for wanting a financial plan*

Financial mission *Broad and enduring statement that identifies the client's long-term purpose for creating a financial plan*

Financial needs approach *Evaluates the income replacement needs of one's survivors in the event of untimely death*

Financial objectives *Statements of financial desire that contain time and measurement attributes, making them more specific than financial goals*

Financial phases *These phases include the asset accumulation phase, the conservation/protection phase, and the distribution/gifting phase*

Financial risk *A risk that involves a monetary loss*

Financial risk *An unsystematic risk based on the inclusion of debt in the capital structure of a firm, which affects the return on equity (ROE) for a company*

Financial success *For most individuals, financial success means accomplishing one's financial goals*

Firm commitment *Equity underwriting in which the underwriter purchases the entire issue at a specific price from the firm and resells it on the open market*

First-to-die policy *Pays the face amount upon the first death of two or more insureds*

Fiscal policy *Taxation, expenditures, and debt management of the federal government*

Fixed annuity *Insurer agrees to credit a specified interest rate over a stated period*

Fixed outflows/expenses *Outflows that remain constant over a period of time and over which the client has little control*

Fixed-amount option *Specifies that a designated amount of income will be provided to the beneficiary on a regular basis until the proceeds and accumulated interest are depleted*

Fixed-income (or bond) mutual funds *A mutual fund that invests in fixed-income securities ranging in maturity of several months to 30 years or longer. Bond funds invest in numerous bond issues to diversify the investment portfolio from default risk.*

Fixed-income securities *Securities with specified payment dates and amounts, primarily bonds*

Fixed-period option *The beneficiary will receive the maximum periodic payments that the death benefit proceeds will purchase for a specified period*

Flexible premium annuity *Allows the insured the option to vary premium deposits*

Flexible spending account (FSA) *An account typically funded by employee salary reductions that allows employees the benefit of paying for their health-care-related expenses with pretax income*

Flow-through or conduit entity *A type of business entity in which the results of business operations are reported directly on the owner's income tax return*

Foreign closed-end funds *Closed-end funds that invest in foreign firms*

Foreign funds *Securities that provide investors with the easiest method of investing in foreign markets in the context of a diversified portfolio*

Foreign securities *Securities issued by non-U.S. firms*

Forfeitures *Employer contributions that are not fully vested and thus revert to the employer in the event that an employee terminates service*

Fourth market *Composed of institutional traders who trade without the help of brokers*

Fraud penalty *A penalty levied against a taxpayer by the IRS after it has proven an underpayment of tax by the taxpayer and proven that the underpayment was attributable to a willful attempt to evade tax*

Free Application for Federal Student Aid (FAFSA) *An application form that must be submitted by a college student to become eligible for federal financial aid*

Free cash flow to equity *Term that describes the available cash after meeting all of the firm's operating and financial needs; used to calculate the value a company*

Front-end load *A sales charge based on the initial investment into a mutual fund*

Fundamental analysis *The analysis of a stock's value using basic, publicly available data, such as the stock's earnings, sales, risk, and industry analysis*

Fundamental risk *An impersonal risk that involves a possible loss for a large group*

Future value of an annuity due *The future value to which a series of deposits of equal size will amount when deposited over a definite number of equal-interval periods, based on a defined interest rate, and the deposits are made at the beginning of each period*

Future value of an ordinary annuity *The future amount to which a series of deposits of equal size will equal when deposited over a finite number of equal-interval periods, based on a defined interest rate, when the deposits are made at the end of each period*

Future value *The future dollar amount to which a sum certain today will increase compounded at a defined interest rate over a period of time*

Futures contract *An agreement between two parties to make or take delivery of a specified amount of a commodity or financial asset at a future time, place, and unit price*

Galloping inflation *Inflation that occurs when money loses its value very quickly, and real interest rates can be negative 50% or 100% per year*

General agent *An independent businessperson who represents only one insurer for a designated territory*

General obligation bonds *A municipal bond backed by the full faith, credit, and taxing power of the municipality*

General partnership *A type of business entity owned entirely by general partners, each of whom can act on behalf of the partnership*

Generation-skipping transfer tax (GSTT) *A tax in addition to the unified gift and estate tax designed to tax large transfers that skip a generation (i.e., from grandparent to grandchild)*

Geometric mean *A method of calculating the internal rate of return based on periodic rates of return*

Gift *In estate planning, a direct transfer of property or cash made during life*

Goals *High-level statements of financial desire that may be for the short term or the long term*

Good-till-canceled order *An order to buy or sell a security at a specific or limit price that lasts until the order is completed or canceled*

Grace period *Amount of time following the premium due date in which the policyowner may pay the overdue premium*

Gross domestic product (GDP) *The value of all goods and services produced in the country; GDP is the broadest measure of the general state of the economy*

Gross estate *All assets included in a decedent's estate, including but not limited to cash, stocks, bonds, annuities, retirement accounts, notes receivable, personal residences, automobiles, art collections, life insurance proceeds, and income tax refunds due*

Gross income *The Internal Revenue Code Section 61(a)defines gross income as "all income from whatever source derived"*

Group supplemental plans *Often attached to basic medical expense coverage, these policies allow the employer to use more than one provider for coverage, offer first-dollar coverage, or use different contribution rates for basic and supplemental coverage*

Growth stocks *Stock issued by companies whose sales, earnings, and market share are growing at higher rates than the average or the general economy*

Guaranteed renewable *The insurer is required to renew the policy for a specified period, regardless of changes in the insured's health (premiums may be increased) by class of insureds*

Hazard *A condition that creates or increases the likelihood of a loss occurring*

Head of household *The filing status that identifies a taxpayer as an unmarried individual who maintains a household for another and satisfies certain conditions set forth in the Internal Revenue Code*

Health savings account (HSA) *Special account that is used to pay for current and future medical expenses in conjunction with a high-deductible health plan (HDHP)*

Hearing panel *Panel that establishes the rules of procedures and evidence to be observed at a complaint hearing seeking disciplinary action against a certificant*

Hedge funds *An unregistered, privately offered, managed pool of capital for wealthy, financially sophisticated investors*

Hedging *A means of trying to match profit on one transaction to the expected loss of another*

Heir *One who inherits; beneficiary*

High-deductible health plan (HDHP) *A health plan, often used in conjunction with a health savings account (HSA); the HSA is used to pay for expenses up to the deductible amount*

Holding period return *Measures the total return an investor receives over a specific time period*

Holographic will *Handwritten will dated and signed by the testator*

Home health care *Part-time skilled nursing care and rehabilitative therapy provided at the patient's home*

Homeowners insurance *A package insurance policy that provides both property and liability coverage for the insured dwelling, other structures, personal property, and loss of use*

Hospice care *Care that provides dignity and comfort to terminally ill patients*

Hospital expense insurance *Provides payment for expenses incurred by the insured while in the hospital*

Housing costs *Principal and interest to pay the mortgage loan, real estate taxes, and homeowners insurance*

Human life value approach *Uses projected future earnings as the basis for measuring life insurance needs*

Hybrid (or balanced) mutual funds *A mutual fund that invests in a combination of cash, fixed-income securities, and equity securities*

Immediate annuity *One in which the first annuity payment is made one payment interval from the purchase date*

Immunization *Minimizing the impact of changes in interest rates on the value of investments*

Implied authority *The authority that the public reasonably perceives the agent to possess, even without express authority*

Income statement *A financial statement that reports a business's income and expenses over a given period*

Income stock *Stock issued by companies in the maturity phase of the industry life cycle and that pay out the majority of their earnings in the form of dividends*

Incontestability clause *Prevents the insurer from canceling the policy after it has been in force for two years in the event the life insurer discovers material misrepresentation or concealment*

Incorporation *Results in limited liability for businessowners*

Independent agent *An agent that represents multiple insurers*

Index of leading economic indicators *A composite index of 10 variables that has had a reasonable track record in predicting recessions; it has accurately predicted every recession since 1950 but has also predicted five that did not happen*

Indifference curves *A graphical representation of the risk-reward trade-off that an investor is willing to make*

Indirect investing *A process of investing where investors invest in companies that invest directly in securities*

Inflation *An increase in the price level of goods and services*

Inflows *All monies received from employment, investments, and other sources*

Information ratio *A ratio of expected return to risk as measured by standard deviation that seeks to quantify the amount of incremental risk undertaken by a portfolio manager to achieve an excess return*

Initial public offering (IPO) *First offering of equity securities to the general public*

Installment payment method *The policyowner receives the cash value and accrued interest over a period, usually in fixed amounts*

Installment refund annuity *The insurer promises to continue periodic payments after the annuitant has died until the sum of all annuity payments equals the purchase price of the annuity*

Insurance *A mechanism through which risk is transferred to an insurer, evidenced by a promise to pay, in exchange for an equitable premium*

Intentional interference *Intentional act committed against another that causes injury*

Interest rate risk *A systematic risk where changes in interest rates will affect the value of securities*

Interest-only option *The insurance company retains the death benefit and pays the primary beneficiary interest on that sum*

Interest-sensitive stock *Stock issued by companies whose performance is largely affected by changes in interest rates*

Intermediate nursing care *Occasional nursing and rehabilitative care ordered and monitored by a physician*

Internal rate of return (IRR) *The discount rate that causes cash inflows to equal cash outflows, thus allowing comparison of rates of return on alternative investments*

Internal rate of return *A measure of return that equates discounted future cash flows to the present value of an asset*

Internal Revenue Bulletin (IRB) *Announces official rulings and procedures of the IRS and publishes Treasury Decisions, Executive Orders, Tax Conventions, legislation, court decisions, and other items of general interest*

Intestacy laws *State laws that direct how a decedent's property will be distributed when the decedent dies without a will*

Intestate *To die without a valid will*

Investment companies *Financial services companies that sell shares of stock to the public and use the proceeds to invest in a portfolio of securities*

Investment policy statement *A written document that sets forth a client's objectives, as well as limitations on the investment manager*

Irrevocable beneficiary *Cannot be changed without the beneficiary's consent*

Itemized deductions *Deductions in excess of the standard deduction that are used in lieu of the standard deduction*

Jensen's alpha *An absolute measure of performance indicating how the actual performance of an investment compares with the expected performance*

Joint and last survivor income option *Provides joint beneficiaries a stated amount of income during their lives, and a continuation of the original or reduced amount for the remaining beneficiaries' lives*

Joint and survivor annuity *Based on the lives of two or more annuitants*

Joint life *Covers two or more lives under one policy at a cost lower than premiums for multiple separate policies*

Joint tenancy *Two or more persons, called equal owners, hold the same fractional interest in a property*

Keogh plan *A qualified plan for unincorporated businesses*

Key person life insurance *After the death of a key employee, used to recruit and train a replacement and compensate the company for lost business*

Ladder strategy *Portfolio immunization strategy that uses a portfolio of bonds with staggered maturities*

Lagging economic indicators *Economic statistics that fall or rise 3–12 months after the general economy*

Last-to-die policy *Makes a death benefit payment upon the last death of multiple insureds*

Law of diminishing marginal utility *As the rate of consumption increases, the marginal utility derived from consuming additional units of a good will decline*

Law of large numbers *The chance that predicted results will reflect true results increases as the number of exposures increases*

Law *Rules of conduct established by a government or other authority that command and encourage behavior considered right and prohibit behavior considered wrong*

Learning styles [auditory, visual, kinetic (or tactile)] *The conditions under which people learn best. Clients whose preferred learning style is auditory learn best by hearing information; clients who prefer a visual learning style learn best by reading and viewing; those who prefer a kinetic, or tactile, style learn best through manipulation and testing information*

Legal reserve *A fund that is accumulated and maintained by the insurer to meet future obligations, such as administrative expenses and mortality charges*

Lending securities *Securities wherein the investor lends funds to the issuer in exchange for a promise of a stream of periodic interest payments and a repayment of the loaned principal at maturity*

Letter Ruling *A written statement issued by the National Office of the IRS that gives guidance on the way the IRS will treat a prospective or contemplated transaction for tax purposes*

Level term *A policy with a level death benefit and a fixed level premium for a stated period*

Liability *Money owed by the client*

Libel *Written statement that causes harm to another*

Life annuity with period certain *Guarantees the greater of a life income to the annuitant or a minimum number of payments to the annuitant's beneficiary*

Life cycle phases *Intervals in a client's life cycle that tend to give a planner insight into the client's financial objectives and concerns (asset-accumulation, conservation/protection, and distribution/gifting phases)*

Life cycle positioning *Using information about a client's age, marital status, dependents, income level, and net worth to help determine goals and risks*

Life estate *An interest in property that ceases upon the death of the owner of the life interest or estate*

Life income option *Allows the beneficiary to receive a specified periodic payment, usually for life*

Life income with period certain option *Provides an income to the beneficiary for life or a specified period, if longer*

Life income with refund option *The life insurance company agrees that if the primary beneficiary dies before the total amount paid under the option equals the proceeds of the policy, the company will pay the difference to a contingent beneficiary*

Lifetime Learning Credit *A tax credit available to pay for tuition and enrollment fees for undergraduate or graduate degree programs*

Limit order *Type of securities order that requires the trade be made at a specified price or better*

Limited liability company (LLC) *A relatively new and versatile form of business entity created under state law by filing articles of organization*

Limited liability partnership (LLP) *A form of business entity similar to a general partnership, except that an LLP provides additional liability protection to the partners*

Limited partnership *In a limited partnership, limited partners are not allowed to participate in the management of operations but generally are allowed to vote on major changes affecting the structure of the partnership*

Limited-payment policy *Permanent life insurance for which premiums are payable for a limited number of years, after which the policy becomes paid up for its stated face amount*

Linear thinking *The initial phase of a client's thinking process when setting financial direction in which a client focuses on accomplishing one particular goal or narrow objective using a very compartmentalized, simplistic, self-designed financial plan*

Liquidity preference theory *Yield curve theory asserting long term bonds have greater yields to compensate investors for increased interest rate risk*

Liquidity *The ability to sell an investment quickly and at a competitive price, with no loss of principal and little price concession*

Living benefits rider *Gives the policyowner access to a portion of the policy's eligible death benefit if the insured is diagnosed with a terminal illness and has a life expectancy of 12 months or less*

Load funds *Mutual funds that charge either a front-end load or back-end load*

Long position *The purchase of a stock in hopes that it will appreciate over time*

Long-term capital gain *A gain from a sale or exchange of a capital asset that has been held for more than one year*

Long-term care insurance *Provides coverage for nursing home stays and other types of routine care that are not covered by other health insurance*

Long-term disability *Provides coverage for specified term greater than two years, until specified age, or until death*

Long-term Equity Anticipation Securities (LEAPS) *Long-term options that generally have expiration dates of up to three years*

Long-term liability *Debt extending beyond one year (long term > 12 months)*

Loss frequency *Expected number of losses that will occur within a given period*

Loss of fair rental value *The gross rental value less charges and expenses that do not continue during the period in which the property is uninhabitable*

Loss of use *Coverage that provides reimbursement to an insured homeowner for additional living expenses or loss of fair rental value*

Loss severity *Potential size or damage of a loss*

Lump-sum payment method *The total cash value of the life insurance policy is paid to the policyowner*

Major medical insurance *Health insurance that provides broad coverage of all reasonable and necessary expenses associated with an illness or injury, whether incurred at a doctor's office, a hospital, or the insured's home*

Malpractice insurance *Used where the deficient conduct of the insured provider of professional services may result in damages*

Management fee *A fee charged by an investment adviser for the management of a mutual fund's assets*

Managers *Individuals who are responsible for the maintenance, administration, and management of the affairs of a limited liability company*

Margin accounts *A type of brokerage account that allows the investor to borrow funds from the broker to purchase additional securities without adding cash to the account*

Marginal utility *The additional utility received from the consumption of an additional unit of a good*

Marital deduction *Unlimited deduction for transfers of property to a spouse during life (gifts) or at death (bequests)*

Market capitalization *The product of the number of outstanding common stock shares and current stock price*

Market order *Type of securities order that requires the trade be made at the best current market price*

Market risk *A systematic risk describing the tendency of stocks to move with the market*

Market segmentation theory *Yield curve theory asserting yields are determined by the laws of supply and demand for specific bond maturities*

Marketability *The ability of an investor to find a ready market where the investor may sell an investment to a willing buyer*

Maturity *The period through which the issuer has control over the bond proceeds and the period it must continue to pay coupon payments*

Maximum family benefit *The limit on the amount of monthly Social Security benefits that may be paid to a family*

Mean-variance optimization model *Used to determine the highest level of return (based on combinations of asset classes and different weightings of asset classes) for a specified level of risk tolerance*

Medicaid *Provides medical assistance for persons with low incomes and resources*

Medical payments *A no-fault, first-party insurance coverage designed to pay for bodily injuries sustained in an auto accident*

Medical savings account (MSA) *Used to pay the out-of-pocket medical expenses of an insured enrolled in a high-deductible insurance plan*

Medicare Advantage *A managed care plan that uses a network of doctors, hospitals, and health care providers approved by Medicare*

Medicare investment tax *A Medicare tax on investment income for taxpayers whose modified gross income (MAGI) exceeds certain thresholds*

Medicare *A federal health insurance plan for those who have attained full retirement age or have been disabled whether retired or still working*

Members *The owners of a limited liability company (LLC) who can be individuals, partnerships, trusts, corporations, or other LLCs*

Misstatement of age or gender provision *If a misstatement is made, the insurer can adjust the face amount to the amount the premium would have purchased had the age or gender been correctly stated*

Moderate inflation *Inflation characterized by slowly rising prices*

Modern portfolio theory (MPT) *A theory created by Harry Markowitz that describes portfolio diversification gained by combining securities with varying characteristics*

Modified adjusted gross income *On the 1040 federal tax return, modified adjusted gross income is the sum of adjusted gross income, nontaxable interest, and foreign-earned income*

Modified endowment contract (MEC) *A life insurance policy that exceeds its net level (7-pay) premium during the first seven years or during the seven years following a material change of the policy*

Modified whole life *Premiums are lower for the first few years after policy issue, typically three to five years, and increase to a higher level premium thereafter*

Money market mutual funds *A mutual fund that invests in money market instruments, such as Treasury bills and negotiable CDs*

Money market *Consists of debt securities that have the following characteristics: short-term maturity, low credit risk, and high liquidity*

Monopoly *A single seller of a well-defined product with no valid substitutes*

Moral hazard *A character flaw or level of dishonesty that causes or increases the chance for loss*

Morale hazard *Indifference to a loss based on the existence of insurance*

Morbidity *Relates to the probability of becoming disabled*

Mortality charge *The amount of money the insurance company charges for providing a death benefit*

Mortgage bond *Bond secured by real property*

Mortgage-backed securities (MBSs) *Ownership claims on a pool of mortgages*

MSCI EAFE Index *An index measuring the international securities markets*

Municipal bonds *Debt instruments issued by municipalities (states, counties, parishes, cities, or towns)*

Mutual funds *Open-end investment companies that sell shares of stock to the public and use the proceeds to invest in a portfolio of securities on behalf of their shareholders*

Mutual insurance company *Owned by policyholders and distributes profit in the form of policy dividends*

Named perils policy *A policy that provides protection against losses caused by the perils specifically listed in the policy*

Named-perils coverage *Protects from perils that are specifically listed in the policy*

Negligence *The failure to act in a way that a reasonably prudent person would have acted under similar circumstances*

Negligence *Tort caused by acting without reasonable care*

Net asset value (NAV) *The price at which shares of an open-end investment company are sold. The NAV of a fund is determined by subtracting total liabilities from total assets of the fund and dividing the difference by the outstanding shares.*

Net cash flow *Money available after all expenses are accounted for*

Net present value (NPV) *The difference between the initial cash outflow (investment) and the present value of discounted cash inflows (i.e., NPV = PV of CF – cost of investment)*

Net worth *The amount of wealth or equity the client has in owned assets*

New comparability plan *A defined contribution plan that maximizes the age-weighted discrepancy permitted under the cross-testing provisions of proposed nondiscrimination regulations*

No-fault insurance *Used in states that require drivers to carry insurance for their own protection; places limits on the insured's ability to sue other drivers for damages*

No-load funds *Mutual funds purchased directly through the mutual fund family without the assistance of a broker*

Nominal interest rate *Stated interest rate without considering the effect of inflation*

Nominal return *The stated return from an investment*

Noncancelable *Insurer guarantees the renewal of the policy for a given period or to a stated age without an increase in premium*

Nonfinancial risk *A risk that involves a non-monetary loss*

Nonparticipating *A policy that does not pay dividends*

Nonqualified plan *A retirement plan that can discriminate in favor of executives but is not eligible for all of the special tax benefits available for qualified or other tax-advantaged retirement plans*

Nuncupative (oral) will *Dying declarations made before sufficient witnesses*

OASDI *Old Age, Survivors, and Disability Insurance, commonly referred to as Social Security*

Objective risk *The relative variation of an actual loss to an expected loss*

Objectivity *Relating to facts without distortion by personal feelings or prejudices*

Occurrence *An accident, including exposure to conditions, which results in bodily injury or property damage during the policy period*

Offer of Settlement *A certificant may tender an Offer of Settlement in lieu of a disciplinary hearing*

Office audit *The audit is conducted at the IRS office near the taxpayer's home and usually involve issues too complicated to be resolved by mail, such as travel and entertainment expenses, income from rents, and large itemized deductions*

Officers *Individuals appointed by a corporation's board of directors to carry out the board's policies and make day-to-day operating decisions*

Oligopoly *Small number of rival seller firms; incentive to collude; high barrier to entry*

Online trading *A method of buying and selling securities over the internet without the use of a broker*

Open market operations *The process by which the Federal Reserve purchases and sells government securities in the open market*

Open perils policy *A policy in which all perils or causes of loss are covered unless they are specifically listed in the exclusions section*

Open-end investment company *An investment company whose capitalization constantly changes as new shares are sold and outstanding shares are redeemed*

Open-perils coverage *Coverage designed to protect against all perils except those specifically excluded from coverage*

Opportunity cost *The highest-valued alternative not chosen; represents what is forgone by choosing another alternative*

Opportunity cost *When faced with investment alternatives, it is the highest-valued alternative not chosen—it represents what is forgone by choosing another alternative; when discounting a future sum or series of payments back to present value, it is the composite rate of return on the client's assets with similar risk to the assets being examined*

Optionally renewable *The insurer may not cancel the policy during the term, but the insurer may decline to renew the policy for a subsequent term*

Options *Derivatives that give the holder, or buyer, the right to sell or purchase the underlying asset*

Ordinary (straight) life policy *A continuous-premium whole life policy in which premiums are paid regularly until either death or age 100*

Ordinary annuity *Deposits or payments are made at the end of each period*

Ordinary income *Any income that arises from services or from property that is not classified as a capital asset*

Other insured rider *Offers level term insurance coverage on the insured's spouse or children*

Other structures *Structures not attached to a dwelling, such as detached garages, small greenhouses, storage buildings, and gazebos*

Outflows *Recurring obligations, or monthly expenses paid*

Own occupation *Definition of disability in which an insured is considered totally disabled if the insured cannot perform the substantial and major duties of the insured's own occupation*

P/E ratio *A measure of how much the market is willing to pay for each dollar of earnings of a company*

Paid-up insurance rider *Increases the whole life death benefit protection and builds additional cash value*

Paid-up policy *A policy for which no future premium payments are due; remains in effect for life*

Paradoxical thinking *The second phase of a client's thinking process when setting financial direction in which a client tries to focus on several simultaneous objectives, causing confusion, goal conflict, and ambiguity. The paradoxical thinking phase is where a client often seeks the advice of a financial planner.*

Parent Loans for Undergraduate Students (Plus Loans) *Loans that allow parents with good credit histories to borrow funds for a child's education expenses*

Partial disability rider *The insured cannot perform all of the substantial and material duties of the job*

Participating preferred stock *Preferred stock that receives dividend based on the performance of the firm in addition to the specified preferred dividend*

Participating *A policy that pays dividends*

Particular risk *Personal risk that involves a possible loss for an individual or a small group*

Partner *An individual, corporation, trust, estate, or other partnership that has an ownership interest in a partnership*

Partnership *An association of two or more entities or individuals that operate as co-owners of a business for the purpose of making a profit*

Passive loss rule *Passive losses may only offset income from another passive activity. If the passive activity is a publicly traded partnership (master limited partnership), losses from that activity may only be offset by income from the same publicly traded partnership.*

Passive risk retention *Being unaware of a risk, but taking no steps to manage it properly*

Payable date *The date that the dividend will actually be paid*

Payments for legal support *transfers to children that are essentially legal support obligations; exempt from gift tax rules*

Peak *The point in the business cycle that appears at the end of the expansion phase when most businesses are operating at full capacity and gross domestic product is increasing rapidly*

Pell Grant *A grant from the federal government awarded to undergraduate students who have not earned bachelor's or professional degrees; the EFC calculation, which is based on one's financial need, is used to determine a student's eligibility for a Pell Grant and how much is awarded to a student*

Pension plan *A qualified plan structured to provide a regularly paid, fixed sum at retirement*

Peril *The proximate, or actual, cause of a loss*

Personal automobile policy (PAP) *Provides physical damage insurance, medical payments, liability coverage, and uninsured motorist protection*

Personal financial planning *The process of formulating, implementing, and monitoring multifunctional decisions that enable an individual or family to achieve financial goals*

Personal liability umbrella policy *Coverage designed to provide a catastrophic layer of liability coverage on top of the individual's homeowners and automobile insurance policies*

Personal service corporation (PSC) *A C corporation in which substantially all of the activities involve the performance of services in the fields of health, law, engineering, architecture, accounting, actuarial science, or consulting*

Personal statement of cash flows *Summary of the client's income and expenses during an interval of time, usually one year*

Personal utility curves *Economic curves that describe the satisfaction that an individual receives from a selected item or additional units of that item*

Physical hazard *A tangible condition or circumstance that increases the probability of a peril occurring and/or the severity of damages that result from a peril*

Physician's expense insurance *Pays for fees charged by physicians that provide nonsurgical care*

Policy loan provision *Allows the policyowner to borrow (with interest) against the cash surrender value of a permanent insurance policy*

Pool-of-money concept *Long-term care coverage provided up to a specific dollar amount, regardless of time*

Power of appointment trust *Allows a terminable interest to be passed to a surviving spouse and the property to still qualify for the marital deduction; unlike a QTIP trust, no election is required*

Practice Standards *The set of standards that (1) establish the level of professional practice that is expected of certificants engaged in personal financial planning, (2) advance professionalism in the practice of financial planning, and (3) enhance the value of the personal financial planning process*

Preemptive right *Allows shareholders to maintain ownership percentage by requiring new issues of stock to be offered first to current shareholders*

Preexisting condition *A medical condition that required treatment during a specified period before the insured's effective date*

Preexisting conditions clause *Excludes coverage for preexisting conditions for a specified period, such as 12 months, after the effective date of coverage*

Preferred habitat theory *Yield curve theory asserting financial institutions prefer to match asset maturities to liability maturities*

Preferred provider organization (PPO) *A contractual arrangement between the insured, the insurer, and the health care provider that allows the insurer to receive discounted rates from service providers*

Preferred stock *A type of stock that has characteristics of both fixed-income investments and of common stock in that dividend payments must be paid each year before paying a dividend to the common shareholders*

Premium *The cost of an option contract*

Prepaid legal services *Under this arrangement, law firms, in exchange for a monthly payment, provide specific legal services at no or greatly reduced cost*

Prepaid Tuition Plans *Plans where prepayment of college tuition is allowed at current prices for enrollment in the future; in other words, a parent can lock in future tuition at current rates*

Prepayment risk *The risk that homeowners will pay off their loans before the scheduled loan maturity date*

Preponderance of the evidence *A measure or degree of proof. With regard to disciplinary rules and procedures, preponderance of the evidence means the evidence as a whole shows what it was intended to prove with a probability of 51% or more.*

Present value of an annuity due *The value today of a series of equal payments made at the beginning of each period for a finite number of periods discounted at a defined interest rate*

Present value of an ordinary annuity *The value today of a series of equal payments made at the end of each period for a finite number of periods discounted at a defined interest rate*

Present value *The current dollar value of a future sum discounted at a defined interest rate over a period of time*

Price elasticity *The quantity demanded of a good in response to changes in that good's price; a good is elastic when its quantity demanded responds greatly to price changes (luxuries) and inelastic when its quantity demanded responds little to price changes (necessities)*

Price index *A weighted average of the prices of numerous goods and services (e.g., the Consumer Price Index, the gross domestic product deflator, the gross national product deflator, and the Producer Price Index)*

Primary beneficiary *The party designated by the policyowner to receive death benefits*

Primary Insurance Amount (PIA) *Amount on which a worker's retirement benefit is based. The PIA determines the amount the applicant will receive at full retirement age, based on the year in which the retiree turns 62. The PIA is indexed to the Consumer Price Index (CPI) annually.*

Primary market *The market where new issues of securities are first offered to the public*

Principal *In a power of attorney document, the person (power giver) who designates another person or persons to act as his attorney-in-fact*

Principle of indemnity *A person is entitled to compensation only to the extent that financial loss has been suffered*

Principle of insurable interest *To have an insurable interest, an insured must be subject to emotional or financial hardship resulting from damage, loss, or destruction*

Principle of utmost good faith *Requires that the insured and the insurer both be forthcoming with all relevant facts about the insured risk and the coverage provided for that risk*

Principles *Aspirational statements expressing the ethical and professional ideals CFP® certificants are expected to display in their professional activities*

Private censure *An unpublished written reproach that is mailed to the censured CFP® certificant by the Disciplinary and Ethics Commission*

Private Letter Rulings *Statements issued for a fee upon a taxpayer's request that describe how the IRS will treat proposed transactions for tax purposes*

Private placement *A corporation selling a new issue of securities to a small group of institutions or sophisticated individual investors*

Pro forma income statement *A financial statement that projects a business's income and expenses for the future rather than reporting the past*

Probate process *Proves the validity of any will, supervises the orderly distribution of assets to the heirs, and protects creditors by ensuring that valid debts of the estate are paid. Probate is also the legal process that performs the function of changing property title from a decedent's name to an heir's name.*

Producer Price Index (PPI) *A group of indexes that measures the average change in the selling prices received by domestic producers of goods and services over time*

Professional eligible for reinstatement (PER) *An individual who is not currently certified by CFP Board but who was certified in the past and has an entitlement to potentially use the CFP® marks*

Profit-sharing plan *A qualified defined contribution plan featuring a flexible (discretionary) employer-contribution provision. Profit-sharing plans are structured to offer employees participation in company profits that they may use for retirement purposes*

Proprietor *The owner of a sole proprietorship*

Proxy voting *Authorizing an agent to cast the votes for the shareholder*

Public letter of admonition *Written reproach of the CFP® certificant's behavior that will normally be published in a press release or other form of publicity selected by the Disciplinary and Ethics Commission*

Purchasing power preservation (PPP) model *A capital needs analysis method that assumes the client will have a capital balance of equal purchasing power at life expectancy as he did at retirement*

Purchasing power risk *A systematic risk where inflation will erode the real value of the investor's assets*

Pure annuity model *The basic capital needs analysis approach that is generally prepared on a pretax basis*

Pure expectations theory *Yield curve theory asserting long-term interest rates are based on expectations about future short-term interest rates*

Pure risk *A risk in which the results are either a loss or no loss*

Put option *A derivative that gives the holder the right to sell the underlying asset, generally a stock, at a specified price within a specified period*

Qualified dividends *Dividends received from domestic corporations and foreign corporations incorporated in a U.S. possession, such as Puerto Rico*

Qualified domestic trust (QDOT) *For a noncitizen spouse who was a U.S. resident at the time of the decedent's death, the marital deduction is allowed if the property is placed in a QDOT that passes to the noncitizen surviving spouse*

Qualified longevity annuity contracts (QLACs) *An insurance option that ensures retirees have a stream of regular income throughout their advanced years*

Qualified long-term care services *As defined by HIPAA, include necessary diagnostic, preventative, therapeutic, caring, treating, rehabilitative services, and maintenance or personal care services required by a chronically ill or cognitively impaired person and provided by a plan prescribed by a licensed health care practitioner*

Qualified terminable interest property (QTIP) trust *Allows a terminable interest to be passed to a surviving spouse and the property to still qualify for the unlimited marital deduction; the election is made by the executor on IRS Form 706*

Qualified transfer *A payment made directly to an educational institution for tuition and fees or to a medical provider for medical expenses for the benefit of someone else*

Qualified Tuition Programs (QTPs) *Also known as 529 plans, QTPs allow individuals to either participate in Prepaid Tuition Plans in which tuition credits are purchased for a designated beneficiary for payment or waiver of higher education expenses or participate in College Savings Plans in which contributions of money are made to an account to eventually pay for higher education expenses of a designated beneficiary*

Qualifying child *A taxpayer may claim an individual as a dependent if the individual satisfies all of the following requirements: relationship, abode, age, support, citizenship, and joint return*

Qualifying relative *A taxpayer may claim an individual as a dependent if the individual satisfies all of the following requirements: relationship, support, gross income, citizenship, and joint return*

Random walk *An unpredictable pattern that describes the movement of security prices over time*

Ratio analysis *The relationship or relative value of two characteristics used to analyze an individual's financial health and to conduct comparison and trend analysis*

Readjustment period *The period of time that lasts for one to two years following the death of a breadwinner*

Real estate investment trust (REIT) *A form of indirect ownership of real estate that invests in real estate, short-term construction loans, and mortgages*

Real interest rate adjustment *The rate of interest expressed in dollars of constant value (adjusted for inflation) and equal to the nominal interest rate, less the rate of inflation*

Real interest rate *Nominal interest rate considering the effect of inflation*

Real rate of return *The nominal rate of return adjusted for inflation*

Recession *A decline in real gross domestic product for two or more successive quarters*

Record date *The date at which an owner of the common stock of a corporation is entitled to receive the dividend payment*

Reentry term *A policy whereby the insurer may renew coverage at a lower premium rate if the insured provides satisfactory evidence of insurability*

Reinstatement clause *Outlines the conditions under which a lapsed policy may be reinstated*

Reinvestment rate risk *A systematic risk where earnings (cash flows) distributed from current investments cannot be reinvested at a rate of return equal to the expected yield of the current investments*

Remaining work life expectancy (RWLE) *The work period remaining at a certain point in time prior to retirement*

Renewable *A feature whereby the policyowner may continue a term policy for an additional period without evidence of insurability at a premium based on the insured's current or attained age*

Replacement cost *The amount necessary to purchase, repair, or replace the dwelling with materials of the same or similar quality at current prices*

Representation *Statement made by the proposed insured to the insurer in the application process*

Res ipsa loquitur *"The act speaks for itself"; negligence can be assumed from the character of the outcome without evidence of wrongdoing on the part of the tortfeasor*

Reserve requirement *The percentage of deposit liabilities that must be held in reserve by a member bank of the Federal Reserve; as the reserve requirement is increased, less money is available to be loaned, resulting in a restriction of the money supply*

Residual benefits provision *Policyowner receives a percentage of the disability benefit on the basis of the percentage of income loss due to sickness or injury*

Residuary clause *A general provision in a will that provides for the transfer of the balance of any assets not specifically mentioned in the will to someone or to some institution named by the testator*

Retirement benefit *The most familiar Social Security benefit, full retirement benefits are payable at full retirement age, with reduced benefits as early as age 62, to anyone who has obtained at least a minimum amount of Social Security credits*

Retirement earnings limitations test *One of the ways in which Social Security benefits are reduced on the basis of earnings*

Return of premium rider *Returns the premium paid for a policy (less any administrative charges, fees, or rider premiums) to the policyowner at the end of the policy term*

Revenue bonds *A municipal bond backed by a specific source of revenue*

Revenue Procedures *Statements reflecting the internal management practices of the IRS that affects the rights and duties of taxpayers*

Revenue Rulings *Official interpretation on how the law should be applied to a specific set of facts*

Revocable beneficiary *Can be changed by the policyowner (who may or may not be the insured) at any time*

Revocation *The Disciplinary and Ethics Commission may order permanent revocation of a certificant's right to use the marks and to publish the revocation in a press release or other form of publicity*

Rider *Provides additional coverage for something specifically not covered within the primary policy*

Riders (endorsements) *Written additions to an insurance contract that modify the original provisions*

Risk avoidance *The avoidance of any chance of loss*

Risk reduction *Taking measures that reduce the frequency or severity of losses*

Risk retention *Bearing all or part of the financial burden in the event of a loss*

Risk tolerance *An estimate of the level of risk an investor is willing to accept in his portfolio*

Risk tolerance *The level of risk exposure with which an individual is comfortable*

Risk transfer *Shifting the probability of loss to another party, such as an insurance company*

Risk *The chance of loss, possibility of loss, uncertainty, or a variation of actual from expected results*

Risk-based capital model (RBCM) *Adjusts an insurer's capital base according to the amount and types of risk to which it is exposed*

Roth IRA *An individual retirement account in which contributions are made on an after-tax basis and qualifying distributions are made tax free*

Roth IRA *An IRA created by the Taxpayer Relief Act of 1997; contributions to a Roth IRA are nondeductible; qualified distributions are excluded from an individual's taxable income; distributions used for qualified education expenses can also avoid the 10% penalty*

Rule of 72 *A method of approximation that estimates the time it takes to double the value of an investment where the earnings (interest) rate is known (by dividing 72 by the interest rate); it can also estimate the earnings (interest) rate necessary to double an investment value if the time is known (by dividing 72 by the period of investment)*

Rules of Conduct *Rules established by CFP Board that establish the high standards expected of CFP® certificants, the violation of which may subject a certificant to discipline*

Russell 2000® Index *A well-known index used to benchmark small capitalization companies*

S corporation *A special type of corporation formed under state law like a regular corporation; however, for income tax purposes, is treated similar to a partnership*

Sale *Transfer of property for an amount of money or money equivalent that is fixed or determinable*

Savings *Deferred consumption*

Scheduled personal property endorsement *Provides open-peril coverage under the same terms as if separate contracts were purchased for each type of property; the amount for which an item is insured is considered the value of the item if a loss occurs*

Secondary market *The market where investors can buy and sell securities with other investors*

Section 1035 exchange *Provides for the replacement of an existing insurance-based contract for a newer insurance-based contract without having to pay taxes on any gain in the original contract*

Section 125 (cafeteria plan) *A plan in which employers offer their employees a choice between cash and a variety of nontaxable qualified benefits that are excludable from the employee's income*

Section 401(k) profit-sharing plan *A defined contribution profit-sharing plan that gives participants the option of reducing their taxable salary and contributing the salary reduction on a tax-deferred basis to an individual account for retirement purposes*

Section 403(b) plan *A retirement plan similar to a 401(k) plan that is available to certain tax-exempt organizations and to public schools*

Securities Act of 1933 *Federal law that provides rules and regulations related to new issues of investment securities*

Securities Exchange Act of 1934 *Federal law that provides rules and regulations related to the purchase and sale of investment securities in the secondary market*

Securitization *The process of transforming nonnegotiable securities into negotiable securities*

Self-employment tax *Tax paid by self-employed individuals that is based on net earnings, not on the individual's wages. Because the self-employed must bear the burden of both the employer and employee portion of FICA, the self-employment tax rate is 15.3% (up to the taxable wage base)—double the employee's rate of 7.65% in 2016. Net SE income exceeding the TWB is taxed at the 2.9% Medicare tax rate, which has no income ceiling, and is added to the SE tax calculated for the SE income up to the TWB.*

Self-insured retention *A payment similar to a deductible that an insured is usually required to pay for each loss under a personal umbrella policy*

Semivariance *Measures the variability of returns that fall below the average or expected return*

Serial payment *A payment that increases at a constant rate (usually, the rate of inflation) on an annual basis*

Series EE United States Savings Bonds (EE Bonds) *If used to pay for qualified higher education expenses at an eligible institution or state tuition plan, EE bonds bestow significant tax savings—that is, no federal income tax is due on the interest*

Settlement options *Allow the policyowner or beneficiary to choose either cash or one of several alternatives to how the death benefit proceeds will be paid*

Shareholders *The owners of a corporation who elect the corporation's board of directors*

Sharpe ratio *A measure of risk-adjusted portfolio performance that uses standard deviation as the risk measure*

Short position *A type of position investors take by selling borrowed shares in hopes that the stock price will decline over time*

Short-term capital gain *A gain from a sale or exchange of a capital asset that has been held for one year or less*

Short-term disability *Provides coverage for up to two years*

Side instruction letter *Also known as a personal instruction letter, separate from a will; details the testator's wishes regarding the disposition of tangible possessions (household goods), the disposition of the decedent's body, and funeral arrangements*

Simplified employee pension (SEP) *A tax-deferred, noncontributory retirement plan that uses an individual retirement account (IRA) as the receptacle for contributions*

Simultaneous death clause *In the event that both spouses die simultaneously, this clause provides a presumption that one spouse (predetermined) predeceased the other spouse*

Single premium annuity *An annuity purchased with a single lump sum*

Single premium whole life *Single lump-sum payment made at policy issue with no future premiums due*

Sinking funds *Funds usually held by trustee to ensure repayment of borrowed principal*

Skilled nursing care *Daily nursing care and rehabilitation services ordered and monitored by a physician*

Slander *Verbal statement that causes harm to another*

Social Security Statement, Form SSA-7005 *A written report, mailed by the Social Security Administration to all workers age 25 and over who are not yet receiving Social Security benefits; provides an estimate of the worker's eventual Social Security benefits and instructions on how to qualify for those benefits*

Sole proprietorship *A business owned and controlled by one person who is personally liable for all debts and claims against the business*

Speculative risk *A risk where a potential for profit as well as loss or no loss exists*

Split gift *A joint gift made by spouses that has the effect of doubling the annual exclusion of gifts to the donee. A split gift requires the consent of the spouse and spouse's signature on Form 709.*

Split limits *Lists the per-person bodily injury limit, the per occurrence bodily injury limit for all bodily injuries, and the property damage limit*

Split-dollar plan *An agreement between an employer and employee who share the costs and benefits associated with a life insurance policy*

Spouse and child insurance riders *Provide life insurance coverage on the lives of the insured's spouse or children*

Stafford Loan *The primary type of financial aid provided by the United States Department of Education; Stafford loans are either subsidized or unsubsidized*

Standard & Poor's Index (S&P 500) *A financial index of 500 U.S. equities chosen for market size, liquidity, and industry group representation*

Standard deviation *Measures both total volatility and total risk (systematic and unsystematic risk) of the portfolio*

Standby underwriting *Equity underwriting in which the underwriter purchases any securities remaining after an initial offering*

Statement of cash flows *A financial statement that reflects the cash inflows and outflows of a business and reconciles the net changes in cash between two balance sheets*

Statement of changes in net worth *Summary of changes from one statement of financial position to the next*

Statement of financial position *A list of assets, liabilities, and net worth*

Static risk *A risk dependent on factors other than a change in society or the economy (e.g., natural disaster)*

Statutory (formal) will *Generally drawn by an attorney and signed in the presence of witnesses, complying with the statutes for wills of the domiciliary state*

Statutory voting *One vote per share of common stock*

Stock bonus plan *A defined contribution profit-sharing plan in which all employer contributions are in the form of employer stock. Distributions to participants can be made in the form of employer stock.*

Stock insurance company *Operate for-profit and owned by stockholders*

Stop limit order *A type of securities order that becomes a limit order when the security's price reaches a specific level*

Stop loss order *A type of securities order that becomes a market order when the security's price reaches a specific level*

Stop-loss limit *A dollar amount of covered benefits to which the coinsurance provision is applied, but it does not include the deductible; once the stop-loss limit is reached, the insurer pays 100% of all covered expenses*

Straight life annuity *Provides a lifetime income to the annuitant regardless of how long the annuitant lives*

Strict and absolute liability *Liability resulting from law; strict liability allows for defense, and absolute liability does not*

Subaccounts *Portfolios of stocks and/or bonds that are professionally managed according to a specific investment objective*

Subjective risk *A particular person's perception of risk; varies greatly from individual to individual*

Subjectivity *Relating to the client's perception of reality*

Subrogation clause *States that the insured cannot indemnify oneself from both the insurance company and a negligent third party for the same claim*

Substitutes *Products that serve similar purposes; an increase in the price of one will cause an increase in the demand for the other*

Substitution effect *The phenomenon in which consumers substitute less expensive goods for similar, more expensive goods; this is one of two reasons why the demand curve slopes downward*

Suicide clause *Asserts that, if the insured commits suicide within a specified period of time, the policy will be voided and premiums will be refunded to the beneficiary*

Supplemental Security Income (SSI) *Program administered by the Social Security Administration and funded by the general Treasury that is available to those at full retirement age or disabled who have a low income and few assets*

Supply curve *The graphic depiction that shows the relationship between the market price of a particular good and the quantity supplied*

Supply *The quantity of a particular good businesses are willing to produce or sell*

Surgical expense insurance *May be added to a hospital expense insurance policy to provide payment of surgeon's fees, even when procedures are not performed in a hospital*

Surplus lines agent *An agent that has the authority to engage in business with out-of-state insurers in order to meet consumer needs*

Survivors benefit *Social Security benefit available to surviving family members of a deceased, eligible worker*

Survivorship clause *Provides that the beneficiary must survive the decedent for a specified period in order to receive the inheritance or bequest*

Survivorship clause *Requires that a beneficiary survive the insured by a specified period (usually 30 to 60 days) in order to receive the death benefit proceeds*

Suspension *May be ordered by the Disciplinary and Ethics Commission for a specified period of time, not to exceed five years, for individuals it deems can be rehabilitated*

SWOT analysis *An analysis that helps the financial planner understand how internal and external environmental factors impact the client's financial situation. The acronym SWOT stands for strengths, weaknesses, opportunities, and threats.*

Systematic risks *Investment risks impacted by broad macroeconomic factors that influence all securities*

Target benefit pension plan *An age-weighted money purchase pension plan; a hybrid between a defined contribution plan and a defined benefit plan*

Tax avoidance *The legal minimization of taxes, which is accomplished by applying knowledge of the IRC and the Treasury regulations to an individual's income tax situation*

Tax evasion *Any of the various fraudulent methods by which a taxpayer may pay less than his proper tax liability*

Tax risk *The uncertainty associated with the tax laws that may impact the ownership and/or disposition of investment assets*

Taxable equivalent yield *A method for investors to compare the yield on municipal bonds with the yield on taxable (e.g., corporate) bonds*

Tax-qualified long-term care insurance *Policies that meet standards established with the passage of the Health Insurance Portability and Accountability Act of 1996 (HIPAA)*

Technical Advice Memoranda *Advice or guidance in memorandum form furnished by the National Office of the IRS to IRS agents who request such advice or guidance during an audit*

Technical analysis *The search for identifiable and recurring stock price patterns*

Technology stocks *Stocks of companies involved in high-technology fields categorized by above-average earnings potential and high risk*

Tenancy by the entirety *Joint tenancy with right of survivorship (JTWROS) that can only occur between a married couple*

Tenancy in common *Two or more persons hold an undivided interest in a whole property*

Term insurance rider *Offers additional term life insurance on the insured*

Term life insurance *Provides temporary life insurance protection for a given period*

Terminable interest *An interest that ends upon an event or contingency*

Testamentary capacity *Having the mental capability to make a will to transfer assets; being of sound mind*

Retirement life expectancy (RLE) *The time period beginning at retirement and extending until death; the period of retirement that must be funded*

Third market *Over-the-counter trading of equity shares that are listed on an exchange*

Time value of money *The concept that money received today is worth more than the same amount of money received sometime in the future*

Time-weighted returns *A method of determining an internal rate of return by evaluating the performance of portfolio managers without the influence of additional investor deposits or withdrawals to or from the portfolio*

Tort *A private wrong; an infringement on the rights of another*

Total return *The sum of the capital appreciation/depreciation on an investment plus any income or earnings generated by the investment*

Treasury inflation-protected securities (TIPS) *Marketable securities whose principal is adjusted by changes in the Consumer Price Index (CPI)*

Treasury STRIPS *Acronym for Separate Trading of Registered Interest and Principal of Securities, a program that permits investors to hold and trade the individual interest and principal components of eligible Treasury notes and bonds as separate securities*

Treynor ratio *A measure of risk-adjusted portfolio performance that uses beta as the risk measure*

Trough *The point in the business cycle that appears at the end of the contraction phase when most businesses are operating at their lowest capacity levels and the gross domestic product is at its lowest*

Trust *A legal arrangement, usually provided for under state law, in which property is transferred by a grantor to a trustee for the management and conservation of the property for the benefit of the named beneficiaries*

Underwriters *Classify proposed insureds in a way as to adequately protect the insurance company from adverse selection*

Underwriting *The process by which investment bankers purchase an issue of securities from a firm and resell it to the public*

Uneven cash flows *Investment returns or deposits that are neither single interval deposits nor equal payments*

Unified gift and estate transfer tax system *Unified tax transfer system created by Congress to ensure that at the time of transfer of property, either during life (gifts) or at death (bequests), the transferor will pay the same tax rate or amount for the transfer*

Uniform Gift to Minors Act (UGMA) *Allows parents to put cash and securities in a custodial account for a child*

Uniform Transfers to Minors Act (UTMA) *Allows parents to put cash, securities, and real property in a custodial account for a child*

Unilateral *Only the insurer agrees to a legally enforceable promise*

Uninsured/underinsured motorist *Motorist without liability coverage or whose insurer cannot or will not pay the claim, hit-and-run driver, or motorist with insufficient liability coverage according to state law*

Unintentional tort *Failure to act in a reasonably prudent manner, thereby causing harm to another*

Unit investment trust (UIT) *A registered investment company that is passively managed and may invest in stocks, bonds, or other securities*

Unit-elastic demand *The percentage of change in quantity demanded is exactly equal to the percentage of change in price, ignoring the direction of the change (PE = 1); a change in price results in no change to total revenue*

Universal life insurance *Gives policyowners the ability to adjust the premiums, death benefit, and cash values up or down to meet individual needs (within certain limits)*

Unsystematic risks *Types of investment risks unique to a single company, industry, or country that can be eliminated by portfolio diversification*

Usual and customary expenses *Health care costs that are consistent with the average rate or charge for identical or similar services in a particular geographic area*

Value stocks *Stock trading at prices that are low given the stock's historical earnings and current asset value*

Variable annuity *Does not guarantee specific payments but has a potential for greater returns*

Variable life *A fixed-premium, whole life policy in which the death benefit and cash values fluctuate on the basis of the performance of subaccounts sometimes referred to as separate accounts*

Variable outflows/expenses *Expenses that fluctuate from time to time over which the client has some control*

Variable universal life (VUL) insurance *Combines the investment component of variable life and the premium, death benefit, and cash value flexibility features of universal life*

Vesting *An employee's nonforfeitable right to receive a present or future pension benefit*

Viatical agreement *The owner of a policy covering a terminally ill insured sells a life insurance policy to a third party without the proceeds being subject to income tax*

Vicarious acts *Negligent acts performed by someone else but for which the individual is held at least partially responsible*

Vicarious liability *One person may become legally liable for the torts of another (e.g., parent/child, employer/employee acting in the scope of employment)*

Voluntary Employee Benefit Association (VEBA) *A tax-exempt trust authorized by IRC Section 501(c)(9); in a VEBA, an employer makes tax-free deposits to the plan on an employee's behalf*

Wage replacement ratio (WRR) *An estimate of the percentage of income needed at retirement compared to earnings prior to retirement*

Wait-and-see agreement *A hybrid version of the cross-purchase and entity purchase buy-sell agreement that allows the businessowners to wait until an owner dies or retires before deciding whether the surviving owners or the business entity will purchase the deceased or retired owner's share*

Waiver of premium rider *Waives the premium due on a policy during the period the insured is disabled*

War exclusion *Allows the insurer to deny a death claim if the insured's death is related to war or military service*

Warrants *A long-term, customized call option to purchase the stock of a given corporation within a specified period of time*

Warranty *Promise made by the insured to the insurer that is part of the insurance contract to which the insurer must adhere*

Whole life insurance *Provides coverage during the lifetime of the insured as long as the premiums are paid according to the policy contract*

Will *A legal document used in estate planning that provides the testator, or will maker, the opportunity to control the distribution of property and avoid the state's intestacy law distribution scheme*

Wilshire 5000 Index *A financial index consisting of over 5,000 U.S.-based companies; often used as a measure of the overall market within the United States*

Work life expectancy (WLE) *The number of years a person spends in the workforce, generally 30–40 years*

Yield curves *Graphical representations that reflect current market interest rates for various bond maturities*

Yield to call (YTC) *The expected return on a bond from the purchase date to the first date that the bond may be called*

Yield to maturity (YTM) *The compounded rate of return on a bond purchased at the current market price and held to maturity*

Zero-coupon bond *A bond that does not pay periodic coupon or interest payments*

Index

Symbols

A

B

C

D

E

Notes